PSYCH

PSYCHOLOGY

OLOGY:

Principles and Applications

Stephen Worchel

Wayne Shebilske

UNIVERSITY OF VIRGINIA

PRENTICE-HALL, INC., ENGLEWOOD CLIFFS, NEW JERSEY 07632

Library of Congress Cataloging in Publication Data

Worchel, Stephen.
  Psychology, principles and applications.

  Bibliography.
  Includes index.
  1. Psychology. 2. Psychology, Applied. I. Shebilske,
Wayne. II. Title.
BF121.W66 1983   150   82-16553
ISBN 0-13-732453-7

To some people whose support, understanding, and patience has helped us appreciate and value learning about others: our parents—Phil and Libby, Larry and Eileen; our siblings—Harvey and Jason, Sheila, Gary, Steve, Kevin, Mark, and Mike; our wives—Frances, Ann; and our children—Leah and Jessica, Sherry, Lisa, and Laurie.

PSYCHOLOGY: PRINCIPLES AND APPLICATIONS
Stephen Worchel/Wayne Shebilske

ISBN 0-13-732453-7

Printed in the United States of America

10 9 8 7 6 5 4 3

Prentice-Hall International, Inc., *London*

Prentice-Hall of Australia Pty. Limited, *Sydney*

Editora Prentice-Hall do Brasil, LTDA, *Rio de Janeiro*

Prentice-Hall Canada Inc., *Toronto*

Prentice-Hall of India Private Limited, *New Delhi*

Prentice-Hall of Japan, Inc., *Tokyo*

Prentice-Hall of Southeast Asia Pte. Ltd., *Singapore*

Whitehall Books Limited, *Wellington, New Zealand*

Development Editor: Susanna Lesan
Production Editor: Jeanne Hoeting
Photo Research: Anita Duncan
Book Design & Page Layout: Joan Greenfield
Assistant Art Director: Linda Conway
Cover Design: Sue Behnke
Cover Photo: Fred Burrell
Manufacturing Buyer: Ray Keating
Line Art: J & R Technical Services

(Acknowledgments appear on p. 621, which constitutes a continuation of the copyright page.)

OVERVIEW

CONTENTS

12 ABNORMAL PSYCHOLOGY   380

PREFACE

Our world is a fast-paced, exciting, and sometimes frightening place in which to live. We read of new inventions and discoveries almost every day. In our own lifetime, medical science has developed drugs that have eliminated such dread diseases as smallpox and polio; certain types of cancer can now be treated effectively; artificial limbs, eyes, and organs prolong life and open new worlds to the handicapped. Science has also developed ways to send people to space or across oceans with amazing speed. And with the mere push of a button, people can talk with and see others who are thousands of miles away. We may marvel at the ingenuity of the human being and experience pride in all that has been accomplished; we have, indeed, come a long way.

However, all these inventions and discoveries mean very little if we do not understand people, who must ultimately determine how these inventions will be used. What good is a prolonged life if people do not find these additional years fulfilling and rewarding? Rapid transportation and communication are of little value if people cannot use them to improve their lives and relationships. And, on the darker side, we have developed such terrible weapons that we have the ability to destroy ourselves. Therefore, it is at least as important, if not more important, that we develop a science that explains people and their behavior.

Psychology is the scientific study of human behavior. By discovering how and why people behave, believe, think, and learn we will be in a better position to understand our own world and anticipate the changes that will occur in it.

The problem that we as textbook writers have is how to present the richness of the field in a way that is meaningful and understandable, but still gives a fair picture of psychology. This problem is not unlike the one that you face when someone says, "Tell me about yourself." Where do you start? How do you tell your story so that you present an interesting and exciting picture of yourself, but still include information about your daily routine?

In writing about psychology we have tried to keep two goals in mind. Our first goal is to teach the theories and research support that constitute the principles of psychology. We do not, however, want to stop here, for while theories and research are interesting, they serve another important purpose. Psychology can be the looking-glass through which we can examine and understand events in our history and our daily lives. Psychology can help us explain and predict the behavior of people around us. Therefore, our second goal in this text has been to show how psychology can be applied to everyday life.

We have stressed application in two ways. First, we begin each chapter with a short account of an incident from history or current events. We chose these events because they represented a wide range of human behaviors. Some involve famous people (President Truman, Helen Keller), while others involve people who will never make the pages of history books (Hondo Crouch, Genie). In some cases, the behaviors include common activities such as making decisions and raising a family, while in other cases the behaviors involve the unusual and the bizarre, such as cannibalism. We refer back to these incidents throughout the chapter to show how psychology can help explain and give insight into the events that occurred. Second, in addition to using the incidents, we also present many examples from everyday life to show how psychology can help us understand ourselves and others.

The incidents and applications are also aimed at presenting psychology in an understandable way. Many people have come to think of science as a set of abstract concepts that are difficult to master. The incidents and applications, however, bring these principles to life and thus make them easier to remember.

PLAN OF THE BOOK

After a brief section on the history and methods of psychology, we begin by examining the structure of the individual (Chapter 2). In other words, we look at the "parts" that make up the body and how they work. We discuss how we see, hear, feel (Chapter 3); think (Chapter 4); learn (Chapter 5); and store information (Chapter 6). Once we understand the parts of the human machine and how they operate, we examine *why* they operate as they do. In other words, what factors influence our behaviors? In answering this question, we present material on how age influences behavior (Chapters 7 and 8). We also examine how people get the energy and direction for their behavior (Chapters 9 and 10). In the next chapter we examine the question of why people are different (Chapter 11). Given that humans are built in roughly the same way and that their bodies work in similar ways, we ask why each person is at the same time a unique individual. In the next two chapters after this (Chapters 12 and 13) our attention turns to the things that go wrong with human behavior. In these chapters we discuss psychological disorders and the treatment of these disorders. Clearly, people are not islands by themselves: We live in a social world that involves daily interactions with others. The next two chapters examine the way other people affect our behaviors (Chapters 14 and 15). We conclude the discussion of psychology by an examination of the way our physical environment influences behavior (Chapter 16). In a sense, then, our organization begins with the smallest scale of behavior (the parts of the body) and continues to increase in perspective to the largest scale of looking at people in groups interacting in the physical world.

While chapters are ordered according to a plan, each one stands on its own. We have made it easy to read chapters in any order, because some instructors prefer different organizations. Furthermore, we have tried to make each topic understandable without outside help, because many instructors ask students to read topics before they lecture on them. Since chapters are self-contained, we hope students will find the book to be a valuable starting point for doing term papers in other courses. To this end, we have supplied more references than probably will be needed in an introductory course. We have also listed suggested readings that expand upon topics covered in each chapter.

LEARNING AIDS

The chapters are clearly divided into sections, with each one focusing on a particular issue in a subfield. Figures, tables, and illustrations are used to highlight important points. Summaries at the end of the chapters are designed to review major issues. Terms appear in colored print the first time they are used, and a definition is given at that point in the text. The terms are repeated in color print in the summary at the end of each chapter. Finally, the glossary at the end of the book serves as a review of main terms used in the field of psychology.

SUPPLEMENTS

The *Study Guide/Practice Tests* seeks to help students check what they have learned and review for tests by presenting multiple-choice, fill-in-the-blank, and essay or discussion questions for each chapter. To aid the student in reviewing or in checking points in the text, each question has been keyed to the text page on which the answer may be found. The *Instructor's Manual* has supplementary lectures, ideas for discussion, and demonstrations that can be used in class to illustrate various points in the text. Finally, the *Test Item File* contains over 125 multiple-choice questions for each chapter, testing both conceptual understanding and factual recall.

ACKNOWLEDGMENTS

Although we as authors must be ultimately responsible for the contents of this text there are many people who made valuable contributions to the project. These people not only helped shape the book, but they turned what could have been a tedious and sometimes dreary job into an enjoyable and educational experience. In general, we would like to thank all those people for working as part of our team.

More specifically, we would like to thank John Isley, Psychology Editor, who was wreckless enough to sign the project and who, despite our most diabolical efforts, never lost faith in us. We appreciate your guidance, patience, and expertise. Susanna Lesan, our Development Editor, played a major role in the project from its inception to its completion. It would be impossible to list her many contributions so we can only say, thank you for your untiring efforts, your golden sense of humor, and your patience. We would also like to thank Marilyn Coco, Jeanne Hoeting, and others at Prentice-Hall who contributed so much of their time and effort and gently helped us conquer our most fearsome problems.

Closer to home, there were many people who not only helped with various phases of the book, but who also cheerfully suffered our moods and anguish during the project. Thanks to Dr. Cecile B. Finley and Roberta Senechal for gathering materials and for critiquing early versions of the manuscript, to M. Elizabeth Wetmore for taking some photographs and writing the appendix, and to Debra Mundie, Louise Spangler, Kristin Vlahas, Lou Carter and Carol Littowitz, who helped type and edit the manuscript. We would like to express our appreciation to the many students at the University of Virginia and Piedmont Community College who read and offered comments on parts of the manuscript. In addition I (Steve Worchel) would like to thank my colleagues and students at the University of Athens, Greece, where I was a Fulbright Research Fellow. Not only were they generous in opening up their libraries and facilities to me, but they also broadened my perspective on psychology.

One of the most important parts of our team was the reviewers. Your efforts and help were tremendous—not only did you help shape the manuscript, but you taught us a great deal about psychology. Although you often reigned as anonymous critics, your help and guidance were much needed and greatly appreciated. Thanks so much to:

James R. Averill, University of Massachusetts
Brian R. Bate, Cuyahoga Community College, Western Campus
David Brodzinsky, Rutgers University
Janice Westlund Bryan, Middlesex Community College
Thomas P. Cafferty, University of South Carolina
Thomas Carr, Michigan State University
Randall Clouser, Montgomery County Community College, Pennsylvania
James C. Coyne, University of California at Berkeley
Patricia Crane, San Antonio College
Stephen Davis, Emporia State University
Joan DiGiovanni, Western New England College
Karen Duffy, State University College of New York at Geneseo
Bernard Gorman, Nassau Community College
Megan Gunnar, University of Minnesota
Leonard W. Hamilton, Rutgers University
Ralph W. Hansen, Augustana College
Richard H. Haude, University of Akron
Maurice Hershenson, Brandeis University

William A. Johnston, The University of Utah
Donald Kaesser, Des Moines Area Community College
Paul S. Kaplan, Suffolk County Community College
Robert F. Kidd, Boston University
Ronald Kopcho, Mercer County Community College
Donald McBurney, University of Pittsburgh
James Mazur, Harvard University
Susan Mineka, University of Wisconsin
Martin M. Oper, Erie Community College
Marion Perlmutter, University of Minnesota
Ronald Peters, Iowa State University
John B. Pittenger, University of Arkansas at Little Rock
Alan D. Poling, Western Michigan University
J. Randall Price, Richland College
Alan Randich, University of Iowa
Damaris J. Rohsenow, University of Wisconsin at Madison
James S. Uleman, New York University
Herbert Van Schaack, State University College of New York at Oswego
Wayne Weiten, College of Du Page
Robert B. Welch, University of Kansas
Stephen West, Arizona State University
Diana S. Woodruff, Temple University

Finally, we would like to express our generally upspoken appreciation to our families. Frances and Ann not only offered constant encouragement, patiently listened to our anguished bellowing, ran the households while we frantically wrote "just one more page," and helped create a working environment; they also served as our most compassionate critics and confidants, helped gather material for the book, and offered invaluable suggestions. Our children, Leah, Jessica, Sherry, Lisa, and Laurie, too often, but with good cheer, took a back seat to "the book." Your encouragement, your smiles, and your understanding sustained us. Thanks.

S. W.

W. S.

Introduction

On the morning of September 28, 1976 the host of a morning radio show in Texas opened with a sad announcement:

"A bit of the twinkle in the eyes of Texas is missing today. Hondo Crouch died yesterday. Hondo was widely known as the mayor of Luckenbach, Texas. He was also the owner of Luckenbach and the chief of police and the city manager. Hondo put Luckenbach on the world's map. He held a world's fair there. Recording artists made their albums there. Chili-cookoffs, tobacco-spitting contests, cow-chip throwing competitions, and no-talent shows were staged there. But mainly Hondo Crouch was there. He was the village attraction." (Patterson, 1979, p. 223)

This is an unusual eulogy about an unusual man. Nothing was really special about Hondo Crouch, yet everything seemed special to him. John Russell Crouch was born in 1915 in the obscure town of Hondo, Texas. Young John Russell lived an uneventful childhood. Most people thought that he would follow the pattern of other young men from Hondo; after high school, most of the boys went to work for the railroad.

But John Russell always told people, "I'm different." And, indeed, he was different. As a child, he was fascinated with the way humans could propel themselves across a body of water. There was no lake or swimming hole near Hondo, so John Russell bought a swimming instruction book with cereal box tops and taught himself to swim by lying on a piano bench, kicking his feet, and moving his arms while reading the book. When it rained, John Russell would practice his swimming in the swollen creeks or in a local cattle-watering tank. Then, when he was 18, he and a friend hitchhiked to Austin and entered the state swimming meet. John Russell won so many events that spectators and other contestants at the meet kept asking, "Who is this Hondo guy?" As a result, John Russell not only came away with a number of gold medals, he also earned a nickname that stayed with him all his life—he became known as Hondo Crouch.

Hondo's performance caught the eye of the University of Texas swimming coach, who offered him a place on the swimming team in 1935. Understandably, Hondo was a little frightened and insecure in the "big city" and at the university. His insecurity was masked by his remarkable swimming ability. Hondo also hid his insecurity with his keen sense of humor; he became a renowned practical joker. For example, he kept a family of baby skunks in a cigar box in his room and would carry them in his pocket when the swimming team went on road trips. When he got to the cash register in a restaurant, he would pull out one of the skunks and ask the cashier to "please hold this for me" while he searched in his pocket for money. With his jokes and swimming Hondo became widely known; he was twice named All-American and had hopes of swimming in the Olympics. But his dreams of an Olympic medal were shattered when he hurt his back while playing water polo in 1940.

After serving in the Army, Hondo returned to the Texas ranch country that he loved so well. He married Helen Stieler, whose father owned a 22,000-acre ranch and was known as the Goat King of the world. Helen was everything that Hondo was not. She was self-assured and refined. Helen (or Shatzie, as Hondo called her) had a serious nature that was in sharp contrast to Hondo's fun-loving spirit.

In the beginning Hondo worked for Shatzie's father, learning the ranching business and getting to know the land. Hondo became part of the land, and the wild animals were his companions. He loved to tell stories about the animals he came into contact with. In a story for a local newspaper, he observed: "The ground is cracking and clumsy baby ants are fallin' in 'em. That's why Mama ants raises so many youngsters to feed some to the cracks they can't stay out of. Ain't nature wonderful? You probably didn't know this went on, because not many folks lay on their bellies across deer and coon trails in the forest at night watchin' baby ants fall in big dark cracks. That's where I do alot of my spare thinkin' " (Patterson, 1979, p. 71).

Hondo and Shatzie had four children, and Hondo delighted in teaching them everything from manners to lessons about nature. As with the rest of his life, his teaching methods were often unorthodox. In order to get his children to drink their milk, Hondo would wrap a nickel in wax paper and drop it into the bottom of the glass; the children eagerly gulped their milk to get the prize.

Hondo worked hard and saved his money. In 1953 he bought a 3,000-acre ranch. The land was hilly and rocky, dotted with sagebrush and small oak trees; it grazed 2,300 goats, 1,200 sheep, and 100 cows. Life as a rancher presented a constant challenge to Hondo; there never seemed to be enough grass or water, and it was a struggle to keep the land clear. Although the weather was hot and dry, a 3-month drought could give way to a flood with a single day's rain brought in by a Texas norther. Hondo loved the challenge of the harsh environment, and he was constantly experimenting, trying to find the best breed of animal for his land. His experiments often resulted in personal triumphs that he could boast about for years.

Although his ranch prospered, it was not ranching that made Hondo Crouch the center of attention in the Texas Hill Country. While he loved the land, Hondo had a need to be with people. He became a writer for the Fredericksburg newspaper. Under the name Peter Cedarstacker, he used wit and humor to comment on issues of local interest.

In addition to his writing, Hondo brought his humor to life on stage. He formed an acting team, and every summer the team would put on plays in the fallen-down dance hall in the ghost town of Waring, Texas. Hondo was a natural actor and he always seemed to know how to make the audience laugh. His fame grew, and many celebrities visited his little theater. Hondo acted and sang with a diverse group that included astronauts Frank Borman and James Lovell, Jr.; singers such as Jerry Jeff Walker and Willie Nelson; and comedian Bob Hope.

Hondo was a grown man who in some ways never outgrew being a little boy. However, all was not happiness and jokes in Hondo's life. His favorite son, Kerry, went to the University of Texas in 1967, a time of turmoil over the Vietnam War. Kerry was a talented artist and a warm, sensitive young man. He idolized his father and this admiration was returned by Hondo. One day in 1969, when Kerry was 21 years old, Hondo received a call from a doctor in Austin. Kerry had developed a severe psychological disorder known as schizophrenia. The once happy, playful boy now lived in a world of his own. He was unable to interact with other people, and he heard voices and saw strange figures. Hondo was crushed. He blamed drugs and Kerry's "hippie" friends for the problem. He loved

Kerry so much, but was hurt so deeply, that he could not bear to visit him in the hospital. Kerry spent much of the next 8 years in hospitals and jails; despite urgings from family and friends, Hondo never visited his son.

Hondo's spirit was broken by this tragedy and his only wish after learning about his son's condition was to die soon. His will to live was restored, however, by a small advertisement in the Fredericksburg paper: "Town for sale; Luckenbach. Benno Engle, owner." The town of Luckenbach stood at the end of Hondo's ranch. Its main street (the only street in town) was 200 feet long, and the whole town consisted of just a general store, which had a saloon in one section and a post office in the other. (A white line painted down the center of the floor separated the saloon from the post office.) Hondo had often admired the little town and the thought of owning it stirred his imagination.

He would put Luckenbach on the map; it would be a place where anyone could feel at home. Most of all, it would give Hondo a place where he could once again be the center of everyone's attention. He bought the town and hung a sign over the general store entrance: "Everybody's Somebody in Luckenbach."

Hondo assumed his role as mayor and foreign minister of Luckenbach and became a champion of the downtrodden. Chili contests were popular in Texas, but women were traditionally excluded. Hondo formed the "Hell Hath No Fury (Like a Woman Scorned) Society" and staged the first women's chili cookoff. In 1973, Hondo held Luckenbach's first "Great World's Fair," which attracted 10,000 people. Contests included tobacco-spitting, chicken-frying, cow-chip throwing, and armadillo races. Hondo encouraged aspiring entertainers to come to Luckenbach; Willie Nelson and Jerry Jeff Walker, who were unknown at the time, performed at the fair and became close friends of Hondo.

Hondo and his creative humor and insight received national attention. The Clown Prince of Texas had found his kingdom in Luckenbach. Here, Hondo, the man who was really no one special, found a way to make all those who visited his town feel a little special.

WHAT IS PSYCHOLOGY?

Even as a young boy, Hondo believed he was different from other people. Indeed, in many respects Hondo was unique. His thoughts, feelings, and actions were different from everyone else's. In fact, each of us is unique. But despite this uniqueness, we all have a large number of things in common. We all learn (some faster than others); we all talk (some more than others); we all have goals that we are trying to reach; each of us experiences emotions such as love, hate, and happiness; and we all interact with other people and belong to groups. Most of us take our thoughts, feelings, and actions for granted. We rarely question how we see objects, learn new material, or feel emotions. We seldom wonder why we are attracted to certain people or why we have bizarre dreams. The exception to this occurs when something goes wrong. We begin to question how learning occurs if we see our child having difficulty reading or writing. We begin to question why people feel emotions when we find ourselves in the depths of a deep sadness or depression.

As you will see in this book, the field of psychology is aimed at discovering the "hows and whys" of behavior. More formally, **psychology** is the scientific study of behavior and the applications gained from that knowledge. The main goals of psychology are to clearly describe, predict, and explain behavior. As with any field of study, psychology has developed methods for investigation, a vocabulary for clearly communicating findings and ideas, and theories that explain the outcomes of psychological research.

Knowing how and why humans behave as they do can have very important consequences for everyone. This knowledge can help us teach the child who is having learning difficulties. It can enable a young couple to resolve their conflicts before they destroy their relationship. And for people who are not having any particular difficulty, this knowledge of human behavior can point the way to creating a more fulfilling and exciting life. As one student said, "Of all the fields I have studied at the University, psychology is the one that is really about *me*. In psychology, I am the center of attention; its findings apply directly to me."

Wilhelm Wundt, a German psychologist, founded the first psychology laboratory in Leipzig, Germany, in 1879.

THE HISTORY OF PSYCHOLOGY

A recent trend in human behavior has been people's interest in finding their roots by tracing their family tree. The reason for these efforts is the belief that understanding one's history will give meaning to the present and help predict the future. Even beginners have little trouble tracing their roots back three or four generations, into the early 1800s. The family tree of psychology is also rather easy to trace, since it is just over 100 years old; the most cited date for the "birth" of psychology is 1879. The clearest way to examine the psychology family tree is by studying the schools of thought or approaches that have developed over the last 100 years.

Structuralism

In 1879, Wilhelm Wundt came to Leipzig, Germany, to start the first psychological laboratory. Wundt developed techniques for studying the laws of the human mind. Most of his techniques involved analyzing sights, sounds, and other sensations, because he believed that sensations are the "atoms" of thought. Many students came to study with Wundt; one of the most famous was Edward Bradford Titchener, who set up his own laboratory in the United States at Cornell University.

Besides setting up laboratories, Wundt and Titchener are credited with developing an analytical approach to studying how we experience the world the way we do. This approach, which is called **structuralism,** is based on identifying the elements of human experience and finding out how those elements combine to form thoughts and feelings. Titchener identified three categories of elements: sensations (such as sights and sounds), feelings (such as joy and sorrow), and images (such as memories and dreams). The main research tool of structuralism is the method of **analytic introspection,** which is a way of isolating the elementary sensations of which experiences are made.

You would have to go through a rigorous training program to learn analytic introspection. As a trainee, you would learn to break down your experiences into their most basic elements. To get some idea of how this works, imagine yourself standing in front of a window looking at a house, trees, and sky. You would divide the window scene, for instance, into separate patches of colors and brightnesses. You might notice different shades of blue and green in the sky and trees, and you might see that the light tan house looks darker in an area covered by a shadow. According to structuralists, in doing this you would be uncovering the sensory elements used to construct your experience. Psychologists no longer rely on analytic introspection, because the method could only be used with trained observers, who were usually the psychologists themselves. Fur-

If you were a trainee in analytic introspection, you would not just describe the scene shown here as a house, trees, and sky. You would learn to notice patches of brightness and darkness and how different colors are affected by shadows or bright sunlight, and you would incorporate this into your description of the scene.

William James, a foremost American psychologist, helped to give applied psychology its scientific status.

thermore, the method gave different results in different laboratories, depending on how observers were trained. But many researchers today carry on the goal of discovering the sensory elements of experiences, using new methods.

Psychologists have developed many new research approaches since the founding of the first laboratory. Some developed in a very different direction from structuralism. Others were motivated by the desire to study aspects of behavior for which structuralism was not well suited. Let's review some of these other approaches.

Functionalism

While structuralist's publications were still "hot off the press," an American psychologist, William James, proposed a different program of research. His new approach was called **functionalism,** because it concerned the way in which mental processes (such as thinking) function to fill needs. While structuralists were asking "What is thinking?" functionalists asked "What is it for?" Emphasis on the function of thought led functionalists to pursue important applications in education. John Dewey, a leading functionalist, strengthened public education in America and was the founder of school psychology, which has become a major subfield. Other functionalists applied their work to a great many pressing problems. For instance, they served as advisors to the United States armed services, they developed tests of personality, and they contributed to the development of child psychology.

Gestalt Psychology

In the 1920s, while Hondo Crouch was in grammar school, a group of German psychologists, Max Wertheimer, Kurt Koffka, and Wolfgang Köhler, established still another approach to psychology. They believed that there are experiences that cannot be broken down into separate elements. They therefore argued that structuralist "elements," or units of analysis, were unnatural. They maintained that some things have to be experienced as wholes—that they cannot be broken down any further. Thus, the units of choice in the earlier example would be trees, house, and sky. These psychologists were so committed to analyzing these "whole" units that they named their approach **Gestalt,** which is a German word meaning "whole." Gestalt psychologists argued that it is the organization of elements, rather than the elements themselves, that is important. In order to understand their point of view, think of your favorite tune. Clearly, the tune is made up of musical notes, but it is not the notes themselves that give melody to the tune. Instead, it is the *arrangement* of the notes that is important. We could take those same notes and make a different melody (or maybe just noise), if we organized them differently. In Chapter 3 we will review Gestalt laws of organization, and we will discuss modern attempts to refine those laws.

Behaviorism

When Hondo's children refused to drink their milk, Hondo found that he could quickly change their behavior by dropping a nickel into the bottom of the glass. They then quickly gulped down the milk in order to get the nickel. In order to understand and predict their behavior, Hondo did not have to worry about what his children were thinking or feeling; it was easy to see that "nickel in glass" resulted in "drinking the milk."

This view is characteristic of the **behaviorist approach** that developed in the 1920s. John Watson, one of the first behaviorists, argued that the

B. F. Skinner, a well-known advocate of the behaviorist approach, is shown in the laboratory with the basic experimental apparatus named after him, the Skinner box.

science of psychology must concern itself only with *observable* events. Watson pointed out that we cannot observe events such as thinking or feeling, nor can we directly observe "the mind." Watson believed, therefore, that psychologists should not try to explain behavior in terms of something we can't observe. Further, he argued that we do not need these "fuzzy" concepts to predict behavior. In the example of Hondo's children we saw that an event could be described by referring only to what could be observed: a stimulus (nickel in the glass) and a response (drinking the milk). Watson argued that we can describe human behavior in the same way, by focusing only on the observable stimulus and response.

In Chapter 5, we will discuss a famous experiment that helped Watson show the power of his behaviorist approach (Watson and Rayner, 1920). In that experiment, he was able to predict and control an infant's responses, such as crying, by systematically manipulating observable aspects of the infant's environment.

The behaviorist approach was well received by many psychologists, because it represented an approach to understanding behavior that could be directly tested and applied in many settings. One of the well-known advocates of this approach was B. F. Skinner, who is still an active researcher and writer. Skinner has applied the behavioristic approach in a number of different areas, from child rearing to teaching pigeons to guide missiles (Skinner, 1960; see also Chapter 5).

While there were many strong points in the behaviorist approach, critics argued that it did not fully take into account the richness of human experience. After all, even though we cannot see a thought or a feeling, we know that people do think and experience emotions. Since these are important parts of the human experience, they should also be material for psychological investigations.

Psychoanalytic Psychology

While many would criticize behaviorism for being too simple, few would accuse psychoanalytic theory of the same thing. As behaviorism was being introduced in the United States, a Viennese physician named Sigmund Freud had the European scientific world in an uproar with his unorthodox

Sigmund Freud is the founder of psychoanalysis, which has played a central role in understanding and treating psychological disorders.

views of human behavior. Freud, the founder of the **psychoanalytic approach** to psychology, not only suggested that much of human behavior is the result of thoughts, fears, and wishes, he also suggested that people are often unaware of these motivating forces, even though they have a strong effect on behavior. Freud argued that many, if not most, of these thoughts and wishes are the result of our experiences during infancy and early childhood. He caused the greatest outcry of criticism when he suggested that infants have sexual fantasies about their parents.

Freud's ideas had a tremendous influence on psychology. Since his early work was aimed at explaining emotional disorders, psychoanalytic theory has played a central role in understanding and treating psychological disorders. We will see this influence in Chapters 12 and 13. Psychoanalytic theory has also been used to explain differences between people. In this role, as we will see in Chapter 11, psychoanalytic theory has been the basis for important advances in understanding personality.

While people no longer express shock and dismay at Freud's ideas, there is still a great deal of controversy about psychoanalytic theory. One of the criticisms of the approach has been that it takes a very dim view of human nature. According to Freud, the unconscious impulses that influence behavior are often destructive and antisocial. Psychoanalytic theory paints a bleak picture of the individual, who is caught in a struggle to control these destructive impulses.

Humanistic Approach

If Hondo had adopted a school of psychology, there is little doubt he would have been comfortable with the humanistic tradition. He strongly believed in the goodness of human nature. He often said that all people need is "half a chance" and they will "do good." And it was in Luckenbach where everyone could have their "half a chance." The ragged sign over the general store proclaimed this: "Everybody's Somebody in Luckenbach."

A number of psychologists objected to Freud's view that humans are basically destructive beasts who are constantly fighting their negative impulses. In the 1950s the *humanistic* movement began. The main theme of the **humanistic approach** is that people are basically good. Instead of being driven by unconscious desires to destroy, people have free will, and, given the proper environment, they will strive to achieve positive social goals. As we will see in Chapter 11, the humanistic psychologists argued that each person is unique, and that psychologists should examine this individuality rather than lumping people into categories. The humanists also reject the behaviorist view that psychologists should only study observable stimuli and responses. Rather, they argue, it is their thoughts, desires, and feelings that make people unique.

SUBFIELDS OF PSYCHOLOGY

By the 1950s psychology had established itself as a major area for scientific study. The field had a rich history; it had developed methods for studying behavior; and it had a rapidly growing library of theory and research. Along with age came a wisdom that only experience can supply. Psychologists began to realize that the study of behavior was so broad that no single approach could be relied on to give the necessary answers to all the questions that were being raised. Each approach had merit, but it would take all of them to solve the puzzle of behavior. For this reason many psychologists began moving away from identifying with one school or approach to psychology. Instead, they began to define areas where many approaches of study could be used. As a result, the branches of the psychology family tree took on a new look. The branches no longer bore the name of approaches to the general area of psychology; instead they took on the name of subfields of psychology. Let us now examine how this new direction has affected the field of psychology.

Physiological and Experimental Psychology

Hondo Crouch was a great swimmer during his college days. As a young boy he spent a great deal of time teaching himself to swim. How was he able to do this and achieve such splendid results? Swimming, like many other complex behaviors, involves many steps. Swimmers must

If Hondo had adopted a school of psychology, there is little doubt he would have been comfortable with the humanistic tradition. The sign over Luckenbach's general store proclaims this: "Everybody's Somebody in Luckenbach."

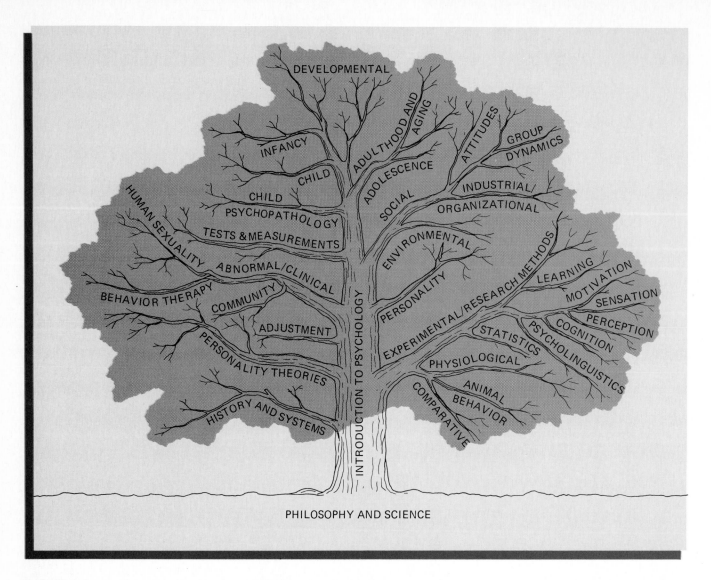

FIGURE 1–1

This psychology family tree shows the various subfields of psychology as they are reflected in course titles in most psychology departments. If you decide to pursue your interest in psychology after the introductory course, you will have many of these courses to choose from.

learn the best way to move their arms and legs; they must develop their muscles; they must deal with their fear of the water; and they must be able to sense where their body is in relation to the water and to the direction they wish to move in. In short, swimming involves learning, memory, perception, motivation, and emotion. The subfields of physiological and experimental psychology are concerned with the scientific examination of these areas.

Physiological psychologists examine these areas by studying the neurobiological events that underlie them. They study the eyes, ears, and other organs that we use to sense our environment. They also investigate muscles and other structures that we use to respond to our environment. Another major concern is the brain, which coordinates information coming from sense organs and going to muscles. They carefully map the brain to determine the function of various parts. Physiological psychologists also probe the pathways that carry information to and from the brain.

Experimental psychology examines the behaviors and cognitions (thoughts) that are related to learning, memory, perception, motivation, and emotion. The name of this subfield is more an historical accident than an identifying characteristic of the field; as you will see, all the subfields of psychology are experimental in that each uses experimental methods to investigate questions. However, experimental studies of perception and learning were some of the first in psychology and, therefore, the subfield was called experimental psychology.

Experimental psychologists brought to psychology the white rat, sometimes referred to as the mascot of the field.

The areas studied by experimental psychologists are amazingly varied, as are the subjects used in these studies. Investigations examine the basic questions of how we see, hear, and feel pain. They study how people learn to perform everything from simple tasks such as sitting upright to more complex things such as emotions and language. Experimental psychologists study both humans and animals. It is the experimental psychologists who brought to psychology the white rat, sometimes referred to as the mascot of the field. Experimental psychologists use animals to investigate a variety of issues, especially those involving learning, memory, and motivation. The use of animals in research allows psychologists to learn about animal behaviors that are important in their own right and to test new directions for human research.

The use of powerful manipulations and fine controls are two advantages of using animals even when the ultimate goal is to learn about human behavior. Psychologists can test drugs and other manipulations that might not be safe for humans. They can also control an animal's ancestry and its environment. These advantages are accompanied by the disadvantage of leaving open the important question, Do the results hold true for humans? This question is answered ideally in follow-up experiments on humans. In later chapters, we will review many examples of animal research that have paved the way for new discoveries about human behavior.

Experimental psychologists concentrated almost exclusively on behavior during the heyday of behaviorism. Today, however, experimental psychologists study cognitions as well as behaviors. In fact, a subgroup of experimental psychologists refer to themselves as cognitive psychologists. They are concerned with the mental events that intervene between stimuli and responses. Their goals are best understood in comparison with those of physiological psychology. Suppose physiological psychologists analyzed an Atari game of Space Invaders in the same way that they analyze humans. The photo on page 12 shows a home version of this popular video game. Its major components are (1) buttons, which send information into the system; (2) a TV, which makes responses; (3) a computer, which coordinates information coming from the buttons and going to the TV; and (4) a Space Invaders program cartridge, which is one of

Cognitive psychologists are concerned with mental events that intervene between stimuli and responses. In the Atari games, different programs cause different responses—for example, in the Space Invaders game, the program causes a cannon to shoot when a button is pressed. In the same way, we can make up our minds, or "program" our brains, to respond differently to the same stimuli.

many program cartridges used with the Atari system. Physiological psychologists would study the electronic components and the pathways between them.

In contrast, cognitive psychologists would analyze the computer events that took place between button pushes and TV responses. Different programs result in different events, so cognitive psychologists would concentrate on the programs. For example, the Space Invaders program causes a cannon to shoot when one button is pressed, while the Football program causes a football player to pass a ball when the same button is pressed. Cognitive psychologists would try to focus on how the programs caused the different responses. Similarly, we can make up our minds, or "program our brains," to respond differently to the same stimuli. We could make many different responses to this page of print, for example. Often we represent information in many forms during the course of making a response. For example, we might first represent this text as letters, then as words, and then as a complete train of thought. Cognitive psychologists try to follow this flow and transformation of information that occurs between stimuli and responses.

As you can see, the subfields of physiological and experimental psychology are very large. Most psychologists in these areas are engaged in research at universities and colleges. Recently, however, more and more have been entering applied settings, where they use their knowledge to help solve a wide range of problems. As we will see later in this book, they have been involved in projects to restore sight to the partially blind and hearing to the partially deaf; they have worked on finding the best methods for teaching; and they are discovering new drugs and treatments to treat people with psychological disorders.

Developmental Psychology

One common gift that parents receive at baby showers is the Baby Book. In this book, they can record when their child first smiles, babbles, crawls, talks, and walks. Many an anxious parent has worried, "Why isn't Johnny smiling? Helen's baby smiled at 6 weeks." The subfield of **developmental psychology** was developed to examine the function of age on behavior. Developmental psychologists are not only concerned with identifying the age at which people should be performing various behaviors; they are also interested in how events that occur at various ages affect behavior. For example, they study the effects on later development of being born prematurely. They examine how family changes (such as births of siblings, divorce, or death) influence the child's development. As we will see in Chapter 8, developmental psychologists are also interested in the changes that take place in middle-aged and elderly adults. Most developmental psychologists work in universities and colleges, although many are employed in hospitals, schools, and day-care centers.

Social and Personality Psychology

In many respects, Hondo was like each of us, and in other ways he was different from any of us. Hondo loved the outdoors; he enjoyed being the center of attention; he had strong attitudes about the way children should be raised; and he was always willing to help someone in distress. Most people liked Hondo, but some were irritated by his clowning.

As we examine the story of Hondo's life, many of us can picture ourselves in similar situations and having similar feelings. In a sense, social psychology is concerned with similarities in people's behavior as they interact with one another. **Social psychology** is the study of the way people are affected by social situations. The field examines questions such as how people form and change attitudes; how they form impressions about themselves and each other; why they are attracted to some people and angered by others; and how being in a group affects their behaviors and beliefs. Social psychologists develop theories that explain why people in general behave as they do in various situations. Although most social psychologists work in university settings, there are many in industry, advertising agencies, political organizations, and hospitals. The research findings from social psychology have been used by lawyers to help in choosing sympathetic juries; by advertisers to plan advertising campaigns; by politi-

Research findings from social psychology have been used by politicians to design political campaigns and by negotiators on both sides of industry-labor bargaining disputes.

cians to design political campaigns; and by negotiators involved in planning bargaining strategies in industry as well as internationally.

While social psychology is concerned with how most people act most of the time, investigators of personality are interested in individual differences. Personality focuses on explaining and predicting the unique ways that people respond to their environment. They would, for example, be interested in why Hondo was always joking, while Shatzie, his wife, was serious most of the time. Personality psychologists have designed tests to measure and describe personalities, and they have developed theories to explain why people are different. Their work has been applied in business and the military to help channel the right people into right jobs.

Clinical Psychology

When people find that you are taking courses in psychology, their first response is often, "Analyze me." Some may begin bringing their personal problems to you and ask you for your advice. Many people believe that all psychologists analyze and treat psychological disorders, and, indeed, the subfield of clinical psychology has more psychologists than any other subfield.

Clinical psychology is dedicated to the diagnosis and treatment of emotional and behavioral disorders. Clinical psychologists are not medical doctors, but some of them work closely with *psychiatrists*, who are medi-

HIGHLIGHT / CAREERS IN PSYCHOLOGY

You can feel at home in a psychology class or be comfortable as a psychology major even if you are not planning to become a psychologist. Psychology classes and psychology majors consist of a good many students who have not yet decided on their career goals. Of those who have fixed goals, many have chosen careers in medicine, law, business, and education, as well as in psychology. Students with a B.A. in psychology find themselves well received in law schools, medical schools, and business schools. Harvard Business School, for example, accepts more psychology majors than students in any other single major, including undergraduate business majors. The diversity of interests served by psychology classes is, in fact, a good reason for considering psychology as a major.

Psychologists seeking jobs in colleges and universities already outnumber the available academic positions. But psychologists have many other job options. Woods

(1976) did a survey for the American Psychological Association that looked into just this topic—where are psychologists employed outside academia? The following are some excerpts from his list of job descriptions of psychologists in innovative roles:

CONSULTANT TO A PUBLIC DEFENDER'S OFFICE

Employer description. I serve as a full-time consultant to the investigators and lawyers in the Public Defender's Office on matters relating to their clients. . . .

Job description. I am employed by the Community Mental Health Center and am placed in the Public Defender's Office. . . . My activities, which are diagnostic, evaluative, and consultative, are not innovative, but the setting in which I provide my services is a relatively new one for clinical psychologists.

Training. I have found my training in psychological diagnostics to be essential in performing my duties. Of course, training and experience in

interviewing have also been essential.

Employment prospects. It seems to me that any large Public Defender's Office could provide more efficient service and enhance the services to defendants if a behavioral scientist with clinical training and experience were added to the staff. . . .

PSYCHOLOGIST IN ACCIDENT RESEARCH

Employer description. The organization gathers and disseminates technical safety information on a nationwide basis.

Job description. The purpose of my job is to review accident literature, to design and execute original research, and to systematically evaluate accident countermeasure programs.

Training. The "traditional" degree is helpful, but I believe more of a "co-op" approach to graduate education is needed, that is, a program in which work in the real world is mixed with academic coursework.

cal doctors that specialize in psychological problems. Those who work closely with psychiatrists are often in private practice, in mental hospitals, or in mental health clinics. It is highly probable, for example, that clinical psychologists worked with Hondo's son, Kerry, after he was hospitalized. Clinical psychologists are also employed by probation offices, prisons, and institutions for the mentally retarded and physically handicapped. Clinical psychologists apply psychological principles, especially those principles related to motivation, emotions, and personality. Chapters 9, 10, and 11 will therefore set the stage for a sound introduction to clinical psychology in Chapters 12 (Abnormal Psychology) and 13 (Therapy).

Counseling and School Psychology

Counseling and school psychology are dedicated to helping people with social, educational, and job or career adjustments. Although most counseling psychologists work in schools, some assist with social and job adjustments in other settings, such as social work offices. Many psychological problems reveal themselves first in schools and homes. School psychologists work with parents and teachers to help individual students before problems become serious. Another important part of their job is administering and interpreting intelligence, achievement, and vocational tests. Seeing a school psychologist is not necessarily a sign of a problem. Many of the best college students take full advantage of school psychologists for

Employment prospects. There is definitely a job market for as many as 1,000 psychologists. They could be employed by indicating the cost-benefit to employers of studying and reducing the tremendous losses caused by accidents, both on and off the job.

COMMUNICATION WORK BETWEEN PEOPLE AND COMPUTERS

Employer description. We are trying to identify design criteria to aid communication between a computer and a lay person. . . . The Office of Naval Research has partially funded our efforts, but my major employer is the research center of a large computer manufacturer.

Job description. We are trying to find ways of making it easy for people in business to tell their problems to a computer and receive some help. We do experiments to investigate features of programming languages, to study how people specify procedures in natural English, and eventually to test our ideas about how a certain set of natural language mechanisms could

be used to provide an exciting, powerful system.

Training. A person should have training in "artificial intelligence," linguistics, and computer sciences in addition to the traditional degree.

Employment prospects. This field is certainly a potentially expandable job market for psychologists. Since costs in using computers are primarily labor costs, that is, labor

for translating a user's problems into computer-compatible form, we can save tremendous sums of money by solving these problems. I suggest contacting industrial companies for funding or cooperative work.

All of these jobs are held by people with a Ph.D. in psychology. That doesn't mean, however, that you need a Ph.D. to get a good job. Some of the people described here hire assistants with bachelor's or master's degrees at salaries comparable to other jobs at those levels.

Many people panicked when the academic job market for psychologists started to dry up. Thanks to the diversity and versatility of the field, however, people are beginning to find alternative careers in psychology. Employment opportunity is not the only reason for choosing any major, of course. But, if you find that you love psychology, you will be happy to know that the chances of being gainfully employed as a psychologist are excellent.

Most counseling psychologists work in schools, aiding individual students before problems become serious.

help with vocational planning. Students who are thinking about careers in counseling and school psychology will be especially interested in the clinical and developmental chapters.

Engineering and Industrial Psychology

Hondo's world was a rather simple one. He ran his ranch on horseback or from his beloved pickup truck. He employed a ranch foreman and a few ranchmen, but each man often spent days working alone. The world in which most people live is not so simple. Many workers operate complicated machines that perform delicate and sometimes dangerous tasks. Most people work with groups, and each day they must deal with other workers and supervisors. The workplace can be a place of great stress and strain. Over the last two decades, psychologists have entered business and industry to help reduce many of the problems that workers face.

Engineering psychology is concerned with making human interactions with tools and machines as comfortable and as error-free as possible. In other words, they work on designing machines that will "fit" people. Engineering psychologists probably played an important role in designing the car you drive; they may have even designed the chair in which you are sitting. The space program employs many engineering psychologists to help design spacesuits, space capsules, and other equipment used by astronauts. Atomic power plants hire engineering psychologists to help design the best control panels for people who operate those plants. The atomic accident at Three Mile Island was caused in part because operators did not respond effectively when a problem first started. Engineering psychologists have been called in to reduce the chance of this problem being repeated and to reduce the probability of human error in power plants.

Industrial psychologists are concerned with selecting, training, and managing employees. People have come to expect not only good paying jobs, but also fulfilling ones. Matching people to jobs that they will learn well and enjoy doing is not only good for people, it is also good business.

Industrial psychologists know what Hondo knew so well: Everyone is special in some way. An important part of an industrial psychologist's job is to make sure that a person's special talents are put to good use. Today, psychologists have more to offer personnel offices than ever before, thanks to intensive investigations of people across the life span.

Other Subfields

The psychology family tree continues to grow. As our world changes and new problems arise, psychologists expand their focus of study to meet these challenges. **Environmental psychology** analyzes how behavior is influenced by environmental factors such as architecture, weather, space, crowding, noise, and pollution. The close relationship between environment and behavior can be appreciated by trying to imagine how Hondo's life would have changed if he lived outside of the Texas ranch country. **Forensic psychology** concerns behaviors that relate to our legal system. Forensic psychologists work with judges and lawyers who are trying to improve the reliability of witnesses and of jury decisions. They consult also on the mental competency of accused people and on the possibilities for rehabilitation of convicted criminals. **Psychology of minorities** examines the behavior of people in minority groups. This subfield is emerging in response to important questions. For example: How important is it for minority children to have minority school teachers for role models? What hiring criterion will give minorities equal opportunities in the business world? What can we do to give minorities equal opportunities in the public school system? **Community psychology** is dedicated to promoting mental health at the community level. Community psychologists prevent and treat psychological problems by working to evaluate and to improve community organizations. They get involved in public programs aimed at such problems as employing the handicapped, rehabilitating juvenile deliquents, and caring for the elderly. These are just some of the new branches on the psychology family tree. We will introduce others later in the book.

As you can see, there are many areas of psychology. Just because they are set off in subfields, you may get the impression that they are

FIGURE 1–2

As can be seen here, most psychologists are engaged in research at universities and colleges, but recently more and more have been entering applied settings, where they use their knowledge to help solve a wide range of problems.

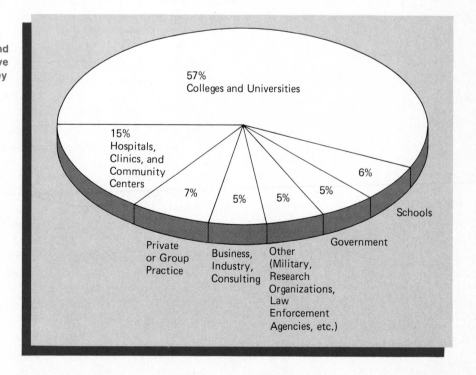

FIGURE 1–3

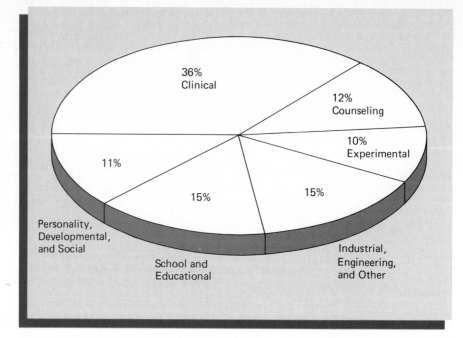

independent of one another. This is far from the case. In fact, the different areas of psychology are very closely related. Research and theory in any one area is important to psychologists in all the other areas. For example, an industrial psychologist must know how people learn (experimental psychology), what workers of different ages are capable of doing (developmental psychology), and the effects of job stress on an employee's emotions and behaviors (clinical psychology). Thus, in order to be a specialist, the psychologist must first have a general background in psychology.

As you read this book, you will see the important links between the various areas of psychology. The differences in the areas are often smaller than the similarities. As is the case in any discipline, psychologists concentrate their study in a subfield because the body of literature in psychology has become so great that it would be nearly impossible to be an expert in all areas. By concentrating in a subfield, a psychologist can best understand the special problems and requirements of that area and will be in the best position to apply the psychological theories and research to that area. The specialization, however, must be built on an understanding of the whole field of psychology.

RESEARCH METHODS IN PSYCHOLOGY

We have seen what psychology is. Now we can ask how psychologists go about studying human behavior. In a sense, all of us are psychologists. We watch other people, guess what they are thinking, and then test out our guesses. Hondo Crouch followed this procedure each time he went on stage. He reports looking over his audience before each show and deciding which jokes they would like. He would then test the correctness of his decisions by watching the audience's reactions to his chosen jokes.

Psychologists follow much the same procedure. They make guesses or **hypotheses** about how people will behave in certain situations. They might hypothesize, for instance, that people will remember notes in a melody better than notes in isolation. Such hypotheses are generally based on a theory. **Theories** are explanations about *why* behaviors occur. The example of remembering a melody better than isolated notes, for instance, could be based on the Gestalt theory that people respond to whole, organized patterns better than to separate elements. Psychologists test hypotheses in experiments. As we will see, there are many kinds of experiments that can be used to examine hypotheses or, in some cases, to help the psychologists develop hypotheses.

In order to see how this process works, let us take an example that was important to Hondo and still is an issue today. Hondo believed that the best way to raise children was to give them a lot of freedom to make their own decisions. However, he was concerned about the effects that television had on his children and he did everything he could to discourage them from watching it. Today, the effect of television on behavior, especially aggressive behavior, is an issue of hot debate. Many people believe that watching violence on television causes people to engage in aggressive actions. Some parents' organizations have called for boycotts of the products of companies who sponsor violent programs on television. On the other hand, there are many people who argue that TV violence does not cause people to act violently. Who is correct? How can psychologists find evidence to resolve this debate?

In Chapter 9 we will discuss in detail the research on this issue. In this chapter, therefore, we will not be concerned as much with the question of who is right; instead, we will simply examine the ways in which the answer can be found.

Case History

One way to look at this question might be to examine newspaper accounts and stories about the lives of some violent criminals. We would want to determine when they started committing violent acts and what television programs they watched. If this information were not available in written sources, we might want to interview people who knew these individuals to get the information. In this way we could learn whether

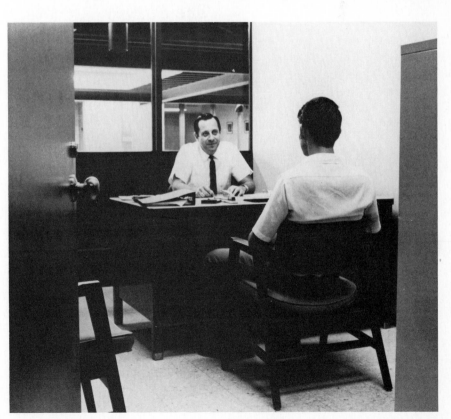

The case study method gathers information by studying in depth a few individuals through interviewing.

these people began acting violently at the same time they began watching many violent TV programs. A different approach would be to examine people's behaviors before and after a violent program was shown. For example, we might know that a very violent movie was going to be shown on nationwide television on the night of December 14. We could examine national crime statistics for the week before and the week after that date to see if there was an increase in violent crime. Both of these approaches are examples of the **case history.**

This method involves studying in depth a few individuals (sometimes only one) or the effects of a single event. The aim is to discover how a certain event affects behavior. The case history method has a number of strong points. It is a relatively easy way to collect a great deal of information in a short time. It examines people's behaviors in their natural surroundings. However, would you be convinced that watching television violence causes people to act aggressively if the case history studies described above reported a relationship between the two events?

Most people would not be convinced. Because the method uses only a few cases, we would not know whether the findings could be applied to everyone. For example, in the first study, we looked only at a few violent criminals. The family and economic backgrounds of these people may have been very different from most other people. If this is the case, two conclusions are possible. First, TV violence may only affect people with these backgrounds. Second, their violent behavior may have been due to their backgrounds and may have had nothing to do with the TV programs they watched. In the second example, it is possible that the violent TV programs caused police to become more concerned about violent crime, causing them to detect and report more crimes. As you can see, it is very difficult to determine the relationship between events using the case history method. For this reason, this method is generally used to help psychologists develop theories and hypotheses. Other methods must be used to make clear tests of the hypotheses.

The Survey

One disadvantage of the case history method is that it focuses on only a few people; we learn a lot about a few people, but we are unable to easily apply the results to a large population. One way around this problem is to design a questionnaire and give it to a large sample of people. In this way we can choose the sample to include people from many different family and economic backgrounds. This is the **survey** method.

We could use this method to look at the effects of television violence. In doing so, we could develop questions that ask people to describe how they behaved after seeing violent TV programs. Then we could have people from all over the country respond to our questionnaire. There are many advantages to surveys. First, we can collect a great deal of information from a large number of people. As we pointed out, we can use people from a number of different backgrounds and ages in our sample. Second, the survey allows for flexibility, so that we can examine a number of questions at the same time. For example, in our questionnaire, besides asking people how they *behaved* after viewing violent TV programs, we might also ask questions about how people *felt* and what they *thought* after seeing these programs. Thus, in addition to finding out how they behaved, we could determine if bad feelings or hostile thoughts were associated with violent programs.

In spite of these advantages, there are a number of problems with surveys. One problem is that people often do not remember their behavior in earlier settings. For example, could you tell someone what you did after lunch last Monday? Another problem is that people may slant their

In the survey method, a questionnaire is designed and given to a large sample of people. Using this method it is possible to interview people from a number of different backgrounds and ages.

answers in order to make themselves look good. In the case of our survey, people may not want to admit that they acted aggressively. A related problem is that people may be responding to the **demand characteristics.** In many cases, people want to be "good" subjects and give experimenters the "right" answers. From the subject's point of view, the right answer is the one that the experimenter is likely to want. Therefore, the subject may look to the experimenter to find cues about what the "right" answer is. For example, you might express very different attitudes toward violence on television to an experimenter from the "Committee to Ban Television Violence" than you would to an experimenter from the "Let's Put Murder Back in Television Committee."

Because of these problems, surveys are often used to obtain preliminary information to guide later research. Surveys in the form of opinion polls are also used to get rough estimates of people's attitudes on issues.

The Psychological Test

Surveys are usually aimed at finding out how people in general react to an event or events. In other words, a survey on TV viewing and behavior might give us an idea about how most people are affected by television. However, what if we wanted to examine how TV violence affected a *specific* group of people? For example, we might believe that TV violence has a different effect on intelligent people as compared to unintelligent people. In order to test this hypothesis, we must first be able to distinguish between intelligent and unintelligent people. A **psychological test** would be used to measure intelligence. Such tests are used to identify individual differences among people. Psychological tests have been developed to measure attitudes, abilities, achievement, and personality traits. They can be very useful tools in both research and applied settings, where the aim is to put people in situations best-suited for their individual abilities and needs.

As we will see in Chapter 11, the construction of tests involves a number of steps. In order to be useful, tests must have **reliability.** That is, they must yield similar results no matter how many times the person takes them. For example, we would expect a person who scores high on an intelligence test one day to also score high a month later. Tests must also have **validity.** In other words, the test must measure what it says it does. A test of capacity to learn is valid, for instance, if it indicates how much people will learn when they are given an equal opportunity to learn.

Naturalistic Observation

There is an old saying that goes, "If you want to know how many teeth are in a horse's mouth, count them." If we were to apply this saying to our question about television, the saying might be changed to, "If we want to know how television affects people, go out and observe people after they have seen violent programs." **Naturalistic observation** is the research method that involves studying people's reactions to naturally occurring events in natural settings. In order to use this method to study the effects of television, we could use hidden cameras to observe children at home and in school settings to see if they aggress after watching violent TV programs.

There are a number of advantages to this method of research. First, the data involves firsthand observations and does not rely on people's memories of events. Second, since people do not know that they are being studied, there are few problems with people wanting to be "good" subjects and somehow doing what they believe the observer wants or expects them to do. Third, people are being observed in their natural environment. This point allows us to feel confident that this is really the way people behave.

Despite these strong points, naturalistic observations have a number of drawbacks:

Naturalistic observation involves studying people's reactions to naturally occuring events in natural settings. Here a psychologist observes parents and children interacting in a classroom.

1. Results are difficult to verify, because natural events seldom reoccur in exactly the same way.
2. They are difficult to analyze precisely because *the amount or degree of a variable such as TV violence may vary considerably in one*

example. The same program, for instance, might have parts ranging from moderately violent to very violent.

3. They cannot establish cause-and-effect relationships. Naturalistic observations can only establish **correlations,** which are measures of the extent to which variables change together. If two variables increase and decrease at the same time, they are *positively correlated.* Watching TV violence and behaving aggressively would be positively correlated if aggressive behavior increased when people watched more TV violence. Measures are *negatively correlated* if one increases while the other decreases. Watching TV violence and behaving aggressively would be negatively correlated if aggressive behavior decreased when people watched more TV violence.

The existence of a correlation does not necessarily indicate a cause-and-effect relationship. If researchers observed a positive correlation between watching TV violence and behaving aggressively, for example, they would be faced with three possible cause-and-effect relationships: (1) TV violence causes aggression; (2) aggressive behavior causes people to watch TV programs that have many violent sequences; and (3) neither factor causes the other (an additional factor, such as grumpiness, could be causing both). That is, grumpiness could cause people to act aggressively *and* to watch more TV violence. These three possibilities are always present when one observes correlations. Despite their drawbacks, however, naturalistic observations are important, especially as a way to come up with ideas that can then be tested in experiments.

The Experiment

When we originally posed our question, we wanted to know whether or not television violence *causes* people to act aggressively. The methods that we have discussed so far may give us clues about the cause-and-effect relationship between these two variables, but we have seen that they cannot definitely establish the cause. In order to determine what events actually cause certain behaviors, psychologists have used experiments.

An **experiment** is an investigation in which a researcher directly manipulates one variable while measuring the effects on some other variable. The manipulated variable is called the **independent variable;** the measured variable is called the **dependent variable.** In one experiment, Liebert and Baron (1972) used TV aggression as an independent variable and play aggression as a dependent variable. Their goal was to test whether or not violent TV programs cause aggressive behavior. The study was made up of boys and girls between the ages of 5 and 9 years. The experimenters assigned half the children to an experimental group in which children watched 3½ minutes of violence on TV (shooting and fighting). The experimenters assigned the other children to a control group in which children watched 3½ minutes of nonviolence on television (racing and high jumping). (A **control group** is made up of subjects who are treated exactly the same as the experimental group except that they are not exposed to the independent variable and thus serve as the basis for comparison.) The experimenters used special procedures to ensure that the two groups were equivalent before they were exposed to the TV programs. After watching TV, both groups had an opportunity to "help" or "hurt" a child playing in another room. The other child was actually an actor who was helping with the experiment. The actor played a game that required turning a handle. Children in the experiment could "help" by pressing one button that supposedly made the handle easier to turn. They could "hurt" by pressing another button that supposedly made the handle

Liebert and Baron's experiment (1972) sought to establish a link between violent TV programs and aggressive behavior on the part of children who watch such programs.

hot and difficult to turn. The actor pretended to be helped or hurt, and the experimenter recorded the length of time that children in the experiment held down each button. Children who had watched violence on TV held down the "hurt" button more and the "help" button less than children who had watched nonviolence. These results suggest that violent TV programs *caused* experimental subjects to act more aggressively than control subjects.

Experimental reports rarely go into detail about how an experiment can test cause-and-effect relationships. The same reasoning would be given repeatedly if they did. Once you know the logic, however, you can read it "between the lines" in every experimental report. The argument can be spelled out for Liebert and Baron's experiment as follows:

The experimental and control conditions were identical except that one group watched violent TV programs and the other watched nonviolent ones. Since there was only one difference, it must have caused the greater aggression in the experimental group. In general terms, the argument is: Since the independent variable is the only difference, it must have caused any effects that were observed in the dependent measure.

Do you agree that Liebert and Baron's experimental and control conditions were identical except for the independent variable? Did the experimenters overlook any other variables that might have differed? Let's examine what Liebert and Baron did, or could have done, to control other variables.

Subject Differences and Randomization. One thing that can differ between experimental and control conditions is the subjects. They can differ in sex, personality, intelligence, and many other variables. Liebert and Baron controlled such subject differences by using random assignments of subjects to groups. This procedure, called **randomization,** ensures that each person has an equal chance of being assigned to each group. This procedure makes it highly probable that subject differences will be equally distributed between groups. One way to make random assignments is to draw names from a list. Put all subject names in a hat; mix them up; draw them blindly, one by one; assign the first draw and all odd-numbered draws to the experimental condition; and finally, assign the second draw and all even-numbered draws to the control condition. Randomization gave Liebert and Baron a basis for saying that their two groups were the same with respect to subject differences. Randomization sometimes fails to equate subjects, which is one reason why it is important to repeat experiments. It is very unlikely that experimental subjects will respond more aggressively in replications of this experiment, if the original results were caused by a failure of randomization.

Subject Expectations and Placebos. We mentioned in our previous discussion of demand characteristics that people's expectations influence their behavior. Perhaps Liebert and Baron's experimental subjects thought that they were expected to be violent, for instance. The experimenters tried to equate such expectations. They did not tell subjects what they were testing until after the experiment. They gave all subjects the same instructions, and they involved all subjects in similar activities before the critical test. Still, one might argue that experimental subjects thought that they were expected to be violent since they had just viewed so much violence. A better control for demand characteristics is possible in drug studies. Experimenters can give both groups pills that look and taste the same. That way both groups can think that they are getting the same drug, when in fact only the experimental group gets a real drug. The control group gets a placebo, which is a look-alike drug substitute made from inactive materials.

Experimenter Bias and Double-Blind Control. Rosenthal (1966) showed that an experimenter's bias can influence the outcome of an experiment. **Experimenter bias** is the expectation on the part of an experimenter that a subject will behave in a certain way. Perhaps Liebert and Baron were biased toward expecting experimental subjects to be more violent. Such a bias would be especially dangerous if the dependent measure had been experimenter ratings of violent behavior. Liebert and Baron reduced this danger by having a machine time the "hurt" and "help" responses. One might argue that some danger remained, however. The experimenters could have unconsciously communicated their expectations to subjects. They might have done this, for example, with facial expressions, gestures, and word selection.

Experimenter bias is controlled best when the experimenter does not know a subject's group assignment until after the experiment. This could have been done in Liebert and Baron's experiment, for example. One experimenter could have controlled the films while another worked with the subjects. In this way, the one working with the subjects would not have to know which film was shown. Ideally, an experimenter should use a double-blind control, which is a procedure in which neither subject nor experimenter is aware of how the independent variable is being manipulated.

Strengths and Weaknesses of Experiments. Liebert and Baron's experiment reveals advantages and disadvantages of experiments. Several strong points are as follows:

1. Experiments can establish cause-and-effect relationships, as we already mentioned. To do so, however, researchers must be sure that they vary only one thing at a time. They must guard against subject differences, subject expectations, and experimenter bias and other hidden differences between experimental and control conditions.
2. Experiments can be repeated by anyone who may wish to verify and extend them. You could get enough information from Liebert and Baron's original report, for instance, to replicate the experiment in detail.

HIGHLIGHT / ETHICAL ISSUES IN PSYCHOLOGICAL RESEARCH

The television set has truly become a member of the American family. It has been estimated that a family is more likely to have a television set than it is to have running water. By the age of 10, a child watches 4–6 hours of television a day. Although there are many topics portrayed on television, one of the most common is violence. On the average, there is a violent act shown on television every 16 minutes; someone is killed on our TV screens every 31 minutes.

These figures are startling enough to motivate even the most ardent TV fan to demand research on the effects of TV violence. Indeed, there has been a great deal of research on this topic; we discuss some of that research in this chapter and will take a closer look at this area in Chapter 9. While we may readily admit the need for research in this area, there is also another issue that must be addressed. That issue is the ethics of research. The question of ethics involves what scientists should be allowed to do to their subjects in order to collect data, and how the rights of subjects can be safeguarded in research.

In order to answer these questions, let us identify some of the potential ethical issues that arise in research. The first is the *invasion of privacy.* In the Liebert and Baron (1972) study, the "invasion" resulted because the experimenters observed and recorded people's behaviors. In other words, they "eaves-dropped" on people and gathered information from them. In this case, the information may not have been considered sensitive. However, in other cases, such as surveys on sexual behavior or illegal activities, the information that is gathered is of a highly sensitive and private nature.

Given that research involves the gathering of information, how can we protect people's rights to privacy? In most studies, subjects' responses are kept *anonymous;* that is, their names or identity are not associated with their data. In the Liebert and Baron study, it would be impossible to find out how a particular child responded, because the children's names were not recorded with their responses. A second safeguard is that the data collected in studies are *not made public.* While a summary of the results of a study may be published, the public is not given access to individual responses. These remain the property of the experimenter. Finally, a policy of *informed consent*

is followed in most cases. Subjects are not forced to answer any question, and they may withdraw from the experiment at any time. Whenever possible, subjects are told about the procedures to be used in the study before they volunteer. When the subjects are children or people in institutions, the procedures of the study are explained to a parent or guardian who must give consent before the subject can take part in the study.

A second ethical issue involves *deception.* In some cases, it would destroy the value of the data if subjects knew *exactly* what the experimenter was studying or what events would occur in the study. For example, if Liebert and Baron (1972) had told subjects that they were interested in studying aggressive behavior, the subjects may have changed their behavior. In this case, the subjects may have become concerned about their own aggression and tried to change their behavior to "look good" to the experimenter. If this happened, the experiment would not have yielded valid data about the effects of TV violence on behavior. However, despite this reason, the point remains that the experimenter has not been truthful with the subject.

3. Experiments can be used to analyze variables precisely, because researchers can control the variables. They could, for instance, make all the TV programs in one experiment moderately violent and all the programs in another experiment very violent.

Experiments also have several weak points:

1. Subjects know that they are being studied, so they may put on a false front. They may, for instance, reduce aggression when they know that they are being observed.
2. Experimental controls sometimes make independent variables unrealistic. Liebert and Baron's experiment suffers from this problem, since 3½ minute segments might not represent normal TV programming or viewing time.
3. Experimental controls can also make dependent variables unrealistic. Critics of Liebert and Baron's study might wonder if pushing a "hurt" button really represents aggressive behavior. We are on solid ground

The ethical rules of psychological research dictate that if deception must be used in research, the experimenter must explain this to the subject after the study is over. During this follow-up session, the experimenter reveals the true nature of the study, what issues were being investigated, and why deception was used. After subjects learn about the study, they are given the chance to demand that their data be destroyed and not be used by the experimenter.

A third ethical problem concerns the possible *harmful consequences* that people may suffer as a result of the study. In studies such as the Liebert and Baron experiment, there are probably very few harmful consequences that can result. At most, some subjects may be stressed by watching the violent activities shown in the TV programs. However, in some psychological experiments, people may be exposed to very stressful procedures. In another area, we are learning today that the United States military conducted studies over 20 years ago in which soldiers were exposed to radiation. In cases like this, severe physical problems may result.

The issue of harmful consequences is a very difficult issue to deal with. In some cases, other procedures that do not involve risk can be used. However, risk may sometimes be necessary in order to investigate the problem at hand. When such a situation arises, the first question to be asked is whether or not the potential benefits of the study are more important than the risks the subjects face. This is clearly a hard question to answer in some cases. Is learning about the effects of TV violence worth the suffering that some subjects may experience while watching this violence? There is no easy formula by which to frame an answer. If the decision is made to proceed with the study despite the risks, at least two steps must be followed. First, subjects must be informed *before* they volunteer to be in the study. Second, the experimenters must "follow up" and examine subjects for some time after the study to see if they are suffering harmful consequences.

Another ethical problem arises from the fact that subjects may be taught something about themselves in the study. For example, subjects in the Liebert and Baron study may have discovered that their behavior is influenced by TV programs. We might argue that this is a valuable lesson for them to learn. However, we must also remember that the subjects did not enter the study wishing to learn about themselves; they may not want to know this information about themselves. And some subjects may be distressed by what they learn about themselves. There is no easy way to deal with this problem. It is important that experimenters be aware of this ethical issue and evaluate their procedures with it in mind.

Ethical issues have long been a concern of psychologists. The issue of ethics is not confined to laboratory studies; it involves all methods. In 1973, the American Psychological Association published ethical guidelines for psychological research. All research that is supported by United States grants must be examined by a panel of qualified experts to ensure that they follow ethical guidelines. In most universities and colleges, investigators must submit their research proposals to "ethics committees" before they conduct their studies. The committees evaluate the risks of the research and the safeguards, and they may suggest alternative procedures. The question of ethics is clearly a difficult one. The ethical standards for research have become more strict over the last decade and researchers are continuing to develop new safeguards for their subjects. As you read about the studies presented in this book, you may wish to examine them in light of our discussion on ethics.

if we conclude that watching violent sequences on television causes children to hold down a "hurt" button longer. We are on thin ice if we try to generalize beyond the experiment to say that violence in normal TV programming causes children to be more aggressive.

Some of these weaknesses can be overcome by moving experiments from laboratories to more natural settings. Liebert and Baron's study is an example of a laboratory experiment, which is done in a controlled environment created for the experiment. In contrast, a field experiment is done in a more natural setting. Chapter 9 will discuss a field experiment on TV violence. Experimenters manipulated TV programming in a juvenile home setting, and they measured aggressive behavior in the same setting. Direct manipulations of TV programming gave more control than one gets in naturalistic observations. Doing the experiment in an everyday setting made the independent and dependent variables more realistic. Such field experiments are becoming increasingly popular.

Research Methods: A Final Comment

As you can see, psychologists have developed a number of ways to study behavior. Each one has strengths and weaknesses. The experiment is the most widely used method because it allows for the greatest amount of control and enables investigators to determine cause-and-effect relationships. However, just as a carpenter cannot build a house with only one tool, neither can psychologists build an understanding of human behavior with only one method of research. Therefore, all research methods are used, often to study the same issue. Imagine what a strong case for the effects of television researchers could make if they found the same results in a case history, a naturalistic observation, and an experiment. Thus, the different research methods are often used to increase the credibility of results. The variety of methods are also important because there are some events that can only be studied with certain methods. For example, you couldn't study reactions to natural disasters in the laboratory, you'd have to use one of the other methods.

Thus, no one method is perfect. There is a time and place for each one. The use of many different methods to study the same problem enables the investigator to build a convincing case.

We have concentrated on methods for collecting results. The Appendix discusses closely related methods for analyzing results. It also gives suggested readings on collecting and analyzing behavioral data.

SUMMARY

1. **Psychology** is the scientific study of behavior and the applications gained from that knowledge. Its main goals are to clearly describe, predict, and explain behavior.

2. The most cited date for the birth of psychology is 1879, which is when Wundt set up the first psychological laboratory in Leipzig, Germany. Wundt and Titchener are credited with developing **structuralism,** which is concerned with identifying the elements of human experience and finding out how those elements combine to form thoughts and feelings.

3. **Functionalism** is concerned with the function of mental processes. This emphasis led to important applications in education and to the founding of educational psychology.

4. **Gestalt psychology** was based on the assumption that many experiences cannot be broken down into separate elements—they must be experienced as wholes, or gestalts. Gestalt psychologists worked at identifying these and other organizational laws of perception.

5. Watson said that we did not need such unobservable events as thinking or feeling to explain behavior. He said that behavior could be explained and predicted by focusing only on observable stimuli and responses, the basis of the **behaviorist approach** to psychology.

6. Sigmund Freud is the founder of the **psychoanalytic approach** to psychology, which focuses on unconscious motivations that control human behavior. Freud thought that many of these unconscious thoughts and wishes are the result of our experiences during infancy and early childhood.

7. The **humanistic approach** to psychology is based on the idea that people are basically good, and, given the proper environment, will strive to achieve positive social goals.

8. By the 1950s psychology had established itself as a major area for scientific study. Since that time a number of subfields of psychology

have developed, in which many of the approaches we have discussed are used. These subfields include the following: **physiological, experimental, cognitive, developmental, social, personality, clinical, counseling** and **school, engineering,** and **industrial psychology.** Some of the most recent subfields to develop are **environmental psychology, forensic psychology,** and **psychology of minorities.**

9. In psychological research, scientists make **hypotheses** about how people will behave in certain situations. These hypotheses, which can be tested experimentally, are based on **theories,** which are explanations about *why* behaviors occur. A number of different research methods were discussed, including: **case history, survey, psychological test, naturalistic observation,** and **experiment.**

10. An **experiment** is an investigation in which a researcher directly manipulates one variable while measuring the effects on some other variable. The manipulated variable is the **independent variable.** The **dependent variable** is measured to see the effects on it of the manipulation of the independent variable.

11. There are a number of other elements or variables in an experiment that must be carefully controlled. For example, **randomization** assures that subject differences will be equally distributed between the control group and the experimental group, and **double-blind controls** assure that **experimenter bias** cannot affect subjects or the researcher's perceptions of what occurs in the experiment.

SUGGESTED READINGS

The following book is about Hondo Crouch:

PATTERSON, B. C. *Hondo, my father.* Austin, Tex.: Shoal Creek Publishers, 1979.

American Psychological Association. *A career in psychology.* This booklet outlines career opportunities and the training required in subfields of psychology. It can be obtained by writing the American Psychological Association, 1200 Seventeenth Street N.W., Washington, D.C. 20036.

Annual Review of Psychology. A separate book each year reviews recent literature in about twenty different areas of psychology. An excellent starting point for those who wish to get into the technical literature of psychology.

BRENNAN J. F. *History and systems of psychology.* Englewood Cliffs, N.J.: Prentice-Hall, 1982. Provides a solid foundation for understanding psychology's present and future by tracing its history and development.

MARX, M. H., and HILLIX, W. A. *Systems and theories in psychology.* New York: McGraw-Hill, 1979. Introduces students to classical and contemporary approaches to the science of psychology.

WATSON, R. I. *The great psychologists: From Aristotle to Freud.* Philadelphia: Lippincott, 1978. Traces the history of psychology through the works of those who shaped the field. Interesting reading for those who enjoy biographies.

WEGENER, B. (Ed.). *Social attitudes and psychophysical measurement.* Hillsdale, N.J.: Erlbaum, 1982. Individual chapters by authorities not only give a solid foundation in psychological measurement procedures, but also relate those procedures to social applications.

Biology and Behavior

BEHAVIORAL NEUROSCIENCE

NEURONS: BASIC UNITS OF THE NERVOUS SYSTEM
Neural Impulses / Synaptic Transmission

ANATOMY OF THE NERVOUS SYSTEM
The Brain / HIGHLIGHT: Close-up on Nobel Prize-Winning Research / The Spinal Cord

FUNCTIONAL SUBDIVISIONS OF THE NERVOUS SYSTEM
The Reticular Activating System / The Limbic System / The Autonomic Nervous System
Control of Skeletal Muscles / Language Control Centers

THE ENDOCRINE SYSTEM
Structure / Function

GENETICS
The Biochemistry of Genes / The Structure and Function of Chromosomes
Genetic Laws of Inheritance
HIGHLIGHT: Genetic Engineering

SUMMARY / SUGGESTED READINGS

Kathy Morris, a pretty 22-year-old singer, lay on an X-ray table, surrounded by massive machinery. Metal clamps gripped her head and orange crosses marked her temples and forehead. She was too drugged to be scared. Even the antiseptic smell did not frighten her today. Still, she tensed when doctors cut a small incision on her leg, and guided a tube into a major artery. Kathy watched X-ray pictures of the procedure on closed-circuit television while the doctors pushed the tube up the artery, into her heart, and out again. The tube slithered on slowly until it came to rest in a neck artery. Then the manmade serpent released a radioactive dye directly into the arteries and veins in her head. As Kathy felt a burning sensation in her head, the X-ray machines began to buzz and click. After a few moments the burning subsided and a doctor turned to Kathy, saying, "It's a very good angiogram."

The tube retreated faster than it had advanced, leaving only a small wound as evidence of its invasion. The wound was closed, and Kathy was wheeled to a waiting room while the doctors examined her X-rays.

As she waited, Kathy wondered, "How could all this happen to me so suddenly?" But was it really so sudden? She knew she had ignored the warning signs before her seizure last night. Several months ago, while driving alone from her home in New York to visit her brother, her memory failed her. All of a sudden she couldn't remember who she was supposed to visit. Perhaps her brother. She tried to phone him, but she couldn't remember his number. In fact, she could not remember his name, or her own name! She did manage to find her nameless brother, however, because she recognized the streets. She knew the way, even though she had forgotten the street names.

"Now, why did I ignore this warning? And earlier warnings, too!" Kathy asked herself. For over a year she hadn't been herself. She had spent money foolishly; she ate like a pig; she seemed as moody and changeable as spring weather—sunshine one day, thunderstorms the next. She had abused her friends, lied at least 10 to 20 times a day, missed appointments, and cut her music classes. "How could *I* miss my music classes?" she wondered, "I'm more than just a student there; I'm a singer. Singing is my life; I live for my music."

While Kathy meditated, her doctors were conferring over her angiogram. They minutely examined every blood vessel in her brain, looking for deviations from normal pathways. As they had feared, the angiogram indicated a brain tumor. There was some good news, however. The tumor they found was not malignant and had not spread throughout her brain. Since it lay on the surface of the brain, the doctors felt fairly certain that it could be successfully removed. But they were still very concerned. The tumor was located just above and in front of Kathy's left ear, directly over the brain's speech center. One slip during surgery might destroy her ability to speak, read, write, and sing.

The task of explaining the dangers to Kathy fell to Dr. Cunnought, the neurosurgeon who was to perform the operation. He spoke with her briefly after the angiogram and again the following day. He thought the operation would be, in his words, "a piece of cake." Dutifully, however, he told her of the possible hazards. She might die—always a possibility in major surgery. Or, she might become a "vegetable," totally or partially paralyzed. Her ability to speak, write, and sing might be lost. Kathy listened, but the full significance of the doctor's words didn't sink in right away. She could not believe or accept the idea that she might lose her voice. Of all the possible dangers of surgery, the loss of her voice seemed to her the most horrible.

Suddenly an uncontrollable rage built up inside her; her right side trembled, her eyes widened, and she burst into a violent temper tantrum. She screamed, "I'd just as soon die as lose my voice!"

Next morning when Kathy saw Dr. Cunnought, all she could say was, "Let's go, I'm ready." Shortly afterward she was in the operating room under a bright light and surrounded by even more machines than she had seen the last time. The last thing Kathy said before the anesthesia took effect was, "Hurry up."

The brain beats. Throbbing with every heartbeat, it looks as mysterious as it is. It looks like a pulsating relief map with several major valleys and many shallow folds. When Dr. Cunnought first saw Kathy's exposed brain, he was delighted, exclaiming, "This looks good, it looks just fine, everything is really fine." Even though it had a tumor, the brain looked healthy, its color a bright pinkish-gray and its "landmarks" were right.

Perhaps the main reason for Dr. Cunnought's optimism at this point was the absence of swelling in Kathy's brain. He had read reports in the medical literature of four cases in which the patients' brains had expanded for no discernible reason. All four patients had died.

Cunnought strapped on a pair of magnifying glasses and focused on his hands to make sure the lenses were adjusted properly. After a few moments he announced, "We seem to be running out of room here. I don't think I can see very well. The space here seems to be getting smaller."

Luddy, the resident who was assisting at the operation, said, "Are your glasses okay?"

Cunnought stepped back and looked at his hands. "The glasses seem to be normal," he replied. Looking at Kathy he said, "I think this brain is swelling up." He mentally reviewed his own procedure. What had he done wrong?

Other surgeons might have given up at this point, but not Cunnought. He knew there was a chance—a small chance—that something in the right half of Kathy's brain might be causing the problem. Now that Kathy was dying, a slim chance seemed better than none at all, and Cunnought was willing to gamble on it. In an unprecedented surgical procedure, Cunnought turned Kathy over and prepared the right side of her head for surgery while the left side was still open. He drilled through her skull again, hoping to see blood, find its source, and stop its flow. He found no blood.

When he looked back at the left side of the brain, Cunnought saw that it had stopped pulsating and had become puffy, yellow, and bloody. The brain had expanded, smashing itself against the skull's abrasive edge. Now there was no way for Cunnought to find and remove the tumor. The machines monitoring Kathy's vital signs said she was alive, but Cunnought thought she was well beyond rescue.

Cunnought, one of the world's finest neurosurgeons, had never learned to lose.

He had successfully completed many far more complicated operations. How could this "piece of cake" have gone wrong? With this question tormenting him, he flew into a rage when he found that Kathy's brain had enlarged so much that even closing up after the surgery was impossible. Plunging his index and middle fingers into the puffy mass, he scooped out a portion of her brain, turned, and threw the bloody tissue at the wall. Turning from the splattered wall he said, "Now there's room to close. We'll prepare the body for autopsy."

Patrick, Kathy's brother, received the shocking news by phone at 4:00 that afternoon. He rushed to the hospital, hoping to get there before she died. When the doctors told him they were almost certain she was dying, he decided to watch over her until the end. But her condition, instead of deteriorating, improved hour by hour. By mid-morning Kathy uttered her first words, repeating what she'd said as she went into the operation: "Hurry up."

During the next several weeks Kathy made steady progress, but then her condition began to get worse again. Dr. Cunnought knew that she would die unless the tumor was removed; however, he also knew that another operation would probably kill her. But the odds seemed to mean little in Kathy's case. The second time, with the decks stacked against surgery, everything went smoothly.

The second operation produced no new side effects. Kathy still was experiencing all the complications caused by the earlier surgery, but she began to improve steadily. Determined to get better, she began physical therapy classes and learned how to sit up

and how to walk again. She relearned how to read and how to write her name by tracing it over and over again on a piece of paper. Though she recalled parts of her past, she had difficulty talking about it. Words would enter her mind, but she could not always express them. She learned to feed herself and began to learn how to take care of herself.

Kathy also learned to accept that she will never do some things again. She will never feel heat or cold on her right side and will never be able to see to the right out of either eye. She will never dance. Though she can visualize dance steps, she cannot perform the complicated sequence of movements involved.

Kathy has learned to accept these handicaps and to compensate for them. Today, a person meeting her for the first time would notice nothing extraordinary about her. Nothing extraordinary, that is, except her magnetism and her beautiful voice. Her rhythm, pitch, tone, and vocal attack are still those of an opera singer. Once again, as before, Kathy is a singer.

BEHAVIORAL NEUROSCIENCE

Kathy's struggle for life raises important questions: Why did Kathy's tumor increase her appetite, make her depressed, disrupt her memory, and alter her personality? How did Cunnought know that Kathy's tumor threatened her singing? Why did the swelling in Kathy's brain blind her only on her right side? Why did it destroy her sense of touch only on her right side? Why did it make it temporarily difficult for her to sit up or walk, and permanently impossible for her to dance? Why did it make it difficult for her to converse, read, and write? Such questions are the concern of *behavioral neuroscientists,* who study the biological underpinnings of behavior. We will address these questions in the second half of this chapter. In the first half we will examine the brain's basic properties. The brain is part of a pervasive system, the *nervous system,* which monitors our outside world, controls our movements, learns, remembers, and generally controls all of our behavior.

The nervous system works in harmony with the *endocrine system,* which controls body chemistry. Some of Kathy's symptoms may have been related to chemical changes. In our discussion of the endocrine system, we will consider the possibility that Kathy's tumor triggered a chain reaction of events in her body's chemistry.

Kathy's struggle brings to mind the many ways that each of us depends on our body. Even a healthy body can impose limitations: A 5 foot, 7 inch male who weighs 147 pounds will probably not be a professional football player, for example. The last section of this chapter discusses how we inherited our body from our parents. That is, it reviews *genetics,* which is the study of how traits are passed on from parent to child.

The first section will discuss the brain in the context of a general overview of the nervous system. Without necessarily denying differences between brains and machines (see Koestler, 1967), neuroscientists analyze brains the way engineers analyze machines. *Neuroanatomists* describe structural elements of the brain and how they are arranged. *Neurophysiologists* study how the parts function. We will describe both structure and function of the nervous system's specialized cells and of the nervous system's major anatomical subdivisions.

NEURONS: BASIC UNITS OF THE NERVOUS SYSTEM

Kathy gave an early sign of recovery when she said, "Hurry up." How did her brain initiate and control this miraculous utterance? We begin our search for an explanation by exploring the brain's basic components, neurons, which are cells that are specialized to send and receive information.

Our brain contains between 100 and 200 billion neurons. As shown in Figure 2–1, they are similar to all other cells in that they have a *cell nucleus* within a *cell body,* surrounded by a *cell membrane.* Unlike other cells, however, neurons have tiny fibers extending out from their body that allow them to communicate with other cells. Many short branches called dendrites receive messages from surrounding cells and carry them to the cell body. A single long extension called an axon carries messages away from the cell body toward terminal branches that reach out to many other cells. Most axons are 1 or 2 inches long, but some are as long as

FIGURE 2–1

Drawing and photographs of some typical neurons.

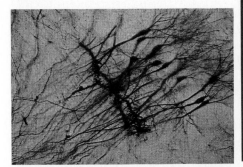

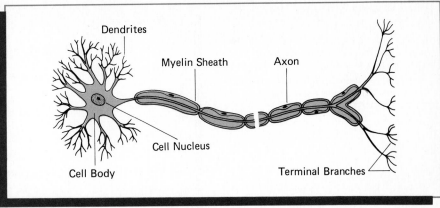

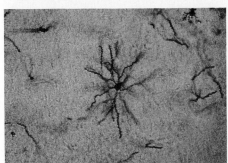

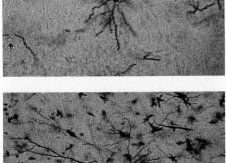

3 feet. Some axons have a fatty covering called a **myelin sheath,** which is pinched in at intervals. Neural messages travel faster on myelinated axons because the messages skip from one pinched spot to the next. Let's look first at what neural messages are, and then discuss the way they are transmitted.

Neural Impulses

Kathy's attempt to communicate with her doctors and nurses depended on a complex communication system operating inside her nervous system. Kathy's message, "Hurry up," began with activity in one or more neurons in the form of a neural impulse or message, spread methodically through a network of neurons, and ended with well-coordinated muscle movements. Understanding neural impulses is the key to understanding the language used within the nervous system.

Neurons "speak" a simple language, consisting of an "off-on" code. A neuron is "off" at all times, except during neural impulses. During the "off" or *resting state*, a neuron has an electric tension, or **membrane potential,** existing between the cell's inside and outside environments. The potential is caused by an attraction that exists between negatively and positively charged particles, or ions. During the resting state, there are more positively charged ions outside the cell, and more negatively charged ions inside the cell. This resting state of tension is sometimes called a state of **polarization.**

Correspondingly, the "on" state, or neural impulse, is called **depolarization.** It happens when the cell membrane momentarily opens to positive sodium ions, causing the charge inside the cell to go from negative to positive relative to the outside. When the charge reaches the critical value shown in Figure 2–2, the membrane closes to sodium ions, and positive potassium ions are pumped out, bringing the charge back to the resting level.

As soon as the firing process ends in one spot on a neuron, it starts at a neighboring spot, spreading the impulse down the entire length of the neuron. In cells with large myelinated axons, the neural impulses travel at speeds of nearly 400 feet per second. Small axons without myelin sheaths carry impulses as slow as 3 feet per second. When neural impulses reach the end of an axon, they are sent on to other neurons.

This off-on firing process can happen spontaneously, but it is usually triggered by electrical impulses from other neurons. The interaction is what spreads neural messages through the nervous system. Sending messages from one neuron to another depends both on the state of the receiving cell and on the strength of the incoming message or stimulation.

Cells are not always responsive. When a cell fires once, it will not fire again for about 1 millisecond. After this **absolute refractory period,**

FIGURE 2–2

Neural impulses occur when a cell membrane momentarily changes. The inside of the neuron goes from negative to positive with respect to the outside when the membrane changes. The graph above shows the magnitude and duration of the voltage changes.

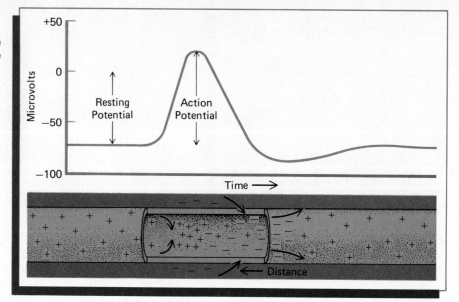

a cell enters a **relative refractory period** for a few milliseconds, during which time it fires only in response to a very strong impulse.

An incoming impulse must be above a minimum level or threshold of intensity or else a cell will not fire. If the threshold is too low, the membrane will not open up to sodium. Cell thresholds are sometimes compared to triggers on a gun. You must pull a trigger hard enough or a gun won't fire. If you pull a trigger even harder, however, the bullet will not travel any faster or any farther. In the same way, cell firing is an all-or-none action. No response occurs for stimuli below the threshold level; a full response occurs for stimuli at or above the cell threshold as long as the receiving cell is ready to fire. A neuron sends different messages, not by changing the strength of its response, but by changing the *rate* of its response. Stronger stimuli are indicated by faster firing rates.

Synaptic Transmission

We have seen how an impulse moves down an axon of one cell; this is called axonal transmission. **Synaptic transmission** occurs as the impulse moves from one neuron to another. It is called synaptic because a junction between two neurons is called a **synapse.** As Kathy's "Hurry up" message raced through her nervous system, it darted through millions of synapses. Let's look at just one of them to see how it works.

Each synapse has four parts: (1) the **axon terminal,** a tiny knob at the end of an axon's terminal branch; (2) the dendrite of the receiving cell; (3) the **synaptic space,** a very small gap between the axon terminal of one cell and the dendrite of the next cell; and (4) the **synaptic vesicles,** tiny oval sacs on the axon terminal filled with a chemical transmitter substance. In most neurons, when an impulse reaches an axon terminal, the synaptic vesicles release a chemical that travels across the synaptic space to a dendrite on a receiving neuron (see Figure 2–3).

Chemical Transmitters. Scientists have learned within the last 60 years that the nervous system contains many kinds of **chemical transmitters.** All carry messages between neurons, but different kinds of chemical transmitters carry different messages. Some excite neurons (that is, they cause the receiving neuron to fire); others inhibit neurons (that is, they keep the receiving neuron from firing). Some transmitters shout loudly and call for a fast response; others speak softly and influence neurons slowly but surely.

FIGURE 2-3

Synaptic transmission occurs when a
neurotransmitter carries a neural impulse
from the axon of one neuron to the
dendrites of another.

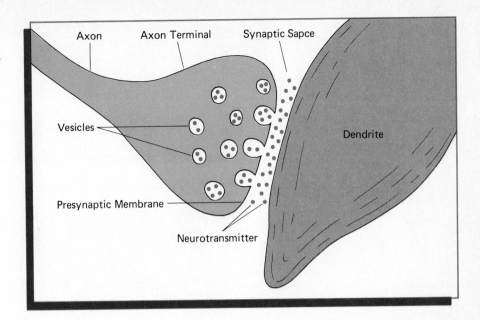

The most common transmitter is **acetylcholine (ACh)**. Synapses using ACh usually transmit strong, fast-acting, excitatory messages. After ACh delivers its message, it is broken down so that it is prevented from activating the receiving neuron again. ACh components are then transported back to the axon terminal, reassembled, and stored again in the synaptic vesicles.

Research on ACh has led to important applications, including a better understanding of such diseases as myasthenia gravis, a deadly disease in which synaptic transmission fatigues rapidly, preventing normal movement and breathing. Botulism, another deadly disease, works by blocking the release of ACh, which results in paralysis. On the other hand, if too much ACh builds up in the synaptic space, which is the effect of certain poisons (such as the venom of the black widow spider), the neuron can no longer respond to it, again causing paralysis and, in extreme cases, death.

Another important kind of transmitter is a class of substances known as **catecholamines**. Synapsis using catecholamines typically transmits slow-acting, inhibitory messages. Unlike ACh, catecholamines are not broken down after they deliver their message. They are cleared out through a powerful transport system that then restores them in synaptic vesicles. This process keeps the catecholamines from activating the receiving neuron again after their message is delivered.

Research on catecholamines has led to important applications, including a better understanding of mental disorders and of commonly used drugs. We now know, for example, that cocaine works by blocking the reuptake process of catecholamines. Cocaine is used medically to render a local area insensitive to pain. It is also misused by some as a recreational drug. Unsupervised use of cocaine can be dangerous because it can have toxic effects, including dizziness, convulsions, and drastic drops in blood pressure. Popular amphetamines or "pep pills" (such as Benzedrine and Dexedrine) not only block reuptake of catecholamines, they also produce an additional chemical response leading to a general state of arousal. Their unsupervised usage is also quite dangerous, especially for people with high blood pressure or women in the early stages of pregnancy.

It is hardly surprising that interference with synaptic transmission can have serious, even fatal, effects when we consider the fact that individual neurons never operate in isolation. Neurons are subsystems whose actions are integrated to form larger subsystems, which in turn are coordinated to form still larger and more complex systems.

In the next section, we will consider some of the major anatomical subdivisions of the nervous system, a major coordinating system in the body.

ANATOMY OF THE NERVOUS SYSTEM

Have you ever tried to place a long distance call on a holiday only to find the lines jammed for hours on end? Telephone operators cannot avoid telephone traffic jams on holidays, even with the help of computers. Yet the brain avoids neural traffic jams, even though "traffic" is much heavier in the nervous system than it is in the Bell System. In fact, if we compare a single message sent between two neurons with a single phone call between two houses, Kathy's simple "hurry up" message produced more "traffic" than that occurring in the telephone system on the very busiest holidays. The nervous system is more efficient because of its highly organized structure. In this section, we will discuss that structure by analyzing major components of the nervous system.

We will necessarily introduce many new terms. The best way to learn them is not as a random list, but as an organized set of interrelated parts. Since the interrelationships can be hard to keep track of at first, Table 2–1 presents an overview of the overlapping contrasts between major components. It gives both structural and functional characteristics, because it is useful to learn how these two aspects correspond. For the same reason, both structure and function are discussed in this and the next section. Use Table 2–1 as we go through both sections. We will begin our discussion with the brain, the master controller.

The Brain

Dr. Cunnought knew exactly where he could cut during Kathy's surgery because he knew the relationship between brain structures and functions. Most of us will not perform neural surgery in the near future, so we don't need to learn brain anatomy in detail. Many of you will continue to study psychology, however, and you will find a basic understanding of brain structures invaluable in your studies.

The human brain is about 3 pounds of soft, spongy, pinkish-gray nerve tissue, made up of billions of neurons. In this section we will discuss divisions and subdivisions of groups of these neurons and the ways in they which are connected. Divisions can be identified on the basis of both structure and function. Here we will focus on structural divisions. It is easiest to see structural divisions in a developing human embryo, where the neural tube is divided into three cores arranged in a row, with one near the bottom (the hindbrain), one in the middle (the midbrain), and one near the top (the forebrain).

Hindbrain. The part of the brain that develops from the bottom core in the embryonic neural tube is called the **hindbrain.** It is shown in Figure 2–4 along with its three main components:

1. The lowest part of the hindbrain is the **medulla,** a slender tube no larger than your finger. It houses nerve centers that control breathing, heartbeat, and posture. For this reason, even slight damage to the medulla could be fatal.
2. Above the medulla is the **pons,** a broader tube formed by a massive cable of nerve fibers. It connects the medulla to the midbrain. If

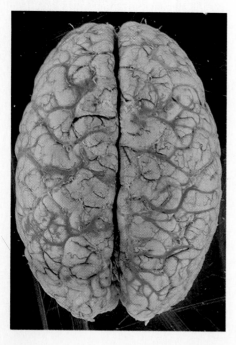

The human brain is about 3 pounds of soft, spongy, pinkish-gray nerve tissue, made up of billions of neurons.

TABLE 2–1: Overview of Endocrine and Nervous Systems

Contrasts between Subdivisions	Structural or Anatomical Characteristics	Functional or Physiological Characteristics
Endocrine System vs. 	A system of internal organs or glands that secrete chemical messengers directly into the bloodstream	Has slow-acting, long-duration effects on the integration and regulation of body activity
Nervous System	A highly organized systems of nerve tissue which is tissue that transmits electrochemical messengers between cells	Integrates and regulates body activity
Central Nervous System vs. 	Nerve tissue within the brain and spinal cord	Collects sensory information about our environment and controls body activity
Peripheral Nervous System	Nerve tissue outside the brain and spinal cord that connects those structures with sense organs, muscles, and glands	Provides pathways for incoming sensory information about the environment and for outgoing commands that control bodily activities
Sensory Portion of Nervous System vs. 	Central and peripheral nerve tissue involved in collecting and analyzing information from specialized receptors such as eyes and ears	Reports and analyzes the nature of conditions around our body
Motor Portion of Nervous System	Central and peripheral nerve tissue involved in controlling muscles	Maintains body posture and makes the body move effectively as a whole
Voluntary Portion of Motor Subdivision vs. 	Central and peripheral nerve tissue connected with skeletal muscles	Controls body posture and movement, often (but not always) with voluntary control
Autonomic Nervous System or Involuntary Portion of Motor Subdivision	Central and peripheral nerve tissue connected with muscles of internal organs and with glands	Controls internal organs and glands, often (but not always) without voluntary control
Sympathetic Division of Autonomic Nervous System vs. 	Contains chiefly fibers that activate their targets to use energy	Prepares our body for action
Parasympathetic Division of Autonomic Nervous System	Contains chiefly fibers that cause their targets to burn less energy	Opposes and compensates for sympathetic effects allowing body to relax

this cable were damaged, you might develop a sleep disorder similar to the "restless-leg" syndrome, which would result in thrashing about during sleep to the point where you would repeatedly wake yourself. This effect on movement makes sense when you consider the third hindbrain component, which is one of the units tied into the massive pons cells.

3. The third part of the hindbrain is the cerebellum, which looks like

FIGURE 2–4

Hindbrain, midbrain, and forebrain.

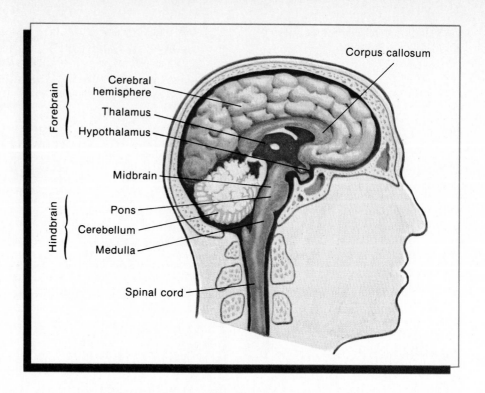

two wrinkled hemispheres strapped onto the back of the pons. It coordinates the force, range, and rate of body movements. If your cerebellum were injured or even destroyed, you would still enjoy all the sensations of the world around you (such as sights, sounds, and smells), but you would lose muscular tone, strength, and coordination.

Midbrain. Above the pons and cerebellum is a still wider tube, the midbrain, which develops from the middle core of the embryo brain. So many vital nerve tracts run up and down it that you would face unconsciousness, if not death, if your midbrain were damaged. The core of the midbrain contains the *reticular formation*, which seems to regulate the strength of responses in surrounding brain areas. The midbrain and hindbrain are together referred to as the brainstem.

Forebrain. The rest of the brain develops from the top core of the embryo brain and is called the forebrain. It is shown in Figure 2–4 along with three main components:

1. Directly over the brainstem, in the central core of the forebrain, lies the hypothalamus. It includes several centers, some of which control body temperature and the rate at which you burn fat and carbohydrates. Since the hypothalamus influences these and other body maintenance functions, injury could be disastrous. Damage to your hypothalamus could hinder your bowel movements, urinary output, sweating, alertness, and reaction to pleasure and pain. The role of the hypothalamus in eating is described in more detail in Chapter 9.

2. Above the hypothalamus are two egg-shaped structures called the thalamus. It is often called a relay station, because sensory pathways from all over the body pass through it. Brain relay stations, including the thalamus, modify incoming information by integrating it with information coming from other parts of the body. Injury to the thalamus would distort your sensations of the world around you.

3. Mushrooming out from the brainstem are two wrinkled hemispheres

FIGURE 2–5

A comparison of cerebrums in a number of different species.

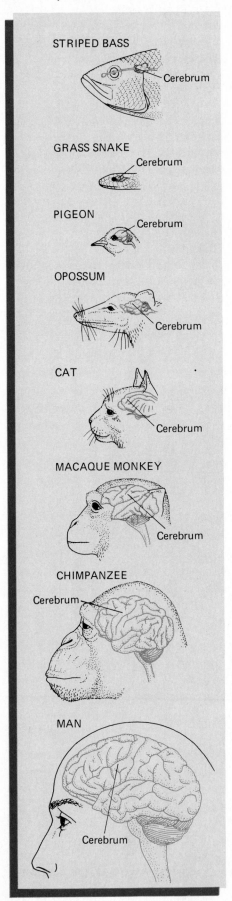

STRIPED BASS
Cerebrum

GRASS SNAKE
Cerebrum

PIGEON
Cerebrum

OPOSSUM
Cerebrum

CAT
Cerebrum

MACAQUE MONKEY
Cerebrum

CHIMPANZEE
Cerebrum

MAN
Cerebrum

called the **cerebral cortex,** or **cerebrum.** This is the part of Kathy's brain that Dr. Cunnought exposed when he drilled through her skull. It is the part that contained her tumor and the part that was partially scooped out in order to close up the skull after the first surgery. It is the crown jewel of our brain, accounting for about 80 percent of the brain's weight. Among other functions, it governs our most advanced human capabilities, including abstract reasoning and speech. It is more highly developed in humans than in other animals, as shown in Figure 2–5. The effects of injury to the cerebrum depend on which area is injured. We have already considered the consequences of damaging Kathy's speech center, which is an area of the cerebrum located above and in front of the left ear. We will examine the speech center and other areas in more detail. But first let's point out some landmarks for our discussion.

The cerebrum is divided into left and right *cerebral hemispheres* which are connected by a large cable of nerve fibers called the **corpus callosum.** Figure 2–6 shows a side view of the cerebral hemispheres. Three deep grooves, or *fissures,* are labeled, as are four well-defined areas called *lobes.* The fissures are: (1) the **longitudinal fissure,** which separates the two hemispheres; (2) the *lateral fissure,* or **fissure of Sylvius,** which, if you view the figure as a boxing glove, defines the thumb of the glove; and (3) the *central fissure,* or **fissure of Rolando,** which runs across the knuckle area of our imaginary boxing glove.

These fissures separate each hemisphere into four lobes. The cortex in front of the central fissure and above the lateral fissure makes up the **frontal lobe.** It receives sensory impulses after they have been processed by other lobes, and it sends out commands to muscles to make voluntary movements. The **occipital lobe** is the hindmost lobe. This lobe receives visual impulses from the eyes. The **parietal lobe** extends back from the central fissure to the occipital lobe, and responds to touch, pain, and temperature. Finally, the **temporal lobe** is below the lateral fissure and in front of the occipital lobe. (It is the thumb of our imaginary boxing

FIGURE 2–6

Side view of a cerebral hemisphere, showing the various lobes and fissures.

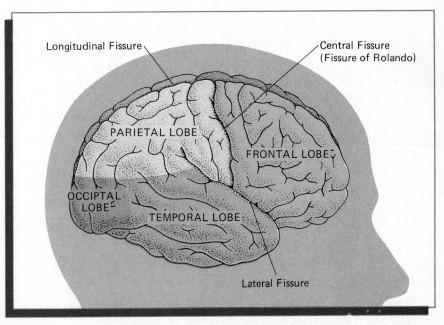

Longitudinal Fissure

Central Fissure (Fissure of Rolando)

PARIETAL LOBE

FRONTAL LOBE

OCCIPITAL LOBE

TEMPORAL LOBE

Lateral Fissure

glove.) The temporal lobe receives sound and smell impulses and has centers that control speech.

There is a band of cerebral cortex at the top of the head, on either side of the central fissure, that controls sensory and motor responses. The **motor cortex,** which is directly in front of the central fissure, controls motor responses of the body. The **somatosensory cortex,** which is directly behind the central fissure, controls sensory responses of the body.

We owe most of what we know about the motor and somatosensory cortexes to the research of Wilder Penfield, a Canadian neurosurgeon. He determined which parts of these cortexes affect which parts of the body. Penfield did his research while surgically treating epilepsy. His technique allowed the patient to remain awake and alert during the operation. Penfield then was able to "map" areas of the cortex by stimulating a certain part and recording the patient's response. When he stimulated the motor cortex, muscles would move; when he stimulated the somatosensory areas, people felt sensations in various parts of their body, which they would report to him. Figure 2–7 shows the specific connections that Penfield discovered; note how much of the cortex is devoted to certain areas of the body, and how little to other areas.

The effects of injury to the cerebrum depend upon which area is injured. Although Kathy's tumor was located in her left temporal lobe, and parts

FIGURE 2–7

Motor and somatosensory cortexes have regions that are associated with specific body parts. The relationships are shown by drawing body parts over the corresponding brain areas. The body parts are drawn smaller or larger to reflect the amount of brain surface devoted to each.

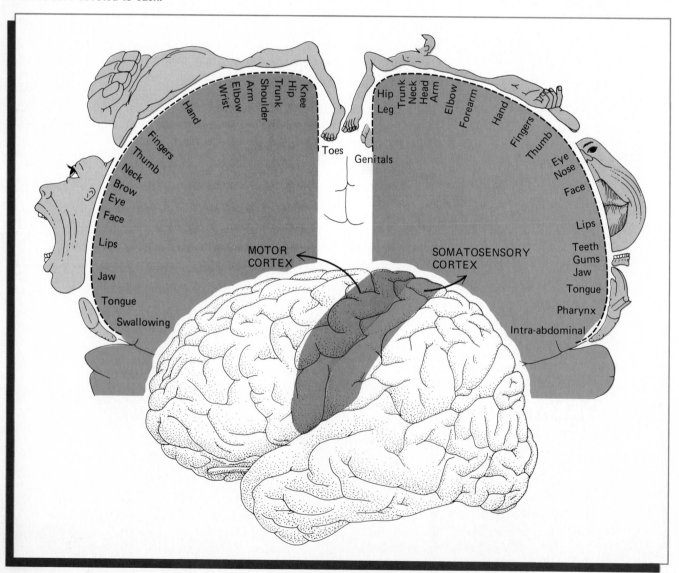

HIGHLIGHT / CLOSE-UP ON NOBEL PRIZE-WINNING RESEARCH

Roger Sperry, 68, of the California Institute of Technology, won half of the 1981 Nobel prize in Medicine for his pioneering brain research, which revealed the separate functions of the left and right hemispheres of the cerebrum. These two halves of the brain usually share information across the *corpus callosum,* a network of millions of nerve fibers. This sharing makes it difficult to determine what each half does. Sperry began his research some 30 years ago by cutting the link between the two hemispheres in test animals. His most revealing experiments came later when humans received the same surgery to reduce epileptic seizures, which can spread across the corpus callosum. After this operation, patients are said to have a *split brain,* and they function well in their everyday lives. Sperry discovered with special tests, however, that split-brain patients often function with the two hemispheres being unaware of what the other is doing. Sperry therefore studied split-brain patients to find out the way each hemisphere functions on its own (Sperry, 1970).

Sperry's experiments took advantage of the fact that each side of the brain services the opposite side of the body. The right hemisphere, for example, receives touch sensations from the left hand and it moves the left hand. Only the right hemisphere receives information, therefore, when objects are placed in the left hand of split-brain patients who are blindfolded. The results were fascinating when Sperry did this experiment with a comb, toothbrush, key case, and other familiar objects. The patients showed how the objects are used by gesturing with their left hand. But they could not *say* how the objects are used and they had no idea of what their left hand was doing. The right hemisphere can apparently

recognize objects, but it cannot speak. When the patients touched the same objects with their right hand, information was sent to the left hemisphere. In that case, they immediately said what the objects were, which indicated that the left hemisphere can speak.

Sperry did similar experiments with visible words and objects. He took advantage of the fact that the two hemispheres see different sides of the world. When a person looks at a point, the right hemisphere sees everything to the left of that point, and the left hemisphere sees everything to the right. Split-brain patients usually move their eyes around in order to send information to both hemispheres. Sperry prevented this strategy in his experiments, however. He flashed a stimulus on one side and then removed it before the eyes could move. Thus, only one hemisphere saw the stimulus.

Sperry found that the left hemisphere understands abstract language, enables people to speak, and performs complicated mathematical computations (see Figure A). The right hemisphere understands only simple nouns and phrases. It can, for example, read the word "nut" and find a nut with the left hand in a pile of unseen objects. It can also find a match when it reads "used for lighting fires." It cannot understand abstract words, it cannot speak, and its mathematical abilities do not go beyond adding two-digit numbers. The right hemisphere is superior to the left in a number of ways, however, such as drawing, assembling blocks to match designs, and recognizing emotions in facial expressions.

Sperry's research formed a foundation for much modern brain research, which in turn guided the development of life-saving techniques of brain surgery.

The left and right brain hemispheres specialize in different functions. Split-brain research suggests that functions are divided as indicated in the figure. Electrical recordings (EEG) support the different functions of the hemispheres in normal subjects. (Ornstein, 1977)

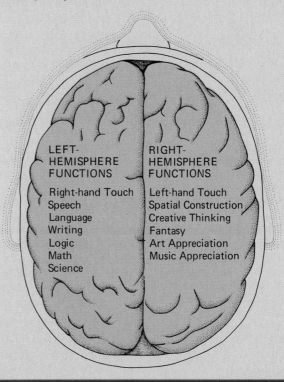

LEFT-HEMISPHERE FUNCTIONS

Right-hand Touch
Speech
Language
Writing
Logic
Math
Science

RIGHT-HEMISPHERE FUNCTIONS

Left-hand Touch
Spatial Construction
Creative Thinking
Fantasy
Art Appreciation
Music Appreciation

of her left motor and somatosensory cortexes were damaged by the swelling of the cerebrum during surgery, these injuries caused Kathy to lose movement control and feeling on her *right* side. Why is this so? Because the left cerebral hemisphere primarily controls the right side of the body, and the right cerebral hemisphere primarily controls the left side of the body. Roger Sperry, a colleague of Wilder Penfield's, also made a number of discoveries while treating epilepsy through surgery; his pioneering work in split-brain research has provided much information about the differences between the left and right hemispheres (see "Highlight: Close-up on Nobel Prize-Winning Research").

The Spinal Cord

The structure that connects the brain with the rest of the body is the **spinal cord,** a cable of long nerve fibers running from the brainstem down through the backbone to the lower back. Fibers on the outside of the cord have myelin sheaths, which give this area a whitish color. (As we mentioned earlier, neural impulses travel faster on neurons covered with a myelin sheath.) Fibers on the inside of the cord are unmyelinated, so the color is grayish. The gray area is shaped like a bent *H* (as shown in Figure 2–8).

Nerve tissue in the brain and spinal cord are called the **central nervous system.** All other nerve tissue is called the **peripheral nervous system.** These two systems work together. At the start of a race, for example, runners listen for the starting gun. Peripheral nerves in their ears respond and send impulses to the central nervous system. The brain interprets the impulses as the waited-for "go" signal, and it sends commands to peripheral nerves in muscles that launch the runner down the track.

Sometimes the spinal cord triggers responses without waiting for commands from the brain. Such responses are called **reflexes,** or automatic actions that require no conscious effort on our part. There are a number of different kinds of spinal reflexes. The gray inner area of the spinal cord plays an important role in all of them, as illustrated in Figure 2–9. The stretch reflex, for example, extends your arms and legs, bringing them toward a straight position. Doctors test this reflex when they tap your knee to make your leg straighten out from a crossed position. Another kind of reflex bends your arms and legs to pull them away from painful stimulation, as when you step on a tack and jerk your leg up. When your leg jerks away from that tack, you do not fall down, because still another type of reflex extends or stiffens your other leg, supporting your weight on it.

The white outer spinal area carries impulses up and down the spinal cord. **Ascending nerves** carry sensory information up to specific areas of the brain; **descending nerves** carry commands to move muscles. Diseases and injuries that damage descending nerves can cause paralysis. Polio, for example, is a viral disease that attacks descending nerves, causing paralysis of leg and other muscles. Since Dr. Jonas E. Salk developed an effective vaccine against polio, the disease is less common than it was in the 1950s, when it reached epidemic levels. Injury is also a common cause of paralysis. If the lower spinal cord is severed, the legs are paralyzed. If the upper spinal cord is severed, paralysis occurs in the arms and legs and in breathing. As of yet, no cure has been developed for paralysis related to these unfortunate injuries.

While an intact spinal cord is necessary for normal muscle control, it's not enough on its own. Kathy's spinal cord was in perfect condition, yet she lost a great deal of motor control after her operation. In the next section we will learn why Kathy's brain injury affected some muscle movements and not others.

FIGURE 2–8

Cross-section of the spinal cord.

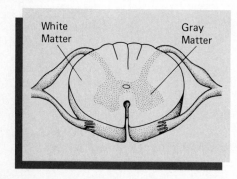

White Matter

Gray Matter

FIGURE 2–9

Spinal cord reflexes: (left) stretch reflex,
(right) flexor reflex, and (below) flexor-
cross-extensor reflex.

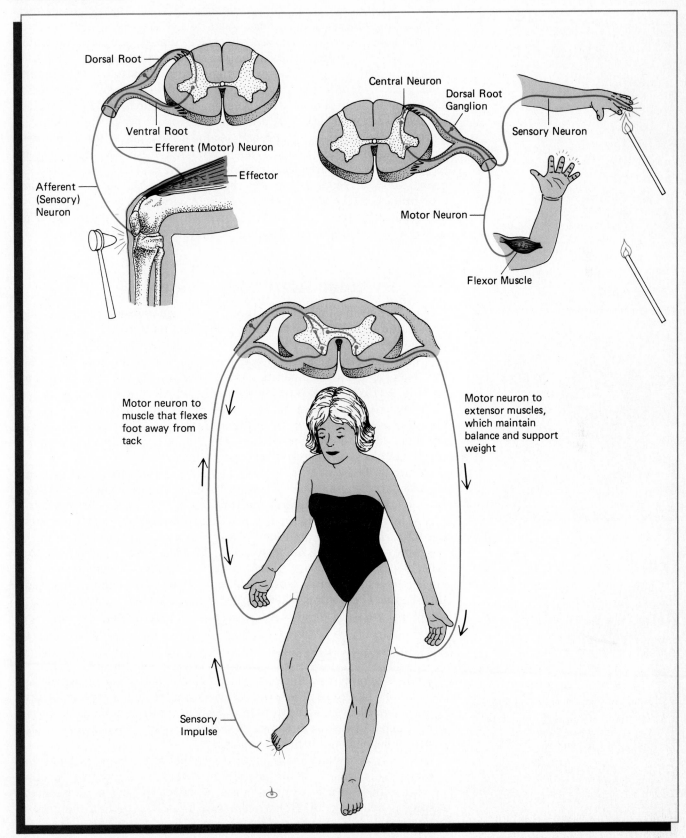

Dorsal Root

Ventral Root

Efferent (Motor) Neuron

Effector

Afferent
(Sensory)
Neuron

Central Neuron

Dorsal Root
Ganglion

Sensory Neuron

Motor Neuron

Flexor Muscle

Motor neuron to
muscle that flexes
foot away from
tack

Motor neuron to
extensor muscles,
which maintain
balance and support
weight

Sensory
Impulse

FUNCTIONAL SUBDIVISIONS OF THE NERVOUS SYSTEM

Kathy's abilities and disabilities after surgery involve coordinated efforts of many anatomical subdivisions. Parts of her forebrain, midbrain, and hindbrain work together, for example, when she sings and plays her guitar. It is useful, therefore, to consider *functional subdivisions*, which are interconnected structures that work together in carrying out certain functions in the body. An everyday example of the distinction between subdivisions can be seen in a bicycle. "Anatomical" subdivisions would include the front section (handlebars, brake controls, front brake, fork, and front wheel); midsection (seat, frame, and peddles); and hind section (rear wheel, rear brake, and chain assembly). A functional subdivision that includes parts from each anatomical section is the braking system. It includes brake controls, peddles, and the chain assembly, as well as front and rear brakes. In the remainder of this chapter we will take up functional subdivisions of the nervous system. We will learn the reasons for some of Kathy's handicaps, and also the biological underpinnings of our own everyday experiences.

The Reticular Activating System

On the morning of her operation, Kathy was awakened at 6 o'clock by a nurse who gave her two small pills and an injection. When Kathy was helped onto a cart 15 minutes later, her mouth felt dry, and she was cold and sleepy. Kathy remembers going into the operating room and easing over onto the operating table. Shortly after that, she remembers nothing. As far as she knows, she suddenly fell into a completely dreamless void beyond time and sensations. This place was created for her by a drug that blocked Kathy's **reticular activating system (RAS)**. The RAS activates all of the regions of the brain for incoming sensory impulses; when it is blocked, no sensations register at all.

Figure 2–10 shows that the RAS ignores the anatomical divisions that we introduced earlier. The system joins the reticular formation with other parts of the brain to perform the function of making the brain alert. A person is awake only when the RAS is operating. Another function of the RAS is *selective* attention. When two or more messages arrive at the same time, the RAS seems to decide which is most urgent. The system then blocks, or tones down, the irrelevant messages and prepares the upper areas of the brain to respond vigorously to the relevant message. (In Chapter 4 we will further explore general arousal and sleep, and in Chapter 5 we will look at ways to concentrate attention.)

The Limbic System

Kathy's symptoms before her surgery—her emotional upheavals and her memory lapses—suggest that her tumor affected her **limbic system.** This system of brain structures includes the structures shown in Figure 2–11. Limbic system interconnections are clearly defined and each part seems to depend on all the other parts.

Limbic system functions are less clearly defined, however; the system does so many things that it is hard to characterize any one function. One way to do this is to observe the behavior of people whose limbic system is disturbed by frontal cortex injuries. One patient laughed at sad things and cried at funny things; another was unable to plan a meal because she kept forgetting how to cook; still another urinated in public

FIGURE 2–10

The reticular activating system (RAS).

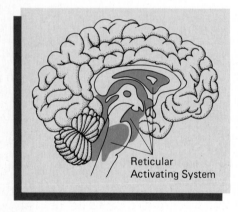

Reticular Activating System

FIGURE 2–11

The limbic system.

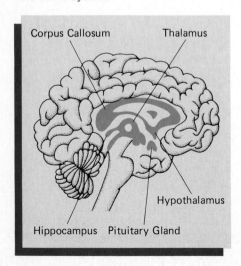

Corpus Callosum

Thalamus

Hypothalamus

Hippocampus   Pituitary Gland

Special x-ray techniques aid the examination of anatomical and functional subdivisions. The top photo shows a *cerebral angiogram.* This x-ray was taken after a dye was injected into cerebral blood vessels. The angiogram indicates the positions of the vessels. Deviations from normal positions can indicate a tumor as it did in Kathy's case.

The bottom photo shows a computerized axial tomography scan, which is better known as a *CAT-SCAN.* This "picture" was taken without injecting dyes and without presenting special risks or discomforts to the patient. An x-ray beam scanned the brain while a computer recorded how much of the beam was absorbed. The computer then projected the "picture" to indicate in a color code its interpretation of varying densities of tissues, fluids, and bone.

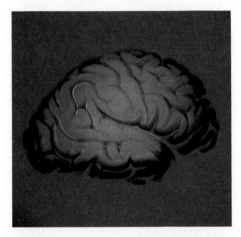

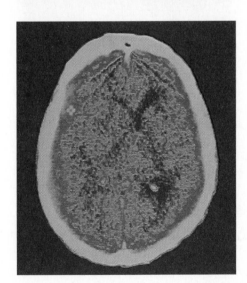

while dressed in evening clothes (Cotman and McGaugh, 1980). The ill-timed urination is one of many examples of inappropriate actions that seem to result from an inability to deal with two conflicting goals at the same time (one goal was to enjoy social interactions with companions; another was to urinate). Normally we cope with conflicting demands by responding at the right time and place. People with disturbed limbic systems often cannot deal with conflicting goals. From this set of bizarre symptoms, we get the impression that the limbic system controls emotions, memories, and goal-directed behavior.

Kathy's memory lapse while driving in New York is consistent with limbic system disturbance. Her inability to recognize streets suggests that her tumor may have affected her hippocampus, which provides us with a spatial map of where we are and where we have been (Best and Ranck, 1982). Her tumor also seemed to hamper her goal-directed behavior. She started to drive to her brother's house, but somewhere along the way she lost track of her goal. She says that it was a very strange experience, since she drove the rest of the way as if she were on "automatic pilot."

The Autonomic Nervous System

Have you ever experienced an uncontrollable rage of the kind that overcame Kathy when she was told that she might lose her voice? We all have, and we have also experienced the peace that follows when we calm down. Such responses are governed by our **autonomic nervous system,** which regulates glands and organs. Rage is triggered by the **sympathetic division** of the autonomic system. This division prepares the body for action. The peace that follows is controlled by the **parasympathetic division,** which allows the body to relax. These two divisions, with their effects on the body, may be seen in Figure 2–12.

Sympathetic Division. Sympathetic pathways work all the time to keep our body functions stable. They are especially busy, however, during stressful situations. Let's look at some of the body changes triggered by Kathy's sympathetic division when she flew into her fit of rage.

1. Her heart worked faster and harder to pump more blood to the muscles.
2. Her breathing rate increased, and her air passage opened to carry more air to her lungs.
3. Her sweat glands produced more sweat to help maintain normal body temperature.
4. Her digestion stopped to save energy for the other functions that were speeded up.

All of these responses prepared Kathy for action. Together they are called the *fight-or-flight* responses, because in emergencies they prepare us either to fight or to flee. Sympathetic responses are very helpful in emergencies, but they can be harmful when they are repeatedly used for minor crises. Students who have fight-or-flight reactions every time they think about exams, for example, put undue stress on their bodies. We will discuss this again in Chapter 10.

Parasympathetic Division. Parasympathetic fibers go to all the same glands and organs as the sympathetic division, but they carry the opposite message, as if to say, "Relax." This *relaxation response* was traditionally regarded as being beyond voluntary control, as were all autonomic responses. For this reason, the autonomic nervous system is sometimes called the involuntary nervous system. Recent studies, however, show that we can voluntarily control our autonomic nervous system, as we will discuss in Chapters 4 and 5. Even when we learn to control our

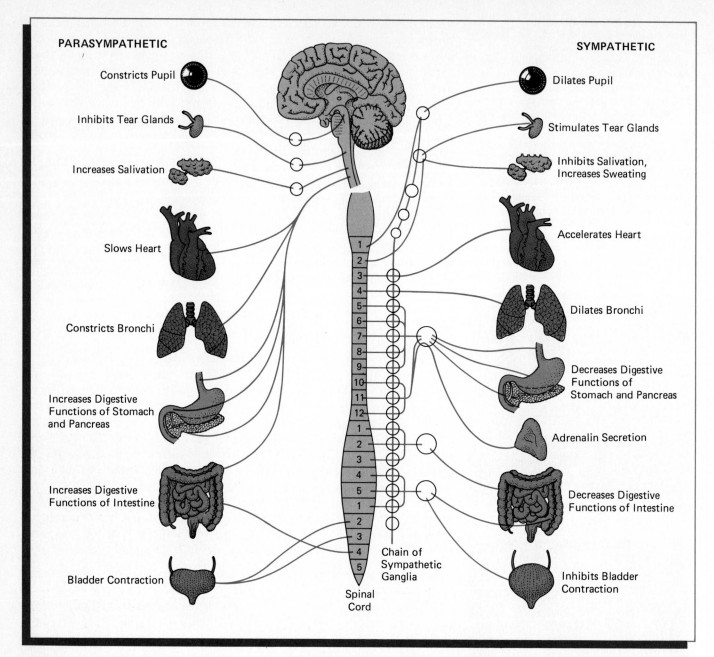

PARASYMPATHETIC

Constricts Pupil

Inhibits Tear Glands

Increases Salivation

Slows Heart

Constricts Bronchi

Increases Digestive Functions of Stomach and Pancreas

Increases Digestive Functions of Intestine

Bladder Contraction

SYMPATHETIC

Dilates Pupil

Stimulates Tear Glands

Inhibits Salivation, Increases Sweating

Accelerates Heart

Dilates Bronchi

Decreases Digestive Functions of Stomach and Pancreas

Adrenalin Secretion

Decreases Digestive Functions of Intestine

Inhibits Bladder Contraction

Chain of Sympathetic Ganglia

Spinal Cord

FIGURE 2–12

The sympathetic and parasympathetic subdivisions of the nervous system serve many of the same organs, but they affect them differently.

organs voluntarily, however, we never achieve the same sort of precise control that we have over our skeletal muscles.

Control of Skeletal Muscles

The bones of our skeleton are rigid, but without the muscles that move and support them we would collapse in a heap. Spinal cord reflexes control most of the work our skeletal muscles do in maintaining our posture against the pull of gravity. We continually control our skeletal muscles, therefore, without being aware of it. At the same time we control the same muscles deliberately and purposefully. Such voluntary muscle control includes simple movements (as when Kathy responded after surgery to the command to squeeze her left hand) and complex sequences of movements (as when Kathy walks or sings). In this section we will examine the neural processes that underlie such voluntary muscle control.

The part of the nervous system that controls muscle movements is called the **motor system.** We have already discussed the spinal reflexes, which are part of the motor system. Here we will consider three higher centers:

1. **Basal ganglia** are four masses of gray matter located deep in the brain. They have a number of functions, which are not well understood. One function is to control "background" muscle tone. When Kathy responded to the command to squeeze her left fist, her basal ganglia first tensed muscles in the upper part of her arm to prepare for the hand movement. In general, basal ganglia perform large, general muscle movements to set the stage for more detailed, controlled movements.

2. The **cerebellum** participates in controlling fine-grain muscle movements. It "puts a brake" on motor impulses to make them smoother and more coordinated.

3. The **motor cortex,** which is in the frontal lobe (see Figure 2–7), is the place where motor impulses originate. The motor cortex contains giant cells, called **pyramidal cells,** which send a long axon through the brain down to neurons in the spinal cord. From there motor impulses go directly to muscles. Most pyramidal cells in the left hemisphere send their impulses to muscles on the right side of the body, and vice versa. They tend to control precise movements such as those of hand movements and speech. A large part of the motor cortex controls a small number of muscles that we often use in precise movements.

Shown here are two basic types of muscle movements. The musician is using pyramidal cells to control precise hand movements. The gymnast is using basal ganglia to control general muscle tone.

FIGURE 2–13

Broca's area and *Wernicke's area* of the brain.

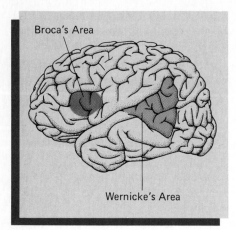

Broca's Area

Wernicke's Area

Language Control Centers

Most of us speak, write, listen, and read with such ease that we do not appreciate the work our brain does. But Kathy's surgery made her keenly aware of her brain's role in language. Her operation left her with *aphasia*, which is difficulty in producing and understanding language. Her case illustrates two well-known types of aphasia:

1. **Broca's aphasia,** which is characterized by speech that is slow, labored, and slightly distorted. It is caused by injury to *Broca's area*, which is a part of the cortex, shown in Figure 2–13.
2. **Wernicke's aphasia,** which is characterized by speech that sounds normal until one pays attention to the meaning. The speech includes the wrong words and nonsense words, and the message seems to shift from topic to topic. Wernicke's aphasia is caused by injury to the upper area of the left temporal lobe (Figure 2-14).

Kathy showed signs of both of these disorders. When asked to repeat words, she did well on "chair," "circle," "fifteen," "brown," and others, but she had trouble with some words such as "hammock," which she pronounced "ham . . . ham . . . ock," and "Methodist," which she pronounced "Metho . . . Meth . . . dister . . . Meth . . . o . . . dist." When asked to say the months of the year, she said, "January, February, January, February, March, January. It's just the first couple of months that I forget."

When Dr. Brust, a language expert, explained the nature of Kathy's disorders to her, she asked, "Am I going to get better?"

Brust answered, "I don't know. You'll see."

Then Kathy asked, "Why can I sing?"

Brust answered, "The lyrics to songs are not only bits of language, but, because you sing them, they are also bits of music. As such, they appear to be stored in your right hemisphere, too. Perhaps not entirely, but at least enough to give you the boost you need." Recent studies support Brust's explanation (Geschwind, 1979).

We have concentrated so far on direct effects of Kathy's brain damage on language and other abilities. We will now turn to possible *indirect* effects of brain damage on Kathy's body chemisty.

THE ENDOCRINE SYSTEM

Kathy's behavior changed gradually before her brain tumor was discovered. The tumor seemed to touch every aspect of her life, including her eating habits, moods, attitudes, and sexual behavior. Research has shown that injuries in the temporal lobe (where Kathy's tumor was located) can influence appetites and emotional aspects of behavior (Cotman and McGaugh, 1980). Such injuries cause these effects indirectly by upsetting the balance in the endocrine system, a major coordinating system that regulates body chemistry.

Structure

The endocrine system is made up of internal organs called endocrine glands. Located throughout the body (Figure 2–14), they touch almost every aspect of our lives. The glands release hormones (chemical messengers) directly into the bloodstream, which carries the hormones to other body tissue. When hormones reach their target, they either directly change

FIGURE 2–14

Glands of the endocrine system release hormones (chemical messengers) directly into the bloodstream.

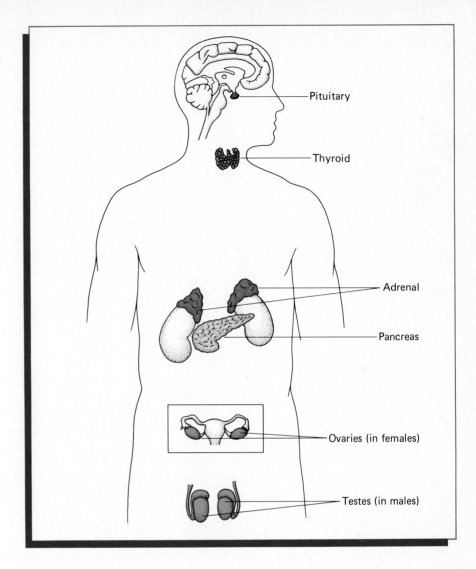

it or they cause it to release other hormones that change tissues elsewhere in the body.

Function

It's easiest to understand the endocrine system's function if we go over each individual gland.

Thyroid Glands. The fact that Kathy ate everything in sight suggests that her **thyroid gland** may have been affected. It is a large butterfly-shaped gland in the front and sides of the throat. It produces **thyroxin,** a hormone that determines the rate at which you transform your food into energy. This rate, called the **metabolic rate,** determines how hungry you feel, how energetic you are, and how fast you gain weight.

If your thyroxin level is too high, you will burn food fast, which makes you hungry, gives you lots of energy, and keeps you thin. It also speeds up and intensifies your reactions to stress.

You burn your food too slowly when your thyroxin level is low. Much of your food consequently turns to fat, and you feel sleepy and sluggish. In Chapter 9 we will discuss other factors that influence why we gain or lose weight. Children with extremely low thyroxin levels suffer from *cretinism,* which is characterized by arrested physical and mental development. If untreated with thyroid extract, they will become dwarfed, mentally retarded, and sterile.

Parathyroid Glands. Other glands may have influenced Kathy's general energy level. One of them is a set of four pea-shaped glands next to the thyroid, called the **parathyroid glands.** The parathyroid hormone causes lethargy when its level is too high, and muscle spasms when its level is too low.

Pancreas. Another gland that may have affected Kathy's general energy level is the *pancreas,* a large gland located behind the stomach. It controls the level of sugar in the blood by secreting two hormones, *insulin* and *glucagon.* Too little sugar in the blood causes chronic fatigue, and too much sugar poisons the blood, causing *diabetes.* A person who has diabetes needs a specially controlled diet and daily injections of insulin to avoid serious complications, which include heart damage, nerve damage, and blindness.

Pituitary Gland. Kathy's elated and depressed moods may have been influenced by her **pituitary gland,** which has the widest-ranging effects of all the endocrine glands. This master gland is only the size of a pea. It, like all the endocrine glands, is influenced by the brain. Its location makes that influence especially easy to see. It lies in a small recess at the base of the brain and is connected to the hypothalamus, which controls it. The pituitary gland secretes many different kinds of hormones. One is the **growth hormone,** which controls development of the skeleton. Too little of it causes dwarfism and too much causes giantism. Other pituitary hormones influence reproductive organs and sexual behavior, often indirectly by regulating another endocrine gland, the **gonads.**

Gonads. Changes in Kathy's behavior suggest that her tumor may have set off a chain of physiological events that ultimately affected her gonads. In females, gonads are called *ovaries,* in males they are called *testes.* Hormones produced by the gonads are called *sex hormones.* Ovaries produce two hormones, *estrogen* and *progesterone;* they control ovulation, pregnancy, and the menstrual cycle. Testes manufacture *testosterone,* which stimulates production of sperm. Gonads also regulate *secondary sex characteristics,* such as the distribution of body hair, development of breasts, and pitch of voice. The whole subject of hormones and sexual behavior will be discussed in Chapter 9.

Kathy's sudden clash with death and her amazing recovery are both related to the organization of her body's two coordinating systems, the nervous system and the endocrine system. On the one hand, Kathy's tumor affected her in many ways, because parts of her nervous system and endocrine system depend upon one another. When one part breaks down, other dependent parts can fail in a disastrous chain reaction. On the other hand, Kathy's recovery indicates an advantage of this organization. Apparently, when one part fails, other parts can sometimes take over. In other words, within limits, parts of these systems are flexible in their ability to take on duties (Cotman and McCaugh, 1980).

GENETICS

Whether we focus on the negative side of Kathy's illness or on the positive side of her recovery, we can hardly help being reminded of our dependence on our own bodies. Some of us have strong, healthy bodies that give us great freedom. Others of us have disabilities that limit what we can do. In this next section we will consider the origin of our bodies and the factors that determined the specific bodies that each of us inherited.

Genetics is the study of how traits are inherited, or passed on, from

FIGURE 2-15

DNA molecules are shaped like a spiral staircase or double helix. The steps of the staircase contain a genetic code. Four chemical bases make up the steps: Adenine (A), Thymine (T), Cytosine (C), and Guamine (G). Each step contains two bases, A and T or C and G. A single gene might contain as many as 2,000 steps. The specific order of A-T and C-G pairs determines a gene's special character.

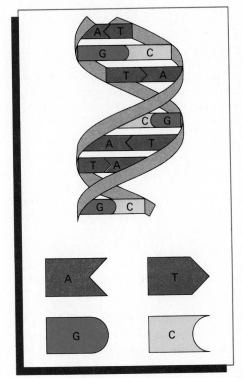

parent to child. The cells from which we started contain **genes**, which are the basic units of heredity. They determine our sequence of growth into a human baby instead of into a turtle, rabbit, or some other animal. Genes determine our blood type, coloration, and many other traits. In general, genes determine the resemblance between newborns and parents. People often observe that a baby "has his mother's eyes" or "has her father's chin," and so on. The resemblance becomes even more striking later on as genes continue to influence development.

The Biochemistry of Genes

Genes are located in the nucleus of every cell in the body. They are composed of **deoxyribonucleic acid (DNA)**, which contains blueprints for life. Living organisms are made of protein, and DNA controls the way in which protein chains are built. Material for constructing protein surrounds cells and DNA sends out messenger molecules, **ribonucleic acid (RNA)**, to control how the material is fashioned into specific kinds of protein chains. James Watson and Francis Crick (1953) made a significant breakthrough in deciphering the chemical "language" in which these genetic blueprints are written (see Figure 2–15).

Every living cell contains between 20,000 and 125,000 genes grouped together in clusters of a thousand or more. They are arranged in threadlike chains called **chromosomes.**

The Structure and Function of Chromosomes

Every plant and animal has a specific number of chromosomes, which are grouped in pairs. Garden peas have 7 pairs, fruit flies have 4 pairs, frogs have 13 pairs, chickens have 39 pairs, chimpanzees have 24 pairs, and humans have 23 pairs. The cells in your body have 46 chromosomes, arranged in 23 pairs. You inherited one member of each pair from your mother and the other from your father. If you have children, you will pass along 23 of your chromosomes to each child; the other 23 will come from your partner.

Genes are transmitted from generation to generation by means of sex cells, which are called **gametes.** A female gamete is called an *ovum*, and a male gamete is called a *sperm*. Your gametes have 23 chromosomes each, only half the number of your other cells. Each gamete is formed by randomly choosing one member from each of your 23 pairs of chromosomes. With 23 pairs to choose from, your body can generate an incredible number of unique gametes.

Ovum and sperm combine their chromosomes when they unite to form one cell called a **zygote.** Thus, zygotes have 46 chromosomes, half from the mother and half from the father. Each of us started from the union of one sperm and one ovum. The resulting zygote contained 46 chromosomes, which determined our **genotype,** or genetic inheritance, for the rest of our lives.

Figure 2–16 shows 23 chromosome pairs for a normal human male (left) and female (right). Scientists have classified chromosomes according to size and shape, and they have identified some pairs that carry (and pass on) specific traits. Pair 23 determines sex, for example. Notice that the male has one large X-shaped chromosome and one small, upside down, Y-shaped chromosome in pair 23. The female has two large X-shaped chromosomes in that pair. One of the important consequences of this discovery was the realization that men alone determine the sex of offspring. A female body always contributes an X chromosome to pair 23. A male body can generate gametes with *either* an X or a Y chromosome. Thus, a female

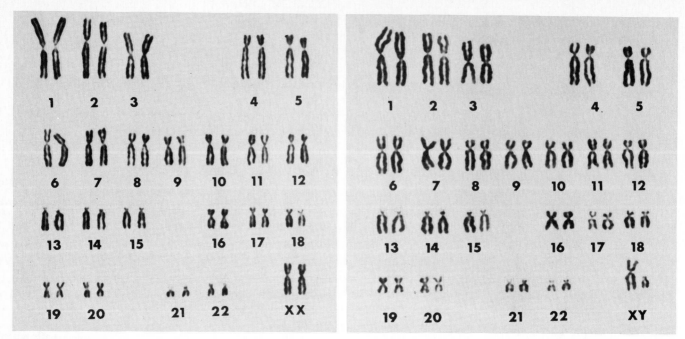

FIGURE 2–16

Human chromosomes grouped into 23 pairs, with female chromosomes on the left and male chromosomes on the right.

is conceived when a sperm carrying an X chromosome unites with an ovum, and a male is conceived when a sperm carrying a Y chromosome does so.

Mutations. Errors are made occasionally in transmitting genes from one generation to the next. As a result, children are sometimes born with abnormal chromosome structures, which are called mutations. Scientists have observed mutations of pair 23, as follows:

1. *Two Xs and a Y.* People with an XXY mutation often have characteristics of both sexes. They might have developed breasts and small testicles, for example. Some superior female Russian athletes have had XXY chromosome structures.
2. *Two Ys and an X.* Males with an extra Y chromosome (XYY) are often taller than other males. Some evidence suggests that they might also be more aggressive, but the evidence is mixed. On the one hand, XYY males are more likely than normal males to be inmates of prisons or mental hospitals. On the other hand, XYY males in the general population (about 1 in every 1,000 births) are no more aggressive than normal males (Owen, 1972; Hook, 1973).

Another kind of genetic mutation is one in which a person has 47 chromosomes because of an extra one added to pair 21. Children with this chromosome abnormality suffer from Down's syndrome, a disorder characterized by mental retardation and a unique physical appearance, including folds on the eyelid corners, a round face, a head with a flattened back, a short neck, and a small nose. Before modern medicine, Down's syndrome children often died during or before their teens because they were very susceptible to leukemia (blood cancer), heart disorders, and respiratory infections. Today, Down's syndrome babies live longer because of better treatments for these diseases. Down's syndrome children are usually affectionate, calm, and cheerful.

Down's syndrome can be detected before birth through amniocentesis, a process in which fluid is taken from a mother's womb. A fetus sloughs off cells into the fluid, enabling doctors to examine an unborn child's genetic structure, which is recorded in each cell. This procedure is only done where there is a reason for concern. A mother who has already had a Down's syndrome child is about three times more likely to have one again, for

This is a Downs Syndrome child, shown taking part in a special education class.

example, and mothers over age 35 are more likely than younger mothers to have a child with this disorder. Such mothers might consider amniocentesis, which is best done in the sixteenth week of pregnancy. Unfortunately, Down's syndrome cannot be treated, so the only option when amniocentesis indicates Down's syndrome is whether or not to induce an abortion.

The causes of mutations are not well understood and are of great concern to modern geneticists. They have identified three causes:

1. Some people carry *mutator genes* that increase the rate of mutations in other genes.
2. High temperatures can increase mutation rate. Males generate sperm in their scrotum, a sac that is usually cooler than the rest of the body in mammals. Research has indicated that wearing tight trousers can raise scrotal temperature to a point that could almost double mutation rate (Lerner and Libby, 1976).
3. Radiation has been linked to mutation rate. X-rays are one source of radiation and pregnant mothers are advised to avoid them. Radiation before pregnancy may also increase mutation rate. Recent evidence suggests that more exposure to radiation may explain the fact that older mothers have more Down's syndrome babies.

Continuing research on mutations will hopefully allow geneticists to understand and treat the more than 2,000 genetic disorders that are known today.

Genetic Laws of Inheritance

Gregor Mendel started modern genetics by formulating laws of how characteristics or traits are inherited. He based his laws on years of sys-

HIGHLIGHT / GENETIC ENGINEERING

On January 4, 1982, Judith and Roger Carr took their daughter, Elizabeth Jordan Carr, home from Norfolk General Hospital, where she was born a week earlier. This seemingly ordinary event was in the news because Elizabeth Carr was America's first "test-tube" baby. That is, she was conceived outside her mother's body. An egg, or ovum, was removed from her mother, placed in a test tube, and fertilized with her father's sperm. The united egg and sperm cells were then placed back in her mother where Elizabeth developed normally.

Elizabeth Carr is the world's nineteenth test-tube baby. Dr. Daniel Petrucci was the first to successfully combine an ovum and sperm in a test tube in 1959. The first test-tube baby, Louise Brown, was born in 1978 at a clinic in England operated by Dr. Patrick Steptoe and Robert Edwards. None of the parents of test-tube babies could have conceived any other way. They and many parents in the future will forever be grateful to *genetic engineering,* the science of applied genetics. The study of how traits are passed on from parent to child led to a basic understanding of how eggs and sperm unite. Elizabeth Carr and other test-tube babies owe their lives to the application of that basic knowledge.

Genetic engineers are also credited with at least three other breakthroughs:

1. Dr. H. Gobind Khorana headed a team that achieved the first chemical synthesis of a gene in 1970 at the University of Wisconsin. This work opened the door for creating any gene in a test tube. A Harvard research team recently constructed genes that produce insulin, an important hormone discussed earlier in this chapter (Gilbert and Villa-Komaroff, 1980).

2. An Oxford team of scientists in 1971 changed the structure of defective cells in mice. They injected healthy chick chromosomes into defective mice cells. The cells used the new material to correct their own defect and to reproduce healthy cells. This research was a first step toward correcting defective human genes (see Anderson and Diacumakos, 1981).

3. J. B. Gurdon produced a frog without fertilizing an ovum with sperm. He destroyed the genes in a frog ovum and replaced them with a full set of genes from an intestinal cell of another frog. The ovum then had a full set of genes and it started to reproduce. This process, which is called *cloning,* resulted in a tadpole that was genetically identical to the frog that donated the intestine cell. The tadpole is called a *clone,* which is an "identical twin" to one of its parents because of the cloning processes by which it is produced. Some researchers speculate that a day will come when scientists will be able to produce human clones.

Genetic engineering has risks. Scientists must exercise extreme caution to avoid creating a "doomsday bug," a bacteria that causes mass infections for which there is no cure. Genetic engineering also raises ethical questions. For example, who could be cloned? Despite the dangers and ethical questions, genetic engineering could obviously be a tremendous benefit to society. It will surely be in the news for a long time to come.

Judith Carr with her newborn daughter, Elizabeth Jordan Carr, who is America's first "test-tube" baby.

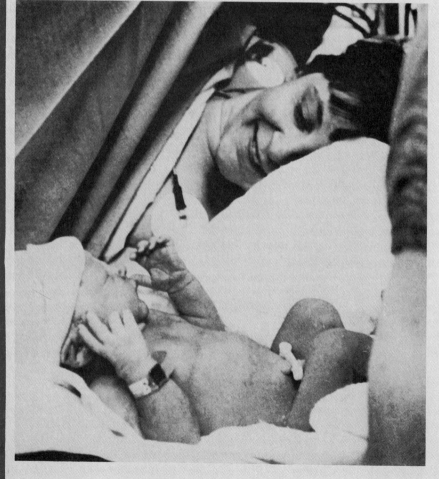

FIGURE 2–17

Dominant and recessive genes control eye color in fruit flies. The gene for red eyes (*E*) dominates the gene for white eyes (*e*). Offspring get one gene from each parent. An offspring will have white eyes only if it gets an *e* from each parent, forming an *ee* pair.

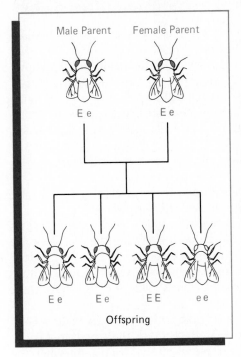

tematic breeding of garden peas. He noticed that peas, like humans, inherit traits from both parents, and he noticed a pattern in the way these traits are passed along.

Single-Gene Traits. Modern geneticists now realize that Mendel studied a special case, known as **single-gene traits.** Some genes single-handedly determine specific traits like eye color in fruit flies. Such genes occur in pairs with each member located in the same position on paired chromosomes and with each parent contributing one member to each gene pair. A single gene may occur in one of several different forms called *alleles*, which geneticists represent by means of letters. Some alleles, called *dominant*, rule over others, which are called *recessive*. Dominant alleles are represented by capital letters and recessive alleles are represented by small letters. Allele *E*, for example, produces red eyes in fruit flies, and it dominates over allele *e*, which produces white eyes. Fruit flies therefore have red eyes if one member of its gene pair is *E* and the other is *e*, of if both members are *E*. Fruit flies have white eyes only if both members of its gene pair are *e* (see Figure 2–17).

Sex-Linked Traits. A complication occurs when the gene for a trait is located on the chromosome that determines one's sex. A human gene is *sex-linked* if it is located on the X chromosome in pair 23. The gene for color vision is an example. Allele *C* produces normal color vision, allele *c* produces colorblindness. Either allele occurs in X chromosomes; neither one occurs in Y. Males have only one X chromosome, which comes of course from their mother and which completely determines their color vision. A male will therefore have normal vision if he inherits *C* from his mother, and he will be colorblind if he inherits *c*. A female, on the other hand, has two X chromosomes and therefore has two chances for normal color vision. She will have normal color vision if either one of her X chromosomes is *C*, because the *C* allele is the dominant allele. She will be colorblind only in the unlikely event that she inherits a *c* from *both* her father *and* her mother.

Polygenic Traits. Another complication occurs when traits are **polygenic,** which means that they are determined by the action of more than one gene pair. Most human traits are *polygenic.* Each human parent contributes a *set of genes*, rather than a single gene, to each chromosome pair to determine specific traits. Rules governing dominant and recessive alleles still apply for polygenic traits. As the number of genes determining a single trait increases, the task of specifying the relationship between genes and traits gets even more complicated.

Today's geneticists cannot even say how many genes go into determining complex traits like intelligence, so they are far from being able to link specific genes to intelligence. Scientists do have evidence, however, that genes influence intelligence. In one experiment, rats were separated into a "bright" group, who were good maze runners, and a "dull" group, who were poor maze runners (Tryon, 1940). "Bright" rats mated together and "dull" rats mated together, for 8 generations. Tyron continued to use maze-running ability as his critical measure. He found that almost every offspring of the "bright" rats was better than the average of the first generation, and almost all of the offspring of the "dull" rats were poorer maze runners than the original group. The results suggest that genetic inheritance influences intelligence, assuming, of course, that we accept maze running as a measure of rat "intelligence."

While Tryon's experiment and others like it justify further investigations into genetic influences on intelligence, other studies suggest that environment also influences intelligence. For instance, Cooper and Zubek (1958) controlled for genetic background and found that raising rats in an enriched, or challenging, environment also increases "intelligence." Traits that interest psychologists, such as intelligence, personality, and emotions, are generally influenced by both heredity and environment. We will therefore keep track of both factors when we follow the course of human development in Chapters 7 and 8.

SUMMARY

1. Behavioral neuroscientists study both the structure and function of body parts that influence our behavior.

2. Neurons are cells specialized to receive and transmit information. They look like other cells except that they have tiny fiber projections that allow them to communicate with other cells.

3. Neurons "speak" a simple language consisting of an "off-on" code. They go off and on at different rates to send messages that can go from neuron to neuron throughout the body.

4. The brain's anatomical subdivisions include the hindbrain, midbrain, and forebrain.

5. The spinal cord connects the brain with the rest of the body. It also controls important automatic responses called reflexes.

6. The brain's functional subdivisions include the reticular activating system (RAS), which controls waking and sleeping; the limbic system, which controls emotions; the autonomic nervous system, which keeps our body functions stable; the motor system, which controls muscles; and the language control centers, which allow us to produce and understand language.

7. The endocrine system consists of glands that regulate body chemistry. The glands send chemical messengers through the bloodstream.

8. Cells contain genes, which determine traits that people inherit from their parents. Genetics is the study of how traits are inherited.

9. Scientists are beginning to understand "blueprints for life," which are contained in the chemical structure of genes.

10. Genes group together in structures called chromosomes, which are key units in the study of reproduction and in the study of errors in transmitting genes from one generation to the next.

11. Geneticists have formulated laws of how traits are inherited. These laws or principles have led to important applications in a new field called genetic engineering.

SUGGESTED READINGS

The following book is about Kathy Morris:

MEE, C. L., JR. *Seizure.* New York: M. Evans, 1978.

COTMAN, C. W., and MCGAUGH, J. L. *Behavioral neuroscience: An introduction.* New York: Academic Press, 1980. This book takes students step by step through the process of using biology, chemistry, physiology, and psychology in the study of behavior.

FULLER, J. L., and THOMPSON, W. R. *Foundations of behavior genetics.* St. Louis, Mo.: Mosby, 1978. A comprehensive survey of how genetics influences behavior.

LUBOR, J. F., and DEERING, W. M. *Behavioral approaches to neurology.* New York: Academic Press, 1981. Explores the application of biofeedback and other behavioral medicine techniques to areas for which traditional medical approaches have not been completely satisfactory.

ORBACH, J. *Neuropsychology after Lashley: Fifty years since the publication of Brain mechanisms and intelligence.* Hillsdale, N.J.: Erlbaum, 1982. Traces the development and current state of the art in neuropsychology through individual chapters presented by Lashley's students.

THOMPSON, R. F. *Introduction to physiological psychology.* New York: Harper & Row, 1975. A wide-ranging introduction to theories and data of physiological psychology.

WHITAKER, H. A. (Ed.). *Brain and cognition.* A new journal presenting research papers, clinical case histories, and reviews on brain structure and function. Topics include visual processes, memory, emotions, sex differences, hemispheric differences, and cognitive processes.

Sensation and Perception

A t 9:08 Central Standard Time on the night of Monday, April 13, 1970, an oxygen tank exploded, tearing away one side of the Apollo 13 service module. John L. Swigert, strapped to his pilot's seat in the command module, felt a shudder. Fred W. Haise, pilot of the lunar module (LM, pronounced "lem"), was in the tunnel connecting the LM and the command module when the whole tunnel violently shook up and down. Captain James A. Lovell, the commander, felt nothing—he was floating, weightless, in front of his seat. He heard a strange noise, but it didn't sound like an explosion—he thought Haise might have dropped something in the LM. Lovell's first clue to the emergency came when the master alarm sounded and Haise scrambled from the LM tunnel, slamming the hatch behind him. All three astronauts knew by then that something was fundamentally wrong, but it would be 15 minutes before they would get a rough idea of what had happened, and about an hour beyond that before they would realize that the odds were now against their ever returning to earth.

Several engineers at the Manned Spacecraft Center near Houston, Texas, 205,000 miles below, saw a tiny flare of light that looked like a distant star exploding, but they did not connect the glow with Apollo 13. They were not the only ones to ignore signs of the disaster. Next door, in the Mission Control Center, other signs were missed. For example, the column of numbers on a television screen that monitored oxygen pressure increased rapidly when the oxygen tank ruptured. The controller looking at the screen didn't notice this because his eyes were directed 3 inches to the right, on the readings from the hydrogen tanks.

The delay in realizing the danger was costly, because during it Apollo 13 passed the point where the spacecraft could easily have returned directly to earth, a trip of about 1½ days. Now it would be necessary to circle the moon before returning, a trip that would take 3 or 4 days. The flight controllers began frantically calculating whether or not the astronauts could possibly last that long. The astronauts had to abandon the command module because it would lose all of its power except for the power in its three reentry batteries. Every bit of that energy would be needed if the astronauts were to return. Before they hit the earth's atmosphere, they would have to get rid of the LM and the service module, because only the command module had the heat shield needed for reentry. Until then, the astronauts could use the LM as a lifeboat because it had power and controls that could maneuver the whole spacecraft. But the LM was designed to support only two men for about a 2-day trip from the command-module to the moon. Could the fuel, water, and oxygen be stretched to last three men for a 4-day trip around the moon and back to earth? The answer was "maybe"—a more definite answer would not be known until the very end.

As the ground crew made their calculations, the astronauts climbed inside the LM to fly their crippled spacecraft. Their world seemed to turn over as they entered because the floor of the command-module was in the position of the ceiling in the LM. Swigert, who knew the least about the LM, was worried most. As he watched the world fall away behind him, he had some very depressing thoughts about never returning to the dust of his planet. Lovell and Haise had less time for worrying because they had to follow a perpetual stream of instructions from mission control. They stood for hours grasping the pistol-grip hand controls of the thruster rockets. Their main job was to continuously change the spacecraft's attitude with respect to the sun, or else one side of their vessel would burn while the other froze. About 24 hours after the accident had occurred, the ground crew finally found a way for the LM's computer to do this rotation for the astronauts.

The astronauts then tried to sleep in the dead command module. Relaxing was difficult, even though they had been awake for 48 hours. Their sleeping area looked as if it were being lit by a slow motion disco strobe until Lovell pulled the shades. After the shades were pulled, however, the temperature dropped into the low 40s. The astronauts slept restlessly for the remainder of the trip, because their clothes and bedding couldn't keep them warm.

By Tuesday afternoon, the moon, which had looked like a small white disc at the time of the accident, now filled the spacecraft's windows. The constant chatter from mission control stopped when the astronauts circled around the moon's dark side, and they lost contact with earth for about 25 minutes.

As it rounded the moon, Apollo 13 was on a path that would swing it back toward earth, missing it by some 40,000 miles. To return safely, the astronauts would have to correct their course with their manual controls, and they would have to guide their spacecraft through a narrow reentry corridor. If they were outside this narrow path, they would bounce off into space without enough power to return. Their predicament was like that of a sailor using the stars as a guide for steering a floundering vessel. Ironically, however, even though they were in the heavens, they had trouble seeing the stars. Gases coming from the spacecraft clouded their view of the sky, making it almost impossible to hold a sextant on a star long enough to get their bearings. The astronauts thus had to settle for less precise targets to steer by—the sun, the moon, and even the earth itself, which would work until they were close to the earth. Before entering the earth's atmosphere, however, they would somehow have to get a fix on a star. To further complicate matters, controlling Apollo 13 now often called for the efforts of all three astronauts—it was like driving a car with one person working the brake, another the accelerator, and the third controlling the steering wheel.

While the fate of the astronauts depended upon their own visual abilities and their own motor coordination, they were not alone. Dozens of mission controllers, most of them in their twenties or thirties, were making heroic efforts to bring Apollo 13 home safely. They tested Apollo's equipment, trying to get it to do things for which it was never designed, and in 3 days they came up with a plan for reentry that would have otherwise taken 3 months to prepare. One of the most demanding jobs fell upon the shoulders of 27-year-old mission controller John Aaron. He had to find a way to stretch the remaining power in the command module over several hours, even though it was designed to last only 45 minutes. Aaron's final plan did not give the astronauts enough power to signal their location if they landed off target. The spacecraft would sink shortly after it landed in the ocean; what was the use of landing safely if it sank before they could find it? Aaron was concerned, but he had run out of options. They would have to hope for a direct hit.

When the earth finally loomed in the spacecraft's windows, it was time for one last try at a star check. One of the flight controllers suggested that Swigert try to locate Altair or Vega, two stars on the side of the spacecraft facing away from the sun, where its shadow could cut the glare. When Swigert tried this he couldn't see anything until a flight controller told him to turn off a nearby light. Meanwhile, Lovell, who could see that they were approaching the earth at an alarming rate, shouted to Swigert to hurry up; unless the adjustments in position were made quickly, they would be too late. With the light out, Swigert found Altair easily. Moments later, the computer compared the actual position with the estimated position of Apollo 13. The astronauts could not believe their bleary eyes. There was no error! Somehow, Haise's and Lovell's rough alignment with the sun and moon had been perfect. The test was quickly repeated on Vega, and Swigert's results were the same. Suddenly, the astronauts, who had been behind schedule, were now slightly ahead. They had 5 minutes to disconnect the LM from the rest of the spacecraft.

With the LM gone, the command module was flying alone. Earlier, when the service module was jettisoned, the astronauts got their only chance to see and photograph the damaged vessel. Lovell, the first to spot it, said, "O.K., I've got her. . . . And there's one whole side of that spacecraft missing." This raised questions in everyone's minds about whether or not the ceramic heat shield on the command module, which had been near the ruptured oxygen tank, was damaged. If it was, the astronauts would burn up during reentry.

This horrible thought returned when radio contact was lost during reentry. The astronauts should have reestablished radio contact 3 minutes and 30 seconds after hitting the atmosphere, but they didn't. Everyone waited anxiously. One minute and forty seconds later, Houston called the spacecraft. There was no answer. Then, 5 seconds later, Swigert called in, "O.K., Joe."

The astronauts splashed down safely near a recovery ship at 12:07 P.M., Houston time, on Friday, April 17. It was an unsuccessful mission, but it was perhaps Apollo's greatest success story.

It took advanced technology to send the Apollo 13 astronauts to the moon, but it took their basic sensory and perceptual abilities to get them back to earth. The astronauts depended upon sight to navigate, hearing to get instructions from mission control, and other senses, such as touch, to maneuver their crippled craft. This chapter is about these sensory and perceptual abilities. As a first step, we will examine methods for measuring sensations and perceptions.

What is the dimmest star visible from Apollo 13? This is a psychophysical question. **Psychophysics** studies the relationship between physical energies and psychological experiences. In this example, the physical energy is light from a star, and the psychological experience or sensation is seeing the star. Psychophysical questions can be grouped into three categories:

1. What is the **absolute threshold,** or the least amount of a certain stimulus energy, that can be detected? Our question about the dimmest star is an example. Table 3–1 shows a method that could be used to measure the absolute threshold for seeing a star.
2. What is the **difference threshold,** or the smallest difference in intensity, that can be noticed between two stimuli? For example, how

TABLE 3–1

The method shown here was used to record responses in a hypothetical experiment on the absolute threshold for seeing a star. On an ascending series, the observer first was given a light too dim to see, and reported, "No, I don't see it." The brightness was then gradually increased in equal steps until the observer reported, "Yes, I see it."

On a descending series, the observer first was given a light bright enough to see, and reported, "Yes, I see it." The brightness was then gradually decreased in equal steps until the observer reported, "No, I don't see it."

Star Intensity (in quanta)	Alternating Ascending and Descending Series (Yes = "I see it"; No = "I don't see it")					
120						
118						
116		Start				
114		Yes				Start
112		Yes		Start		Yes
110		Yes		Yes		Yes
108		Yes		Yes		Yes
106		Yes		Yes		No
104		Yes		Yes		
102		No		Yes		
100			Yes	No		
98			No		Yes	
96			No		No	
94	Yes		No		No	
92	No		No		No	
90	No		Start		No	
88	No				No	
86	No				No	
84	Start				No	
82					No	
80					Start	
78						
76						
Absolute threshold on each series	93	103	99	101	97	107

Average Absolute Threshold: 100

bright must a star be in order to appear just noticeably brighter than another star?

3. How do the intensity and other qualities of a stimulus relate to the intensity and other qualities of our sensations and perceptions?

Throughout this chapter we will be asking this sort of question about all of our sensations and perceptions: How does a stimulus get translated into a psychological experience that is seen, heard, tasted, smelled, or felt? We will begin with seeing, which is perhaps our most highly developed sense.

SEEING

The Apollo 13 crew had excellent vision, as this is a requirement for being an astronaut. As part of their mission, they were called on to navigate by dim stars, read information on their instrument panels, and identify important land formations on the moon. While some people enjoy good vision, many do not; some see poorly without corrective lenses, and some do not see at all. The main causes of visual problems and blindness are in the eyes themselves. We will briefly study the eyes and the physiology of the visual system. We will then turn to psychophysical facts that explain some of the things that the astronauts saw on their trip around the moon.

The Eyes

Figure 3–1 shows the structure of the human eye, which includes the following structures:

1. The **cornea** is the window of the eye. A healthy cornea is transparent and shaped like the side of a crystal ball. The **sclera** is the white, opaque, outer wall of the eye. The cornea is attached to the sclera. Two diseases of the cornea occur when the cornea becomes pointed, like the end of a football, or becomes cloudy. These diseases rarely cause blindness, however, because they can be corrected by corneal transplants.

2. The **aqueous humor** is a clear fluid that carries nourishment to the cornea. Have you ever seen spots hovering in front of your eyes?

FIGURE 3–1

This cross-section drawing shows the basic structures of the human eye: the cornea, iris, pupil, lens, vitreous humor, retina, fovea, and optic nerve.

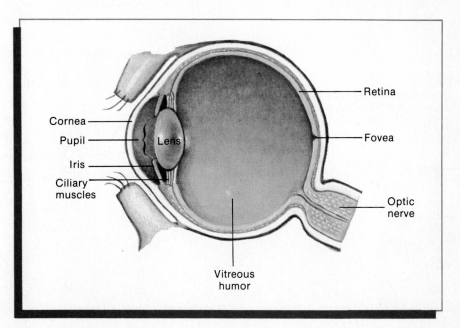

Cornea
Pupil
Lens
Iris
Ciliary muscles
Retina
Fovea
Optic nerve
Vitreous humor

FIGURE 3-2

Nearsightedness and farsightedness are caused by abnormal eye shapes. For clear vision, light must be focused directly on the eye's back wall, as it is in the normal eye. The nearsighted eye is too long, so light focuses in front of the back wall; the farsighted eye is too short, so it focuses behind the back wall.

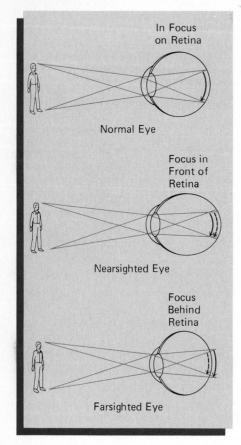

In Focus on Retina

Normal Eye

Focus in Front of Retina

Nearsighted Eye

Focus Behind Retina

Farsighted Eye

They can be caused by impurities floating in the aqueous humor. The "spots" can disappear and reappear because the aqueous humor is completely recycled every 4 hours. The most common cause of blindness is a problem with the recycling system, which causes pressure to build up inside the eye. The pressure can destroy the eye's critical structures. In America, this disease, called **glaucoma**, threatens more than 1½ million people with blindness. It can be treated with special eye drops and other methods. Early treatment is important, so it is wise to get periodic checkups.

3. When you are asked the color of your eyes, you are really being asked the color of your **iris**, which is a flat, doughnut-shaped network of muscles behind the aqueous humor. What appears to be a black spot in the center of the iris is actually an opening called the **pupil.**

Eye doctors examine the eye's internal structures with an **ophthalmoscope,** which uses mirrors or prisms to direct light through the pupil. This important instrument allows doctors to detect eye diseases and other diseases such as high blood pressure.

4. The **lens** is directly behind the pupil. It helps the cornea focus light onto the back of the eye. The lens does the critical fine adjustments or **accommodations** required to focus objects at various distances. It accommodates by changing its shape; it gets rounder for near objects and flatter for far ones.

The near point of accommodation is the nearest point at which print can be read distinctly. As we get older, we all lose some of our ability to accommodate. As a result, the near point of accommodation gets farther and farther away, until reading requires bifocals (or an extra-long arm!).

The most widespread disease affecting vision is **cataracts,** a condition characterized by cloudy lenses. Blindness results if the lenses become too cloudy, but, fortunately, surgical procedures provide a very effective treatment.

5. The **vitreous humor** is a semiliquid gel that fills the eye's main chamber and gives it a spherical shape. **Nearsightedness** results when an eye is elongated like a horizontal egg. Nearsighted people see near objects well, but see far objects poorly. **Farsightedness** is caused by an eye that is flattened, like a vertical egg (Figure 3–2). Farsighted people see far objects well, but see near objects poorly. Both of these problems are easily corrected by wearing glasses.

6. The **retina** is tissue covering most of the eye's interior wall. It contains receptors that respond to light, blood vessels, and a network of neurons that transmit information to the brain. One area of the retina is blind. This **blind spot** contains no light receptors, which are needed to see. You can find your blind spot with the simple test shown in Figure 3–3. There are no light receptors in this area because the space is taken up by the *optic nerve*, which is a bundle of nerve fibers that carry neural signals to the brain. In contrast to the blind spot, another retinal area, called the **fovea**, is especially sensitive. Most blood vessels and nerve

FIGURE 3-3

To locate your blind spot, close your left eye and stare at the X. Slowly move the book toward you and away from you at a distance of about a foot until the dot disappears.

fibers are routed around this sensitive area. In addition, the fovea has special light receptors, called *rods* and *cones*, which we will discuss in detail in the next section.

Light Receptors: Rods and Cones

The retina has two kinds of receptors: (1) **cones,** which are located mostly in the fovea and which are best for seeing details, and (2) **rods,** which are located mostly on the sides or periphery of the retina, and which are best for seeing in dim light.

Cones enable us to see sharp details. When you want to look at something, you move your eyes so that the image of the object you want to see is focused on your fovea, where most of your cones are. If you want to know what the world would be like without a fovea, look at a flashbulb when someone takes your picture. Almost all you will see with your fovea for the next several minutes is a bright silver spot. You will see the rest of the world only from the periphery or sides of your retina, where details are hard to make out. Try reading while you are still experiencing this and you will find out how hard it is to see details from the sides of the retina. Rods are best-suited to seeing in dim light—indeed, they are the only receptors that function at night. When you are using only your rods you cannot see color, which is why you see shades of black and white, but not color, in dim light and at night. Rods are located on the periphery or sides of the retina. As a result, you can see best at night if you look at something to your left or right rather than straight on. This is called **peripheral vision,** because you use the receptors on the periphery of the retina. Pilots who fly at night are trained to use their peripheral vision by looking at the sides or edges of what they want to see. You can use a TV set to demonstrate that peripheral vision is better than central vision for seeing dim lights. Watch the TV set for about 10 minutes in a room with all the lights out. Then turn off the set. The screen's glow will gradually fade. Soon it will be too dim to see when you look directly at it, but it will still be bright enough to see out of the side of your eyes when you look to either side.

Why are cones best for seeing details, while rods are best for seeing dim light? The answer is found in the neural pathways between these receptors and the brain.

Pathways to the Brain

The visual pathways connect the eyes with the brain's cortex, which we discussed in Chapter 2. But these pathways are more than passive cables; they contain cells that actively participate in the process of coding or interpreting the information contained in light. This coding process begins in the retina. Here all cones and rods are connected to bipolar cells, which are in turn connected to ganglion cells that send signals out of the retina to the brain (see Figures 3–4 and 3–5).

Cones and rods have different functions, in part, because they are connected to bipolar cells differently. Cones are best for seeing detail because almost every cone in the fovea has its own bipolar cell. The one-to-one connections give each cone a way to report to a bipolar cell. Two cones can thus report different messages when the light falling on them is in any way different. The separate messages enable us to discern small differences or details in what we see. Cones do not function in dim light because each cone's message gets too weak for bipolar cells to receive it.

Whereas each cone has its own bipolar cell, many rods share the same bipolar cell. These many-to-one connections allow rods to add their messages together to make a signal strong enough for a bipolar cell to receive.

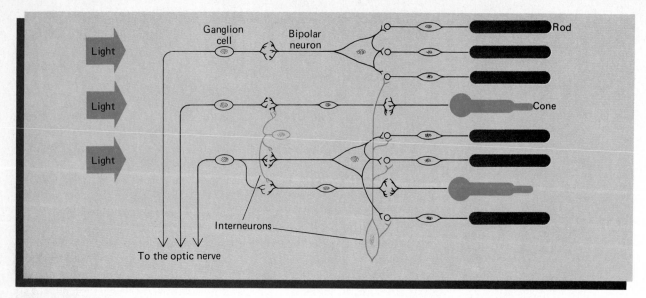

FIGURE 3–4

The visual pathways go from the retina to other brain structures. Messages first go from receptor cells to bipolar cells. Each cone sends a message to a separate bipolar cell. Many rods send messages to the same bipolar cell. Messages go from bipolar cells to ganglion cells, and then exit from the retina as part of the optic nerve.

For this reason, rods do much better than cones in dim light. The many-to-one connection also means, however, that each rod does not really send a separate message. Rods are therefore poor at discerning details, because of the way they are connected to bipolar cells.

Most cells in the visual pathways to the brain receive messages from many other cells and send messages to many other cells. Information is thereby added and subtracted, coded and recoded, in a series of processes that determine vision. These processes somehow turn poor optical information into clear perceptions. Optical information is poor because the eye's lens creates distorted images like those you see through a cheap magnifying glass. To make matters worse, light must pass through blood vessels and nerve fibers before reaching light receptors. Cells in the visual pathway and cortex work together to "clean up" the information (Campbell,

FIGURE 3–5

Messages from the left visual field travel to the right occipital lobe; messages from the right visual field of each eye go to the left occipital lobe. The place where they cross is called the optic chiasma.

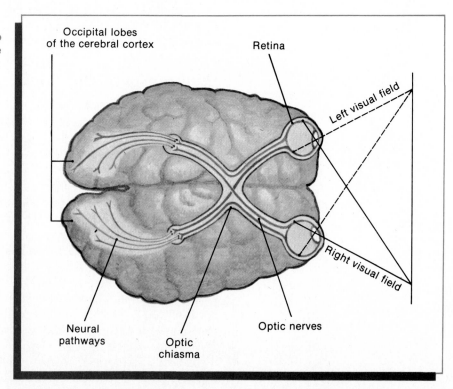

FIGURE 3–6

Can you tell whose portrait this is? Block portraits have two parts: a blurred picture of a famous person and a set of sharp edges outlining the blocks. A glance will tell you that this is poor optical information. Your visual system can clear up the information, however, with a little help. Have someone jiggle the picture slightly at a viewing distance of about 8 feet while you squint your eyes to blur your vision.

1974; Pollen and Ronner, 1982). Figure 3–6 illustrates what your visual system can do with poor optical information. Scientists are only beginning to understand how cells in the visual pathways and in the cortex join forces to determine what we see (see the Highlight, "The Eye Is Not a Camera").

Light and Dark Adaptation

Apollo 13 astronauts navigated by dim stars that sent very little light into their eyes, and they saw without pain the bright light reflected from the moon's surface. Similarly, we can see dimly lit faces in a movie theater, and we can see the light reflected from snow on a bright sunny day. But this large range of sensitivity is never available at any one moment. When we walk from sunlight into a dark theater, for example, we are almost blinded until our eyes adjust. We are again almost blinded until our eyes adjust when we leave the dark theater to go back out into the sunlight. If we can understand how this happens, we will have a partial explanation for why Swigert had difficulty seeing that dim star that was so important for the navigation of the Apollo 13 spacecraft on its return journey.

When the eyes are exposed to light, their sensitivity continually changes. If the amount of light remains fairly constant for about 15 minutes, the eyes will become most sensitive to that amount of light and will be unable to see lights that are about 100 times brighter or 100 times dimmer. Thus, while the overall range of sensitivity is enormous, the range *at any one moment* is relatively narrow. When we enter a movie theater on a sunny afternoon, we encounter more than a 100-fold decrease in light, far outside our momentary range of sensitivity, so we cannot see well. An adjustment in sensitivity starts immediately and continues for about 15 minutes until our eyes become as sensitive as possible to the level of light in the theater. This adjustment of sensitivity is called **dark adaptation.** The adjustment that takes place when we go from the dark theater into sunlight is called **light adaptation.**

Aboard Apollo 13, Swigert adapted to the level of light in the command module. Because these lights were very bright, the brightness of the stars was too dim until Swigert's eyes dark-adapted enough to bring the stars within his momentary range of sensitivity.

Color Vision

Part of the astronauts' excellent vision is the ability to tell the difference between green and red lights on Apollo's control panels. All the lights would look yellow to people who are *colorblind;* **colorblindness** is the inability to distinguish between colors. Imagine walking through a grocery store and seeing yellow beefsteaks and hams, yellow cabbage, yellow radishes, and yellow spinach. Now you leave the store on a bright summer day, walk across a well-manicured yellow lawn and past tall yellow pine trees, and approach a traffic signal containing three vertically arranged yellow lights. This is how the world looks to about 2 out of every 100 males and to about 2 out of every 10,000 females who have red-green colorblindness. (We would have no idea how the world looks to colorblind people if it were not for a few people who had red-green blindness in one eye and normal vision in the other. Things that look red and green to the normal eye look light yellow to the colorblind eye.) There are other less common kinds of colorblindness. For example, some people have yellow-blue blindness; that is, they can't tell the difference between yellows and blues. Others have total colorblindness. We are not sure how their world looks, but it might be like watching black-and-white TV. Some people

HIGHLIGHT / THE EYE IS NOT A CAMERA

Scientists used to think that our eyes worked like a camera. Cameras produce images of objects by recording light intensities at each point. If you enlarged a photograph many times, you would see that it is made-up of dots ranging in brightness from light to dark. Until fairly recently, scientists compared the dots in such pictures with the response of each retinal receptor in the eye; thus they thought that eyes send dotlike pictures to the brain, where they are interpreted.

In the 1950s researchers in a number of different laboratories tried to find out exactly what the frog's eye tells the frog's brain. The answer electrified the scientific community. One kind of cell in the retina responded best when a small black disk was moved about in front of a frog's eye. When this was done, frogs jumped and snapped at it as if they were trying to catch a bug. This class of retinal cell was called a "bug detector." The point was that this response was cued by a cell in the retina—not in the brain.

Those who had been thinking about eyes as cameras suddenly realized that the retina did much more than they thought. It does not just project a picture for the brain to recognize and interpret—it does some of the recognizing and interpreting itself.

David Hubel and Thorsten Wiesel won half of the 1981 Nobel prize for medicine for their research in this field. They found cells that might be called feature detectors because they respond to specific aspects or features of a visual stimulus (just as the frog's bug detector responded to the buglike aspects of certain stimuli). Hubel and Wiesel (1970) gained special recognition by investigating the development and organization of feature detectors.

They discovered that feature detectors develop shortly after birth, and that their development depends upon visual experience. Detectors are permanently altered if kittens get distorted visual experience during critical early stages of life (see Chapter 7). Such studies of altered development depended upon years of research on the normal organization of feature detectors. Hubel and Wiesel (1965) had found, for instance, that detectors of different complexities are neatly organized in the brain (see Figure A). One layer of cells near the brain's surface has *simple cells,* which respond only if a line of a specific orientation falls on a specific retinal location. A deeper layer has *complex cells,* which respond to a line of a specific orientation no matter where it falls on the retina. A still deeper layer has *hypercomplex cells,* which detect angles and other features. One of Hubel and Wiesel's greatest contributions was a model of how such detectors might work together. The accompanying figure shows how cells might be connected, for example. Such models provided the foundation not only for Hubel and Wiesel's subsequent research, but also for the work of many modern researchers in vision and development.

FIGURE A. Organization of feature detectors.

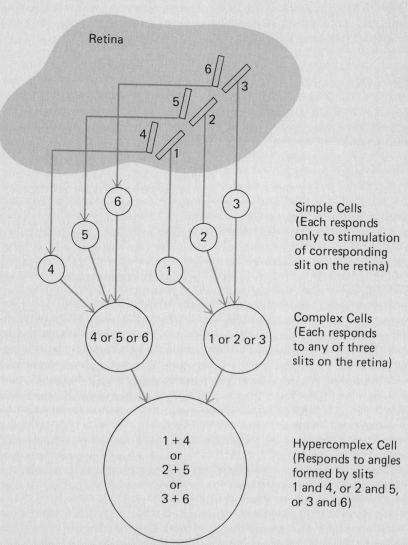

Simple Cells (Each responds only to stimulation of corresponding slit on the retina)

Complex Cells (Each responds to any of three slits on the retina)

Hypercomplex Cell (Responds to angles formed by slits 1 and 4, or 2 and 5, or 3 and 6)

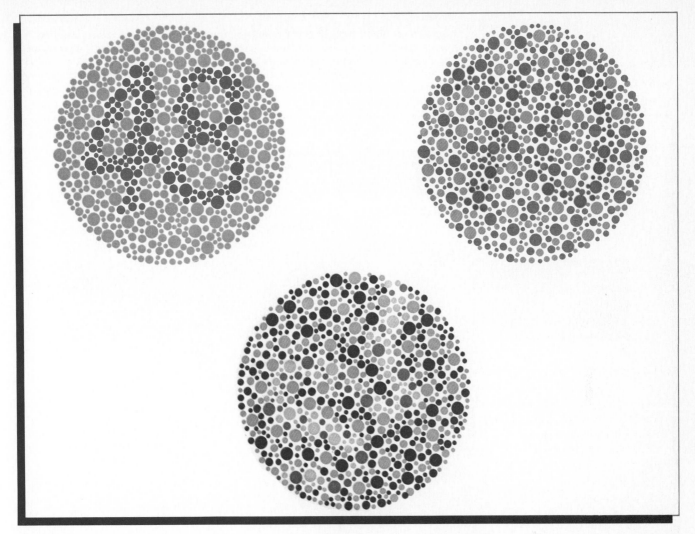

FIGURE 3–7

A common colorblindness test is contained in these figures. If you don't see numbers in two of the circles you have red-green color blindness. If you don't see a pattern in the other circle, you have yellow-blue colorblindness.

do not realize they are colorblind until they are tested with the pictures shown in Figure 3–7.

The high value placed on color is illustrated by the popularity of color television. Today Americans buy more color than black-and-white televisions, even though color sets cost quite a bit more. In this section, we will discuss some of the research that lead to the development of color television.

The first major breakthrough was Isaac Newton's (1642–1727) discovery that white light from the sun is a compound of all colors. We now know that light travels in waves, with different wavelengths for each color. Figure 3–8 shows the electromagnetic spectrum forming the entire range of wavelengths of electromagnetic radiation. The wavelengths corresponding to visible colors cover only a small part of the whole spectrum. For example, we do not see X-rays, which are much shorter in wavelength than light waves, and we do not see radio waves, which are much longer. Objects have particular colors because they absorb some wavelengths and reflect others. We see the reflected wavelengths; a red apple, for example, reflects red wavelengths.

The next major breakthrough occurred when Thomas Young (1773–1829) tackled the problem of how the nervous system responds to different wavelengths. He began with experiments on color mixture, which are illustrated in Figure 3–9. Three colored lights (violet, red, and green) are projected onto a screen in an otherwise dark room. The resulting pattern reminds one of an insignia on a color TV. This is no accident—experiments on color mixing led to the development of color TV. The most unusual

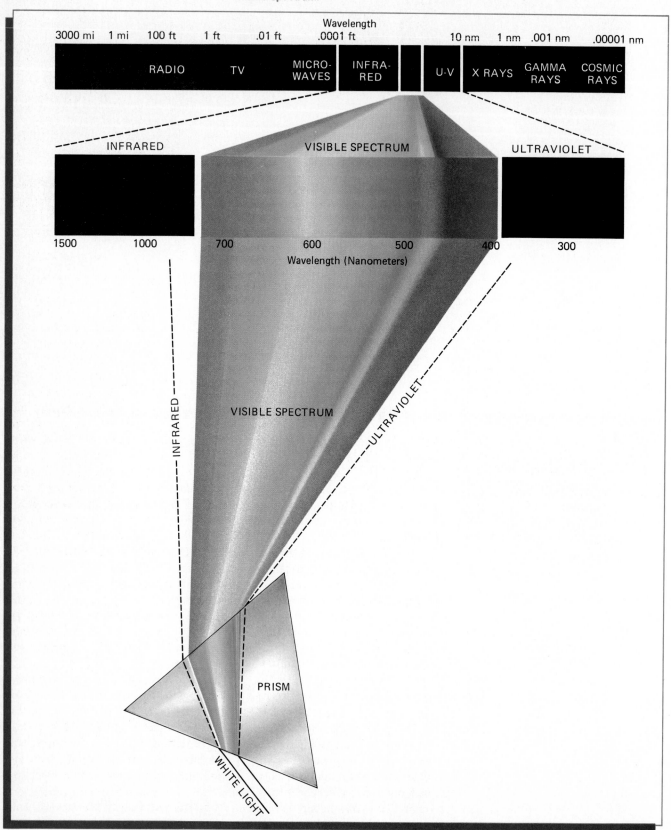

FIGURE 3–8

Sunlight, or white light, contains all the colors that we can see. A prism separates white light into its component colors. Each color in this visible spectrum corresponds to a specific wavelength. Light travels in waves, and wavelength is the distance between wave crests. The visible spectrum is only a small part of the electromagnetic spectrum, which consists of energy traveling in wavelengths that are shorter or longer than the visible spectrum.

FIGURE 3–9

Color mixture of three lights is shown here—red, green, and violet; they are widely spaced on the spectrum. Any color on the spectrum can be produced in the overlapping areas by adjusting the intensities of the three lights. Here we see yellow where green and red mix, and we see white where all three mix.

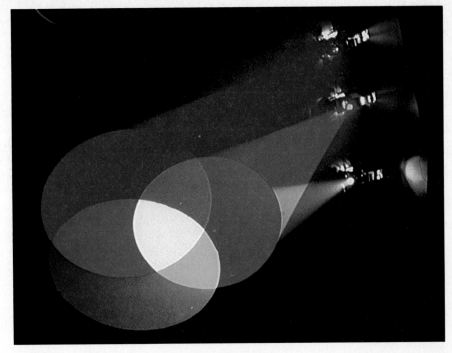

FIGURE 3–10

This green, black, and yellow flag will turn red, white, and blue in an afterimage. You can make an afterimage by staring at the lower right-hand star for about 45 seconds. You will then see the afterimage when you shift your gaze to a bright white piece of paper.

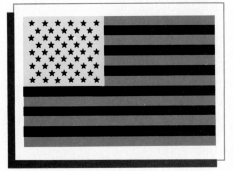

aspect of Figure 3–9 is that white is seen where all three colors overlap and yellow is seen where red and green overlap. Young could produce every color of the visible spectrum in the overlapping areas by varying the intensity of the lights. He theorized that the retina contains three kinds of color receptors and that the signals from these merge to produce our sensations of color. With further developments by Hermann von Helmholtz (1821–1894), this theory, called the *trichromatic receptor theory,* led physiologists to verify that the retina does indeed have three kinds of color receptors. Each kind responds differently to colors. One responds most to blue-violet, another responds most to green, and another favors yellow-red (Marks, Dobelle, and MacNichol, 1964; Brown and Wald, 1964).

This is an important fact, but it doesn't explain all aspects of color vision. For example, it does not explain what you see in Figure 3–10. If you stare at the picture for about 45 seconds and then shift your gaze to a white surface, you will see red where green had been, white where black had been, and blue where yellow had been. What you see is an afterimage. It occurs because some activity continues in the retina after you look away from the picture. The trichromatic receptor theory does not account for the colors of afterimages.

To explain this and other observations, Hering (1877) offered the *opponent-process theory,* which states that receptor cells are joined in opposing pairs. The color we see depends upon whether a pair responds positively or negatively. For example, blue is seen when a blue-yellow pair responds negatively; yellow is seen when it responds positively. This explains why afterimages appear blue when yellow is in the original. When we look at yellow, the receptor that is sensitive to yellow gets *fatigued;* that is, it responds less to the same stimulus. When cells are not fatigued, light from a white surface stimulates the blue-yellow pair equally so that neither color is seen. But when the yellow side is fatigued, it does not respond as strongly, upsetting the balance in favor of blue. As a result, we see blue. The theory also proposes the existence of a red-green opponent pair and a black-white pair, which explains the other colors we see in the afterimage (Hurvich and Jameson, 1974).

We turn now to the role of organization, and how it affects our visual sensations and perceptions.

FIGURE 3–11

These drawings illustrate four Gestalt laws of organization. (A) The law of proximity. We group together elements that are close together. (B) The law of similarity. We group together elements that are alike. (C) The law of good continuation. We group together line segments that form straight or smoothly curving lines (thus you will see a circle and a square in the left figure rather than the two objects shown in the right figure). (D) The law of closure. We tend to fill in gaps in straight lines or smooth curves.

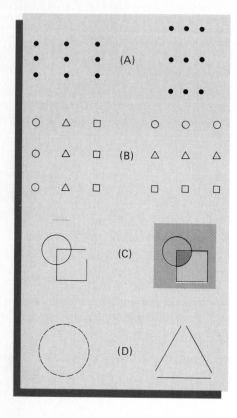

FIGURE 3–12

The reversible goblet can be seen as a white cup against a blue background or as two blue faces against a white background.

The Role of Organization in Vision

Think for a moment about the flood of light rushing into your eyes when you stand at a window and see a house, trees, and sky. Millions of receptors are stimulated by the light stream, which contains many different wavelengths, colors, and intensities. Receptors register these separately, but you do not see separate patches of colors and brightnesses. Somehow separate sensations are organized into wholes so that you see a house, trees, and sky. You would have a hard time seeing other groupings of these stimuli. For example, you could not easily see the trees as part of the house, because you unconsciously follow a set of rules for organizing sensations.

Gestalt Laws of Organization. In the 1920s a group of German psychologists, called the Gestalt school, attempted to describe the rules by which we organize sensations. "Gestalt" means a structure that forms a unit or a whole, and the Gestalt laws of organization describe the way in which we tend to group objects or stimuli according to certain characteristics that they have. For example, one such law, the **law of nearness or proximity**, says that we group elements that are close together. In Figure 3–11 we see three vertical columns of dots when the vertical dots are closer together than the horizontal ones. When the horizontal dots are closer, then we see three horizontal rows of dots.

Another law is the **law of similarity**, which states that we group elements that are similar, or look alike. In Figure 3–11 we see three vertical columns of figures when the vertical elements are similar, and three horizontal rows when the horizontal elements are similar. Other Gestalt laws of organization are illustrated and briefly described in Figure 3–11.

It was also the Gestalt school that pointed out our basic tendency to divide what we see into **figure** (an object) and **ground** (the background or surroundings of the object). But what happens when figure and ground suddenly reverse, as they do in Figure 3–12? When you look at this figure, you see a goblet at one moment and a pair of silhouetted faces the next. This phenomenon is called **figure-ground reversal** or **multistable perception,** since you perceive more than one image in the same figure (Attneave, 1976).

The fact that figure and ground seem to reverse in this way points up something that we often overlook: *We* impose organization on objects, we do not just passively take in what's there. How else could we see two different pictures in Figure 3–12? The basic drawing, the sensory input, remains the same. Our perception changes.

Organization of Moving Patterns. We actively impose organization on moving objects. As shown in Figure 3–13A, when people view a light on the rim of a rolling wheel in an otherwise dark room the light appears to hop along, making a series of arches. The same physical motion path looks quite different, however, if a light is added to the opposite side of the rim of the wheel. Both lights then appear to roll smoothly along, spinning around an invisible hub. The same physical motion looks different when the other light is added because viewers impose different organizations on it. Scientists are learning the rules that we use to impose organization on wheel motions, and these same rules explain how we organize more complicated motions as well, such as those made by a walking person or a waving hand, as shown in Figure 3–13B (Johansson, 1973, 1976; Proffitt and Cutting, 1980; Cutting and Proffitt, 1981).

In the next chapter, we will follow up on the theme of our active contribution to perception. There we will discuss dreams and other experiences in which we seem to construct perceptions out of nothing.

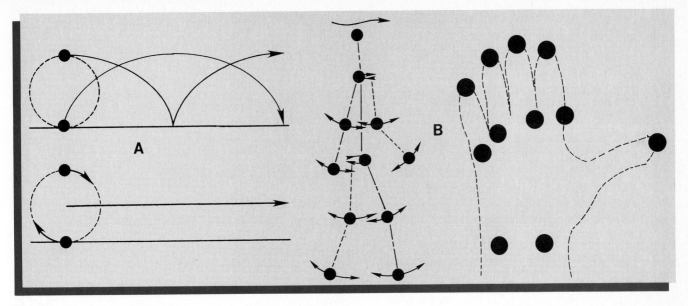

FIGURE 3–13

This figure shows the various ways that we actively impose organization on moving objects, such as a rolling wheel, a person walking, or a hand waving.

FIGURE 3–14

The identical twins, Evangeline and Jacqueline Motely, look the same size in this picture, even though the image of the farther one is only half as large as that of the closer one. This illustrates the law of size constancy.

Constancies

If figure-ground reversals make you dizzy, you may find relief in the stability, or constancy, of our perceptual world. We depend on this constancy even to recognize a friend. For example, we may look at a friend from a number of different angles, close up and far away, in bright light or in dim light, and still recognize him or her as the same person under all these different conditions. In the same way, Apollo 13 astronauts depended on constancy as they circled the moon. They identified important land formations even though they saw them under continually changing conditions. This seems simple enough, but there really is nothing simple about it—in fact, scientists still do not understand how it is done. How can perceptions remain constant when optical information changes? Let's look at what scientists have come up with in answer to this question for size, shape, and other perceptual constancies.

Size Constancies. Look at the twins in Figure 3–14. The twin on the left was 4 feet away when the picture was taken, and the one on the right was 8 feet away. Their picture illustrates the **law of size constancy,** which states that we see an object's size as constant even if the object's distance from us changes.

Figure 3–15 explains how **retinal image** sizes change. Light reflects off the twins into the observer's eye. The critical light rays for this discussion are those coming from the feet and the top of the head. They are represented by two lines that cross over inside the eye's lens. The angle between these lines is called the **visual angle.** It gets smaller as an object moves farther away. When the visual angle gets smaller, the retinal image also gets smaller. The closer twin's visual angle is twice as big, and therefore her retinal image is twice as big as the farther twin.

So why do we perceive the twins as being the same size? Scientists don't really know. We might suppose that the perceived size remains constant because we *know* the approximate true size. (For example, we know the twins in Figure 3–14 are the same size.) However, this explanation can be ruled out for two reasons. First, size would be seen as constant even if unfamiliar objects, such as boards, were seen in place of the twins. Second, if a picture contains misleading information about distance, we will be fooled, even if we know the true size of the objects. For example, the Ames Room (see Figure 3–16) is designed to provide misleading information about distance. As can be seen in the diagram in Figure 3–16, the left corner of the room is actually much farther away than the right

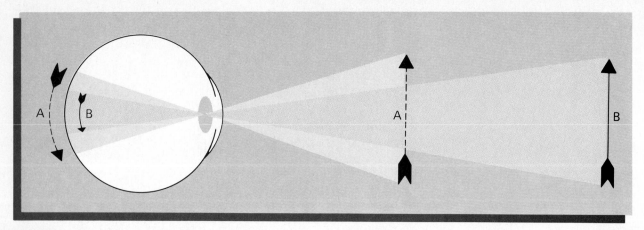

FIGURE 3–15

Retinal image size is determined by the visual angle, which is defined at the eye's lens by the angle between light rays coming from the top and bottom of an object. As an object gets closer, its visual angle and its retinal image size get larger.

FIGURE 3–16

The Ames room, shown here, distorts the apparent size of three men. Your eye is fooled in this picture because the room looks square, but is actually not. The diagram illustrates the actual shape of the room, which causes the men to seem to be such different sizes.

corner, yet the corners appear equally far away. People in the far corner of an Ames room look like dwarfs, while those in the close corner look like giants. Obviously, seeing objects with familiar sizes does not guarantee accurate size perception.

There are two opposing theories of size constancy: the unconscious inference theory (Epstein, 1973; Rock, 1977), and the ecological theory (Gibson, 1979). Unconscious inference theory states that we unconsciously make accurate inferences about object size when we have accurate information about retinal image size and object distance. It follows that perceived size should be consistent with perceived distance. In the Ames Room we saw distorted sizes *because* we saw distorted distances. Specifically, the person on the left has a smaller image and he looks just as close as the person on the right. Therefore, we unconsciously infer that he is smaller.

In contrast, the ecological theory states that we see a constant size because we see some aspect of the visual scene that remains unchanged when distance changes. For example, the twins are the same size with respect to the walls near both of them. If we respond to such relationships, we would be fooled by Ames's trick room because basic relationships

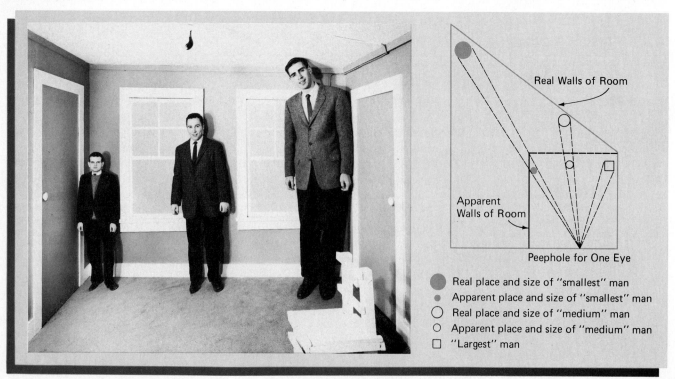

Real Walls of Room

Apparent Walls of Room

Peephole for One Eye

● Real place and size of "smallest" man
• Apparent place and size of "smallest" man
○ Real place and size of "medium" man
○ Apparent place and size of "medium" man
□ "Largest" man

are distorted. Notice, for example, the size of the people with respect to the sizes of doors and windows. Accordingly, the trick room misleads us by distorting relationships that are critical for constancy.

Other Constancies. The issues raised about size perception also apply to other constancies. The **law of shape constancy** states that we see an object's shape as constant when the object's slant changes, or when we view it from a different angle. Figure 3–17 shows how this might occur. The checkers are round and the board is square in the top picture; the checkers are shaped like footballs and the board's side edges are shorter in the side view. Because of shape constancy, however, the checkers look round and the board looks square in both views.

Unconscious inference theory says that we unconsciously infer the correct shapes when we see the correct slants. Ecological theory states that we see a constant shape because we see some aspect of the visual scene that stays the same when the slant changes. For example, the same number of squares run along the left and right edges of the checkerboard, whether it is slanted or not.

The **law of brightness constancy** states that we see an object's brightness as constant when the amount of light striking it changes. For example, you see the ink on this page as black and the paper as white in dim light or in bright light. The ink reflects about 5 percent of the light that strikes it; the paper reflects about 80 percent. Thus, when 100 units of light strike the page, the ink reflects 5 units and the paper reflects 80 units. When 10,000 units of light strike the page, the ink reflects 500 units and the paper reflects 8,000 units. Hans Wallach (1948) showed that the appearance of black and white remains constant because our perceptual system responds to the *ratio* of the light from an object divided by the light from what surrounds it. In our example, this ratio is the same in dim light, 5/80 = .0625, and bright light, 500/8,000 = .0625.

How do our two theories explain this? The ecological theory says that we perceive a constant because some aspect of the visual scene remains constant (in this case, the ratio of light reflected remains constant, even though the light itself may change). Unconscious inference theorists (Gilchrist, 1975), however, argue that unconscious inferences must also play a role. They note that changes in brightness do not always affect objects and backgrounds equally. When the sun comes out from behind a cloud, for instance, more light might shine on the ground than on a tree trunk growing out of the ground. We take into account such differences in lighting, according to unconscious inference theory.

FIGURE 3–17

The photograph on the right here shows a quite distorted view of the same checkerboard shown on the left, but, because of shape constancy, the checkers look round and the board looks square in both photographs.

FIGURE 3–18

Can you trust your eyes to distinguish craters from hills in the area indicated on this photograph? Turn the book upside down and try again. Many people see a depth reversal in the two ways of looking at the photo. That is, they see hills where they had seen craters and vice-versa.

Depth Perception

As Lovell, Swigert, and Haise rounded the back side of the moon, they were presented with a breathtaking sight. For them this was the most important part of their flight. It gave them a chance to bring back some scientific data that would, in some minds, justify the expense of the mission. In order to recognize the hills and craters they were looking for, the astronauts had to be able to see the relative depth between the tops and bottoms of the land formations. Figure 3–18 shows how difficult this can be. At first glance, the craters and hills are readily distinguished. But, turn the book upside down and look again. Now, what you had identified as craters are seen as hills, and vice versa. This depth reversal is related to shading cues. While shadows have a powerful effect on depth perception, they are by no means the only source of depth information available to us.

We will discuss three kinds of depth information in this section: binocular, monocular, and kinetic. Binocular information is available through the use of both eyes. Monocular information is available even when we use only one eye. And kinetic information is available only when we move or when the environment moves.

Seeing Depth with Two Eyes. Because our eyes are separated by several centimeters, we get a different view of the world from each eye. This difference is called **binocular disparity.** You can see disparity for yourself by closing one eye while holding your right index finger about 12 inches in front of your nose, and your left index finger about 6 inches in front of your nose. Look at the far finger first with one eye and then the other. Your near finger will appear to be in different places as you look with each eye. Now look with both eyes—you will see a double image of the near finger.

When you look at distant objects, binocular disparity (the different view from each eye) is so small that you usually are not aware of it. Even though you see a single image, however, you notice the disparity at an unconscious level. When disparity is very large, people see double images. When disparity is small, the brain fuses or integrates the images, using the disparity as a source of information about depth. The brain can use even small disparities as a depth cue. In fact, most of us are very sensitive to disparity, and we use it to help us see depth.

Seeing Depth with One Eye. You can get a feeling for **monocular** cues for depth by looking around you with your hand over one eye. You can still see depth, but you are using different cues than you would be if you were using both eyes. Monocular cues are used not only to see depth (the relative distance between objects), but also to see how far away objects are from you. A number of the most common monocular cues are shown in Figure 3–19: clearness, linear perspective, and texture.

One monocular cue is *clearness.* We look at objects on earth through air filled with tiny particles, which causes far objects to look blurry. This cue wouldn't have helped the astronauts on the moon, however, because in that environment there is no air or suspended particles. As a result, far objects look as sharp as near ones on the moon.

One of the most important monocular cues is **linear perspective.** Artists use linear perspective to create the impression of depth in their paintings. Notice, for example, how railroad tracks in Figure 3–19 seem to converge or come together in the distance. We often use linear perspective unconsciously to see depth in our environment.

Usually linear perspective is used in close conjunction with *texture.* Some surfaces, such as plastics and metals, have very little texture—they have smooth surfaces. But most surfaces have noticeable elements, or texture; for example, carpets, lawns, and foliage have texture, and

A   B   C

FIGURE 3–19

Monocular cues: (A) clearness, (B) linear perspective, and (C) texture gradient.

certainly the moon's surface has texture. As we look at something with texture, the nearer elements are spaced farther apart than the more distant elements, forming what is known as a **texture gradient.** Some natural examples of texture gradient are shown in Figure 3–19C.

Seeing Depth Through Motion. As the astronauts flew over the moon, their viewpoint changed continuously, giving them a powerful source of depth information. We learned earlier that the brain can determine depth from the two views of the world it gets from each eye. The brain also detects depth by using different views it gets when a person moves. You can see the power of motion or **kinetic depth** information while looking at a bush. You will not be able to tell which branches are in front of which when you look with only one eye and with your head held still. As soon as you swing your head back and forth, however, you will notice the depth of the bush. James Gibson and Hans Wallach did important experiments on motion and depth (Gibson, 1957; Wallach and O'Connell, 1953).

Visual Illusions

The human sensory and perceptual abilities are reliable enough to bring astronauts back from the moon, but they are far from perfect. They are, in fact, very undependable in some situations. An example of this is **illusions,** which are perceptual distortions. Illusions not only endanger astronauts, they also threaten airplane pilots. Kraft and Elworth (1969) found evidence, for example, that visual illusions cause about 16 percent of all airplane accidents.

Boeing officials had turned to Kraft for help after four Boeing 727s crashed within a 4-month period; there were no apparent mechanical causes for any of these crashes. Dr. Conrad Kraft, Chief Scientist for the Personnel Subsystem of Boeing's Commercial Aircraft Division, combined a thorough knowledge of aviation with the data and methods of experimental psychology. In their experiments, Kraft and Elworth built a device to simulate night visual approaches. The simulator included a stationary cockpit and a model airport that moved in response to the cockpit controls. The device simulated distances from 34 to 4.5 miles and altitudes from 16,000 feet to *minus* 2,500 feet. Kraft asked 12 experienced pilots to make simulated visual approaches. The simulator reproduced the visual conditions faced by the pilots who crashed in the Boeing 727s. Had the simulated flights been real, all but one of the pilots would have crashed short of the runway. The one successful pilot was an ex-Navy pilot who had gained his early experience landing on aircraft carriers. Kraft did not explain exactly what kind of illusion caused the others to "crash," but he did explain how the angle of approach distorted important visual information, increasing the pilots' susceptibility to visual illusions.

Psychologists studied visual illusions long before they knew that these could bring down an airplane. Let's look at some of their findings.

Geometrical Illusions.   The illusions shown in Figure 3–20 are line drawings that produce perceptual errors. Look at them and then measure them. In contrast to what the drawings look like, your ruler will tell you the following: the two horizontal lines are the same length in both the Müller-Lyer illusion and the Ponzo illusion; the oblique lines are parallel in the Zollner illusion; and the inner circles are the same size in the Titchener illusion. Scientists have studied such illusions for over 100 years in an attempt to gain a better understanding of perception (Gillam, 1980). In one important experiment Schiller and Wiener (1962) found that illusions are almost full strength when their parts are presented to each eye separately, indicating that the distortions are in the brain and not in the eye. Psychologists study illusions in the hope of better understanding the perceptual system. Whether or not illusions fulfill this hope, they do teach an important lesson. Those who maintain that "seeing is believing" are putting their eggs in the wrong basket. Sometimes "seeing is deceiving" (Coren and Girgus, 1978).

UFOs and Illusions: The Autokinetic Effect.   The autokinetic effect is the tendency for a stationary light viewed against darkness to look as if it's moving. The light seems to glide, jerk, and swoop through space. The autokinetic effect could be responsible for some reports of unidentified flying objects (UFOs). Word spreads fast about UFO sightings, causing people's imaginations to run wild. This could set the stage for the autokinetic swooping of some distant house light to become a UFO in the mind of some well-intentioned witness (Geldard, 1972).

The autokinetic effect is extremely dangerous for aviators. Planes flying in formation at night have collided because pilots saw autokinetic movement of another plane's wing light. Pilots have also crashed while trying to fly next to what appeared to be another plane but what turned out to be a street light or marker buoy.

You can demonstrate the autokinetic effect by setting a dim penlight on a table edge in an otherwise dark room. This demonstration is fun, especially in a group. If each of you draws the motion path you see, without talking about it, you will all draw different paths. If one of you reports the light's apparent motion out loud, though, most of the rest of the group will tend to see the same path (Sherif, 1936). This shows the power of suggestion and group pressure on the illusion, which we will discuss in more detail in Chapter 15.

Psychologists have debated the cause of the autokinetic effect for over 100 years. The most popular explanation is that eye movements somehow cause the illusion. When we look at a light, our eyes seem motionless, but they actually move about randomly over a tiny area. As a result, the image of the light moves slightly over the retina. Matin and MacKinnon (1964) tested for the autokinetic effect when these small image movements were stopped by a special device. This device greatly reduced the autokinetic effect, suggesting that eye movements do play a part in the illusion. It has been suggested that eye movements produce autokinetic motion of a light because the brain fails to keep track of eye movements unless the light has a fixed relationship to other objects (Worchel and Burnham, 1967).

Psychologists have also attempted to find practical ways to reduce the autokinetic effect. One way is to replace single lights with a cluster of several lights (Royce, Stayton, and Kinkade, 1962). Another way is to

FIGURE 3–20

These drawings show several geometrical illusions, which cause a disagreement between what you see and what you can measure with a ruler.

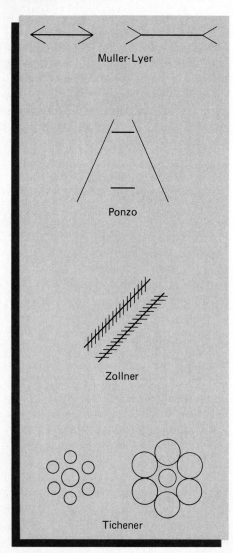

Muller-Lyer

Ponzo

Zollner

Tichener

Understanding visual illusions is an important part of making modern air travel safe.

flash the light source. A group of researchers showed that autokinetic motion is greatly reduced for lights flashing between 4 and 10 times per second (Page, Elfner, and Jarnison, 1966). No one completely understands why the clusters and flashes work, but the results have practical value. Today lights on towers and aircraft blink. Undoubtably, this has saved many pilots who would have otherwise fallen victim to the autokinetic illusion.

HEARING

If seventeenth century scientists could have imagined the possibility of Apollo 13's explosion in airless outer space, they could have made predictions about whether or not the astronauts would hear the sound. In 1650 their predictions would have been wrong. A decade later, they could have correctly predicted the silent explosion. Around 1650, a German scientist, Athanasins Kircher, tried to determine whether sound could be heard in a vacuum. He put a bell in a glass tube and pumped out as much air as he could. When he heard the bell, he mistakenly concluded that sounds can travel through empty space. Ten years later Robert Boyle, a British scientist, challenged this conclusion. Boyle repeated the experiment with an improved method for creating a vacuum. With all the air removed, the bell was silent inside Boyle's vacuum tube. It could be heard again when a slight amount of air was pumped back into the tube. Boyle correctly concluded that sound needs a medium—that is, a substance such as air to carry it. Outer space lacks air, so Apollo 13's explosion was silent.

We now know that sound travels through air like waves travel through water. A stone dropped in a pond sends out ripples in all directions. Similarly, when objects vibrate in air, they create waves in air. To understand hearing we must learn how these sound waves affect the ears.

The Ears

The word "ears" brings to mind flaps on the sides of the head. But, as Figure 3–21 shows, these flaps are just one of three basic subdivisions of ears:

1. The *external ear* captures sound traveling through the air. The pinna is the elastic flap we usually are referring to when we talk about the ear. The ear canal is a tubelike passage that funnels sound. The eardrum is a fine membrane stretched over the inner end of the ear canal; it vibrates when sound waves strike it.

2. The *middle ear* is a small air cavity containing three small bones: the hammer, the anvil, and the stirrup. This delicate chain of bones transmits sounds from the eardrum to the inner ear.

3. The *inner ear* is the part of the ear that transforms sound vibrations into neural impulses, which we discussed in Chapter 2. It receives sounds through the oval window, which is a membrane stretched over the opening of the inner ear. Attached to the oval window is a structure that

FIGURE 3–21

As can be seen in this diagram, the ear has three parts: the external ear or pinna, which includes the ear canal and the eardrum; the middle ear, which contains the hammer, the anvil, and the stirrup; and the inner ear, which contains the oval window and the cochlea.

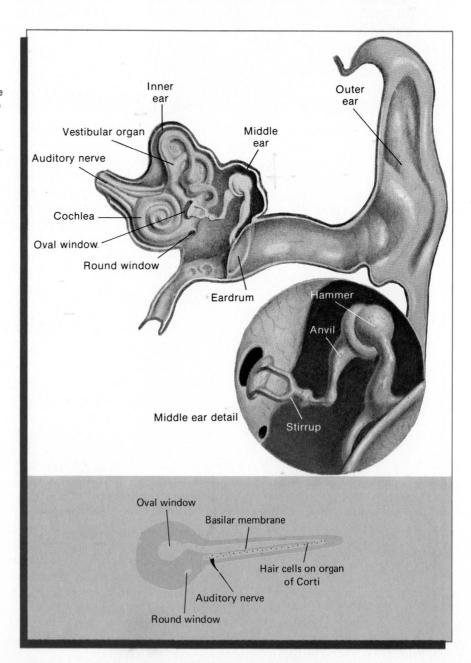

looks like a snail. It is called the **cochlea,** which is the Latin word for snail. It is a coiled tube that makes about three turns, like a spiral around a central core. Inside the cochlea is a flexible membrane, called the **basilar membrane.** It is attached to the oval window at one end and to the tip of the cochlea at the other end. Vibrations in the oval window cause hair cells on the basilar membrane to vibrate. When the hair cells are bent, they send nerve impulses along the acoustic nerve to the brain.

To sum up, the external ear collects and focuses sound, causing the eardrum to vibrate. Three delicate bones carry these vibrations to the oval window, which vibrates receptors in the cochlea, triggering nerve impulses to the brain.

Bone conduction is another way that sound is transmitted. When you speak, your jaw bones conduct vibrations to the cochlea. Thus, you hear your voice through bone-conducted sounds and air-conducted sounds. Others hear your voice only through air-conducted sounds. Your tape recorded voice sounds strange to you because you are not used to hearing only your air-conducted sound, which is the way everyone else hears your voice. Some hearing aids use bone conduction when the middle ear cannot conduct sound. Other hearing aids simply amplify air-conducted sound.

Characteristics of Sound

Sound waves are easier to study when they are converted to visible waves. Figure 3–22 shows a way to do this with an **oscilloscope,** which is similar to a television. We can learn relationships between psychological and physical characteristics of hearing by listening to a sound while watching it on an oscilloscope. Let's imagine taking an oscilloscope to a concert.

Frequency and Pitch. We have all delighted in the mellow low notes of a bass singer and the trilling high notes of a soprano. But have you ever wondered how we hear the difference between low and high notes? Such differences are referred to as differences in **pitch.** In Figure 3–23 we see that changes in pitch correspond to changes in **frequency** of sound waves, which is the number of wavecrests that occur in a second. The distance between two wavecrests is called a *cycle,* so frequency is measured in cycles per second. One cycle per second is called a *hertz* (Hz). As most stereo buffs know, frequency is often reported in hertz. A piano plays frequencies ranging from 27.5 Hz (low note) to 4,186 Hz (high note). A bass singer sings notes as low as 82.4 Hz, and a soprano sings notes as high as 1,046.5 Hz. You might want to consider this before buying stereo speakers. Today, a good pair of speakers capable of reproducing sounds as low as 35 Hz costs about $100; a good pair of speakers capable of reproducing sounds down to about 25 Hz costs about $1500. That's

FIGURE 3–22

The device shown here, an oscilloscope, makes pictures out of sound waves. A tuning fork makes a sound wave, which, as shown here, consists of compressions and expansions of air molecules. A microphone makes an electrical response to these compressions and expansions. The oscilloscope changes the electrical response into a moving picture on a screen similar to a TV screen. The picture is a wave with high points and low points. A high point in the picture represents a compression of air molecules; a low point represents an expansion of air molecules.

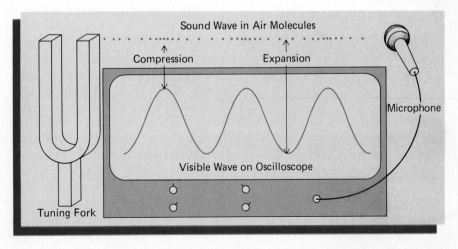

FIGURE 3-23

Each oscilloscope shows 1/100 of a second (.01 second) from two sound waves: (A) a low-pitched sound, with 600 cycles per second, and a higher pitched sound, with 1,200 cycles per second; (B) a soft note and a loud note; (C) a note played on a trumpet and on a clarinet.

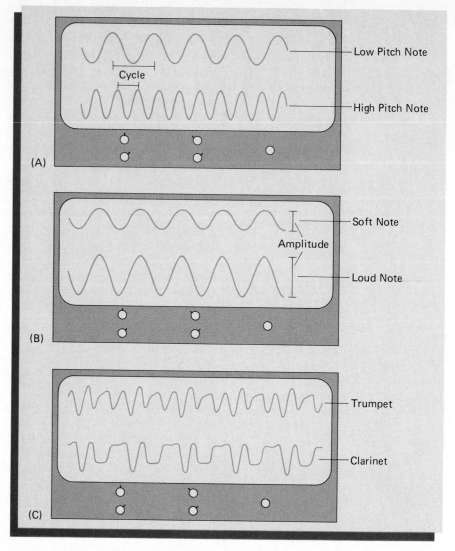

an expensive 10 Hz—especially when you consider that there is very little music written in that range!

Humans hear sounds ranging from 20 to 20,000 Hz. This means that the ears somehow give different neural responses for different frequencies within this range. Scientists are debating two rival theories of how this is done. According to the *place theory*, one hears different pitches because different frequencies stimulate different places on the basilar membrane According to the *frequency theory*, one hears different pitches because receptors send pulses up the auditory nerve at the same frequency as the sound wave.

Nobel laureate George von Békésy used a powerful microscope to show that different frequencies vibrate different parts of the basilar membrane. His work convinced most scientists that the place theory explains how people hear frequencies above 3,000 Hz. On the other hand, almost everyone agrees that the frequency theory explains how we hear frequencies below 50 Hz. Thus, the debate concerns how we hear frequencies between 50 and 3,000 Hz. The major proponent of the frequency theory in this range is E. G. Wever. He realized that single nerve fibers cannot respond faster than 1,000 times per second, so he advocated the *volley principle*, which states that the combined response of different fibers corresponds to the frequency of sound waves. In other words, cells take turns firing, similar to the way Revolutionary War soldiers alternated so that one group fired a round, or a volley, while another group reloaded. With the help of the volley principle, the frequency theory could explain hearing up to 3,000 Hz. But no one knows for sure whether or not it does in fact explain it. In the 50 to 3,000 Hz range, the place theory, the frequency theory, or some as yet unspecified theory may be correct. Most speech sounds are in this range, so settling this theoretical issue will have practical consequences for helping the deaf.

Amplitude and Loudness. There is another change in sound waves that occurs as volume is increased. Figure 3–23 shows this change for the same note played softly and loudly. Notice that the frequency is the same, but the **amplitude** of the waves differs. The amplitude, which can be measured as the distance between a wave's top and bottom, gets larger as sounds get louder. The scientist's unit for measuring loudness is called the *bel*, after Alexander Graham Bell. Often scientists prefer to use a unit one-tenth as large as a bel. They call this a **decibel.** Each tenfold increase in sound level adds 10 decibels.

From what has been said so far, we would expect to hear the same pitch when we listened to the sound waves illustrated in Figure 3–23. After all, they have the same frequency. Unfortunately, hearing is not that simple. A wave's amplitude also influences the brain's interpretation of pitch. As a tone gets louder, its pitch sounds lower. Thus, the higher amplitude wave in Figure 3–24 would seem to have a slightly lower pitch than the other wave, even though the frequencies are the same. When buying a stereo system, you might ask whether or not the system electronically compensates for this distortion; better systems do.

Loud sounds can be irritating and even damaging. For example, riveters and others who work in extremely noisy environments often suffer from **boilermaker's deafness.** This is a partial hearing loss caused by spending long periods of time amid loud noises. Experts warn that no worker should be exposed to a continuous sound level of 85 decibels (about the loudness of a vacuum cleaner) for more than 5 hours a day without using protective devices. Loud rock bands have sound levels between 125 and 135 decibels. Thus, it is not surprising that college students who frequently listen to loud rock bands suffer some hearing loss (Lipscomb, 1969). We will discuss sound and noise (and noise pollution) in more detail in Chapter 16.

Waveform and Tone Quality. If we watched our oscilloscope during a trumpet solo and then during a clarinet solo, we might notice another way that sound waves change. Figure 3–23 illustrates this change for a trumpet and a clarinet playing the same note at the same sound level. Notice that the frequencies and amplitudes are the same, but the shapes are different. It is this difference in shape, or **waveform,** that allows us to distinguish between the two sounds.

Waveforms differ because most sounds contain more than one frequency. While it is possible to generate **pure tones** containing a single frequency, most musical instruments generate **complex tones** containing many frequencies. The higher ones are called *overtone frequencies*. A trumpet and clarinet sound different because they have different overtone frequencies. The different frequencies within each complex get combined into a single wave. But, as we see in Figure 3–23, the resulting waves have different shapes when the sounds have different overtones. Both of these waveforms sound quite pleasant. However, sometimes waves combine to create unpleasant sounds. This can happen, for example, in a poorly designed auditorium.

Locating Sounds

The ability to tell where a sound is coming from is sometimes a matter of life or death. How many times do you think our ancestors were saved, for example, by hearing a twig cracked by the foot of a stalking beast?

A Doppler shift in sound is demonstrated by race cars. The high-pitched whining sound of an approaching car drops to a low pitch when the car zooms by.

How many lives have been saved on today's highways because a driver was able to tell where a blasting automobile horn was coming from? One way to study this important ability is by taking a mental trip to an imaginary race track. If you close your eyes at the race track you will notice that you can locate the cars simply by listening to them. How?

If you listen carefully, you might notice that *loudness* plays a role in hearing a car's distance. In general, you hear louder sounds as being closer than softer ones. You might also notice that moving sounds provide more information. As the race cars roar toward you, their engines have a high-pitched, whining sound. When the cars zoom by, their engines' sounds drop sharply to a lower pitch. This is called the **Doppler shift.** It happens because sound waves bunch up as the cars approach and spread out as the cars speed away. The bunched-up waves have a shorter distance between their wave crests (higher frequency); the spread-out waves have a longer distance between their wave crests (lower frequency). You can hear both the loudness changes and the frequency changes without special instruments. In contrast, we would need to bring special equipment to the race track if we hoped to study the other ways we can localize sounds. All the other ways depend upon tiny sound differences between the two ears.

When a sound is straight ahead, it reaches both ears at the same time, it sounds equally loud in both ears, and it has the same waveform in both ears. When a sound comes from one side, all three of these things change because the sound is farther from one ear: (1) the sound arrives *later* at the farther ear; (2) the sound is *softer* in the farther ear; and (3) the *phase* is slightly different in the farther ear. That is, the wave is closer to its highest point when it strikes one ear. Researchers have found that we are extremely sensitive to differences in time, loudness, and phase. When we close our eyes at a race track and localize the cars by sound, we are using these three sources of information, even though we are not aware of it. We apparently have this ability from the moment we are born (Castillo and Butterworth, 1981).

OTHER SENSES

The Apollo 13 astronauts depended mostly upon seeing and hearing, but their other senses were also active. They tasted and smelled their food, and they felt cold, for example. In this section we will briefly review the senses of taste, smell, touch, and body orientation.

Taste

Today we rarely eat cakes "made from scratch" because cake mixes are much easier to prepare. Dinners are prepared for us in advance and frozen, or else all the ingredients are boxed for us in the exact quantities needed. We simply heat and eat, or stir and serve. Whether we like it or not, food preparation has become a big business. As a result, shrewd executives are hiring psychologists to make sure that the company's food tastes good to as many customers as possible. In this section, we will examine some of the factors that determine taste.

The primary sense organ for taste is the tongue. As shown in Figure 3–24, the tongue has small elevations called **papillae.** Our taste sensors are called **taste buds.** They are located inside of papillae away from direct contact with food. We taste solid foods by first dissolving them in saliva. The liquid solution runs down pits in the papillae and stimulates sensory cells in the taste buds. The sensory cells then send messages to the brain, giving rise to our sensation of taste. Taste cells die and are replaced about every 11 days. As people age, taste cells begin to die and are not replaced, which is why the elderly lose some of their taste sensitivity.

There are four primary tastes: sweet, sour, salt, and bitter. Different parts of the tongue are sensitive to different tastes, as shown in Figure 3–24. Our sensitivity to all of these is greatest when the food or drink temperature is between 22° and 32°C. (about 71° to 89°F.). Since temperature of a substance changes your sensitivity to it, it is important to season food at the temperature at which you intend to eat it. For example, soup salted at room temperature may need more salt when it is warmed up, and lemonade sweetened at room temperature may taste sour when it is chilled (see McBurney and Collings, 1977).

This cotton candy registers as "sweet" through the taste receptors located on the front of the tongue, which are most sensitive to sweetness.

FIGURE 3–24

The tongue's taste receptors are called taste buds, which are located inside small elevations or papillae on the surface of the tongue. Different locations on the tongue are most sensitive to the four basic taste qualities: sweet, sour, salty, and bitter.

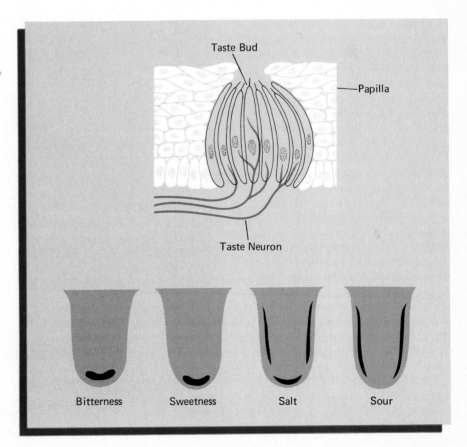

Smell

Smell is important in taste, which is why food tastes strange (or seems to have no taste at all) when you have a head cold. Also, some foods taste different to the elderly because of changes in the ability to smell. As people age, they lose olfactory cells, which reduces not only their ability to smell, but also their ability to taste. For example, the elderly often lose their fondness for chocolate. Taste receptors register chocolate as very bitter, while smell receptors register chocolate as sweet. For this reason, chocolate has an unpleasant, bitter taste to the elderly with a reduced sense of smell.

The passageway between the nose and the throat contains the odor-sensitive cells called **olfactory cells.** Gases we breathe are dissolved in a fluid covering the receptors, causing the cells to send messages to the brain. We rapidly detect a new odor, but we lose our ability to smell it after several minutes, because olfactory cells respond rapidly and fatigue rapidly. We have more to learn about the sense of smell than any of the other senses.

The fragrance of a flower can make us appreciate our sense of smell, about which scientists still have much to learn.

Touch

Our skin responds to pain, temperature, and pressure. Research on skin sensations has led to important theoretical and practical advances. Let's review these research developments for each kind of skin sensation.

A better understanding of pain is being sought in order to find better ways to relieve those who have chronic pain, and to find better ways to restore pain perception to those who have lost it. You might think, "Who needs it?" But pain perception is actually quite important. Diseases that reduce or eliminate pain perception have caused people to inflict injuries inadvertently upon themselves, including serious cuts and burns; one woman, for example, even chewed off the tip of her tongue (Cohen et al., 1955). Most of us use "pain-killing" drugs from time to time, but we may depend upon them less in the future because medical doctors are finding new ways to control pain without drugs, which we will discuss in Chapters 4 and 13.

The skin may contain specialized pain receptors, but physiologists have not identified any yet. An alternative theory is that pain results from overstimulation of temperature and pressure receptors. However, many facts argue against this. For instance, some drugs reduce pain sensations in the skin without reducing temperature or pressure sensation (Candland, 1968).

Imagine that you are sunbathing at the beach and decide to go swimming. You approach the water with confidence because it is filled with swimmers who seem to be enjoying the water as much as you were enjoying the sun. You touch the water with one toe just to make sure—*Brrr*, how can they stand it! Moments later, after much hesitation, a little coaxing, and many goose bumps, you are enjoying the water as much as the others are. Thanks to our skin's ability to adjust, we can be comfortable over a wide range of temperatures. To date, no one physiological theory can explain all the known facts about temperature perception.

One popular theory is the *vascular theory*, which states that thermal receptors are actually sensory nerves that detect the contraction and dilation of blood vessels. This is a clever theory, because blood vessels contract when the skin is cooled and they dilate when the skin is warmed. However, according to the vascular theory we should be able to experience hot and cold on all regions of our body. This is a problem for the theory, because only hot is felt in some areas, called **warm spots,** and only cold is felt in other areas, called **cold spots.** We have about six cold spots and one or two warm spots on the average square centimeter of skin. When a warm object stimulates a cold spot, it feels cold. This is called **paradoxical cold.**

Such results lead to another popular theory, the *specific receptor theory*. According to this theory, distinct receptors exist for the sensation of hot and cold. The problem with this theory is that both hot and cold are experienced on skin areas that have few or none of one kind of receptor. For example, cold can be felt on hairy skin where there are few if any cold receptors. Thus, for now, we have no satisfactory theory of how we experience temperature on the skin.

The blind depend heavily upon their sense of touch, and psychologists have teamed up with engineers to help the blind capitalize as much as possible on this important sense. Psychologists laid the foundation for helping the blind by doing basic research on the sense of touch. For example, they mapped the skin's sensitivity to slight amounts of pressure. They found, among other things, that the face is the most sensitive, and that females are more sensitive than males to the pressure of touch. Scientists also noticed that two objects touching the skin produce two distinct sensations of pressure if the objects are far enough apart. However, if the objects are too close, they produce a single sensation of pressure. The least distance between two stimuli that can be perceived as separate is called the two-point threshold. You can see this for yourself through the following experiment.

Push two pins into a cork one centimeter apart. Push one pin into another cork. Blindfold a friend and touch his or her finger tip lightly

HIGHLIGHT / OTHER SENSES HELP THE BLIND "SEE"

Technological advances have led to exciting applications of sensory research, including restoring sight to the blind. In a visual substitution system planned by Dr. Dobelle at Columbia University in New York, a subminiature television camera will be mounted in a glass eye. The artificial eye will be attached to eye muscles so that a blind person will point the camera as easily as we point our eyes. The camera will send optical information to the brain via a tiny computer mounted in a pair of eyeglasses. The computer will translate the information into a pattern of stimulation that will be experienced as a black and white picture when it is sent to the brain. Microelectrodes mounted on the surface of the visual cortex will be used to stimulate the brain. The best Dr. Dobelle expects in the foreseeable future are low-resolution, slow-scan, black and white images that are like the early television transmissions sent by astronauts from the moon (Dobelle, 1977).

Another new device, the Tactile Visual Substitution System (TVSS), which was developed by Bach-Y-Rita (1982) and his colleagues at the Smith-Kettlewell Institute of Visual Science in San Francisco. A miniature television camera is mounted on spectacle frames allowing the camera to be pointed by head movements. The camera's picture is analyzed into 400 dark or light dots, such that each dot represents a small area of the camera's field of view. Each dot's brightness depends upon the amount of light falling on the

corresponding part of the visual field. Once the brightness of the dots is determined, they are translated to frequencies of vibrations on a matrix of 400 tiny skin vibrators mounted on the abdomen. When the corresponding dot is dark, the vibrator is off; when the dot is gray, the vibrator oscillates at a low frequency; and when the dot is bright, the vibrator oscillates at a high frequency. At first, it takes 5 to 8 minutes to recognize common objects such as telephones, cups, and chairs, but after only 1 hour of training, blind people can identify 25 common objects in about 5 to 20 seconds each. After several weeks of training, blind people learn to negotiate hallways, open doors, and locate and pick up small objects with TVSS.

One of the most promising sensory substitution systems is the

Sonicguide, a device developed by Professor Lesley Kay, an imaginative electrical engineer, at the University of Canterbury, New Zealand (see Sterlow, Kay, and Kay, 1978). The Sonicguide shown in the photos here emits high frequency sounds beyond the human hearing range. These hit objects in the environment and reflect back to the Sonicguide. Here they are converted to audible slashings, "wheeps," and rushing sounds. A user of the Sonicguide must learn to interpret this futuristic electronic "music." The sound's pitch indicates the distance of an object; it goes lower as an object moves farther away. Loudness indicates size; larger objects make louder sounds. Clarity indicates texture; when the "music" sounds like a poorly tuned radio, the object is rough; when it sounds like a well-tuned radio, the object is smooth. The time of arrival of the

with either cork. Have your friend say whether or not two distinct sensations of touch are felt. Repeat the experiment on the palm and the forearm. You should observe no mistakes on the finger tips, some mistakes on the palm, and many mistakes on the forearm. Such results provided important information used to develop sensory substitution systems for the blind (see the Highlight, "Other Senses Help the Blind 'See' ").

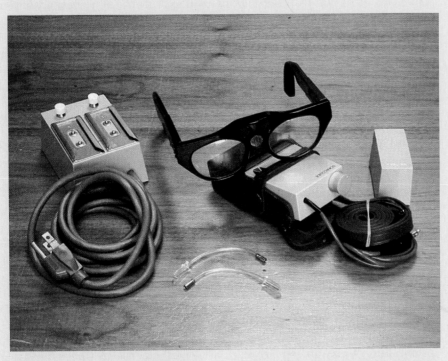

sounds in the two ears indicates location; objects to the right are heard first by the right ear and objects to the left are heard first by the left ear.

Even infants who are blind can learn to interpret this code. During his first session with a Sonicguide, a 16-week-old baby boy learned to reach out and grab a small object waved in front of his face. Dr. Tom Bower (1977) swung an object by a thread toward the baby until it tapped his nose. After the third presentation, the baby moved both eyes toward his nose as the object approached and moved both eyes away from his nose as the object receded. On the seventh presentation, the baby blocked the object by putting his hand in front of his face. The object was then moved from right to left. The baby tracked it with his head and eyes and he swiped at it with his hands, hitting

it four times. The baby also learned to enjoy a game with his mother. Standing on her knee, he turned his head, bringing her in and out of the Sonicguide's sound field. The baby's smiles and giggles suggested that he enjoyed this game as much as most babies enjoy the "peek-a-boo" game.

The baby's development after the initial session was similar to a sighted baby's. He was able to identify favorite toys without touching them, and he reached for them with both hands when he was about 6 months of age. By 8 months he searched for objects that were hidden, and by 9 months of age he reached out his hand when lowered toward a surface.

The Sonicguide is also used in the United States. For example, in Pennsylvania, James Newcomer (1977) is using the Sonicguide with blind children in public school.

Under his direction, Dana, a 5-year-old kindergarten student, is using the device to find her way around school. Already she can locate water fountains and doorways, and she knows when to stop to reach out for objects. Gerry, an 8-year-old second grader, uses the Sonicguide to maneuver between a maze of poles in a room without touching them. He can also find a person "hiding" in the room between the poles. Fourteen-year-old Wally is the first high-school student to own his own Sonicguide. He has learned to thread his way through congested corridors with few collisions, and he can follow other students at a distance if he chooses.

Looking into the future is always dangerous, so no predictions will be made about the course of psychological research on the senses. But after such an encouraging start, it will certainly be disappointing if in the 1980s a major effort is not made to continue basic and applied research on sensory substitution systems.

In May, 1961, President John F. Kennedy declared, "I believe that this nation should commit itself to achieving the goal, before this decade is out, of landing a man on the moon and returning him safely to earth. . . ." On July 24, 1969, that mission was accomplished. And with that success came the "new frontiers in science, commerce, and cooperation" that Kennedy promised in his 1962 State of the Union message. What would happen if an equally strong commitment were made now to rescue the blind and deaf from their prisons of sightlessness and soundlessness before this decade is out?

Body Orientation

How do we know where we are in relation to the world around us? Basically two kinds of senses are involved here: **equilibrium,** our sense of overall body orientation (for example, the difference between standing upright or tilting backwards), and **proprioception,** our sense of the position and motion of body parts.

Equilibrium. Equilibrium is based on the body's reaction to gravity. The space program inspired a lot of research in this area, because astronauts wanted to know what to expect in outer space, where they would be free from earth's gravitational pull. In space, vision plays an important part in equilibrium; on earth, **vision** and gravity usually work together. Gravity affects equilibrium through the **vestibular system,** which is an inner-ear structure that detects body orientation and changes in body orientation. Figure 3–25 shows the vestibular system. The three arching structures are the **semicircular canals,** which detect changes in head position. Fluids move in the canals when the head rotates in any direction. The fluid motion causes neural messages about head movements.

Semicircular canals stop responding shortly after the head stops moving. Other gravity detectors continue to report head position, however. They are the **otolith structures,** which are organs that signal head orientation with respect to gravity. The otolith apparatus consists of two sacs located near the junction of the semicircular canals. The inside of one of those sacs contains hair cells and a tissue that holds tiny stones over the hair cells. The stones change position when the head changes position. The semicircular canals and the otolith apparatus are idle in outer space, but they are continually active on earth. Disagreements between vision and vestibular information, is in fact, a major cause of **motion sickness,** a dizzy, nauseous feeling.

Proprioception. Knowing where our head is at is only part of body orientation. We also need **proprioception,** the sense of where our other body parts are. Proprioception is determined by sense organs in joints, muscles, and tendons, which connect muscles with bones (Matin, 1982). An experiment by Rock and Harris (1967) illustrates proprioception. It also illustrates people's ability to adjust to an altered environment.

In this experiment, subjects held their arm under a glass table top, and they pointed at targets that were slightly above the table (see Figure 3–26). The experiment had three parts:

FIGURE 3–25

The semicircular canals of the vestibular system are located in the inner ear. Fluids move in the canals when the head rotates in any direction, sending neural messages to the brain.

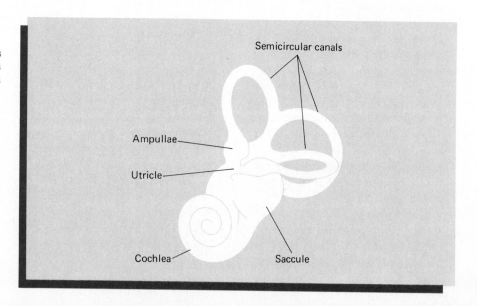

FIGURE 3–26

This is the apparatus used in the Rock and Harris experiment.

1. On pretests, subjects pointed at targets with the glass covered. They pointed accurately with both arms, even though they could not see their arm or hand under the table. Proprioception is indicated by the fact that people knew where their arms were even though they could not see them.

2. During an exposure condition, subjects wore goggles that displaced vision. The goggles made targets seem to be about 4 inches to the right of where they actually were. The cover was then removed from the glass table. Subjects practiced pointing at targets with one arm while they rested the other arm. They pointed off to the right at first. Within a few minutes, however, they saw and corrected their mistake.

3. The goggles were removed for posttests. The procedures for these final tests were identical to pretest procedures. Subjects pointed accurately when they used their rested arm. This result suggests that subjects still saw the targets in the correct places. It also suggests that they still knew where their rested arm was without looking at it. They pointed off to the left, however, when they pointed with their practiced hand. This result suggests that subjects had adjusted their arm's proprioception; that is, the goggle exposure caused them to feel that their arm was in a different place than it actually was. When the goggles were on, this adjustment in proprioception helped them coordinate their pointing with the displaced vision. When the goggles were removed, however, the adjustment caused errors until subjects had a chance to readjust to normal vision.

Recent investigations show that people can adjust to a distorted world in many ways (Ebenholtz, 1981; Shebilske, 1981; Welch, 1978). Scientists are not sure why we have this ability, but astronauts are glad that we do, because it helped them adapt to outer space.

SUMMARY

1. The study of sensation and perception raises many **psychophysical** questions, that is, questions about relationships between physical energies and psychological experiences.

2. The eyes convert light energy into neural responses that we experience as sight. The actual conversion is done by two kinds of receptor cells in the **retina: rods** and **cones.** They send neural messages through visual pathways to other brain structures. The pathways contain cells that participate in the interpretation of these messages.

3. The eyes can adjust their sensitivity to light. They become more sensitive in dim light through a process of **dark adaptation.** They become less sensitive in bright light through a process of **light adaptation.**

4. Light receptors are specialized so that they are more sensitive to some colors than to others. Cells in the visual pathways also participate in the coding of colors.

5. We actively impose organization on what we see, according to various rules. The Gestalt laws of organization attempt to describe some of those rules. Our active contribution is clear when appearances alternate back and forth in **multistable perceptions.** Scientists are beginning to understand the rules according to which we organize perceptions of moving objects.

6. We have perceptual constancies; that is, perceptions remain constant when visual information changes. For instance, apparent size remains constant when we move farther from an object, even though our movement shrinks the **retinal image** of the object. **Unconscious inference theory** and **ecological theory** offer opposing explanations of the constancies.

7. We respond to many sources of information about depth. **Binocular** information is available through the use of both eyes. **Monocular** information is available even when we use only one eye. **Kinetic** information is available when we move or when the environment moves.

8. Sometimes, as is the case with **illusions,** seeing is deceiving. In geometric illusions (such as the Müller-Lyer, Ponzo, Zollner, and Titchener illusions) our eyes tell us one thing, but a ruler tells us something different. Other illusions, such as the **autokinetic effect,** are more serious—the study of such illusions is helping to reduce the number of airplane accidents caused by them.

9. The ears convert sound waves into neural responses that we experience as hearing. The external ear collects and focuses sound, causing the **eardrum** to vibrate. Three delicate bones carry these vibrations to the **oval window,** which vibrates receptors in the **cochlea,** triggering nerve impulses to the brain.

10. **Pitch** (high notes versus low notes) is determined by the **frequency** of sound waves. **Loudness** is determined by the **amplitude** of sound waves. Tone quality is determined by how sound waves combine. We hear the location of sounds in part because we are sensitive to tiny sound differences between the two ears.

11. Our tongue has **taste buds** that convert chemical stimulation into neural responses, which we experience as taste. Different regions of the tongue are sensitive to the four primary tastes: sweet, sour, salt, and bitter.

12. The throat and nasal passages contain **olfactory cells,** which convert the gases we breathe into neural responses that we experience as smell. Olfactory cells also influence taste.

13. The skin responds to pain, temperature, and pressure. Scientists have not yet identified all the receptor cells that underlie these sensations. The understanding that they have gained so far, however, has already helped to relieve pain for many people, and it has helped the blind to "see" with their skin.

14. There are two types of body orientation senses, equilibrium and proprioception. **Equilibrium** is our sense of overall body orientation; it is affected by gravity through the **vestibular system,** which consists of the **semicircular canals** and the **otolith** structures. **Proprioception** is the sense of where our other body parts are. It is determined by sense organs in joints, muscles, and tendons.

Suggested Readings

The following books are about the Apollo 13 mission:

Cooper, H. S. F., Jr. *Thirteen: The flight that failed.* New York: Dial, 1973.

Lewis, R. S. *The voyages of Apollo: The exploration of the moon.* New York: Quadrangle, 1974.

Gregory, R. L. *Eye and brain.* New York: McGraw-Hill, 1977. This book is interesting reading and very informative; perhaps the most popular book available on the psychology of seeing.

Hochberg, J. E. *Perception.* Englewood Cliffs, N.J.: Prentice-Hall, 1978. This book capitalizes on the power of pictorial displays to illustrate principles of perception. Figures and their captions are an integral part of this text on "why things look as they do."

KUBOVY, M., and POMERANTZ, J. R. (Eds.). *Perceptual organization.* Hillsdale, N.J.: Erlbaum, 1981. Chapters by authorities on theory, history, philosophy, methodology, and recent discoveries in sensation, perception, and cognition. Many illustrations and auditory phenomena are demonstrated on an optional cassette tape.

McBURNEY, D. H., and COLLINGS, V. B. *Introduction to sensation/perception.* Englewood Cliffs, N.J.: Prentice-Hall, 1977. Uses everyday examples to awaken one's curiosity about the sensory world. The structure and function of all the senses are covered.

REED, E., and JONES, R. (Eds.). *Reasons for realism: Selected essays of James J. Gibson.* Hillsdale, N.J.: Erlbaum, 1982. Explores James J. Gibson's revolutionary theory of how we see the world.

WALLACH, H. *On perception.* New York: Quadrangle, 1976. One of the outstanding visual scientists of our day reviews his research, which has contributed significantly to our understanding of perception.

4

Alternate States of Consciousness

olding his alarm clock near the hospital night light, Private George Ritchie saw that he could start his long-awaited trip home in 1 hour. One hour, that is, if the Army nurse did not take his temperature again. His condition had gotten much worse during the night. About 2½ hours earlier, at midnight, he had started to cough up bright red blood. Now his chest, throat, and head ached, his legs trembled, his heart pounded, and his body was covered with sweat. But he was going to try to slip out of the hospital unnoticed; he didn't want to pass up the chance of a lifetime because of a stupid cold.

Ritchie had come to Camp Barkeley, Texas, for basic training in September, 1943. He was 20 years old, tall, slender, and ready to whip the Nazis, but he was less prepared to fight the cold, rainy Texas weather. Then, shortly after Thanksgiving, he got the break of his life—he was offered a chance to start classes in the Army Specialized Training Program on December 22, at the Medical College of Virginia.

Now it was 2:20 A.M. on December 20, and he was determined to catch the last possible train that could get him to Richmond on time. Quietly, he dressed. "Just what is my temperature?" he wondered, as he felt his clothes become soaked with sweat. He walked down to the supply room and asked the night ward boy for a thermometer, which he then tried to read in the light from the supply room doorway. He couldn't make sense of it. The silver mercury seemed to go past the numbers. The night ward boy came up behind him and slipped the thermometer out of his hand, checked the temperature reading, and raced down the hallway to find a nurse.

Within the next few minutes both a doctor and a nurse were examining Private Ritchie. The doctor listened to his chest while the nurse repeated the temperature reading. They quickly sent him by ambulance to another wing of the hospital for X-rays. While standing in front of the X-ray machine, Ritchie collapsed. He was taken to a small isolation room where his condition was diagnosed as double lobar pneumonia.

Twenty-four hours later, Ritchie sat up in bed with a start. "The train—I must catch the train," he thought. He jumped out of bed and looked for his clothes. Suddenly he froze, realizing that someone was lying in the bed he had just gotten out of. That puzzled him for a moment, but then he decided it was too strange to think about. Besides, he had to hurry. Perhaps the ward boy had his clothes. Running out into the hallway, he was relieved to find a sergeant coming toward him carrying a cloth-covered instrument tray.

"Excuse me, Sergeant," he said. "You haven't seen the ward boy for this unit, have you?"

The sergeant didn't seem to hear or see him—he kept walking toward Ritchie.

"Look out!" Ritchie yelled, jumping out of the way.

This too was strange, but Ritchie had no time to figure it out now. He had his mind on one thing: getting to Richmond.

Before he knew what was happening, he found himself outside of the hospital on his way to Richmond, not traveling by train as originally planned, but speeding over the dark, frozen desert a hundred times faster than any train could carry him. He was flying—not in a plane or any other vehicle—he was just flying. Soon he was beyond the desert, passing over snow-covered wooded areas and an occasional town.

Suddenly he slowed down and found himself hovering about 50 feet over a red-roofed, one-story building. A blue neon "Cafe" sign was over the building's door and a "Pabst Blue Ribbon Beer" sign was propped up in the front window. The next thing Ritchie knew, he was down on the sidewalk in front of the cafe walking next to a middle-aged man wearing a topcoat.

"Can you tell me, please, what city this is?" Ritchie asked. Then he shouted, "Please sir! I'm a stranger here and I'd appreciate it if. . . ." He stopped; the man obviously had heard nothing.

In desperation Ritchie tried to grab the man's shoulder, but he felt nothing, as if the man were only a mirage. Now Ritchie began to think about all of the strange things that were happening to him. He remembered the young man he had seen in the hospital bed. Could it have been him? Could it have been the material, concrete part of himself? He had to find out.

In a flash, he was flying again, this time back toward Texas. Before long he was standing next to the bed from which he had started his bizarre journey, but now the person lying in the bed was covered with a sheet from head to toe. Only the arms and hands were exposed. On the left hand was a ring containing a gold owl on an oval, black onyx and the words, "University of Richmond." Ritchie fixed his eyes on the ring. Could this be *his* ring? How could it be? This man was obviously dead. Ritchie asked himself, "How could I be dead and still be awake?"

Suddenly the room glowed with a light that seemed too bright for mortal eyes, radiating from a man who appeared to be made of light. The man seemed to put thoughts directly into Ritchie's head. "Stand up! You are in the presence of the Son of God." Ritchie stood up and became filled with a mysterious inner certainty that this all-powerful person loved him. At the same time the room filled with a giant, three-dimensional, moving mural showing every episode in Ritchie's life. It normally would have taken weeks to see so many events, but Private Ritchie seemed to be outside of ordinary time.

A question filled Ritchie's head: "What have you done with your life to show me?" Ritchie knew that the all-loving being in his presence was asking, "How much have you loved with your life? Have you loved others as I am loving you?" For Ritchie, having to answer this question was like having to take a final exam for a course he had never taken. "If that is what life is all about, why didn't someone tell me?" he protested. The man who seemed to be made of light answered that he had tried to tell Ritchie and that he would show him more. With that they started to move toward a distant pinpoint of light that rapidly grew into a large city. It could have been any of several cities in the United States. The streets were crowded with living humans and many substanceless beings that were similar to Ritchie.

These nonphysical beings were unable to perform any physical acts, yet were completely and futilely absorbed in some worldly activity. One spirit constantly begged for cigarettes, while another begged for beer. Another spirit tried to manage a business as he had once done, and still another followed her middle-aged son, nagging constantly without being heard.

Ritchie realized that this was hell—a place where people were powerless to obtain those things for which they had a burning desire.

Suddenly Ritchie and the spirit guiding him were in an immense void traveling toward a seemingly endless city where everything and everyone seemed to be made of light. As he approached, Ritchie thought he might be entering heaven, the home of beings who had incorporated the man made of light and his love into their lives to such an extent that they had been transformed into his very likeness.

But a glimpse is all Ritchie got, because in a flash he was back in the room with his sheet-covered body. The man of light explained that Ritchie had to return to his body.

As Ritchie pleaded to stay with this man, his mind blurred. He was now aware of nothing except his burning throat and aching chest. He tried to move his arms, but only his hands would move. He felt his ring and began to twist it around his finger.

Just then the ward boy, preparing Ritchie for the morgue, noticed Ritchie's hands and ran to get the doctor who had pronounced him dead about 10 minutes earlier. Doctor Francy repeated his exam and again pronounced Ritchie dead.

The ward boy refused to accept this diagnosis and pleaded with the doctor to inject adrenalin directly into the heart muscle, which he did.

Today, George Ritchie is a psychiatrist at the University of Virginia Medical School. Dr. Ritchie has told many about his close encounter with death (see Ritchie, 1978). Skeptics assume that he was dreaming, or hallucinating. But even skeptics recognize that his experience profoundly affected his life. He is characterized by a remarkable depth of kindness, understanding, and loving concern for others.

STUDYING THE MIND

George Ritchie believes that he died for about 10 minutes and that his mental activities continued to exist after his body died. That is, he continued to have sensations, mental images, thoughts, desires, emotions, and wishes. Without a body, however, his mind could not contact physical things. Is it possible for a mind to exist without a body? Clearly, ancient Egyptians thought so in the fourteenth century B.C. when they filled the tomb of their dead boy-king, Tutankhamen (King Tut), with food, water, furniture, jewelry, and tools. Egyptians sought eternal life beyond all else, and they believed that King Tut's spirit would enjoy his entombed treasures forever. Hippocrates, the "Father of Scientific Medicine," also thought the mind could continue to exist after death. In the fifth century B.C., on the Greek island of Cos, he taught that the brain and mind are separate entities and that careful observations of people would clarify the relationship existing between mind and body. In this chapter we will: (1) review the debate of modern scientists on the nature of the conscious mind; (2) examine some scientific observations suggesting that George Ritchie's experience is not unique; and (3) entertain the possibility that we have hidden mental powers, such as the ability to project our minds out of our bodies as Ritchie may have done.

WHAT IS CONSCIOUSNESS?

Is it possible that what you are experiencing right now is just a dream? Will you soon wake up and find that you have been dreaming instead of reading? Charles Tart (1977) asks similar questions at the beginning of his lectures on consciousness, but his students rarely answer yes. Sometimes dreams seem real, but we hardly ever mistake waking states for dreaming states. We distinguish between mental states easily, even though we would be hard pressed to say how we do it. Researchers studying consciousness start with people's intuitions about mental states and then study the basis for them. In so doing, they hope to precisely define the nature of consciousness.

Alternate States of Consciousness Defined

John Locke (1960) defined consciousness as "the perception of what passes in a man's own mind" (p. 138). Locke's definition is fine for everyday usage, but it's not enough for our purposes, because it does not distinguish among different kinds of consciousness, such as waking states and dreaming states. Scientists refer to different mental states as alternate states of consciousness (Zinberg, 1977), which they define as "a specific pattern of physiological and subjective responses" (Shapiro, 1977, p. 152). By *physiological pattern*, Shapiro means such things as brain activity, eye movements, heart rate, blood pressure, and oxygen consumption. By *subjective pattern*, Shapiro means sensations, thoughts, and emotions. Table 4–1 is a questionnaire that may help you identify patterns in your own experiences. You might enjoy answering the questions to describe your most recent dream, and then going back to answer the same questions with respect to your present state of consciousness. Notice that questions 1, 6, and 7 refer to aspects of sensations; questions 2, 4, 5, and 8 analyze thoughts; and question 3 is about emotions. Zinberg (1977) used an extended version of this questionnaire to help his subjects scan the contents and qualities of their experiences. He found unique response patterns associated with waking states, dreaming states, and other alternate states of consciousness, such as drug-induced states. As we discuss various states of consciousness in this chapter, we will focus on both physiological and subjective patterns for each.

TABLE 4–1: Alternate States of Consciousness Questionnaire

1. How vivid are each of the following kinds of sensations?

	None	Barely Detectable							Very Vivid
Sight	0	1	2	3	4	5	6	7	8	9
Sound	0	1	2	3	4	5	6	7	8	9
Taste	0	1	2	3	4	5	6	7	8	9
Smell	0	1	2	3	4	5	6	7	8	9
Touch	0	1	2	3	4	5	6	7	8	9

2. How sure are you that you are in an ordinary waking state of consciousness?

Absolutely Convinced I Am Not								Absolutely Convinced I Am
1	2	3	4	5	6	7	8	9

3. How much are you feeling the following:

	None	Barely Detectable							Strong Feeling
Joy	0	1	2	3	4	5	6	7	8	9
Rage	0	1	2	3	4	5	6	7	8	9
Surprise	0	1	2	3	4	5	6	7	8	9
Interest	0	1	2	3	4	5	6	7	8	9
Sadness	0	1	2	3	4	5	6	7	8	9

4. How much are you in control of your experiences?

Events Passing by Without My Control							I am in Complete Control
1	2	3	4	5	6	8	9

5. To what extent are your experiences ordered logically?

Experiences in a Seemingly Random Order								Experiences in a Very Logical Order
1	2	3	4	5	6	7	8	9

6. To what extent are you experiencing unusual sensations?

Many Strange Sensations								All Ordinary Sensations
1	2	3	4	5	6	7	8	9

7. To what extent do you believe that your experiences are being caused by something located outside of yourself?

Absolutely Sure that My Experiences Are in My Mind Only								Absolutely Sure That My Experiences Are Being Caused by Something Outside of Myself
1	2	3	4	5	6	7	8	9

8. To what extent are you aware of your awareness?

I Am Not Thinking about the Fact that I Am Experiencing Things								I Am Thinking a Great Deal about the Fact that I Am Experiencing Things
1	2	3	4	5	6	7	8	9

Philosophies and Theories of Mind

Ritchie never doubted for a moment that he actually walked with God. He believes there exists a reality beyond what we can see—another dimension in which our spirits will live on after our bodies die. For centuries people have held similar beliefs. Let's look at some modern theories.

Monism vs. Dualism.   Recently, Wilder Penfield (1975), who carefully observed the connection between brain and behavior in epileptic patients for more than 40 years (see Chapter 2), echoed Hippocrates's claim that brain and mind are separate entities. Penfield took into consideration two philosophies: monism, which states that the mind and brain are one organic whole; and dualism, which describes the mind and brain as separate things. Monism rules out the possibility that Ritchie's mind continued to exist after his brain stopped functioning. Monists hold that brain functions completely account for mental functions. When the brain dies, the mind dies. Perceptual release theorists are likely to be monists. Dualism, on the other hand, allows for the possibility that Ritchie's mind existed outside of his body. Dualists believe that brain and mind draw upon different energy sources (neither of which is understood). Thus, when the brain dies, the mind could in principle continue to function, but dualists are not committed to the view that it does.

Penfield favored dualism, knowing full well that scientific evidence does not provide proof on the issue. Some neurobiologists, such as Nobel prize winner Sir John Eccles (1973) and Karl Pribam (1977), realize that they cannot explain all that the mind does on the basis of what is currently known about brain functions, and they favor Penfield's dualistic view. Other scientists, such as Rose (1973), favor monism, believing that someday brain research will explain all mental experiences. Despite their inability to offer firm answers, Penfield and other scientists are optimistic that at some future time science will be able to answer conclusively the age-old question about the relationship between mind and brain.

Perceptual Release vs. Mysticism.   For the sake of discussion, let's assume that Ritchie had his experience while in an alternate state of consciousness. (As we shall see, this assumption can be made whether or not we believe that Ritchie actually was in the presence of God.)

A theory that challenges Ritchie's convictions is *perceptual release theory,* which holds that experiences during alternate states of consciousness are actually caused by the actions and reactions of our central nervous system. This theory compares alternate states of consciousness to a man looking out of a window at dusk. Inside, a fireplace is lit, but it goes unnoticed as the man pays attention to things outside the window. Gradually, the outside world becomes dimmer and is replaced by a reflection of the fire and the room it illuminates, which then appears to be located out-of-doors. Thus, during alternate states of consciousness, external stimuli fade, and at the same time the perceptions that originate in our minds seem now to come from outside. To give an example of this, when we sleep our senses are dimmed (our sensors are not receiving sensations from outside), so we respond to our *internal* brain activity, which we experience as dreams.

Perceptual release theory has had important practical applications. Looking inward to explain drug-induced states, for example, scientists have better understood the relationship between brain chemistry and drug-related experiences. This in turn has given scientists a better understanding of communication within the brain (Gillin, Kaplan, Stillman, and Wyatt, 1976; Cotman and McGaugh, 1980).

Despite the obvious value of looking inward for explanations, perceptual release theory cannot explain alternate state experiences in detail yet—and some critics think it never will.

Opponents of perceptual release theory hold an alternate view, **mysticism,** which suggests that alternate state experiences are caused by stimulation in a part of external reality that is not apparent to our usual senses of hearing, sight, taste, touch, and smell. Those sympathetic to mysticism agree with perceptual release theorists about the importance of shutting off interference from sensory stimulation, but they do not agree about what happens next. Mystics believe that when our sensory system is silenced, our minds respond to an external reality that exists beyond the visible and understandable universe. We experience a divine presence, as George Ritchie did, not because of our own mental activity, but because our mind is actually in touch with God. The nature of supernatural reality is thus beyond words, and is for this reason often described in what seems to be a contradictory way. An example is the Christian belief that there are three persons in one God. Even if our language is inadequate for describing mystic theories, some psychologists argue that mysticism *is* compatible with science. Mystics use scientific methods of advance knowledge about alternate states of consciousness in the hope of overcoming the Western tendency to reduce human consciousness to only rational thinking. They believe life will be more satisfying when we learn to be more aware of all of our experiences, including those that lie beyond our senses and beyond our rational intellects (Zinberg, 1977).

Nonmystics who look within the central nervous system for explanations agree that alternate states of consciousness should be investigated, but they believe further studies will reveal that mystical experiences are nothing more than tricks of the brain. You will have a chance to form your own opinion as we review available data on consciousness.

SCIENTIFIC OBSERVATIONS OF ALTERNATE STATES OF CONSCIOUSNESS

Dr. Ritchie's book, *Return from Tomorrow*, in which he describes his out-of-body experience, is not a scientific document, nor was it intended to be. Experiences similar to Ritchie's have been studied scientifically, however, and we will analyze existing data after briefly summarizing standard methods of studying alternate states of consciousness.

Methods for Studying States of Consciousness

In the beginning of *Return from Tomorrow*, Ritchie relates a case of a dying patient who is unprepared to face death. The reader learns about Ritchie's experience as it is told to the patient, who is at first skeptical, but who is later inspired, as are many readers. *Return from Tomorrow* goes to one's heart, as Ritchie intended. If Ritchie had chosen instead to objectively examine his experience in order to determine its nature, he could have used his encounter with death as a basis for a scientific inquiry. Such an investigation would be self-experience, the first of three methods used to study subjective patterns in various states of consciousness.

Self-Experience. Many researchers believe that the best way to experiment with alternate states of consciousness is to experience them firsthand (see Highlight: "Inside a Sioux Indian Sweat Lodge"). Some have applied the self-experience approach to the investigation of conscious-altering drugs; they include Havelock Ellis (1902), Aldous Huxley (1952), and Carlos Castaneda (1972). Such drug research has made important contributions, but it has been extremely dangerous even for well-prepared

HIGHLIGHT / INSIDE A SIOUX INDIAN SWEAT LODGE

Andrew T. Wiel, a Harvard researcher, and many other scientists believe that the best way to experiment with alternate states of consciousness is for investigators to experience the states themselves. In one interesting self-experience experiment, Wiel analyzed states of consciousness induced by religious ceremonies inside a Sioux Indian Sweat Lodge. Wiel planned his experience in advance and he prepared himself for it with the help of a Sioux medicine man on the Rosebud Reservation in South Dakota. When Wiel was ready, the medicine man led him into a circular lodge about 5 feet in diameter and 4 feet high. Wiel, the medicine man, and four other Indians sat unclothed in the lodge while attendants filled a shallow pit in the center of the floor with red-hot rocks and sealed the hut from the outside, leaving the participants in total darkness and increasing heat. The medicine man began the ritual with prayers to the Great Spirit of the Universe, asking for the well-being of the participants. He sprinkled sage sprigs and cedar incense on the hot rocks and passed around a sacred pipe filled with aromatic tobacco and red-willow bark. As each person prayed and

smoked the pipe, the medicine man chanted and threw water on the glowing rocks. When the water hit the rocks an explosive hiss filled the air, accompanied by a wave of intense heat. As soon as one wave passed, the medicine man added more water, creating a continuous flow of waves, each one slightly stronger, until no one could stand any more. At this point all shouted a special phrase meaning "All my relations!" and the attendants opened the lodge to the cooling winds.

Wiel participated in this ritual several times and summarized his experiences as follows: "On coming out of sweat lodges I have felt high in many of the same ways I have felt on using psychedelic drugs. The high lasts an hour or so and gradually gives way to great relaxation and a desire to rest. Increased awareness of one's own strength and a sense of well-being may persist for a long time" (Wiel, 1977, p. 45). Wiel also commented on why he didn't get burned by temperatures that reached almost 212°F:

. . . curiously enough, one's mental state seems to be the most important determinant of the fate of

one's skin. Burning occurs only when you lose contact with the psychic energy of the group. . . . When the steam explodes from the rocks there is no time for thinking; all mental effort is focused on the wave of heat about to break. Coping with that wave, receiving it, and riding over its crest take full concentration. . . . The chanting of the medicine man brings about an initial degree of concentration. . . . It seems to work by occupying the ordinary mind that is usually busy thinking and paying attention to multifarious external stimuli. In a similar way the sharp noise of the steam focuses awareness on a specific auditory sensation, increasing the depth of concentration. (Wiel, 1977, p. 45)

Wiel's suggestion that he was in touch with the psychic energy of the group implies the existence of a distinct source of mental energy. The theme of special mental abilities based on psychic energy will recur in this chapter, as will Wiel's emphasis of directing attention away from distracting external stimuli. We have already observed that focusing attention is a key factor in both perceptual release theory and mysticism.

---

scientists such as Timothy Leary, whose famous research on LSD resulted in tragedy (Cohen, 1976).

We will encourage you in this chapter to use the self-experience approach, but only for safe conscious states, such as sleep and deep relaxation. These states are every bit as fascinating as the more highly publicized drug-induced states. We will also encourage you to use questionnaires and interviews, as discussed in the next section.

Questionnaires and Interviews. We have already seen and used a questionnaire earlier in this chapter. Similar questions could be asked in an interview. You can control exact wording better in a questionnaire, but you can often learn more in an interview by following up on a person's interesting comments.

Timing is important in this method. For example, say you want to interview people about their dreams. There are three ways to do this. First, you can ask people without any advance warning to describe the dreams they can remember having during the past week. Second, you can ask them ahead of time to pay special attention to the dreams they have during the next week, because you will ask them to describe them afterwards. Warning them ahead of time has an advantage—they are not as likely to forget their dreams if they make a conscious attempt to remember them in order to report them to you. But this kind of ahead-of-time warning can also have a disadvantage. Suppose we told you to report every time you think about pink elephants for the rest of the day. Would your reports reflect how much you usually think about pink elephants? The third way is to administer the questionnaire or interview during or immediately after an experience. An advantage is that the experience is easier to remember. A disadvantage is that the experience usually must take place with the experimenter on hand, often in an artificial laboratory setting. Can people have normal dreams when they know scientists are observing them?

Laboratory Experiments. Despite the fact that they may seem artificial, laboratory experiments are valuable for studying alternate states of consciousness. Laboratory researchers enjoy several advantages: (1) They can control factors such as drug dosage that might influence the alternate state of consciousness; (2) they can obtain immediate reports from subjects; and (3) they can supplement subjective reports with other measures such as observations of physiological changes during alternate states.

We will draw on all three approaches (self-experience, questionnaires and interviews, and laboratory experiments) in the following sections on various alternate states of consciousness, looking in each section at both physiological and subjective patterns of response. As we review available data, you might want to consider how you would classify alternate states of consciousness.

NEAR-DEATH EXPERIENCES

Raymond Moody (1975) interviewed George Ritchie and hundreds of other people who had had similar near-death experiences. Moody presented his results in his book *Life After Life*. Besides being catchy, his title skirts the question of whether or not his subjects had actually died. Moody plays down this issue and emphasizes instead the fact that his subjects are experts on what we all are likely to experience when we encounter death.

Physiological Patterns

Ritchie was pronounced dead because he lost his vital signs: His eyes dilated, his body temperature steadily dropped, his blood pressure became undetectable, and his heartbeat and breathing stopped for an extended period of time. Today, doctors have added a new standard by which to judge, the absence of electrical activity in the brain as determined by EEG records. Doctors still cannot be certain, however, whether or not a person can be brought back to life in any given case. People with no vital signs for about a half-hour have been brought back to life without brain damage. Moody, a physician, suspects that some as yet unmeasurable biological activity continues to supply the brain with oxygen and nourishment for some time after vital signs are gone. He acknowledges that this hypothesis leaves open the possibility that such residual brain activity may also account for near-death experiences. Until we learn to measure this residual function, we will know little about physiological patterns that accompany near-death experiences.

In the meantime, Moody encourages us to think about the possibility that minds are released from bodies at death and that they continue to exist and to experience. Ritchie's mind and those of Moody's other subjects may have been released before their bodies reached the point of no return and rejoined when their bodies recovered. According to Moody's mystical speculation, we would not expect future research to reveal any correspondence between physiological and subjective patterns during near-death experiences, since they are entirely *separate* during these experiences.

Subjective Patterns

Various reports of near-death experiences are so similar that Moody was able to identify fifteen elements that turn up again and again. None of Moody's subjects reported all fifteen elements, but every element was reported frequently. The elements are as follows:

1. The experience seems beyond words, leading to the feeling that descriptions are inadequate. One woman said, "That's as close as I can get it, but it's not really adequate. I can't really give you a complete picture."
2. People often hear their doctors pronounce them dead.
3. Pain and anxiety are relieved, creating a very pleasant feeling during the early part of the experience.
4. Many subjects reported hearing sounds ranging from extremely unpleasant buzzing to very beautiful music.
5. Upon leaving their bodies, people often feel as if they are pulled through a dark space of some kind, often described as a well, a trough, an enclosure, a tunnel, a funnel, a vacuum, a void, a sewer, a valley, or a cylinder.
6. After a rapid passage through the dark tunnel, people find themselves viewing their own physical body, seeing everything going on in the room as if they were watching it from above.
7. Quite a few subjects told Moody that they saw dead friends and relatives during their experience.
8. Many also saw the being of light reported by Ritchie. Not everyone thought the being was the "Son of God," as Ritchie did, but all thought that the being was loving.
9. The being of light presents people with a panoramic review of their life.
10. Some people report approaching a border of some kind near the end of their experience. Ritchie approached a city made of light; others have reported approaching a body of water, a gray mist, a door, a fence across a field, and a line.
11. All Moody's subjects "came back," of course. Many people resist the return and long to stay with the being of light.
12. People feel certain that their near-death experiences were real, but they are reluctant to tell others about them.
13. Their vision left Moody's subjects with new moral goals and a determination to pursue them, but with no feelings of instant or moral infallibility. Like Ritchie, many developed a deep caring for others.
14. Most of Moody's subjects were no longer afraid of death after their experience.
15. Many people have accurately reported events that occurred while they were supposedly dead. One girl went out of her body and found her sister in another room of the hospital crying. Later she told her sister where she had been sitting and exactly what she had been saying: "Oh, Kathy, please don't die, please don't die." (Moody, 1975, p. 99)

Moody's data is important and fascinating, but it is not proof of mystical theories. Mystics argue that people have similar near-death experiences because they contact the same mysterious external reality. Perceptual release theory suggests, on the other hand, that people have similar near-death experiences because they have similar brains, and that these brains remain at least minimally active for a certain amount of time after "death." Whether we prefer mystical or psychological explanations, we are faced with deciding how to categorize near-death experiences. Moody argues that they are a novel phenomenon, but we should also consider the possibility that they are closely related to other experiences. We shall see that many of the fifteen elements identified by Moody also characterize other alternate states of consciousness.

SLEEP AND DREAMS

Ritchie regained waking consciousness 3 days after the doctor injected adrenalin into his heart. Is it possible that Ritchie was mistaken in thinking that his experience took place before the doctors injected the adrenalin? Could his tour of hell and his glimpse of heaven have been only a dream occurring sometime during the 3 days after he was revived? Let's consider this question in light of the literature on sleep and dreaming. **Sleep** is defined as a period of rest for the body and mind during which bodily functions are partially suspended and sensitivity to external stimuli is diminished but readily or easily regained. **Dreams** are series of images, thoughts, and emotions occurring during sleep. Was Ritchie *only* dreaming? The question's emphasis shows a current attitude that dreams do not reflect a dreamer's direct contact with the supernatural. But dreams were not always regarded as being so "down to earth."

Egyptians, Romans, and Greeks believed that we receive messages from God during dreams. Throughout the Middle Ages as well, Greeks slept in churches in order to contact God. Toward the end of the Middle Ages, however, most religions took an official stand against dreams as a means of contacting God. At the same time, science dismissed dreams as unreal or worthless because they could not be studied "objectively" (Cohen, 1976). As a result, the ancient theory was never disproved—it was merely displaced. An objective scientist is free to accept or reject the possibility that Ritchie walked with God *during a dream*. There is no proof one way or the other and perhaps there never will be.

While scientists have little or nothing to say about the possible mystical nature of sleep and dreams, they know a great deal about the physiological and subjective activities that accompany these important states. Two separate research programs sparked scientific interest in sleep and dreams. First, Sigmund Freud (1900) used special interview procedures to record dreams. The contents of the dreams were varied and often bizarre. Freud, however, felt that dreams must have some function for the individual. After intensive study of dream reports, he concluded that there were two levels in dreams. The first, which he called manifest content, is the part that the dreamer remembers. For example, a patient might report that she dreamed of being chased by a big snake with a face much like her father's face. There is also a hidden or latent content in dreams. The latent content of the dream is determined by impulses of which the individual has no awareness. For example, the latent content in the dream presented above may have been the patient's wish to have a sexual relationship with her father. Freud felt that the latent content generally involved an unacceptable desire that would create pain or anxiety if it were expressed directly. It would probably be very threatening to our dreamer if she dreamed that she was having a sexual relationship with her father. The unacceptable impulse is, therefore, disguised in the dream. Thus, Freud felt that dreams were vehicles through which individuals could express their unacceptable impulses in disguised or acceptable forms. Freud's work contradicted the notion that dreams are worthless.

Second, Eugene Aserinsky and Nathaniel Kleitman, using laboratory techniques to measure physiological responses, demonstrated that sleep is accompanied by a complex and ever-changing pattern of physiological activity (see Kleitman, 1963). In addition, they discovered physiological patterns that occur when a person is dreaming. This means that when this pattern occurs, researchers can wake up people to get immediate and usually vivid recall of dreams. Aserinsky and Kleitman helped undermine the view that sleep and dreams cannot be studied objectively. Since then scientists have measured physiological patterns and recorded dreams of thousands of people. Let's look at some of the patterns that emerged.

Physiological Patterns During Sleep

In "sleep and dream laboratories" (Figure 4–1) volunteers sleep with electrodes attached to their head and body, providing data on brain waves, eye movements, muscle tension, heart rate, and respiration. Figure 4–2 shows the pattern of brain waves and other bodily functions during conscious resting and during the five stages of sleep.

Stage 1 is characterized by the presence of low voltage, low-frequency brain waves called theta waves, and by slow, side-to-side, rolling eye movements, which we discussed in Chapter 2. Stage 2 is marked by the onset of sleep spindles, which are medium-voltage, medium-frequency brain waves. Sleep spindles diminish in stage 3 and are replaced in stage 4 by delta waves, high-voltage and extremely low-frequency brain waves. During the first four stages, heart rate, respiration, and muscle tension steadily decline. Stage 5 is marked by the onset of rapid eye movements (REM, pronounced "rem") and is referred to as **REM sleep.** During REM sleep, muscles twitch in the face and limbs, and sometimes the whole body moves. Brain waves show increased alpha activity, and there is an increase in heart rate and respiration. If people are awakened during REM sleep, they almost always say they have been dreaming, and they are able to recall their dreams in vivid detail. When people are awakened during stages 2 through 4, they rarely claim to have been dreaming and they never remember many details.

FIGURE 4–1

This subject is taking part in an experiment at a sleep laboratory at New York University. As he sleeps, a number of bodily functions are being measured, as shown in Figure 4–2 below.

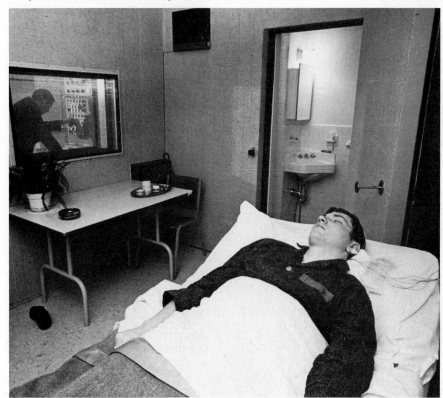

FIGURE 4–2

Brain waves, eye movements, muscle tension, heart rate, and breath rate are shown here for the waking state and for the five stages of sleep. (Sterman, 1972)

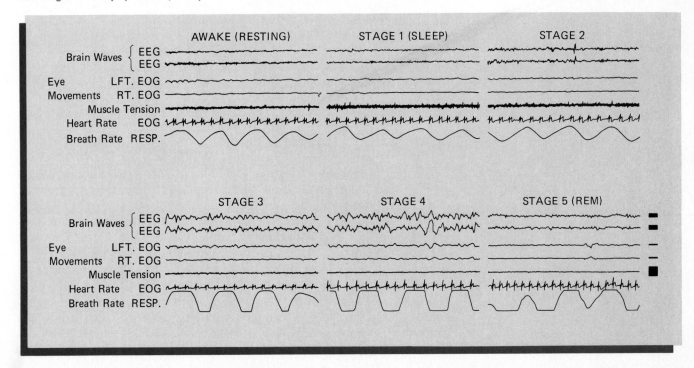

FIGURE 4–3

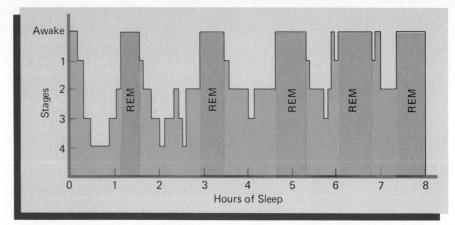

We pass repeatedly through these various stages of sleep during the night (Figure 4–3). As we approach sleep, we enter stage 1, the transition stage. It occurs only when we go from waking to sleeping, and usually lasts just a few minutes. Within 90 minutes after falling asleep, we pass through stages 2 through 4, and then begin REM sleep. We enter REM sleep for 10-to-20-minute periods throughout the night, alternating with stages 2 through 4. REM intervals become longer and stages 2 through 4 become shorter toward morning. When we were infants we required 16 to 20 hours of sleep. As adults most of us need between 6 and 9 hours, 25 percent of which is spent in REM sleep.

When we go without sleep for long periods, the pattern of stages that occurs when we finally do sleep changes. In one case, a young man went without sleep for 264 hours in order to qualify for the *Guinness Book of Records*. When he finally gave up his quest, he went to sleep in a sleep and dream laboratory, where scientists observed that on the first night he spent much more time in stage 4, at the expense of stage 2. On the second recovery night, his REM sleep increased sharply at the expense of stages 2 through 4. The phenomenon of increased REM sleep after sleep deprivation is called **REM rebound.**

Total sleep deprivation leads to irritability, fatigue, poor concentration, memory failure, and reduced muscle coordination. Some people behave in bizarre ways associated with mental illness, but usually these symptoms do not last after a person sleeps through a recovery period. The ill effects of total sleep deprivation can also be created in sleep and dream laboratories, where it is possible to deprive a subject only of stage 4 and REM sleep. The selective recovery of stage 4 and REM sleep along with the ill effects of such selective deprivation suggest that these stages are especially significant. It remains to be seen whether or not dreams are what make REM sleep so important.

Subjective Patterns During Dreams

As most of us know, dreaming can be an intense experience, accompanied by unusual images and extreme emotional responses such as joy and fear. If dreams in sleep and dream laboratories are representative of our usual dreaming behavior, however, such intense dreams are the exception rather than the rule. The hundreds of thousands of dreams recorded immediately after subjects are awakened from REM sleep suggest that we dream four or five times every night, and that most of our dreams are rather ordinary. We dream about playing ball, riding buses, taking exams, and other everyday activities. Scientists have also recorded some exotic dreams, as well as terrifying nightmares. Despite all of this, no dream as exotic as Ritchie's experiences has ever been recorded in a sleep and dream laboratory.

Failure to record similar dreams does not rule out the possibility that Ritchie was dreaming. As mentioned earlier, Freud maintained that dreams reflect memories and feelings. Accordingly, we would expect Ritchie's dreams to be unusual since his prior experiences were unusual. For instance, he had a great desire to go to Richmond—he was even willing

HIGHLIGHT / SLEEP DISORDERS

The Association for the Psychophysiological Study of Sleep may be your salvation if you are one of the millions of people who suffers from a serious sleep disorder. The association's researchers have established research laboratories and clinics and have both improved the basic understanding of sleep and developed important clinical applications. Their clinical contributions include spelling out dangers associated with the most common medical treatment, sleeping pills, and advancing more effective therapies. These applications grew directly out of research aimed at distinguishing the many different kinds of sleep disorders. Two broad categories can be separated: *insomnia,* which is abnormal wakefulness, and *hypersomnia,* which is abnormal sleepiness. A sleep clinic may be your best bet if you are one of the 15 percent of all Americans who fall into one, or both, of these categories (Mayer, 1975).

The estimate of 15 percent includes only those who have serious and persistent sleep disorders. You should not count yourself among them if you cannot sleep as long as your roommates, for example. One woman went to a sleep clinic after being treated unsuccessfully with sleeping pills. She took the pills in an effort to get a full 9 hours of sleep a night like her husband. It turned out that she only needed 6 hours, which she could get without pills. It is not unusual for one person to require 6 hours of sleep while another requires 9. A 6-hour sleeper need not try to become a 9-hour sleeper. In the same way, you need not worry if you occasionally have sleeping

problems associated with specific events. You might have had trouble sleeping, for instance, on the night before an important exam or on the night before an exciting trip. You might also experience extreme sleepiness during temporary periods of depression. These experiences are common, and they do not indicate that you should tag yourself as one of the 15 percent with sleep disorders.

One serious form of insomnia is an inability to breath properly during sleep, which can eventually lead to heart damage. When breathing is interrupted, the person usually makes loud snoring sounds and wakes up momentarily. One researcher can identify this problem simply by listening to a tape recording of a person's snoring. It might be useful to educate the public about the sound of snores that indicate interrupted breathing, because people who suffer from this problem are often unaware of it. Frequently they complain of being unable to get a restful night's sleep without knowing why. A spouse or friend trained at sizing up snores might be able to warn the afflicted person. Such warnings could help medical doctors avoid the use of sleeping pills, which would only worsen the breathing problem.

A serious form of hypersomnia is indicated in the following case report of a 40-year-old businessman:

I began to experience a sudden drop of my head and my upper arms when I laughed or was under stress. . . . Recently, I had two very frightening experiences. I took my car to go back home near 4 P.M. I remember driving out and turning on the freeway. Then I had a complete

amnesia. I found myself 70 minutes later somewhere in Oakland. . . . A similar episode occurred recently . . . and when I "came back" I was once again lost, with a complete feeling of disorientation. (Guilleminault and Dement, 1977, p. 444)

Guilleminault and Dement have studied some 80 patients with similar conditions. The patients seem to have a malfunction in the brain mechanisms that control sleep. It is hoped that understanding those mechanisms will lead to a cure. Many experts believe that the problem involves chemicals (neurotransmitters) that increase or decrease the transmission of nerve impulses (see Chapter 2).

Sleep experts are identifying and treating many kinds of insomnia and hypersomnia (Cotman and McGaugh, 1980). Some specialists are working toward safer and more effective drug treatment, while others are developing new approaches. One new therapy involves teaching people to control what are ordinarily involuntary bodily actions. Barry Sternman, for example, is trying to train people to make their brain waves resemble those of normal sleepers. He teaches with *biofeedback,* which is a procedure that uses instruments to inform people about the effects of their efforts to control body functions. Such applications are emerging from research that was originally aimed at understanding the psychophysiological processes that underlie sleep. The work of sleep experts is therefore a prime example of how research on basic principles can lead to applications that might benefit you personally.

to jeopardize his health. His dreams could have been influenced by these wishes that existed before sleep. Many students are quite familiar with daily events influencing dreams, since they often dream about exams during finals week.

Ritchie was also surrounded by a strange environment and he was being prepared for the morgue during the time that he might have been dreaming. These conditions could have influenced his dreams because we are not cut off from external stimuli during sleep. In one famous series of experiments, Alfred Maury arranged for an assistant to stimulate him while he slept. When the assistant tickled his lips and nose, Maury dreamed he was being tortured. When the assistant waved perfume in the air, he dreamed he was in a bazaar in Cairo. When part of the bed accidentally fell on the back of Maury's neck, he dreamed he was being beheaded (Cohen, 1976). Ritchie's experience has themes consistent with what we might expect for a dream under his unusual circumstances.

The profound effect of Ritchie's experience on the rest of his life is also consistent with the possibility that he was dreaming. Many people claim to have had their lives changed by dreams. In fact, Fritz Perls, a pioneer in Gestalt psychotherapy (see Chapter 13), tried to get his patients to use their dreams to discover ways to change their lives. Dreams also can solve problems that we are unable to solve in our waking hours. A classic illustration is Friedrich August Kakule's dream of a snake eating its tail. Kakule, a German chemist, had been unsuccessfully pondering the structures of benzene. His dream suggested a ring structure that provided the correct solution. Many others have tried to utilize the creative potential of dreams, but without much success.

An objective scientist is free to accept or reject the possibility that Ritchie walked with God during a dream. Scientists have not *disproved* this mystical explanation, and perhaps they never will. They have, however, made a strong case for a perceptual release theory, which, as mentioned earlier, is a logical alternative to a mystical theory. Hobson and McCarley (1977) maintain, for instance, that dreams are caused by brain activity during REM sleep. Specifically, they argue that dreams are caused by the firing of giant cells, which are large nerve cells in the brainstem (see Chapter 2). The firing of giant cells is associated with all the physiological patterns that are characteristic of sleep. In addition, giant cells activate parts of the brain that are associated with vision and emotions. This activation could explain the things we "see" and "feel" during our dreams, according to Hobson and McCarley. We might say that giant cells "release" perceptions that we experience as dreams. This theory is consistent with the fact that direct electrical stimulation of the brain by means of electrodes causes people to "see" and "feel" things (see the discussion of Penfield's work in Chapter 2). Studying the biological correlates of sleep and dreams has led to a better understanding of sleep disorders (see Highlight: "Sleep Disorders"). The theory needs further development and testing, however, because it does not yet explain *subjective* patterns in detail. It does not explain, for example, why dreams correspond to memories and to daily events. Perhaps future research will show exactly how it is that the firing of giant cells causes memories to be "released" and to be experienced as dreams.

George Ritchie may have been dreaming, but that doesn't reduce the importance of his experience. Dreams are much more important and far richer than many of us realize. We don't have to solve problems or have psychic powers to benefit from them. Simply by paying attention to them, we take a giant step toward an understanding of other forms of consciousness. In the next section we will discuss another state of consciousness that is quite common and safe to explore.

VISIONS DURING DROWSINESS

During the drowsy interval before sleep (stage-1 sleep), we sometimes see visions, hear voices, or feel ourselves falling without any apparent external stimuli to support these sensations. Such sensations are hallucinations, or false sensory perceptions in the absence of an actual external stimulus. Hallucinations may be caused by emotional factors, drugs, alcohol, or stress, and may occur in any of the senses. Hallucinations that occur during the drowsy interval before sleep are called hypnagogic images. ("Hypnagogic" comes from the Greek words *hypnos*, which means sleep, and *agogos*, which means causing.) We will briefly summarize the physiological patterns of stage-1 sleep and then look at its interesting cognitive patterns.

Physiological Patterns

Transitions from waking to sleeping are gradual, with no sharp break between the two states. There is, however, an identifiable transition stage (stage 1) between waking and sleeping. Hypnagogic images occur during this drowsy transition interval, which begins with the onset of theta waves and ends with the onset of sleep spindles in EEG patterns. The interval is also characterized by the occurrence of slow, side-to-side eye movements, which are quite different from the rapid eye movements associated with REM sleep.

Subjective Patterns

Hypnagogic images occur in all senses, including smell. For example, one student smelled bacon frying before she fell asleep. When she got up to investigate, she found that she was the only one awake in her apartment. Furthermore, the smell that seemed so strong only moments earlier was gone. She had hallucinated the smell. The most common hypnagogic images, however, are those that we seem to see, hear, or feel.

Visual hypnagogic images occur in a consistent sequence of stages. In the first, we see flashes of color and light; in the second, we see geometric patterns; faces and static objects appear in the third. Finally, landscapes and more complex, prolonged scenes appear in the fourth stage (cf. Schacter, 1976). Stages 3 and 4 are the most interesting. Dreamlike faces, occurring in stage 3, are notorious for their vividness, detail, and novelty. Hypnagogic faces usually are not familiar and they often take on unusual and even grotesque qualities. Stage 3 hypnagogic images may be responsible for the popularity of night lights among children (cf. Schacter, 1976). Presleep visions of landscapes occurring in stage 4 are often beautiful, and frequently contain a great deal of activity and movement. Sometimes the landscape appears as if it were being viewed from a moving car or train.

Visual images are sometimes combined with auditory hypnagogic images. We might hear imaginary faces speak or hear road noises associated with visual hypnagogic landscapes. Auditory images also occur by themselves. We might hear our name called or hear music, which can be unfamiliar and bizarre (perhaps similar to the music George Ritchie heard during his experience), or it can be familiar. In one case, a woman tried to turn off her radio after listening to several popular songs. She was amazed to discover it was already off. The music she "heard" was an auditory hypnagogic image.

The feeling of being touched and of being in motion are other possible presleep images. A rich image of riding a horse might include the sight of the landscape passing by, the sound of hooves, and the touch sensations of the reins and saddle. More typical is the sensation of falling with no associated visual or auditory images, sometimes accompanied by severe involuntary jerks of the body.

If you have never experienced a hypnagogic image, it may be because you pass through stage 1 too quickly. Some people go through the transition between waking and sleeping much faster than others. You might consider using procedures developed in sleep and dream laboratories to prolong the drowsy interval before sleep. You could, for example, set a "snooze alarm" on a modern alarm clock to go off every 5 minutes unless you push a button to stop it. Also, you might position a clock so that you must hold your forearm up to hold a button or else the alarm will go off. Either procedure will keep you awake and, if you are tired, you should slip into stage-1 sleep long enough to experience hypnagogic images.

You need not go to such extremes to experience the stage of consciousness discussed in the next section. In fact, some of you may be in it right now.

DAYDREAMS

Imagine going to an emergency clinic with a wound in your right forearm. As the doctor sews up the cut, you wonder what she is thinking about. Most of us would like to believe that her mind is fixed on the stitches she is putting in our skin; more than likely, however, she is daydreaming. One researcher (Csikszentmihalyi, 1974) found that 14 out of 21 surgeons interviewed in his study reported daydreaming during routine aspects of surgery. Their daydreams were about music, food, wine, and women, among other things. Daydreams can be defined as "thoughts that divert attention away from an immediately demanding task" (Singer, 1975). We all daydream, and scientists are beginning to study carefully this important aspect of our mental life.

Physiological Patterns

Unlike night dreams, daydreams are not characterized by unique physiological patterns. Physiological responses during daydreams are not very different from those of ordinary waking consciousness. One physiological response that is characteristic of daydreaming is a blank (or unfocused) stare of the eyes, but many daydreams occur without this characteristic "staring off into space." Surely the surgeons in the study reported earlier had no such blank stare. Thus, physiological responses are not useful in distinguishing daydreams from ordinary waking states.

The lack of unique physiological patterns supports Jerome Singer's claim that daydreams are an aspect of ordinary waking consciousness.

Subjective Patterns

Singer (1975) believes that daydreams are an extremely important part of our private mental life. He found that daydreams can be divided into three categories: *unhappy, uncontrollable,* and *happy.* The first category includes fantasies involving guilt, aggressive wishes, and fear of failure. The second includes fleeting, anxiety-laden fantasies that make it hard

We all daydream sometimes. One characteristic of a person who is daydreaming is a rather blank or unfocused stare of the eyes, as can be seen in the photo here.

to concentrate and to hold attention on outside events. Finally, happy daydreams are characterized by vivid visual and auditory imagery, and by fantasies used for planning future activity. In one study of happy daydreams, Hariton and Singer (1975) reported that many women daydream during sexual intercourse. They found that these fantasies promote arousal during the sex act, are not associated with sexual conflict, and are characteristic of women who are generally given to happy daydreaming. Each of us might engage in all three kinds of daydreams, but we are likely to experience one kind more often.

An intriguing relationship between daydreaming patterns and alcohol abuse has been observed (Singer, 1975). People prone to unhappy daydreams are more likely to abuse alcohol. This correlation does not mean that unhappy daydreams cause alcohol abuse (see Chapter 12). Singer speculates, however, that happy daydreams may help *prevent* it. Alcohol and other drugs induce intense, novel sensations, but they are not necessary for experiencing rich, attractive stimulation. Singer maintains, for instance, that someone practiced at attending to his or her "inner" experiences can achieve a "high" while listening to music without the use of drugs. People who learn to enjoy such natural "highs" may have no need to seek artificial ones.

DRUG-INDUCED STATES

Drugs that produce subjective effects are called **psychoactive drugs**. The most widely used psychoactive drugs in America are caffeine, which is in coffee and many soft drinks; alcohol; and nicotine, which is in tobacco.

Americans use these drugs for such subjective effects as pepping up, reducing inhibitions, and relaxing. Even though the dangers of smoking are well known, Americans continue to light up. They also continue to consume alcohol and caffeine even though the dangers of those drugs are also widely publicized. Why?

The Drug Abuse Council, which was established by the Ford Foundation in 1972, addressed this question along with questions about the use of illegal drugs. They did not answer the question, and we cannot do so here, either. They did suggest in their final report, however, that illegal drug use must be considered in the context of the use and misuse of *legal* psychoactive drugs (Drug Abuse Council, 1980). We will go over physiological and subjective responses associated with some legal and illegal psychoactive drugs. In later sections, we will show that similar effects can be achieved without the use of dangerous drugs.

Psychoactive drugs fall into three categories: (1) depressants, which slow body functions or calm nervous excitement; (2) stimulants, which excite body functions; and (3) hallucinogens, which cause hallucinations. Subjective effects are difficult to predict because they are affected by non-drug factors. Cross-cultural comparisons illustrate this point. Psychoactive drugs are used recreationally at social events in our culture, and some of them have gained a reputation for producing heightened enjoyment from food and sex. In contrast, other cultures use psychoactive drugs during religious ceremonies. Ancient Hindus used a hallucinogen called *soma* to feel at one with God, and Aztecs "became one with the Great Spirit of the Universe" by chewing the dried tips of peyote cactus (a source of a hallucinogen). Hallucinogens are associated with reduced sexual appetites and self-denial in these religious contexts. The same drug can increase or decrease sexual activity depending upon the culture in which it is taken, because culture influences the expectations and desires in people using drugs.

Personality also influences subjective responses. Some people have pleasant drug-induced experiences, knowing that their unusual mental state is caused by drugs. Others have terrifying experiences during which they act like they are mentally ill. They might, for example, be unable to distinguish between reality and drug-induced hallucinations. In the worst cases, mentally ill behaviors persist after the drug effects have worn off. Scientists generally cannot predict subjective responses unless nondrug factors are carefully controlled. We can nevertheless characterize typical responses.

Depressants

Three common depressants are alcohol, nicotine, and heroin. You might be surprised to see alcohol listed as a depressant. This classification seems inconsistent with the use of alcoholic drinks to "liven up" a party. The reason for the classification is clear, however, when we consider physiological patterns associated with alcohol consumption.

Physiological Patterns. Alcohol, nicotine, and heroin depress body functions. Alcohol is consumed in beer, wine, and liquor. The alcohol in three beers is enough to dilate the pupils, to slow response time, and to impair motor functions. Extreme doses can cause death. Nicotine is very poisonous, but the amount inhaled while smoking tobacco is too little to cause death. Excessive smoking, however, can cause weak, rapid pulse, sense of exhaustion, and poor appetite. Initially, nicotine acts as a stimulant, but ultimately it depresses the central and autonomic nervous system. Smoking is also associated with heart disease and lung cancer. Heroin comes from the juice of the opium poppy. It is sold illegally in the United States to users who either sniff or inject it. Heroin reduces sensitivity

Alcohol is this country's most popular drug, and the source of many drug-abuse problems.

to pain and it depresses respiration. An overdose can cause death. Alcohol, nicotine, and heroin are all *physiologically addictive*, which means that body functions can become dependent upon the drug's effects and that the body can require increasingly larger doses to obtain the desired effects.

Subjective Patterns. Depressants have highly variable subjective effects. One of alcohol's main effects is to make one feel uninhibited in social behaviors. This release from social inhibitions explains the party effect mentioned earlier. Large doses can cause anger and aggression in some individuals, and it can cause depression and drowsiness in others. Nicotine's subjective effect is slight in comparison with other drugs. It is characterized by a subtle relaxing response. Heroin, on the other hand, has dramatic subjective effects. In some people it produces a "rush," which is an intensely pleasurable response. It causes some people to forget their troubles. They also feel no hunger, pain, or sexual urges and they often get drowsy. Heroin's dominant effect is a feeling of well-being, which is part of the lure that attracts people to this highly addictive and very dangerous drug.

Stimulants

Stimulants are quite popular in America. A common one is *caffeine*, which is available without prescription, as mentioned earlier. *Amphetamines* stimulate the central nervous system and are available in pill form by prescription under such trade names as Methedrine, Dexedrine, and Benzedrine. These pills are also sold illegally as "speed," "uppers," or "bennies." *Cocaine* is another stimulant that is sold illegally.

Physiological Patterns. Caffeine, amphetamines, and cocaine all stimulate body functions. Caffeine increases heart rate, and causes restlessness and sometimes tremors. Amphetamines increase blood pressure and breath rate. They also act as an appetite suppressor and they can cause rapid and irregular heartbeats, tremor, and dryness of mouth. Cocaine also stimulates the central nervous system. It can cause dizziness,

Cocaine is an illegal drug that stimulates the central nervous system and is physiologically addictive. Produced from the coca plant, it is believed to be the strongest natural stimulant known. Most users inhale cocaine, but it can also be injected.

low blood pressure, and even convulsions. All three of these drugs are physiologically addictive.

Subjective Patterns. Subjective effects are highly variable in stimulants, as they are in other drugs. The main effect for all stimulants is a feeling of energy, which is often accompanied by a feeling of restlessness. Caffeine can also cause irritability. The possible subjective side effects for amphetamine and cocaine use are much worse. They can cause a pleasant "rush," followed by irritability. The stimulating effect can end with a "crash," which is sleep followed by a period of fatigue and depression. Finally, both amphetamines and cocaine can cause behaviors that are indistinguishable from certain kinds of mental illness.

Hallucinogens

Four common hallucinogenic drugs are *marijuana, mescaline, psilocybin,* and *LSD.* Hallucinogenic drugs are sometimes called *psychedelic,* which means "mind-manifesting." The nature of psychedelic experiences is illustrated in the following quote, which shows a partial transcript of a person who took 20 milligrams of psilocybin.

> It looks like several different whirlpools, with lots of spirals divided up into checks. It's pretty black. There's purple and green glowing areas in the middle of the spirals, kind of clouds around. There are lines going from top to bottom, kind of a grid, but the lines squiggle around. There's odd shapes, but still lots of right angles in them. Seems really bright. . . . There's like an explosion, yellow in the middle, like a volcano gushing out lava, yellow, glowing. There's a black square with yellow light coming behind it. There's a regular pattern superimposed on everything, lots of curlicues, with dots in the middle. Lots of little paisley things that fill up the spaces between the patterns of triangles, squares, or crown-shaped things. And there's a little white star that floats around the picture and sometimes goes behind what's on the screen and illuminates from behind.
>
> Now there's a kind of landscape. Very flat, flat country. The picture is very narrow. In the middle part a tree at the left and then flat with green grass and blue sky above. There are orange dots, oranges hanging all over, in the sky, on the tree, on the ground. A bicycle! Oh, my! It's headed down, not horizontal, like someone's holding it up on end. . . . There's a checkerboard superimposed on everything like the flags they wave at the races.
>
> I can see the street out there. . . . Well, it's old-golly-interesting! It's like in the forties, I guess, or maybe the fifties. . . . And there are people riding their bicycles, and there are, like, boys, in plaid vests and those funny kind of hats. . . . I was at the side walking on the sidewalk, so it wasn't like I was in the middle of the street and [laughter] you can't laugh very long in the middle of the street in the city, so that image kind of went away [laughter]. (Siegel, 1977, p. 139)

Not all drug-induced sensations are as pleasant. Sometimes people imagine that their limbs are distorting and their flesh decaying, or they see sickly greens or ugly dark reds and experience gloom and isolation. Despite the variability of drug-induced experiences, consistent patterns are present, some of which share characteristics with George Ritchie's experience, even though he was not on hallucinogenic drugs.

Physiological Patterns. Marijuana is the least potent of the four hallucinogenic drugs mentioned above. After ingesting THC, a person's EEG shows a higher percentage of alpha brain waves, heart rate increases, eyes redden, and the mouth goes dry, while blood pressure and respiration are unaffected. LSD is the most potent hallucinogen. Brain waves and other physiological responses during LSD intoxication indicate intense activity similar to physiological response patterns during REM sleep. However, the most interesting effects of hallucinogenic drugs are subjective responses.

Subjective Patterns. When we suggested that Ritchie's experience may have been influenced by his background and his immediate situation, we introduced a theme that is especially important in drug research. We cannot yet predict the course of psychedelic experiences because we do not understand all the factors influencing them.

Figure 4–4 shows a model used to help analyze drug-induced states (Tart, 1977). According to his model, we must know what drug a person has taken, how much of the drug was taken, and how the drug was taken, if we want to predict responses to the drug. Even more important, we must know many nondrug factors.

Tart's model suggests, first, that a person's mood, expectations, and desires are important short-term or immediate factors influencing drug-induced states. People who are afraid of drugs, for example, will probably have a more anxiety-laden experience than people who are comfortable with them. In addition, the context in which the drug was taken also plays a role. People taking drugs with strangers in an unfamiliar environment are more likely to be afraid, and their fear response itself can modify the situation by making others around them more anxious. Tart's model suggests, second, that culture, personality, physiology, and learned drug-use skills are long-term factors influencing drug-induced states.

Despite these factors, however, it has been found that drug-induced hallucinations have four stages in a carefully controlled laboratory setting (Siegel, 1977). The first stage is characterized by vague black-and-white forms moving about in one's visual field. You can probably see the same thing by simply closing your eyes, or by gently rubbing your closed eyelids. What you see then are **phosphenes,** visual sensations arising from spontaneous discharges of light-sensitive neurons in your eyes. Apparently, drugs make people more aware of phosphenes.

The second stage begins with the appearance of geometric forms. Siegel created a special keyboard to help people report on second-stage images. He divided the keyboard into three sections (corresponding to form, color,

FIGURE 4–4

This model shows the many variables that should be taken into account in analyzing drug-induced states. (Zinberg, 1977, p. 200)

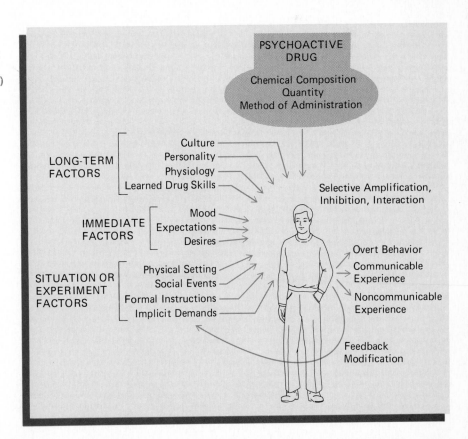

FIGURE 4–5

In the second stage of drug-induced hallucinations, the color red dominates, along with the appearance of a spiral-shaped tunnel covered with a graph paper design.

FIGURE 4–6 (Below, left)

In this stage images are sometimes superimposed on the spiral-shaped tunnel that is shown above.

FIGURE 4–7 (Below, right)

Images in the third stage often include unusual vantage points, such as this one, showing a view from the bottom of a swimming pool.

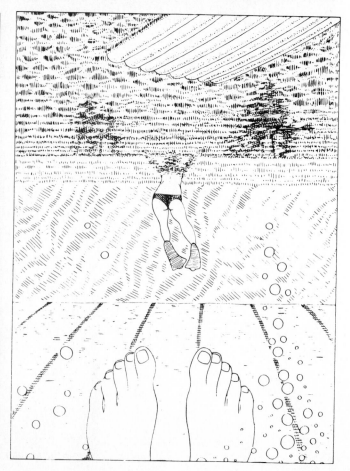

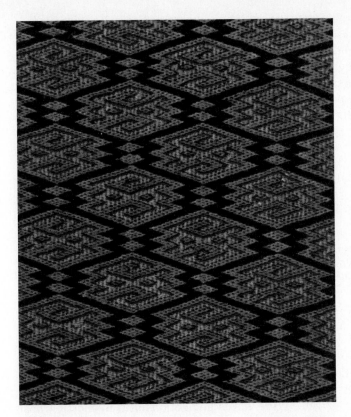
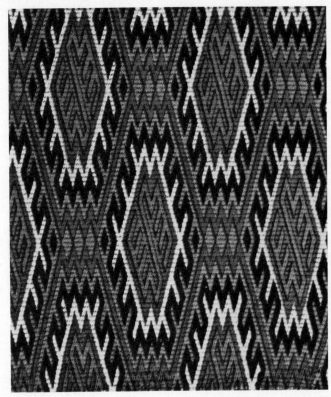

FIGURE 4–8

Huichol Indians show hallucinated patterns such as these in their art and weaving, and report other patterns of hallucinations similar to those of Americans.

and movement), and put eight keys into each section. The keys offered the following options: form (random, line, curve, web, graph paper, tunnel, spiral, and kaleidoscope); color (black, violet, blue, green, yellow, orange, red, and white); and movement (aimless, vertical, horizontal, oblique, explosive, concentric, rotational, and pulsating). People who were trained on the keyboard reported new images 20 times per minute. Untrained observers could only report 5 times per minute. Both trained and untrained subjects indicated that second-stage images are colored geometric forms that usually pulsate or rotate. All colors occur, but blue is the most frequent at first. Later, red dominates, and with the shift to red comes the appearance of a spiral-shaped tunnel covered with a graph paper design (Figure 4–5). Often a bright light seems to pulsate in the tunnel's center. The third stage usually begins shortly after the appearance of the spiral tunnel.

The third stage is characterized by meaningful images that sometimes appear superimposed on a spiral tunnel, as in Figure 4–6, and sometimes seem to be images drawn from memory. One student saw the backyard in which she played as a child. Images in this stage often include unusual vantage points, such as George Ritchie's view from about 50 feet directly above a cafe (Figure 4–7). If Ritchie's visual experiences can be identified by any stage, however, it would be the fourth.

Stage-4 images seem more like moving pictures than snapshots—that is, they are more like dreams. Sometimes fourth-stage hallucinations share with Ritchie's experience a feeling that one is part of the imagery and a feeling of being dissociated from one's body.

The four stages of drug intoxication seem to be consistent across cultures. Siegel noted, for instance, that Hindu religious symbols are similar to commonly hallucinated geometric patterns. Furthermore, Huichol Indians show hallucinated patterns in their art and weaving (Figure 4–8). They also report patterns of hallucinations almost identical to those of Americans, even though Huichol Indians have been relatively isolated in Mexico since the Aztec era.

One could argue from a mystical or psychological point of view that drug-induced experiences and near-death experiences are closely related. People who use a drug in religious ceremonies, as Huichols do, obviously believe that it puts them in touch with a sacred external reality, presumably the same reality that Ritchie claimed to have experienced. The similarities between drug experiences and near-death episodes do not rule out the perceptual release theory. A perceptual release theorist would try to explain the similar experiences in terms of similar brain reactions. It remains for future research to determine what the common brain responses might be. A good starting point for this future research would be to explore the possibility of similar effects on brain chemistry. Scientists are already beginning to understand how hallucinogens affect brain chemistry (Cotman and McGaugh, 1980).

HYPNOSIS

George Ritchie took a chance with his professional reputation when he comforted his dying patient with a personal report about life after death. In the same way, Oscar N. Lucas (1975), a dentist, went out on a limb to help his hemophiliac patients, who have a tendency to bleed uncontrollably when they have a tooth pulled. At the risk of appearing unprofessional, Lucas tried to control bleeding with **hypnosis,** which is a state of consciousness induced by the words and actions of a hypnotist whose suggestions are readily accepted by the subject. Lucas suggested during hypnosis that his patients' mouths were filled with ice that would control bleeding. The effect was astonishing. When hemophiliacs have teeth pulled, they usually receive 5 pints of blood, spend 6 days in the hospital, and do not heal for about 2 weeks. With hypnosis, Lucas's patients received no blood, were not hospitalized, and waited about 4 days to heal. Such results are slowly swinging the professional community in favor of hypnosis.

Successful control of pain has been influential in the acceptance of hypnosis as a professional tool. In the mid-nineteenth century, England's medical society rejected as a hoax claims that hypnosis can control pain during surgery. Today, medical doctors recognize many well-documented cases of pain control by means of hypnosis. Many hypnotized patients who could not use drugs as pain killers have felt little or no pain when having a tooth pulled, after being severely burned, during childbirth, and during the final stages of terminal cancer. Hypnosis has also been used to speed the recovery of heart-attack patients, to cure skin diseases, and to eliminate allergies.

While hypnosis is being used more, as an issue it remains controversial. The controversy has shifted emphasis, however. Originally, it was about what hypnosis can and can't do. Now it is about how hypnosis works. The debate is fueled by data on physiological patterns; it is calmed by data on subjective patterns.

Physiological Patterns

No consistent physiological patterns accompany hypnosis. Blood pressure, heart rate, and breathing can vary with the suggestions of the hypnotist. In some cases, EEG patterns resemble REM sleep patterns, but they are often indistinguishable from normal waking consciousness.

The lack of distinct physiological patterns raises two possibilities. One is that hypnosis does not induce an alternate state of consciousness. Barber (1970) maintains, for instance, that hypnosis leaves people in a waking state, but it highly motivates them to cooperate with the hypnotist's suggestions. Accordingly, anything people can do under hypnosis, they can also do in a normal waking state, as long as they are highly motivated. Another possibility is that distinct physiological patterns do exist, but scientists have not yet found them. Those who favor the view that hypnosis induces an alternate state of consciousness point to the distinctive abilities that are possible under hypnosis, such as reduction of bleeding and severe pain (Orne, 1972).

Subjective Patterns

Although scientists do not agree about how hypnosis works, they do agree about basic subjective and behavioral patterns associated with it. Even those who deny that hypnosis induces an alternate state of consciousness accept that hypnotists can cause the following changes:

1. Hypnotists can influence judgment and suggestibility. A susceptible subject will disregard his or her own judgment and accept a hypnotist's suggestions. People vary in susceptibility. Some will not yield to a hypnotist's suggestions at all, and, therefore, they cannot be hypnotized. Wallace (1979) maintains, on the other hand, that most people can be hypnotized to some extent, and particularly if they are trained to do so. He estimates, however, that only 10 percent of us could follow a hypnotist's suggestions well enough to undergo surgery without using drugs as pain killers. A major problem, then, is predicting the extent to which people can be hypnotized. **Hypnotic susceptibility tests** are used for this purpose. They indicate the extent to which people are willing to yield to a hypnotist's suggestions (Barber and Glass, 1962; Shor and Orne, 1962; Weitzenhoffer and Hilgard, 1962).

2. Hypnotists can influence relaxation. They often suggest that people are falling asleep. A susceptible subject begins to feel drowsy and then appears to be very relaxed. The subject is awake, however, because he or she can respond to the hypnotist's suggestions. Relaxation is typical, but it is not necessary. Hypnotists can induce increased tension and alertness while at the same time getting subjects to follow suggestions.

3. Hypnotists can influence attention. They sometimes help subjects relax by getting them to concentrate most of their attention on some target, such as a small light. Subjects can also direct their attention to the hypnotist's voice while ignoring other voices. Hypnotists can also get subjects to divide their attention between two tasks in order to reduce interference between tasks. This channeling of attention has been demonstrated with two tasks that ordinarily interfere with one another (Knox, Crutchfield, and Hilgard, 1975). The tasks were pushing buttons in a repetitive pattern and naming colors. People usually do not push the buttons as well when they name the colors. But hypnotized subjects could push the buttons as well with or without color naming.

4. Hypnotists can influence memory. They can, for instance, persuade subjects to regress back in age. In one experiment, a hypnotist suggested that adult subjects were 5 years old, and he asked them to recall the children in their kindergarten class; many subjects recalled the names of most of the children that had been in their class (Ferguson, 1973). Hypnotists sometimes use their influence on memory to recover critical information in criminal investigations. An example occurred in a 1976 kidnapping case in California. A bus driver, who was nabbed along with his 26 young passengers, was unable to remember details. Under hypnosis, however, his memory improved enough to recall the kidnapper's license plate number (Wallace, 1979). Hypnotists can also use their power over memory to cause people to forget temporarily what happened during hypnosis. Memory returns when a prearranged signal is given.

Frank Ray, the driver of the school bus in the Chowchilla kidnapping case, was at first unable to remember details that would aid police. Under hypnosis, however, he was able to recall the kidnappers' license plate, which led to their eventual arrest.

5. Hypnotists can use **posthypnotic suggestions,** which are suggestions that are carried out after hypnosis has ended. A hypnotist might suggest that a subject will scratch her ear when she hears a bell after hypnosis has ended. A susceptible subject will scratch her ear when the bell rings. If asked why, she will probably say that it itched. Subjects usually forget that posthypnotic suggestions were given. Sometimes they claim to remember, however. A man accused of robbing a bank, for example, recently pleaded innocent on the grounds that he was following a posthypnotic command. It is thought to be unlikely, however, that hypnosis could cause people to commit crimes they would not otherwise commit (Barber, 1961; Orne, 1965; Coe, 1977).

While the debate goes on concerning the mechanisms that underlie hypnosis, new applications are being found. Applications in addition to those already mentioned include: treating irrational fears and other behavioral problems; improving athletic skills; and controlling overeating and other bad habits. The use of hypnosis is expected to increase as the public becomes aware of its many beneficial uses.

MEDITATION

Many of the basic elements or characteristics of hypnosis are also essential to **meditation,** a state of consciousness similar to hypnosis except that the hypnotist's authority is transferred to the meditators themselves. Some meditators encounter many of the experiences reported by George Ritchie. They feel united with God, sometimes their minds seem to leave their bodies, they see into the future, and often they see into the past with unusual clarity. After one 2-hour meditation session, Aldous Huxley reported a fantasy that brings to mind the part of Ritchie's experience in which his life "passed before his eyes." During meditation, 26-year-old Aldous Huxley found himself on a hill with 6-year-old Aldous Huxley. During the confrontation, the adult Huxley experienced in vivid detail the child's growth. As day after day passed, Huxley felt the anguish, relief, and elation of the growing boy. Huxley called his meditation procedure *deep relaxation,* which is an apt term, given recent evidence that meditation is an effective way to cope with fatigue, anxiety, and stress.

We will discuss physiological and psychological patterns associated with two kinds of meditation, transcendental meditation and Benson's relaxation response method.

Eastern forms of meditation are the source of most other procedures. Zen Buddhist monks in Japan practice *Zen* meditation, in which enlightenment is obtained by thinking about paradoxical or nonlogical things such as the "sound of one hand clapping." In India, *yoga* is practiced as part of ancient Hindu efforts to give people control over their minds. Many forms of yoga exist. One emphasizes complete relaxation, another uses strenuous exercise, and still another concentrates on controlling body functions such as breathing. Yoga requires extensive training and is not easily grasped by westerners. **Transcendental meditation (TM)** is a simplified yoga technique that allows people to meditate after a short training course. The technique is simple. An instructor gives you a secret word, sound, or phrase that is called your **mantra.** You can mentally repeat your mantra over and over again while sitting in a comfortable position. If distracting thoughts enter your mind, you disregard them and return your thoughts to your mantra. You are advised to meditate 20 minutes before breakfast and 20 minutes before dinner. TM was developed by Maharishi Mehesh

Meditation is an effective way to cope with fatigue, anxiety, and stress. There are several different types of meditation, including Zen, yoga, and transcendental meditation, which is a simplified form of yoga.

Yogi, an Indian guru. In the 1960s, TM gained popularity, and over 2 million people now practice it.

Herbert Benson (1975), Associate Professor of Medicine at the Harvard Medical School and Director of the Hypertension Section of Boston's Beth Israel Hospital, westernized TM even further. Instead of concentrating on your own secret mantra, in Benson's procedure you are asked to keep your thoughts on the number "1." Benson's procedure has six steps:

1. Sit quietly in a comfortable position.
2. Close your eyes.
3. Deeply relax all your muscles, beginning at your feet and progressing up to your face. Keep them relaxed.
4. Breathe through your nose. Become aware of your breathing. As you breathe out, say the word, "one," silently to yourself. Breathe easily and naturally.
5. Continue for 10 to 20 minutes. You may open your eyes to check the time, but do not use an alarm. When you finish, sit quietly for several minutes, at first with your eyes closed and later with your eyes opened. Do not stand up for a few minutes.
6. Do not worry about whether you are successful in achieving a deep level of relaxation. Maintain a passive attitude and permit relaxation to occur at its own pace. When distracting thoughts occur, try to

ignore them by not dwelling upon them and return to repeating "one." With practice, the response should come with little effort. Practice the technique once or twice daily, but not within 2 hours after any meal, since the digestive processes seem to interfere with elicitation of the relaxation response. (Benson, 1975, pp. 114–115)

Physiological Patterns

Herbert Benson (1975) uses the phrase relaxation response to refer to the physiological patterns observed during meditation. The relaxation response decreases oxygen consumption, respiratory rate, heart rate, blood pressure, and muscle tension. At the same time, it increases alpha waves to levels observed during other alternate states, including REM sleep. The relaxation response is the opposite of the fight-or-flight response (Cannon, 1914) which involves increased oxygen consumption, respiratory rate, heart rate, blood pressure, and muscle tension (see Chapter 2). Fight-or-flight responses seem to have evolved to prepare animals for emergencies. Perceived danger automatically triggers the response, preparing an animal to run or fight. In humans, stressful situations trigger the response, often needlessly, as when you panic before an exam. Frequent inappropriate responses may be a fundamental cause of strokes, heart attacks, and other stress-related diseases, as we discuss in Chapter 2 and Chapter 10.

Benson's book, *The Relaxation Response*, makes a strong case for our ability to improve our physiological and psychological well-being by learning to elicit the relaxation response through meditation.

Subjective Patterns

You could encounter out-of-body experiences, hallucinations, and other psychic phenomena through meditation. You probably will not do so, however, if you limit your meditation to two 20-minute sessions per day. Cognitive patterns obtained with moderate use of the relaxation response are illustrated in the following quote, which shows a report of a woman who used Benson's procedure to treat her high blood pressure.

The Relaxation Response has contributed to many changes in my life. Not only has it made me more relaxed physically and mentally, but also it has contributed to changes in my personality and way of life. I seem to have become calmer, more open and receptive especially to ideas which either have been unknown to me or very different from my past way of life.

Intellectually and spiritually, good things happen to me during the Relaxation Response. Sometimes I get insights into situations or problems which have been with me for a long time and about which I am not consciously thinking. Creative ideas come to me either during or as a direct result of the Relaxation Response. I look forward to the Relaxation Response twice and sometimes three times a day. I am hooked on it and love my addiction. (Benson, 1975, p. 119)

Many students have had similar experiences, finding the relaxation response helpful, especially before exams. You might try it.

SENSORY DEPRIVATION

The apparent psychological benefits of meditation are consistent with Peter Suedfeld's suggestion that isolation can have positive effects (Suedfeld, 1981). Meditators isolate themselves by focusing on a word or process

FIGURE 4–9

This shows a sensory deprivation chamber, in which goggles, earphones, and padding to cover hands and arms eliminate almost all sensory stimuli. (Heron, 1961, p. 9)

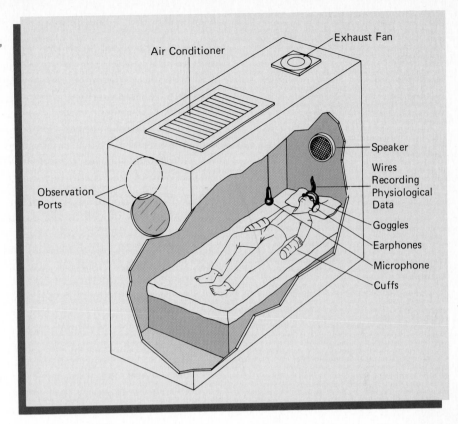

to block out other sensory stimulation. Suedfeld studies another kind of isolation called **sensory deprivation,** which is a condition in which sensory stimulation is drastically reduced in quantity and intensity. Experiments induce sensory deprivation in various ways. Some submerge people in a dark, silent tank of water that is at body temperature. The subject's only connection with stimulation outside of the tank is through an air hose (Lilly, 1956). Other experimenters use less extreme procedures, as shown in Figure 4–9. They cover people's eyes with translucent goggles, which let them see constant but formless light. They cover the ears with earphones that play a constant buzzing sound. Finally, they cover the hands and arms with padding to reduce touch stimulation (Heron, 1961). Research done during the early 1960s associated sensory deprivation with negative reactions such as high anxiety. Suedfeld maintains that these reactions occurred because subjects were not properly oriented to the conditions. He finds that with appropriate orientation, sensory deprivation can induce relaxation and calm. He has used sensory deprivation to treat drug addictions, hypertension, and alcoholism. Let's examine the physiological and subjective responses associated with sensory deprivation.

Physiological Patterns

Researchers have recorded many physiological responses during sensory deprivation. Their measures include breath rate, heart rate, blood pressure, brain waves, eye movements, and muscle tension. Their results suggest conclusions similar to those drawn for hypnosis. Sensory deprivation causes changes in physiological patterns, including changes in brain waves. But the changes do not establish a distinct pattern that can be used to identify a unique state of consciousness. Sensory-deprived subjects alternate between states of being alert, drowsy, and asleep. Physiological measures keep track of these changes.

Subjective Patterns

One of the most publicized results of sensory deprivation research is that alert subjects experience hallucinations and dreamlike episodes. Suedfeld (1975) acknowledges these effects, nothing that some subjects think they see tiny spaceships buzzing around and shooting at them. Suedfeld thinks that it is regrettable, however, that these and other negative effects have been sensationalized, while positive effects have been ignored. He presents a more balanced review that includes negative and positive effects. We can group the results into perceptual, cognitive, and suggestibility effects that appear temporarily after sensory deprivation:

1. Certain aspects of perception are distorted. People are off in their perception of colors and spatial orientation, for instance. But they do better on a wide variety of perceptual tasks. They estimate weights better, hear softer sounds, and see more detail.
2. Some cognitive abilities are dulled, but others are sharpened. People do worse on arithmetic and concept formation tasks, but they learn word lists faster and they score higher on IQ tests.
3. People are more open to suggestions. On the negative side, some fear that sensory deprivation could be used to "brainwash" subjects. In one experiment, sensory-deprived subjects were more influenced than control subjects by messages about humans having hidden mental powers, including abilities to read minds and to "see" into the future. Some worry that similar techniques could be used to influence people about political views that they would not otherwise believe. On the positive side, people are more susceptible to suggestions to make changes that they want to make. In one experiment, sensory deprivation helped people who were eager to quit smoking. They listened to antismoking messages after sensory deprivation. Then, over the next 2 years, they reduced smoking much more than a group who heard the same message without experiencing deprivation (Figure 4–10).

Sensory deprivation procedures not only reduce sensations, they also confine subjects and eliminate social contacts. Sensory reduction, confinement, and social isolation can all contribute therefore to effects of the procedure. Research is underway to separate the influences of these three variables (Zubek, Bayer, and Shepard, 1969; Zuckerman, 1969). Research

FIGURE 4–10

Sensory deprivation has been shown to have positive effects in some cases. In one experiment, subjects who were trying to stop smoking cigarettes were able to reduce their intake more after sensory deprivation than those subjects who had not experienced sensory deprivation.

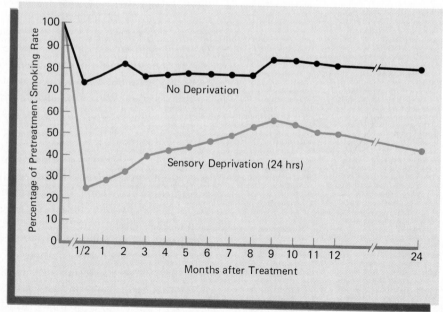

is also being done with sensory deprivation to test theories of motivation, personality, and social psychology.

Earlier, we mentioned attempts to "brainwash" people about reading minds and "seeing" into the future; in the next section we will consider such abilities. We do not want to wash any brains or even twist any arms one way or the other. We invite you, however, to test objectively the possibility that you might have hidden mental powers.

HIDDEN MENTAL POWERS

By virtue of being born human, we have a wide variety of behaviors and experiences available to us. Many of us have the potential for running a 4-minute mile, using advanced calculus, and enjoying Beethoven's symphonies. We develop only a fraction of our human potentialities, however. Most of us never run a 4-minute mile, and many of us never get beyond basic calculus. Our ability to do more remains hidden inside of us.

What are our hidden abilities and how can we discover them? It has been suggested that we might have to enter alternate states of consciousness to find some of them (Tart, 1977). Many of us discover, for instance, that we can create in our dreams bizarre images and weird stories that are beyond our waking imagination. If we are highly motivated, we may also find in our waking consciousness the ability to control severe pain and other such hidden abilities (Barber, 1970; Olshan, 1980). We will conclude this chapter with some tests that are designed to test two kinds of hidden mental powers. One kind is **extrasensory perception (ESP)**, which is the reception of information by means other than our usual senses of hearing, sight, taste, touch, and smell. George Ritchie's alleged communication with the being of light by direct thought transference is an example. The other kind is **psychokinesis (PK)**, which is direct mental influence over physical objects or processes. A person with *PK* could supposedly "will" dice to come to rest at desired numbers, for instance. Evidence for the existence of these abilities does not meet usual scientific standards (Diaconis, 1978; Hansel, 1980; Hyman, 1977). *There is, therefore, no scientific basis for expecting that you will have these powers.* The tests will cost you little more than your time, however, and they might clear up sensationalized half-truths that are spread about these abilities.

Extrasensory Perception

Scientists who study ESP and PK are called *parapsychologists.* One parapsychologist, Dr. Joseph Banks Rhine of Duke University, developed simple laboratory procedures that we can use to test our powers of ESP and PK. To do the tests you will need to make a deck of cards out of heavy, opaque paper. Make 25 cards, 5 each of the patterns shown in Figure 4–11. Draw the patterns on the cards, being careful not to make distinguishing marks on the backs. When you finish you will have **Zener cards,** and you will be able to test the various kinds of ESP.

Telepathy Tests. One kind of ESP is **telepathy,** the perception of another's mental state or emotion by means of ESP. You can test your telepathic powers with your Zener cards and a friend. Sit back to back with your friend and shuffle the cards. Turn the cards over one at a time. Look at each card, while trying to "send" a mental image of the card to your partner, and then have your partner say which of the five patterns you were looking at. Go through the whole deck without telling whether his or her answers are right or wrong. If your friend gets 10 or more

FIGURE 4–11

Zener cards, which are used to test various kinds of ESP, consist of 25 cards, 5 each of the patterns shown here.

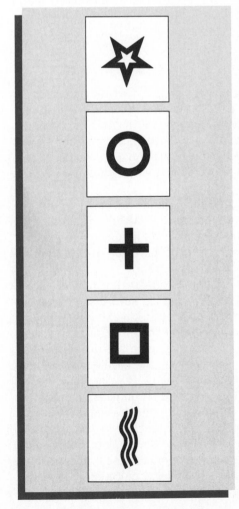

correct, you probably have telepathic powers. Less than 10 correct will happen quite often by chance. For example, wild guesses will give five correct answers about half the time. You can get a more sensitive test of ESP versus chance if you are very patient. Soal and Bateman (1954), for example, reviewed a study in which a woman got a total of 707 correct answers after 2,600 times through a deck. This was 187 more than would have been expected by chance. The results surpassed standards that statisticians use to test chance, even though the average number correct was only 6.8 on any one time through the deck.

Clairvoyance Tests. If you fail with telepathy, do not give up—you may have a different hidden mental power called **clairvoyance,** which is the perception of an object, action, or event by means of ESP. You can test your powers of clairvoyance with the help of a friend who serves as the experimenter. Do everything that you did when you were the receiver in telepathy tests, but with one important modification. Before turning over a Zener card, your friend will ask you what card is on top of the deck, without looking at the card until after you announce your choice. Your friend should record your answer without telling you if you were right or wrong. If you get 10 or more correct, you may have powers of clairvoyance.

Precognition Tests. Another kind of ESP is **precognition,** the perception of future thoughts, events, or actions. You can test your powers of precognition with Zener cards. Have a friend hold the deck while you write down the order in which you feel the cards will be dealt. After your guesses are recorded, your friend should shuffle the deck and deal it, checking the actual first card with the predicted first card, the actual second card with the predicted second card, and so on, through all 25 cards. If you get 10 or more correct, you may have hidden powers of precognition.

Psychokinesis—Mind over Matter

We all have some psychokinetic power. That is, we can exert direct mental influence over a physical object—our body. We can, for instance, decide to move our little finger and then move it. Our *will* to move is a mental process that causes a physical activity. Apparently, we have mental energies, sometimes called psychic energies, that move our bodies. Some people, however, claim that they can move objects *other* than their bodies with psychic energies.

Unfortunately, when we investigate such claims we must be on the lookout for frauds. Some masters of illusion and sleight-of-hand enjoy perpetrating a hoax. Time after time careful investigators have exposed as frauds people who are alleged to have used psychic powers to move tables and other objects (Cohen, 1976; Randi, 1975).

To test your own hidden powers of psychokinesis, try to influence a compass needle. Set the compass on a table, making sure that you cannot accidentally bump the table. Concentrate on the compass, noting as many aspects of it as possible. Then close your eyes and try to visualize every detail. When you get a clear mental picture, imagine the needle moving between NNW and NNE. Once you clearly "see" the needle moving, consciously "send" your image to the compass. That is, imagine your mental compass shooting from your head to the physical compass, overlapping it exactly and causing it to move. As soon as your message is "sent," clear your mind completely. If you fail, you might recall the words of Yoda to Luke Skywalker in *The Empire Strikes Back:* "You fail because you do not believe it is possible." There might be something to this fictional character's claim, since positive results appear to be more likely in people who have a positive attitude (Wolman, Dale, Schmeidler, and Ullman, 1977).

A FINAL COMMENT

Could George Ritchie's mind have continued to function after his body died? We cannot answer this question. We took a step toward scientific classification by observing many similarities between his near-death experience and other alternate states of consciousness. But scientific theories have a long way to go in this area before they will be able to explain existing facts and predict new ones. They must tell us why alternate states occur when our normal sensory sensitivity is reduced by drowsiness, sleep, drugs, hypnosis, or meditation. They must also account for the following responses shared in common by various states:

> feeling outside of normal time,
> feeling united with the universe, and
> experiencing hallucinations that develop in four stages.

Two theories are consistent with known facts: *perceptual release* and *mysticism*. According to perceptual release, excitations originating within the central nervous system cause experiences during alternate states of consciousness. According to mysticism, alternate state experiences are caused by stimulation originating in a part of external reality that is not apparent to our usual senses.

The perceptual release theory raises a fundamental question: Is it possible that states of consciousness exalted by mystics throughout history are really nothing more than tricks played on us by our brain? On the basis of scientific evidence we cannot say. We cannot rule out the possibility that stimulation originating without our nervous system causes alternate state experiences, nor can we disprove the possibility that we can experience another side of the universe during alternate states—a side George Ritchie may have seen.

SUMMARY

1. **Consciousness** is perception of what is in a person's own mind. Some psychologists attempt to distinguish **alternate states of consciousness** in terms of specific patterns of physiological and subjective responses that are brought on by sleep, drugs, meditation, and other causes.

2. **Monism** is the theory that the mind and brain are one unitary organic whole. **Dualism** is the theory that the mind and brain are separate entities.

3. Perceptual release theory holds that visions and other experiences during alternate states of consciousness are subjective responses to internal *brain activity*. **Mysticism** is an opposing position that suggests that experiences occurring during alternate states of consciousness are subjective responses to an external reality that is hidden from us during normal waking consciousness.

4. Methods for studying consciousness include self-experience, questionnaires, interviews, and laboratory experiments.

5. Many people have lost all measurable vital signs and then have been revived. Some of them report having subjective responses while they were supposedly dead. These near-death experiences have aspects that turn up repeatedly.

6. **Sleep** has five stages that are distinguished by distinct patterns of brain waves and other physiological responses. Increased understanding

of sleep is leading to better treatment of sleep disorders.

7. Sleep has distinct subjective patterns that include dreams and visions during drowsiness.

8. Daydreams do not have physiological patterns that distinguish them from waking consciousness, but they have subjective patterns that may make an important contribution to our lives.

9. Drugs that produce subjective effects are called psychoactive drugs. Three kinds are depressants, stimulants, and hallucinogens. Each kind produces unique physiological responses. They also produce distinct subjective patterns that can be analyzed in experiments that control the many nondrug factors that ordinarily make subjective responses highly variable.

10. Hypnotists can control both physiological and subjective responses in susceptible subjects. Physiological measures do not distinguish hypnosis from waking consciousness, which leaves room for debate about whether or not hypnosis induces an alternate state of consciousness. While scientists debate this, they agree that hypnotists can influence judgment, suggestibility, relaxation, attention, and memory, both during and after hypnosis. Important applications include the reduction of severe pain.

11. Meditation reduces oxygen consumption, respiratory rate, heart rate, blood pressure, and muscle tension. It also induces subjective responses characterized by feelings of calm and well-being.

12. Sensory deprivation changes physiological responses but not in a way that distinguishes a unique state of consciousness. Subjective effects include positive and negative influences on perception, cognition, and suggestibility. Important applications include helping people to break bad habits such as smoking.

13. You can objectively test the possibility that you have hidden mental powers. You can test for extrasensory perception (ESP), which is the reception of information by means other than our usual senses of hearing, sight, taste, touch, and smell. You can also test for psychokinesis (PK), which is direct mental influence over physical objects or processes. Evidence of such powers does not meet usual scientific standards, but many are continuing to seek better evidence.

SUGGESTED READINGS

The following book is about George Ritchie:

RITCHIE, G. G. (with Elizabeth Sherrill). *Return from tomorrow.* Waco, Tex.: Chosen Books, 1978.

BENSON, H. *The relaxation response.* New York: William Morrow, 1975. Reviews the psychological and medical research that led to the development of a simple meditative technique that helps people relax. It also describes the technique in detail.

DEMENT, W. C. *Some must watch while some must sleep.* San Francisco: San Francisco Book Company, 1976. This book introduces the diagnosis and treatment of sleep disorders. It is intended primarily for students who have no prior background in sleep and dream research.

Drug Abuse Council. *The fact about "drug abuse."* New York: Free Press, 1980. A comprehensive final report of the Drug Abuse Council of Washington, D.C., analyzes the illegal use of drugs in the context of the uses and misuses of legal drugs.

GIBSON, H. B. *Hypnosis, its nature and therapeutic uses.* New York: Taplinger, 1978. A refreshing discussion of what hypnosis is, how it works, and why some people are more susceptible than others.

PENFIELD, W. *The mystery of the mind.* Princeton, N.J.: Princeton University

Press, 1975. A leading neurosurgeon and scientist gives a clearly written analysis of the extent to which the current state of knowledge about the brain can explain the actions of the mind.

ZINDBERG, N. E. (Ed.). *Alternate states of consciousness.* New York: Free Press, 1977. Experts from diverse fields present multiple perspectives on the study of consciousness. The book includes many fascinating reports of experiences during alternate states of consciousness.

Learning and Intelligence

On April 5, 1887, 19-year-old Anne Sullivan made a dramatic breakthrough in the education of her 7-year-old deaf and blind pupil, Helen Keller. Anne described the event in a letter:

We went out to the pump-house, and I made Helen hold her mug under the spout while I pumped. As the cold water gushed forth, filling the mug, I spelled "w-a-t-e-r" in Helen's free hand. The word coming so close upon the sensation of cold water rushing over her hand seemed to startle her. She dropped the mug and stood as one transfixed. A new light came into her face. She spelled "water" several times. Then she dropped on the ground and asked for its name and pointed to the pump and the trellis, and suddenly turning round she asked for my name. I spelled "teacher" . . . in a few hours she had added thirty new words to her vocabulary. (Lash, 1980, p 5 6)

In a moment of insight, Helen learned that the manual alphabet used to spell words in her hand was the key to release her mind from what she later called her "prison-house" of darkness and silence. This was a landmark event in what became a lifelong dedication to teaching and learning.

Helen had not always lived in her "prison-house." Born June 27, 1880, in Alabama, she was a bright child, walking at the age of 1 and beginning to speak fairly early. At the age of 19 months she was struck by a high fever that almost killed her, and she was left deaf and blind. She had been a very lively baby, gay and affectionate; now there was a sad unresponsiveness of tone and look.

Helplessly the family watched her baffled attempts to deal with her world, the things she could touch, but which meant nothing to her. Nothing was a part of anything, and frequently there blazed up in her fierce anger. Helen did whatever she wanted, and the family went along with her, for though she raged and stormed, she was also a loving and lovable child. As she grew older, however, her thwarted passion to communicate produced increasingly violent tantrums, and some members of the family said she should be put away in an institution. Luckily, her parents sought advice from Dr. Alexander Graham Bell, inventor of the telephone, who was deeply concerned with teaching the deaf. He suggested they contact Dr. Samuel Gridley Howe, who was director of the Perkins Institute for the Deaf and Blind.

Until the end of the eighteenth century, no special education programs existed for the deaf and blind. Most people avoided the handicapped because they were thought to have been (justly) punished by God. About 100 years before Helen's birth, schools for the deaf and blind were started in France. Dr. Samuel Gridley Howe promoted this idea in America in 1831 when he became director of the Perkins. Laura Bridgman, who lost her sight and hearing through scarlet fever at the age of 2, was his most famous student, but she only obtained a language ability equivalent to that of a 6-year-old child. Dr. Howe concluded after 20 years of study that the blind as a class are inferior to other persons in mental power and ability.

Anne Sullivan, a pupil at the Perkins Institute, disagreed with this conclusion. She herself had been nearly blind until she was 15, when eye surgery was performed, restoring most of her sight. Before her surgery, she was a student at the Perkins Institute, and she had learned the manual alphabet from some of the deaf students there. Anne doubted that Laura and other blind people were mentally inferior. She believed, instead, that the blind simply faced far greater obstacles, which interfered with learning.

After she graduated from the Institute, Anne Sullivan agreed to go to Alabama to work with Helen. This is her first impression of the child: "I remember how disappointed I was when the untamed little creature stubbornly refused to kiss me, and struggled to free herself from my embrace" (Lash, 1980, p. 50). Helen later always celebrated March 3, the day Anne had arrived, as her "soul's birthday."

But things did not go smoothly between teacher and student. Although Helen quickly imitated the signs that Anne spelled into her hand, she made no connection between them and the objects they symbolized. Finger spelling was just a game that she soon tired of, since she couldn't see the point of it. To make matters worse, she was entirely undisciplined, because of her family's indulgence of her slightest whim. Her father sided with Helen in any battle against Anne. Battles soon became the rule and cooperation the exception. No progress was being made because of this, and so Anne was able to persuade the Kellers to allow her and Helen to live by themselves for awhile, in a little garden house a quarter of a mile away. Here Anne hoped to get Helen to trust and obey her, so that she could focus her attention on learning instead of fighting. It worked: "The little wild creature of two weeks ago has been transformed into a gentle child" (Lash, 1980, p. 54). Unfortunately, Helen's parents were unhappy over the separation, and within a month Anne and Helen had moved back to the Kellers' house. There the battles began again, because Helen soon found that her family would still let her do just as she wanted.

All this time Anne practiced finger spelling with Helen constantly placing articles in Helen's hand and then spelling the name into her hand. She continued doing this even though Helen showed no sign of understanding that there was a connection between an object and the name that was immediately spelled into her hand.

Then, 2 weeks after they moved back to the main house, the landmark break-through happened. They went for a walk by the well-house. Someone was pumping water. Anne placed one of Helen's hands under the spout and spelled "water" in the other hand, as she had done with so many other names. But this time was different. Helen remembers it this way:

> As the cool stream gushed over one hand, she (Annie) spelled into the other the word water, first slowly, then rapidly. I stood still, my whole attention fixed upon the motions of her fingers. Suddenly I felt a mistly consciousness as of something forgotten—a thrill of returning thought; and somehow the mystery of language was revealed to me. I knew then that W A T E R meant the wonderful cool something that was flowing over my hand. . . . I left the well-house eager to learn. Everything had a name, and each name gave birth to a new thought. As we returned to the house every object which I touched seemed to quiver with life. (Lash, 1980, p. 55)

This was the beginning of the remarkable education of Helen Keller, who was the first blind and deaf person to ever attain the full use of her faculties and to pursue a higher education. She went to the Perkins Institute and learned Braille, always accompanied and taught by Anne Sullivan. Next she prepared for and entered Radcliffe College, where she carried a full course load.

Helen attended lectures, with Anne Sullivan by her side every minute. Anne spelled the lectures into Helen's hand. Others tried to substitute for Anne, but no one else could translate lectures as effectively. Others knew the manual alphabet as well as Anne, but no one knew as much about how Helen thought. Anne knew exactly how to edit lectures in order to make them as clear as possible. At the end of the day, Helen wrote notes on what she remembered of the day's lectures. After finishing her notes, she read whatever assignments had been copied in Braille for her. Most of her assignments were not available in Braille, however, so Anne read to her, usually 4 or 5 hours a day.

Helen's academic schedule would have been challenging even for students with no handicaps. But somehow, working against all odds, Helen and Anne not only finished the schoolwork, but they also published a book, *The Story of My Life,* one of five books that Helen published in her lifetime.

Helen received recognition from many sectors. Mark Twain said that "the two most interesting characters of the nineteenth century are Napoleon and Helen Keller." Helen and Anne were both awarded the degree of the Doctor of Humane Letters on Founder's Day at Temple University, and Helen received the degree of Doctor of Laws at the University of Glasgow in Scotland. The Glasgow *Herald* reported:

> Yesterday will long be remembered as Helen Keller's day . . . [an] occasion on which honour was paid to one who, partly by her own magnificent character, partly by the help of loving friends, has achieved what is little short of a miracle.

If everyone had viewed Helen's accomplishments as a miracle, the impact of her life would have been diminished. Fortunately, Alexander Graham Bell and others were able to persuade educators that, with the proper teaching methods, they, too, could produce similar results in other deaf and blind children. In *The Silent Educator* for June, 1892, Bell wrote:

> It is, then, a question of instruction we have to consider, and not a case of supernatural acquirement. Among the thousands of children in our schools for the deaf . . . there are some who are intellectually as capable of mastering the intricacies of the English language as Helen herself.

Helen strongly agreed with this point of view. She did not consider herself a genius. She credited her accomplishments to the availability of education and to her willingness to take advantage of it. She expressed this best, perhaps, at her speech to the alumnae shortly before her graduation from Radcliffe. She said: "College has breathed new life into my mind and given me new views of things, a perception of new truths and of new aspects of the old ones. I grow stronger in the conviction that there is nothing good or right which we cannot accomplish if we have the will to strive" (Lash, 1980, p. 315).

LEARNING: WHAT IS IT?

For Helen Keller, learning is what released her mind from a "prison-house" of darkness and silence. Helen's facial expression in the photo we showed reflects the "life that learning breathed" into her mind.

The transformation that took place in Helen as a result of her learning experiences inspire our definitions of learning. We define **learning** as the process by which experience or practice results in a relatively permanent change in what one is capable of doing. Many books define learning in terms of permanent changes in behavior. The problem with such definitions is that they ignore differences between what we are capable of doing and what we in fact do. If we define learning in terms of what we do, that is, in terms of our performance, we have trouble accounting for learning that is not immediately shown in behavior. Ask yourself, for example, whether or not you learned anything in the last 10 minutes of reading. You might have learned some new things about Helen Keller, but this learning probably has not changed your behavior yet. It changed what you are capable of doing, such as answering test questions, but it probably has not changed anything that you have done so far. It might not change your behavior for weeks, or even months, and probably not until you are asked about Helen Keller, or until you act upon your knowledge for some other reason. Tolman and Honzik (1930), who were leaders in the learning field, introduced the term **latent learning** to describe learning that is not manifested until some later time. The concept of latent learning recognizes the difference between *learning* and *performance*. Our definition of learning itself makes a clear distinction between the two.

Growth of Helen's human potential inspired our definition, but it applies equally to our own learning. Helen's learning process was not unique; it was only more obvious because of the handicaps she had to overcome before she was able to learn. We learn from the time we are born until we die. We learn what we can and cannot eat and what we can and cannot touch. We learn to walk, talk, ride bicycles, and play games. We learn how to relate to parents, brothers, sisters, friends, and teachers. We learn how to read and write, and how to think and reason. Some of what we learn is useless, such as the infectious mannerism of saying "you know" after every sentence. Some of what we learn is even harmful, such as racial prejudice. But for the most part, learning expands our potential as human beings every bit as much as learning expanded Helen's potential.

In this chapter we will learn about learning. We will study basic theories of learning, and we will see how these theories apply in our everyday lives. We will find that no one theory explains every kind of learning—in fact, much remains to be learned about learning.

Ideally, one theory would explain every kind of learning. Although some theorists have tried this, all have failed. Some theories account well for many important kinds of learning, but no one theory explains every important type. Therefore, we will break down our discussion of theories into separate sections on different types of learning. The first section is on a simple kind that sets the stage for more advanced learning.

CLASSICAL CONDITIONING

In 1904, the year that Helen Keller graduated from Radcliffe, Ivan Pavlov won the Noble prize for his research on digestion. In some of his experiments, Pavlov (1927) measured the amount of saliva that flows when food is placed in a dog's mouth. This automatic, or *reflexive*, response to food was not surprising. But Pavlov also noticed that saliva often flowed before food was presented. It flowed at the sight of food, for example, and even at the sound of Pavlov's footsteps. Shortly after winning his Noble prize, Pavlov turned to the question of why dogs salivated in response to sights and sounds. The work that followed revolutionized the study of learning.

Pavlov studied a kind of learning that now is called **classical conditioning,** the process by which an originally neutral stimulus (such as footsteps) comes to elicit a response (such as salivating) that was originally given to another stimulus (such as food). This learning process takes place when the neutral stimulus (footsteps) is repeatedly paired with the other stimulus (food). Classical conditioning is only one kind of learning that we will study. But it is such an important kind that we must consider it in detail.

Pavlov's Learning Experiments

Pavlov knew that a dog's mouth waters automatically in response to food. A dog doesn't have to learn this response. Pavlov figured, however, that dogs salivate in response to other stimuli because they learn to do so. He assumed, for example, that his dogs learned to respond to the sight of food and to the sound of his footsteps. He decided to investigate this learning process by training dogs to salivate to some stimulus that ordinarily does not cause a dog's mouth to water. He found that a bell served his purpose. Before training, dogs did not salivate to the sound of a bell; after training, they did. Figure 5–1 shows the apparatus that he used to test this.

His experiment included the four basic elements of the training procedure known as classical conditioning:

1. Food causes salivation without conditioning, so it is called the **unconditioned stimulus (US).** Food automatically or reflexively causes a dog's mouth to water.
2. The salivation response to food also happens without conditioning, so it is called the **unconditioned response (UR).** It happens automatically or reflexively in response to food, or the *US*.
3. The bell does not cause salivation until after conditioning, so it is called the **conditioned stimulus (CS).** It is a stimulus to which an animal learns to respond.

FIGURE 5–1

Pavlov's basic training apparatus.

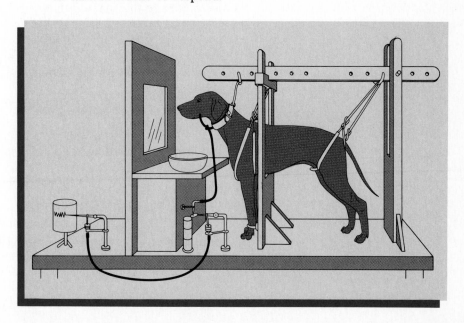

FIGURE 5–2

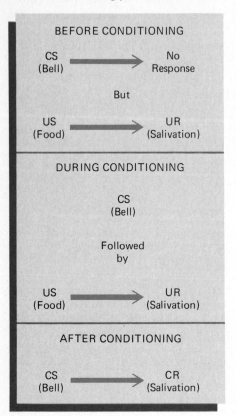

BEFORE CONDITIONING

CS
(Bell) ⟶ No Response

But

US
(Food) ⟶ UR
(Salivation)

DURING CONDITIONING

CS
(Bell)

Followed by

US
(Food) ⟶ UR
(Salivation)

AFTER CONDITIONING

CS
(Bell) ⟶ CR
(Salivation)

4. The response to a CS, such as Pavlov's bell, is not identical to an unconditioned response. It is therefore called a **conditioned response (CR)**, to distinguish it from a UR. One way that a CR often differs from a UR is in the strength of the response. In Pavlov's experiment, for instance, the CR contained fewer drops of saliva than the UR. That is, after conditioning, a dog's mouth watered less in response to a bell than it did in response to food.

Figure 5–2 summarizes Pavlov's conditioning procedure. Before classical conditioning, the CS (bell) did not cause salivation. But the US (food) did cause a UR (salivation). During conditioning, the CS and US were paired. That is, Pavlov rang the bell and then, shortly afterwards, gave food. After conditioning, the CS (bell) was presented alone and Pavlov's dogs salivated (CR). By pairing the food and the bell, Pavlov established in the dogs a salivation response to the bell.

Classical conditioning is a simple kind of learning that has many important applications in its own right (see "Highlight: Applying Classical Conditioning"). In addition, it may at times provide a temporary stepping stone for more complicated learning processes that will be discussed later in this chapter. To illustrate this, let's consider the possibility that classical conditioning paved the way for Helen's famous insight about finger spelling the word "water."

Recall Anne's description of the events leading to Helen's insight: "As the cold water gushed forth, filling the mug, I spelled "w-a-t-e-r" in Helen's free hand. The word coming so close upon the sensation of cold water rushing over her hand seemed to startle her. She dropped the mug and stood as one transfixed. A new light came into her face." Perhaps it was a coincidence that Helen's insight came at that moment. But perhaps there was something special about the pairing of cool water and finger spelling.

To relate this learning experience to conditioning, we might call water the US and finger spelling the CS. Before conditioning the US (the water) led to a UR, which was a set of automatic responses, such as shivering. The CS (the finger spelling) led to no response. During conditioning the US and CS were paired. After conditioning the CS lead to a CR, a response similar to the UR. That is, we might speculate that after the water and finger spelling were paired, finger spelling caused Helen to shiver and make other responses that she had previously made to the cold water. This new stimulus-response connection might have provided a building block for her realization that the finger spelling stood for water. After having made the connection, she repeated the finger spelling, which now had a new meaning for her. We are only speculating, of course, because we cannot be sure that classical conditioning was part of Helen's learning process. One way to evaluate our speculation is to analyze factors that are necessary for establishing and losing classically conditioned responses.

Important Factors in Classical Conditioning

Pavlov's work established many of the factors that are important for establishing and losing classically conditioned responses.

Establishing a Response. The likelihood of establishing a conditioned response depends on five factors:

1. The CS must be *strong and distinctive*. Pavlov's dogs heard his bell easily and were readily conditioned to it. Pavlov probably would have failed, however, if he had tried to condition his dogs to salivate whenever he lightly touched their back. Helen's learning experience passes this criterion, for finger spelling is strong and distinctive.
2. The *order* in which the CS and US are presented makes a difference. Conditioning is best when the CS comes slightly before the US. Pav-

HIGHLIGHT / APPLYING CLASSICAL CONDITIONING

Psychologists have used classical conditioning techniques to improve the well-being of their patients. In one case, classical conditioning was used to treat alcoholism (Davidson, 1974). Davidson paired the sight, taste, and smell of alcohol (CS) with a drug (US) that caused vomiting (UR). After many such pairings, Davidson's patients developed a nausea response (CR) to alcohol itself. This treatment is called *aversion therapy*, and it can help break a bad habit when used in combination with other treatments.

In another case, classical conditioning was used to treat irrational fears, such as the fear of harmless bugs (Wolpe, 1962). Wolpe assumed that bugs were a CS and that fear was a CR. Working from that assumption, he experimentally extinguished the undesirable CR. He first asked patients to think about bugs. This produced a mild fear response. But the response soon extinguished, because it was never paired with a bite or any other US. After the response was extinguished, Wolpe introduced pictures of bugs, which again elicited mild fear. This fear, too, was extinguished. Wolpe gradually extinguished one CR after another, until finally patients could even touch bugs without being afraid. Wolpe's procedure is called *systematic desensitization therapy*, and it has helped many patients overcome irrational fears.

Classical conditioning research has also helped save wild coyotes, an endangered species. Ranchers wanted to destroy coyotes because they prey on lamb and other livestock. Environmentalists, who wanted to save coyotes, realized that they somehow had to force coyotes to leave livestock alone. A solution emerged from classical conditioning laboratories. In one laboratory, John Garcia found that rats learned to avoid food that made them sick. In another laboratory setting, it was learned that the "Garcia effect" could be used to solve the coyote problem

(Gustavson et al., 1974). The experimenters fed coyotes either poisoned lamb meat or poisoned rabbit meat. The poison (US) made the coyotes sick (UR), but it did not kill them. Afterwards, the coyotes developed an aversion (CR) to the kind of food that had been poisoned (CS). They would eat rabbit meat if lamb had been poisoned, or lamb if rabbit had been poisoned, but they would not touch the kind of meat that had made them sick. The same procedure worked in the wild, forcing coyotes to return to their natural prey and leave livestock alone.

lov, for instance, rang the bell before giving food. Conditioning is less effective when the CS and US are presented at the same time, and conditioning is weakest if the CS is presented after the US (backward conditioning). Anne presented water and finger spelling at the same time, which is not the most effective pairing, but it doesn't rule out classical conditioning.

3. Classical conditioning also depends on the time lapse between the CS and US. Usually, conditioning is best if the interval is between a fraction of a second and a few seconds. Pavlov's dogs did not learn to respond to his bell when Pavlov waited too long to give them food after the bell. Helen's interval was zero, which is acceptable, but not the best.

FIGURE 5-3

The strength of a CR gradually decreases if the CS is always repeated alone. This is called extinction. Spontaneous recovery occurs if the response reappears again without any further pairings of CS and US; but the response will eventually extinguish again if the CS is repeatedly presented alone.

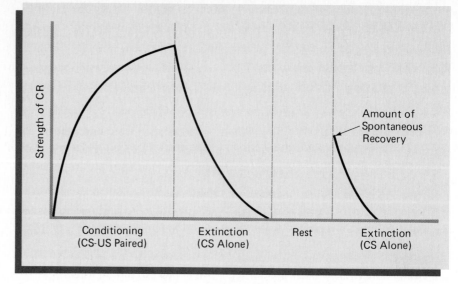

4. Most classical conditioning requires *repeated pairings* of the CS and US. Pavlov paired the bell and food several times before his dogs salivated at the sound of the bell. Once salivation occurs in response to a bell, one can measure the strength of the CR by recording the drops of saliva, the more drops the higher the strength. One finds that strength of the CR grows gradually with each presentation, until the CR is almost as strong as the UR. Anne noticed a sudden response to finger spelling, but we cannot rule out the possibility that weaker responses built up gradually before that. If we want to argue that classical conditioning was involved, we must assume that a CR strengthened gradually until Anne noticed what only appeared to be the first response.

5. The rate at which a classically conditioned response strengthens depends upon how the experimenter *spaces* the pairings of the CS and US. Conditioning will be slower if pairings follow each other too quickly or too far apart. This factor does not help us categorize Helen's experience.

Losing a Response. Classically conditioned responses need not last forever. Going back to Pavlov's dogs, we find that the dogs stopped salivating to the sound of a bell when the bell was rung many times without food being given. Figure 5-3 shows that the strength of a CR gradually decreases to no response at all if the CS is repeatedly presented alone. This falling off is called **extinction.** Once a response has been extinguished it can reappear again without any further pairings of the CS and US. Pavlov called this **spontaneous recovery.** He conditioned dogs to salivate when they heard a bell, and then he extinguished the response so that his dogs' mouths did not water when they heard the bell. Several days later, Pavlov tested his dogs again. As soon as the dogs heard the bell, their mouths began to water. The response reappeared without any retraining. Figure 5-3 shows that spontaneous recovery does not bring a response back to its full strength and the response extinguishes again if the CS is repeatedly presented alone.

After the first pairing of finger spelling with water, finger spelling was undoubtedly presented alone many, many times. Thus, if conditioning played a part in Helen's learning, it was only a temporary role. Because of conditioning, Helen might have shivered in response to finger spelling and this might have helped her learn the connection between it and water. But this was only a stepping stone to other types of learning, which supplemented and built upon the original conditioning that had taken place.

Generalizing Conditioned Responses

Staying with the idea that conditioning might have set the stage for Helen's learning, we can ask other questions about the conditioning. For example, would Helen shiver only in response to Anne's finger spelling, or would a similar stimulus also elicit the conditioned response? Pavlov's experiment provided an answer. After Pavlov's dogs had been conditioned to salivate to the sound of a bell, their mouths also watered when they heard a buzzer and a metronome. This reaction to similar stimuli is called **stimulus generalization.** Conditioned responses are elicited not only by the conditioned stimulus, but also by similar stimuli.

John Watson demonstrated stimulus generalization in an experiment that surely would not be allowed today (Watson and Rayner, 1920). Before the experiment, Albert, an 11-month-old boy, was not afraid of white rats. When he saw one, he crawled toward it and wanted to play with it. During conditioning, Watson and Rayner presented the white rat (CS), waited for Albert to approach, and then made a loud noise by clanging steel bars behind him (US). The earsplitting sound made Albert cry (UR). After several such pairings of the rat and noise, Albert developed a conditioned fear of the rat. When he saw it, even if there was no noise, he immediately started to cry, and he tried to crawl away. The experimenters then showed Albert a white rabbit, a fur coat, and a Santa Claus mask. All of these things terrified him; he had generalized from the white rat to the rabbit and other white furry objects.

Discrimination

If stimulus generalization were carried too far, conditioning would not be a useful building block for learning. In finger spelling, for instance, it is necessary to discriminate between different patterns. Pavlov showed that his conditioned dogs could make **discriminations.** Pavlov presented one sound followed by food and a similar sound without food. The dogs learned to salivate to the sound that had been followed by the food, and they learned not to salivate to the other sound. In this way, they learned to discriminate between the stimuli.

Higher-Order Conditioning

Animals and humans often base new learning on old learning—for example, Helen Keller learned new finger spellings based on old ones. If conditioning is a building block for learning, then we should expect Pavlov's dogs to be able to base new conditioned responses upon old ones. What happens is that a well-established conditioned stimulus (CS) comes to act like a US in establishing a *second* conditioned stimulus (CS). Thus a dog or a person learns conditioned responses without getting food or any other US.

In testing this, Pavlov first conditioned his dogs to salivate in response to a bell (CS). He then paired a black square (CS) with the bell. He presented the square and then the bell over and over again, occasionally pairing the bell with food. The dogs learned to salivate in response to the black square, even though *it* was never paired with food. Pavlov called this a second-order conditioned response, and he went on to establish a third-order conditioned response (Kehoe et al., 1981). Pavlov speculated that all learning might be nothing more than long chains of conditioned responses.

Modern psychologists reject the notion that classical conditioning explains all learning. Instead, they see classical conditioning as one of several kinds of learning (Resorla and Holland, 1982). They would go beyond classical conditioning, for instance, to explain all of Helen Keller's learning. In the next section we will see, in fact, that another kind of conditioning played an important role in changing Helen's behavior.

OPERANT CONDITIONING

A major limitation of Pavlov's work on classical conditioning is that his dogs were restrained and made to respond reflexively to external stimuli. His dogs learned to transfer responses from a stimulus that naturally elicited it to other stimuli that previously did not. When all is said and done, Pavlov's dogs were only making passive responses to stimuli that came from outside them. This limitation is serious, because many of our behaviors are internally motivated active responses. We search for food, seek companions, and ask questions. Psychologists call these actions *operant behaviors* because they actively *operate* on the environment.

Edward L. Thorndike (1913, 1932) began research on operant behaviors in cats at about the same time that Pavlov began his classical conditioning research with dogs. Figure 5–4 shows Thorndike's apparatus, which he called a "puzzle box." The idea was to escape from the box; the puzzle was to find out how to do it. Thorndike made sure that a cat was hungry, then he put it in the puzzle box with a small dish of food on the outside in open view. The cat could not get the food unless it could somehow get free. Thorndike rigged the box so that it opened when a cat brushed up against a string. When the cat escaped and ate the food, Thorndike put the cat back in the box and filled the dish again. Since the dish was small, the cat was still hungry, so it tried to break out again. Each time the cat solved the puzzle, Thorndike set it up again. Gradually, the cat took less and less time to open the box and escape.

Thorndike interpreted the decrease in escape time as evidence of learning. He noticed that a cat usually tried a number of actions that didn't work, such as clawing at the sides of the box, before it brushed up against the string. Thorndike explained his observations by proposing that animals learn according to the **law of effect.** This law states that animals tend to repeat behaviors that are followed by "good effects" and they tend to stop behaviors that are not followed by desirable results.

About 20 years later, B. F. Skinner (1938) expanded upon Thorndike's observations, and he translated the law of effect into the theory of **operant conditioning.** This theory states that operant behaviors are learned when desired responses are reinforced and undesired responses are either ignored or punished. Notice that Skinner replaced the idea of "good effects" with the notion of reinforcement, which has a special meaning in the theory of operant conditioning. An event is a **reinforcement** if its occurrence just after the response increases the likelihood that the response will be repeated. The theory of operant conditioning allowed Skinner to study learning without speculating about whether an animal considered an event to be "good" or "bad." As we discussed in Chapter 1, Skinner was a follower of John Watson's school of behaviorism. Skinner thought, therefore, that he should stick to the observable facts—stimuli and responses made to the stimuli.

Helen's education provides many examples of operant conditioning. Anne Sullivan devoted her life to Helen's education long before psychologists formalized principles of operant conditioning, yet her ingenious instincts guided her toward operant conditioning methods. In fact, she could not have followed them any better even if she had studied modern teacher's manuals, which are loaded with operant conditioning techniques. We will

FIGURE 5–4

Thorndike's experimental apparatus, which he called a "puzzle box," is shown here. In order to escape from the box, a cat had to brush against the string inside the box, which in turn opened the door so that it could get out.

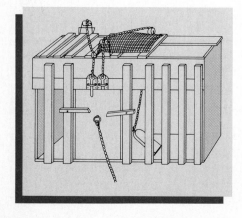

therefore find many illustrations of operant conditioning in Helen's education.

Acquisition of Operant Behaviors

Skinner (1938, 1966) studied operant behaviors with a procedure that was similar to Thorndike's. Skinner placed a hungry rat in a small cage that contained a food cup with a bar over it (Figure 5–5). The cup was empty until the rat pushed the bar, which made a small pellet of food drop into the cup. This apparatus became known as a *Skinner box*. A cat in a puzzle box had to learn to break out in order to get food; a rat in a Skinner box had to learn how to bring food into the box.

The learning process for Thorndike's cats and Skinner's rats were similar. At first Skinner's rats explored the cage, making a number of ineffective responses until they happened to press the bar. The rat then ate the food pellet that was delivered and continued to explore until it again hit the bar and brought in more food. After two or three bar presses, the rat stopped most of its ineffective responses and started to push the bar repeatedly.

FIGURE 5–5

Skinner's experimental apparatus, which became known as a Skinner box, is shown here. In order to get food, the rat had to press the bar inside the box, and a food pellet was delivered into a cup in the box. The elaborate setup in the background of the photo is for recording the number of bar presses, how frequently they occurred, and other data of that nature.

About 30 years earlier Anne Sullivan had used a similar procedure to teach Helen Keller. Anne and Helen sat at a table containing familiar objects such as a cup and a doll. Anne placed an object in one of Helen's hands and spelled its name in the other. She then guided Helen's fingers to spell the same name. As soon as Helen finished spelling a name correctly, Anne gave her a small bit of cake. If Helen made a mistake, she got no cake. Gradually, Helen stopped making mistakes and started making spelling responses quickly and correctly. The parallels between Anne Sullivan's procedure and Skinner's procedure are amazing. Skinner's rats and Helen Keller both stopped making responses that were not reinforced and continued making responses that were.

Positive and Negative Reinforcement. There are several different kinds of reinforcement. The basic definition we gave of reinforcement is an event that increases the likelihood that a response will be repeated. In this context, psychologists distinguish between "positive" and "negative" events. A *positive event* occurs when a stimulus is added to an environment. A *negative event* occurs when a stimulus is taken away. When a positive event serves as a reinforcer, it is called **positive reinforcement.** The rat's food pellets and Helen's cake are examples of positive reinforcement. When a negative event serves as a reinforcer, it is called **negative reinforcement.**

Skinner demonstrated negative reinforcement by using an electric shock grid on the bottom of his Skinner box. He turned on the grid and put a rat in the cage. The rat received a mild shock continuously until it pushed a bar that turned off the grid. After a short time the shock grid went on again until the rat again pushed the bar. The rat soon learned to press the bar to turn off the shock. Turning *off* a shock is a negative event, because it *takes away* a stimulus. It is a reinforcing event because its occurrence increases the likelihood that a rat will push the bar. Thus, it is a negative reinforcer.

Skinner used negative reinforcement in two kinds of training programs. The rat that learned to press a bar to turn off electric shock participated in **escape training.** Skinner also used **avoidance training,** in which a negative reinforcer can be avoided altogether. He placed a rat in a Skinner box, sounded a buzzer, and then turned on a shock a few seconds later. The shock did not go on if the rat pressed the bar after the buzzer and before the shock started. Pressing the bar after the shock started did no good. The shock stayed on for a fixed time, and then it went off until a few seconds after the buzzer sounded again. Gradually, rats learned to press the bar to avoid being shocked.

Primary and Secondary Reinforcers. Besides positive and negative reinforcers, psychologists distinguish between **primary reinforcers,** which are reinforcing in and of themselves, and **secondary reinforcers,** which are reinforcing only after they have been paired with other, primary reinforcers. All the examples that we considered so far (rat pellets, cake, and electric shock) are primary reinforcers. An electric shock is an effective negative reinforcer, for example, even for rats who never experienced it before. In contrast, secondary reinforcers work only after they are associated with other reinforcers. Skinner found that a rat who has had no experience in a Skinner box will not learn to press a bar if the bar turns on a light and nothing more. That is, a light is not a primary reinforcer. Skinner showed that a light can become a secondary reinforcer, however. He rigged his Skinner box to deliver food and turn on a light every time a bar was pressed. After many pairings of the food and the light, Skinner discontinued the food and continued to turn on the light whenever the rat pushed the bar. The rat continued to push the bar because the light had become a secondary reinforcer.

As a child, Helen spelled for cake, a primary reinforcer. But she probably

Credit cards are not in themselves reinforcing—you can't eat them or drink them, for example. But they are secondary reinforcers, because they allow us to obtain food, drink, and other primary reinforcers.

would not have responded as well for money, because it didn't mean anything to her. Later, after money was associated with food and other rewards, Helen worked for money. In fact, she wrote her autobiography, *The Story of My Life*, primarily to earn money for her college education. Money is an effective secondary reinforcer for most of us.

Schedules of Reinforcement. Considering money as a reinforcer brings to mind the fact that we usually are not reinforced every time we do something. We work a certain time interval (a week or a month), and then we get our paycheck. Or we finish a fixed amount of work (mowing the lawn) and then we get paid. When Helen received cake for every correct spelling, she was on a **continuous reinforcement schedule.** Later, when she received royalty checks from the sale of her book (these came twice a year), she was on a **partial reinforcement schedule.**

Psychologists have studied schedules that are based upon time (weekly paychecks) and schedules that are based upon the amount of work done (mowing the lawn). They have also studied schedules that are fixed (e.g., a weekly allowance) and schedules that are variable (e.g., an allowance given whenever parents see fit). The following are four common schedules:

1. **Fixed-interval schedules** reinforce the first response after a constant time interval. Skinner observed a rat responding to a fixed-interval schedule. He trained the rat to press a bar for food. Then he rigged his Skinner box so that it would deliver food after a bar press, wait 5 minutes, deliver food to the next bar press, wait another 5 minutes, and so on. During the 5-minute waiting intervals, bar presses were useless; they did not deliver food. After being on this schedule for a short time, rats stopped responding immediately after food was delivered, they responded again at a high rate as the end of the 5-minute interval approached (Figure 5–6A). This response pattern is similar to what students do when exams are given at fixed intervals. They rarely study immediately after exams, but they often cram like mad right before the next exam.

2. **Variable-interval schedules** reinforce the first response after varying time intervals. The first time interval might be 9 minutes, the second one 2 minutes, the third one 4 minutes, and then 3 minutes, 3 minutes, 7 minutes, 5 minutes, and so on. Skinner found that rats give a slow, steady rate of response when they are reinforced on a variable-interval schedule (Figure 5–6B). This pattern is similar to students' study habits in a course in which "pop quizzes" are given at unpredictable times.

FIGURE 5–6

These two graphs show the rate of responding under fixed-interval and variable-interval schedules of reinforcement.

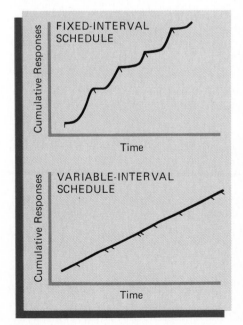

They study at a steady rate because they have to be prepared for a quiz at any time.

3. **Fixed-ratio schedules** reinforce the first response after a certain number of responses have been made. A fixed ratio of 1 in 10 would reinforce every tenth response. Rats on fixed-ratio schedules respond at a fast, steady rate. They have to push a bar many times to get one reinforcer, and they find that the faster they push, the more reinforcers they get. Factories sometimes pay workers on a fixed-ratio schedule. Knitting mills, for example, may pay workers for every 100 mittens finished. The more mittens workers finish, the more money they get, so they usually work at an incredibly fast rate. A job with a fixed-ratio schedule is called *piecework;* it can work out well for both the employer and the employee.

4. **Variable-ratio schedules** reinforce the first response after a varying number of responses. A variable-ratio schedule might reinforce the tenth response, then the fourth response after that, then the seventh response after that, and so on. Rats on this kind of schedule respond at a very fast steady rate, as do people. Slot machines are a good example of a variable-ratio schedule. They are set to pay off after varying numbers of attempts. Gamblers might win two in a row, or they might have to play a hundred times before winning. What seems to be important is that the next time *could* always bring the jackpot; one never knows. Gamblers seem to treat each attempt as if it will be the one to pay off. They respond rapidly with hardly any pause, and they continue to respond over and over again for a long time.

Kenny Rogers, in his song "The Gambler," warns us that we "have to know when to walk away and when to run." The best time to run

Gambling is a good example of a variable-ratio schedule of reinforcement. The best way to avoid being hooked by gambling as Kenny Rogers warns in his song "The Gambler," may be to know when to walk away.

away from slot machines may be before you deposit a single coin. That way you can avoid getting caught up in its captivating reinforcement schedule. Knowing this, some gambling casinos give each customer a few coins to get them started (and hooked). This ploy is one solution to the general problem we will discuss next: How do you get someone to make that first operant response so that the behavior can be brought under the control of a reinforcement schedule?

Encouraging a First Operant Response

Once Helen started finger spelling, Anne could reinforce her with cake. But how did Anne get Helen started? Indeed, how does any parent or teacher get children to perform desirable behavior the first time? Let's look at some ways this can be done.

Hurry-Up-and-Wait. Some responses occur without special coaxing. To bring such behaviors under control of operant conditioning, teachers are faced with a hurry-up-and-wait routine. They must hurry up and reward a response when it occurs; then they must wait patiently for the next time it occurs. If a response is ignored, it will stop; if it is reinforced, it will recur over and over again.

Anne Sullivan used a hurry-up-and-wait procedure to teach Helen to ask questions. Anne believed that "Why?" would be the door through which Helen would enter the world of reason and reflection. She therefore waited watchfully for her to ask questions and she immediately greeted every question with warm encouragement as well as with answers. Soon Helen was asking questions all day long. "Who put chickens in eggs?" "Can flies know not to bite?" "Why is Viney black?" Helen's questions were not all as intelligent as these. In fact, Anne always insisted that Helen's mind was not superior to that of others. All children seem to crack open the "Why?" door. Parents and teachers have the power through operant conditioning either to slam the door by ignoring questions or to aid its opening by reinforcing them.

Increasing Motivation. Another way to encourage a first response is to increase the motivation to make the response. Anne did this with Helen; Helen had been refusing to use her napkin, and Anne anticipated another protest. Anne therefore cut down on Helen's snacks, making sure that Helen was hungry before dinner. Helen's hunger increased her motivation for food, which had been paired with proper use of a napkin in earlier battles. That night Helen used her napkin properly, and she was immediately reinforced with a delicious dinner.

Verbal Instructions and Modeling. There is, however, a limit to what one can do by increasing motivation. Even if Helen had been craving cake, she would not have started finger spelling out of the blue if Anne had not been "talking" to her constantly. They went for long walks during which Anne described in finger spelling everything that they encountered. These walks not only provided instructions in how to form sentences, they also provided a model of the desired behavior. Parents and teachers often must describe and demonstrate operant behaviors in order to get them started in children.

Increasing Restraints on Other Possible Behaviors. Anne was every bit as strong willed as Helen, but the child's parents eventually gave Helen her way if she misbehaved long enough. Helen would grab food from her parent's plate, throw her napkin on the floor, and kick the table until she got exactly what she wanted. Anne figured that her war over table manners was being drawn out because Helen had too many options and too many distractions. Anne therefore insisted that she be allowed to spend time alone with Helen in a nearby guest house. It was in this more controlled environment that Anne finally gained control

This photograph shows a scene from the movie "The Miracle Worker," which is the story of Helen Keller and Anne Sullivan. Here Anne and Helen are engaged in one of their frequent early battles at the table. Once Helen learned that her tantrums were to no avail, she started to learn rapidly in response to positive reinforcement.

over Helen. At first Helen "kicked and screamed herself into a sort of stupor" everytime she disagreed with a command (Lash, 1980, p. 51). But when Anne demanded a certain behavior she allowed Helen no other choice, even if it meant physically restraining her. One night they struggled for 2 hours before Helen finally stayed in bed. Eventually Helen realized that her tantrums were to no avail, and she started to learn rapidly in response to positive reinforcement.

Decreasing Restraints. Anne was strong-willed when she had to be, but she was a flexible person by nature. She disagreed with the rigid methods used to teach language to deaf children in schools. She believed that

> the schoolroom is not the place to teach any young child language, least of all the deaf child. He must be kept as unconscious as the hearing child of the fact that he is learning words, and he should be allowed to prattle on his fingers, or with his pencil, in monosyllables if he chooses, until such time as his growing intelligence demands the sentence. Language should not be associated in mind with endless hours in school, with puzzling questions in grammar, or with anything that is an enemy to joy. (Lash, 1980, pp. 201–202)

Once Helen learned basic obedience, Anne removed any restraints that might have stood in the way of learning. She did not require Helen to use complete sentences or proper grammar. At first she reinforced her for using single words to express sentences. For example, she praised Helen for using "milk" to express "Give me more milk." Later she reinforced Helen for using poorly constructed word strings. Once Helen was trying to express "Baby cannot eat because she has no teeth." Anne praised her for spelling "Baby teeth-no, baby eat-no." A school teacher might not have praised this poorly constructed word string. By allowing Helen more freedom than deaf children generally had in schools, Anne started Helen down a learning path that led to much greater ease with language than any deaf child had ever had before.

Shaping. Gradually, as Helen's language skill increased, Anne became more discriminating with her reinforcement. Looking back, we can see that she used a procedure that is now called shaping. That is, she

In the circus, animal trainers use the technique of shaping to teach animals to perform various tricks. In shaping, they reinforce each step of a series of behaviors until eventually the animal can perform the complete behavior chain.

reinforced each part of a behavior that eventually led to the whole behavior. She realized that Helen had to go through intermediate steps before she would master the whole of forming sentences, so she shaped the whole by reinforcing the intermediate steps.

Skinner (1938) used shaping to teach a bird to walk in a figure eight. He first reinforced the bird for turning its head in the right direction. When the bird learned that, Skinner withheld reinforcement until the bird stepped in the right direction. Gradually, Skinner demanded more and more before he gave rewards. The pigeon had to take several steps in the right direction. Next, it had to do that and also make the appropriate turn. After doing those two things, the pigeon then had to take a few more steps. Skinner continued with this procedure until the bird was making a figure eight to get its reward.

Benji, a lovable dog who starred in several children's movies, learned his tricks with the help of shaping. In one episode, he climbed a stack of boxes, walked a narrow plank to a roof, climbed the roof, and finally jumped through an open window into a house. Benji's trainer taught the trick by first shaping the last feat of the series, jumping through the window. He then shaped the second to last part, using the window as a secondary reinforcer. That is, Benji had to run across the roof in order to get to the window, which had already been paired with a reward. Benji's trainer kept working backwards through the steps. Soon Benji could perform the whole behavior chain to the delight of his young audience.

Loss of Operant Behaviors

So far, we have examined operant conditioning when it was being used to establish certain desired responses or behaviors. It can also establish undesirable behaviors. These must then be extinguished. Anne's war with Helen over manners was difficult, because Helen's obnoxious behavior had been firmly established by operant conditioning. Her father was the inadvertent trainer. He couldn't stand to see Helen unhappy, so he gave her what she wanted. When she threw her napkin on the floor, he let her eat anyway. When she grabbed food from his plate, he let her have it. When she resisted going to bed, he let her stay up, and he gave her a little treat to quiet her down. Each time, he provided an immediate reward, thereby reinforcing her behavior. We can examine some of Anne's battles with Helen in more detail to learn general principles of wiping out or extinguishing operant behaviors.

Extinction. Operant behaviors are extinguished by withholding reinforcement. But they do not decrease immediately when reinforcement is withheld. In fact, they increase and become more forceful for a brief period after reinforcement stops. The first few times that Anne failed to reward Helen's tantrums, Helen unleashed fits of rage that lasted for up to 2 hours. Anne made sure that Helen was cut off completely from any rewards for such frenzies. Gradually the outbursts stopped.

Four factors affect how difficult it is to extinguish operant behaviors. Helen's behaviors made extinction difficult on all four counts:

1. The stronger the original learning, the harder it is to extinguish. Helen's tantrums had been stamped in by years of inadvertent, but effective, conditioning.
2. Behaviors are harder to extinguish when they are learned in a variety of settings. Helen's tantrums had worked for her at bedtime, mealtime, and playtime. They had worked inside or outside the house, in public or in private. In fact, they had worked at any time and in any place.
3. Complex behaviors are more difficult to extinguish. Helen's tantrums consisted of many actions that had to be stopped. She cried, kicked, screamed, hit, scratched, and pinched. Each of these actions had to be extinguished.
4. Behaviors learned by partial reinforcement are harder to extinguish. Helen's father had unintentionally put her on a variable ratio schedule. Sometimes he rewarded her first action; sometimes he held out until Helen went through 10 or more actions. Helen learned not to expect a reward for every action. She learned to continue to respond until she eventually got rewarded. As a result, when Anne permanently withdrew rewards, Helen continued to respond for a long time.

With the deck stacked against her, Anne made no attempt to tip toe around Helen's behavior. She rapidly issued one command after another, forcing Helen to comply each time. We can now see that Anne's instincts had taken her in the right direction again. Many experiments with animals have shown that extinction is easier when nonreinforced behaviors occur in rapid succession. Modern studies also show that responses are weaker and easier to extinguish in a new environment. Anne's move to the garden house was therefore another factor working in her favor.

Even though Anne was able to even the odds to some extent, she was not able to eliminate Helen's tantrums simply by withholding rewards. She was forced to use punishment.

Punishment. A punishment is a stimulus that *decreases* the likelihood of a response when it is added to an environment. Spanking and scoldings are common punishments. Parents may be wise to use these when a dangerous behavior, such as running out into traffic, must be eliminated fast.

Skinner (1938) demonstrated the effectiveness of punishments in experiments on rats who had learned to press a bar for food. Bar pressing was extinguished when Skinner withheld food, but it was eliminated much faster when he shocked rats every time they pushed the bar. Again, notice that electric shock used as a punishment is quite different from electric shock used as a negative reinforcer. Punishments are imposed to eliminate responses; negative reinforcers are stopped to increase responses.

Anne used punishment wisely. Every time Helen hit her, Anne immediately slapped her hand. Studies with animals have shown that both immediacy and consistency are important. Animal studies have also shown that punishments are much more effective when they are not accompanied by rewards. Anne's instincts served her well with respect to this variable also. She never followed punishments with rewards. Some parents make the mistake of hugging and kissing their children immediately after a spanking. Anne was wise enough to avoid such mixed messages.

Thanks to her superior teaching skills, Anne was able to punish Helen without terrifying her. Less skilled teachers disrupt learning by frightening children with punishment. The key to Anne's success was her ability to provide Helen with acceptable, alternative behaviors. Helen soon learned that Anne was as quick to reward her good behaviors as she was to punish her bad ones. Anne's unfailing responsiveness to Helen paid off in extremely rapid learning. Less than 2 weeks elapsed between Helen's 2-hour tantrum at bedtime and her finger spelling breakthrough at the pump house.

Spontaneous Recovery. Helen moved back to the main house shortly after she started to learn names. She explored everything around her with such enthusiasm that she seemed to have no time for tantrums. One might have thought that they were extinguished for good. But when dinnertime came, Helen refused to use her napkin and threw it to the floor. This mild outburst was an example of *spontaneous recovery*. It occurs in animals as well as humans. Skinner extinguished bar pressing responses in rats and then he tested them again after a delay. The rats pressed the bar again with no retraining.

The spontaneous recovery of Helen's tantrums did not last long. For the most part, she left her spoiled behavior in her "prison-house." With keys provided by her teacher, Helen emerged from her prison of isolation a new person eager to explore every facet of her new-found world.

Implications for Parents and Teachers. Let's review what we have just discussed by looking at the implications for parents and teachers of the following operant conditioning principles:

1. *Avoid reinforcing undesirable behaviors.* Few parents reward tantrums to the extent that Mr. Keller did, but some parents inadvertently condition tantrums in public. Parents who would not dream of giving in to a tantrum at home do so in public to avoid an embarrassing scene. Such parents are soon asking why their child is an angel at home and a devil in public. The best way to avoid this Jekyll-and-Hyde behavior is to ignore or punish public tantrums right from the start. One or two uncomfortable situations in the beginning will avoid many more later on.

2. *Immediately reward desirable behaviors.* Children love attention, so a smile or a hug is often reward enough. Anne used lots of this kind of attention to reinforce Helen. In the same way, alert parents can direct most of their attention toward positive reinforcers, which greatly reduce the need for punishment.

3. *Supplement punishments with rewards of desirable responses.* Never reward and punish the *same* behavior by giving hugs and kisses immediately after a punishment, but do watch for good behaviors to reward. If Anne had not rewarded good behaviors, her punishments might have terrified Helen. In the same way, children may become too afraid to learn if teachers do not praise correct responses as often as they criticize wrong ones. Today, teachers' manuals in-

clude these and other principles of operant conditioning. As a result, formal applications of operant principles have found their way into the classroom.

Generalization

About 1½ months after Helen started to learn names, she demonstrated an interesting example of **stimulus generalization,** which means giving the same response to similar stimuli. One day, shortly after learning to call her little sister "baby," Helen ran up to Anne and spelled "dog-baby" over and over. She also pointed to her five fingers one after another and she sucked them. Anne's first thought was that a dog had bitten Helen's sister, but Helen seemed too delighted to be carrying bad news. Anne followed Helen to the pump-house where she found that the Keller's setter had given birth to five adorable puppies. Helen had generalized the response "baby" to include the puppies. Anne taught Helen the word "puppies," which Helen used correctly after that. Stimulus generalization is common in children and Helen's example is typical.

HIGHLIGHT / APPLYING OPERANT CONDITIONING

One specific application of operant conditioning is a *token economy,* in which children are given play money or plastic chips for good performance. Once a week or so, children turn in their tokens for candy and other primary reinforcers. Token economies are effective at producing short-term changes in behavior. They provide immediate rewards and children learn quickly what is expected of them. Once initial learning is established, however, teachers must substitute rewards that spring from the learning situation itself. The reward for learning how to read new words, for example, might be the ability to read something enjoyable. Children who read to get tokens may stop reading when the tokens stop. But children who enjoy what they read will continue to read even when they get no tokens. Token economies for adults will be discussed in Chapter 13.

Another classroom application of operant conditioning is *programmed instruction,* which is a set of materials specially arranged to be easily mastered. B. F. Skinner used operant principles to produce programmed instruction sequences

in the 1950s. The program leads students to make correct responses and then immediately reinforces those responses. Such programs are often presented in *programmed textbooks,* which present one frame at a time. A frame contains a statement and a fill-in-the-blank question. Answers to the questions are in the margin. Students cover the answers with a slider, answer a question, and then move the slider down to uncover the correct answer

and next frame. Skinner also developed *teaching machines* to present his programs. Students turn a knob to expose a frame, write their answer, and then turn the knob again to expose the correct answer and the next frame.

Modern technology is replacing Skinner's teaching machines with *computerized interactive display systems.* Figure A shows a system that presents an instructional program on a TV screen. Students

Children also demonstrate **response generalization,** which is giving different, but similar, responses to the same stimulus. A child who is reinforced for saying "bye-bye" may also say "gye-gye" or "pye-pye." Parents can eliminate such inappropriate response generalizations by reinforcing only the correct responses.

Discrimination

The opposite of stimulus generalization is **stimulus discrimination,** which means making different responses to different stimuli. Helen demonstrated discrimination when she gave the response "baby" to her sister and the response "puppies" to her new pets.

You are discriminating whenever you stop for a red traffic light and go for a green one. Skinner (1938) showed that even pigeons can learn simple red-green discriminations. He taught pigeons to peck at a white disc and then he presented two discs, one red and one green. He gave food every time the pigeon pecked the green disc, and he gave nothing when the pigeon pecked the red one. Soon the pigeon pecked only the

respond by operating a typewriter keyboard or by touching an electronic pencil to a screen. A large computer can teach several hundred topics at once to several thousand students, each of whom learn at their own pace. Skinner's teaching machines were limited to *linear programs,* which move students through the same sequence of frames no matter how they answer questions. Computers, on the other hand, can teach with *branching programs,* which give students different frames depending on their answers. Computerized systems give remedial lessons to students who are doing poorly, or they give advanced lessons to students who are doing well. Armed with branching programs, computers provide students with learning tasks that are adjusted to individual interests and abilities.

Earlier in this book (Chapter 4) we discussed Dr. Benson's *relaxation response,* which may be the most important application of operant conditioning research for college students. Dr. Benson's procedure has helped many students cope with the stresses of college life (Benson, 1975). Although Benson's procedure resembles techniques that have been used in Eastern cultures for

centuries, it found its way into Western culture through operant conditioning laboratories.

In earlier discussions of our autonomic nervous system (Chapter 2), we learned that our bodies automatically prepare for emergencies by means of a fight-or-flight response. Our heart rate and breathing rate increase along with other changes, giving us more energy to meet emergencies. The relaxation response works in the opposite direction, allowing our bodies to relax after we are out of danger. A problem is that flight-or-fight responses often occur when people are in no real danger, as when they panic before an exam. The repeated occurrence of such inappropriate responses leads to high blood pressure and heart damage. Dr. Benson showed that we can avoid this unnecessary wear and tear on our bodies by learning to control relaxation responses.

Dr. Benson based his work on the operant conditioning research of Miller and DiCara (1967) and others (e.g., Schwartz, 1977). Miller and DiCara reinforced rats whenever they spontaneously decreased their heart rates. Soon the rats learned how to decrease their heart rate voluntarily. Other rats learned how

to increase their heart rate when they were reinforced for doing so. Schwartz showed that humans can also learn to control heart rate voluntarily. Schwartz flashed a light and played a tone at every heartbeat to give subjects immediate information about their heart rate. Such immediate information about biological responses is called *biofeedback.* Schwartz rewarded subjects for either increasing or decreasing the light and tone on/off rate, and his subjects learned to control their heartbeat accordingly. Schwartz also reviewed other biofeedback experiments in which people learned to control skin temperature, blood pressure, electrical activity of the brain, and muscle tension. We will discuss the uses of biofeedback again in Chapter 13, Therapy.

Dr. Benson carried this line of research forward another step by showing that we can learn to relax at will without the aid of flashing lights or beeping tones. Scientists have a long way to go in explaining the psychobiological mechanisms that underlie self-regulation. In the meantime, we can all enjoy a more relaxed life thanks to this important application of basic research on operant conditioning.

green disc. Skinner's procedure is valuable for parents to remember. When children first learn the word "mama" they often apply it to all women. Mothers can teach the appropriate discrimination by ignoring incorrect applications and by reinforcing the correct one.

Preparedness

In our previous examples, cats learned to brush up against a string, rats learned to press bars, pigeons learned to peck, and children learned names. Does it matter which animals learn which responses? Traditional and modern theorists disagree about this. Traditional theorists would have said that operant conditioning can link any stimulus with any response, and that will hold true for all animals. Modern theorists say that **preparedness** is also involved here—that animals are more prepared to make certain responses than others, and may find other responses more difficult to make (Timberlake, Wahl, and King, 1982).

Evidence favors preparedness. Rats learn to jump to avoid foot shock faster than they learn to press a bar to avoid the same stimulus. This may be because rats are biologically prepared to jump when they are frightened. Pigeons learn to peck a disc for food faster than rats learn to press a bar for food. One might argue that pigeons are smarter. But this explanation seems ruled out by another fact. It takes pigeons longer to learn *not* to peck than it takes rats to learn *not* to press a bar. Apparently, pigeons are more biologically prepared to peck for food than rats are prepared to press a bar for food. These and other results support the theory of preparedness (Wickelgren, 1977).

Preparedness also applies to humans. We are, of course, prepared to learn speech and other behaviors that animals never learn. We are also prepared to learn different things at different times in our lives, as we will discuss in Chapter 7. Anne Sullivan noticed, for instance, that at 15 months Helen's baby cousin could obey verbal commands such as "Go to papa," "Shut the door," and "Give me the biscuit." At the same time, the baby was not producing sentences. When she gave a command of her own, she combined single words and gestures. "Go" with a gesture meant "I want to go outside." Anne assumed that Helen would also be able to understand sentences long before she could produce them. Therefore Anne spent many hours a day spelling complete sentences into Helen's hand without requiring Helen to reproduce them. In this way, Anne took advantage of the fact that Helen could understand sentences before she was prepared to produce them.

SOCIAL LEARNING THEORY

Conditioning theories are limited to learning by experience. Nobody would deny the importance of their own experiences, but people do not learn everything that way. In fact, learning by experience is sometimes called learning the hard way. Helen learned the hard way, for example, that her temper tantrums were to no avail in the garden house. Often, instead of learning directly through experience, however, it is much easier to learn indirectly, by observing others. Children learn many things by imitating their parents, for instance, and Helen learned many things by imitating Anne. Albert Bandura (1962, 1977) proposed **social learning theory** to account for such learning. Chapter 11 presents social learning theory in detail, so we will not discuss it further here. We will return instead to our consideration of various kinds of direct learning.

We often learn things suddenly and irreversibly, as opposed to the gradual strengthening and weakening of responses that occurs in conditioning and extinction. Helen's learning experiences provide many examples. We have already considered her sudden understanding of finger spelling. Another example happened one day when Anne saw Helen trying to correct an error that she had made while trying to string beads. Noticing her concentration, Anne spelled "t-h-i-n-k" on Helen's forehead. In a flash, Helen realized that the word was the name of the process that was going on in her head. Her insight came suddenly, on Anne's first attempt to teach this abstract concept, and Helen never forgot what she learned in that moment.

Conditioning theories try to explain learning without taking into account unobservable mental processes. Yet, as Helen's insights reveal, unobservable thought processes often play an important role in learning. We therefore need to supplement conditioning theories with a theory about thought processes. **Cognitive learning theory** fills the bill. It attempts to explain the function of thought processes in learning. As mentioned in Chapter 1, cognitive theories did not become a dominant force in psychology until the 1960s. Its roots go back much farther than that. One root was early work on insights.

Insight

Wolfgang Köhler (1925), a founder of Gestalt psychology, was among the first to demonstrate the importance of insight in problem solving. An **insight** is the discovery of relationships that lead to the solution of a problem. In Köhler's experiments, chimpanzees had to solve the problem of getting bananas that were hung out of reach of the chimps. The relationship between three boxes that were also in the room was essential to the problem's solution. No one box was high enough, but all three together allowed the chimp to climb up and reach the bananas (Figure 5–7).

In another experiment the bananas were placed out of reach outside the chimp's cage. In this case it was the relationship between two sticks

FIGURE 5–7

In one insight experiment, a chimp had to pile three boxes on top of one another in order to reach some bananas that were hung out of reach from the ceiling.

that formed the solution. One stick, inside the cage, was too short to reach the bananas, but it was long enough to reach a second stick outside the cage, which in turn was long enough to reach the bananas. Köhler described the behavior of one of his chimps, Sultan, in this situation:

> Sultan tries to reach the fruit with the smaller of the two sticks. Not succeeding, he tears at a piece of wire that projects from the netting of his cage, but that, too, is in vain. Then he gazes about him (there are always in the course of these tests some long pauses, during which the animals scrutinize the whole visible area). He suddenly picks up the little stick once more, goes up to the bars directly opposite to the long stick, scratches it towards him with the "auxiliary," seizes it, and goes with it to the point opposite the objective (the fruit), which he secures. From the moment that his eyes fall upon the long stick, his procedure forms one consecutive whole. . . ." (pp. 174–175)

Köhler set the two-stick problem up again after that and Sultan solved it immediately.

Unlike Thorndike's cats, who *gradually*, through trial and error, learned to solve the puzzle-box problem, Köhler's chimpanzees suddenly learned how to solve the two-stick problem all at once and irreversibly. Köhler explained that his chimpanzees had learned by insight, and that Thorndike's cats were denied the possibility of doing so. Köhler's chimps saw the relationship between the sticks, and once they did, the insight guided their behavior. Thorndike's cats could not see the relationship between the string and the door to their puzzle box, because the relationship was complex and hidden. Without the benefit of insight, the cats slowly decreased the time needed to solve their problem through many attempts. With the benefit of insight, the chimps learned to solve their problem quickly, without hesitation, time after time. The same thing happened with Helen. Once she understood what finger spelling meant, she never looked back—it was an instantaneous and irreversible insight.

Insights are common in human learning. We have all experienced the sudden emergence of solutions after the pieces of a problem fall into place in our minds. Such moments of insight are so pleasurable that they are often accompanied by an "Aha!." Cognitive psychologists consequently refer to human insights as "aha" experiences.

Latent Learning

While cognitive psychologists have made their major contributions in analyses of complex human behaviors, such as learning to speak sentences (Chapter 7) and learning from textbooks (Chapter 6), the cognitive approach is not limited to human behaviors. In fact, animal learning experiments laid the basic foundation for cognitive psychology.

Edward C. Tolman and his associates led the way in showing the importance of cognitive factors in animal learning. Figure 5–8 illustrates the apparatus that Tolman used in a classic experiment on the role of cognitive structures in animal learning (Tolman and Honzik, 1930). Tolman placed a hungry rat in a start box and the rat had to find its way through a maze to an end box. Tolman recorded an error every time the rat entered a blind alley in the maze. Tolman and Honzik ran three groups of rats in their experiment:

1. Group 1 ran the maze only to find an empty end box day after day for 16 days. They made about nine errors on the first day and reduced that only slightly to about seven errors by the sixteenth day.
2. Group 2 ran the maze and ate food that was provided in the end box each day for 16 days. They also made about nine errors on the first day, but they greatly reduced errors to about two per day by the sixteenth day.
3. Group 3 started out like Group 1. They received no food reward

FIGURE 5–8

Tolman's experimental apparatus for testing
cognitive structures in animal learning is
shown here. (Tolman and Honzik, 1930)

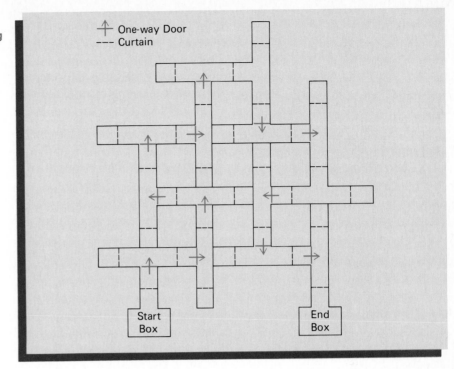

for the first 10 days. Then they were treated like Group 2 rats, with food provided in the end box, for the last 6 days. They started with about 10 errors per day and reduced that only slightly to about 7 errors by the tenth day. Tolman and Honzik observed their critical result on the twelfth day. The number of errors dropped sharply to about two and stayed at that level until the end of the experiment. A single reinforcement on day 11 had a powerful effect. It reduced errors to about the same number that were made by rats in Group 2, who had been reinforced every day.

Tolman and Honzik argued that conditioning theories could not explain their results. Conditioning theories hold that performance errors indicate learning strength, and that learning strength increases gradually with reinforcement. Accordingly, learning strength was very low after rats in Groups 1 and 3 ran a maze for 10 days without reinforcement. In other words, their performance suggested that rats in Groups 1 and 3 had *not* learned their way around the maze after 10 days. If that's true, then why did Group 3 rats do so well on the twelfth day after receiving only a single reinforcement? Operant conditioning theory provides no satisfactory answer. Tolman and Honzik therefore broke ranks with operant conditioning theorists.

Tolman and Honzik proposed that performance does not necessarily reflect learning strength. As mentioned earlier, they introduced the term **latent learning** to refer to learning that does not show itself immediately in performance. While latent learning makes an important distinction between learning and performance, it leaves open a question: What, then, *is* learned, if it is not *observable* responses? Tolman and Honzik answered this question with the proposal that cognitive structures are learned. Specifically, they suggested that Group 3 rats had learned a **cognitive map,** or mental picture, of the maze. When the rats found food in the end box on the eleventh day, they used their cognitive maps to run the maze almost without errors on the twelfth day.

Tolman and Honzik's experiment suggested a need for psychologists to turn away from conditioning theories and toward cognitive learning theories. The proposal of cognitive maps was out of step with conditioning theories not only because cognitive maps are unobservable mental events, but also because they are learned without reinforcement. But psychologists were slow to give up what they hoped would be a general learning theory. Almost 3 decades passed before a significant number of psychologists broke ranks with operant conditioning theory and turned toward cognitive learning theory. Today, cognitive maps make good sense to cognitive psychologists, who assume that we constantly explore and store information about our world.

Learning Sets

Anne taught Helen at home, which may have made it easier for her to compare Helen's learning to that of other children who learn language at home. Most teachers of deaf children work in school, where it is natural to compare deaf children with other school children. Cognitive psychologists would say that the different experiences may cause different **mental sets.** A mental set is a readiness to view a problem in a particular way— a readiness to see certain relationships. Research shows that past experience affects readiness to solve problems (Harlow, 1949). Harlow gave monkeys the problem of finding food under one of two covers, a square one and a round one. He always placed food under the square cover, and the monkeys gradually learned to look under the square cover whether it was on the right or left side. Harlow then did his critical manipulation. He changed to different covers, such as a red triangle and a green triangle. The monkeys again learned that food was always under one of the covers, but this time they learned faster. After solving hundreds of problems with different covers, the monkeys learned to solve them in one trial. They looked under one cover; if food was there they kept looking under that cover, never bothering to lift the other one. If food was not under the first cover, they looked under the other one on the next trial, and then they stayed with that one. The monkeys had established a mental set, or what Harlow called a **learning set.** Their previous experience made them ready to solve a particular kind of problem.

Sometimes mental sets put us on the wrong track. When they do, they are called a **negative set,** which is one that reduces our chance of learning

In an experiment by Harlow, monkeys established a mental set in which they could solve a certain problem in one or two trials.

a new relationship. Luchin's water jar problem is an example. Table 5–1 illustrates the problem. You can solve the first six problems in four steps:

1. Fill the largest jar
2. Fill the next largest jar with the water in the largest jar
3. Fill the smallest jar with the water in the largest jar
4. Fill the smallest jar again with the water in the largest jar

The water remaining in the large jar is the required amount.

The next two problems can be solved in the same way or they can be solved much more easily with two steps:

1. Fill the second largest jar
2. Fill the smallest jar from the water in the second largest jar

The water remaining in the second largest jar is the required amount. This simple two-step solution is the only one that works for the last problem.

We would solve the last three problems easily if we had not worked on the others. We would have trouble, however, if we had worked on the first six. People who solve the first six problems tend to use the harder four-step solution on the next two problems and they get stuck on the last one. The first six problems establish a negative set that blinds them to the simple solution for the last three problems.

Dunker (1945), a latter-day Gestalt psychologist, looked into a fascinating kind of negative set called **functional fixedness.** This form of mental set reduces our ability to learn new uses of something that has served a specific function in the past. One researcher set up a problem that is useful in demonstrating functional fixedness (Maier, 1931). The problem is to tie together two strings that hang from a ceiling. When the strings hang straight down, you cannot reach both of them at the same time. When you grab one and walk toward the other, you still cannot reach both at once. Can you think of a solution? (*Hint:* there are tools in the room such as pliers, a screw driver, and a hammer.) The solution is to tie a tool to one of the strings and swing it. Grab the other string and walk as close as possible to the swinging string. When it swings toward you, grab it and tie the two strings together. If this problem were actually set up for you, you would have a harder time solving it if an experimenter had you build something with the tools first. Your experience with tools in their normal function reduces your chance of seeing them as weights.

Teachers at schools for deaf children may have been victims of functional fixedness. They had always used schools to teach language in a certain way. Their past experience with language lessons in school always

TABLE 5–1: Luchins's Water Jar Problems

How do you measure out the right amount of water using any or all Jars A, B, and C?

Problem Number	Jars Available for Use			Required Amount
	A	B	C	
1	27	3	2	20
2	21	127	3	100
3	14	163	25	110
4	18	43	10	5
5	9	42	6	21
6	20	59	4	31
7	23	49	3	20
8	15	39	3	18
9	28	76	3	25

Source: Luchins (1942).

involved drills on vocabulary and grammar. Their experience with a school's usual function reduced their chance of seeing schools as a place where children could be stimulated to acquire language naturally. Anne Sullivan's first teaching job was in Helen Keller's home. Ironically, Anne's lack of teaching experience may have contributed to her teaching effectiveness with Helen.

INTELLIGENCE: THE CAPACITY TO LEARN

Up until now we have been considering general principles of learning. Now we will consider individual differences in **intelligence,** which may be defined as the capacity to learn. People differ widely in intelligence. At one extreme are people who are totally dependent on others for basic care. They are unable to learn how to care for themselves. At the other extreme are people who are highly successful in college and in professional careers. They seem able to learn whatever society can teach, and they usually add to what society can offer. Most of us fall between the extremes, but it is difficult to pinpoint just where.

The task of specifying the capacity to learn would be relatively easy if we all had an equal opportunity to learn. Differences in accomplishments would then directly reflect differences in capacity. Unfortunately, people do differ in their opportunities to learn. As a result, different achievements can indicate either different capacities or different opportunities. And to make matters worse, opportunities themselves are hard to evaluate. Take Helen Keller, for example. Her accomplishments were outstanding indeed. But does that mean that she had an outstanding *capacity* to learn or an outstanding *opportunity* to learn? Surely her opportunity was reduced by her blindness and deafness, but just as surely it was increased by the constant attention of a highly responsive and insightful teacher, Anne Sullivan. Helen would not have graduated from college if she had not had a high capacity to learn. But, how high was it compared to other deaf and blind people who did not have the advantage of Anne Sullivan's wise tutorship? How high was it compared to all other college graduates? Such questions may never be answered, because it is so difficult to evaluate Helen's opportunity to learn. In general, whenever it is difficult to compare opportunities to learn, it is difficult to compare intelligence.

Psychologists formally recognize the problem of different opportunities by distinguishing between two kinds of tests: (1) **achievement tests,** which are designed to measure a person's current knowledge and skills, and (2) **aptitude tests,** which try to predict capacity for future performance. Some achievement tests are **standardized;** that is, they have been given to many people so that one person's score can be evaluated with respect to a large population. Many achievement tests are not standardized, however. Examples are the tests and quizzes used in most college courses. They enable teachers to evaluate a class, but they do not enable comparisons with a general population.

Most aptitude tests are standardized. You may take standardized aptitude tests on many specific skills, including artistic, musical, mechanical, physical, foreign language, and mathematical skills. Your score in each case would be compared with those of people who are successful in that specific area. You may also take standardized aptitude tests to measure a broad range of aptitudes. An example is the General Aptitude Test Battery (GATB), which measures 10 aptitudes, including verbal, numerical, clerical, and motor speed. Finally, you may take, and probably have taken, intelligence tests, which are broad-range aptitude tests that are designed to predict capacity for future school performance. Let's look at the history of intelligence tests.

The History of Intelligence Testing

Sir Francis Galton developed the first intelligence tests. He administered them to 9,000 people in London in 1884, 4 years after Helen Keller was born. Many of his tests were invalid, since they did not do what they were designed to do. Specifically, they did not distinguish eminent British scientists from ordinary citizens on the basis of their intelligence. In 1905, Alfred Binet, a French psychologist, published the first useful intelligence test. He based his test on the idea that mental ability increases with age. He tested many children on mentally demanding tasks, recording each child's **chronological age** (the age in years and months) and then defining **mental age** as the average performance of children at a specific chronological age. A mental age of 10, for example, is the *average* performance of 10-year-olds. He converted each child's performance score into a mental age. Average children received a mental age that was the same as their chronological age. Below-average children received lower mental ages, and above-average children received higher mental ages. Binet recommended that children should get special educational attention when their mental age was 2 years below their chronological age.

Lewis Terman introduced in the United States in 1916 a modified version of Binet's test under the name of the Stanford-Binet test. Terman also popularized the concept of **intelligence quotient,** or **IQ,** which is determined by a formula that divides mental age by chronological age and then multiplies the resulting sun by 100. For example, a child with a mental age of 12 and a chronological age of 10 would have an IQ of 120:

$$IQ = \frac{\text{Mental Age}}{\text{Chronological Age}} \times 100 = \frac{12}{10} \times 100 = 120$$

Binet assumed that his test measured general intelligence, which he defined as the ability to judge, to comprehend, and to reason. Charles Spearman (1927) also argued that intelligence test items measure general mental capacity, which he called g. But he said that test items also measure some specific ability, s, although these specific influences cancel out when many items are combined. Later on, Louis Thurstone (1946) concluded that intelligence test items measure seven independent factors. The seven were: verbal comprehension, word fluency, number, space, memory, perceptual speed, and reasoning. J. P. Guilford (1967) stated more recently that intelligence includes at least 120 separate abilities. Despite these efforts to identify separate mental skills, however, the most popular tests remain those that yield a general IQ score. Such tests predict school performance as well or better than tests yielding multiple scores. See Table 5–2 for sample questions from modern IQ tests.

IQ and Age

Binet introduced the concept of mental age because his research showed that mental abilities increase with age. His investigations were limited to children, however. Modern researchers are only beginning to understand what happens to intelligence in adulthood and old age. Early studies used *cross-sectional* designs that measured different people at different ages; for example, one group at age 15, another at age 30, another at age 60, etc. (Jones and Conrad, 1933). These studies were contaminated by the fact that different age groups had different educational experiences, and

TABLE 5–2: Sample Questions from a Modern IQ Test

Verbal Scale	
Information	What is steam made of? What is pepper?
Comprehension	Why is copper often used in electrical wires? Why do some people save sales receipts?
Arithmetic	It takes three people nine days to paint a house. How many people would it take to do it in three days? An automobile goes 25 miles in 45 minutes. How far would it go in 20 minutes?
Digit Repetition	Repeat the following numbers in order: 1,3,7,2,5,4 Repeat the following numbers in reverse order: 5,8,2,4,9,6
Similarities	In what way are a circle and a triangle alike? In what way are an egg and a seed alike?
Vocabulary	What is a hippopotamus? What does "resemble" mean?
Performance Scale	
Picture Arrangement	A story is told in three or more cartoon panels placed in the incorrect order; put them together to tell the story.
Picture Completion	Point out what's missing from each picture.
Block Design	After looking at a pattern or design, try to arrange small cubes in the same pattern.
Object Assembly	Given pieces with part of a picture on each, put them together to form such objects as a hand or a profile.
Digit Symbol	Learn a different symbol for each number and then fill in the blank under the number with the correct symbol. (This test is timed.)

Source: Sample questions from Wechsler Adult Intelligence Scale.

thus researchers could not say whether differences between groups were due to differences in age or to differences in education. Later studies used *longitudinal* designs, which measured the same people as they grew older. Overall IQ scores showed gain to age 32, little or no change until age 60, and significant decline thereafter. The decline after age 60 did not include declines in important subtests such as verbal meaning and reasoning (Schaie and Labouvie-Vief, 1974).

Recently, the use of one overall IQ score to represent intellectual changes with age has been criticized (Horn, 1978). Horn argues that the declining scores observed after age 40 represent only one aspect of intelligence. He calls this aspect **fluid intelligence,** which we can roughly define as general mental skills, such as the ability to make inferences.

IQ scores do not decline with age until after age 60, and in fact only decline in fluid intelligence at that point. Crystallized intelligence, on the other hand, steadily increases with age.

Horn and Donaldson (1980) state that fluid intelligence declines with age mainly because of a decline in physical and neurological functioning. They also feel that part of the decline is due to reduced practice of certain mental skills. Horn's main point, however, is that there is another aspect of intelligence that steadily increases with age. He calls this ever-improving aspect **crystallized intelligence,** which we can define as specific mental skills, such as one's vocabulary, or the ability to define words. Figure 5–9 helps clarify the distinction between general and specific skills by showing test questions that tap either fluid or crystallized intelligence. Crystallized knowledge is specific, in the sense that it depends upon exposure to a specific environment. People in different cultures would learn

FIGURE 5–9

These are sample test items used to measure fluid intelligence and crystallized intelligence. Answers to the items are given below. (Educational Testing Service, 1962, 1976)

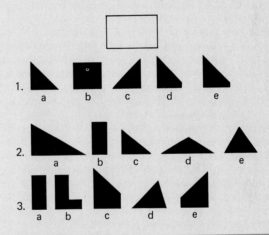

SAMPLE TEST ITEM: FLUID INTELLIGENCE

Below is a geometric figure. Beneath the figure are several problems. Each problem consists of a row of five shaded pieces. Your task is to decide which of the five shaded pieces will make the complete figure when put together. Any number of shaded pieces from two to five may be used to make the complete figure. Each piece may be turned around to any position, but it cannot be turned over.

1. a b c d e
2. a b c d e
3. a b c d e

SAMPLE TEST ITEM: CRYSTALLIZED INTELLIGENCE

Choose one of the four words in the right-hand box which has the same meaning as the word in the left-hand box.

1.	bizarre	market imaginative	conventional odd
2.	pecuniary	involving money trifling	esthetic unusual
3.	germane	microbe relevant	contagious different

Answer:
Fluid intelligence item: (1) a, c, d, e; (2) a, d, e; (3) b, c, e

Crystallized intelligence item: (1) odd; (2) involving money; (3) relevant to define different words, for instance. Horn and Donaldson (1980) imply that such culturally specific knowledge "crystallizes in the mind," so that it is less affected by physical and neurological deterioration. People thus retain culturally based knowledge through the years, and they continually learn new specific facts. Figure 5–10 shows the end result. While fluid intelligence first increases and then decreases with age, crystallized intelligence steadily increases.

IQ: The Extremes

Intelligence tests have been most successful at identifying the extremes of intelligence (Isaacson, 1970). At one extreme, people with IQs below 30 are the totally dependent, to whom we referred earlier. About 1 out of every 1,000 people fall in this category. Those with IQs between 30 and 50 are trainable; that is, they can learn to take care of their daily needs in a sheltered environment. About 3 out of every 1,000 people are in this category. People with IQs between 50 and 70 are educable; that is, with special training, they can learn to support themselves in the community (Zucker and Altman, 1973).

At the other extreme, people with IQs of 140 or above are classified as mentally gifted. In 1921, Terman and his associates started a longitudinal study that followed mentally gifted people from early childhood through adulthood (see Sears, 1977; Sears and Barbee, 1977). The results supported two conclusions. On the one hand, high IQ scores are associated with good health, outstanding school performance, and leadership. On the other hand, a high IQ is not a perfect predictor of success, because other factors are also important. Some of the mentally gifted people in the study, for example, failed in college and in their careers. Many factors are important in determining differences between the least and most successful mentally gifted individuals, including motivation, perseverance, and creativity (Crockenburg, 1972).

IQs: The Controversies

Classifying people at the low and high extremes of intelligence is an important contribution, for it helps educators provide programs that are best suited for individual needs. Few would deny that people and society are well served when educable individuals and mentally gifted individuals receive different education programs. Nevertheless, grouping people for different educational programs is a sensitive issue, as indicated by several recent controversies. One major public concern is whether or not IQ tests are fair to minority groups. Let's consider this controversy.

Culture Fairness. Those who question the validity of IQ tests for minorities argue that the tests are not fair to blacks, poor whites, and other cultural subgroups. As mentioned earlier, differences in performance on IQ tests could be caused by differences in opportunity to learn the tested material, or by differences in capacity to learn. If everyone has the same opportunity, then differences can safely be attributed to capacity. If, however, a cultural subgroup has had less of an opportunity to learn the tested material, then the IQ test is an invalid test of capacity for that group.

Test-makers have tried to develop "culture-fair" tests. Most often this has meant cutting down on the use of verbal materials, since there are obvious language differences between subcultures. Nonverbal tests usually involve geometric relationships of some kind. The tasks on such tests include fitting pegs into holes, judging relationships between geometric forms, making designs with blocks, and completing drawings (Cattell, 1949; Raven, 1947). Unfortunately, test-makers have too little data to back

FIGURE 5–10

The graph shows how fluid intelligence first increases and then decreases with age, while crystallized intelligence steadily increases. (Horn and Donaldson, 1980)

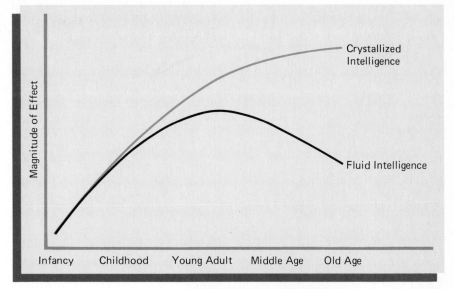

The children shown here are in a class for the educable mentally retarded, those with IQs between 50 and 70. With special training they will eventually be able to support themselves in the community.

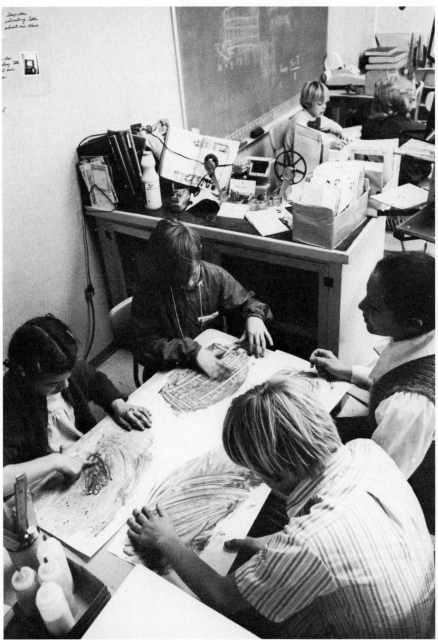

up their assumption that everyone has an equal opportunity to learn even the skills required for these tasks. Developmental psychologists are only beginning to understand the effects of experience on cognitive development. What they have learned so far suggests that environments during infancy and childhood do make a difference, but many questions remain unanswered: At what age do children learn aspects of geometric relationships? What elements of the environment are essential for providing an opportunity to learn geometry and other skills that are examined on IQ test? If there are critical environmental factors, how are they influenced by the complex and subtle differences between subcultures? Until these and other questions about opportunities to learn are answered, it will be impossible to establish the validity of even culture-fair IQ tests for cultural subgroups. A closely related controversy concerns the role of heredity and environment in determining IQ.

Nature and Nurture Issue and IQ. What is the relative contribution of heredity and environment to IQ? In the study of genetics one estimates the heritability of traits in plants and animals by controlling environment while manipulating the proportion of genes held in common. Such experiments cannot be done with humans, of course. Although human families vary systematically in the extent to which they share genetic makeup, they also differ systematically in their environments. Specifically, those who have similar genes (parents and children) also have similar environments. Those who have less similar genes (grandparents and grandchildren) also, for the most part, have less similar environments. Some authorities argue, in fact, that genetic similarity is so interwoven with environmental similarity that scientists cannot make meaningful heritability estimates for humans (Feldman and Lewontin, 1975).

Many investigators have nevertheless studied genetic relatedness in humans. They use three procedures:

1. *Studies of identical twins who are raised apart.* These have often failed to separate effects of heredity from effects of environment (for example, Shields, 1962). The twins were reared in separate but similar environments and often had contact with each other. One study that claimed to avoid this problem (Burt, 1966) is now regarded as fraudulent. Burt apparently invented much of this data (Kamin, 1973).

2. *Studies comparing identical and fraternal twins.* As we discussed in Chapter 2, identical twins come from the same egg, and thus their genes are exactly the same. Fraternal twins, on the other hand, come from two separate eggs, and thus their genetic makeup differs. If correlations of IQs were higher with identical twins than with fraternal twins, this would say something about the heritability of IQ. Such tests, however, are also inconclusive. Correlations between IQs are higher for identical twins (Erlenmeyer-Kimling and Jarvik, 1963), but this result has two interpretations. The higher correlations could be due to heredity, or to the fact that identical twins are more likely than fraternal twins to share a similar environment—to play together and to have the same friends and teachers (Loehlin and Nichols, 1976).

3. *Studies of adopted children, which compare their IQs to those of both their biological parents and their adopted parents.* Such studies suggest that IQ heritability is low to moderate (Horn et al., 1979; Scarr and Weinberg, 1977). This conclusion is supported by the fact that the IQ correlation between parent and biological child is not consistently higher than that between parent and adopted child. Furthermore, IQ correlation between genetically related broth-

ers and sisters is not consistently higher than that between brothers and sisters who are only related by adoption.

The controversy is far from settled. Jensen (1969) reviewed the literature on genetic relatedness and concluded that heredity is about four times as important as environment in determining IQ. More recent reviews maintain that heredity is no more important than environment, or that it is perhaps not even as important as environment (Kamin, 1979; Plomin and DeFries, 1980).

Race and IQ. The most heated debate about intelligence concerns the fact that in the United States black people average 10 to 15 points lower on IQ tests than white people. A number of researchers (Eysenck, 1971; Herrnstein, 1973; Jensen, 1969, 1973; Shockley, 1972) have used this and other selected results to argue that blacks are innately less intelligent than whites. Other scientists (Kagan, 1973; Kamin, 1976, 1979; Scarr-Salapatek, 1971) rebut this conclusion with one or more of the following arguments:

1. Even if IQ has a hereditary element, that refers only to heredity within the group being studied—it does not say anything about differences *between* groups, such as blacks and whites.
2. IQ tests are biased against black people and other minorities.
3. Average IQ differences can be attributed entirely to environmental differences.
4. Differences in heredity and environment are so interwoven that IQ differences cannot be attributed to one or the other at this time.

IQ and You

You probably know your IQ or your scores on scholastic aptitude tests (SAT), which also are used to predict school performance. You are advised to interpret this information cautiously. On the one hand, don't let a high IQ score give you a false sense of security. Remember that a number of Terman's mentally gifted subjects failed in college. On the other hand, don't give up if you have a modest IQ score. Standard IQ scores predict school performance, but not perfectly.

Some school counselors advise students against a college career unless they have an IQ of 120. This advice amounts to a prediction that people with lower IQs will not succeed as scholars. The uncertainty of this prediction is illustrated by the case of Nobel prize winner James Watson. After having his IQ measured as 115, he not only succeeded in college, he also discovered the structure of DNA (as we discussed in Chapter 2), which is one of the major scientific breakthroughs in modern history. Watson's success brings to mind Helen Keller's earlier quoted graduation speech: "There is nothing good or right which we cannot accomplish if we have the will to strive."

SUMMARY

1. **Learning** is a process by which experience or practice results in a relatively permanent change in what one is capable of doing.

2. **Classical conditioning** occurs when an originally neutral stimulus comes to elicit a response that was originally given to another stimulus. It takes place when the neutral stimulus (CS) is repeatedly paired with the other stimulus (US).

3. A number of factors help in establishing conditioned responses: The CS being strong and distinctive; the CS being presented shortly before the US; the time lapse between the CS and the US being brief; there being many pairings of CS and US; and the pairings of CS and US must be spaced properly.

4. **Extinction** occurs if the CS is repeatedly presented alone, without the US. But in **spontaneous recovery,** the conditioning effect appears again without any further pairings of CS and US.

5. **Stimulus generalization** occurs when responses are made to stimuli that are similar to, but not the same as, the original CS. **Discrimination,** on the other hand, occurs when subjects learn to respond only to certain stimuli, but not to other, similar stimuli.

6. **Operant conditioning** is a type of learning that occurs when desired responses are rewarded or reinforced and undesired responses are ignored or punished. **Reinforcement** is an event whose occurrence just after a response increases the likelihood that the response will be repeated; **positive reinforcement** is the presentation of a stimulus, **negative reinforcement** is the removal of a stimulus.

7. Schedules of reinforcement can be either continuous (rewarding every response) or partial (rewarding only some responses), based on reinforcement of a certain *number* of responses or reinforcement after a certain *interval of time*. There are four basic schedules: **fixed interval, variable-interval, fixed ratio,** and **variable ratio** schedules of reinforcement. Each type affects the rate of responding in different ways.

8. **Extinction** and **spontaneous recovery** occur in operant as well as in classical conditioning (extinction in operant conditioning occurs through the withholding of reinforcement). **Generalization** and **discrimination** also occur in operant as well as classical conditioning. **Punishment** is a stimulus that decreases the likelihood of a response when it is added to an environment.

9. **Shaping** is a procedure used in operant conditioning in which each part of a behavior is reinforced, eventually leading to the whole behavior that is desired.

10. **Social learning theory,** or learning indirectly through observing others, occurs through imitation. It is discussed in detail in Chapter 11.

11. Cognitive learning theory attempts to explain the function of thought processes in learning. It includes such concepts as **insight** learning, **latent learning, cognitive maps, learning sets,** and **functional fixedness.**

12. **Intelligence** has been defined as the capacity to learn. It is difficult to measure intelligence as a capacity, however, since people differ greatly in their opportunities to learn, and it is not easy to see whether test scores reflect capacity or opportunity.

13. **Achievement tests** are designed to measure a person's current knowledge and skills, reflecting past learning. **Aptitude tests** try to predict the capacity for future performance. Many tests are **standardized,** that is, they have been given to many people so that one person's score can be evaluated with respect to a large population.

14. **Intelligence quotient,** or **IQ,** is *mental age* divided by *chronological age,* with the product then multiplied by 100. It is a concept that was popularized through the introduction of the Stanford-Binet test early in this century.

15. It is difficult to estimate the effects of aging on IQ, because it depends on whether one is talking about **fluid intelligence** (general mental skills) or **crystallized intelligence** (specific mental skills). Fluid intelligence first increases and then decreases with age; crystallized intelligence steadily increases.

16. Several controversies of IQ and IQ testing were discussed. They included culture-fair testing, the question of whether heredity or environment is more important in its effect on IQ, and race and IQ.

SUGGESTED READINGS

The following books are about Helen Keller and Anne Sullivan:

KELLER, H. *Story of my life*. Garden City, N.Y.: Doubleday, 1954.

LASH, JOSEPH P. *Helen and teacher: The story of Helen Keller and Anne Sullivan Macy*. New York: Dell, 1980.

BRODY, E. B., and BRODY, N. *Intelligence: Nature, determinants, and consequences*. New York: Academic Press, 1976. A balanced coverage of the nature-nurture controversy and related controversies is given in this thorough review.

ESTES, W. K. (Ed.). *Handbook of learning and cognitive processes* (Vols. 1–6). Potomac, Md.: Erlbaum Associates, 1976. This series covers all aspects of learning and cognition at an advanced level.

HILGARD, E. R., and BOWER, G. H. *Theories of learning*. Englewood Cliffs, N.J.: Prentice-Hall, 1975. Presents principal points of view toward learning in their historical settings and summarizes typical experiments to which each theory has led.

HORTON, D. L., and TURNAGE, T. W. *Human learning* (5th ed.). Englewood Cliffs, N.J.: Prentice-Hall, 1981. Presents a broad cross-section of theory and evidence, with an emphasis on recent developments. The book is divided into three parts: traditional learning approach, information-processing approach, and learning of language and concepts.

RACHLIN, H. *Introduction to modern behaviorism* (2nd ed.). San Francisco: W. H. Freeman & Company Publishers, 1976. Places facts and concepts of classical and operant conditioning in a historical context.

WICKELGREN, W. A. *Learning and memory*. Englewood Cliffs, N.J.: Prentice-Hall, 1977. The book focuses on explaining concepts and principles, which are illustrated with everyday experiences and practical applications.

6

Memory and Cognition

O n December 24, 1919, three bandits attacked a payroll truck in broad daylight, firing at it as it skidded down an icy street in Bridgewater, Massachusetts. The bandits, unsuccessful in their robbery attempt, drove off in a getaway car. No one was injured.

Several months later, there was a similar crime in the neighboring town of South Braintree. At about 3 o'clock on the afternoon of April 15, 1920, armed robbers ambushed and shot two guards in a truck that was carrying the payroll of a local shoe company. The gunmen grabbed the cash box containing $15,000 from the dying guards and jumped into a car that had pulled up while the shooting was going on. Two days later the getaway car was found abandoned in some nearby woods, with the tracks of a smaller car leading away from it. During the investigation that followed, the police theorized that the tracks of the smaller car might have been made by the vehicle used in the earlier crime at Bridgewater. This theory would later form the net that snared Sacco and Vanzetti.

To understand how these two rather ordinary men (one a factory worker, the other a fish peddler) came to the center of national and international attention and why they were ultimately electrocuted in 1927, one must consider the social backdrop as well as the details of the case itself.

The two crimes and the Sacco-Vanzetti trial took place during a period of acute social unrest and upheaval in America. Labor strikes had shocked the nation in 1919, and prominent figures in government and business were targets of radical assassination attempts. Americans blamed their troubles on the strangers (the immigrants) in their midst. Partly for this reason, Congress established in the late 1920s a quota system to drastically cut down on immigration, especially limiting the influx of people from southern and eastern Europe. More than other groups, they were viewed as a main source of America's troubles.

Faced with charges of robbery and murder, Sacco and Vanzetti found themselves doubly handicapped. Both were Italian immigrants; both were anarchists. (The term "anarchist" in those days was used very loosely. It did not necessarily mean that one was a member of an efficient, ruthless organization bent on the overthrow of government. Sacco and Vanzetti's rebellion against authority was a general, poorly organized expression of dissatisfaction with the lot of immigrant industrial laborers.) Neither man had a background of crime or violence.

Eyewitnesses at both the Bridgewater and South Braintree crimes said that the bandits were foreigners. This was enough to convince Bridgewater's chief of police that the crimes had been the work of "Reds and Bolshevists." At the time of the Braintree murders, he was working under the assumption that the culprits were Italians who owned a car in a nearby town. He located an Italian-owned car that was in a nearby garage for repairs and theorized that whoever came for the car must be involved in the two crimes. On the night of May 5, 1920, Sacco and Vanzetti arrived at the garage. They roughly fit the description of the bandits, and they were carrying guns, so they were arrested. Only Sacco had an alibi for the day of the unsucessful Bridgewater holdup. Neither Sacco nor Vanzetti had an airtight alibi for the day of the Braintree murders. Thus Vanzetti was charged with the Bridgewater attempt, and both men were charged with the killings at Braintree.

Vanzetti stood trial from June until August of 1920, charged with assault as one of the gunmen who shot at the payroll truck in Bridgewater. The testimony of witnesses for the prosecution was riddled with contradictions and inconsistencies. The district attorney relied heavily upon the testimony of three witnesses to establish the identity of Vanzetti as one of the gunmen. Two of these men had been passengers in the payroll truck and therefore the targets of the shooting. The third man was a bystander, also close to the action and in danger of being shot. The actual exchange of gunfire—the moment when the men in the truck had the best opportunity to see the robbers—lasted only for a matter of seconds and was viewed at a speed of about 20 miles an hour. Afraid of being shot, the driver had hunched so low in the seat that he lost control of the truck. The other passengers scrambled for the steering wheel, and, in the confusion, ran the truck into a telephone pole. Thus the attention of the passengers in the truck was divided between the gunmen and keeping control of the truck.

The three witnesses gave three reports of the incident: the first on the day of the crime (December 24); the second at a preliminary hearing on May 18; and a third at the trial in late June. The first reports were as follows:

1. Alfred Cox (a passenger in the payroll truck):
"The man with the shotgun was a Russian, Pole or Austrian, 5'8", 150 lbs., dark complexion, 40 years of age, was without a hat and wore a long, dark overcoat with the collar up. He had a closely cropped moustache which might have been slightly gray."

2. Benjamin Bowles (an armed guard who returned the fire from the truck):
"I can positively identify two of the bandits. The man with the shotgun was 5'7", 35 or 36 years, 150 lbs., had a black, closely cropped moustache, red cheeks, slim face, black hair and was an Italian or Portuguese. He had no hat on and had a black overcoat with collar up."

3. Frank Harding (a bystander):
"The man with the shotgun was slim, 5'10", wore a long black overcoat and derby hat. I did not get much of a look at his face but I think he was a Pole."

Vanzetti, who was accused of being the shotgun bandit at Bridgewater, had a distinctively full, long, and droopy moustache, and he had always worn it so. The moustache originally seen on the shotgun bandit was apparently smaller than Vanzetti's, but as time passed and the witnesses had the chance to see Vanzetti, the moustache "grew to fit the man." Other details changed also. For example, Cox changed his description from "dark" complexion to "medium" complexion—closer to Vanzetti's coloring. Bowles added at the trial that the gunman had a "high forehead," moving closer to a description of Vanzetti.

Other confusions were apparent. Under cross-examination, Bowles (the armed guard) revealed that he was unsure of whom he shot at, and therefore unsure of whom he got a "good look" at. He also was unsure about which of the gunmen had fired first. Inconsistencies in his testimony suggested that he had altered his story (possibly unconsciously) to please his questioners. Adding to the confusion, the district attorney called other witnesses who gave questionable testimonies—for example, that of a 14-year-old newsboy: "By the way he ran I could tell he was a foreigner; I could tell by the way he ran." Despite its defects, the testimony persuaded the jury, for they found Vanzetti guilty. Ruthless news coverage of the conviction added another strike against Sacco and Vanzetti. Because of this, Sacco requested a separate trial, which was denied.

The joint trial of Sacco and Vanzetti began a year later, on May 31, 1921, at Dedham, Massachusetts. It lasted nearly 7 weeks. Only one question was relevant: Were Sacco and Vanzetti the assailants of the two men at Braintree? There was a mass of conflicting evidence regarding this question. The discord in the testimony was summed up by Francis Russell (1962) in his book *Tragedy in Dedham:*

> Scarcely a minute had elapsed from the first shot until the getaway car vanished, but with its disappearance the actuality faded and the myth took over. All in all there were more than fifty witnesses of the holdup in its various stages, yet each impression now began to work in the yeast of individual preconceptions. The car was black, it was green, it was shiny, it was mud-streaked. There were two cars. The men who did the shooting were dark, were pale, and had blue suits, had gray suits, wore caps, were bareheaded. Only one had a gun, both had guns. The third man had been behind the brick pile with a shotgun all the time. Anywhere between eight and thirty shots had been fired. (pp. 41–42)

Apparently, the witnesses at Braintree could do no better than those at Bridgewater. But again it was good enough for the jury. On July 14, 1921, Sacco and Vanzetti were found guilty of murder in the first degree.

Many who studied the trial carefully were unconvinced. Because of the inconsistencies in the testimony and other irregularities, many thought (and many still think) that Sacco and Vanzetti did not get a fair trial. Six long years passed, taken up with appeals for a new trial. All this was to no avail, however—on August 22, 1927, Sacco and Vanzetti were executed.

HOW MEMORY IS STUDIED

Memory is a system that allows people to retain information over time. Human memory is far from perfect, as we have seen: Why did the Sacco and Vanzetti witnesses remember some facts and forget others? Why do you remember some answers on tests and not others? This chapter will examine the cognitive processes that underlie memory successes and failures. It will test your memory several times by asking what you read earlier in the chapter, so stay alert! The first test will show how good your memory can be; some of the others will probably reveal weaknesses in memory. We will end the chapter with suggestions for improving memory.

Test Yourself

The best way to analyze the relationship between memory research and eyewitness testimony is to take part in a memory experiment. Then you will be able to compare your experience with those of the eyewitnesses in the Sacco and Vanzetti case. Miller, Galanter, and Pribram (1960) outlined an experiment that is fun to experience firsthand. You must first learn the following verse: "One is a bun, two is a shoe, three is a tree, four is a door, five is a hive, six are sticks, seven is heaven, eight is a gate, nine is a line, and ten is a hen." This verse will provide a mental framework for learning a study list. (Psychologists call such mental frameworks *schemata*.) Study the following list of numbers and words, using the verse to help you learn which word goes with each number. You already know that "bun" goes with the number 1. Now you must learn that "ashtray" goes with 1. Try learning this new relationship by forming a bizarre image in your mind of a bun with an ashtray—you might imagine a pipe spilling ashes into a bun, for example. Follow the same procedure for every number until you have formed an image relating the right verse word to every word on the study list.

Study List

1 ashtray
2 firewood
3 picture
4 cigarette
5 table
6 matchbook
7 glass
8 lamp
9 shoe
10 phonograph

When you finish going through the list once, take the following test. Next to each number write the word that was next to it on the study list.

3 _____
8 _____
6 _____
4 _____
9 _____
1 _____
7 _____
2 _____
10 _____
5 _____

How many did you get correct? People often get all the words correct after one time through the list (Miller et al., 1960).

Methods of Testing Memory

You can assume from your performance that you remember all, or nearly all, of the study list. But it is not always safe to assume that performance reflects memory exactly or completely. We have all taken tests in school that have either overestimated or underestimated what we remember. The relationship between performance and memory is a theme that weaves its way through the research on memory. We will follow this important theme better if we understand the different kinds of performance that psychologists often use to measure memory.

Recall Tests. **Recall tests** measure a person's ability to reproduce material. The test you just took gave a number as a cue, and you had to reproduce the rest of the number-word pair. When part of an item is provided as a cue for the other part, the test is called *cued recall*. Teachers use cued recall tests when they ask fill-in-the-blank questions, such as "Mental frameworks are also called _____."

Another kind of recall test is *free recall*, in which no cues are provided and any order of recall is allowed. A teacher might say, "List three technical terms used in last night's homework assignment." Similarly, police asked Cox, Bowles, and Harding to give free recalls of what they had witnessed during the attempted payroll robbery at Bridgewater.

Recognition Tests. **Recognition tests** measure a person's ability to pick the correct answer when several answers are given. Teachers use recognition tests in the form of multiple-choice questions, such as "Mental frameworks are also called: (a) conditioned stimuli, (b) schemata, (c) operant responses, or (d) primary reinforcers." Recognition is usually, but not always, easier than recall (Hulse, Deese, and Egath, 1975). The difficulty depends on the answers you have to choose from. You might have had more trouble, for example, if the answers had been: "(a) schematics, (b) schemata, (c) schemes, or (d) schemas."

You would be taking a recognition test if you tried to select the word that goes with 7 on the earlier study list: Is it firewood, lamp, glass, or table? Witnesses at the Slater and Morrill holdup took recognition tests when they tried to identify the shotgun bandit from a number of pictures of suspects.

Savings Tests. **Savings tests** measure people's ability to take advantage of what they have learned before in order to relearn material faster. You rely on savings every time final exams roll around. By the time you get to the end of a course you have probably forgotten some of the facts you learned in the beginning, so you must relearn them for the final exam. You might not recall the name of one of the founders of structuralism, for example, even though you learned it in Chapter 1 of this book. You might not even recognize the correct name from the following list: Skinner, Watson, Wundt, James. But if you learned it earlier, you will probably learn very quickly that Wundt is the correct answer. The fact that you relearn old material faster than you learned it the first time shows that you remember something about it even if you cannot recall or recognize the information. To measure your savings in the earlier list you would have to record how long it took you to learn the list the first time and how long it took you to relearn the list at a later time. The difference between your original learning time and your relearning time is your **savings.** (If you waited long enough, you would probably find a time at which you could neither recall nor recognize the list, but you would still show savings.)

Notice that all three tests—recall, recognition, and savings—measure memory indirectly, through performance. Inferring memory from performance is no simple matter. Lawyers know full well that performance is not a perfect indicator of memory. A good question will often bring forth key evidence that a witness failed to produce on earlier occasions. Students also know that tests do not always reflect what they learned in a course. As our analysis of memory research unfolds in this chapter, we will learn many reasons why performance does not perfectly reflect memory.

TYPES OF MEMORY

There are basically two different theories about memory. One theory, called the *multiple memory theory* (Atkinson and Schiffrin, 1971, 1977), states that there are three types of memory (see Figure 6–1): sensory memory, which holds sensory impressions for only 1 or 2 seconds; short-term memory, which holds information for less than 30 seconds; and long-term memory, which holds information for long periods of time (perhaps permanently).

Another theory, the *levels of processing theory*, agrees about the existence of sensory memory. But, beyond that, these theorists argue that we have only *one* kind of memory, which holds different kinds of information. We get the different kinds of information by using different levels of processing what is stored in memory (Craik and Lockhart, 1972). According to this theory, we recode information into more and more abstract forms as we process it at deeper levels. At a surface level, we code visual properties when we read. At a deeper level, we recode visual properties of letters and words into word meanings. At a still more intense level, we recode word meanings into sentence meanings. With these deeper levels of processing, we get different kinds of information, but every kind is retained in the same unified memory.

We'll come back to these two theories as we discuss different kinds of memory and different ways of processing it. First let's look at what the multiple memory theorists call sensory, short-term, and long-term memory.

Sensory Memory

Sensory memory holds visual sensations long enough for recognition processes to operate. We often continue to look at a stimulus until we recognize it, but sometimes our view is disrupted by blinks and other disturbances. Sensory memory holds visual information *through* these disruptions so that recognition processes can operate without interruption. You can see evidence of your sensory memory by waving a pencil in front of your eyes. The shadowy image that trails behind the pencil means that your sensory representation of the pencil in one position stays on after the pencil moves to a new position. This information fades or decays from sensory memory within 1 or 2 seconds.

Sperling (1960) used an interesting method to study visual sensory memory. In this experiment, he presented 12 letters in three rows with 4 letters in each row (Figure 6–2). He flashed the letters for 50 msec., then asked subjects to name as many letters as they could. They were able to name only four or five letters, even though they claimed that they had seen more than that. From this Sperling formed the following hypothesis: Subjects did not see all the letters, because the flash was too brief. They saw more letters than they could report, however, because they forgot some before they could say them.

FIGURE 6–1

Multiple memory models include sensory memory, short-term memory, and long-term memory. The arrows show the flow of information between these three types of memory.

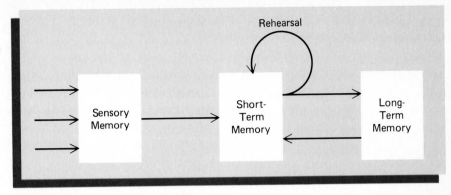

Sperling ran a second experiment to test his hypothesis. This time he directed his subjects to view only a portion of the 12-letter display. He did this by using various tones as stimuli, sounding the tones after the letters were presented: A high-pitched tone meant that they should name the letters in the top row; a medium tone cued the middle row; and a low tone indicated that the subjects should concentrate on the bottom row. Sperling called this a *partial report procedure*, because subjects only report part of the display that is shown to them. The procedure is based on the same logic that teachers use to determine course grades. Teachers sample only part of a course's material on exams. They then use the percentage correct on the exam to estimate what percentage you know of all the material in the course. If you get 90 percent correct on the exam, the teacher assumes that you know 90 percent of all the material. Sperling found that subjects knew 75 percent of the letters in his display (3 out of 4) when they were cued immediately after the display went off. This suggested that they saw 9 of the 12 letters that were briefly flashed.

FIGURE 6–2

Sperling's partial report technique is shown in the upper part of the figure. Below it is a graph of the results: The number of letters recalled decreases as the signal to report is delayed. (Sperling, 1960)

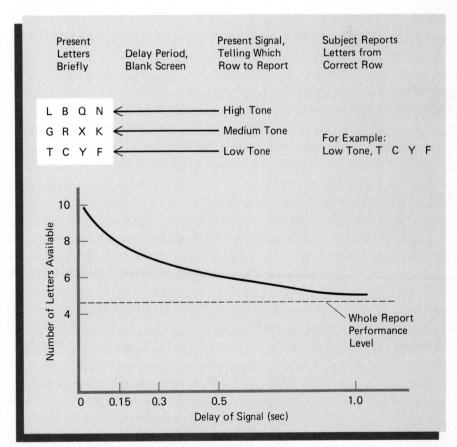

In other conditions, Sperling delayed the cue 150 msec., 300 msec., or 1,000 msec. after the letters were presented. This forced subjects to remember all the letters until they got the cue. The percent correct gradually dropped (Figure 6–2). With a 1,000 msec. delay, the cue was useless, since subjects did no better than when they received no cue at all. From this Sperling concluded that sensory memory held visual information for a short time after the display went off, and that the memory gradually faded.

Sperling determined these important properties of sensory memory in related experiments:

1. Visual properties of a stimulus, such as brightness, determine the length of sensory memory. The brighter the stimulus, the longer sensory memory lasts. Usually sensory memory lasts less than 1 or 2 seconds.
2. Sensory memory for one stimulus is wiped out when another stimulus is presented after the first one is out of sight. The ability of a stimulus to wipe out the sensory memory of a preceding stimulus is called *backward masking.*
3. Sensory memory contains visual information that has not yet been recognized or named. Based on physiological evidence reviewed in Chapter 2, we can assume that sensory memory contains information represented in terms of visual features such as angles, curves, and straight lines.

Massaro (1970) showed that auditory sensory memory has similar properties.

Short-Term Memory

We take in a vast number of sensations in sensory memory, but we only identify a small part of this information. What we do not identify is lost. What we do identify is transferred to short-term memory for further processing. Transfer to short-term memory, therefore, usually involves a considerable loss of information. We retain information in short-term memory by repeating it to ourselves, a process called **rehearsal.** If we do not rehearse the information, the memory decays or fades rapidly. A good example of this is the way you repeat or rehearse a phone number that you have just looked up. If you do not repeat it, or if someone interrupts you before you can make the call, you will probably forget the number almost immediately.

Peterson and Peterson (1959) developed a way to measure how long information is held in short-term memory when it is not rehearsed. They divided their procedure into three intervals: presentation, retention, and recall. During presentation, subjects looked at a three-letter unit called a trigram, such as XNT. During retention, subjects did a math problem that was designed to keep them from rehearsing the trigram. During recall, subjects simply attempted to say the trigram that had been presented. Figure 6–3 shows the results. Subjects recalled trigrams correctly about 50 percent of the time after 3 seconds, about 25 percent of the time after 9 seconds, and about 8 percent of the time after 18 seconds. This and many other experiments show that we forget new, isolated facts (such as trigrams) in less than 30 seconds if we do not rehearse them.

Any acceptable memory theory would have to explain Peterson and Peterson's results. Multiple memory theory says that we retain isolated facts in short-term memory until we transfer them to long-term memory. Transfer is impossible without rehearsal, so we quickly forget facts that we do not rehearse. Levels-of-processing theorists offer a different explanation for the same results. They assume that facts are remembered longer

FIGURE 6–3

Research has shown that people rapidly forget isolated facts if they do not rehearse them. In the graph here we see a rapid decline in the amount of correct recall of trigrams. (Peterson and Peterson, 1959)

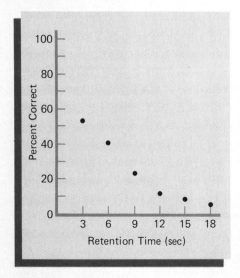

when they are processed more deeply, not because they are transferred to a different type of memory. Peterson and Peterson's subjects only had time to do surface-level processing of trigrams, so they forgot them quickly. Both multiple memory theories and levels of processing theories pass the test of being able to explain the Peterson and Peterson results. We will have to consider other ways to distinguish the two theories.

Long-Term Memory

Long-term memory holds information that is transferred from short-term memory through rehearsal or some other such process. The longer that information stays in short-term memory, the more likely it is to be transferred to long-term memory. Some researchers assume that our long-term memory is virtually permanent—that is, we lose nothing from long-term memory, although we may sometimes fail to retrieve information from it (Atkinson and Schiffrin, 1971, 1977).

Types of Long-Term Memory.   We store concrete information about sensory aspects of our experiences in long-term memory. We remember the sound of voices over long periods, as when an old friend calls and we immediately recognize his or her voice. We remember body movements. If you drive a car with a bright-light switch on the floor, for instance, you will probably hit the switch rapidly on your first try, even if you haven't used it for some time. Keele and Ells (1972) showed that we remember both the switch's position and how far we have to reach to hit it.

We also remember smells extremely well. In one experiment, people recognized smells as accurately after 30 days as they did after 30 seconds, and they forgot very few smells over a period of one full year (Engen, 1980).

Evidence of long-lasting memories does not necessarily prove that the multiple memory theory is right, however. As mentioned earlier, levels of processing can also explain long-term retention. Let's look at some support for the levels-of-processing theory.

Deeper Processing Means Longer Memory.   Many experiments show that memory depends upon levels of processing—the deeper the level, the better the memory (cf. Wickelgren, 1979). There is one experiment that is of particular interest with respect to eyewitnesses' testimony (Bower and Karlin, 1974). The experimenters showed pictures of faces and they manipulated the levels of processing that people engaged in while looking at the pictures. Sometimes subjects used surface levels of processing to make judgments about simple things, such as sex of the pictured person. Other times subjects used deeper levels of processing to make more difficult judgments, such as likeableness or honesty. Subjects recognized pictures better on a later test when they had processed the pictures more deeply, even though they looked at all pictures for the *same* amount of time. This and other experiments suggest that theories of memory must take into account levels of processing.

We will continue to review evidence for multiple memory theory and levels-of-processing theory as we go on to discuss the processes of encoding, retention, and retrieval in short-term and long-term memory.

ENCODING

Video and audio tape recorders passively take in everything that is bright enough or loud enough to record. A lawyer's job would be much easier if human witnesses did the same. But, of course, people don't; they decide what to take in and how to represent it. For instance, you used a special plan to **encode,** or represent, the study list at the beginning of this chapter. Similarly, Frank Harding may have used a special encoding strategy when he observed the ambush of the payroll truck that caused him to remember a derby hat that wasn't worn by either gunman. Cognitive psychologists include analyses of encoding as a major part of their research on memory. They find that encoding comes into play in sensory memory, short-term memory, and long-term memory. Let's discuss each of these in turn.

Encoding in Short-Term Memory

We have already said that much information is lost between sensory memory and short-term memory. Let's take a closer look at the selective way in which most of us encode information.

Attention. Put yourself in the place of Benjamin Bowles on Christmas Eve in 1919. You are riding shotgun in a payroll truck when suddenly it comes under fire. Your first instinct is to hit the floor, but you have committed yourself to defending the money, so you return the fire. Moments later the truck swerves out of control and hits a telephone pole. Think about the rush of stimuli you would encounter—the gunmen, the smoke from their guns, the smoke from your gun, bystanders running, the background spinning by, the smell of the truck's heater and of rubber burning, the bumps against your body as you and the other passengers are bounced around, the bangs, the squeals of tires, the shouts. You would not experience all of these to the same extent. Your mind would zero in on some and ignore others. Just by imagining the situation you probably have a good idea about which stimuli would get your attention.

The process by which we notice important stimuli and ignore irrelevant stimuli is called **attention.** Without it, our minds would surely drown in

In traffic, our senses are often flooded with more information than our minds can handle at one time. We manage in this sort of situation because we pay attention only to important stimuli, which, in the case here, would most likely be the stop sign.

FIGURE 6–4

This is the apparatus used in a typical shadowing experiment. Separate messages are played to each ear of a subject, who tries to ignore one message and to repeat the other.

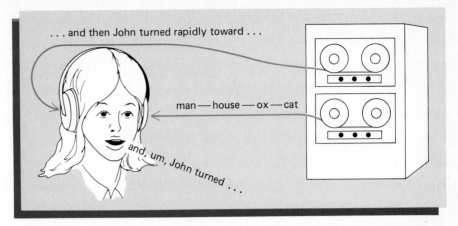

. . . and then John turned rapidly toward . . .

man — house — ox — cat

and, um, John turned . . .

a churning, muddled ocean of stimuli. In traffic, on disco floors, and at cocktail parties our senses are flooded with more information than our minds can handle at one time. We manage in these situations because we attend selectively to important information.

Figure 6–4 illustrates one of the artificial laboratory settings used to study attention. Each earphone carries a separate message. The subject is asked to ignore one message and to *shadow* the other, that is, to repeat it aloud as it is heard, staying as "close behind" the speaker as possible. This procedure allows the experimenter to examine two questions: What happens to the message that the subject is asked to ignore? When does this irrelevant message interfere with perception of the relevant one?

Before looking at the answers, try to guess. What do you think happened to the irrelevant smells, sounds, and bumps rushing in on Bowles when his truck was attacked? Do you think they were ever noticed in the first place? Surely the irrelevant stimuli excited his sensory receptors, but perhaps the signals from the receptors were filtered out before his brain recorded them. If they did reach the brain, and if they were noticed, perhaps they were remembered for only a very short time.

One way to find out is to give subjects a surprise test on their ability to recall the irrelevant message in a shadowing experiment. Research has shown that 30 seconds after the material is presented, the content of the irrelevant message is forgotten (Moray, 1959). In some experiments the irrelevant message was alternately presented in English and an unfamiliar foreign language, or in English and gibberish; 30 seconds later subjects had no recollection of these changes.

In contrast, the physical characteristics of the irrelevant message are remembered. For example, people remember whether it was a man's voice or a woman's voice, whether or not it stopped completely, and whether or not it was replaced by some other sound. Apparently people attend to an irrelevant message enough to determine its physical characteristics, but not enough to determine its meaning, or at least not enough to remember the meaning 30 seconds later.

The second question also deserves some thought before we look at the answers regarding the shadowing experiment. We all know that irrelevant stimuli sometimes interfere. For example, try listening to a lecture while someone next to you cracks his or her knuckles. Sometimes, however, irrelevant stimuli don't seem to matter. The background hum of an air conditioner, for instance, probably does not take your mind away from a lecture.

As you might have guessed, the content, or meaning, of an irrelevant message can make a difference. For example, if a subject's name is mentioned, shadowing of the attended message is disrupted. This is similar to losing track of your own conversation when hearing your name mentioned in a nearby discussion. Hearing one's name mentioned is distracting because people are somehow predisposed to hear their names. A researcher found that other words also become distracting when we are inclined to hear them (Treisman, 1960). For example, one sentence in the attended message started with the words "Poor Aunt. . . ." Consequently, subjects expected to hear a woman's name. A woman's name (Jane) was then played in the unattended message and something else was played in the attended message. Subjects suddenly started shadowing the unattended message. The mistake was often noticed and subjects stopped to apologize. These subjects had a hard time ignoring the distracting message when they were predisposed to hear it.

Encoding, of course, is more than selecting certain information; it is also representing it in a certain form. If you had seen the license plate number on the getaway car at the Braintree armed robbery, would you have tried to form a mental picture of the license plate, using a visual code, or would you have repeated the number to yourself? How would you have tried to remember the bandit's face? Would you have repeated facial features to yourself—black hair, red cheeks, slim face—or would you have formed a mental picture of it? Evidence suggests that you would have used both kinds of codes.

Verbal Codes. Many experiments have shown that we prefer to use verbal codes for verbal materials such as digits, letters, and words. In one study, Conrad (1964) found evidence for verbal codes in the errors that people make. He briefly exposed six consonants and then asked people to write down all six letters in order. When people made mistakes, the incorrect letters were usually ones that *sounded* like the correct ones. For the list R L T K S J, a subject might substitute a B for a T, recalling R L B K S J. It is hard to imagine why subjects would have made this mistake if they had remembered the letters by means of a visual image. After all, a B does not *look* like a T. The mistake makes good sense, however, if people are using verbal codes, because B does *sound* like T. Such mistakes, therefore, support people's claims that they remember strings of letters by repeating the letter names to themselves. If we tried to remember a license plate number on a getaway car, we would probably repeat it to ourselves several times until we had a chance to write it down.

Visual Codes. While we *prefer* verbal codes for verbal material, we don't always use them. For example, we used visual codes to memorize the words in the study list at the beginning of this chapter. Furthermore, we seem to prefer visual codes for memorizing stimuli that are difficult to describe. Kosslyn, Ball, and Reiser (1978) found evidence suggesting that people use visual codes when they are asked to memorize maps. After subjects memorized a map similar to the one in Figure 6–5, they seemed to have a mental image of it. They could use their image to visualize a dot moving from one object (the hut) to another (the pond). The farther the dot had to move, the longer it took to visualize the movement, suggesting that subjects "saw" the dot move across a remembered image of the map. This and other evidence (Kosslyn, 1981; Wickelgren, 1977) suggest that we use visual codes. We would certainly use them to remember a robber's face if we happened to witness a crime.

Our choice of codes depends to some extent on how long we must remember something. So far we have only talked about experiments on memory for short intervals. Experiments on memory over longer intervals suggest that we *recode* information for long-term memory.

Encoding in Long-Term Memory

Which of the following sentences was the first sentence in this section on encoding?

FIGURE 6–5

People can use visual images to memorize maps. They can also imagine a dot moving from one object to another on the map's image. The reaction time from the beginning to the end of the imagined movement increases as objects on the map are shown farther apart. (Kosslyn et al., 1978)

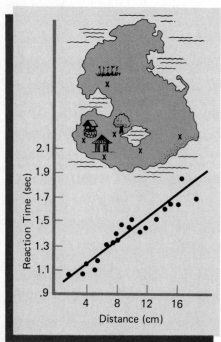

1. Video and audio tape recorders actively decide what bright or loud information should be recorded.
2. Audio and video tape recorders automatically record everything that is bright enough or loud enough to take in.
3. Video and audio tape recorders passively take in everything that is bright enough or loud enough to record.

Sentence 1 is easy to eliminate because its meaning is different from the first sentence in this section. You may have had more trouble, however, deciding between sentences 2 and 3. Sacks (1967) read sentences to subjects such as "The author sent a long letter to the committee." Two minutes later subjects remembered sentence meanings, but they did not remember exact words. They could not choose between the actual sentence and a different one that had the same meaning: "A letter that was long was sent to the committee by the author." In the same way, you may be representing the meaning of sentences that you are reading here, but you probably are not representing the exact words in long-term memory. Will you remember the meaning at test time? That will depend on many factors that are discussed in the next section.

RETAINING AND RECODING

Retention in tape recorders is uninteresting. Tape recorders retain whatever information they pick up, and they play it back in the same form in which they have recorded it. Retention in humans is quite another matter. Humans alter some memories and forget others during retention. Testimonies by Cox, Harding, and Bowles during the Vanzetti trial illustrated the changeable nature of human memory. Over time their descriptions of the bandit changed in many ways; they altered their statements about characteristics such as moustache length, complexion color, and forehead shape. Here we will review experiments that shed light on what might have caused these changes.

Will you remember what you have been reading here at test time? That depends on how the information was encoded and organized in your long-term memory.

We have already discussed the kind of coding that takes place when information is transferred from sensory memory to short-term memory. In this section, we will more closely follow the path of information to explore how it is *retained* after it is encoded in short-term memory and long-term memory.

Capacity of Short-Term Memory

Memory theorists try to distinguish short-term and long-term memory on the basis of how much each holds or *retains*. Try to dial the following number without looking back at it: 924–3401–5732–816. Most of us can't do it. We're used to handling 7 digits without much trouble, but we find 14 almost impossible. Why? Multiple memory theorists say that we have trouble dialing 14 digits because our short-term memory has a limited capacity, or a limit to how much information it can hold. While long-term memory can hold almost any amount, short-term memory can only hold a limited number of digits. Fourteen is well beyond that limit.

Our memory span is the number of items that we can read through one time and then recall in sequence with no mistakes. Experiments have shown that seven-digit numbers seem to mark the limit of our memory span. Ebbinghaus (1885) was one of the first to estimate his memory span at seven items. Many years later Miller (1956) saw the estimate of seven coming up so often in experiments that he wrote a paper entitled "The Magical Number Seven, Plus or Minus Two." While people differ greatly in their ability to remember facts for exams or lines for plays, virtually all normal adults have a memory span that falls between 5 and 9 items.

Multiple memory theorists explain this "magical number" with the assumption that short-term memory has a limited storage capacity of 7 ± 2 items. It is as if short-term memory is a small filing box with only 7 ± 2 slots. When all the slots are filled the only way we can get new information into short-term memory is by displacing some item that is already there (see Waugh and Norman, 1965).

Levels-of-processing theorists explain limited memory span not in terms of *limited storage capacity*, but in terms of *limited processing capacity*. They assume that we are limited in the rate at which we can perform the processes of holding items and of repeating them back. Since storage limitations and processing limitations are both plausible, the existence of memory span limitations does not help us choose between multiple memory theories and levels-of-processing theories.

Chunking. We can say that memory span is limited to 7 ± 2 items, but what exactly is an item? Experiments have shown that our memory span can correspond to 7 ± 2 digits, letters, syllables, words, or even sentences. The letter string NOSPMAS HPLAR is well beyond our memory span, but the same string in reverse order, RALPH SAMPSON, is well within our span. In fact, we could manage five or six more names. When we process information, we group elements together to form units that function as wholes. We group visual features into letters, letters into words, and words into sentences. This process is called chunking. Miller (1956) labeled the units *chunks* and concluded that memory span corresponds to 7 ± 2 chunks. We can appreciate the economy of chunking information when we compare memory span for different kinds of items. Our memory span is about seven letters when we try to memorize letter strings that are unpronounceable and meaningless. It is 7 ± 2 sentences, which corresponds to about 80 letters, when we try to memorize sentences (Craik and Lockhart, 1972).

Sometimes we try to memorize information for very short intervals, as when we dial a new telephone number. Most of the time, however, we try to remember things for longer periods, as when we study for exams. Let's look now at the special characteristics of retention in long-term memory.

Retention in Long-Term Memory

The eyewitness testimony at Sacco and Vanzetti's trial illustrates two principles of retention in long-term memory: organization and reconstruction. People organize the information that they store in long-term memory, and they continue to work on or reconstruct that organization as time passes. Initial organization is revealed in reports by Cox, Bowles, and Harding to police at Bridgewater. These descriptions of the "shotgun bandit," which we quoted earlier, depended upon long-term memory, because the police did not arrive immediately. The reports were highly organized. Specifically, all three witnesses used organizations that grouped together facts into four categories: body build, facial features, clothing, and nationality. As time passed, all three witnesses changed their testimony in a way that might have indicated a reconstruction of their original memory. Let's take up this example in more detail and relate it to research on principles of organization and reconstruction.

Organization in Long-Term Memory. People store a wealth of general knowledge, and they use this background knowledge to organize memories for episodes that they witness. Cox, Bowles, and Harding, for instance, already knew the categories that they used to organize their memories of the "shotgun bandit." Tulving (1972) formalized the distinction between the long-term retention of background knowledge and specific episodes as follows:

1. **Semantic memory** refers to a person's general background knowledge about words, symbols, concepts, and rules.
2. **Episodic memory** refers to a person's memories about events, including the time and place they occurred.

All three witnesses in the Sacco and Vanzetti case changed their testimony from the time they first talked to the police to the time they actually testified at the trial. Their memories of the body build, facial features, clothing, and even nationality of the "bandits" may have been affected by the process of reconstruction in long-term memory.

We will use this distinction in the following discussion, even though researchers are still debating its value for theories of memory (McCloskey and Santee, 1981).

The extent to which semantic memory can impose itself on episodic memory is illustrated by Harding's testimony. He did well, remembering details such as a black overcoat, but he got one fact wrong. He reported that the "shotgun bandit" wore a derby hat, when he actually wore no hat at all. Overcoats and derby hats were probably closely associated in Harding's semantic memory, and he may have mixed up his semantic memory with his episodic memory of the event he witnessed. We are, of course, just speculating about the reason for Harding's error. For better evidence of the interaction between semantic and episodic memories, we should turn to the research in this area.

Galton (1879) studied semantic memory with a **free association test,** which is a procedure in which a person looks at, or listens to, a target word and then reports other words that come to mind. Deese (1959) combined free association tests with free recall tests to show that we use semantic memory to organize episodic memory. Free association tests measure semantic memory, because they reflect the way our general knowledge about words is organized. Free recall tests measure episodic memory, because they reflect the organization of memory for a list learned at a specific time and place. Deese first measured free associations in one group. He then gave a list of words in random order to another group. The second group was allowed to recall the words in any order. The subjects recalled the list not in its original order, but in an order that grouped together things that were related in earlier associations. Apparently, associations that were present in semantic memory imposed themselves on episodic memory.

Other researchers used a clever procedure to study semantic memory (Collins and Quillian, 1969). They measured how long it took people to answer simple true-false questions. Consider one of their questions: A canary can fly, true or false? The question asks about general knowledge; it doesn't ask about a specific piece of information (that is, you can answer it without saying when or where you saw a canary fly, or without ever having seen a canary fly). They used such questions to test a model of how people organize semantic memory. Figure 6–6 shows an example of their model. Information about canaries is stored in different places, according to the model. Some is stored under a high-level category, "animal"; some is under a lower level or subordinate category, "bird"; and some is under a still lower category, "canary." This organization, which is called a **hierarchy,** arranges information into levels of categories and subordi-

FIGURE 6–6

This is a model of semantic memory. This type of organization of ideas is called a hierarchy, as is described in the text. (Collins and Quillian, 1969)

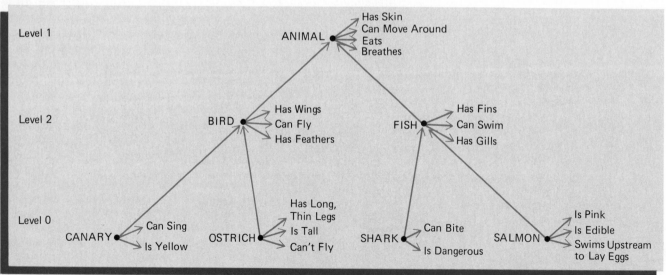

TABLE 6–1: Scrambled Sentences Test

Unscramble these sentences and put them in the proper order to form a story about a farmer and a donkey.

But the cat replied, "I would gladly scratch the dog if only you would get me some milk."

Thus, the farmer went to the haystack and got some hay.

The barking so frightened the donkey that it jumped immediately into its shed.

So, then, the farmer asked his cat to scratch the dog so the dog would bark loudly and thereby frighten the donkey into the shed.

Then the farmer pushed the donkey, but still the donkey wouldn't move.

As soon as he gave the hay to the cow, the cow gave the farmer some milk.

As soon as the cat got the milk, it began to scratch the dog.

But the cow replied, "I would gladly give you some milk if only you would give me some hay."

Finally, the farmer asked his dog to bark loudly at the donkey and thereby frighten him into the shed.

But the dog refused.

First, the farmer pulled the donkey, but the donkey wouldn't move.

So the farmer went to his cow and asked for some milk to give to the cat.

There once was an old farmer who owned a very stubborn donkey.

As soon as the cat scratched the dog, the dog began to bark loudly.

Then the farmer went to the cat and gave the milk to the cat.

One evening the farmer was trying to put his donkey into its shed.

nate categories. Collins and Quillian assumed that it would take time to move between categories. They found, in agreement with this prediction, that it takes longer to decide "A canary can fly" than it does to decide "A canary can sing." It takes even longer to decide "A canary has skin." Today many models of semantic structure include similar hierarchical structures (Anderson and Bower, 1973).

Bower and his associates (1969) showed how such hierarchies benefit recall. They gave two groups of subjects free recall tests on four lists of words. One group saw all four lists arranged in hierarchies, while the other group saw all four lists arranged randomly. The first group, who could easily organize the list according to preexisting categories, recalled 65 percent of the words. The other group recalled only 19 percent. This and other studies (Horton and Turnage, 1976) show that we use our knowledge of categories and hierarchies to organize and, thereby, to improve our episodic memory.

Our semantic memories contain, in addition to associations and categories, rules for structuring stories. The sentences in Table 6–1 can help demonstrate your knowledge of such rules. The sentences can be unscrambled to form a short story about a farmer and a donkey. Try it, and your story will probably be almost identical to the original. How did you know the correct order? You knew because of your semantic memory, which contains rules for structuring stories. Most of us started learning these rules as young children by listening to stories our parents told. We can use those rules to make a story out of a scrambled list of sentences (Shebilske and Reid, 1979).

Researchers have developed formal grammars for diagramming story structures (Frederikson, 1975; Kintsch, 1974; Norman and Rumelkart, 1975; Schank, 1973; Yekovich and Thorndyke, 1981). Figure 6–7 shows a story diagrammed in a hierarchical tree structure according to one of the grammars. Notice that general ideas are near the top of the tree, and specific details are near the bottom. These same tree structures are used when people try to summarize a story from memory. Figure 6–7, for example, shows that the likelihood of including an idea in a summary is directly related to the level that the idea holds in the story's structure. Psychologists generate tree structures and predicted rank orders according to specific rules. The fact that recalls fit the predicted rank orders

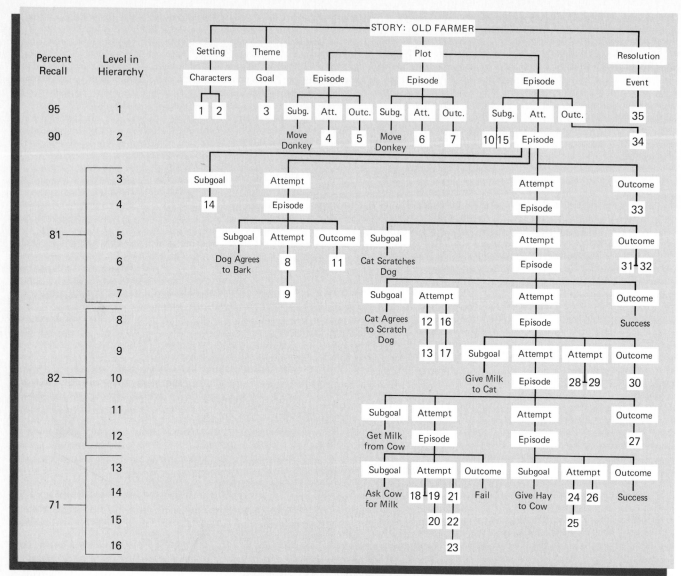

FIGURE 6–7

This is a model for how stories might be stored in a hierarchy. As shown on the left, people recall a higher percentage of ideas from high levels in the hierarchy than they do from low levels. (Thorndyke, 1977)

Most college students follow unconscious rules when they read textbooks, which allow them to study and remember important information and ignore and forget unimportant information.

suggests that we unconsciously follow similar rules for remembering stories.

We follow unconscious rules when we read textbooks. The rules are different than those we use for stories, because textbooks are different. But the rules are similar in the sense that they distinguish between important and unimportant ideas. Most college students tend to study and to remember important information, while they ignore and forget unimportant material. In contrast, many high school students study textbooks as if all material is of equal importance, or, worse yet, they tend to remember only unimportant information (Deese, 1980; Estes and Shebilske, 1979; Shebilske, 1980). Efforts are being made to help students who cannot learn well from textbooks. A goal is to teach them rules that will assist them in effectively organizing their memory.

Reconstruction in Long-Term Memory. We start organizing material when we first encounter it, and we continue to organize and reorganize as time passes. We are often unaware of our efforts to reorganize, or recode, material in long-term memory. Such unconscious reconstruction of memory is a major source of unreliability in witness testimony.

After witnesses saw Vanzetti during his trial, their description of the shotgun bandit moved closer to a representation of Vanzetti. We might think that the witnesses were deliberately trying to frame Vanzetti. But research suggests another possibility; witnesses may have unconsciously distorted their memories.

In one experiment, Loftus found that exposure to new information can distort a witness's memory (Loftus, 1975, 1981; Loftus and Palmer, 1974). Subjects were shown a film of a traffic accident, and they then answered one of five questionnaires. The questionnaires were all the same except for the wording of a question about speed. One questionnaire asked, "About how fast were the cars going when they smashed into each other?" The other questionnaires substituted the verbs "collided, bumped, contacted, or hit" in place of "smashed." Loftus had two ways to measure how much influence the verbs had. One measure, the estimate of speed, showed that the verb "smashed" drew higher speed estimates than the other verbs. A second measure came a week later, when Loftus asked, "Did you see any broken glass?" Subjects who had the questionnaire with the verb "smashed" in it were more likely to say yes, even though there had been no broken glass. Apparently, memory was altered to include details that did not actually exist, but which were consistent with an accident at higher speeds.

In courtrooms, questions that "lead" a witness to a particular answer are called "leading questions," and there are rules against them. However, the rules may be inadequate. Leading questions asked well in advance of a trial seem to alter memory for an event. Consequently, answers to "fair questions" during the trial might be unreliable.

What exactly is a "leading question?" To get at a precise, unambiguous definition, researchers must show exactly how and when people can be led by questions. Loftus has begun to explore the kinds of questions that cause memory distortions. For instance, she conducted an experiment similar to the one above, except she used a different leading question. Immediately after showing a film of a fast-moving event, she asked a question that presupposed the existence of an object that was not in the film. For example, in a film showing no barns, the leading question was "How fast was the white sports car going when it passed the barn while traveling along the country road?" One week later, nearly one-fifth of the students who heard this question "remembered" a barn being in the film.

Even without leading questions, memory changes in predictable ways. For example, memory tends to have standardized representations. Gordon W. Allport (1958) demonstrated this by showing students a roughly trian-

FIGURE 6–8

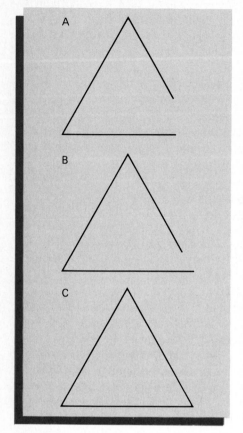

People reconstruct their memories to fill in details. Subjects who were shown A and were later asked to draw what they had seen, reproduced drawings B and C after 1 and 3 months respectively. (Allport, 1958)

gular drawing (Figure 6–8A). He then varied the time at which he asked students to draw what they had seen. Those who were asked immediately after they were shown the picture drew very good reproductions; those who were asked 1 month later produced drawings like Figure 6–8B; and those who were asked 3 months after the original viewing produced drawings like Figure 6–8C. With time, the student's memories tended to leave out the details that made the original drawing unique. In the end, memory contained a standardized representation of a triangle.

Memory standardization affects witness testimony as well. To test this, one researcher staged an assault on a college campus (Buckhout, 1974). A student "attacked" a professor in front of 141 witnesses, and sworn statements were then obtained from each witness. Buckhout found that witnesses tend to give standardized estimates. For example, heights and weights are overestimated for short or thin people and underestimated for tall or heavy people because memory tends toward the average.

RETRIEVAL

Push a button and mechanical recorders play back all the information that they have recorded. Human **retrieval,** the process of getting information out of memory, is not as reliable. We sometimes fail to retrieve, or get back, information that is stored in our memory. You might be unable to recall a date on a history exam, for example, but then it comes to mind right after the exam. This suggests that the date was in your memory all along, but you failed to retrieve it during the exam. Such retrieval failures increase unreliability stemming from inattentiveness during encoding and from memory loss during retention.

Memory researchers would have a fairly easy time studying retrieval if all of our retrieval efforts were open to conscious inspection, but they are not. We often search through our memory without being aware of it, which makes memory research both more difficult and more interesting. Let's turn to some of the special techniques used to study conscious and unconscious retrieval processes.

Retrieval from Short-Term Memory

Sternberg (1966) conducted an experiment that shed light on retrieval from short-term memory. You can get a feeling for his experiment easily enough with the following test. Memorize the numbers 2, 3, and 8, and then cover them. Now, ask yourself whether or not the following numbers were on the list: 3, 7, 1, 2, 9, and 8. The answers "yes, no, no, yes, no, yes" come to mind so quickly and effortlessly that it is hard to realize that we have to search our short-term memory at all. Sternberg found evidence, however, that we do, in fact, search our short-term memory for such information.

He recorded how long it takes people to respond "yes" or "no" in a task like the one that you just tried. He had subjects memorize numbers, ranging from one to six items on a list. He tested a list only once, then asked subjects to memorize another list. On each test he presented a digit, and subjects pushed a "yes" button if the digit was on the memorized list and a "no" button if it was not.

Sternberg found that response time depends on the length of the original list (Figure 6–9). It takes about 440 msec. with one item, about 480 msec. with two items, about 520 msec. with three items, and so on, with each

FIGURE 6-9

The time to decide if an item is in one's memory increases as the number of items in short-term memory increases. This result shows that it takes time to search through items in short-term memory. (Sternberg, 1966)

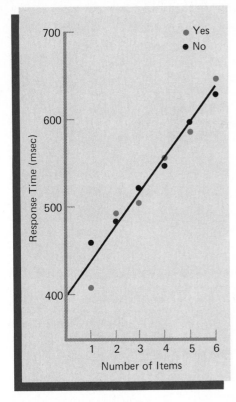

additional item taking about 40 additional msec. Sternberg concluded that we retrieve the test digits one at a time, with each comparison taking about 40 milliseconds.

Retrieval is not open to conscious inspection in Sternberg's experiment. Yet he was able to make a strong case that retrieval from short-term memory involves a search process. His experiment goes beyond our intuitions about retrieval from short-term memory. Similarly, cognitive psychologists have been able to go beyond what introspection reveals about retrieval from long-term memory.

Retrieval from Long-Term Memory

We are often unaware of our efforts to search long-term memory (Raaijmakers and Schiffrin, 1981). Sometimes, however, we are aware of our attempts to retrieve information from long-term memory and we deliberately control our search (see Norman, 1973). For instance, imagine yourself in place of Sacco and Vanzetti having to account for your whereabouts during the Bridgewater and Braintree crimes. If that seems too farfetched, imagine yourself in the predicament faced by the two similar-looking young men on the left and the right in Figure 6-10. On the basis of eyewitness testimony, both were accused of crimes until the man in the center in Figure 6-10 confessed. Suppose you are questioned in connection with a crime because it was committed by someone fitting your description. All you have to do to put a rapid end to this unfortunate case of mistaken identity is account for your whereabouts any time between 3:00 and 5:00 P.M. on the first day of last month. Can you do it? If you try, you will probably find yourself consciously reconstructing the events of that day. You might say to yourself, "I get paid on the first of the month and I usually deposit my check shortly before the bank closes. Oh, yes, I remember now. I deposited my check at about 4:30 on the first of last month. In fact, that was the day I complained to the service manager about an unexplained service charge on my account. I hope she has a record specifying the time of my complaint." But maybe you are not so lucky. Perhaps you can remember classes you attended in the morning and the play you saw that night, but you cannot remember what you did that afternoon. The point is that you are sometimes aware of your efforts to search your memory.

We are not always aware of our retrieval processes, however. Researchers, therefore, cannot rely entirely on people's direct reports of efforts to search memory. One way that researchers investigate retrieval processes that are not always open to consciousness is by manipulating cues that are designed to aid retrieval.

Organization and Retrieval Cues. Tulving and Pearlstone (1966) argue that we can take advantage of organization when we retrieve information from episodic memory (see also Masson and McDaniel, 1981). They showed subjects long lists containing words from common categories such as animals, colors, and professions. The words were presented in random order, and then subjects attempted to recall the lists. Half the subjects were told the category names at the time of recall; the other half were not. Subjects who were given category names did much better than the other subjects. Both groups were given category names in a later test, and they both recalled the same number of words. Both groups must have had the words in memory, but subjects could not retrieve as many without the help of category names. The category names served as aids to retrieval, or what psychologists call **retrieval cues.** We apparently use retrieval cues to organize our search through memory.

Tip-of-the-Tongue Phenomenon. We reveal other aspects of our retrieval processes when we come close to information in our memory

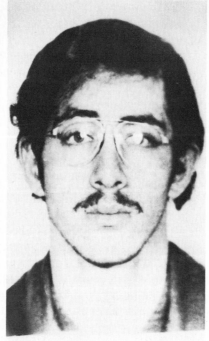

FIGURE 6–10

Mistaken identifications by witnesses can have serious consequences. The men on the right and the left were picked out of police lineups by victims of rapes and a robbery that actually were committed by the man in the center. Both innocent men were arrested, but were later cleared when the actual criminal, the one in the center, was found.

without actually finding it. Try to recall the words corresponding to the definitions shown in Table 6–2. You will know some immediately; you will not know some at all, and you will hopefully think you know some without being able to recall them right away. This uncomfortable state of being on the verge of recalling something is called the **tip-of-the-tongue (TOT)** state. Brown and McNeill (1966) produced over 200 TOT states in students who tried to recall words for definitions similar to those in Table 6–2. When students indicated that a word was on the tip of their tongue, Brown and McNeill asked them questions about the word. Students knew the number of syllables in the word over 60 percent of the time; they knew the word's first letter over 50 percent of the time; and they could give words that sounded like the words being defined (for example, *secant* instead of *sextant*). Brown and McNeill suggested that we retrieve information by sound as well as by meaning.

Anxiety and Retrieval. Most of us have panicked on an exam at one time or another. Panic is especially likely when there is a lot at stake. Consider a particularly crucial exam that you have taken. Passing means that you finally reach a long sought after goal; failure prevents you from

TABLE 6–2: Definitions Used to Produce a Tip-of-the-Tongue State

1. A fanatical partisan; one who is carried away in his pursuit of a cause or object.
2. Lying on one's back, with the face upward.
3. Selecting, choosing doctrines or methods from various sources, systems, etc.
4. A conciliatory bribe, gift, advance, etc.
5. An instrument having 30 to 40 strings over a shallow, horizontal sounding box and played with picks and fingers.
6. A hiding place used by explorers for concealing or preserving provisions or implements.
7. To clear from alleged fault or guilt; to absolve, vindicate, acquit, or exonerate.

Words corresponding to definitions.

1. Zealot	5. Zither
2. Supine	6. Cache
3. Eclectic	7. Exculpate
4. Sop	

Source: Brown and McNeill (1966).

HIGHLIGHT / STATE-DEPENDENT MEMORY

State-dependent memory refers to the fact that a memory is more easily recalled when a person is in the same emotional state in which the memory was acquired. Gordon Bower (1981) studied state-dependent memory in an American veteran of Vietnam, who turned to a psychiatrist for treatment of depression. The psychiatrist put the veteran under hypnosis and encouraged him to recall his combat days. At first the former soldier calmly recalled episodes. Suddenly, however, he became agitated, and he started to relive a traumatic event that he had previously blanked out of memory. His blackout had occurred when he saw the remains of his girlfriend who had been killed by a mortar shelling. Some might say

that hypnosis helped this patient overcome *repression,* which is the tendency to avoid anxiety-provoking memories. Bower maintains, however, that the case exemplifies state-dependent learning. Accordingly, hypnosis brought out memories because it helped the veteran return to the same emotional state in which the memories were acquired.

Bower conducted several experiments to test his theory. In one experiment, he used hypnosis to induce bad moods or happy moods. Figure A shows the results. People recalled a list of words much better when they were in the same mood they had been in when they learned the list. Repression theory and state-dependent theory can

explain the results with sad moods, but only state-dependent theory can explain the results with happy moods.

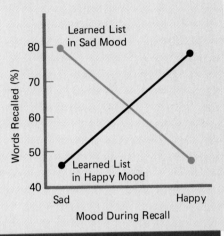

FIGURE A

Effects of mood on recall.

getting something you really want. Suddenly you become overwhelmed by a fear of failure, even though you know the material. Your anxiety level rises as each difficult question is reviewed until finally you are so panicked that you cannot remember a thing. Anxiety does not wipe out your memory. Things you couldn't remember during the exam often start coming to mind when you calm down after the exam.

Holmes (1974) argues that anxiety does not in itself prevent retrieval. Anxiety produces extraneous thoughts, such as, "I'll never be able to face my dad," or "This is unfair because I've worked so hard." Holmes argues that these thoughts are what stand in the way of retrieving answers to exam questions. You might try to control such distracting thoughts, or you might try to control your anxiety level directly. Chapter 4 outlines procedures that you can use to relax before taking exams. You should use the same procedures before studying. Maintaining lower anxiety levels during both study periods *and* tests may improve your performance (see Highlight, "State-Dependent Memory").

Decision Factors. Tape recorders report everything that they retrieve. With human retrieval, however, we *decide* what we want to say before we report anything. This intermediate decision allows us time to edit what we report.

Imagine yourself on a television game show. You are asked to name the children in the Walton's television family. How would you answer? If you think about it a minute, you will be able to determine your confidence in your memory. But, assuming you have some uncertainty, you still will not be able to say how you would answer the question. That would depend upon the *cost* of wrong answers and the *rewards* for correct answers. If you had everything to gain for correct answers and nothing to lose for errors, you would probably include some guesses. You might say "John Boy, Jim Bob, Mary Ellen, I think there was a Jason, maybe an Aaron, how about a Beth?" If, on the other hand, your winnings were taken away for each error, you might be more cautious. For example, you might say, "John Boy, Jim Bob, and Mary Ellen—that's all I can remember."

Costs and rewards also influence the testimony of witnesses in a trial. The cost in such a situation might be guilt associated with identifying the wrong person; the reward might be the satisfaction of seeing justice done. Buckhout (1974) maintains that two witnesses with the same memory might decide to say quite different things, and he developed a test to identify good witnesses. He based his test on **signal detection theory,** which makes it possible to measure memory and decision factors separately (Green and Swets, 1966). To give the test he shows a film of a staged "crime" and then presents 20 true statements about the incident and 20 false statements. Witnesses score a *hit* whenever they say "yes" to a true statement, and they score a *false alarm* whenever they say "yes" to a false statement. The percentage of hits and false alarms are used to calculate the witnesses' measure of sensitivity. If witnesses say "yes" as many times to true statements as they do to false statements, they obviously have no sensitivity about the truth of the statements, and their score is 0. If, on the other hand, witnesses almost always say "yes" to true statements and almost never say "yes" to false statements, they are very sensitive and they get a high score. Generally, observers who score high on Buckhout's test prove to be the best witnesses in other situations. For example, they do better at picking suspects from a lineup. For about 80 years, psychologists have warned about the unreliability of witness testimony. Now they are taking positive steps toward identifying reliable witnesses.

FORGETTING

Forgetting is defined as an inability to remember. You probably remember what it is like to forget, but in case you don't, let's probe for some reminders. What was the name of your third-grade teacher? Can you name five students who were in your fourth-grade class? What is the formula for figuring the area of a circle? What is your social security number? Can you name five glands in the endocrine system along with the hormones they secrete (see Chapter 2)?

If you answered all these questions correctly, please call the University of Virginia, Department of Psychology (804–924–0656). A number of researchers there would love to find out how you did it. If you answered some of these questions wrong, you might ask yourself why your memory failed you. If you knew why, you might be able to improve your memory. With that in mind, let's review the possibilities.

Trace Decay

When we memorize something, we produce a change within our nervous system. The nature of that change is highly debatable. Some argue that the change is confined to some specific location in the brain; others claim that it is dispersed throughout the nervous system (cf. Wickelgren, 1977). Either way, we can use the term **memory trace** to refer to the change that occurs as a result of memorizing. One of the earliest theories of forgetting, **trace decay theory,** holds that memory traces fade away in time. The theory's appeal to early theorists is apparent. Memories are natural, and things of nature change. Trees grow leaves only to lose them again; grass turns green only to fade back to a tawny brown; the sun rises and sets; we wake up fresh only to get tired again.

In the same way, according to trace decay theory, memory traces start out strong, and their strength is maintained through use. But traces gradually weaken and fade away if they are not used. Trace decay theory would explain a failure to recall the name of your third-grade teacher as follows: You once had a strong memory trace for the name and you refreshed the trace regularly by using it. Your trace gradually lost strength, however, when you stopped using it, and it became so weak that you could no longer recall the name.

Wickelgren (1977) argues that trace decay may contribute to forgetting, but other factors are also involved. For example, you learned many names since the third grade, and these may have interfered with your ability to remember your third-grade teacher's name. The next section presents an interference theory of forgetting.

Interference

When we learn different things, we create the possibility that learning one thing will hinder our memory of something else. A popular theory of forgetting, **interference theory,** holds that we forget information because other information gets in the way. Two kinds of interference are as follows:

1. **Proactive inhibition** is interference of previous learning with memory for new learning. Suppose historians suddenly discovered that Columbus really discovered America in 1534. Our previous memory of Columbus discovering America in 1492 would hinder our learning of the new date. The hindrance would be proactive interference. Researchers study proactive interference with experiments similar to the one illustrated in Table 6–3. The experiment has three steps and two groups of subjects.

   In the first step, the experimental group learns a list of words, List A; the control group does some unrelated activity. In step two, both groups learn a list, List B. In the third step both groups recall List B. Proactive inhibition is shown by lower recall of List B for the experimental group, who had previously learned List A.

2. **Retroactive inhibition** is interference of new learning with memory for previous learning. Suppose you went away for 6 months and you did not use your phone number during that time. You might have trouble recalling your number, but you would probably have even more trouble if you had acquired a new phone number during that time. The interference of the new number with your memory for the old one would be retroactive inhibition. An experiment for studying retroactive inhibition is outlined in Table 6–4. It has three steps and two groups.

   In the first step, both groups learn List A. In the second step, the experimental group learns List B, and the control group does some unrelated activity. In the third step, both groups recall List

TABLE 6–3: Proactive Inhibition

	Experimental Group	Control Group
Step 1	Learn List A	Rest or engage in unrelated activity
Step 2	Learn List B	Learn List B
Step 3	Recall List B	Recall List B

TABLE 6–4: Retroactive Inhibition

	Experimental Group	Control Group
Step 1	Learn List A	Learn List A
Step 2	Learn List B	Rest or engage in unrelated activity
Step 3	Recall List A	Recall List A

A. Retroactive inhibition is shown by lower recall of List A by the experimental group, who learned List B after learning List A.

Old and new material do not always interfere with each other in our memory, of course (see Shebilske and Ebenholtz, 1971). Sometimes old memories help us learn new material, as in the "one is a bun" experiment cited in the beginning of this chapter. Similarly, new learning sometimes helps us remember things that gave us trouble in the past. Isolated dates in history are often difficult to remember until we learn enough facts about a period to provide a frame of reference. Determining when memories will help or hinder the recall of other memories is one of the major challenges facing memory researchers today.

Another challenge is explaining how one memory interferes with another. Some theorists argue that a memory can be erased or dissolved by other memories. Other theorists claim that interfering memories do not distroy other memories, they only make them harder to locate during attempts to recall them.

IMPROVING YOUR MEMORY

"You can remember all the things that make the vital difference in your everyday existence, eliminating the unnecessary loss of so much knowledge and information that should be yours to keep and use forever" (Lorayne and Lucas, 1975, p. 1). So begins *The Memory Book*, which is filled with ways to improve your memory for things you do in school, such as giving speeches and taking exams. It also helps you remember people's names, shopping lists, playing cards, and important numbers such as telephone numbers. The book promotes a general understanding of how memory works and it gives hints on how to apply this insight to your own memorizing. We have already discussed how our memory operates. Now let's see how we can make that understanding work to our advantage in our everyday lives.

You can take steps to improve your memory when you first encounter new material, when you review and rehearse, and when you try to recall. These three times correspond to the three basic processes of memory: encoding, retention, and retrieval.

Encoding Efficiently

A key to encoding is attention. You must pay attention to important material if you want it to stay with you. We have all had experiences that help drive home the importance of attention. Perhaps you have failed to pay attention during a social introduction. Then you realized immediately afterwards that you did not catch the name of the person to whom you were introduced. Or perhaps you have found yourself at the bottom of a page without any idea of what you have just read. You can take steps to overcome these common problems of not paying attention.

You can ask yourself two questions during an introduction that will heighten your attention:

1. Is there anything unusual about the name?
2. Does the name go with the face?

The first question is easy to answer for some names that have obvious peculiarities, such as Mr. Katz Meow. Finding unusual aspects will be harder for other names. What's unusual about the name Shebilske? Different people will notice different things, of course. Did you notice, for example, that if you allow for misspelling, the name can be broken down into three common words—"she," "bill," and "ski"? With practice you will get good at finding something unique about any name. The second question is also easy to answer for some names. Mr. Katz Meow might have a moustache that looks like cat whiskers. You will have to be more imaginative to link other names with faces. You might notice, when being introduced to Mr. Shebilske, that his "bill" (nose) looks like a ski slope. Get in the habit of asking yourself these questions during every introduction. They will sharpen your attention to details, even if you don't have time to answer them right away.

You might also get in the habit of using the person's name immediately after hearing it. "It's a pleasure to meet you, Mr. Shebilske." You will force yourself to pay attention if you hold yourself responsible for saying the name. Be careful not to get these two habits mixed up, however. You don't want to find yourself saying, "It's a pleasure to meet you, Mr. Ski Face."

You can also develop special study habits that will help you overcome inattentiveness during reading. First of all, admit that you do not have a will of iron. Certain things are going to capture your attention despite your best efforts to ignore them. You will be distracted by radios, televisions, and nearby conversations when you read. You may do well at first if you try to read in the presence of these distractors. Sooner or later, however, something will capture your attention, and your mind will be taken away from your reading. You will improve your memory if you get in the habit of reading in a quiet place.

The next step is to develop the habit of focusing your attention on important parts of your reading. Your memory will increase significantly

Good study habits can help you get the most out of what you read. One of the most important of these habits is to study in a quiet place without a lot of distractions.

if you identify important ideas and concentrate on them (Shebilske and Rotondo, 1981).

There are certain steps that will help you put your attention in the right places. These steps are as follows:

1. Survey material before reading it carefully. You can determine important ideas better after you see a whole passage. You should therefore go over a passage quickly, keeping an eye out for the main ideas. Topic headings often identify main points. Summaries are also helpful. Read them before you read whole passages, even if summaries are placed at the end of chapters, as they are in this book.
2. Ask yourself, "What are the main points?" Come up with a temporary list that can be refined as you read more carefully. Also ask yourself questions that you think the text will answer.
3. Read the text carefully, noting the main points and answering your self-generated questions.
4. Recite the text in your own words after you finish reading. Note the main points that you do and do not know.
5. Review, firming up what you do know and learning main points that you may have missed the first time.

Organization is another key to efficient encoding. You find information better in an organized memory, just as you find things better in an organized home. Disorganized people spend more time looking through their homes for things they have misplaced than organized people spend returning things to their proper places after each use. In the same way, organizing your memory will take time during encoding, but it will save time during retrieval. It will also save time because you won't need to relearn forgotten material.

The trick in organizing is to relate new material to things that you already know. You can organize shopping lists, for example, according to familiar categories. Consider this shopping list: milk, bananas, spinach, oranges, cheese, lettuce, radishes, apples, and butter. You will have an easier time remembering it if you reorganize it according to categories: milk, cheese, butter, bananas, oranges, apples, spinach, lettuce, radishes (see Bower et al., 1969).

You can reduce organization time by using one of many preestablished systems. Memory-aiding systems are called **mnemonic systems.** The "one is a bun" experiment at the beginning of this chapter taught you an effective mnemonic system. You can use the whole system to learn other lists, or you might simply use the image-forming part of the system. To remember that B. F. Skinner did experiments on operant conditioning, for example, you might visualize a hunter skinning wild game on top of a rat cage. Wallace, Turner, and Perkins (1957) found that people can learn to form images for most word pairs in less than 5 seconds and they can remember about 95 percent of 700 pairs after a single exposure to each. Obviously, imagery can be a quick and effective organizing system.

Imagery is used in the **key-word method** of learning foreign vocabulary. Let's use this method to learn that *muleta* means *crutch* in Spanish. We first look for part of the foreign word that sounds like an English word. "Mule" is an obvious choice, so it becomes our key word. We then form an image between the key word and the English equivalent of muleta. We might visualize a mule hobbling along with its front legs propped up on crutches. Figure 6–11 illustrates this image and gives a vocabulary list. Key words are provided so that you can practice the key-word method. You should find that the key-word method will help you with the list and with any foreign language you try to learn (Atkinson, 1975).

Many medical students have learned the twelve cranial nerves by remembering, "On old Olympus' towering top, a fat armed German viewed

FIGURE 6–11

Imagery is used in the key-word method of learning foreign vocabulary. Forming an image like the one shown here will help you remember that *muleta* means *crutch* in Spanish.

Spanish	Key Word	English
Muleta	Mule	Crutch

some hops." The first letter of each word reminds them of the first letter in each nerve: olfactory, optic, oculomotor, trochlear, trigeminal, abducens, facial, auditory vestibular, glossopharyngeal, vagus, spinal accessory, hypoglossal. Similarly, students have learned the Great Lakes by remembering HOMES: Huron, Ontario, Michigan, Erie, Superior. These students are using a memory-aid called *verbal mediation*. They relate new material to **verbal mediators** which are words that have easy-to-remember structures.

Mediators are extremely powerful. In one study, Bower and Clark (1969) asked 84 subjects to use mediators to learn 12 lists of 10 words each. Subjects made up 12 short stories to connect the words in each list. Afterwards they recalled 90 percent of the words. You can make up your own mediators to improve your memory for facts in school.

You should consult *The Memory Book* for other easy-to-use memory aids. You should also make up your own memory aids. Anything you do to organize your memory at the time of encoding will be to your benefit. No matter how good your encoding procedures are, however, you will often find it necessary to review. It is therefore also important to learn special review procedures.

Better Retention through Better Review

How do you review for exams? Reviewing for some people is characterized by repetition. They reread material, paying special attention to parts that they highlighted or underlined the first time. Such selective rereadings are better than no review at all. But if your reviewing tends to be selective repetition, you are not getting as much out of your reviewing hours as you could be. Effective reviewing is characterized by *organization* and *depth of processing*. You should approach your reviewing with a two-part plan.

The first part of your review plan should be to improve upon the organization you started during encoding. The more organization you can get done at first the better, and the more practice you get, the more you will get done. But it is not essential to finish all your organizing during your first study session. You can use review time to put lists in order, to form verbal mediators, and so on. The techniques used during reviews are identical to those used during encoding, except that you can spend more time on them.

The second part of your review plan should be to increase your depth of processing. Earlier we learned that the more deeply we process material, the better we remember it. You can increase your depth of processing of textbooks in three ways:

1. First, list all the main topics (for example, theories, encoding, retention, retrieval, forgetting, applications). Under each topic, write as many subheadings as you can remember. If you don't remember some, look them up. Under each subheading write as many facts as you can remember. Again, look up facts you don't remember. Make sure you see how the facts, subheadings, and main topics relate to one another. You will be writing to yourself, so you need not use complete sentences or even complete words.

2. After you know what is in a passage, think up good test questions for the material and then write out answers. Your questions should cover the material as thoroughly as possible. Your answers should be short notes on key ideas related to each question. You will be processing more deeply because you will be forcing yourself to think about relationships existing in the material. You need not guess the exact questions that will be on an exam. The deeper processing will make you better prepared for any exam.

3. Another way to think about relationships is to criticize the text. Do you think it makes sense to compare human memory with computer memory? What are the strengths and weaknesses of this approach? Does it make sense to distinguish between multiple memory theories and levels of processing theories? Can you think of an experiment that would test the two theories? Does the text contain gaps? Have you learned things in other books that fills in gaps in the present text? Perhaps this chapter failed to mention your favorite memory-aid system. How does your favorite memory aid relate to the ones reviewed here? Critical thinking of this sort will increase your depth of processing and thereby improve your retention.

Reviewing is important outside of school as well. You might be introduced to several people at once during your first day on a new job. You would do well to review their names before going to work the next morning. If you memorized a shopping list, you would do well to review it on the way to the store. Follow the same principles outlined above. Your review should improve your organization and your depth of processing. If you didn't have time to link names with faces or to organize your list, do it during your review. You might improve your depth of processing by having an imaginary conversation, using the names of the people you met. Or, you might imagine making a meal out of the things on your shopping list. If, for some reason, you don't have time to organize or to process deeply during encoding and retention intervals, don't panic. There are things you can do during retrieval to improve your memory.

Retrieving Information Effectively

We learned earlier that retrieval cues aid recall. People remember lists better, for example, when they are given category names during retrieval. We set up retrieval cues in advance when we form images, key words, and mediators during encoding. The payoff for the extra work comes during retrieval, when all we have to do is use our preestablished memory aids. Planning is recommended but you still can use retrieval cues even if you did not develop memory aids in advance.

What do you do when a memory demand catches you completely off guard? Suppose you lose a shopping list, and you did not commit it to memory because you wrote it down. What do you do? Two things will improve your recall in this situation.

1. First, search your memory systematically. Try to think of categories. If you recall one vegetable, try to think of others.
2. Second, try to reestablish the context in which you wrote the list. Lawyers sometimes return witnesses to the scene of a crime because the original context helps them remember details (see Norman, 1973). You may not be able to return to where you wrote a shopping list, but you can at least mentally take yourself back. You might mentally retrace the steps you made when you searched your cupboard to see what you needed.

You can follow these two procedures on exams, too. If a question seems to come out of the blue, search your memory systematically and try to remember the context in which you might have studied the relevant information. Suppose you draw a blank when you are asked to define *mnemonics*. You should try to figure out which main section might have included this word. If you can correctly place it in the section on improving your memory, you will greatly increase your chance of coming up with the definition. Try to remember as much as you can about the session in which you studied the material. What was the first thing you reviewed? What questions did you ask? You still might not remember, but you will

HIGHLIGHT / COMPUTERS IMPROVE EYEWITNESS MEMORY

Police photograph all convicted criminals and keep their "mug shots" on file. Eyewitnesses are often asked to look at hundreds of such mug shots, and sometimes they correctly identify the culprit. Unfortunately, they too often pick out the wrong person. Computers can reduce these errors. For example, an interactive display system has been developed in which a witness and a computer exchange information. This witness-machine system can remember faces better than either the witness or the computer can do alone.

To test his system, Harmon (1973) set up a mug-shot file containing photos of 256 white males between the ages of 20 and 50 (Figure A shows the most and least similar of the photos in the set). For each photo, subjects rated 21 basic facial features, such as hair texture (straight, wavy, curly); chin profile (receding, straight, jutting); or forehead (receding, vertical, or bulging). The computer used the average of these ratings as its "official" description. Armed with this information, the computer was ready to help witnesses.

The computer starts the dialogue by asking the witness to describe the suspect, and the witness chooses one feature to start with—for example, eyebrows. The computer gives a range of numbers that stand for thin, medium, or bushy eyebrows, and the witness selects "1" for "thin." The computer prints the numbers of the five pictures that best fit the description of thin eyebrow weight. The witness then selects the next feature that comes to mind, ear length, and the dialogue continues until the witness cannot remember additional conspicuous features.

At this point, the witness calls for "automatic feature selection," which allows the computer to select features for the witness to rate. The computer selects only those features that discriminate between photos that fit the description given so far. The computer allows the witness to ask 21 questions, but a dialogue may end much sooner than that, because a certain photo turns out to be the only one that comes close to fitting the description.

This system puts the target picture among the top 10 suspects 99 percent of the time and picks the target picture as the number one suspect 70 percent of the time, which is far better than witnesses do on their own. Computers cannot completely overcome witness fallibility, but they can help.

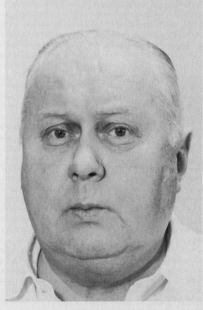

FIGURE A: Most similar and least similar pairs of faces, as determined by computer comparison of facial features.

at least be improving your chances.

Based on the overwhelming success of *The Memory Book*, we can assume that it has helped people. Hopefully, this is one application that you will be able to put to use immediately. Someday you may be able to strengthen your memory further with the help of computers. Computerized memory aids are already available on a limited basis. The Highlight here ("Computers Improve Eyewitness Memory") discusses one example that might have changed the outcome of the Sacco and Vanzetti trial, for it uses computers to improve eyewitness memories.

SUMMARY

1. **Memory,** a system that allows people to retain information over time, is measured with three tests: recall, recognition, and savings.

2. Multiple memory theorists distinguish three kinds of memory: sensory memory, which lasts 1 or 2 seconds; short-term memory, which lasts less than 30 seconds; and long-term memory, which may be permanent. Levels-of-processing theorists reject the distinction between short- and long-term memories as separate memories. They believe that all abstractions are held in the same memory no matter how deep the level of abstraction.

3. **Sensory memory** represents, or **encodes,** information in a form, or code, that is similar to sensations. **Short-term memory** uses verbal codes and other abstract codes to represent only a small part of the original information. **Long-term memory** uses even more abstract codes to represent meaning.

4. People recode, or change the representation of, memories during retention intervals. They group or chunk information in short-term memory. They organize long-term memories according to preexisting categories. They sometimes reconstruct these organizations, including new things that were not part of the original memory.

5. People sometimes fail to recall, or to **retrieve,** information that is present in memory. Retrieval from short-term memory involves a search that takes additional time for each item in memory. Retrieval from long-term memory also involves a search that is often very organized.

6. When a search process locates something in memory, we must decide whether or not it is what we were looking for.

7. **Forgetting,** the inability to remember, may be caused by trace decay and/or by interference. There are two kinds of interference: **proactive,** the interference of things learned earlier; and **retroactive,** the interference of things learned later.

8. You can improve your memory by improving your **attention** and organization when you first encounter new material. You will remember textbook material better, for example, if you identify important ideas and concentrate on them when you read. You should also organize new material by relating it to things you already know.

9. You can improve your memory through effective reviewing. Do not just repeat what you have learned—organize it, test yourself, and criticize it.

10. Suppose a test asks for information that you only skimmed at first and that you never reviewed. You can still improve your memory when you try to retrieve the information for the test. For instance, it will help to search your memory systematically, by thinking of a chapter section by section.

SUGGESTED READINGS

The following books are about the Sacco and Vanzetti case:

FEUERLICHT, R. S. *Justice crucified: The story of Sacco and Vanzetti*. New York: McGraw-Hill, 1977.

FRANKFURTER, F. *The case of Sacco and Vanzetti: A critical analysis of lawyers and laymen*. Boston: Little, Brown, 1927.

LOUIS, J. G., and MORGAN, E. *The legacy of Sacco and Vanzetti*. New York: Harcourt Brace Jovanovich, 1948.

BOURNE, L. E., DOMINOWSKI, R. L., and LOFTUS, E. F. *Cognitive processes*. Englewood Cliffs, N.J.: Prentice-Hall, 1979. The organization of this book is especially compatible with the present chapter. It has separate chapters on encoding, retention, and retrieval, and also relates these basic processes to topics of language, text comprehension, concept formation, problem solving, and reasoning.

LOFTUS, E. *Eyewitness testimony*. Boston: Harvard University Press, 1980. Loftus outlines a theoretical framework for research on perception and memory. She also relates that framework to applications in the legal process.

LORAYNE, H., and LUCAS, J. *The memory book*. New York: Ballantine, 1974. Based on results and principles that have emerged from research laboratories, this is primarily a practical book that outlines many techniques for improving one's memory.

NEISSER, U. *Cognition and reality: Principles and implications of cognitive psychology*. Neisser clearly presents modern theories of schemata and attention. He also makes a strong case for relating principles to applications.

NORMAN, D. A. *Memory and attention: An introduction to human information processing* (2nd ed.). New York: John Wiley, 1976. Undergraduates can understand and enjoy Norman's clear and lively presentation of results and theories on multiple memories and attention.

WICKELGREN, W. A. *Cognitive psychology*. Englewood Cliffs, N.J.: Prentice-Hall, 1979. This book teaches theoretical concepts and principles about how the mind works. It begins with what we already know about the mind through everyday experience, and relates these common experiences to laboratory results.

YARMEY, D. A. *The psychology of eyewitness testimony*. New York: Free Press, 1980. Yarmey has created a much needed resource book for both the psychological and legal professions. He covers all aspects of eyewitness testimony with special emphasis on how people perceive others, memory for faces, and verbal and visual descriptions.

7

Infancy and Childhood

STUDYING DEVELOPMENT
Methods of Studying Development / Theories of Development

PRENATAL DEVELOPMENT
Stages of Prenatal Development / Prenatal Environmental Influences

BIRTH TO 1 YEAR
Physical Growth / Motor Development / Perceptual Development
HIGHLIGHT: The Baby as Interior Decorator

CHILDHOOD
Physical Growth / Cognitive Development / Language Development
HIGHLIGHT: Are Human Language Abilities Unique?
Personality and Social Development

SUMMARY / SUGGESTED READINGS

S pringtime means rebirth. Flowers, trees, and grass come back to life after lying dormant all winter. The sun becomes noticeably brighter and it shines for a longer period each day. Everywhere there is the promise of new life. Most parents realize that promise to its fullest when they themselves give birth to a child. But this was not so with the birth of Genie in the spring of 1956. She was her parents' second daughter and their fourth child within 5 years. The fates of her sister and brother forebode a dim future for Genie.

Genie's sister was born after her parents had been married for 5 years. Her father, who was adamant about not having children, couldn't stand his new daughter's crying, so he put her in the garage where he couldn't hear her; she died of pneumonia and overexposure at the age of 2½ months.

Genie's first brother was born a year later, but died when he was 2 days old, allegedly from choking on his own mucus. Genie's second brother was born 3 years later. His father allowed him in the house, but forced the child's mother to keep him quiet. The boy was late to walk and talk and was not toilet-trained at 3 years of age, when his grandmother started to care for him in her home. The boy thrived under his grandmother's care and returned home toilet-trained and in much better developmental condition.

Genie was born by Caesarean section, as were her brothers and sisters. She received a blood transfusion the day after her birth because of an inherited blood condition, which her brothers had also had. She recovered nicely from the transfusion and within 3 months she grew from 7 pounds, 1¼ ounces, to 12 pounds, 2¼ ounces. At 11 months she was underweight for her age, but otherwise she seemed to be in good shape. Her teeth development was normal, she could sit alone, and she was alert. At 14 months, Genie developed an acute respiratory illness and was taken to a physician who noticed that she was listless and unresponsive. The doctor reported that it was difficult to assess her development because of her illness, but he suggested that she might show signs of retardation. At 20 months Genie's grandmother, who had helped the little girl's brother, died. Genie's life took a tragic turn for the worse shortly after that.

Genie's father moved his family into his mother's home following her death and isolated them from the outside world. Genie's mother was fast becoming blind and was finding it difficult to care for her baby, so the father confined Genie to a small bedroom. During the day, he harnessed her to an infant's potty seat. The harness allowed Genie to move only her hands, fingers, feet, and toes. At night, when he didn't forget, he put her in a crib containing a sleeping bag, which was specially designed to hold her arms stationary. This extreme confinement continued for the next 12 years!

Most of the time Genie saw only her crib and potty chair, dirty salmon-colored walls, a bare ceiling light bulb, a wall of closets, a wall with a closed door leading to the rest of the house, and two covered windows. Gaps at the bottom of the windows allowed her to see the sky out of one and the side of a neighbor's house out of the other. Occasionally, Genie was allowed to play with two plastic raincoats, a TV magazine, a cottage-cheese container, or empty spools.

Genie was not allowed to make any noise. In fact, her father had a large piece of wood that he beat her with whenever she was noisy. Genie's father never spoke to her, even to scold her. Instead, he barked and growled at her like a dog. He growled and bared his teeth to threaten her. He didn't bite, but he did grow his nails long so that he could scratch. He taught his son to treat Genie in the same way, and gradually the brother became her primary caretaker, feeding her cereals, baby food, and an occasional soft-boiled egg.

Genie's father thought that his daughter would die before she was 12. He therefore told his wife that she could seek help for Genie if she lived longer than that. The mother waited until Genie was 13½ years old before she took any action. She finally escaped with Genie, who was taken into police custody shortly after. The police brought charges against the parents, and on the day of the trial, Genie's father killed himself. He left a note, stating, "The world will never understand."

Genie was admitted to a hospital in the winter of 1970 suffering from extreme malnutrition. At the age of 13 years, 7 months, she weighed 59 pounds and was 54 inches long. Her hair was sparse and stringy. She could not stand erect, could not straighten her arms and legs, and could not walk more than about 10 feet, which she did by swaying from side to side while shuffling her feet. She could not chew and she swallowed with difficulty. She could not control her feces or urine. She salivated copiously and she spit often. She suppressed almost all vocalization. Even during temper tantrums she remained silent while flailing about, scratching, spitting, and blowing her nose. She demonstrated interest in people by maintaining eye contact, but she did not speak except for a few words that she heard and imitated when she first arrived at the hospital. As winter passed, Genie's strength returned and spring brought hope of a new life.

The hospital transferred Genie to a rehabilitation center where she had a greater opportunity to interact with a warm, loving staff. She gained weight, grew taller, stood more erect, and walked more steadily. In fact, before summer had begun she was able to take long walks during which her adult companions tired out long before she did.

Genie also began to grow socially. At first she responded cooly and passively to everyone. But gradually she developed affectionate relationships with several adults, including her mother, who visited her twice a week, and Dr. James Kent, who supervised her activities. She whooped with delight when she saw her favorite people and she protested when they left. She seemed to keep track of time because she never protested after her mother's first weekly visit, but she always did after her second. When Dr. Kent tried to leave, she would grab his hand and try to pull him to sit down. Generally, however, her fussing when people left was mild in comparison to the ecstatic greeting she gave when they arrived.

Genie's curiosity about her new world steadily increased. She became especially fond of daily outings to stores, homes, office buildings, and so on. Once she visited a place, she could direct Dr. Kent back to it by pointing. When she arrived, she could immediately locate things she wanted to see again. Genie relaxed on the passenger's side of the seat when Dr. Kent drove along a familiar route. She scooted over in the seat, grabbed his hand, and worriedly scanned her surroundings, however, when he turned onto an unfamiliar road.

Genie encountered many patients and sensitive people during her outings. A butcher at a supermarket, for instance, noticed Genie's great interest for the meat counter. He watched her looking at packages of meat for a long time on several occasions. One day he held out a piece of unwrapped meat for her to touch and smell. On later visits he brought out bones, fish, chicken, and many kinds of meat for her to examine as long as she wished. He accepted her on her own terms without knowing anything about her, and he gave to her without asking anything in return, not even a greeting.

Genie began to internalize the caring she experienced from others. On one occasion, a teacher at the rehabilitation center asked a child who had two balloons how many he had. He said, "Three." Genie looked startled and gave him one of her balloons. This event revealed not only Genie's caring for another, but also her understanding of language. Relative to her first coming into the world she was obviously behind; relative to her second coming, she was making steady progress.

Genie has continued to progress. In fact, her mental age has increased one year for each year that she has been free to experience the world. Dr. Susan Curtiss has carefully observed Genie's development. In 1977 she summarized Genie's progress as follows: "My work with Genie continues, and Genie continues to change, becoming a fuller person, realizing more of her human potential. By the time this work is read, she may have developed far beyond what is described here. That is my hope—that I will not be able to keep up with her, that she will have the last word" (Curtiss, 1977, p. 42).

STUDYING DEVELOPMENT

Human development is a process by which the genes that we inherit from our parents come to be expressed as specific physical and behavioral characteristics. Development is controlled by a continuous interaction between *heredity* and *environment*. Genie, for example, inherited genes that together with her environment determined the characteristics that she developed.

The relative influence of heredity and environment varied from characteristic to characteristic. Heredity dominated to control the development of Genie's blood condition at birth, as well as other physical characteristics such as skin, hair, and eye color. Genie's extremely deprived environment played a major role in determining the development of her bent-over posture, strange eating habits, and limited language ability. Genie advanced developmentally when she entered a normal environment. Today, heredity and environment continue to work together to determine her development.

Methods of Studying Development

Susan Curtiss (1977) and other psychologists studied Genie for many years. They interviewed her mother and hospital staff. They made videotapes and audiotapes of her several times a week for the first year and frequently after that. They repeatedly administered about 100 different psychological tests, and they saved her many drawings, which she loved to produce. Genie entered the hospital a severely underdeveloped human being. Throughout the following years psychologists sought any clues that could be used to help Genie tap her human potential. They assisted and observed as Genie grew physically and emotionally stronger and as she became more knowledgeable in social and psychological aspects of normal human life. While Genie's welfare always remained of central importance, psychologists also brought their observations to bear on issues of general concern, such as the relationship between cognitive development and language development. Can one legitimately formulate general principles based upon observations of only one person? Surely there are problems in doing so, especially when circumstances are as unusual as Genie's. But are there any better ways? Are there any completely trustworthy ways to study development?

Longitudinal versus Cross-Sectional Research. The study of Genie is an example of **longitudinal research,** in which investigators periodically test the same person or group of people over a period of time. Another approach is **cross-sectional research,** in which investigators compare the responses of different people of different ages. Each has both advantages and disadvantages:

1. *Measuring stability of behavior* is a main advantage of longitudinal research. Kagan and Moss (1962) studied the same people from birth to the twenties. They found, for example, that children who were passive and dependent at age 6 were also that way as adults. Cross-sectional research cannot examine stability, because it does not measure the same people at different ages.

2. *Cultural and historical experiences* are better controlled by longitudinal research, because investigators can keep track of many aspects of a person's experience. Cross-sectional studies compare people who may have had very different experiences. Suppose you did a cross-sectional study in 1960 to compare thriftiness of 10-, 20-, and 30-year-olds. These people grew up in the 1950s, 1940s, and

1930s respectively. You would wonder, therefore, if differences between groups existed because of different ages or because of different early experiences. Being raised during the economic depression of the 1930s was surely very different from being raised during the booming economy of the 1950s.

3. *Lack of practicality* is a major disadvantage of longitudinal designs. It takes 20 years to do a longitudinal study on people from birth to 20 years old, and keeping track of people for that long is very expensive. You could do a cross-sectional study on the same age range in about a month for much less money.

4. *Loss of subjects* is another disadvantage of longitudinal designs. People die, move away, or quit because they are tired of the experiment. Such losses can greatly restrict your ability to generalize from the results. The only ones left to study might be those who were not mobile and who were patient enough to see your experiment through. Cross-sectional studies reduce this problem by collecting data over a short period.

5. *Flexibility* is another consideration that weighs against longitudinal research, since it must use the same tests over many years in order to provide comparable measures between ages. If improved tests are developed, you cannot go back in time to give the new test to your subjects at earlier years. You would have to continue to use the old test with which you took original measures, or else you would lose the ability to compare different ages. Cross-sectional research allows you to try various measures until an appropriate one is found, and you are always free to use the most up-to-date tests.

No single design is best for every purpose; researchers must select the right design for studying the problem at hand. Ideally, researchers strive to apply both longitudinal and cross-sectional designs to the same problems. They can be more certain that they are on the right track when results from both designs agree. Both designs have been valuable in testing theories of development, which we will discuss in the next section.

Theories of Development

Two kinds of theories have guided the study of development. One theory, called *nativism*, emphasizes the role of heredity in the development of mind and behavior. Thus, using perception as an example, nativism would say that infants are born with innate capacities to experience the world pretty much as adults do. Extreme nativism holds that development is nothing more than **maturation,** which is the unfolding of genetically determined abilities. Another theory, called *empiricism*, holds that experience is the source of all knowledge. Thus, in the example of perception, this theory would state that newborns experience the world as very confusing until they learn to perceive as adults do. Extreme empiricism holds that all development is determined by learning through experience.

Neither extreme theory can explain a phenomenon called a **critical period,** which is a stage of development during which an organism must have certain experiences or else it will not develop normally. Researchers demonstrated critical periods experimentally by carefully suturing closed the eyelids of kittens to deprive them of visual stimulation (Hubel and Wiesel, 1970). They varied the age of the kittens at the beginning of deprivation and they manipulated the length of deprivation. The kittens learned to get along quite well while they were deprived. But, depending on the timing, deprivation sometimes caused permanent damage to the kittens' visual system. Hubel and Wiesel tested development of the visual cortex after deprivation by placing tiny electrodes in cells of anesthetized kittens (see Chapter 2). Deprivation damaged cortical cells only if it came between the fourth and twelfth week of life. Deprivation in kittens younger than 4 weeks caused no noticeable damage, nor did deprivation in kittens older than 12 weeks, even if it lasted for months. In contrast, 3 to 4 days of deprivation during the fourth and fifth week of life caused irreversible damage. Weeks 4 through 12 bound a critical period during which kittens must have visual experience or else their visual system will not develop normally.

We cannot explain critical periods without assuming that heredity (maturation) and environment (learning) interact. Genes regulate a timetable that determines the critical period for developing cortical cells. The environment must then provide certain experiences or development will be knocked off track. Traits that interest psychologists, such as intelligence, personality, and emotions, are generally influenced by both heredity and environment. We will therefore pay attention to both factors when we follow the course of human development in this and the next chapter.

PRENATAL DEVELOPMENT

Prenatal refers to the 9-month period of development before birth. Mothers carry the developing organism in a hollow muscular organ called the **uterus** or **womb.** In this section we will outline stages of normal prenatal development and discuss environmental forces that affect that development.

Stages of Prenatal Development

We have very little firsthand information about Genie's prenatal development, but we can assume from her healthy condition at birth that it was normal. She grew from a microscopic cell through a naturally determined sequence into a 7 pound, 1¼ ounce baby. Let's look at some of the highlights of this stage of development.

Period of the Ovum.   During the first 2 weeks of prenatal development the organism is called an **ovum.** A fertilized ovum, or zygote, immediately divides, forming new cells that cluster together in a ball. The cell ball grows to about the size of a poppie seed and implants itself in the wall of the womb.

Period of the Embryo.   From the third week through the eighth week the organism is called an **embryo.** This period is characterized by extremely rapid growth, in which the embryo grows to a weight of about 1 ounce and is about 1 inch long. By that time, it is dependent on the **placenta,** which is a special filter that allows for the exchange of food and waste with its mother. The embryo develops internal organs, limbs with separate fingers and toes, a face with a prominent nose, and external sex organs (although it is difficult to distinguish males from females at the end of the second month).

Period of the Fetus.   From the third month through birth the organism is called a **fetus.** The following is a breakdown of this period, month by month:

1. By the end of the third month, a heart starts pumping blood through the fetus, and its beat can be heard by a stethoscope. Teeth begin to develop, and males can be distinguished from females.
2. A mother often feels fetal movement during the fourth month. Weight increases to nearly half a pound, and the fetus is about 8

These photos show a fertilized ovum (top left), an embryo at 5 weeks (top right), and a fetus at 12 and 18 weeks (middle and bottom photos).

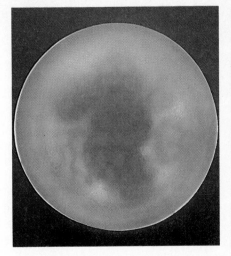
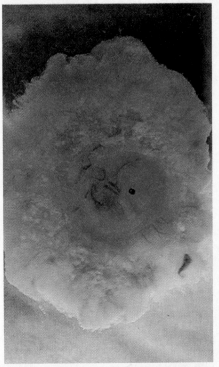
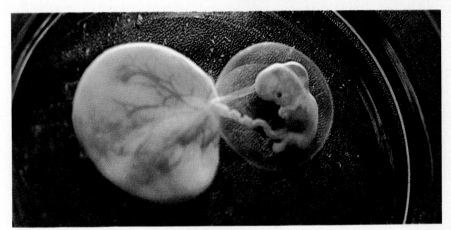
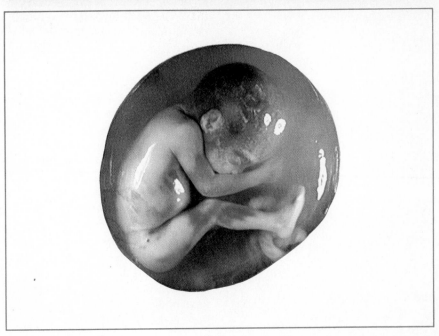

inches long. He or she develops eyebrows, eyelashes, fingerprints, and footprints.

3. During the fifth month the fetus gains about half a pound and grows about 4 inches longer; sucking, swallowing, and hiccoughing reflexes develop.

4. The sixth month adds 1 additional pound and about 2 inches in length. The skin is wrinkled with the first evidence of fat beginning just beneath the skin. Eyes are well developed and they open and close.

5. After 7 months, the fetus reaches the *age of viability*, a time at which the fetus might survive if born prematurely. At this important point, the fetus is about 16 inches long and weighs about 3 pounds, with more fat under his or her skin.

6. Fat continues to develop during the eighth month and the skin loses some of its wrinkles. The fetus gains about 2 pounds and grows another 2 inches longer. The arms and legs move about strenuously, often kicking, or punching the uterine wall. Mothers feel this movement inside them, and others can feel it by placing a hand over the uterus. The fetus will probably survive if it is born after the eight month.

7. The fetus is fully prepared for birth after the ninth month.

Average birth weight is about 7 pounds, and average length is about 20 inches. Genes determine birth size, for the most part. Mothers who eat more because they are "eating for two" find that the extra food is not used by the baby, but is stored in the mother's body as fat. Mothers do have to be careful about what they eat and drink, however, as we shall see in the next section.

Prenatal Environmental Influences

Heredity and environment start interacting long before birth. A host of environmental influences can prevent an unborn infant from achieving its full inherited potential. Mothers who take the time to learn some fundamental precautions can provide an optimal prenatal environment for their baby. Let's go over some of the major environmental influences in prenatal development.

Nutrition. A good diet is essential for healthy fetal development, including brain development. A baby's brain can be 60 percent smaller than normal at birth if he or she is seriously malnourished during prenatal development (Wyden, 1971). Doctors emphasize adequate amounts of protein in a pregnant woman's diet and they prescribe iron and vitamin supplements.

Diseases. Many diseases, including heart disease, diabetes, and hypertension, have a bad effect on fetal development. Mothers are warned to avoid exposure to German measles during early pregnancy; it can cause many birth defects, including impaired vision and hearing, heart malformation, and mental retardation. *Venereal diseases*, which are contagious diseases that are transmitted by sexual intercourse, also have tragic effects. One venereal disease, *syphilis*, can infect the fetus carried by a woman with the disease, usually causing both physical and mental defects. Fetal infection can be prevented, however, if the mother's infection is successfully treated by the fifth month of pregnancy.

Drugs. Drugs taken by the mother during pregnancy can have disastrous effects on fetal development. A well-known example is the use of *thalidomide*, a drug that had been prescribed to calm nervousness (it has been taken off the market). Its use during pregnancy caused serious developmental deformities of the baby's limbs. Many other drugs are dangerous during pregnancy—even aspirin in high doses can cause fetal blood

TABLE 7-1: The Apgar Scoring Method

Sign	0	1	2
Heart Rate	Absent	Below 100	Over 100
Respiratory Effort	Absent	Minimal; Weak Cry	Good; Strong Cry
Muscle Tone	Limp	Some Flexion of Extremities	Active Motion; Extremities Well Flexed
Reflex Irritability (response to stimulation on sole of foot)	No Response	Grimace	Cry
Color	Blue or Pale	Body Pink; Extremities Blue	Pink

Source: Apgar (1953).

disorders. Nicotine and alcohol also harm fetal development. Both lead to higher rates of abortions, premature births, and low birthweight. Researchers have also found abnormal behavior patterns in the offspring of moderate drinkers (Landesman-Dwyar, Keller, and Streissguth, 1977).

Delivery Complications. Most births (over 90 percent) occur without serious complications, but sometimes infants get injured during the birth process. The most serious injuries involve too much pressure on the brain and too little oxygen being supplied to the brain. These disorders occur during abnormal deliveries, when the head is squeezed too hard or when the baby is cut off from the placenta's nourishment too soon. Both of these factors can cause neurological damage leading to mental deficiencies (Pasamanick and Lilienfeld, 1955). Such injuries can be detected shortly after birth. Many hospitals assess the condition of newborns with the Apgar scoring system, which is shown and described in Table 7-1. Low Apgar scores indicate possible neurological damage.

This discussion of environmental factors can create a misleading impression that the odds are against us. In fact, the odds are overwhelmingly in our favor. Our species would not have survived if we were unlikely to produce healthy offspring, so the odds have been in our favor for some time. The odds are even greater today, because doctors are continually improving their ability to prevent, detect, and correct prenatal problems. Most parents who enter hospitals to have babies leave for home several days later to assume full care of a healthy infant. Let's examine some of the many developmental changes that take place during the first year of that infant's life.

BIRTH TO 1 YEAR

Susan Curtiss was able to get a brief sketch of Genie's first year from medical records and interviews with her mother. In this section, we will review what little information we have about Genie's early physical, motor, and perceptual development. We will analyze normal patterns of development in detail in order to establish a standard for comparison with Genie. We will also discuss the extent to which heredity and environment influence each aspect of development.

Physical Growth

Genie's isolation from 20 months of age to 13½ years of age accounts for much of her poor development. There is some evidence, however, that

At the age of 12 months, the average height for an infant is 30 inches and the average weight is 22 pounds (girls tend to weigh slightly less than boys in the first year).

she had already started to fall behind during her first year.

Height and Weight. There is a simple rule for height at this stage: An infant grows about 1 inch per month in the first 6 months and about ½ inch per month in the next 6 months. Susan Curtiss reported Genie's height as 25½ inches tall at 6 months, which is normal.

Genie's weight was not normal, however. It was normal at birth, but it fell far below average by 11 months. She should have gained 5 to 7 ounces a week during the first 6 months and 3 to 5 ounces a week during the second 6 months. She therefore should have weighed about 20 to 21 pounds at 11 months, but she only weighed 17 pounds. Three or four pounds below average may not seem like much, but it could be reason for concern when you consider that less than 15 percent of all children are that far below average after 11 months. A reason for Genie's falling behind was suggested by her mother, who reported that Genie was reluctant to chew and that she would not eat solid foods, even moderately soft foods specially prepared for infants. Low weight and poor eating habits suggest that Genie might not have had adequate nutrition during her first year.

Other aspects of physical development also follow timetables that provide valuable frames of reference. Psychologists refer to normal patterns to detect deviant cases and to learn when infants are likely to be physically able to interact with their environments in particular ways. They might want to know, for example, when an infant's muscles and bones are strong enough for the infant to explore its environment.

Muscle and Bone Growth. An infant's bones are soft at birth, and they harden at different rates. Hand and wrist bones harden early, making it possible for babies to pick up objects and move them around at about 4 or 5 months of age. Skull bones develop more slowly. Newborns have "soft spots" on their heads where skull bone does not cover the brain. These spots disappear over the first 2 years as the skull bone gradually grows.

Babies are born with a complete set of muscle fibers. They only gradually learn how to use their muscles, however, to control their movements. Development of muscle control is so important that we will devote a separate section to it later on in the chapter, when we discuss development in childhood.

The Nervous System. Muscle development serves as an interesting contrast to neural development, which we discussed in Chapter 2. At birth, infants have every muscle they will ever have, and muscles grow and develop for a long time, especially during teenage years. In contrast, infants are born with an incomplete nervous system, but it develops very rapidly, finishing its growth sometime between the second and fourth year. This rapid growth makes the first several years very important in neural development.

The nervous system at birth is "unfinished" in three ways:

1. Parts of the brain that are present at birth are smaller than they will be later in life. The brain is much nearer to its final size, however, than are muscles and other structures.
2. A newborn's cortex is very underdeveloped. During the first year, new cortical cells are formed, cells become larger, and new interconnections are formed between cells. Parts of the cortex develop at different rates. Areas controlling hearing and seeing develop within 6 months, as do areas controlling movement of the head, upper trunk, arms, and hands. Areas controlling movement of the lower trunk and legs develop slowly over almost 2 years. Rosenzweig (1966) found that raising rats in enriched environments (with "toys"—wheels, ladders, platforms, and so on) greatly increases cortical development.

3. Newborns lack some important nerve coverings called *myelin sheaths*, which we discussed in Chapter 2. Development of myelin sheaths, a process called myelinization, determines control over body parts. For instance, a child has poor control over lower body parts until spinal cord myelinization reaches a critical stage at about 2 years of age.

The nervous system is most vulnerable to diseases, malnutrition, and other environmental influences while it is developing. The fact that Genie may have been malnourished during her first year raises the possibility that she could have suffered permanent neural damage because of it.

Motor Development

Motor development refers to a baby's growing ability to control muscles in order to move around and to manipulate objects. We do not know much about Genie's early motor development. What we know suggests that she was not too far behind schedule, however. Her doctor noticed that she could hold her head steady at her 4-month checkup, make hand-to-mouth movements at her 5-month checkup, and sit alone at her 11-month checkup. To make a proper evaluation, we would need much more information about both her reflexive movements and her voluntary movements, as described in the next sections.

Reflexive Movements. Infants are born with many reflexes, which are movements that are made automatically in response to a stimulus. The presence or absence of reflexes can indicate normal or abnormal development. Some reflexes are protective, such as *coughing* and *sneezing*, which clear the respiratory tract. Other reflexes are involved with eating. The rooting reflex causes infants to turn their head toward anything that touches their cheek. It helps in feeding because it moves the mouth closer to a nipple. The sucking reflex causes sucking when anything touches the lips. It is, of course, essential for getting milk from a breast or bottle. Four other common reflexes are:

1. The grasp reflex, which causes infants to close their fingers tightly around an object that touches their palm (thumbs do not respond in this reflex). An infant's grip is so strong that you can insert your index fingers into a newborn's palms and then lift the baby into a standing position. The reflex is present at birth, but disappears at about 6 months after conscious control takes over grasping.
2. The dancing reflex, which causes babies to prance with their legs in a "tip-toe" stepping motion when they are held upright with feet touching a surface. (Perhaps there is some truth to the saying that we are "born to boogie.") This reflex is usually no longer seen by the seventh or eighth month.
3. The Moro reflex or startle reflex, which causes a motor reaction of infants' legs, arms, and trunk in response to a sudden loud noise or loss of support. You can observe it best by suddenly slapping a baby's mattress. The newborn will draw up his or her legs with the soles of the feet turned toward each other. The arms will stretch out into an embracing position, and the back will arch. This reflex disappears by the fifth month.
4. The tonic neck reflex, which causes infants who are on their back to move their arms and legs into a "fencing" position when the head is turned to one side. Newborns extend the arm and leg on the side that they are facing and draw up the other arm and leg into a flexed position. This reflex disappears by the fourth month.

The lack of any of these reflexes at birth can mean that there is an abnormality in the nervous system. Continuation of these reflexes for too long after they should have disappeared can also be a sign of abnormal neural development.

Voluntary Movements. A major accomplishment in the first year of life is the replacement of motor reflexes with voluntary motor control. This achievement greatly increases an infant's ability to explore its environment. A baby begins to successfully reach for and grasp objects at about 4 or 5 months of age. As noted, 1-year-olds like to feed themselves with their fingers, and they are able to scribble with a crayon.

Figure 7-1 summarizes landmark achievements in a baby's ability to move around. Some infants reach each stage ahead of others, as can be

(Top, right) The sucking reflex causes the baby to suck when anything touches the lips.
(Bottom, left) In the tonic neck reflex, when the head is turned to one side, infants who are lying on their back move their arms and legs into a "fencing" position.
(Bottom, right) The grasp reflex causes infants to close their fingers tightly around anything that touches their palm.

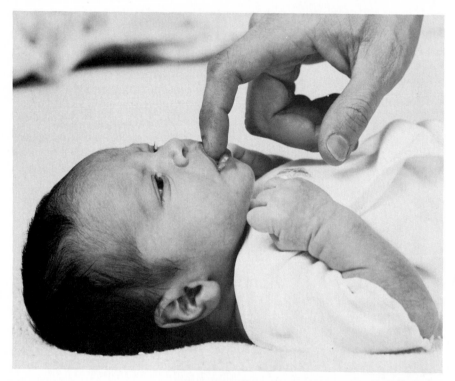

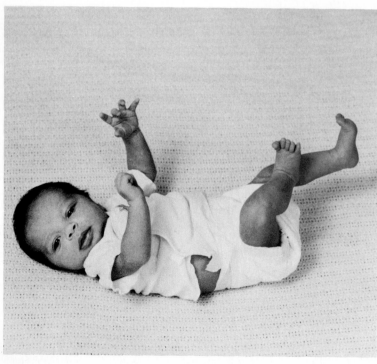

FIGURE 7–1

This diagram shows some landmarks in an infant's ability to move around. Each line shows the age range, and the "X" shows the average age, at which the achievement occurs. (Frankenburg and Dodds, 1967)

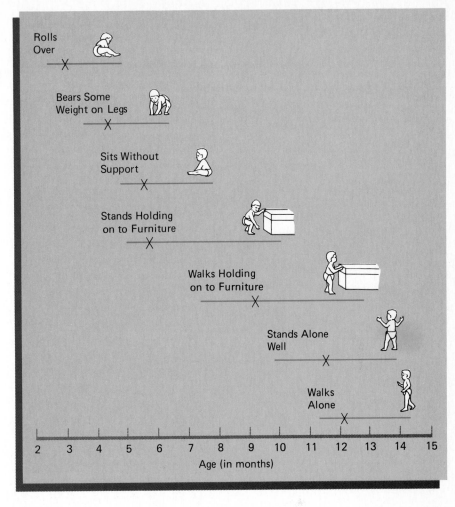

Rolls Over

Bears Some Weight on Legs

Sits Without Support

Stands Holding on to Furniture

Walks Holding on to Furniture

Stands Alone Well

Walks Alone

Age (in months)

seen in the figure. Most babies learn to roll over sometime between the second and fifth month. They sit alone between the fifth and eighth month. They stand alone between the tenth and thirteenth month, and many walk alone by the end of their first year.

Perceptual Development

Perceptual development involves the increases in one's ability to experience the world. Chapter 3 introduced many aspects of sensation and perception, almost all of which develop mostly during the infant's first year. Unfortunately, we do not know any details about Genie's perceptual development. The questions we would ask about her perception are the same as those we might ask about infants in general: Do babies see depth? Can they tell the difference between a large object that is far away and a small one that is close? What do babies like to look at?

Visual Cliff Experiments.   Walk and Gibson (1961) designed a clever device for studying infant depth perception. Their apparatus, which is called a **visual cliff,** consists of a special table divided into three parts (Figure 7-2). A mother places her baby on a solid board in the center and then she encourages the infant to crawl to one side or the other. The "visual cliff" side has a solid surface covered with a checkered pattern about 4 feet below the center board. It also has a strong glass surface about 1 inch below the board. The other side has a solid surface covered with a checkered pattern about 1 inch below the center board.

Infants between the ages of 6 and 12 months refuse to cross the visual cliff despite their mother's encouragement. In contrast, they eagerly cross

FIGURE 7–2

This device, called a "visual cliff," is used for studying depth perception in infants.

the other side. Apparently, infants see depth, but a warning is in order. Parents should not place infants who can crawl on high beds or other high surfaces. Visual cliff experiments show that babies try to avoid a drop-off, but the same experiments show that they are very clumsy—many of the 36 babies that Gibson and Walk tested would have fallen over the cliff if glass hadn't been there. A common mistake was to back off of the "cliff" while looking in the other direction.

Gibson and Walk showed that chicks and lambs avoid the visual side of the cliff 1 day after birth. Experimenters cannot give humans the crawling test at such a young age, because human babies do not crawl until they are at least 4 months old and usually older. Other researchers, however, figured out a way to test younger humans (Campos, Langer, and Krowitz 1970). They placed 1½-month-old babies over each side of the cliff and measured heart rate. They found changes in heart rates when babies were placed over the visual cliff, suggesting that babies see depth long before they learn to crawl.

Reaching Experiments.   Researchers also observe reaching behavior to study the perceptual world of infants. In one experiment, Bruner and Koslowski (1972) observed reaching to study infant size perception.

If you were asked to grasp a tennis ball held 4 or 5 inches in front of your eyes, you would extend your hands, bringing them closer together and closing them around the ball. If a large beach ball were held in the same position, you would extend your arms, bringing them farther apart and wrapping them around the ball. Before you would begin either movement, you would see that one ball was small and the other large, and you would know what movements were needed to grasp them. What do babies do in this situation? In one study, infants (between 10 and 22 weeks old) looked at a small ball or a large ball placed within arm's reach (Bruner and Koslowski, 1972). The main finding was that babies who had not yet learned to reach and to manipulate objects nevertheless showed size discrimination. They brought their hands to the center and moved them while they were at the center, doing so more often when they saw the small ball. They made more forward sweeps with their arms spread apart when they saw the large ball. Apparently, then, they could see that one ball was small and the other large, and were responding to this.

The babies seemed uncoordinated because they did not order their movements in the proper sequence; they often brought their hands to center and closed them before they extended their arms, for instance. This lack of coordination caused some theorists to argue that babies are confused by what they see. They cannot see size, they argued, until they add to visual information the knowledge they gain from manipulating objects (see Hochberg, 1978). Bruner and Koslowski's experiment is contrary to this theory because the experiment suggests that babies see size *before* they learn to manipulate objects. They are uncoordinated *not* because they are visually confused, but because they do not yet know how to control the order of their arm movements.

In earlier decades, limited response capabilities in infants led many to assume that babies see a "blooming, buzzing confusion." Today, opinions are changing. Modern experiments suggest that babies see more than we had previously realized. Parents can directly apply research findings on the perceptual world of infants, as indicated in the accompanying Highlight, "The Baby as Interior Decorator."

A baby's first year is also important for cognitive development as well as for social and personality development. Infants lay a foundation in these developmental areas upon which they build in following years. Most theories in these areas tie together the first year with later years of development, so we will take up these fascinating aspects of development in our next section on childhood.

HIGHLIGHT / THE BABY AS INTERIOR DECORATOR

What would infants ask for if they could choose decorations for their room? Would pastel blues and pinks remain in vogue for nurseries if infants could choose for themselves? What about the mobiles that are found in most nurseries? Would they go or stay? Research into the perceptual world of infants suggests answers to these questions.

"LOOKING BOX" EXPERIMENTS

An infant cannot directly answer our questions about its experiences. As a result, the perceptual world of infants remained a mystery until the middle of the 1950s, when Robert L. Fantz showed that psychologists can coax even a newborn into answering questions about what it sees (Fantz, 1963).

Fantz used a "looking box" to peek into the perceptual world of infants. The photo below shows a looking box in which an infant is placed on its back. Pads beside the head keep the eyes directed upward toward two pictures on the ceiling of the box. The pictures are 2 or 3 feet from the infant. An experimenter can determine which picture the infant is looking at by peering through a peephole in the top of the box. Whatever the baby looks at is reflected in the center of its pupil.

Fantz used a looking box to establish that babies have definite preferences in what they choose to look at. Fantz's results and those from other laboratories indicate the following looking preferences:

1. Infants as young as 1 week old prefer pattern pictures over unpatterned ones (Greenbert and O'Donnell, 1972).
2. Infants as young as 2 months prefer curved lines over straight ones (Ruff and Birch, 1974).
3. Infants as young as 2 months prefer bright colors to pastels (Haith and Campos, 1977; Schaller, 1975).
4. Infants as young as 4 days old prefer a human face over an

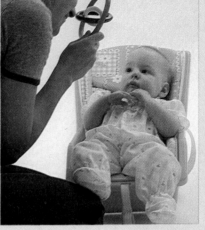

equally complex pattern (Fantz, 1963).
5. Newborns and older infants prefer things that move over things that don't (Carpenter, 1974; Gregg, Clifton, and Haith, 1976).

So what do looking preferences suggest about decor preferences? The results suggest that we might see some changes if babies could pick their own decorations. The popular pastels would be replaced by bright colors and pictures of faces would be all the rage. Some popular decorations would remain, however. Mobiles, for instance, would probably stay, because infants enjoy moving objects. Furthermore, since infants enjoy brightly colored, curved lines, the increasing popularity of rainbow decorations would be cheered.

Parents need not wait for their own children to speak up. Representative infants have been allowed to choose in carefully controlled experiments. Although silent, the infants cast their votes decidedly with their eyes. This is one research result to which parents might want to attend before their own children are old enough to speak for themselves.

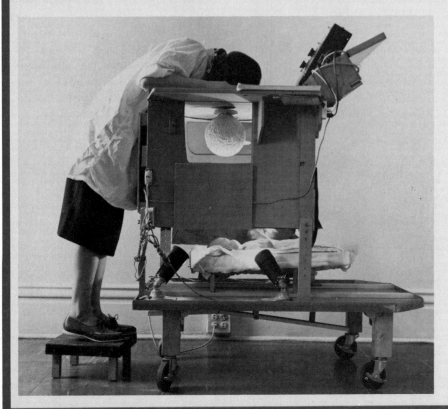

CHILDHOOD

Genie spent her childhood years in isolation. She therefore fell far behind on many charactersitics that usually develop between the second and thirteenth years. She fell behind in areas of physical growth, cognition, language, personality, and social development. Susan Curtiss and other psychologists carefully observed Genie's development in these areas after she entered a supportive environment. We can therefore compare Genie's development to normal patterns, which we will discuss in detail. We will continue to evaluate the extent to which heredity and environment influence development.

Physical Growth

We don't know Genie's growth rate during her isolation, but we know that her height (54 inches) and weight (59 pounds) were far below average by the end of her childhood. Children grow rapidly during their first year, as we saw. This rapid growth rate continues through the second year, and then it becomes slower until the end of childhood, when it increases again. Children usually grow about 3 inches and gain about 5 pounds per year between their third birthday and the end of childhood. A typical 13½-year-old girl is about 62 inches tall and about 104 pounds (Lowrey, 1978). Parents need not worry when their children differ from these averages, because "normal" childhood heights and weights cover a wide range. Genie was alarmingly below the normal range, however.

Cognitive Development

Cognitive development involves changes in how children understand and think about their world as they grow older. This section will review evidence that children understand and think about their world in qualitatively different ways as they pass through various stages of cognitive development. The data on normal development provide a frame of reference for evaluating abnormalities. After considering normal patterns of development, for instance, we will be in a better position to evaluate Genie's cognitive development. She obviously had limited knowledge when she came out of isolation. But did she understand and think about the world in a vastly different way from other people her age?

Historical Overview.   As we discussed in Chapter 1, American behaviorists in the early years limited their research to discovering relationships between stimulus and observable responses. Their theories held that learning at all ages can be explained without considering what goes on in a person's mind. In contrast, Jean Piaget, a Swiss scientist, made observations precisely in order to figure out what goes on in a child's mind. He argued that: (1) we cannot understand learning without understanding thinking, and (2) that children think differently from adults. We will cover his methods and theories in detail, because they had a tremendous impact on modern psychology.

Piaget's Approach.   Piaget used open questioning sessions with his own three children and with other children to find out how they interpreted objects and events in the world around them. He concluded that children of the same age make similar incorrect responses, which are different from errors made by both older and younger children. This pattern of errors suggested that children develop qualitatively different ways of organizing and responding to experiences. He used the term schema to refer to a mental structure that organizes responses to experiences. He proposed that newborns inherit *schemata* (plural of *schema*), which are simple reaction patterns and reflexes, such as a sucking schema and a grasping schema. Gradually, these independent schema become integrated through the process of *organization*, an inherited predisposition to organize simple schema into higher-order ones. A higher-order schema would control a response pattern for grasping a bottle, bringing it to the mouth, and drinking it, for example.

A child also inherits two other processes: (1) **assimilation**, which is the process of responding in a way that fits existing schema; and (2) **accommodation**, which is the process of adjusting a schema to fit environmental demands. Consider a baby with a schema to control bringing a bottle to his or her mouth. Suppose a bottle was placed behind a plexiglass barrier. The barrier allowed the baby to see the bottle, but did not allow the baby to reach the bottle directly. Assimilation would be shown if the baby responded according to its existing schema, that is, if the baby tried to reach directly for the bottle. Accommodation would be shown if the baby changed its schema by reaching around the barrier.

Piaget (1960) is perhaps most famous for his assertion that the sequence of cognitive development is divided into a series of stages. He assumed that stages are organized around a dominant theme and that each stage contains qualitatively different behaviors. He did not claim that all children go through stages at exactly the same ages, but he did state that all children go through the same stages in the same *order*, and he identified four stages.

1. *The* **sensorimotor stage** extends from birth to about 2 years old. its main theme is discovering relationships between sensations and motor behavior. As we mentioned earlier, children replace reflexes with voluntary actions during the first 2 years. At first, reflexes supply the means for infants to gain nourishment by sucking. Later they learn that they can grasp a bottle and bring it to their mouth at will. They learn that they can cause other sensations as well, such as making noise by shaking a rattle.

You could easily observe unique behaviors during a babysitting session with an infant who is in the first 4 months of the sensorimotor stage. Simply place a favorite toy in front of the infant. He or she will express interest by looking, moving both arms, and so on. Now, drop a screen in front of the toy, hiding it from view. The infant will act as if the toy no longer exists! He or she will not search for it visually or manually (out of sight, out of mind). Piaget claims that infants act this way because they lack the concept of *object permanence*, which is knowledge that

If a screen is put in front of a toy, blocking it from view, infants in the first 4 months will act as if the toy no longer exists, and will not try to find it behind the screen. Piaget says infants do this because they do not yet have the concept of object permanence.

objects continue to exist even when they can no longer be experienced. Object permanence is developed during the sensorimotor stage. Infants start searching for concealed objects somewhere between 8 and 12 months of age.

2. *The* **preoperational stage** extends from 2 to 7 years of age. Its dominant theme is discovering *operations*, which are plans, strategies, and rules for solving problems and for classifying information. Preoperational children have the basic mental abilities for doing mental operations: They can form mental images and they can represent things symbolically with words. But preoperational children are only beginning to discover the logical mental operations that will characterize their later thinking.

Their immature thinking leads to unique responses, which you might observe during an interview. Striking up a conversation about the sun might reveal two characteristics of preoperational thought: *animism*, which is the tendency to attribute life to inanimate objects, and *egocentrism*, which is the belief that everything is centered around one's self.

One characteristic of preoperational thought is lack of conservation—a lack of the understanding that amounts do not change when shapes change. To test this, Piaget poured water from a short wide glass into a tall narrow glass and asked if the amount of water was the same. Preoperational children tend to say that there is more water in the taller glass.

The following conversation between Piaget and a child illustrates both characteristics (Piaget, 1960, p. 215):

Piaget: Does the sun move?
Child: Yes, when one walks it follows. When one turns around it turns around too. Doesn't it ever follow you too?
Piaget: Why does it move?
Child: Because when one walks, it goes too.
Piaget: Why does it go?
Child: To hear what we say.
Piaget: Is it alive?
Child: Of course, otherwise it wouldn't follow us, it couldn't shine.

Another characteristic of preoperational thought is lack of conservation—a lack of the understanding that amounts do not change when shapes change. For example, if you rolled out a ball of clay into a log shape, the preoperational child would say that the log has more clay than the ball. If you spread out a row of five chocolate candies next to a bunched-up row of five pieces, this same child would say that the longer row had more candy, and he or she would be much happier to get it as a prize. If you poured orange juice from a short wide glass into a tall, narrow one, the child would say that the taller glass has more juice in it. Again, he or she would be much happier to have the taller glass, even after watching you pour the liquid from one glass to the other without adding a drop.

3. The **concrete operational stage** extends from about ages 7 to 12. Its main theme is extending mental operations from concrete objects to purely symbolic terms. Concrete operational children have learned most of the principles of conservation, which means that they correctly use mental operations about concrete objects. They also use operations to form mental maps of their environment. Although preoperational children can find their way to a friend's house by learning a specific place to turn, they do not have an overall picture of their surroundings. Concrete operational children, on the other hand, can draw maps of their environment. They are only beginning to form operations about abstract concepts, however, so their reasoning process differs from those of older children and adults.

For example, concrete operational children would have much more trouble than an adult with the following problem:

Andy, Bob, Charles, and Doug are close friends. How many groups of two, three, or four of these friends can be formed with Andy in each group? In a few minutes, you would be able to figure out that the answer is 7, as follows:

1. Andy, Bob
2. Andy, Charles
3. Andy, Doug
4. Andy, Bob, Charles
5. Andy, Bob, Doug
6. Andy, Charles, Doug
7. Andy, Bob, Charles, Doug

Preoperational children would probably find this problem to be very difficult for two reasons. First, they have trouble thinking about hypothetical examples. They might wonder why Andy gets to be in every group, for instance, even though that is irrelevant to solving the problem. Second, they have trouble thinking of all the possible combinations of things. The ability to consider many possibilities readily doesn't come until the last stage of development.

4. The **formal operational stage**, Piaget's last stage, extends from

about 13 years of age on into adulthood. Its main theme is the ability to consider many possible solutions to a problem and the ability to systematically test those possibilities. Formal operations are required to understand many of the concepts introduced in this text.

Environmental Influences. Maturational processes and environmental influences interact to determine the way that stages of cognitive development unfold. Knowing what we do about her environment, we would expect Genie's cognitive development to be quite abnormal, and in fact it was.

In 1977 Susan Curtiss gave 20-year-old Genie standard tests to determine her development with respect to Piaget's stages. The results indicated that Genie understood and thought about the world in a qualitatively different way from other young adults. Genie appeared to be in the concrete operational stage. She showed some egocentrism, but much less than pre-operational children. She formed mental maps of her surroundings, and she knew some principles of conservation. Genie failed the test for conservation of substance and liquid, however. Genie's understanding and thinking as a young adult was limited to concrete events and she was in fact still struggling to master all concrete operations. Unlike most young adults, Genie could not yet think in terms of formal operations. This limitation was related to her extremely underdeveloped language ability.

Language Development

When Genie arrived at the rehabilitation center she did not respond to simple commands and questions. She seemed to understand some isolated words such as "rattle," "bunny," "red," "blue," "green," "brown," and "mother," but she demonstrated no understanding of how words are used in sentences. She responded to gestures, but she did not respond to speech. Gradually, she began to understand more and more words and she learned to name many objects in her environment. She learned to understand sentences long before she produced them, and when she did finally start to string words together, what she said was grammatically primitive and ill-formed. Some examples are as follows: she said "Cow tongue meat" meaning "A cow's tongue is meat"; she said "No more ear hurt" meaning "My ear doesn't hurt anymore"; she said "Boy is pinch" meaning "the boy pinched me"; and she said "Graduation to buy presents" meaning "At my graduation, people will buy me presents." These examples come from statements that Genie made when she was between the age of 14 and 16 years old. On the one hand, Genie made remarkable progress. On the other hand, she remained far behind people her age. Just how far behind will be shown in detail in the next section, which considers normal patterns of language development.

Patterns of Language Development. Children move in a few years from absence of speech to exhibiting an amazing mastery of language. Before starting school at the age of 5, children understand and say thousands of words. They also can combine words to express thoughts in well-formed sentences. Some landmarks in language development are as follows:

1. About 2 months old: Children make cooing sounds, which are pleasant sounds made in response to pleasant stimuli. During their second month many babies also start to express happy feelings by smiling.
2. About 6 months old: Children start making babbling sounds, which are nonsense sounds containing many different speech sounds. At first, babbling contains speech sounds from many languages that babies have not heard as part of their environment (for example, they will make the French "eu" sound, or the German "ü," even

TABLE 7–2: Two-Word Sentences in Child Speech

Function	Two-Word Sentence
Locate, Name	there book that car see doggie
Demand, Desire	more milk give candy want gum
Negate	no wet no wash not hungry allgone milk
Describe Event or Situation	Bambi go mail come hit ball block fall baby highchair
Show Possession	my shoe mama dress
Modify, Qualify	pretty dress big boat
Question	where ball

Source: Slobin (1971).

Interaction with parents is of course important in language learning, but psychologists do not agree on exactly how children learn to speak sentences.

though their parents or those around them have never made those sounds). Within several months, however, babbling includes mostly sounds from only those languages that babies hear spoken.

3. About 10 months old: Children distinguish between a few adult words. They might, for instance, give different responses to the words "cookie" and "bed." Thus, comprehension of words seems to start before production of words. The ability to understand speech stays far ahead of the ability to produce it throughout a child's development.

4. About 12 months old: Children utter single words to name people and objects around them. They might, for example, say "dada" and "block."

5. About 15 months old: Single words begin to be used in a new way. They are used in what is called **holophrastic speech,** which is the use of single words to express whole phrases. For example, a child might say "out," meaning "I want to go outside."

6. About 24 months old: Children combine words into two-word statements. Table 7-2 gives examples of some two-word statements and their function.

7. During second year: Children rapidly learn to expand two-word statements into longer, grammatically correct sentences. To illustrate, Limber (1973) reported the following sentence spoken by a 34-month-old child: "When I was a little girl I could go 'geek-geek,' like that; but now I can go, 'This is a chair.'"

The statement in this last example contrasts sharply with the simpler, ill-formed sentences that Genie uttered at the age of 16. The difference indicates that Genie was behind not only in the words she knew, but also in the rules for combining words to make sentences. We will consider these rules in the next section, as we review theories of language development.

Theories of Language Development. How do children learn to speak sentences? Psychologists have considered three possible answers. First, social-learning theory suggests that children might learn to speak by imitating adults. Indeed, some children do learn some *words* by imitating elders (Bloom, Hood, and Lightbown, 1974). However, children apparently do not learn *sentences* by imitating. If they did, they would say word combinations that are similar to sentences used by adults. But children constantly say things that adults never say. Table 7-2 gives other examples of primitive sentences uttered by 2-year-olds. These observations seem contrary to the idea that children learn sentences by imitating adult utterances.

Second, operant conditioning suggests that parents might teach children to speak by reinforcing correct utterances and by ignoring or punishing incorrect ones. B. F. Skinner (1957), in his book, *Verbal Behavior*, tried to explain language acquisition strictly in terms of such stimuli and response patterns, without reference to cognitive representations. Skinner argued that science has no room for speculations about mental processes, because scientists cannot actually observe them. Most psychologists agreed with Skinner at that time. Gradually, however, evidence was gathered in opposition to this view. Scientists found, for example, that parents rarely pay attention to grammar when children are learning to form sentences (Brown, Cazden, and Bellugi, 1969). Parents do not ignore or punish grammatically incorrect statements. Yet incorrect sentences usually stop anyway, and they are replaced by correct ones.

Third, Chomsky, who was a leading critic of Skinner's views, and an advocate of cognitive theories, had his own views regarding language development (Chomsky, 1975). He pointed out that operant conditioning cannot explain the fact that we speak and understand sentences that are novel in the sense that we have had no prior experience with them (Chomsky, 1975). He argued further that scientists must postulate cognitive representations to explain language acquisition. He proposed that children learn cognitive representations that include units of thought and rules for combining those units. For instance, one rule is that "ed" is added to verbs to change them from present tense to past tense (look-looked). Children give evidence of having formed a rule when they overgeneralize it, producing utterances that they have never seen or heard. They might say, "I goed outside," or "I taked the cookie." Later on, they learn that irregular verbs are exceptions to the rule, and they learn the correct past tense form of irregular verbs. Cognitive psychologists must observe children's speech to infer the rules that children learn. It does no good to ask children what rules they use, because they cannot say. Children learn to verbalize the rule about "-ed" endings, for example, only after the rule is taught in grammar school. By that time, of course, children have been using it for years.

As mentioned earlier, at the age of 16, Genie was behind in using language rules. The next section analyzes her language deficiencies in more detail, and it suggests an explanation of them.

Critical Period in Language Development.   In this section, we will take up the idea of critical periods and language development. Lenneberg (1967) proposed that human brain development passes through a critical

HIGHLIGHT / ARE HUMAN LANGUAGE ABILITIES UNIQUE?

We can raise two questions about the uniqueness of human language: (1) Do any naturally occurring nonhuman communication systems have the properties of human language?, and (2) Can scientists teach human language to nonhuman animals? Let's take up each of these questions in turn.

Nonhuman animals communicate in nature. But even the more complex communication systems are simple in comparison to human language. Honey bees do a dance, for example, to tell other bees in the hive the distance and direction of nectar that they have just found (von Frisch, 1974). Their dance is quite involved, but it lacks important properties of human language. Humans use relatively few symbols to express endless ideas. How do humans get so much meaning from so few symbols? A key is a powerful grammar, which is a set of rules for combining symbols. For instance, all human languages have word order rules. They can be used to change meaning (for example, The Dodgers

beat the Yankees, versus The Yankees beat the Dodgers). Honey bees have symbols, but they can only be used to indicate the direction and distance of nectar. They do not have a powerful grammar. As a result, their use of symbols is limited. They cannot, for instance, vary symbol order to change meaning. Thus, human language is superior to the honey bee dance. In fact, human language has properties that set it above all other animal communication systems found in nature so far. The answer to the first question is, therefore, "no." Naturally occurring nonhuman communication systems do not have the powerful properties of human language.

What about the second question? Can scientists teach human language to animals? Early attempts clearly failed. For example, Keith Hayes and Cathy Hayes (1951) tried, without success, to teach a chimpanzee to speak English. The results of later attempts are far more interesting.

Researchers suggested that chimps might lack human vocal abilities without lacking human language abilities (Gardner and Gardner, 1975). To test their idea, they tried to teach a chimp, Washoe, the American Sign Language, which is a human language used by many deaf people. It is based on hand gestures, which Washoe was able to learn. Once she learned the gestures, Washoe used them in a way that resembled human language. She answered questions with simple statements like "Me Washoe." She made requests such as "Gimme flowers," and she commented on her feelings ("Washoe sorry").

Other scientists have achieved similar results with chimps. In one project, Ann Premack and David Premack (1972) taught Sarah, a female chimp, to read and write using plastic symbols. Other researchers taught Lana, another female chimp, to read and write on a special plastic keyboard (Rumbaugh, 1977).

period between 2 years and about 13 years. During this period children learn language "from mere exposure" to it. Genie is a test case for this theory because she did not receive adequate exposure to language during the alleged critical period.

The theory has two versions. One version suggests that people cannot acquire language from mere exposure before or after the critical period; the second version states that people cannot acquire *normal* language from mere exposure before or after the critical period. Genie's case argues against the first version, since Genie learned language from "mere exposure" long after the critical period. On the other hand, Genie's case supports the second version, since her language is far from normal.

Genie's language is marked by characteristics that are found in people with brain damage. She rarely makes use of some rules that she knows, such as rules for forming plurals. She also exhibits an abnormal degree of variability in applying rules. Genie never learned about certain aspects of language, such as asking WH-questions (e.g., who, what, where). And her rate of language development is far slower than normal. Genie is acquiring language, but she may never speak normally because her brain may have matured past a critical period for normal language development. While some scientists ask whether human brains pass through a critical period for normal language learning, others ask whether nonhumans can learn human language at all (see "Highlight: Are Human Language Abilities Unique?").

More recently, gorillas have gotten into the act. Francine Patterson (1978) taught Koko, a female gorilla, to use a sign language based on hand gestures. Koko now seems to construct original sentences. For instance, one day she broke a sink by jumping on it. When asked about it, she seemed to blame the damage on a researcher (Kate). She signed, "Kate there bad."

What do the chimp and gorilla results say about our second question? Can scientists teach human language to nonhuman animals? The results suggest a qualified "yes." The qualification is that chimps and gorillas can learn only *parts* of human language; they can learn words, but they may not be able to generate sentences by combining those words in different ways, a basic property of human language (Limber, 1977; Terrace et al., 1979). The present results, therefore, provide only a partial answer. They also raise new questions: Are the language skills of specially trained animals too undeveloped to qualify as "human language"? If they are, will they remain so? Research aimed at these questions will give us not only a better understanding of animals, but also a better understanding of ourselves.

The Gardners taught their chimp Washoe to use American Sign Language. Washoe is shown here using two of the over 30 different signs she eventually learned.

Personality and Social Development

Language communication is an important part of our social relationships (our interactions with others). It is not surprising, therefore, that Genie was underdeveloped in both her use of language and her social behavior. She was often unresponsive in conversations, as if she heard nothing, even when she was in fact capable of hearing and understanding everything that was being said. This conversational incompetence seemed to be related to a general pattern of social abnormality. In this section, we will discuss Genie's underdeveloped social abilities and her unique way of reacting and adjusting to her environment—that is, her personality. We will, as usual, contrast Genie's development with normal patterns, which we will review in detail.

Early Social Responses. The only information we have on Genie's early social responses is her mother's report "that Genie was a noncuddly baby, [and] that she didn't coo or babble very much" Curtiss (1977, p. 4). Did Genie inherit this unresponsiveness or did she learn it? Literature on early social responses suggests that both genetic makeup and environment played a part.

Heredity. Smiling is an often studied social response. Evidence suggests that genetic factors influence the age at which infants start social smiles. Not all smiles are social responses. Infants sometimes smile as a reflex when someone strokes their lips, for instance (Gewirtz, 1965). Smiles are not considered to be social responses until they are elicited by social stimuli, such as faces and voices. Social smiles start between 3 and 8 weeks of age. Fraternal twins, who have different genotypes, start smiling at different ages; identical twins, however, who have the same genotype, start smiling at similar ages. The higher correlation of starting age for identical twins suggests that genes influence the onset of social responses. Genie may have therefore inherited her early unresponsiveness. It seems unlikely, however, that genetic factors alone influenced her social behavior.

Environment. Environmental conditions also influence early social responses. Institutionalized infants decrease their smiling rate when they receive little social stimulation. They smile more again when caregivers play with them regularly (Brackbill, 1958; Dennis, 1973). We know that Genie's father discouraged special attention for his babies. It is quite

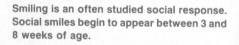
Smiling is an often studied social response. Social smiles begin to appear between 3 and 8 weeks of age.

likely, then, that Genie's early unresponsiveness was caused both by genetic factors and by an extremely deprived environment.

Attachment. Heredity and environment also interact to determine later social behaviors. An important one is **attachment,** which is the tendency of youngsters to seek closeness to certain people. Attachment normally develops in a series of three steps during the first 6 months of life: (1) infants first begin to show a preference for any human over any object; (2) they then show a preference for familiar people over unfamiliar ones; and (3) finally, they become attached to certain people, usually their mother or other primary caregiver. These attachments provide a foundation for social and personality development. Genie apparently became attached to Dr. Kent and others. Let's look at some of the research available to Dr. Kent that may have helped him to establish Genie's attachment.

Determining Factors. The three-step pattern of developing attachments is found not only in Western society (Schaffer and Emerson, 1964), but also in cultures with greatly different child-rearing practices, such as Uganda (Ainsworth, 1963) and a Hopi Indian reservation (Dennis, 1940). This developmental consistency across different cultures suggests that genes play a role in developing attachments (Bowlby, 1973). Environmental factors are also important, especially in determining the choice of attachment figures and the quality of attachment.

Early theories on attachment held that a mother's presence becomes satisfying because it is associated with food. Accordingly, attachments should develop only to those who provide nourishment. This prediction was challenged in famous experiments on attachment in monkeys. Harlow and Zimmerman (1959) raised monkeys in the presence of two artificial mothers. One substitute "mother" had a bare wire body and the other had a cuddly terrycloth body. Either one could supply milk from a bottle attached to the "chest." No matter which one provided food, infant monkeys became attached to the terrycloth "mother." They clung to the cloth substitute, for example, in strange environments or in other stressful

In Harlow's study, infant monkeys became attached to the terrycloth "mother" and their typical response when frightened was to cling to it. This occurred even if they had only been fed by the wire "mother."

situations. Harlow and Suomi (1970) showed that infant monkeys also prefer artificial mothers that rock over ones that don't move, and they prefer warm substitute mothers over cold ones. The fact that the mother provides food is neither necessary nor enough to establish attachment.

This conclusion also applies to human infants. Although attachments usually form between infants and their primary caregiver, it is not the giving of routine care, as such, that determines choice of attachment figures. A father who responds appropriately to his child in play is more likely to be an attachment figure than a mother who limits her interactions to mechanical feeding and cleaning (Schaffer and Emerson, 1964). You are more likely to become an infant's attachment figure if you provide appropriate visual, auditory, and tactual stimulation, and if you are responsive to smiles and to other social signals (Gewirt, 1965).

The importance of factors other than feeding was good news for Dr. Kent. He was able to establish himself as an attachment figure to Genie by responding appropriately to her. But is mothers' nonexclusive role good news for those with children in day-care centers? Do mothers "lose their children" to day-care center staff? Some researchers addressed this question in a longitudinal study of infants enrolled in day-care centers and infants reared at home (Kagan, Kearsley, and Zelanzo, 1977). They found that day care did not weaken attachments to mothers. Another study showed that although children prefer their day-care teachers over strangers, they still prefer their mothers over their teachers (Farran and Ramey, 1977).

Quality and Consequences of Attachment. Studies on day-care centers also addressed the consequences of multiple attachments on later social development. One study found that infants with day-care experience play more with other children and adapt more quickly to new environments (Kagan et al., 1977). These researchers also observed that the quality of attachments at home and in day-care centers influenced later social development. These results raise two general questions: (1) What determines quality in social attachments; and (2) What are the consequences of early social attachments?

Mary Ainsworth and her colleagues argue that quality of mother-infant attachment depends on the responsiveness of the mother to the infant's needs. Ainsworth (1973) analyzed mothers' responsiveness to their babies in several situations, including face-to-face play and feeding. Responsive mothers continually adjust their actions to maintain their baby's attention in play. They also respond to their baby's hunger, allowing the baby to influence when feeding begins, its pacing, and when it ends. One study periodically observed the same infants from birth to about one year old (Ainsworth et al., 1967). The experiment used a method called the *strange situation procedure*, in which researchers unobtrusively observe an infant in the presence or absence of several combinations of the child, mother, and a stranger. In the study, attachments were divided into two categories:

1. Some infants were characterized as *securely attached*. They sought closeness and contact with their mother, but they did not whine and cling. They were not too disturbed by brief separations, and they enthusiastically greeted their mother's return with hugs and affection.
2. Other infants were characterized as *anxiously attached*. If they had any interest in contact with their mother at all, it was often ambivalent: They would seek her contact, and then reject and push her away, especially after she returned from a brief separation. These babies were often upset in the strange situation whether their mother was present or not.

The infants were observed for a year, during which time it was clearly indicated that responsive mothers tend to have securely attached infants, and unresponsive mothers tend to have anxiously attached babies.

Early attachments influence a child's later development. Sroufe (1978) argues that "securely attached" infants are more likely to enjoy problem solving at the age of 2 and 3 years: They get more involved in problems and they work on them longer. Leiberman (1977) found that "secure" mother-infant attachments are associated with better relationships with other children. Securely attached children show more sharing or giving, and less crying or fighting in social relationships with other children at the age of 3 years. Apparently, a healthy attachment to parents encourages curiosity in problem solving and generosity in social relationships with others.

Critical Periods in Attachment. We have already suggested that Genie may have passed by a critical period in language development. Did she also bypass a critical period in social development?

Animal research suggests that critical periods do in fact exist in the development of attachments. Ducklings, for example, show attachments by following their attachment figure. A newly hatched duckling will follow almost any moving object that it first sees, including a wooden decoy or a human. Hess (1958) showed that after following a wooden decoy for ten minutes a newly hatched duckling becomes attached, or imprinted. That is, the duckling will stay close to the decoy in preference to any other object (including a live duck). A duckling is most likely to form attachments during its first 14 hours of life; after 2 days, attachment will probably not occur.

Critical periods in human attachments are not as simple, if they exist at all. Stendler (1952) argues that humans may go through critical periods for attachment during the eighth and ninth months and again during the second and third years. Stendler's measure was the failure to develop mature relationships later on in life. Perhaps humans pass through a critical period in life, beyond which they cannot use attachments as a foundation for developing mature social relationships. This possibility is consistent with the fact that Genie became attached to Dr. Kent, but she did not develop mature relationships with others. Let's examine what leads to or what is involved in developing a mature personality and social relationship.

Identification, Imitation, and Reinforcement. Attachment is one of several processes that is important in personality and social development. Genie's failure to develop normally may have been caused in part by other processes. For instance, her problems may have had something to do with identification, which is the process of acquiring personality and social behaviors by taking on characteristics of others. Sigmund Freud felt that identification involves more than just copying. He proposed that when children identify with their parents they unconsciously respond as if they *were* their parents. You might, for example, remember feeling proud when your father or mother received an award, as if you yourself had been honored. Genie's identification process could have been seriously distorted by the fact that she had no one to identify with, because of her isolation from both her parents and the outside world.

Modern psychologists recognize the importance of copying the behavior of others, but they do not necessarily agree with all that the term "identification" stands for in the Freudian sense. They therefore often use the term imitation to refer to the process of copying other people's behavior. Preschool children in our society often imitate their parents and other family members. They also imitate TV characters. Once children enter school, at the age of 5 or 6, they find other important models in their friends and teachers.

Preschool children often imitate their
parents and other family members, as well
as TV characters; once they enter school
they find other important models in their
friends and teachers.

Family members, friends, and teachers influence children not only by modeling behaviors, but also by *reinforcing* them. Praise is often an effective reinforcer. If you praise children for a job well done, you will increase the probability that they will repeat their efforts. Reinforcement, then, is another important mechanism for shaping personality and social development.

Genie, of course, was severely deprived of guidance from family members, friends, or teachers. Let's look at some of the important influences that she missed.

Parents. Mothers and fathers influence almost every aspect of their children's personality and social development. Children adopt their parents' values and standards and try to live up to them even when their parents aren't watching. One area of parental influence that has received much attention lately concerns the development of *sex roles*, which are a society's approved ways for men and women to behave (see Chapter 15). Societies assign distinctive roles to males and females. Traditionally, American men were expected to be self-sufficient, powerful, and tough, while American women were supposed to be dependent, weak, and tender. Those expectations are changing. Today, for example, more and more women are becoming equal breadwinners in families, and, in general, men and women are exchanging or sharing many responsibilities. Behavior standards still differ for males and females, however, and parents help transmit those standards.

Parents treat boys and girls differently long before the children realize the difference between sexes. Most children cannot use the labels "boy" and "girl" correctly until about the age of 3 years. The labels are first used on the basis of external differences in dress and hair styles. Children are usually 5 or 6 before they relate their concept of boys and girls to genital differences. Parents, however, start treating boys and girls differently at birth. They describe newborn daughters as *delicate, beautiful,* and *weak.* But they describe newborn sons of the same height and weight as *robust, coordinated,* and *strong* (Rubin et al., 1974). The descriptions apparently reflect parents' expectations. Parents express their expectancies in other ways as their children grow. Mothers and fathers handle their sons more roughly, protect them less from physical harm, and punish them physically more than they do their daughters (Maccoby and Jacklin, 1974). Parents also model sex roles, of course, and by the age of 6 years children prefer to imitate the parent of the same sex. Parents therefore transmit sex roles both through differential treatment of their sons and daughters and through modeling.

Teachers. Personality and social development are also shaped by teachers who transmit personal attitudes and beliefs in addition to academic lessons (Walter and Ashton, 1980). Teachers shape development both through modeling and through reinforcement (Ringness, 1975). In fact, the roles of reinforcer and model seem to be interrelated. In one study, Portuges and Feshbach (1972) demonstrated that children are more likely to imitate teachers that reward successes as opposed to teachers that punish failures. Both reinforcement and modeling may be responsible for the fact that students of warm and friendly teachers tend to be less aggressive, and to be more conscientious in their attitudes toward school (Cronbach and Snow, 1977). Because it is easier for students to imitate teachers who are similar to them, many think that having more black teachers will cause black students to develop a more positive attitude toward school.

Peers. Entrance into schools also brings children into contact with many other children, their *peers*. School-age children acquire friends in whom they find security. As a result, they learn important social skills such as sharing and cooperating.

FIGURE 7–3

The graph shows how, between the ages of 1 and 11, children have more and more contact with other children, and less and less contact with adults. (Wright, 1967)

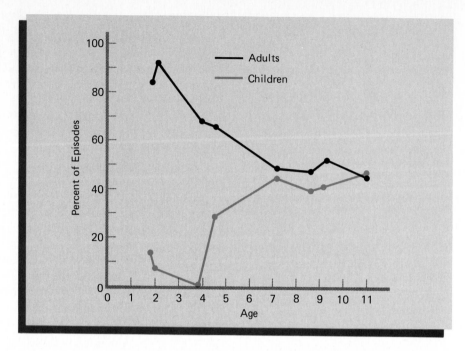

Genie had no friends until she was 13 years old. She was denied contact with peers at a time in her life when other children learn to enjoy the company of friends. Suomi (1977) did an experiment that sheds light on the possible effects of such deprivation. He raised monkeys with their mothers, but without an opportunity to play with other young monkeys. Later on, he introduced the deprived monkeys to other monkeys. Some of the deprived monkeys screamed with fear when strange monkeys approached; others were overly aggressive. Apparently, early play activity between young monkeys is essential to normal social development. Genie's social development remained stunted even after she entered a supportive environment. The difficult time she had with others was probably caused in part by her early isolation from peers.

In the normal course of development between the ages of 1 and 11 years, children steadily decrease their contact with adults and increase their contact with other children, as shown in Figure 7-3 (Wright, 1967). They prefer friends of the same sex, especially between the ages of 8 and 11. "Fitting in" with their friends becomes very important. Children want to conform to the trends established by their peers. They try to be as similar as possible in dress, hair styles, language, and mannerisms. Peers gradually take over more and more both as models and reinforcers.

Between the ages of 8 and 11, children prefer friends of the same sex—girls tend to play with girls, and boys with boys.

Birth, interactions between siblings, and the sex of older siblings, as well as the way parents treat them, all have an effect on personality and social behavior.

Brothers and Sisters.   Effects of birth order on personality and social behavior suggest that brothers and sisters (*siblings*) influence development. Firstborn children or only children tend to be more cooperative, conscientious, and cautious than later-born children (Altus, 1966). They also score higher on intelligence tests, go farther in school, and obtain more honors. Sex of older siblings seem to make a difference: For example, boys with older sisters tend to be less aggressive than boys with older brothers (Longstreth et al., 1975). Direct interactions between children probably causes some of the effects. Younger siblings, for example, are notorious for being pests to older brothers and sisters. Older children often control their younger siblings through acts of aggression. The aggressive acts reduce an annoyance and are therefore reinforced (Patterson, 1979).

Parents also contribute to birth-order effects by treating siblings differently. In one study, researchers found that parents spend more time with firstborn infants and talk to them more (Thoman et al., 1972). Parents also exert more pressure on firstborn children to achieve (Rothbart, 1971). Birth order does not affect everyone in the same way, of course. Family situations are different, as are individuals. Consequently, children with older brothers and sisters often have qualities that are associated with firstborns, and many later-born children have achieved great accomplishments. One example is Georgia O'Keeffe, a famous American artist, whose life story will be told in the next chapter.

Genie and Georgia O'Keeffe faced different obstacles in life. As a result, their achievements are quite different. It we measure success, however, not in terms of what one achieves, but in terms of the obstacles one overcomes in life, then Genie is every bit as successful.

SUMMARY

1. Development is a process by which the genes that we inherit from our parents come to be expressed as specific physical and behavioral characteristics.

2. *Nativism* emphasizes the role of heredity in the development of mind and behavior. *Empiricism* holds that learning through experience is the source of development. Neither theory, however, can explain the existence of a critical period, which is a stage of development during which an organism must have certain experiences or it will not develop normally. It requires both heredity and environment to explain this phenomenon, and, indeed, it is through the interaction of these two elements that most development occurs.

3. Prenatal development refers to the approximately 9-month period of development that precedes birth. The stages of prenatal development are divided into the periods of the ovum, the embryo, and the fetus. A number of factors can influence development in this stage, including nutrition, disease, drug use by the mother, and delivery complications.

4. The next stage of development, from birth to 1 year, is marked by the development of the nervous system, including myelinization, which determines control over body parts. Motor development is marked by the disappearance of various reflexes that the baby is born with, and the development of voluntary movement, such as sitting up, crawling, and standing. Perceptual development has been studied in the visual cliff experiment and various reaching experiments, which test both size and depth perception and motor control.

5. Childhood is most notably marked by increases in cognitive development. Piaget studied two processes in children that account for much of this development: assimilation and accommodation. As a result of his years of observation and research on children, he divided cognitive development into a series of stages: sensorimotor (birth to 2 years), preoperational (2 to 7 years), concrete operational (7 to 12 years), and formal operational (13 years and older).

6. Language development is an important element of cognitive development. It progresses in the first two years of life from cooing and babbling, through holophrastic speech, which is the use of single words to express whole phrases, to two-word statements. During the second year children rapidly learn to expand two-word statements into longer, grammatically correct sentences.

7. There are three basic theories of how language development occurs: social-learning theory, which suggests that children learn to speak by imitating adults; operant conditioning theory, which states that parents teach children to speak by reinforcement; and Noam Chomsky's view, which is that children learn units of thought and rules for combining them as the basis of speech.

8. An important part of personality and social development in infancy is attachment, the tendency to seek closeness to certain people. Attachment normally develops in a series of three steps during the first 6 months of life; the quality of attachment, usually between infant and mother, affects later personality and social development in children.

9. Another important element in personality and social development in childhood is identification, which is the process of acquiring personality and social behaviors by imitating those around us.

10. Parents transmit sex roles to their children both by treating boys and girls differently from an early age, and by modeling different behaviors for each sex.

SUGGESTED READINGS

The following book is about Genie:

CURTISS, S. *Genie: The psycholinguistic study of a modern-day "wild child."* New York: Academic Press, 1977.

ASLIN, R. N., ALBERTS, J. R., and PETERSEN, M. R. *Development of perception: Psychobiological perspectives. Volume 1: Audition, somatic perception, and the chemical senses. Volume 2: The visual system.* New York: Academic Press, 1982. A broad coverage of recent progress in understanding perceptual development from physiological, behavioral, and evolutionary perspectives.

BEE, H. *The developing child.* New York: Harper & Row, 1978. A brief textbook on child development, this is a good source of facts about sex differences in development.

BROWN, R. *A first language: The early stages.* Cambridge, Mass.: Harvard University Press, 1973. An excellent book on early language development.

FLAVELL, J. H. *Cognitive development.* Englewood Cliffs, N.J.: Prentice-Hall, 1977. An easy-to-understand presentation of Piaget's research and theories.

HELMS, D. B., and TURNER, J. S. *Exploring child behavior.* New York: Holt, Rinehart and Winston, 1981. A comprehensive textbook on development; a good source of information on development in the school setting.

HETHERINGTON, E. M., and PARKE, R. D. *Contemporary readings in child psychology.* New York: McGraw-Hill, 1981. A collection of readings organized to complement Hetherington and Parke's *Child psychology: A contemporary viewpoint.* Together these books provide a springboard for those who are preparing to take the plunge into the depths of research on child psychology. A refreshing style makes the books enjoyable as well as informative.

Adolescence, Adulthood, and Aging

On November 15, 1887, in Sun Prairie, Wisconsin, Ida and Francis O'Keeffe gave birth to their second child and their first daughter. Ida named her baby Georgia Totto after Count George Totto, Ida's father, a political refugee who had escaped from Hungary after fighting in a hopeless Hungarian uprising against Austrian rule. Ida and Francis had no way of knowing that their daughter, who looked more like her Irish father than her Hungarian grandfather, was to become one of the world's outstanding artists. Nobody would have guessed that for many years—nobody, that is, except Georgia herself. At the age of 12, after less than a year of private art lessons, she announced to a friend that she was going to be an artist. In 1976, Georgia reflected back on that statement and wrote in her autobiography that it was inspired in part by a small illustration of a beautiful Grecian maiden in one of her mother's books. She wrote, "I believe that picture started something moving in me that kept on going and has had to do with the everlasting urge that makes me keep on painting."

Ida and Francis had three more daughters after Georgia. As Francis worked his dairy farm, Ida tended to the education of her five children. She read to them constantly, and every Saturday she took her daughters 7 miles round trip by horse and buggy to have private art lessons. Shortly before Georgia turned 14, Ida entered her in an exclusive convent boarding school, paying an eighty-dollar tuition and an extra twenty dollars so that Georgia could take art lessons.

Georgia, who was eager to please her dignified mother, excelled in school. The following year, Ida sent Georgia and her brother Francis to live with their aunt in Madison, where they could attend Madison High School. One day, as she passed an art classroom, she stopped to watch a teacher who was instructing the class to observe the unusual shapes and subtle shades of a jack-in-the-pulpit plant; she realized for the first time that one could paint living things rather than just copy pictures.

Georgia spent much of her childhood freely roaming the family farm, and could often be found at the side of her jovial father, who kept his pockets full of sweets and played Irish melodies on his fiddle. Georgia never lost her rural roots; whenever she counted her blessings, she put at the top of her list having been born a farmer's daughter.

In March, 1903, while Georgia was attending Madison High School, Ida and Francis sold their Wisconsin farm and moved to Williamsburg, Virginia. Georgia went to Chatham Episcopal Institute, a girl's boarding school about 200 miles from Williamsburg. There she was lucky to have a sensitive art teacher, Elizabeth May Willis, who let Georgia work at her own pace. Sometimes Georgia worked intensely; at other times she refused to work for days. When others complained about Georgia not working, Mrs. Willis would reply, "When the spirit moves Georgia, she can do more in a day than you can do in a week" (Lisle, 1980, p. 34).

During the next few years Georgia attended various art schools, and then, when her parents could no longer afford the tuition, she began to earn her own living. She worked first as a freelance illustrator in Chicago (one of the images she created, a bonneted Dutch girl chasing dirt with an upraised broom, is still used today to sell a cleanser); later she taught art in several public schools in Texas.

In 1914, at the age of 27, Georgia resumed her academic career in New York at Columbia Teacher's College. After one year at Columbia, Georgia accepted a teaching position at a teachers' college for women in South Carolina. She taught four classes a week and spent many hours each day painting. Throughout the year she corresponded with Anita Pollitzer, a friend she had made at Columbia. In one letter she described her frustration with having taken on the painting styles of her teachers. She wrote, "I feel disgusted with it all and am glad I'm disgusted" (Lisle, 1980, p. 82). Georgia decided to start learning all over again, so she put away all colors and worked only in black and white. She committed herself to stay with those two colors until she had exhausted all their possibilities. During the weeks that followed, Georgia created charcoal drawings unlike anything she had been taught. She saw abstract shapes in her mind that were an integral part of her imagination; she had always seen them, but she had not paid attention to them before. Georgia mailed some of her drawings to Anita, who later recalled, "[I] was struck by their aliveness. They were different. Here were charcoals on the same kind of paper that all art students were using, and through no trick, no superiority of tools, these drawings were saying something that had not yet been said."

Anita took the drawings to a little art gallery run by photographer Alfred Stieglitz, who was famous for showing unconventional art. Georgia had visited Stieglitz's "291" gallery many times while she was a student in New York. She had written to Anita in an earlier letter that she "would rather have Stieglitz like something—anything I had done—than anyone else I know of—I have always felt that—If I ever make anything that satisfies me even ever so little—I am going to show it to him to find out if it is any good" (Lisle, 1980, p. 81). Anita found Stieglitz alone in his gallery and she unrolled the charcoals for him. He looked at each sheet closely, saying nothing. Then he looked at Anita and declared, "At last, a woman on paper!" (Lisle, 1980, p. 85).

When Georgia heard the news, she wrote Stieglitz a letter, the first of more than 3,400 letters and telegrams that they would exchange. Georgia met with Stieglitz a month later in New York. He told her that her drawings were so wonderful that he simply had to show them, which he did, creating the sensation that he had predicted.

Georgia and Stieglitz corresponded, often exchanging paintings, photographs, and ideas. Although Stieglitz was about 25 years older, it became apparent that the two had much in common. They valued candor and genuineness, they burned to express themselves in art, and they shared a passion for excellence. Georgia joined Stieglitz in New York in the spring of 1917. During the long romance that followed, Georgia became the favorite subject for Stieglitz's photographs. Many critics recognize his photographs of Georgia as the height of his artistic achievement. The photographs have been compared to the joyous biblical love "poem," the Song of Solomon, and one woman standing in front of the photographs was observed to tearfully murmur: "He loves her so" (Lisle, 1980). The couple married on December 11, 1924.

Several years later, at the age of 41, Georgia returned to the West to seek inspiration. She found what she was looking for in Taos, New Mexico. She returned to New York after a few months with enough paintings to put on an exhibition in February, 1930. Georgia returned to New Mexico during the next two summers, each time returning with paintings that amazed New York art critics. They were especially fascinated by paintings of white animal skeletons, which Georgia had found scattered over the desert and had decorated with artificial cloth flowers of the type found in New Mexican cemeteries. Friends worried that the paintings indicated depression and morbid concern with death. Their concerns proved valid, for Georgia suffered a nervous breakdown and was admitted to a hospital on February 1, 1933, at the age of 45.

Georgia left the hospital 7 weeks later, spent a quiet winter with Stieglitz, and then once again headed West. Gradually, Georgia started painting again. Although friends saw in her work signs of a triumphant convalescence, Georgia suffered a brief relapse in 1939. Some attributed her rapid recovery after that to Stieglitz's unwavering support and to the fact that she was now widely recognized as America's most successful female painter.

A combination of factors slowed Georgia down considerably in the 1950s. First, Stieglitz died in 1946 at the age of 82. Even though Georgia had spent many months away from him each year, she missed him intensely after his death. Furthermore, his passing put new demands on her time. She put long hours into settling his estate, and she took on the business end of selling her paintings, which he had always handled for her.

Georgia made an incredible comeback in the 1960s after taking an around-the-world trip. Her paintings of this period captured her fascination with the extraordinary spectacle of earth and clouds from jet airplanes. At the age of 77 she completed the largest painting of her life, *Sky Above Clouds IV,* a 24' × 8' "chunk of heaven" depicting clouds viewed from above floating off into infinity. She exhibited her new painting in

1966 along with 96 other paintings at the biggest exhibition of her lifetime in Fort Worth. The reviews of her exhibition indicated that, at the age of 78, Georgia had captured the hearts and imaginations of yet another generation of Americans.

Georgia's productivity was slowed once again late in 1971 when she lost her central vision because of an irreversible degenerative eye disease found among the elderly. Her blurred vision stopped her from painting between the ages of 84 and 88. But by 1976, at the age of 89, she again started painting. She proudly stated that her shadowy vision gave her an interesting new way of seeing light and it gave her new painting ideas. By 1980, her paintings were back in the news.

For years Georgia predicted that she would live to be 100. Now that she is in her nineties she has changed that prediction to 125.

A LIFE-SPAN APPROACH TO DEVELOPMENT

Georgia O'Keeffe's career as an artist puzzles those who attempt to classify artists and their works. Georgia joked that critics had tried to place her "in every movement that came along—expressionism, precisionism, regionalism, surrealism, and all the rest—until pop art came along, and then they gave up" (Lisle, 1980, p. 392). She fits no ready niche. In the same way, her incredibly fluid and dynamic life clashes with traditional development theories, which assume that development moves in one direction until maturity, at which point a person remains basically the same until old age causes a decline (Harris, 1957). Such theories do not seem to explain Georgia's life very well. They offer little or no framework for explaining her adaptive responses to life in places as varied as New York City and the desert of New Mexico. They have little to say about the adjustments Georgia made to her husband's death, or about the comeback she made in her career late in life.

A defender of traditional developmental theories might argue that Georgia's life is too exceptional to be captured by theories about ordinary people. It is indeed, unusual to find so much dynamism in one lifetime. But when we observe people throughout their life span, we find that change is the rule, not the exception. Thus a developmental framework is needed to integrate changes that occur within an individual over time and the differences in such changes between individuals. That need may be met by a life-span developmental approach, which is concerned with the description and explanation of changes in behavior within an individual and differences between individuals from conception to death (Hultsch and Deutsch, 1981, p. 15).

This chapter adopts the life-span approach to development in adolescence, young adulthood, middle age, and old age. If you do not already identify with Georgia O'Keeffe, you may come to feel a bond with her by virtue of being a developing individual. In fact, the life-span perspective on physical, social, and cognitive changes may show you the common themes as well as individual differences running through the lives of all people.

ADOLESCENCE

Adolescence, which extends from about age 12 to the late teens, is a time of passage from childhood to adulthood. Georgia's favorite childhood toy was a dollhouse, but she set it aside at about the age of 12. She announced her desire to be an artist at about the same time, marking the beginning of her transition from a dollhouse world to the real world beyond her home. Let's follow some of the many significant events that happened to Georgia during this period and that happen to each of us during adolescence.

Physical Changes

At 12 Georgia looked like a little girl. By the time she was 16, however, Georgia was the very image of herself as a woman. Such a rapid physical transformation is characteristic of adolescence.

Height and Weight. The accelerated growth rate during adolescence (often referred to as a "growth spurt") is apparent in Figure 8–1, which

The graph here shows average heights and weights for girls and boys from birth to 17 years. Note that on the average the adolescent growth spurt occurs earlier for girls than for boys. (Tanner, 1978)

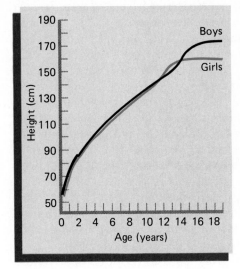

The timing of the adolescent growth spurt, as well as the onset of puberty, varies considerably among individuals.

shows average heights and weights for girls and boys from birth to 17 years of age. Girls increase their growth rate earlier than boys, so that most girls are larger than boys between the ages of 11 and 13. Once boys start their growth spurt, however, they rapidly overtake girls. By the age of 17, boys are, on the average, about 4 inches taller and about 17 pounds heavier than girls. Boys and girls also differ in the extent to which their muscles and strength change during adolescence. At the age of 10, girls and boys are generally of equal strength. But, while girls stay about about the same strength, boys almost double their strength during their teen years. At the end of the "adolescent growth spurt," adolescents have adult body proportions.

Puberty and Sexual Characteristics. Adolescence is also associated with **puberty,** the time when sexual reproduction is possible. Development occurs in all **primary sexual characteristics,** which are traits directly concerned with reproduction. For instance, girls begin to produce ovum and boys start manufacturing sperm. Puberty starts between 11 and 13 for most girls and between 13 and 15 for most boys. The timing varies considerably among individuals, however. The development of secondary sexual characteristics provides external signs of the approach of puberty. **Secondary sexual characteristics** are those traits typical of a sex, but not directly concerned with reproduction.

The first visible sign for girls is usually breast development, followed by appearance of pubic hair. The onset of puberty is often assumed to be **menarche,** the beginning of *menstruation,* which is the periodic discharge of blood and tissue from a nonpregnant uterus. Using menarche as a dividing line is only an approximation, however, since the ability to reproduce is often not present for 1 or 2 years after menarche.

The first external indicator for boys is growth of the scrotum and appearance of pubic hair. Beard growth is another sign, but this is often delayed for several years. Growth rate and muscular development is the most obvious visible evidence of puberty in boys.

Complex changes in hormones (see Chapter 2) cause both the adolescent growth spurt and the development of sexual characteristics. They also

cause behavioral changes, such as interest in the opposite sex. There are also important psychological and social changes that take place during adolescence.

Moral Development

Moral development refers to development that is related to principles of right and wrong in behavior. Societies have rules about the rightness and wrongness of behaviors, and various authorities enforce a society's rules through rewards and punishments. Parents rely heavily on such external controls to maintain appropriate behaviors in children. Teenagers require less supervision because part of their moral development involves internalization, which is the process of bringing behavior under the control of inner, personal standards that make people obey rules even if there are no external restraints. The development of moral reasoning and moral behavior is the focus of research that we will review in this section.

Moral Reasoning. Jean Piaget (1932) and Lawrence Kohlberg (1963, 1969, 1978) have done a great deal of research on the development of internalization and moral reasoning. Both investigators asked children to comment on stories containing moral dilemmas; both proposed theories that related moral development to cognitive development. Here we will concentrate on Kohlberg's more recent, and more refined, theory.

The following is an example of a story used in Kohlberg's research:

In Europe, a lady was dying because she was very sick. There was one drug that doctors said might save her. This medicine was discovered by a man living in the same town. It cost him $200 to make it, but he charged $2,000 for just a little of it. The sick lady's husband, Heinz, tried to borrow enough money to buy the drug. He went to everyone he knew to borrow the money. But he could borrow only half of what he needed. He told the man who made the drug that his wife was dying, and asked him to sell the medicine cheaper or let him pay later. But the man said, "No, I made the drug and I'm going to make money from it." So Heinz broke into the store and stole the drug.

Kohlberg asked children of various ages, "Should Heinz have done that? Was it actually wrong or right? Why?" Answers to these questions suggested three levels in the development of moral reasoning, with two stages in each level (Table 8–1). A typical answer in the first level (preconventional) might be, "The man was wrong because he could be sent to jail for stealing." Or it might be, "The man was right because he would get in trouble for letting his wife die." Both answers characterize the preconventional level, because right or wrong is decided in terms of possible punishment. Children often give this kind of answer, but teenagers rarely do. A typical answer in the second level (conventional) might be, "The man was wrong because people don't like thieves." Or it might be, "The man was right because his friends wouldn't like him if he let his wife die." Both answers characterize the conventional level, because right or wrong is decided in terms of being liked or disliked for one's actions. Teenagers often give this kind of response. A typical answer in the third level (postconventional) might be, "The man was wrong according to social law, but he was right according to divine law, which holds that human life is sacred." This answer characterizes Kohlberg's highest level, because it is based upon abstract principles. Less than 10 percent of teenagers reach this level by the time they are 16, which was the oldest age included in Kohlberg's study. Kohlberg speculates, in fact, that many people may never reach this level.

Moral Behavior. Thought does not always guide actions. A person who knows it is wrong to cheat might still do so. Children, for instance, show little relationship between moral reasoning and moral behavior (Podd,

TABLE 8–1: Stages and Levels of Kohlberg's Theory of Moral Development

Level I	Preconventional morality
Stage 1	Obedience and punishment orientation
Stage 2	Naive hedonistic and instrumental orientation
Level II	Conventional level: Morality of conventional rules and conformity
Stage 3	"Good boy/Good girl" morality
Stage 4	Authority and social order morality
Level III	Postconventional level: Morality of self-accepted moral principles
Stage 5	Morality of contract, individual rights, and democratically accepted law
Stage 6	Morality of individual principles and conscience

1972), and evidence is mixed on this relationship in teenagers. In one study, a substantial correlation was suggested by the finding that adolescents in Kohlberg's third level of moral reasoning were less likely to cheat than those at lower levels (Grim, Kohlberg, and White, 1968). Other studies raise questions about this, however. Teenagers are more likely to be at higher levels of moral reasoning, yet academic cheating does not seem to decrease with age. Changes in important factors may explain these seemingly contrary results. The gains involved in cheating increase at higher educational levels. University students, for instance, say that they cheat to gain vocational opportunities and admission to graduate school (Smith, Ryan, and Diggins, 1972). Teenagers may indeed be more resistant than children to cheating, but they still cheat when the pressures are great enough, and those pressures tend to increase as they get older. Researchers have much to learn about how internalized moral standards interact with external pressures.

There are also many psychological and social changes taking place during the teenage years. Let's go over some highlights of these changes.

Personality Development

As we will discuss in detail in Chapter 11, personality has many aspects that determine the unique way that we adjust to and respond to our environment. This section will deal with questions about the development of personality: How did our personality develop to what it is today? Is it still developing? Will it ever stop developing?

Georgia O'Keeffe's nonconforming nature illustrates that some personality traits can remain stable throughout a person's lifetime, as evidenced in her childhood: "From the time I was a little girl, if my sisters wore their hair braided, I wouldn't wear mine braided. If they wore ribbons, I wouldn't. I'd think they'd look better without it, too" (Lisle, 1980, p. 11). Her inclination to do things her own way was strengthened by her experiences as a northern teenager who came to live in the South. Southern classmates described 16-year-old Georgia in the school yearbook as "a girl who would be different in habit, style and dress; a girl who doesn't give a cent for men—and boys still less" (Lisle, 1980, p. 36). Her friends also teased her because of her flat midwestern accent. Teasing didn't bother Georgia, however, because she was certain that her way was correct. As an adult, Georgia continued as a nonconformist. This strong personality trait may have been responsible for launching her career, since she achieved her first widely acclaimed work by consciously breaking with the traditions in which she had been trained. Georgia's popularity survived the coming and going of many different trends in the art world, perhaps because she always had a style of her own. The survival of one personality trait in one person does not mean, of course, that our personality remains the same throughout life, or even that certain traits will stay with us throughout life. In fact, modern theories assume that our personalities continue to develop and change as long as we live. Let's turn to one such theory.

Erik Erikson's Theory. As we will discuss in Chapter 11, Freud and his followers argued that our personality is determined by the time we are 6 or 7 years old; the remainder of life is spent following the script written during these "formative years." Erik Erikson, who studied with Freud, acknowledged that early childhood is an important period for personality development. However, he believed that our personality continues to grow and change throughout our lifetime. Erikson, again like Freud, suggested that people go through stages where certain issues or events are critical, but, unlike Freud, he did not believe that these issues were always sexual in nature. He also felt that many of these stages occur well after childhood. According to Erikson, the way in which each crisis is resolved not only shapes the personality, but also influences how the person will approach and resolve the crisis at the next stage.

As you can see in Table 8–2, Erikson listed eight stages of life; the first four correspond to those suggested by Freud, and the other four stages occur after puberty. The first, and probably most critical, crisis involves issues of trust and mistrust. The way in which this crisis is resolved will determine whether a person approaches the world in a trusting, open way or with a suspicious, cautious, outlook. According to Erikson, it is the mother who determines whether people will have a predominantly trusting or mistrusting personality. Social trust will develop to the degree that infants have an inner sense of security that their mother will love and take care of their basic needs.

An important stage in Erikson's theory is the **identity crisis,** which occurs during puberty. The search for an identity is particularly difficult in our complex Western culture. The sheer number of choices facing the adolescent is bewildering, and, to complicate matters even further, there are few guides to help someone make these choices. During adolescence, people begin to confront issues concerning career, education, marriage, and place of residence. The decision about each of these issues will influence how people view themselves. In earlier, more traditional societies, the search for an identity was not so difficult. People rarely moved away from the area in which they were raised; male children were generally expected to adopt the occupation of their fathers; and females "naturally" got married, raised a family, and kept house. The difficulty of the identity crisis in our present-day society is reflected in the fact that this period is characterized by a great deal of trying out and testing of different roles as adolescents struggle to "discover" themselves. College students may change their major a number of times as they attempt to discover "their niche." Even by graduation, many college students have not settled

TABLE 8–2: Stages of Erikson's Psychosocial Personality Theory

Age	Stage
First year of life	Trust vs. mistrust
1–3 years	Autonomy vs. doubt
3–5 years	Initiative vs. guilt
6–12 years	Industry vs. inferiority
Adolescence	Identity vs. role confusion
Young adulthood	Intimacy vs. isolation
Middle adulthood	Generativity vs. self-absorption
Late adulthood	Integrity vs. despair

on an identity, and an increasing number of them choose to "take a year off" to travel, work at different jobs, and learn about themselves.

Thus, Erikson argues that our personality changes throughout our lifetime. Erikson's theory also includes a certain amount of continuity in personality, however, since the way one crisis is resolved affects later stages. We will return to Erikson's theory and compare it with other theories as we come to other stages of adult life. Here we want to emphasize the identity crisis that must be resolved by adolescents. We will end our discussion of the developing teenage personality by considering how physical changes affect the identity crisis.

Influence of Physical Changes. A teenager's search for identity is influenced by the adolescent growth spurt, which we discussed earlier. Late maturing boys and girls have an especially difficult time. Researchers found that boys who mature late often feel inadequate, and this feeling persists into adulthood (Mussen and Jones, 1957). Early maturers take over as leaders, especially in sports, because of their greater strength. Later maturers try to compensate with immature, attention-seeking behaviors such as bossiness. Reactions of others to these annoying behaviors tend to reinforce the low self-image of the late maturers. These researchers also found that late-maturing girls face similar adjustment problems, but to a lesser extent. High-school girls who are physically mature early on tend to be leaders among girls. Late-maturing girls tend to be less self-confident and less relaxed in social relationships. These effects carry over into adulthood, but they are small in comparison to the influence of late maturing on boys.

One effect these physical changes have is on the way parents, teachers, and friends treat teenagers. The less teenagers *look* like adults, the less they are treated like adults, which could contribute to low self-esteem in late maturers. In addition, many other social variables change dramatically during adolescence.

Social Changes

Think back to the interpersonal, or social, relationships that you had as a 12-year-old. In all likelihood you lived at home, and your parents kept a fairly close eye on your activities. If you got into trouble at school, they found out almost immediately; they decided when, where, and with whom you could date; and they were close at hand when you needed encouragement. Contrast that to your social situation at the age of 19. Many 19-year-olds move away from home and enter college or begin working. Most make their own decisions about school, dating, and careers. Parents care as much as ever, but their involvement is generally limited. Georgia O'Keeffe followed this pattern of assuming more freedom and responsibility during adolescence. At the age of 12, she lived in a sheltered home environment, but by the time she was 19 she was living alone while attending the Art Students League in New York City. Much research has been done on various aspects of the movement towards independence during adolescence. Parental control is one important factor.

Methods of Parental Control. There are basically three kinds of parental control.

The first type, *authoritarian* control, is characterized by harsh and forceful discipline with an emphasis on hard work and obedience. Authoritarian parents set rules without explaining them and without taking their children's views into account. Research seems to show that this type of discipline may lead to maladjustment in college students (Perove and Spielberger, 1966) and to juvenile delinquency (Kagan and Freeman, 1963).

Second, *permissive* control is characterized by little or no control at all. Permissive parents are willing to explain the few rules that they have, but they are relatively uninterested in their children's input into decision making. You might expect children from permissive households to be very self-reliant, because they often have to fend for themselves. The opposite seems to be true, however; they tend not to be self-reliant and they also tend to be selfish (Baumrind, 1971).

And finally, *authoritative* control is characterized by democratic policy making, with children included in decision making, but with parents having the final say. Authoritative parents discipline mostly on a verbal basis, and they give teenagers a fair share of independence. Research has been done on the link between authoritative control and children's traits (Baumrind, 1968, 1971). The research looked at this link in two different ways:

1. Children with various characteristics were identified and then the kind of control used by their parents was examined; well-adjusted children tended to have authoritative parents.
2. Parents who used various kinds of control were identified and then their children's traits were categorized. Authoritative parents tended to have children who were cooperative, achievement-oriented, and independent.

Besides studying specific control techniques, researchers have focused on other aspects of parental behavior. In one study, Hetherington, Cox, and Cox (1978) found that marital disharmony and inconsistency in discipline are associated with aggressive or delinquent behavior in juveniles. On the brighter side, parental warmth and nurturance is associated with security and healthy development in youths.

Peer Groups. As children approach their teen years, contact with other children, that is, their peers, becomes more and more important.

Peer-group structures of teenagers seem to develop through several stages. In an early stage, separate cliques of boys and girls start interacting as groups.

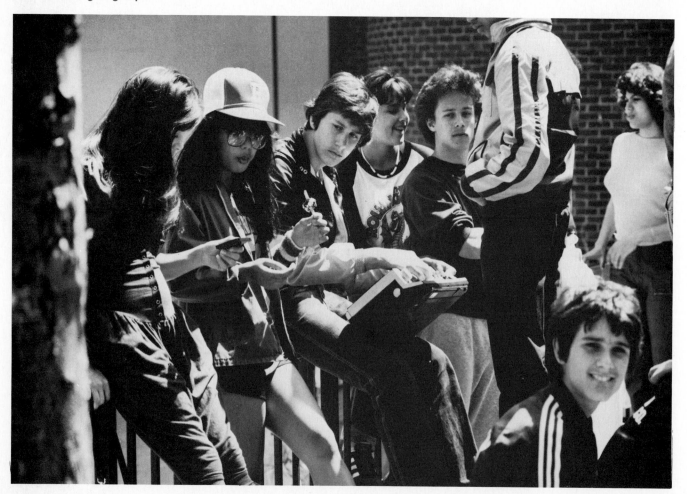

Adolescent peer groups often take on highly organized structures. Dunphy (1963) observed, for instance, that peer-group structures of urban teenagers develop through five stages. Boys and girls remain separate in the first stage; they form small groups with members of their own sex. These groups, which are called *cliques*, contain members that share common interests and emotional attachments. Boy and girl cliques start interacting as groups in the second stage. Dating starts in the third stage, causing boy and girl cliques to merge. The isolated sex groups often maintain their identity as well during this stage. The fourth stage is characterized by larger groups, called *"crowds,"* which are made up of several merged boy-girl cliques closely interacting. These "crowds" dissolve in the fifth stage, and fully mixed boy-girl cliques reappear. The cliques during this last stage consist of loosely associated couples.

Sexual Behavior. Intimacy during dating includes sexual behaviors ranging from light embracing to sexual intercourse. Almost all American teenagers experience light embracing (Luckey and Nass, 1969), and slightly more than 50 percent experience sexual intercourse (Gordon and Scales, 1977). One nationwide survey of 13- to 19-year-olds found that 59 percent of the males and 45 percent of the females reported having had sexual intercourse (Sorenson, 1973). In the same survey, 37 percent reported having experienced intercourse before they were 16 years old. When these figures are compared with earlier surveys, one sees a trend of increasing sexual activity at younger ages (Fox, 1979). Adolescent sexual activity seems to be restricted when parents provide sex education, but 85 to 95 percent of today's parents do not discuss sexual behavior with their children, according to a recent survey (Fox, 1979; *Time,* 1978).

Some of the statistics about adolescent sexual behavior in the United States are alarming. For instance, there has been a dramatic increase in *venereal disease (VD)*, which is any infectious disease transmitted by sexual intercourse. The common cold is the only infectious disease that occurs more frequently today. About 11 percent of females and 12 percent of males contract VD before they are 19 years old (Katchadourian, 1977). Venereal diseases can be cured if they are treated early; if not, they can lead to blindness, sterility, brain damage, heart disease, and death.

Teenage pregnancy is another current problem in the United States, which has the fourth highest teenage pregnancy rate in the world. According to a Planned Parenthood (1976) report, girls under the age of 15 give birth to about 30,000 babies a year. Approximately 1 million girls between the ages of 15 and 19 become pregnant annually. Almost 60 percent of these give birth; nearly 40 percent have abortions. Two-thirds of teen pregnancies are accidental and only about one-third of all teenage mothers are married when they deliver (Castleman, 1977). Those who do get married often get divorced later on (Presser, 1977). Not only do teenage pregnancies cause considerable emotional trauma, they also increase the risk of physical complications for both mother and child (Moore, 1978).

Cox (1974) argues that mass media is seducing teens into earlier sexual activity. Mass media does probably contribute to what Gordon and Scales (1977) call the "myth of the normal outlet." This myth causes some teenagers to wonder if they are "normal" if they delay sexual activity. The reality is that going steady and being sexually active in early teens is associated with less maturity (Helms and Turner, 1981).

Career Choices

Georgia O'Keeffe faced many critical decisions during her teen years. She had to turn down many modeling opportunities, for example, in order to dedicate her time to art. In the same way, adolescents today make many decisions that affect or limit their career choices: They learn good or poor work habits, they stay in school or dropout, they take college preparation courses or they specialize in some trade. Our rapidly changing society is also creating a need for better career counseling for teenagers. Parents are important role models and they can provide sound advice, but job markets are changing so fast today that even full-time counselors have trouble keeping up with all the options. Additional counseling outside the home is especially important for girls and for teenagers from economically disadvantaged homes. The work world is changing especially fast for women (Hanes, Prawat, and Grissom, 1979), and disadvantaged children are often unaware of the full range of career possibilities (Laska and Micklin, 1979).

Children are unrealistic about careers, often thinking that they will be able to have any job they want. Teenagers begin to appreciate that most jobs require certain qualifications. They then try to come to grips with their own job-related qualities and abilities. This self-evaluation process continues on into adulthood.

YOUNG ADULTHOOD

Georgia O'Keeffe's life is a valuable reminder that adults do not necessarily experience the same life events in the same order. Many adults marry and have a first child between the ages of 20 and 25. Georgia's parents are examples of this, but Georgia herself did not marry until she was 37, and she never had children. She did, however, dedicate herself at about this time to what became her lifework, her career in art. This became the most important commitment of her life.

Lowenthal (1977) provided a valuable framework for investigating development during young adulthood. She proposed that researchers could unify various aspects of development by studying commitments. She suggests that young adults make three particularly important commitments: moral, interpersonal, and mastery. *Moral commitments* relate to development in Kohlberg's highest stage of moral development, the postconventional stage, which we discussed earlier. *Interpersonal commitments* relate to Erikson's sixth stage of development, "intimacy versus isolation." Most young adults at this point commit themselves to intimate relationships that are characterized by deep caring and mutual respect. Avoiding this type of commitment may lead to a deep sense of isolation from other people. To illustrate this stage we will discuss marriage and child rearing, which are the most common ways for adults to develop intimate relationships. *Mastery commitments* refer to occupational commitments, such as the one Georgia made to her career in art.

Family Commitments

Georgia's mother, Ida, moved away from her parent's home at the age of 20. She married and had her first child within the next 2 years, and her last of five children was born before she was 30. Much of Ida's young adulthood was therefore committed to starting and raising her own family. About 93 percent of today's women make the same commitment during young adulthood, although recent trends suggest an increase in alternative life styles (see Hultsch and Deutsch, 1981). For example, an unmarried man and woman may live together in a relationship that is very similar to that of a married couple; this is called **cohabitation** (Stafford, Backman, and Dibona, 1977). Communes offer another alternative in which members try to live as one large family (Stinnet and Walters,

1977). Despite the increasing popularity of these alternatives, we will concentrate on marriage, because it affects the vast majority of young adults.

Marriage and the Family Cycle.   Marriage and child rearing create a *family cycle*, which is a sequence of family events that repeat themselves generation after generation. Major events in the family cycle are: (1) leave parental home; (2) marry; (3) have first child; (4) bear last child; (5) first child leaves home; (6) last child leaves home; (7) children marry; (8) grandchildren are born. These events are among the important influences that interact to produce unique patterns of adult development. Researchers therefore observe the timing, duration, and clustering of family-cycle events.

You can compare with your friends to see that there is considerable variability in the age at which family events occur. Psychologists have nevertheless found interesting trends by observing average ages for these events. Figure 8–2 shows the results of one study that compared averages for women of different social classes (Olsen, 1969). Upper-middle-class women were 4 to 8 years older than lower-class women for each event, with lower-middle class and working-class women falling in between. A notable difference between groups was the time span between first and last child. The average age for upper-middle-class mothers at the time their first child was born was 26, and it was 29 for the last. The comparable averages for lower-class mothers were 18 and 27. Beyond those differences, the sequencing of events was similar between classes. The average woman left her parents' home 1 to 2 years after finishing her formal education; she got married 1 to 3 years later; and she had her first child 1 to 3 years after that.

Some evidence suggests that timing of family events may be related to marital and parental satisfaction. One researcher found, for instance, that middle-class women who marry between 20 and 30 years of age report happier marriages than those who marry earlier or later (Nydegger, 1973). Being "off-schedule" is not always associated with dissatisfaction, however. Most men become fathers before they are 40, but those who wait longer tend to be happier with their parental role. Nydegger suggested that men who wait to have children may experience less conflict between family life and career demands. His explanation is consistent with the

FIGURE: 8–2

These are the results of a study that compared the average age at which certain family events had occurred in the lives of women of different social classes. (Olsen, 1969)

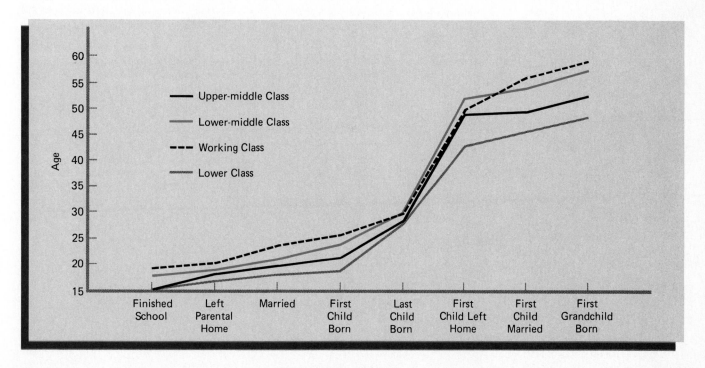

existence of heavy career demands during young adulthood, as we shall see in the next section.

Occupational Commitments

Georgia O'Keeffe launched her career as an artist with her first showing in Stieglitz's gallery at the age of 28. By the time Georgia reached middle age she was recognized as "the greatest woman painter in America" (Leslie, 1980). Not everyone becomes the greatest in their field, of course, but many young adults achieve high levels in their chosen occupation before they enter middle age. Young adults usually dedicate themselves to the mastery of knowledge and skills, which they achieve through occupational commitments. Typical life events include not only getting married and having children, but also trying several jobs and advancing in a chosen occupation.

Mastery of specific knowledge and job-related skills is only a fraction of the total developmental changes necessary for successful career commitments. White (1975) outlines four aspects of personality and social development that are also associated with careers. Young adults must learn to: (1) respond to people warmly and respectfully without anxiety; (2) base decisions upon their own beliefs; (3) respect cultural values; and (4) care about society and the people in it. Accordingly, career commitments depend upon cognitive, social, and personality development during young adulthood. As mentioned earlier, Lowenthal (1977) maintains that the commitment to mastery in an occupation is a very important aspect of development in young adults.

Career Women. An increasing number of women in America are lining up for their paychecks. Women constituted 25 percent of the labor force in 1940 and 50.7 percent in 1980 (U.S. Department of Labor, 1981). Married women account for most of the increase. Their rate of working, however, still is behind that of single women. The difference is especially large during young adulthood, as indicated in Figure 8–3, which shows working rate by age for single and married women. The figure also reflects the tendency for married women to have two entry points into the work force. Their rate of working peaks in their twenties and again in their fifties. The double peaks correspond to women working before their children are born, taking a break while rearing children, and working again when their children leave home. This interruption partially explains why

FIGURE: 8–3

The graph shows working rate by age for single and married women. (U.S. Department of Labor, 1975)

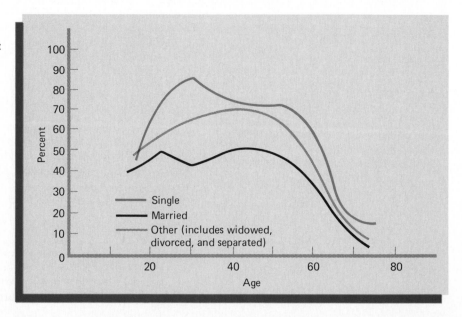

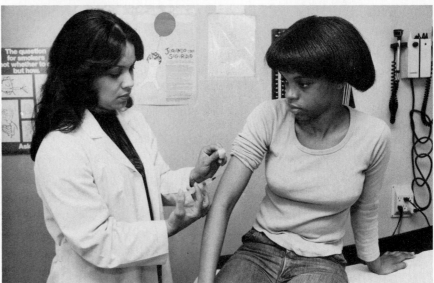

women receive 20 to 25 percent less pay than men in the same occupations. It is only a partial explanation for the pay difference, however. The discrepancy also exists because the American economic system discriminates against women, although this discrimination is decreasing (Hoffman and Nye, 1974; Kreps, 1976).

Housewives versus Career Women. Who is happier—the full-time homemaker or the career woman? This question is most meaningful when asked about career women with multiple roles of worker, wife, and mother. The answer may surprise you in light of portrayals in modern media. Magazines, television, and movies suggest that careers for women are enriching, liberating, and satisfying. In contrast, the role of homemaker is often pictured as boring, lonely, and demeaning. Accordingly, career women should be happier. In fact, there is no difference! Two separate and extensive studies showed no difference in general life satisfaction or in self-esteem (Baruch and Barnett, 1980; Wright, 1978). This important finding dramatizes a pervasive theme in life-span psychology—there is no single path to happiness.

The paths to life satisfaction for full-time homemakers and for women with careers are indeed distinctive. The two groups spend their time quite differently, of course. One study suggests that working women spend only half as much time doing housework (Kreps, 1976). Working women do not feel that they pay less attention to their husbands, and they are happiest when their husbands are supportive of their careers (Rappaport and Rappaport, 1971). The main source of satisfaction and esteem for the career woman is her work; the main source for the full-time homemaker is her husband's approval (Baruch and Barnett, 1980). Neither path guarantees happiness.

Profile of a Successful Career Woman. Henning and Jardin (1976) identified characteristics of 25 women who had established themselves as successful executives by the end of young adulthood. These women tended to be first born in their families, and they tended to excel in college. Their fathers were extremely supportive of their careers, encouraged them to develop their abilities, reinforced them for breaking away from sex-role stereotypes, and financially assisted the launching of their careers. The women accepted assistance from senior male executives in the beginning, but they became independent by the time they reached middle-management positions. This profile of the successful career woman is adequate, but it is sketchy in comparison to the more detailed observations that are available on the successful career man.

Becoming One's Own Man. Daniel J. Levinson (1978) and four colleagues at Yale University conducted one of the most comprehensive studies of development in young male adults. The research team studied 140 men who were either executives, biologists, novelists, or hourly wage earners. The team interviewed the men for a total of 10 to 20 hours, in sessions that were spread over about 1½ years. All men were between 35 and 40 years of age at the first interview; 2 years later the team conducted a follow-up interview. As part of the sessions the men were asked to recall the events of their young adulthood. The results suggested that males go through three periods during young adulthood:

1. Men go through a phase Levinson called *entering the adult world* between their early and late twenties. In this phase they seek a balance between keeping options open and establishing a stable life

According to Levinson, most men experience an age-30 transition, during which they carefully evaluate their lives and their careers. For some this may be a smooth transition; for others it may be a crisis, leading to divorce or career change.

structure. A good balance results in a wide exploration of alternatives, followed by strong commitments. As part of this, most men get married, have children, and choose an occupation during this period.

2. Most men experience an *age 30 transition* within several years of their thirtieth birthday. They think then that it will soon be too late to make changes, so they carefully evaluate their commitments. Some men make a smooth transition, reaffirming their earlier decisions; others face a severe crisis accompanied by divorce and occupational change.

3. Between the early thirties and about age 40, men go through an important period that Levinson called *settling down*. They emphasize stability and security now, often fixing on some key goal, such as a promotion. The end phase of *settling down* is called *becoming one's own man*. As men grow out of early adulthood, they urgently strive to advance as far as possible in their careers, to gain greater authority, and to be independent. Most men advance within a stable life structure. Changes in residence, job, or life style usually represent advancements rather than basic changes in their established life structure. For some men, however, this is another time for a severe crisis. Like those who went through a crisis at age 30, those who have them at this point try to drastically alter their existing life structure, through divorce or career changes. The phase of becoming one's own man, whether smooth or rocky, usually ends at about 40 years of age, as new developmental demands usher in middle age.

MIDDLE ADULTHOOD

The adage "Life begins at 40" seems to miss the mark with respect to a person as dynamic as Georgia O'Keeffe. She seemed to "begin" over and over again throughout her life. The adage is not entirely inaccurate in her case, however, since one of her fresh starts came at about the age of 40. "Having abandoned the idea of having a child, and approaching her fortieth birthday, Georgia began planning precisely every detail of her daily existence to eliminate anything unnecessary to art. . . . She set new goals for herself and became absorbed in solving various technical problems after the critics had given her high praise for her technical virtuosity" (Leslie, 1980, pp. 182–184). Her experiences between 40 and 60 years of age provide an interesting frame of reference for our discussion of middle adulthood.

Sequence of Development in Middle Years

Erikson's Generativity versus Stagnation. Erikson (1959, 1963) maintains that one of two feelings dominates at this age: (1) *generativity*, a sense of producing and contributing to the world, or (2) *stagnation*, a sense of not fulfilling what was expected of one. A sense of generativity can be gained through family, job, or community involvement. Georgia clearly gained a sense of generativity through her career; her mother gained it by rearing children. People who feel no sense of worthwhile accomplishment form an impression of being bogged down in a life without meaning. People can get beyond this sense of stagnation, however, and doing so can make them more compassionate about the weaknesses and suffering of others.

Levinson's Periods of Middle Adulthood. Levinson (1978) proposed a universal sequence of periods during middle adulthood. They are as follows:

1. Men experience a *midlife transition* between the ages of 40 and 45. This is the period of the so-called midlife crisis, which we will discuss in the Highlight, " 'Midlife Crisis,' 'Empty Nest Syndrome,' and Other Myths."
2. Forty-five- to fifty-year-old men settle into a new life structure during a period called *entering middle adulthood*. Those who created a satisfactory structure during the previous transitional period enjoy one of the happiest times of their lives. (Levinson's conclusions about life after 45 is more speculative because it is based on biographies instead of interviews.)
3. Another transitional period, *age 50 transition*, occurs between 50 and 55. It is analogous to the *age 30 transition*, in which men reevaluate previous commitments.
4. A stable period, *culmination of middle adulthood*, is enjoyed between 55 and 60. Levinson has very little data on this period, but he suspects it is similar to the settling down period discussed earlier.

Levinson is the first to acknowledge that it is too early to tell if he is correct in postulating a universal sequence. You might judge the appropriateness of his periods for yourself as we consider physical, family, and occupational events during middle adulthood.

HIGHLIGHT / "MIDLIFE CRISIS," "EMPTY NEST SYNDROME," AND OTHER MYTHS

Magazines are filled with stories about people going through various crises in middle age, such as the "empty nest syndrome," which occurs to parents when their last child leaves home, or "midlife crisis," a period of conflict and stress in the mid-forties. As a result, one could easily get the impression that these crises are the common fate of most middle-aged people. When we look at the primary research that is behind these articles in the popular press, however, we get a different picture.

Research indicates, for example, that there is a distortion of parental reactions to children leaving home. The media exaggerates the negative feelings connected with "empty nest syndrome" and plays down the positive responses that parents experience when their children leave home (Hagestad, 1980). National surveys indicate, furthermore, that there is a strong positive side. Parents actually look forward to the "empty nest," and they report high levels of life satisfaction after their youngest child leaves home (Glen, 1975; Lowenthal and Chiriboga, 1973). One reason for these positive feelings is that sons and daughters who set up their own home continue to be a source of satisfaction for their parents (Hagestad, 1980).

Research also indicates that the term "midlife crisis" may be a distortion of what most people experience during middle age. The theoretical background for the idea of a midlife crisis can be traced back to Erikson's theory, which includes the stage called generativity versus stagnation. During this period the adult's interests expand and he or she "looks" both backwards ("What have I done with my life?") and forward ("What do I want to do for the rest of my life?"). This period is marked by considerable conflict and vacillation. Some people try to make dramatic changes in their life style and occupation. Others adapt a very different set of values (either much more conservative or liberal than before).

Modern researchers are suggesting, however, that such a crisis is the exception rather than the rule (Brim, 1976; Neugarten, 1970; Vaillant, 1977). The rule, according to these researchers, is a relatively smooth tranisition through the middle years. A study by Costa and McCrae (1980), supports this transition view and argues against the idea of a universal crisis confined to midlife. These researchers found no relationship between age and crisis in a sample of 33- to 79-year-old men. They did, however, identify crisis-*prone* middle-aged people, who were also not well adjusted as adolescents or as young adults. On the one hand, then, midlife crisis is real enough for some people, and groundwork is in fact being laid for predicting who those people will be, based on patterns of crises at earlier

Physical Changes

Georgia's appearance during the middle years portrayed years of joy, laughter, pain, and sorrow, which, together with the harsh southwestern sun, etched character into her face. Physical alterations in middle age call attention to the aging process. Changes that affect appearance (e.g., baldness, wrinkles, and weight gain) are accompanied by reduced physiological capacities. Muscle strength, lung capacity, and cardiac output all decline (de Vries, 1970). There is also a slight increase in the time it takes to make simple responses, such as braking a car in an emergency (Hodgkins, 1962). People who are middle-aged also start noticing visual loss caused by changes in the eye's lens (Fozard et al., 1977). The lens becomes yellower, cloudier, and less able to focus light for close work such as reading. All these biological changes remind people that their life span is limited (Levinson, 1978).

Physical decline causes professional athletes and others with physically demanding jobs to make radical career adjustments during middle age. Biological changes have little effect, however, on the everyday lives of most middle-agers. Yet, most middle-aged adults, especially men, express considerable concern about their decreased physical efficiency (Neugarten, 1968).

Some changes must be accepted, of course, but currently many more middle-aged men and women are taking steps to stay in shape than in

stages. On the other hand, "midlife transition" may be a more accurate term for what most people experience in middle age.

Whether there is a crisis or a transition, there does seem to be a universal sequence of development during middle years. Erikson, Levinson, and others seem to find a common behavioral pattern that emerges through people's interactions with society. Middle-aged people face physical changes, and most face changes in family and career as well. In response, they look back at certain decisions that they have made, and they look ahead to future commitments. Studies of these patterns have practical applications. They might guide employers in the selection of people who will be dependable, for example, and they might help clinicians work with people having adjustment problems. Studies of universal patterns lend themselves to misinterpretation, however, especially by those whose only exposure to them is through the popular press.

Magazine articles often give the impression that they are providing a sure guideline to happiness. This could create a serious misconception about what life-span research can and cannot do. Life-span research often reveals universal or behavioral patterns without providing any basis for saying what behaviors are "best" or "right." They do not necessarily indicate a "best" way to live. The life-span approach recognizes the importance not only of common patterns, but also of individual differences in our behavior. Look to the research to provide a frame of reference for comparing yourself with others if you like, but do not turn to it for a rule of how to live. It is just possible that your way is both different and better than "normal."

In what is a fairly recent trend, many middle-aged men and women actively pursue exercise programs aimed at staying in shape.

previous years. Exercise programs including calisthenics, running, and swimming can be very effective (de Vries, 1970). Physicians highly recommend such rigorous programs for those who can pass a careful physical examination (de Vries, 1975; Woodruff, 1977). Less strenuous programs also help. People can, for instance, take short brisk walks that will help them stay in good physical condition.

Family Commitments

Georgia's family commitments were unusual, as mentioned before. She had only been married 8 years on her forty-fifth birthday, and she had no children. Most middle-aged people have about 20 years of marriage behind them at this age, and they find themselves sandwiched between the needs of two generations. Their, children, generally teenagers, have special needs as they seek greater independence, while their aging parents have special needs as they become more dependent.

Middle-aged Parents and Their Children. Parent-child relationships change at various points in the family cycle. One transitional phase begins with adolescence and ends when children leave home. We already examined this passage into adulthood from a teenager's point of view. Now we will consider it from the perspective of middle-aged parents.

Some parents need to be reminded that children have rights. They have the right to love as well as discipline (West, 1967); they have the right to respect for their concerns, interests, goals, and freedoms to the extent that they can handle responsibilities (Elkind, 1979). Popular magazines bombard parents with reminders about children's rights. In *Redbook*, Spock (1977) told "How Loving Parents Can Discipline Their Child"; in *McCalls*, Salk (1979) discussed "The Right and Wrong Way to Discipline Children"; and *Parents*, McCall (1980) explained, "Babies Are Real People!" This emphasis is fine as long as we remember that parents are real people, too.

Parents also have rights that are every bit as important as children's rights. Middle-aged parents and their adolescent children are likely to encounter some conflicts as their relationship evolves toward greater independence. The key to parent-child harmony is mutual respect for the rights of both children and parents (Baumrind, 1971, 1982; Elkind, 1979).

The Middle-Aged and Their Parents. In addition to being parents themselves, many middle-aged people have a special relationship with their own parents. Adult sons and daughters maintain strong ties with their parents. Much as parents value independence, aging parents gradually become more and more dependent upon their offspring (Blenker, 1975). People meet their aging parents' needs in many ways. They visit, do household tasks, run errands, and give physical care (Sussman and Burchinal, 1962). Some even take their parents into their homes (Spark and Brody, 1970). Research has indicated that 80 to 90 percent of parents studied have children living within an hour's driving distance. Of these, 80 percent had seen their children within the past week (Riley, Johnson, and Foner, 1972). Such interactions are best when elderly parents are allowed to preserve their personal dignity and when middle-aged sons and daughters are allowed to pursue their other commitments (Blenker, 1965).

People at this age are truly the "middle" generation—they are parents themselves, and they usually have their own parents living within visiting distance. As their children grow and become independent, their aging parents often begin to become more dependent.

TABLE 8–3: Effects of Personality and Situation on Occupation

Personality Factors	Situational Pressures	Stability or Change in Occupation
Low self-direction	Little pressure to change	Routine career; advancement follows seniority
High self-direction	Little pressure to change	Flexible career; initiative for change and type of work assumed by person
Low self-direction	Much pressure to change	Disjointed career; technologically oriented reasons for unemployment (e.g., blue-collar workers), no skill or experience (e.g., widow)
High self-direction	Much pressure to change	Orderly, sequential career; well-planned effort in making changes by person

Source: Murray et al. (1971).

Occupational Commitments

Georgia made stronger commitments to her career, and she became more successful in it, during her middle years. Many people follow this pattern. An increasing number, however, change careers at this age. Clopton (1973) calls those who stay with the same careers *persisters*, and he calls those who change careers *shifters*. Let's look at the developmental patterns of men and women who fall into these two categories.

Career Men. Evidence indicates that there is a strong positive side to midlife career shifts. Researchers found, for instance, that such shifts can be satisfying, productive, and orderly (Murray, Powers, and Havighurst, 1971). This positive pattern is more likely in white-collar workers than in blue-collar workers (Schein, 1975). It is also associated with certain personality and situational factors, as shown in Table 8-3.

Males who persist in a career are not always highly successful. In one study, Bray and Howard (1980) found considerable variability in success of managers who had stayed with the Bell Telephone System for over 20 years. The successful managers were more intelligent, more motivated, and more aggressive than less successful ones. They were also happier with their jobs, but they were not necessarily happier in their overall life situations. The most and the least successful managers found happiness through different life patterns.

Career Women. We have already identified various career patterns: women who stay with the same company through young adulthood and middle adulthood, women who remain full-time homemakers, and women who interrupt their outside-the-home careers to raise children. We might call the first two groups *persisters* and the third one *shifters*.

The shifters are especially interesting. Many of these women return to school during their middle years for a wide range of reasons. At one extreme, some women merely brush up on previously held skills before reentering the work world. At the other extreme, some women complete graduate degrees in order to become full-time professionals. Middle-aged women tend to enter graduate school with fire in their eyes. Their confidence often diminishes midway through the program, as both school and family pressures mount. The original determination usually wins out, however, and the women emerge with increased self-esteem and assertiveness (Lefevre, 1972). These shifters tend to be happy despite unfortunate discrimination against them in wages and job opportunities (Blau, 1975; Ritzer, 1977). In fact, shifters seem to be as happy as persisters, which is consistent with an important theme that emerges from life-span research: There are many ways to be happy.

LATE ADULTHOOD

Georgia's ability to emerge triumphantly from a trying struggle was shown again in late adulthood when her husband died. Georgia virtually retired from her career during her first 10 years of widowhood; then she made an incredible comeback. The spirit that enabled her to rekindle her blazing career is catching on today with more and more elderly adults. That spirit is symbolized in one of Georgia's adventures: In 1961, at the age of 74, she took a 10-day, 185-mile raft trip down the Colorado River. She handled her own equipment, helped with the rowing, and remained cheerful through very hot days, freezing nights, and drenching thunderstorms. Her keen insights heightened the experience for her companions. She didn't have time to paint on the first trip, but she returned many times after that, trying to capture on canvas the beauty she had seen.

Georgia's elderly years, like her earlier ones, are typical in some respects and unusual in others. Having to face the death of a spouse is typical. Having a zest for life is also prevalent. Her mental and physical agility, however, are uncommon, as is her persistence in the same career. In this section, we will examine current trends in aging and we will try to predict future ones. As we progress, you might ask yourself whether Georgia's river trip was something that only she would do at that age, or whether it forecasts the adventures that could well be ours in late adulthood.

Physical and Mental Abilities

Georgia has always taken an active part in maintaining her good health. She has an organic garden that forms the basis of her carefully planned diet. A typical day begins with a big breakfast that includes beef butchered to her specification, a morning snack of homemade yogurt, a lunch consisting of an organic salad, and a light dinner of little more than fruit and cheese. She especially loves the strong flavors of garlic, raw onion, and chili peppers. She maintains her weight at 127 pounds, and she is very healthy for her age.

We all understand the qualifier, "for her age," to some extent through our experience with grandparents and other elderly adults. We know that our health will decline. Physical changes will eventually touch nearly every aspect of our lives, including our mental abilities. We may have to give up things that we now enjoy; we may have to slow down. But we can follow Georgia's example in taking steps to maximize our health as we age. We can stack the deck in our favor by knowing what to expect and by planning for it.

Biological Theories of Aging. Not everyone accepts aging as a natural and inevitable process. Bjorksten (1968), for example, argues that aging is a disease. He maintains that humans might live for 800 years or more in good health if that disease could be cured. Few researchers express such optimism. Many believe, however, that the maximum life span, which is now about 110 to 120 years, will increase as researchers discover the basic mechanisms of the aging process (Medvedev, 1975). Cell malfunctions in elderly people is caused in part by mutations that damage genes, as we discussed in Chapter 2, according to Sinex (1974). Abnormal cell functioning interferes with the normal operation of physiological systems such as the endocrine system. This in turn leads to the physical changes we know as aging. Knowing the physical changes associated with aging can be valuable if you ever care for an elderly person (see the Highlight, "Sensory Changes and Caring for the Elderly").

Georgia O'Keeffe is shown here at age 75, shortly after her rigorous raft trip down the Colorado River. When this photograph was taken, she had just been elected a member of the American Academy of Arts and Letters, the nation's highest honor society of the arts.

Cognitive Changes. Elderly people are often the first to admit a decline in their cognitive abilities. Those who work with the elderly also notice declining mental abilities in their patients. Experimenters, however, have had trouble analyzing cognitive changes because of certain methodological pitfalls.

A study by Jerome (1959) illustrates some of the snags. He tested problem-solving abilities with a logical analysis device. People had to

HIGHLIGHT / SENSORY CHANGES AND CARING FOR THE ELDERLY

Stephen Cohen (1981) has described sensory changes in the elderly, and he has also outlined procedures that will help if you ever care for an elderly relative or some other elderly person. Some of his main points are as follow:

1. Vision is impaired in the elderly because of structural changes in the aging eye (which we discussed in Chapter 3). When you assist an elderly person, you should be aware that there are reductions in abilities to see depth (for example, distance of floor from bed), to see objects located off to the side, and to see detail. Old eyes also take longer to adjust when going from dark to dim places. The elderly have trouble seeing blues, greens, and violets; they have an easier time seeing reds, oranges, and yellows. You should, therefore, select lighting, positioning, and coloring of objects carefully, especially critical objects such as stairs, handrails, doorknobs, and light switches.

2. Aging also causes hearing problems. One reason for this is a decrease in the number of nerve fibers that carry sound information (see Chapter 3). Hearing loss especially affects the ability to hear high-pitched sounds, such as high notes on a piano. Thus elderly people hear low-pitched sounds better than high-pitched sounds. You can help an aging person hear important sounds such as doorbells, smoke alarms, and telephone bells not only by

increasing the volume, but also by lowering the pitch. You can help an aging person understand speech by teaching yourself and others how to modify your voice. You should speak loudly, but do not shout. Shouting conceals high-pitched speech sounds that the elderly person already finds difficult to hear. You should slow down, to space your sounds as far apart as possible. Finally, you should lower the pitch of your voice as much as possible. A deep male voice is easiest for a hard-of-hearing person to understand.

3. Other sensory impairments must be overcome. The sense of smell and taste are reduced, so that foods with intense aromas and flavors will be appreciated by the elderly. Avoid piping hot food, however, because an elderly person's ability to detect heat is dangerously reduced. For the same reason, protect the aging from hot surfaces such as faucets, radiators, pots, and pans. The sense of touch and of pain is reduced to the point where the elderly might not realize that they are cutting off blood circulation. They should be encouraged, therefore, to wear loose clothing and to change positions every so often when lying or sitting for long periods.

Cohen convincingly demonstrates that knowing the nature of sensory changes can make life safer for the aging.

gather information piece by piece and then integrate it to solve problems. A group of subjects who were about 66 years old did much worse than a group of subjects who were about 23 years old. The older people tended to ask for the same information over and over again. Jerome tried to cut down on the need to remember information by allowing subjects to write notes. Younger people made good use of the notes, but older people did not. Jerome's experiment left no doubt that the older subjects had greater difficulty solving problems because they approached the problems haphazardly, but its meaning is nevertheless uncertain. This is because we cannot be sure that age caused the difference that was observed between young and old subjects. The two groups might have differed in motivation. Perhaps older people considered the problems meaningless and irrelevant and therefore may have exerted themselves less. Furthermore, the two groups might have had different educational experiences. Schools for the younger subjects may have put greater emphasis on problem solving. As a result, the younger subjects may have been better problem solvers than the older people were at *any* point in their lives. For these reasons, Jerome's experiment does not prove that age causes a decline in problem-solving ability.

Whenever researchers compare different age groups, age is not the only difference. Motivation and education are two other factors that often differ. Researchers do not agree on how to define motivation or on how to measure it. Until they agree on these issues, there will be little hope of controlling motivation in studies of aging (Botwinick, 1977). Motivational changes could cause changes in performance even when researchers study the same people at different ages. Education is also difficult to control for because the educational system keeps changing. Despite these methodological problems, however, researchers have gathered important data on cognitive changes.

Botwinick (1977) has outlined six cognitive changes that occur with age and aids to counteract them:

1. Older people need more time to respond in learning situations (Canestrari, 1963). The pacing of learning tasks should be slowed to allow for this.
2. Older people are prone to have high anxiety, which limits responses in learning tasks (Eisdorfer, 1968). Researchers should take steps to reduce anxiety as much as possible in learning and testing situations.
3. Elderly people tend to resist learning things that seem to them to be irrelevant and meaningless (Hulicka & Grossman, 1967). It's a good idea to make sure an elderly person wants to learn something or understands why it is important before teaching is begun.
4. The elderly often fail to take advantage of organizational strategies that could help them learn. We learned in Chapter 6, for instance, that list learning is easier when similar items are grouped together. Elderly learners do not try such groupings on their own (Denny, 1974). They may improve considerably if they are helped to organize in this way (Hultsch, 1971).
5. Elderly people tend to be insecure. They will therefore respond much better if they are praised rather than criticized.
6. Elderly people's short-term memory (Chapter 6) is better for things they hear than it is for things they see (Arenberg, 1967). If you want to help an aging person remember a phone number long enough for a single dialing, say it for them.

Most of you will not personally experience sensory or cognitive declines for many years. You may, however, be able to help aging relatives counteract such sensory and cognitive changes. We mentioned earlier, for instance, that aging parents often depend upon support from their sons and daughters (Spark and Brody, 1970). In the next section, we will reexamine this important phase of the family cycle from the aging parents' perspective.

Family Commitments

Georgia's decision not to have children meant that she had few family commitments during late adulthood, especially after her husband died. She made up for this, however, by becoming a "foster grandparent" to children in her village. These children visited her regularly. They ate with her, colored with crayons in her studio, and sometimes they even helped her prepare canvases. She took some of her favorites camping with her, and she sent several to private schools. She supplied a Little League team with uniforms, balls, and bats. She provided funds to bring educational programs to local television stations, and she supported the construction of a local recreational center with a donation of about $60,000. She may have been motivated by the fond memories of her grandmothers, who in her childhood lived nearby until she was about 10 years old. Psychologists are only beginning to gather data on grandparenting. They are finding that this important role enriches the lives of grandchildren *and* grandparents.

Being a Grandparent.   Clavan (1978) called grandparenting a "roleless role" because its rights and responsibilities are not clearly defined in our society. In agreement with this conclusion, a variety of styles of grandparenting have been found (Neugarten and Weinstein, 1964). The most common styles are "formal" and "fun-seeking." Both are characterized by special interest in grandchildren and by giving treats to them. The fun-seeking style has the additional quality of mutually satisfying leisure activities for grandparents and grandchildren. Less common styles are: "surrogate-parent," in which care-giving responsibilities are assumed; "reservoir of family wisdom," in which instruction for special skills are dispensed by an authoritarian grandparent; and "distant figure," in which there is little interaction between grandparents and grandchildren.

Grandparents and grandchildren mutually enrich each others' lives. Ninety-two percent of grandchildren in one study thought that grandparents contribute much to growing up (Robertson, 1976). Children like doing things with their grandparents, and they value love and gifts from them (Kahana and Kahana, 1971). In return, they give their grandparents great satisfaction. The majority derived pleasure from a feeling of renewal, from meaningful companionship, and from being able to contribute to

Grandparents and grandchildren mutually enrich each others' lives.

the development of their grandchildren. Grandparents also enjoy seeing their grandchildren accomplish things that neither the grandparent nor their children were able to do. Grandparenting can become especially important when death of a spouse deprives an elderly person of one of his or her most important sources of life satisfaction.

Elderly Husbands and Wives. Marital satisfaction is very high for elderly couples. In fact, it may reach its highest level during late adulthood (Miller, 1976). Older husbands and wives find happiness in companionship, mutual expression of true feelings, and economic security, among other things (Stinnett, Carter, and Montgomery, 1972). Contrary to common belief, they also enjoy sexual relations to the age of 80 years and beyond (Rubin, 1966). Reduced occupational commitments enable elderly couples to spend more time together. In the best situations, husbands help more around the house and women become more loving and understanding (Troll, 1971). Such adjustments increase marital satisfaction for those who had happy relationships during younger years (Peterson and Payne, 1975).

Occupational Commitments

Georgia O'Keeffe widely exhibited new paintings as she advanced in years through her eighties and into her nineties. She remained in the mainstream of art when others her age had long since retired. Many people cannot stay engaged in their careers as Georgia did. But most people can make up for career retirement by increasing involvement in other activities (Neugarten and Hagestad, 1976). Retirement, from this point of view, can be as fulfilling as Georgia's late-life career. In this section, we will consider how people plan for retirement, how they adjust to it, and how satisfied they are with it.

Planning for Retirement. Retirement in the United States is usually mandatory at the age of 65 or 70 years. The mandatory versus voluntary retirement issue will probably be debated for some time to come. On the one hand, mandatory retirement seems to discriminate against older people who are ready and able to work. On the other hand, Botwinick (1977) argues in favor of mandatory retirement on several grounds, one of which is that a fixed age limit will better enable people to plan for retirement.

To what extent do people actually plan under the present mandatory system? There is no simple answer, because many variables influence the extent of planning. A tendency for men to plan is positively associated with high socioeconomic status, leisure-time interests, financial security, and good health (McPherson and Guppy, 1979). These same variables are associated with a positive attitude toward an upcoming retirement in men. The variables of socioeconomic status and financial security affect women differently. Women with high-status jobs and high income do *not* want to retire (Streib and Schneider, 1971). This sex difference is ironic, because women often adjust more easily than men when they do retire.

Adjusting to Retirement. Lowenthal (1972) suggests that the trick to a successful retirement is substituting activities for the time previously spent on an occupation. Career women are often better prepared to make this adjustment because the role of homemaker is a traditionally acceptable substitution. Men also adjust better when they share in household tasks. Some men, however, especially working-class men, consider "women's work" demeaning. As a result, adjusting to retirement can be more problematic for this group (Troll, 1971). A second popular substitution is another job. Streib and Schneider (1971) observed that 73 percent of people who consider work to be a major source of satisfaction find another job after retirement. A third substitution is well-planned leisure activity, which can be especially fulfilling for those who have a history of sharing recre-

Most people plan to make up for retirement by increasing their involvement in other activities, such as painting or attending sports events.

ational interests with their spouses. Whatever the substitution is, a redistribution of energy seems to be basic to a satisfying adjustment.

Retirement and Life Satisfaction. The impact of retirement is often not as negative as people anticipated, according to Streib and Schneider (1971). They measured attitudes of 4,000 people before and after retirement. Their sample included people from many walks of life, ranging from unskilled laborers to professionals. The results indicated that about 33 percent found retirement to be better than they had anticipated. Only about 5 percent found it to be worse. Most people in the sample adjusted well to retirement and were satisfied with life.

Streib and Schneider's study raises the question of why so many people are overly pessimistic about retirement. One reason may be that some of the negative feelings are not actually related to retirement itself. A worker inevitably associates retirement with old age, and that in the end is associated with death. Older people have had a chance to come to grips with aging and they are less fearful of death (Kalish and Reynolds, 1976). After retirement we would therefore expect a reduction in some of the pessimism that was associated with the fear of aging and death.

DEATH AND DYING

Georgia was almost 60 when her husband died. Many friends and relatives also died as she advanced through her sixties. These deaths not only depressed her, they also made her aware that she had to make plans for her estate after her own death. She assigned some paintings to be left to several museums and universities. She wants most of her art to be displayed, however, in an O'Keeffe art museum in New Mexico. As Georgia planned her museum, it was apparent that she loved life, but accepted the reality of death. In terms of Erikson's (1963) theory, she faced the last stage of development, the crisis of *integrity versus despair*. Resolution of this crisis determines whether one faces the end of life with a feeling that a full and meaningful life has been led or with a feeling that life has been wasted. Georgia emerged with wisdom that is related to integrity. She achieved the wisdom to be pleased with her accomplishments and to be accepting of her death. We will conclude our life-span investigation with a brief discussion of the processes of accepting the deaths of others and accepting one's own death.

Adjusting to the Death of Loved Ones

Georgia grieved over the deaths of her parents, other relatives, and friends. But the death of her husband seemed to be most devastating. Death of a spouse requires more than an emotional adjustment. It also requires adoptations of new roles and responsibilities. Life-satisfaction ratings of widows and widowers correlate highly with having skills necessary for making these adaptations (Rux, 1976). Another important factor is the extent of involvement in a spouse's life. Lopata (1973a b c) observed, for instance, that widows report more life disruption when they identified strongly with their husband's activities. Widows and widowers experience severe loneliness and grief, however, whether or not they are forced to make drastic life-style changes.

Psychologists are only beginning to learn about the grief process (e.g., Parkes and Brown, 1972). Glick, Weiss, and Parkes (1974) outlined distinct phases of grieving:

1. The *initial response* is a phase characterized first by shock and then by an overwhelming sorrow.
2. The second phase, *coping with anxiety and fear*, is characterized by worry of a nervous breakdown. Some people depend upon tranquilizers during this period.
3. The third phase, the *intermediate* phase, consists of obsessional review of how the death might have been prevented and a review of old memories of times with the loved one.
4. *Recovery* is the last phase, which usually begins after 1 year. People become proud that they survived an extreme trauma, and they begin to develop a positive outlook once again.

Accepting Your Own Death

How often do you think about your own death? Can you face it without fear or despair? Your answers probably depend upon your age. Young people think about death much less than old people, and they are more fearful of it (Kalish and Reynolds, 1976). The question of accepting one's own death becomes especially relevant to those who are told that they have a terminal illness. In her book, *On Death and Dying*, Elizabeth Kübler-Ross (1969) summarized results of interviews with over 200 people in this situation. She identified five stages in the adjustment process:

1. *Denial and isolation* is first. A common initial statement is "No, not me, it cannot be true." Some denials are long lasting and are accompanied by conviction that the doctors are wrong. Other denials are soon replaced by isolation, which is the ability to talk about one's own death as if it were happening to someone else.
2. The second stage is *anger*, which typically stems from resentment and from concern about being cast aside. One patient reported wondering, "Why couldn't it have been old George instead of me?" Another patient cried out "I am alive, don't forget that. You can hear my voice, I am not dead yet!"
3. Anger is often replaced by *bargaining*. This third stage usually involves private promises with God. For "a little more time," patients

promise "a life dedicated to God" or "a life in the service of the church."

4. Most people move quickly from bargaining to *depression*, the fourth stage. Kübler-Ross distinguishes two kinds of depression: *Reactive depression* is feeling downcast because of people and things that need to be taken care of. A mother will be depressed, for instance, until she knows the kind of care that will be provided for her children. *Preparatory depression* is a sense of impending loss of everything and everybody one loves. Patients at this time are grateful to those who can sit with them in silence.

5. People who work through their depression reach the final stage, *acceptance*. It is not a happy stage, but it is a time of peace. Most patients in the Kübler-Ross study died in this stage without fear or despair.

Kübler-Ross (1974) warns that her "stages" are not invariant or universal. She was not trying to perscribe a "best way" to prepare for death. She is disturbed that some health caretakers are trying to manipulate patients through her stages. It is far better to accept an individual's response pattern.

If you were told that you had a terminal disease and had 6 months to live, how would you want to spend your time? One study obtained answers to this question from people in three age groups: 20 to 39 years old, 40 to 59 years old, and 60 years old (Kalish and Reynolds, 1976). More younger respondents thought that they would change their life styles, and more older people thought that they would reflect on spiritual needs. Such reflection may be adaptive since people with strong religious beliefs have less fear of death (Nelson and Nelson, 1973; Templar, 1972).

Georgia O'Keeffe revealed that she reflects on spiritual beliefs. In fact one wonders if her desire to display her art in New Mexico is related to a view she once expressed about death: "When I think of death, I only regret that I will not be able to see this beautiful country [the New Mexico countryside] anymore, unless the Indians are right and my spirit will walk here after I'm gone" (Lisle, 1980).

SUMMARY

1. The life-span developmental approach deals with changes that occur within an individual over time as well as the differences in such changes among individuals.

2. In **adolescence** the physical changes include the adolescent "growth spurt," **puberty,** and the development of **primary** and **secondary sex characteristics.** In moral development teenagers generally progress through Kohlberg's conventional level of moral reasoning. In personality development, adolescents are concerned with what Erikson calls the **identity crisis,** which occurs during puberty. Peer groups become very important on the social scene, and early sexual activity seems to be becoming more common.

3. One way of looking at development in young adulthood is in terms of commitments that are made at this time: moral commitments (Kohlberg's postconventional stage is usually reached at this point), interpersonal commitments (Erikson's stage of intimacy versus isolation, in which marriage and family commitments are a major theme), and mastery commitments (the establishment of and mastery in a career or occupation).

4. Levinson's framework for development of young adulthood includes

several stages, including a transition stage at about age 30, and a settling down stage, in which in terms of occupation the person seeks a certain amount of independence.

5. Middle age is concerned first with Erikson's generativity versus stagnation stage, in which one's involvement in family, job, or community work can either be fulfilling or leave one with a sense of being meaningless. In the same way, Levinson's framework at this age includes a kind of midlife transition (often called a midlife crisis, but not necessarily so). In terms of family commitments, this is a time when children begin leaving the home, while, at the same time, middle-aged people often become more involved in caring for their elderly parents.

6. Late adulthood involves many physical changes, which affect sensory abilities as well as general health and mobility. There are also changes at this age in cognitive abilities, but only of a certain type. Family commitments at this point include being a grandparent, and there is often an increase in marital satisfaction for elderly couples. In terms of occupation, one of the major themes is planning for and adjusting to retirement. The elderly face Erikson's final crisis, the stage of integrity versus despair, which determines one's final outlook on life.

7. Just as there are stages that we go through adjusting to life, there seems to be stages in adjusting to death—the death of those close to us and our own death. Kübler-Ross has outlined what seem to be five distinct stages in this adjustment process: denial and isolation, anger, bargaining, depression, and, finally, acceptance.

SUGGESTED READINGS

The following book is about Georgia O'Keeffe:

LISLE, L. *Portrait of an artist: A biography of Georgia O'Keeffe.* New York: Washington Square Press, 1980.

ERIKSON, E. E. (Ed.). *Adulthood.* New York: Norton, 1978. Various authorities have written separate chapters on adults in contemporary society. The writers take many perspectives, including cultural, historical, and medical.

KÜBLER-ROSS, E. *Living with death and dying.* New York: Macmillan, 1981. A warm, sophisticated, and sensitive sequel to Kübler-Ross's *On death and dying,* which is reviewed in this chapter.

MCKENZIE, S. C. *Aging and old age.* Glenview, Ill.: Scott, Foresman, 1980. This text is an integrated, multidisciplinary analysis of psychological, social, and biological aspects of aging.

SARASON, S. B. *Working, aging, and social change.* New York: Free Press, 1977. An analysis of career commitments and how they are affected by aging and social policy.

STEVENS-LONG, J. *Adult life.* Palo Alto, Cal.: Mayfield, 1979. A chronologically organized analysis of developmental processes from young adulthood through old age. The book reviews both basic and applied research on adult development in modern society.

Motivation

As dawn broke, the airport in Uruguay was filled with the excited chatter of the 40 passengers who waited to board the plane for the 4-hour trip to Santiago, Chile. Fifteen of the passengers were members of the Old Christians Club rugby team, which had organized the trip and chartered the airplane. They were going to Chile to play a number of rugby matches with the tough Chilean national teams. At one point they feared that the trip would be cancelled because the plane was not filled. However, after much scurrying around they had managed to entice others to come, and all 40 seats had been sold. While most of the passengers were young men between the ages of 18 and 26, a middle-aged woman was going to attend her daughter's wedding in Chile, and there were two other middle-aged couples and the sister of one of the players. All the passengers were from prominent Uruguayan families.

At 8:05 A.M., on October 12, 1972, the plane taxied down the runway and took off for the 900-mile trip. The flight plan took them through Argentina and over the snow-covered peaks of the Andes. Their first view of the Andes brought gasps of wonder. The mountains were awesome, with jagged snow-capped peaks reaching into the clouded heavens. The plane bounced savagely in the light air as it tried to climb above the clouds. Among the passengers there was a holiday atmosphere as the boys joked at each lurch of their tiny aircraft. The atmosphere in the cockpit, however, was not so jovial; the pilot fought to maintain control of the plane and searched for landmarks that would show whether they had passed over the Andes.

Suddenly the plane swooped out of the clouds just in time for everyone to see a massive rock outcropping not more than 10 feet from the wing tip. The wing slammed into the mountain, ripped off, and sliced into the tail section. The torn body of the plane hurtled down the snowy mountainside like a toboggan. Finally it came to rest in a snowbank. For a moment, there was utter silence, and then the moans of the injured filled the air. One by one, those who were not hurt climbed out of the plane and sat in a dazed and bewildered state in the snow.

Soon the survivors began a gruesome survey of what was left of the plane. Five people, including the pilot and copilot, were dead, and many of the others were so badly injured it was clear that they, too, would soon be dead. Mustering all of their physical and psychological strength, they untangled the injured and dead from the wreckage; the dead were dragged out of the plane and the injured were carefully laid inside.

The subzero cold of the Andes quickly made the survivors realize that their first task must be to clear an area inside the wreck for shelter. Seats were dragged out and a makeshift wall was built over the gaping hole in the tail area. No one was prepared for the cold; many of the passengers wore only short-sleeved shirts. As the sun began to set, they huddled together inside the shelter; some tried to sleep, although the piercing cries of the injured made this almost impossible.

By morning, more of the injured had died, leaving 28 survivors to share the 20-foot section of the plane. The morning also brought another problem; many of the survivors began to complain of thirst. This problem was especially acute for those who had lost a lot of blood. A careful search was made and an odd assortment of food and drink was discovered, including some bottles of wine, brandy, whiskey, and creme de menthe; eight bars of chocolate; three jars of jam; and two cans of mussels. With all the snow around, they felt that water would not be a problem, but they were wrong. They soon found that it was hard to melt the snow, and eating snow did little to quench their thirst. Finally, they found they could get water by putting a little snow in some pans and placing the pans in the sun.

The survivors organized themselves into three teams. Some of the men were in charge of melting ice to provide water. A second team included the three medical students, who were responsible for the injured. A third team had the duty of clearing more space in the wrecked plane. In the area they had, it was impossible to stretch out—each time someone moved, he intruded on the others around him. This brought screams of pain from the injured and anger and cursing from others who were trying to sleep.

One of the men found a transistor radio; on it they were excited to hear that search parties had been sent out to find them. But no help came that day, and the survivors trudged into the plane as night came and temperatures again plunged below zero.

The expected rescue did not come the next day, or the day after that. As time wore on, many of the survivors became more and more irritable; the slightest frustration was met with a stream of curses, and conflicts between survivors led to violent confrontations. During the day, they could not stray far from the plane because the snow was soft and they would sink into it over their waists. They spent the time exploring the area immediately around the plane and talking about their families.

Day after day passed and they began to realize that no help was coming. By the ninth day, another realization began to sink in, one that was even more frightening than the diminished prospects for a speedy rescue. As the survivors looked at one another they became aware of wrinkled skin, protruding bones, and sunken eyes; they were all slowly starving to death. Their meager food supply was nearly gone. The strength of even the strongest survivors had dwindled to the point where a walk around the plane left them panting and exhausted. A few of the boys at this point cautiously raised the idea of eating the dead whose bodies had been preserved in the frozen snow outside the plane.

At first this idea was met with shock and disgust. But by day nine their situation was desperate, and a meeting of the 28 survivors was called. Most of them realized that eating human flesh was the only way they could survive, however much they might dislike the thought of it. One of the rugby players argued, "I know that if my dead body could help you stay alive, then I would want you to use it. In fact, if I do die and you don't eat me, then I'll come back from wherever I am and give you a good kick in the ass" (Read, 1974, p. 84). Another of the men argued that it was like Holy Communion: "When Christ died he gave his body to us so we could have spiritual life. My friend has given us his body so that we can have physical life" (Read, 1974, p. 91).

One of the medical students walked to a body that was sticking through the snow and cut a number of slices of frozen flesh. He thawed these on the outside of the plane and forced some meat into his mouth. One by one, over the next few days, the starved survivors forced themselves to eat human flesh. Finally only an older couple the development of their grandchildren. Grandparents also enjoy seeing their grandchildren accomplish things that neither the grandparent nor their children were able to do. Grandparenting can become especially important when death of a spouse deprives an elderly person of one of his or her most important sources of life satisfaction.

Elderly Husbands and Wives. Marital satisfaction is very high for elderly couples. In fact, it may reach its highest level during late adulthood (Miller, 1976). Older husbands and wives find happiness in companionship, mutual expression of true feelings, and economic security, among other things (Stinnett, Carter, and Montgomery, 1972). Contrary to common belief, they also enjoy sexual relations to the age of 80 years and beyond (Rubin, 1966). Reduced occupational commitments enable elderly couples to spend more time together. In the best situations, husbands help more around the house and women become more loving and understanding (Troll, 1971). Such adjustments increase marital satisfaction for those who had happy relationships during younger years (Peterson and Payne, 1975).

Occupational Commitments

Georgia O'Keeffe widely exhibited new paintings as she advanced in years through her eighties and into her nineties. She remained in the mainstream of art when others her age had long since retired. Many people cannot stay engaged in their careers as Georgia did. But most people can make up for career retirement by increasing involvement in other activities (Neugarten and Hagestad, 1976). Retirement, from this point of view, can be as fulfilling as Georgia's late-life career. In this section, we will consider how people plan for retirement, how they adjust to it, and how satisfied they are with it.

Planning for Retirement. Retirement in the United States is usually mandatory at the age of 65 or 70 years. The mandatory versus voluntary retirement issue will probably be debated for some time to come. On the one hand, mandatory retirement seems to discriminate against older people who are ready and able to work. On the other hand, Botwinick (1977) argues in favor of mandatory retirement on several grounds, one of which is that a fixed age limit will better enable people to plan for retirement.

To what extent do people actually plan under the present mandatory system? There is no simple answer, because many variables influence the extent of planning. A tendency for men to plan is positively associated with high socioeconomic status, leisure-time interests, financial security, and good health (McPherson and Guppy, 1979). These same variables are associated with a positive attitude toward an upcoming retirement in men. The variables of socioeconomic status and financial security affect women differently. Women with high-status jobs and high income do *not* want to retire (Streib and Schneider, 1971). This sex difference is ironic, because women often adjust more easily than men when they do retire.

Adjusting to Retirement. Lowenthal (1972) suggests that the trick to a successful retirement is substituting activities for the time previously spent on an occupation. Career women are often better prepared to make this adjustment because the role of homemaker is a traditionally acceptable substitution. Men also adjust better when they share in household tasks. Some men, however, especially working-class men, consider "women's work" demeaning. As a result, adjusting to retirement can be more problematic for this group (Troll, 1971). A second popular substitution is another job. Streib and Schneider (1971) observed that 73 percent of people who consider work to be a major source of satisfaction find another job after retirement. A third substitution is well-planned leisure activity, which can be especially fulfilling for those who have a history of sharing recre-

Most people plan to make up for retirement by increasing their involvement in other activities, such as painting or attending sports events.

ational interests with their spouses. Whatever the substitution is, a redistribution of energy seems to be basic to a satisfying adjustment.

Retirement and Life Satisfaction. The impact of retirement is often not as negative as people anticipated, according to Streib and Schneider (1971). They measured attitudes of 4,000 people before and after retirement. Their sample included people from many walks of life, ranging from unskilled laborers to professionals. The results indicated that about 33 percent found retirement to be better than they had anticipated. Only about 5 percent found it to be worse. Most people in the sample adjusted well to retirement and were satisfied with life.

Streib and Schneider's study raises the question of why so many people are overly pessimistic about retirement. One reason may be that some of the negative feelings are not actually related to retirement itself. A worker inevitably associates retirement with old age, and that in the end is associated with death. Older people have had a chance to come to grips with aging and they are less fearful of death (Kalish and Reynolds, 1976). After retirement we would therefore expect a reduction in some of the pessimism that was associated with the fear of aging and death.

DEATH AND DYING

Georgia was almost 60 when her husband died. Many friends and relatives also died as she advanced through her sixties. These deaths not only depressed her, they also made her aware that she had to make plans for her estate after her own death. She assigned some paintings to be left to several museums and universities. She wants most of her art to be displayed, however, in an O'Keeffe art museum in New Mexico. As Georgia planned her museum, it was apparent that she loved life, but accepted the reality of death. In terms of Erikson's (1963) theory, she faced the last stage of development, the crisis of *integrity versus despair*. Resolution of this crisis determines whether one faces the end of life with a refused to eat it. Their strength slowly ebbed and finally on day 16 they too gave in and ate the flesh. A group was chosen to find the rest of the bodies and prepare the meat and fat for eating.

Then another disaster struck: Suddenly a wall of snow broke through the barrier at the back and swept through the plane. The buried survivors began frantically clawing their way out as the snow pressed down on them. As each person found his way out of the white tomb he began digging furiously to help others get out. Tears filled their eyes as they uncovered the dead bodies of their companions. Nine people died in the avalanche, leaving a grieved group of 19 survivors.

Slowly they regrouped, and all agreed that they could not wait for rescue; they must send out their own search party. A new group was formed for this purpose, made up of the four most physically able young men. They were allowed to eat as much meat as they wished and were assigned no other duties except to build up their strength. In the weeks that followed the avalanche, this group began to explore the area around the plane in order to find a way out of the mountains.

On the fifty-sixth day after the crash, the boys saw their first signs of outside life; two giant birds circled lazily over the wreck. That same day a bee flew into the plane. These signs brought the realization that the snow was melting as summer came to the Andes. The melting snow meant that the bodies of the dead would thaw and rot, and the only source of life for the survivors would then be gone. The search party would have to go for help now, or it would soon be too late.

It was with some reluctance to leave their friends that three of them, dressed

in many layers of clothing and carrying socks full of meat, began their journey. They found after three days of walking that the trip would be more difficult than expected, and one of them was sent back to the plane so that the other two could use his food. After struggling through the mountains for nine days, they saw a peasant tending his cattle. The young men screamed and wept with joy; they had been saved.

The other survivors (16 out of the 45 who had begun the trip) were soon picked up by helicopter and taken to Santiago. The world buzzed with excitement as news spread that the 16 young men had survived for 70 days in the subzero temperatures of the Andes. The excitement, however, gave way to horror when pictures of human bones scattered around the wreckage were published and it became known that the survivors were forced to eat the flesh of their dead friends to stay alive. Their survival was truly remarkable, but the moral questions raised by their methods of survival were debated for many years afterward.

MOTIVATION: THE ENERGIZER AND DIRECTOR OF BEHAVIOR

As you read the story of the rugby team survivors, you are likely to find yourself asking: "What would I do in their situation?" Would I eat human flesh rather than starve to death? Would I be the person to encourage the group about the hope of survival, or, as some of the survivors did, would I give up? Would I try to keep the peace or would I become involved in violent confrontations with other survivors? Each of us has the ability and knowledge to behave in any of these ways. But given a particular circumstance, how would we actually behave?

It is on this question of how people behave and why that we now focus our attention. We have already examined the human being much as we would a machine. In Chapter 2 we discussed the physical makeup of the human machine. In Chapter 3 we looked at how these parts work together, and in other chapters we have seen how humans learn to behave. Now we will examine what energizes this wonderful machine and guides its actions.

As an analogy, we might consider a jukebox. It has the necessary parts to play music and it has a wide selection of tunes. However, in order for the jukebox to play, someone has to plug it in (that is, give it energy) and select a tune. In the same way, the human machine has a wide variety of behaviors that require energy and some selection device to determine which behaviors will be performed in a particular situation.

Psychologists have used the term motive to describe the condition that energizes and directs the behavior of the organism. In this way motivation explains why an organism acts a certain way. For example, we may ask why, on the ninth day, did some of the survivors turn to eating human flesh? The bodies of the dead were there right after the crash, and those who survived could have eaten them at any time. To answer this question we talk about motivation; the survivors were driven to this act by the motive of hunger.

The concept of motivation is widely used in our everyday world. In courts of law, lawyers argue about the motive behind criminal acts, and penalties for crimes may vary according to the motive behind the crime. For example, murder performed in self-defense or for humanitarian motives (mercy killing) may go unpunished, while murder motivated by desires of personal gains will be severely punished. First-degree murder is defined as a killing where a person thought about and intended to murder his or her victim. In most states this crime is punishable by death or a sentence of life in prison. On the other hand, manslaughter generally involves situations in which the victim was killed accidentally and without intent. Such a crime carries a shorter prison sentence. The victim has been killed in both cases; it is the intent or motivation that is different.

Even our own behavior toward others is strongly influenced by what we think are their motives. We will be strongly attracted to people who do something nice for us if we feel that they are truly interested in our own well-being. However, the same behavior may bring repulsion if we feel that they have been motivated solely by self-interest. As we will see in Chapter 14, we spend a great deal of time and energy trying to determine the motives behind the behaviors of others.

When we speak of motives, we can loosely place them in one of two groups. On one hand, we have primary motives, which concern our biological needs. These motives are usually unlearned, common to all animals, and vital for the survival of the organism. Motives such as hunger, thirst, the need for air and rest, and sex fall in this category. The second type of motive is the social motive. These motives come from learning and social interaction and include affiliation, aggression, and achievement. We will see, however, that almost all motives are influenced to some extent by our environment and learning. However, before looking at specific motives, let us take a quick look at some of the theories that explain how and why we have motives.

THEORIES OF MOTIVATION

Instinct Theory

During the 70 days after the crash, the survivors did many different things. In addition to eating, drinking, and breathing, they spent a lot of time together talking about home, fighting and arguing, exploring the plane and the area around it, and even hoarding bits and pieces of objects they found. Where did the motives come from for each of these behaviors?

A view that was popular at the turn of the century would have suggested that the survivors acted as they did because they had the instincts to do so. Instincts are innate or inborn predispositions to act in specific ways. According to these early views, "nature" supplied organisms with a pattern of behavior *and* the energy to perform these actions. Thus, the conditions inside the organism push it to action as these instinctive behaviors seek an outlet.

However, the idea of instinct began to fade by the late 1920s. A major reason for the decline of instinct theories for humans was the great variety found in human behavior. If a certain instinct exists in a species, then we should find similar behavior in all members of that species. However, this is not true with humans; for example, we can find some societies where a behavior such as aggression is very common, while in other societies the behavior is almost nonexistent. Even within a society, there are wide differences in behaviors.

A second problem is that it is difficult, if not impossible, to clearly identify specific instincts. In other words, how do we prove that a certain behavior is caused by an instinct? Holt (1931) clearly showed this problem by saying:

> Man is impelled to action, it is said, by his instincts. If he goes with his fellows, it is the "herd" instinct which activates him; if he walks alone, it is the "anti-social instinct"; . . . if he twiddles his thumbs, it is the "thumb-twiddling instinct"; if he does not twiddle his thumbs it is the "thumb-not-twiddling instinct" (p. 4).

One researcher was so taken aback by the wide use of the instinct concept that he wrote an article subtitled "The instinct of belief-in-instincts" (Ayres, 1921).

Drive Theory

In a room filled with photographers and reporters, one of the survivors told of the dreadful ordeal in the Andes. He described the physical pains caused by the intense cold and the mental torment he experienced as he watched his best friend die. He also told of how hunger gnawed at his body and drove him to eat the flesh of the dead passengers.

The idea that the living organism is driven to actions by the needs of its body has served as the basis for many theories of motivation. This point of view suggests that *needs* result when the body has gone without

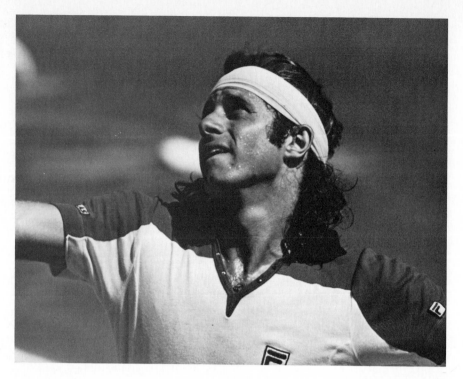

According to the principle of homeostasis, our bodies try to keep a constant internal state. When we are physically active, our bodies heat up. Sweating is the natural air conditioner that brings down body temperature.

something for a period of time and is thus in a state of deprivation. The need creates a tension or **drive** that compels the organism to satisfy the need. Once the need is satisfied, the drive is reduced, and the organism is no longer motivated to act. Looking at the plight of the survivors, we can see that the nine days of starvation created a need for food. This need created a tension and drove them to find food. When a food source had been found and their hunger had been satisfied, the survivors were no longer motivated to search for food.

The basis of drive theory is the principle of **homeostasis.** According to this principle, the body tries to keep a constant internal state. When changes occur, the homeostatic mechanism "turns on" the organism to act in ways that will return the internal state to what it was. This mechanism works much like the thermostat in your home. The thermostat is set to maintain a certain temperature. When the temperature in the home goes too high, the thermostat will turn on the air conditioner; when it drops too low, the thermostat will turn on the heater. With this mechanism, the temperature in your house can be kept at a certain level. In the same way, when your body temperature drops, the homeostatic mechanism may cause your body to shiver and constrict your blood vessels. If these actions do not make you warm enough, you may be motivated to seek shelter. On the other hand, if you become too hot, the homeostatic mechanism may stimulate your body to sweat, which causes cooling. If this fails to reduce your body temperature, you may find yourself seeking out a cool swimming pool.

As we can see, drive-reduction theories view deprivation as the source of motivation and do not presume that organisms are born with patterned behaviors (instincts) to reduce their drives. They readily admit that learning can influence the way an organism reduces drives.

Incentive Theory

For some time the drive theory served as the basis for explaining all motivation. However, if we look at many of the survivors' actions, we will find that much of their behavior cannot be explained easily by drive reduction theories. For example, there were many cases where, after the

Incentive theories agree that behaviors can be motivated by external events rather than internal needs. The incentive of a tempting dessert may motivate eating even when the person is not physiologically hungry.

boys had eaten and were fairly warm inside of the plane, one or another of them spent time looking into small nooks of the plane that clearly could not hold objects useful for survival. At other times the young men aimlessly fooled with objects around them or tied and untied knots in a rope. These behaviors were adopted to increase stimulation rather than to reduce it. There are many everyday examples of our own behavior aimed at increasing arousal. Some of us engage in dangerous sports such as mountain climbing or sky diving; others spend money on movies guaranteed to scare or sexually arouse them.

In addition to finding that drive reduction is not the aim of every motive, investigators have also realized that not all motives are aroused solely by internal states. For example, we sometimes eat when we are not hungry, simply because food is there. Strange objects or novel events often motivate people to explore. Sir Edmund Hillary, a famous explorer and mountain climber, was asked why he climbed mountains. To this question he responded, "Because they are there." In each of these cases, it is not an internal bodily need that motivates behavior. Rather, it is an *incentive* outside of the organism that motivates it to act. Thus, we can view drive theories as "push" theories; they argue that internal states push the organism to act. On the other hand, incentive theories are "pull" theories, since they suggest that external stimuli pull behaviors from the organism. Incentives can be either positive or negative. In either case, the incentive motivates the organism to move toward or away from a situation.

As you can see, motivation can be the result of either internal drive states or external incentives. Further, not all motivation is aimed at reducing stimulation or arousal. Rather, living organisms seem to have a preferred range of arousal, and either too much or too little stimulation can motivate the organism to act (Berlyne, 1969; Cofer, 1974).

A Hierarchy of Motives?

Immediately after the crash, the survivors turned their attention to clearing out the wreck of the plane and trying to warm themselves. After doing this, they worried about finding a water supply and seeing what food there was. The survivors seemed to care very little about what others

FIGURE 9–1: Maslow's Hierarchy of
Needs

Maslow believed that motives at each
level must be satisfied before motives at
the next higher level will direct
behavior.

thought of them during these early days. Some openly wept, some reverted
to childish behavior, and others performed such socially disapproved behaviors as wetting their pants. After their hunger and thirst had been satisfied,
the survivors began organizing themselves into groups, leaders emerged,
and people who broke loosely defined rules were reprimanded. Later in
the ordeal, after the decision had been made to eat the dead, some of
the boys began thinking about their families and sweethearts. Some even
wrote letters expressing their love for their families.

Looking over this sequence of behaviors, we can ask why the survivors
did certain things in this order. Why did it take them so long to think
about their families? Why didn't the survivors organize into effective working groups right after the crash?

It has been suggested that our motives are organized into a hierarchy,
like the rungs of a ladder, with the stronger biological motives at the
bottom and the more complex psychological motives at the top (Maslow,
1954, 1970). Maslow further believed that the motives at the lower level
must first be satisfied before the motives at the next higher level will
influence or direct one's behavior. For example, if you look at Maslow's
hierarchy (see Figure 9–1), you can see that hunger and thirst must be
satisfied before you will begin to direct behavior at satisfying security
or social order needs. You might have had your own experiences with
this hierarchy of motives if you have ever tried to study when you were
hungry. It is likely that this was a difficult, if not hopeless, undertaking.
You probably interrupted your studies frequently to search your room
for food. If you didn't find any, your mind may have wandered as you
stared at the pages of your books while visions of a thick, juicy steak, a
steaming baked potato, and chocolate pudding kept flashing in your mind.
The behaviors of the survivors fit nicely into Maslow's scheme. Their first
actions were aimed at satisfying their physical needs (warmth, liquid,
and food), while later actions seemed to be directed by desires for social
order, thoughts of their families, and the need for respect from their
companions.

Maslow's specific hierarchy has received some criticism because of the
order of motives. For example, there seems to be little evidence that the
motive for order and safety is lower or more basic than the desire to be
with other people or belong to a group. In spite of these criticisms, however, the general idea of a hierarchy of motives is appealing. It is likely
that some motives are stronger than others and that it is hard to pay
attention to certain needs until others have been satisfied.

We have now examined the general nature and theories of motives.
With this background in mind, let us turn our attention to specific motives.
We will begin by looking at hunger, which is a physiological and drive-reducing motive. Next we will examine the sex motive, which, although
it is largely physiological, has a very strong incentive element. We will
then briefly turn to the exploration and manipulation motives, which are
even more clearly activated by incentives. Finally, we will focus on three
psychological or social motives—affiliation, aggression, and the need to
achieve.

HUNGER

As time passed and hunger gripped the survivors, they began to look
for food. Their first efforts turned up a meager assortment of candies,
jam, and some tins of canned fish. Soon, however, this supply began running out, and their search intensified. Squabbles over food became more
frequent, and best friends angrily accused each other of "stealing" a

square of chocolate or a crumb of bread. By the ninth day, the once stout and husky rugby players became aware of their deteriorating physical conditions (one of them lost 80 pounds during the ordeal). The gnawing hunger made them decide to eat the flesh of their dead companions.

Clearly hunger was the motivating force behind many of the survivors' behaviors. Much of our own behavior is also aimed at satisfying our desire for food. In order to prove this, make a note of the amount of time you spend in food-related activities: eating, shopping for food, talking about food, worrying about your weight, and so on. **Hunger**, then, is a motive common to us all.

The Experience of Hunger

The Gut Reaction. When most of us think about hunger we think of cramping and pangs coming from an empty stomach. Most of us believe that the stomach signals hunger. This was, in fact, the position accepted over 200 years ago when one scientist wrote that hunger arises when "the naked villi of nerves on one side (of the stomach) grate against those on the other (side) . . ." (Cofer and Apley, 1964). Cannon and Washburn (1912) set out to experimentally demonstrate that contractions of the stomach cause people to feel hungry. Washburn swallowed a balloon, which, when it reached his stomach, was inflated and hooked to an amplifying device (see Figure 9–2) to record the contractions of his stomach. Washburn sat with this balloon in his stomach and pressed a key each time he felt hungry. The results showed that feelings of hunger often occurred at the same time as strong contractions of the stomach.

This experiment was seen as strong support for the internal cause of hunger. However, later experiments cast doubt on this theory. For example, researchers (Tsang, 1938; Penick et al., 1963) found that rats whose stomachs had been removed and whose esophagi were connected to their small intestines searched for food and ate as much as those with normal stomachs. The only difference was that the former group of rats ate less food; however, they ate more often. In the same way, human patients whose stomachs have been removed report feeling hungry (Janowitz, 1967). Other researchers have found that if the nerves to an animal's (rat or dog) stomach are cut so that the animal's brain cannot know of stomach contractions, the animal continues to eat normally.

The most recent conclusion is that while stomach contractions may play some role in signaling our hunger, the role is probably a minor one. However, while our stomachs may not motivate us to start eating, there is evidence that a full stomach plays a large part in getting us to stop eating. McTeer (1972) reports a number of studies showing that a full (distended) stomach leads a person or animal to stop eating.

Blood-Sugar Level. If we can't blame our stomachs for making us

FIGURE 9–2

In this experiment, Washburn swallowed a balloon, which was inflated once it reached his stomach. The balloon was attached to an amplifying device to record contractions. Washburn pressed a key every time he felt hungry. The results showed that Washburn's feelings of hunger often occurred at the same time as strong contractions of the stomach. (Cannon and Washburn, 1912)

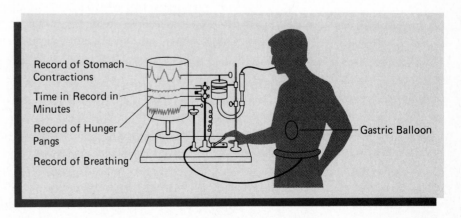

Record of Stomach Contractions

Time in Record in Minutes

Record of Hunger Pangs

Record of Breathing

Gastric Balloon

eat, what can we blame? One answer seems to be the glucose level in our blood, or, more correctly, the blood-sugar level. Some researchers found that if they injected a hungry animal with the blood of one who had been well fed, the hungry animal either did not eat or ate less when offered food (Davis et al., 1967, 1971). Other studies found that humans injected with insulin reported feeling hungry. Insulin, which is often used to treat diabetes, lowers the concentration of glucose (blood sugar) in the bloodstream.

Thus, it seems that the level of glucose in the blood affects our feeling of hunger. But how do we become aware of the glucose level? One answer is the *hypothalamus* and the cells located around it (Ziegler and Kurten, 1974). As we saw in Chapter 2, the hypothalamus is a small structure that is richly supplied with blood vessels and located at the base of the brain. This area contains glucoreceptors, which monitor the glucose content of the blood. If they find the blood low in glucose, they send out signals that, among other effects, cause hunger and motivate us to seek food.

Two types of experiments have shown the important role of the hypothalamus in eating. In one type, areas of the hypothalamus are stimulated with electrical current from implanted electrodes. When these "eating centers" are stimulated in this way, even an animal that has been well fed starts to eat (Hoebel and Teitelbaum, 1962). Such studies have also shown that there are areas of the hypothalamus that, when stimulated, will cause the animal to stop eating, even if it is hungry. The other type of experiment involves destroying cells in the hypothalamus. Results from these studies have shown that destruction of certain areas will cause the animal to refuse food. Destruction of other areas will result in the animal eating continuously. In some cases the animal will eat until it has doubled or even tripled its body weight.

Using these techniques, investigators have found evidence that some areas of the hypothalamus may be responsible for causing organisms to start eating while other areas cause them to stop eating (Powley and Keesey, 1970; Gold, 1973). In other words, we may have different "on" and "off" centers that monitor the level of glucose in our blood and regulate our eating. Researchers were able to produce very obese rats by destroying parts of the hypothalamus that stop eating behavior (Hetherington and Ransom, 1939).

The hypothalamus is not the only place where blood-sugar levels are monitored. One researcher found that the liver is also sensitive to the content of the blood, and that the liver regulates eating behavior (Russek, 1971). In fact, the liver may supply us with the first signals of hunger or satiation because it is "the first to know" the content of our blood. After food is broken down in our stomachs and small intestines, nutrients are absorbed into the blood. The blood then flows to the liver before going to other parts of our body, including the brain. Thus, the liver is the first organ to examine the content of the blood. Research has shown that there are indeed centers in the liver that monitor the blood-sugar level of the blood and transmit signals to the brain (Nijima, 1969).

Temperature.   There is another theory of hunger, which, if true, helps us understand why the survivors' behavior was motivated by hunger. Brodbeck (1957) suggests that food intake is partly regulated by cells in the hypothalamus that are sensitive to body temperature. The digestion of foods, especially those high in protein, causes body temperature to rise. Brodbeck suggests that as the body temperature falls, we become motivated to eat; he even went so far as to suggest that we eat to keep warm.

Andersson and Larsson (1961) did an interesting experiment to gather support for this theory. They implanted a small hollow wire in the hypothalamus of a goat. When the wire was cooled, causing a drop in the temperature in the hypothalamus, the goat began eating. The goat stopped eating, however, when the wire was warmed. Warming the hypothalamus also caused the goat to start drinking water.

There are still some questions about the role of temperature and eating. In line with this theory, though, you may notice that your own eating behavior is affected by the weather; most people eat less during the warm summer days than during the colder winter season.

Body Weight and Long-Term Eating. Thus far we have focused on short-term mechanisms of hunger; they are short-term in the sense that they control our behavior from meal to meal. There is another interesting phenomenon of eating behavior, however, that cannot easily be explained by these short-term mechanisms. Most animals, including humans, tend to keep a stable body weight for long periods of time even though the availability of food may vary over this time. If you think about your own weight, you will probably find that it varies by less than 5 percent annually. You may also notice how difficult it is to gain or lose weight, even with effort.

Our bodies have a certain energy requirement to keep them going. The exact amount of energy (measured in the form of **calories**) varies from one person to another and is dependent on such factors as size, level of activity, and metabolism. When we take in more calories than our bodies need, these calories are converted to fat and the fat is stored in our body tissues.

Investigators have suggested that there are cells in the hypothalamus that keep track of fat deposits in the body (Keesey and Powley, 1975). When changes in the level of deposits are noted they motivate changes in the overall eating pattern to return the fat deposits to their normal level. Although the exact nature of this system is not clear yet, it is generally accepted that different systems control short-term and long-term eating behaviors.

What We Eat: The Role of Learning

Learning plays an important role in determining what we eat. In France, for example, snails are a delicacy.

Thus far we have been discussing why we eat. Our focus has mainly been on how deprivation causes us to become hungry and to search for food. It is also believed that the type of foods we choose to eat are, to some degree, controlled by our needs. In support of this position, Davis (1928) allowed newly weaned infants to choose their diet over a period of months from a cafeteria-like selection of foods. On any given day the infants might choose a "bad diet," but over a long period of time they selected foods that met their nutritional needs. In one case, a child who had rickets chose foods that had high concentrations of cod-liver oil and in so doing helped cure the rickets. In another study, rats were fed a diet that did not have enough calcium in it (Rozin and Kalat, 1971). When these rats were later given a choice of things to eat, they chose high-calcium foods. We can also see a wise selection of foods in the example of the crash survivors who at first ate only the flesh of the dead victims. After a time, however, many of the survivors began eating kidneys and liver, which were high in necessary vitamin and mineral content, even though the high-protein flesh was still available.

It seems logical to conclude that people eat because they are hungry and that they eat the foods needed to nourish their bodies. Unfortunately, this is not always the case; animals and humans, even at early ages, learn to prefer certain foods, and they even learn when to be hungry. Often these learned preferences go against the body's needs. For example, Harriman (1955) found that rats learned to prefer sugar over salt. Even when these rats had their adrenal glands removed and needed to eat salt to survive, they continued choosing the sugar diet. Some of them died as a result of this choice. The survivors of the crash in the Andes had all learned to avoid human flesh as a suitable food, and some of them resisted eating it until they became so weak that others had to force them to eat. Thus, when we eat and what we eat are influenced by our bodily state *and* by our learned habits and preferences. And in many cases learning can override our physiological needs.

Obesity

While our bodies may have natural selection processes that help ensure our nourishment, those of us who have struggled with diets know that our eating patterns can present major problems for our body weight.

Incidences of obesity have reached epidemic proportions in the Western world; over half the people in the United States can be classified as being significantly overweight. In humans, **obesity** can be defined as more than 15 percent over the "ideal" weight, given a person's height and overall body build. Obesity is a major factor in many physical and psychological disorders. It is also big business; hundreds of millions of dollars are spent by people on weight-reducing drugs, diets, health plans, and spas.

In recent years psychologists have turned their attention to the causes of obesity. In some cases these causes can be traced to physical, hormonal, or emotional disorders. But in most cases the problem is overeating; that is, taking in more calories than are used or needed by the body. The important task is, then, to identify why obese people have such a difficult time controlling their food intake.

The Role of External Cues.   If we ate only when our bodies signaled the need for food, few of us would ever have to worry about being obese. Unfortunately, many people, especially obese people, do not eat only when their bodies command. Rather, their eating behavior is triggered by external cues such as the sight or smell of food. Researchers have speculated that obese people do not know when they are hungry but, instead, eat whenever they are stimulated by external cues (Schachter, 1971a, 1971b; Rodin, 1975, 1977).

For example, Schachter and Gross (1968) suggested that obese people are more likely than normal-weight people to "eat by the clock"; that is, obese people will eat because the clock says it's dinner time. In order to show this, the investigators had normal-weight and overweight subjects arrive at the laboratory at 5:00 P.M. The subjects were told that their physiological responses would be measured while they worked on tasks. Their watches were removed and electrodes were strapped on their arms; then the experimenter left the room so that they could work. There was a large clock in front of the subjects, which, unknown to them, was controlled by the experimenter. The experimenter returned to the room 30 minutes later (5:30) eating crackers. However, in some cases, the clock in front of the subjects had been slowed to read only 5:20, while in other cases it had been moved forward to read 6:05. The experimenter asked the subjects to complete questionnaires and left the box of crackers with them so that they could munch while they worked. The number of crackers eaten by the subjects were counted. As can be seen in Table 9–1, obese subjects ate more crackers than did normal-weight subjects when the clock read 6:05 (dinner time), but they ate fewer crackers than the others when the clock read 5:20.

There are a number of other external cues that affect the eating behaviors of obese people. Many of these cues can be found in the food itself. For example, Nisbett (1968) found that obese subjects ate more than thin subjects if the food tasted good, but less than the thin subjects if it had an unpleasant taste. Overweight subjects will also increase their food

TABLE 9–1

Amount eaten by obese and normal subjects in each of two conditions: slow (when the clock has been slowed to read 5:20 P.M.) and fast (when the clock has been speeded up to read 6:05 P.M.).

Subjects	Amount Eaten	
	Slow	Fast
Obese	19.9	37.6
Normal	41.5	16.0

Source: Schachter and Gross (1968).

HIGHLIGHT / BORN TO BE FAT?

For dieters who work and sweat to lose a few pounds, the tendency to regain lost weight is a curse. The ease with which weight is regained, along with the fact that obesity tends to run in families, has led investigators to look for a physiological basis for many cases of obesity.

After many years of careful study, such a link has been identified. Richard Nisbett (1972) points out that weight is a function of the *number* and *size* of fat cells. The size of these fat cells is determined by daily food intake. Thus, it is possible to control the size of your fat cells by controlling your diet. However, the *number* of fat cells is not affected by your daily diet. The number of fat cells that you have is partly an inherited trait and partly determined by your diet during the first two years of life (Knittle, 1975). Eating a great deal as a youngster, then, may increase a person's

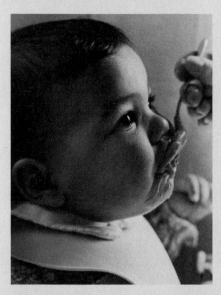

number of fat cells; what one eats as an adult will not affect their number.

Björntorp (1972) found that obese people have more than double the number of fat cells compared to normal-weight people. Thus, regardless of how they try to starve themselves, obese people will not be able to reduce the number of fat cells in their body. They will always have a tendency to be obese because they have a large number of fat cells eagerly waiting to store up fat. For the obese, keeping their weight down will be a constant battle. On the other hand, thin people will have a very difficult time gaining weight no matter how much they eat; these people do not have a large number of cells for storing fat.

intake if the food looks attractive (Hashim and Van Itallie, 1965) and is easily available (Schachter and Friedman, 1974). Obese people will actually eat less than normal-weight subjects if they have to work in order to get their food. A good example of this is shelling nuts.

While it is likely that everyone's eating behavior is influenced to some degree by external cues, these cues play a more important role for obese people than for others.

Further, more recent research has suggested that attention to external cues is not the only factor, in overeating behavior (Nail et al., 1981; Rodin, 1981). This research has found that in many situations normal-weight people are not less sensitive than obese people to external cues such as time. As Rodin (1981) points out, this situation suggests that other, as yet unidentified, characteristics of the overweight population are important and may be more crucial in motivating overeating behavior than external cues. Findings such as these indicate that the reasons behind overeating are complex and varied, and research is just beginning to uncover additional factors related to obesity.

Arousal and Eating. What red-blooded American can resist the lure of popcorn and other munchies while watching an exciting movie? In an interesting study, White (1977) had normal-weight and obese subjects watch four different movies; three of the movies were arousing and one was a nonarousing travelogue. After each session, the subjects were allowed to sample crackers under the guise of consumer-preference research. While normal-weight individuals ate about the same amount no matter which film they had seen, obese subjects ate a lot more after seeing the arousing films than after the travelogue.

These results suggest that obese people are not insensitive to their internal cues. Rather, they may have a hard time figuring out or understanding the cues their bodies are sending them (McKenna, 1972). In the experiment just mentioned as well as in others, obese subjects respond to most types of arousal by eating. In a sense, they may be misinterpreting the arousal as hunger rather than as anxiety, fear, or anger. This type of misinterpretation is not as common in thin or normal-weight people.

To sum up, there are clearly a number of factors associated with obesity. The most important of these are an increased sensitivity to external cues to eat, a difficulty in interpreting internal cues, and the sheer number of fat cells in the body (see "Highlight: Born to Be Fat?").

SEXUAL BEHAVIOR

Sex is a powerful drive that involves a set of unique characteristics. Unlike hunger, sex is not necessary for the survival of the individual. Not all aspects of the sex drive are as yet fully understood. In fact, it is only in recent times that discussions of sex were considered acceptable, even in textbooks. However, the research that has been completed shows that sexual behavior is strongly affected by both physiology and environment.

The Biological Basis of Sex

It may seem like a simple question to ask if biological changes regulate sexual behavior. However, an examination of research in the area shows this to be an exceedingly complex issue; the answer depends on whether we are interested in the sexual behavior of animals or humans (and other primates), and whether we are interested in males or females. There are some general statements that should be made before we begin our discussion. First, sexual behavior in animals is strongly influenced by the levels of certain hormones in the blood; human sexual behavior is not. Second, although sexual behavior is evident in young animals and children, the strongest sex drive occurs when the organism reaches sexual maturity. In humans, *puberty* is the period when this sexual maturity begins. Interestingly enough, the age at which puberty occurs has been decreasing over the last 150 years. As Figure 9–3 shows, in 1840 the average age at which women reached puberty (signaled by the onset of menstruation) was about 17 years, while in 1960 it was 12½ (Tanner, 1962). With these points in mind, let's examine separately the biological basis of male and female sexual behavior.

When the male reaches sexual maturity, the *pituitary gland* (as discussed in Chapter 2) located at the base of the brain stimulates the testes (the male reproductive gland) to secrete androgens into the bloodstream. These androgens, or male sex hormones, increase the sex drive in men. In humans, androgens also influence the development of *secondary sex characteristics*, such as the growth of pubic hair and the deepening of the voice. Androgens are found in their highest concentration shortly after the male has reached sexual maturity. While the concentration of androgens may vary a bit over long periods of time, androgen concentration over the shorter time span is fairly constant. In other words, there are no definite biological cycles for male sexual behavior; given the proper stimuli, sexual behavior from both animal and human males can be elicited at almost any time.

In support of this position, Goldstein (1957) found that castration of male dogs before they reached sexual maturity stopped the development of sexual behavior. However, if castration was performed after the dogs reached maturity and had had sexual experience, they continued to respond sexually. Thus, androgens are necessary for the development of sexual behavior, but they do not control the sex drive after maturity.

FIGURE 9–3

The graph shows the average age of first menstruation for girls in Western countries in the last 150 years. As can be seen, the average age has gone from 17 years in 1840 to 12½ years in 1960. (Tanner, 1962)

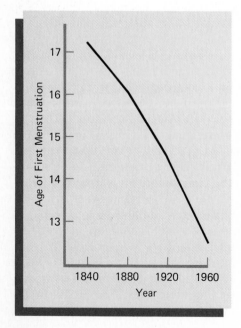

Female sexual behavior has a more complicated biological basis. First, hormones play a very different role in female animal and human behavior. On reaching sexual maturity, the pituitary gland stimulates the **ovaries,** which are the female reproductive glands, to secrete **estrogen** (the female sex hormone). However, unlike males, the rate of secretion of estrogen rises and falls in a cyclical way. The secretion of estrogen is at its highest level during the period of **ovulation,** the time when the egg is available to be fertilized. In most animals, this time is called being "in heat," and it is only during this time that the female animal is receptive to sexual advances. Therefore, the level of hormones controls the animal's sexual response patterns. Removal of the ovaries for these animals eliminates sexual behavior (Carlson, 1977). This, however, is not the case for humans. Many women who have had their ovaries removed or who have reached menopause still have strong sex drives and are sexually active. Thus, while the level of estrogen determines the onset of menstruation and the period of fertility, it does not determine the human female's sex drive. The human female may engage in sex at any time; as we will see, human sexual behavior (both male and female) is more influenced by learning and external stimuli than by hormone levels.

The Importance of External Cues. Even with lower animals, it takes more than hormones to elicit sexual behavior. The existence of sex hormones only primes the animal or places it in a state of readiness for sexual behavior. In order for sexual behavior to occur, some added stimulation is necessary. In animals, this comes from the partner. One of the most common forms of external stimulation for males involves cues of smell. Receptive females in many species discharge a vaginal substance that has a particular odor; when the male catches scent of this odor, he becomes sexually aroused. However, despite advertisements insisting that Brand X perfume or Brand Y cologne will drive your mate wild, there is no evidence that human sexual behavior is innately influenced by odors (Doty et al., 1975).

On the other hand, humans certainly have plenty of other external cues that are capable of sexually arousing them. Almost any object that people have learned to associate with sex is capable of arousing them. These objects can include anything from high-heeled shoes and black leather pants to a particular song. The principle, however, is the same; even with the proper amount of hormones flowing in the veins, external cues are needed to initiate sexual behavior.

The Human Sexual Response

The Role of Learning. In much of the discussion thus far regarding sexual behavior, we have had to qualify statements by saying "except with humans."

Human sexual behavior is neither as dependent on hormones nor as stereotyped as animal sexual behavior. Because of this, humans have to learn the "when and how" of sexual behavior. This seemingly simple fact of life has many important consequences. One consequence is that human sexual behavior is widely varied, being limited only by a person's imagination and physical capabilities rather than a predetermined plan set by nature. A second consequence, as we have pointed out, is that humans can learn to be sexually aroused by an almost inconceivable range of stimuli.

While these points add to the excitement and variety of human sexual behavior, the important role of learning adds a third consequence that is anything but exciting. That is, if the proper learning situations do not occur, normal sexual behavior will fail to develop. Much of this learning takes place through social interaction and play with peers during childhood.

It has also been reported that early childhood experiences in humans influence the development of later sexual behavior (Rosen and Rosen, 1981).

Four Phases of Sexual Response. In the early 1920s, the well-known behaviorist John B. Watson decided to investigate the physical effects of sexual behavior on the human body. He placed electrodes on his own body and that of his partner and recorded their responses during various stages of intimacy. His valiant effort was met with dismay and disgust by his colleagues and little attention was given to his data.

It was not until the late 1950s, when the team of William Masters and Virginia Johnson began their studies, that much of the mystery of the human sexual response was lifted. Masters and Johnson carefully monitored the responses of a large number of subjects engaged in both intercourse and masturbation. They found that male and female sexual responses were alike in a number of ways.

These researchers found that it was possible to roughly categorize the human (male or female) response into four phases (Masters and Johnson, 1966, 1975). The first phase is the *excitement phase*, which may last anywhere from a few minutes to several hours. During this phase, arousal increases and the genital areas become engorged with blood. The *plateau phase*, the second stage, is characterized by increased body tension, heart rate, and blood pressure. In males there is an erection of the penis, and in females the glands in the vagina secrete lubricating fluid. The *orgasm phase* is accompanied by rhythmic contractions in the genitals of both sexes and by ejaculation in the males. These contractions occur every eight-tenths of a second and last for varying lengths of time. The orgasm is experienced as a pleasurable sudden release of sexual tension. Masters and Johnson exploded some earlier myths by finding that women were not only capable of having orgasms, but that these orgasms were pleasurable experiences.

The final phase is the *resolution period*, during which the body gradually returns to its normal state. One major difference between men and women is that women are capable of multiple orgasms in quick succession. Males usually are not; instead they enter a *refractory phase*, which may last from a few minutes to several hours. During this time males are incapable of sexual arousal or orgasm.

Human Sexual Behaviors

Throughout much of time, many a parent resorted to the "ultimate threat" to control their child's sexual behavior: "Nice girls (boys) don't do that (e.g., masturbate or engage in premarital sexual intercourse)." This type of statement could hardly be challenged before 1948 because we had little idea of the type or frequency of sexual activities of humans in general, let alone that of "nice girls and boys." However, attitudes began to change in the late 1940s when Kinsey and his colleagues (1948, 1953) interviewed a large sample of American males and females on a wide range of topics regarding their sexual habits. Because of this study and those that followed, we now have a clearer picture of the nature of human sexual activities.

Autosexual Behavior. The first and most common sexual experience for most people is **masturbation,** or autosexual behavior, the self-manipulation of one's genitals. Masturbation is common among both children and adults; Kinsey found that more than 90 percent of males and more than 60 percent of females masturbate. A later survey supported these findings (Hunt, 1974). This researcher also found that 72 percent of married men over the age of 30 and 68 percent of married women over age 30 continued to engage in masturbation.

For a long time, masturbation was not only thought to be a shameful practice, it was also seen as dangerous. Some physicians suggested that masturbation caused such maladies as feeble-mindedness and nervousness (Kellogg, 1902). Children have been told that masturbation leads to blindness and, for males, the eventual separation of the penis from the body. Kinsey (1948) summed up early feelings toward masturbation: "Every conceivable ill, from pimples to insanity, including stooped shoulders, loss of weight, fatigue, insomnia, general weakness, neurasthenia, loss of manly-mindedness, genital cancer, and the rest, was ascribed to masturbation" (p. 513). Today we know that masturbation is not physically harmful; in fact, the most damaging results come from the emotional trauma and guilt instilled in children to prevent masturbation. In some cases, masturbation is recommended by therapists treating sexual disorders (McMullen and Rosen, 1979).

Along similar lines, another group of researchers found that women who had positive attitudes toward masturbation were more easily aroused by sexually explicit pictures (Abramson et al., 1981). The investigators also suggested that women with these attitudes would be more likely to reach orgasm during intercourse.

Heterosexual Behavior. The Kinsey report also shed light on heterosexual behavior, the sexual desire for people of the opposite sex. Despite religious and social taboos and the fear of pregnancy, 27 percent of college-educated women and 49 percent of college-educated men said that they had engaged in premarital sex. This was considered by many to be a high figure for those times. The last two decades have seen vast changes in social attitudes toward premarital sexual behavior. In addition to these changing attitudes, there has been the introduction of "the pill" and other safe and easy means of birth control. These changes have also been accompanied by changes in sexual practice. Surveys done in the 1970s found that between 60 and 85 percent of the males interviewed and 43 to 80 percent of the females had engaged in premarital sexual intercourse (Hunt, 1974; Bauman and Wilson, 1974; Jessor and Jessor, 1975). In one study, an investigator interviewed married people and found that of those under the age of 25, 95 percent of the males and 81 percent of the females had engaged in premarital intercourse (Hunt, 1974).

Simply looking at the numbers gives the impression that the sexual experience of males and females is becoming a great deal more alike than was the case 20 years ago. To a degree this is true; however, there are some important differences in the way in which males and females regard sexual behavior. Women who engage in premarital sexual intercourse tend to do so with more emotional involvement and with fewer partners than do men; Hunt reports that the average number of premarital partners for men was six, while it was generally two for women. Further, male and female attitudes toward sex are different. Females tend to voice concerns about pleasing their partner, while males are often more concerned about their own pleasure in a sexual relationship (Tavris and Offir, 1977; Bardwick, 1971); in essence, it seems as if "females aim to please and males aim to be pleased." However, just as similarity in the sexual practice of males and females has increased over the last few years, it is likely that in the next decade there will be a greater similarity in attitudes and beliefs about sex held by males and females.

In addition to studying when people engage in sexual intercourse, investigators have examined how often this occurs. The median frequency of sexual intercourse for married males in the United States was three times a week; median frequency means that half of all married males had sex more often than this and half had sex less often than this (Hunt, 1974). In this same survey, Hunt found that some people reported having intercourse more than once a day, while others reported averaging less than

TABLE 9–2: Frequency of Marital Coitus in the United States, 1938–1949 and 1972

1938–1949		1972	
Age	Median	Age	Median
16–25	2.45	18–24	3.25
26–35	1.95	25–34	2.55
36–45	1.40	35–44	2.00
46–55	0.85	45–54	1.00
56–60	0.50	55 and over	1.00

Source: Hunt (1974), p. 196.

once a year. Also, as can be seen in Table 9–2, frequency of sexual intercourse declines as people get older. Clearly, then, heterosexual behavior has changed over time and varies widely between individuals.

Homosexual Behavior. Recently, the Gay Rights movement has focused national attention on **homosexuality,** the sexual desire for those of the same sex as oneself. For years homosexuality was treated as a mental or physical disorder. In many states homosexual behavior is still considered a "crime against nature," and jail sentences can be given to people convicted of the "crime" even when it occurs between consenting adults.

In terms of percentages, the number of people who engage exclusively in homosexual behavior is rather low; it has been estimated that about 4 percent of men and slightly over 1 percent of women in the United States are exclusively homosexual (Gebhard, 1972). However, Kinsey and others have estimated that possibly as high as 45 percent of all people in the United States have had some homosexual encounter during their lives, often during childhood. Further, most people who are labeled homosexuals are not exclusively homosexual; rather, they are bisexual and are attracted to members of both sexes.

There is still not a clear understanding of why some people engage in homosexual behavior. In some cases, it is possible to point to a hormonal imbalance. For example, researchers found lower levels of the male sex hormone in males who were exclusively homosexual than in males who

practiced only heterosexual behavior (Kolodny et al., 1971). However, they were quick to point out that this finding does not demonstrate that the level of hormones *causes* homosexual behavior. It is possible, too, that the stress and anxiety associated with a homosexual life style causes the reduction in hormone level.

Social and psychological factors also influence a person's sexual preference. For example, a child growing up may form a number of close attachments to members of the same sex, while he or she has difficulty forming such relationships with members of the opposite sex. As a result, the person may focus all efforts into developing satisfying homosexual relationships.

While the causes of homosexuality still remain a mystery, it has become clear that homosexuality is not a mental disease or disorder and does not demand treatment." In fact, in a recent study Masters and Johnson (1979) reported that homosexuals have no inadequacy in sexual functioning and, in some cases, achieve greater satisfaction for themselves and their partners than do heterosexual couples.

STIMULUS-SEEKING MOTIVES

After dealing with the immediate perils of the crash, many of the survivors began to get restless; they wanted something to do while they waited for rescue. As a result, despite the bitter cold, some of them spent their daytime hours searching the area around the plane, and several set out to explore the larger area around the crash site. Others spent time wandering through the plane. When a new object was found, such as a broken piece of radio, the discoverer spent hours examining and fingering it.

Many animals have this same desire to explore and manipulate new objects, which is also referred to as a **stimulus-seeking motive**. When rats, cats, or dogs are put in a new environment, their immediate response is to explore the area. Dember (1965) even found that rats will choose a new environment when given the choice between a familiar area and a new one.

The motive to explore is found in animals and humans. Harlow observed that monkeys will spend long periods opening and closing locks in their cages. Exploring behavior seems to be an end in itself.

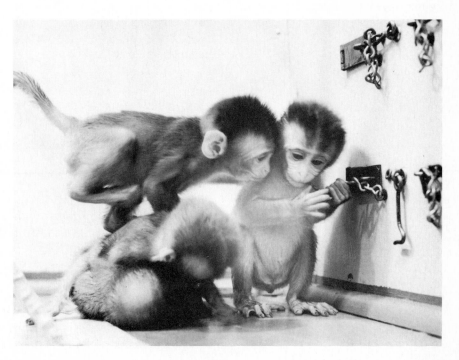

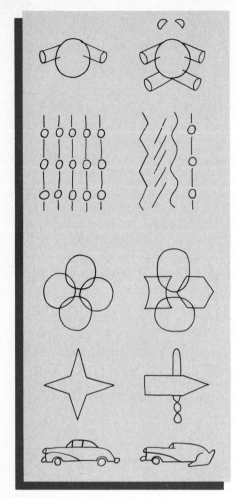

FIGURE 9–4

In this study, Berlyne found that most people, when presented with the figure pairs shown here, preferred the more complex figures on the right to those on the left in each pair. Subjects showed their preference by focusing more quickly and for a longer period on the right-hand figures. (Berlyne, 1958)

In the animal kingdom the monkey has emerged as the "King of Curiosity." Monkeys will inspect, kick, taste, handle, and smell any new object that is put in their cage. Some researchers found that young monkeys would spend hours opening and closing locks and other mechanical devices in their cages (Harlow, Harlow, and Meyer, 1950). Others observed that monkeys spent a lot of time opening a window in their cages so that they could look out (Butler and Alexander, 1955). In neither of these experiments were the animals given any extra reward for their behavior; their satisfaction seemed to come from simply having the opportunity to "monkey" around with a new object or explore a new view.

Anyone who has been around young children for any length of time will agree that they are major contenders for the "King or Queen of Curiosity" title. A walk through a home lived in by a young child will often show that every moveable object has been placed on shelves high above the floor and out of the child's reach, and every passageway has been barricaded. However, despite all such precautions, these mobile destruction units still seem to find some new area to explore or new object to manipulate. Taking note of this and the sometimes tragic consequences, the Food and Drug Administration has required drug manufacturers to use "child-proof" caps so that children cannot eat dangerous drugs if they find the bottles.

What is behind this common and seemingly insatiable behavior? Two important elements are novelty and complexity. Researchers have found that infants spend more time looking at complex figures than at simpler figures (Berlyne et al., 1957, 1958, 1966). They also discovered that adults focus their attention more quickly and for a longer period of time on complex and novel pictures (see Figure 9–4).

The motive to explore and manipulate is an important one for the individual's survival. It is through searching new areas and feeling, touching, and manipulating objects that people learn about their environment and how it works. In addition, exploration and manipulation help people learn how to control their environment. This mastery is important if they are to survive and thrive. The motives to explore and manipulate do not easily fit the drive-reduction models of motivation. First, they do not seem to be caused by some internal state or lack. Rather, it is new and complex stimuli that elicit these responses. Second, the aim of these motives is to increase arousal or tension, not to reduce it. Seeking out new objects or areas to explore excites people. Thus, the study of these motives has made it clear that all motivation cannot be explained by a simple drive-reduction theory.

SOCIAL MOTIVES

Affiliation

The crash caused many drastic changes in the lives of the survivors. No longer were they faced with a familiar environment and a routine daily schedule. Their lives were filled with fear: fear of the cold, fear of going hungry, fear that they would never be found, and fear that each day might be their last. Their response to this situation was to seek comfort in one another. The survivors sat together, talked together, slept together, ate together, and even went outside together to go to the bathroom.

The **affiliation motive**, the desire to be with others, does not only occur in the cold isolation of the Andes. If you look around your own environment, most of the people you see will be in pairs, trios, or other

Research shows that fear leads to affiliation. The plane-crash survivors spent almost all their time in groups. They discussed their feelings together and tried to calm their fears.

small groups. And if you talk to those people, you are likely to find that most of them spend a great deal of their time with other people.

Social affiliation seems to be a favorite human pastime. Some investigators have said that humans have a basic drive to affiliate (French, 1958; Gewirtz and Baer, 1958). According to Gewirtz and Baer, the affiliation drive is aroused by social deprivation.

While it may seem that humans have a natural drive to affiliate, other research suggests that learning and early experiences strongly affect our desire to be with others. As we mentioned earlier, Harry Harlow (1971) did a study of infant monkeys who were raised in social isolation. Although they were well fed, they lacked the comfort of a mother and the opportunity to play with peers. When these isolated monkeys were 1 year old, Harlow placed them in a cage with other young monkeys who had been raised in a normal environment. Instead of joining the others in play, the isolated monkeys avoided social contact and cringed in a corner of the cage. If one of the other monkeys approached, the isolated monkey would react viciously. Thus, it seems that without the early experience of social comfort and interaction, the desire to affiliate does not develop.

Taking another approach, a number of experiments were performed to show that fear often leads to the desire to affiliate (Schachter, 1959). Imagine yourself in the following situation. You and some other subjects report for an experiment and are met by a very serious-looking man dressed in a white laboratory coat with a stethoscope hanging from his pocket. He introduces himself as Dr. Gregor Zilstein, and as he points to a ghastly array of electrical equipment, he informs you that you are in a study concerning the effects of electrical shock. He says that you will have electrodes placed on your hand and will be given a series of electrical shocks so that your reactions can be studied. In a very somber manner he confesses: "Again, I do want to be honest with you and tell you that these shocks will be quite painful, but, of course, they will do no permanent damage" (Schachter, 1959, p. 13). These were the instructions you would have received if you had been assigned to the high-fear group.

TABLE 9–3: Effect of Fear on Affiliation

	Number Choosing		
Group	Waiting Together	Didn't Care	Waiting Alone
High fear	20	9	3
Low fear	10	18	2

Source: Adapted from Schachter (1959).

If, on the other hand, you had been randomly placed in the low-fear group, you would have been met by a friendly Dr. Zilstein wearing sports clothes. Electrical equipment would not have been present in the room. After greeting you, Dr. Zilstein would tell you that the experiment concerned the effects of electrical shock. However, he would quickly add: "We would like to give each of you a series of very mild electric shocks. . . . It will resemble more a tickle than anything unpleasant" (Schachter, 1959, pp. 13–14).

After manipulating fear in this way, Dr. Zilstein told the subjects that there would be a 10-minute delay before the experiment would begin. He then gave the subjects (all of whom were women) the option of waiting alone, waiting with others, or stating no preference. What would be your desire in the two conditions? As can be seen from Table 9–3, subjects in the high-fear group had a much greater desire to be with others than did low-fear subjects. Thus, Schachter demonstrated that fear leads people to affiliate.

There was another interesting result in the Schachter study. Schachter found that the fear-affiliation link occurred only in subjects who were firstborn or only children. Fear did not make later-born subjects want to affiliate. This finding suggests that the fear-affiliation relationship is learned. According to Schachter, firstborn children are more likely than those born later to receive attention and comfort from their mothers in crisis situations; mothers tend to be particularly attentive to the needs of their first child. As a result, firstborns learn to seek out companionship when they are fearful. Later-born children do not receive the same degree of attention from their mothers and thus do not learn to seek companionship to deal with fearful situations.

Given that fear does lead to affiliation, we can now ask whether the presence of other people is effective in reducing fear. Research suggests that being with other people and receiving social support from them can indeed reduce fear (Sarason, 1981). In order to demonstrate this, Sarason chose college students who had test anxiety and, therefore, performed poorly in test situations. Some of the subjects were allowed to talk with other students before taking a test, while others were not given the opportunity for social interaction. The results indicated that the subjects with social support did better on the test and were less anxious than subjects not given social support.

Humans clearly have strong desires to affiliate. However, both their past experiences and the situation they are in at the time will influence the strength of this motive.

Aggression and Violence

In addition to hunger, thirst, and cold, the plane-crash survivors were forced to deal with one another's reactions to the crisis. From the very beginning there were fights. Many a night's calm was suddenly shattered by angry shouts and fighting. Some of the boys fought easily and often, while others rarely, if ever, participated in a fight.

Examples of violence and aggression constantly surround us. Nearly every page of a newspaper carries a story of violence; even the comics are liberally sprinkled with it. As a case in point, count the number of aggressive incidents or stories of aggression that occur around you in one day. It seems, then, that while humans have a desire to affiliate, many of their social encounters are characterized by aggression. The question of why people aggress has long intrigued psychologists.

Instinct Theories. One of the earliest views was that aggression is an instinct. Influenced by the human destructiveness that he witnessed in World War I, Sigmund Freud held that humans have a basic instinct to aggress. To Freud, the motivation to aggress arises within the person.

The instinct position was further developed by those who argued that while an organism may be naturally endowed with the readiness to aggress, an external cue is necessary to release the response. According to these theorists, only certain stimuli are capable of releasing aggression. This external trigger is viewed as a key that opens the door for aggression; just as only the proper key can open a lock, so it is that only certain predetermined stimuli can trigger aggression.

While such theories are of value in explaining aggression in some animals, it is hard to apply them directly to human behavior. Human aggression varies from culture to culture. For example, in Tokyo, a city with a population of 11 million people, there were 213 homicides in 1970, while during that same year in New York City (with a population of 8 million) there were 1,117 murders. Even looking at the experiences of the survivors, we find that in the same situation some of them acted aggressively and others did not. Thus it is difficult to argue that humans are instinctively aggressive.

Frustration-Aggression Theory. Despite attempts to show that the motivation for aggression arises from within the individual, most investigators believe that violence is set off by external events. One of the most widely studied theories was developed by a group of psychologists at Yale. John Dollard and his colleagues (1939) stated, "aggression is always a consequence of frustration," and "frustration always leads to some form of aggression" (p. 1). **Frustration** results when people are blocked from getting what they want when they want it. This frustration-aggression theory fits many of the incidents of aggression we discussed that occurred among the survivors in the Andes. A survivor's desire to sleep was clearly thwarted when he was stepped on or kicked in the face by a neighbor. In many cases, the result of this frustration was aggression.

While many of the survivors directly fit the model, there are some that did not. Canessa was one of the strongest of the survivors, and he was also the one who tended to bully the smaller boys. While there were some direct attacks on him, his actions often set off a chain reaction; he attacked one boy who, in turn, took out his anger on another, smaller boy. This fits a common stereotype of a man or woman who, frustrated by the boss at work, comes home and yells at the dog for no apparent reason. This behavior has been labeled **displaced aggression** (Dollard et al., 1939). Dollard and his colleagues argue that when we are frustrated, our first tendency is to attack the person responsible. However, if that person is either unavailable or feared (as in the above example), we will displace our aggression onto another target. In Chapter 15 we will discuss how displaced aggression may be at the root of some cases of prejudice.

Another important but controversial part of the theory deals with reducing the urge to aggress. According to the theory, as we face various frustrations in our daily lives, tension builds up inside us. This tension must be released in some way. One of the quickest ways to do this is through aggression. Dollard and his colleagues suggest that if people

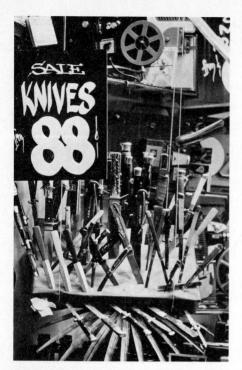

Berkowitz suggests that aggressive cues elicit aggressive behavior. An aggression cue can be any object that people have learned to associate with aggression—for example, knives.

behave aggressively they will release the tension and thus be less likely to aggress in the near future. **Catharsis** is the term used to describe this release of tension. This is a very important concept, because it argues that aggressive behavior can have a good effect on people and, in some cases, should be encouraged.

There has been some support for the catharsis effect. A group of investigators found that, under some conditions, behaving aggressively reduces a person's general state of arousal, as measured by blood pressure and heart rate (Hokanson and Shelters, 1961; Hokanson et al., 1963). However, while catharsis may occur after some acts of aggression, more recent surveys and research indicate that the effect is, at best, limited to a very narrow range of conditions (Geen and Quanty, 1977; Konecni and Doob, 1972). In many cases, the expression of aggression not only fails to reduce future aggression, but actually increases the probability of it.

The frustration-aggression theory has received both support and criticism. It has been generally accepted that frustration often sets off aggression. However, frustration is not the only source of aggression, nor does it always lead to aggression. Further, the theory does not adequately explain the wide variety in human aggressive behavior. For example, why did some of the plane-crash survivors respond aggressively to their frustrations while others did not? Why did some of the young men use physical violence as a response to frustration while others resorted to verbal abuse?

Leonard Berkowitz (1965) offered one explanation for this variation in reactions. He suggested that frustration leads only to *anger*, or the readiness to aggress. However, once a person has become angry, he or she will not aggress unless there are **aggression cues** present in the environment to elicit the behavior. An aggression cue is a stimulus that the person has learned to associate with aggression. For example, guns, knives, and brass knuckles are aggression cues for most of us. According to Berkowitz, in many cases it is "the trigger that pulls the finger."

While the availability of aggression cues may influence our aggression in some situations, it is clear that people do aggress without such cues. It is equally clear that frustration does not always cause aggression, nor that all aggression is the result of frustration. Hence, there must be other roots of human aggression.

Social-Learning Theory. It has been argued that aggression, like most other behaviors, is the result of learning, rather than some natural link with frustration (Bandura, 1973, 1977; Bandura and Walters, 1963). The *social-learning theory* suggests that we learn both when and how to aggress. The theory focuses on two major mechanisms for the learning of aggression: *reinforcement* and *imitation.*

As we have seen in Chapter 5, we tend to repeat behaviors that bring positive rewards. According to Bandura and Walters, children in our society are often rewarded for behaving aggressively; the rewards come in many forms. In one case, the reward may be a direct result of aggression. For example, Johnny may find that no matter how much he begs and pleads, little Billy will not give him any marbles. However, Johnny may quickly find that one sure way to get the marbles is to beat Billy to a pulp. In another case, rewards may come as an indirect result of aggression. For example, Suzy may find that the teacher never pays attention to her in class; no matter how often she holds up her hand, the teacher fails to notice her. However, the teacher's attention (and even that of the principal) is quickly captured if Suzy pulls the hair of the girl sitting in front of her.

A second important way to learn aggression is through the imitation of models. If we look at the world through children's eyes, we find that many of the successful models available to them achieve success through aggressive behavior. On television, the children see such stars as the Bionic

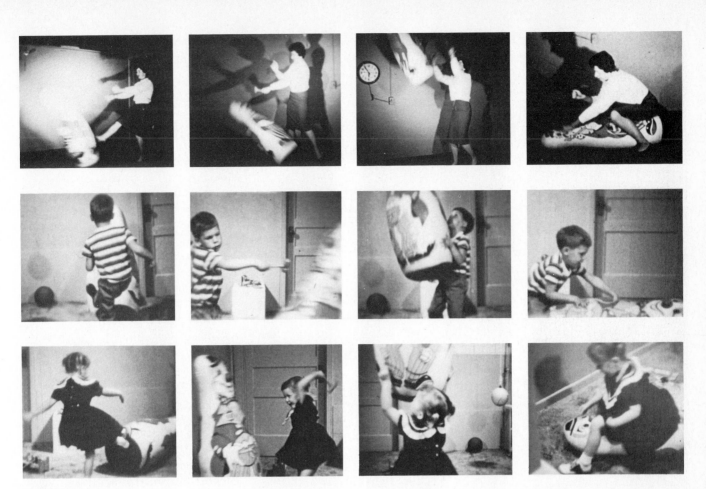

FIGURE 9–5

These photos were taken during Bandura's study of modeling and aggression. After watching an adult model kick and beat up the Bobo doll, boys and girls repeated these actions when they were allowed to play with the doll. (Bandura et al., 1963)

Woman and Agent 007 achieve fame through strength and aggression. Even at home, children see their parents use strength and aggression (spankings) to control their offspring. All these models broadcast the lesson that successful people use aggression to achieve their success.

In order to demonstrate the effectiveness of models, Bandura, Ross, and Ross (1961, 1963a) had nursery school children observe an adult model aggressively playing with an inflated doll ("Bobo doll"); the model kicked, hit, and beat the doll with a hammer (see Figure 9–5). When the children were later allowed to play with the doll, they too kicked, hit, and beat the doll with a hammer, just as the model had done. Bandura and his associates (1963b) also found that children imitated an aggressive model even when the model was seen on film or in a cartoon. Another important feature of this kind of learning is that children are more likely to repeat the behavior of a high-status model (Turner and Berkowitz, 1972) or a model that is rewarded for aggressive behavior (Bandura, 1965).

Social-learning theory also helps us understand why different people respond to the same situation in different ways. For example, Canessa may have learned that physical aggression was an effective way for him to deal with people who annoyed him. Thus, when people bothered him or got in his way during the mountain ordeal, his response was a violent one. Other survivors, on the other hand, may have had very different experiences and models and, as a result, learned to approach problems with reason and calm.

In addition to explaining why people aggress, social-learning theory can also be used to develop ways to reduce aggression. Bandura and Walters (1963) point out that when parents use physical violence to punish their children, they are providing them with aggressive models. In fact, studies show that children who were severely punished at home for aggression were likely to act aggressively outside the home (Sears et al., 1953).

HIGHLIGHT / MEDIA VIOLENCE AND AGGRESSION

The television set has become a family member in almost every household in this country; a family is more likely to have a television than it is to have running water. By the age of 10, the average child watches four to six hours of television a day, more time than is spent interacting with parents.

Aggression is very frequently shown on TV. An act of violence is shown every 16 minutes; a murder is shown on the average of once every 31 minutes. If you grew up in an average family, you probably saw 13,000 murders on TV by the time you were 16 years old (Waters and Malamud, 1975).

These startling figures lead to an obvious question: What effect does this have on behavior? In general, the evidence from both laboratory and field studies is that viewing violent programs increases the tendency to behave aggressively (Liebert et al., 1973). Let's look at just two of these studies.

A group of researchers studied the effects of viewing aggression on a group of juvenile delinquents in minimum custody institutions (Parke et al., 1977). The boys were divided into two groups: one group watched aggressive movies every night for a week, while the other group saw only nonaggressive movies during

the week. As can be seen in the figure shown here, the effect of the aggressive movies was to increase aggressive behavior—those who saw the violent films behaved more violently than those who had seen the nonviolent films.

The second study showed that, in addition to affecting our behavior, the regular viewing of aggression on TV also affects our *general* reactions to violence (Thomas et al., 1977). In this study, children watched either an aggressive episode of a TV program or a nonviolent film showing a game of volleyball. After this they were all shown a scene of "real-life" aggression that was supposedly taking place as they saw it. Those who had seen the aggressive film first were less affected by the "real" violence than those who had seen the nonviolent film. Such results suggest that viewing aggression on TV may make us less sensitive to and less bothered by aggression in our own lives.

In 1969 the National Commission on the Causes and Prevention of Violence did an extensive review of the literature on human aggression. It stated: "It is reasonable to conclude that a steady diet of violent behavior on television has an adverse effect on human character and attitudes. Violent behavior fosters moral and social values about violence in daily life that are unacceptable in a civilized society."

The graph shows that aggressive movies increase aggressive behavior in boys. In the case of boys who are normally aggressive, there was increased violence even during the weeks after seeing the films. (Parke et al., 1977)

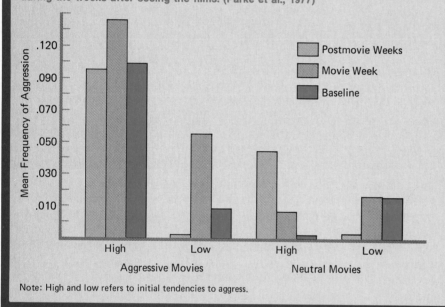

Note: High and low refers to initial tendencies to aggress.

Thus, it follows that parents should punish their children by withholding love or other rewards rather than by using aggression (Bandura and Walters, 1963). Social-learning theory also argues strongly against the catharsis notion: If people learn aggression, then allowing them to participate in aggressive activities will increase their future aggression, not reduce it, as suggested by the catharsis hypothesis. In the next section, we will see yet another implication of social-learning theory for the control of aggression.

The Role of Arousal in Aggression. The survivors were in a constant state of tension during their mountain ordeal due to fear and anxiety about keeping alive and about being rescued. Outside of the airplane nearly every step taken was a major ordeal as they sank into snow up to their waists. A walk around the outside of the plane would leave them gasping for breath. Is it possible that these additional sources of arousal increased the aggressiveness of the survivors?

Researchers have suggested that arousal of any type can cause people to act more aggressively when they are frustrated (Zillman, 1971, 1979; Zillman et al., 1974). In one study, Zillman (1971) showed subjects either an aggressive film, a sexually arousing film, or a nonarousing film. The subjects were then either angered or not angered by an experimental confederate. Finally, they were given the chance to shock the confederate under the guise of a learning task. The results showed that subjects who were sexually aroused and later angered were the most aggressive (delivered the highest amount of shock), and subjects who watched the nonarousing film were least aggressive. Zillman et al. (1981) also found that watching arousing but displeasing sexual films increased later aggression.

Other research has shown that arousing exercise (Zillman et al., 1974), humor (Mueller and Donnerstein, 1977), and noise (Donnerstein and Wilson, 1976) can also increase aggression when subjects are frustrated. There are two possible explanations for this effect. First, the heightened state of arousal may serve to energize people's responses. A second explanation is that people may misinterpret the cause of their arousal, as we shall discuss in Chapter 10. That is, the person who is first sexually aroused and then frustrated may feel that all the arousal is a result of anger. Thus, he or she may feel more angry than someone who was not aroused before the frustration. Whatever the reason, this research offers one explanation for the intensity often found in "lover's quarrels," and it should make you think twice before angering someone who has just seen an arousing movie.

The Achievement Motive

After Fernando Parrado recovered from the injuries he received in the crash and the shock of finding that his mother and sister had died, he carefully assessed the situation. He realized that the immediate problem faced by the group was simply to stay alive. He began building a wall to keep out the cold. He was the first of the survivors to suggest the eating of the dead. But above all, Parrado knew that the group was unlikely to be rescued if they simply sat on the mountain and waited. Parrado suggested that an expedition be organized to go down the mountain and find help. He knew there were risks involved, but he felt it must be done. Despite attempts by the other survivors to persuade him not to go, Parrado began making careful plans for the expedition. And in the end, it was this expedition, led by Parrado, that resulted in the group's rescue.

If you think of your own friends, you can probably identify a number of them who have the same traits that were shown here by Parrado. They enjoy struggling with challenging tasks and they don't quit until they have successfully solved the problem. They are not easily sidetracked, even by social pressure. On the other hand, you can probably identify some of your friends who respond very differently. They are happy just to finish a task, regardless of how well they do it. The challenge to them is to get by with doing as little as possible.

Many years ago, Harry Murray (1938) suggested that some people are driven by the motive "to do things as rapidly and/or as well as possible." Later, McClelland (1958) argued that people can be identified by the strength of their **achievement motive (nAch)**. People with high nAch are driven by the general desire to set and achieve high standards of excellence. These people seek out challenging tasks and do their best to perform well even if the task holds no special interest for them. These

Traditional views of women in Western society discourage them from striving for independent achievement. These views are slowly changing,and women are demonstrating that the desire to achieve is not determined by sex.

people have an internal standard of excellence that they strive to meet.

Measuring the Achievement Motive.   How can we tell if someone has a high need to achieve? One way is simply to ask. However, McClelland felt that the achievement motive is largely an unconscious one, and people are unlikely to know whether or not they have it. In order to measure the strength of this motive, McClelland and his colleagues (1953) adapted the *Thematic Apperception Test (TAT)*. This approach involves showing people a picture (such as a boy daydreaming) and having them tell a story about what is happening in the picture and what led up to these events (we will discuss this test in more detail in Chapter 11). The subjects' responses are then examined to identify themes involving achievement and success. McClelland felt that people who had a high nAch would tell stories involving themes of achieving and striving to obtain high goals, but that people with a lower nAch would not develop stories around achievement themes. For example, let us assume that a picture of a boy daydreaming was shown to subjects. In this case, we might expect those high in nAch to say that the boy is thinking about becoming a successful lawyer and winning important cases, or he is thinking about solving a difficult math problem. Those scoring low in nAch, on the other hand, might say that the boy is thinking about what he will have for lunch or about what his girlfriend is doing at that particular moment. The TAT cards have been widely used to tap the achievement motive.

Basis for the Achievement Motive.   Given that everyone does not have equally high motives to achieve, we can ask where this motive comes from. As with so many things in life, it seems that the blame (or praise) rests with our parents. Research shows that family characteristics and life style influence the development of the achievement motive. Winterbottom (1953) found that the mothers of those high in nAch raised their children to act independently. The children were allowed to make decisions on their own and were rewarded with affection for independent actions.

Other researchers found that both the opportunity for independence and the reward for independent behavior were necessary for developing high nAch (Teevan and McGhee, 1972). Children who are forced to act independently but are not rewarded for these behaviors do not develop high achievement motive; they may learn to act on their own, but they do not strive for excellence. Thus, it is clear that early childhood experiences have a strong influence on the achievement motive.

Characteristics of People Scoring High on Achievement Motive. For the most part, a strong drive for achievement is a good thing to have. A number of studies found that people with high nAch outperform those who are low in achievement motivation even though the IQ scores of both groups are the same (Lowell, 1952; Morgan, 1951). People with high achievement motive tend to get better grades in school (Raynor, 1970) and be more successful in business (Andrews, 1967) than those who have a low need to achieve.

Research has shown that the strength of a person's motive to achieve is related to the type of occupation he or she chooses (McClelland, 1955). McClelland found that people scoring low on the need to achieve chose jobs that involved few risks and few opportunities for independent decision making. However, people scoring high in nAch chose entrepreneurial positions such as sales, or were self-employed; in either case they had to make decisions and their salary and success were dependent on their own actions.

The reason for these differences are not entirely clear. However, it seems that people scoring low in nAch tend to be most concerned with either succeeding or having an excuse for not succeeding. To the contrary, those higher in nAch desire a challenge that they can work and succeed at, with success measured by their own ability and work.

While having a high need to achieve has many positive consequences, it does have its drawbacks. Recent evidence suggests that people scoring high in nAch take everything as a challenge. In their drive for perfection, they run the risk of becoming "workaholics." In some cases, they have difficulty "letting go" and relaxing and are prone to getting ulcers (as we will discuss in Chapter 10).

Sex and Racial Differences in nAch. The strong desire to achieve and be successful in school and business is encouraged for males, but what about females? Researchers point out that the traditional view of women in our society discourages success and striving for achievement (Frieze et al., 1978). Women are not encouraged to seek independent careers, and, when they do so, they are often the object of social scorn and discrimination. As a result of these values, Matina Horner (1968) argued that women learn to avoid and fear success.

In order to demonstrate this position, Horner asked male and female subjects to write a story about the following situation: "After first-term finals, Anne (John) finds herself (himself) at the top of her (his) medical school class." As can be seen in Table 9–4, when males wrote about John, they described him in positive terms with a happy future. However, when females wrote about Anne, their descriptions were far from flattering and they expressed concern about her future. Interestingly enough, Feather (1975) found that women's fear of success disappeared when the job involved a typically female role such as nursing. In this case, males expressed fears about succeeding. Hence, the desire to achieve may be affected by both gender and situation.

In addition to sex, racial variables have been related to the achievement motive (Katz, 1967). In many educational settings, educators have complained that black students lack the desire to achieve. In some recent work, it has been found that racial differences in achievement were related to the type of task being undertaken (Banks and McQuater, 1976; Banks,

TABLE 9–4: Sex Differences and the Achievement Motive

Sample Male Response

John is a conscientious young man who worked hard. He is pleased with himself. John has always wanted to go into medicine and is very dedicated. His hard work paid off. He is thinking that he must not let up now, but must work even harder than he did before. His good marks have encouraged him. . . . He eventually graduates at the top of his class.

Sample Female Response

Anne has a boy friend in the same class and they are quite serious. Anne met Carl at college and they started dating. . . . Anne is rather upset and so is Carl. She wants him to be higher in school than she is. Anne will deliberately lower her academic standing next term, while she does all she subtly can to help Carl. His grades come up and Anne soon drops out of medical school. They marry and he goes on in school while she raises their family.

Source: Horner (1968).

McQuater, and Hubbard, 1977). On boring tasks, black children did show less desire to achieve and succeed than did white children. However, on interesting tasks, both black and white children expressed high achievement motivation. Thus, once again, it seems that the particular situation interacts with an individual variable (race, in this case) to influence achievement motive.

SUMMARY

1. The study of **motivation** is concerned with how and why people behave as they do—what energizes and directs their behavior.

2. A distinction is made in the chapter between **primary motives** (such as hunger, thirst, the need for air and rest, and sex) and **social motives** (such as affiliation, aggression, and achievement).

3. Maslow has suggested that our motives are organized into a hierarchy, like the rungs of a ladder, with the stronger primary motives at the bottom and the more complex social motives at the top. Motives at the lower level must first be satisfied before the motives at the next higher level.

4. **Hunger** is one of the most basic primary motives. In looking for what controls eating and hunger, researchers have studied contractions of the stomach, the level of glucose in the bloodstream (as monitored by the hypothalamus and the liver), and body temperature.

5. There are a number of factors associated with **obesity** and overeating. The most important of these are an increased sensitivity to external cues to eat, a difficulty in interpreting inner cues of hunger (or lack of hunger), and the sheer number of fat cells in the body.

6. Unlike hunger, sex is not necessary for the survival of the individual; but it is necessary for the survival of the species. The biological basis of male and female sexual behavior is hormonal (**androgens** in the male, **estrogen** in the female), which also influences the development of secondary sex characteristics. Human sexual behavior is neither as dependent on hormones nor as stereotyped as animal sexual behavior. Because of this, learning and external cues play an important role in human sexual response.

7. Masters and Johnson have categorized the human sexual response into four phases: the excitement phase, the plateau phase, the orgasm phase, and the resolution phase. Males then usually enter a refractory phase, which may last from a few minutes to several hours, during which time they are incapable of sexual arousal or orgasm. Women, on the other hand, are capable of multiple orgasms in quick succession.

8. The desire to explore and manipulate new objects is called a **stimulus-seeking motive.** It is important for our survival, because it causes us to learn about our environment, how it works, and how to control it.

9. The **affiliation motive,** the desire to be with others, is a social motive. As noted in experiments by Schachter, fear often increases one's desire to affiliate with others.

10. The question of why people aggress has long intrigued psychologists. Among the theories considered here are instinct theories, frustration-aggression theory, and social-learning theory. Two factors that are thought to influence aggressive behavior are media violence and arousal.

11. The **achievement motive (nAch)** can be defined as the general desire to set and achieve high standards of excellence. McClelland devised the Thematic Apperception Test to measure the strength of this motive.

SUGGESTED READINGS

The following book is about the Andes survivors:

READ, P. T. *Alive: The Story of the Andes Survivors.* Philadelphia: Lippincott, 1974.

ARNOLD, W., and LEVINE, D. (Eds.). *Nebraska symposium on motivation.* Lincoln, Neb.: University of Nebraska Press. Issues are published once a year. They include original articles on a wide range of topics related to motivation. The articles are timely and focus on both theory and research.

BECK, R. *Motivation: Theories and principles,* 2nd ed. Englewood Cliffs, N.J.: Prentice-Hall, 1983. Discusses the major theories of motivation; also focuses on many specific motivations, such as aggression and achievement.

COFER, C., and APPLEY, M. *Motivation: Theory and research.* New York: Wiley, 1964. An excellent and complete discussion of a wide range of motivation theories. The volume presents research associated with each theory and examines the strengths and weaknesses of the theories.

DOLLARD, J., DOOB, L., MILLER, N. E., MOWER, O., and SEARS, R. *Frustration and aggression.* New Haven, Conn.: Yale University Press, 1939. Presents the frustration-aggression theory and discusses applications of it.

ROSEN, R., and ROSEN, L. *Human sexuality.* New York: Knopf, 1981. A general discussion of all aspects of human sexual behavior.

SCHACHTER, S., and RODIN, J. *Obese humans and rats.* Hillsdale, N.J.: Erlbaum, 1974. Discusses the major theories and research on obesity. The emphasis is on the relationship between obesity, attribution, and eating behavior.

10

Emotions and Stress

ave you ever wondered what people in the United States did for entertainment before television? During the first part of this century and for much of the last century the circus brought joy and excitement to residents of large cities such as New York and Boston and to small towns such as Cabool, Missouri and Old Dime Box, Texas. The young and young-at-heart eagerly awaited the arrival of John Robinson's Circus, Howe's Great London Circus, Hagenbeck-Wallace Company, or the Sells-Floto Circus. Some of these circuses were so small that they traveled on a few makeshift horse-drawn wagons, while others, such as the Ringling Brothers and Barnum & Bailey Circus, needed over a hundred railway cars to transport the show.

Emmett "Tater" Kelly became a part of the circus tradition in the early part of the twentieth century, and his name quickly became a household word for the patrons of The Greatest Show on Earth. Kelly had a rather usual and uneventful childhood. He was born in Sedan, Kansas on December 9, 1898. One of his earliest recollections was his first spanking. At the age of 5, he climbed a tall telegraph pole and sat surveying the world from the crossbeam. Suddenly the serenity of his world was broken by the shrieking of his terrified mother and neighbors. Seeing their fear caused Emmett to reassess his own situation; his own exhilaration quickly changed to fear.

Kelly, like other children in this Kansas farming community, was fascinated by the circus, and he looked forward to the arrival of the traveling companies. However, his main interest lay in art; he wanted to draw cartoons. While his parents did not understand this desire, they encouraged him and even paid the $25 tuition to enter Kelly in the Landon School of Cartooning correspondence course. Kelly worked hard; he carefully studied people's expressions and learned to draw humorous pictures of people in many different moods.

In 1917 he headed for Kansas City with $20 in his pocket and visions of earning a fortune as an artist. He soon found that realizing his ambitions as an artist would be more difficult than he expected. His first "art job" was painting letters on signs. His next job involved painting faces on plaster kewpie dolls that were given as prizes in circus sideshows. Then he painted horses for circus merry-go-rounds. Kelly's work thus brought him into contact with the circuses that traveled through Kansas City. He became intrigued with the work of the aerial trapeze acts, and he began practicing on the trapeze in his spare time.

The persistent Kelly finally got a job as a trapeze artist with Howe's Great London Circus. He was delighted with his job until he was told that he would also have to do a clown act. He had no desire to be a clown, but he reluctantly acted the part.

The typical clown act of the time was called "whiteface." The clown painted his face white with a mixture of zinc oxide and lard. Next, grease paint was used to outline the eyes and exaggerate the nose and mouth. Kelly's costume included a white wig and comic, oversized shoes. The goal of a clown was to capture an emotion such as joy, surprise, or sadness, exaggerate the expression of the emotion, and portray it in situations that made it funny. For example, a favorite act of the time was a sad-faced clown who searched for his dog, who secretly trailed along behind him during the search.

Kelly loved the circus and the people in it. He was captivated by their approach to life. "They (circus performers) may die broke or sick or unhappy, but they seldom give up hope. . . . They just can't quite settle for the idea that the deck is stacked, the wheel is fixed, the dice frozen or the whole game rigged against them. Show people are hopeful people" (Kelly, 1954, p. 97).

While Kelly loved the circus and the people, he was not happy being a clown. When the chance arose, he switched to the John Robinson Circus, where his only job was on the trapeze. There he met Eva Moore, who did a double trapeze act with her sister. Eva was a tiny, slim blond who dazzled the circus patrons with her daring acts

high above the big top. He proposed to Eva at the top of the Ferris wheel at a carnival in Canada, and they were married a few days later. The Kellys worked up a double-trapeze act and stayed with Robinson's Circus.

However, times were getting hard. When the Depression began to grip the Western world, a number of circuses were forced to close, including Robinson's Circus. The Kellys searched desperately for a job, but none of the other circuses needed a trapeze act. Finally, in 1933, another circus offered Kelly a job, but they would only hire him as a clown. He reluctantly accepted the job, but he decided that he would do a different kind of clown act.

He wanted an act that would turn people's attention away from their own sadness and depression and cause them to laugh as they watched someone less fortunate deal with hard times. He wanted to show people that there was both humor and hope in their situation. So, "Weary Willie" was born. In

Kelly's own words, Willie was "a sad and ragged little guy who is serious about everything he attempts—no matter how futile or how foolish it appears to be. I am the hobo who found out the hard way that the deck is stacked . . . but there is always present that one tiny, forlorn spark of hope still glimmering in his soul which makes him keep on trying" (Kelly, 1954, pp. 125–126). Willie was a tramp with a dirty face, exaggerated frown, and ragged clothes who delighted circus fans when he tried to crack a peanut with a sledge hammer or sweep away light rays with an old broom.

Kelly (or Willie, as he became known throughout the United States) won the hearts of thousands even though he never said a word in his act. Kelly clowned around the world. He found that he could get his greatest laughs when he performed after the most dangerous circus acts, such as the lion-taming or trapeze acts. He also found that no matter what language circus patrons spoke, they all understood the silent antics and sad face of Willie.

Kelly continued his act until the 1960s. He became a featured performer in the world's largest circus, the Ringling Brothers and Barnum & Bailey Circus. He brought his clown act to Broadway, where he acted in a show with Jackie Gleason and Jimmy Durante, and he found his way into the hearts of millions in the movie *The Greatest Show on Earth.* Even in the complicated world of the 1980s, clowns who imitate many of Willie's antics bring laughter and tears of joy to circus audiences.

A Search for a Definition

Emmett Kelly spent his life influencing people's emotions. As Willie, the little tramp, Kelly could make the audience feel sad when he smashed his peanut into an inedible pulp with his sledge hammer. And just as quickly, Willie could make the audience feel happy and burst out laughing as he frantically chased the light beams with his frayed old broom. All of us are familiar with emotions; we talk about emotions and we experience them many times each day. We seek out situations that arouse certain emotions and avoid other situations because they will arouse unwanted emotions.

Despite this everyday familiarity, the concept of *emotion* has a certain mystery for those studying it. Some investigators argue that emotions are not different from motives (which we discussed in Chapter 9), while others see a clear distinction between the two. Despite these disagreements, **emotions** are generally conceived of as affective states (or feelings) accompanied by physiological changes that often influence behavior (Izard, 1977; Strongman, 1973). The emphasis in the definition is on feeling; emotions, unlike motives, are something that we feel. As Cofer (1972) points out, "We usually say 'I am hungry' or 'I am thirsty,' not that we *feel* hungry or thirsty" (pp. 56–57). Emotions, on the other hand, such as happiness or sadness, are states that we *feel*.

Another distinctive feature of emotions that tends to separate them from motives is that emotions are usually aroused by events outside us. You are likely to feel happy because you get a good grade in class or a large raise at work. In each of these cases the emotion is the result of an outside event. As we pointed out in Chapter 9, motives are often caused by our inner, bodily states.

The Physiology of Emotion

In 1937, Emmett Kelly was invited to perform in England. It was the first time he had been out of the United States. He reports the "strange" responses of his body as he "peeked through that curtain separating the American clown from his foreign audience" (Kelly, 1954, p. 33). His mouth was dry and felt like paste, his knees shook, and his stomach tightened up like a fist.

It has been recognized for centuries that bodily changes are associated with emotions. Modern research has shown that there are definite physiological changes that accompany emotions.

As we pointed out in Chapter 2, the *sympathetic nervous system* is concerned mainly with preparing the body for action and using energy. It increases heart rate and blood pressure, stimulates the adrenal glands to secrete adrenalin, increases breathing rate, and increases perspiration (Carlson, 1977). The *parasympathetic nervous system*, on the other hand, works to conserve energy. It returns the body to a normal resting state after the sympathetic nervous system has aroused the body for action.

Since most of our emotions, such as anger, fear, joy, and even love, are states that prepare us for action, the physiological effects associated with most emotions are influenced by the sympathetic nervous system. You may recall the exhilaration you felt the first time you fell in love. Or you may remember running faster than you believed possible after you disturbed a bee's nest. Occasionally we can read stories of people performing superhuman feats while being gripped by a strong emotion such as fear or anger. In each of these cases, the physiological effects that make the actions possible are the result of the sympathetic nervous system's activity. In most cases, after the situation that gave rise to the emotion passes, the parasympathetic nervous system takes over to return the body to its normal state.

For the most part, this cooperative relationship between the sympathetic and parasympathetic nervous systems is elegantly adaptive. The systems prepare the individual for action and then "close down" when the need for action has passed. Unfortunately, the relationship is not a perfect one and, as we will see later, the physiological changes associated with emotions can create problems for the individual.

GETTING THAT FEELING: THEORIES OF EMOTION

On the afternoon of July 6, 1944, Kelly was busy getting into his costume for the first performance of the day in Hartford, Connecticut. The show had started and the big top was packed. Suddenly, someone ran past Kelly's tent and shouted "Fire!" Kelly ran outside and saw a column of black smoke billowing from the main tent. His heart quickened its beat and fear gripped him as he ran to the big top. A sickening sight greeted Kelly; hundreds of people ran screaming from the tent, circus animals stampeded in wild panic through the smoke, and the stench of burning flesh settled over all. The disaster was one of the worst in circus history; scores of people were killed and hundreds were seriously injured.

Kelly experienced a wide variety of emotions in a short period of time during that tragic day. He reported feeling *fear* when he heard about the fire and saw the smoke, *hope* that the fire was not in the main tent, *anger* as he grabbed a bucket of water to fight the fire, and *sadness* as he cried when he saw some charred shoes and part of a clown doll lying in the smoldering ashes. Why did Kelly experience these particular emotions in this situation? How did Kelly know he was "feeling" fear when he heard the scream of "fire" and saw the smoke? The question of how we feel specific emotions has been a source of interest and debate for nearly a century. The debate is far from settled. Despite this disagreement, there are some basic viewpoints that have shaped much of our thinking about emotions.

James-Lange Theory

Kelly vividly described his feelings of fear and sadness on the day of the Hartford fire. The common-sense view of emotions suggests that the feeling of emotions caused Kelly to react in certain ways. For example, we might argue that when Kelly saw the charred shoes and doll he felt sad, and *because* of this feeling the corners of his mouth turned down, his throat tightened, and he began to cry. This sequence of events makes sense to most of us, but it did not to William James, writing in the 1880s. James argued that it is difficult to imagine feeling an emotion without experiencing a bodily change *at the same time*. (The common-sense view suggests that the emotion comes *before* the bodily change.) He also pointed out that people often feel emotions without knowing exactly what has caused the emotion (James, 1890). For example, you may be suddenly overcome with feelings of sadness while you are sitting quietly in your room. You may not know why you feel sad, but you can clearly identify your feelings.

HIGHLIGHT / TRUTH IN EMOTIONS: LIE DETECTION

As we have seen, emotions are reflected in physiological arousal. This fact has long intrigued researchers who wanted to find a way to tell when a person is lying. The basic assumption in the search for the perfect lie detector is that people experience a twinge of guilt or stress when they tell a lie. This "twinge" should be reflected in their physiology, which, unlike verbal behavior, is not under their control. Thus, all that is needed to detect lying is some way to measure a person's physiological responses.

Like so many of our "modern" inventions, a search of history reveals that the concept of the lie detector was conceived hundreds of years ago. The ancient Chinese had a suspect chew rice powder while being questioned (Rice, 1978). After the questioning period, the wad of powder was carefully examined. If it was found to be dry, the suspect was found guilty. The Chinese reasoned that lying would create tension, which would slow or block the flow of saliva. Thus the dry mouth resulted in dry rice powder, which, in turn, resulted in a guilty verdict. Interestingly enough, the basic theory behind this test was quite sound; strong emotions such as stress are associated with less secretion of saliva.

The modern lie detector, called a **polygraph,** does not use rice powder. Instead, it records changes in heart rate, blood pressure, respiration, and galvanic skin response (GSR). Suspects are hooked up to the polygraph, and the operator asks them a number of questions (see Figure A). The first questions are unrelated to any crime; by using such questions as "What is your name?" or "How old are you?" the operator can establish a baseline that shows how the individual responds to truthful answers. The operator then begins to ask carefully worded questions about the crime. Lies are identified when there is a *change* from this baseline response; there is no absolute level of physiological responding that is associated with telling a lie. The operator generally avoids asking the "did you do it" question, since this question may cause even innocent suspects to feel stress. Rather, the operator asks questions that are related to the crime but would create stress only in someone who was familiar with the crime (Lykken, 1975). For example, David Lykken (1959) had subjects act out a crime that involved stealing an object from an office and hiding it in a locker in the hallway. The subject in each case was then given a polygraph test in which the operator asked questions about where the object was hidden. "Was it (a) in the men's room, (b) on the coat rack, (c) in the office, (d) on the window sill, or (e) in the locker?" (p. 386). The mention of the locker would have meaning only for

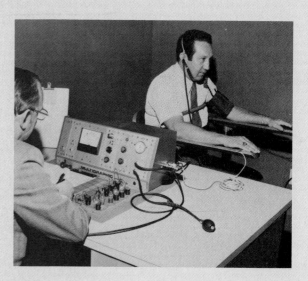

FIGURE A

The polygraph records heart rate, blood pressure, respiration, and galvanic skin response (GSR). The basic assumption is that people's physiological functioning changes when they tell a lie. There are still many questions about the accuracy of the polygraph in detecting lies and about the ethics of forcing people to submit to a lie detection test.

Because of these and other considerations, James (1884) argued that events cause bodily and behavioral changes in people, and the emotion lies in the *perception* of these physiological and behavioral changes. According to this investigator: "Common sense says that we lose our fortune, are sorry, and weep; . . . (My) hypothesis . . . is that we feel sorry because we cry, angry because we strike, afraid because we tremble . . ." (James, 1890). The Danish psychologist Carl Lange arrived at the same conclusion, which has become known as the James-Lange theory of emotion. An example of this theory that is familiar to many of us occurs in "near miss" accidents. In such cases, when you are confronted with the possibility of an accident, you respond almost without thinking: you swerve and brake your automobile. After the danger has passed, you notice yourself trembling or sweating. Only then do you feel overcome with fear. It was not the emotion that guided your actions or affected your physiological someone who was familiar with the crime. Thus, if the suspect showed a change in physiological response at the mention of the locker, the operator could detect his or her guilt.

What a marvelous machine that can determine guilt or innocence! Unfortunately, the polygraph is not infallible. People naturally vary in the amount of stress they show; an innocent person may show tension when certain questions are asked. Or guilty subjects may intentionally make themselves tense when neutral questions are being asked. In this case, it would be difficult, if not impossible, to establish a baseline from which change can accurately be measured. Careful laboratory studies of the polygraph show that it is accurate about 70 to 85 percent of the time (Lykken, 1975). This is a considerable error, especially when a person's life or liberty is at stake. Because of this, polygraph results are not admissible as evidence in most courts of law, and a person cannot be forced by police to take a polygraph test. The business world, however, has been more willing to accept this margin of error, and many businesses screen job applicants with the polygraph or routinely have their employees take such tests.

Recently, a new method of lie detection has been introduced. During the Vietnam War, the Army searched for a simpler, more covert way to detect lies, one that could be used during the interrogation of prisoners (Rice, 1978). At one point, they experimented with measuring body odors, believing that the body would give off a different odor under stress. However, this didn't work, and they then turned to voice analysis. The theory behind this method is that the muscles controlling voice tremor are affected by stress. The voice can be recorded and a visual picture of voice tremor can be made on graph paper, as shown in Figure B, by a machine called a voice stress analyzer. Subjects can be asked questions the same way they are in the polygraph test. A lie can be detected when the voice stress analyzer indicates tension in the individual's voice (that is, when the voice tremor decreases) in response to the critical questions.

The beauty, and the frightening feature, of this method is that it can be used to analyze any voice that can be recorded. This includes personal conversations, telephone conversations, and even speeches by politicians. And people can have their voices recorded without their knowledge or consent. This raises an important ethical question about the use of lie detection. There is, in fact, considerable study of this issue before the United States Congress, and it is likely that within the next few years laws will be passed concerning the use of these devices.

In addition to the question of ethics, there is also the question of how accurate the voice stress analyzer method is. There have only been a few carefully controlled studies and the results are often contradictory.

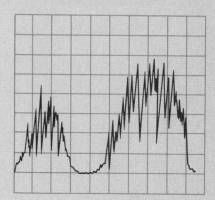

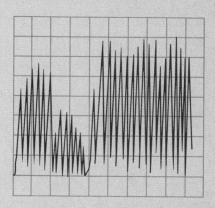

FIGURE B

The voice stress analyzer measures voice tremor. It has been found that the arousal produced by telling a lie changes the voice tremors. The graph on top is the voice tremor of a relaxed speaker. The graph on the bottom shows the voice tremor of a speaker under stress. (After Holden, 1975)

responses. It was your perception of these responses that caused you to feel fear.

One assumption of the James-Lange theory is that we have different physiological arousal patterns for each emotion. Supposedly the perception of these arousal patterns "tells" us what emotion we are feeling. More recent research, however, shows that this is not the case (Izard, 1977). With few exceptions, there do not seem to be specific patterns of arousal for different emotions. For example, fear, rage, fever, and exposure to cold all lead to increases in heart rate, blood-sugar level, adrenalin secretion, pupil size, and the erection of body hair (Plutchik, 1980). Thus, the James-Lange theory is not completely correct. However, it played an important role in shaping the way investigators examined emotions, by focusing attention on the physiological changes that accompany emotions.

Cannon-Bard Theory

It was this focus on physiological changes that led another Harvard professor, Walter B. Cannon (1929), to criticize the James-Lange theory and offer another point of view. Cannon argued that physiological changes in bodily organs occur too slowly to be the basis of emotions. He further pointed out that such organs are relatively insensitive, and people are not normally aware of changes in them, such as contractions or relaxations in their stomachs, intestines, or other organs. Cannon performed a number of experiments in which he removed the sympathetic nervous system tract in cats. As a result of this operation, the sympathetic nervous system cannot increase heart rate, body hairs cannot be erected, and "the liver cannot be called upon to liberate sugar into the blood system" (Cannon, 1929). In short, these animals were not able to receive information about what was happening in their organs. However, Cannon found that these animals continued to show typical emotional reactions of fear, anger, and pleasure. Given these criticisms, Cannon argued that emotions could not be simply the perception of physiological changes.

Cannon proposed a theory that was later extended by Bard (1938). He suggested that events activate the thalamus (see Chapter 2), which sends messages to the cerebral cortex and to organs such as the heart and the stomach. The stimulation of the cerebral cortex leads to the emotional experience, while the excitation of the organs leads to the accompanying physiological arousal. Thus, Cannon argued that the emotional experience and the arousal occur at the same time, rather than one after the other, as proposed by James.

More recent research has shown that Cannon's theory was not entirely correct (Plutchik, 1980). The hypothalamus and limbic system, and not the thalamus, play central roles in the experience of emotion. Also, emotions are not simply quick events that we experience only for the moment. Thus, while Cannon was correct in pointing out the complexity of the process involved in emotions, there were problems with his theory.

Cognitive Theories: A Two-Factor Theory

As can be seen from the discussion so far, most of the early theories of emotion focused on the specific role and timing of physiological arousal. In 1962, Stanley Schachter and Jerome Singer proposed a theory that focused on the cognitive element of emotions. These researchers argued that the physiological arousal accompanying emotion is very diffuse and that the same arousal patterns can be found in many different emotions. Because of this, they felt that physiological arousal cannot determine the *specific* emotion that we experience. Rather, Schachter and Singer argued that people become aware that they are aroused and *then* they look around them to find the reason for this unexplained arousal. The decision about the reason for the arousal serves as the basis for labeling the emotion.

In order to illustrate this theory, let us take the example of Emmett Kelly at the circus fire. Kelly fought the fire and helped people and animals escape from the burning tent. Surely, all these activities caused a heightened arousal state. Kelly was probably not completely aware of how aroused he was until it was over and he had time to look back on the situation. At this point, Kelly saw the charred shoes and the doll. According to the Schachter and Singer theory, Kelly may have used the sight of these pitiful remains to label his emotional state as sadness. These cues "suggested" to Kelly that his arousal state was sadness. If, on the other hand, Kelly had seen a happy scene such as a little girl being reunited with her joyful family, Kelly might have interpreted his arousal state as being happiness or relief. It is important to understand that the theory predicts that the same arousal state can lead to very different emotional labels depending on the cues in the environment.

In an effort to demonstrate this point, Schachter and Singer (1962) designed the following experiment. In order to better understand it, place yourself in the role of a subject. When you arrive to take part in the experiment, you are greeted by an experimenter who explains that the study is designed to examine the effects of a vitamin supplement called Suproxin. You are then injected with the drug and taken to a room where another subject is waiting. The experimenter says that you both must wait for a short period of time so that the drug can take effect and then you can go on with the second half of the study. When the experimenter leaves, the other subject jumps up and begins to throw paper wads into the wastepaper basket. As you watch this bizarre behavior, you feel your heart beating faster and your face begin to flush. Soon, the other subject turns his talents to making and flying paper airplanes, and he follows this act by playing with a hula hoop he found in the corner. After a few minutes, the experimenter enters and asks you both to fill out a questionnaire on your present mood.

This may sound like a bizarre study, one that could hardly be used to test a theory of emotions. However, it begins to make more sense when you realize that the injection was actually epinephrine, a drug that leads to heightened physical arousal. Given the procedure, subjects could not know that the injection would arouse them, and, according to the Schachter and Singer theory, this unexplained arousal should motivate them to search the environment to find a label for their arousal. It is at this point that the actions of the other subject, actually an experimental confederate, become significant. Schachter and Singer predicted that the confederate's euphoric behavior would serve as a cue for subjects to label their arousal as happiness.

This was only one of the conditions in the study. While all subjects were told the story about the Suproxin, half were given the injection of epinephrine and the other half of the subjects were given an injection of a saline solution that would not arouse them. Some of the subjects were told nothing about the effects of the injection (as in the above condition); others were informed that the injection would indeed arouse them, causing an increase in heart rate and respiration. A third group was misinformed and told that the drug might cause them to feel numb and itchy, and that they might possibly experience headaches. All subjects were then placed in the room with the confederate who acted euphoric (as explained above) in half of the conditions. However, in the other half of the conditions, the confederate acted angry, complaining about the experiment and tearing up papers.

Schachter and Singer felt that subjects in the no information and misinformed conditions would have unexplained arousal sensations. This arousal should cause them to search the environment to label this arousal. Those paired with the euphoric confederate would use his happy behavior to label their own state as happiness, while those paired with the angry confederate would label their arousal as anger. Subjects in the informed conditions would already have a reason for their arousal and, hence, their emotional state should not be influenced by the confederate's behavior. Finally, subjects who were in the placebo condition would not experience arousal and would not be concerned with the confederate's behavior.

The results of the experiment generally supported Schachter and Singer's hypotheses. One of the most interesting results was that subjects in the no information and misinformation condition labeled their emotions in line with the confederate's behavior. That is, subjects with the happy confederate reported that they felt happy and subjects with the angry confederate labeled themselves as being angry. This difference in emotional label occurred despite the fact that both groups of subjects had received the same injection of epinephrine and should have been experiencing the same arousal. This study and others (Schachter and Wheeler, 1962; Schachter and Latané, 1964) seem to support the position that emotion is the result of labeling arousal states.

Criticisms of the Two-Factor Theory. There have been, however, a number of criticisms of the Schachter and Singer position. One researcher argued that actual physiological arousal may not be necessary for the experience of emotions (Valins, 1966, 1972). Rather, he suggested that individuals need only to think they are aroused. In order to demonstrate this point, Valins hooked up male subjects to a machine that was supposed to measure their heart rate. In addition to measuring their heart rate, the machine also broadcast their heart beat so subjects "overheard their heart rates." Subjects were then shown a series of centerfold pictures of nudes taken from *Playboy* magazine. At various intervals, the subjects heard what they believed was their heart rate increasing or decreasing. Actually these were fake and had no relation to the subject's actual heart rate. At the end of the study, subjects were allowed to take home any of the nude pictures they wanted. Most of the pictures chosen had been accompanied by a change in heart rate during the earlier procedure. Thus, subjects were using their perceived, not actual, arousal as the basis for labeling their likes and dislikes.

The Schachter and Singer theory has also been criticized for suggesting that all unexplained arousal has no qualitative character of its own and simply motivates individuals to seek an emotional label (Maslach, 1979). This researcher found that subjects who had high levels of unexplained arousal tended to view this arousal as negative and uncomfortable.

Finally, Pennebaker (1980) suggested an alternate relationship between emotional label and arousal. He argued that sometimes individuals "*first* become aware of a label and *then* seek out internal information that pertains to the label" (Pennebaker, 1980, p. 94). In order to test this idea, Pennebaker and Skelton (1981) told subjects that they would listen to an ultrasonic noise and then be asked questions about it. Some subjects were told that earlier research had shown that ultrasonic noise caused increased skin temperature, while other subjects were told that the noise might lower skin temperature. A control group of subjects were told nothing about the effects of the noise. The subjects then listened to a noise while the experimenter measured their skin temperature. After the study, the experimenter asked subjects to discuss the effects of the noise on their skin temperature. As predicted, those subjects who expected the noise to increase their skin temperature reported being warmer during the study than those who expected the noise to lower their skin temperature. While the self-reports were not related to actual skin temperature, they were related to changes in temperature. That is, subjects who expected the noise to increase temperature interpreted any change in temperature as an increase. On the other hand, subjects who expected to have decreased temperature believed that the same changes represented a decrease in temperature. Thus, subjects began with an expectation of how they should feel and they interpreted any change in their bodies as supporting their expectation.

Baumeister and Cooper (1981) also found that expectancy influences the emotion of embarrassment. They told some subjects that they would probably be embarrassed while singing a solo; other subjects did not expect to be embarrassed while performing this task. As predicted, subjects who expected to be embarrassed did report this feeling, and they stopped singing sooner than subjects who did not expect to be embarrassed.

You may have had such an experience on a day when you woke up feeling fine and ready to face the world. However, a number of your friends commented that you looked very tired. After a few such comments you began to "feel" tired and then examined your body to support this feeling.

While the Schachter and Singer theory may not describe how we feel all emotions, it has played an important role in shaping the way investigators examine emotions. The theory has focused attention on the role of cognitive process and environmental cues in the experience of emotion. Clearly, our emotions are determined not only by body cues but also by environmental cues.

The Role of Appraisal

It is easy for all of us to imagine how Emmett Kelly felt when he saw smoke coming from the big top. His heart rate probably increased tremendously, his muscles tensed, and he may have felt like running from the scene as the fear of fire and the thoughts of the potential tragedy gripped him. However, would Kelly's emotions and his actions have been the same if he had known that this was all part of another clown's act (for example, a clown performing an act that involved a little dog jumping out of a smoking house into a fireman's net)? If he had thought this, it's unlikely that he would have become tense and filled with fear when he saw the smoke and heard a few screams. He may even have been amused by the screams as he imagined the success of the act in thrilling the spectators.

This example shows that the way we evaluate a situation affects not only our response but also our emotions related to it. It has been suggested that the first step in experiencing emotions is appraising (judging or interpreting) the situation (Arnold, 1960; Lazarus, 1968). The appraisal determines whether we view the situation as threatening or nonthreatening. This appraisal also determines our response to the situation. Finally, our emotion surfaces as we examine both our appraisal of the situation and our responses to it.

In an effort to demonstrate this effect, Speisman and his colleagues (1964) showed subjects a film of the gory and painful circumcision rites practiced by an aboriginal Australian tribe to initiate boys into adulthood. While all subjects saw the same film, Speisman varied the soundtrack that went with the picture. In one track (stress), the narration emphasized the pain associated with the rites. In another track (intellectual) the ceremony was described in a detached, clinical manner. A third track (denial) glossed over the pain and focused on the boy's happiness at becoming a man. Finally, in a control condition, subjects saw the film with no soundtrack. The experimenters recorded subjects' arousal (heart rate and GSR, or galvanic skin response) while they watched the film. As can be seen in Figure 10-1, subjects who watched the film with the soundtrack emphasizing pain were significantly more aroused than the other subjects. The investigators reasoned that the soundtrack influenced the subjects' judgment of the event, and so influenced their emotional response to it. The appraisal theory may explain the popular saying, "If you expect something to make you feel bad, chances are it will."

Theories of Emotion: A Concluding Note

While it is clear that investigators disagree to some extent about how we experience emotions, it is also clear that they have identified some important variables that affect our emotions. The research and theories demonstrate that emotions are a function of our physiological arousal, our behavior, and our interpretations of events. No single factor is responsible for our feelings; rather, it is a combination of all three that leads

FIGURE 10–1

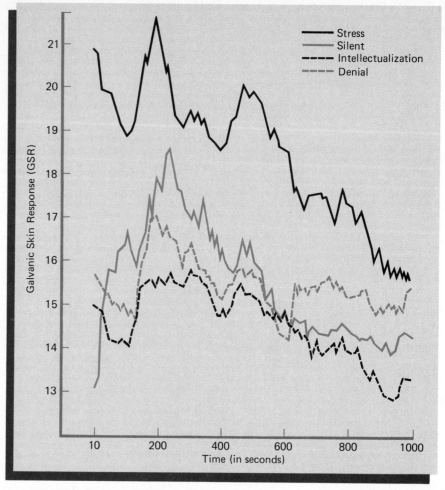

to a specific emotion. Investigators do not disagree about the components of emotion; the major concern is how these components combine to yield a specific feeling. Additional research is necessary to answer this, but it is evident that the theories and the research have made significant progress in telling us why we feel the way we do.

NONVERBAL COMMUNICATION OF EMOTIONS

After Kelly joined the Ringling Brothers and Barnum & Bailey Circus, he had the opportunity to take his clown act to Cuba. He was a little frightened by the prospect, since he had heard that the Latin Americans were hot-tempered and impatient. He also wondered whether they would be able to understand his act; would they recognize sadness in Willie's drooping eyes and turned-down mouth? Since Willie never spoke a word, it was very important that the audience respond to his actions and facial expression. On opening night, he bravely walked into the ring and began sweeping at the little white puddle that the spotlight threw at his feet. He heard some laughs and his spirits rose. After his sweeping act, he turned toward the audience and gave them the sad stare that had made Willie famous in the United States. At this point, he heard the crowd hissing and waving him away. As the hissing and waving gathered momentum, Kelly turned and ran off the stage, feeling that for the first time in his life he had found a group of people he couldn't communicate with (or who didn't like his act).

Once off the stage, Kelly sought out a clown that spoke Spanish and told him what had happened. The other clown laughed and explained, "In Cuba, that waving means they want you to come closer." He also told Kelly, "That isn't hissing as we know it in America; that's part of the handwaving—to get your attention, just as we do when we yell Hey" (p. 238).

Kelly's adventures in Cuba tell us two things about nonverbal communication. First, that it *is* possible to communicate without words, and communicate across national boundaries—the Cuban audience understood immediately what Willie was all about. The second thing is that the nonverbal communication used in some cultures may be misunderstood in others—Kelly certainly did not understand what the Cuban audience was trying to tell him. How much of nonverbal communication is universal and how much is learned as part of one's culture?

Emotional Expression: Innate or Learned?

Almost 100 years before Kelly's experience in Cuba, Charles Darwin studied how humans express emotions. Darwin believed that the human expression of emotion is inborn and has definite survival value. Darwin pointed out that many animals bare their teeth and the hair on their neck becomes erect when they are angry and ready to attack. This has survival value because other animals of the same species can readily interpret it and avoid the angered animal. Darwin pointed out, too, that humans also grit their teeth and the hair on their neck becomes erect when they are angry.

At the base of Darwin's evolutionary theory of emotion was the hypothesis that some, but not all, of the ways in which humans express emotions are innate or inborn. In order to support this position Darwin needed to show two things: (1) emotions are expressed the same way by all people regardless of their background, and (2) people inherit rather than learn the tendency to express emotions in these patterned ways.

In order to show the universality of emotional expression, Darwin made careful observations of the people he met on his voyages around the world. He found many similarities in the way people from different cultures expressed specific emotions. For example, he reported that Australian aborigines, African Kafirs, Malays, "Hindoos," and South American Guaranies frown when they are puzzled, and they express grief using similar facial signs. Darwin's observations were supported by Ekman, Sorenson, and Friesen (1969), who showed pictures of faces expressing various emotions to subjects in the United States, Brazil, Japan, New Guinea, and Borneo. The subjects were asked to identify the emotion expressed in each photo, and there was relatively high agreement in the judgments of the pictures. In a follow-up study, Ekman and Friesen (1971) found that even members of the Fore tribe, a preliterate group who led an isolated, almost Stone Age existence in New Guinea, were able to judge the facial expressions correctly. The high degree of agreement found in these studies suggests that there is some universality in the way people in different cultures express emotions. This universality was observed by Emmett Kelly, who found that his Cuban audience could understand the message in Willie's silent act. However, none of the cross-cultural studies found complete agreement, which suggests that culture and background also influence the way emotions are expressed. Kelly learned this painful lesson when he interpreted the waving hands in the Cuban audience as signs of anger or disapproval.

While these cross-cultural studies demonstrate some degree of universality in emotional expression, they do not prove that this expression is inborn. It is conceivable that people in the various societies simply learn to express themselves in similar ways. How would you go about demonstrating that the nonverbal expression of emotions is innate rather than learned? Darwin answered this question by observing children who had been blind from birth. He reasoned that it would be impossible for these children to have learned the intricacies of nonverbal expression of emotions, since they could not observe others. His observations and those that followed showed that the emotional expression of both blind and blind-and-deaf children was similar to that of sighted children for a number of emotions (e.g., Thompson, 1941; Eibl-Eibesfeldt, 1973). For example, the blind children cried when unhappy, laughed and smiled when happy, frowned and stamped their feet in defiance, and shook their heads as a gesture of refusal.

These and other studies suggest that many of the ways in which we express emotions are inborn. While our experiences and learning do modify the way we express emotions, there is a large degree of similarity in the way emotions are expressed around the world.

Given that there is some universality in emotional expression, the next question concerns the exact nature of this universality. In other words, what are the nonverbal signs of emotions? Are some nonverbal channels more important than others in expressing emotions? It is to these questions that we now turn our attention.

The Face

The most important part of a clown costume is the face. Kelly would spend hours getting his face ready for a show; he worked on accentuating his mouth and eyes, building up his nose, and emphasizing the wrinkles in his brow. Research indicates that this concern with the face may be well placed; Izard (1977) points out that the face is most important in communicating emotions.

In an interesting study, researchers cut apart photographs of faces into three partial pictures; brow-forehead, eyes, and mouth (Boucher and Ekman, 1975). These partial photos were then shown to judges who were asked to guess which of six emotions (surprise, anger, fear, disgust, sadness, or happiness) were being shown. The results showed that different parts of the face were important for communicating different emotions. For example, the eyes are most important in communicating sadness, while the mouth best communicates happiness and disgust, and the forehead sends signals of surprise. Interestingly enough, all three parts of the

TABLE 10–1: Characteristic Facial Patterns for Eight Primary Emotions

Emotion	Facial Pattern
Interest-Excitement	Eyebrows down, eyes track, look, listen
Enjoyment-Joy	Smile, lips widened up and out, smiling eyes (circular wrinkles)
Surprise-Startle	Eyebrows up, eyes blink
Distress-Anguish	Cry, arched eyebrows, mouth down, tears, rhythmic sobbing
Fear-Terror	Eyes frozen open; pale, cold, sweaty face; trembling; hair erect
Shame-Humiliation	Eyes down, head up
Contempt-Disgust	Sneer, upper lip up
Anger-Rage	Frown, clenched jaw, eyes narrowed, red face

Source: Tomkins and McCarter (1964).

face are necessary to clearly communicate anger. In a recent study, Ekman and his colleagues were able to determine which of two films their subjects preferred simply by examining the subjects' facial expressions (Ekman, Friesen, and Ancoli, 1980). According to these investigators, we can accurately determine what other people are feeling if we can learn the "language of the face." However, this may not be an easy task—Ekman reports that there are over 7,000 different combinations of muscle movements in the face!

In an earlier study, Tomkins and McCarter (1964) tried to map out how the face communicates eight primary or basic emotions. As can be seen in Table 10–1, they found that each emotion has a characteristic facial pattern. It is interesting to note that their description of distress involves just those features that were drawn on Willie's face.

According to some research, the face not only shows other people what emotion we are feeling, but it also helps us identify our own emotions (Izard, 1977, 1981; Tomkins, 1979, 1981). These investigators argue that

The face shows others the emotion we are feeling, and may also help us to determine our own emotions.

events arouse us *and* cause our facial expression to change. This information is transferred to the brain and it is taken into account when we determine what emotion we are expressing. This is an interesting theory, but it has so far proved difficult to develop studies that clearly show how this information about facial expression is used (Ellsworth and Tourangeau, 1981).

Body Language

Not only does our face speak, but, according to one researcher, our bodies are also expressive (Birdwhistle, 1967). Birdwhistle used the term **kinesis** to mean the study of body language. He argued that no body movement is accidental or meaningless, and that something is communicated in even the slightest movement. Mehrabian and Weiner (1967) found that positive feelings were communicated by moving closer to an object and leaning and turning the body toward it. Beier (1974) studied 50 newlywed couples and found that conflict and insecurity were expressed by frequent self-touching, sitting with arms and legs crossed, and the avoidance of eye contact.

Physical distance also sends emotional messages (see Chapter 16 for a more complete discussion). An anthropologist found that people feel a sense of ownership of the space that directly surrounds them (Hall, 1966). They attempt to protect such *personal space* by "keeping their distance" from other people, and they feel uncomfortable if someone intrudes into this space. People will move to restore the proper space, the size of which is largely a function of the type of interaction and attraction involved. People allow friends to come closer than strangers. Thus, one way in which we communicate love and attraction is to get physically close to others. And we can communicate our dislike by keeping a large distance between ourselves and others.

An interesting feature of body language is that we are often unaware of it. We usually do not consciously decide that we will smile, dilate our pupils, and move closer to someone to show our attraction. Because of this lack of awareness, people may give themselves away through nonverbal cues when they are lying. Albert Mehrabian (1971) asked subjects to tell a lie while he studied their body language. He found that people who are telling a lie show less frequent body movement, smile more, keep a greater distance from the listener, and lean backwards more than people telling the truth.

What does body language communicate? Efforts to decode specific messages from body movements have met with only moderate success. After reviewing the literature and observing many communicators, Mortensen (1972) suggested that our bodies may not communicate specific emotions. Rather, he suggested the body indicates the *strength* of emotion, while the face expresses the *quality* of emotion being experienced. This is an interesting possibility that has not yet been fully explored.

SPECIFIC EMOTIONS

We have examined the basic theories of emotions and learned how people express emotions. Up to this point, we have been talking in general terms. Now we can try to illustrate these points by examining some specific emotions. Rather than making comments on an endless list of emotions, we will look at two: fear and love. These two emotions represent extremes on many levels. Fear is considered to be negative, while love is viewed as positive, and many of us will go to great lengths to experience it. Fear has been studied a great deal, while love has, until recently, been seen as the domain only of poets and playwrights.

Fear and Anxiety

Fear and the related concept of anxiety is one of the most carefully studied emotions. Sigmund Freud built much of his psychoanalytic theory around the concept of anxiety (Freud, 1933). He believed that there are two types of anxiety: objective anxiety and neurotic anxiety. *Objective anxiety* is the response to a specific danger in the environment. In other words, people know (or think they know) what is causing the anxiety. Objective anxiety is more popularly referred to as **fear,** which is a reaction to a specific object or event. On the other hand, Freud viewed *neurotic anxiety* as resulting from unconscious conflict within the person. Because the person is unaware of the roots of the anxiety, it is experienced as a general state of apprehension or dread with no definable object. While we may distinguish between fear and anxiety based on the causes of each, the feelings and the physiological responses associated with the two states are very similar. Because of this, many investigators use the terms fear and anxiety interchangeably, and we will follow this practice in this text.

If you were to write down every object or event that leads to anxiety in people, the list would be endless. People can, and do, learn to fear almost anything. As we will see in Chapter 12, irrational fears (phobias) cause some people a great deal of suffering.

While we can develop new fears at almost any time in our lives, some fears are age-related. For example, infants develop a fear of strangers between 6 and 9 months of age (Sroufe and Waters, 1976). The fear of noises tends to decrease between the ages of 1 to 6 years, while the fear of animals increases until the age of 4 and then levels off (Jersild and Holmes, 1935). One fear that does seem to increase with age is the

Many fears are age-related. The fear of strangers develops in infants between the ages of 6 and 9 months.

fear of imagined situations. An example of this age-related fear can be seen in the reaction of Emmett Kelly's mother upon seeing her 5-year-old son sitting atop the telegraph pole. She was overcome by fear because she imagined the numerous disasterous consequences that could result from the situation. However, the brave 5-year-old showed no fear because his imagery process had not developed to the extent that he could conjure up these consequences.

The Functions of Fear.   Imagine a life without fear. You could go into the exam for which you had not studied feeling fine and confident. You could walk through the most wicked of neighborhoods on the darkest night feeling secure and safe. You could drive your automobile at breakneck speed without your heart clogging your throat, and you could tell your chemistry professor what you really thought of his incomprehensible lecture on amino acids. Sound nice? As hard as it may be to believe, a life without fear could be far more dangerous than Emmett Kelly's trapeze act. Fear has important functions in our life; it leads us to avoid certain objects and situations that are dangerous. For example, driving your automobile at 120 mph down a busy highway can be hazardous to your health, and your fear of such high speeds may cause you to be more careful in your driving habits. Similarly, taking an exam for which you have not prepared is not good for your survival as a student.

Fear also prepares the body for action. The heart rate increases, muscles tense, digestive functions slow, and epinephrine (adrenalin) pours into the bloodstream when we face the object of fear. These physiological changes enable us to act quickly and decisively.

Researchers also argue that fear often leads to the strengthening or forming of social bonds (Suomi and Harlow, 1976). Children seek out their parents when they are fearful and, as we will see in the next section, fear leads adults to affiliate with others.

Thus, while the experience of anxiety may be unpleasant, it can play a constructive role in our lives. Of course, fear can become destructive. Problems occur when we develop irrational fears of objects that are not real dangers. Fear can also be destructive when we are consumed by it and are unable to direct our behavior to deal with the object of the fear.

Results of Fear.   Research has shown that fear influences our perceptions, our performance, and our social behavior. With regard to our perceptions, Izard (1977) states that fear is the most limiting of all emotions. It leads to "tunnel vision," where people block out all stimuli except the object of their fear. Thinking also becomes rigid and concentrated on the objects related to the fear. This rigidity may lead to tragic results.

Anxiety also affects performance, but not in the way many people might expect. As we have shown, anxiety arouses us. According to the **Yerkes-**

FIGURE 10–2: The Yerkes-Dodson Principle

The graph shows the relationship between arousal and performance. A certain amount of arousal is necessary to function, but a very high degree of arousal, such as that caused by excess anxiety, makes it difficult to perform at all. The most effective level of arousal for performance depends on the difficulty level of the task. (After Hebb, 1955)

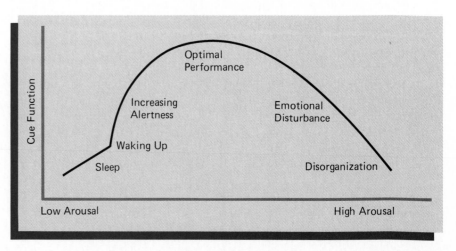

Dodson principle, the most effective level of arousal for performance depends on the difficulty of the task. Some degree of arousal is necessary for a good performance on any task; high levels of arousal will aid work on an easy task, but will hinder work on difficult tasks (see Figure 10–2). Thus, the high arousal caused by anxiety is disruptive for difficult tasks.

In addition to perception and performance, our social interaction is influenced by fear. In Chapter 9 we discussed in some detail an interesting experiment by Schachter (1959) demonstrating that fear causes people to want to be with other people. In some additional research, Schachter refined the finding that "misery loves company." He reported that people who were experiencing fear preferred to wait with others who were also experiencing fear. Therefore, we can conclude that "misery loves miserable company." There are many other effects of fear on our social interactions. We will tend to avoid others whom we fear. If we cannot avoid them, Jones and Wortman (1973) suggest that we may try to win over people of high status who may potentially make us uncomfortable.

Love

In 1923 sisters Eva and Mitzie Moore brought their double trapeze act to John Robinson's Circus. Kelly watched with a pounding heart as Eva hurled her tiny, slim body through the air. This young woman had talent and courage. There was only one problem: She also had a protective father. Mr. Moore did not want his children to get married and break up their circus act. However, Kelly fell in love, and soon he and Eva were arranging secret meetings. The romance progressed quickly despite the interferences, and when the circus set up in Charlottesville, Virginia, the couple sneaked off to the home of a preacher and got married.

While **love** is a common theme in our history, our literature, and even in our own daily lives, it has generally eluded the careful eye of the scientific researcher. Only recently have investigators begun to study love.

There are at least two reasons for this. One reason has been the popular feeling that love should not be the subject of scientific study. Love seems to have a mysterious and almost holy quality for many people, and there is an undercurrent of feeling that the scientific study of love would remove these qualities. Senator William Proxmire voiced this position when he criticized the National Science Foundation for "wasting" money for the investigation of love: "I believe that 200 million Americans want to leave some things in life a mystery and right at the top of things we don't want to know is why a man falls in love with a woman and vice versa."

Another reason why love has not been widely studied is the difficulty encountered in defining love. Investigators are not the only ones who have had trouble with this endeavor. The Random House Dictionary gives 24 definitions of "love," while it gives only 5 of "hate." There are at least two reasons for the confusion surrounding the concept. First, unlike fear, shame, or anger, there are many components of love. For example, Zick Rubin and his colleagues (Rubin, 1973; Rubin, Peplau, and Hill, 1978) define love as an emotion involving three components:

1. *Caring:* The feeling that another person's satisfactions are as important to you as your own. In Erich Fromm's words, "It is the active concern for the life and growth of that which we love."
2. *Attachment:* The need or desire to be with the other, to make physical contact, to be approved of and cared for by the other.
3. *Intimacy:* The bond or the link between two people. It is shown by close and confidential communication between people.

There is difficulty in defining love, too, because there are many types

Love is an emotion involving caring, attachment, and intimacy. Research is just beginning to identify the factors that influence love.

of love. For example, Berscheid and Walster (1978) distinguish between *romantic love* and *mature love*. According to these researchers, romantic love is an intense feeling that involves physical arousal. It generally develops quickly, but fades with time. Romantic love is accompanied by a high level of fantasy and often involves jealousy, sexual arousal, and fear of rejection. Mature love, on the other hand, has less emotional intensity, but, while it begins rather slowly, it continues to grow. It is characterized by openness and interpersonal communication.

Effects of Learning. Love is an emotion that most of us regard as positive and desirable, and many people spend much of their lives in search of it. An interesting but sad feature of love is the fact that some of these "searchers" have a very difficult time experiencing love. This is not because they do not have the opportunity to form a loving relationship, however. Many researchers believe that people must learn to love (Harlow, 1971; Fromm, 1956). The ability to experience love and form loving relationships is strongly influenced by past experience. Harlow (1971) demonstrated this by removing infant monkeys from their mothers shortly after birth. These monkeys received adequate care and feeding, but because they were reared in isolation they were deprived of maternal love. At 3 months, 6 months, and 2 years of age these monkeys were introduced to other monkeys their own age, and their interactions were observed. The isolated monkeys could not form friendships or play with their own age-mates. Nor were they receptive to sexual advances from other monkeys. Harlow impregnated some of the isolated female monkeys in order to study whether or not they could develop maternal love for their own offspring; the results were startling. The isolated mothers failed to feed or care for their young, and in many cases the mothers treated them so brutally that the infants would have been killed had the experimenter not removed them. This study suggests that the ability to experience love may be very dependent on past experiences.

Emmett Kelly recalls "falling in love" with Eva as he watched her flying through the air on the trapeze. His story is reminiscent of romantic cases of "love at first sight." This "instant love" phenomenon, however, seems to be found more frequently in novels and poems than in actual life. In one study 226 engaged couples were interviewed, with only 8 percent of the men and 5 percent of the women revealing that they felt "strong physical attraction" for their partner during the two days following their first meeting (Wallin, 1953). Thus, love does seem to be an emotion that takes some time to develop.

Effects of Arousal. There are, however, certain conditions that are conducive to falling in love. Berscheid and Walster (1978) suggest that it often follows the same course as any other emotion. That is, people experience arousal when they are together, and they attribute this arousal to love. This hypothesis leads to an interesting prediction that was tested by Dutton and Aron (1974). Half of the male subjects in this experiment were asked to walk across an old wooden bridge that swayed above a 230-foot precipice. The remaining subjects walked across a sturdy bridge that crossed a stream 10 feet below. After crossing the bridge, both groups of subjects were met by an attractive female who said she was working on a psychology project. She showed them a picture of a woman covering her face with her hand and asked the subjects to make up a story about the picture. After they finished, she gave the subjects her name and telephone number and said they could call her if they had questions. Two differences were found in the responses of the two groups. First, the subjects who had just crossed the rickety bridge told more sex-related stories about the picture than subjects who had crossed the sturdy bridge. Second, subjects who had walked across the old wooden bridge were more likely to call the interviewer after the study than were subjects who had used the sturdy bridge. How can we explain these results? Dutton and Aron argued that crossing the swaying bridge aroused subjects. In most circumstances individuals would interpret this arousal as fear. However, when the subjects met the attractive female, they attributed their arousal as attraction or sexual arousal. On the other hand, individuals crossing the sturdy bridge would not be aroused and, hence, they were less likely to experience attraction when met by the female experimenter.

The possibility that passionate love may result from the misidentity of arousal has some intriguing applications. Often, young lovers are faced with interference and disapproval from their parents. These interferences and frustrations may arouse the lovers, who may misidentify the cause of the arousal as being love. Thus, the attempts by parents to break up a love relationship may unwittingly increase the feelings of love between the thwarted adolescents. Another intriguing possibility derivable from the cognitive theory of passionate love was suggested by the Roman author and philosopher Ovid in his first century Roman handbook on romantic conquest. Ovid suggested that an excellent time to arouse passion in a woman was while she was engrossed in watching gladiators attack each other. The modern interpretation of this advice would be that the exciting gladitorial event arouses the woman, and the task of the amorous-minded male is to have the woman interpret the arousal as love or sexual excitement. It is, in fact, interesting that Kelly's love for Eva bloomed while he watched her perform dangerous and exciting feats on the trapeze.

Certainly, love is a complex emotion. Social scientists are just scratching the surface in understanding the pathways to love. It is, however, important to notice that a familiarity with the basic theories of emotion may help in understanding the more complicated emotions such as love.

STRESS

When Emmett Kelly was 19 years old, he decided he had had enough of life on the farm; he wanted the excitement and fortune offered by the city. He packed his bag and off he went to Kansas City. However, life in the city was not what Kelly had imagined it would be. First he had to find a room. After several hours of searching, he found a place in an old boarding house; for 5 dollars a week he shared a room and a double bed with a young fellow from Texas. Everything about the city was different from his Kansas farm life, and Kelly spent the first few days exploring his surroundings. His early life in Kansas City involved one change of job after another. He made sign frames, he painted the inside of steel tanks, he tried to drive a lumber truck, and he painted kewpie dolls. Kelly rarely had much money, and at times he went to bed hungry because he couldn't afford to buy food. The fast life of the city and the numerous changes in job and life style most certainly created a great deal of stress for this young man from the farm.

The concept of stress is one that we are all familiar with. Many of us use the term "stress" to describe a feeling or emotion. **Stress,** however, is not an emotion; rather, it is the general response of the body to any demand made on it (Selye, 1976). Hans Selye, a Canadian physician, spent years examining the body's response to stressors (stimuli or events that threaten us). He found that the stress response, which he called **general adaptation syndrome,** was very systematic and could even be charted in three phases. The first phase (the *alarm reaction*) involves the release of substances into the bloodstream and is often accompanied by headaches, loss of appetite, and fatigue. Recent research (Stone, Cohen, and Adler, 1979) has identified this substance (adrenal cortical hormones), and efforts are presently being directed at artificially producing the compound. The body's resistance to disease is associated with the specific stressor lowered by this reaction. This may explain why the threat of an upcoming exam causes so many students to fall prey to a variety of sicknesses! The vulnerable condition of the body during the alarm reaction could have severe consequences if it were prolonged, but the alarm stage is rather short-lived. If the stressor continues, the body responds by entering a *stage of resistance*. In this phase, the body bounces back and the symptoms of the alarm reaction disappear. The body returns to normal functioning and the person may feel increased vigor. While the body may be able to deal with the specific stressor during this stage, there is decreased resistance to other stimuli. If the stressor disappears during this stage, the person will quickly recover from the stress. On the other hand, if the stress-producing situation continues, the *stage of exhaustion* begins. This is the point where the body begins to wear down, and many of the symptoms of the alarm reaction reappear. If the stress is extreme and the stressor is not removed quickly, the person will die.

The Causes of Stress

The range of events that give rise to stress is almost unlimited. While the list of potential stressors is almost inconceivably long, there are certain characteristics that increase the degree of stress arising from a situation. We will quickly examine four of these factors: change, unpredictability, lack of control, and conflict.

Change. There are many ways to describe Kelly's life in the city, but it clearly involved a great deal of change. He changed his home, his life style, and his diet; his friends changed; and he changed jobs many times during the 3 years he spent in Kansas City. Kelly enjoyed some of these changes, but some were not as pleasant as others. All of us experience a great deal of change in our lives; we look forward to some of the changes, while we would prefer to avoid others. It may, however, come as somewhat of a surprise to learn that change itself, whether positive or negative, is a stressor.

Thomas Holmes and his colleagues (Holmes and Masuda, 1974; Holmes and Rahe, 1967) studied thousands of medical histories and interviews and then questioned over 400 men and women in an effort to identify stressful events. Based on their research, the investigators developed the Life Change Scale (see Table 10–2), which attempts to give stress values to life events. As can be seen from the list, the common thread is that each event involves some *change* in an individual's life. Although many of the events are negative (death of a spouse, being fired from a job), some are clearly positive changes (outstanding personal achievement, vacation). Holmes argued that stress is directly related to major illness, and he suggested that the scale could be used to predict when an individual is most likely to suffer a severe illness. Specifically, he predicted that individuals who score over 300 points of stress during a 1-year period run a high risk of being struck down by a major illness during the following year.

In general, the research has supported the position that major life changes create stress. But there have been some interesting qualifications of this. For example, it has been found that changes involving undesirable consequences were more likely to result in physical illness than those that had positive consequences (Liem and Liem, 1976).

Most of the work on the relationship between change and stress has focused on major life events. The research with Holmes and Rahe's Life

TABLE 10–2: Life Change Scale

Life Event	Stress Value	Life Event	Stress Value
Death of spouse	100	Son or daughter leaving home	29
Divorce	73	Trouble with in-laws	29
Marital separation	65	Outstanding personal achievement	28
Jail term	63	Wife begin or stop work	26
Death of close family member	63	Begin or end school	26
Personal injury or illness	53	Change in living conditions	25
Marriage	50	Revision of personal habits	24
Fired at work	47	Trouble with boss	23
Marital reconciliation	45	Change in work hours or conditions	20
Retirement	45	Change in residence	20
Change in health of family member	44	Change in schools	20
Pregnancy	40	Change in recreation	19
Sex difficulties	39	Change in church activities	19
Gain of new family member	39	Change in social activities	18
Business readjustment	39	Mortgage or loan less than $10,000	17
Change in financial state	38	Change in sleeping habits	16
Death of close friend	37	Change in number of family get-togethers	15
Change to different line of work	36	Change in eating habits	15
Change in number of arguments with spouse	35	Vacation	13
Mortgage over $10,000	31	Christmas	12
Foreclosure of mortgage or loan	30	Minor violations of the law	11
Change in responsibilities at work	29		

Source: Holmes and Rahe (1967).

Change Scale has shown a relationship between changes in one's life and physical illness. This relationship, however, has not been as strong as many expected it would be.

Recently Richard Lazarus (1981) and his colleagues examined the effects of minor but frequent daily events on illness. Lazarus identified two types of daily events involving change. On the negative side are *hassles*, which are the "irritating, frustrating, or distressing incidents that occur in our everyday transactions with the environment" (p. 58). Common hassles include misplacing or losing things, too many things to do, and concern about physical appearance. On the positive side are *uplifts*, which include such pleasures as completing a task, visiting or phoning a friend, and feeling healthy.

Hassles may have a number of sources. Major life events may create continuing hassles, what Lazarus calls the "ripple effect." For example, divorce or the death of a spouse might force people to do countless tasks that they are unfamiliar with. A man may have to fix meals, get the kids off to school on time, and deal with laundry and housecleaning chores. A woman may have to handle household finances, buy a car on her own, or replace a blown fuse for the first time. Thus there is a major life event topped off by the daily hassles connected with it.

Lazarus selected a sample of 100 people (48 men, 52 women) who were mainly middle-aged, middle-class, and white. At the beginning and at the end of the year-long study, the subjects filled out the Holmes and Rahe Life Change Scale. Each month during the study the subjects indicated

Change, even positive change, leads to stress.

the hassles and uplifts that had occurred to them during the month. Lazarus also collected information on the subjects' physical health and mood during the study.

A number of interesting findings came out of this study. First, Lazarus found that hassles "turned out to be much better predictors of psychological and physical health than life events" (1981, p. 62). People who suffered frequent and intense hassles had the poorest health, while the link between major life events and health was weak. Lazarus also found that uplifts did not offset the negative impact of hassles. In fact, the study found that, for women, uplifts had a negative effect on emotions and mental health.

While this study supports the position that change itself can be stressful and contributes to physical and mental illness, Lazarus concludes, "It is not the large, dramatic events that make the difference, but what happens day in and day out, whether provoked by major events or not" (1981, p. 62). Clearly more research needs to be done in this area; and this study suggests that research should focus on the effects of the small hassles in life as well as the more infrequent dramatic life changes.

Stewart and Salt (1981) studied women who had graduated from an elite, competitive women's college. They found that the different types of life stress were related to different responses. For example, women who scored high in life stress related to work tended to report being ill. However, women who reported high life stress in family situations reported being depressed but not physically ill.

Another researcher reported that if a person expects change, *no* change may actually be more stressful than the expected change (Graham, 1974). You can understand this if you have ever spent time preparing for an exam only to find out that it has been postponed, or if you have had an expected vacation cancelled.

Finally, Richard Lazarus and his colleagues (Coyne and Lazarus, 1981; Lazarus and Launier, 1978) have argued that the degree of stress created by change is often a function of how a person appraises or interprets change. For example, two men may learn that they are to be transferred to another city by the company that they work for. One of them may interpret the change as a sign that his boss likes his work, and he may begin to imagine making new friends and having new experiences. The other man may view the transfer as a sign that his boss is unhappy with his work, and he may think sadly about leaving his old friends and about the problems of adjusting to a new position. In this case, the change is the same for both men, but the latter one will experience more stress.

What is it about change that is so stressful? Change, whether positive or negative, requires that the individual make psychological and physical adjustments. These adjustments place certain demands on the body and, hence, each is experienced as stress. Clearly, some changes are more stressful than others, but all demand some accommodation.

Unpredictability. While all change is stressful, we are able to predict and prepare for some change while others are unpredictable. For example, you know that you will graduate college on a certain date and you probably will know many months in advance the date on which you will get married. Many other events, however, happen in a very unpredictable fashion.

Unpredictability is stressful because you cannot plan for these random events. You have to be constantly "on your toes" and you have no "safe" period in which you can rest and relax (Cohen and Weinstein, 1981). One of the most vivid examples of unpredictability occurs in the job of air-traffic controllers. Imagine yourself as a controller at Chicago's O'Hare Airport, where an airplane lands or takes off on the average of every 20 seconds. While some of the flights are scheduled, many others are not. It is difficult to predict how many planes may be circling overhead waiting for you to make a potentially life-or-death decision. Martindale (1976) compared the medical records of 4,000 air-traffic controllers with those of second-class Air Force airmen who generally have regular and predictable jobs. The controllers were significantly more likely to suffer from high blood pressure, attacks of anxiety, peptic ulcers, and depression.

You may wonder exactly how stressful unpredictability really is. The answer seems to be that it is highly stressful. In an experiment, rats were allowed to choose between predictable and unpredictable shock (Badia, Culbertson, and Harsh, 1973). If a rat pushed a button at the start

Lack of predictability leads to stress. One reason that air-traffic controllers are stressed is that they often cannot predict when an airplane will request landing or take-off permission, and they cannot anticipate when trouble may develop.

of the study, all the shocks received would be preceded by a warning tone. If the lever was not pushed, no warning tone preceded the shocks. The tone allowed the rat to predict when the shock would come. Not only did the rats prefer the signaled shocks, but they maintained their preference even when the predictable shocks were longer and stronger than the unpredictable shocks.

Lack of Control.   After overcoming his early fears, Kelly loved the city life. He could choose where and what he ate because of the wide variety of restaurants. He could decide what type of entertainment would fill his evenings. He had a wide variety of people from which to choose his friends. And he found that if he became bored with one job, he could always find other types of work. In short, Kelly found that the variety of the city offered him a chance to control his own destiny and life.

These opportunities for control may well have reduced the stress that Kelly might otherwise have experienced in the city. Numerous investigators have pointed out that uncontrollable situations are stress-producing (Baum, Singer, and Baum, 1981). Judith Rodin and her colleagues (Rodin, Solomon, and Metcalf, 1978) conducted an interesting experiment showing the importance of control. A team of four experimental confederates waited in the Yale University library until they spotted a single individual waiting for the elevator. When the elevator arrived, the confederates followed the subject into it. In half the cases, the confederates positioned themselves so that the subject was in front of the control panel of the elevator and could determine at which floors the elevator stopped. During the other incidents the confederates placed themselves in front of the control panel so that the subject was not able to physically control the elevator. When a subject arrived at his or her desired floor, an experimenter questioned the person about the library and about the elevator service. Subjects who had access to the control panel reported being more comfortable and less crowded in the elevator than did subjects who did not have access to the control panel.

In another study, a group of elderly residents in a nursing home were given more control over their day-to-day lives (Langer and Rodin, 1976). These residents were able to do such things as choose their own meals, care for plants in their rooms, and decide how to arrange the furniture in the rooms. A second group of residents were treated according to the standard nursing home routine where staff members make all decisions on these issues. The results of the study showed that residents given control over their own lives became more alert and more involved in activities than residents who did not have this control. The residents given control also showed significantly greater improvement in their health than residents who did not have control. In fact, during the 18 months of the study, only 15 percent of the patients with control over their daily lives died; 30 percent of the comparison group died.

It is not entirely clear why control reduces stress. One view is that having control increases the predictability of events and allows people to feel more prepared to deal with their environment (Pervin, 1963). Whatever the reason, we do know that the degree of control people have over their lives influences the amount of stress that they experience.

Conflict. Kelly had an important choice to make when he found that he would have to be a clown in the circus: Would he do a white-face act like other clowns, or would he develop a whole new character? While there were strong points in favor of each of the acts, Kelly had to choose one—he couldn't do both. This is an example of **conflict,** which is a state that occurs when a person is motivated to choose between two or more mutually exclusive goals or courses of action. Events are mutually exclusive when choosing one automatically eliminates the other. Kelly's dilemma about his clown act involved two mutually exclusive courses of action because choosing one meant that he couldn't do the other.

Some conflict occurs almost every time you make a choice; the degree of conflict is determined by how attractive each choice is and by how equally they are matched in attractiveness. (For example, there would be little conflict in choosing between a new Rolls-Royce and a broken-down 1962 Ford.) Conflict has been found to be one of the conditions that causes stress for people. While there are many situations in which a person will experience conflict, investigators have identified four major types of categories of conflict (Lewin, 1931; Miller, 1944). In defining these types, they have focused on people's tendencies to either approach or avoid a goal.

1. Approach-Approach Conflict. After Kelly had become famous as the clown Willie, he was offered a chance to act in the movies. This excited him, because it meant that millions of people could see Willie, and it also offered him financial rewards. However, becoming an actor would force Kelly to give up the circus for a certain amount of time. He loved working with circus people and dealing with live audiences. Thus, Kelly was faced with making a choice between two very attractive alternatives.

This is an example of an approach-approach conflict, which involves a choice between two attractive goals. In theory, this conflict should be easy to resolve, because it is a ''no lose'' situation—either choice brings rewards. However, anyone who had had to make the choice between two good job offers or two attractive dates knows that this type of conflict can be stressful.

2. Avoidance-Avoidance Conflict. This type of conflict results when people must choose between two unattractive goals. Kelly faced this type of conflict when he considered divorcing Eva. He felt that he was unhappy with Eva, but he also knew that he would be unhappy without her. Thus the choice between whether to stay married or get divorced involved two

FIGURE 10–3

The graph shows approach and avoidance tendencies as one nears a goal. Both approach and avoidance curves increase the closer one gets to the goal, but the avoidance curve increases more rapidly than the approach curve.

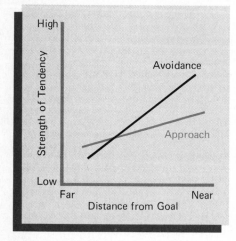

unattractive goals. This type of conflict is difficult to resolve. For this reason, people faced with this situation often try to delay making a decision. They sometimes hope that if they delay long enough, they can either escape the situation or something will happen that will make the decision for them.

3. Approach-Avoidance Conflict. Kelly's first job offer in the circus involved being a clown. This created a great deal of conflict for him. On the positive side, he would be with the circus, and he would be earning a regular salary. On the negative side, however, Kelly knew nothing about clowning and he really wanted to be a trapeze artist. The approach-avoidance conflict involves only one goal, which has both attractive and unattractive qualities. People's desire to both obtain the goal and avoid it traps them in conflict.

4. Double Approach-Avoidance Conflict. This type of conflict results when a person has to choose between two goals, each of which has both positive and negative qualities. For example, as a teenager, Kelly had to choose between staying on the farm or going to the city. Kelly had many friends (+) and security (+) at home on the farm, but he was bored (−). On the other hand, Kansas City offered excitement (+) and jobs (+), but he had no friends there (−). The double approach-avoidance conflict is the most common of the four types we have discussed, because it is rare that people are faced with goals that are completely positive or negative. In fact, many conflicts that appear to be simple approach-approach conflicts can actually be viewed as double approach-avoidance conflicts, because choosing one goal (+) means giving up the other (−).

As we all know, conflicts can be hard to resolve. An interesting point about most conflicts is that the closer we get to a goal, the stronger the approach and avoidance forces become. Unfortunately, as can be seen in Figure 10–3, the strength of the avoidance tendencies increases at a faster rate than the strength of the approach tendencies. In other words, the closer you get to making a decision, the more you will be disturbed by the negative qualities of the choice. You may have experienced this in choosing what college to go to: When you first learned that you had been accepted at your two top choices, you were very happy and felt the decision would be easy. However, as the decision deadline approached, you found the choice increasingly hard to make. This fact not only increases the stress associated with conflict, but, as we will see in Chapter 14, it increases how hard we must work to justify our final decision.

The Reactions to Stress

All of us experience stress many times each day. In fact, some of us seek out stress-producing situations by engaging in sports such as sky diving or going to scary movies. In most cases, the level of stress is not particularly high, and if it becomes too uncomfortable, we take the necessary steps to reduce the stressor. However, some people are subjected to such high levels of stress or to such long periods of stress that they develop severe physical or psychological symptoms. Let us examine some of these symptoms.

Psychophysiological Disorders. Few college students need to be told that stress can make people physically sick. Anyone who has had to prepare for a big exam knows that stress can lead to a loss of appetite, insomnia (the inability to fall asleep), and tension headaches. **Psychophysiological disorders,** often called psychosomatic illnesses, are real physical illnesses in which stress is a contributing factor. The list of psychophysiological disorders is long and includes a surprising range of illnesses.

One of the most common disorders associated with stress is the *peptic ulcer.* Ulcers are lesions or holes that develop in the stomach or upper

FIGURE 10–4

Brady and his colleagues (1958) found that monkeys faced with the need to respond quickly in an uncertain situation developed ulcers. The monkey who could not actively respond was less likely to suffer from ulcers.

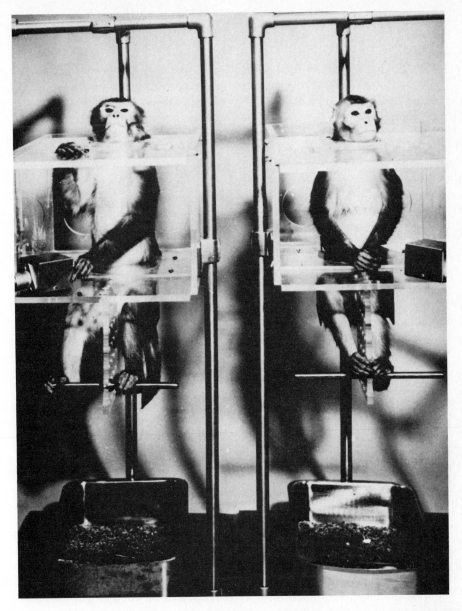

part of the small intestine. These holes are caused by the oversecretion of stomach acid, which literally eats through the lining of the digestive tract. Ulcers are often referred to as the "executive's disease," and it was once thought that the stress associated with making decisions was responsible for the oversecretion of the acid. In a classic study, Brady and his colleagues (1958) placed pairs of monkeys in restraining chairs (Figure 10–4). The monkeys were to receive electric shock on a programmed schedule. One of the monkeys (the "executive"), however, had a lever that could be pressed to eliminate the shock to both himself and his partner for 20 seconds. However, if the executive did not press the lever within the 20 second period, both monkeys were shocked. The second monkey had no lever and, thus, his fate was in the hands of the executive. The executive monkey learned very quickly to push the lever and avoid the shock. After a period of time, though, he failed to respond and both monkeys received the same shocks. Interestingly enough, the executive monkeys developed ulcers, while the partner monkeys did not. This study, along with the finding that ulcers are most likely to be found in males between the ages of 35 and 45, suggests that the stress associated with decision-making is responsible for ulcers. However, more recent research (Weiss, 1972) indicates that control and decision-making are not responsible

HIGHLIGHT / LONG-TERM EFFECTS OF THE STRESS OF CAPTIVITY

Of all the stressful events a person can experience, being taken captive must rank as one of the most stressful. After the Vietnam War was over, heart-rending scenes of POWs who had been held prisoner for years were commonplace news items. In 1976, the world was puzzled by the bizarre actions of Patricia Hearst, a wealthy heiress, who had been kidnapped by the Symbionese Liberation Army, an underground political group. In 1979, threats of war filled the air when 52 U.S. State Department employees were taken hostage in Iran. In each of these cases and many other hostage situations, the change, uncertainty, and lack of control in the situation is extreme. Given the degree of stress, people are amazed to see how fit many captives look after their ordeals.

However, recent observations suggest that surviving captivity may only be the first step on a rocky road to recovery for hostages. These people must undergo a great deal of psychological and social adjustment, which may take months and even years. One problem is the so-called *delayed stress reaction.* This response includes depression, anxiety, an inability to concentrate, insomnia, edginess, and night sweats (Lagone, 1981). What is unusual about this condition is that it may occur months or years after the captivity has ended and after the person seems to have readjusted to his or her environment. The delayed stress response is not only suffered by victims of captivity; many veterans of the Vietnam War who were not captives have suffered such reactions. Psychologists do not completely understand why these delayed reactions occur or what factors bring on the attacks. There is some evidence that suggests that people who were already predisposed to anxiety disorders before the stressful

situation are most likely to suffer from delayed stress reaction (Committee of Veterans' Affairs, 1981).

A second problem shown by some ex-captives is the *Stockholm syndrome.* In this case the hostage develops a strong attraction for his or her captor after having been held captive. This attraction is strongest if the hostage has been well treated and watched by the same guards over a long period of time. This syndrome occurred in the case of Patty Hearst, who seemingly chose to remain with her captors and participate in some of their terrorist activities. Bruno Bettelheim (1960) observed that even *during* captivity a similar process of identifying with one's captors can occur. He reports that some prisoners in Nazi concentration camps adopted many of the mannerisms, behaviors, and even speech patterns of their Nazi guards. One possible reason for this syndrome is that the captor-captive relationship is in many ways like the parent-child relationship: Hostages are totally dependent on their captors for their food, clothing, and, most important of all, their lives. This dependence can cause some to develop an infantile emotional state and respond to the captors the way children respond to their parents.

Flashbacks or sudden memories

of the captive situation may occur for long periods of time after release. There is no way to control or even anticipate when such flashbacks will occur. The ex-captive may have nightmares about the time spent in captivity. Or the ex-hostage may see a picture on television or a person on the street that triggers a flashback. Along with the flashback comes the arousal and emotions that were experienced during the period of captivity.

During captivity, many hostages may experience a sense of bewilderment and anger that their country, family, or friends have not come to their rescue. The question "Why don't they do something to get me out of here?" may constantly be in the back of a hostage's mind. However, hostages cannot express these feelings during captivity because the captors will take such feeling as signs of weakness. In many cases, immediately after being released the hostage is made the center of attention. The expression of anger at the assumed inactivity of others would at this point be viewed as inappropriate, so these feelings must be repressed. As a result, some ex-hostages have been found to experience a delayed anger reaction long after their captivity has ended. Because of the time delay, many people cannot understand the reasons for this response, and the anger seems to be without cause.

The study of hostages has given psychologists a better understanding of the unique problems faced by these individuals. This increased sensitivity has led to new methods of helping them re-enter society. As we saw with the Iranian hostages, even those who showed no immediate effects of captivity were isolated for a period of time. During this time, they were encouraged to express their feelings and were made aware of the potential problems of re-entry.

for ulcers. Rather, it is the pressure arising from the need to respond quickly over an extended period of time, and the uncertainty associated with choosing an effective response, that cause ulcers.

Stress contributes to getting sick in a number of ways. First, because the body must mobilize to deal with the stress, the resistance to diseases is lowered. Second, people may become so preoccupied with or depressed about the stress that they fail to notice or deal with symptoms of impending illness. We do not know exactly what factors determine the specific psycho-physiological illness a person will suffer. That is, why does one person get colds when distressed while another suffers from ulcers? Part of the answer may involve constitutional weakness. That is, people may be born with or develop a weak spot in their stomach. When these people encounter stress, the symptoms find expression in the already weak stomach and an ulcer appears. Other people may have a high susceptibility to colds, and, when stress lowers their immunity, they catch colds. Another factor may be the environment or culture in which we live. Certain bacteria or viruses are more common in some environments than in others, and lowered immunity will allow these more common bacteria to take control of our systems, giving rise to specific diseases associated with particular bacteria or viruses.

Coronary-Prone Behavior Pattern. Stress not only causes changes within our bodies, it also may move us to action. Some people seek to "get away from it all" when they feel the pressure building. These people may take a relaxing drive or engage in a hobby to relieve the pressure. Others may turn to alcohol or drugs when they feel pressured. However, some people, especially males in high-pressure businesses, may respond to stress by becoming increasingly competitive and hostile. When these people become stressed they feel increasing time pressures to "get the job done" and they feel overwhelmed by external demands. Their desires for achievement increase and their actions and speech patterns become more animated and abrupt. These individuals give the impression of someone running on "nervous energy" with the single goal of achievement (Friedman and Rosenman, 1974; Jenkins, 1976). This constellation of behaviors has been labeled as Type A behavior or *coronary-prone behavior pattern* because people who behave this way are more likely to become the victims of heart attacks than those who do not respond to stress in this manner. The Type B pattern has been defined as an absence of these behaviors (see Table 10–3).

Glass (1977) argued that this coronary-prone behavior pattern is a learned response to stress. Type A behavior is more common in men than in women. However, this coronary-prone behavior pattern is more likely to be found in women who are employed outside the home than in housewives. It is also interesting to note that Type A individuals are more common in industrial societies than in less industrialized nations. In fact, heart disease first became a major problem in the United States in the

TABLE 10–3: Research Findings on the Type A Personality

Type A people are more likely than Type B people to:

1. Be more aggressive when frustrated (Carver and Glass, 1978).
2. Judge that a time period has passed more quickly (Burnam et al., 1975).
3. Show more impatience when slowed down in making a decision (Glass et al., 1974).
4. Be more motivated to win in conflict situations (Smith and Brehm, 1981).
5. Be more likely to exaggerate the meaning of information from an opponent in conflict (Smith and Brehm, 1981).
6. Show higher blood pressure when performing a competitive task (Goldband, 1980).

early 1920s, the period when industrialization took a firm hold on the country. Interestingly enough, the Type A behavior pattern may be related to productivity. Mathews and his colleagues (1980) found that social psychologists with Type A behavior published more articles in scientific journals than Type B social psychologists.

There have been a number of interesting experiments demonstrating the unrelenting drive of these Type A people. Burnam, Pennebaker, and Glass (1973) identified Type A and Type B (not showing coronary-prone behavioral patterns) people. They presented them with 240 simple arithmetic problems ($6 + 9 - 2 = $ _____). Half the subjects were told that they had only 5 minutes to solve as many problems as they could, while the other subjects were given no time deadline. The results indicated that Type A and Type B subjects solved an equal number of problems when working under a time deadline. However, when there was no time deadline, Type A subjects solved significantly more problems than Type B subjects. Thus, Type A subjects worked fast regardless of whether or not there was a deadline. These Type A subjects could not relax; they imposed their own time deadlines when there was no external deadline. In another study, rewards were offered to Type A and Type B subjects if they responded slowly (Glass, Snyder, and Hollis, 1974). They found that the Type B subjects had little difficulty learning to respond slowly. However, the Type A subjects had a great deal of difficulty learning to slow down their response rates.

Learned Helplessness. As you can see, the picture of the Type A personality is of someone who is constantly striving to achieve and change his or her environment. Stress causes this person to burst into a wild frenzy of action that may be misdirected. Many other people, however, do not respond to prolonged stress in this manner. These people may try to change their environment and reduce their stress. If they are not successful with these first attempts, these people develop the feeling that their actions do not affect their environment. They develop a state of **learned helplessness** (Maier and Seligman, 1976; Seligman, 1975), and they stop trying to control events. They become apathetic and depressed.

Martin Seligman (1975) demonstrated this effect with dogs. He strapped a group of dogs into harnesses and gave them repeated shocks that they could not escape. Later, he placed these dogs in a shuttle box that had two compartments separated by a low barrier. These dogs were then given a signal that a shock was coming; if they did not jump to the other compartment, they were given a shock. The dogs who had been given the previously inescapable shock failed to avoid the shock in the shuttle box. When they saw the warning, they ran around the box and then laid down, whimpered, and took the shock. However, dogs that had not been given inescapable shock in a previous session quickly learned to jump the barrier and avoid the shock. Seligman argued that the experience of the inescapable shocks led to a state of learned helplessness; the dogs learned that they could not control their environment. As a result, they stopped trying to influence events around them even when they were placed in a different situation.

Hiroto (1974) showed that humans, too, can learn to be helpless. In his experiment, some subjects were placed in a condition in which they had to listen to inescapable noise. In another condition, the subjects could stop the loud noise by pushing a button, and in a third condition, the subjects were not exposed to any noise. In the next phase of the study, all subjects were given a finger shuttle box. The box was designed so that loud noise was played when the subject's finger was on one side of the box. A subject could stop the noise by moving one finger to the other side of the box. Subjects who had been in the escapable or no noise conditions in the first phase of the study quickly learned to control the noise.

However, subjects who had been in the inescapable noise condition did not learn to stop the noise in the finger shuttle box. It was reasoned that this latter group had learned in the first phase that they could not control stressful events and thus they ceased trying and remained apathetic in the second phase.

COPING WITH STRESS

Eva and Emmett Kelly lived an event-filled life after they were married. They traveled the country doing their double trapeze act, and Emmett also did his clown act. However, this happy life began to falter as the Depression gripped America. The strain of constant travel and worry about finding a job slowly destroyed the Kellys' relationship. As the stress increased, their marriage deteriorated, until in 1935 Eva filed for divorce. The divorce hit Kelly hard and he experienced periods of melancholy. At first, he quarreled with other performers, but soon he bounced back. He developed new routines for "Willie" and did 15 numbers 6 days a week. He found new joy in his work and became even happier with his circus life.

It might seem a little odd that a person could react to the stress of divorce by developing new clown acts. But think about your own responses to situations that arouse stress. How did you react when you failed a final exam for which you had spent many sleepless nights studying? What was your response when your girlfriend or boyfriend told you that he or she was in love with your best friend? Or, how did you handle your own feelings when you discovered that you were in love with your best friend's fiancee?

Most of us would be quick to agree that people should respond directly to stress. By looking honestly at our feelings, we can learn effective ways to cope with them and we can learn how to avoid their unpleasant recurrences in the future. For example, Emmett might have examined the events that led to the deterioration of his relationship with Eva. This examination could have shown him more effective ways to deal with other people in his life.

Defense Mechanisms

People, however, do not always deal with stress in a direct way, because the discomfort associated with stress makes it difficult to deal directly and constructively with it. Sigmund Freud became aware of this problem when he observed people struggling with their anxieties. He found that people often distort reality in order to defend against painful conflicts and anxieties. This distortion is done unconsciously in order to cope with a situation. The **defense mechanisms** are normal ways of coping with anxiety, and they help us handle difficult situations. However, because they involve self-deception and distortions of reality, they keep us from dealing with the basic causes of stress. Let us examine a few of these defense mechanisms. Which of these mechanisms do you use and what has been the result?

Rationalization. **Rationalization** means finding logical or desirable reasons for our behavior. In this way we try to justify our actions by giving them good reasons (or excuses). Rationalization reduces anxiety by: (1) limiting the person's responsibility or guilt for undesired events, and (2) decreasing the person's disappointment for failure by belittling the goal. A review of your own behavior should demonstrate how common this method is for dealing with anxiety in everyday life. How often have you soothed yourself about a grade by arguing, "Grades aren't important—it's what you learn in a course that is important." Or how often have you tried to convince yourself that you are "better off" without that friend you just lost or that job you didn't get? These efforts to reassure ourselves are generally harmless, and they help us get over disappointments. However, we must also realize that too much reliance on rationalization can keep us from dealing with the reasons for failure or from taking helpful steps to avoid future failures.

Repression and Suppression.   After their divorce, Emmett and Eva Kelly met occasionally. Kelly reports that their meetings were always cordial and that he had no ill feelings towards his ex-wife. Some of us may question the last statement. Regardless of the reasons for the divorce, it is difficult to conceive of one that does not lead to some hurt feelings, a tendency to assign blame, and some hostility. It is possible that Emmett had these feelings but that he *repressed* them and thus was not aware of them. **Repression** means blocking or keeping unpleasant thoughts or memories from conscious awareness.

How can we ever know about another person's thoughts and feelings if they themselves are unaware of them? Freud faced this question. He felt that he could "unlock" people's unconscious through hypnosis. Later, he discovered that he could also uncover people's repressed feelings by focusing on their dreams.

Although Freud was convinced that individuals do repress threatening thoughts, others have questioned this concept. They argue that these thoughts are merely suppressed. **Suppression** involves a conscious effort to block or avoid thinking about events. You have probably told yourself at times, "I don't want to think (or talk) about that." In other words, you'd rather forget "about the whole thing." These cases are different from true repression, since you are aware of the thoughts and events. As we pointed out, repression occurs when you are *un*aware of the thoughts hidden in your unconscious. The controversy surrounding repression and suppression has not been resolved, and both concepts are still widely used in the clinical literature.

Displacement.   After the divorce, Kelly went through a period in which he was irritable and he quarreled with other members of the circus on slight provocation. Some of these actions may have been the result of displacement (see Chapter 9). **Displacement** involves redirecting feelings from the individual that caused them to a, safer or more available target. Thus, Kelly may have felt angry at his wife, but since she was not with him, he displaced his anger onto the people around him in the circus. Students may use displacement when they are angered by a professor's assignment of an unfair grade. It is, however, somewhat risky to express this anger toward the professor, so students may take it out on their friends. Displacement allows people to work the stress out of their system and, thereby, reduce tension. However, it does not allow a person to deal with the real cause of the stress.

Sublimation.   Kelly threw himself into his work following the divorce. He planned new routines, did extra acts, and was determined to be the best possible clown. This behavior may seem strange if we expect the problems associated with disappointment to interfere with our work. In many cases disappointment and depression do interfere with other activities, but sometimes people channel the energy associated with one activity or event into a seemingly unrelated activity. This rechanneling is called **sublimation**. It differs from displacement because it does not merely redirect feeling from one target to another; it involves changing the whole nature of the feeling. It is considered a defense because it keeps the individual from focusing on the earlier stress or unpleasant activity.

Projection. All of us have qualities or feelings that we would rather not recognize or acknowledge. One way to protect ourselves from focusing on our own shortcomings is to *project* these shortcomings or undesirable traits on other people. **Projection** reduces our stress because it helps justify our actions or feelings: "If other people feel that way, it's not so bad for me to feel that way." Thus, people who are filled with hostility often see the people around them as being very hostile—this justifies their own actions and feelings, because it means they are reacting to other people's hostility.

Reaction Formation. Earlier, we pointed out that Kelly's relationship with Eva continued to be friendly after their divorce. This cordiality seemed to be somewhat of a surprise even to Kelly, who expected to respond with tenseness and hostility in his later meetings with her. As we suggested, he may have been suppressing or repressing his hostility and simply not recognizing it. There is, however, another possibility. Kelly's cordiality and even expressed friendliness toward his ex-wife may have been his way of dealing with his guilt and hostility. **Reaction formation** is a defense mechanism used to conceal unacceptable impulses by expressing instead the opposite impulse. For example, a man who fears that he has impulses to sexually molest children may react by voicing strong support for laws to severely punish child molesters. Or a woman who feels guilty about her negative feelings toward her mother may go out of her way to send her mother expensive gifts and cards on her birthday and, other holidays. It is important to realize that these actions are not motivated by caring for the mother. Rather, they are attempts to hide negative feelings and reduce the guilt associated with these feelings. Admittedly, it is difficult to determine if an action is influenced by reaction formation or is an expression of true feelings. However, reaction formation is characterized by excessiveness in behavior. Thus the woman might not send her mother just any gift; the gift would probably be expensive to the point of straining her budget.

Defense Mechanisms: A Concluding Note. These are just a few of the defense mechanisms used to deal with uncomfortable feelings or stress. You can probably think of many more. After reading about defense mechanisms, you may be shaking your head and thinking that people do funny things. It is, however, important to realize that we live in a complex physical and social environment and that we sometimes face difficulties adjusting to that environment. Pressures may build up slowly or we may be suddenly overwhelmed by a situation. In these cases we may need a temporary safety valve to help us cope with the difficulty. Defense mechanisms are safety valves that we all use. They redirect, reinterpret, or block out difficult situations and anxiety. Some may seem more unusual than others, but the basic purpose of all the defense mechanisms is the same. They can be helpful when used as a temporary crutch to help us stand up to difficult situations.

Because defense mechanisms do cover up much emotional experience, people who rely *solely* on these defenses are doomed to an unhappy life. They must constantly battle to keep their hidden anxiety under control. These people are often described as suffering from psychological disorders called neuroses (which we will discuss in Chapter 12). In Chapter 13, "Therapy," we will examine a number of the techniques that psychologists have developed to help people deal more directly and effectively with stress.

SUMMARY

1. **Emotions** are feelings that are usually caused by events outside of us. Methods of measuring emotions include self-report, behavioral observations, and changes in physiological responses. One such method, the modern polygraph, uses physiological changes in order to tell if a person is lying.

2. Several viewpoints have contributed to the present theories of emotions. James and Lange argue that external events cause physiological changes in people and that it is the perception of these changes that leads to emotions.

3. Cannon, however, showed that emotions can occur in the absence of physiological responses. Cannon and Bard propose that emotions and physiological changes occur together.

4. Schachter and Singer introduced cognitions as most important in labeling emotions. They suggest that once people are physiologically aroused, they will search for environmental cues to determine the nature of their emotional arousal.

5. Another theory assumes that the way we interpret a situation influences the emotion we experience. In other words, interpretation or appraisal comes before emotion.

6. Although many theorists disagree on the exact mechanism by which specific emotions are evoked, they generally agree that emotions are the result of physiological arousal, behavior, and interpretations of events.

7. Two emotions, **fear** and **love,** have been examined in this chapter. Fear, which may be either inborn or learned, serves two important functions. Fear causes us to avoid situations that may be dangerous and, when danger is encountered, prepares the body for action. Although love has not been as widely studied as fear, it has been suggested that romantic love differs from mature love and that our ability to love may be affected by our past experiences.

8. **Stress** was defined not as an emotion, but as a general response by the body to any demand made on it. Several factors that affect the amount of stress experienced in a situation are change, unpredictability, and lack of control. Change, whether positive or negative, may be stressful; however, the stress is lessened if we are able to predict and control the situation.

9. Another element of stress is **conflict,** which is a state that occurs when a person is motivated to choose between two or more mutually exclusive goals or courses of action. Some of the various types of conflict are approach-approach, avoidance-avoidance, approach-avoidance, and double approach-avoidance.

10. When people are exposed to a great deal of stress, they may develop **psychophysiological disorders,** ranging from insomnia and headaches to ulcers and heart attacks.

11. When people repeatedly find themselves unable to control a stressful situation, they may develop a state of **learned helplessness,** in which they become apathetic, depressed, and do not make any effort to control their environment.

12. People often cope with their emotions by using unconscious **defense mechanisms** such as **rationalization, repression, suppression, displacement, sublimation,** and **projection.** Although these mechanisms may help to temporarily redirect or block out anxieties, they are seldom effective over an extended period.

SUGGESTED READINGS

The following book is about Emmett Kelly:

KELLY, E. *Clown.* Englewood Cliffs, N.J.: Prentice-Hall, 1954.

IZARD, C. *Human emotions.* New York: Plenum, 1977. A discussion of the major theories of human emotions. A careful examination is given to the role of nonverbal (especially facial) cues used in determining emotions.

PLUTCHIK, R. *Emotion: A psychoevolutionary synthesis.* New York: Harper & Row, 1980. Examines the parallels in emotional development in animals and humans. Draws on material from psychology, biology, ethology, and psychiatry to show how emotions evolve.

SELIGMAN, M. *Helplessness: On depression, development, and death.* San Francisco: Freeman, 1975. Discusses the theory of learned helplessness, showing how a loss of control can lead to depression and contribute to death.

STONE, G., COHEN, F., and ADLER, N. (Eds.). *Health psychology.* San Francisco: Jossey-Bass, 1979. Presents original chapters discussing the role of psychology in health and health care. The chapters discuss topics ranging from how people determine when they are sick to the factors that determine when people will seek and follow medical advice.

WALSTER, E., and WALSTER, G. *A new look at love.* Reading, Mass.: Addison-Wesley, 1978. Discusses the differences in passionate and mature love. Examines the research on love and attraction.

11

Personality: Theories and Assessment

By Monday, the *Augusta* had slipped into the Gulf Stream off the New Jersey coast. The group of officers had just sat down to lunch when the watch officer handed a telegram to the old man at the head of the table: HIROSHIMA WAS BOMBED VISUALLY WITH ONLY ONE TENTH COVER AT SEVEN FIFTEEN PM WASHINGTON TIME AUGUST FIVE. THERE WAS NO FIGHTER OPPOSITION AND NO FLAK. FIFTEEN MINUTES AFTER DROP CAPTAIN PARSONS REPORTED "CONDITIONS NORMAL IN AIRPLANE FOLLOWING DELIVERY. RESULTS CLEAR CUT SUCCESSFUL IN ALL RESPECTS. VISIBLE EFFECTS GREATER THAN IN ANY TEST." The old man nodded in deep thought as he carefully read and reread the telegram.

The "old man," who had made the decision to drop the atomic bomb on Hiroshima, was President Harry S. Truman. And, three days later, he would make the decision to drop a second atomic bomb on Nagasaki. The destruction caused by the two bombs was tremendous; over 100,000 people died immediately, and countless others were affected by radiation sickness that would slowly and painfully end their lives.

Was the use of the atomic bomb necessary? This question was asked and debated around the world. Even today, historians continue to argue about the wisdom of that decision. One man, however, never took part in these debates. That man was Harry S. Truman. He felt that he had made the best decision possible based on the facts available at the time. He would not labor over a past decision nor become involved in second guessing.

Truman took a similar attitude toward the other decisions he made during his eight years as president. While his other decisions may not seem as momentous as the one involving "the bomb," many of them still play a dramatic role in our lives today. Truman helped develop the Marshall Plan, which rebuilt Western Europe and made it one of the closest allies of the United States. He took part in the Potsdam Conference, which divided Europe into a free Europe and a Communist-controlled group of countries, forming the Iron Curtain around the Soviet Union. During his second term of office, Chinese and North Korean troops invaded South Korea and Truman sent United States troops into battle. With the hope that nations might be able to handle their conflicts through negotiation rather than war, Truman entered the United States as a charter member of the United Nations.

Many historians rate Truman among the greatest presidents of the United States. This praise is particularly striking in light of several facts. First, Truman probably never would have been president except for the death of Franklin D. Roosevelt; Truman was a rather obscure politician before being named Roosevelt's vice president. Second, Truman had one of the most humble and least glamorous backgrounds of all our modern presidents. In fact, only four years before Truman became president, the banks foreclosed on his mother's farm because there was no money to make the mortgage payments. How did this rags-to-riches story come about and who was Harry S. Truman?

Harry S. Truman was born on a small farm outside of Independence, Missouri in 1876. His parents could not agree on a middle name for their first child, so they simply gave him the initial "S." Truman's father was a farmer with an eye for speculation and he was also a mule trader. He had a reputation of being the most honest man in Jackson County. Although he was a small, neatly dressed man, the elder Truman was a fighter: ". . . he could whip anybody up to two hundred [pounds] if they got in his way" (Miller, 1973, p. 66). Harry's mother was a strong woman who was very concerned with her children's education. She was very strict and insisted on obedience and honesty.

Truman's early childhood was fairly normal. He received a great deal of warmth and affection from his parents. At the age when other boys were becoming interested in sports and outside games, Harry developed a fondness for books. He read the Bible twice through before he began school. His choice of the Bible as his reading material was not, however, due to his religious devotion. Rather, Truman states, "I guess I read the Bible because the type was large, but then it developed about the time I was six years old, it was then that we first noticed it, that I had flat eyeballs" (Miller, 1973, p. 52). Truman's eyesight was so bad that he had to be fitted with thick eyeglasses.

The glasses had a major influence on his life. They set him apart from the other kids and kept him from joining in their games. As a result, he became even more absorbed in books. His eye defect also brought him closer to his mother. She encouraged his reading and, later, his interest in the piano. She looked after him in a special way and young Truman responded to this attention. "Harry was a sort of mamma's boy, oddly more like a little old woman than a sissy child. He helped in the kitchen with neither reluctance nor boyish clumsiness. He learned to cook" (Daniels, 1950, p. 50).

Although he dreamed of becoming a concert pianist, economic considerations forced him to change his plans. Truman's father lost the family farm and most of their cash savings in a grain speculation deal. Thus, after he graduated from high school, Truman took a job as time keeper for a railroad construction crew. This job presented quite a picture of contrast as the small, owlish-looking young man worked with the burly construction workers. Truman, however, found that his size was no handicap, and he got along well by treating the workers honestly and directly. After working at the railroad, Truman then went to Kansas City, where he worked as a bank clerk and joined a field artillery unit. By the beginning of World War I, he had risen to the rank of first lieutenant. Truman soon became a captain and was sent to France to command Battery D. The battery, known as "Dizzy D," had already had four commanding officers, none of whom could control the outfit. Truman took charge of the unit and won the trust of his men.

On his return from the war, Truman married his childhood sweetheart, Bess. He had known her since he was 4 years old. Truman had always been painfully shy around women; this shyness, combined with feeling that Bess deserved more, kept him from proposing until he was 35 years old. Bess was much the opposite of her new husband. She came from a well-to-do family, had an outgoing personality, and was an athletic woman.

The marriage forced Truman to become more concerned with his financial status. He started a clothing store with a war buddy, but economic times were bad and the business went bankrupt. Thus, 1922 found Harry Truman with a wife, a bankrupt business, and no future plans. But he did have a number of friends in Jackson County, and a reputation for honesty. Soon after the store closed, Mike Pendergast persuaded Harry to run for a county judge post. The Pendergast family headed a strong political machine in Missouri; with the help of the Pendergast machine, Truman was elected county judge.

Truman served in this capacity (with the exception of a two-year period) until 1934. One of his major jobs was overseer of the road system in the county. The previous judges had been corrupt, taken bribes, and given contracts to political friends. Truman attacked the job with a zeal and honesty that surprised even the Pendergasts. While controversy and accusations of graft swirled around the Pendergast machine, Truman remained an impeccably honest man. When he left his county office, Jackson County had the best road system in the state, and finances were well in the black.

In 1934 the Missouri Democratic party, headed by the Pendergasts, ran Truman for United States senator. He won the election and went to Washington, D.C. He thought he was the poorest senator in Congress, and he was very self-conscious about not having a college education. Truman became a champion of the "common man" in Washington. He served on a committee to investigate graft in the nation's railroads, and he gave a stirring criticism of big business on the floor of the Senate in 1937. "One of the difficulties as I see it is that we worship money instead of honor. A billionaire in our estimation is much greater in the eyes of the people than the public servant who works for the public interest. It makes no difference if the billionaire rode to wealth on the sweat of little children and the blood of unpaid labor. . . . No one ever considers the Carnegie libraries steeped in the blood of the Homestead steelworkers, but they are. We do not remember that the Rockefeller Foundation is founded on the dead miners . . ." (Miller, 1973, p. 152).

Truman's work earned him the reputation of being an honest politician. However,

he was also a modest man who never boasted of his power and who made light of his accomplishments. Thus, Truman was surprised to learn that he had been chosen to be Franklin D. Roosevelt's running mate in 1944. Eighty-two days after Roosevelt was elected to his fourth term, he died, and Truman became the thirty-third President of the United States. It has often been argued that power has a way of corrupting those who hold it, but Truman proved to be an exception to this rule.

The debates about what type of president Truman was will probably rage on for many years to come. Eric Sevareid, however, expressed the opinion of many. "A man's character is his fate, said the ancient Greeks. Chance, in good part, took Harry Truman to the presidency, but it was his character that kept him there and determined his historical fate. He is, without any doubt, destined to live in the books as one of the strongest and most decisive of the American Presidents."

DEFINING PERSONALITY

". . . but it was his *character* that kept him there and determined his historical fate." The concept of character or personality is often used to explain, excuse, or justify people's actions. Eric Sevareid used the concept of character to explain why Truman achieved a great place in history.

What do we mean when we talk about Truman's personality, or Jane's personality, or your own personality? Most of the work of psychologists is aimed at studying and developing theories about how "people in general" behave. We have already discussed the basic principles of learning, perception, motivation, and emotion. The major aim in each of these areas is to identify the most likely response that people will make to a particular situation, stimulus, or event. In each case, we lump people together and try to find rules to explain how they behave or why they behave in a particular manner.

We know, however, that all people do not act the same, even when faced with the same situation. For example, think of how people behave in a restaurant when the service is very slow. Some sit waiting patiently to be served, others "make a scene" and grumble loudly at the waiter, while still others simply get up and leave. Why do these people act differently when they are all faced with the same bad service and are all unhappy about it?

The study of personality is aimed at answering questions like these. The basic question of personality research is to explain why people act differently in the same setting; in other words, the focus is on *individual differences*. There have been many attempts to define personality. Gordon Allport (1937) suggested the global view, that personality "is what man really is." Most other definitions, however, are not so ambitious; they focus on personality as organized, enduring, and characteristic of the individual (Forgus and Shulman, 1979). We will define **personality** as the unique set of behaviors (including thoughts and emotions) and enduring qualities that influence the way a person adjusts to his or her environment. In this definition personality is seen as influencing, guiding, and motivating behavior. Presumably, personality is what makes people unique and causes them to act or see situations differently from anyone else.

The task of explaining why people act differently in situations is clearly a big one. It is not concerned with a single type of behavior such as learning, perception, or social interaction. Theories of personality must cover all these areas and more. Because of the huge size of this task, there are many varying approaches to and theories about personality. Some of these approaches are concerned with identifying and describing different forms of personalities. We will examine this approach when we discuss type and trait theories. A second approach focuses on the structure and dynamics of personality. This approach is interested in identifying the forces or dynamics of personality and explaining how these components influence behavior. The emphasis of this approach is to identify forces such as drives, motives, or goals that arise within the individual and to relate these forces to behavior. The psychoanalytic theories of Sigmund Freud and his followers and the humanistic theories are examples of this type of theory. A third approach that we will examine is concerned with the way in which external events influence behavior. These learning approaches suggest that we can understand individual differences without a great deal of theorizing about the structure or dynamics of personality. Rather, learning theories argue that we can explain many individual differences by focusing on the learning process. According to this approach, each of us has a unique history and this history influences the way we respond to the world.

The similarities and differences of these three approaches will become clearer as we discuss them in the chapter. What is important to remember is that each approach is aimed at explaining why people act differently in similar situations.

A Question of Situational Consistency

Truman came to enjoy giving speeches during his terms as president. At the end of his speeches he would hold question-and-answer sessions. In one of these sessions a small, red-haired boy meekly asked him, "Mr. President, was you popular when you was a boy?" Truman smiled and slowly replied, "Why no, I was never popular. The popular boys were the ones who were good at games and had big, tight fists. I was never like that. Without my glasses I was blind as a bat, and to tell the truth, I was kind of a sissy. If there was any danger of getting into a fight, I always ran. I guess that's why I'm here today" (Miller, 1973, p. 32). Truman's answer shows a modesty that characterized him throughout his life. He rarely boasted about his accomplishments. He was always willing to praise others, but slow to take credit for himself.

One of the basic assumptions of many personality theories is that individuals behave consistently across many situations. This assumption is based on the belief that personality is a relatively stable part of the person that guides behavior. Thus, if we believe that modesty is a component of Truman's personality, we would expect him to display modest behavior in situations where he was dealing with an audience of children as well as in situations where he interacted with dignitaries or generals.

If people do act with such consistency across situations, we should be able to predict an individual's behavior if we know his or her personality. However, the case for situational consistency in behavior is not particularly strong. In a classic study, children's moral behavior was examined in a wide variety of situations (Hartshorne and May, 1928). Each child was given the opportunity to commit dishonest behavior (lying or cheating) in a number of settings (home, classroom, party, and athletic contest). If we believe that behavior is consistent across situations, we would predict that a child who acted dishonestly in one setting would do so in other settings. The results of the study, however, did not strongly support this position. There was only a slight tendency for children who were dishonest in one setting to be dishonest in other settings.

Does this finding mean that our personalities have no influence on our behavior? One group of researchers answers this question by pointing out that personality is only one determinant of behavior. Characteristics of the situation and the way in which the individual interprets the situation also influence behavior. Thus, an individual's personality may predispose him or her to act in a certain way, but situational variables will also influence behavior. For example, Truman may, indeed, have been a modest person who was reluctant to be pushy or boastful. However, during the Potsdam Conference he had to negotiate the division of Europe with Joseph Stalin, the stubborn, strong dictator of Russia. In this situation, Truman may have felt that modesty would be taken as a sign of weakness. Thus, in order to gain the respect of Stalin, he may have voiced his accomplishments and power as President of the United States. Thus, personality is one of the dimensions that influences behavior, and an understanding of an individual's personality can help in predicting his or her behavior. However, predictions of behavior cannot be made according to an individual's personality alone.

Bem and Allen (1974) have taken another approach to the question of situational consistency in behaviors. They argue that certain traits may show more situational consistency than others. Further, they point out that the specific traits in which consistency is evident will be different for different people. For example, modesty may have been an important or central trait of Truman's and, hence, he may have shown this modesty in many situations. On the other hand, while you may consider yourself modest, this may not be of primary importance to you. Therefore, you are unlikely to show strong situational consistency in this trait. In order to demonstrate this position, the investigators asked subjects to rate themselves on a friendly-unfriendly dimension and to indicate how consistent their behavior was on this dimension (Bem and Allen, 1974). The subjects' actual behaviors were then rated by observers across a number of situations. The results indicated that those subjects who rated themselves as being consistently friendly, did, in fact, respond in a friendly manner across a range of situations. However, the subjects who described themselves as variable in friendliness did not respond consistently. Thus, for each individual there may be traits that influence behavior across situations, but there will also be traits that are not evidenced consistently in different situations.

TYPES AND TRAITS

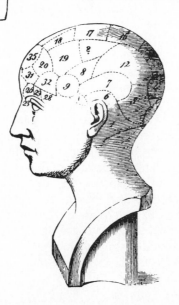

Some of the earliest personality theories were not really theories in the proper sense. That is, they did little to explain how personality develops or functions. Rather, they were attempts to describe or categorize personality. Some of these theories attempted to discover the connection between physical characteristics and personality.

Type Theories

In the eighteenth century, a Viennese doctor, Franz Joseph Gall, argued that physical formation of the skull is directly related to personality and intelligence. His basic assumption was that we can determine an individual's personality by examining the bumps and contours in his or her skull. Gall called this the science of *phrenology*. Many an anxious mother carried

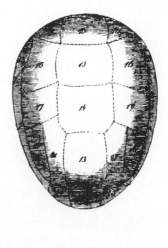

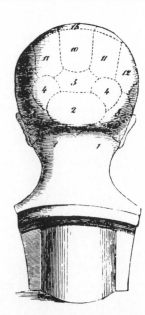

her child to a phrenologist, who, after feeling the child's head, told the mother what type of personality the child would have.

Almost a century later, Cesare Lombroso, an Italian psychiatrist and criminologist, suggested that criminals could be identified by the structure of their face. He argued that some people were born with the physical features of primitive man; these features showed that such people were destined to lead a life of crime: "The face of the criminal, like those of most animals, is of disproportionate size. . . . The eyes and ears are frequently situated at different levels and are of unequal size, the nose slants towards one side, etc." (Ferrero, 1911, p. 12). Although it offers some interesting possibilities, Lombroso's work has been largely discredited.

While not adopting phrenology or accepting Lombroso's theory, William Sheldon, a Harvard psychologist, offered the rather radical position that biological structure or body build determines behavior (Sheldon, 1942; Sheldon, Hartl, and McDermott, 1949). As a boy, Sheldon was trained to judge livestock. He not only learned that the body type of animals could be judged by a rating scale, but he also noticed that there was a relationship between an animal's body type and its temperament. In order to test his theory that there is a relationship between human body type and personality, Sheldon photographed thousands of students. After carefully examining these photographs, he developed three dimensions along which body builds could be rated: endomorphic (soft, round, fat); mesomorphic (muscular, hard, rectangular); and ectomorphic (tall, thin, fragile). Sheldon argued that each body could be rated on a seven-point scale according to these three dimensions. Each person could, therefore, be given a three-number rating (for example, 1:2:7, 6:4:1) that would describe his or her body build or **somatotype.**

Sheldon's next step was to relate somatotype or body build to personality. After observing people with various body types, Sheldon arrived at the following conclusions:

1. Endomorphs love comfort and food; they are relaxed and need social approval and affection.
2. Mesomorphs are assertive, physical, aggressive, and active.
3. Ectomorphs are restrained, socially inhibited, artistic, and oriented toward intellectual activities.

Thus, Sheldon argued that a person's body type determines his or her personality. It is interesting to look at Truman in light of Sheldon's types. As can be seen from Figure 11–1, Truman tended toward ectomorphy,

FIGURE 11–1: Sheldon's Somatotypes

Sheldon argued that body type determines personality. According to him, endomorphs love food and comfort, and need social approval and affection; mesomorphs are assertive, physical, aggressive, and active; and ectomorphs are restrained, socially inhibited, artistic, and oriented toward intellectual activity.

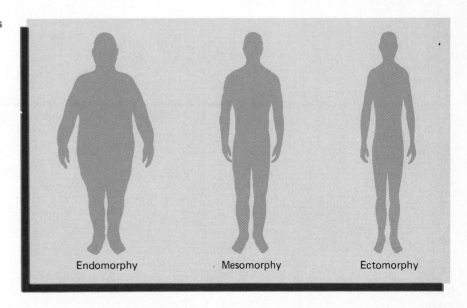

Endomorphy   Mesomorphy   Ectomorphy

being thin and rather fragile in build. And as we might expect from Sheldon's classification, Truman was a shy person whose major interests were artistic (piano) and intellectual (reading).

While on the surface it may seem that Sheldon's type theory is useful, a closer look reveals a number of problems with his basic approach. First, Sheldon assumed a direct relationship between body type and personality: a specific body type causes a certain personality. However, investigators pointed out that the relationship between body build and personality is neither as simple nor as direct as Sheldon suggested (Hall and Lindzey, 1978). Instead, we often have ideas about how people with certain body builds should behave—we expect a strong, muscular man to be an athlete; a fat person *should* be jolly; a skinny person who wears thick glasses *should* be an "egghead" who would rather read a good book than play football. These expectations influence the way we respond to others and, consequently, they influence the way others behave (Rykman, 1979). Thus, it is possible that people's expectations, rather than body build, influence behavior.

A second problem with Sheldon's theory and other type theories is the assumption that people can be placed in categories or "boxes" so easily or neatly. People are not so easily categorized. That is, they are not either passive or aggressive, introverted or extroverted, honest or dishonest. We may describe some of our friends as more aggressive or more honest than others, but few, if any, of them are *always* aggressive or honest. People cannot be categorized as being one type or another; instead, they have certain degrees of one trait or another.

Trait Theories

Another way of discussing personality is to assign traits. For example, Merle Miller describes Truman as being modest, loyal, honest, optimistic, shy, and decisive (Miller, 1973). This list of traits gives us a concise picture of Truman, while it can also serve as the basis for predicting his behavior.

Traits are relatively permanent qualities that people may possess to

FIGURE 11–2: Cattell's 16-Factor Questionnaire

Shown here are scores from three quite different groups: Olympic athletes, clergymen, and sales representatives. Cattell tried to identify the 16 basic traits that describe personality. (Cattell, 1965, pp. 242, 347)

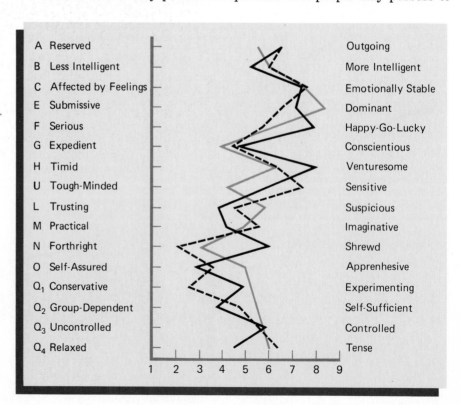

A Reserved	Outgoing
B Less Intelligent	More Intelligent
C Affected by Feelings	Emotionally Stable
E Submissive	Dominant
F Serious	Happy-Go-Lucky
G Expedient	Conscientious
H Timid	Venturesome
U Tough-Minded	Sensitive
L Trusting	Suspicious
M Practical	Imaginative
N Forthright	Shrewd
O Self-Assured	Apprenhesive
Q₁ Conservative	Experimenting
Q₂ Group-Dependent	Self-Sufficient
Q₃ Uncontrolled	Controlled
Q₄ Relaxed	Tense

1 2 3 4 5 6 7 8 9

a greater or lesser degree. For example, to say that there is a trait called honesty means that we can rate people on a scale ranging from very honest to very dishonest. This contrasts with the "either-or" classification used with types. According to Gordon Allport (1937), one of the early trait theorists, traits are "the building blocks of personality." An individual's personality is made up of a number of traits, some more central or dominant than others. Thus people can differ according to the number and specific traits they have as well as according to how much of a certain trait they have. According to this view, you may have some traits (shyness, laziness) that your best friend doesn't have. On the other hand, you may both have the same trait (honesty), but possess it in different degrees.

One of the major issues faced by trait theorists is the identification of traits. Researchers have pointed out the size of this problem by drawing up a list of 17,953 English words that could be used to indicate personal traits (Allport and Odbert, 1936). Imagine having to describe Truman by showing where he falls on 17,953 dimensions! Raymond Cattell (1965, 1973) set out to reduce this unmanageable number and to identify the "basic traits." He spent a number of years collecting data on the personality and behavior of thousands of subjects. Cattell identified 16 basic traits that could be used to describe people. He also developed a questionnaire, the "Sixteen Personality Factor Questionnaire," to find out where an individual was located on these 16 dimensions (see Figure 11–2). Despite Cattell's work, there is still a great deal of disagreement about the nature and number of the basic traits.

The Trait Approach: An Evaluation

The trait approach became popular for a number of reasons. First, it suggests that personality can be measured. Indeed, a number of scales have been developed to measure specific traits. Second, the view that behavior is caused by an individual's personality traits and that people can be described with these traits seems logical. In our everyday interactions, all of us use traits to describe other people. Your roommate is friendly, kind, and studious; your professor is absent-minded, humorous, and indecisive; your local politician is smooth-talking, suspicious, and tense. In fact, investigators (Jones and Nisbett, 1972; Nisbett and Ross, 1980) found that we tend to view other people's behavior as being caused by their personality traits (see Chapter 14). On the other hand, we generally see our own behavior as being determined by the situation. For example, you may explain your friend's low test scores by saying that she is not very smart. However, if you receive a low grade, you are likely to reason that the exam was very hard or that you had a bad headache when you took the test. There are a number of factors that influence such attributions (Brehm and Aderman, 1977; Miller, 1977), but the important point is that we often see people's behavior as being influenced by their personality traits.

Despite the appealing nature of the trait approach, there have been some important criticisms. First, the use of traits to explain behavior can lead to circular reasoning (Mischel, 1968). Traits are not something that we can see or directly measure. Rather, we must infer them from behavior or answers to personality tests. Thus, we may infer that Bill is aggressive because we see him hit other people or verbally abuse them. This may, indeed, be a reasonable conclusion to draw from his behavior. However, we then get into trouble if we conclude that Bill acted aggressively because he is an aggressive person. In essence, we would be saying that Bill is aggressive because he acts aggressively and he acts aggressively because he is aggressive.

A second problem is that many trait theories do not pay enough attention to the influence of the situation on behavior. For example, we might conclude that Harry Truman was a shy and modest person; he once stated, "The most peaceful thing in the world is riding a mule, plowing a field." However, in 1948, Truman was in danger of losing his bid for reelection. He chartered a train and went across the country giving speeches about his accomplishments and shaking hands with thousands of people. In these situations he acted neither shy nor modest. Clearly, then, situations play a large role in determining behavior. Trait theories, however, have not really taken this fact into account, and this limits their ability to predict behavior.

Finally, trait theories have been criticized because they are designed to identify traits and measure them, but they are not involved with how personality develops or changes.

PSYCHOANALYTIC THEORY

Trait theories are criticized because they take too simple a view of personality and because they generally avoid the issue of how personality develops. Psychoanalytic theory certainly avoids these criticisms; it is not simple, and its major focus is on the development of personality. In fact, psychoanalytic theory is one of the most comprehensive and ambitious theories in psychology, but it is also one of the most controversial. The man who first proposed the theory spent much of his life in the center of controversy, emerging as the best-known figure in psychology.

Sigmund Freud

Sigmund Freud was born in 1856 in Freiburg, Moravia (Czechoslovakia). As a boy, Freud was a serious student who enjoyed science and did very well in school. He continued his education at the University of Vienna, where he studied medicine. Although he was not thrilled at the idea of practicing medicine, he was interested in the scientific approach used to study medical problems. While at the university he worked as a laboratory assistant examining the nervous system of animals.

Freud would have been content to continue research in the laboratory, but his plans to marry demanded that he find a position that offered financial security. He therefore began a private medical practice. Two years later, however, he was awarded a fellowship to study the treatment of nervous disorders with the famous French neurologist, Jean Charcot. This proved to be a turning point in Freud's career. Charcot used hypnosis to treat patients classified as hysterics. These patients suffered from paralysis of limbs or from partial or total loss of sight or hearing. The cause of these symptoms was not physical; the paralysis was the result of psychological stress. Charcot discovered that he could relieve the physical symptoms through hypnotic suggestion.

Freud became dissatisfied with hypnosis as a tool because not everyone could be hypnotized. Freud found, however, that he could uncover the events that were related to the hysterical symptoms by having patients express every thought (no matter how unimportant or irrelevant) that came into their mind during the therapy session. Freud used this method of free association to discover the traumatic (painful, emotional, shocking) events that were the root of his patients' problems.

Most of Freud's patients were women from middle- and upper-class Victorian society. As Freud listened to them talk, he noticed a striking similarity in their stories. Many of his patients talked about traumatic

Sigmund Freud, founder of psychoanalytic theory.

events related to sexual experiences in early childhood. The patients talked about strong sexual urges and fantasies that they had experienced as children. This was especially surprising because the people of Freud's time believed that children did not have sexual urges or fantasies.

His discussions with patients led Freud to draw two conclusions. First, early childhood is a critical time for the formation of personality. Second, children, indeed even infants, have sexual urges, and much of their behavior is motivated by these urges. This second idea shocked people, and Freud was looked on as what we today would call "a dirty old man."

The Unconscious

In addition to having patients free associate, Freud also had them report their dreams (Jones, 1957). The contents of the dreams were varied and often bizarre. Freud, however, felt that dreams must have some function for the individual. He believed that dreams represented thoughts and feelings of which people were unaware. Thus, Freud felt that dreams were vehicles through which people could express their unacceptable impulses in disguised or acceptable forms.

This conclusion reinforced Freud's feeling that much of our behavior is the result of unconscious desires. He divided the personality into three parts or processes. The **conscious** includes what the person is perceiving or thinking at the moment. The **preconscious** is essentially one's memory; it includes thoughts that people may not be aware of but that they can retrieve from memory. Finally, the **unconscious** is the "storehouse of unacceptable images, including past events, current impulses, and desires of which one is not aware" (Byrne and Kelley, 1981). The unconscious makes up the largest part of our personality. Impulses are "filed" in the unconscious because people find them painful or threatening. Examples of these impulses might be the sexual desire to possess one's mother or an intense hatred of one's brother or sister. Once these images are *repressed*, or forced into the unconscious, they are removed from our awareness. However, the fact that we are not aware of these images and desires does not mean that they do not influence our behavior. According to Freud, these desires "push" for expression, but because of their threatening nature they are expressed only in disguised form.

As we discussed earlier, one of these disguises is dreams. Unconscious impulses can also find expression through "Freudian slips." Imagine the unconscious message in the following exchange. Mary sees her friend Jane, who is recently divorced and has also been on a diet. With all the best intentions of complimenting Jane for the success of her diet, Mary rushes up and says: "I haven't seen you for ages. You really have lost a lot of *face*—I mean weight." Accidents are still another way in which

"Freudian slips" are one way that people express unconscious feelings.

unconscious impulses are expressed. According to Freud, there is likely to be a "hidden message" when your roommate "accidentally" spills coffee on your psychology term paper, or when your neighbor "accidentally" loses control of his 1962 Ford station wagon and demolishes your new Porshe.

The Structure of Personality

Freud believed that the individual's personality was the scene of a never-ending battle; on one hand there are the primitive and unacceptable drives striving for expression, while on the other hand there are the forces trying to deny or disguise these impulses. Freud not only viewed the personality as a battlefield, but he also identified the participants in this battle: the id, the ego, and the superego (see Figure 11–3).

The Id.   What is your concept of a savage? Most of us would describe savages as those who eat when hungry, engage in sexual behavior whenever they desire, attack when angry, and defecate whenever and wherever they please. Freud believed that each of us has a savage quality to our personality. He labeled this part of the personality the **id.** According to Freud, people are born with two instinctual drives that serve as the basic motivation for all behavior. One, called *Eros,* is the drive for survival. Included in this drive are the needs to eat and drink, be warm, and above all, to engage in sexual activity. The energy force that propels the person to satisfy these drives is called **libido.** The second innate drive, *Thanatos,* is a destructive drive. The aim is not only to destroy others; there is also a self-destructive aspect to it. This self-destructive impulse is not only seen in suicide, but in the harmful excesses in which so many people engage, such as drinking alcohol, smoking, and overeating. According to Freud, it is the unconscious desire for self-destruction that motivates people to drive an automobile at dangerously fast speeds; to get drunk at parties, and to smoke cigarettes, which have been proven to be harmful.

The id, like the savage, wants to satisfy these primitive drives in the most direct and immediate way. It is not concerned with reality, logic, or manners. It functions on what Freud called the **pleasure principle,** which dictates the immediate satisfaction of drives. We are not aware of these drives because the id operates at the unconscious level of our personality.

The Ego.   Infants are controlled by the id. They demand pleasure without concern for the situation or the people around them. While each of us may have these primitive desires, it is clear that we could not function long in our social world if we gave free expression to the savage within ourselves. Thus, Freud suggested that at the age of 6 months another dimension of the personality develops. This dimension, which he called the **ego,** works to control the impulses of the id. The ego is the person's view of physical and social reality, and it tries to satisfy the id impulses in a realistic way. In other words, it works on the **reality principle.** Thus, the ego attempts to satisfy the desires of the id by taking into account the possibilities of reward and punishment that exist in the situation. For example, suppose you are very thirsty and see a nice, cold beer sitting on a table in a restaurant. Your id impulses would tell you to grab the beer and drink it. The ego, however, would calculate the possible results of this action, the worst being that the 200-pound man at the table will punch you and the bartender will call the police. Thus, the ego would direct your behavior to order and pay for your own beer. It is important to understand that the ego is only concerned about the consequences of actions; it does not ask such moral questions as "Is this the right thing to do? Is it ethical?"

The job of the ego is a tough one. Sometimes the id impulses come

FIGURE 11-3

Freud divided the personality into three parts—the conscious, preconscious, and unconscious. As shown here, the unconscious is the largest of the three, because Freud believed that much of our behavior is the result of unconscious desires. Personality is also divided into three dimensions—the id, ego, and superego. The id is made up entirely of unconscious motives and impulses, while both the ego and superego are more evenly divided among the conscious, preconscious, and unconscious.

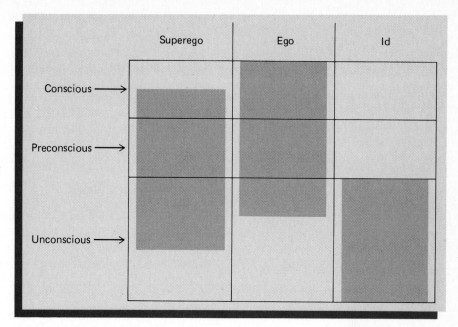

dangerously close to taking control of a person. In these cases the person will feel anxiety, and the ego will have to use defense mechanisms to redirect behavior and protect the person. As we pointed out in Chapter 10, there are a number of these defenses, such as projection, rationalization, reaction formation, and identification. The specific defense mechanism "chosen" by the ego will be a function of the situation and of the person's past experience. And the specific defense mechanisms chosen by the person become a part of his or her personality. For example, you may have a friend who always tries to rationalize when things go wrong.

Before leaving this issue, let us see how we might use the concept of the unconscious and the dynamics of the id and the ego to explain some of Truman's behaviors. Throughout his life, he basically disliked those who were in positions of power. As we pointed out, he did not like wealthy, influential business people and spent much of his life searching for corruption in business organizations. He had few kind words for leaders in the military: "You always have to remember when you're dealing with generals and admirals, most of them, they're wrong a good deal of the time. . . . They're most of them just like horses with blinders on. They can't see beyond the ends of their noses, most of them" (Miller, 1973, p. 220). Truman could list a number of very justifiable reasons for his dislike of military people. If we wanted to psychoanalyze Truman's behavior, we might suggest that his behavior was the result of his unconscious dislike of his father. Taking this line of reasoning, we might argue that Truman had repressed his feelings for his father into his unconscious because he found it unacceptable to hate him. Despite being forced into the unconscious, these feelings "pushed" for expression. As a result, the ego turned the hatred toward figures that stood for his father; military officers served as such figures because they, like fathers, have authority, power, and prestige.

In this application of psychoanalytic theory we see how an unacceptable impulse is expressed in a way that is more easily tolerated by a person. Clearly, this is only an exercise in speculation, but it does show how the theory can be used to explain behavior.

The Superego. We can view the id as operating on the signal "I want it now." The ego answers this demand by saying, "Let's be realistic and get it in a way that won't cause trouble." These two partners, however, must also deal with the superego, which says, "Think. Is it *right* to want it?'' The superego represents our conscience. It includes the moral values of right and wrong that are largely instilled in us by our parents. The superego makes us feel guilty when we have done the wrong thing. As you might imagine, people who are dominated by the superego will be very up-tight and self-conscious; they must constantly ask themselves, ''Is it right to feel or act this way?'' It is also the superego that motivates us to better ourselves and to live up to our ideals. As can be seen in Figure 11–3, the superego operates in both the conscious and unconscious regions of our personalities.

The Emergence of Personality

We have set the stage (unconscious, preconscious, and conscious) and introduced the cast of characters (id, ego, and superego). Now we must turn our attention to the play itself. What determines the specific type of personality that someone will have? Given that each person has a similar personality structure, how do individual *differences* develop? Freud believed that the major ''battles'' of the personality are fought during childhood. Events that occur during childhood mold and form the personality, which then remains basically stable throughout the rest of the person's life. Freud argued that there are certain critical events during childhood; these events occur in a fixed order and in distinct time periods or stages. The important issue at each of these stages is the expression of the libido, or sexual energy. At each stage, the libido seeks an outlet through a different part of the body. According to Freud, if people suffer a traumatic experience or are overprotected in a particular stage, they may become *fixated* at that stage. The personality will then take on the characteristics of the stage in which the fixation occurred. While most of Freud's specific assumptions about the stages of childhood have been criticized (e.g., Byrne and Kelley, 1981), his suggestion that traumatic events in early childhood can influence personality has received some support. Let us, therefore, examine Freud's view of how the personality develops.

Oral Stage. According to Freud, the infant is born with the general desire for physical pleasure, which quickly becomes focused on the mouth region. This is known as the oral stage. The infant satisfies these impulses by eating, sucking, and biting. In addition to satisfying the need for food, these behaviors also are a source of sexual pleasure. At this stage, infants are totally dependent on others to fulfill their needs, parents are usually the primary caretakers.

Fixation at this stage can occur in two ways. On one hand, mothers may overindulge their infants' sucking desire, feeding them on demand and catering to all their wishes. This overindulgence will result in the development of an oral personality characterized by excessive trust, unreasonable optimism, and a strong dependence on others (Blum, 1953). Further, this type of individual will admire strength and leadership, but will not generally take a leadership role (Tribich and Messer, 1974). According to Freud, fixation can also occur at the oral stage if the mother is underindulgent and abruptly weans the infant. The underindulged infant will develop into an aggressive, sadistic person who exploits others for his or her own benefit. Orally fixated people may also orient much of their later life around the mouth. This can be seen in people who always seem to be eating or who smoke a great deal. The oral person may be someone who spends a large amount of time talking (a politician, a professor, a gossip, a lawyer) or singing (a performer).

Anal Stage. During the second and third years, the child enters the anal stage. The main focus of pleasure shifts from the mouth to the anal area. During this period children are faced with the trauma of toilet training. A major battle between the child and parents occurs during this

The oral personality focuses on the mouth. People who always need to have something in their mouth, whether it is food, drink, or a cigarette, are good examples of this.

stage. The parents assert their authority by forcing the child to control his or her bowels. The child, on the other hand, resists this authority and tries to be independent. The child takes a negative attitude toward the parents and is determined to do just the opposite of what the parents want. Two types of anal personalities can result from fixation during this stage. The *anal retentive* is compulsively neat, stingy, and orderly. The *anal expulsive* is rebellious and very messy. Using a psychoanalytic approach, we could argue that Truman showed many of the characteristics of the anal retentive personality. Truman paid careful attention to detail in most areas of his life; he dressed neatly, showed great concern about keeping his home and office perfectly ordered, and followed a well-scheduled routine in his daily life. He was very self-controlled and showed great opposition to being influenced by others.

Phallic Stage. The phallic stage begins at the age of 4. During this stage the child discovers his or her genital organs and delights in masturbation. The trauma of this stage is different for males and females. According to Freud, boys desire a sexual relationship with their mother. This desire, however, is thwarted by the realization that the father already possesses the mother. The little boy becomes fearful that the father will discover his lust and castrate him as punishment. In order to get rid of these fears, the child identifies with and tries to be like his father. This identification with the father helps form the superego, because the child internalizes the father's values. Freud called events occurring to males during the phallic stage the Oedipus complex, since they reminded Freud of the Greek play, *Oedipus Rex*, in which the hero, Oedipus, kills his father and marries his mother.

If you find it difficult to understand the Oedipus complex, Freud's view of the female's conflict during this stage will stretch your powers of imagination even further. According to Freud, during the phallic stage girls discover that they are biologically inferior to males; to their horror, girls find out that they lack a penis. While girls were sexually attracted to their mothers earlier, they now blame her for this "anatomical inferiority." They envy their father's penis and become attracted to him. The little girl now begins to fantasize about having a male baby by her father; in this way she can deliver an individual into the world who possesses the desired penis. Freud delivered the crowning blow by concluding that because females never experience castration anxiety, they must have inadequate superegos and, hence, cannot be as morally strong as males. Some of Freud's followers refer to this situation as the Electra complex after a story in Greek mythology in which Electra induces her brother to kill her mother and feels love for her father.

An inadequate resolution of the Oedipus complex leads to a personality that is reckless and self-assured. The phallic-type male overvalues his penis and seeks to prove that he is a "real man"; he has a constant need to sexually conquer women. This individual is also likely to be vain and boastful. The female who becomes fixated at this stage will develop the "castrating female" syndrome. She will strive for superiority over males and may seek out "typically male professions." The castrating female will delight in criticizing and dominating males. As we will see later in this chapter, the Oedipus and Electra complexes are among the most criticized and least empirically supported of Freud's ideas.

Latency Stage. The latency stage begins during the child's sixth year and lasts until puberty. Freud felt that the individual's personality is generally determined by this time. During this period children lose interest in sex-related activities and focus their energy on other things, such as schoolwork and hobbies. There is also a tendency for children to confine themselves to all-male or all-female groups at this age.

Genital Stage. The genital stage begins at puberty, when sexual tension erupts. If the person has successfully weathered the earlier stages, he or she will seek to marry, raise a family, and join the work force. However, people who have become fixated at one of the earlier stages will have a great deal of difficulty adjusting to puberty.

Psychoanalytic Theory: An Evaluation

When we look at psychoanalytic theory, it is impossible to simply ask, "Is the theory right?" The theory is so broad and covers so many areas that a definite answer cannot be given. Psychoanalytic theory has influenced the study of human behavior. Freud was one of the first to point out the enormous importance of infancy and early childhood in the formation of the personality. Freud's emphasis revived the study of early childhood, and in a very real sense, his work served as a foundation for the emergence of developmental psychology (see Chapters 7 and 8). In our own examination of Truman's life, we can see how his experiences as a child influenced his personality. His poor eyesight forced him to be very close to his mother, and as a result, he acquired typically feminine characteristics. He took on many of his mother's concerns about cleanliness and orderliness and he developed her stubbornness; these traits were characteristic of Truman throughout his life. Freud also pointed out that our behavior can be influenced by motives of which we are unaware. While there is still a great deal of disagreement about how the unconscious works, research has shown that hidden motives can influence us.

While Freud was clearly a major figure in the study of modern psychology, his theory has been criticized on a number of levels. The broadest criticism concerns whether or not Freud's work is really a theory in the scientific sense. It is difficult, if not impossible, to test many parts of psychoanalytic theory. For example, we suggested that Truman's dislike of military officers may have been the manifestation of his unconscious hatred for his father. While this may sound reasonable, how can we prove or disprove it? It is equally reasonable that Truman's dislike of powerful people resulted from the fact that he was bullied or rejected by his stronger peers when he was a child. Another broad criticism was raised by some of Freud's very close followers (Alfred Adler, Carl Jung, and Karen Horney). They argued that Freud overemphasized the role of sex in the development of personality. While guilt and conflict about sexual matters may be an issue that influences the formation of personality, there are many issues that have at least as much, if not more, influence. In the next section we will see some of the other factors that were focused on by these Neo-Freudians.

In addition to the broad criticisms, a number of questions have been raised about specific parts of the psychoanalytic theory. Freud's theory that women are biologically inferior to men and, therefore, doomed to have inadequate superegos was first questioned by Karen Horney (1937). She pointed out that Freud's argument was typical of the male point of view. This researcher argued that women may envy the *status* that society has given men, but not the penis that fate has given them. She also attacked the position that penis envy is the basis for the "castrating female" personality, saying that the drive for power is at least as common in men as it is in women. Cross-cultural research (Malinowski, 1927; Mead, 1928) has produced results that question Freud's idea that the Oedipus complex is universal and based on sexual dynamics. Finally, research has not found strong support for Freud's identification of specific stages of personality development (e.g., Kline, 1972; Rykman, 1979).

Thus, while the psychoanalytic position is creative, radical, and rich in ideas, many of the specific hypotheses of the theory are incorrect.

NEO-FREUDIANS

In 1902 Freud formed the Vienna Psycho-Analytic Society, which consisted of a small group of scholars who met to discuss and advance psychoanalytic theory. However, it was not long before dissension among the members resulted and some of them broke away from the group. Carl Jung disputed Freud's emphasis on the sex instinct and felt Freud was too preoccupied with the abnormal personality. Jung developed his own, very complex theory built partly on the belief that people adopt one of two basic approaches or attitudes toward the world: introversion (a reflective, defensive, and mistrustful approach) or extroversion (an outgoing, socially oriented, adventuresome approach). Jung also took a positive view of people, believing that much of their striving was to reach goals and fulfill themselves.

Karen Horney, another member of the Society, accepted Freud's view on the structure of the personality and his emphasis on the importance of early childhood in personality development. However, as we have pointed out, she rejected the view of women as biologically inferior beings and she questioned Freud's position on instincts. Horney argued that one of the major forces in personality development is the *basic anxiety* experi-

HIGHLIGHT / ORGAN INFERIORITY

An interesting concept developed by Adler was organ inferiority. Adler felt that people who are born with organ defects have feelings of inferiority centering on these deficiencies. He felt that it was likely that they would develop a life style to compensate for these defects.

In fact, the history of sports is filled with athletes who overcame organ inferiorities to become stars. For example, Wilma Rudolph had polio as a child, but she went on to become one of the greatest women runners of all times, winning three gold medals in the 1960 Olympic games. As a young boy, Johnny Weissmuller was frail and sickly. Many childhood diseases sapped him of his strength, and it was feared that if he survived through childhood, he would be bedridden the rest of his life. Weissmuller was determined to prove the doctors wrong. This frail boy went on to set 67 world swimming records and lead the United States team in the 1924 and 1928 Olympics. And this was not the end of the story. After his swimming career Weissmuller became an actor, and, as the first actor to play Tarzan in the movies, he became a universal symbol of health and strength around the world.

At the age of 8, Walt Davis was stricken with infantile paralysis that left both legs and one arm paralyzed. Learning to walk would have been an unbelievable accomplishment for someone with this condition. Davis not only learned to walk, but he became a world class high jumper, winning a gold medal at the 1952 Olympics and setting five world records. After his career as a high jumper, Davis became a professional basketball player.

The list of famous people who

were motivated to overcome organ inferiorities is long. Recently, the newspapers were filled with the heart-rending story of someone whose accomplishments were equally as great as those found in the history books. Terry Fox was a 22-year-old student in Canada when his right leg was amputated below the knee to stop the spread of bone cancer. After a long recuperation period spent learning how to walk with an artificial leg, Terry learned that his cancer was spreading. Rather than waiting to die, he set out to raise money for cancer research. On April 12, 1977, he dipped his artificial leg in the Atlantic Ocean off Newfoundland and began jogging across Canada. For 4½ months he did what he called his "Fox trot," averaging almost 30 miles a day. Terry ran 3,339 miles before lung cancer made him too weak to continue and eventually took his life. His heroic efforts raised 20 million dollars for the Canadian Cancer Society.

Stories such as these make Adler's ideas about organ inferiority seem more believable. It must be remembered, however, that there are countless other cases in which people become overwhelmed by their defect. It remains an interesting research question—why do defects motivate some people to strive for accomplishment and have the opposite effect on others?

enced by young children who find themselves helpless in a bewildering world. Horney also thought that children develop a *basic hostility* that at first comes from resentment of their parents' indifference and interference. The way in which parents structure their children's social and physical environments and help them deal with these "basic" emotions will determine their personalities.

Alfred Adler was another of the early members of the Psycho-Analytic Society and one of the first to break with Freud. While Adler believed in the importance of early childhood, he rejected Freud's pessimistic view of people and his focus on sexual instincts. Adler felt that people direct their lives toward reaching perfection and dominance. These strivings are motivated by *feelings of inferiority* that all people experience to some degree. Early childhood is important because during the first 5 years of life the child identifies personal inferiorities and develops a "life style," or plan for overcoming them. Each person develops a unique life style that makes him or her different from other people. The life style is strongly influenced by the child's interactions with parents and others during the crucial first 5 years.

HUMANISTIC THEORIES

Harry Truman lived during a difficult period in United States history. The country and its people experienced two World Wars, the Korean War, and the Great Depression. It was a time when a person, especially one in politics, had to be tough and fight hard to survive. Truman had these qualities, but biographies of Truman show another side of him; he was also a person who genuinely cared about others and who tried to solve problems in creative ways. During the First World War he showed this concern for his men and their families. A soldier who served with Truman said: "He used to get a lot of letters from the old Irish mothers of the boys in the outfit, and most battery commanders, company commanders, wouldn't pay any attention, but not Harry. I don't think he ever went to bed at night before he answered every one of those letters" (Miller, 1973, p. 97).

The fact that so much of human behavior has a positive, caring overtone led a number of personality theorists, such as Abraham Maslow, Carl Rogers, and Rollo May, to form the humanistic movement, which rejected the position that humans are inherently evil savages who must be controlled by society. Instead, the humanists argued that people are basically good and worthy of respect. Humanistic psychology stresses the creative aspect of people and argues that they are driven by the desire to reach their true potential. Oftentimes, society serves only to force people to act in a conforming, conventional way and inhibits them from reaching their true potential.

The humanists argue that the study of personality should include human virtues: love, humor, creativity, joy, and personal growth (Maslow, 1968). In light of the gloomy outlook projected by psychoanalytic theories, the humanistic approach stands as an optimistic testimony to human personality. Let us briefly examine two of the more widely known humanistic theories of personality.

Abraham Maslow

Abraham Maslow, one of the leaders of the humanist movement, believed that humans have a natural motivation to be creative and reach their highest potential. Maslow argued that people cannot begin to achieve their highest potential until their more basic needs have been met. As we pointed out in Chapter 9, Maslow suggested that human needs are arranged in a hierarchy like the rungs on a ladder. The bottom rungs are the basic or lower-order needs, while the top rungs include the *meta* or growth needs. People must satisfy the lower needs before they can deal with the higher needs. The lowest needs include the basic necessities of life, such as the requirement for food, water, and oxygen. The next level of needs involves the concern for personal safety (the need to be secure and avoid pain). Once these basic needs are satisfied a person can focus on the meta needs, which include the desire to belong to groups and experience love; the wish to be competent and develop a positive self-esteem; and the need to be creative and become self-actualized. The concept of **self-actualization** is a bit fuzzy, but it is conceived of as the process by which people strive to learn, create, and work to the best of their ability.

Maslow believed that to strive for self-actualization is an aspect of human nature. In other words, people have an innate, inborn drive to be good, to be creative, and to grow. Therefore, the role of society should be to create an environment that will encourage these natural tendencies.

If the environmental conditions are right and if people are willing to take the risks to achieve their full potential, personal growth will result. As people move toward self-actualization, they will experience periods of increased insight and feelings of completeness and of being in harmony with their surroundings. These feelings, which Maslow called **peak experiences,** are fleeting moments in people's lives where they feel truly spontaneous and unconcerned with time or other physical constraints. You may have had such a peak experience while walking in a peaceful forest or viewing a beautiful picture; the feeling is one of being totally absorbed in the situation, in the moment, without cares from the past or concern for the future.

Maslow, unlike many personality theorists, felt that research in personality should focus on healthy individuals. He identified a group of historical figures whom he considered self-actualized (Maslow, 1954). Included in his list were Abraham Lincoln, Thomas Jefferson, Eleanor Roosevelt, Ludwig von Beethoven, and Albert Einstein. He later extended his research to college students and concluded that less than 1 percent of all people are truly self-actualized. Thus, the state of self-actualization is one to which we all aspire, but it seems that few of us ever reach it.

Carl Rogers

While Maslow focused on the importance of satisfying needs, Carl Rogers identified another hurdle that had to be overcome before people could reach their full potential. Rogers believed that people had to accept themselves (their feelings and behaviors) first. This may sound simple, but, according to Rogers, most people hide or deny parts of their own personality and behavior. This is because there are rules or norms in society that outline a wide range of behaviors and thoughts that are "permissible." When people do not act "in the right way," they are scorned by those around them. According to Rogers, all of us have a need for *positive regard* from others; that is, we want other people to like and value us. Not only do we try to think and behave in the "correct way," but we also may deny or reject those parts of ourselves that do not conform to the way we think we ought to be.

We develop our self-concept by accepting certain values and behaviors and rejecting others. **Self-concept** consists of our judgments and attitudes about our behavior, ability, and even our appearance; it is our answer to the question, "Who am I?" The self-concept is very important, because it determines how we act and how we perceive our world. Many studies have shown that people with positive self-concepts also tend to be high in achievement (Green et al., 1975). Because our self-image is so vital to the way we behave, it is crucial that it include an honest representation of our feelings, values, and experiences, not just those that society or the people around us find "acceptable." In fact, Rogers believes that people can become self-actualized only to the extent that they can accept all of their personal experiences as part of their self-concept.

Sound complicated? Let's take an example from Truman's life. As a young boy, he enjoyed rather domestic activities, such as reading, cooking, and playing the piano. His father and peers pressured him to engage in more "manly" activities such as sports and farming. These pressures con-

It is important for our self-concept to reflect our own abilities and inclinations rather than just the values and attitudes that others find "acceptable."

flicted with Truman's true feelings and experience and could have made him deny his own desires. Fortunately, Truman did receive support from his mother and some other friends, and he was able to include his love for reading, cooking, and playing the piano in his self-concept.

Truman was fortunate compared to many other people. According to Rogers, many people react to similar pressures by denying parts of their experience in an effort to gain positive regard from others. These people may refuse to accept certain feelings and experiences. They try instead to adopt the values and attitudes of others and, as a result, they lose touch with themselves. They become defensive, depressed, tense, and unable to form close relationships with others. Rogers believed that this damaging situation could be reversed by getting people to recognize and accept a broader range of their own experience.

In order to do this, a different social environment must be created; this environment must include **unconditional positive regard** from others. People must be made to feel accepted and liked regardless of their behavior. This does not mean that one must be told that everything he or she does is "good." Rather, the message must be, "While we may not like that specific behavior or agree with that attitude, we still like and accept *you*." In this way, the person can learn to accept more of his or her experiences as part of the self-concept and can move closer to or begin to work toward self-actualization.

As you can imagine, it is often difficult to shape our everyday environment into one that includes unconditional positive regard. Rogers, however, felt that the therapy sessions could do this. As we will see in Chapter 13, Rogers developed *client-centered therapy*, in which the therapist offers unconditional acceptance of the client. It is important to see how Rogers, like Maslow, believes that, given an open and accepting environment, people will naturally strive for positive personal growth and self-improvement.

Humanistic Theories: An Evaluation

Compared to the gloomy positions taken by other personality theories such as psychoanalytic theory, the humanistic theories are like a bright light on a dark night. In a broad sense, the humanistic concern with people's integrity and uniqueness has influenced research in many areas. Many theories and much research (Wegner and Vallicher, 1980) have been aimed at examining just how people form self-concepts and what influences them in doing this (Wegner and Vallicher, 1980). Since the 1940s, well over 2,000 studies on self-concept have been completed (Bergen, 1971). The humanistic values have been adopted in applied settings such as clinical therapy (client-centered therapy) and in the T-group or encounter group movement, which is aimed at providing environments to aid "personal growth." We will discuss these in detail in Chapter 13.

There have also been criticisms of the humanistic approach. Some investigators have argued that the humanists have failed to clearly define the important terms of their theories. For example, what is self-actualization and how can we measure it (Hall and Lindzey, 1978)? This kind of vagueness makes their theories difficult to test. A second criticism is that the humanistic approach is mostly concerned with human nature. In doing this, it takes such a broad view that it is impossible to make predictions about behavior in specific situations. Finally, Rykman (1979) argues that humanistic theories rely on too few concepts to explain the complexity of human behavior. The theories fail to take into account situational variables that can affect behavior. Thus, while the humanistic position is appealing, more attention must be given to making the theories more testable and more applicable to specific situations and behaviors.

LEARNING THEORIES

While each of the theories we have discussed so far explains behavior in a different way, they all have one point in common: They start from an internal drive or need. In all of them, people are seen as acting because of a motivation arising from inside of them. As we have pointed out, it is difficult if not impossible to measure these internal forces. We are placed in the position of guessing that these internal drives exist because we see the results in the person's behavior. Because we cannot actively "see" or measure such drives, we can never truly prove that they exist. At best, we can argue that people act "as if" these internal states or drives existed. The learning theory approaches to personality were developed to avoid this problem. Learning theorists not only point out these measurement difficulties, but they also argue that we do not need to assume the existence of these "internal forces" to explain behavior and individual differences. They argue that much, if not all, human behavior can be explained by looking at environmental conditions and examining the rewards or punishments the person receives or expects to receive for certain behaviors.

Behaviorism

B. F. Skinner (1953, 1974, 1978) argued that we can explain a wide range of human behavior by examining the rewards and punishments associated with situations. Skinner proposed that people will continue to perform behaviors that are rewarded and avoid performing behaviors that are not rewarded or that are punished. In Chapter 5, we reviewed a number of Skinner's experiments in which he shaped the behavior of pigeons through a carefully controlled reward schedule.

According to Skinner, we do not need to "invent" ambiguous inner forces such as the unconscious, the self, or personal traits to explain why humans behave in certain ways. He believed that we can explain human behavior by looking only at behavior and reinforcement schedules. Skinner argued that the environment determines an individual's behavior, and he rejected the idea that people have "free will" and are masters of their own actions. Individual differences occur in behavior because each of us grew up in a slightly different environment and were rewarded for different behaviors. Taking Skinner's approach, we would not attempt to explain Truman's entry into politics by referring to Truman's unconscious conflict or his desire to be creative; in fact, we would not even describe his behavior as involving choice. Rather, we would examine Truman's environment to see what rewards and punishments were present.

In his book *Walden II*, Skinner (1948) painted the picture of a society based on the principles of behavior modification. Here people's behavior was skillfully manipulated by careful control of rewards and punishments. While Walden II was a fictional society, Skinner's concept of the *token economy* where rewards or tokens are used to shape behavior has been incorporated in therapeutic techniques (see Chapter 13) and in the management of institutions such as prisons and mental hospitals.

As you can see, Skinner's model is a radical departure from most personality theories. According to Skinner's view, a person is little more than a lump of clay in the hands of the environment, which can shape and reshape it by varying rewards and punishments. As you might imagine, Skinner has been strongly criticized by humanists who attack the position that people have no free will. Skinner's description of a society of people totally controlled by rewards and punishments has also pricked the sensitivity of many who view this possibility as dangerous and as having facist overtones.

Social-Learning Theories

Another reaction to Skinner's position is based not on philosophical or moral grounds, but on the concern that the behavioristic approach does not adequately account for human behavior. The **social-learning approach** (Bandura, 1977) does not deny that external rewards and punishments play a role in determining behavior. Rather, it argues that individuals can learn in many ways; trial-and-error learning is just one of them. Further, social-learning theorists point out that we learn more than behaviors; we learn rules, languages, and expectancies. These concepts or cognitions can also influence the way we interpret and behave in situations.

Social-learning theory states that people's personalities develop by imitating models. New behaviors and knowledge are acquired through imitation, and the situation determines when people will perform these behaviors.

In other words, behavior is dependent on both environmental (external) and personal (internal) influences.

Bandura and his colleagues argued that behavior should be seen as two processes, learning and performance (Bandura, 1971, 1977; Bandura and Walters, 1963). We *acquire* knowledge and behavior in many ways— one of the most important is through imitation. We learn by watching other people act and observing the consequences of their actions. We can also imitate behavior that we read about or that has been explained to us. This type of learning is called observational or cognitive learning; it occurs without external reinforcement or without even performing the behavior. The list of behaviors that are learned by observing models is almost endless. One of the behaviors that has received much attention is aggression, as we discussed in Chapter 9.

Does this mean that external reinforcement has only a slight effect on human behavior? Obviously not. According to the social-learning approach, reinforcement may not be necessary for learning, but it does determine the actual *performance* of what has been learned (Bandura, 1969, 1971). For example, you certainly know how to yell loudly. It is, however, unlikely that you will demonstrate your talents during a psychology lecture or church service; you would be punished for yelling in these situations. On the other hand, you would probably yell until you were exhausted if you entered the annual hollerin' contest at Spivy's Corner, North Carolina; your loud yell in this situation could bring you a trophy, fame, and a reward. Bandura (1965) demonstrated this principle under more rigorously controlled conditions. As we discussed in Chapter 9, he had subjects observe an adult model hitting and kicking the Bobo doll. In some conditions the model's behavior was punished, in other conditions it was rewarded, and in a third set of conditions there was no reinforcement. The children were then placed in a room with the Bobo doll and their behavior was observed. The children who had seen the model rewarded acted most aggressively toward the Bobo doll. We might wish to conclude that those children had learned more aggressive behavior than did children who had observed the punished or unrewarded model. This, however, was not the case. When Bandura offered the children rewards for imitating the model's behavior, there was no difference in the aggression displayed by the children who had observed the different models. Therefore, all the children had learned from the model; whether or not they were reinforced determined whether or not they *performed* the behaviors they had learned.

Bandura focused largely on the learning and performance of specific behaviors. Other social-learning theorists, most notably Walter Mischel and Julian Rotter, examined person or internal variables that influence behavior. These person variables, like behaviors, are acquired through the social-learning process and are influenced by the individual's past history of reinforcement. They are stored as cognitions (beliefs, attitudes, assumptions) and they influence the way the individual interprets and responds to situations.

Mischel (1968, 1973, 1977) identified five person variables. These variables are different for each individual and they can account for why people in the same situation may respond differently. Mischel's person variables include the following:

1. *Competencies.* The individual's social skills, task accomplishments, and abilities.
2. *Encoding strategies.* The way the individual categorizes and interprets events and the features of the environment to which the individual attends.
3. *Expectancies.* What the individual expects will happen in different situations and the rewards or punishment he or she will receive for certain behaviors.
4. *Subjective values.* The value or importance the individual attaches to various outcomes.
5. *Self-regulatory systems and plans.* The rules that guide the individual's behavior, his or her goals, and the self-imposed standards for behavior.

Julian Rotter (Rotter and Hochreich, 1975) argued that certain personal characteristics are important in determining behavior. This researcher believed that people learn to expect certain outcomes from their behaviors. The probability that a certain behavior will occur is determined by what the person expects as a reward for that behavior, and what the reward means to the person. Rotter worked with the premise that it is our general expectancies that lead us to act in consistent ways. He has done some interesting work in identifying, measuring, and examining how these expectations affect behavior. (These expectancies are like traits, but they are viewed as *learned*, and thus can be influenced by the environment, unlike the traits we discussed earlier.) Let us briefly examine one of the more widely researched expectancies, locus of control, to see how it can affect our behavior.

Locus of Control. When Truman became president, he placed a sign on his desk that read "The Buck Stops Here." One of his favorite sayings was, "Things don't just happen, you have to *make* them happen" (Ferrell, 1980). Truman was a man of action and he was a man who believed that his actions had consequences. Truman's attitude is characteristic of an internal locus of control position. According to Rotter (1966), individuals learn generalized expectancies to view reinforcing events either as being directly dependent on their own actions or as being beyond their control. In other words, people develop expectancies about the locus of control of reinforcements. At one extreme are *internals* who believe that they control their own fate. Internals feel that they can have an effect on the environment through their actions and they feel responsible for the results of their behavior. To the other extreme are *externals*, who believe that what happens to them is the result of luck and chance; they believe that they can do little to directly influence their own surroundings. Rotter (1966) developed the I-E Scale (see Table 11–1) to measure people's perceptions of locus of control.

Expectancies about locus of control are not inherited, they are learned. One investigator found that internals grew up in families where the parents were warm and supportive and gave praise for accomplishments (Crandall, 1973). This atmosphere encouraged the child to learn to accept blame for failure and praise for success. Crandall also found that as the child grew up, the parents became more detached and encouraged the child to become independent. This withdrawal forced the child to exercise more control over his or her surroundings and gave the child the opportunity to see the behavioral outcomes.

An individual's perception of locus of control not only influences the way he or she interprets situations, it also affects behavior. For example, Seeman and his associates (Seeman, 1963; Seeman and Evans, 1962) found that internals are more likely to seek out information to help them cope with problems than are externals. In one study, the investigators found that internal tuberculosis patients were more likely than external patients to ask their doctor for information about their disease. This finding was expected because internals believe they can influence their own fate; the information should help them decide on behaviors to further their cure. Externals, on the other hand, believe that their fate is out of their control; hence, what good would the information be to them?

Locus of control also influences the attribution one makes about the reasons for success and failure. It was found that internals believed that their failures were due to their own lack of ability or effort (Phares, 1976). Externals, though, felt that their failures were due to task difficulty or bad luck. As a result of these attribution differences, internals felt more shame for their failures than did the externals. These attribution differences extend beyond explaining the individual's own behavior. Phares

TABLE 11–1: Sample Items from Rotter's Internal/External (I-E) Scale

1A. Many of the unhappy things in people's lives are partly due to bad luck.

*1B. People's misfortunes result from the mistakes they make.

2A. No matter how hard you try, some people just don't like you.

*2B. People who can't get others to like them don't understand how to get along with others.

*3A. In the case of the well-prepared student, there is rarely if ever such a thing as an unfair test.

3B. Many times exam questions tend to be so unrelated to course work that studying is really useless.

*4A. Becoming a success is a matter of hard work, luck has little or nothing to do with it.

4B. Getting a good job depends mainly on being in the right place at the right time.

*5A. The average citizen can have an influence in government decisions.

5B. This world is run by the few people in power, and there is not much the little guy can do about it.

---

* These items represent an internal locus of control outlook; the others reflect an external locus of control view.

Source: Rotter (1966), p. 11.

(1976) also found that internals felt that other people are in control of their own outcomes. As a result of this feeling, the internals judged others more severely than did externals and they were more likely to deliver harsh punishment for failures of rule violations.

Learning Theories: An Evaluation

The learning theories have had a great impact on the study of personality. The emphasis on environmental factors has caused researchers to pay more attention to the context in which behavior occurs. The learning approach enabled investigators to explain why there is not a high degree of situational consistency in many behaviors; reinforcement contingencies are not the same across situations and, therefore, behaviors may differ from situation to situation. A second point of impact has been the emphasis on research by learning theorists. Of all the personality theories, those in the learning tradition are most strongly based on research. For the most part, the theories are so built that hypotheses can be developed for testing. Finally, the learning approach represents one more voice for the position that personality develops *throughout* a person's life, not just in the first 5 years. While learning theories show agreement that early childhood is an important time for the formation of personality, these theories argue that personality can be influenced and changed by the experiences one has as one matures—you *can* teach an old dog new tricks.

In a sense, the strengths of the learning approach have also been its weakness. Critics argue that environmental factors have been overemphasized and that learning theorists pay too little attention to individual differences. According to these critics, learning theories don't explain certain consistencies in a person's behavior in many different types of situations. Others argue that in their attempt to deal only with what can be observed (such as behavior and reinforcement) learning theorists have taken too simple a view of the individual. For example, it is difficult to see how learning theory can explain complex behavior patterns such as creativity or innovation. Finally, some critics feel that learning theories are theories of specific behaviors, not of people. In other words, we might be able to explain why a person behaves in a certain way in a certain situation, but we do not get a picture of the person as a whole; we cannot see how all these behaviors "fit together" to make up the total personality.

PERSONALITY THEORIES: A CONCLUDING REMARK

This brief introduction to personality theories may have left your head spinning, wondering which one is right. There is no one theory that explains personality. As we have pointed out, each of the theories has its strengths and weaknesses. The answer to the question of what makes people act differently is found in all the theories together and in none of them on its own. Research is even now going on to define and redefine the theories. Few investigators are willing to adopt one theory and exclude the others.

The human personality is wonderfully complex and the various theories offer different routes to follow in the effort to understand it. Psychoanalytic theory suggests that we can best understand human behavior by identifying internal forces that are set into action during infancy and childhood. Humanistic theories argue that we can understand personality by looking at the "good side" of people and examining how the desire for self-fulfillment guides behavior. Learning theories add that our quest to understand personality must take into account external events; these theories also suggest that personality changes throughout the person's life and that present situations are at least as important as past events in directing behavior. These different theories are guesses about how personality works, and they are also guides that influence the direction of research. For example, an investigator guided by psychoanalytic theory will focus his or her attention on early childhood experiences, while a researcher who adopts learning theory will study external variables that occur in the person's present environment. While the different methods of study uncover different characteristics of the personality, we cannot conclude that one method is more correct than the others; each has a purpose and helps us understand personality.

PERSONALITY ASSESSMENT

We began this chapter asking the question, "What was Harry Truman really like?" How was he different from other people and why was he different? Our discussion of personality theories focused on the *why* issues. We used the various theories to explain why Truman chose to enter politics or why he became a modest, studious individual. We will now turn our attention away from the issue of *why* Truman was the way he was, and focus on identifying what Truman was like.

Personality assessment is the description and measurement of individual characteristics. We all make personality assessments, almost every day. On the first day of class, for example, you might anxiously assess the personality of your professor. Is she a hard person who will be a tough grader, or a rather easygoing, vague type who will grade easily? There are many ways you can make your assessment. You can concentrate on what the professor says: "There will be no curves in my class and I am willing to fail half the class." Or, you can review the professor's behavior; last semester she failed 72 percent of the class. Still a third way of learning about the professor is to see how she interprets some rather ambiguous information about grading at your university or college. For example, what does the professor say on learning that last semester over half the students at the school had an A average? If your professor comments that this is a sign that grading has become too easy, you had better figure on spending many hours in the library. On the other hand, you might breathe a sigh of relief if she says, "We've got bright students at this school and this grade average is a good sign of it."

Each of these methods (looking at behavior, examining verbal or written responses, and studying the interpretations given to ambiguous information) is used to assess personality. The method a researcher will use often depends on the particular theory or approach to personality that he or she holds. Also, just as there are strengths and weaknesses associated with each theory, the different personality tests are blessed with certain strengths and cursed with certain weaknesses.

Before discussing the specific methods of assessment, let us look at some requirements for any test, whether it is measuring personality characteristics or what you learned in class last week.

Requirements of a Test

Any test that measures stable dimensions, whether it be personality or one's college ability, must have two qualities before it can be considered a good test. First, the test must be **reliable**. In other words, it must give similar results each time the individual takes the test. For example, imagine that you took the college entrance examination twice in a 2-month period. The first time you took it, you scored 1200; the second time you scored 650. Since it is unlikely that your ability to do college work changed that much over time, you could rightfully argue that the test was not reliable.

On the other hand, supposed you took the test and scored 640 the first time and 650 the second time. In this case, you could not criticize the test's reliability. However, before you completely give up the goal of becoming a college student, there is another ground on which you could question the test. Granted that the test gives a good (reliable) estimate; but what is the test estimating? Does it really measure one's ability to do well in college? In other words, is the test **valid,** in that it measures what it is designed to measure? One of the most popular ways to determine the validity of a test is to see if it is a good predictor of the behaviors it was designed to test. With the college entrance examination, we could examine the college performance of students who had scored high or low on the test. If we found that the high scorers did better in college than the low scorers, we could argue that our entrance examination was a valid test; it proved to have predictive validity. In the same way, if we designed a personality test to measure aggressiveness, we could determine validity by examining the behaviors of people who had received different scores on the test.

A useful measure of personality must have both reliability and validity. The test must give consistent scores and it must measure what it is designed to measure.

Behavioral Assessment

Since one of the aims of personality tests is to predict behavior, a number of investigators have examined an individual's present behavior to predict future actions, which is known as **behavioral assessment.** Behavioral assessment can also be used to assign traits to individuals. There are a number of techniques of behavioral assessment. One involves observing an individual's behavior in natural settings.

This *natural observation* method has many advantages. It is unobtrusive in the sense that people do not know they are being studied. There is a great deal of research (Orne, 1962) showing that people are likely to change their behavior if they are aware that they are being studied. The natural observation method may also have a high degree of predictive validity because it offers a sample of behavior in a number of real settings.

Despite these important strengths, there are also problems with the natural observation method (Kent and Foster, 1977). First, it takes a great deal of time. In many cases, the researcher may have to observe a single individual for many days in many settings. Second, it may be hard to get a high degree of interjudge reliability. For example, the acts that one judge rates as "friendly" may not be rated the same by another judge. One might categorize a person's behavior as friendly when he or she smiles and says hello to a professor; another person might score this behavior as manipulative.

The Interview

There is an old story about two philosophers who wanted to know how many teeth were in a horse's mouth. These two learned individuals spent days arguing about such issues as how many teeth the horse needed, the optimal arrangement of teeth in the horse's mouth, and the probable

Interviews are used to assess personality. In the unstructured interview, the examiner's questions are influenced by the subjects' responses. In the structured interview, the examiner has a set of predetermined questions that the subject answers.

size of the horse's teeth. In the middle of their heated argument, a small child walked up to the horse, forced its mouth open, and counted the teeth. This solution was so simple that it had not occurred to the two philosophers. We might apply the same type of reasoning to the measurement of personality; if we want to know what people are like, why not ask them? Psychologists do use the "asking" method, in the form of the **interview.** Two main types of interviews have been used.

In the *unstructured interview,* the interviewer has a particular area in which he or she is interested, and the interview begins with some planned questions. However, the later questions and probes are determined by the subject's responses. The unstructured interview is often used in clinical settings or in other situations where the interviewer is interested in getting a broad picture of what the person is like.

In the *structured interview,* the interviewer has specific questions that are asked according to a set plan. This type of interview is aimed at getting specific information from someone. Employers often use this type of interview to get information before hiring someone. Some personality tests are also conducted in the form of structured interviews. For example, Cantril's Self-Anchoring Scale is aimed at assessing an individual's personal and national goals and has been used in many different cultures (Cantril, 1965). The advantage of asking all respondents the same questions is that responses can then be directly compared. In this way, Cantril was able to directly compare the goals of people from different cultures.

The interview is a direct method of obtaining information and is very useful. It does, however, have its drawbacks. In some cases it may have little validity, because respondents are reluctant to present themselves in a bad light. For example, imagine how you might respond if an interviewer asked you to discuss your problems with your sex life. Reliability may also be low, because people's responses can be affected by their feelings about the interviewer. An interviewer who seems cold and critical may get very different responses from those that a warm and understanding interviewer would get. Finally, interviews are very time-consuming.

Generally only one person can be interviewed at a time, and someone must spend time reviewing and scoring the responses.

Thus, assessing personality is not as simple as counting a horse's set of teeth; the most direct method may not always give us the most useful information. However, valuable information can be obtained from an interview. The interview can also be used to make someone feel more at ease before taking some other personality test. Because of this, interviews, like behavioral assessments, are often used along with other tests.

The Questionnaire

In order to get around the time and reliability problems associated with behavioral assessment and interviews, many questionnaire personality tests have been developed. The **questionnaire** involves a standard set of questions; often people respond by indicating their answers on computer forms. The questions are often true/false or multiple choice. The strengths of the questionnaire are: (1) They can be given to groups of people at the same time; (2) all people answer the same questions under the same conditions; and (3) the tests can be scored quickly, in many cases.

There are also some potential problems with this method. The first problem concerns understanding; because people may fill out the questionnaire either alone or in groups, we can't be sure that they understand each question or even interpret the questions in the same way. A second problem is that we can only assume that people answer honestly. In some cases people may be motivated to give the answer that makes them look good or the answer that they feel the examiner wants. It would be difficult for some people to answer "true" to the following question, even if it honestly reflected their feelings: "Sometimes I feel intense hatred toward my mother." The third problem of this test is *response bias*. Some people have a tendency to agree to almost any position presented in almost any question.

With the strengths and weaknesses of personality questionnaires in mind, let us examine one specific example.

Minnesota Multiphasic Personality Inventory (MMPI). One of the most popular personality questionnaires used by clinicians in diagnosis is the **Minnesota Multiphasic Personality Inventory (MMPI)** (Hathaway and McKinley, 1942, 1943). The MMPI was designed to identify specific psychological disorders. Hathaway and McKinley developed the scale by preparing a number of one line statements to which the individual could respond true, false, or cannot say. The items concerned a wide range of issues such as attitudes, past experiences, emotions, and psychological symptoms. For example, the following statements were offered to people: "I tire easily," "I believe there is a God," and "My mother often made me obey even when I thought it was unreasonable." The investigators then presented these items to patients in mental hospitals who had been diagnosed as suffering from specific psychological disorders (e.g., depression, hysteria, paranoia). They also had a control group of nonpatients answer the questions. Their next step was to choose the items that distinguished patients from nonpatients. For example, they would look for an item that most depressed patients answered in the same way, but that was answered differently by the control group. This item would be included in the test as one that could identify depression. Through this procedure, Hathaway and McKinley eventually chose 550 questions to be included in the MMPI. The MMPI has sets of items or scales aimed at identifying 10 different disorders (for example, hysteria, depression, or schizophrenia). The investigators also added some items to determine the validity of responses. For example, the Lie Scale included an item, "I do not always tell the truth." It is, indeed, a rare individual who never tells a falsehood;

HIGHLIGHT / MEASURING SELF-CONCEPT

How do you measure what people think of themselves? Self-concept is one of the basic dimensions of the humanistic theories of personality, and people have tried through the years to develop a test or scale of self-concept.

One way is simply to present people with incomplete sentences, each starting with "I am _____," and see how they respond. The first time this was done, in the 1950s, most responses referred to social status ("I am a student, parent, dancer," etc.). More recently, in the 1970s, most people used traits or other abstract terms to describe themselves ("I am aggressive, shy, outgoing," etc.).

The questionnaire that follows is designed to measure self-concept, but it also asks questions about what people would like to be (their self-ideal). People filling out this questionnaire are asked to give two answers to each question: "I am" and "I would like to be." The answers show not only a positive or negative self-concept, they also show how close to the "ideal" people perceive themselves to be. This in turn can be used to determine people's general level of frustration: The closer they are to their own self-ideal, the less frustrated they are.

	I am a person who:					II I would like to be a person who:				
	very often	often	sometimes	seldom	never	very often	often	sometimes	seldom	never
1. feels he must win an argument.	1	2	3	4	5	1	2	3	4	5
2. plays up to others in order to advance his position.	1	2	3	4	5	1	2	3	4	5
3. refuses to do things because he is not good at them.	1	2	3	4	5	1	2	3	4	5
4. avoids telling the truth to prevent unpleasant consequences.	1	2	3	4	5	1	2	3	4	5
5. tries hard to impress people with his ability.	1	2	3	4	5	1	2	3	4	5
6. does dangerous things for the thrill of it.	1	2	3	4	5	1	2	3	4	5
7. relies on his parents to help make decisions.	1	2	3	4	5	1	2	3	4	5
8. has periods of great restlessness when he must be on the go.	1	2	3	4	5	1	2	3	4	5
9. seeks out others so they can listen to his troubles.	1	2	3	4	5	1	2	3	4	5
10. gets angry when criticized by his friends.	1	2	3	4	5	1	2	3	4	5
11. feels inferior to his friends.	1	2	3	4	5	1	2	3	4	5
12. is afraid to try something new.	1	2	3	4	5	1	2	3	4	5
13. gets confused when working under pressure.	1	2	3	4	5	1	2	3	4	5
14. worries about his health.	1	2	3	4	5	1	2	3	4	5
15. has difficulty in starting to get down to work.	1	2	3	4	5	1	2	3	4	5
16. is dissatisfied with his sex life.	1	2	3	4	5	1	2	3	4	5
17. bluffs to get ahead.	1	2	3	4	5	1	2	3	4	5
18. goes out of his way to avoid an argument.	1	2	3	4	5	1	2	3	4	5
19. makes quick judgments about other people.	1	2	3	4	5	1	2	3	4	5
20. wonders whether parents will approve of his actions.	1	2	3	4	5	1	2	3	4	5
21. is afraid to disagree with another person.	1	2	3	4	5	1	2	3	4	5
22. ignores the feelings of others.	1	2	3	4	5	1	2	3	4	5
23. feels angry when his parents try to tell him what to do.	1	2	3	4	5	1	2	3	4	5
24. likes to gossip about the misfortunes and embarrassments of his friends.	1	2	3	4	5	1	2	3	4	5
25. takes disappointment so keenly that he can't put it out of his mind.	1	2	3	4	5	1	2	3	4	5

thus, a "false" response to this question would cast some doubt on the validity of the individual's responses to other items in the questionnaire.

The MMPI is most effective in separating those suffering from mild disorders from people suffering from more serious personality disturbances. Subscales of the MMPI have also been developed to predict alcohol and drug abuse (Zager and Megargee, 1981). The California Psychological Inventory (CPI) was developed to measure more normal traits: poise and self-assurance, sociability and maturity, achievement and aptitude. The CPI is similar in form to the MMPI; in fact, half of the CPI items are taken from the MMPI.

Projective Tests

As we discussed earlier, Freud believed that people have unconscious drives that motivate their behavior. Some of these drives are very threatening and, consequently, they are repressed or disguised. In fact, people may not be aware of these drives even though they affect their behavior. One of the disguised ways in which these drives are expressed is through projection; people see others as having these forbidden drives and desires. According to this position, we might have difficulty learning about an individual's personality by asking direct questions about his or her personal feelings and desires. However, these unconscious drives will be expressed if we ask the individual questions about others or about ambiguous events. In these cases the individual will *project* these unconscious desires onto the ambiguous and unthreatening stimulus.

This is the reasoning behind projective tests. In these projective measures of personality, the individual is asked to discuss an ambiguous or vague stimulus. The individual's responses are analyzed to determine what they tell about him or her. A big advantage of the projective tests is that there is no right or wrong answer. Thus, it is impossible for the person to give the answer that he or she assumes the examiner wants. And, unlike many of the questionnaires, projective tests can be used with people who do not read or write.

There are, however, problems with the projective tests. First, they are often difficult to interpret or score; the same response may be interpreted differently by different judges. Second, responses to projective tests have not proven to be good predictors of specific behaviors. For example, we might find that certain people have a strong unconscious aggressive drive. However, they may rarely act aggressively. Finally, because most projective tests are given individually, the administering and scoring is very time-consuming.

Despite these problems, projective tests are used by many clinicians to aid them in diagnosis. Let us examine two of the most widely used projective techniques.

Rorschach Inkblot Test. Have you ever become absorbed in watching clouds floating lazily through the sky and suddenly realized that you "saw" pictures in the clouds? In one cloud you might have seen a fat woman sitting on a broken chair, and another cloud showed the perfect outline of a lion attacking a small lamb. While these represent the pictures that you saw in the clouds, another person may see completely different scenes in the same formations. These "pictures" are projections that are being made onto ambiguous stimuli.

Hermann Rorschach, a Swiss psychiatrist, was aware that people "see things" in ambiguous stimuli, and he felt that much could be learned about individual personalities from the things that people "saw." In 1911, Rorschach began showing cards containing inkblots to his patients. He asked them to describe what they saw in the blots. After using many different inkblots for over a decade, he chose the 10 blots that brought

FIGURE 11–4

The Rorschach inkblot test involves subjects stating what they see in ambiguous inkblots. It is assumed that subjects will project their feelings in their responses.

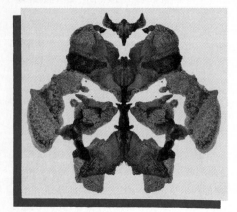

out the most vivid and emotional responses. These blots make up the Rorschach test.

Each blot has a different shape; some are colored and others are black-and-white (Figure 11–4). The blots are printed on cards and presented to subjects in a set order. The individual is asked to describe what he or she "sees" in the blot.

Controversies about the Rorschach test do not so much center on the gathering of responses as they do on the scoring or interpretation of these responses. There are a number of techniques used for scoring the Rorschach test (Holtzman, 1975). However, regardless of the specific method, the scoring focuses on the same general questions. The scorer examines whether the response was concerned with the whole blot or only part of it; the shape, color, and amount of activity present; and the subject of the response (human figure, animal, plant, or inanimate object). In addition to the responses given to the inkblot, the tester notes the individual's behavior while taking the test. Was the individual nervous? Did he or she take a great deal of time studying the blot before responding? As you might imagine, it takes a great deal of training to interpret the Rorschach test. The Rorschach test has been used almost exclusively for the diagnosis of personality and emotional disturbances.

Thematic Apperception Test (TAT). While the Rorschach test was developed to identify psychological disorders, the Thematic Apperception Test (TAT) was originally constructed to identify people's needs and their achievement motivation (see Chapter 9). In the test, the subject is shown a picture of an ambiguous scene (see Figure 11–5) and asked to tell a story about it. The subject is asked to discuss what is happening in the scene, what led up to the situation, what the people in the picture are thinking, and what will happen in the end. The TAT is a projective test because it is assumed that people will reveal their own concerns about achievement in the story. While the TAT was first used to measure achievement motivation, other scoring techniques have been developed to measure such areas as affiliation and personal fears. Variations of the TAT have also been used as research tools in other cultures. As can be seen in

FIGURE 11–5

The Thematic Apperception Test (TAT) is a projective test. Subjects are asked to describe what is happening in the picture. This picture was used in Vietnam to examine the affiliation needs and personal needs of villagers.

Figure 11-5, it may be necessary to redraw the pictures to make them more suitable to the culture being examined.

There has been a great deal of effort put into developing a scoring system for the TAT. As a result, scoring reliability is fairly high. However, the TAT suffers from the same problems of validity found with the Rorschach test; it has proven very difficult to predict specific behaviors from responses on the TAT. Therefore, the TAT, along with most projective tests, is often used as only one of the tools in a whole group of tests aimed at assessing personality.

Choosing an Assessment Technique

As you can see, there are a number of ways to measure an individual's personality. Given this wide range of methods, how do you decide which ones to use? One of the major factors that will determine your decision is the personality theory in which you most strongly believe. For example, if you adopt psychoanalytic theory, you will be interested in measuring unconscious drives that influence people's behavior. Given this approach, you will most likely choose projective tests as the basis for your assessment. However, if you are a learning theorist, you will use behaviorial assessment. As you will recall, learning theories argue against the importance of internal drives; instead they focus on observable events such as behavior. If you adopt the humanistic point of view, one of your main interests will be to identify goals; you will want to learn what type of person the individual desires to be. The most direct way to determine these goals is to ask the person. Therefore, you will use the questionnaire method.

In addition to theoretical considerations, you must also take into account the characteristics of the people who make up your sample. Can they read or write? If they cannot, you will not use a questionnaire.

Clearly there are many factors that will influence your choice of an assessment technique. It should, however, be remembered that in almost all cases, the psychologist will not rely on only one method. Rather, a battery of techniques will be used. This battery will often include an interview, behavioral assessment, and questionnaire or projective test. Just as we pointed out that no single theory can account for the complexity of human personality, no single assessment method can adequately measure personality.

SUMMARY

1. **Personality** is defined as a unique set of behaviors and enduring qualities that influence the way a person adjusts to the environment. The study of personality involves examining individual differences and explaining why people act differently in similar situations.

2. Many personality theories assume that people tend to act the same way in many different situations. Research, however, has shown that situational variables may determine a person's behavior. It therefore seems that personality factors predispose the individual to act in a certain way, but this predisposition may be overridden by situational factors.

3. Some of the earliest theories of personality were type theories, which tried to place people into "either/or" personality categories. A related approach occurs in trait theories, which try to determine the structure of personality by identifying relatively permanent qualities that people may possess.

4. **Psychoanalytic theory** was developed by Sigmund Freud. It focuses on the internal, often unconscious forces that cause people to act in certain ways. Freud described personality as the result of a constant struggle between the **id, ego,** and **superego.** Freud argued that an individual's personality is formed during the first 6 years of life.

5. Neo-Freudians, who accepted much of Freud's psychoanalytic theory, argued that Freud focused too heavily on sex. They suggested other motives, such as power, that influence personality.

6. **Humanistic theories** "look on the bright side" of human behavior. These theories argue that people desire to become **self-actualized** and experience personal growth. Humanists encourage people to learn about and accept themselves rather than trying to live up to standards set by others.

7. Learning theorists argue that outside events determine human behavior. According to learning theories, people act only to obtain rewards and avoid punishment. Their personality is dependent on the rewards available in their environment, and because of this personality is formed and changed throughout people's lives.

8. **Social-learning theory** suggests that people learn new behaviors by **imitating** others. One thing that people can learn is a generalized expectancy to perceive events either as being dependent on their own actions or as out of their control. People with an internal **locus of control** believe they control their own fate; those with an external **locus of control** see their fate as determined by chance.

9. **Personality assessment** is the description and measurement of individual characteristics. While there are many techniques used to assess personality, a good measure must be both reliable and valid.

10. One of the most common assessment techniques is **behavioral assessment.** This method involves observing how people act and determining what their actions indicate about their personality.

11. Both structured and unstructured **interviews** are used to obtain information about an individual's personality.

12. A number of **questionnaires** have been developed to examine specific parts of the personality. For example, the **Minnesota Multiphasic Personality Inventory (MMPI)** includes 550 questions aimed at identifying personality disorders.

13. **Projective tests** are based on the psychoanalytic theory position that unconscious motives influence behavior. These tests attempt to identify these unconscious motives by allowing people to project their feelings onto ambiguous stimuli. For example, the **Rorschach inkblot test** involves having people describe what they see in inkblots. With the **Thematic Apperception Test (TAT),** people tell stories about what is happening in a series of pictures.

14. Most personality assessments involve using many assessment techniques together. However, the main focus of the assessment is often based on the examiner's preference of personality theories and on the characteristics of the subject. For example, an examiner who was strongly influenced by psychoanalytic theory may rely on projective tests, while one who agreed with learning theory would emphasize behavioral assessment.

SUGGESTED READINGS

The following books are about Harry Truman:

DANIELS, J. *The man of Independence.* Philadelphia: Lippincott, 1950.

MILLER, M. *Plain speaking: An oral biography of Harry S. Truman.* New York: Berkley, 1974.

BANDURA, A. *Social learning theory.* Englewood Cliffs, N.J.: Prentice-Hall, 1977. Bandura presents an overview of social-learning theory and applies it to many areas, including the development of personality.

HALL, C. S., and LINDZEY, G. *Theories of personality* (3rd ed.). New York: Wiley, 1978. This book presents a summary of the major theories in personality and some of the important criticisms of each. It is widely used as a reference for personality theories.

MISCHEL, W. *Introduction to personality* (2nd ed.). New York: Holt, Rinehart and Winston, 1976. This text focuses on research and applications in the area of personality. It also discusses the development of personality and the interrelation of personality and environment.

SKINNER, B. F. *Beyond freedom and dignity.* New York: Knopf, 1971. Skinner discusses behaviorism and how it can be applied to many situations.

VERNON, P. *Personality assessment: A critical survey.* New York: Wiley, 1964. This volume presents many of the major methods for assessing personality. It shows how these methods relate to the major theories of personality and examines the merits and problems with the methods.

WOLLHEIM, R. *Sigmund Freud.* New York: Viking Press, 1971. This book discusses Freud's life and psychoanalytic theory.

Abnormal Psychology

DEFINING ABNORMALITY
The Scope of Abnormality / Classifying Psychological Disorders / Insanity: The Legal Label
The Danger of Labeling

APPROACHES TO PSYCHOLOGICAL DISORDERS
The Early Views / The Medical Model / The Psychoanalytic Model / The Learning Model
The Cognitive Model / The Systems Model / Concluding Comment

THE MEDICAL STUDENT SYNDROME

CHILDHOOD DISORDERS
Infantile Autism / Anorexia Nervosa

NEUROTIC BEHAVIOR
Anxiety Disorders
HIGHLIGHT: Case Study of a Generalized Anxiety Disorder
Somatoform Disorders / Dissociative Disorders / Affective Disorders
HIGHLIGHT: Case Study of a Manic Disorder / Psychosexual Disorders

PSYCHOSIS
Schizophrenia / Symptoms of Schizophrenia
HIGHLIGHT: Case Study of Paranoia / Theories of Schizophrenia
Schizophrenia: Normal Adjustment to an Abnormal World?

PERSONALITY DISORDERS
Antisocial Personality

ALCOHOL AND DRUG ADDICTION
Alcoholism / Drug Addiction

SUMMARY / SUGGESTED READINGS

he little man's eyes blazed as he watched the jurors file into the courtroom. Everyone was strangely silent; the longest criminal trial in American history was about to end. The trial had lasted 9½ months, cost over a million dollars, and produced 31,716 pages of transcript. The clerk solemnly accepted the written verdict from the jury foreman. He paused a moment and then read, "We, the jury in the above-entitled action, find the defendant, Charles Manson, guilty of the crime of murder. . . ." It took 38 minutes for the clerk to read all the verdicts; Manson and his three female codefendants were found guilty of murdering seven people, including pregnant actress Sharon Tate. After the clerk finished reading the verdict, Charles Manson, an intense man with piercing eyes, leapt to his feet and shouted at the judge: "We are still not allowed to put on a defense? You won't outlive that, old man!"

The trial had uncovered the gruesome details of how four members of the Manson Family had followed Manson's orders to break into two fashionable Beverly Hills homes and murder all the residents. Five people inside one of the homes were beaten, shot, and slashed to death, and the raiders wrote the word "PIG" on the walls of the house with the blood of their victims. Later the Manson Family members entered the house of a wealthy businessman and slaughtered him and his wife and scrawled the words "Helter Skelter" with the victims' blood. Nothing was taken from either house and the murderers did not know their victims; their sole purpose was to kill whomever they found in the houses.

The trial not only revealed the details of the bizarre and shocking deeds of this band of killers, it also sketched a picture of the man who ordered this senseless slaughter. Charles Manson was born "No Name Maddox" on November 12, 1934; he was the illegitimate son of a 16-year-old girl named Kathleen Maddox (Bugliosi, 1974). According to Manson, his mother was a prostitute, and he was not sure who his father was. His mother, who lived with a number of men, was, however, married to a William Manson for a short time and for this reason Charles was given the name Manson.

Kathleen was not to be tied down by her child; she would leave her young son with a neighbor "for an hour or so" and then disappear for days or weeks. In 1939, Kathleen and her brother were caught robbing a service station and were sentenced to a state penitentiary. Charles went to live with a very strict aunt who thought that all pleasures were sinful, but who gave him love. Three years later Kathleen reclaimed him, and she spent the next few years dragging him from one rundown rooming house to another. At the age of 12, he was placed in an institution for boys because his mother was unable to care for him. The school records indicate that Manson "had a tendency toward moodiness and a persecution complex. . . ." Ten months later he ran away from the institution and began his life of crime.

Over the next 4 years, Manson was arrested eight times for crimes ranging from auto theft to armed robbery. By the age of 16, Manson was a hardened criminal. His behavior was erratic and unpredictable. For example, less than a month before his parole hearing at one institution, he held a razor blade against the throat of another inmate while he raped him. Prison authorities labeled Manson as a dangerous homosexual and he was transferred to the Federal Reformatory at Petersburg, Virginia. Here, Manson's behavior suddenly changed. He took an active interest in the work and educational programs, learning to read and to solve simple arithmetic problems. He was granted parole, but in less than a year he was back in the penitentiary for stealing an automobile. At times he was so depressed that he avoided all social contact; at other times he sought out others and tried to impress them.

Manson spent the next several years in and out of prison. During this time he developed three obsessions. One of these obsessions was with mystical religions; he became an avid reader of literature on different religious philosophies such as Buddhism and Scientology. He was not a believer in these religions; rather, he studied them and used quotes from them to impress others. His second obsession was with music. He learned to play the guitar in prison and he would spend hours each day practicing. His third fascination was with the Beatles, the British singing group that rose to fame in 1964. Manson studied their music, listened to their songs over and over, and tried to find the hidden message in the words of their songs.

On March 21, 1967, Charles Manson was released from prison. He was 32 years old and had spent over 17 years in prison. On his release, he begged prison officials to let him remain in prison. He said that prison was the only home he knew and he was afraid of the outside world.

The authorities refused Manson's request, and, on obtaining his parole, he went to San Francisco. There Manson found free food, music, drugs, and love; in 1967 the hippie movement was at its peak and San Francisco was the center of the flower culture. Manson was fascinated with the whole scene. ". . . I started playing my music and people liked my music and people smiled at me and put their arms around me and hugged me—I didn't know how to act. It just took me away. It grabbed me up, man, that there were people that are real" (Bugliosi, 1974, p. 222). Unfortunately, Manson did not know how to accept the warmth that was offered to him. He did, however, see a way to use the situation. He began playing up to a number of the young women who had "made the scene." Manson charmed these vulnerable flower children with his mystical quotes and soft music. In a very short time, he had 18 followers, all of whom he controlled through the use of drugs, sex, and his almost hypnotic personality. He used the women to lure men into his fold, and the Manson Family was born.

The Family bought an old bus and traveled up and down the West Coast picking up more converts. Manson was overjoyed with his power over the Family, and his thinking and behavior became more and more bizarre. He developed the belief that he had lived before, nearly 2,000 years ago, and that he had died on the cross. He reinforced his belief that he was Jesus Christ by highlighting his name, "Man Son." His obsession with the Beatles grew. He believed that they were angels of God who spoke to him through the words of their songs. He was especially fascinated with the Beatles' *White Album* and with the song "Helter Skelter." He was convinced that the song predicted a black revolution, which "would begin with the black man going into white people's homes and ripping off the white people, physically destroying them, until there was open revolution in the streets. . . . Then the black man would assume white man's karma" (Bugliosi, 1974, p. 331). According to Manson, the blacks would destroy all the whites except for the Manson Family, who would be hiding in the desert and multiplying while the revolution was going on. After the revolution, Manson and his Family, which would then number 144,000, would emerge and assume control over the inferior blacks. Manson's whole life began to revolve around Helter Skelter, the black-white revolution that he had imagined.

He started training the Family for the revolution. One of his favorite tactics was to "creepy-crawly" houses. This involved sneaking into a home while the unsuspecting residents slept, rearranging furniture and other items, and then leaving, all done without waking the residents.

Manson soon decided that he must be the one to start the revolution. Therefore, he ordered his family members to break into two houses on the nights of August 9 and 10, 1969, and murder whoever was in those houses. He further instructed his followers to make the scene look like black people had committed the crime. According to Manson's thinking, this tactic would serve two purposes. First, it would teach black people how to revolt. Second, it would cause the white establishment to turn against the blacks and bring the black-white conflict to a head. Charles Manson believed that he could bring about Helter Skelter, a national racial revolution, by murdering seven in Hollywood.

It was this Charles Manson who sat in court on March 29, 1971, and heard the clerk read, "We, the jury . . . do fix the penalty as death." Because of later changes in the California laws concerning the death penalty, Charles Manson instead remains in a California prison awaiting his next parole hearing.

DEFINING ABNORMALITY

The nation was shocked and outraged by the Manson Family crimes; as the trial went on, people around the country were aghast at details of Manson's behavior. Newspapers described Manson as weird, crazy, and subhuman. This man believed he was Jesus Christ and lived by stealing food out of garbage cans; he believed a British rock group spoke to him through their songs; and while he would go into a rage if one of his followers killed a snake or spider, he thought nothing of ordering them to kill people. Few of us would argue with the statement that Manson's behavior was *abnormal*.

However, while we might be comfortable in labeling Manson's behavior abnormal, there are many other cases where labeling may be more difficult. Let's take some examples:

1. You may know fellow students who stay up studying all night and sleep during the day. Are they normal?
2. And what about a woman who, on giving birth to twins, proceeded to kill one of the infants? Would we consider her abnormal?

Situations like these call into question the way we define **abnormal.**

One of the definitions of "abnormal" in the Random House Dictionary is "not average, typical, or usual." This is a statistical definition, describing as normal what most people do, and as abnormal any deviation from the average. According to this position, Manson's belief that he was Jesus was abnormal, because most people do not hold this belief. College students who sleep during the day and study all night are also abnormal, because most people do not follow this pattern. At first glance, you may accept the statistical definition of abnormality. However, you may begin to feel uneasy when you find yourself having to label Christopher Columbus abnormal because he believed the earth was round when others "knew" that it was flat. The uneasiness may persist when you find that the abnormal "night-owl" students we mentioned are earning straight As. If we use statistics to define normality, then any behavior that is outstanding or different is abnormal—this will be the case even if the behavior is outstandingly good.

Another problem with the statistical definition of abnormality is that it does not take into account cultural differences in behavior. For example, using the statistical standard, we would call the woman who kills one of her infant twins abnormal. However, if we examine the Zhun/twa culture of Zambia, we find that killing a twin is standard practice. It is not done out of cruelty; on the contrary, it has a humanitarian base. Practice has taught Zhun/twa people that there is not enough food to keep both children alive. Hence, rather than run the high risk that both infants will slowly starve to death, one is killed in infancy to increase the chances of survival of the other child. Thus, statistics alone does not offer a satisfying basis for defining abnormality.

Psychologists must consider the consequences of a person's behavior in addition to examining the behavior itself. That is, does the bizarre, unusual behavior cause distress to the individual or those around him or her? Manson's belief that he was Jesus made it difficult for him to fit into society. Because of this belief, Manson felt that he could do no wrong; everything belonged to him and all people should obey him. Thus, his beliefs and his actions were not only unusual, but they caused distress to others and made it difficult for Manson to adjust to his environment. On this basis we can label Manson's beliefs and behavior abnormal. On the other hand, students who study all night seem to have adjusted to the demands of academic life, and their behavior does not bother others. Therefore, their behavior may be unusual, but we would not generally consider it abnormal.

The Scope of Abnormality

Charles Manson's abnormal behavior was reported in newspapers around the world. The sensational abnormal behaviors of others also periodically make the news. However, this is only the tip of the iceberg, and it gives no indication of the amount of mental illness in this country. In one study, the President's Commission on Mental Health (1978) estimated that 25 percent of the population suffers from mild to moderate depression and other emotional disorders. Twenty to thirty million Americans are in need of some type of mental health care; eight million of these are children. There are 200,000 child-abuse cases reported each year, and 500,000 Americans are addicted to heroin. These staggering figures include only the cases that come to the attention of authorities; when we include unreported cases, the actual numbers are likely to be four or five times higher. When we add the income loss of patients receiving mental health care to the salaries of mental health professionals, the annual cost of mental health care can be figured in the tens of billions of dollars (Sarason and Sarason, 1980). Thus, while we may recoil at the acts of a Charles Manson, the scope of behavioral and emotional disorders is so large that it is almost impossible to comprehend.

Classifying Psychological Disorders

The list of Manson's bizarre behaviors is certainly quite long. Included in such a list would be the murders of at least 12 people, which he either ordered or directly participated in; his inability to form close relationships with others; his moodiness and erratic behavior; his belief that he was Jesus; and his obsession with Helter Skelter. If someone were to ask you to describe Charles Manson, it would be inconvenient to recite such a long list of his specific actions. It would be a great deal simpler if you could use a single word or two to classify Manson's behavior; this classification would serve as a shorthand summary of a number of behaviors or traits.

Almost every field of science and even our own everyday language involves classification systems. If someone asks you how you are feeling, it is unlikely that you will reply that you have been sneezing, your nose has been "running," you have a slight fever, and your head feels stuffy. You are more likely to reply that you have a cold. The classification *cold* is a short way to summarize your symptoms.

Modern attempts to classify psychological disorders date back a hundred years to the German psychiatrist, Emil Kraepelin. Although he believed that psychological disorders could be traced to specific organic causes, Kraepelin's focus on symptoms is still used in today's classification systems. The most commonly used system is the **Diagnostic and Statistical Manual (DSM),** which was developed by the American Psychiatric Association. Psychologists and psychiatrists are continually refining the classification system and shaping it to be more in line with current views and research on psychological disorders. The third edition of the manual (DSM III) was published in 1979.

DSM III focuses on describing the symptoms of disorders rather than interpreting them or speculating about their causes. It is unusual in the sense that it does not place people in a single category. Rather, it identifies disorders by using five axes or criteria to classify people's symptoms.

DSM III is a complex and involved classification system. Its complexity is both a curse and a blessing. On the negative side, the system is difficult to use and says little about the *causes* of disorders. On the positive side, because of its complexity, DSM III allows professionals to achieve greater reliability in their diagnosis. One of the major problems with earlier versions of the DSM system was that it was imprecise, and those using it often arrived at different labels for the same patient (Garfield, 1978; Schacht and Nathan, 1977).

Because it is new, the verdict is still out on the value of DSM III. It is likely that it will undergo many changes as practitioners identify its weaknesses. Regardless of the changes in DSM III, it should be remembered that a classification system is only an attempt to arrive at a shorthand method for communicating and keeping records on psychological disorders; it does not dictate the treatment of these disorders.

Another point to keep in mind is that people will often suffer from symptoms associated with a number of disorders. There are few "pure" obsessive compulsives or paranoid schizophrenics. As we examine Charles Manson's behavior, we will see this point very clearly; Manson showed behaviors that could be associated with a number of different disorders. Therefore, people are placed in categories that most nearly represent their symptoms.

Finally, a useful classification can only be made by carefully considering a great deal of information about the individual. In order to arrive at a classification, clinicians and counselors review the individual's life history, examine test results, interview the individual and his or her acquaintances, and consider the individual's environment. It takes a great deal of training and practice to correctly diagnose Charles Manson. We will, however, use his case to illustrate the symptoms associated with various disorders.

Insanity: The Legal Label

The bizarreness of Manson's history and his behavior prompted his lawyers to suggest that he plead not guilty by reason of insanity. Manson was appalled by this suggestion and refused to consider it; such a plea would cause him to lose the blind obedience of his followers in the Manson Family. Others, however, have not been so reluctant to use the plea of not guilty by reason of insanity. Jack Ruby, who killed President Kennedy's assassin, Lee Harvey Oswald, appealed his death sentence on the basis that he could not determine right from wrong at the time of the slaying. John Hinckley, who shot President Reagan and three others as they left the Hilton Hotel, used the insanity defense.

Insanity is a legal term, not a psychological one. It was used in English law as early as the thirteenth century; the prevailing feeling was that a person who was "mad" was not responsible for his or her actions and, therefore, could not be held accountable. In 1843, Daniel M'Naghten, a Scottish woodturner, was found not guilty by reason of insanity of assassinating the secretary to the prime minister of England. The judges stated that M'Naghten "did not know he was doing what was wrong." The *M'Naghten rule* became the legal standard for defining insanity; it argued that an individual must be able to determine right from wrong at the time of the crime before he or she can be judged responsible and therefore guilty.

There have been numerous revisions of the M'Naghten rule. The present standard used in United States courts is the Brawner rule, which states that a person is not responsible for an act committed while, "as a result of a mental disease or defect, he lacks substantial capacity to appreciate the wrongfulness of his conduct or to conform his conduct to the requirements of the law." As you might imagine, it is exceedingly difficult to "prove" insanity, and such court trials often result in a battle between

Insanity is a legal term, not a psychological one. In order to prove insanity, it is necessary to show that the person did not know right from wrong at the time of the crime. Because of the bizarre motives behind John W. Hinckley's assassination attempt on President Reagan, some people believe he was insane. Despite the outcome of the case, insanity is very difficult to prove and rarely used as a defense.

the conflicting testimony of experts (psychologists and psychiatrists). Because of this problem, many judges, including the chief justice of the Supreme Court, have suggested that the insanity ruling should be abolished or drastically restricted.

Thomas Szasz (1970), a psychiatrist, argues for abolition of the rule on other grounds. First, he points out that the label of "mentally ill" or "insane" is a much worse label to pin on someone than the ruling of "guilty" or "not guilty." Further, a person who is judged "insane" under the law can be sentenced to a mental institution until he or she has "recovered sanity." In some cases this sentence keeps a person in the institution for a longer period of time than would result from a prison sentence for the crime. In other cases the person may be kept in the mental hospital only a short time and then set free. Both of these alternatives present dangers to the individual and to society.

The Danger of Labeling

As we have seen, a classification system can be a handy, time-saving device. However, using a label to describe an individual's behavior can also have some rather dire consequences. Imagine that a man who lived down the block was suddenly classified as "violently antisocial." Chances are good that your behavior toward him would change rather dramatically. You would avoid meeting him as much as possible. If you did run into him you would find it awkward to talk to him and look him in the face, and you would probably warn your kids not to play near his house. Everyone else in the neighborhood would react the same way. Naturally he would notice that everyone was treating him differently. He might react with hurt and anger to the new situation, perhaps seeking confrontations with his formerly friendly neighbors. This would play into their and your expectations and would further convince you all that the "violently antisocial" label was correct.

This type of vicious cycle has been labeled the **self-fulfilling prophecy,** a situation in which one's expectations cause to happen what one expects to happen. Researchers have done a series of studies demonstrating how the self-fulfilling prophecy works (Rosenthal, 1973; Rosenthal and Jacobson, 1968). In one study, teachers were led to believe that certain students had scored very well on tests and that they had a great deal of intellectual potential. Actually, these students were selected at random and had no greater potential than other students in the class. However, at the end of the semester when students were retested, the students who had been labeled as having great potential showed greater achievement than the other students. Rosenthal suggests that because teachers believed that certain students had great potential, they devoted more time to them than to other students and they were more likely to reinforce the good performance of this group of students. Even though the teachers were unaware of their changes in behavior, they did create a situation that led to a confirmation of their expectancies and a support of the label. We will come back to this again in Chapter 14.

Another potential problem with labels is that observers may interpret behavior to fit the label. In a controversial study, eight people, including a pediatrician, a psychiatrist, and three psychologists, requested permission to enter psychiatric hospitals (Rosenhan, 1973). Each pseudopatient complained, "I hear voices, unclean voices. I think they say 'empty, howwow, thud.'" The pseudopatients gave false names and occupations to the hospitals as well. They were admitted to the hospitals and, in all cases except one, were given the diagnosis of "schizophrenic."

After being admitted, all the pseudopatients acted normally and stopped faking the symptom of hearing voices. Rosenhan states that, "Despite their public 'show' of sanity, the pseudopatients were never detected." They stayed in the hospital from 7 to 52 days, with the average stay being 19 days. Even when the pseudopatients were discharged, their records carried the label of "schizophrenia in remission." It was difficult for the pseudopatients to overcome their label, and even their normal behavior was interpreted to support it. For example, one pseudopatient took notes of what happened in the hospital during his stay. A nurse noted on this patient's record that "patient engages in writing behavior." Thus, even normal behavior became interpreted as symptomatic.

Rosenhan (1973, 1975) argues that psychologists should avoid labeling their patients. If a label must be used, it should focus only on the specific symptom or symptoms that are shown by the patient. This would reduce the problem of observers "seeing" normal behaviors as supporting a label and it could help in identifying specific problems rather than misidentifying more broadly based disorders. Rosenhan's position has, however, been criticized by a number of investigators. Spitzer (1975, 1976) argues that the fact that Rosenhan's pseudopatients were able to lie their way into the hospital should not invalidate the system of diagnosis. Clinicians do not expect patients to lie about their symptoms, and it is considered important to observe individuals who have the symptoms reported by the pseudopatients. He also points out that the pseudopatients actually had very short hospital stays for people diagnosed as schizophrenic. Therefore, the diagnosis did not interfere with the treatment or the observation of the pseudopatients.

In summary, it seems that labeling can aid communication about psychological disorders and can help in record keeping. It is important, however, to remember the possible negative consequences of a label and to attempt to guard against these problems.

APPROACHES TO PSYCHOLOGICAL DISORDERS

How can we explain Manson's bizarre behavior? What caused his moodiness and erratic behavior? Why was he unable to form close relationships with others? From where did he get the belief that he was Jesus and that the Beatles spoke to him through their songs? And what caused him to plot the gruesome murders of people he didn't even know? Throughout history, people who showed unusual and bizarre behavior and beliefs were regarded with curiosity and a mixture of awe and fear. During the sixteenth century in England, people visited the "insane asylums" to watch the unusual antics and ravings of the patients, much as we visit zoos today to look at the unusual animals. In one such institution, St. Mary of Bethlehem (or Bedlam, as it was called), the public watched plays put on by the patients. The plays were so disorganized and chaotic that the word "bedlam" came to be used to describe confused and disorganized situations.

A large part of this fascination with bizarre behavior results because we have difficulty explaining why people act in this way. Psychological disorders are mysterious and their causes represent intriguing unknowns for many people.

The Early Views

A rather simple explanation for Manson's unusual behavior would be that he was possessed by some supernatural or demonic force. In other words, "the devil made him do it." The view that a supernatural or spiritual force is responsible was one of the earliest explanations for abnormal behavior and it is still held today by some primitive tribes. An interesting feature of the "supernatural explanation" is that some societies believed that the force was godlike and good, while others believed that it was an evil demon. In societies where the spirit was believed to be a good one, the "possessed individual" was given a special position and received good treatment. In some Plains Indian tribes the "touched" person was felt to have special healing powers and he was made the shaman or medicine man. In ancient Greece, girls suffering mental disturbances were taken to the temple at Delphi and consulted before important decisions were made (Zilboorg and Henry, 1941). Their confused rantings were believed to have special meaning, since they had "direct communication with the Gods." If, on the other hand, the people believed that the spirit was evil, the possessed person was subjected to torture to drive out the evil spirit (see Chapter 13).

The Medical Model

When we read of Charles Manson's terrible deeds, few of us are likely to accept the idea that he was possessed by the devil. We may, however, be more willing to conclude that Manson was "sick"; only someone with a sick mind could order those senseless murders and truly believe he was Jesus. If we view Manson as mentally *ill*, we are likely to feel a certain amount of pity for him and believe that he might be "cured." This point of view represents the medical approach, which explains mental disorders in somewhat the same way we explain physical disorders. In fact, even the vocabulary takes on a medical flavor: mental illness, diagnosis, cure, mental hospital.

The medical approach has been accepted by many people. Treatment for psychological disorders often includes drugs, and the search for causes centers on biological and physical bases. There have, however, been many criticisms of this model (Bandura, 1977). In many cases, it has proved impossible to identify an organic or biological cause for disorders. Rather, research has shown that personal and social variables are the root of many disorders. Also, the medical definition of "abnormal" behavior is based on social norms and, as we will see, social norms can change over time (Szasz, 1961, 1970). Finally, Szasz argues that it is demeaning to label someone as "mentally sick"; this label implies a great deal more than simply identifying certain abnormal or unusual behaviors.

The Psychoanalytic Model

It is clear that Manson suffered a rough childhood. His mother lived with one man after another and she would leave young Manson whenever

TABLE 12–1: Approaches to Psychological Disorders

Approach	Critical Period	Importance of Determining Cause	Main Focus
Medical	Past	Very important	Physiological function
Psychoanalytic	Past	Very important	Childhood conflicts
Learning	Present	Not important	Present behavior
Cognitive	Present	Not important	Present behavior and beliefs
Systems	Present	Important	Person's role in social network

she could. The psychoanalytic perspective focuses on early childhood and argues that abnormal behavior is the result of unresolved conflicts that occur during infancy and childhood. As we saw in Chapter 11, Sigmund Freud believed that personality is formed in early childhood as an individual attempts to resolve conflicts concerning aggression and sexual behavior. Freud argued that if these conflicts are not successfully resolved during childhood, the person will repress them into the unconscious and not deal with them. However, these repressed conflicts will influence the person's behavior later in life because they will try to push their way into the person's consciousness. When this happens, the person experiences anxiety and tries to cope by using defense mechanisms such as rationalization, projection, or reaction formation, as we discussed in Chapter 10. However, if these efforts are not successful, the anxiety will increase and the individual will develop *neurotic* patterns of behavior. In some cases, the disturbance caused by these unresolved conflicts may become so great that the person can no longer deal with reality; the person then develops his or her own world and behaves in ways that make it difficult to adjust to the real world. This poor contact with reality is called *psychosis.*

As you might imagine, it has proved very difficult to establish clear evidence that specific abnormal behaviors are the result of childhood conflicts. How could we "prove" that Manson developed antisocial behavior because he experienced conflicting feelings of love and hate for his mother during childhood? While it may be difficult, there are many reports in the scientific literature supporting the position that some cases of abnormal behavior may, indeed, have their roots in early childhood experience.

The Learning Model

According to the medical and psychoanalytic models, we must find the cause of the illness before we can treat it. This follows good medical practice; we would be foolish to continue to treat a persistent headache when that headache could be the signal that something more serious is wrong. While this approach may be effective for medical problems, learning theorists argue that it is not necessarily the best method for treating psychological disorders. The learning model suggests that we learn abnormal behaviors in the same way in which we learn other behaviors. Thus, Manson may have learned his antisocial behavior by imitating people in his environment or by being rewarded for this behavior. If we adopt this position, we will not view abnormal behaviors as a symptom of some underlying disease or deep-rooted conflict. Rather, the abnormality is the product of the individual's learning environment.

The Cognitive Model

The cognitive approach also focuses on people in their present setting. According to this view, people's behavior is strongly influenced by their beliefs and attitudes. The basis for irrational or bizarre behavior is irrational beliefs or attitudes. Therefore, the way to change behavior is first to change the underlying attitudes. Using the cognitive approach we would argue that Manson's belief in Helter Skelter caused him to develop irrational rules for the Family and led to many of his antisocial actions. Further, we would try to change Manson's behavior by first trying to change his beliefs. As you can see, the cognitive approach is similar to the learning approaches in that both deal with the present and both involve retraining. The difference is that while learning approaches work directly with behavior, the cognitive approach works on teaching the person new attitudes or beliefs in order to change his or her behavior.

The Systems Model

Thus far, we have examined theories that explain abnormal behavior by focusing on the individual and his or her weaknesses. This focus gives rise to treatment procedures that also concentrate on the individual. In the last 20 years, a new perspective on mental health has become popular. The systems approach, as represented by community and ecological psychology, regards the individual as part of a social network made up of family members, friends and acquaintances in the community, and various community organizations. The individual plays a role in relation to each of these people and agencies. For most people, the social network supports and maintains their behavior. However, for some people, the social network is filled with stress and conflicting demands, which play a major role in fostering abnormal and maladaptive behavior. Thus, the community-ecological approach suggests that abnormal behavior may be caused as much by a "sick" system as by a "sick" person.

Investigators using this social network approach have pointed out that certain psychological disorders are often associated with certain socioeconomic groups (Kohn, 1972). For example, schizophrenia is most prevalent in lower socioeconomic areas. Hollingshead and Redlich (1958) argue that the stress associated with the substandard housing, high crime rates, and broken families in these low socioeconomic areas cause this high rate of mental illness. Others, however, dispute this position, saying that people who suffer behavior disorders drift downward into the lower class (Dunham, 1965; Levy and Rowitz, 1973). A resolution to this disagreement has still not been reached. However, it does seem reasonable to conclude that additional stress associated with lower economic conditions and certain cultural environments may create maladaptive behavior.

Concluding Comment

As we will see, the types of psychological disorders are many and varied. Anyone searching for quick or simple answers may become frustrated by examining the research and theories of psychological disorders. While medical research on physical illness has a long history, careful research on psychological disorders is a relatively new field of study. Therefore, psychologists do not know many of the answers to questions about the cause of psychological disorders. The present theories serve as guidelines by pointing out ways to examine the disorders and areas where research is needed. It is unlikely that any single model or approach can explain all disorders. More probably, each of the modern perspectives explains certain disorders, and any single maladaptive behavior may have many causes. As we examine the disorders, we will give examples of different explanations that have been advanced as the "roots of abnormality."

THE MEDICAL STUDENT SYNDROME

Before examining specific psychological disorders, there is one additional point that we should address. As the symptoms of the psychological disorders are reviewed, you may find yourself growing increasingly uneasy. The symptoms of some of the disorders will include depression, a difficulty in falling asleep, a loss of appetite, headaches, and sexual dysfunction. As you read these, you may recall that you have periodically felt depressed, suffered headaches, lost your appetite, been unable to sleep, and not functioned sexually according to your expectations. These realizations may cause you to leap to the conclusion, "I've got it!" In a near panic you may decide that you are schizophrenic, or that you have an affective disorder, or that you suffer from a psychosexual disorder.

This "I have it" conclusion is often found among medical students as they study different diseases. They remember times when they felt dizzy and had no appetite, and conclude that they are suffering from cancer, or they recall a time when they had a burning sensation when they urinated and conclude that they have venereal disease. Still other students remember when their heart beat wildly and they were short of breath and decide that they have heart disease. They rush to the emergency room in a state of panic and fearing the worst, only to find out that they are in fine physical shape.

It is important to remember that most of us have displayed some of the states associated with the psychological disorders, just as we have had some of the symptoms of severe medical ailments. However, in most cases, our psychological symptoms are not intense and do not occur with any great frequency. Experiencing symptoms of this kind is normal and does not suggest mental illness or psychological disorder. The symptoms associated with the psychological disorders are generally intense and enduring, and they interfere with people's adjustment to their physical and social worlds. With this thought in mind, let us examine some specific psychological disorders.

CHILDHOOD DISORDERS

Psychologists have identified a wide variety of severe psychological disorders that occur during childhood. While the nature of these disorders varies, they tend to show an interesting pattern: The childhood disorders occur with greatest frequency during two rather distinct age periods (Rutter, 1974). The first period is between 6 months and 3 years of age and the second period is during early adolescence (12–14 years old). These two "high risk" periods are not confined to American children; research in Great Britain, Japan, and the U.S.S.R. also found a strong tendency for childhood disorders to begin during these two periods. While there are many childhood disorders, let us examine two: one that occurs during early childhood and the other that begins during adolescence.

Infantile Autism

In 1943, Leo Kanner, a child psychiatrist, observed that some very young infants seemed to live in a world of their own. These infants were suffering from **infantile autism.** They were placid and showed no interest in social stimulation. They would not hold eye contact with others and showed no reaction to noise or to the speech of others. By the age of 18 months or 2 years, when most children begin increasing their vocabulary and interacting with others, these *autistic* children would not talk and became preoccupied with inanimate objects. They were particularly fascinated with spinning objects and formed attachments to these objects much as normal children form attachments to other people. The autistic child spent hours on end touching objects or engaging in other motor activities such as rocking back and forth. These children developed very rigid schedules and showed strong resistance to change; they refused new foods and new activities. One of the most serious symptoms of this disorder is self-destructive behavior; autistic children will often bang their heads on floors or walls with such force that they suffer severe concussions.

Autistic children live in a world of their own. They are not responsive to other people and they will often spend hours on end engaged in various actions, such as rocking back and forth.

Because of the failure to develop speech, these children often have been diagnosed as mentally retarded. However, it has been found that while autistic children do show retardation on some skills, they do not generally have subnormal intelligence (DeMeyer, 1976).

There are some rather interesting statistics on autism. Autism usually begins during the first year, and certainly by age 3 (Stafford-Clark and Smith, 1978). It is relatively rare, occurring an average of 4.5 per 10,000 children. It is four times as likely to be found in boys as in girls, and it is most common in firstborn children (Stone and Church, 1973). The parents of autistic children are generally in the higher social classes and of above-average intelligence.

The prognosis for autistic children is not good. No specific treatment has been found effective in dealing with autism. Drugs have been used with some success and behavior modification programs have been applied to increase language and social skills. However, the autistic child rarely improves enough to be placed in regular schools. In fact, Stafford-Clark and Smith (1978) report that most autistic children stay in institutions, with only about 10 percent making some social adjustment to life outside the institution.

What could cause such an unfortunate condition in infants? Most current theories (e.g. Lotter, 1974; Ornitz, 1976; Routtenberg, 1968) focus on damage to the central nervous system (see Chapter 2). Organic diseases that can cause damage to the central nervous system have been associated with autism. For example, a child who contacts encephalitis or meningitis during infancy is more likely to become autistic than a child who does not have these diseases. Present research efforts are aimed at identifying exactly what nervous system damage leads to autism and determining how the social environment influences the probability of autism.

Anorexia Nervosa

Anorexia nervosa is a condition in which a person loses his or her appetite, eats little, and slowly "wastes away." Bachrach, Erwin, and Mohr (1965) report a case where their patient's weight fell from 118 to 47 pounds. At first, anorexia was thought to be relatively uncommon, but a recent study found that 1 out of every 200 adolescent females suffers from a severe case of anorexia nervosa (Crisp et al., 1976). The condition is most commonly found in adolescent females, although males in early adolescence make up about 10 percent of the cases. It has been reported that about 15 percent of the cases actually end in death (Van Buskirk, 1977).

Recent investigators have identified two categories of anorexia (Strober, 1981). One type is characterized by reduced food intake; in this case, the person slowly starves by eating very little food. The second type is represented by the person who goes on binge-eating episodes in which she consumes great quantities of food and then vomits what has been eaten.

Anorexics starve because they are unhappy with their physical appearance. Casper and Davis (1977) identified three phases of anorexia. In the first phase, people develop a low self-esteem and an increasing concern for their physical appearance. The second phase is characterized by an intense fear that eating will make them very fat. They adopt a very restricted diet and begin to lose weight. In some cases, they may eat and then stick their finger down their throat to vomit the just eaten food. When hunger pains occur, anorexics exhaust themselves through strenuous exercise. The severe loss of weight is accompanied by constipation, cessation of menstruation, and a slowing of the pulse and respiration. Interestingly enough, no matter how thin they are, they still feel fat. In the third phase, anorexics admit that they have a problem and they increase food intake. However, at the first sign of weight gain, they begin to fear that they will become fat, and the slow starvation process may begin again.

There are many theories about the causes of anorexia. Some focus on the possibility that the cause may be a hormone disorder or a malfunctioning of the hypothalamus. Others (e.g. Minuchin, Rosman, and Baker, 1978) suggest that the problem may be the result of family conflict. Many anorexics report feeling intense pressure from their parents to attain high goals, including standards involving physical appearance. Their cessation of eating may be an attempt to rebel against these demands; they adopt the "I'll show you" attitude.

Other researchers argue that anorexia results as a means of coping with depression and feelings of helplessness (Sugarman et al., 1981). According to this point of view, anorexics attempt to demonstrate control over the environment by showing that they have mastered their own bodies.

NEUROTIC BEHAVIOR

Charles Manson spent a great deal of his life in prison. For most of us, this would be a horrible experience and we would probably do almost anything to keep from going back behind bars. Manson, however, had a somewhat different reaction. Prison gave him some security, which he did not get in the outside world; in prison he lived by a schedule, had a roof over his head, was fed, and had a group of associates (other inmates) with whom he could interact. It was also a world whose rules he understood and could live with. The outside world was filled with conflict and uncertainty. On several occasions, Manson admitted fearing freedom, but he also said he wanted freedom "more than anything." The fear of freedom and conflict about it led him to develop some seemingly bizarre behavior patterns that kept him in prison. He invariably escaped or tried to escape a short time before each of his parole hearings; in most cases he was caught, denied parole, and sent back to prison. When he did win his freedom, he would quickly violate the law—not just any law, but federal laws that carried long prison sentences.

Clearly Manson's bizarre criminal behavior had a purpose. It helped reduce his anxiety about entering the outside world by keeping him in prison. However, it was maladaptive in that it increased his conflict about freedom, and he was forced to experience the anxiety each time a new parole hearing came up. **Neurosis** is the term that has been used to describe maladaptive behaviors aimed at dealing with anxiety and stress. The behaviors are maladaptive because they do not completely succeed in controlling the anxiety and they keep a person from developing more effective ways of reducing the anxiety. They often take the form of exaggerated versions of the normal defenses, which we discussed in Chapter 10.

While the term *neurosis* has been used by psychologists for a number of years, it has proved to be rather vague and confusing in some situations. Because of this, DSM III has dropped the term as a diagnostic category. Instead, DSM III uses separate categories to identify the wide variety of "neurotic disorders." These categories include anxiety, somataform, dissociative, affective, and sexual disorders. We will look at disorders from each of these categories.

Anxiety Disorders

We have all experienced anxiety. Remember how you felt when you were in your first school play, went out on your first date, had an important job interview, or jumped out of an airplane for your first skydiving attempt? You probably had trouble falling asleep the night before each of these events. And as the time for the event approached, you probably felt uneasy, tense, and were afraid to open your mouth for fear that the butterflies in your stomach would escape. While you may not have enjoyed the feeling of anxiety, you probably found a way to control it and were able to complete the task at hand.

Unfortunately, this is not the case for some people. These people experience anxiety that is far out of proportion to situations they are in, and their responses to these anxiety-arousing situations are exaggerated and interfere with normal daily functioning. These characteristics are common to a group of conditions classified as **anxiety disorders.** It has been estimated that 2 to 4 percent of the population suffers from anxiety disorders. As we will see, there are a number of behavior patterns classified as anxiety disorders; the common thread, however, is that each is a maladaptive reaction to excessive anxiety.

Generalized Anxiety Disorder. Charles Manson knew that he feared leaving prison and trying to adjust to the outside world. While we might feel some sympathy for Manson, imagine the plight of the people who suddenly experience overwhelming anxiety but cannot identify its source.

This "free-floating anxiety," (also called a **generalized anxiety disorder**), keeps people in a constant state of agitation and dread. They have trouble falling asleep, suffer a loss of appetite, feel tense and keyed up, and may have increased heart rate and faintness. They will also have trouble concentrating and their work will suffer because of this. At times, this generalized anxiety may turn into panic, at which point victims are overwhelmed by fear; their heart races and shortness of breath results. They may think that they are going to die or that they are going crazy. These panic attacks can last anywhere from a few seconds to many hours. The most disturbing aspect of the generalized anxiety disorder is that those suffering from it cannot identify the cause.

We do not know the reasons why some people suffer anxiety disorders. We do know that they are twice as common in females as in males and that they run in families (Sarason and Sarason, 1980). Research on this last point suggests that people learn to experience these attacks by imitating other family members. On the other hand, psychoanalytic theorists suggest that the cause may be repressed feelings or conflicts that threaten to surface. The anxiety that this causes makes people repress the feelings rather than let them surface, which would force them to deal with these feelings.

Phobia. Phobia occurs when people have an irrational fear of an object or event. The name is derived from Phobos, who was the Greek god of fear, and most phobias have Greek names (see Table 12-3). Phobics know what causes their fear; it is attached to a specific, identifiable object. They can control their anxiety by avoiding that object or situation. While this may seem to be a simple solution to anxiety, many phobias can be very disruptive. For example, people suffering from agoraphobia (fear of open or unfamiliar places) may be so overwhelmed by their fear that they will not leave their home; people who suffer a fear of crowds may be unable to go to parties, the movies, the library, class, an office, or other places where crowds may be found. As can be seen from the representative list in Table 12–2, phobias can involve a wide range of objects. In most cases, phobics recognize the irrationality of their fear, but they are

TABLE 12–2: Familiar and Rare Phobias

Acrophobia	Fear of heights
Agoraphobia	Fear of open spaces
Haphephobia	Fear of touching or being touched
Hematophobia	Fear of blood
Melanophobia	Fear of bees
Ophidiophobia	Fear of snakes
Panophobia	Fear of everything
Phonophobia	Fear of speaking aloud
Scopophobia	Fear of being stared at

FIGURE 12–1

Specific phobias tend to occur at certain ages.

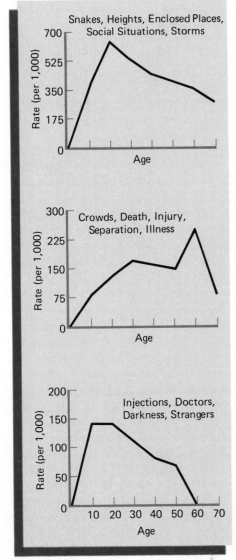

powerless to do anything about it. This realization only makes the phobia more troublesome.

There are some interesting statistics regarding phobias. Women are more likely to suffer phobias than men. For example, it has been estimated that 95 percent of all zoophobics (fear of animals) are women (Davison and Neale, 1978). Phobics tend to be of average or above-average intelligence, and in many cases they show few signs of any disorder outside of the phobia. While phobias occur most often around the age of 50, specific phobias tend to have very distinctive age peaks (see Figure 12–1).

Freud was one of the first psychologists to study phobias. He believed that the phobic object is chosen to symbolize the real source of fear or conflict. For example, a woman may harbor a deep resentment and fear of her father. However, these feelings can be very threatening to her and make her feel guilty. Further, each time she sees her father she is reminded of her resentment. She may, therefore, displace these feelings onto some other object, such as an animal, a color, or a situation that can be avoided more easily. The chosen object may only be remotely associated with the real, feared object. However, she can now control the anxiety by avoiding the new, substitute object.

Other theorists (e.g., Bandura, 1969) believe that phobias, like other behaviors, are learned. Some phobias may result from classical conditioning (see Chapter 5). For example, a boy wakes up one dark, stormy night fearing that his parents have left him. After a frantic search of the house, he finds his parents, but the trauma of the experience leaves the child with a fear of the dark or of lightning. Phobias can also be learned by watching other people showing fear of certain objects or situations (Hygge and Ohman, 1978), or by hearing people express their fear of objects (Bootzin and Max, 1981). Imagine how you might respond to a snake if you grew up in a home environment where the sight of even a garter snake sent your father into a wild panic.

Obsessive-Compulsive Disorders. One of the most bizarre points brought out in Manson's trial was that he had ordered the killing of seven innocent people on the belief that it would start a black revolution. Thoughts of this revolution, which he called Helter Skelter, were never out of Manson's mind. Members of the Manson Family described how he constantly dwelled on Helter Skelter, which would destroy all white people in the United States. Manson planned his whole life around the coming revolution; in short, Manson was obsessed with Helter Skelter. In psychological terms an **obsession** is a recurring, irrational thought that cannot be controlled or banished from one's mind. Some obsessions are quite harmless. For example, you may have had the experience of hearing a catchy tune on the radio that you then hummed for the next few days. No matter where you went or what you did, you couldn't seem to get it out of your mind. While this type of obsession is at worst annoying, other obsessions can cause a great deal of stress. Imagine constantly having thoughts of murdering your brother or being obsessed with the belief that your house is going to burn down. No matter where you go, these troubling thoughts enter your mind. Not only is the content of the thoughts disturbing, but their constant occurrence keeps you from concentrating on anything else. You might realize that the fears are irrational, but no matter what you do, you cannot control them or block them out. These types of obsessions can greatly interfere with people's adjustment to their environment.

A related problem involves **compulsions,** which are irrational behaviors or rituals that people cannot control; people feel a recurring compulsion to perform an act but cannot determine why they feel this desire. Children often become caught up with harmless compulsive actions such as not stepping on the cracks in the sidewalk: "Step on a crack and break your mother's back." Just as is the case with obsessions, many compulsions can seriously intrude on a person's life and make adjustment very difficult. In one of Shakespeare's plays, Lady Macbeth experiences a hand-washing compulsion; she must continuously wash her hands in an effort to wash away the guilt she feels for taking part in a murder. Hand-washing compulsions also occur in real life; Davison and Neale (1978) report the case of a woman who washed her hands over 500 times a day. Another common compulsive behavior involves the desire for neatness and orderliness; people suffering from this compulsion may spend every day cleaning their room and putting things away. No matter how neat and tidy the room is, these people feel compelled to clean it. Obsessive-compulsive behavior not only interferes with people's own life, it also makes life miserable for others who have to associate with them.

This latter point may be one reason why surveys have found that almost half of all people suffering from obsessive-compulsive disorders remain unmarried. It has also been found that obsessive-compulsive behaviors are most commonly found in people of high intelligence and socioeconomic status. Further, unlike many other anxiety reactions, this disorder occurs about equally in men and women.

What could cause people to spend the whole day washing their hands or counting every step they took? Many explanations for obsessive-compulsive disorders are based on psychoanalytic theory. One view is that people try to keep unwanted thoughts or feelings from entering into consciousness by performing compulsive acts or engaging in obsessive thinking. By constantly engaging in such activities, these people do not have the chance to focus on threatening thoughts. It has been suggested that guilt may underlie obsessive-compulsive disorders (Rosen, 1975). People may experience guilt over actions they did or thought about doing; obsessions or compulsive behavior are adopted as a form of self-punishment. The use of repetitive acts as a punishment is similar to a school teacher's favorite punishment of ordering a student to write "I will not talk during a test" 1,000 times on the blackboard.

More recently, cognitive theorists have suggested that irrational anxiety that underlies this disorder may be the result of faulty judgments that people make about objects or situations. They may overestimate the danger in a situation and become obsessed with this danger. Obsessive thoughts may be warnings that people give themselves about the possible dangers in a situation, and compulsive behaviors may be aimed at avoiding these dangers. According to the cognitive approach, treatment of obsessive-compulsive disorders involves restructuring thoughts about a situation or teaching people to control their thoughts.

Somatoform Disorders

Anxiety often leads to the bizarre changes in behavior that we discussed in the previous section. There is, however, another class of disorders in which anxiety affects the person's physical well-being. Most of us have felt sick and experienced stomach problems before an important event such as a final exam or a singing debut. We might look to others for sympathy only to be told that our problem is "psychological." In Chapter 10 we examined psychophysiological disorders, in which a person suffers actual physical damage such as an ulcer or migraine headache as the result of stress and anxiety. There is, however, another group of disorders (**somatoform disorders**) in which people feel ill or show other symptoms such as blindness or paralysis, even though there is no evident organic damage. For example, stress may cause an ulcer; if we examine the person's stomach, we will actually see a hole in the stomach wall. On the other hand, stress may also result in a somatoform disorder such as paralysis of a hand, but close inspection of the hand will show no physical damage. There are a number of types of somatoform disorders, but we will examine two of the most distinctive.

Somatization Disorder. This condition, **somatization disorder,** is characterized by a number of vague but dramatic complaints. People having this disorder may experience headaches, nausea, vomiting, stomach pains, tiredness, and menstrual problems. These people often believe that they are sick; this belief may cause them to feel depressed and threaten suicide. They will make frequent trips to the doctor and may demand surgery even though the physician can find no organic cause for the complaint. The fact that there is no organic problem does not mean that these people do not feel bad; quite the contrary, they do feel sick. Stress may bring on the feeling, but there simply is no physical problem on which the doctor can work. As you might expect, people with somatization disorders have long medical histories, and they prove to be some of the most difficult patients with whom a medical doctor deals. Somatization disorders are more common in women than in men; it has been estimated that almost 1 percent of all women suffer from this disorder to some degree (Sarason and Sarason, 1980).

Conversion Disorder. While the somatization disorder involves a number of vague problems, the **conversion disorder** almost always concerns one specific symptom. The most common symptoms involve paralysis of a limb, loss of sensation in a part of the body, blindness, or deafness. There are some distinct factors that make conversion disorders rather easy to diagnose. First, as with other somatoform disorders, there is no organic damage: A patient may be unable to move her left arm, but there is no physical reason for this immobility. Second, the disorder often appears shortly after some stressful event and has a sudden onset. For example, Malamud (1944) reports the case of a man who became blind after a minor traffic accident that resulted in only a few scratches. Third, the symptoms do not make anatomical sense. For example, people with **glove anesthesia** report losing sensation in a hand although they have normal feelings in the arm (see Figure 12–2). Given the system of nerves in the hand and arm, this symptom would be impossible without loss of sensation in parts of the arm as well. Fourth, and most interestingly, the symptoms (paralysis, deafness, or blindness) disappear when people are asleep or hypnotized. It has also been found that the symptoms may disappear when people are in an emergency situation; "deaf" people will hear the scream "FIRE!" if they are in a burning building. A final symptom that distinguishes conversion disorders from real physical problems is that those who have them often show little concern or anxiety about the disabling symptoms. You can probably imagine your reaction if you suddenly found that you were blind. In the case of Malamud's blind man, the patient responded in a matter-of-fact tone, saying that he would probably be blind for the rest of his life and that his wife should consider divorcing him so he would not be a burden on her.

At this point, you may be thinking that people with conversion disorders are simply faking it. This, however, is not the case. The paralyzed person cannot move the affected limb. With people who have lost sensation in a particular area, it is possible to stick pins in that area without getting a response. Thus, the person truly experiences the symptom and has no control over it and yet there simply is no organic cause for the problem.

There have been many theories about the causes of conversion disorders. Freud believed that the symptoms were people's way of controlling threatening impulses. For example, people who have been taught that masturbation is wrong may develop arm paralysis to control their urges to masturbate. The paralysis solves the problem by making it physically impossible for them to masturbate. Learning theorists argue that conver-

FIGURE 12–2

The symptoms involved in a conversion disorder do not make anatomical sense. On the left is shown the loss of feeling complained of by people with glove anesthesia; on the right is shown the loss of feeling that would occur if there were actual nerve damage.

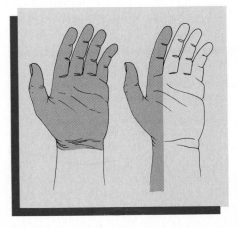

sion disorders are the result of reinforcement patterns. People may find that they can gain attention from others (positive reinforcement) by having these conversion symptoms. Sometimes they receive more direct rewards because of the disorder; for example, escaping family or job pressures, and getting sympathy and attention at the same time.

Dissociative Disorders

An interesting characteristic of Charles Manson's personality came to light during the trial. The district attorney asked Susan Atkins, one of the Family members who took part in the Sharon Tate murder, to describe how Manson reacted after the murder. Susan told how Manson would have periods during which he "tuned out the world" and seemed to forget where he was. He was also very unpredictable, having one personality at one moment and another one a short time later. "Charles Manson changes from second to second. He can be anybody he wants to be. He can put on any face he wants to put on at any given moment" (Bugliosi, 1974, p. 243). **Dissociative disorders** are characterized by "tuning out" or dissociating a part of the person from the situation at hand. It is almost as if part of the person has split off and taken on its own identity.

Most people who suffer dissociative disorders do not have control over the onset of the disorder; the symptoms tend to occur after a stressful period or a traumatic event. The most common explanation for dissociative disorders involves repression of unwanted thoughts or urges. People try to control these threatening urges by psychologically separating the stressed parts of their personality. It is almost as if they tie a number of unwanted thoughts or feelings in a package and store them in some part of their personality. This solution enables them to avoid dealing with these unwanted thoughts or feelings—*most of the time*. However, the price for this solution is that this "package" of unwanted thoughts may suddenly open up and take control. If the unwanted feelings do not actually take control, they may threaten the individual to such an extent that he or she blocks out *all* thoughts, feelings, or memories. Dissociative disorders are quite rare, but they are fascinating to study. Let us briefly examine four types.

Psychogenic Amnesia. A favorite movie theme involves a person who suddenly forgets who he or she is and spends the rest of the movie trying to discover a true identity. **Amnesia** is a selective forgetting of past events. Interestingly enough, memory loss is limited to certain events or areas. For example, a man may forget who he is or where he lives, but remember how to perform acts such as driving an automobile. Some forms of amnesia are caused by physical injuries, such as a blow to the head. However, the term psychogenic indicates that the cause of the memory loss is stress rather than physical injury.

Psychogenic Fugue. On September 13, 1980, a park ranger patroling a wooded area in Birch State Park in Florida found a naked, half-starved young woman lying in the brush. The woman could not remember her name or events about her past. She was also unable to remember how she got to the park. Authorities named her "Jane Doe" and an exhaustive search was launched to discover her true identity. With the help of a drug used as a sedative and hypnosis, Jane Doe began to recall details of her childhood. She had lost her memory and wandered away from her home after having some difficulty with her boyfriend. This is an example of a **fugue** (from the Latin word meaning "to flee"), which involves not only the loss of memory, but also physical flight in which the person wanders away from his or her home. The person may leave for a matter of hours or even for years. Often the person will suddenly "come to" and remember his or her past. What is interesting is that once the person

"Jane Doe" was found naked, filthy, and dehydrated in a Florida park. She did not know who she was or how she had come to the park. After weeks of investigation, it was determined that she suffered from a fugue state.

has "snapped out" of the fugue, he or she will not remember events that occurred during it (Cameron, 1963)—it's like trading one memory loss for another.

Somnambulism. **Somnambulism** means walking in one's sleep. Many of us may talk or walk in our sleep, but somnambulism is viewed as a disorder when it consistently occurs and leads people into embarrassing situations.

Multiple Personalities. Susan Atkins's description of Manson suggests that he often took on different personalities. It is, however, unlikely that Manson suffered from a **multiple personality disorder,** which is quite rare. In this disorder, as we will see at the beginning of the next chapter, a person assumes two or more personalities. Each personality has its complete set of memories, and one is often "unaware" of the existence of the other. When in control, the personality completely dominates the person to the exclusion of the other personalities. A favorite example of the multiple personality is found in the story of Dr. Jekyll and Mr. Hyde. Dr. Jekyll was a good kind doctor who developed a drug that could transform him into the wicked Mr. Hyde.

Affective Disorders

As we have seen, Charles Manson displayed a wide array of unusual behaviors that would lead us to believe he was psychologically disturbed. As a young man Manson showed another symptom that is often the signal of psychological disorders. This symptom involved his mood. At times Manson was depressed and sullen; during these periods he showed an almost pathetic sadness and became withdrawn. At other times, he was happy and became wildly elated. These shifts in mood were noted by his caseworker, who indicated that Manson should receive counseling to deal with these wide shifts in mood.

Affective disorders represent a major category of psychological disorders that involves problems with emotions and moods. While we all have periods when we feel down or up, some people are consumed by their moods and have trouble functioning because of them. It is these people who are classified as suffering from an affective disorder.

Depression. Think about the last time you felt depressed. How did you feel and act? For most people, **depression** causes a loss of interest in many activities, including eating and sex. They cannot concentrate, and falling asleep is difficult. They feel sad, worried, and irritable, and have periods of uncontrollable weeping. They may feel hopeless and begin to wallow in self-pity. In some extreme cases they may wish that they were dead and even plot their own death.

None of this is much fun, but for most of us the depression soon passes and we get back into the swing of things. However, some people are not able to shake feelings of depression. They become consumed with sadness and cannot function. The depression hangs over them like a dark cloud, and it can last for weeks or even months. For most people who suffer from a depressive disorder, their feelings are often the result of a sad event such as the loss of a job, the end of a romance, or the death of someone close to them. For some people, depression occurs without any external event. Feeling depressed after a sad event is normal, and everyone suffers through some depression. However, depression is considered a disorder when it lasts an unusually long time and interferes with the person's functioning. Depression can become so severe that hospitalization is necessary.

Depression is the most common disorder; it has been estimated that 15 percent of all adults may suffer from a depression disorder in any single year, and at any one time 2 to 4 percent of the population has impaired functioning due to depression (Secunda et al., 1973). Depressive disorders tend to reappear; a person who has had one episode has a 50 percent chance of suffering another one at some time in his or her life. While the average length of a depressive episode is about 6 months, many people can suffer depression for periods of 2 years or more (Keller, 1981). There is also evidence that some people may spend their lives in a chronic state of low-level depression; traumatic events increase the depth of depression for these people. At one time it was believed that older people were most likely to have depressive episodes. However, more recent evidence shows that depression is also common among younger people, especially college students. Researchers report that 46 percent of college students will seek professional help during their college career as the result of depression (Beck and Young, 1978). Depression is more common among women than among men; in fact, two-thirds of those who suffer a depression disorder are women.

In addition to the problems of adjustment created by depression, another concern is suicide. People who are depressed often get the feeling that

Suicide is the ninth most common cause of death in the United States. Although women are more likely to attempt suicide, males are more likely to succeed at it.

nothing will ever go right and there is little point in going on with life. As a result of these feelings, they may contemplate suicide. Research has found that the best indication that people will attempt suicide is that they talk about it; few people attempt suicide without first talking about it (Stafford-Clark and Smith, 1978). Interestingly enough, the greatest risk of suicide is not when people are in the grips of a depressive episode. Rather, people are most likely to try to kill themselves when they are pulling out of an episode.

Suicide is a major problem; it is the ninth most common cause of death in the United States (National Center for Health Statistics, 1977). Although women are more likely to attempt suicide than men, males are four times as likely to succeed at it (Frederick, 1978). Suicide is most frequent in adults over 45 years of age, but the rate for younger people, especially college students, is increasing. In fact, the rate for college students is almost 50 percent higher than for the general population. Thus, disorders involving depression have an added risk factor and deserve special attention.

Theories of Depression. One of the earliest explanations of depression was based on *psychoanalytic theory*. According to this theory, people may suffer the loss of a loved one or the loss of self-esteem during childhood, but instead of expressing their natural feelings of grief, sadness, or anger, they inhibit them. Then, later in life, they may suffer a loss that reminds them of the earlier loss; in other words, the recent loss symbolizes the earlier event and brings up those repressed feelings of guilt and sadness. These people now respond to the current event, which may be the death of a pet or the loss of a job, not only with the feelings aroused by it, but also with the repressed feelings that surrounded the childhood loss. In short, they experience a double dose of depression, which is clearly a more extreme reaction than most people would show in their current situation. In an interesting study, researchers found that women who had lost their mothers before the age of 11 were more likely to suffer adult depressive disorders than women who had not experienced such a loss (Brown et al., 1977).

Learning theories identify reinforcement schedules as the cause of depression. Some investigators argue that depression results because people find few positive rewards in their environment (Lewinsohn, 1974; Lewinsohn et al., 1980). Life loses its zip and excitement because they find little to be happy about. As a result, they become sad, irritable, and self-pitying. This depression, by itself, would certainly make them uncomfortable, but it is only the beginning of a vicious cycle. As they become depressed, other people avoid them; few of us enjoy being around people who are sullen and depressed. As friends flock away, they become even more depressed and develop feelings of self-worthlessness. Research has indeed shown that people who are depressed cause others to feel hostile and anxious (Coyne, 1976).

Hammen and Peters (1977) suggest a somewhat different relationship between reinforcement and depression. They argue that the reason that fewer men than women show depressed behavior is that male depression is more negatively reinforced than female depression. That is, a depressed female may receive attention and sympathy, while a depressed male is treated with indifference and the lecture that it is ''unmanly'' to be inactive and sulk. Males, therefore, find other ways to respond to stress and anxiety.

According to learning theory, individuals learn to behave in depressed ways and feel depressed because of their reinforcement schedules. *Cognitive theories*, on the other hand, add one extra step to this process; these theories take the position that people learn negative views of the world and of themselves. It is these negative views that lead to depression.

This position may not seem very different from the traditional learning position, but it has important implications for treatment. According to cognitive theories, treatment for depression should focus on changing people's cognitions or views rather than being aimed directly at changing emotions or behaviors. Aaron Beck (1967, 1978) believes that depression-prone people often set unrealistically high goals for themselves and then blame themselves for their subsequent failure. They also tend to overgeneralize from failures and focus on their negative characteristics. They become overwhelmed with a sense of worthlessness or personal failure and this leads to depression. For example, depression-prone people who receive a D on a very difficult test might react by deciding that they are dumb and don't belong in college. The fact that they have As in all their other courses is overlooked and they begin to review all their "other faults." It is not difficult to see how this approach to life could lead to depression.

Other investigators combine learning and cognitive theories to explain depression (Seligman, 1974, 1975). In Chapter 10, we discussed a study in which dogs were placed in a situation where they could not escape electric shocks (Seligman et al., 1968). The dogs first responded by yelping and trying to find a way out. After a time, however, they "gave up" and no longer sought to escape. Later, when they were put into a situation where escape from the shock was possible, they remained passive and did not try to get away. In the earlier session they learned that their responses could not influence the shock, and this learning generalized to other situations. In short, they learned to be helpless. Seligman suggested that some people also develop a feeling of **learned helplessness,** and this leads to depression. These people feel that they cannot change their environment and they give up. They become passive and inactive; they feel depressed; they develop a feeling of "What's the use of trying if the things I do have no effect on what happens to me?"

This position suggests that people who feel helpless in one situation will feel helpless in many other situations. However, some research suggests that this does not always occur; many people feel helpless in certain situations but not in others (Cole and Coyne, 1977).

Another related question concerns why some people respond to helplessness by blaming themselves and becoming depressed, while others blame the situation and experience only a mild and short-lived twinge of depression. Seligman and his colleagues have modified their theory in order to answer these criticisms (Abramson, Seligman, and Teasdale, 1978). They argue that what people see as being responsible for their helplessness will determine the degree of depression. If they attribute the lack of control to their own lack of ability, a general and deep depression is likely to develop. However, if they feel that their problems are due to the situation they are in, they will experience only mild depression. They will be comforted by the feeling that the helplessness will pass when the situation changes, and their depression will probably be confined to that situation and be short in duration.

While most investigators agree that some types of depression result directly from a combination of stress and learning, there is a growing body of evidence that *biological factors* play a major role. This position is based in part on the finding that depression seems to run in families; people who have a depression disorder are likely to have relatives who have also suffered from depression (Rosenthal, 1970). Recently a number of investigators have uncovered evidence that depression is linked to an unusual structure in the genes (*New York Times* News Service, 1981). This structure is inherited and therefore is likely to be found in many members of certain families. The researchers, however, emphasize that this gene abnormality does not *cause* depression. Rather, it predisposes the person to suffer from this disorder under certain environmental conditions. This finding is exciting because it offers the possibility that doctors can identify and treat depression-prone people before they ever suffer depression.

It is still somewhat of a mystery how the gene structure can make a person prone to depression. A number of theories have focused on the neurotransmitters. In Chapter 2 we discussed how neurons transmit messages. As you will remember, neurons do not touch one another. Rather, there is a very small gap between the end of one neuron and the beginning of another. Electrical impulses are passed between this gap by a chemical substance called a neurotransmitter. Many substances serve as neurotransmitters, but the two associated with depression are *norepinephrine* and *serotonin*. One biological view is that depression is the result of lack of these neurotransmitters (Berger, 1978). Another theory argues that depression is the result of too much sodium, which slows the transmission of nerve impulses (Depue and Evans, 1976). It has been found that exercise reduces the level of sodium in the blood, and some clinicians suggest that jogging and other physical exercise may reduce depression.

Mania and Bipolar Disorders. While depressives seem to drag around and have no interest in becoming involved in any project, people in a state of mania have the opposite problem. Manics are a fountain of energy who feel ready to take on the world; they have very positive self-images. Unfortunately, they often fail to stay with a project until it is completed, jumping from one thing to another. They are easily distracted; in fact, they may begin a sentence and fail to finish it because they begin a sentence on a new topic. People in a manic state often have an increased sex drive and seem to need less sleep than usual. These

HIGHLIGHT / CASE STUDY OF A MANIC DISORDER

As seen on the ward the morning after admission, Mrs. L. J., aged 38, presented a striking picture. She had been too excited to eat breakfast, but after gulping a cup of coffee she had taken several daisies from the centerpiece on the table and entwined them in her hair. She paced briskly up and down the hallways singing snatches of popular songs, and she paused briefly from time to time attempting to get other patients and personnel to join in the singing. . . .

Mrs. J. took the initiative in greeting everyone she encountered, patting the women on the back in a familiar manner and putting her arms around the men. It was, however, almost impossible for personnel to maintain a conversation with her. She responded with smiles and laughter to most remarks addressed to her and often talked volubly, but she

was too distractible to give attention to any one subject for more than a moment. If an effort was made to detain her or to hold her attention, she would break away with a transient flash of anger.

A brief excerpt from the patient's stream of talk was as follows: "How do I feel? I feel with my hands. How do you feel? No, seriously, everything's wonderful. Couldn't be better. Going 'From Bed to Worse,' Benchley said." (Laughs.) "Really, honey, this is a marvelous place you've got here, mar-ve-lous. 'Marvelous *Vel.*' I really must shampoo my hair." . . .

In the course of the diagnostic evaluation and subsequent treatment of Mrs. J., a full background history was obtained, of which two features may be mentioned here. (1) The present illness had begun about ten days prior to admission upon the patient's

having received the information that an ambitious volunteer-service project of which she had been chairman had failed to gain the approval of the community agency on which it depended. (2) Her initial response had been one of low spirits and irritability, lasting two or three days and then giving way to a mood of unusual cheerfulness, accompanied by various erratic activities and gaining in intensity until it reached the reckless and irrational gaiety shown on admission. On the previous day, the patient had stopped at a travel agency where, despite her confusion, she had arranged passage for five on a luxury cruise at a cost which was wildly beyond the family's means.

From C. K. Hofling, *Textbook of Psychiatry for Medical Practice*, 1975, pp. 351–352.

manic periods may last for days or even weeks. Pure cases of mania are relatively rare. In most cases, people suffer from a **bipolar disorder,** which means alternating between manic and depression stages. Interestingly enough, people with this bipolar disorder generally behave normally in the periods between the extreme affective states. In many cases, the extreme mood states appear for only a short time.

Recent research suggests that heredity plays a strong role in the cause of bipolar disorders. Evidence has been discovered linking the bipolar disorders to the X chromosome (Cadoret and Winokur, 1975). As we discussed in Chapter 2, females have two X chromosomes and males have only one. This situation would lead us to expect that more females than males have the bipolar disorder, and that transmission of the disorder must be from an affected mother. Research has generally supported these predictions. It has, however, proved difficult to pinpoint exactly *what* is inherited. Bunney and his colleagues (1972) have suggested that the inherited feature involves a condition at the nerve endings that allows for a build-up of norepinephrine. During the "build-up" phase, little of this neurotransmitter passes between the neurons, causing vulnerability to depression, as we discussed earlier. However, at some point, the level of norepinephrine reaches a certain concentration at which a stressful event causes the neuron to "dump" the neurotransmitter, resulting in a high level of neuron activity and mania.

Psychosexual Disorders

The history of Manson's sexual behavior falls somewhere between an X-rated movie and a horror story. As an adolescent inmate, Manson repeatedly engaged in homosexual behavior—he sometimes found willing partners, but he forced others by threatening them with a knife. Outside prison, Manson engaged in heterosexual behavior, married twice, and fathered two children before he formed the Family. Sex in these relationships was not an intimate union based on love. Instead, Manson used sexual behavior to dominate his partners; in his second marriage, he forced his wife to become a prostitute to support him. Manson continued to use sex to lure young women into the Family. Once a woman joined the Family, Manson insisted that she participate in group sex and engage in sex while pretending to be an animal; Manson felt that these activities would rid her of her middle-class sexual hang-ups (Sanders, 1974).

Should we consider Manson's sexual activities clinically abnormal, or are they simply deviant? The question of normality of sexual behavior is very difficult to answer. We have very little data on current sexual practices. As we pointed out in Chapter 9, it was not until the work of Ellis and Kinsey in the late 1940s that investigators began to collect information on sexual behavior.

A second factor complicating the issue is that social views of "normal" and "abnormal" sexual behavior are constantly changing. This change has also been reflected in the classification of systems. For example, DSM II classified homosexuality as a maladaptive sexual behavior; homosexuality is not even considered a disorder in DSM III. This difference in the two classification systems is largely the result of greater acceptance of homosexuality in today's society as compared to the attitudes that were common just a few years ago.

With these issues in mind, the most common position is that sexual behavior is considered maladaptive only if people are disturbed by their activities or if other people are hurt by them. Admittedly, this definition is not as precise as we might like, but it can serve as a guideline in many cases. The list of psychosexual disorders is long and includes some rather unusual practices. Let us briefly examine some of these disorders.

Gender Identity Disorders. Imagine parents' reaction as their rugged young son strides into the living room sporting a dress and hugging a doll. Equally upsetting to some parents is their little girl who insists on dressing like a cowboy and beating up the little boy next door. We discussed the development of sex roles in Chapters 7 and 8, and pointed out that at a certain age these cross-gender behaviors are indeed normal. In fact, there is now recognition that sex-typing children and forcing rigid sex-role behavior is not advisable. While a rigid view of the role prescribed for one's sex may have undesired consequences, the problems created when people rigidly adopt the role of the opposite sex are even greater. This relatively rare childhood **gender identity disorder** is more often found in males than in females. Boys who suffer this disorder often shun playing with other boys, develop female gestures, and engage solely in female play activities. Girls with a gender disorder join male groups and engage in male play activities. While it is often difficult to distinguish between a gender disorder and a healthy ability to avoid stereotyped sex-role behavior, the gender disorder is characterized by an exclusive or near-exclusive attraction for the opposite sex role.

People who have a gender disorder are likely to be ridiculed and rejected by peers and punished by parents. These responses often lower their self-esteem and create a great deal of unhappiness. There is some disagreement about the cause of the disorder. Some investigators believe that hormone disturbance is responsible for this behavior. Others, however, argue that the root of the problem lies in the family. Boys who develop the disorder often have mothers who smother them with affection and are protective and fathers who are absent or very submissive. In this case, the boy identifies with the mother and begins to model her behaviors. Girls with gender disturbances come from families in which the mother is either absent or cold. Their fathers, on the other hand, are affectionate and serve as their role model. It is likely that future research may show that the disorder results from a combination of hormonal disturbances and family patterns. This would explain why every child who lacks the right role model does not develop a gender disorder. As we have seen, Charles Manson, who from birth did not have a father, did not show signs of gender disorder.

Transsexualism. Gender identity disorders often disappear at an early age. However, in some cases, the disorder persists into adulthood and becomes stronger. In such cases, people progress from wanting to play and dress like members of the opposite sex to actually wanting to be a member of the opposite sex (**transsexualism**). This longing may lead them to seek a sex-change operation that changes their anatomical features to be like those of the desired sex. Transsexuals may also take the necessary legal steps to become members of the opposite sex.

Recent advances in medical surgery techniques have made possible both the male-to-female and female-to-male anatomical changes. Before such an operation is performed, transsexuals are interviewed and given an extensive battery of tests to ensure that they understand the procedure and have made a careful and thoughtful decision to have the operation. These tests and interviews eliminate between 80 to 90 percent of the applicants (*Newsweek*, November 22, 1976). After having been accepted as a candidate for the operation, it is required that they dress and live as members of the opposite sex for at least 2 years. During this time they are given a series of hormone treatments. Males are given hormones that reduce the growth of body hair, round the figure, and cause the breasts to enlarge. Women are given hormones that stimulate the growth of body and facial hair, deepen the voice, and thicken the skin. The male-to-female operation is the more simple of the two. The procedure involves reducing the size of the Adam's apple, removing the testicles, and forming a vagina lined with skin from the penis. Nerve endings in the penile skin are kept, so it is possible for the person to achieve orgasm during intercourse. The female-to-male procedure is a great deal more complicated and may require as many as six separate operations. The procedure involves the removal of the ovaries and uterus and reducing the size of the breasts. In some cases a penis is fashioned out of plastic material, while in others a penis is made from abdominal and thigh skin. These operations have proved so successful that an active sex life is often possible.

Transsexualism is a relatively rare condition, affecting less than 1 out of every 100,000 people. In most cases transsexuals have suffered from a gender disorder as children. The condition persists and they begin experiencing feelings of self-doubt and depression; they "feel" like the member of one gender but have been "born into" the body of the opposite gender. There have been few studies of transsexuals, but there is some evidence that suggests that positive adjustment often follows the sex-change operation (Pierce et al., 1978). Others, however, argue that psychiatric counseling rather than surgery is the best treatment for transsexuals (Restak, 1979). Because of uncertainty about the best way to treat transsexuals, some clinics have stopped performing transsexual operations.

The absence of research on transsexuals makes it difficult to determine the cause of the disorder. Many professionals believe that genetic or hormonal disturbances are at the base of transsexualism. Others, however, argue that learning plays a major role. Research has indicated that male transsexuals often have fathers who are passive and cold and mothers who have strong desires to be male and encourage feminine behavior in their sons. Clearly more research is needed to understand this dramatic and surprising disorder.

Sexual Dysfunctions.   The most common group of sexual disorders falls under the category of sexual dysfunctions. For males, these dysfunctions include **impotence** (inability to have an erection or maintain one long enough for ejaculation), *premature ejaculation*, and *retarded ejaculation* (inability to ejaculate during intercourse). For females, the most common disorders include the inability to achieve orgasm, **dyspareunia** (experiencing of pain during intercourse), and **vaginismus** (involuntary tightening of the vagina so that intercourse is impossible). Most of these dysfunctions are disorders of degree rather than kind. That is, many people have temporary dysfunctions in sexual behavior. For example, it has been estimated that half the male population has experienced periodic impotence, and dysfunctions in both sexes may occur during periods of stress, tiredness, or drunkenness (Kaplan, 1974). While these dysfunctions are troublesome, they quickly pass and there is little reason to be overly concerned about them. Some people, however, experience dysfunctions that last an extended period of time; these problems are distressing and inhibit normal adjustment. In some of cases, the root of the dysfunction may be physiological, such as diabetes or a hormone inbalance. Most of the time, however, the dysfunction has a psychological cause. LoPiccolo (1978) found that many of the psychological roots result from childhood experiences or teaching. For example, a child may be taught that premarital intercourse is evil and morally wrong; this lesson may conflict with the person's present desires and result in impotence. An early sexual trauma, such as being the victim of rape or child molesting, may also interfere with satisfying sexual experiences after a person has reached adulthood.

Masters and Johnson (1970, see Chapter 9) have joined together in a pioneering effort to treat sexual dysfunctions and to help people have fulfilling sexual experiences. They encourage patients to first discuss their feelings and concerns, and then to engage in sexual activities in a nondemanding situation where anxiety about performance will be minimal. While there is some disagreement (Zilbergeld and Evans, 1980) about the exact failure rate of this method, the Masters and Johnson technique has proved very successful in reducing or curing these sexual dysfunctions.

PSYCHOSIS

The disorders that we have previously described involve interference with people's basic adjustment to their world. In most cases people realize that they are acting or feeling "abnormally" and are distressed by this realization. They try to deal with reality and the social world in spite of their disorder.

People suffering from **psychosis,** on the other hand, have lost touch with reality. They no longer attempt to adjust to the world as others see it. Instead they create their own world, different and apart from others, and they respond only to their own reality. When this occurs their bizarre behavior and perceptions severely impair their functioning, and they usually must be hospitalized. In most cases psychotics can no longer care for themselves. In the everyday world, it is the psychotic that we call "crazy," "mad," or a "lunatic."

Some investigators believe that psychosis is simply a severe case of the neurotic disorders that we have previously discussed (Mayer-Gross, Slater, and Roth, 1960). Indeed, some neurotic disorders do have their psychotic counterpart. For example, there is a manic-depressive psychotic disorder in which people become so overwhelmed by their mood that they lose touch with reality, cannot function, and must be hospitalized. There are, however, psychotic disorders, including the most common one, schizophrenia, whose symptoms do not resemble those of the less severe disturbances. Further, many people who suffer from psychosis never show signs of neurotic behavior. These points have led many researchers to conclude that psychosis is really a different type of disorder and not just the extreme end of a continuum going from normal to neurotic to psychotic.

We will examine the most common psychosis, schizophrenia. As we do this, compare this disorder with the others we have discussed and determine for yourself whether psychosis is a distinct category of psychological disturbances.

Schizophrenia

A study of Charles Manson's life reveals bizarreness in almost every aspect of his personality. The most pronounced area involved his thinking. We have already pointed out that Manson believed that he was Jesus Christ and that he felt that the Beatles were angels of God who spoke to him through their songs. Manson also had some unusual perceptions. At times he heard the voice of God giving him instructions to prepare for Helter Skelter. Manson's emotions showed such wide variation that it was impossible to predict how he would act next. During his trial, he would sometimes sit for hours smiling at the most damaging testimony; this calmness might then be shattered by a wild outburst as Manson leapt on top of the table and angrily denounced the court, the witness, and the world. Members of the Family reported how Manson at times would berate them for "killing rattlesnakes, picking flowers, even stepping on a blade of grass" (Bugliosi, 1974).

Many of Manson's bizarre feelings, thoughts, and behaviors are considered symptoms of the psychotic disorder known as schizophrenia. **Schizo-**

phrenia is actually a group of disorders characterized by disorganization in (1) thoughts, (2) perceptions, (3) communication, (4) emotions, and (5) motor activity. Over half the beds in all psychiatric hospitals are occupied by people diagnosed as schizophrenic (Kramer, 1976). It has been estimated that 2 percent of the population will suffer from schizophrenia at some time during their lives. The peak onset period for schizophrenia is between the ages of 25 and 35, and it is most common in people from a lower socioeconomic class. Unlike some of the psychological disorders we have examined, schizophrenia is not a product of our modern stressful society; there is evidence that it has occurred throughout history, and today it is found in simple primitive societies as well as in more modern industrial countries.

Schizophrenia is a complex disorder that is characterized by a wide variety of symptoms and types. Table 12–3 on page 413 gives a summary of the most common subtypes and the most common symptoms of each. People may show all or only a few of the symptoms. Whatever the array of symptoms or the subtype of disorder, schizophrenia is a disabling condition that often requires long periods of hospitalization. Let us briefly examine some of the most common symptoms.

Symptoms of Schizophrenia

Disorganization of Thought. One of the most common symptoms of schizophrenia is **delusions**, irrational beliefs that are held in spite of the existence of contrary evidence. In other words, these beliefs have no base in reality. There are many types of delusions. One is the *delusion of grandure*, which is the belief that the person is special or different from other people. Manson's belief that he was Jesus and his view that the Beatles sent special messages to him through their music are examples of delusions of grandeur. Those with *delusions of persecution* believe that people are "out to get" them and that such people are controlling their thoughts or behaviors. Examples of this type of delusion can be seen in Manson's belief that all blacks were plotting a revolt and that society itself was against Manson. At one of his court appearances, Manson passionately spoke of this persecution: ". . . I have done my best to get

HIGHLIGHT / CASE STUDY OF PARANOIA

A prosperous builder aged forty-four was refused a very substantial overdraft from a local bank against the collateral of his firm and property. This was his first serious business reverse in sixteen years of independent building; and he became morose and disturbed about it.

After some months he suddenly expressed the conviction that people were talking about him because the loan had been refused; and that the basis of its refusal was the fact that the Bank Manager believed that he had syphilis, and had passed it on to his wife and children. He then went about demanding legal action against the Bank Manager, and various other people, and accusing his General Practitioner of having falsified and then published medical reports about him. He was admitted to the hospital, having refused to see any doctors, after a suicidal attempt in which he had tried to hang himself; leaving a note saying that no one man could stand up to the devilish and calculated campaign of mind reading, calumny, and persecution to which he had been submitted.

During the course of treatment in the hospital he disclosed that his mind was still being read by an electronic machine, in which his thoughts were transcribed into a formula for a new and more terrible atomic bomb. He made a partial remission in response to treatment, and returned to take control of his firm and property; seen for outpatient follow-up and assessment he remains deluded, but can discuss and accept support and re-assurance about his general predicament while remaining a competent builder and manager of his business.

From D. Stafford-Clark, and A. C. Smith, *Psychiatry for Students,* 5th ed.

along in your world and now you want to kill me, and I look at you, and then I say to myself, You want to kill me? Ha!" (Bugliosi, 1974, p. 526). People with delusions of persecution are called **paranoid;** they are mistrusting of others and interpret their actions as plotting.

Disorganization of Perception.   When you look at a tree, what do you see? Probably you see some green leaves clinging to some branches and a large trunk supporting this structure. This is the way most us view a tree. Now imagine looking at that tree in much greater detail. You look at every leaf. Is the leaf dark green or light green? You look at each branch. Is the branch thick or thin, long or short, bent or straight, brown or grey? Now you examine the trunk closely. At this point you might be throwing up your hands, exclaiming that this is "crazy"! At this rate you could spend the whole afternoon looking at just one tree, and regardless of the time involved, there is no reason to examine every tree with such care. Of course you are correct on both counts. However, this is an example of the perceptual process used by some schizophrenics. They become engrossed in minute details and are unable to block out irrelevant stimuli. They can spend hours looking at a simple object. They may pay this same deep attention to noises. They hear each and every noise in their environment. When someone talks, the schizophrenic notices each change in pitch and tone. The schizophrenic may become engrossed in his or her own body, listening to each heart beat and feeling each surge of blood through the veins. In each of these cases, the schizophrenic pays attention to the smallest detail of stimuli or events without trying to organize them into larger, meaningful wholes.

Another perceptual phenomenon experienced by some schizophrenics is **hallucination,** which, as we discussed in Chapter 3, involves having

Hallucinations are often associated with schizophrenia. These are paintings done by schizophrenics showing their hallucinations.

a sensory experience without the external stimuli. Hallucinations can involve vision, hearing, taste, touch, or smell. The most common types are auditory; people "hear" voices that are not there. Many times the voices accuse these people of doing or thinking bad things. Manson stated that God actually talked to him in the desert. Visual hallucinations can involve seeing people, even those who died many years earlier, or seeing monsters that have come to punish the person. Clearly, the perceptions of the schizophrenic are strange and troubled.

Disturbances in Communication. Talking to a schizophrenic is often like communicating with someone who is talking in his or her sleep. The schizophrenic talks in a dreamy tone of voice and does not seem to be paying attention to anything anyone says. For example, if you asked a schizophrenic how he or she is feeling, you might get the following response.

> Yesterday I was *fine*. The *fine* head of a pin can fit into a very small *hole*. The *whole* group of birds landed in the field and ate corn.

In this case, the schizophrenic's speech follows no train of thought. Instead, each sentence follows from an association with a word in the previous sentence. The schizophrenic may also show completely irrelevant replies to questions or may launch into a highly intellectual and complex reply to a very simple question. In this case, the schizophrenic, when asked how he is feeling, may discuss the distinction between being physically healthy and feeling well. Needless to say, communication with a schizophrenic is often difficult and forces people to stretch their imagination.

Inappropriate Emotions. Schizophrenics may giggle and laugh when talking about the death of a close friend or relative. On the other hand, they may sob uncontrollably when talking about matter-of-fact issues. Overall, it is difficult to predict what emotions they will show, because their feelings seem to have little connection with the situation or what is happening to them. Another rather common emotional pattern of schizophrenics is apathy. No matter what is happening, they show almost no emotion or feeling. In some cases, they might not even move when pricked with a sharp object or when burned.

Unusual Motor Activities. There is a wide variety of unusual motor activities associated with schizophrenia. In some cases, people may move in slow motion, as if every movement is achieved only with the greatest effort. They may slowly move their head and stare around the room with an almost vacant glance. In the most extreme instances, they may spend hours without moving. If they move their arms, they let them remain in the new position; it is like molding wax, since schizophrenics exercise no control over how their body is manipulated. In other cases, they may repeat the same motor activity for hours on end. For example, in one reported case a schizophrenic spent 4 hours touching first the end of her nose and then touching her ear. Whatever the particular motor activity, the major characteristic is that it has no connection with the physical reality of the situation and is not aimed at achieving any identifiable goal.

Theories of Schizophrenia

Schizophrenia is one of the most studied of all the psychological disorders. There are many reasons for this. The first is the seriousness of the disorder; it is one of the most severe disorders and it is therefore important to understand it. Second, schizophrenia is a very widespread disorder. As we pointed out, it is found in almost every culture and is the most common disorder of patients hospitalized for a mental disorder. Despite the large amount of research, we will see that investigators have not reached agreement as to the cause of schizophrenia. There are many

TABLE 12–3: Major Types of Schizophrenia

Type	Description
1. Disorganized (Hebephrenic)	This type is characterized by many delusions, hallucinations, and inappropriate emotions. People may laugh and giggle for no apparent reason. They become childlike, urinate and defecate on the floor, and refuse to wear clothing.
2. Catatonic	The major characteristic of this type is disturbance of motor activity. People may remain in one position for long periods of time without moving, their body almost waxy; if someone moves them, they will remain in the new position. In agitated cases, they will show wild, constant movement, often becoming violent and destructive.
3. Paranoid	The major problem in this type is cognitions or thoughts. People believe that others are trying to destroy or control them (delusions of persecution), and they trust no one. They will not let others get close to them for fear that these others will harm them. In some cases, there may be delusions of grandeur, in which people believe that they are a famous person or powerful figure who controls the world. These people may have difficulty functioning because they are concentrating on the "sinister" acts of others.
4. Undifferentiated	This type involves delusions, hallucinations, and disorganized emotions. This is really a "catchall" category for cases that are characterized by extreme disorganization but do not fit any of the other types.

theories about its cause; it is likely, in fact, that there are many causes of schizophrenia.

Biological Theories. The story of attempts to show a biological cause of schizophrenia reads much like a Sherlock Holmes mystery. When we talk about biological cause, we focus on the issue of inheritance. Each of us has many clearly visible traits that we have inherited from our parents. For example, your blue eyes, curly hair, bushy eyebrows, large chest, and bony knees are features you received through a combination of your parents' genes. In these cases it is rather easy to show the relation of these features to your parents and to show that these features are not the result of the environment. It is unlikely that your eyes turned blue because you moved to Texas as an infant or that your hair became curly because you spent many cold winters in Kansas. But how can we prove that a psychological disorder like schizophrenia is inherited in the same way as these physical features?

Some evidence for a biological cause comes from studies of identical twins. Identical twins have the same genetic makeup, so we would expect to see schizophrenia in both twins if one developed the disorder. In fact, research has found that if one twin has schizophrenia, the other twin has almost a 60 percent chance of developing the disorder (Ban, 1973; Gottesman and Shields, 1972). While this may be strong evidence, we might argue again that not only do these twins have identical genetic structure, but they also grew up in similar or very similar environments. Thus, learning and other environmental factors could still be responsible for the disorder.

In a further effort to counter this environmental argument, investigators examined the development of schizophrenia in people who were born to schizophrenic parents but were adopted as infants by nonschizophrenic parents (Kety et al., 1968; Rosenthal, 1973). Such studies found that these people are more likely to develop schizophrenia than adoptive children who did not have schizophrenic parents. Taken together, these studies suggest that genetic factors can be *one* cause of schizophrenia. We must emphasize that genetics can only be one of the causes, since schizophrenia does not always occur in both twins of an identical pair when one has schizophrenia, and not all, or even most, of the adopted children whose natural parents were schizophrenic develop the disorder.

Given that schizophrenia can be inherited, our next question concerns how the disorder is passed on. More directly, what does the defective gene do to people that causes them to develop schizophrenia? One study focuses on a neurotransmitter called *dopamine* (Davis, 1974). This research suggests that schizophrenics have too much dopamine and that this dopamine overstimulates the brain, causing schizophrenic behavior (Paul, 1977). Another set of theories focuses on chemicals in the blood. Early research produced some excitement by showing that tadpoles died when placed in the blood serum of schizophrenics (Lazell and Prince, 1929) and that spiders injected with a schizophrenic's blood built inadequate and bizarre webs (Bercel, 1960). While these results have been disproved, Wagemaker and Cade (1977) reported a recent discovery that has revived interest in the blood chemistry theories. These investigators treated a schizophrenic woman for a physical disorder by filtering her blood through a dialysis machine. To their surprise, her schizophrenic symptoms almost disappeared after this treatment. When dialysis was tried on three other schizophrenics, their symptoms were also reduced after a short period of time. The investigators argued that the filtering may have removed some substance from the blood that is responsible for schizophrenia. Research in this area is still continuing. In summary, it does seem that schizophrenia or the tendency to develop schizophrenia may have its roots in biological conditions that are inherited. It is also clear that biological abnormalities are not the only cause of schizophrenia. There must be other factors that create schizophrenia either by themselves or in combination with biological conditions.

Learning Theories. Schizophrenics have been described as living in a world of their own. Learning theorists have suggested that schizophrenics may have learned that being in their own world is more rewarding and less stressful than living in the real world. They argue that schizophrenics are rewarded for escaping into their own world and acting in bizarre ways. One type of reward is attention. If you were to sit in the corner of your room for a long period of time, it is likely that your roommate would soon approach you and ask, "What's wrong?" If you continued with this behavior, other people might be called in to do something about you. It has been reported that the bizarre behavior of schizophrenics diminished when they were ignored by hospital personnel (Agras, 1967). Ayllon (1966) found that he could reduce schizophrenic behavior by rewarding the individual for "normal" behavior. Therefore, learning may be responsible for some of the schizophrenic's actions.

Cognitive Theories. As we have pointed out, one of the main characteristics of schizophrenics is the way they perceive and think about the world. They often spend large amounts of time focusing on small details and cannot "block out" irrelevant stimuli. One researcher suggests that one cause of schizophrenia may be that people develop faulty ways to perceive the world; they learn a certain set of expectations that causes them to focus on unimportant parts of their environment (Shakow, 1977). Their adjustment is, therefore, retarded because they are responding to a world that is different from the one that you and I perceive. Treatment

The double bind.

Martin, 1981.

should, therefore, focus on changing the way schizophrenics perceive situations.

Maher (1970) offers another interesting view. He suggests that schizophrenics suffer from a biochemical disturbance that causes them to experience distorted sensations that are different from those experienced by other people. Their seemingly bizarre behavior and beliefs are their efforts to deal with this unusual stimulation. Therefore, there may be nothing wrong with schizophrenics' reasoning or belief systems. They are simply using logical processes to deal with the unusual sensory stimulation that they experience.

Family Approach. If we return to the example of Charles Manson, we can see that his early childhood was filled with family stress. His mother fought very hard with his aunt and the courts to retain custody of her son. However, once she had custody of Manson, she would leave him with neighbors and friends for days at a time. Did she love her son or dislike him?

Research on families suggests that certain types of stress can lead to schizophrenia. A **double-bind conflict** results when children receive contradictory messages from their parents. These messages create a "no-win" situation for the person. The example of Manson's mother fighting for him and then giving him away creates a double-bind. The following is another example:

> A young man who had fairly well recovered from an acute schizophrenic episode was visited in the hospital by his mother. He was glad to see her and impulsively put his arm around her shoulders, whereupon she stiffened. He withdrew his arm and she asked, "Don't you love me anymore?" He then blushed and she said, "Dear, you must not be so easily embarrassed and afraid of your feelings." The patient was able to stay with her only a few minutes more and following her departure he assaulted an aide . . . . (Bateson et al., 1956, p. 144)

Children faced with a double-bind situation will begin to withdraw and cease trying to form close relationships with people. The family situation teaches them that dealing with people is confusing; people's words and actions are often very different. Therefore, they often retreat into a world of their own.

Other family conflicts have been identified that can lead to schizophrenia (Lidz, 1967). One occurs when parents who do not get along with each other fight for their children's support in their battles. The father may buy the children candy, take them to the zoo, and show other affections as he tells them, "I just don't understand your mother." On the other hand, the mother works to gain the children's support against the father; she cuddles them, and does favors for them, while she delivers the message, "You should love me and fear your father." Neither parent acts out of love for the children; each has the ulterior motive of gaining an ally. In this case, the children are faced with the difference between actions and intentions. They can't win, because to support one parent is to deny the other.

Taken together, the family theories argue that stress and conflict present in family situations can cause people to develop a distorted view of reality and force them to retreat into a private world. The question that is still unanswered is why some people faced with this type of conflict develop schizophrenia while others do not.

Schizophrenia: Normal Adjustment to an Abnormal World?

The usual reaction to schizophrenic behavior is, "These people are really crazy." Certainly, people have to be crazy to believe they are Jesus, to hear voices coming out of light sockets, to repeat the same word five times in each sentence, and to spend hours touching their navel. R. D. Laing, a humanistic psychologist, presents an alternate view. Maybe schizophrenics are not so crazy; they are simply trying to adjust to a crazy family situation and social environment (Laing, 1964). Laing argues that schizophrenic behavior may actually be a resonable response to a bizarre environment. He believes that we can understand schizophrenics by examining the environment that they are responding to. According to Laing, we need to try to perceive schizophrenics' environment in the same way that they perceive it. By doing this we can then understand schizophrenic behavior. In short, Laing suggests that it is the world, not the schizophrenic, that is crazy.

There are certainly times when many of us would agree with this last statement. It does not, however, explain why certain people develop schizophrenia and others do not, even when they face similar environments. Despite this problem, Laing's radical view has forced investigators to examine more closely schizophrenics' environment and try to find out how schizophrenics interpret that environment.

PERSONALITY DISORDERS

We have used Manson's behavior to illustrate symptoms related to many disorders. Indeed, Manson's life represents a cafeteria of unusual and maladaptive activities. As we pointed out in the beginning of this chapter, we do not have enough information to definitely categorize Manson as suffering from one of the disorders we have discussed. Considering the amount of time Manson spent in prison, he had surprisingly little contact with psychologists and other counselors. The lack of a professional perspective on Manson further complicates any efforts to determine Manson's psychological problems. However, a review of the records that do exist shows that the clinicians and counselors who had contact with Manson described him as having an antisocial personality disorder.

Personality disorders are rigid and maladaptive ways of dealing with the environment. They are not so much characterized by a specific behavior as they are a general approach to dealing with events. They usually become evident during adolescence and remain with people throughout their life. Unlike many of the disorders we have discussed, most personality disorders are not characterized by wild or bizarre behaviors. In fact, in most cases, people with a personality disorder can function and seldom require hospitalization. However, their behavior is strange enough that other people avoid interacting with them or are distressed by the interactions. The most noticeable characteristic of the personality disorder is that people tend to react to stress in a patterned way. This response is seldom affected by the requirements of the situation. For example, if someone intentionally stepped on your toe, you would most likely shout and make your anger known. However, if that someone happened to be a 280-pound, 6'7" male, chances are your shouts would not be so loud. However, people with an antisocial personality disorder would probably respond to this intimidating person in the same way they would respond to someone of more manageable size.

There are a number of types of personality disorders; in fact, DSM III lists 12 types. However, let us examine only one, the antisocial personality. This is the type most characteristic of Manson, and it is the type most commonly found in Western society.

Antisocial Personality

Vincent Bugliosi, the prosecuting attorney, reported being most amazed at two of Manson's characteristics. The first was that Manson never seemed to learn from his mistakes. He continued to violate federal laws even though this resulted in long prison sentences. The second characteristic was Manson's total disregard for anyone other than himself. Manson felt no remorse or guilt in ordering the murder of at least nine people whom he did not know. And during the trial Manson showed that he felt nothing for his three female codefendants, who had killed for him. He told Bugliosi that he was more than willing to let the girls go to prison if it would save him.

These characteristics are common in people with *antisocial* personalities (often referred to as *psychopaths* or *sociopaths*). Research shows that people with **antisocial personality disorders** perform violent and hurtful acts without the least bit of guilt or remorse (Cleckley, 1976). They are incapable of forming close relationships with others, and they are manipulative and insincere. They also seem to be incapable of learning from their mistakes. Many antisocial people serve prison terms, but, once released, they continue with the same kind of behavior that got them in trouble to begin with. One of the more frightening aspects of this disorder is that antisocial people are often very intelligent. They use this intelligence to "get away" with their behavior. It is very revealing that Manson was not the one who actually murdered Tate or the others; he manipulated the devoted members of the Family to do the killing.

Antisocial personality is a relatively common disorder. It has been estimated that 3 percent of American men and 1 percent of American women have this type of personality. In fact, this estimate may be low, since antisocial people seldom seek professional help, and many of the statistics must be based on cases that have come to the attention of law enforcement officials (Widom, 1978).

What causes people to treat others with such indifference? The most direct answer is that we don't know. There is some evidence that people may inherit an antisocial personality. One investigator found that children of antisocial parents who were adopted at birth were more likely to show antisocial behavior than adopted children who did not have antisocial parents (Cadoret, 1978). Learning theorists, on the other hand, believe that children learn antisocial behavior from very punitive parents who are quick to punish, but who seldom reward positive behavior. Psychoanalytic theorists also place the blame on the parents. They suggest that children who feel rejected and unloved by their parents develop a lack of caring about other people.

ALCOHOL AND DRUG ADDICTION

The prosecuting attorney told the court that Manson controlled the minds of his followers by his almost hypnotic words and he controlled their bodies through the use of drugs. Throughout the trial, witnesses told of the Family's wild sex orgies and abuse of drugs. Manson was portrayed as the typical "hippie" of the time; he had long hair, wore sandals, played no productive role in society, and began his conversion to the hippie cult in the Haight Ashbury area of San Francisco. During the 1960s and early 1970s hippies served as the symbol of drug abuse to many people, particularly the older generation.

As the preoccupation with hippies passed, society realized that the problem use of drugs and alcohol was not confined to a handful of hippies. Addiction occurred in the old as well as the young, the rich as well as the poor, whites as well as blacks, females as well as males. It also became clear that the range of substances to which addiction occurred was far wider than just "hard drugs."

Drug addiction is the physical dependence on a substance; in short, the body develops a need for the drug (Jaffe, Peterson, and Hodgson, 1980). The need is generally a growing need in that the body builds up a tolerance for a dose of the drug and demands ever increasing doses. Once the need has developed, people experience painful symptoms if the drug is not taken. These painful symptoms, often referred to as *withdrawal*, may include headaches, cramps, nausea, uncontrollable trembling, and restlessness.

The range of substances to which people can become addicted is wide. Let us briefly examine some specific addictions.

Alcoholism

You probably do not consider alcohol a drug. It is, however; addiction to alcohol (alcoholism) is the most common addiction in today's society. One of the reasons that it is difficult to think of alcohol as a drug is that most of us use it on occasion; in fact, two-thirds of adult Americans drink alcohol at times. In low or moderate doses, alcohol may have a relaxing effect, help in sleeping, lower pulse rate, and aid in social interaction. There is, in fact, evidence that small doses of alcohol may reduce the risk of heart attack, and nursing mothers may be encouraged to drink a glass of beer or wine to help their milk flow (Turner, 1981).

It may seem hard to believe that a drug that has these positive effects could have so many negative ones when taken in large doses. Large amounts of alcohol lead to impaired judgment, slowed reflexes, nausea, fainting, and possibly death. Extended use of large quantities of alcohol results in liver damage, hypertension, and malnutrition. Coleman (1980) states that alcohol is associated with over half of all deaths and major injuries in automobile accidents, 50 percent of all murders, and 30 percent of all suicides. He also points out that nearly one-third of all arrests in the United States are the result of alcohol abuse. In addition, countless marriages are destroyed and billions of dollars in lost work time are wasted each year as a result of alcoholism.

When we talk about alcohol abuse, we are really talking about two categories of people. The larger category is the **problem drinker.** This includes people who often drink too much and whose drinking has undesirable effects. Problem drinkers may be people who have learned to deal with stressful situations by drinking, or they may be people who enjoy drinking or getting drunk. A small number of these problem drinkers fall under the subcategory of the alcoholic. **Alcoholics** are addicted to alcohol. They have an uncontrollable urge to drink, and, because of an increasing tolerance, they must continue to increase the dosage of alcohol. Because of the large amount of alcohol consumed, alcoholics are often in poor physical health and social relationships suffer.

The number of problem drinkers in the United States is surprisingly high; 10 percent of adult males and 3 percent of adult females are problem drinkers. Less than half these problem drinkers are alcoholics. With these large figures, it is surprising to learn that the United States ranks only fifteenth in amount of alcohol consumed; France ranks first. Although today much attention and concern is focused on "hard drugs," the problem of alcohol abuse is increasing. For example, in England and Wales, the number of individuals admitted to hospitals for alcoholism is 20 times greater today than 25 years ago. It has been estimated that alcoholism costs industry $10 billion a year in the United States (Jaffe et al., 1980).

Why would some people become addicted to alcohol and develop an uncontrollable urge to drink when others neither become addicted nor feel the need to drink? As with most other disorders, there are many theories. One view is that alcoholism is inherited. For example, Goodwin (1979) found that sons of alcoholic parents are four times more likely to become alcoholics than sons of nonalcoholic parents. This figure occurs even if the children are not reared by their natural parents. Interestingly enough, daughters of alcoholic parents do not run a greater risk than daughters of nonalcoholic parents of being alcoholic. While there is evidence that alcoholism is inherited, we are still unsure of how it works. It may be that individuals inherit an allergy-like response to alcohol. Other theories adopt the position that alcoholism is learned. The individual finds that alcohol reduces stress and, therefore, "turns to the bottle" when stressful situations arise. Still other theories take the psychoanalytic approach, arguing that alcoholism is the result of childhood trauma during the oral stage (from birth to 2 years old). According to this theory, people fixated at the oral stage focus on their mouth area; they try to satisfy their oral need by putting things in their mouth. In some cases they may smoke a great deal; in other cases they may be compulsive gum-chewers; and in still other cases they turn to alcohol.

Drug Addiction

The term "drug" has become a catchword in today's society. Making the statement that "drugs" were used heavily by members of the Manson Family could have many meanings. On one hand, we might be referring to **narcotics** (morphine, heroine, opium). Narcotics are drugs that in small doses reduce pain, cause drowsiness, and give the individual a feeling of happiness and well-being. The term drug might also be referring to *amphetamines* (speed and pep pills) or *cocaine*, which are **stimulants** causing the individual to feel excited and full of energy. Another category of drugs is the **hallucinogens** (LSD, STP, mescaline, peyote—see Chapter 3), which cause the individual to feel happy and see visions and illusions. *Barbiturates* and *tranquilizers* are **depressants** that slow the body functions, reduce anxiety, and have a relaxing effect. We could even interpret the statement about the Manson Family's use of drugs to mean that they drank coffee, tea, or colas (*caffeine*) and smoked cigarettes (*nicotine*).

The use of drugs seems almost as old as civilization itself. There is reference to the use of marijuana in China in 2737 B.C. and to the use of opium in the Middle East before the eighth century B.C. In most cases, the substances that we term "drugs" have medical importance when used in small doses in prescribed ways. Narcotics, for example, reduce pain and marijuana has been used to treat glaucoma (a disease of the eye). However, used in large doses most of the drugs that we listed can cause serious physical and psychological impairment and even lead to death.

Although addiction is possible with most of the drugs, it seems to have different characteristics depending on the specific substance being used. For example, the body builds up a tolerance for each of certain drugs. This means that people must increase the dose to get the desired effect from the drug. However, research suggests that while a physical dependence develops for narcotics, amphetamines, barbiturates, and nicotine, there is no physical dependence on hallucinogens. Thus, withdrawal from the former set of drugs will be *physically* painful. This finding seems to argue that we need to have little concern about addiction to hallucinogens because withdrawal will not be physically painful. However, closer examination of the issue reveals that there are actually two types of depen-

The tragic effects of drug abuse can be seen in the death of John Belushi, actor and comedian, at the age of 34.

dence that can develop. The first, *physical dependence*, involves the body developing a need for the drug. The second, *psychological dependence*, results when people feel that they must have the drug; in other words, the dependence is in the mind. In this case, withdrawal may not cause physical pain, but will result in the psychologically painful symptoms of anxiety, depression, and uneasiness. These symptoms are often as difficult to cope with as the physical withdrawal symptoms. Psychological dependence develops to each of the drugs we have discussed.

Today a great deal of controversy surrounds the drug called *cannabis*, which is found in marijuana. Cannabis can be smoked, eaten, or drunk in tea. It generally causes people to feel relaxed and happy, and reduces inhibitions. The majority of research (Stafford-Clark and Smith, 1978) suggests that people do not develop a physical dependence to cannabis. However, psychological dependence can result from prolonged use.

The problem of drug addiction has physical, social, and psychological effects. The physical effects include the possibilities of malnutrition, infection, and other physical diseases such as hepatitis. There are two categories of psychological problems. The first includes the direct effect of the drug.

It has been argued that marijuana causes people to lose motivation, become apathetic, and reduce striving for future goals. Hallucinogens can cause people to experience psychotic episodes where they lose touch with reality and cannot function. These episodes may last a long time and flashbacks can occur, where the symptoms of an earlier episode suddenly return and overwhelm the person without warning and without having taken the drug again. Another issue here involves the long-term effects of drugs. Because concern about many drugs is a fairly recent issue, there is little research aimed at examining how the use of drugs for a period of years may affect people. The issue of long-term effects has become especially important with marijuana; some people have argued that its use be legalized, while others demand stiffer prison sentences for users.

The second category involves psychological problems such as depression and feelings of helplessness, which people who are addicted may experience. In essence, people's dependence eliminates their freedom to control their lives and makes them a slave to the drug.

The social effects are many also. On one hand, there is the direct loss of productivity, high absenteeism, and impaired performance that may be caused by the drug. Social relationships may suffer as people retreat into the world of drugs. Another problem is legal. Because most of the drugs are illegal, the cost of supporting a habit may run well over $200 a day. Most people do not have this amount of spending money and must turn to crime to pay for their drugs. The Manson Family, in fact, participated in many burglaries to pay for the drugs they used. Our jails and prisons have become overcrowded as a result of the large number of people serving time for drug or drug-related offenses.

Drug addiction is widespread in our society and is not confined to individuals in any particular class, race, or sex.

A great deal of research is being conducted to identify factors that determine addiction and the effects of addiction. This research is complicated by the legal, social, and moral issues surrounding drug use. It will probably take many years to completely understand the effects of drugs on people. Even with this information, the controversy surrounding the complex questions about the legalization of drugs may continue. This is because the research is unlikely to paint a completely negative or positive picture of these substances. While some drugs may be shown to be less harmful than others, the exact effect of a substance will be influenced by the characteristics of the person using it. As we have seen, this is the case with alcohol, where an overuse has negative consequences for everybody. But even in moderate doses, some suffer negative effects while others do not.

SUMMARY

1. A behavior is labeled as **abnormal** when it causes distress to others and hinders people from adapting to their environment. The most commonly used system of classifying psychological disorders today is the **Diagnostic and Statistical Manual (DSM III).**

2. Five approaches for explaining deviant behavior were discussed in this chapter: the medical, psychoanalytic, learning, cognitive, and systems models.

3. Childhood disorders are most likely to occur between 6 months and 3 years or during early adolescence. **Infantile autism** is characterized by social withdrawal, the failure to develop language and communication skills, and a rigid use of schedules. **Anorexia nervosa** is most often

found in adolescent girls. It involves a slow starvation that can sometimes result in death. It has been suggested that family conflict and depression contribute to the disorder.

4. **Neurotic behaviors** are attempts to cope with anxiety. **Anxiety disorders** occur when people experience fear that is out of proportion to the situation they are in. In **generalized anxiety disorders,** the person does not know what is causing the anxiety; he or she simply feels overwhelmed with anxiety. **Phobias** are irrational fears of objects or events that not only cause people to psychologically suffer, but may strongly influence their behavior. **Obsessive-compulsive disorders** occur when the person feels an overwhelming need to think a certain thought (obsession) or perform a certain behavior (compulsion).

5. **Somatoform disorders** involve physical symptoms that are caused by stress and have no physiological basis. Included under this category is the **somatization disorder,** in which people have a wide variety of general complaints, such as headaches, nausea, and stomach pains. **Conversion disorders** are characterized by one specific and often dramatic symptom. This may include blindness or paralysis.

6. In **dissociative disorders,** people separate or dissociate part of their personality from the situation. These disorders include **amnesia, fugue, somnambulism,** and **multiple personalities.** In each of these cases, the person tries to escape anxiety by removing part of his or her personality from consciousness. The disorder results when the person must deal with the anxiety because it is pushing into the conscious.

7. **Affective disorders** are disturbances in mood. The most common affective disorder is **depression.** There are numerous theories about how depression develops, ranging from early childhood experiences to a lack of positive reinforcement in people's present environment. The **learned helplessness** approach combines learning theory and cognitive theory by arguing that depression occurs when people feel that they have no control over their environment. Finally, there is some evidence that biochemical imbalances either in neurotransmitters or in the blood cause depression.

8. **Bipolar disorders** occur when the person shows wild swings in mood between depression and **mania** (elation). Recent evidence suggests that this disorder is inherited.

9. It is difficult to determine abnormality in sexual behavior because we have little knowledge about people's sexual practices and social views about sexual behavior are continually changing. Sexual dysfunctions are the most common sexual disorders. Included in this group are **impotence** and **premature ejaculation** in males and **dyspareunia** and **vaginismus** in females.

10. **Psychoses** are disorders in which people lose touch with reality and have difficulty functioning in their environment. **Schizophrenia** is the most common psychosis. There are many types of schizophrenia; symptoms include disturbances in thinking, disorganized perceptions, disturbances in communication, inappropriate emotions, and unusual motor activities. Theories of schizophrenia have focused on biological problems, disturbances in learning, and conflict in the family setting.

11. **Personality disorders** involve rigid and maladaptive ways of dealing with the environment. People with this disorder can function, but they often have problems forming close relationships with others. The **antisocial personality** is characterized by performing violent or hurtful acts without experiencing guilt or regret.

12. People can develop psychological and physiological dependences on drugs. The most common addiction in our society involves alcohol.

Drug addiction has physical, psychological, and social effects. Research is being conducted to determine the short- and long-term effects of a wide variety of drugs.

SUGGESTED READINGS

The following book is about Charles Manson:

BUGLIOSI, V., and GENTRY, C. *Helter Skelter: The true story of the Manson murders*. New York: Norton, 1974.

American Psychiatric Association, *Diagnostic and statistical manual of mental disorders* (3rd ed.). Washington, D.C.: American Psychiatric Association, 1980. This book presents the latest classification system of psychological disorders.

DAVISON, G., and NEAL, J. *Abnormal psychology: An experimental clinical approach*. New York: Wiley, 1978. This textbook takes a learning approach in discussing the causes of maladjusted behavior. It outlines controversies and other approaches to studying psychological disorders.

JAFFE, J., PETERSON, R., and HODGSON, R. *Addictions*. New York: Harper & Row, 1980. An easy-to-read and informative overview of addiction to a wide variety of drugs. In addition to presenting statistics on addictions, the book examines theories of why people become addicted.

SARASON, I., and SARASON, B. *Abnormal psychology* (3rd ed.). Englewood Cliffs, N.J.: Prentice-Hall, 1980. This textbook examines the historical approaches to abnormal psychology and also presents a broad coverage of the psychological disorders.

STAFFORD-CLARK, D., and SMITH, A. *Psychiatry for students* (5th ed.). London: Allen & Unwin, 1978. This text examines the psychological disorders and modern approaches to treatment. The discussions are illustrated with actual case histories.

SZASZ, T. *The myth of mental illness: Foundations of a theory of personal conduct*. New York: Harper & Row, 1961. Szasz presents a controversial view of abnormal behavior. In short, he offers the position that in some cases the behavior represents reasonable ways to cope with chaotic environments.

13

Therapy

It was with fear and uncertainty that Chris entered Dr. Thigpen's office. According to the country lore with which Chris had been raised, psychiatrists were doctors for crazy folks; they often locked these crazy people in dark padded rooms and let them scream until they exhausted themselves. Was this going to happen to her? Dr. Thigpen sensed Chris's uneasiness and he greeted her with a smile and a simple description of what Chris could expect. "Mrs. White, I work a little differently from other doctors. I don't physically examine my patients. I talk to them, and they talk to me. They tell me things about themselves: what is worrying them, what they feel, what they think" (Sizemore and Pitillo, 1977, p. 288).

During the first few sessions, Chris talked about her troubles with her husband; she revealed that she did not like living in her present home and she talked about her feelings toward her child and her parents. She portrayed herself as a timid woman with little self-confidence, and she cared little about her appearance. Sometimes she felt hesitant to discuss a topic; during these periods Dr. Thigpen would hypnotize her and ask her questions, often about her childhood, which had been a rather stressful one.

An early memory of Chris's was watching with awe as her mother stepped out of the car holding her newborn twin sisters. She was delighted to have not one but two new sisters. But her delight began to fade as her relatives rushed to admire the matched pair; no one was paying any attention to 6-year-old Chris. She knew then that she was destined to lose her favored spot as the center of attention.

Chris's chance for revenge came one day when she was alone in the house with the twins. Chris walked quietly to the side of the little green bed and peered down at the sleeping girls. Suddenly she felt her stomach churn and her vision blur. She shut her eyes tightly and when she opened them again she saw a thin girl with a bony face standing by the bed. The girl looked familiar, but Chris could not recognize her. This other girl threw the bed covers off the twins; she poked her finger into their eyes, grabbed their legs, and fiercely bit their toes. Chris's mother heard the twins shrieking and rushed to the bedroom to find Chris terrorizing the little girls. Her frantic cries snapped Chris out of her daze. She looked around, but the terrible little girl who had tortured her sisters had disappeared.

Mrs. Costner examined the babies and then turned her wrath on Chris. "Look what you've done!" she cried, as she wrenched Chris's arm. Chris was astonished; it was not she who had hurt the twins. The other girl had done it. "But, Mother, you saw her, you saw her do it!?" (Sizemore and Pitillo, 1977, p. 118). Her mother's anger increased; not only had Chris hurt her sisters, but now she was lying about it. But Chris persisted: "No, no, I didn't do it, she did it. That ugly little girl did it. She bit your babies, Mother."

This was one of the first of a series of bizarre incidents that were to plague Chris throughout much of her life. When stressful events occurred, Chris would feel faint or suffer a severe headache; then a "different" Chris would appear and respond to the situation. One Chris was often unaware of how the other Chris behaved. During her childhood, this created quite a problem, because other people did not know that at least two "Chrises" resided in the body of the young girl. They would stare disbelievingly when they observed Chris perform a certain behavior and only a few minutes later heard her deny having behaved in that way.

Chris's childhood was a nightmare; she never knew which personality would dominate. Oftentimes the "naughty" Chris emerged to commit some mischevious act and then quickly retreated, leaving the "ugly, freckled" girl to take the blame and to explain behaviors of which she was unaware. These multiple personalities were an even greater problem when Chris became an adult.

When Chris was 19 she married Ralph White, and the couple soon had a daughter. Ralph had a difficult time holding a steady job, and the family moved often. She began having fights with Ralph, and then the headaches came. These were headaches of such intensity that Chris often fainted from the pain. The headaches signaled the coming out of a new personality; one that hated Ralph and cursed him. Chris's pain and confusion had become so great that her family decided she should see a psychiatrist, at which point she began sessions with Dr. Thigpen.

One day, Chris abruptly interrupted her therapy session to ask, "Doctor, does hearing voices mean you're going insane?" Dr. Thigpen was surprised by this question and asked Chris to explain more about the voices. Chris said that she often heard a strange voice coming from inside her head. The next few sessions were spent talking about the voice, examining what it said and when it appeared. Dr. Thigpen was intrigued by this strange complaint, but his interest sharply increased a few months later, when Chris revealed another problem.

On that day, the session began with Chris discussing her feelings. Suddenly, her face tightened, she grabbed her temples, and she began to moan. The pain was terrible and Chris's world began to whirl. Dr. Thigpen was about to comfort her when Chris raised her head. Dr. Thigpen was surprised as Chris sat up in her chair with her eyes glowing; there was an unusual spark of life in the usually drab Chris. "Hi, Doc," she chirped as she assumed a sexy slouch in the chair. "Gimme a cigarette," she asked, as she winked at Dr. Thigpen. The psychiatrist could hardly contain his surprise as he asked, "Who are you?" As she inched her skirt higher up her leg, Chris answered, "I'm Chris Costner. Chris White is *her*," she said as she pointed off into space.

After talking to this new Chris Costner, Dr. Thigpen was convinced that Chris was not faking; there were indeed two personalities. One was the dutiful but unhappy Chris White who struggled to please her unreliable husband. The other was the sexy Chris Costner who enjoyed flirting, loved expensive clothes, and who truly believed, ". . . I ain't married to that jerk, *she* is." Dr Thigpen soon found that he could cause Chris to change personalities simply by calling for either Chris White or Chris Costner. He also found that Chris White was unaware that Chris Costner existed, but that Chris Costner was well aware of Chris White. He diagnosed Chris as suffering from the rare psychological disorder called dissociative personality, which we discussed in Chapter 12.

Dr. Thigpen continued to question Chris about her childhood in an effort to determine how the "split personalities" developed. He made Chris White aware of Chris Costner, and he often served as a negotiator for the two personalities. At times he even had the two personalities write notes to each other. Dr. Thigpen structured therapy sessions so that good behavior by each of the personalities was rewarded.

However, just when it seemed that the two personalities might be united, Chris began to experience headaches and blackouts again. She had entered into another difficult period in her life. Her marriage had broken up and she was now trying to make it on her own. Was she now having a psychotic break with reality that would require hospitalization? As Dr. Thigpen's concern for Chris increased, another personality emerged. Jane emerged as a cultured and self-assured young woman. She was not frivolous like Chris Costner nor weak like Chris White. It was Jane who got a job as a bookkeeper and managed the money. However, even Jane's best-laid plans were sometimes ruined when Chris Costner "came out" to create havoc.

Dr. Thigpen continued to probe Chris to determine how Jane fit in. More tests were given. An EEG (electroencephalogram), which measures brain waves, revealed that Jane was the most relaxed of the personalities and that Chris Costner did show signs of a psychopathic personality (see Chapter 12).

After 14 months of treatment, Chris was significantly improved. She had fallen in love with Don Sizemore, and after discussing her unusual psychological problem, the couple decided to get married. At this time, both Chris White and Chris Costner faded into obscurity, and only Jane was present. Dr. Thigpen and his associate Hervey Cleckley wrote a book, *The Three Faces of Eve,* in which they described Chris's unusual case; in an effort to protect her identity, the therapists referred to her personalities as Eve White, Eve Black, and Jane. The book was instantly popular and a movie of the same title was made.

But just as it seemed that Chris would now lead a normal life, she suffered a setback; other personalities began to appear. In fact, 12 new personalities "emerged" during the next few years.

Don encouraged Chris to see another psychiatrist near their new home in Virginia.

This psychiatrist attempted to show Chris that all her personalities were the same person. He suggested that Chris reveal herself to her friends and explain what she had been going through. Chris began working on a book, *I'm Eve,* in which she described her life. With the help of her family, her new therapist, and her new project, Chris gained confidence and showed tremendous improvement. At the end of her book, Chris stated, ". . . I am in control of my life, I am comfortable in my world" (Sizemore and Pittillo, 1977). And in a newspaper interview, she reported, ". . . You don't know how wonderful it is to go to bed at night and know that it will be you that wakes up the next day" (*New York Post,* September 15, 1975, p. 4).

It was clear at an early age that Chris needed special help and guidance to adjust to her surroundings. Even as a young child, she was unhappy and bewildered by her own actions. She had difficulty making friends and interacting with other people. Overall she was unable to change her behavior; she did not know what to do to make others like her and she could not stop the "other Chris" from emerging and causing problems for herself and others. Chris needed therapy to help her adjust to her environment and have fulfilling interactions with others.

There are two broad classifications of therapy that are aimed at dealing with psychological disturbances. One is **psychotherapy,** which is the use of psychological techniques by a professionally trained individual to help a client change unwanted behavior and adjust to his or her environment. In short, it is the use of language to make positive changes in the life of another (Davison and Neale, 1978). Dr. Thigpen used psychotherapy to treat Chris; he talked to her about her problems, attempted to show Chris why her different personalities emerged, and discussed methods that Chris could use to control her behavior. A second type of therapy is **biotherapy,** which may be used together with psychotherapy. This therapy includes the use of drugs, surgery, or electric shock to induce behavior change.

As we will see, there are many types of biotherapy and psychotherapy. All, however, have three basic goals. According to Millon (1969), the first goal of the therapist is to be sure that his or her techniques do not bring harm or intensify the problems of the client. The second goal is that the therapist should seek to reduce the individual's present discomfort. And finally, the therapist should attempt to aid in the development of a healthier and more adjusted individual. It is important to keep these goals in mind as we examine the many techniques that are used to relieve psychological suffering.

Historical Background of Psychotherapy

In order to understand the psychotherapy of today, it is useful to turn back to its beginnings. The treatment of psychological disorders is not a modern invention; throughout time people have been intrigued, bewildered, and often afraid of the "strange" or "different" behaviors of people. The treatment prescribed for disordered behaviors was generally based on the "theories" people had about the cause of the disorders. As we pointed out in Chapter 12, the ancient view of psychological disorders was that they were caused by demons who inhabited the person. These demons had to be coaxed out of the person and destroyed. Those who were "possessed" were beaten, burned with hot irons, starved, or had holes chipped in their skull (a process called *trephining*) to allow the demon to escape. In 1500 B.C. the Egyptians used magic potions, which included lizard's blood, crocodile dung, and fly specks, to combat the evil spirits. Although Hippocrates and his followers (about the fifth century B.C.) urged a more humane treatment of the mentally ill, the belief in demons persisted through the Middle Ages. In many societies, large asylums were built to keep the "possessed" from interacting with and contaminating other people. These asylums were really prisons characterized by filthy conditions where the mentally ill were often mistreated.

One of the first major changes in the treatment of people suffering from psychological disorders occurred in the late 1700s and early 1800s. These changes were aimed at reforming the asylums. Philippe Pinel in

Early views on psychological disorders were that they were caused by demons and evil spirits that were inside the person. Treatment focused on getting rid of these spirits. In trephining, a hole was chipped in the head to allow the demon to escape. In the photo on the right is shown a 16th century physicians treatment of "fantasy and folly."

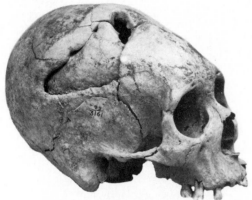

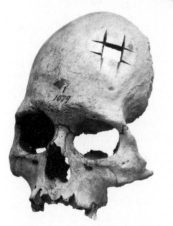

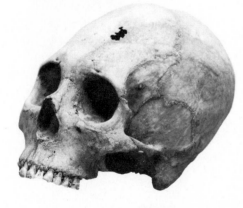

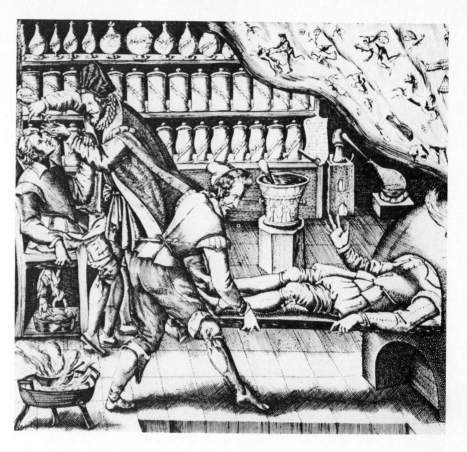

France and Dorothea Dix in the United States campaigned to improve the treatment of disturbed people in institutions. They criticized the inhumane conditions of the asylums and fought hard to eliminate the corruption and torture that was present in many of them. Through their efforts and others like them, changes were slowly made. In some institutions patients were given sunny, bright rooms; they were allowed more freedom and exercise; their diets were improved; and they were treated with greater kindness and understanding. As a result of these advances, many patients made dramatic recoveries and were able to return to society.

While there were some important changes in the living conditions of institutionalized patients, there was little advance in therapy techniques until late in the nineteenth century. At this time a young Viennese physician named Sigmund Freud began developing his psychodynamic model (see Chapter 11) of personality. Freud believed that many psychological problems were the result of feelings and emotions that had been repressed during childhood. According to this position, treatment of these disorders would be best achieved by helping the person recognize and deal with these repressed feelings. Freud's psychoanalytic therapy was characterized by treatment techniques that involved a professional working with one patient at a time in the professional's office. While therapists adopted many different styles, the psychotherapy of the early twentieth century was mainly individual therapy involving a single patient.

The early 1900s were also the time of advances in biotherapy. The assumption underlying much of the work in biotherapies was that mental disorders were diseases much like other physical diseases and, as such, they should be treated in a similar manner. Since the seat of mental diseases was supposedly in the brain, the focus of biological cures was on techniques involving manipulation of the brain. In 1938, Ugo Cerletti reported therapeutic effects from electric shock therapy. This technique involved administering electric shocks to the patient's brain, causing him or her to experience epileptic-like convulsions. Cerletti believed that the electric shock brought the patient close to death; as a result, the body's natural defenses were aroused and these defenses not only fought the effects of the shock, but also worked on eliminating the mental disease. This work was the basis for *electroconvulsive therapy* (ECT), which was widely used during the early 1900s and is still used today. During this same period, Egas Moniz, a Portuguese psychiatrist, reported the use of a surgical technique known as a prefrontal lobotomy to treat psychological disorders.

World War II was responsible for the next chapter in the history of therapy. An alarming number of psychological deferments were given, and many soldiers suffered stress disorders from combat (Sheras and Worchel, 1979). These facts led to the realization that psychological difficulties were more common than previously believed. Unfortunately, there was a serious shortage of professionals who could treat psychological disorders. These conditions led to a reexamination of the field of clinical psychology and a concentration of resources to train more professionals. *Group therapy* techniques were also developed, and many individual therapy techniques were adopted for use with groups of people who suffered from similar problems. Not only was there a strong theoretical rationale for this practice, but it also allowed for more economical and widespread use of professional resources.

The end of World War II also saw significant advances in biotherapy. Doctors working with patients suffering from hypertension and high blood pressure accidentally discovered two drugs that had a calming effect on patients suffering some psychological disorders. These drugs were known as *tranquilizers;* their discovery led to the widespread use of drugs to treat both mild and severe psychological disturbances. In fact, the use of *drug therapy* is so popular today that many professionals have voiced concern that this use of drugs has actually become a misuse of drugs.

At present, a new page in the history of therapy is being written. With new understanding about the causes of psychological disorders came the realization that therapy did not have to be confined to the treatment of disorders; therapy could also be used to prevent disorders from occurring. The Community Mental Health Centers Act was passed by Congress in 1963 to set up 600 community-based mental health centers. These centers were aimed at supplying outpatient and emergency services to people suffering from stressful situations. People working in these centers help others deal with crises and stress before severe and deep-seated disorders develop. Many of these centers have "hot lines" where people can call in and receive help and advice. Since the centers are located in the community, people needing help can receive it on an outpatient basis without disrupting their lives. The field of community psychology is still in its infancy, but it offers a new and bright hope for dealing with psychological disturbances.

The Therapists

Once Chris and others realized that she needed professional help in adjusting to her environment, the next decision concerned who could provide this help. If her problem had been a medical one, this decision would have been relatively easy. She would seek help from an orthopedist if her complaint involved bones; she would consult an obstetrician if she were pregnant; she would call a dermatologist if her problem concerned a skin rash. There are, however, a number of professionals who could be consulted for a psychological disorder.

The **psychiatrist** is a medical doctor who has received a degree in medicine and has taken part in a residency program (usually 3 years), specializing in emotional disorders. Psychiatrists may specialize in any of the psychotherapy techniques, and they are the only professionals who can prescribe drugs or conduct psychosurgery. Dr. Thigpen, Chris's first therapist, was a psychiatrist.

The **psychoanalyst** is often a psychiatrist who has had a great deal of training in psychoanalytic techniques. As part of this training, psychoanalysts must themselves undergo psychoanalysis, which involves between 200 and 2,000 sessions. As we will see, psychoanalytic therapy is very time-consuming and involves some very specialized techniques.

The **clinical psychologist** has received a Ph.D. or Psy.D. in clinical psychology from a graduate school. This training generally takes from 3 to 6 years after receiving an undergraduate degree. The clinical psychologist receives extensive training in therapy techniques, methods of testing, and interpreting psychological theories. Many clinical psychologists have also received training in conducting research. Most practicing clinical psychologists have interned for a year, during which time they work with a wide range of clients under the close supervision of other clinical psychologists and psychiatrists. Dr. Thigpen consulted a number of clinical psychologists and had them administer psychological tests to Chris in an effort to arrive at a clear identification of her disorder.

The **counseling psychologist** has earned either a M.A. or Ph.D. Most counseling psychologists take a 1-year internship, during which time they work with clients under the direction of a practicing counselor. Generally, counseling psychologists are trained to deal with adjustment problems rather than psychological disturbances. For example, the counselor may work with adjustment problems in a school or college setting or work situation. The aim of counseling is to help the person adjust to the situation rather than "treat" a specific disorder.

The **psychiatric social worker** has a master's degree in social work and often has served an internship. Social workers have special training in interviewing techniques, and they may visit individuals in their home to collect information, interview relatives and friends, and make assessments. Social workers are often called upon by juvenile courts to make reports about the family environments of delinquents.

The **psychiatric nurse** is a registered nurse who has received special training in dealing with psychological disorders. Psychiatric nurses are employed by mental institutions, where they are responsible for a wide variety of activities, including patient care and making careful observations of patient behavior.

These are the professionals who administer therapy to the 6 million Americans who seek professional help each year (Gross, 1978). There is, however, an even larger group of people who are called upon to deal with those who are emotionally disturbed. These people include the police officer who must "defuse" a family conflict or calm a distraught victim of crime; the paraprofessional who receives training to handle crisis calls on a "hot line"; the minister, rabbi, or priest who counsels disturbed individuals or families. Even the neighbor or friend who lends a sympathetic ear so that a distressed individual can "talk out" his or her problems plays a vital role in the effort to deal with psychological disorders. In fact, Chris credits her understanding husband, Don, and her cousin Elen with helping her cope with some of her biggest crises.

Now that we have given a brief history of therapy and reviewed the cast of professionals who practice it, we can turn our attention to some of the specific types of therapy that are in use today. As we will see, each type is based on a theory of the cause of psychological disturbances. For example, client-centered therapy has its roots in humanistic psychology (see Chapter 11), while psychoanalysis grew out of Freud's psychodynamic theory of personality. Although many therapists have favorite types of therapy with which they are most comfortable, few practice only one type. Rather, after carefully evaluating a client, therapists choose the techniques that they feel will be most effective with that person. The chosen therapy usually involves techniques taken from a number of the types of therapies, which we will examine.

BIOTHERAPY

Ancient history is filled with examples of attempts to treat psychological disorders with physical methods. These early methods were based on the assumption that the disorder was caused by some physical or supernatural invader in the individual's body. As medical science developed, the uselessness of these methods was recognized. However, the desire to treat psychological disorders by physical methods remained. In some cases, this desire was based on the medical model, which viewed all psychological disorders as diseases or illnesses whose causes were due to a malfunction of the body. In other cases, the desire for a physical treatment was not based on the medical model, but on the belief that even problems of a psychological nature could be treated quickly and effectively with drugs (Millon, 1969).

The quest to find medical cures for psychological disorders, however, did not lead to a careful, concentrated effort to develop these cures. Rather, until recently, the story of biotherapy has been one of *serendipity*, or accidental, lucky discoveries. A procedure or drug that was being used to treat one type of medical illness was accidentally discovered to have therapeutic effects on a psychological disorder. In most of these cases, the discoverers had no idea why the procedure was effective; they only knew that it seemed to work. As we will see, even with the improved techniques and methods of study used today, scientists are still unsure of why many drugs are effective.

Biotherapy includes a wide range of treatments that involve some type of physical treatment. Most of these treatments must be administered under the direction of a psychiatrist or other medical doctor. In many cases, the individual who receives biotherapy is also given some type of psychotherapy.

Electroconvulsive Therapy

When Chris first visited Dr. Thigpen, she was very depressed and had considered suicide. After talking to Chris for several sessions, Dr. Thigpen suggested that Chris undergo electric shock treatment. Chris recoiled in fear—she had visions of jerking in pain on a cold steel table while electric shocks were sent through her head. Because Chris began to recover from her depression and because of her extreme fear of the treatment, Dr. Thigpen decided against shock therapy.

Chris's fears were somewhat mislaid. **Electroconvulsive therapy (ECT)** has been developed to the point where it does not cause the patient great discomfort. However, the preparation for the procedure can frighten some patients. Before receiving ECT, patients are given a sedative and a muscle relaxant to reduce the risk of injury. They are then placed on a well-padded mattress, and electrodes are attached to the head. A current of 70 to 130 volts is given for a period of .1 to .5 seconds. The shock causes the patient to go into convulsions similar to those suffered in an epileptic seizure. Following the convulsion, most patients remain unconscious for 5 to 30 minutes. ECT generally involves 8 to 20 treatments at the rate of 3 per week. All this may sound terrible, more like something from a horror movie than a humane treatment for psychological disorders! However, people generally awake feeling only a little hazy; they have no memory of the procedure.

While patients are not harmed by the procedure, that alone is not enough—does it relieve their psychological suffering? Research suggests that electroconvulsive therapy has short-term benefits for those suffering from depressive disorders (Scovern and Kilmann, 1980). In fact, 60 to 90 percent of those who receive this therapy show rapid signs of improvement, as opposed to 40 to 50 percent recovery rate found in those who are not treated (Millon, 1969). The beneficial effects are the result of the convulsions rather than the shock itself, since convulsions brought on by drugs also yields these short-term benefits.

While the research is encouraging, it also points out the limits of electroconvulsive therapy. First, the procedure has little effect on disorders other than depression. Second, there are few *long-term* benefits from the procedure. In fact, people who receive ECT for depression suffer a relapse (become depressed again) more frequently than those who recovered without therapy (Millon, 1969). Finally, some people experience considerable

Electroconvulsive therapy involves administering an electric shock of 70 to 130 volts for .1 to .5 seconds. It is a controversial procedure and is generally used for people suffering from severe depression.

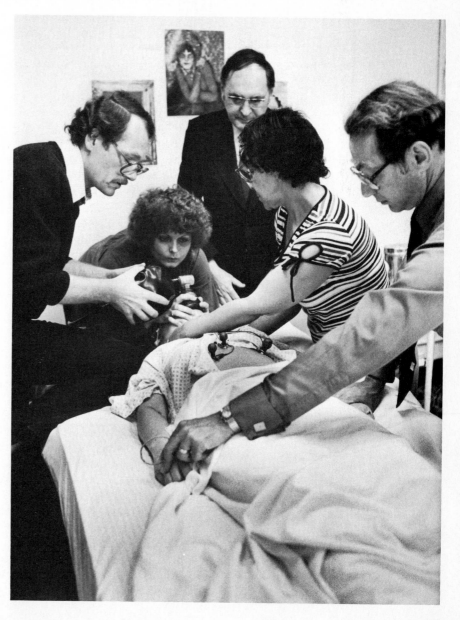

stress and uncomfortable side effects such as headaches, nausea, and memory loss that can last for days or longer.

Clearly, there are pros and cons to electroconvulsive therapy. After reviewing both sides of the issue, the American Psychiatric Association (1979) concluded that this therapy should be regarded as a useful procedure when used under the right circumstances. Electroconvulsive therapy is given to over 100,000 Americans each year. These people are suffering from severe depression, and in many cases the therapist has concluded that they may attempt suicide if not relieved of their depression.

Psychosurgery

For many decades it has been known that certain parts of the brain control different functions (see Chapter 2). In the early 1930s, Egas Moniz, a Portuguese psychiatrist, reasoned that people suffering from emotional disorders might be helped by destroying the connections from the parts of the brain that control emotions. He developed a surgical technique, **psychosurgery**, that became known as the **prefrontal lobotomy**, which involved cutting the connections between the thalamus (emotional center) and the frontal lobes (thought center). Moniz reported that this procedure calmed patients and helped many recover from severe psychological disturbances. Psychosurgery was hailed as a major breakthrough in the treatment of emotional disorders, and Moniz was awarded a Nobel Prize for his work. Thousands of prefrontal lobotomy operations were performed during the 1940s and 1950s. Other psychosurgery techniques were also developed.

However, it was not long before research began to cast doubt on the effectiveness of psychosurgery. It seemed that psychosurgery does succeed in reducing the intensity of people's emotions. As such, it can help people suffering from high levels of anxiety or agitated emotions. However, the research also showed that many people became human vegetables after the operation; they went through the motions of life without showing any emotional reaction to their environment or expressing any ambition or hopes. Further, the effects of psychosurgery cannot be undone; once the connections are severed, they cannot be reattached. For these reasons, psychosurgery is seldom used today; it has become the procedure of last resort, used only when all other methods have failed.

Chemotherapy

Drug therapy, **chemotherapy**, began in 1952 in a very accidental way. Indian doctors had used reserpine, an extract of the Rauwolfia Snakeroot plant, as a general medicine since 1920. As the use of the drug became more widespread, physicians noticed that reserpine had a calming effect on patients. More importantly, this calming effect occurred without making the patient drowsy or reducing alertness. Thus, in 1952 reserpine and another drug (chlorpromazine), which had also been used for medical purposes, were introduced as *tranquilizers*, medication for the treatment of emotional disturbances. Chemotherapy was readily embraced by the medical and psychological world as a major advance in treatment. Drugs seemed to be a quick and inexpensive way to treat psychological disturbances. These discoveries launched the field of **psychopharmacology**, which is the study of drugs to treat psychological disorders.

Drugs are currently divided into three categories. **Antianxiety drugs** (minor tranquilizers) reduce anxiety and tension without causing drowsiness or a loss of mental alertness. The most popular antianxiety drugs are Valium, Librium, and Miltown. Since almost everyone suffers attacks of anxiety and tension at some time, antianxiety drugs have become the

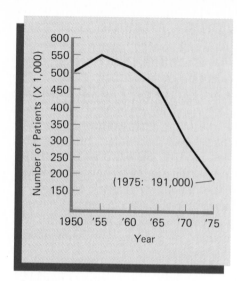

FIGURE 13–1

Reduction of patients hospitalized for mental disorders, 1950 to 1975.

most widely used prescription drugs in the United States. In fact, almost 60 million prescriptions were written for Valium in 1975 (Reinhold, 1980). Dr. Thigpen, for example, gave Chris tranquilizers to calm her during fits of anxiety. These minor tranquilizers are not only prescribed by psychiatrists for people suffering from diagnosed disorders; family physicians and other doctors tend to prescribe the drugs to help people cope with stressful situations. The wide use of tranquilizers recently has been viewed with alarm. There is a fine line that separates wise use from abuse, and people must be careful not to rely on these drugs to solve all their problems. This warning is particularly important because scientists have not yet discovered exactly how these drugs work. There has been some information suggesting that prolonged use can lead to dependency. Further, people may use the drugs to treat the symptoms of stress without trying to uncover and deal with the causes of their tension.

A second category of drugs is made up of antipsychotic drugs (major tranquilizers). These drugs, which include Thorazine and Stelazine, are used to calm and relieve the delusions of schizophrenics. They do not "cure" schizophrenia, but they do calm the person so that he or she can be helped or reached by psychotherapy. Further, these drugs reduce the symptoms of some schizophrenics to such a degree that they can leave the hospital and live in a home environment while receiving other treatment (see Figure 13–1). Antipsychotic drugs are so effective that nearly 87 percent of all patients hospitalized for psychological disorders receive some form of such medication (MacDonald and Tobias, 1976).

In spite of the value of the antipsychotic drugs, they are not without their critics (MacDonald, Lidsky, and Kern, 1979). One of the criticisms of drug therapy is the issue of side effects. Many people who take these drugs suffer from headaches, nausea, blurred vision, drooling, stiff muscles, and fainting. There is even some evidence that prolonged use of the drugs can result in permanent brain damage (MacDonald et al., 1979). Another criticism is that drugs are often used to control patients rather than to actually treat their disorders. Patients taking antipsychotic drugs become docile and easily controlled by hospital staff. Thus there is a strong temptation to use drugs when a patient is acting in a disruptive manner (Sobel, 1980). Despite these issues, many clinicians agree that the careful use of antipsychotic drugs along with psychotherapy can have very positive effects. Research efforts are now being aimed at developing drugs that do not have undesired side effects and determining exactly how these antipsychotic drugs work.

Tranquilizers are drugs that bring people "down" from highly anxious or agitated states. Antidepressant drugs, such as Tofranil and Elavil, work by lifting the person's spirits and increasing his or her activity level. Generally, the antidepressant drugs are given to people who are suffering from deep states of depression. It is interesting that the antidepressant drugs do not work equally well with all depressed individuals; in some cases, they are very effective, while in others they have almost no effect (Gelenberg, 1979). Unfortunately, there are a number of unpleasant side effects associated with antidepressant drugs; these include nausea, restlessness, and insomnia.

There is another drug, lithium carbonate, that has been introduced in the last decade. Lithium is used to treat people suffering from bipolar disorders (see Chapter 12), which are characterized by wide swings in mood. The drug, used in the proper dosage, is effective in keeping people from becoming too elated or too depressed. Lithium, however, is a dangerous drug that can cause death if its concentration in the blood becomes too high. Thus, people who receive lithium treatment must take regular blood tests.

The advancements in chemotherapy have both exciting and frightening implications. On the positive side, drugs offer the possibility that people suffering from psychological disorders can be treated quickly, efficiently, and inexpensively. Further, there is evidence that drugs can be used to treat people who suffer disorders such as schizophrenia, which are difficult to treat with psychotherapy. These points suggest that drugs can be invaluable in the treatment of psychological disorders. There are, however, some issues that must be considered before adopting chemotherapy. *First, drugs generally reduce only the symptoms of the disorder and not the cause of it.* Because patients can receive quick relief of unpleasant symptoms, they may be tempted not to deal with the underlying problem. If people take this position, they will lose control over their lives; they become dependent on drugs to make them feel good. A second problem related to chemotherapy is that the drugs can be used simply to control people's behavior rather than treat their problems. People who work on wards in mental health institutions are often faced with the simultaneous demands of a number of patients. Because they cannot help all the patients immediately, they may use drugs to quiet disruptive patients and bring peace to the wards. This is clearly a misuse of drugs.

These issues are all important and must be considered before using drug therapy. Another issue is that scientists are still unsure of how these drugs work and what their long-term side effects might be. Research is now being conducted to gain more information about the way these

HIGHLIGHT / BIOFEEDBACK: BRIDGING THE TWO TYPES OF THERAPY

Our present generation has often been called the "generation of the pill." For any disorder, physical or psychological, there seems to be at least three pills that can be used to treat it. We have pills that get us started in the morning, calm us down if we get tense during the day, pick us up if we get depressed, control our appetities at mealtimes, and help us sleep at night. There is little doubt that drugs can play a very valuable role in therapy when they are used properly; however, one of the problems with using pills is that people often lose control and come to depend on them.

Many drugs work by regulating physiological functions such as heart rate, blood pressure, and body temperature. For many years it was believed that drugs were necessary because people could not control these physiological functions on their own (Ivey and Simek-Downing, 1980). However, more recently investigators have found that people do have some degree of voluntary

control over these functions. One of the problems with teaching people how to control their bodies is that most people are not good at monitoring physiological messages such as heart rate or muscle tension. For example, it is unlikely that you are aware of how fast your heart beats at different times during the day.

Biofeedback therapy is designed to help people control their physiological functions without the use of drugs. It attempts to control people's physiological functioning without the use of biotherapy techniques.

In biofeedback training, people are connected to devices that measure physiological functions such as heart rate, muscle tension, skin temperature, blood pressure, and even brain waves. These devices not only monitor these responses, they also give people information about the state of the responses. Through a series of lessons, the person is then taught

how to control these functions and achieve a more relaxed state (Tarler-Benlolo, 1978). These lessons include breathing exercises and muscle relaxation techniques. Physiological recording devices are used so that the person can receive feedback about how effective his or her efforts are in reducing tension. In this way, they can determine by themselves just what types of behavior are successful in achieving the desired effect, such as decreasing blood pressure or muscle tension.

Biofeedback therapies have been used to help people reduce tension and stress, control phobic reactions, and control headaches. Biofeedback techniques have been combined with other psychotherapies such as desensitization to increase the effectiveness of therapy. Although the technique offers some exciting possibilities for treating problems without the use of drugs, there is still controversy about the conditions under which it will be effective.

drugs bring about their effects. At present, chemotherapy is most effective when it is coupled with careful observations of the person's behavior and with some form of psychotherapy.

PSYCHOTHERAPY

During her long battle to deal with her problem, Chris went to a number of psychiatrists and psychologists. These interactions were characterized by discussions between Chris and the therapist. In some cases, the therapist attempted to review Chris's background to see what was causing multiple personalities. In other cases, the aim of the session was for Chris to gain insight into her problem and to give her a chance to vent emotions that may have been building inside her. Still other sessions were aimed at showing Chris how she could change her behavior, and she was rewarded for positive changes. All of these techniques are examples of *psychotherapy*, which involves social interaction between a therapist and client aimed at changing the client's behavior. As we will see, there are many types of psychotherapy. Some types stress helping clients gain insight into their problems; others stress having clients express feelings that have been repressed; and still others focus on teaching clients how to change their behavior. Each type of therapy is based on a theory of the cause of psychotherapy disorders.

As we pointed out earlier, most therapists use techniques taken from a number of types of therapy. In this way, they can design the particular therapy to fit the client's specific problem. With this point in mind, let us examine some of the types of therapies that have been developed to deal with psychotherapy disorders.

Psychoanalysis

As we discussed in Chapter 11, Sigmund Freud believed that our personalities are shaped by events in early childhood. According to Freud, as children each of us go through stages. A traumatic event that occurs at any of these stages can have a lasting effect on us. Many of us witness events, have thoughts, or experience emotions that we have been taught are bad and unacceptable. As a response to these teachings, we attempt to defend against these unacceptable thoughts or feelings by forcing them into the unconscious; in other words, we repress them. These thoughts or emotions, locked in the unconscious, fight to enter our conscious. Therefore, we must constantly use energy to keep these unacceptable feelings in the unconscious. According to Freud, anxiety results when these unconscious thoughts threaten to break into our consciousness.

Freud developed the method of psychoanalysis to treat these anxiety disorders. According to Freud, people can be helped only when they recognize and deal with (work through) the repressed feelings. Hence, the aim of therapy is to help people identify these "hidden emotions," bring them into the open, and deal with them. This may sound like a difficult task for a therapist; after all, these feelings have been repressed since early childhood. How can they be identified?

Freud believed there were two methods that could be used to identify repressed feelings. One is the technique of free association. This method involves having clients talk about whatever thoughts come to their mind. Clients are told to talk about every thought that comes to mind without worrying about how much sense it makes or its structure. While this may sound easy, it often becomes rather difficult, especially when the thoughts are embarrassing or sensitive. Sometimes clients resist expressing certain thoughts or associations. This resistance may be shown by the client "forgetting" to attend sessions or simply refusing to talk. Freud believed that this resistance indicated that the client was close to revealing the repressed emotions and these delaying actions were a way to keep these feelings repressed. The therapist listens to the free associations, observes the resistance, and attempts to *interpret* their meaning. These interpretations are the basis for identifying the repressed emotions.

The second method used to uncover repressed feelings is **dream interpretation.** Freud believed that our defenses are relaxed during sleep, and the repressed feelings come close to the level of consciousness. However, because our defenses are not completly lifted, the repressed emotions are expressed in a disguised form in dreams. Thus, the therapist must look beyond the expressed content (*manifest content*) to determine the true meaning (*latent content*) of the dream (as we discussed in Chapter 4). For example, a man might report dreaming that he stands by helplessly as a young boy burns in a fire (manifest content). The therapist might interpret this dream to be an expression of the client's resentment of his younger brother (latent content).

As psychoanalysis progresses, people reveal many intimate and usually secret details about their life to the therapist. In a sense, the therapist learns as much, if not more, about clients than their parents ever knew. Because of this, clients develop strong feelings about their therapist; some of these feelings may be positive, while others are very negative. Freud believed that clients *transfer* to the therapist feelings that were originally aimed at their parents or other authority figures; in this way clients "relive" these early relationships. **Transference** is a very important part of therapy. It gives people the chance to voice emotions that may have been repressed during childhood. According to psychoanalytic theory, these repressed emotions are the cause of anxiety. The expression of these repressed feelings allows the therapist to help clients deal with them in a constructive way. When these feelings are brought from the unconscious to the conscious and worked through with the therapist, they will no longer cause anxiety attacks.

The practice of classical psychoanalysis has an almost mystical quality to it. The client is given a comfortable couch to recline upon and the lights of the therapy room are usually dimmed. The therapist sits in a chair out of the line of sight of the client. These conditions are designed to relax the client and promote free recall. The therapist takes a neutral role, becoming involved only to encourage the client to talk, or to offer an interpretation of a dream or recalled materials. The client meets with the therapist 4 or 5 times a week over a period of time that ranges from one to several years. Needless to say, classical psychoanalysis is a very expensive procedure that may cost over $10,000 a year. It is also apparent that the procedure is designed for the relatively well-educated who can express themselves well in free recall and in reporting dreams (Luborsky and Spence, 1978).

Psychoanalysis is most successful for disorders involving anxiety. Since Freud introduced psychoanalysis, there have been many changes in the basic procedure. Many psychoanalysts have patients sit in chairs facing them; the therapists argue that because this is a more "normal" arrangement, clients are more comfortable with it. Further, the number of sessions is often shortened so that the client attends therapy only once or twice a week.

It is important to remember that psychoanalysis focuses on the experiences of early childhood. It is aimed at discovering conflicts people had as children and showing them how these long-repressed experiences or feelings cause anxiety. Psychoanalytic therapy can be viewed as helping

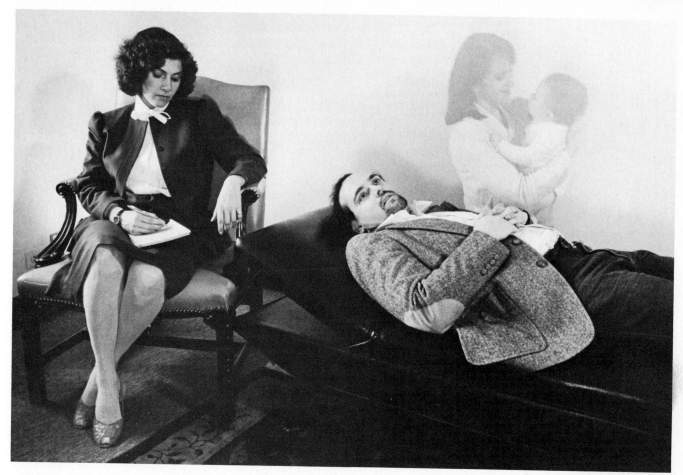

Free association is one technique used in psychoanalysis. This method involves having clients talk about whatever thoughts come into their mind.

people gain *insight* into their personality. In our example at the beginning of the chapter, Dr. Thigpen's approach was basically a psychoanalytic one. He had Chris talk about her childhood and her feelings toward her parents for hours. He attempted to interpret Chris's dreams as they related to her childhood experiences. Through therapy Dr. Thigpen discovered that as a young child, Chris had seen a number of people die in various accidents. She became terrified of death and viewed herself as responsible for the deaths of these people. Was anxiety and guilt about these early deaths responsible for Chris's multiple personalities? While we cannot be sure of the cause, it is evident from her book that Chris believed that repressed feelings about death did influence her condition.

Client-Centered Therapy

As we have seen, psychoanalysis focuses on "reconstructing" people's childhood and interpreting their problems in light of this. Carl Rogers (1941, 1951, 1970) and other humanistic psychologists also believe that the root of many disorders is in childhood. However, their approach is very different from that of psychoanalysts. The humanists argue that we naturally strive to reach our potential and lead a fulfilling life. However, as children we often learn that other people have expectations about how we should behave. We also learn that the way to get rewards is to live up to others' expectations. If we follow these lessons, however, we may lose touch with our own desires and feelings. When this happens we become unhappy and experience anxiety.

According to Rogers, given the proper conditions people will become more self-aware and happy, and they will strive to meet their own goals. In short, Rogers suggests that people will reduce their own anxiety and mature by their own efforts if they are given the right opportunities. Therefore, the aim of therapy is to provide the proper setting for this self-growth to occur. The "proper setting" is one in which people do not fear social rejection for expressing themselves. The goal of the therapist is to create this condition by giving clients **unconditional positive regard;** that is, accepting and caring for them no matter what feelings or behaviors are revealed in the sessions. Therapists need to show a genuine warmth and concern for their clients. In this way, their clients will gain enough confidence to begin the self-exploration process and strive toward personal fulfillment.

The emphasis in therapy is on the client rather than on the therapist. The client determines what will be discussed during therapy; in other words, the therapy is **client-centered.** The therapist does not attempt to diagnose or interpret the client's condition. According to the humanists, a diagnosis serves no purpose and only places the client in a dehumanized category. Instead, the therapist responds to the person as a unique individual and attempts to experience the world from the client's position, as the client sees it. In doing this, therapists mirror and rephrase what they hear the client saying.

Unlike psychoanalysis, client-centered therapy focuses on the here-and-now. While difficulties may have begun in childhood, people must deal with them in the present. According to the humanistic position, there is little value in spending time tracing problems to the client's past. The cause of present difficulties is not as important as how the person is now responding to these difficulties. Thus, the therapist helps the client focus on present feelings.

If Chris had seen a client-centered therapist, her therapy sessions would have gone very differently. Unlike Dr. Thigpen, the therapist would have spent little, if any, time discussing her early childhood. Instead, he or she would have supported Chris as she examined her present feelings and attempted to deal with her multiple personalities. The therapist would not have tried to diagnose Chris or probe for the hidden meaning in what she said. He or she would have treated Chris as a unique individual and not just as a patient who had come to be cured.

We cannot determine if this type of therapy would have been successful in Chris's case. There is, however, a mounting body of research (Mitchell, Bozarth, and Krauft, 1977; Truax and Mitchell, 1971) that indicates that therapist characteristics have a strong effect on the progress of therapy; therapy is most successful when the therapist is perceived as genuine, warm, and caring. Research has also shown that client-centered therapy leads to improvement in the client's self-concept and better interpersonal relationships outside of the therapy setting (Rogers and Dymond, 1954; Rubin, 1967).

Gestalt Therapy

While it may seem that the theories behind psychoanalysis and client-centered therapies are very different, **Gestalt therapy** borrows ideas from both theories. It has been argued that our actions are often influenced by emotions and thoughts of which we are unaware (Perls, 1969). These unconscious motivations can lead to unsatisfying social interactions. For example, you might find yourself becoming very angry as you wait a long time for a waitress to take your order. You believe that your anger is the result of the waitress's incompetent actions (*figure,* in Gestalt terminology). However, much of your emotion may actually be the anger aroused by a professor who criticized your work earlier that day. That anger, which was repressed at the time, serves as the *background* for your feelings in the restaurant. Perls agrees with the psychoanalytic position that we need to become aware of the unconscious influences on our behavior. Putting it in Gestalt terms, people need to bring together awareness of both figure and background in order to become "whole" and reduce anxiety.

While accepting these psychodynamic positions, Perls also adopts many humanistic principles. He believes that we can take responsibility for our own actions. Like Carl Rogers, Perls feels that we become sidetracked from personal growth and self-awareness when we try to live up to the expectations of others rather than following our own desires. Perls (1969) makes this position explicit in the following statement:

> I do my own thing and you do your thing. I am not in this world to live up to your expectations. And you are not in this world to live up to mine. You are you and I am I. And if by chance we find each other, it's beautiful. If not, then not.

Finally, Perls argues that while the past may shape our feelings, we can only live and experience in the present. "The past is no more and the future not yet. Only the *now* exists" (Perls, 1970, p. 14). A person who is preoccupied with the past or too concerned with the future cannot function well in the present.

Thus, the aims of Gestalt therapy are to make people more aware of the feelings and thoughts that influence their behavior and to help them express these emotions in the present. Gestalt therapy also forces the person to accept responsibility for these emotions rather than trying to excuse them. In other words, *why* someone feels angry is of little importance; what is important is that the individual *be aware* that he or she is angry and *express* this anger.

Gestalt therapy uses a number of interesting techniques to help people develop greater self-awareness and responsibility. For example, there is heavy emphasis on using *first person pronouns*. A person might say, "It really makes you mad when people don't do the things they promise." The therapist in this situation would then challenge the person by asking, "Who does it make mad?" The person must then "claim" his or her emotion by replying, "I really get mad when. . . ." In this way, people are forced to take responsibility for their feelings.

In the "empty chair" exercise, the client places a part of her personality in the empty chair and attempts to explore it and deal with it.

Role playing is often used to clarify a feeling. For example, the therapist might take the role of the client's mother and encourage the client to act out his or her feelings toward the mother. This exercise can make the client more aware of these feelings and demonstrate how these feelings are affecting his or her present interactions with the mother. Another interesting technique is the **empty chair technique.** In this case, the clients place different parts of their personality in chairs and act each of these parts. For example, the client may feel conflict about being aggressive. "Aggression" is put in one chair and "passiveness" is placed in the other chair. The individual alternates sitting in the two chairs and taking the role prescribed to that chair. He or she acts aggressively and talks to the passive part of the personality when sitting in the aggression chair. This technique allows the person to become more aware of the conflict between these two parts of the personality. It also makes the person actually experience both emotions. Gestalt therapy is often conducted in a group setting, but the focus of attention is aimed at one individual at a time.

Unfortunately, there has been little research on Gestalt therapy. The goals of being aware of one's emotions and being more expressive are assumed to be positive. The Gestalt therapy techniques have been used in a number of different types of therapy. There are, however, still many questions about the effectiveness of the therapy and the conditions under which it is best used.

He: "Want to go to the movies tonight?"
She: "I'm sorry, I'm afraid I can't make it."

Ellis believes that the way we feel depends on the way we interpret events rather than on the events themselves. The man shown here can interpret this event in one of two ways, and it is the way that he interprets it, not the event itself, that will determine how he feels.

Oh, well, maybe next time.

Gee, what's wrong with me, she must not like me.

Changing Thoughts: Rational Emotive Therapy (RET)

Had Chris been involved in any of the previous therapies we have discussed, the focus would have been on her feelings. The therapist would have been very concerned in identifying how Chris felt and encouraging her to express these feelings. According to Albert Ellis this is not the best way to treat anxiety (Ellis, 1962; Ellis and Grieger, 1977). Ellis believes that our problems are not the result of how we feel; rather, he suggests that how we *think* and *believe* determines how well we will adjust to our environment. In fact, Ellis argues that the way we feel depends on the way we interpret events rather than on the events themselves. For example, imagine that a friend turns down your invitation to go to the movies. According to Ellis, this refusal by itself will not make you too unhappy. However, if you interpret the refusal as a sign that the friend really does not like you and that you are thus an unlikeable person, you will feel very depressed.

There are a number of irrational and destructive attitudes that can lead to depression. Among the most common are:

1. It is necessary that I be loved by every significant person in my environment.
2. It is absolutely necessary that I be completely competent, adequate, and achieve in all areas or I am worthless.
3. If something is dangerous, I must be constantly concerned about it.
4. It is a terrible disaster if things do not turn out the way I want them to turn out.

We can see from Chris's report of her childhood that she felt that she was a failure if everyone did not always express approval of her. She was always striving to please others because she feared their rejection.

Since it is these attitudes that are the root of anxiety, Ellis argues that therapy should be aimed at restructuring the way people think. In order to do this, therapists must take an active and direct teaching role.

They must point out people's irrational beliefs and identify more rational attitudes to hold. For example, a therapist might point out to Chris how her irrational fear of rejection makes her adjustment so difficult. The therapist might challenge her belief, asking, "What's so bad about being rejected by others? What's the worst thing that can happen if someone doesn't like you?" The therapist attempts to substitute or replace the person's beliefs that behaviors or events *must* or *should* occur with beliefs that "it would be nice if they did occur, but all will be well even if they do not happen." The therapist who practices this type of therapy, **rational emotive therapy (RET),** acts in a directive and challenging manner and is not concerned about forming a warm, caring relationship with the client (George and Cristiani, 1981). The therapist may also use techniques like role playing to demonstrate the irrationality of many of the client's beliefs. As you can see, RET focuses on the present; while the irrational attitudes may have been learned in the past, the problem (and its solution) is in the present.

RET is widely practiced with people who suffer from anxiety. This form of therapy has the advantage of working faster than other therapies, which focus on insight and developing warm relationships between therapist and client. Despite this advantage, there is criticism that too much insensitivity to the client's feelings on the part of the therapist can be destructive in some cases (George and Cristiani, 1981). In responding to this issue, many therapists combine techniques of RET with those from other therapies in dealing with clients.

Behavior Therapies

We might refer to the therapies that we have been discussing as "inside" therapies. They are "inside" in that they attempt to change how the person thinks or feels. These theories are based on the assumption that inner processes are responsible for the person's stress and failure to adjust. Changing these inner processes will result in positive changes in behavior. If Chris had been treated by any of these therapies, many hours would have been spent examining how she felt or thought.

Behavior therapies take a very different approach. These therapies are based on the assumption that maladaptive behavior is learned through the same process that other behaviors are learned. Given that abnormal behavior is learned, it can also be unlearned, and new, more adaptive behavior substituted in its place. According to behavior therapies, it is a waste of time to focus on internal events like emotions and attitudes. Therapy will be more effective if it concentrates on behavior, an external and observable factor.

Behavior therapies, which are derived from experimental psychology, argue that maladaptive behavior can be changed by changing the reinforcement patterns and/or the models in the person's *present* environment. While the problem behavior may have been learned in the past, it is the present environment that maintains it. Further, many behavior therapists believe that changes in emotion and attitudes will follow changes in behavior (Sheras and Worchel, 1979).

There are a number of therapies based on the principles of learning theories. We will examine four of the most common therapies in an effort to show the broad range of behavior therapies.

Aversive Conditioning. From the moment the twin girls were born, Chris felt that people stopped paying attention to her. The little girls received everything, including Chris's bed. However, on the day that the thin, bony-faced girl appeared and hurt the sleeping girls, Chris got attention from her mother. After that, Chris found that she quickly got others to pay attention to her when a different personality emerged. Thus, despite the problems that resulted, there may have been some pleasure associated with the emergence of a different personality.

According to **aversive conditioning therapy,** the way to handle this type of difficulty is to reverse the process. That is, the person must learn that the presence of a target behavior is associated with an unpleasant event. Thus, the therapy is designed so that the person receives unpleasant consequences for undesired behavior.

Aversive conditioning has been used to help people break undesirable habits such as smoking and drinking and to treat sexual deviations. For example, people with drinking problems may be given a drug that will cause nausea if they drink alcohol. The drug can be given before the drink (Lemere and Voegtlin, 1950) or mixed with the drink (Nathan, 1976). In this way, drinking alcohol becomes associated with an unpleasant feeling. Your parents may have used a form of aversive conditioning to prevent you from smoking after they found you hiding in a closet taking a few puffs. Their "cure'" may have been to force you to smoke the whole cigarette, the result being that you became violently sick. After that, you remembered your "near-death" feeling every time you were tempted to smoke. A similar technique, called *rapid smoking*, has been used to help adults stop smoking (Lichtenstein et al., 1977). The technique involves having people smoke rapidly until they become sick. While this technique has proved useful in some cases, critics argue that it may be dangerous, leading to problems such as nicotine poisoning.

A form of aversive conditioning has been developed where people only *imagine* a negative event being associated with a certain behavior (Cautela, 1977). For example, if you wished to stop eating sweets, you might be asked to imagine that candy is actually sugar-coated worms that will invade your stomach when you bite into the candy.

There has been a lot of controversy about the effectiveness of aversive conditioning. Some therapists report that the technique is very successful. Others argue that the technique does not produce lasting results; people return to the undesired habits after the therapy is over (Conway, 1977). There has also been some concern that the technique results in overgeneralization, in which the person stops performing many positive behaviors. For example, if you imagined worms in candy, as we just mentioned, you might not only stop eating candy, but you might also give up eating other good foods that remind you of candy. In spite of these questions, aversive conditioning is used to help people change undesired behaviors.

Systematic Desensitization. Two-year-old Chris watched in horror as her father and the other men pulled the bloated body of the old man from the irrigation ditch. "It's ole man Williams, I think he's dead." At the word "dead," Chris gasped and felt her body tremble. From that moment, Chris developed an irrational fear of death that may have been one of the causes of her multiple personalities.

A number of behavioral techniques have been developed to treat phobias (irrational fears) and other anxiety disorders. One of the techniques is known as **systematic desensitization** (Wolpe, 1958, 1974). The technique is based on the assumption that it is impossible to be relaxed and anxious at the same time. The therapist's aim is to make the client relax in the presence of an object or event that used to cause anxiety. Systematic desensitization involves three steps. First, on the basis of interviews and psychological tests, events or objects that cause stress are identified. These events are arranged in a hierarchy based on the amount of anxiety that they cause. Table 13–1 shows a hierarchy that Wolpe (1958) developed from a client's fear of death; a similar hierarchy might have been created if Chris had been involved in systematic desensitization.

The second step involves teaching the client deep muscle relaxation.

TABLE 13–1: Systematic Desensitization Hierarchy

This hierarchy was developed by Wolpe from a client's fear of death. Events that cause stress are identified and arranged according to how much anxiety they cause.

a. Seeing first husband in his coffin

b. Attending a burial

c. Seeing a burial assemblage from afar

d. Reading an obituary notice of a young person dying of heart attack

e. Driving past a cemetery

f. Seeing a funeral

g. Passing a funeral home

h. Reading an obituary notice of an old person

i. Being inside a hospital

j. Seeing a hospital

k. Seeing an ambulance

Source: Wolpe (1958)

This method calls for clients to focus on and relax different parts of their body. The therapist might first have clients relax the muscles in their arms by letting them go completely limp and heavy. Next, they may practice relaxing leg or stomach muscles. After a number of sessions, clients should be able to deeply relax their whole body.

The third phase pairs relaxation with the events listed in the hierarchy. The therapy starts with the least stressful event. Clients are told to remain relaxed and calm while vividly imagining the event. If they are successful in doing this, the therapist moves on to the next event in the hierarchy. If they show signs of anxiety or tension, the therapist will move back to the next lower event and begin the relaxation process again. After some time, clients are able to relax even when imagining the most stressful event in the hierarchy.

According to Wolpe and others (Denney and Sullivan, 1976), people who can relax while imagining feared events can also relax when they encounter these events in their everyday lives. Other investigators have changed the procedure to include real contact with the feared objects or events. For example, Moss and Arend (1977) have used *contact desensitization* to treat clients who have a fear of snakes by having them first relax while holding a rope. Later they practice relaxation while watching a live snake in the room, and in the final sessions they use their relaxation techniques while handling a live snake. As you can see, desensitization involves learning a new response to a stimulus that previously aroused fear and stress. It is also a technique that focuses only on the present situation; there is no attempt to trace the cause of the anxiety. The technique has been used with a wide range of problems, including phobias, alcoholism, and insomnia (Rimm and Masters, 1979).

Operant Conditioning Therapies. Dr. Thigpen used positive reward to reduce the frequency of Chris's multiple personalities. When he wanted to talk with the "Jane" personality, he would reward Chris with kind words and sweets if she would produce this other personality. If one of the other personalities surfaced, Dr. Thigpen would scold Chris and withhold rewards until Jane reemerged. In this way, Dr. Thigpen was able to call the personalities at will and keep them for a long time.

The process of rewarding desired behaviors is based on **operant conditioning,** which we discussed in Chapter 5. As you will remember, this type of learning involves rewarding the desired behavior after it has occurred. People soon learn that they can obtain the reward by performing the "right" behavior. As we saw previously, this technique has been used to condition and shape a wide variety of behaviors.

Operant conditioning therapy can be used in an individual therapy setting, as it was with Chris and Dr. Thigpen. It has also been used in a variety of institutional settings such as mental hospitals and prisons. When used in this type of setting, it involves designing a **token economy** (Kazdin, 1976). People taking part in a token economy are given rewards such as poker chips for performing certain behaviors. They can use the tokens to purchase things they want, such as candy or cigarettes. One of the authors conducted research in a juvenile prison that was based on a token economy. When a juvenile entered the prison, he lived first on the top floor, in a room that was bare except for a bed and a sink. He was given plastic tokens for performing such duties as cleaning his room. When he had earned a certain amount of tokens, he could "buy" his way to the next lower floor, which had larger rooms with more attractive furnishings. A new set of behaviors was reinforced with tokens; for example, he might receive tokens for reading books. Once again, when the prescribed amount of tokens was collected, he could move to a lower floor that had other attractive features such as curtains on the windows and

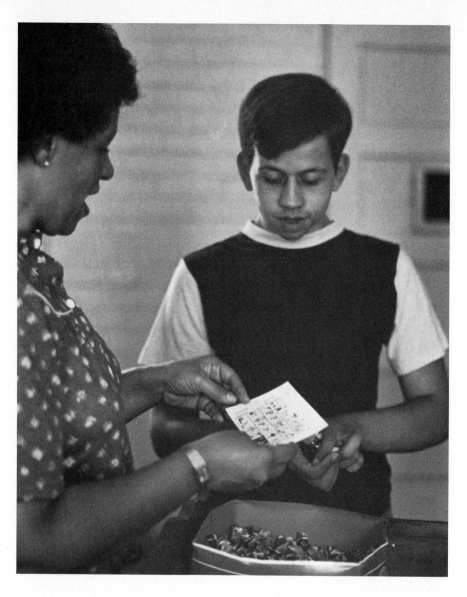

a television. The token economy continued on each floor, with the ground floor being set up so that the boy could obtain his freedom with the proper number of tokens.

Other token economies have been used in mental hospitals. For example, Ayllon and Azrin (1968) used a similar type of token economy in a mental institution to get schizophrenic patients to perform such behaviors as eating, taking care of personal hygiene, and doing chores. Another researcher used the technique to get autistic children to talk (Lovaas, 1977). A number of investigators have reported great success using token economies (Goldfried and Davison, 1976).

Other investigators, however, have criticized the technique on a number of grounds. First, the technique gives a great deal of control to the person who gives out the tokens. This person determines the "desired" behaviors and exercises complete control over the others in the economy. Many humanists view this control as a negative situation. They feel that it is wrong for one person to have so much control over another. A second criticism is that the desired behavior sometimes stops when the reward is no longer available. For example, inmates in the juvenile prison that we just discussed perform behavior for the rewards or tokens. Outside the prison, no one is going to give them a reward each time they make their bed or clean their room. As a result, the positive behavior may not occur outside the prison. In order to increase the probability that the behaviors will occur outside the token economy, small rewards or self-rewards are often used (Krasner, 1971). These rewards do increase the likelihood that the person will continue performing the desired behavior outside the token economy setting. A third criticism is that the token economy teaches people to perform behaviors only for rewards; because of this, there is the possibility that they will fail to appreciate or value the behavior in its own right. For example, if you are given a reward each time you read a book, you may learn to read simply to obtain the reward and never develop pleasure from reading.

While there are a number of criticisms of operant conditioning therapies, it is clear that such therapies can be used to bring about behavioral change. In some cases this technique may be the only way to change someone's behavior (Davison and Neale, 1978). A therapist who uses this technique must take into account the ethical and methodological considerations that we have discussed.

Modeling. Clearly people learn new behaviors through reinforcement; they also learn by watching other people and *imitating* their actions. Statements such as "like father, like son" and repeated requests to "set a good example for others" remind us that modeling is an effective teaching technique. The human tendency to imitate has been used as the basis of the therapeutic technique of modeling aimed at teaching clients new behaviors or strengthening existing behaviors (Dustin and George, 1977).

Albert Bandura and his associates have used the modeling technique to reduce a wide range of phobic behaviors, such as fear of dogs and snakes (Bandura, 1968; Rosenthal and Bandura, 1978). The procedure generally involves showing clients a series of pictures of a model interacting with the feared object. For example, people who are afraid of snakes may first see the model watching a snake from a distance. In the next picture, the model may move closer to the snake. As the sequence progresses, the model will touch the snake and finally handle it. Research has found that watching these models over a period of time does reduce the strength of clients' phobias (Bandura and Menlove, 1968; Rosenthal and Bandura, 1978).

The modeling technique can also be used to get clients themselves involved by asking them to perform the behavior that is modeled by the therapist or other model. In our snake example, after people watch the model handle the snake, they will be asked to handle a live snake them-

Modeling can be used to change many behaviors. Here, a young boy overcomes his fear of dogs by watching the model handle the dog, and then trying it himself.

selves. This participant modeling is effective in reducing fears and teaching new behaviors (Bandura, 1977). Further research has found that modeling is most effective when the model is similar to the client. For example, Kornhaber and Schroeder (1975) found that children were more likely to handle a snake after watching a child model this behavior than after seeing an adult handle the snake.

The use of modeling in therapy offers a number of exciting possibilities because the technique is relatively easy to use and almost any behavior can be modeled. There is, however, still some question about why the technique is effective (Sherman, 1979). Does the model teach a new behavior? Does watching the model allow the viewer to imagine performing the behavior? Does the model show the observer that no negative consequences will follow the feared behavior? These questions will have to be answered in future research so that the most effective modeling techniques can be identified.

Group Therapies

If we examine Chris's life, we find that many of her problems resulted from her attempts to interact with other people. As a child, Chris lived in an extended family, which included not only her parents, but her grandparents, uncles, aunts, and cousins. Chris longed for attention and often felt neglected. The beginning of her multiple personality problem came at a time when she felt most neglected. As a school-aged youngster, Chris had difficulties making friends and interacting with her schoolmates. She was poorer than many of the other children and she felt different. Still later in life, Chris had difficulties interacting with her own family, and family stress caused a new personality to emerge. Chris entered psychotherapy with Dr. Thigpen in the late 1940s. Dr. Thigpen used the individual, or one-on-one, therapy method that was widely practiced at that time. This method involved a single patient discussing his or her problems with the therapist in much the same way as you might interact with a physician if you have a medical problem.

However, the late 1940s and early 1950s saw the emergence of a different style of therapy, called **group therapy.** This type of therapy usually involved one therapist and a group of clients (usually 6 to 12 clients). The clients discussed their problems in the group and received feedback from the therapist and other group members. There was no single therapy technique used in the group; in fact, almost all the techniques that we have discussed have been adapted for group settings.

The role of the therapist differs in groups from what it is in individual therapy. In groups, the therapist must focus on creating and building a good group climate. Group members look to the therapist to define the basic rules of therapy (Korchin, 1976). The therapist must teach by setting examples for other members to follow; in a sense, the therapist must play two roles—that of therapist and that of group member. The relationship of the therapist to group members is important, but so is the relationship between group members. Because of these many demands, some groups may be run by two therapists.

As time passes, the therapist works on developing a trusting and cohesive relationship within the group. Cohesiveness is the solidarity and "we-feeling" that binds groups together, as we will discuss in Chapter 15. Members of cohesive groups are more open in their feelings, more committed to group goals, and more likely to attend therapy regularly. One patient recalled: "The most important thing in it (group therapy) was just having a group there, people that I could talk to, that wouldn't walk out on me. There was so much caring and hating and loving in the group and I was part of it" (Yalom, 1975, p. 48).

Group therapy allows the therapist to work with many clients at the same time. It also allows the clients to receive feedback from other people who have similar problems.

Group therapy offers a number of advantages over individual therapy (Yalom, 1975). First, as we pointed out earlier, it is more economical. One therapist can work with a number of clients at the same time. Second, since many of the clients' problems involve interpersonal relationships, the group setting is the best place to examine these problems and "practice" interpersonal behaviors. Third, Yalom points out that other group members often serve as a source of hope and encouragement for individual members. Group members encourage one another to deal with their problems and offer hope for improvement. Fourth, the other group members show each individual member that he or she is not alone in having problems. People who suffer psychological disorders often fall into the trap of thinking they are the only ones who ever had this problem. In the group they can see that others also have similar problems. Finally, other group members can serve as a source of information. They can point out problems and give helpful feedback. Thus, group therapy can have very positive results for both clients and therapist.

After this long list of advantages, you might naturally ask why all therapy is not practiced in groups. Despite the many positive characteristics of group therapy, there are some important limitations. Researchers point out that many clients may need individual therapy before they can function well in a group setting (Shertzer and Stone, 1974). These clients may be too insecure to interact with others. Some clients find it difficult to develop trust in a group interaction. Without trust, they are unwilling to openly discuss their problems and feelings. In some groups, the therapist's attention may be spread too thin to give each client the help that he or she needs. Finally, the pressure to conform to group rules may limit the therapy process (Corey and Corey, 1977).

Clearly, there are advantages and disadvantages to group therapy. While group therapy may be appropriate for many people, individual therapy will be best-suited for others. Just as we cannot argue that chemotherapy is always better than psychotherapy, we cannot say that group therapy is always better than individual therapy. The old saying that there is a time and a place for everything applies to therapies as well. In some cases chemotherapy is most appropriate, in other cases individual therapy may be called for, and in still other situations, group therapy will be most effective. Let us now examine a specific use of group techniques that aids personal adjustment and changes behavior.

Family Therapy

If Chris had consulted a family therapist, her experience in therapy would have been very different from that which she received from Dr. Thigpen. The family or systems approach views the family as a unique organization having roles, rules of behavior, and identifiable communication patterns (Perez, 1979). Although members may be unaware of the family structure, a trained therapist can often identify the structure by watching family members interact in a therapy setting. The family therapist believes that the family system can create stress and contribute to the development of psychological disorders. In Chapter 12 we discussed how double-bind communications (Bateson et al., 1956) in the family setting can be a factor in schizophrenia. In addition to causing psychological disorders, the structure of some families can maintain maladaptive behavior in family members. For example, when Chris began suffering her multiple personalities, she took on the role of "problem child" in her family. Her mother became the "protector" who cared for Chris and tried to explain her behavior to others. Her father took on the role of "concerned parent" who worried about Chris and talked about her problem to other family members. Chris's sisters became "helpers" who had to aid in the daily chores because Chris's problems took up much of the parents' time and energy. As you can see, a system of roles developed in the family around Chris's problem. While the system was designed to help Chris, it could also have contributed to maintaining her behavior by labeling her the "problem child." Further, if therapy were to change Chris's behavior so that she no longer fit the role of "problem child," all the other members of the family would have to change their roles, too. There would no longer be a need for a "protector" or "concerned parent."

With these considerations in mind, the family therapist attempts to work with the whole family. The therapist sees all the members of the family together and observes their behavior (Epstein and Jackson, 1978). He or she attempts to identify the family role structure and communication patterns. In "treating" the family, the therapist will take an active role, requesting family members to behave in certain ways (Haley, 1980). He or she will have the members work on open communication and encourage the expression of repressed emotions. The "rules" of the family will be identified and openly stated. These unwritten rules will be examined, and the therapist will point out how many of these rules exist only through habit and have outlived their usefulness. The therapist may also have family members play different roles so that others can see how they are perceived in the family. Through this process, the family system is changed so that it encourages more adaptive behavior from its members. While the family therapy approach has been found to be of particular value in helping adolescents, it has also been used in helping couples deal with interpersonal conflicts (Foley, 1974).

Community Psychology

As we have seen, the treatment of psychological disorders is generally a long process that involves several weeks or months of therapy. Even in the medical profession, the treatment of physical illness is often very involved and time-consuming. One way to treat a physical illness is to inoculate people to prevent its occurrence; an example is the use of vaccinations to prevent polio or measles. Unfortunately, there is no vaccine against psychological disturbances. However, in the last decade more attention has been paid to the prevention of disorders. The **community psychology** movement studies how environments can be altered to reduce stress and promote mental health. Community psychologists try to anticipate problems and take appropriate action to avoid them. For example, the school setting can be very stressful for many children. Children entering school for the first time are often faced with an unfamiliar environment and with the anxiety of being separated from their parents. With this in mind, many schools have set up programs to help children adjust to the academic setting and to deal with specific stressful events that may occur during the school day (George and Cristiani, 1981). For adults, *self-help groups* are organized to help people through difficult periods in their lives (Goethals and Worchel, 1980). Groups such as Parents Without Partners allow divorced parents to discuss their problems and seek solutions from one another. There is a wide variety of self-help groups; groups exist where the aged can discuss their special problems, where alcoholics can seek help, and where handicapped people can work through their stresses.

Changing the environment and preventing stress and disorders is an ideal goal, but often it is not possible to achieve it. Thus, a second aim

A veteran discusses his problems with a counselor in a government-sponsored "Vet Center" in Chicago. These community-based programs are aimed at helping veterans adjust and deal with potential problems before they develop into severe disorders.

of the community psychologist is to give aid to those suffering mild disorders before these disturbances become severe. Congress passed the Community Mental Health Centers Act in 1963. The act stated that one mental health center should be developed for every 50,000 people. The centers would be located in the local communities where they could offer a wide variety of services in a convenient and nondisruptive manner. For example, a person could walk into the center during a lunch break or after work and receive psychotherapy on an outpatient basis. If the person required hospitalization, he or she could be accommodated in the local center where frequent visits by family members would be possible. Many of the centers would operate "hot lines" where people suffering a crisis could call and talk with a professional or trained paraprofessional. Over 600 of these centers have been established.

The community mental health centers have offered counseling to many people who would not normally be able to afford it or seek it out. The centers have also made people more aware of the value of counseling and therapy. The aim of prevention is indeed a valuable one. There have, however, been a number of criticisms of the mental health centers (Holden, 1972). Often there is not a large enough staff to meet the problems of the community. Priority treatment may be given to one group, while inferior treatment is given to members of other groups. The goals of the centers may not be clearly stated, so that people are confused about the purpose and types of service offered by the center (Lamb and Zusman, 1979). Clearly, there are improvements to be made in the community mental health movement. The centers, however, can and are playing a vital role in the prevention and treatment of psychological disorders.

Personal Growth Techniques

When we think of therapy, we immediately think of techniques used to treat people suffering from an emotional or behavioral disorder. Indeed, the therapies that we have discussed are generally used for this purpose. There are, however, many people who seek professional help for a different reason. These people are not suffering from any severe disorder, although they often express discontent or unhappiness with their present lives (Korchin, 1976). In most cases these people have adjusted to their physical and social environments, but, in spite of their "normal" lives, they feel that something is missing. They may be unsatisfied with their relationships or unfulfilled in their jobs; they want to learn more about themselves; they want to be able to form closer relationships with others; and they want to have a wider variety of experiences. They turn to *personal growth techniques* to help them achieve this.

There are many different techniques that have been developed to help people in their quest for personal growth. Some are aimed at helping people develop greater understanding of themselves. There are techniques, on the other hand, that focus on developing greater sensitivity to others. In some cases, the techniques have been designed to help people learn how groups function. Many of these latter techniques have been used in business and industry to develop more effective leaders and managers.

The techniques are extremely varied. Some are based on theory and careful research, while others come from a dubious background. In many cases, the professionals have received extensive training and are experts in their area; in other cases, the people using these techniques have not had adequate training. In most states there are laws requiring that psychologists be licensed and trained before they can conduct therapy with people suffering from disorders. This is not always the case for people conducting personal growth therapies. In a strict sense, personal growth techniques are not really viewed as therapy, so it is often unclear just how they should be regulated. For this reason it is important to use some care when choosing a personal growth technique and leader.

Transpersonal Psychology. As the demands of our world become more complex, many people feel that they are losing touch with themselves—they pay so much attention to the things that are going on around them that they don't take the time to experience the things that are going on inside them. They also become overly concerned with the practical and rational aspects of their lives and scoff at the intuitive and the imaginative. Transpersonal psychology attempts to increase people's awareness of themselves. It seeks to expand people's experiences and teach them how to become completely absorbed in these experiences. The transpersonal movement represents a mixture of psychological theory, religion (including the teachings of Buddha, Lao Tzu, and the Dali Lamas of Tibet), and modern philosophy. Transpersonal psychology operates on the assumption that physical, emotional, intellectual, and spiritual growth are interrelated (Ivey and Simek-Downing, 1980). The movement argues that intuition, imagination, and altered states of consciousness (dreams, meditation, and drug-related experiences) are all part of human experience and should be examined.

Transpersonal psychologists attempt to develop all parts of the person, including the physical, emotional, mental, intuitive, psychic, and mystical aspects of personality (McWaters, 1975). In order to develop the physical parts, exercises such as jogging, dance, and massage are used. Yoga is also practiced; it involves tightening and relaxing exercises designed to

Transpersonal psychology attempts to increase people's self-awareness. Art is one of the mediums used to increase personal expression and understanding.

increase the blood supply to various parts of the body. The aim of these physical exercises is to make people more aware of their bodies and to help them relax. Emotional development is encouraged through the use of various psychotherapy techniques such as Gestalt therapy and personal expression in music and art. Mental development takes the form of lectures from leaders on topics ranging from philosophy to language and math. The psychic and mystical functions are developed through meditation, biofeedback training, prayer, and astrology.

Because of its emphasis on mystical experiences and its cultlike nature, many psychologists remain skeptical of the value of transpersonal psychology. Only recently has research begun to focus on some of the techniques used in this field, and it is thus too early to determine its effectiveness. Questions have been raised about the background and training required to practice transpersonal psychology. The movement, however, has captured the interest of many people who desire to expand their range of experiences and personal growth; only time and future research will determine whether it represents a valuable method or only a passing fad.

T-Groups and Encounter Groups. At about the same time that therapists realized that group therapy could be used to help people overcome specific psychological problems, others began using the group setting to help "healthy" people. They pointed out that although we work, play, and live in groups, few of us really examine how groups function or how we affect those groups (Bradford et al., 1964). These investigators argued that people could become more effective group members if they were more aware of how groups function. With this goal in mind, the **T-group,** or training group, was developed. These groups are generally made up of 8 to 15 members and 1 or 2 trainers. These trainers are not leaders in the sense that they set group goals or structure the group. Rather, trainers make observations about the process of the group, focusing on such issues as how decisions are made, how group roles and norms form, and how individual members contribute to the process. The group itself begins with no structure and no assigned task. Because of this, individual members are forced to develop this structure and define the group's goals. This process not only gives the members additional insight into how groups operate, but they can also get feedback about the ways in which each of them helps or hinders the group process. T-groups have been widely used in industrial and educational settings to aid group performance (Heller and Monahan, 1977).

The National Training Laboratories (NTL) have been the major organizer of the T-group movement. NTL operates a number of centers where T-groups meet. People interested in being in a T-group go to these centers, where they may live for a few weeks while they are in the group. Such centers are generally removed from urban centers so that there are few distractions. NTL also has an extensive training program, where people can learn the ethical standards and methods for running a T-group. Most of the people who become T-group trainers come from academic rather than clinical backgrounds. Many of these trainers are research-minded, and there has been extensive study of the T-group.

While the aim of the T-group is to help members examine the group process, the aim of the encounter group or sensitivity group is to expand personal awareness and growth (Brammer and Shostrom, 1977; Shapiro, 1978). Encounter groups provide intense, personal interactions in a setting where self-expression is encouraged. In a sense, encounter groups attempt to rid people of their interpersonal "hang-ups." There are numerous exercises often emphasizing nonverbal expression. For example, someone may be asked to express his or her feelings about another person without saying a word. It is from such exercises that encounter groups have gotten the label "touchy-feely" groups.

The variations on the encounter group are almost unlimited. In the marathon group, members interact and live together for 2 or 3 days. It is believed that this will increase the intensity of interaction and remove many inhibitions about interpersonal communication. Nude encounter groups (Bindrim, 1968), in which people interact in the nude, and encounter groups in which participants live in a minimal survival setting are some other varieties that have been used.

Many people profit from encounter groups by becoming freer in their expression and more sensitive to their own feelings (Dies and Greenberg, 1976; Golembiewski and Blumburg, 1973). However, during the 1960s the encounter group became something of a fad; groups were led by unqualified leaders and variations were tried not because they served a purpose, but simply because they were different or unusual. Because of the intensity of interaction, "casualties" resulted from encounter groups. A casualty was someone who suffered a negative effect from the group experience; sometimes these negative effects caused long-term suffering for the person. It has been estimated that from 9 to 33 percent of the participants had negative experiences from encounter groups (Lieberman, Yalom, and Miks, 1973; Yalom and Lieberman, 1971). Some of these causalties resulted because participants were not properly selected for the group. The encounter group is *not* a therapy group designed to help people suffering through a psychological disorder. Thus, encounter groups can be misused, and it is important to choose one that has a competent leader.

Does Psychotherapy Work?

We have traveled through the complex and sometimes confusing world of psychotherapy. As we have seen, there are long-term and short-term therapies; therapies that focus on the client's emotions; therapies that focus on changing behaviors; and therapies that use drugs and therapies that use words. Regardless of the type of therapy, the aim is the same: to help people deal with psychological disorders and change maladaptive behaviors. Now we must ask the basic question: "Is psychotherapy effective in treating psychological disturbances?"

At first glance, this seems like a simple question to answer. All we need to do is give psychotherapy to one group of people suffering from a disorder and withhold therapy from another group of people suffering the same disorder. At the end of a certain period of time, we can check to see which group has improved the most.

This solution seems so simple that it is hard to believe that there is still so much controversy as to the effectiveness of psychotherapy (Dodosh, 1981). However, as is so often the case in scientific investigations, the simple often turns out to be very complex. As we review the experimental program we outlined above, the first question that is raised deals with the issue of improvement. What does it mean to say someone is improved? For example, after many sessions with Dr. Thigpen, Chris understood her problem of multiple personalities and felt better about herself. However, she continued to suffer the emergence of different personalities. Would we say that Chris was improved because she felt better, or would we say that she showed no improvement because the multiple personalities still existed? It seems possible to make a strong argument for either position. A second issue involves the duration of improvement (Meltzoff and Kornreich, 1970). How are we to compare the effectiveness of a therapy that results in a quick but temporary change in the person's behavior with the effectiveness of a therapy that takes a long time but results in a more permanent change? A third issue concerns who is to determine the success of therapy. The therapist's opinion may be biased because he or she has a strong interest in believing that the therapy is successful.

Throughout modern and ancient history, the physician has been one of the most respected people. Stories of miracles worked by physicians are commonplace in every age. When we look at the history of medicine, it becomes amazing that even the most hardy patient could survive, let alone improve, under early medical techniques. Patients took almost every known organic and inorganic material, including crocodile dung, teeth of swine, powder of precious stones, furs, feathers, human perspiration, oil of ants, blood, and earthworms. The patients were purged, poisoned, punctured, cut, blistered, bled, leached, heated, frozen, and sweated (Shapiro, 1971). Today we know that most of these treatments have no medical value. Yet there are carefully documented stories of patients improving. How could this happen?

A number of investigators have suggested that these miraculous recoveries are examples of the placebo effect (Honigfield, 1964; Shapiro, 1971). Simply put, the placebo effect describes the situation in which a treatment that has no curative value of its own has a healing effect on the patient because of the patient's belief in its effectiveness. While the placebo effect has been most frequently applied in medicine, some clinicians (Wilkens, 1973) have suggested that the placebo effect may be one of the reasons that psychotherapy works. According to this position, almost any method of psychotherapy should show positive results if the client believes it will be effective. In other words, it is the client's belief that the method will work that causes the positive results. If this is the case, it is clear that the therapist must convey to the client that the method will be successful.

There are a number of possible reasons for the placebo effect. One of the most common explanations focuses on the "self-fulfilling prophecy," which we discussed in Chapter 12. According to this position, people are motivated to interpret events to support their expectancies. In order to illustrate this, let us suppose that we have two people, Bob and Mary, who are in group therapy to overcome shyness. Mary strongly believes that the therapy will be effective, while Bob does not. After two sessions of therapy, Mary and Bob meet a stranger on the bus and strike up a short conversation. For Mary, this becomes a sign that therapy is working; even though it was hard, she would never have been able to talk to a stranger before therapy. Her new confidence motivates her to talk to other people. Bob, on the other hand, focuses on the fact that he felt uncomfortable talking to the stranger. For Bob, this is a sign that reinforces his belief that the therapy was not helping him. His trust in the therapy decreases even further, and he eventually drops out of the group. In this example we can see that the expectancy not only influenced the way Mary and Bob interpreted their behaviors, but it also had future consequences for their efforts in therapy.

A second reason for the placebo effect involves the feelings of control. In Chapter 10 we discussed how a lack of control can cause stress. Many people enter therapy because they believe that they have no control over their feelings or behaviors. Gatchel (1980) suggests that the expectancy that therapy will be effective gives people a feeling of control over their lives. This perceived control reduces their stress and anxiety.

A third explanation for the placebo effect focuses on effort justification. As we will see in Chapter 14, research on cognitive dissonance theory has found that people are motivated to justify their effort; the more effort they choose to expend, the greater the need to justify it. One way to justify effort is to change one's attitudes to believe that the effortful behavior was a positive and valuable experience. Cooper and Axsom (1982) point out that therapy often involves a great deal of effort on the part of clients. Not only is it often difficult to talk about one's problems, but clients must also sacrifice their time and money. It would be even more difficult to continue making these sacrifices if the clients believed that the therapy was not helping them. Therefore, in order to justify their sacrifices and efforts, clients may become motivated to believe in the effectiveness of the therapy.

The important point of the placebo effect is that it can be applied to any type of therapy; the effect can influence clients' responses no matter what technique is used in therapy. It also shows how important it is for the therapist to show that he or she has confidence and faith in the therapy.

At first glance, it may seem that the placebo effect suggests that therapy is simply a process of self-deception. This is not the case. Rather, both physicians and therapists have known for a long time that a patient's attitudes and beliefs are very important in determining the effectiveness of treatment. Any treatment will be more effective if the patient believes in it and is willing to use it in the proper manner. Research on the placebo effect suggests that the way in which the treatment is presented to the patient or client is one major factor in determining the effectiveness of that treatment.

The client's opinion may also be influenced by expectations and desires to see the therapy as successful. Objective measures such as test scores or behavioral measures may be the most unbiased, but they are difficult to use on a long-term basis.

A related issue is *why* therapy works. If we can determine that psychotherapy is successful, we would also like to know why this is so. Does the success of therapy depend on characteristics of the client, characteristics of the therapist, the specific techniques used in therapy, or simply the expectations of those involved? Suddenly, the simple question "Does it work?" becomes very complicated.

Given the complexity of the issue, it is easier to see why clinicians have sometimes been reluctant to conduct evaluation research and why there are disagreements as to the meaning of the results that have been obtained. In 1952, Hans Eysenck created a furor when he concluded that people receiving psychotherapy showed no more improvement than those receiving no treatment. Eysenck based his conclusion on a review of 24 studies of people suffering moderate psychological disturbances (neuroses). Eysenck's shocking conclusion led a number of investigators to review his data and to conduct additional research (Bergin, 1971; Smith and Glass, 1977). These more recent reviews of a larger body of research suggest that psychotherapy does have positive effects, although it does not work for everyone (Smith and Glass, 1977). Further, Smith and Glass found that psychoanalytic, behavioral, and humanistic therapies were about equally effective.

While specific techniques might not determine the success of therapy, research has shown that both client and therapist variables influence the outcome of therapy. For example, a client who is physically healthy, strongly motivated to improve, and of relatively high intellegence is most likely to be helped by therapy. Further, certain disorders, such as phobias, can be treated more effectively than other disorders such as personality disorders. Mitchell, Bozarth, and Krauft (1977) found that the personal characteristics of the therapist influence the effectiveness of therapy. Therapists who can project warmth and caring had the greatest positive effect on their clients. This position was supported in a study that found that male college students suffering from neurotic disorders showed equal improvement when treated by an experienced therapist or a college professor who was chosen for the personal characteristics of warmth and understanding (Strupp and Hadley, 1979).

An overall picture of the effectiveness of psychotherapy is difficult to form based on the present research. At this point, we can conclude that psychotherapy is effective in some cases and that the degree of effectiveness is influenced by the disorder, the client's characteristics, and the personal traits of the therapist. Clearly, more research is needed on this complex issue. Careful research in this area can not only clear up confusion about the value of current techniques, but it can also serve as the basis for developing new and more effective ways of working with psychological disorders.

SUMMARY

1. Many methods of therapy have been developed for dealing with psychological disturbances. These methods may be broadly divided into psychotherapy and biotherapy. **Biotherapy** involves some type of physical treatment, including the use of drugs, surgery, electric shock, and biofeedback to induce behavior change. **Psychotherapies** involve a trained professional who uses verbal interactions to bring about behavior change

and positive adjustment in an individual or group.

2.   There is a wide variety of biotherapies **Electroconvulsive therapy (ECT)** involves electric shock; it is used most often with severely depressed patients. **Psychosurgery** involves cutting connections between different parts of the brain; the **prefrontal labotomy** is the best-known type of psychosurgery. **Chemotherapy** is the use of drugs (antianxiety, antipsychotic, and antidepressant drugs) to treat psychological disorders. **Biofeedback** is a method that teaches people to control their physiological functions by giving them feedback about these functions.

3.   Many types of psychotherapy were discussed in this chapter. **Psychoanalysis,** developed by Sigmund Freud, is based on the notion that events in early childhood are important determinants of one's personality. Feelings or events associated with early childhood may be **repressed,** leading to anxiety later on. Freud believed that these repressed feelings enter the person's **unconscious** and can be released through the use of **free association** or **dream interpretation.**

4.   Carl Rogers and other humanistic psychologists propose that **client-centered therapy** will help people through a process of self-growth. Client-centered therapy involves creating an atmosphere of **unconditional positive regard** in which the therapist relays warmth and concern for the client. In this setting the client is able to gain the confidence necessary for self-exploration and personal growth.

5.   **Gestalt therapy,** developed mainly by Fritz Perls, proposes that unconscious thoughts and emotions (background) may lead to behaviors (figure) that are inappropriate to the situation. In Gestalt therapy people are helped to take responsibility for their actions, while understanding the emotions that are influencing their behaviors.

6.   According to **rational emotive therapy (RET),** irrational thoughts are responsible for the way we feel about ourselves and others. RET therapists are concerned only with the present, and use a challenging, directive approach to help clients discover their anxiety-producing irrational thoughts.

7.   **Behavior therapies** assume that abnormal behaviors are learned, and thus can be unlearned by changing the events that reinforce maladaptive behaviors. Behavior therapists may use **aversive conditioning** to break undesirable habits, or **systematic desensitization** to help overcome phobias. With **operant conditioning,** positive rewards are used to motivate people to perform desirable behaviors. These rewards often take the form of **token economies.** A fourth method of changing behaviors involves **modeling.** With this type of behavior therapy, the client watches someone else engage in the desired behavior.

8.   In psychotherapy, a therapist may see only a single client at a time, or may work with a group of clients. In **group therapy,** clients not only receive feedback from the therapist, but the other group members also contribute. **Family therapy** involves seeing the family unit as a whole during the therapy session. Family therapy assumes that the family system can create stress and contribute to the development of psychological disorders.

9.   **Community psychology** attempts to prevent stress by changing the environment. When environmental change is not possible, community psychologists strive to help those people suffering from mild disorders before their disturbances become severe. These goals are often met through the use of self-help groups of community mental health centers.

10.   There are a number of techniques used to help people achieve greater personal growth. These methods are not really therapies, since they are not aimed at treating a specific disorder. Included in this category are **transpersonal psychology, T-groups,** and **encounter** and **sensitivity groups.**

SUGGESTED READINGS

The following books are about Chris Sizemore:

SIZEMORE, C., and PITTILLO, E. S. *I'm Eve*. Garden City, N.Y.: Doubleday, 1977.

THIGPEN, C. H., and CLECKLEY, H. M. *The Three Faces of Eve*. New York: Popular Library, 1974.

EGAN, G. *The skilled helper: A model for systematic helping and interpersonal relating*. Monterey, Calif.: Brooks/Cole, 1975. Presents a three-stage helping model to teach readers to be better counselors and increase interpersonal sensitivity. It also examines theories of learning, social influence, and behavior modification.

GARFIELD, S., and BERGIN, A. (Eds.). *Handbook of psychotherapy and behavior change: An empirical analysis*. New York: Wiley, 1978. Presents a number of original chapters examining a wide range of types of psychotherapy.

KORCHIN, S. *Modern clinical psychology*. New York: Basic Books, 1976. A comprehensive overview of the field of clinical psychology. Korchin focuses on testing, therapy, and community psychology.

LEITENBERG, H. (Ed.). *Handbook of behavior modification and behavior therapy*. Englewood Cliffs, N.J.: Prentice-Hall, 1976. This book is a collaboration of chapters dealing with the use of behavior modification and other learning techniques in therapy.

SHAPIRO, J. *Methods of group psychotherapy and encounter*. Itasca, Ill.: Peacock Publishers, 1978. An examination of the various methods of group psychotherapy, the book presents cases and exercises for using groups in therapy and for personal growth.

14

Interpersonal Relations

Young Malcolm listened carefully as his father preached to the small group: "No one knows when the hour of Africa's redemption cometh. It is in the wind. It is coming. One day, like a storm, it will be here" (Malcolm X, 1965). Reverend Little continued his militant stance on black-race purity, urging his audience to take pride in their African heritage and return to their African homeland. While this radical position shocked many blacks, it threatened many whites. The Ku Klux Klan warned Reverend Little against continuing his inflammatory sermons. Then one afternoon in 1931, the warnings turned into actions; the preacher was beaten to death. Malcolm was 6 at the time and understood little about the racial hatred that had suddenly turned his world into a nightmare.

Malcolm's nightmare did not stop there. Over the next several years, the family survived on the brink of starvation. Mrs. Little was committed to a mental institution and her eight children became wards of the state. Although Malcolm lived in detention and foster homes, he made good progress in the nearly all-white Mason, Michigan school. But despite having many friends and being elected class president, he felt out-of-place.

After the eighth grade, he went to Boston to live with his half-sister. Boston was both exciting and frightening. At first he felt helplessly alone: "I looked like Li'l Abner. Mason, Michigan was written all over me. My kinky, reddish hair was cut hick style, and I didn't even use grease in it" (Malcolm X, 1965, p. 39). The blacks in Boston were different from any he had seen in Michigan. They "conked" their hair to make it straight and shiny like white men's hair. They used slang expressions such as "cat," "chick," "cool," and "hip." He saw 12-year-olds shooting craps, playing cards, and fighting.

One day, Malcolm met a young man named Shorty in a pool room. Shorty was well acquainted with the Boston scene, and if anybody could get Malcolm a job, he could. The two talked for a while and Malcolm described his background. When he said he was from Lansing, Shorty jumped up and shouted: "My homeboy. Man, gimme some skin! I'm from Lansing." This basic similarity cemented their friendship and Shorty took Malcolm under his wing. He got Malcolm a job shining shoes at Roseland, the famous dance hall. Famous bands such as Count Basie's played there, and blacks and whites flocked there in droves to enjoy the music and dance.

Malcolm was in the midst of the action and he began to make use of it. He conked his hair, bought a wild-looking zoot suit, and was soon making friends with the musicians who played at the hall. At that time, it was prestigious for a black man to have white, female friends. Malcolm began dating Sophia, one of the most beautiful white women who came to Roseland.

He soon quit his job at Roseland and took a job selling sandwiches on the train that ran from Boston to New York. This job introduced him to Harlem, the hub of activity. Money flowed like water in Harlem and the hundreds of bars and restaurants were the focus of people dealing in drugs, gambling, and prostitution. With his status and connections, Malcolm was well suited for these activities. He began dealing drugs and running numbers in Harlem, living at a fast and furious pace.

Drug dealing was a dangerous business, and Malcolm had come close to being arrested several times. Knowing that his luck would not hold out much longer, he decided to change his "line of work." He called Shorty, Sophia, and Sophia's sister together and they decided to form a burglary gang.

Success made him careless, and one day he was caught. In February, 1946, just before his twenty-first birthday, Malcolm Little was sentenced to 8 to 10 years in prison. Although at first he had almost welcomed his prison sentence, Malcolm soon longed for his freedom. It was this longing that made him read a letter from his brother with curious delight. In the middle of the letter from his youngest brother, Reginald, he read, "Malcolm, don't eat any more pork, and don't smoke any more cigarettes. I'll show you how to get out of prison." He couldn't figure out the connection between these actions and getting out of prison; perhaps the game was to convince the prison psychiatrist that he was crazy. Whatever the angle, it was worth a try.

A few months later, he learned that his brother's instructions were based on religious beliefs, not some secret angle to get him out of prison. Reginald visited the prison and informed Malcolm that his brothers and sisters had joined the Nation of Islam. This was a Muslim sect led by the Messenger of Allah, the Honorable Elijah Muhammad. He explained the Muslim religion to Malcolm and also told him, "The white man is the devil." He pointed out that the white man had destroyed a marvelous black civilization and had raped and enslaved the blacks until they no longer had their own identity. Reginald told him that blacks could begin to regain their identity by following the laws of Allah, which were taught by Elijah Muhammad.

This discussion overwhelmed Malcolm. He had been a drug pusher, a pimp, a burglar, and a gambler. He had mocked religion. But his brother's words kept running through his mind as he lay in his cell. Maybe, just maybe, he was right. In order to be a Muslim, he would have to live a very strict and disciplined life: no smoking, narcotics, or liquor, strict codes for eating and styles of dress, and few luxuries. "The key to a Muslim is submission, the attunement of one toward Allah." Malcolm pondered these words. The more he read, the more he began to believe.

His next step was to write to Elijah Muhammad, and to his delight and surprise, he received a quick reply. He then began doing something he had never done in his life; he began praying. Each day he wrote to Elijah Muhammad. He studied and prayed in the solitude of his cell. When he entered prison, he had associated mostly with white inmates, but his conversion to Islam brought a change of friends. Now he associated almost solely with black inmates, and he tried to convert them to his new faith.

In 1952, Malcolm was released from prison. He immediately went to Elijah Muhammad and pledged his loyalty. His mission in life was to start new temples for the Muslim faith and recruit followers for Elijah Muhammad. He would stand on the street corner "fishing" for converts. When someone listened, Malcolm would invite him to attend one of the services. Once this small commitment was made, the potential convert would be invited to take an increasingly more active role in the temple. Malcolm Little became Malcolm X. The "X" symbolized the true African name that he never could know. Malcolm X became a minister in the service of Elijah Muhammad. He sounded the message "Black is beautiful" and said that blacks should band together to demand their rightful place on the throne of history. He followed the strict code of behavior demanded by Elijah Muhammad. He did not gamble, dance, date, attend movies or sports events, or take long vacations. Any domestic quarreling or discourtesy, especially to women, was forbidden. No lying, stealing, or insubordination was allowed. The more he adhered to these rules, the more devoted he became to Elijah Muhammad. Malcolm X's fame grew as he defended the militant stand of the Black Muslims. He became the main spokesman for Elijah Muhammad.

However, with his new fame, problems also began to surface. Many Black Muslims began to feel that Malcolm X was becoming too powerful. The rift widened and at one point erupted into a feud between Elijah Muhammad and Malcolm X. The once-devoted follower of Elijah Muhammad announced that he was breaking away from the Nation of Islam to found his own movement: the Muslim Mosque, Inc. Now, Malcolm X not only had to defend his position against whites and non-Muslim blacks, but he was also in a struggle with other Muslims who followed Elijah Muhammad.

At this point, Malcolm X decided to make a pilgrimage to Mecca, the holiest city of the Muslim faith. With a great deal of effort, he obtained the necessary passport and started for Mecca. When he arrived in Saudi Arabia, he was surprised to find that he attracted a great deal of attention. After the excitement of his arrival in Saudi Arabia had worn off, Malcolm X realized that he would need a great deal of help getting to Mecca. To his surprise, many people were willing to help him, and some of these people were white. His confusion continued when he arrived in Mecca; here people of white, yellow, brown, and black skin prayed together in harmony and peace. He did report, "There was a color pattern in the huge crowds. I saw that people who looked alike drew together and most of the time stayed together. This was entirely voluntary; there being no other reason for it. But Africans were with Africans. Pakistanis were with Pakistanis. And so

on" (Malcolm X, 1965, p. 344). But despite this voluntary segregation, the people from different races got along very well together. These observations had a profound effect on Malcolm X; his antiwhite attitude changed. He now believed that the plight of blacks was the result of the American system rather than the inherent evil of whites.

He was the source of almost daily verbal blasts of criticism in the media. Many, both blacks and whites, saw him as a real threat to American society. But in his words, he tried to instill a new pride in American blacks. As his popularity grew, so did the feud between his sect and that of Elijah Muhammad.

Malcolm X had said many times that he would meet with a violent death either as the result of a plot by whites, or from the Black Muslim followers of Elijah Muhammad. Malcolm X's prediction of a violent death came true; on February 21, 1965, he was gunned down by three assassins as he began to deliver a speech.

THE SCOPE OF SOCIAL PSYCHOLOGY

The story of Malcolm X raises many fascinating questions. How could a man from a rural background who had been a gambler, pimp, drug pusher, and convict, become a devout member of a religion that forbade drinking, smoking, gambling, and dating? Why did Malcolm X adopt an extreme antiwhite attitude? What determined Malcolm X's choice of friends? What was this complex man really like?

One way to examine these questions about Malcolm X is to study him as a unique case. That is, we could look at his history and attempt to determine the specific personality characteristics that influenced him. In fact, Malcolm X himself suggested this approach. "But people are always speculating—why am I as I am? To understand that of any person, his whole life, from birth, must be reviewed" (Malcolm X, 1965, p. 150). As you will recognize, this is the approach used by personality psychologists (Chapter 11, "Personality: Theories and Assessment"). The aim of this approach is to identify the individual differences that influence the way a particular person behaves.

While there are many strengths in this method of study, there is another way to examine this case. Although Malcolm X lived in a different time and in a different environment from that facing us today, the general dynamics of social interaction were the same then as now. In other words, in the story of Malcolm X, we find the same issues that are of concern to each of us in our daily lives. Therefore, if we can grasp an understanding of the broad conditions that influence human behavior, we can begin to gain some insight not only into Malcolm X's behavior, but also into our own behavior.

Social psychology is the branch of psychology that takes this approach to understanding social behavior; its aim is to develop general laws of human behavior. Social psychologists are interested in identifying factors that influence most people, most of the time. For example, we will review research showing that people are generally attracted to those who are like them. This is a general rule of human behavior. It does not mean that you will always be attracted to someone who is like you. It does mean, however, that in *most* cases, *most* people will be attracted to people who are like them.

Social psychology is a relative newcomer to the family of psychology. It began to develop in the late 1930s with the research and theories of Kurt Lewin, who believed that much of a person's everyday behavior is influenced by other people in the environment. Thus, in order to develop a deeper understanding and appreciation of human behavior, we must study how people are affected by their social situations. Lewin also emphasized the need for a systematic and scientific approach to study social behavior, and stressed the importance of developing theories of behavior and testing these theories in carefully controlled experiments. Therefore, we can define **social psychology** as the scientific study of the way in which people are affected by social situations and social relationships (Worchel and Cooper, 1979). Or we might say that social psychology is the scientific study of the way most people act most of the time.

With this introduction in mind, let us now look at some of the specific areas of interpersonal behavior that have been investigated by social psychologists. In reviewing these areas we will see that the broad approach of social psychology can be used to help explain such different areas as attitudes, social influence, impression formation, interpersonal attraction, and helping behavior.

ATTITUDES

When we observe the people around us, we see that much of their conversation and behavior is concerned with attitudes. People discuss their attitudes toward nuclear arms, President Reagan's policies, premarital sex, and abortion. Conflicts between people often begin over differences of opinion, and people with similar attitudes often find themselves attracted to one another. Attitudes played a large role in Malcolm X's life. His attitudes about blacks and whites made him the spokesman of many and a threat to many others. His attitudes about religion led him to make his pilgrimage to Mecca. And his attitudes made him a target for the assassins' bullets.

Although there are many definitions, most present **attitudes** as learned, relatively enduring feelings about objects, events, or issues (McGuire, 1968). It is generally agreed that attitudes have three components.

1. The first is *evaluation;* that is, attitudes place a positive or negative meaning on the object or event in question. Clearly, Malcolm X evaluated whites negatively.
2. Attitudes have a *belief* component. Beliefs are statements that express a relationship between events or objects (Zimbardo and Ebbesen, 1970). Imbedded in Malcolm X's attitude about whites was his belief that whites had destroyed black civilization.
3. The third component is *action*. Attitudes often describe how people should act toward an object or event. Looking again at Malcolm X's attitude about whites, we see that he advocated a separation of blacks and whites. Later, when his attitude changed, he felt that blacks and whites could live together if American society were changed.

The Development of Attitudes

As we move from the general definition to looking at the attitudes that people actually hold, two points become very clear. First, people are not born with attitudes; attitudes are developed and formed as we grow up. Second, people hold attitudes, often very strong attitudes, about subjects that they don't know much about. For example, most of us do not really understand nuclear energy, nor do we know the federal standards that nuclear power plants must meet. However, we do have attitudes about the use of nuclear energy. Where did such attitudes come from?

The Influence of Parents. Many of your attitudes are like those of your parents. For example, you and your parents probably support the same political party, and you probably share similar religious beliefs as well. It is interesting to see that the attitude about whites that was first adopted by Malcolm X was close to that held by his father.

Parents influence their children's attitudes in two ways. First, they use rewards and punishments. Children who voice the "right" attitudes are likely to get praise and smiles, while children who express the "wrong" attitudes are likely to be greeted with frowns and scolding. Parents are especially powerful sources of influence for young children because they have almost total control over the rewards and punishments in their childrens' world. Second, parents are able to control the information that reaches their children. Many parents decide which television programs and books their children watch and read. In some cases they even try to control what their children learn in school. In this way, they influence attitudes by controlling outside information that will affect those attitudes.

Parents have a strong and lasting effect on our attitudes. They are usually the first sources to shape our attitudes.

For example, it is unlikely that a young child will have a positive attitude towards blacks if he or she has only seen television programs depicting blacks as being lazy or stupid, or has read books associating them with crime.

Parental influence on attitudes is strong and lasting. There are several reasons for this. One is that children tend to believe their parents; they see them as the best and smartest people in the world. A second reason is that it's much easier to create new attitudes than it is to change old ones. Parents in this sense are in at the start, because they help their children form attitudes to begin with—they don't have to change their preexisting ones. Finally, attitudes formed when young tend to persist because for the rest of their lives people tend to seek out information that upholds their attitudes and ignore information that conflicts with them. Thus, once an attitude is formed, we tend to behave in a way that will protect and preserve it.

The Influence of Peers. As we discussed in the development chapters, beginning at around age 6 and continuing through at least the early teen years, children become more and more affected by their peers. From the time they start school, they begin to spend more time with peers in the classroom, on the playground, and in other formal and informal groups such as cub scout or brownie troops and little league baseball teams.

These peers supply the child with new information and present different ways to look at issues. This, by itself, could influence the child's attitudes. There is, however, another way that peers shape attitudes. That is the threat of rejection. Children quickly learn that the way to be accepted by other children is to act and believe as they do. Rejection is often the penalty for taking a position that is different from the group. Thus, both children and adults often adopt the attitudes of their peers because they fear rejection if they do not.

The Influence of the Media. Malcolm X was very aware of the power of the press. He started his own newspaper, and he invited media coverage of his speeches. He willingly accepted invitations to appear on talk shows. In other words, he effectively used the media to spread his message to the public. In modern day revolutions and armed conflicts, one of the most prized targets by both sides are the mass communication sources (radio, television, newspapers), because of the view that whoever controls the media can control the people.

One of the reasons for the power of the press is that the media are able to reach so many people. For example, 97 percent of the homes in the United States have at least one television set. This is a higher percentage than the number of homes that have indoor plumbing! By the age of 12, most children in the United States have spent more time watching television than in school (Gerbner and Gross, 1976).

A second reason for this influence is that the media are often the only source of information we have about events. For example, most of us have never visited Russia, nor have we talked to anyone who has been there. However, we have very definite attitudes about the Russians. These attitudes are based on information we have received from the media.

While it is generally accepted that the media do influence us, there has been some disagreement over which medium has the greatest influence. Our first response on this question might be that television should have the greatest effect; television allows us to both see and hear the communicator. However, a recent review of the research has failed to find that one medium is always more persuasive than any other medium (Taylor and Thompson, 1982). Rather, it seems that the effectiveness of a medium is determined by such factors as the audience, the type of message, and the communicator.

Peers are able to influence attitudes by supplying new information and threatening rejection if these attitudes are not adopted.

Attitude Change

Up to this point, we have focused on the agents that influence the development of new attitudes. In a sense, we can view these agents as the pioneers of our attitudes; they tread on new territory, trying to get us to accept new information about issues that are often unfamiliar to us. Since we may have only few preexisting attitudes in these cases, the decision facing us is whether or not this new information is reasonable and the source is credible.

As we grow older, the focus changes. Often we are no longer dealing with the formation of new attitudes. Rather, efforts are aimed at changing our existing attitudes. The task facing those who wish to change our attitudes is somewhat different and more difficult than that faced in the development of new attitudes. In changing our attitudes, we must not only accept a new position or new information, we must also give up our old position. We may be reluctant to do this because our existing attitudes form an interlocking or balanced system (Heider, 1946). If we change one attitude, there is often pressure to change other attitudes. For example, a young woman may believe that her parents are smart and trustworthy. Her parents may have taught her that women should be housewives and that she should avoid taking a job outside the home. If this person were to change her attitude about women, she would also feel pressure to change her attitude about her parents.

A second difference between the development of new attitudes and changing attitudes is that people involved in attitude change must not only decide if the new information and communicator are trustworthy, they must decide whether or not the new information and communicator are *more* trustworthy than the original information and communicator.

Although the issue of attitude change has always been central to social psychology, it received added interest during World War II. While a war of bullets and bombs raged in many parts of the world, a war on attitudes was being waged in the United States. In order to be prepared for war, Americans had to change many of their habits and attitudes. Since the war was being fought in Europe, many Americans felt that there was little danger to their homeland. A successful war effort required that this attitude be changed. Other attitudes of concern involved people's daily habits. For example, although the war created a shortage of beef, there was no shortage of beef entrails such as kidneys, brains, and sweetbreads. There was a great deal of food value in these items, but Americans tended to resist eating them. Therefore, it became important to change attitudes about what foods were edible (Lewin, 1943).

Given this important need, investigators began to carefully study attitude change. Their research focused on three factors: The communicator, the message, and the audience. In other words, research on attitude change examines who says what to whom. Let us briefly look at some of the more important findings in each of these areas.

The Communicator. One of the first questions that we can ask is who should deliver the message? It does seem to make a difference if the communicator is highly credible (that is, easily believable). For example, Hovland and Weiss (1952) found that an audience was more likely to believe an eminent scientist than the Communist newspaper *Pravda* on the subject of building nuclear submarines. Interestingly enough, however, this effect disappeared over time (see Figure 14-1). That is, the more credible source had a greater effect on people's attitudes than the less credible source right after the message was given. But the credibility of the communicator made no difference when people were asked their opinion 4 weeks after hearing the message. This pattern of results has been called the **sleeper effect** (Kelman and Hovland, 1953; Gruder et

The events following the Watergate break-in demonstrate how difficult it is to change attitudes. Many people believed that a President of the United States could not become involved in such events. Despite all the evidence showing Nixon's involvement, it took many years before most people were convinced that he indeed took part in the Watergate coverup.

FIGURE 14–1

The sleeper effect occurs when people separate the source from the message over time. As a result, the influence of communication credibility on attitude change is reduced or eliminated.

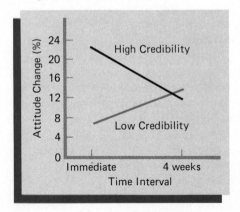

al., 1979). It seems to occur because people tend to separate the source from the message as time passes. In other words, they forget who said what, and the early advantage of the more credible communicator is reduced.

There is another factor that affects how persuasive a communicator is: his or her similarity to the audience. Imagine that you are interested in buying some paint to redecorate your apartment. You walk into a paint store and choose your paint, and, while waiting at the cashier's counter you meet a salesman who tells you that he recently completed a painting job using about the same amount of paint that you are using. After noticing the brand of paint you have chosen, he states that he used another brand and was very happy with it. He suggests that you switch brands. Now, imagine yourself in a similar situation, but this time you are met by a paint salesman who informs you that he recently completed a painting job that was very different from the one you are planning and his purchase of paint was much larger than yours. He, too, notices your brand of paint and suggests you change to another brand. In which case would you be more likely to buy the brand being pushed by the salesman? Brock (1965) conducted this study in a paint store and found that the salesman who presented himself as being similar to the customer was more persuasive than the other salesman. Other research (Goethals and Nelson, 1973) has found that similar communicators are most effective when the issue involves evaluations, what is good or bad, rather than facts.

The Message. Moving from the communicator to the message, we can ask whether or not there are certain types of messages that are more effective than others. There are many factors that can increase persuasiveness of a message. We will look at two: the mood and the structure of a message.

Messages associated with events that make people feel good are more persuasive than ones not associated with such events. For example, one study had subjects read persuasive messages about a number of topics (Janis, Kaye, and Kirschner, 1965). Half the subjects read the messages in a typical laboratory setting. The other half were given a tasty snack

HIGHLIGHT / ADVERTISING, THE ULTIMATE IN ATTITUDE CHANGE

The advertising industry can be viewed as the industry of attitude change. Imagine the huge task facing advertisers; they have only a small space in a magazine or a 30-second spot on television to convince the audience to buy their product. Given our discussion on the difficulty of changing attitudes, this would seem to be an impossible task. However, a great deal of money is riding on the possibility that the advertising industry can succeed in its task: More than $25 billion was spent during 1973 for advertising in the United States (Rice, 1974). Advertisers have developed very sophisticated techniques to convince us to drink Coke when thirsty, eat Big Macs when hungry, and take Alka Seltzer when our stomachs don't agree. And Wells (1975) points out that advertisers are often able to change our attitudes without teaching us anything about their product. How are they able to do this?

When we examine advertising techniques, we find that they use many of the theories that social psychologists have studied.

Communicator similarity is frequently used in advertisements. For example, we often see the "average American family" using brand X soap and proclaiming how

clean and refreshed they feel after using this soap. Or we find the "typical housewife" exclaiming how clean brand Y laundry powder gets her wash. The message clearly is that if the product works well for these people, it will certainly work well for the majority of people.

The "hidden camera" technique is used to give the impression of a *trustworthy communicator.* In these types of advertisements, the audience is led to believe that the communicator does not know that he or she is being taped, and is therefore speaking honestly.

Credible communicators are often created. For instance, we may see a person dressed in a white laboratory coat proclaiming that "three out of four doctors" recommend a certain brand of aspirin. An interesting twist on the expert approach is to use an expert in one field to advertise products in another. We may find a famous baseball player advertising an automobile or a well-known actor or actress advising us to buy a certain breakfast cereal. In each example, the aim is to enhance the product by associating it with an "expert" source.

Emotional appeals are often used to sell a product. One favorite ploy is to play a catchy tune while

advertising a product. Another plan is to use a communicator who will sexually arouse the audience. It is common to see a scantily dressed woman or a handsome male recommending a certain automobile, wine, or shave cream. In all these cases, the aim is to have the audience associate the product with a pleasant feeling (sexual arousal).

Conversely, a number of advertisements use *fear appeals* to get their message across. A common ad for wearing seat belts shows a terrible automobile accident and presents the message that injury could have been avoided if the driver had worn a seat belt. As we pointed out, arousing a moderate degree of fear and then presenting a means to reduce the fear is an effective persuasive technique.

Repeated exposure is another common advertising technique. The aim here is simply to have the audience see the product as often as possible. This approach is consistent with research showing that the more people are exposed to an object, the more attractive they find it (Zajonc, 1968).

It is obvious that the research in social psychology can help explain the effectiveness of advertising campaigns.

to munch on while they read the messages. Afterwards, subjects' attitudes were measured, and it was found that those who were provided with a snack were more likely to adopt the position of the message than the others. An example of this in real life is the "business lunch," in which business people often invite clients to join them for a nice lunch or dinner over which they can negotiate contracts.

There are also messages that are used to try to change our attitudes by making us fearful. Malcolm X used fear when he spoke of how the whites were destroying the black race. He painted grim pictures of what would happen to blacks if they allowed this to continue. Studies show that a moderate amount of fear is more effective than either a low or a very high amount. The moderate amount of fear grabs the audience's attention, but is not so great that it causes them to reject the message because they are uncomfortable thinking about it (Janis and Feshbach, 1953).

Focusing more directly on the message itself, we can examine whether some structures are more effective than others. Basically this comes down to whether it is better to present only one side of an argument or both sides. Which one of these messages is the most persuasive? It has been repeatedly shown (Hovland et al., 1949; Jones and Brehm, 1970) that the answer to this question in part depends on the audience. The two-sided message would be more persuasive than the one-sided one if the audience initially disagrees with the position taken. However, if the audience is already in favor of the position advocated in the speech, the one-sided message would be most persuasive.

The Audience. We have already seen that the early attitude of the audience affects whether a one- or two-sided message will be most effective. Taking a somewhat different approach to audience effects, Freedman and Fraser (1966) asked whether people's opinions of themselves will affect how they respond to attempts to change their attitudes. The investigators reasoned that people who saw themselves as action-oriented people would be more likely to respond to a request for involvement than people who did not view themselves as action-oriented. In this study, the experimenters approached some residents of Palo Alto, California and asked them to either place a small sign that read "Be a safe driver" in their window or sign a petition for safe driving. Two weeks later a second experimenter approached these same residents and a group of residents who had not been asked to comply with the small request. This second experimenter asked these people if they would allow a large "Drive carefully" sign to be placed in their front yard. On the average, 55.7 percent of the residents who had gone along with the small request allowed the sign in their yard, while only 16.7 percent of the residents who had not received the earlier request allowed the sign. The investigators reasoned that by agreeing to the small request, residents came to view themselves as action-oriented and were, therefore, more willing to get involved in the second request. This is known as the foot-in-the-door technique. We can see this approach in Malcolm X's attempts to "fish" for converts to the Muslim faith. His first step was to get a person to make a small commitment: Attend one Muslim service. Later he would try to get the person to make larger commitments.

It is interesting to find that the opposite approach, the door-in-the-face technique, also works. Researchers (Cialdini et al., 1975) have found that people who at first refuse a large request will be more likely to go along with a smaller request than people who are not given the chance to refuse the earlier request. This effect may be because people feel a bit guilty about turning down the first request; they therefore go along to reduce their guilt. It is also possible that, compared to the large first request, the second request seems quite reasonable.

Good salespeople know that the chances of getting people to make large commitments are improved if they can first get them to agree to smaller commitments.

The Relationship between Attitudes and Behavior

Before leaving our discussion of attitudes, we need to address one more issue. When we defined attitudes, we pointed out that attitudes have an action component. In other words, they have a tendency to direct behavior. Clearly, for example, advertisers' interest is not only for people to have a positive attitude about their products; they want people to *buy* their products. They assume that people's behavior is often guided by their attitudes.

Given this, we might expect to be able to predict people's behavior if we know their attitudes. While this may be true in some situations, it is not always the case. In the early 1930s, LaPiere (1934) took a Chinese couple on a 10,000-mile tour of the United States. This was during a time when anti-Chinese feelings were common in this country. They stopped at over 250 hotels and restaurants and in only one case were they not given full service. After the trip, LaPiere wrote the owners of the places where they had stopped and asked about their attitudes toward serving Chinese people. Over 90 percent of the people who answered said that they were against serving Chinese people in their establishments, and yet this had not been their response when they were face to face with a Chinese couple. Results such as these show that attitudes do not always or totally determine behavior.

More current research (Fishbein, 1974; Fishbein and Azjen, 1975) has shown that there are many things to consider when you try to predict behavior from attitudes. One important consideration is the situation. In many cases, the particular situation may play a larger role than attitudes in determining behavior. Another important factor involves how the attitudes were formed. Fazio and Zanna (1981) argue that attitudes formed through direct personal experience are better predictors of behavior than attitudes not based on experience. Thus, in LaPiere's study, it may have been that most of the hotel operators had never had direct experience with Chinese people. Therefore, even though they may have been prejudiced against them, their attitudes were not good predictors of their behavior.

Thus, while attitudes may influence behavior, they do not determine it. In fact, in the next section we will see that the opposite relationship often occurs; that is, behavior influences attitudes.

Behaving Is Believing: Cognitive Dissonance

Malcolm X's conversion to the Muslim religion followed an interesting pattern. On his brother's advice he began to practice many of the rules of the religion even before he became a believer. He gave up smoking, stopped eating pork, and prayed. After making these sacrifices, he began to adopt the faith. He also reports that his faith was further strengthened when he underwent additional hardships and made public speeches for the Nation of Islam.

At first glance, this may seem like an odd chain of events. We might expect that having to make these sacrifices would have made Malcolm X question his desire to be a Muslim. However, according to Festinger's (1957) cognitive dissonance theory, this series of events is very understandable. According to Festinger, people strive to have their attitudes, beliefs, and behaviors support one another. When these components (*cognitions* in Festinger's terminology) come into conflict with one another, a person will become uncomfortable and experience a state of **cognitive dissonance.** In order to relieve the dissonance, the person will try to change the cognitions so that they will again be in agreement.

In order to illustrate this principle, consider the case of Bob, who runs a small business. Bob considers himself to be liberal minded, and he has always believed in equal rights for men and women. Economic times get a little hard, however, and Bob looks for ways to cut costs in his business. He decides to reduce the salaries of some of his employees; but whose salary shall he reduce? He cannot cut Bill's salary because Bill has a family to support. Sally, on the other hand, has a working husband, so Bob decides to cut her salary, even though she and Bill do the same job. This action should create cognitive dissonance for Bob; the fact that he is paying a woman less money for doing the same work as a higher paid male employee is not consistent with an attitude of equal rights for men and women. How can this dissonance be reduced? Bob cannot change the fact that he has paid different wages to his male and female employees, but he can change his attitude about equal rights. Thus, we would expect that in order to reduce his dissonance, Bob would change his attitude about equal rights.

The most interesting cases of cognitive dissonance involve the relationship between attitudes and behaviors (Wicklund and Brehm, 1976). We desire consistency between our attitudes and behaviors, and if we cannot justify our behavior by external factors, we change our attitudes to justify the behavior. When we believe that we have freely chosen to perform a particular act, we will become motivated to realign our attitudes to justify that behavior.

In Malcolm X's case, the fact that he was making drastic changes in his life style and undergoing hardships would be inconsistent with doubts about the value of the Muslim religion. Therefore, one way to reduce this possible dissonance was to change his attitude about the Muslim religion. The belief that the Muslim religion was very good would be consistent with the hardships he endured for this religion. As this example illustrates, dissonance theory suggests that our behavior may determine our attitudes. This seemingly simple theory has been the foundation for a number of creative experiments. Let us now examine some of these to show the breadth of the theory.

Effort Justification.   According to dissonance theory, we love those things for which we suffer. Consider the case of the young man who chooses to join a fraternity that is notorious for its difficult initiation rites. In order to become a full member, the man must eat many kinds of disgusting foods, take long hikes without his shoes, spend many sleepless nights doing exercises, and suffer humiliation for attending classes dressed as a chicken! Certainly no sane person would voluntarily place themselves in this position. These behaviors are dissonant with his belief that he is indeed a sane individual. According to dissonance theory, the man will be motivated to reduce his dissonance by justifying his behavior. He can do this by changing his attitude about himself; that is, he can believe that he is really insane. However, this attitude would be dissonant with many other attitudes he already holds. On the other hand, he can form an attitude that his suffering is justified because the fraternity is a great organization. It is not so unusual to suffer in order to achieve a great reward.

Aronson and Mills (1959) conducted a study showing that people who suffer (or work hard) to obtain an object will value that object more than people who do not suffer for it. Women were told that they would soon be joining a group discussion on sex. However, before joining the group, they would have to pass a test to see if they could participate in the discussion without embarrassment. Subjects in the *severe initiation condition group* had to read lurid sexual passages and recite very obscene words in front of a male experimenter. Subjects assigned to the *mild*

Choosing to help others may increase our attraction to them. Dissonance theory suggests that the more effort we use to help someone, the more we will like them.

initiation condition group were given less embarrassing passages and sex-related words to recite. A *control group* was given no initiation task. After the initiation, subjects were asked to listen to a discussion by their group before entering the group. The "discussions" were the same for all subjects and were actually tape recordings of a dull exchange on the sexual behavior of lower animals. Finally, subjects were asked how interesting they found the discussion and the group members.

Subjects in the severe initiation condition rated the group higher than did the other subjects. It seems that the severe initiation subjects justified their embarrassing initiation by saying that they did it because the discussion group was very good. The other subjects did not have to justify their behavior, and for this reason they gave a more accurate rating of the uninteresting group. It is important to notice that the behavior (the initiation, in this case) created the attitude.

It is interesting to examine the life required by the Nation of Islam in light of the work on effort justification. In order to become members, people have to undergo a great deal of hardship and change. It may well be that as a result of this effort the Muslims become even more committed to their faith. This additional commitment would justify their efforts.

Insufficient Reward. Most of us are raised in a world where we are rewarded for hard work and good performance. If we work hard in our jobs, we get a good increase in pay. In these situations, people can justify their work because of the reward: "I worked hard for the reward." However, what about the person who works hard for little or no reward? The cognitions "I worked hard" and "I got nothing for it" are dissonant.

How does a person in this situation reduce dissonance? According to dissonance theory, this person could increase the value of the particular behavior. Thus, the unrewarded student may say, "I worked hard in school because I really enjoy the subjects." In this sense, then, the less a person is rewarded for behaving in a certain manner, the more he or she will value the behavior.

In a number of studies (Cooper et al., 1974; Cooper and Worchel, 1970; Festinger and Carlsmith, 1959) subjects were enticed to volunteer to perform rather dull tasks for either a small reward or a large reward. Even though the tasks were the same, those performing them for little or no reward stated that they enjoyed the tasks more than subjects who received large rewards. Since the rewards did not justify the behavior in the low-reward conditions, it is obvious that subjects changed their attitudes about the tasks.

In an interesting variation of this theme, Brehm and Crocker (1962) asked subjects to skip breakfast and lunch before coming to the experiment. Half the subjects were given no incentive to do this, while the other subjects were offered five dollars for fasting. When subjects arrived at the study, they were asked to rate how hungry they were. The subjects who were paid five dollars reported being more hungry than the subjects who were given nothing for fasting. The rewarded subjects could justify their fasting by saying that they were getting five dollars for not eating. The no-reward subjects could not do this. When they asked themselves why they had chosen not to eat, they could only justify their behavior by believing that they were not hungry. Thus, dissonance theory predicts that the smaller the reward we get for choosing to do something, the more we should value the behavior for itself.

A Just Barely Sufficient Threat. Let's look at another situation that would arouse dissonance.

In this experiment, children were tested individually. Each young child was brought into a room filled with toys. After the child had played with all the toys, the experimenter entered and picked up an attractive mechanical robot. He put the robot on a table and told the child that he or she should not play with this toy. In the *severe threat* condition, the experimenter told the child that if he or she played with the robot, severe punishment would follow. In the *mild threat* condition, the experimenter said that he would be annoyed if the child played with the robot. After giving these instructions, the experimenter left the room. None of the children played with the toy in his absence. In each case the experimenter allowed some time to pass before returning to ask the subjects to rate the attractiveness of the robot. Based on your knowledge of dissonance theory, which group of children (severe or mild threat) rated the robot *lowest?* The results of this study by Aronson and Carlsmith (1963) showed that children in the mild threat condition rated the toy lowest in attractiveness. According to cognitive dissonance theory, the children in the mild threat condition were faced with two dissonant cognitions: (1) I did not play with the toy, and (2) The toy is attractive. They could not justify their behavior by the external conditions, as they had not been threatened enough to explain why they did not play with the toy. Hence, in order to justify their behavior, they were forced to change their attitude and downgrade the attractiveness of the robot. It is not dissonant to believe, "I did not play with an unattractive toy." The children in the severe threat condition did not have to change their attitude toward the robot. The high threat justified their not playing with the robot.

Thus, dissonance theory predicts that the greater the threat used to keep people from performing a certain activity, the *less* likely it will be for them to change their attitude about that activity. This is another example of a case where behaving (or not behaving) motivates attitude change.

Our discussion of dissonance theory centered on how we are affected by our own behavior. Let us now change our focus from ourselves to our relations with other people. As we turn our attention outward, one of the first issues that arises concerns how we decide what other people are really like. In other words, how do you *know* that your roommate is moody, your spouse is friendly, or your professor is intelligent? In each of these cases, you have moved from observing the person's behavior to inferring traits or characteristics about him or her. The process of inferring characteristics from observable behavior is called the **attribution process.** In a sense, assigning certain qualities to others represents our way of trying to explain their behavior. Each of us forms attributions to describe others many times a day. Even though the process may be automatic to us, it is a complex process in which we can make many errors. This complexity is shown by the fact that often the impression you form of another person may be very different from the impression others form about that same person.

In order to illustrate the attribution process, let us return to the Malcolm X example. Many people observed Malcolm X's conversion to Islam and his behavior after this. They saw him speak out for black pride and power, heard him praise Elijah Muhammad, and read about his pilgrimage to Mecca. Despite observing these same behaviors, the impressions that people formed about Malcolm X were often very different. Some saw him as a man who had truly changed his ways; they saw him as a true believer of Islam and as being concerned with the plight of blacks. Others saw him as a cunning scoundrel who saw a chance for personal gain in the Black Muslim movement. Some people felt that Malcolm X was a madman who delighted in the possibility of an open war between blacks and whites. Each of these people attributed characteristics to Malcolm X based on the behavior they observed. No one could see inside Malcolm X to know the traits that he really possessed, but each person was convinced that they could determine what Malcolm was like based on his behavior.

The interesting questions that arise from this example concern the process by which people move from observing behavior to inferring traits, and the factors that influence the attributions they make. How did Malcolm X's varied audience determine what was really going on inside him? How do you decide that your neighbor is hostile or your child is intelligent? And how do people make attributions about you?

Internal vs. External Causes

One of the first objectives in getting to know people is to figure out what causes their actions. For example, did they act because of some inner need, attitude, or ability? Or did outside events or situations cause their behavior? If we think there is an internal cause, then we learn something about that particular person. However, if we decide that there is an external cause, then we learn something about the situation the person is in, but not about the characteristics of the person.

Harold Kelley (1967) uses the example of seeing a woman, Mary, laugh while watching a movie. We have two choices in deciding what caused Mary's laughter—it could be caused by Mary herself (she has a good sense of humor, she laughs at anything and everything) or by the situation Mary is in (the movie is so funny that anyone who saw it would laugh).

According to Kelley (Kelley, 1973; Kelley and Michele, 1980), we can make our decision based on the answers to the following three questions:

1. How distinctive is the behavior? Does Mary respond this way to all situations (all movies) or only to this particular event (this movie)? If Mary laughs only at this movie, it is a funny movie. If Mary laughs at most movies, however, we are more likely to decide that the behavior is caused by a personal characteristic of Mary's.
2. How do other people respond to the same situation? If everyone responds in the same way to an event, we assume that the behavior is caused by the event. But if Mary is the only person responding this way to this particular event, we assume that the behavior is caused by something in that person.
3. How consistent is the person's behavior? Does Mary laugh every time she sees this movie? If there is no consistency in behavior, then we can't really infer anything about the person from this behavior.

Assigning Specific Traits

Determining that an action is internally caused is only half the battle in making an attribution. We also have to decide what the particular action tells us about the person. For example, we may believe that Malcolm X's conversion to Islam was the result of his own decision. However, we would like to know what this conversion tells us about the man. Was he a true believer, a cunning schemer, or a madman?

What was Malcolm X really like? Because we cannot "see inside him" we must make attributions based on his behavior. The attribution process involves assigning traits to people on the basis of their behavior.

Jones and Davis (1965) developed a model to show how we determine a person's specific attributions of personality. They point out that actions and the effects of actions are the only samples of solid evidence that can be observed. According to these investigators, we must make two decisions after viewing the actions. The first is whether or not the person, known as the actor, had *knowledge* of the effects of his or her actions. If the action had effects that were not anticipated by the actor, these could not have been the reasons for the behavior.

For example, one of the effects of Malcolm X's conversion to the Muslim religion was that he gained power. Therefore, one step in the attribution process must be to decide whether or not he knew that he would gain power by becoming a Muslim. If we decide that he had no knowledge of this effect, then we cannot use the desire for power to explain his conversion. In addition to knowledge, the observer must determine whether or not the actor had the *ability* to produce the desired effects. If the actor did not have the ability, then the observer will conclude that the effects were due to luck and, therefore, nothing is learned about this person.

Based on the decisions about knowledge and ability, the observer attempts to determine the *intentions* of the actor. In other words, what results did he or she expect when performing the act? In Malcolm X's case, the people observing his actions had to decide whether he intended only to live a simple life as a follower of Elijah Muhammad, or if his intentions were to ultimately gain power. Based on the decision about intention, dispositions can then be assigned to the actor.

As we pointed out, the ultimate aim of the attribution process is to explain other people's behavior. Once we can explain their behavior, we can also begin to predict their future actions (Shaver, 1973). Therefore, assigning a trait or disposition to a person not only explains their present behavior, but also predicts their future behavior. As you can see, we would expect very different behaviors from Malcolm X if we decided that he was power hungry as compared with deciding that he was a devoutly religious man who was only interested in the welfare of blacks.

Biases in Attribution

Attribution models present people as scientists who are seeking to determine the causes of behaviors. In going through this process, they carefully consider the relevant information and arrive at an unbiased attribution. While we might like to consider ourselves in this light, we also know that people are not always completely rational or unfeeling, like a computer or a robot. Just as our feelings and biases affect how we act, they also influence how we make attributions about other people. Since these biases are very interesting and revealing, let us quickly examine how some of them affect our attributions.

Hedonic Relevance. Consider this situation: You observe a young man break into the front of a long line of people waiting to purchase the few remaining tickets to a Rolling Stones concert. If you were merely passing by, you might see this action as somewhat rude, but you might also try to explain it by saying that other people in the line were "saving his space." However, if you were one of the people in line, your attribution would probably not be so kind; you would probably see this man as being terribly rude and uncaring. The difference in the two cases is that in the first situation the behavior would not have affected you, while you would have been directly affected in the second situation. **Hedonic relevance** refers to the degree to which a person's behavior is rewarding or costly to the observer.

Hedonic relevance influences attributions in two ways. First, it increases the likelihood that a person's behavior will be seen as representing an underlying trait or disposition (Lowe and Kassin, 1978). In our previous example, this means that the person waiting in line would be more likely to attribute a trait to the line-breaker than would the passer-by. The second consequence of hedonic relevance is that it increases the extremity of the evaluation. While the passer-by may see the line-breaker as somewhat rude, the person waiting in line would see this same behavior as very rude. The important point to remember in this example is that the behavior of the person is exactly the same in both cases. Therefore, a completely rational attribution would not take into account whether or not the observer was affected by it.

Fundamental Attribution Error.   Imagine that your professor assigns you to argue the position in a debate that the tuition in your school should be raised so high that only the rich can attend. Not wishing to fail the course, you comply with the assignment. At a later time you may be surprised to find a number of your classmates believing that you truly feel that higher education should only be for the rich. In this case, your classmates are attributing an attitude to you based only on your behavior; they have failed to give sufficient weight to the situation in which your behavior occurred. This bias is so common that Ross (1977) has called it the **fundamental attribution error**. A truly accurate attributor would carefully review the behavior and the context under which the behavior occurred.

Although these people may have many good reasons for dressing as they do, we are likely to think they are a little unusual. This represents the fundamental attribution error, whereby we pay more attention to behavior than to the situation when making attributions about others.

Actor and Observer Difference. In a recent press interview, President Reagan argued that the presence of Cuban advisors and revolutionaries in Central America was proof that Fidel Castro was aggressive and wanted to control Central America. Reagan also pointed out that he had sent military advisors into the same area in response to Castro's aggression. This example shows a difference in actor and observer attributions that occurs in many situations. President Reagan sees Castro as acting because he is warlike; he sees himself as taking similar actions because of the situation. While we will not question the validity of these attributions, Jones and Nisbett (1972) report that there is a general tendency for people to view the behavior of others as being caused by internal traits, while they see their own behavior as being situationally determined. A number of possible reasons have been suggested to explain this interesting bias.

One reason is that people have more *information* about themselves than they do about others (Monson and Snyder, 1977). In other words, we know that we tend to behave differently in different situations. However, since we do not know the history of other people, we may assume that their behavior is less varied than our own and, therefore, caused by their personal traits. A second reason involves *salience* (Wyer, Henninger, and Hinkle, 1977). When we observe other people, our attention is focused on them. However, when we behave, our attention is focused on the situation. Therefore, personal cues are most salient when we watch others act, while situational cues are most salient when we consider our own behavior.

Primacy Effects: The Order of Information. The people that Malcolm X met after he got out of prison learned that he was a devout follower of Elijah Muhammad and that he endured many hardships for his religion. Only later did many of them hear that he had been a gambler, drug dealer, and burglar. On the other hand, people that knew Malcolm X before he went to prison knew of his wild life and then learned that he was a Muslim and black power advocate. Was the impression of Malcolm X different for these two groups of people and were their impressions of him affected by the order in which they received information? This type of question has been the basis for research on order effects in impression formation.

If we were to follow strictly logical rules, the order by which we receive information should make no difference in our final impression. However, once again, the research suggests that we do not follow the rules of science when making attributions. In general, the first information we receive has a greater influence than later information; in other words, there is a **primacy effect** influencing our attributions. In order to demonstrate this effect, consider the following two descriptions:

Person A	Person B
intelligent	envious
industrious	stubborn
impulsive	critical
critical	impulsive
stubborn	industrious
envious	intelligent

What is the general impression you get of these two people? Solomon Ash (1946) gave these descriptions to subjects and asked them to give their impression of the person described. Despite the fact that the information is the same in both lists, people gave Person A a more positive rating than Person B. The subjects rated Person A as being more sociable, humorous, and happy than Person B. As you can see, the only difference in

In most cases there is a primacy effect in attributions. First impressions are often very lasting.

the two lists is that the positive traits come first in Person A's description, while they come last in the list for Person B.

These results support the influence of a primacy effect in impression formation, which means that people tend to base their impressions on what they hear first. In addition to general impressions of personality, there is also evidence for a primacy effect in impressions of intelligence. A group of researchers had subjects observe a person answering 30 multiple-choice questions (Jones et al., 1968). In all conditions, the person answered 15 questions correctly. However, in one condition the person started off very well, but missed a number of questions toward the end. In the other case, the person began slowly, but did very well at the end. After observing the person, subjects were asked to rate his or her intelligence and predict how well he or she would do on the next series of problems. The person who did well in the beginning was rated as more intelligent and more likely to succeed in the future than the person who did poorly in the beginning.

In general, primacy effects are strongest when we are judging stable traits such as personality or intelligence. Clearly, the message here is that if you wish to have someone form a good impression of you, it is most important that your first encounter be the best. The first information they receive about you will have the strongest influence on their overall impression.

Consequences of Forming Impressions: The Self-Fulfilling Prophecy

In examining the attribution process, we may feel that is is unfortunate that people form impressions based on so little information. On the other hand, we may argue that impressions are a personal thing and that no one is hurt by an impression. We may also believe that first impressions should be easy to change as more information is provided. These statements, however, prove to be far from the truth. First impressions often prove difficult to change because they set into motion a chain of events known as the **self-fulfilling prophecy**.

Research has found that a teacher's expectancy about a student can influence his or her behavior toward that student. This behavior often serves to confirm the expectancy and creates a self-fulfilling prophecy.

The self-fulfilling prophecy follows this pattern:

1. Person A develops a first impression of Person B.
2. Person A then acts towards Person B in a way consistent with the first impression.
3. Person B responds to Person A's behavior in a way that confirms the first impression.
4. Person A's first impression becomes more rigid in light of Person B's behavior.

Rosenthal and Jacobson (1968) present a dramatic example of how this process may intrude into the classroom. These investigators told elementary-school teachers that tests had indicated that some of their students could be expected to out-perform other students. These "high achievers" were clearly identified to the teachers. In fact, no tests had been given, and these "high achievers" were simply chosen at random. At the end of the school year, the students' IQs were measured. As can be seen from Figure 14–2, the "high achievers" dramatically outperformed the other students in the classroom. This is despite the fact that there were no real differences in the ability of any of these students. The only difference was the expectancy of the teacher.

The teachers could have fulfilled their expectations in a number of ways. They may have smiled at and given more reinforcement to the "bright" students. Because of this reinforcement, the "bright" students may have begun trying harder than students who did not receive this support. The teachers may have assigned more challenging and difficult tasks to the "bright" students. In this way, the students were encouraged to use their abilities to the fullest. Finally, the teachers may have given more feedback and spent more time with the "bright" students. Each of these efforts would have helped the students perform better and, thereby, reinforced the teacher's first impression. The interesting point in this and other similar research is that the teachers were totally unaware that they were responding more favorably toward some students. Thus, the self-fulfilling prophecy occurs without the awareness of the parties involved.

The self-fulfilling prophecy is found in a wide range of situations including both positive and negative expectations (Crano and Mellon, 1978). As you can see, these events help cement first impressions and give importance to the study of how people make attributions from minimal information.

FIGURE 14–2

In this study, the teacher's expectation about students' ability created a self-fulfilling prophecy and led to the "high achievers" performing better.

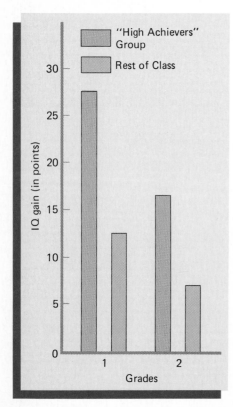

INTERPERSONAL ATTRACTION

Attribution theories are concerned with how we determine what other people are really like. Research in interpersonal attraction focuses on how we determine who we like. As we will see, there are many different factors that influence whether or not we will be attracted to someone. This point becomes very clear when we review the many relationships that Malcolm X had throughout his life and question why he was attracted to various people.

Reward

After Malcolm X got out of prison, he spent a great deal of time with Elijah Muhammad. As Malcolm X worked to build new temples and gain converts for the Nation of Islam, their friendship grew. Clearly, religion and spiritual guidance was one basis for the attraction between these two men. However, another possible foundation for their relationship may have been the rewards that they each received from their interaction. Malcolm X received a new sense of identity, a role of importance, and power from his relationship with Elijah Muhammad. In return, Elijah Muhammed received a tireless worker who was very successful in establishing new temples and gaining converts to the Nation of Islam. Therefore, both men received rewards from their friendship.

Researchers have suggested that we view our social relationships in terms of a profit motive (Homans, 1974). We weigh the rewards and costs and are attracted to those people who provide the greatest profit for us. The rewards and costs include many items, such as emotions, materials, power, and security. According to this position, social relationships are similar to business transactions; we are attracted to people who reward us and are repelled by those who are a burden.

There is considerable evidence supporting the view that we like people who reward us, and there have been many interesting extensions of the reward hypothesis. One extension is that we not only like people who directly reward us, but we also like people who are around us when good things happen. This occurs even when that person had nothing to do with the positive event. For example, Veitch and Griffit (1976) found that a stranger who appeared in a room after a subject had heard good news was liked better than one who appeared after the subject had heard bad news.

The strategy that we use to give rewards also influences attraction. Investigators had subjects hold a conversation with another person (who was actually an experimental accomplice) (Aronson and Linder, 1965). The subjects then "overheard" the accomplice on a number of occasions making evaluative statements about them. Some subjects heard the accomplice make only positive and rewarding statements (positive-positive). Other subjects heard the accomplice making only negative comments (negative-negative). In the negative-positive condition, the accomplice began by making negative statements about the subjects, but the evaluations became increasingly positive as the conversations continued. The final group of subjects (positive-negative) heard the accomplice begin with positive evaluations, but the remarks became increasingly negative.

After the conversations had ended, the subjects were asked to rate how much they liked the accomplice. In which condition do you think attraction was highest? As can be seen in Table 14–1, subjects were most attracted to the other person when she began making derogatory comments, but later switched to positive rewarding evaluations. Interestingly,

TABLE 14–1 The Gain-Loss Effect on Ratings in the Aronson and Linder Study

Experimental Condition	Mean
Negative-positive	+7.67
Positive-positive	+6.42
Negative-negative	+2.52
Positive-negative	+0.87

Source: Aronson and Linder (1965).

the number of rewarding statements were less in this condition than in the positive-positive condition. The results indicate also that subjects were somewhat less attracted to the accomplice when she began with positive comments, but later switched to negative evaluations. This phenomenon is referred to as the *gain-loss effect*. One explanation for the effect is that a need for positive reward was created when the accomplice began by making negative statements. The later positive comments satisfied this need. In the positive-positive condition, the subject did not have as strong a need for positive reward.

Birds of a Feather . . . Similarity

One of the first people Malcolm X became friendly with when he arrived in Boston was Shorty. In their first meeting, Shorty was a bit uneasy with this "hick," but the friendship quickly blossomed when he learned that Malcolm was from his hometown. This basic similarity served as the foundation for a long friendship. Taking another example, Malcolm X observed at Mecca that people from similar cultures or of similar skin color tended to stay together. Here, again, similarity seemed to be the bond of attraction.

There has been a large amount of research showing that similarity on a number of dimensions leads to attraction (Byrne, 1971). Some of these dimensions include ability, intelligence, economic condition, race, height, physical attractiveness, and sometimes, personality. As with most rules, there are also some exceptions to the similarity-attraction relationship. It seems that we are not attracted to people who have a characteristic that we do not admire in ourselves (Goldman and Olczak, 1976). For example, if you are unhappy with the fact that you weigh 345 pounds, you will not necessarily be attracted to another person who weighs 345 pounds. There is also evidence that having certain opposite personal needs and motives may lead to attraction. If you have a strong need to be dominant, for example, you may be attracted to a submissive person. In this relation-

Similarity in attitudes, interests, background, and behavior often serves as the basis for attraction.

ship, your needs will not be in conflict with your partner's needs. Despite these exceptions, similarity often leads to attraction.

There are a number of possible reasons for this similarity-attraction effect. First, similar others tend to validate our own opinions and actions, and this validation is rewarding. For example, if you have just purchased a new jeep, it is gratifying to find someone else who has also just bought a jeep. Seeing that others have done the same thing makes you feel that your own action was not unusual or incorrect. A second reason for the similarity-attraction relationship is that we often expect to have a positive interaction with similar others. For example, if you were raised on a farm, you would have a great deal to discuss with another person raised on a farm. You may have a somewhat more difficult time conducting an engaging conversation with someone who was raised in a large city and who has very different opinions and interests. A third reason is that we expect similar others to like us. Since we enjoy being liked, we will be attracted to those similar others. Thus, there are a number of reasons why "birds of a feather flock together" (and like each other).

To Be Near You . . . Proximity

When Malcolm X quit his shoeshine job, he worked for a while as a soda-fountain clerk. Almost every afternoon, a shy girl would sit at the end of the fountain, reading her books. At first, Malcolm paid little attention to her, but, as time wore on, he began talking with her. They became close friends and would often go dancing at Roseland. It seems that one of the keys to this relationship was that Malcolm and Laura saw each other frequently.

As far back as 1932, Bossard noticed that there was a relationship between physical closeness (proximity) and attraction. In examining the application for marriage licenses in Philadelphia, he found that an overwhelming number of the engaged people tended to live close to their partners-to-be (Bossard, 1932). Clearly, these results could occur for two

We are often attracted to people who are physically close to us. Proximity increases familiarity and offers the opportunity to exchange rewards.

reasons. It is possible that people who like each other choose to live close together. On the other hand, it is also possible that simply being close together leads people to like each other.

In order to test this latter prediction, Festinger, Schacter, and Back (1950) studied friendships that occurred in a married-student housing project. Couples in this project were randomly assigned to apartments so that there was no chance that previous attraction could influence where the couples lived. During the course of the year, the residents were asked to indicate who they were most friendly with. The results showed that 44 percent of the couples were most friendly with their next-door neighbor, while only 10 percent were most friendly with people who lived down the hall. The fact that proximity leads to liking has been found in dormitories, intercity housing projects, and surveys of residential neighborhoods.

There are many reasons why proximity may lead to liking. Simple familiarity is one reason. Earlier, we reviewed research that showed that people tend to be attracted to people and objects that are *familiar* to them and repelled by strange people or objects. Another reason for the proximity effect is that people who are physically close are more likely to reward each other than people who are not physically present. Finally, it is a fact that people must interact with those who are physically close to them. It is certainly more comfortable to like these people than to dislike them (Berscheid and Walster, 1978). Thus, we may try harder to like people who are physically close because we have to interact with them.

Certainly, proximity does not always lead to liking. FBI statistics show that muggings, murders, robberies, and assaults are most likely to be committed by members of the same family or neighborhood (Berscheid and Walster, 1978). However, there are pressures that often result in our liking people who are physically close.

The Way You Look . . . Physical Attractiveness

Prior to his conversion to Islam, Malcolm was often concerned about his physical appearance and the appearance of his friends. Light skin color and straight hair were considered attractive. Malcolm had light-colored skin, but straight hair took some doing. In order to get straight hair, Malcolm "conked" his hair: He made a mixture of potatoes and lye and poured this mixture on his head. Although it nearly burned off the skin on his scalp, it did remove some of the kink from his hair. Malcolm X looked back with sad amusement at the number of times he conked his hair and the money he spent on expensive clothing so that he would be "in style." At the time he felt that fitting this model would not only show that he was successful, but it would attract new friends. When he began to preach the black militant position, physical appearance was one of his topics. He attempted to change blacks' view of what was beautiful; he stressed that dark skin and native dress were the ultimate in beauty.

We pointed out earlier that we often use physical appearance as the basis for attributions about people's personality and intelligence. Research has also shown that our attraction for others is affected by their physical appearance. Several studies found that physically attractive people are liked better and judged to be more pleasant than less attractive people (Kleck and Rubenstein, 1975; Walster et al., 1966a). For example, Walster and her colleagues arranged dates for subjects at a dance. Before the dance, a panel of judges rated the physical attractiveness of each subject. At the intermission of the dance, subjects were asked how much they liked their partners. The results indicated that liking was directly related

HIGHLIGHT / JUDGING PEOPLE BY THEIR COVERS

Of all the biases in attribution, the tendency to use physical appearance to determine traits is one of the strongest. Throughout our lives, we are cautioned against judging people by their looks: "Don't judge a book by its cover." General George Patton is said to have bought his daughter the ugliest dog he could find in order to teach her that ugly things can be loveable. Despite the wisdom in these cautions, research shows that people make a number of attributions based on physical appearance. As we will see, almost any physical trait can be used as the basis for attributions.

BEAUTY

Being physically attractive may serve as the gateway to eliciting a wide range of positive attributions from others. Attractiveness is often associated with intelligence. For example, fifth-grade teachers were shown a number of report cards (Clifford and Walster, 1973). Although all report cards carried the same information, a picture of an attractive boy or girl was attached to some cards, and a picture of an unattractive student was attached to other cards. Teachers rated the attractive students as more intelligent and more likely to do good work than the unattractive student. In addition to intelligence, research has found that physically attractive people are seen as being happier, more pleasant, more sensitive, kinder, more poised, and more outgoing than unattractive people (Adams and Huston, 1975). Remember that the raters in this research have never met or interacted with the people; they are making these attributions based solely on seeing pictures.

Another somewhat startling effect is that physically attractive people are often seen as being less guilty of committing a crime than are unattractive people. Efran (1974) asked subjects to decide the fate of a defendant in a college cheating case. The facts of the case were held constant, but in some conditions the defendant was attractive, while in other cases the defendant was unattractive. Physically attractive defendants were liked better, judged less guilty, and received less punishment than unattractive defendants. One exception to this finding is that attractive people are seen as guiltier and receive stronger sentences when the crime is one that involves taking advantage of one's attractiveness, such as a confidence game or swindle (Sigall and Ostrove, 1975).

EYEGLASSES

For many people, wearing of eyeglasses is inconvenient and annoying. However, for observers, the eyeglasses serve as the basis for attributing intelligence. In one study, subjects were shown a videotape of a person sitting at a desk (Argyle and McHenry, 1971). In some cases, the person was wearing eyeglasses, while in others he was not. Subjects rated the person wearing glasses as more intelligent than the person not wearing glasses.

BODY AND FACIAL HAIR

The amount and color of hair serves as the trigger for a number of attributions. Verinis and Roll (1970) found that college students felt that men with a lot of body hair were more virile, active, and potent than men with less body hair. Bearded men are seen as more masculine, dominant, liberal, and courageous than men with cleanshaven faces (Pellegrini, 1973).

We are all familiar with the old advertisement for hair coloring that proclaimed that "blondes have more fun." Apparently, we as observers take this into account in our attributions. Research shows that people perceive blonde women as being more warm, beautiful, and entertaining than brunettes. On the other hand, brunettes are seen as being more intelligent than blondes. Interestingly, dark-haired men are seen as being more masculine, ambitious, and rugged than blonde or red-haired men (Lawson, 1971).

DRESS

In an interesting study, Darley and Cooper (1972) set up two tables for political candidates at a shopping center. The tables contained no information about the positions of the two candidates. However, three well-dressed college students sat at one table, and three long-haired students dressed in jeans and work shirts sat at the other table. When passers-by were questioned about the positions of the candidates, they saw the candidate supported by the long-haired group of students as being more liberal with regard to gun control, legalization of marijuana, and the Asian policy of the United States than the candidate supported by the well-dressed students.

This research shows that while our physical appearance may only be skin-deep, it serves as the basis for making attributions about characteristics deep inside us: intelligence, personality, and attitudes. These attributions are made despite the fact that people have little control over whether or not they have blonde or brunette hair, wear glasses, have a great deal of body hair, or are physically attractive.

TABLE 14-2: Gateways
to Friendship

We like people who:
1. reward us
2. like us
3. are similar to us
4. live close to us
5. are physically attractive
6. are around us when good things happen
8. like the same people and things we like
9. satisfy all needs

to the partner's physical attractiveness; attractive subjects were liked more than unattractive subjects.

Results such as these might suggest that a person of average or less than average attractiveness is doomed to a life of loneliness. This, however, is not the case. While research shows that we may be attracted to the most physically attractive people, other research shows that we tend to choose to become romantically involved with people whose physical attractiveness is about equal to our own (Murstein, 1972). This *matching rule* probably results because we fear that we will be rejected by someone who is "out of our league" in terms of physical attractiveness. Thus, while we may desire the most attractive person around, we are most likely to wind up with someone who is about as attractive as we are.

The Many Roads to Attraction

The previous discussion should make one point very clear; there are many reasons why people are attracted to each other. This explains why a single individual may have a variety of friends. He or she may be attracted to some of them because they live close by; others may be friends because they have similar attitudes or backgrounds; still others may be included in the circle of friends because of ability to reward. Table 14-2 lists many of the reasons why we are attracted to others. A review of your own history may give you additional reasons.

HELPING BEHAVIOR

As a militant follower of Elijah Muhammad, Malcolm X believed that whites had never helped blacks. His opinion was that what often appeared as helping was really an attempt for the whites to take advantage of the blacks. One incident, however, had such impact on Malcolm X that it caused him to make a major shift in his position. Because of his criticism of the United States, he had trouble getting a passport and the necessary papers to make his pilgrimage to Mecca. To his surprise, some whites went out of their way to help him. Once arriving in Saudia Arabia, Malcolm X found out that he would need additional papers and help to get to Mecca. Again, he was surprised to find that some of the people who helped him were white. These cases of helping had a lasting impact on Malcolm X.

We might find it odd that such simple acts of helping could be viewed as so unusual. Certainly, people go out of their way to help each other many times a day. Unfortunately, this is not always the case. A look at the newspaper will provide us with many examples of situations where help has not been given. One of the more publicized cases involved a young woman named Kitty Genovese.

At 3:20 A.M. on March 13, 1964, Kitty Genovese got off the subway in the borough of Queens in New York City and began walking home. Out of the dark a man brandishing a knife grabbed Kitty and began beating her. Kitty screamed for help, broke away, and began running down the street. The man followed her and stabbed her. Again the young woman escaped screaming, "He stabbed me! Please help me!" Lights went on in apartments overlooking the scene. The attacker again caught Kitty and this time the attack was final. Kitty Genovese lay dead on the sidewalk. It was estimated that the incident lasted almost 45 minutes and at least 38 people heard the screams for help, yet not a single person came to the aid of the young woman or even lifted the telephone to call the police.

Had one person given some type of help, it is likely that Miss Genovese would have been saved.

More recently, newspapers in February, 1982, carried the story of a 62-year-old grandmother who was beaten and tied in a chair. She managed to inch her way out of the office and into the middle of a busy street. However, there she sat in disbelief as numerous cars passed her by. It was two hours before anyone stopped to help her.

Stories such as these give us reason to wonder: Are humans really as uncaring and insensitive as these examples suggest? Certainly, helping someone in need should be a simple behavior, and it should occur almost automatically. If this is the case, why don't people help?

A recent study of helping behavior was begun to answer this question. As we will see, the act of giving help is only the end result of a relatively complex chain of events. In other words, the decision to help is influenced by a number of personal and interpersonal factors.

The Decision to Help

Latané and Darley (1970) suggest that the decision to help involves a number of steps. If any one of these steps is not taken, the individual will not help. First, the individual must *notice* the person in distress. Second, he or she must *interpret the situation* as an emergency and decide that the person does, indeed, need help. Next, the individual must decide that he or she has a *responsibility* to help. Fourth, the individual must have the ability to supply the *appropriate form of assistance*. For example, if you see someone having a heart attack, you may be reluctant to help because you do not know how to help the victim. Finally, the individual who has gone through each of these steps must decide to *implement the decision to help*.

Each of these steps is necessary before an individual will help. Let us examine now the factors that influence helping.

Noticing the Victim. In order for bystanders to help, they must notice the victim. This seems so trivial, and yet it is often overlooked. The more salient or noticeable the victim is, the more likely it is that they will receive help. In an interesting study, a confederate was placed on a subway (Piliavin, Rodin, and Piliavin, 1968). At one point during the ride, the confederate collapsed on the floor, either because he was drunk (smelled of alcohol) or because he was ill (he carried a black cane). A number of results from the study are of interest. The one most relevant to this discussion is that passengers seated near the victim were more likely to offer help than those seated farther away. In fact, in some cases, passengers who did not offer help moved farther away from the victim. Thus, when the victim was clearly visible to the passengers, he was more likely to receive help. Bystanders who wanted to avoid helping moved so that the victim would be less salient to them.

Interpreting the Situation as an Emergency. Not only must people see the victim, but they must also know that the person needs help. For example, assume you notice a man and a woman fighting on a street corner. Is this a simple family squabble, or does the woman (or man) need rescuing? If the situation is the former and you decide to help, you may be embarrassed. Researchers set up just such a situation in which a woman was attacked by a man (Shotland and Straw, 1976). In one condition, she yelled, "I don't know you," in the middle of the fight, and in the other she made no reference to her relationship to the attacker. In the first case, 65 percent of the male bystanders intervened to help, while in the latter case only 19 percent helped. When the assailant was unknown to the woman, it was clear that this was not a "lover's quarrel" and she needed help.

Interpreting a situation as an emergency is an important step in the decision to offer help. In this situation it is difficult to determine if the person is in need of help, is being helped, or is just fooling around with friends.

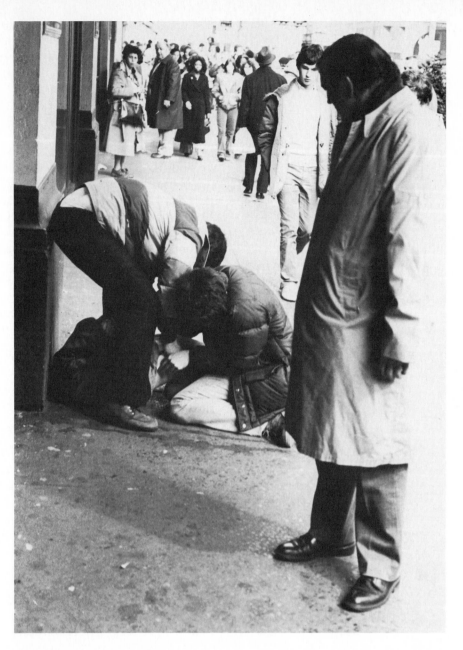

Assuming Responsibility: Is There Safety in Numbers? Assume you knew that at 3 P.M. on a given day you were going to faint and that you would need the help of others to revive you. As the fateful time approached, would you rush to a busy street corner where there were many passers-by, or would you choose a less popular side street where fewer people passed? Most of us would probably choose the busy street thinking that in a crowd there would be at least one person who would stop and help. Research however indicates that the majority choice may not be a wise one (Bar-Tal, 1976; Latané and Darley, 1970). In fact, indications are that when there are fewer people present when an individual needs help, there is a greater chance of receiving it.

In order to illustrate this phenomenon, Darley and Latané (1968) asked college students to participate in a discussion about their problems in adjusting to college life. When the subject arrived, he or she was told that in order to prevent embarrassment, subjects would communicate to each other from private booths over a sound system: There would be no face-to-face interaction. The subject was then led into a booth. In some cases, the subject believed that there would be only two people in the

FIGURE 14–3

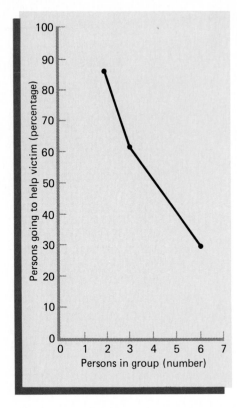

group. In other cases, the subject thought that there would be three people in the group. In the third condition, the subject believed that six people would participate in the discussion. Actually, there was only one subject in the study. The voices of other discussants were tape-recorded.

In the discussion, one tape-recorded voice, designated as the "future victim," spoke first. He talked about some of his difficulties and then mentioned that he was prone to seizures in times of stress. After the other subjects spoke, the "victim" began to speak again. Suddenly he seemed to be having a seizure and said: "I-er-um-I think I-I need-er-if-if-could-er somebody er-er-er-er-er-er give me a little-er give me a little-er give me a little help here because I-er-I'm . . ." (chokes, then quiet) (Darley and Latané, 1968, p. 379). The experimenter, sitting outside the booth, recorded the amount of time it took the subject to search for help for the victim. As can be seen from Figure 14-3, the larger the group, the less likely the subjects were to help. In fact, 85 percent of the subjects helped if they felt that no one else knew of the victim's plight, while only 31 percent helped when they felt that four others (in the six-person group) knew of the victim's need.

How can we explain such an effect? One possible explanation is based on the notion of responsibility. When the subjects felt that they were the only ones who knew of the problem, they were likely to feel responsible for helping the victim. However, when there were other people present, the subject was not as likely to feel responsible for helping the victim. It was easy for the subject to think that "others must be doing something." How many times have you passed an accident on the road and said to yourself, "Someone must have already called the police"? Another possible reason for the effect involves the interpretation of the problem. In the large group, the subject may have felt that the victim did not really need help because he or she did not hear anyone else making an effort to aid the victim. In this case, the subject used the response of the others to determine the extent of the emergency. When the subject was alone, however, he or she had to make a decision about the urgency of the situation based solely on a personal interpretation of the victim's plight.

Thus, simply having a number of people present does not increase the likelihood of helping behavior. In such cases, bystanders may *diffuse* responsibility for helping.

Knowing How to Help. Imagine finding an unconscious woman on the sidewalk who is bleeding from the mouth and ears. You can see clearly that she needs help and that no one else is available. What do you do in this case? For most of us, this would be a very threatening situation. Many of us have heard that it is dangerous to move an unconscious person. But do we leave the woman lying on the sidewalk and go search for medical help? Or do we stay with her, hoping someone will come along? This type of dilemma may cause people to feel helpless and lead them to take no action (Bar-Tal, 1976). In order to be of assistance, people must decide that they can take some action that will help the victim. Since many people do not have specific training in how to help in emergencies, they may decide that there is nothing that they can do.

Taking Action

Even after going through all the earlier steps, the bystander must finally decide to take action. There are a number of variables that determine whether or not a person will actually decide to help. One involves his or her belief as to whether or not the victim actually deserves to be helped. In one study that was discussed earlier, subway riders were more likely to help the ill victim than the drunk victim (Piliavin et al., 1969). Presumably they felt that the ill person was deserving of help, while the drunk person

In order to be of assistance, people must know how to help the victim. The people shown here are being trained in cardiopulmonary resuscitation in case of a heart attack. They will be much more likely in the future to help in such a situation, simply because they know what to do and how to do it.

should have taken control of himself and therefore did not deserve help.

Another factor involves the costs of helping. Bystanders are less likely to help if they feel that they may be injured if they offer help or if helping may cost them a great deal of time or money (Gruder et al., 1975). It is very possible that many people who witnessed the Genovese attack did not directly intervene because they may have fallen victim to the attacker. Further, if they called the police, they may have become involved in later court proceedings.

Even the mood of the individual influences whether or not he or she will offer help. For example, in one study subjects leaving a theater were asked to donate money to the Muscular Dystrophy Foundation (Underwood et al., 1977). They found that moviegoers were more likely to donate if they had seen a happy movie rather than a sad movie.

The results of these studies offer us greater understanding of why people do not rush to help victims in situations such as the Genovese attack. Clearly, helping behavior is complex and involves many decisions on the part of the helper. The social psychological research has identified many of the factors that influence helping behavior and this research can serve as the basis for creating situations in which people will offer help.

Recipient Reactions to Helping

Most of the attention on helping behavior has been focused on the helper. We have been asking questions about why people help or do not help, and we have assumed that the victim wants help and will be glad to receive it. This may well be the case in dire emergencies such as the Genovese example. But most situations of helping do not involve such immediate danger. You may offer to help your roommate with his home-

One consequence of helping is that it shows a difference in power and competency between the helpers and the person they are helping. This man may prefer to forget later that he was in need of help, because it reminds him that he was unable to finish the race and had to be helped by others who were in better shape than he was.

work, or help a stranded stranger change a tire. Even though you offer aid in these situations with the best of intentions, you may be surprised at the response you get. Instead of a friendly acceptance, the other person may tell you that your help is not needed, or they may accept your help with reluctance. Although, this response may puzzle you, social psychologists have begun to uncover the reasons behind such reactions.

In order to understand this situation, we must view helping in the broader context of social interaction. Greenberg (1980) points out that receiving help often obligates the person to return help at some later time: "One good deed deserves another." Therefore, if someone does something nice for you, it is likely that you should feel indebted to that person. The feeling of indebtedness will create a tension that will not be reduced until you have returned the favor. Looking at helping in this way, we can see that some people will be reluctant to accept aid because they will feel obligated to reciprocate in the future.

Another consequence of helping is that it demonstrates a difference in power and competency between the helper and the recipient (Fisher, Nadler, and Whitcher, 1980; Worchel, 1982). In the helping relationship, the helper is demonstrating power and competency over the situation. In essence, the helper indicates that he or she knows what should be done and how it should be done. On the other hand, by receiving help, the recipient may be admitting that he or she is incompetent to perform the task alone. In support of this position, research has shown that people like others with whom they can cooperate on an equal basis better than they like people who give them help (Worchel, 1982). This point is also observed in international relations. Investigators interviewed foreign-aid officials and found that they were concerned with their country's national pride if they accepted foreign aid (Gergen and Gergen, 1972).

These findings increase our understanding of how people react to help, and they also offer another reason why people may be reluctant to give help. That is, people may not help because they fear that the recipient may feel uncomfortable or resent their help. As you can see, helping can be a complex social interaction that involves many decisions and has implications for social relationships.

SUMMARY

1. **Social psychology** is the scientific study of the way in which people are affected by social situations and social relationships. Social psychologists attempt to develop theories to explain factors that influence most people, most of the time.

2. **Attitudes** are learned, relatively enduring feelings about objects, events, or issues. They have three components: evaluation, belief, and action. Parents, peers, and the media all play a role in the development of attitudes.

3. Attitude change involves substituting new attitudes for old ones. Research in this area has focused on the communicator, the message, and the audience. Although there have been few personality traits associated with persuasibility, both **foot-in-the-door** and **door-in-the-face approaches** have been found to change attitudes. These approaches are aimed at changing the way people feel about themselves.

4. **Cognitive dissonance** theory is based on the assumption that people strive to have their attitudes, beliefs, and behaviors support one another. Dissonance theory suggests that changing behavior often causes people to change their attitudes.

5. **Attribution** involves inferring personal characteristics from observable behavior. In order to determine that an act tells us something about a person, we must decide what the person intended to achieve by a behavior. Intentions are determined by deciding whether the actor knew the effects of a behavior and whether or not the actor had the ability to achieve these effects.

6. There are many biases in the attribution process. People make stronger attributions when the behavior affects them, and there is also a bias toward giving more weight to the behavior than to the situational context it occurred in. First impressions are difficult to change because they set into motion the self-fulfilling prophecy.

7. We are attracted to people who reward us directly or who are present when good things happen to us. We like people who are similar to us in any one of a number of ways. There is also a tendency to like people who are physically close to us, although proximity can also lead to disliking. Although we may be most attracted to physically attractive others, we often choose to become romantically involved with people whose physical attractiveness is about equal to our own.

8. The decision to help is only the end result in a complex chain of events. Before helping will occur, people need to notice the person in distress, interpret the situation as an emergency, feel responsible to help, know the appropriate way to help, and decide to offer aid. Research has shown that an individual is less likely to help in a group situation because responsibility is diffused in the group setting.

9. Oftentimes recipients are unwilling to accept help. By accepting help, they may feel indebted to the helper. Further, helping often distinguishes the helper as powerful and competent and shows the recipient to be incompetent in the particular situation.

SUGGESTED READINGS

The following book is about Malcolm X:

Malcolm X and Alex Haley. *The autobiography of Malcolm X.* New York: Ballantine, 1973.

ABLESON, R., ARONSON, E., McGUIRE, W., NEWCOMB, T., ROSENBERG, M. & TANNENBAUM, P. (Eds.) *Theories of Cognitive Consistency: A Sourcebook.* Chicago: Rand McNally, 1968.
A collection of original chapters on the cognitive consistency theories in social psychology including balance theory, dissonance theory, and decision-making theories. The chapters examine the strengths and weaknesses of the theories and the application of research.

BERKOWITZ, L. (Ed.) *Advances in Experimental Social Psychology.* New York: Academic Press.
A new edition of this series is published each year. It includes contributed chapters on areas of social psychology that are timely. It includes chapters on new theories, revisions of older theories, new areas of study, and reviews of research in focused areas.

LINDZEY, G. & ARONSON, E. (Eds.) *Handbook of Social Psychology 2nd Edition.* Reading, Mass.: Addison-Wesley, 1969.
These five volumes offer an indepth examination of the areas of social psychology, its research, and the methods used in this research. Each volume focuses on a specific topic such as methods, groups, and applied social psychology. (A third edition is scheduled for publication in 1983.)

SHAW, M. & COSTANZO, P. *Theories of Social Psychology Second Edition.* New York: McGraw Hill, 1982.
This book discusses the development of theory in social psychology and examines each of the major theories. It is up-to-date and complete.

WORCHEL, S. & COOPER, J. *Understanding Social Psychology Third Edition.* Homewood, Ill.: Dorsey Press, 1983.
This textbook discusses the major theories and research in social psychology and applies this work to understanding everyday events. It introduces the major topics with stories from classical literature and current events and shows how social psychology can be applied to these situations.

WRIGHTSMAN, L. & DEAUX, K. *Social Psychology in the 80's 3rd Edition.* Monterey, Calif.: Brooks/Cole, 1981.
This textbook presents an extensive review of the major theories and research in social psychology. It also includes a discussion of the philosophical basis of social psychology and chapters on organizational psychology and sexual behavior.

15

The Individual in Groups

A s the bus rolled south, Josh Gibson reflected on the events that had taken place over the last few weeks. Despite the fact that he was just 20 years old, he had already earned a reputation as one of the most powerful long-ball hitters in the Negro National League. By the end of the 1931 season, Josh was an established star, hitting in the clean-up spot for the Homestead Grays. He had been happy to sign a new Gray's contract for the 1932 season. Soon after he had signed this contract, however, he was approached by Gus Greenlee.

Greenlee was a newcomer to baseball, but he had decided to build the best team money could buy. Greenlee's money was much needed in the Negro National League, which was struggling to stay alive after the Great Depression. This was an era when blacks were barred from playing on white major league teams. As a result, two leagues existed in the United States—one for white players and one for black players. The white league had the superior organization and superior facilities, and stars such as Babe Ruth, who received wide publicity. Thus, while both leagues struggled to survive the Depression, the black league was hurt more by it. Greenlee, however, promised to bring new life to black baseball; he offered his players higher salaries, new uniforms, and a brand new Mack bus for touring. Thus, when Greenlee made his offer, Josh Gibson had eagerly signed the contract, forsaking his commitment to the Grays.

Josh was now headed for Hot Springs, Arkansas to begin spring training with the newly formed Pittsburgh Crawford Giants. There he would join some of the greatest black players. Greenlee had signed the already famous Leroy "Satchel" Paige to pitch. Judy Johnson would play third, while Oscar Charleston would play first base and coach. Also on the 1932 team were Ted "Double Duty" Radcliffe, Jimmie Crutchfield, and Walter "Rev" Cannady. These stars would have been quickly taken into the white league were it not for the rigid color barrier. In fact, four members of the Crawfords, including Josh Gibson, would be inducted into the Baseball Hall of Fame when the baseball establishment finally decided to judge a player by his ability rather than his color.

Spring training began in mid-February. Josh was just recovering from an operation, so he really needed the time to work himself back into shape and regain his fluid swing and sharp hitting eye. Spring training offered such an opportunity, since the players were isolated from the demanding crowds of spectators and there were no long bus rides to interfere with their training. Josh, like many of the players, spent a great deal of time alone concentrating on his batting and practicing his fielding.

On March 25 the season began in Monroe, Louisiana. The fans marveled as the Crawfords rolled into town in their new bus and took the field dressed in brand new uniforms. Black baseball had not witnessed such extravagance since its beginning in the early 1920s.

Josh was proud of his team and he enjoyed the company of the players on and off the field. As the season wore on, they became a close-knit group. In the early part of the season, the games were played in the South. Here, although the weather was good, the social climate was not always welcoming. In some small towns, the Craws would have to leave town immediately after the game because there was no hotel that allowed blacks. At some parks they were allowed to play on the field, but they could not use the locker rooms for showering or changing clothes, because they were for "Whites Only." Despite (or possibly because of) these problems, the Craws worked hard together and played excellent baseball.

After the games, Josh and a number of his teammates would often go out on the town. Even off the field, it was not hard to tell that the players belonged together. The dress fad of the time was sport caps and "plus fours" (baggy pants). When the players went out after the games, they wore this town uniform. Josh, at first, had been reluctant to dress in plus fours. These baggy pants on his huge frame often made him look like an out-of-control sailboat. However, after a great deal of good-natured pressure from his teammates, Josh adopted the fashion of the day.

The long bus trips between games gave the players a chance to get to know one another. They often talked of their problems, and the younger players were given baseball pointers by the old timers. In order to break the boredom of the long rides, practical jokes were often the order of the day. On one long trip, Josh and some others stole "Tincan" Kincannon's fried chicken while he slept. After devouring the chicken, they tied the remains to his neck. Of course, they were careful to remove the bullets from Tincan's gun, which he had placed in his lap to prevent such thievery.

The 1932 season was a good one for the Craws. They quickly established a reputation as being an excellent team, and they drew good-sized crowds. In fact, in cities such as Cincinnati, which had a weak white team, the Craws were able to draw larger crowds than the white major league team. Their good fortune was in contrast to many other teams in the black league. During that season, teams in Baltimore, Cleveland, Philadelphia, and Newark folded.

By the end of the season, the Craws had not only developed a style of baseball, they had also adopted a clearly identifiable structure as a group. Satchel Paige, who was by far the best-known player on the team, had become an outsider on the team (Brashler, 1978). He was the one player who most often "played to the fans" both on and off the field, and he rarely spent his free time with the other players. Josh, who had become a star in his own right, became one of the leaders of the team. On the field and off, he continued to associate with the team members, and he was rarely seen without them. Because he played catcher, Josh was able to observe the other players on the field, and so could give them advice on how to play their positions. The players looked up to Josh, and by the end of the 1932 season, Josh was being billed in black newspapers as the "Black Babe Ruth."

The long season finally ended, with the Craws having compiled an amazing 99–36 record. Many of the players had looked forward to going home to be with their families. However, the end of baseball season in the United States marked the beginning of winter baseball in the Latin American countries. Scouts from the Latin teams followed both the black and the white leagues and many of the Craws, including Josh, were offered contracts to play in Puerto Rico, Mexico, Cuba, and the Dominion Republic.

When these offers came, the Craws gathered together to discuss the winter leagues. There were many advantages to playing on the Latin teams. First, there was money; in many cases, the salaries offered the Craws were better than those they received in the United States. The second advantage was that there was no color barrier in the Latin countries; blacks, whites, and Latin players were on the same teams. This offered the black players an opportunity to directly compare themselves with white major league players.

In spite of these advantages, there were also many drawbacks to the winter leagues. First, it meant that the ball players would be away from their families for many months. It also meant continued travel and living in hotels. Language was a problem, since few of the Craws spoke Spanish.

Josh and his teammates discussed the pros and cons of winter baseball and decided to give it a try. Josh played in Puerto Rico that year and enjoyed it so much that he traveled south every winter after that to play winter baseball. He delighted the fans with his booming homeruns, and he found out that he could play as well as any of the white major league players.

Despite lucrative offers to stay in Latin America during the summer, Josh returned to the United States to rejoin the Crawfords for the 1933 season. He had enjoyed winter baseball, but he missed being with his teammates. Josh continued this pattern of playing in the United States in the summer and Latin America during the winter. He stayed with the Crawfords until they began to break up in 1937. The Crawfords, however, had become a close-knit group, and even though the players eventually began playing for other teams, they kept in contact with one another. They had shared many successes, hardships, and happy and sad times.

Forty years later, the players had a reunion to discuss old times. The color barrier had been broken in 1945 when Branch Rickey signed Jackie Robinson to play with the Brooklyn Dodgers. Unfortunately for the Craws, this action had come too late for them to have their shot at the big leagues. Only Satchel Paige was given a chance to play with the major league teams. The breaking of the color barrier also came too late for

Josh Gibson, who died in 1947 at the age of 35. The acceptance of black players into the major leagues spelled the end of the Negro National League. Thus, when the Craws gathered in 1972, the Pittsburgh Crawfords, the New York Black Yankees, and other black teams had long ceased to exist. However, the memories of common friends and the feeling of being a special group still existed among the players. The men who gathered in Chicago in 1972 still considered themselves to be the Pittsburgh Crawford Giants.

There are many outstanding aspects of Josh Gibson's life. One of the clearest is the important role the Craws played in his life. This group was the center of his life during his adult years. He worked and played with members of this group; his attitudes, behavior, and even his dress were influenced by the group members.

Josh's devotion to a group is not unusual. The human being is clearly a "social animal." People are born into groups, they go to school in groups, they worship in groups, they work in groups, and when they die, a group is usually present when they are laid to rest. At any one time, the average person belongs to five or six different groups.

People's behavior and attitudes are profoundly affected by the groups to which they belong. A **group** is generally defined as "two or more persons who are interacting with one another in such a manner that each person influences and is influenced by each other person" (Shaw, 1981, p. 8). Because of the importance of groups in our daily lives, psychologists in many areas have devoted a great deal of study to the subject of group dynamics. Social psychologists have focused on finding out what kinds of influence groups have on people. Organizational psychologists, who often work in business and industry, have been especially interested in learning how groups affect people's performance and adjustment to their jobs. Organizational psychologists' interest goes beyond theory and research; they are also concerned with applying principles to help organizations run more smoothly and increase productivity. As we saw in Chapter 13, clinical psychologists have also become increasingly interested in group psychotherapy. In order to increase the effectiveness of the therapy sessions, they must understand how groups function and be able to apply this knowledge in a therapy session. Educational psychologists have developed new teaching methods that center around students learning in small groups. As you can see, an understanding of group dynamics is important in many areas of psychology.

In this chapter we will review some of the research in such areas as conformity, obedience, leadership, group decision making, and group performance. However, before doing this, let's focus on two important questions: Why do people belong to groups? What characteristics are common to most groups?

WHY BELONG TO A GROUP?

Take a few minutes to list the groups you belong to. What can you learn from this? First, you belong to a number of groups. Second, the groups you belong to vary a lot in size, function, and types of members. Some are small, others are large. The functions of the groups you belong to are probably very different; on your list you probably included work groups, social groups, study groups, and religious groups. Given that so many of our activities are performed in groups, it is important to ask why people join groups.

Rewards

Most groups offer their members a wide range of rewards. In Josh's case, he joined the Craws because of the attractive salary. In your own case, it's likely that you have joined some groups for the material rewards offered by the group. For example, one study revealed that workers joined unions for higher wages and job security (Rose, 1952). However, in addition to material rewards, there are a number of other benefits that come from group membership. Prestige and recognition are two such rewards. Josh enjoyed prestige as a member of the Craws. People would often point him out as a member of the famous Craws team, and fans flocked to get his autograph. Willerman and Swanson (1953) interviewed college women and found that prestige was the main reason they joined sororities. Another reward provided by groups is security. People are often comforted by knowing that other group members will come to their aid if it is needed. This sense of security was very important to Josh as he traveled in many small southern towns where a lone black could become the target of verbal and physical abuse. However, people would think twice before attacking a group of young, physically fit blacks. Clearly, people are attracted to groups for rewards, and the range and variety of rewards are often very great.

Social Comparison

How good a baseball player was Josh Gibson? This was a question that bothered him all his life. It drove him to join his first sandlot team. Practicing with his father had shown Josh that he could hit and throw a baseball. But was he really good? In order to answer this question, he would have to compare his abilities with others. He soon found out that he was better than the kids in his neighborhood; he was then anxious to see if he was as good as the major league players. Thus he joined the Homestead Grays and later the Craws, where he found out that he was as good as, and in most cases better than, other black major leaguers. Still, Josh wanted to know whether he was as good as the white major leaguers who got so much publicity. This desire for comparison was one of the main reasons he joined the Latin American teams during the winter season. Here was the one place he could play with white major leaguers to find out how good a player he really was.

Festinger (1954) suggested that one of the main reasons people join groups is for just this kind of social comparison. There are many aspects of our lives that we can evaluate on our own by observing their physical reality. For example, we can find out how much money we have by counting the number of dollars we have in the bank. The number of dollars is a physical reality; we don't need to consult anyone else to find out how much money we have. But if we want to know whether or not we are rich, we can't simply rely on the physical reality of how much money we have; we also need to know how much money other people have. In this case we need to compare our position with that of other people in order to make a decision.

There are many situations in which physical reality can serve as the basis for our judgments. For example, if we want to know if an electric bulb will give out light, we can put it in a lamp socket. While physical reality often can be used, there are many times, including those instances when we are judging ourselves, when physical reality is not a useful guide. In these cases, we need to compare with other people. For example, how can you find out if you are a good tennis player? How do you know whether your beliefs about God are reasonable? How do you know how attractive you are? For these and other questions, there is no physical reality that will give you an answer.

In order to answer these questions, you must turn to **social reality**— the beliefs, attitudes, and behaviors of other people. **Social comparison** means using social reality to evaluate ourselves. Since social comparison clearly involves other people, and people often group together to make such social comparisons, the desire for self-evaluation becomes a strong reason for joining groups.

Goethals and Darley (1977) have argued that the desire for self-evalua-

We must use social comparison to determine how good we are at certain activities. According to the theory, people will seek to compare themselves to others with similar experience.

tion not only motivates people to join groups, but also influences which group they will join. These researchers point out that people want to compare their abilities and values with others who are similar on important dimensions. For example, if you are a beginning tennis player, you would want to compare your ability with other beginners. It would be of little value for you to compare abilities with professional tennis players. This desire for social comparison will thus affect which groups you choose to join. According to this view, you will choose to join groups made up of people who are similar to you in areas that you consider important.

Achieving Goals

Another reason people join groups is to achieve certain goals. In some cases, these goals cannot be achieved without belonging to a group. Josh Gibson could not have played baseball without belonging to a team. A mountain climber needs a team to reach the summit of a cliff. In other cases, people join groups because membership makes achieving the goal

One reason for joining a group is to achieve a goal. Goals such as mountain climbing could not be achieved by one person alone.

easier. Thus, many people join Weight Watchers because they find it easier to stick to a diet if others are also doing it. It's not impossible to diet on your own, but it's easier if you're part of a group.

Clearly, then, there are a number of reasons for joining groups. It is unlikely that any one group will satisfy all these motives. For this reason we seek membership in a wide variety of groups. But no matter how many different groups we belong to, they all share a somewhat similar structure, which we will look at next.

THE STRUCTURE OF THE GROUP

At first glance it may seem that a baseball team has little in common with other groups such as families or social clubs. There are, however, similarities in the structures of most groups. In almost every group there are norms and roles that guide the behavior of its members and contribute to the smooth functioning of the group.

Norms

In general, the Craws were a loosely run team in which a great deal of individual freedom was allowed. However, there were certain rules that applied to everyone. All team members were expected to be in uniform and at the ball park some hours before the game. All team members were expected to be at the bus with their bags packed at a certain time. Moving from the Craws to other groups, we find that they too have general rules. Families, for example, often have agreements about what time everyone will eat meals. Social clubs such as fraternities and sororities may have rules about the acceptable dress or acceptable behavior. Professional societies generally have rules of ethics that guide the conduct of all members.

Rules that govern specific behavior and apply to all members of the group are called **norms.** Norms may be written, as is the case of the bylaws of many groups, or they may be unwritten but clearly understood codes. Whatever the form, norms "specify *what* must, or must not, be done *when*" (Steiner, 1972, p. 171).

In an interesting experiment on norms, Roethlisberger and Dickson (1939) observed work groups on a production line. They found that these groups developed unwritten rules about how much each worker should produce. These norms allowed the men to work at a comfortable rate. Any worker who produced too much or too little was treated to a "binging" ritual that was designed to force him to produce in line with the group norm. Binging involved the other workers joking about the man's work and then playfully but forcefully hitting him on the shoulder. The "bing" was not strong enough to severely hurt him, but it was strong enough to give him the message to change his work habits. In this case, there were not only norms about how much a man should work, but also norms about how the group members should go about changing deviant behavior. These types of informal norms are found in many work groups (Swenson, 1973).

Roles

In addition to norms that apply to everyone, groups also have rules that apply only to people in certain positions. These are called **roles,** and they define the obligations and expectations of that specific position (Shaw,

On many sports teams, an individual or individuals will adopt the role of "enforcer." In the case shown here, Rudy Tomjanovich was punched by Kermit Washington. He later sued Washington and his team, the Los Angeles Lakers, claiming that Washington was the team's enforcer, and that the team should have taken adequate steps to control their enforcer.

1981). For example, on a baseball team there is the role of catcher. The rules applying to where the catcher plays and how this position is played are different from those applying to the pitcher or the first baseman. The formal roles on a baseball team are easily learned from a rule book. In addition to these roles, there are also informal roles in groups. For example, in the late 1970s there was a great deal of discussion about the role of the "enforcer" on athletic teams. The enforcer was supposedly the person who would protect other team members when they were in trouble. In 1976, there was an incident on the basketball court where a scuffle broke out between members of the Houston Rockets and the Los Angeles Lakers. During the fight, Kermit Washington, a Laker who had the reputation of being the enforcer, rushed down the court and punched one of the opposing players, Rudy Tomjanovich. The punch severely injured his face and resulted in a 6-month hospital ordeal for him. In a subsequent lawsuit, Tomjanovich was awarded $4.5 million. The Lakers were ordered to pay the bulk of the damages because, it was argued, they were aware of the enforcer role on their team and they did not take adequate steps to control their own enforcer.

Together, roles and norms give the group structure and let members know what is expected of them. This knowledge also helps group members predict the behavior of other group members. Thus, roles and norms help the group function smoothly. Clearly, there can also be disadvantages to a rigid system of roles and norms. Group roles may severely limit the freedom of members and may force people to take positions that they are not suited for and do not enjoy. In Highlight: "Sex Roles: When Roles Can Be Harmful," we look at one case in which the role system has created friction.

HIGHLIGHT / SEX ROLES: WHEN ROLES CAN BE HARMFUL

Our society has developed traditional stereotypes of men and women. Men are viewed as being logical, competitive, aggressive, ambitious, and domineering. Women, on the other hand, are viewed as being the "weaker sex"—sensitive, emotional, dependent, and talkative. The traditional view of women is also that they have little business sense (Frieze et al., 1978). These stereotypes are held by both men and women alike (Broverman et al., 1972) and are often used as the basis of assigning roles to men and women in various groups. In families, for example, the "logical, competitive, aggressive" male has traditionally been given the role of providing financial security for his family. As such, it is he who must work outside the home. In addition, the "domineering" male is expected to be head of the family: "A *man's* home is his castle." The woman is given the role of managing the household and supporting her husband. If she does seek work outside the household, she is expected to take on more "feminine" occupations such as secretary, nurse, or sales clerk. Further, if she does seek employment, she is not expected to, nor is she usually given the opportunity to, compete with her male counterparts for high salaries.

Children are taught these stereotypes in a variety of ways and places. Parents teach their children how to be a boy or girl. These lessons include allowing children to play only sex-appropriate games, giving instructions about who can express what emotions, and supplying the correct models for sex-related behavior. In school, children read stories in their textbooks that show males as strong, active, and adventurous, while females are shown as gentle and dependent (Wirtenburg & Nakamura, 1976). Even on television, children are shown that the "typical" woman is a housewife with a bunch of kids, while the "typical" man works, fights, plays, and rules the world outside the home.

This assignment of sex roles is not only based on stereotypes about the personality and temperament of men and women, it also *reinforces* those stereotypes. The male who is placed in a competitive job situation must become competitive, domineering, and aggressive if he is to survive in this position. Similarly, the female who is forced into the dependent role cannot function if she seems aggressive and ambitious. Thus a cycle of self-fulfilling prophecy results from the assignment of roles based on stereotypes of males and females (see Chapter 14).

The underlying problem in this situation is that males are not necessarily domineering, logical, ambitious, and businesslike. And all females are not necessarily gentle, sensitive, and not mechanically inclined. The assignment of roles based on these rigid stereotypes has had bad consequences from both the individual's and the group's point of view. For individuals, it has meant that they are often forced to try to fulfill a role that is distasteful and not suited to their abilities. This has been particularly unfortunate for women, who are stereotyped in a more negative light than men

(Deaux, 1976) and who have, consequently, been offered the less attractive alternatives. For the group, whether it is the family or work group, this misguided procedure for assigning roles has often limited effective performance by the group.

Assigning people to roles because of their sex makes no more sense than assigning them to play positions on a baseball team based on their shoe size. There has recently been an increased awareness of the unfairness and negative impact of traditional sex roles. Stereotypes about women are becoming less negative (Der-Karabetran and Smith, 1977). The number of women taking jobs outside the home has increased so that now 52 percent of all women over 16 years of age hold jobs (Bureau of Labor Statistics, *Employment and Earnings,* January 1981).

These changes are viewed with alarm by some people. It is argued that the destruction of traditional sex roles will lead to a state of confusion and chaos that is avoided when everyone knows his or her place. The individual, both male and female, is now faced with a wider variety of alternative roles, occupations, and life styles to choose from. For some, this variety is overwhelming, and being forced to make a personal decision is frightening. However, despite these problems, the ultimate result of this change will be to allow people to adopt roles that are more suited to their personal abilities and preferences. And, consequently, groups will function more smoothly and effectively.

ENSURING ADHERENCE TO NORMS

In order for a group to function smoothly, it must make sure that its members follow its rules or norms. It would have been impossible for the Craws to play games if the team members failed to show up at the park at game time. In the same way, it would be hard for a family to function as a unit if members decided to eat and sleep at all different times. On a larger scale, imagine trying to drive in a city if no one followed the norm that a red light means "stop" and a green one signals "go." There are several types of group pressure aimed at ensuring that group members adhere to the group's norms. We will look at some of them as we discuss conformity, obedience, and leadership. But not all group pressures push people to follow norms. As we will see in our discussion of deindividuation, there are some pressures that can work in the opposite direction, by reducing the pressure to follow norms.

Conformity

Josh Gibson's teammates pressured him to wear the fashion of the day when they went out on the town after a game, even though, as mentioned earlier, baggy pants on his huge frame made him look like an out-of-control sailboat. So despite his better judgment, he gave in to pressure from his teammates to dress as they did. If you think about it, it's probably not hard to find similar examples where you acted in a certain way or wore a certain outfit because everyone else was doing it.

For example, many smokers say that their habit began as a result of their desire to be one of the group. They often report that they hated their first few cigarettes; in some cases, they even became violently sick after the first few puffs. However, they stuck it out and first learned to tolerate and later to crave cigarettes. This torturous journey began in an effort to be like and to be liked by other group members. Similar stories are often told by people who are heavy users of alcohol and other drugs.

What Is Conformity?   Each of these cases is an example of conformity. Conformity occurs when a person changes his or her behavior or attitudes as a result of real or imagined group pressures, despite personal feelings to the contrary. In short, conformity involves *changing* attitudes or behaviors in an effort to be more accepted by a group. In order for conformity to occur, we must be able to say that the person would have acted differently without group pressure (Kiesler and Kiesler, 1969). Josh's behavior represents conformity because he adopted a mode of dress so that the other team members would more readily accept him; without this group pressure, he would not have chosen this outfit—in fact he resisted for a while before he gave in and dressed the way they wanted him to.

The word "conformity" creates negative pictures for most of us. In some cases we view conformity in the everyday sense as squeezing out people's individuality and creativity. Jokes are often made about conformity in American suburbs where families have 2.3 children, live in the same type of house, drive the same kind of car, wear the same types of clothes, belong to the same clubs, and think the same thoughts. On a more serious level, we might think of the role of conformity in such tragic events as My Lai in Vietnam, where a company of American soldiers conformed to each others' example and massacred a village of innocent civilians. Indeed, conformity has a tragic and negative side. On the other hand, conformity is also one of the main reasons that people can live together. Because people conform to norms, we can usually predict how

The fear of being rejected by peers motivates people to conform. People often begin smoking in an effort to be accepted by members of their peer group.

others will behave. For example, we can usually predict that members of our family will wear their clothes rather than ours, or that people will wait in line to buy tickets to a movie rather than rushing all together to the ticket window. Thus, while too much conformity can create problems, too little conformity can also make life difficult and hazardous. And because of the central role that conformity plays in our lives, it is important that we understand it and identify the conditions that affect when people will conform.

Why Do People Conform? Examples of conformity are very easy to find. Each one of us conforms to group pressures many times each day. Our decisions about what to wear, where to park our car, and even about the time we eat can be examples of conformity. What motivates people to conform?

Most theories of conformity have focused on the types of pressure that groups bring to bear on people to change their behavior. Two such pressures have been identified. Both are strong and both are often used together to induce conformity.

One of these pressures is based on the group's value as a source of information. Consider, for example, your attitude toward nuclear power. Most of us know very little about the topic; to really understand the details involved we would have to take many courses in physics, engineering, and economics. How, then, can we form an attitude on this issue and make decisions about it? One way is to find out what other people believe. Even as children we learn to seek information from groups and we generally find that if most people tell us something, it is true. For example, a young boy may be told by his mother, father, and older sister that the lighted stove is hot and he will get burned if he touches it. Being unwilling to accept this information, he touches the stove and quickly learns that the group was right. After that he becomes more willing to accept the group's information. This same process happens repeatedly and people come to rely more and more on others to serve as sources of information. As a result, groups develop power to influence a person's attitudes and behavior because of their informational value. This type of influence has been labeled **informational pressure** (Kelley, 1952), and it is the basis of much conforming behavior.

The second type of pressure is **normative social pressure**. The basis for this pressure is the desire to belong to the group. Or, as some investigators have suggested, it is the desire to receive rewards and avoid punishment (Krupat, 1982). As we grow up and are members of many groups, we learn an important lesson about the "personality" of groups. Groups accept members as long as these members conform to the group norms and standards. People who do not conform are often ridiculed, rejected, and in some cases they are quickly made ex-members of the group (Freedman and Doob, 1968; Schachter, 1951). The general moral to this story is that conformity leads to acceptance. Because belonging to groups is so important in everyone's life and because rejection and ridicule by the group is often painful, the group possesses great power to influence the behavior of its members. Returning to the Josh Gibson example, it is clear that his conversion to "plus fours" was in a large part due to normative pressure; his friends teased him and poked fun at him until he adopted the style. His behavior was aimed at keeping his membership in the group.

Before leaving this discussion of conformity, some additional points need to be made. First, in most cases, groups use both informational and normative pressures to make their members conform. Often one type of pressure may be more effective than the other, but both types are generally used. Second, the two types of pressure cause different types of conformity. People who react to normative pressure are acting on the fear that the group will reject them if they don't conform; conformity is only used as a means of being accepted by the group. In these cases, the normative pressure leads only to simple compliance. An example of this relationship is prisoners of war who may openly criticize their own country while in the hands of their captors. Once they are free, however, they no longer voice these opinions. As captives they responded to normative pressure, believing that the expression of certain positions would lead to better treatment for them. When a person uses the group as a source of information to decide the correct course of action or belief, private acceptance is more likely to result.

Investigating Conformity.   Now that we have clearly defined conformity, we can begin to study the phenomenon. One means might be to take an existing group like the Crawfords and measure how much uniformity in behavior and attitudes existed among the players. In doing this we might find that many of the players dressed in a similar manner, they did similar things in their spare time, and their attitudes on many issues were the same. However, could we use these cases as examples of conformity? Remember that the definition of conformity involves a *change* in behavior or attitudes. It is possible that the members of the Crawfords believed and behaved as they did before they became a team. In fact, it would be very plausible to assume that one of the reasons they joined together was because of their similarities (see Chapter 14). Further, even if we could show that there were changes in behavior after joining the team, it would be difficult to determine if these were the result of normative or informational pressures.

In 1951 Solomon Asch developed a method for studying conformity that controls the problems mentioned above. Imagine yourself as a subject who has volunteered for a psychological experiment. You arrive at the experimental room and see six other subjects seated around a large table. You take the only empty seat and nod a slight hello to the other subjects. The experimenter enters and explains that the study is concerned with perceptual accuracy. He shows the group two large cards (see Figure 15–1). On one card is a single line. On the other card are three lines of varying lengths marked A,B,C. The experimenter says that the group will see a number of these cards and that the task of each member is to identify the line that matches the length of the single line. Each person

FIGURE 15–1

Cards used in the Asch experiment.

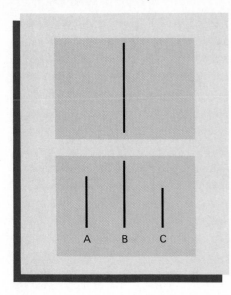

will give their answer in turn; you find that you will be the sixth person to answer.

The experiment begins. On the first card, the single line is 4 inches long, while on the comparison card, line A is 3 inches, line B is 4 inches and line C is 2 inches. Each subject responds in turn calling out "line B." Another pair of cards is held up and you can see that the correct answer is line A. Again, each subject before you calls out "line A." At this point, you are beginning to think that the experiment is stupid and you wonder what these psychologists will dream up next. A third set of cards is held up and again you can easily see that the correct answer is line B. You sit back feeling smug and await your turn. Suddenly you are startled by the first subject's response; he has identified line A. Is he nuts or blind? Maybe he is neither, because you have just heard the second and third subjects identify line A. The two subjects before you confidently identify line A and it is now your turn. What do you do?

This is the question that Asch wished to answer. Actually, the six other "subjects" are Asch's confederates, who have been trained to respond in a certain way: on 12 of the 18 trials they all give incorrect responses. The second-to-the-last person (you in this case) is the only person who is unaware of the conspiracy. This situation allows the experimenter to examine your response to the group; do you conform to the majority opinion or is the correct answer given despite the unanimously incorrect group? This is clearly a study of conformity, since all subjects are able to identify the correct answer. An incorrect response would, therefore, represent a yielding to the group position.

In the first study, Asch found that 35 percent of the responses were conforming ones. He was somewhat surprised at this high rate of conformity with such a simple task. Ross, Bierbrauer, and Hoffman (1976), however, point out that subjects in this situation are under quite a bit of normative pressure to conform to the group opinion. If people do not give the same answer as the other group members, they will be challenging their "competence, wisdom, and sanity. . . ." In such a case you as the subject must be concerned with how the group will respond if you do not conform. Will they laugh at you and be angry with you for questioning their competence? There are, in fact, six of them and only one of you. Thus, even though you can see the correct answer, you will still feel pressure to conform.

Although there have been many variations in the method, the Asch technique has served as the model for conformity research.

Factors Influencing Conformity. Just as we know that each of us conform at times, we also know that there are many other times when we do not conform. Therefore, there are a number of interesting research questions concerning the factors that influence conformity. In examining these factors, we find that they fall into three categories: characteristics of the individual, characteristics of the group, and nature of the task.

If you observe your friends and acquaintances, you are likely to find that some of them conform to group pressures more often than others. This observation leads to the conclusion that there must be characteristics that influence their conformity. Surprisingly, research on this question has failed to identify personality traits that are strongly associated with conformity (Wheeler et al., 1978). Another body of research has examined the stereotype that women are more conforming than men. Overall, research seems to indicate that women give in to group pressures more than men do (Cooper, 1979). However, many of these studies have been tainted with a bias that even the researchers were unaware of. Sistrunk and McDavid (1971) pointed out that much of the early research on this issue involved tasks that were more familiar to males than to females. These investigators suggested that the results may not be reflecting a

In the Asch studies on conformity, one naive subject (Subject #6 in the photos here) was placed in a group of experimental confederates. The subjects were asked to make simple judgments in turn. In the top photo, Subject #6 listens in surprise as the confederates give the incorrect answer. When it is his turn he must decide whether to give the correct answer or follow the example of the other group members. The results of the research showed that subjects would conform to the group and give an incorrect answer over one-third of the time.

sex difference; rather, the results could be due to familiarity with the task. These investigators ran a number of conformity studies using tasks that were more familiar to either male or female subjects. The results showed that while females conformed more than males on "male-related" tasks, the reverse results were found for "female-related" tasks. Therefore, we cannot conclude that one sex is more conforming than the other until more research is conducted controlling problems like task-familiarity.

A number of other studies have examined how people's position in their group affects their behavior. In general, the research suggests that conformity will be greatest among people who (1) expect future interaction with group members (Lewis, Laugan, and Hollander, 1972); (2) are strongly attracted to the group (Sakurai, 1975); and (3) do not feel completely accepted by the group (Dittes and Kelley, 1956). It is interesting to note that this description fits Josh Gibson when he first joined the Crawfords. He knew he would be interacting with the team members over the long season, and he looked forward to playing baseball for the Craws. Because he was so young, he was concerned about how he would be accepted by the other veteran players. Further, when he joined the team, he was recovering from an operation and he was not certain how well he would perform in his weakened state. Research on conformity has shown that people who are unsure of their ability are more likely to comply with group pressure than those who are confident of their ability (Geller, Endler, and Wiesenthal, 1973). Thus, based on the research on individual characteristics, we would expect Josh to conform to team pressures when he joined the Craws. And there is evidence that during this early time Josh changed a number of his behaviors to meet the demands of the team (Brashler, 1978).

In addition to individual characteristics, the nature of the group influences the degree of conformity. Asch (1951) and Gerard et al. (1968) varied the size of the group that confronted the subject. They found that conformity increased as the size of the group increased until it consisted of four others (see Figure 15–2). However, more recent research suggests that four may not be a magic number for conformity. One investigator had two, four, six, or eight persons line up at a bus stop in Jerusalem (Mann, 1977). He then observed how other people would respond to these lines of different lengths. He found that only 17 percent of those who first arrived joined lines of two or four persons. However, 58 percent and 83 percent of the first arrivers took their place in the six- and eight-person lines, respectively. Therefore, it seems that the maximum number of people producing the maximum conformity will be a function of the setting and other task and group variables.

Another important group characteristic involves whether or not the group is unanimous in its opinion. In order to demonstrate this effect, Asch (1956) had subjects judge the line comparison task under three conditions. In one condition, the group of confederates unanimously chose the same incorrect line on 12 of the 18 trials. In a second condition, one of the confederates always gave the correct answer even when the remainder of the group responded incorrectly. In a third condition, one confederate gave an incorrect answer that also differed from the answer given by the other confederates. The results were dramatic. When subjects were confronted with a unanimous majority, they conformed on about 35 percent of the trials. However, when there was one other nonconformer in the group, conformity dropped to about 9 percent. This drop occurred even when the other confederate gave an *in*correct response!

A final important effect involves the influence of the task characteristics on conformity. It has been repeatedly shown that the more difficult the task, the greater the degree of conformity. Asch (1952), for example, was able to vary task difficulty by making the comparison lines more and more similar in length. This finding clearly makes good sense, as people are more likely to rely on the group for information when they

FIGURE 15–2

Asch found that conformity increases until group size reaches three and then levels off.

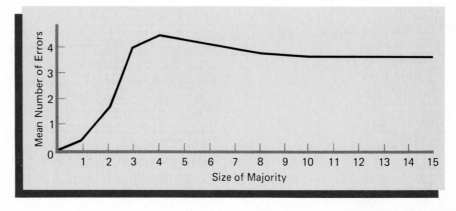

don't know the correct answer. Of course, this does not mean that there will be no conformity when the correct answer is evident; people are simply more likely to conform when the correct position is not evident.

Obedience to Authority

There was another pressure, besides peer pressure, that influenced Josh's behavior and that of his teammates. This pressure was the orders from Oscar Charleston, the manager of the team. It was up to Charleston to blend the talents of the players into a team; a club could have a great deal of talent, but it would not be a winner if the players did not play together as a single team. When necessary, Charleston was a strict and demanding coach, and there was no question who was in charge. He told players where to play, when to bat, how often to practice, and how to wear their uniforms. Josh and the others followed Charleston's orders; they respected his judgment as a player and they knew he could fine them or bench them if they did not obey.

Obedience involves the following of direct and explicit orders of a person in a position of authority. In some cases, the result of obedience is positive. The Craws were a better team because they followed the directions of Oscar Charleston. You can probably point to examples where you followed the orders of an authority figure with positive results.

Because it is possible to point to so many examples where obedience to orders has positive results, many people become all too willing to follow the demands of authority figures. Unfortunately, blind obedience can have disastrous consequences. Six million innocent men, women, and children were tortured and killed during World War II by Nazis who confessed they were only following the orders of their superiors. In November, 1978, over 900 members of the Peoples Temple committed suicide by drinking Kool-Aid laced with cyanide; they were following the orders of their leader Jim Jones. When most of us read of events such as these, we comfort ourselves by saying it could never happen to us—"those other people" were either stupid or under a great deal of stress. A "normal" person in "normal" times would not follow orders that would directly harm another innocent person.

Unfortunately, Stanley Milgram (1963, 1965) found that this is not the case; "normal" people in "normal" times often will blindly follow orders even if it hurts innocent people. In order to comprehend the impact of the Milgram demonstration, imagine yourself in the following situation. Upon arriving at the experimental room, you sit down and begin talking to a middle-aged man who is also waiting for the experiment. Soon, the experimenter, dressed in a white laboratory coat, enters and explains that he is studying the effects of punishment on learning. He further explains that one of the subjects will be the teacher who will be asking the learner questions and delivering electrical shocks when the learner gives incorrect answers. You become a little concerned at the mention of electric shock as you remember the jolt you once recieved when touching a bare wire. The other subject is also concerned and voices his fear of shock. The experimenter reassures him that the shock will not be dangerous. At this point you draw lots to determine who will be the "teacher" and "learner"; it is with some relief that you find that you will be the teacher.

The other subject is led to an enclosed booth where the experimenter straps him into a chair and attaches electrodes to his wrists. The experimenter returns and begins showing you the "teaching machine." The machine contains a row of levers and under each lever is a shock level. The first level reads 15 volts, and each level thereafter increases by 15 volts, with the last lever being marked 450 volts. The lower levels are marked "Slight Shock," while the upper levels are labeled "Danger: Severe

TABLE 15–1: Maximum Shock Levels in Milgram's Obedience Study

Verbal Designation and Voltage Indication	Number of Subjects for Whom This Was Maximum Shock
Slight shock	
15	0
30	0
45	0
60	0
Moderate shock	
75	0
90	0
105	0
120	0
Strong shock	
135	0
150	0
165	0
180	0
Very strong shock	
195	0
210	0
225	0
240	0
Intense shock	
255	0
270	0
285	0
300	5
Extreme-intensity shock	
315	4
330	2
345	1
360	1
Danger—severe shock	
375	1
390	0
405	0
420	0
XXX	
435	0
450	26

Source: Milgram (1963).

Shock." The 450-volt switch carries the ominous sign "XXX." The experimenter explains that you are to read a prepared list of questions and wait for the learner's answer. If he answers incorrectly, you are to give him a shock and call out the correct answer. You should then go on to the next question. Each shock you deliver to the learner must be 15 volts higher than the previous shock; the first shock will be 15 volts, the second will be 30 volts, and so on. In principle, the procedure seems quite simple to you and you inform the experimenter that you are ready to start.

Before beginning, the experimenter gives you a sample shock from the lower end of the scale. Even this level hurts and you become increasingly thankful that you are the teacher rather than the learner. Now the experiment begins. You begin reading the questions and waiting for the learner's answers. He gives an incorrect answer and you deliver the 15-volt shock. After each incorrect answer, you increase the shock level as instructed. When you deliver the 90-volt shock, the learner gives a cry of pain. At 150 volts, the learner screams and asks to be let out of the booth. You look to the experimenter who calmly instructs you to "proceed to the next question." At 180 volts, there is another cry of pain and the subject begs to stop the study. Your concern for the learner increases and you ask the experimenter to check on him. The experimenter instructs you to continue, and despite your uneasiness, you go on to the next question. When you deliver the 300-volt shock, the learner cries that he is getting sick and refuses to answer any additional questions. From this point on there is no response from the booth; your questions and shocks are met only with silence.

What would you do in this situation? Would you continue to follow the orders of the experimenter and deliver shocks to the maximum 450-volt XXX, or would you refuse to continue and disobey the experimenter? What percentage of the "average, normal" subjects in this study do you think would continue to the maximum shock level? These were the questions that Milgram wished to answer.

He ran the first study at Yale University, using male subjects between the ages of 20 and 50. The subjects came from a variety of backgrounds and occupations; 40 percent held unskilled jobs, 40 percent had white-collar sales jobs, and 20 percent were professionals. As can be seen from the Table 15–1, 26 of the 40 subjects (65 percent) went all the way and gave the maximum shock; not a single subject stopped before the last level of intense shock.

In actuality, the "learner" in the study was an experimental confederate who was trained to play a role. He did not actually receive any shocks; he merely recorded the level of shocks which the subjects administered. It is, however, important to note that the subjects did not know of this trickery; they believed that they were shocking the innocent learner. Though many of the subjects expressed concern about the learner, they still followed orders to shock him. The degree of obedience is surprisingly high. In fact, Milgram asked a group of senior psychology students at Yale University and a group of psychiatrists to predict how many subjects would go to the maximum level. They predicted that less than 2 percent would follow orders to give the 450-volt shock.

Why did so many subjects obey the experimenter's orders? One possible reason could be the setting; the subjects knew they were in a psychological study at a prestigious university and may have felt the experimenter would not let them do anything wrong. In order to test this reason, Milgram moved his experiment to a rundown office building in Brockport, Connecticut. The experimenter did not wear the white laboratory coat and subjects were not told of any affiliation with Yale University. Even in this setting, Milgram found that 48 percent of the subjects obeyed the order to give the maximum shock.

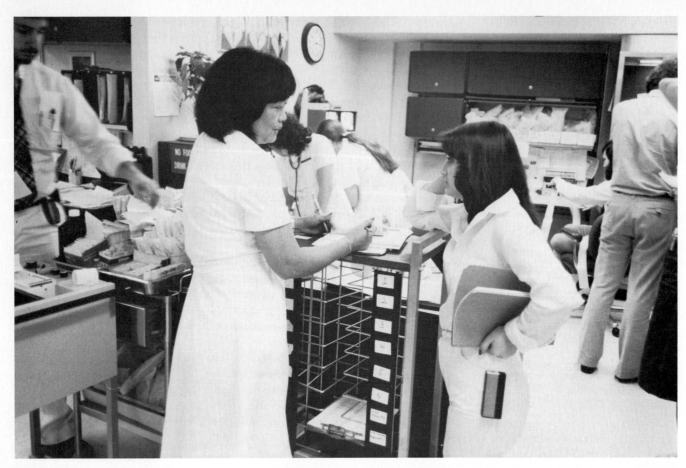

Obedience involves following the direct orders of an authority figure. Research has found that nurses would follow the verbal orders of an unknown doctor even when the orders required actions clearly against hospital policy. One reason that people obey orders is that they do not feel responsible for their actions—the person who gave the orders is responsible.

In a very different setting, Hofling and his colleagues (1966) studied whether nurses in a hospital would follow orders to violate hospital rules and deliver a potentially harmful dosage of a drug to a patient. Nurses on duty received a telephone call from a doctor they did not know. He ordered them to administer 20 milligrams of a drug for which the maximum stated dosage was 10 milligrams a day. This order not only was higher than the maximum safe dosage, but it violated hospital policy that no nurse was to give a patient drugs without the doctor being physically present. Despite these violations, 21 of the 22 nurses who were telephoned followed the doctor's orders.

These studies demonstrate the power of orders. People seem to be willing to follow the orders of an authority figure even when their behavior brings harm to others. The reports of subjects in these and other studies suggest that this willingness occurs because people do not accept responsibility for actions they perform under orders. They feel that the person giving the orders has taken the responsibility for the results of their actions (Kilham and Mann, 1974; Milgram, 1977). This sentiment was clearly echoed at the Nüremburg trials after World War II when many of the Nazi war criminals stated that they felt their actions were wrong, but it was not their fault, because they were merely following orders. Findings such as these should cause us to pause and question our own behaviors. How often do we justify our own actions by convincing ourselves that we are not responsible because we are only doing what we are told? History has proven that this is a dangerous logic to follow, and that the ultimate responsibility for our actions must rest on our own shoulders.

A Question of Ethics. The research on obedience is eye-opening for a number of reasons. The results are certainly quite startling, but the methods used to obtain the results also give us reason for reflection.

Was it fair and ethical to place the unsuspecting subjects in such an uncomfortable position? In the Milgram studies, the subjects had volunteered to be in a study on learning. In the study conducted by Hofling and associates, the nurses had not even volunteered to be in a study. Subjects in the Milgram study suffered a great deal of psychological stress. Even though they continued to give the ordered shocks, Milgram reports that many of his subjects sweated profusely, fidgeted incessantly, fell into uncontrollable fits of nervous giggling, and showed other signs of discomfort and stress.

Another disturbing by-product of the Milgram study is that the subjects were forced to learn about an unpleasant aspect of themselves—namely, that they would follow orders to hurt an innocent person. Certainly the subjects were relieved to find that the learner did not actually receive electric shocks. However, they were still left with the unpleasant realization that they had given the shocks thinking the learner was being hurt. Most of us can comfort ourselves by saying that we would not hurt another person simply because we were ordered to do so. The subjects in the Milgram studies could not protect their self-image with such thoughts; they had just learned that they would do this. They had not volunteered for the study in an effort to learn this about themselves; in fact, it is probable that many of them would just as soon not ever learned about this aspect of themselves.

While there are a number of reasons to question the procedure, there were some positive outcomes. In a follow-up questionnaire sent to subjects after they had been in the Milgram study, 84 percent reported that they were glad they had been in the study. In addition, the results obtained from the studies on obedience have furthered our understanding of human behavior. We now know the power of orders and we have a greater comprehension of why people act as they do. The impact of the results would have been considerably less if Milgram and others had used a less powerful task, such as ordering subjects to write random numbers or write uncomplementary stories about another person, rather than administering electric shocks.

The question of ethics is difficult to answer, especially in regard to designs such as those used in the obedience studies. On one hand, we need to use designs that have strong impact on subjects if we wish to obtain valid results. On the other hand, we need to constantly keep in mind our responsibility as researchers to protect the rights and welfare of subjects. While there is no single answer as to what is an ethical design, today most psychologists submit their studies to ethics committees. Such committees review the design to ensure that subject's rights are protected and they suggest different procedures for greater protection, if necessary. Guidelines for the ethical conduct of research have been devised by the American Psychological Association, and federal and state laws protecting human experimental subjects have been passed. The effort to guarantee the rights and safety of human subjects is a continuing one, and, with the whole-hearted cooperation of researchers, experimental designs that are sensitive to the subject's welfare have become the rule, as we discussed in Chapter 1.

Leadership

The discussion of obedience demonstrates how readily people follow the orders of leaders. Because leaders can have such a strong influence on group members' behaviors, it is important that we understand how someone becomes a group leader and what factors play a part in making someone an effective leader.

A **leader** can be defined as the person who has the greatest influence

The trait theory of leadership says that certain traits make people leaders. However, research has failed to clearly identify traits that are common to all or even most leaders.

on the activities of the group (Shaw, 1981). The use of this definition has given rise to two interesting observations. As far back as 1904, Terman pointed out that each member of a society is both a leader and a follower. It is unusual to find a group where the same person is always the leader; different people at different times are able to influence the activities of the group. If you review the structure of your own groups, it is likely that you will find different people in the role of leader over the history of the group. Some people may lead more than others, but, depending on the time and circumstances, we are all leaders and we are all followers.

A second point is that at any one time there are often two leaders in a group. One of these leaders is generally concerned with solving the tasks facing the group; he or she is most concerned with getting the job done and presenting the group with guidance on solving problems. We might call this person the *task specialist* (Bales and Slater, 1955). The other person who has a strong influence on the group is concerned with the person-oriented activities of the group. This person is usually most concerned with seeing that other group members are happy and that they are allowed to contribute to the group. This *socioemotional* leader may be the clown in the group, since he or she is often reducing group tension, diffusing interpersonal conflicts, and influencing the emotional tone of the group.

It is interesting to find that the Craws' pattern of leadership fit this scheme. Oscar Charleston, the player-manager, was clearly the task specialist. He was older and more experienced than the other players, and even without the title of manager his main concerns were for the Craws to play a good "brand" of baseball. He set the rules for the team, instructed the players about hitting techniques, and advised them about how to play their positions. But Charleston, because of his age and focus, was not the person who set the emotional tone of the team. Players like Josh and Jimmie Crutchfield were the social/emotional leaders. They kept the team members from becoming too depressed when they were playing badly, and they would think up jokes to reduce the tension when personal conflicts threatened the team spirit. These two types of leadership helped the team function more smoothly.

Theories of Leadership. Once we understand the concept of leadership, we can ask why some people have more influence on groups than others. Why did Josh Gibson, Oscar Charleston, and Jimmie Crutchfield occupy the leadership roles on the Craws? On a more global level, why have such people as John F. Kennedy, Martin Luther King, Jr., Golda Meir, Abraham Lincoln, and Ayatollah Ruhollah Khomeini emerged as leaders? Did they rise to leadership positions because of some special characteristics, or did they become leaders due to the situations they were in at the time?

Some of the earliest theories of leadership (for example, Terman, 1904) argued that leaders have certain traits that propel them into positions of influence. These *great man theories* or *trait theories* of leadership often hold that leaders are born, not made. Literally hundreds of studies have sought to identify the traits that make people leaders. These studies have examined physical, intelligence, and personality traits, but they have generally failed to identify specific traits that set off leaders from nonleaders. For example, some studies found that leaders are older than average group members; others have found leaders to be younger. Some studies found that leaders have more emotional control than the average group member, while others found that the leader has equal or even less emotional control.

One interesting finding is that leadership seems to be associated with height; people who are taller are more likely to hold leadership positions than people who are short. Keyes (1980) compared the average salaries

TABLE 15–2: Relationship between Height and Salary, 1943–1968

Height	Mean 1943 Salary	Mean 1968 Salary
5′3″–5′5″	$3,500	$14,750
5′6″–5′7″	3,750	16,500
5′8″–5′9″	3,900	17,000
5′10″–5′11″	3,900	17,500
6′0″–6′1″	4,100	19,000
6′2″–6′3″	4,000	18,500
6′4″–6′6″	3,700	19,500

Source: Adapted from Keyes (1980).

of 17,000 Air Force cadets in 1943 and 1968. As can be seen from Table 15–2, although the cadets had roughly equal salaries in 1943, the salaries attained by these men 26 years later were related to their height. The taller men had higher incomes; in fact, every inch over 5′3″ was worth about $370 in annual income.

Another unusual variable related to leadership is talkativeness—leaders talk more than the average group member. Some studies (Ginter and Lindskold, 1975; Sorrentino and Boutillier, 1975) suggest that any group member who monopolizes group discussions can rise to the position of leader. This "blabbermouth" rule seems to hold even when the quality of the person's conversation and suggestions is low!

Although we can point to certain traits that may be related to leadership, the research has not identified traits that clearly set leaders apart from followers. It is generally agreed that we cannot identify who will emerge as a leader by looking at personal traits (Hollander and Julian, 1975). In other words, the research suggests that people are not "born to lead."

Despite the failure of research to find specific leadership traits or qualities, the search still goes on. Many businesses and military organizations use tests to help identify those with leadership potential. And many of us still believe that there is something special that sets leaders apart from other people. Napier and Gershenfeld (1981) argue that people have a need to believe that their leaders possess some special traits. There seems to be some comfort in believing that our leaders are unusual or superhuman. In many cases, the media reinforces these views by building up the images of leaders. While this belief may make us secure in some cases, it also may increase our disappointment when we find out that one of our trusted leaders has his or her share of human faults. A very good example of this is the disappointment and disillusionment experienced by many people when they learned that President Nixon lied about Watergate.

The failure to find traits that identify leaders led psychologists to examine how the group situation influences who becomes a leader. The *situational theory* assumes that the needs of the group change from time to time and, as a result, the type of person who will lead the group will change. Thus, it is the situational factors that determine who will lead and for how long. For example, one researcher suggests that it was the conditions that prevailed in the United States that determined when John Kennedy and Lyndon Johnson would be accepted as leaders (Toynbee, 1965). At the time of Kennedy's election, there was a need for a president who could deal with questions regarding the international nuclear test ban and mounting problems in Cuba. However, the situation changed when Johnson was running for election; at that time, there was a need for a tactician who could manipulate the Congress to pass important legislation on human rights. In each case a person who had the qualifications fitting the needs of the situation emerged as leader. Toynbee points out, "It is one of the ironies of history that President Johnson had been more successful than Kennedy himself in getting the Kennedy Program enacted. If

The situational theory of leadership states that conditions rather than personal traits determine who will emerge as the leader. Research has shown that a person seated at the head of a table often becomes the group leader.

Kennedy had lived to be re-elected it seems probable that a good deal less of his program would be on the statute books by now."

There has been some research showing that situations do affect who will emerge as leader. For example, several studies have found that the person seated at the head of the table often becomes the leader because he or she can maintain eye contact with most of the other group members (Howells and Becker, 1962; Lecuyer, 1976). It is interesting to note that Josh Gibson, who played the position of catcher, became a leader of the Craws; catcher is the head position on the team, and it is the one position where a person can see all the other team members and they can see him.

Looking at another issue, it seems that the specific requirements of the task facing the group will influence who emerges as the leader (Shaw, 1981). Again, we can see this situation with the Craws. When the team was concerned with playing baseball, the best players were looked to for leadership. However, when the team was interested in relaxation and entertainment, they looked to the members who had the best social skills for leadership.

This discussion leaves us with the question of which theory is right, the great man theory or the situational theory. The answer is that neither theory is correct by itself. More recent approaches to the question of leadership have focused on combining these theories. For example, Hollander (1978) argues that it is a combination of the characteristics of the leader, the followers, and the situation that determines who will emerge as the leader. Each of these factors plays an important role in determining the leader.

The Effective Leader. Overall, the research suggests that we cannot rely only on traits or only on situational variables to predict who will be a leader. More recently, Fiedler has taken a somewhat different approach to the study of leadership (Fiedler, 1973, 1978). Instead of asking who will emerge as a leader, he has concentrated on determining who will be an effective leader. Fiedler's *contingency model of leadership* says that the answer to this question is a function of both individual traits and situational factors. Based on a large body of research, Fiedler points out that there are two styles of leadership. A leader who is motivated by task considerations feels that the best way to get the job done is to focus on the task at hand; such leaders will attempt to get group members to concentrate on working and solving any problem related to the task. On the other hand, leaders who take a relationship approach will try to get the job done by focusing on the feelings of group members and trying to develop a good working relationship with their group. Thus, while both leaders want to solve the problems of the task, they take a different approach to doing this. Fiedler has developed a questionnaire that can be used to determine a person's style of leadership; a sample is shown in Table 15–3. People who score high on this questionnaire are social relationship-oriented leaders; people scoring low tend to be task oriented.

TABLE 15–3: The Least Preferred Co-Worker (LPC) Scale

Think of the person *with whom you can work least well*. He may be someone you work with now, or he may be someone you knew in the past.

He does not have to be the person you like least well, but should be the person with whom you had the most difficulty in getting a job done. Describe this person as he appears to you.

Confident	8 7 6 5 4 3 2 1	Not confident
Distant	1 2 3 4 5 6 7 8	Close
Hardworking	8 7 6 5 4 3 2 1	Not hardworking
Warm	8 7 6 5 4 3 2 1	Cold
Not ambitious	1 2 3 4 5 6 7 8	Ambitious
Happy	8 7 6 5 4 3 2 1	Sad
Not productive	1 2 3 4 5 6 7 8	Productive
Not sociable	1 2 3 4 5 6 7 8	Sociable
Dependable	8 7 6 5 4 3 2 1	Not dependable
Tense	1 2 3 4 5 6 7 8	Relaxed
Creative	8 7 6 5 4 3 2 1	Not creative
Satisfied	8 7 6 5 4 3 2 1	Not satisfied
Not intelligent	1 2 3 4 5 6 7 8	Intelligent
Friendly	8 7 6 5 4 3 2 1	Not friendly
Nervous	1 2 3 4 5 6 7 8	Calm
Pleasant	8 7 6 5 4 3 2 1	Not pleasant

Source: After Fiedler (1967).

Identifying the leader's style is only half the battle in determining an effective leader. Fiedler argues that both types of leader can be effective. In fact, it is the situation that determines which type of leader will be most effective. The model suggests that some group conditions are very positive for the leader, while others are very negative. For example, a positive situation exists when leader-member relations are good, when the task for the group is clearly defined, and when the leader's position is very clear. A negative situation exists when the leader and group members do not get along well, the task is very unclear, and the leader's position is not well defined. According to Fiedler, groups can be graded along these three dimensions to determine the group climate.

After examining leaders in many groups, including sports teams, fire departments, and tank crews, Fiedler concluded that task-oriented leaders are most effective when the group climate is either very favorable or very unfavorable. On the other hand, relationship-motivated leaders are most effective when the group climate is scored as moderate. Thus, both situational and personal factors determine who will be an effective leader.

Fiedler's model has some important implications for choosing a leader. Many organizations spend a great deal of time and money trying to train people to be leaders. Fiedler argues that this may be a waste of resources. It is very difficult, if not impossible, to get people to change their style of leadership. Therefore, Fiedler suggests that we should carefully examine the situation and then choose a person whose style of leadership is right for the particular conditions. More recently, Fiedler has developed a program aimed at teaching leaders to change the group climate to be most compatible to their own style of leadership (Fiedler, 1978). While there have been many criticisms of the contingency model (Graen et al., 1970), it does seem clear that many variables will influence who will be an effective leader.

DEINDIVIDUATION: RELINQUISHING RESPONSIBILITY FOR BEHAVIOR

Earlier, we suggested that one of the reasons why people follow orders given by a leader is that they do not feel responsible for their own behavior while they are following someone else's orders. As we saw, when people place the responsibility for their behavior on a leader, they may engage in blind obedience and perform destructive acts. Investigators who have studied group behavior have found that even without a strong leader, being in a group may reduce people's feelings of personal responsibility.

As far back as 1903, the sociologist Le Bon realized that groups often change people into "primitive beings," causing them to do things that they would not think of doing on their own. A number of years later, Zimbardo (1970) examined the reasons why groups have such an effect on people. He suggested that in some groups people tend to lose their personal identity and assume the identity of the group; in more psychological terms we refer to this as deindividuation. Because they no longer seem to have a personal identity, group members lose the feeling of responsibility for their own behavior, and they no longer feel the same restraints against socially disapproved behavior. The behavior of people in such a situation is generally emotional, impulsive, and intense. People who are deindividuated show little concern about the results of their actions, because they feel that they cannot be personally identified and that the group will assume responsibility. Further, when people are in these deindividuation conditions, they are less self-aware of their feelings and behavior and less concerned with social evaluation (Prentice-Dunn and Rogers, 1980).

It is clear that deindividuation does not occur in all groups. Zimbardo (1970) listed a number of factors that are likely to make people in groups feel deindividuated. The first is that they are anonymous; when people feel they cannot be personally identified, they are most likely to feel deindividuated. This can often be achieved by having everyone in a group dress alike so that no one person stands out. A second factor is group size; the larger the group, the more likely it is that people will feel deindividuated. Deindividuation is also more likely to result when people are aroused and in a new or unstructured situation.

The feeling of not being responsible for one's behavior can have many effects on people (Diener, 1977). Some of these effects can be viewed as positive. For example, Singer and his colleagues (1965) found that deindividuated subjects were less likely to conform to group opinions than were subjects who were more identifiable. It seems that the reduced concern with social evaluation freed people to hold their own opinions rather than conform to group pressure. Still looking at the positive side, in some cases people find being deindividuated an exhilirating experience that frees them to act more spontaneously. As an example of this, we often find the meekest person screaming and shouting during a football or basketball game where he or she is an anonymous face in the crowd. This person would never dream of behaving in this way were he or she alone or in a small group. Thus, in some cases, deindividuation can be fun and have positive results.

However, there is a darker side to deindividuation. Milgram (1977) reports that people who live in large cities often feel deindividuated. As a result, they interact in an impersonal way, and this type of interaction can lead to feelings of loneliness and alienation. Many people are uncomfortable with the loss of personal identity associated with deindividuation. In many cases, these people will try to regain their uniqueness by wearing clothing that separates them from the crowd, putting their name on their automobile license plate, or decorating their home in an unusual way.

In addition to causing people to feel uncomfortable, deindividuation may release people to behave in destructive and tragic ways. People acting in mobs were responsible for racial lynchings in the South during the early 1900s, for rioting and looting during race riots in the 1960s and in 1980, and for attacks on defenseless embassies during the 1970s. Numerous spectators, officials, and players have been injured at sporting events by anonymous fans who have become carried away, hurling rocks and bottles to express their anger.

Zimbardo (1971) explored the bad effects of deindividuation by setting up a mock prison in the basement of the psychology building of Stanford University. The "prison" was complete with a number of tiny barred cells that allowed only enough room for three bare cots. Zimbardo hired 24 male undergraduate students for this study, and he described them as "mature, emotionally stable, normal, intelligent college students from middle-class homes throughout the United States and Canada." Half of the subjects were assigned to be guards, chosen at random from the group of 24 men. They were given khaki uniforms, night sticks, and dark sunglasses, and they were informed that the prisoners and prison were their responsibility. They were told that their control over the prisoners would be absolute.

The other half of the subjects were prisoners. On the appointed day, they were picked up at their homes, taken by squad car to a precinct headquarters for booking, and then placed in the mock prison. They were given white hospital gowns to wear and a prison number to be used in place of their name. At night each inmate had to sleep with a chain around his leg. These procedures should have deindividuated *both* guards *and*

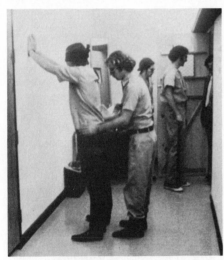

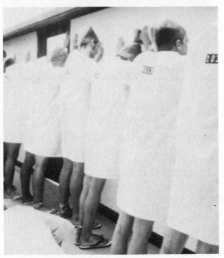

These photos were taken during the Zimbardo "mock prison" study (1971) at Stanford University.

prisoners. Both groups were relatively anonymous because they did not use their names, and they did not stand out as individuals because they all wore uniforms. The situation was a new one for both groups, and it was unstructured for the guards, at least, since they had few rules to follow.

The results of this experiment were shocking. Zimbardo reports with disbelief that the situation "undid (temporarily) a lifetime of learning; human values were suspended, self-concepts were challenged, and the ugliest, most base, pathological side of human nature surfaced." Many of the guards became tyrannical and brutalized the prisoners. The prisoners were allowed little sleep and sometimes the guards withheld their food. The inmates, on the other hand, became "servile, dehumanized robots" who thought only of their own comforts. Conditions became so bad that Zimbardo ended the experiment after only 6 days rather than the planned 2 weeks.

The Zimbardo study should be looked at as demonstrating some of the possible effects of deindividuation. It is clear that his mock prison was very different from real prisons. In some cases, real prison conditions are worse than those in the mock prison; in many cases the conditions are better. In all cases, the conditions in real prisons are *different* from those in the Zimbardo study; therefore it would be unwise to use the results obtained by Zimbardo to make definite conclusions about the effects of real prisons on guards and inmates.

The research on deindividuation presents another example of the subtle effects that groups can have on our behavior. As with conformity and obedience, the result of this influence can have either good or bad results.

GROUP DECISION MAKING

The preceding discussion on deindividuation may leave you with the impression that when people enter groups, they suddenly lose their inhibitions and ability to reason and resort to wild and unorganized behavior. We know, however, that this is not usually the case. Groups of people organize, work together, and interact in a normal way. And in each of these cases, group members must make decisions that affect the group as a whole and themselves as individuals. In some situations, the decisions involve group goals and how to achieve them. In other situations, such as juries, the group is faced with the problem of deciding about the outcome of a particular task or case (see the Highlight, "The Jury Is Out").

How do groups of people make decisions? Is the decision that is made by individual members affected by the presence of the group? Is the group decision generally better or worse than the decision that one person makes? These questions and others have intrigued psychologists for a number of years.

Group Polarization

An important dilemma faced by many of the Craws at the end of the 1932 season was whether or not to play winter baseball in Latin America. Josh didn't know what to do. He loved playing baseball and he needed extra money; playing winter baseball would satisfy both of these desires. On the other hand, he had heard stories about the political unrest in many Latin American countries and about the rowdy fans whose wild enthusiasm sometimes resulted in serious injury to the players. Many of the other players felt the same way, so they came together to discuss the situation.

HIGHLIGHT / THE JURY IS OUT

The work on group dynamics can be applied to many areas of our lives. Recently psychologists have begun to apply the research on group decision making to explain how juries reach their verdicts. For centuries, the traditional jury in England, Canada, and the United States has involved 12 people who must arrive at a unanimous decision of guilt before a defendant can be convicted of a crime. What factors are important in determining the jury's decision and how does this group come to a decision?

One factor is the size of juries. Is it necessary to have 12 people, or would a smaller number arrive at the same decision? Also, is it important for the jury to arrive at a *unanimous* decision, or would a simple majority rule give the same results? Researchers examined these questions using mock juries of college students (Davis, Bray, and Holt, 1977). In these studies the juries listened to a staged trial and then were asked to decide the guilt or innocence of the defendant. Davis compared the verdicts from 12- and 6-person juries, and also the verdicts reached by juries who were told that a unanimous decision was necessary as opposed to juries who were told that a two-thirds majority could convict the defendant.

The results indicated that 6-person and 12-person juries generally arrive at the same verdict. For example, on one rape trial, 89 percent of the 6-person juries and 83 percent of the 12-person juries arrived at an innocent verdict.

Further, the verdicts reached by the juries who had to make a unanimous decision were generally the same as juries who only had to reach a two-thirds majority agreement. Davis also found that the unanimous juries took a longer time to reach their verdict than did the two-thirds majority juries. These results seem to suggest that the court system could be run more cheaply and more efficiently with smaller juries who did not have to reach unanimous decisions. Davis cautions, however, that most of the juries had a two-thirds majority on the first poll of votes; if they were allowed to submit a verdict at this point, discussion of the case would be greatly reduced and many important issues might be overlooked.

The value of jury discussion was dramatically demonstrated in the movie *Twelve Angry Men,* which starred Henry Fonda. In the film, a 12-person jury listened to a murder trial and then retired to reach a verdict. On the first vote, 11 jurors voted guilty, while one, Henry Fonda, argued that the defendant was not guilty. As the group discussed the case, it became clear that many of the jurors had failed to consider important aspects of the case; some voted guilty so that a speedy decision would be reached and they could go home. In the film, Fonda was able to convince each jury member that the defendant was not guilty, and finally, the jury delivered a not-guilty verdict. Is this just a Hollywood fantasy, or can the minority really influence the final

jury decision? Two important factors seem to be involved here. First, the minority must take a clear and consistent position. The other group members must be able to understand exactly what the minority believes. Second, the minority must remain firm and uncompromising in its stance. Despite pressure from other group members, the minority members must steadfastly cling to their position and not show signs of readiness to compromise or change. Thus, while the majority will usually determine the final verdict of a jury, in some cases the minority will influence the decision.

There have been some other interesting findings about juries. For instance, what do jurors talk about when they are deciding a case? James (1959) found that at least half of their discussion is devoted to personal experience, while only about 15 percent is about the actual testimony presented during the trial. Other researchers have found that high-status members of a jury participate more and are more influential than low-status members (Strodtbeck and Mann, 1956). Finally, a group polarization effect has turned up in jury discussions. In one study, mock juries were given information that was either strongly suggestive of guilt or weakly in favor of guilt. When the evidence was strong, juries tended to make very harsh guilty verdicts. When the evidence was weak, the group shifted toward very lenient decisions.

Given the feelings of the individual players, it was somewhat surprising that after these discussions, Josh's whole circle of friends decided to play winter baseball despite the risks. Could the group discussion have influenced the players, who had many personal doubts, to make what seemed to be an extreme decision?

An early opinion was that groups should have exactly the opposite effect on individuals. In his discussion of organizations and business bureaucracies, William Whyte (1956) speculated that people become less creative and less risky in groups because they fear being ridiculed for taking extreme positions. A graduate student in the School of Industrial Management at M.I.T. decided to show the conservative effect of groups. This investigator wrote stories about people's problems or dilemmas and asked groups to discuss them and arrive at a solution (Stoner, 1961). He then compared the group solutions with the solutions that the people developed while working on their own. To his surprise, he found that the group solutions were more risky and extreme than the individual solutions!

Wallach, Kogan, and Bem (1962) developed additional case problems and had people suggest solutions by themselves. After deciding on these individual solutions, the subjects met in groups of five to discuss the cases and arrive at group decisions. Later the subjects were again asked to give individual solutions for the dilemmas. Two interesting results emerged from this study. First, the group decisions were more extreme and risky than the average individual decisions. Second, when the subjects made their own decisions after the group discussion, their solutions were more risky than their individual solutions made before the group discussion. Thus, not only did the groups make more risky decisions, but participating in group discussions made the subjects take more risks when they later acted on their own. In another study on a different problem, researchers found that groups made riskier bets in a blackjack game than did individuals (Blaskovitch, Ginsburg, and Howe, 1975).

For a number of years, investigators believed that groups free members to make more risky decisions, and this area of research was referred to as the "risky shift." However, more recent research has found that people did not always become more risky when placed in groups (Lamm and Meyers, 1978). This research showed that groups tended to polarize people and move them to believe more strongly in the position that they initially held (Moscovici and Zavalloni, 1969). For example, if someone were inclined to make a risky decision on a particular issue, discussing the issue in a group would probably push him or her to take an even riskier position. However, if the person preferred a conservative position, the group discussion would push him or her to take an even more conservative position. Further, the research showed that the **group polarization effect** occurred in a wide range of areas, including attitudes, intersonal impressions, and judgments about the importance of values. For example, Paicheler (1976) measured groups of French students' attitudes toward equal rights for women and found them moderately favorable on the issue. She then had them discuss the topic in groups and remeasured their attitudes. The results indicated that as a result of the discussion the student groups reported being more in favor of equal rights for women. Given this new evidence, we can argue that the team discussion resulted in a decision for the Craws to play baseball in Latin America because most of the individual members were already leaning in this direction. If most of the players had had serious reservations, the group discussion would have strengthened these reservations and they would have decided not to play in Latin America.

There seems to be a number of reasons for this group polarization effect. One explanation involves the diffusion of responsibility. People in groups do not have to feel individually responsible or accountable for the group decision. Therefore, they can afford to let themselves go and push for a strong and extreme position without worrying that someone will later question their individual wisdom. If an individual makes a bad decision, others will point a finger at him or her, saying, "*You* made a bad decision." When the group makes the decision, the person can respond by saying, "Gee, it was the other people in the group who decided this."

Another explanation focuses on social comparison theory (Goethals and

Discussing issues in groups tend to cause members to take more extreme positions than they held before a group discussion. The direction of change can be either more risky or more conservative.

Zanna, 1979). According to this theory, individual group members compare their viewpoint to the positions held by the others in the group. When they find that their position is not as extreme as those of the other members, they change their position to be more extreme. According to the social comparison approach, the positions held by the other members is the most important information influencing the decision making of an individual group member.

However, a third approach takes a rather different view (Burnstein, in press). The persuasive argument hypothesis argues that it is the information about *why* people hold certain positions that is most important. People examine the arguments that others use to support their positions, and they change their position in the direction of the most persuasive arguments. One study (Burnstein, Vinokur, and Trope, 1973) found that increasing information about *why* people adopted a certain position led to greater polarization than simply increasing information about the position of other people. As is the case with many social behaviors, it is probable that all these factors (diffusion of responsibility, social comparison, and persuasive arguments) influence the polarization of attitudes in groups.

Groupthink

We have seen that groups often make more extreme decisions than people acting on their own. This finding leads us to ask another question regarding such decision making: Are the decisions made by groups of better or worse *quality* than those made by one person? At first glance, we might expect to find that groups make better decisions than individuals. Groups are usually made up of people who have different information and who may present different ways to look at a problem. This diversity should allow groups to consider the many aspects of a problem and arrive at the best alternative. This seemed to happen when the Craws considered the possibility of playing winter baseball in Latin America. Each of the players had heard different stories about the pros and cons of baseball "South of the Border," and through an exchange of information the players were able to make a decision. In this case, it was a wise decision, since most of the players enjoyed the experience and returned to play on Latin American teams for many years after.

Unfortunately, groups do not always make the best use of the information available to them. The results of such an unfortunate decision were seen on April 17, 1961. On that date 1,400 Cuban exiles landed at the Bay of Pigs in Cuba. They planned to set up a beachhead there, and unite with Cuban rebels in the Escambray Mountains to overthrow Premier Fidel Castro. They felt that their plan could not possibly fail. Their mission had been devised by one of the best intelligence organizations in the world, the United States Central Intelligence Agency (CIA), and the plan had been approved by President John F. Kennedy and his personal advisors.

However, the impossible happened. Nothing went as planned; instead of being greeted by friendly rebels, the exiles were met by a well-prepared Cuban Army that quickly killed or captured the whole group. The United States suffered a severe political setback, and the world wondered how such a respected group of men as Kennedy and his advisors could have decided on such a foolish plan.

Irving Janis (1971, 1972) carefully analyzed the Bay of Pigs fiasco and concluded that it was the decision-making process that was responsible for the poor decision. Janis suggested that the Kennedy group, like many other decision-making groups, were victims of groupthink. **Groupthink** occurs when group members become so concerned with reaching agreement among all members of the group that they fail to critically evaluate their ideas. Because they are so worried about keeping a happy group atmosphere, they fail to make good use of the information available to them. Groupthink is most likely to occur in close-knit groups in which group members like one another and are proud to be members of the group. Thus an illusion of agreement exists in the group; because no one is openly expressing disagreement, group members feel that everyone must be feeling the same way. The group also develops the illusion that it can do no wrong. James Schlesinger (1965) points out that the Kennedy group had such an illusion; they were euphoric about winning the presidential election against all odds and they enjoyed the popular support of the country. A strong and respected leader reinforces groupthink, since group members are unwilling to "buck" his or her authority and they have a false confidence that their leader could not be wrong. Research indicates that a strong directive leader could produce groupthink even in newly formed experimental groups (Flowers, 1977).

Can groupthink be avoided? Janis says yes. He cites many examples, including one involving Kennedy and his advisors, where groupthink did not occur. Just over a year after the Bay of Pigs incident, Kennedy learned that the Russians were positioning nuclear missiles with atomic warheads in Cuba. Kennedy called a series of meetings with his advisors; many of them had been involved in the Bay of Pigs decision. However, Kennedy was determined to avoid the pitfalls of that earlier decision. This time he encouraged the advisors to consider numerous alternative plans and to critically evaluate each one. Persons outside the group were called in to give advice. Kennedy himself kept from taking an early stand and even stayed away from several meetings. As a result of these actions, groupthink was avoided and the advisors settled on an effective and successful plan of action.

How can groupthink be avoided? Janis (1972) suggests the following:

1. Group members should be encouraged to carefully consider each alternative and to play the role of devil's advocate.
2. The leader should refrain from stating a preference and encourage group discussion.
3. Outsiders should be invited to give their opinions on the issues.
4. Several meetings should be called to reassess new information and review the most preferred decision.

Thus, it is clear that a number of factors affect the quality of group decisions. Even groups with the brightest, most well-informed people can make poor decisions if they fail to properly utilize their resources. The presence of groupthink can handicap the group. However, by effectively utilizing its members, groups can be used to make the best possible decisions.

PERFORMING IN GROUPS

Social Facilitation

Thus far we have seen that groups strongly influence the way in which people interact and make decisions. Before leaving the discussion of groups, we will ask one more question: Does being in a group or acting in front of a group influence the way in which people perform on tasks? This is an important question; its answer has implications in many areas. For example, it is likely that you will soon be preparing for an examination or final test in this course. Will the fact that you will take this examination with other people influence your performance? Or would you do better on it if you were taking it alone?

According to social facilitation theory, performance of well-learned behaviors is enhanced by an audience. Josh hit his longest homeruns when he was in front of large crowds of screaming fans.

This same question is an important one for athletes. Their crucial tests must come in front of audiences who watch their every move. How does the presence of the audience affect their performance? A related question is, How can they best prepare for these crucial tests? The Craws, like many other athletes, felt that they could best prepare if they were not distracted by their attentive fans. Each year the Craws gathered in Hot Springs, Arkansas for spring training. Here the players could practice their hitting and fielding without the hordes of fans that would be present during their regular games. Josh Gibson enjoyed spring training, but he was always anxious for the season to start. He usually hit his longest homeruns and made his best defensive plays when he was in front of large crowds of screaming fans. In fact, Josh hit his longest homerun in Yankee Stadium in front of a nearly packed house; it is said to be the longest ball ever hit in Yankee Stadium (Brashler, 1978).

The fact that a group affects people's performance was recognized before the turn of the century. Triplett (1898) observed that cyclists raced more rapidly when they were in head-to-head competition with other cyclists than when they were simply trying to beat the clock on their own. Triplett devised one of the first social psychological experiments to examine the effect of groups on task performance. Children were given the task of winding string on a fishing reel as fast as possible. On some of the trials, the children worked alone; on others, two children competed while working side by side. Triplett found that the children worked faster when others were there than when they worked alone.

A number of early studies (Allport, 1924; Travis, 1925) also showed that people work faster when in the presence of others than when alone.

Investigators found that this effect even transcends human beings. Chen (1937) studied ants digging tunnels and building nests. In some cases he had the ants work alone, while in other cases the subject ant worked with one or two other ants. Chen examined the balls of dirt excavated by the ant to determine the speed of work. He found that the ant worked harder (removed more dirt balls) when other ants were present. In addition to supplying such practical information as to how to get lazy ants to work, these early studies suggested that working in the presence of others increased individual performance.

On the face of it, these results seem to suggest that people should set up situations so that they can learn and perform with other people. Other studies, however, show that sometimes groups are good for people's performance and sometimes they are bad. For example, Pessin (1933) also found that the presence of an audience inhibited the learning of a maze task and a nonsense-syllable task. However, Pessin made another interesting discovery: After subjects had learned the tasks on their own, their performance increased when they were placed in front of a group.

Robert Zajonc (1965) attempted to make sense out of these contradictory results. He suggested that the presence of other people tends to arouse and excite people. This arousal creates an additional pool of energy that aids the performance of well-learned behaviors. We call this social facilitation. However, this additional arousal hinders the learning of new and complex responses. We call this social inhibition. Thus the presence of others leads to social facilitation of well-learned responses but leads to social inhibition for learning new and complex behaviors.

While Zajonc's reasoning could explain some of the social facilitation

There are many explanations for the social facilitation effect. One suggests that audiences increase the person's concern with being evaluated.

results, it could not explain others. For example, Martens and Landers (1972) found that audiences were most likely to cause social facilitation when the actor felt that he or she was being evaluated. This prompted Cottrell (1972) to suggest that social facilitation is caused by the concerns about evaluation rather than by the simple presence of the audience.

The implication of the research on social facilitation is that people should learn new responses while they are alone and then perform these responses in front of a group. The presence of a group should aid the performance of these well-learned behaviors. Returning to our opening examples, we would expect that taking an examination in the presence of a group should help the student who has learned the material well beforehand, but it will hurt the student who has not learned the material well.

Social Loafing

In most of the research on social facilitation, subjects work on a task where their individual performance is visible and measurable. This is similar to the situation faced by a baseball player; although he is a member of a team, people can easily determine how well he is playing. The research shows that in situations like these the group often has a positive effect on the person's performance. However, what happens when the person performs in a group where his or her contribution is not easily observable? The research shows that in this type of situation the group has a very different effect.

In one experiment, groups of one to eight people were instructed to pull on a rope, and then the total force was measured (Ringelmann, as reported in Moede, 1927). When Ringelmann looked at the average force exerted by each member, he found that as the group size increased, the force supplied by each individual member decreased. That is, as the group size increased, the effort of the individual members decreased. More than 50 years later, Latané, Williams, and Harkins (1979) had people cheer as loudly as they could. Sometime after this they were placed in groups ranging in size from two to six members. The groups were asked to cheer as loudly as they could. Again, the results showed that while more noise was produced by groups, each individual cheered less loudly in the groups than when alone. The larger the group, the less loudly each person cheered.

It has been argued that peoples' motivation to work decreases when they are in groups where their individual performance cannot be observed (Kerr and Bruun, 1981; Latané, Williams, and Harkins, 1979). Being in a group allows members to hide, and they can reduce their efforts without being detected. Also, the larger the group, the less likely that people will pay attention to the individual's performance. This general effect has been called **social loafing.** Kerr and Bruun argue that the social-loafing effect could be reduced if group members felt that others could identify their contribution to the group. Therefore, it is clear that, depending on the nature of the task, groups may either increase an individual's performance or decrease it.

PREJUDICE AND DISCRIMINATION

As we have seen, groups are wonderously complex. Groups affect our lives in many ways. On the positive side, groups help us establish our identity; they help establish order in our world; they offer us protection and comfort; and they can increase our performance on tasks. These advantages are, however, often achieved for a price. Being in a group often

Discrimination is negative, often aggressive, behavior aimed at the target of prejudice. Racial discrimination meant that Josh Gibson could only play on black teams during his lifetime.

means that we have to conform to group rules, and we may lose a bit of our uniqueness. But these costs are minor compared to another effect that often accompanies the formation of groups; that cost is prejudice and discrimination.

Josh Gibson was well acquainted with prejudice and discrimination; his life was greatly influenced by these social phenomena. Because of the racial prejudice that existed during his lifetime, he could only play baseball on black teams in the United States; he was forced to go to South America in order to have the opportunity to play with white players. Racial prejudice determined the restaurants where Josh could eat, the dressing rooms where he could change his clothes, and the hotels where he could sleep. Racial prejudice meant that Josh had to fear for his life and safety in the same towns where he entertained baseball fans.

Before examining prejudice more closely, there are a few points that must be made. The terms "prejudice" and "discrimination" are often used interchangeably. This usage, however, is incorrect. **Prejudice** is an unjustified negative attitude toward an individual based solely on that person's membership in a group. It is generally based on incomplete information and is very hard to change. **Discrimination,** on the other hand, is negative, often aggressive, *behavior* aimed at the target of prejudice. Exclusion from social clubs, neighborhoods, or jobs are examples of discrimination. Everyone who holds prejudicial attitudes does not practice discrimination. However, such attitudes do make discrimination more likely.

Prejudice and discrimination have a number of characteristics that make them more difficult to understand than many other attitudes and behaviors. First, prejudice is baseless. These attitudes are not formed from facts or personal experience—it is not unusual to find someone who is racially prejudiced despite having limited interaction with blacks. Second, discrimi-

Discrimination is often practiced even when it hurts the person practicing it; employers may hire a less qualified white male even when they have applications from more qualified blacks or females.

nation is often practiced even when it hurts the person practicing it. For example, employers may hire a less qualified white male even when they have applications from more qualified blacks or females. Finally, the person who is the target of prejudice often takes on these prejudicial attitudes. For example, Goldberg (1968) asked female students to evaluate a manuscript. Half the students were told that the article was written by a man and half were told that it was written by a woman. Despite the fact that the articles were the same, even women rated the manuscript higher if they thought it was written by a man.

The Roots of Prejudice

How do people develop prejudicial attitudes? There are a number of theories about the roots of prejudice. Some of the earlier theories (Adorno, Fenkel-Brunswick, Levinson, and Sanford, 1950) tried to lay the blame for prejudice on the individual's personality. These investigators had some success in identifying certain personality traits that made people more likely to develop prejudicial attitudes. However, all people with these traits do not hold prejudicial attitudes, and many people without these traits are prejudiced. Thus, we cannot blame prejudice on personal characteristics. As a result, most theories of prejudice are aimed at identifying situational causes of prejudice.

Group Formation and Discrimination

In the opening of this section, we hinted at the possibility that prejudice was somehow related to the formation of groups. This may seem like an odd suggestion, but a number of investigators (Tajfil, 1981; Milner,

The formation of a group leads members to prefer ingroup members and discriminate against outgroup members. There is also a tendency to see less similarity between ingroup members than between outgroup members.

1981) have suggested that prejudice and discrimination may be one of the products of group formation. These investigators argue that groups develop an identity by having group members compare their group with other groups. Because members are motivated to present their group positively, they also become motivated to paint a negative picture of other groups. A number of studies have found that simply placing people into groups leads them to discriminate against other groups. This occurs even when people are randomly assigned to groups, and when they have never met the members of their own group or of the outgroup. For example, Tajfil (1970) assigned subjects to two groups based on their judgment of some paintings. He then gave the subjects the opportunity to award money to members of their own group and members of the outgroup. He found that subjects gave more money to ingroup members than to outgroup members. This effect occurs even when subjects do not anticipate meeting members of either group (Turner, 1981).

Recently, researchers found that group formation also affects the way in which people perceive members of their own group as well as of the outgroup (Jones et al., 1981). In a series of studies, these investigators found that people tend to see outgroup members as being relatively similar, while they see greater variability in members of their own group. In other words, people tend to believe that their own group is made up of people with many different traits, while members of the outgroup are all the same. These biased perceptions lead people to draw another conclusion: They believe that one can generally determine what all the outgroup members are like by observing the behavior of only a few members of the outgroup (Quattrone and Jones, 1980). In other words, the formation of groups not only leads members to conclude that the outgroup members are all alike, but they also tend to adopt the position of "seen one, seen them all."

This research suggests that the simple formation of groups may sow the seeds of prejudice. There does seem to be a strong tendency to prefer members of one's own group over members of the outgroup. However, while this research suggests one of the bases for prejudice, it does not describe why certain groups become the object of prejudice. As we have seen, people belong to many different groups at any one time. Why is it that only certain groups become the object of prejudice?

Learning. In Chapter 14 we examined how parents influence their children's attitudes through their control of rewards and information. Just as parents can teach other attitudes to children, so, too, can they teach their children to be prejudiced against specific groups. The child who hears his or her parents criticize a particular group of people may mimic this position. In some cases, the parents will even directly reward their children for expressing prejudicial attitudes. But oftentimes, the prejudice can be transmitted in a less direct way. For example, a child may hear his or her father characterize women as being poor drivers. Even though the father may have done this in jest, the child may not distinguish the humor. He or she may consequently adopt the position that women are poor drivers. The strong influence of parents is seen in the fact that prejudicial attitudes are observable in many children as young as 3 years old (Milner, 1981).

Prejudicial attitudes are also reinforced by the media, which presents certain groups in a negative way. In many cases this portrayal may be done in an indirect way. This occurred some years ago, when the media habitually reported the race of a criminal if he or she were black. However, no mention of race was used for white criminals. A person reading the news might easily have gotten the impression that most criminals are black.

Thus, like many other attitudes, prejudice may be taught. The prejudicial

Prejudice can be learned from parents and from peers.

attitude will be very difficult to change if it is further supported by peer groups. For instance, children who see that most of their friends have a negative attitude towards blacks or Chicanos will express similar attitudes. In doing this, they are accepted by the group; to do otherwise would lead to rejection. It will be extremely difficult to change these people's prejudice as long as they continue to associate with that peer group.

Scapegoat Theory. Aronson (1976) relates an interesting story about the origin of the term **scapegoat.** In ancient times during the Hebrew days of atonement, a rabbi would place his hands on the head of a goat while reciting the sins of his congregation. The intent of this was to symbolically transfer the sins from the people to the goat. The goat was then chased into the wilderness, taking the sins of the congregation with him. This animal became known as the scapegoat.

One of the earliest theories of prejudice suggested that prejudice and discrimination are the result of scapegoating (Dollard et al., 1939). In Chapter 9, we discussed frustration-aggression theory, the view that frustration motivates aggression. Once frustrated, people will aggress *unless* the cause of the frustration is unavailable or too powerful. In such cases, the frustrated person may displace his or her aggression onto a safer target, even if this target (like the goat of the ancient Hebrews) is not directly responsible for the frustration. According to this theory, then, a minority group may be singled out as the target or the scapegoat for aggression and hostility (Konečni, 1979). The minority group is chosen as the target because it is safe to attack and it often has highly visible characteristics (color, accent, name, etc.) that separate it from the more powerful majority.

There has been some research to support this theory. For example, Miller and Bugelski (1948) frustrated workers at a civilian work camp by not allowing them to attend a movie. They then measured the workers' attitudes towards Mexicans and Japanese. The workers were more hostile toward these minority groups after being frustrated than before the frustration. It seems that the workers displaced their anger onto these minority groups. It is interesting to note that the greatest violence against the Jews in Russia occurred during times of economic hardship.

Reducing Prejudice

It is clear that there are a number of causes of prejudice. Just as important, if not more important, as identifying the roots of prejudice is learning how to reduce it. In the 1950s the Supreme Court ruled that "separate but equal" schools for blacks and whites are basically inherently unequal and unfair. Schools were ordered to integrate. A number of people argued that in order for integration to work, attitudes had to be changed first. According to these people, chaos, fighting, and rioting would result if prejudiced white children were put into schools with black children. Thus the nation held its breath waiting for widespread rioting as the first black students began entering previously segregated schools. There was, in fact, some violence, and governors Ross Barnett of South Carolina and George Wallace of Alabama stood in front of schoolhouses to prevent desegregation. But the widespread violence that many predicted did not materialize, and schools across the country were desegregated. And another interesting result occurred. As time passed and blacks and whites worked together in the school setting, prejudice also decreased (Karlins et al., 1969).

This incident brings up an important point: The most direct way to reduce prejudice is to change behaviors that reinforce these attitudes rather than to simply try to change the attitudes (Cooper and Fazio, 1979). This statement sounds like a page out of dissonance theory, which we discussed in Chapter 14. Prejudice is self-perpetuating. People who hold prejudicial attitudes will avoid contact with the object of their prejudice. Then, in order to justify this segregation, such people will develop even more deep-seated prejudicial attitudes. If we wish to break this cycle, we must change people's behavior (see Cook, 1978).

In a classic study, Sherif and his colleagues (Sherif et al., 1961) created hostility between two groups of children at a summer camp. The groups competed against each other on a series of tasks and soon they were openly fighting against each other. Sherif then decided to find out if simple contact between the two groups would reduce their hostility against each other. Accordingly, the two groups were brought together in a number of situations that did not involve competition: for example, eating together in the dining hall. This did not, however, lead to less hostility—it just gave them an additional chance to fight, and insults as well as apples and other food stuffs were hurled. Clearly simple contact cannot reduce intergroup hostility or prejudice.

The researchers then had the two groups come together in situations where their combined efforts were needed to solve problems that involved both groups. For example, the groups went on a camping trip together, and the truck bringing their food became stuck. In order to move the truck, members from both groups had to push together. After a series of such events, where the groups had to work on a common problem, the hostility between the two groups decreased markedly. Further research found that cooperative efforts aimed at a common goal reduce intergroup hostility only when those efforts succeed in obtaining the goal (Worchel, Andreoli, and Folger, 1977; Worchel, Axsom, Ferris, Samaha, and Schweitzer, 1978).

This research suggests that prejudice can be reduced if people can be

One way to reduce prejudice is to have people work for a common goal with those they may be prejudiced against.

placed in situations where they must work with the people or groups they are prejudiced against. It is also important that these efforts are successful in reaching the common goal. Aronson (1976) has used this approach to develop an approach aimed at reducing prejudice in the classroom. Aronson calls his method the *jig-saw approach*. Students are divided into groups and given a problem to solve. Each member of the group is given only one part of the answer; in order for the group to solve the problem, all members have to contribute their part. A weak group member will hurt the whole group. Thus, the group members must help one another in order for the group to be successful. Aronson has used this method with ethnically mixed groups and found that as a result of working together, children of different ethnic groups came to like one another better.

Again, it is clear that the most effective way to reduce prejudice is to change behaviors that support it. Given a choice, people who are prejudiced avoid interacting with the object of their prejudice. This cycle must be reversed and people must be brought into contact with those against whom they are prejudiced. The contact must involve people working with others on an equal basis to solve problems of mutual concern.

SUMMARY

1. People belong to **groups** for many reasons. In some cases, they get rewards such as money, prestige, and security. In other cases, they join groups in order to evaluate their attitudes, values, and abilities. A third reason is that groups may be necessary for a person to obtain his or her goals.

2. Almost all groups develop **norms,** which are rules that apply to all members. Norms define what must be done and when. **Roles** are norms that apply only to people occupying a specific position in the group. While norms and roles can help a group run smoothly by making the behavior of members predictable, they can sometimes be harmful. For example, people who follow rigid sex roles may not be able to use their own creativity or behave in a way that is most comfortable for them.

3. **Conformity** occurs when people change their attitudes or behaviors as a result of real or imagined group pressure, despite personal feelings to the contrary. Conformity may involve only a change in behavior, or it may include changing both public behavior and private attitudes.

4. **Obedience** involves following the direct and explicit orders of a leader. Research conducted by Stanley Milgram showed that a surprising number of people would follow the orders of an authority figure even when they were ordered to hurt someone.

5. The **leader** is the person who has the greatest amount of influence in the group. Both personal and situational factors influence who will become the leader of a group. The contingency model of leadership suggests that leaders who are task oriented will be most effective when the group climate is either very positive or very negative. Leaders who are concerned with social relationships will be most effective in moderate group climates.

6. **Deindividuation** occurs when the person becomes submerged in the group and loses his or her individual identity. Deindividuation is most likely to result in large groups where uniforms are worn and members are anonymous. As a result of deindividuation, people may not feel responsible for their behavior.

7. Being in a group leads people to take stronger stands on issues than they would outside the group. This effect has been referred to as **group polarization.** It has been argued that this effect occurs because information is exchanged in group discussion and because people in groups do not feel personally responsible for their attitudes or behaviors. It also seems that people in groups compare their attitudes and behaviors, and since no one wants to be seen as the most undecided, each group member tries to adopt a position that is at least as strong as that of the other group members.

8. **Groupthink** results when people are more concerned about arriving at a group consensus than in making the best decision. In order to avoid groupthink, group members must be encouraged to express their opinions even if they disagree with the position of the other group members. The group also needs to seek outside information and opinions.

9. A person's performance is also influenced by the group. Research has shown that while people can learn new and complex tasks better if they are alone, their performance of well-learned tasks is aided by being in front of a group. However, **social loafing** may result if people perform tasks as part of a group effort and if their individual input on the task is not identifiable.

10. **Prejudice** is an unjustified negative attitude toward an individual based solely on that person's membership in a group. **Discrimination** is negative, often aggressive, behavior aimed at the target of prejudice. There are a number of theories about why prejudice and discrimination develop: one places the blame on the formation of a group; another suggests that people learn how to be prejudiced and against whom they should direct their prejudice; a third argues that prejudice and discrimination are the result of displaced aggression.

11. It is very difficult to change prejudice. In order to change biased attitudes, it is important to have people work together to achieve common goals. The effects of cooperation are most positive when the combined effort is successful in obtaining the desired goal.

SUGGESTED READINGS

The following book is about Josh Gibson:

BRASHLER, W. *Josh Gibson: A life in the Negro Leagues.* New York: Harper & Row, 1978.

AUSTIN, W., and WORCHEL, S. (Eds.). *The social psychology of intergroup relations.* Monterey, Calif.: Brooks/Cole, 1979. This is a volume of original papers in the area of intergroup conflict. The chapters focus on causes, effects, and ways to reduce intergroup conflict.

NAPIER, R., and GERSHENFELD, M. *Groups: Theory and experience*, 2nd ed. Boston: Houghton Mifflin, 1981. The text examines theory and research in group dynamics and offers suggestions about the ways in which people can improve their skills as group members and leaders.

SHAW, M. *Group dynamics: The psychology of small group behavior*, 3rd ed. New York: McGraw-Hill, 1981. Presents an up-to-date review of theory and research on small group behavior. Topics of discussion include leadership, social facilitation, group performance, the group environment, and methods for studying group behavior.

TURNER, S., and GILES, H. (Eds.). *Intergroup behavior.* Chicago: University of Chicago Press, 1981. This is an edited volume of papers by British psychologists working in the area of intergroup relations. It is up to date and presents a broad view of the field.

WHEELER, J., DECI, E., REIS, H., and ZUCKERMAN, M. *Interpersonal influence*, 2nd ed. Boston: Allyn & Bacon, 1978. A short but informative discussion of social influence. The book focuses on theories, examining such topics as conformity, group polarization, obedience, power, and social comparison.

16

Living with Our Environment

The United States had broken yet another promise to the Apache. In the summer of 1876, Indian Agent Philip Clum arrived with the calvary to force the Indians off their own reservation and onto the neighboring San Carlos reservation. As Chief Tahza prepared his tribe for the move, he swore that he would not allow all of the tribe to become captives on another pitiful reservation. He carefully planned for the 38 members of his own clan, led by his wife, to escape into an ancient mountain stronghold of the Apache in Sonora, Mexico. These "Nameless Ones" would never be forced to suffer the confinement of the reservation, and they would not be tagged or tatooed for military records. They would be free to continue the Apache way of life deep in the heart of the Sierra Madre mountains.

Nino Cochise, the son of Tahza and the grandson of the famous Chief Cochise, was 2 years old when the Nameless Ones settled in the Sierra Madre. The clan carefully chose the location for their rancheria, Pa-Gotzin-Kay. Water and trees were abundant, and there was plenty of space for everyone. The place was a natural fortress, with sheer cliffs protecting two sides and narrow trails winding around huge rocks insuring that intruders could not surprise the camp from the other two sides.

These refugees quickly built the typical Apache wikiup (a round, one-room dwelling) from sticks and stones they found nearby. Everyone began searching for food. Since they had no guns, the clan was forced to live off the fruits and nuts of the land; they ate cactus fruit, pine nuts, acorns, and skunk cabbage roots. Flint stones were used to start fires; once started, a fire was rarely allowed to die out. After a while, the men made bows and arrows and the boys became experts at throwing stones. Because of their skilled use of these natural weapons, the clan was soon eating deer, bear, rabbits, wolves, and squirrels.

Nino Cochise grew up in this happy and safe environment. He soon learned where game was abundant and where he could find water. He learned to waste no part of the game he killed; the meat was eaten, the skin used to make clothes, and the guts used for bow strings and to sew with. Cochise's clothing was designed for his surroundings. His *kabuns,* Apache moccasins, were made of soft leather so that they could be rolled down below the knees in the summer; in the winter or when riding through cactus forests they could be rolled up as far as the hips. Also, when hunting in the thorny brush, Cochise wore *armas,* a pair of blanket-sized leather skirts that protected his legs and feet and the underside of his horse from the painful cactus needles.

Pa-Gotzin-Kay became a haven for Apaches who were on the run after escaping from the reservation. In the early years, Nino's uncle, Geronimo, often stopped at the rancheria with his raiding parties. From these warriors and hunters, Nino learned how to live off the desert by eating the fruit of the cactus and mashing the pulp to get water. He also learned to track and shoot. He was impressed with the feats of Geronimo and his raiders, but those who live at Pa-Gotzin-Kay were also concerned about these exploits. They wanted to live in peace and they feared that *Los Goddammies,* the Apache term for whites, might follow the raiders into Mexico and destroy their home.

When he reached the age of 15, Cochise was named chief of the clan still living at Pa-Gotzin-Kay. He had learned much, and he meant to improve conditions at the rancheria. Later that year, he was given corn seed by a neighboring tribe, and Pa-Gotzin-Kay became a farming community. The clan now had a stable food supply, and much of the life in the rancheria became centered on planting and harvesting corn. Soon a herd of cattle was added, and the community began to take on a new appearance. With this new source of food, they could allow more people to join them. Before, the clan had discouraged other Indians from settling with the tribe because there was not enough wild game to support a larger group.

Good fortune continued to smile on Pa-Gotzin-Kay when the residents discovered a rich vein of gold in an old tribal mine. With their wealth, the clan began trading with the residents of neighboring towns. They made friends with some of these Mexican settlers and with the Americans who had large ranches in the area. There were no law enforcement authorities in this remote region of Mexico, and the townspeople and ranchers often called upon the Apaches to help rid the area of bandits and lawless prospectors.

For years the Apaches lived in peace with their environment and their neighbors. The calm, however, was soon shattered. Because of the remoteness of the region, Sonora and neighboring states became the breeding ground for Mexican revolutionaries who wished to overthrow the government. Governor Generals Terrazas and Torres hoped to overthrow Mexican President Diaz, but in order to do this they needed a large army. And in order to raise such an army, they needed money and land. They plotted to wipe out Pa-Gotzin-Kay and steal the gold there. Their first attempt to destroy Pa-Gotzin-Kay involved getting a band of Yaqui Indians to settle in the Apache hunting grounds and crowd out the Apaches. The invasion of Apache territory infuriated Cochise and he led his warriors to destroy the invaders.

Seeing this plan fail, Torres and Terrazas decided to directly attack the Apaches and their rancher friends. With a force of 1,500 well-armed men, the generals began their attack on Apache territory. Although they were outnumbered, the Indians and ranchers knew the territory and manuevered the invaders into an ambush. The result was total destruction of the Mexican army and an end to the armed threat on Pa-Gotzin-Kay. The year was 1900; this was one of the last Apache battles.

At the turn of the century, times were quickly changing in northern Mexico. Colonel William Greene had discovered a rich deposit of copper, and Cananea, a town that was a few days' ride from Pa-Gotzin-Kay, had turned into a boom town. Men and supplies poured into Cananea and the railroad linked this northern Mexican town to the copper-hungry United States; Cananea developed and prospered.

In the late winter of 1902, Cochise met William Greene on a hunting trip. Cochise was growing restless at Pa-Gotzin-Kay, and he still mourned his wife, who had been killed in the war with Torres. Greene had heard about the feats of the Apache leader and he offered him a job as his personal body guard. Cochise accepted and, together with his mother and aunt, moved to Cananea.

The move presented Cochise with a completely new environment and way of life. He was given a six-room frame house complete with furniture and beds. Cochise was taken to a clothing store and outfitted from head to toe; boots replaced his moccasins, and his rough range clothing was replaced by a brown Levi-Strauss suit, a fancy black vest, and a new hat. When Colonel Greene saw that Nino wore no underwear, he ordered him a set of BVDs, which Nino reluctantly wore despite the terrible itching they caused. Cochise learned that the whites kept time by the hour and minute hands on their watches; at the rancheria they had counted time by the days, moons, and seasons, since this was the only time that really mattered. At Cananea he found people protecting their land with fences and guarding their privacy by locks on their doors. He saw huge machines moving mountains of dirt and rock so that buildings and tracks could be built; this was certainly very different from Pa-Gotzin-Kay, where they built around these natural barriers. This approach was bewildering to Cochise and he felt uncomfortable with all the noise, activity, and the constant stream of strange people passing through the town. How strange it was to live in a place without knowing all the people who lived there!

However, these problems were child's play compared with Cochise's first trip to New York City. A few days after he arrived at Cananea, Colonel Greene went to New York to sell stock in his mine; he took Cochise along for protection and for the attention he thought Cochise would attract. They took the long trip across country by train, and when they arrived in New York, Colonel Greene ordered a suite in the Waldorf-Astoria, "a heap big, no-stoop-door wikiup" (Cochise and Griffith, 1971). Cochise followed Colonel Greene on his rounds, and he was surprised to find that the men largely ignored him, despite his unusual and striking dress and appearance. Nino was tense and ill at ease in New York; in his own words, he felt there were "too many big buildings, too much noise, too cold, too much smoke, and too many Los Goddammies" (Cochise and Griffith, 1971).

After working for Colonel Green for a number of years, Cochise became restless. He felt that he must move on. He was becoming unhappy with life at the mine, but he did not feel he could again settle at the rancheria. At age 43, he no longer felt part of the land on which he had spent his younger days.

In 1920, Nino went back to Pa-Gotzin-Kay, collected his possessions, and moved north to the United States. He continued to live one adventure after another as he

searched for an environment and an occupation with which he could live. He went to Hollywood and played bit parts in such films as *Robin Hood, Tumbleweeds, The Big Trail,* and *Cimarron.* From there, he moved further north, where he first took a job as a lumberjack, and then, after selling some of his Indian relics, he bought an airplane and started a crop-dusting business in the state of Washington. In 1947, at the age of 73, he learned to fly. Soon, however, the business turned sour, and Cochise decided to return to California. On his way, his plane crashed, and, though he survived, he lost a leg and half of his left hand. After another stint in Hollywood, and a try at setting up a museum, Nino Cochise, who was in his late nineties, settled down in Tombstone, Arizona and opened up the Cochise Trading Post.

OUR RELATIONSHIP WITH THE ENVIRONMENT: A NECESSARY PARTNERSHIP

The story of Chief Nino Chochise is indeed fascinating. During his lifetime, which covered nearly a century, the world experienced almost uncomprehensible progress and change. For example, when Cochise was a boy, the fastest way to travel was on horseback. As a young man, Cochise witnessed the coming of the automobile ("horseless carriage") and train. An as older man, he thrilled to the wonders of the airplane; and now, along with most of us, he watches in amazement as rockets take humans far into space.

There has been another dramatic change in Cochise's lifetime; it has been more subtle than the advances in transportation, but it is equally, if not more, important. That change involves the relationship between humans and their environment. In the early days at Pa-Gotzin-Kay, life was ruled by the environment. The type of house that could be built, the type of clothing that could be made, and the food that could be eaten were determined by nature. When game was abundant, the Apaches ate well and could make new clothing; when there was a drought and game became scarce, Cochise and his clan were forced to eat a diet of cactus fruit and wear whatever clothing they had made at an earlier time. The environment was the master, and it was feared and worshipped. In fact, Nash (1967) suggests that this "environment is master" attitude was held during the Middle Ages and earlier. This attitude is seen in myths and fairy tales of the times, with the environment pictured as dangerous and the forests as being inhabited by monsters, witches, and werewolves. For example, recall the wolf that plagued Little Red Riding Hood or the witch that captured Hansel and Gretel in the woods.

However, with progress and industrialization, life and the view of the environment changed. Food, materials, and clothing could be sent from one place to another. The residents of Pa-Gotzin-Kay, like most other people, could buy their food, clothing, and housing materials from a store; no longer did they have to rely on their own environment for these objects. Desert land could be irrigated in order to grow crops. Bridges could be built over rivers that once stood in the way of travel. Huge man-made machines, like those at the copper mines of Cananea, could literally move mountains or dig gaping holes into the belly of the land. Humans, not nature, could now decide where houses and cities could be built and where rivers would flow. These advances led to changes in the ways humans viewed their environment. No longer was the land seen as being the master; humans had taken over this role, and the environment became their servant, to be molded and shaped.

However, as Cochise began to approach old age, a new idea of the environment emerged; the servant rebelled. The forests that were destroyed by humans were no longer able to grow new trees and they became unusable wastelands. Houses that were built on the sides of hills were washed away in floods and mudslides. In fact, Cochise lost many of priceless relics that had been stored in a California hillside home when it became prey to a landslide. Lakes and rivers that had served as dumping grounds for human waste and chemicals became unfit for drinking. For years, humans carelessly spewed pollutants into the air, believing that natural air currents would carry away this dangerous waste. But again, the environment refused to be the willing servant, and the air in many cities became dangerous to breathe.

Thus, by the late 1950s, people slowly began to realize that even with

Cochise spent his younger days in an unpolluted environment; the environment controlled much of his life. As an older man, Cochise witnessed people's attempts to master their environment—one unfortunate result of these efforts was that much of the natural beauty was destroyed.

advanced technology they are not the rulers of their environment. Rather, they must live in a partnership with their surroundings. Researchers point out that this has been a central view of Oriental philosophy and religion (Altman and Chemers, 1980). The central theme of Oriental thought is that "all things in nature are sacred and not to be unduly exploited by people" (Altman and Chemers, 1980, p. 21). Rather, people must become a part of nature, understand its changing patterns, and adapt to natural events.

Certainly, people can affect and alter aspects of their environment, but the environment can also affect people. Nino Cochise had seen that pendulum swing to both extremes and, in his later life, he saw a newly emerging respect for the human-environment partnership and a greater concern for understanding and protecting the environment.

The Scope of Environmental Psychology

This new concern for the environment has been a major factor in the development of environmental psychology. The aim of this field is to examine the relationship between the physical environment and human behavior. If we understand this relationship better we may be able to make it more harmonious. Although environmental psychology is a relative newcomer to the family of psychology, we are already aware of some important characteristics of the human-environment interaction.

First, the environment influences a large range of human activities. As we will see in this chapter, our environment affects our everyday behavior, our emotions, and our social interactions. Some of these influences are quite subtle. For example, a people's language is both influenced by and influences the perceptions of their environment. The Eskimos, whose environment is often dominated by snow and ice, have nearly 20 words to describe these objects; most of us use only two, calling the white stuff "snow" and the frozen stuff "ice."

A second characteristic is that people often take their environment for granted and resist changing their own behavior even when it is demanded by the environment. In other words, we seem to have a difficult time accepting the fact that we are partners with, rather than rulers of, our environment. Americans became painfully aware of this problem during the energy crisis of 1973. At that time it became clear that our environment (even if the free flow of oil from the Middle East resumed) could no longer supply the typical forms of energy to meet our growing appetite.

Another important point concerns the features of the environment that

HIGHLIGHT / ENERGY CONSERVATION: SAVING OUR ENVIRONMENT TO SAVE OURSELVES

In the last decade we have witnessed almost unconceivable changes in our world. Robots have begun to replace people in factories; computers send us bills, guide our airplanes, and monitor our automobiles. Dreaded diseases like smallpox have vanished. But of all the changes, one of the most dramatic has been people's concern with energy. Before 1973, gasoline sold for around 29¢ a gallon in the United States; many cars got less than 10 miles to a gallon of gasoline; monthly electric bills of under $15 were not unusual. In 1973 all this changed. This was the year of the Arab embargo on oil shipments to the West. People waited in long lines to purchase a few gallons of gasoline. The price of gasoline jumped to over $1 in this country and close to $3.50 in some European countries. The energy crisis was upon us. Along with these skyrocketing prices came the realization that conservation of energy was necessary if we were to keep our comfortable lifestyle.

While some people immediately adopted conservation measures, many others did not; energy conservation was a painfully slow process in the United States during the mid-1970s. Recently a number of psychologists have pointed out

some of the reasons for this reaction.

Becker and Seligman (1981) argue that people feel little control over their own energy usage and even less control over the bigger problem of worldwide energy conservation. People believe that the energy problem is so large that it will not be helped by their saving a few gallons of gasoline. Brechner and Linder (1981) identify another reason by viewing the energy question as a social trap. Social traps arise when behaviors that help the individual hurt the group. For example, driving your automobile 3 blocks to the grocery store may be convenient for you, but it reduces the amount of gasoline that will be available for others. In many cases, energy conservation forces people to decide whether nor not they will sacrifice their own comfort and convenience for the good of the larger group.

Other researchers have outlined steps to aid energy conservation. One of the more novel approaches has involved giving people feedback on how their behavior saves energy. In many cases, people are unaware of how much they save by turning off the lights in their home or reducing the temperature of their hot water. Most people receive a

utility bill only once a month, so there is no immediate information on the savings of these behaviors. In order to show the importance of immediate feedback, Seligman and Darley (1977) recorded the amount of electricity used by a sample group of residents. Half of the residents then received a letter telling them that air conditioning uses the greatest amount of energy in the summer. This group was also told that each day they would receive information shown in their kitchen window about how much electricity they had used the day before. A control group received the same letter but was not told about and did not receive daily information about their energy use. Over the next month, the group receiving daily feedback used less electricity than the group that did not receive daily feedback. The information not only allowed people to see how much energy they used, it also showed them that they did have control over their energy consumption.

Clearly, we have a long way to go in teaching people to conserve energy. However, this research does show that effective programs can be developed and the use of psychological knowledge can help in the fight to conserve our environment's resources.

influence people's behavior. When most of us think about the environment affecting our behavior, we focus on specific factors such as loud noises, extreme heat, or high density. As we will see in our examination of environmental psychology, while the extremity or absolute level of a variable is important, some of the most striking effects are created by more subtle dimensions. For example, the degree of *predictability* and the amount of *control* a person has over the environment is often more important than the physical intensity of the environment. We will see that people can adjust to a very harsh environment if they feel that they have control over that environment. Another important factor involves the *meaning* that people place on environmental variables. For example, a low level of noise can be very stressful and disruptive if a person believes that it signals an impending danger. Therefore, when we study the environment, we must be concerned with the psychological properties as well as the physical properties of stimuli. This point applies to almost any quality of the environment, including density, heat, noise, and the design of buildings.

The aim of this chapter is to illustrate the range of areas where environment and human behavior interact. As we will see, our lives are influenced every day by both the natural and human environments.

PHYSICAL SPACE AND BEHAVIOR

One of the most basic elements of our environment is physical space. Whether our focus is on the small area that directly surrounds our bodies, the larger space on which our homes are built, or the far more immense area of our country, our own lives are very much affected by the way we and others treat physical space. Many people spend their lives working so that they can afford to buy a piece of land they can call their own. Countless other people have lost their lives in wars and disputes over territory. If we look at the story of Cochise's life, we can readily see how he was influenced by spatial behaviors. For example, the decision by the government to move the Apaches to the San Carlos reservation in 1876 was partly due to American settlers who claimed part of the territory in the old reservation. While living at Pa-Gotzin-Kay, Cochise fought a number of battles with people who trespassed on the Apache hunting ground. And as an older man, Cochise found that he felt uncomfortable living in large cities that did not give him enough space and privacy.

As we will see in this section, much of our behavior has to do with the space around us and how we react to it. Much of this behavior is second nature to us now which is exactly why it is important for us to understand it.

Territoriality

When we speak of "physical space," most of us think about a room, a house, or a building lot. As far back as 1920, Eliot Howard noted that birds often lay claim to a certain area and will fiercely protect it against other members of the same species. Indeed, the bird songs that have gladdened all our ears are often a bird's way of announcing "ownership" of a certain area. From this and other early studies emerged the idea of territoriality, which is the claiming of control or ownership of areas or objects (Porteous, 1977). Once the claim is made, the territory must be defended against other members of the same species. Animals and birds in general avoid trespassing once a claim is made—or face the consequences.

Animals have fascinating ways of "staking their claim" to areas. For example, deer rub glandular secretions on trees to mark the boundaries of their property; bears and members of the cat family often scratch trees to show the boundaries of their claimed area; and most of us have observed dogs "marking" their territory by urinating around the edge of it. A Canadian biologist, found that wolves, like dogs, also claim an area by urinating on its boundaries (Mowat, 1963). With this in mind, he decided to test animals' respect for territory. He spent a number of months in the wild observing the movements of a wolf family. Each night, the wolf family would faithfully make the rounds of their territory, urinating in the appropriate spots. One night, when the family went off to hunt food, Mowat staked his own territory the same way the wolves had done. (He reports having to drink large amounts of tea to store up the necessary supply of territorial markers!) Part of the territory that he marked crossed the trail that the wolves would use when they returned from their hunting trip. He then waited for the wolves to return home. As expected, dawn brought the wolf family trudging homeward over the usual trail. However, when they reached the part marked by Mowat, they stopped, surveyed the area in bewilderment, and then carefully forged a new trail home around Mowat's territory.

Human Territoriality. You need only take a stroll through your own neighborhood to see the variety of ways in which humans mark their territory. Fences, hedges, walkways, and signs of almost every conceivable size and shape dot the landscape to separate territories and identify the owners. Many laws spell out the rights of the owner of the territory and the punishment that will be suffered by trespassers.

Although both animals and humans mark their territory, there are important differences in the way territory is treated. First, animal territorial behavior seems to be innate or inborn, while much of the human response to territory is learned (Roos, 1966). Take dogs, for example: whether they live in the United States, South America, or any other country, dogs urinate on boundaries to mark their territory. But humans' way of marking territory varies with a culture or area. The Apaches of Nino's generation used a tribal totem or symbol to signify their territory at the same time that many other people in the United States were using fences. Urban gangs often mark their territory by placing their mark and writing graffiti on walls along the boundary lines (Ley and Cybriwsky, 1974).

Another difference involves the concept of ownership (Ittleson et al., 1974). Animals claim territory only for the period during which they occupy it. If they move on to new areas, the old territory is up for grabs. Humans, on the other hand, own territory; they may possess an area whether they occupy it or not, and they even try to control what happens to their territory after they die.

Humans also consider more things and places as part of their territory than animals do. The territory of most animals involves a single piece of land. Humans, on the other hand, may have a home, a beach house, a mountain retreat, and an office. They may also have an automobile, a boat, a snowmobile, a huge assortment of furniture, and other objects such as tennis rackets, golf clubs, and guns. It was not so long ago that a person's territory could even include other humans.

Even if we focus only on territoriality involving space, we find a variety of human responses. One researcher suggests that humans actually have three types of spatial territory (Altman, 1975). **Primary territories** are owned and controlled by people and are central to their lives. Uninvited trespassing into primary territories is likely to meet with aggression. For example, your home is your primary territory, and an unwanted intruder is likely to provoke a strong response from you. Humans also have **secondary territories,** which are not as central to their lives and which are

Public territory is space that people do not own but control while they occupy it. A spot on the beach is an example of public territory—as can be seen, people mark their public territory in many ways to show that they are occupying it.

now "owned" by them. However, people often become emotionally attached to these areas and try to control them. Secondary territories may include the private country club or social club and the neighborhood street. Even the neighborhood bar often becomes a secondary territory. Cavan (1966) found that frequent patrons of a bar often control who can use it. Outsiders who stray in may be subjected to hostile glances or questions. If you have a regular seat in a classroom you can understand the meaning of secondary territories. You are likely to feel that this is your space even though you don't own it, and you may feel upset if someone "steals" your space in class. People often have secondary territories at the dinner table or in front of the TV set. Finally, humans have **public territories,** which do not involve feelings of ownership, but people do feel that they control these areas while they are occupying them. For example, when you are at a table at a restaurant in the United States, you will feel that it is your territory, and you will react with surprise and possibly anger if a stranger walks over and sits down in an empty chair at your table. Western Europeans, on the other hand, have a very different concept of public territory in a restaurant, and Americans in Europe may be shocked to find strangers invading "their" table.

Because people are more familiar with their own territory, they have an advantage over intruders. Statistics show that the home team is more likely to win a sports contest than the visiting team.

The Functions of Territory.   Clearly, territoriality is deeply rooted in our lives and society. In today's society we often go to great trouble and expense to establish and advertise our ownership of areas. Cochise and his people risked their lives to punish trespassers. A behavior so widely practiced must have important functions.

One important function of territoriality is *spacing*. Territory is a place where an individual or group can carry on the basic functions of survival: raising food and reproducing. Any one area will only be able to sustain a limited number of people or animals. Thus, allowing outside members into one's territory can be a direct threat to survival. The members of Pa-Gotzin-Kay knew this very well. Apache custom demanded that they welcome other Apaches into their area, but the clan often suffered from hunger after doing this. Although they had to welcome other Apaches, they were very careful not to allow *non*-Apache intruders into their territory.

One of the most familiar functions of territorial behavior can be summed up by the term "home court advantage." In athletics, many sports fans swear that the outcome of a game is determined by where it's played, not by the skill of either team involved. In the same way, professional gamblers generally figure the odds to reflect an advantage to the "home team." The belief in home court advantages is supported by Schwartz and Barsky (1977), who found that such advantages do exist in professional basketball, football, and baseball. Their advice might well be that if you know little about the abilities of the teams involved in a game, bet on the team playing on its home territory. There is also a definite home court advantage in military conflicts. A clear example of this is Cochise's defeat of General Torres. The Mexican army was better supplied and far outnumbered the Indians, but the Apaches were familiar with the territory and lured the invaders into an ambush. This is one basis of the home court advantage; a person or group who occupies an area can learn about the characteristics of that area. And this knowledge can prove very valuable when it becomes necessary to fight an invader. Thus, territoriality functions as an aid to the *protection* of an individual or group.

There is also a *psychological advantage* to being in one's home territory. People feel more comfortable within their own area and thus are able to act more effectively. This advantage is manifested in many ways. For example, in one study, pairs of subjects were asked to work on tasks in the room of one of the subjects (Edney, 1975). The researcher found that the subject on whose territory the experiment was conducted dominated the interaction and assumed the role of leader. Other researchers have had people discuss issues in the room of one of the subjects (Conroy and Sundstrom, 1977; Martindale, 1971). They found that when the subjects disagreed on an issue, the resident spoke longer and exerted more influence than did the visitor. This psychological advantage of territory also seems to have an important effect on children. Even young children are affected by territorial factors. Terrence Lee (1970) studied the behavior of school children and found that those kids who were bused to a school outside their neighborhood performed more poorly than students attending school in their own area. After ruling out a number of possible explanations for this effect, Lee concluded that the children felt more uncomfortable when they were outside of their familiar area and this discomfort negatively affected their learning in school.

Territorial behavior may increase social order (Edney, 1975). If people have clearly staked out their own territories, they are less likely to fight over questions of ownership. The poet Robert Frost stated this position when he wrote, "Good fences make good neighbors." Along similar lines, researchers point out that people use territory to gain privacy (Altman et al., 1981). By controlling an area, people can determine with whom they will interact by letting certain people come onto their territory while keeping others out. In another interesting study, Rosenblatt and Budd (1977) found that married couples tended to be more territorial than did people who were not married and living together. For example, married couples were more likely to have clear understandings about who sleeps on what side of the bed and who sits at a particular spot at the dining table. Presumably married couples realize that they will most likely be together for a long time and wish to take steps to avoid future conflict in their relationship.

It has been suggested that territory is also used by people to *identify* themselves and establish their uniqueness (Altman and Chemers, 1980). In a way, a person's territory becomes a representation of the individual. A walk through a dormitory or office building will highlight this function. For example, the person who loves to ski will have skiing pictures and posters of snow-covered mountains on his or her wall. The country music fan may have posters showing Waylon Jennings, Johnny Cash, and Dolly Parton. In this way, people use their territory to set themselves apart from others and to present attitudes, traits, or values that are important to them.

Thus territorial behavior has important functions for our survival and well-being. A knowledge of these functions makes it easier for us to understand why we might become upset when others trespass on our territory. It also gives us a better understanding of why Cochise and his people so jealously guarded their own area.

People use territory to establish their self-identity and "advertise" who they are.

Personal Space

When we speak of territoriality, we refer to the use of fixed or tangible pieces of property that remain even when the person goes away. A number of years ago, another type of territorial behavior was identified in humans (Hall, 1959, 1966). After observing people in many cultures, Hall reported that people act as if they "own" the space that directly surrounds them. Hall found that no matter where they are, people maneuver to keep others from trespassing on the area directly surrounding their bodies. This area, or **personal space,** is like a bubble surrounding the person wherever he or she goes. Even though we are generally unaware of our spatial behavior, we tend to follow very regular and predictable rules concerning it. The term **proxemics** was coined to describe the study of this personal space.

Hall was most interested in our use of space when we are with other people. He watched people from a number of different cultures interacting in various situations, and concluded that the **interaction distance** is influenced by the relationship between people. For example, Hall described four different interaction distances, each with a close and far phase, used by people in Western cultures like the United States. The *intimate distance* is the closest, ranging from touching to 18 inches away. This distance is used for loving, protecting, comforting, and exchanging secrets. The *personal distance* (18 inches to 48 inches) is used by friends when talking. You may notice that this distance is about an arm's length, and it is used when people are close but do not want physical contact. The third distance is *social distance*, which runs from 4 to 12 feet. This distance is used by people discussing business and for conversations at casual social gatherings. Finally, there is the *public distance*, which is used on formal occasions and when interacting with important people, such as a president or head of state.

Hall's work was followed by literally hundreds of studies aimed at testing and expanding his ideas. For the most part, these studies have confirmed not only the existence of these interaction zones but also their size (Little, 1965). There have, however, been some interesting modifications. For example, in a review of the findings from 106 of these studies it was reported that people generally use the social or personal distances when interacting from a seated position (Altman and Vinsel, 1977). However, when standing, the personal and intimate zones are most frequently used. One group of researchers attempted to determine the shape of a personal space zone (Horowitz, Duff, and Stratton, 1964). Was it a circular bubble as implied by Hall, or did it have some other configuration? In order to find out, they had an experimental confederate approach subjects from different angles. The subjects were instructed to stop the confederates when they came "too close" for comfort. As can be seen in Figure 16–1, the investigators found the bubble to be more egg-shaped than circular; the greatest distance is maintained on the front, while less distance is considered personal when approaching from the sides.

The Functions of Interpersonal Distance. It's not hard to see why we claim fixed pieces of property. But why do we need to have a bubble of space around us?

The fact that most interaction distances (except for the intimate distance) are large enough to keep people out of one another's reach led Evans and Howard (1973) to suggest that personal space plays the important function of *controlling aggression.* Keeping a "neutral zone" between people may inhibit physical violence by keeping people away from one another. Two interesting research findings emphasize this role of personal space. First, through a series of interviews with police officers it was found that violent attacks on the law officers generally occurred when

FIGURE 16–1

Personal space zones tend to be egg-shaped rather than neat round bubbles.

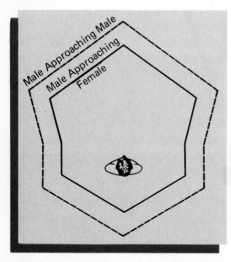

the personal space of suspects was invaded. In another study, Kinzel (1970) found that violent inmates had larger personal spaces than did nonviolent inmates. The violent prisoner did not trust others, and the large personal space zone served as a buffer of protection. It has also been reported that people keep greater distances when they are angry (O'Neal et al., 1980).

Personal distances also play two important functions in our everyday communication. First, the distance at which we interact determines the way we communicate. In order to see this, talk with a friend at the intimate distance (about 12 inches away). What do you see and hear at this distance? Clearly, you can hear the person's voice, but you should also be able to hear his or her breathing. In addition you can see facial details, such as wrinkles and muscle twitches, observe the focus of your friend's eyes, and even spot drops of sweat on his or her forehead. Each of these channels may be used to communicate a message, as we discussed in Chapter 10. While greater clarity exists for some channels, at the intimate distance you cannot observe your friend's hands, feet, or body posture. Thus, while the intimate distance opens some channels, it closes others. Now, try talking at the social distance (5 or 6 feet). At this distance, hand and body movements are easily observed, but eye contact is more difficult and you cannot observe small changes in muscle tone. Thus the distance between you and another person determines how you transmit a message.

The distance between you and another person can itself be a message. You often show the *degree of intimacy* by how close you get to another person (Argyle and Dean, 1965). It has been shown repeatedly that we stand closer to people we like than to people we dislike. You can show this by putting a larger than normal interaction space between you and a very close friend. The friend's first response may be to "close the gap" between the two of you. However, if you continue to back off, he or she will probably ask, "What's the matter with you—are you angry at me?"

What Affects Interaction Distances? What determines how close you get to other people? In some cases, such as in a crowded subway, you have little choice about your distance. However, in most cases, you do determine the size of the space bubble that separates you from others. We have already seen that the nature of our relationship with other people has a major influence on our interaction distance. Mood, age, sex, culture, and physical surroundings influence the distance people keep between themselves. Let's look at how two variables, culture and sex, influence our personal space.

Cultural Background. In his early research into personal space, Hall studied people from many cultures. He found that Latin Americans, Arabs, Greeks, and French people interact at closer distances than Americans, Germans, and English people. In another study, Noesjirwan (1977) observed Indonesians and Australians in a waiting room of a doctor's office. He found that Indonesians chose seats closer to strangers and talked more with them than did the Australians.

This information may seem to be only a small bit of trivia, but there is an amusing story, often called the "Latin Waltz," that shows why such cultural differences can be important. The story involves two men, one from Mexico and one from the United States, who met at a party. After exchanging customary pleasantries, the two began to discuss a topic of mutual interest. As the conversation progressed, the Mexican moved closer to his new acquaintance in order to establish a "comfortable" interaction distance. The American, however, quickly felt uneasy with this close distance, and moved backward to establish a spacing that was comfortable for him. This backward movement brought the Mexican charging in to close the gap between them. Like two dancers in perfect step, the conversationalists waltzed around the room, the American retreating and the Mexican in hot pursuit. Neither was trying to be impolite and neither was even conscious of his behavior. Each was simply trying to establish a distance that was comfortable.

It's funny to imagine these two men dancing around the room, but cultural differences in spatial behavior can have important consequences. In many large cities, people from different cultural backgrounds interact on a daily basis. Differences in language and customs can sometimes make these meetings difficult or stressful. Additional discomfort is added to these interactions if people must silently battle for comfortable interaction distances. Further, since most people are unaware of their spatial behavior, they are likely to have a difficult time realizing the real source of stress in these cross-cultural encounters.

Sex. It seems that somewhere in our early learning on how to be a boy or girl, there is a lesson on spatial behavior, and that lesson seems to be different for each sex. The most generally observed sex difference is that females have smaller personal spaces than do males (Aiello and Aiello, 1974; Heckel and Hiers, 1977). Also, mixed-sex pairs interact at closer distances than do same-sex pairs. There is one interesting exception to this rule. When women start an interaction with a stranger, they keep a greater distance from a man than from a woman (Dosey and Meisels, 1969). As we have seen, intimacy can be communicated by spacing, and it is likely that women are especially careful not to communicate nonexistent feelings of attraction to a strange man. A similar line of reasoning has been used to explain why men have greater interaction distances in same-sex dyads than do women (Hall, 1966). He points out that in Western societies, taboos against male homosexuality are strongly stressed, and as a result men are particularly sensitive about "keeping their distance" when interacting with other men.

In addition to distance, there seems to be another page in the lesson book on sex and spatial behavior. Imagine yourself seated at a library table, minding your own business, when suddenly a stranger takes a seat too close to you. The stranger invades your personal space by taking either the seat next to you or the seat opposite you. Which type of invasion would make you most uncomfortable? Byrne and his colleagues (1971)

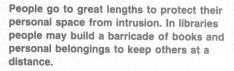

People go to great lengths to protect their personal space from intrusion. In libraries people may build a barricade of books and personal belongings to keep others at a distance.

found that men reacted more negatively to frontal invasions, while women were most upset by invasions from the side. In an interesting observation related to this finding, Fisher and Byrne (1975) found that when men sat down at a library table they most often placed their personal belongings on the table in front of them. This acted as a barrier against frontal invasions. Women, on the other hand, placed their belongings in adjacent chairs, thus ensuring against invasions from the side.

Responses to Invasion of Personal Space. You may want to try the following experiment—it won't win friends, but it will show something about what it means to violate someone's personal space. During a conversation, slowly move closer to your companion, if the other person retreats, continue your charge. How does the other person respond to this?

The most common response to your violation is likely to be *stress.* The other person will probably feel tense and uncomfortable and you may observe some fidgeting (Worchel and Teddlie, 1976). What you cannot observe is the "internal fidgeting" your attack is likely to set off. Your victim's heart rate and blood pressure will increase and muscles are likely to become taut (McBride et al., 1965).

Another common response is *flight:* Your victim is likely to move away from you. This reaction was dramatically demonstrated by Sommer (1969) in a university library setting. When a female seated alone at a table was spotted, an experimenter approached and took a seat immediately next to the unsuspecting subject. In 70 percent of these cases the subject had left the table within a 30-minute period after the intruder arrived. In a control condition where there was no invasion of the area, only 10 percent of the subjects abandoned their table in the same time period. Thus, the flight of the violated subjects appears to be a response to the invader.

If your own victim does not flee or if you're successful enough to maneuver him or her into a corner where flight is impossible, you should begin to see *blocking movements.* Earlier we discussed the fact that close distance communicates intimacy. Researchers reported that a number of other nonverbal behaviors also communicate intimacy (Argyle and Dean, 1965). For example, you can signal that you like other people by maintaining eye contact with them, leaning towards them, and facing them directly rather than placing folded arms or shoulders between them and you. According to Argyle and Dean, all of these channels are used together to signal the degree of intimacy you wish to have. In fact, they form an equilibrium system so that too much intimacy in one channel can be compensated for by reducing intimacy in other channels. Thus, if you move into other people's personal space, which signals intimacy, their response might well be to reduce eye contact or turn their bodies away from you ("giving the cold shoulder"). In order to show this, Argyle and Dean had subjects converse with a confederate at distances of 2, 6, or 10 feet. As can be seen in Figure 16–2, the closer the subjects were to the confederate, the less eye contact they maintained (Argyle and Dean, 1965).

Finally, you will probably find that your inappropriate closeness to another person is likely to cause him or her to dislike you. This reaction has been found even in situations where the violation was not deliberate. One exception to this finding occurs when people interpret the violation as a sign of friendliness on the part of the invader (Schneider and Harsuick, 1979).

There are, then, quite a few responses when you invade someone's personal space. It is likely that your invasion also illustrated another lesson: It is uncomfortable to break spatial norms, even in the guise of an experiment. Didn't you find it so? Did you have to force yourself? This shows that the norms and behaviors regarding the space around us are deeply ingrained.

FIGURE 16–2

When interpersonal distances are violated, people engage in other behaviors, such as avoiding eye contact, to reduce intimacy.

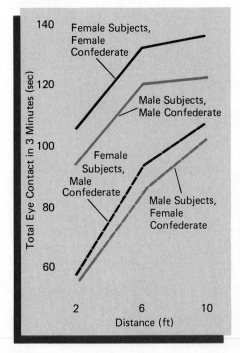

Density and Crowding

In his lifetime, Nino Cochise witnessed a huge amount of change in the world. In the 1870s, a person would have a hard time traveling 100 miles a day; in the 1970s, a person could fly around the world in a day. In 1897, Cochise was delighted with a heliostat system that could send messages from Pa-Gotzin-Kay to the valley below using light reflection; by the 1970s, Cochise could send a message to the other side of the world by telephone. But of all these changes, one of the biggest and most frightening has been the rapid increase in the world's population. When Cochise was born, the population of the United States was about 40 million (Poplin, 1978). By the time he reached his ninetieth birthday, there were over 200 million people in the United States. And, as can be seen from Table 16–1, North America has one of the world's slowest-growing populations. Paul Ehrlich, who refers to the rapid growth in the world's population as the *population bomb*, pointed out that in the 200 years between 1650 and 1850, the world's population doubled, reaching the 1 billion mark. By 1980 the world's population was over 4 billion, and only 38 years will be needed to double it again.

This exploding population growth has many implications. First, there are the obvious economic factors. Second, many of our natural resources are in limited quantities. Ehrlich (1968) estimates that at current levels of consumption, the world's known reserves of petroleum will last only 31 years, tungsten will last 40 years, and nickel will last 150 years. A third consequence of the increasing population is that people will be living closer together, and each person will have less space in which to live.

Recently, social scientists have begun to investigate the social and psychological effects of this rapid growth. Before looking at this research, it is important to explain the difference between two terms: density and crowding. **Density** is a measure of the space available to people in a given area. For example, you can find the density of your city by dividing its population by its area. In 1973, the density of New York was about 450 people per acre, while Hong Kong had a density of 2,000 people per acre. **Crowding,** on the other hand, is a psychological state rather than a physical measure (Stokols, 1972). You can *feel* crowded, but you cannot feel density. Density and crowding are often related; but, as we will see later, this is not always the case.

Density and Behavior. In 1962 John Calhoun published the results of a study that shocked social scientists and added a new urgency to the study of density and crowding. Calhoun built a rat colony (see Figure 16–3) designed to hold about 48 animals. He let the population grow until it reached 80, however, and then he removed young rats after they had been weaned. The colony dwellers were given enough food, water, and nesting material to maintain a "high standard of living," but problems

TABLE 16-1: Doubling Times of Population under Various Rates of Natural Increase

	Crude Birth Rate (per 1,000)	Crude Death Rate (per 1,000)	Rate of Natural Increase (annual, percent)	Number of Years to Double
World	30	12	1.8	38
Major Regions				
Africa	45	19	2.6	27
Asia	32	12	2.0	35
Europe	15	10	0.4	173
Latin America	36	9	2.7	26
North America	15	9	0.6	116
Oceania	22	9	1.3	53

Source: Population Reference Bureau (1977).

soon began to develop. Some dominant rats laid claim to pens 1 and 4, and the rest of the animals were forced to live in pens 2 and 3. As a result of overcrowding, these two pens became **behavioral sinks,** which "aggravated all forms of pathology that can be found within a group." Females often abandoned their young and failed to build nests. Many of the rats became cannibals and devoured the unattended young. Aggression was frequent, and the pens became smeared with the blood of the injured animals. Abnormal sexual behavior was observed as male rats tried to mate with immature females or engaged in homosexual acts. Females suffered a large number of miscarriages, and many developed cancer of the sex organs and mammary glands.

Is this the fate that awaits humans as a result of their population explosion? In order to examine this question, a number of investigators conducted studies comparing the behavior of individuals living in different densities. The results of these studies were largely inconclusive; some found bad effects (high rates of mental illness and juvenile delinquency) associated with high density; others did not. Further, even in the studies that reported negative behaviors related to high density, it was not possible to know for sure that density was the cause of the problems. For example, the highest density areas are usually found in the inner cities, and residents of these areas are often poorer, less educated, and have less job security than people living in the less dense suburbs. Any one of these differences might cause physical, mental, and social difficulties, rather than density alone. In order to isolate the effects of density, researchers devised laboratory studies where the behavior of college students in high-density or

FIGURE 16–3: Calhoun's Rat Colony

The study by Calhoun showed that abnormal behavior resulted when the pens became overcrowded. (Calhoun, 1962)

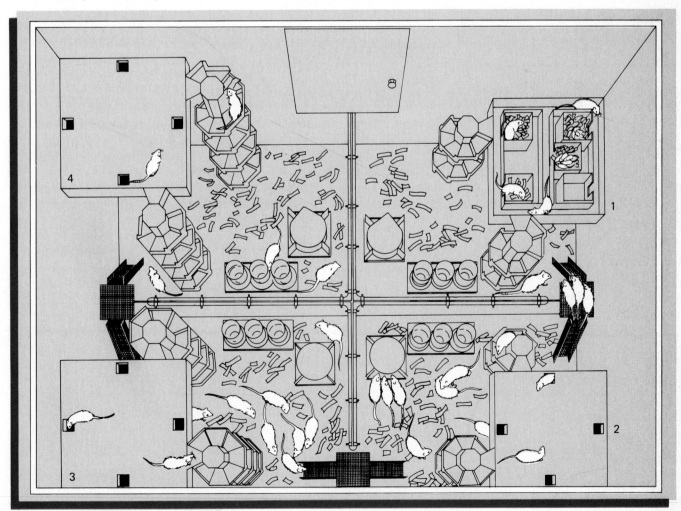

low-density situations was compared (Freedman 1975). The groups were given problems to solve and tasks to work on. Generally, these studies did not find that high density led to problems. In some cases, Freedman reported that female subjects even enjoyed the close environments. The general picture that emerged was that high density, by itself, was not necessarily damaging to humans.

Crowding. This conclusion may cause many of us, especially those living in high-density areas, to breathe a sigh of relief. However, before becoming too complacent, we must examine the research on crowding. As we pointed out earlier, crowding is a feeling or a psychological state that often, but not always, accompanies high density.

Since we are often accustomed to viewing crowding and high density together, let us consider an example that should separate the two. Remember trying to shop for gifts around Christmas time? The stores were jammed with people (high density) and you probably felt very crowded as you searched for items or made your way to the cashier to pay for the gifts. Here, then, is a case where density and crowding are closely related. Now think of a time when you attended a rock concert or athletic event. In these situations people were also packed around you; in some cases, you may have even found strangers hugging you or pounding your back in wild excitement. However, even though the actual density may have been higher at these events than in the stores, you probably did not feel crowded. If someone asked you how you felt at the rock concert or athletic event, you would probably report being excited or happy.

Given that high density does not always lead to overcrowding, investigators have recently begun identifying the conditions that do influence the density-crowding relationship. A number of factors have been found to influence the amount of crowding people will experience. First, some researchers have found that the *focus of our attention* determines when we will experience crowding (Worchel et al., 1978; Worchel and Yohai, 1979). When other people who are violating our personal space become the center of our attention, we will attribute arousal and discomfort as being caused by their closeness. This will result in the feeling of crowding. However, if our attention is not focused on other people, we will not experience crowding, even in high-density situations. For example, at an athletic event, people's attention is focused on the competition and not on the other spectators. As a result they are not likely to experience much crowding. On the other hand, in the busy store, crowding will result because people must focus their attention on other shoppers as they make their way to the cashier.

It has also been suggested that high density will lead to crowding when people feel that they have lost *control* over their environment (Rodin and Langer, 1977; Rodin and Baum, 1978). Again, if you remember your experiences at a store filled with customers, you may recall feelings of utter helplessness; you weren't able to get the attention of the salesperson, the dressing room was always occupied, and you didn't dare go against the flow of traffic for fear of being trampled. At the athletic event, the need for control is not as important; you only want to be able to see the contest. Further, there is some order to the seating of the crowd, and if you wish to leave you can walk through the aisles to get out.

Third, crowding is likely to be felt when people cannot achieve the desired amount of *privacy* (Altman, 1975). Privacy involves being able to choose whether or not to interact with others. Altman believes that when high density forces us to interact with others against our will, we will experience crowding.

Finally, Wicker (1979) takes a somewhat different approach to the issue of crowding. He focuses on the task on which a group is working and suggests that crowding results when there are more people present than

Crowding is a psychological state. Even when density is high, as it often is in sporting events or rock concerts, people may not necessarily feel crowded.

are required to perform the task. For example, if you are trying to build a house out of cards, one or two other people may be able to help you complete the task. However, if there are more than this number of people, they are likely to get in your way and hinder your progress. When the number of people begins to interfere with your efforts, you will feel crowded. It is interesting to note that Wicker's theory views crowding as being affected by the number of people in an environment rather than the amount of space.

Responses to Crowding.   Earlier we saw that high density does not necessarily lead to negative responses from humans. Unfortunately, the research on crowding presents a different picture; the experience of crowding often leads to bad effects on human emotions, performance, and interpersonal relations.

One theory suggests that crowding results when there are more people present than required to complete a task.

Crowding is an unpleasant experience. People who feel crowded generally report feeling stressed, anxious, and uncomfortable (Epstein, 1981). Crowding can lead to physiological arousal. For example, Paulus, McCain, and Cox (1978) found that inmates who lived in crowded cells and reported feeling crowded had higher blood pressure than inmates who did not experience crowding. Cochise reported that being crowded in New York made his "skin crawl" and kept his nerves "constantly on edge" (Cochise and Griffith, 1971). He had never felt so confined, and everywhere he went there were more people. Most of us who have experienced extreme crowding can sympathize with him.

People not only dislike being crowded, they also dislike *people who make them feel crowded.* For example, when dormitory residents were interviewed, those who lived in crowded rooms (three people in a room designed for two) reported being less attracted to their roommates than the noncrowded residents (Baron et al., 1976b). A somewhat puzzling finding is that crowding has a more negative effect on the mood and social relationships of males as compared to females. In one study, groups of males and females were placed in either crowded or noncrowded rooms (Freedman et al., 1971). The groups listened to tapes of court cases involving violent crimes and then decided on the length of sentence that should be given the defendant. Males assigned harsher sentences when they were crowded, while females gave longer sentences when they were not crowded. The exact reason for this sex difference is not yet clear.

Given the list of negative effects of crowding that we have already discussed, we might expect that crowded individuals would not perform well. To a certain degree this is true. Research (e.g., McClelland, 1974) has shown that crowding *interferes with performance of complex or detailed tasks.* On the other hand, people sometimes perform simple tasks better when they are crowded than when they are not crowded. At first glance, this might seem like a curious pattern of results. However, if you will recall our discussion of social facilitation in Chapter 15, we found that the heightened arousal caused by an audience inhibited performance of complicated tasks, but aided work on easy and well-learned tasks. The effect of crowding may be the same; crowding may arouse individuals to such a degree that they cannot concentrate on details, but can quickly deal with simple problems. The message from this work is that you should attempt to choose your environment to suit the type of problem on which you will be working.

Reducing Crowding. The distinction between density and crowding has some very important implications for managing our environment. The first implication is that bigger is not necessarily better. That is, simply giving people more space may lower density, but it will not necessarily reduce crowding or the effects of crowding. For example, imagine that you have had a very hectic day and want to spend some time by yourself. In this situation, you will probably feel crowded in either a large or small room if other people are present. In fact, you might prefer to hide in a closet where you have little physical space but a great deal of privacy.

A second implication of the density-crowding distinction is that crowding can be reduced without reducing density. For example, Sherrod (1974) found that people who believed they could leave a tightly packed room felt less crowded than people who did not feel free to leave the room. The density was the same in each case, but the people who could leave felt some control over their environment. Those who could not leave did not have this control. In another study, Worchel and Teddlie (1976) found that people felt less crowded and performed better in a room with pictures on the walls than in a room with no pictures. This effect was found even though the density in the room was the same for both groups. The investigators argued that the pictures made the presence of other people less obvious and, thereby, reduced crowding.

The finding that crowding and density are not the same has led researchers to identify a number of nonspatial methods that can be used to reduce crowding and help people adjust to their environment. It has also highlighted the point that both physical and psychological features must be considered in determining the relationship between people and their environment.

OTHER ENVIRONMENTAL VARIABLES

Noise

If we close our eyes and think of Pa-Gotzin-Kay perched in the Sierra Madre, we can visualize the domeshaped wikiups with the smoke of fires rising lazily into the sky in front of them. We also see children playing while the adults are working in the fields or tanning skins and making clothing in the village. This scene is very appealing, but what is probably more appealing are the imaginary sounds that strike our ears. The air may occasionally be filled with the laughing of children, conversations in a strange language; the bellowing of mules or braying of the cattle, and the swish of the wind. On the whole, however, we would be struck with the quietness of the place. Quiet was important to the residents because they feared that noise would lead unwanted guests to the rancheria; even dogs were not allowed in Pa-Gotzin-Kay because they were too noisy.

Our own society has come a long way from the Pa-Gotzin-Kay of 1890. If we were to visualize our own town or city, we would have to include busy sidewalks with people hurrying to unknown destinations; cars, buses, trucks, and motorcycles making their way down crowded streets; and occasionally the reflection of a silver airplane in the sky. Regardless of how detailed a picture we paint, it would not be complete without the sounds of our civilization: noise. It would just seem wrong to leave out the rumble of engines, the symphony of honking horns, the music blaring from the record stores, and the scream of a low-flying jet. The variety (and level) of sound in our environment is astonishing. It would probably be easy to make a short list of all the things that were capable of making noise at Pa-Gotzin-Kay. Try doing this for your own environment!

The increasing noise in our environment has led scientists to examine the effects noise has on us. As we review this research, you should keep in mind that most of the sounds in our environment are made by humans and their inventions. Thus this is one environmental variable that humans may be able to control.

One of the first steps in the investigation has been to distinguish between sound and noise. As we discussed in Chapter 3, **sound** is a physical property caused by changes in air pressure. We measure sounds in units called decibels (for example, 55 db is the sound of light traffic; 120 db is equal to a jet taking off at 200 feet). **Noise,** on the other hand, is a "psychological concept and is defined as sound that is unwanted by the listener because it is unpleasant, bothersome, interferes with important activities, or is believed to be physiologically harmful" (Cohen and Weinstein, 1981). While extremely loud sounds can cause physical damage, most of the research in this area has concentrated on the effects of noise. As you can see, the sound-noise distinction is similar to the density-crowding distinction. Sound and density are physical properties, while noise and crowding are psychological concepts. With this distinction in mind, let us examine some of the effects of sound and noise.

Physical Effects. Most of the work on physical effects has focused on high-intensity sounds. If you have, at times, been concerned that your own hearing is not as sensitive as it was when you were younger, your concerns may be well founded. In 1972, the Environmental Protection Agency estimated that 3 million Americans suffer hearing loss caused by loud sounds. In hearing tests for high frequency sounds, the EPA found that 3.8 percent of sixth graders, 10 percent of ninth and tenth graders, and a staggering 61 percent of college freshmen showed hearing impairment. Anspacher (1972) studied the hearing of rock musicians, who are often exposed to noise levels of over 125 db. He found that 41 of the 43 musicians studied had permanent hearing loss. In possibly the most revealing study, it was reported that 70-year-old tribesmen living in quiet Sudanese villages have hearing sensitivity comparable to 20-year-olds in the United States (Rosen et al., 1962). Thus, it is very likely that residents of Pa-Gotzin-Kay did have more sensitive hearing than residents of the large noisy settlements in the area.

Welsh (1979) reviewed a number of studies that examined the effects of loud industrial sounds on workers' health. He concluded that long-term exposure (3 to 5 years) increased the likelihood of cardiovascular problems. Other research suggests that prolonged exposure to loud sounds increases the possibility of ulcers and other digestive tract problems (Kangelari et al., 1966). Because the concern about the effects of sound on health is relatively recent, there is not yet enough evidence to make strong conclusions. However, the results that we do have suggest that we need to pay more attention to the problem.

Effects on Performance. If you were asked whether noise affects a person's ability to work on tasks, your first response might be a quick "yes." However, after giving this question some thought, you might remember a friend who could only study with the stereo blasting.

This pattern of thought parallels the progression of an interesting series of studies by Glass and Singer (1972) on the effects of short-term noise. The investigators created a noise by superimposing the following sounds on a tape: two people speaking Spanish, one person speaking Armenian, a mimeograph machine spitting out copies, an old desk calculator that sounded like a machine gun, and an electric typewriter. Subjects worked on different tasks while this noise was played in the room. In some cases the noise was played loudly, while in others it was played softly. In some of the studies subjects could predict or control the noise, while in others, they could not.

Surprisingly, these studies showed that the noise had little effect on arousal *or* performance. It seemed that subjects reacted to the onset of the noise, but they were able to quickly adapt to it, especially when it was predictable. Even the physiological measures shown in an initial stress response (increased heart rate and blood pressure) were followed by a return to normal levels.

The investigators were, however, not willing to conclude that their subjects were unaffected by the noise. In an effort to further study the possible effects of noise, researchers had subjects listen to a loud or soft noise that was either predictable or unpredictable (Glass et al., 1977). Following this, subjects were asked to perform tasks in a quiet room. This procedure brought to light the effects of noise on performance. The "effects" of noise are really *aftereffects;* after the subjects had been exposed to noise, especially unpredictable noise, their performance suffered. The investigators suggested that people can adjust to noisy conditions over a short

Noise that is unpredictable and uncontrollable is the most damaging type of noise. People who live close to busy airports cannot predict or control the noise in their environment. Research has found that students who live close to the Los Angeles International Airport have higher blood pressure and perform more poorly than students living in a quieter environment.

period of time. However, this adaptation requires the use of a great deal of energy, which makes them less able to cope with later environmental or task demands.

Noise may present an even bigger problem for children. In order to find this out, Cohen, Glass, and Singer (1973) examined the reading abilities of children living in a high-rise apartment building built directly over a New York City freeway. The children living on the lower floors were exposed to a great deal more highway noise than the children on the upper floors. The children on the upper floors had a higher reading ability than those students who lived on the lower floors.

In another important study, children whose school was in the flight path of Los Angeles International Airport were observed and examined (Cohen et al., 1981). Compared to children in quiet schools, these pupils had higher blood pressure, were more likely to fail in a puzzle-solving task, and were more likely to give up when faced with a difficult task. The longer the child had been in the noisy school, the more distractible he or she was. One of the more disturbing factors was that these problems tended to remain even after the children's school had been insulated and the noise level reduced. This suggests that the effects of noise are not easily eliminated.

Taken together, these studies suggest that noise does have a bad effect on performance. The most damaging noises are those that are loud or whose onset and duration cannot be predicted or controlled. Unfortunately, this is the type of noise most likely to assault someone living in a city or close to a busy street. Traffic noise is often loud, and you can't predict when a noisy truck or motorcycle will pass or when horns will begin blowing.

Effects on Social Relationships. Noise also seems to affect our interactions with other people. Appleyard and Lintell (1972) compared the everyday life of people living on a busy, noisy street with that of residents of a quiet block. People who lived on the noisy street rarely interacted with neighbors outside their apartments, and they reported that their street was a lonely place to live. On the other hand, people who lived on the quiet street often sat on their doorsteps chatting with neighbors, and they reported a great deal of contact with other residents of the area. In another study, it was found that people are less likely to stop and offer help in a noisy environment than in a quiet area (Mathews and Cannon, 1975). In one set of conditions they had a confederate, wearing a cast on his arm, drop a load of books in front of a subject who was walking down a sidewalk. In some cases, the area was quiet, while in others a lawn mower was running close by. While 80 percent of the subjects helped in the quiet environment, only 15 percent helped in the noisy environment.

Theories on the Effects of Noise. It may be easy to understand why loud deafening sounds decrease performance and hurt the quality of social interactions. However, it is more difficult to understand why lower intensity sounds that are experienced as noise have these effects. A number of theories have been proposed. Some are relatively straightforward; for example, Isen (1970) suggests that noise puts people in a bad mood, and Poulton (1978, 1979) argues that intermittent noise is distracting. When people are continuously distracted, it is difficult for them to concentrate on tasks or on social interactions.

A number of other investigators (Broadbent, 1971; Cohen and Weinstein, 1981) suggest that noise causes people to narrow their focus of attention. They focus their efforts on trying to explain or control the noise and they do not pay attention to other features in the environment. Therefore, they are less likely to pay attention to other people or task requirements. Noise that is either unpredictable or uncontrollable demands the most attention and, therefore, is most disruptive.

Overall, these theories point out that the noise level of our environment can have a great deal of influence over a large part of our lives.

Air Pollution

The fact that the air could be so polluted that it is unsafe to breath certainly never crossed the minds of those who lived at Pa-Gotzin-Kay. They, like most of us a few years ago, could not conceive of the possibility that humans could pollute their environment to such an extent that people would sell their homes and move away because they were afraid to breathe the air in certain places. Yet that has happened, and with good cause. The breathing of "dirty air" has been found to be a contributing factor in a number of illnesses, including heart disease, cancer, and respiratory diseases. It has been found that the air in many big cities is unsafe for humans, and warning systems, called pollution alerts, have been developed to warn residents when the air is particularly bad. In fact, the President's Council on Environmental Quality (1978) reported that the air quality in 43 major cities, where half the population of the United States lives, is unhealthy.

Despite the evidence, some people have argued that it takes years of inhaling polluted air before its effects are evident. According to a study by Lewis, Baddeley, Bonham, and Lovett (1970), this is not the case. These investigators collected air from 15 inches (the level of automobile exhaust) above the ground level of a fairly busy English road. They had people breathe either this air or pure, unpolluted air. The subjects then performed a number of tasks. Subjects who had breathed the polluted air performed

Air pollution has become a major environmental problem in many large cities. There is some evidence that breathing polluted air can reduce task performance.

Concern for the quality of air has led many people to take steps to improve the air in their own environment. Smoking has been banned in many public places in an effort to reduce inside air pollution.

more poorly than subjects who inhaled the clean air. Thus, there may be important short-term as well as long-term effects from breathing polluted air.

Fortunately, action has been taken in the United States to improve the quality of our air. The Clean Air Act established emission standards for automobiles. Factories and power plants have been ordered to reduce the amounts and types of particles they release into the air. Even air pollution by individuals is being reduced by rules prohibiting smoking in certain areas. However, efforts to reduce pollution in our environment are often slowed because people do not believe that they have any control over the problem (Evans and Jacobs, 1981). Many people reluctantly adopt the view that pollution is bound to increase in the future, and all we can do is try to adapt to it. Campaigns to clean up the environment have been aimed at changing this mistaken belief (Cone and Hayes, 1980).

One of the major problems with changing people's attitudes toward air pollution is that many people are not aware that it exists in their environment. Barker (1976) found that people use six cues to detect air pollution. These cues are dust, odor, discoloration and damage to property, respiratory irritation, eye irritation, and poor visibility. In other words, people use their perceptions of changes in physical conditions to identify pollution. Unfortunately, Evans and Jacobs (1981) point out that some of the most dangerous pollutants, such as toxic gases, cannot be seen or smelled. Therefore, many people remain unaware of pollution that is affecting them.

Weather

Almost every aspect of life at Pa-Gotzin-Kay was very strongly influenced by the weather. The weather determined what clothes would be worn, what foods would be available for eating, and whether or not the trails could be used to visit surrounding ranches and settlements. Even the time and place for battles was influenced by the weather conditions, since it was difficult to travel during the rainy, cold winter. In today's air-conditioned and artificially heated world, with its indoor tennis courts and covered sports arenas, we often overlook the role that weather plays in our lives, unless, of course, a planned picnic or beach outing is rained out. However, many studies have suggested that weather conditions influence more than our choice of clothing or weekend plans.

Effects on Performance. Mackworth (1961) had military personnel work on tasks such as visual tracking and receiving and sending Morse code messages. The humidity in their room was kept constant, but the temperature was varied. The results showed that subjects made more errors as the temperature increased. Since this study, many others have been done, and the overall conclusion is that human performance on tasks involving concentration and psychomotor skills is reduced by long periods of exposure to either very hot (over 100°F.) or very cold (under 50°F.) temperatures (Bell, 1981). These results probably come as no surprise to anyone who has tried to study in either a very hot or very cold room.

Effects on Interpersonal Relations. One of the first people to write about the effects of weather on social interaction was Aristotle. He theorized that climate affected people's temperament. He felt that the cold temperatures of northern Europe made the inhabitants brave warriors, but dull in wit and skill. The inhabitants of Asia were characterized as intelligent, but the warm weather there was thought to make them lazy and inactive. The Greeks, who lived in a climate that was neither extremely hot nor cold, were both brave fighters and intelligent. Of course, Aristotle was a Greek, and his views may seem self-serving. Yet more careful studies have indicated a relationship between weather and social behavior.

Most research has focused on the relationship between heat and aggression. The U.S. Riot Commission (1968) reported that the large portion of civil disorders occur in the hot summer months, and their report speculated about a link between heat and violence. Researchers examined subjects' interactions in either a hot (93.5°F.) or cool (73.5°F.) room; most hostility and aggression was expressed in the hot room (Griffitt and Veitch, 1971). Further, Baron and Lawton (1972) found that people were more likely to imitate an aggressive model in a hot room as opposed to a cool room. While in most cases increasing temperatures seem to be associated with increasingly hostile tempers, Baron and Bell (1976a) report that excessive heat combined with other frustrations actually results in a decline in social interaction and aggression. Under such unpleasant conditions, subjects think more about quickly escaping the situation than in increasing their discomfort by aggressing against others.

Heat may not be the only weather factor that influences human aggression. As children, most of us were frightened out of our wits by stories of vampires who arose during a full moon to stalk the countryside for unsuspecting victims. As we grew older and more cynical, we laughed at the idea that the moon could influence behavior. But some data have been presented that may make us think twice before dismissing the possibility of moon influences (Lieber and Sherin, 1972). They point out that the moon has an important effect on the earth, since the ocean tides are determined by the gravitational pull of the moon. The strength of this pull varies with the phase of the moon (it is strongest during the new and full moon phases). Further, the human body has much the same composition as the earth's surface (80 percent water and 20 percent organic and inorganic solids). So why shouldn't the moon have an influence on humans? In order to test this possibility, Lieber and Sherin looked at the relationship between homicides in Cuyahoga County, Ohio and Dade County, Florida and phases of the moon. In fact, they found that the rate of homicides was significantly higher during the new and full moon phases, the same phases that cause the greatest ocean disturbances. It is an intriguing possibility that the moon may influence human behavior. However, at this point it must remain only speculation, since we do not have sufficient data to draw a definite conclusion. It is interesting, however, to find that the Apaches believed that the full moon brought out braveness in warriors (Cochise and Griffith, 1971).

Clearly, the study of the effects of weather on human behavior has just scratched the surface. Future research may uncover some strong links between weather and behavior.

THE BUILT ENVIRONMENT

At Pa-Gotzin-Kay, Cochise lived in the typical Apache wikiup. This was a round, beehive-shaped, one-room dwelling made of branches and grass. There were two openings in the structure: a door located at the side away from prevailing winds and a smokehole in the top. The total furnishings of the wikiup could be loaded on the back of a horse. They included blankets for sitting and sleeping, and baskets and pots for cooking. Hooks on the walls of the wikiup were used for hanging weapons, clothing, and utensils.

When Cochise moved to Cananea, he lived in a six-room frame house completely furnished with easy chairs, tables, and "the world's softest bed." Later, when he visited New York, Cochise found still another type of dwelling: the high-rise apartment. Here people could spend most of their time high above the ground, and they would have to expend some time and effort to reach the streets when they wished to go out.

Today, few people live in wikiups, but modern architecture allows us to design and build dwellings of almost every conceivable size, shape, and height. Rooms, too, can be shaped and colored with amazing variety and can be furnished in an almost endless array of schemes. Recently, psychologists have begun to examine how our lives are influenced by the environment we have built for ourselves. As we review the findings in this area, examine your own "built" environment and try to imagine how it influences your behavior and that of the people whom you invite into it.

Rooms

Shape. One of the characteristics of a room easiest to describe is its shape. Is it square or rectangular? How many doors and windows does it have? When constructing a dwelling, decisions about the shape of rooms and numbers of windows and doors are often made on the basis of money alone. This, however, may be an unfortunate mistake, since research has shown that these room variables influence human behavior and perception. For example, Ruys (1971) interviewed 139 female workers in windowless offices and found that 47.5 percent felt that the lack of windows had a bad effect on them. These workers felt that the lack of windows caused them to suffer more headaches and physical discomfort, and they worked more slowly and erratically in this environment. Deser (1972) found that room shape and number of doors influenced the feeling of being crowded. He designed two model rooms of the same overall size but varied the shape (square or rectangular) and the number of doors in the room (two or six). Subjects placed stick figures that represented people in the rooms until they felt the room to be "crowded." The subjects felt that more figures (people) could fit comfortably into the rectangular room than into the square room (even though the space was the same). Further, more people were placed in the two-door room than in the six-door room.

Color and Beauty. We have nearly an unlimited range of colors to paint our own rooms. Usually, we choose colors according to our personal taste. We probably do not realize that the colors we choose may affect us both psychologically and physically. For example, Wilson (1966) found that subjects became more physiologically aroused (as measured by GSR) when viewing red slides as opposed to seeing green ones. In another study, women worked in either a "cool blue" room or one painted in "warm yellows and restful greens" (Seghers, 1948). Even though the temperature was the same in both rooms (75°F.), the workers tended to complain of being too cold in the blue room, but too warm in the yellow and green room.

The beauty of a room also affects us. Mintz (1956) had examiners work in either a beautiful or an ugly room. The beautiful room was decorated with bright colors and comfortably furnished, while the ugly room was drab and cluttered. Examiners who worked in the ugly room seemed more hostile and irritable and they complained of more physical ailments such as headaches than did examiners in the beautiful room. Hence, beauty in our environment is not only something to behold, it also can affect our mood and behavior.

Furniture Arrangement. The placement of furniture in a room can have a marked effect on both the amount and type of social interaction. In an interesting demonstration of this, Sommer and Ross (1958) observed patients in a newly remodeled geriatric ward. In the hopes of encouraging more interaction among patients, the hospital administration painted and carpeted the dayroom and put in new furniture. Much to their disappointment, however, the patients continued to sit in the dayroom "like strangers in a train station waiting for a train that never came." Sommer and Ross felt that one reason for this lack of social interaction was the arrangement of the furniture: Chairs were lined up in long straight rows so that the patients had to sit side-by-side or back-to-back. The researchers changed this pattern by grouping four chairs around small tables. The result was quite striking. In a few weeks, interaction among the patients had nearly doubled, and the dayroom was used more often. Thus, the furniture arrangement affected the social interaction among patients.

The type of interaction that people expect to engage in has also been found to influence their preference for seating arrangements (Sommer, 1969). People involved in casual conversation prefer to be seated either corner-to-corner or face-to-face. If the people plan to cooperate, they want to sit side-by-side. But if they are going to compete, they want to be able to keep an eye on each other and thus choose a face-to-face arrangement.

Thus, the shape, color, and arrangement of furniture in a room can affect the way you feel and the way you interact with others.

Buildings

Living in a High-Rise. Many Americans feel that the ideal living arrangement is a house and a yard with trees and flowers. However, in large cities where land is scarce and it is expensive and inconvenient to live some distance away, many people rent or buy apartments in high-rise buildings. As the populations of the cities increase, apartment buildings grow higher. For some people, the high-rise is an answer to their dreams; no yards to water, no grass to cut, and no cars blocking their driveways. However, for many other people, high-rise living is full of problems and discomforts.

One of the clearest examples of the problems of high-rise living occurred in St. Louis, Missouri in the late 1950s. As a result of efforts to improve housing conditions for the poor, 43, 11-story apartment buildings were built on a 57-acre tract. The Pruitt-Igoe complex was praised for its beauty, and with much fanfare the 12,000 residents moved into their new homes. There was, however, a great deal less celebration when, in April, 1972, the last occupants had moved out of the buildings and the city was forced to order the project demolished. The Pruitt-Igoe complex was a good idea turned bad because it had been designed without proper thought for the human problems of high-rise living. Families in the project grew unhappy because parents could not supervise their children, who wanted to play in the playground several stories below their apartments. The long hallways in the buildings did not allow the type of interaction that residents had enjoyed before on the doorsteps of their houses or small apartment buildings. There were areas such as elevators and stairwells, that were unguarded and not well lit; these became prime areas for rape and robbery, and residents became afraid of going out of their own apartments. These problems were not special to the Pruitt-Igoe complex; Cappon (1971) reports similar problems in many high-rise buildings throughout the world.

In addition, McCarthy and Saegert (1979) found that high-rise residents tend to form fewer relationships with other building residents than did those of low-rise buildings. High-rise residents also seem to be more distrustful of their neighbors and less willing to give help than residents of low-rise buildings (Bickman et al., 1973). These feelings are reflected in statistics showing that the higher the apartment building in which people live, the greater is the chance that they will fall victim to a crime (Newman, 1972).

This discussion paints a rather bleak picture of high-rise buildings, but that is no reason to write them off entirely. There have been some suggestions about how to make these buildings safer and more enjoyable for their residents. Newman (1972, 1975), for example, argues that crime can be reduced and social interaction increased by doing away with indefensible spaces in the apartment complex. **Indefensible spaces** are areas that are not open to observation, such as enclosed stairways and alleys, where it is not clear who controls them. These areas invite intruders and breed crime. Newman suggests that stairways and elevators be enclosed in glass

Building for beauty rather than for people has reduced the desirability of many buildings. One extreme example of this was the Pruitt-Igoe complex. In spite of the fact that the buildings won a number of design awards, people found them difficult to live in, and the complex had to be destroyed after only a few years.

It is especially important to provide defensible spaces in high-rise buildings. These buildings are often threatening because people feel that they have little control over their environment.

so that people can see who is inside before they enter. Outside the building, hedges or low fences can be used, which not only allows residents to claim and use these areas, but it also makes it easy to observe the areas. Common meeting areas can be created in certain apartments to get residents to gather and interact socially on a regular basis. Research has shown that such changes may indeed cause residents to feel safer and to enjoy the facilities of their apartment buildings (Kohn et al., 1975). This, then, is an example of using research and theory to *improve* the environment rather than just giving up on it as a hopeless task.

The Dormitory. A building with which many of us have had some experience is the college or university dormitory. Most of these buildings are built in a corridor design: a long hall with rooms on either side and a communal bathroom somewhere on the corridor. Oftentimes there is a community lounge at the end of the corridor. Recently, many institutions have been experimenting with a different type of dormitory. The suite dormitory is built with three or four bedrooms surrounding a common lounge or living-room area, with a bathroom serving all residents of the suite.

While the amount of living space for each resident is often the same in the corridor and suite dormitories, the designs seem to have different effects on residents' behavior. Andrew Baum and Stu Valins (1977) questioned residents of the two types of dwellings (see Figure 16–4). They found that suite residents tended to have more friends and work together as groups more often than did residents of corridor dorms. Corridor residents complained of constantly seeing strangers on the floor, suite residents seldom had this problem. Overall, suite residents felt that they had more control over their lives and environment than did corridor residents. Students living in the corridor rooms reported feeling more crowded and having less privacy than did suite residents.

FIGURE 16–4

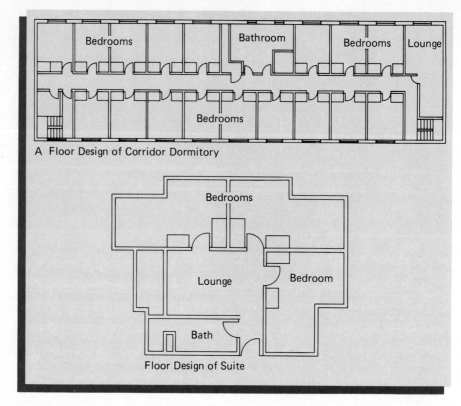

This again is an example of how the architectural design of our environment affects our feelings and actions. We can aid adjustment to our environment by designing our buildings and rooms to fit our needs. On the other hand, if we ignore the fact that we are influenced by our own handiwork and continue to design our buildings with only cost and architectural beauty in mind, we will become our own enemies and we will be making our adjustment and enjoyment of our environment more difficult.

The City

Cochise's first visit to a big city was a bewildering experience. In 1903, he had just settled in Cananea when Colonel Greene decided that Cochise's presence might help him impress potential investors in New York City. Thus, off they went to New York, where Cochise, dressed in his best Indian costume, accompanied Colonel Greene through a round of meetings. Even in 1903, Cochise reported that New York was crowded, noisy, impersonal, and the air was polluted by smoke. He did not like big cities, and even as an older man, he questioned whether cities represented progress in living. Even though he lived in large cities such as Los Angeles and Seattle, as an old man he returned to a more rural environment in Arizona.

The urban environment has come under closer scrutiny in the last decade. Through much of this century, Americans flocked to the cities, where jobs were abundant. In fact, in 1980 over 70 percent of the people in the United States lived in cities (U.S. Bureau of the Census, 1981). This flow of people led to rapid increases in density, noise, and air pollution, and crime in the cities skyrocketed. In an effort to avoid these problems, many of the middle-class residents abandoned the city for the suburbs; in some cases these people had to spend many hours traveling from their suburban home to their urban job. This flight to the suburbs led to increased problems, since the poor were trapped in the urban areas and the cities had a difficult time raising the necessary money to run services such as schools, hospitals, police and fire departments, and social services.

There are now indications that the flight from the cities may be reversing. With a severe energy crisis already on us, many people cannot afford the cost of traveling great distances to their place of employment. Thus, there is increasing urgency to understand how the urban environment affects individuals.

The one term that seems to fit almost every city is "diversity." A walk down a city street will present you with buildings of almost every architectural style imaginable and a mind-boggling array of noises, smells, and sights. Further, the number and types of people you will see will be enormous. One researcher reports that a person working in midtown Manhattan can meet 220,000 people within a 10-minute radius of his or her office (Milgram, 1970). On one hand, this diversity can be a huge barrier for human development. Cohen (1977) points out that a person can attend to only a limited amount of stimuli in his or her environment. When there are too many events occuring in the environment, people become **cognitively overloaded;** it becomes impossible to respond to each stimulus. An environment that is overloaded with stimuli is a stressful place to live. In some cases, the response to this overload is a psychological or social breakdown. Incidences of mental disease have been reported to be the highest in the busiest and most crowded parts of the city (Factor and Wildron, 1974). Crime statistics show a similar pattern.

While some people cannot cope with the overstimulation of the city, most residents do take steps to adapt to their environment. Milgram (1970, 1977) examined how people in cities respond to the overstimulation. He reports that people often give less time to each event; they deal with situations more quickly and pay less attention to details. They also filter incoming stimuli and disregard inputs that are unimportant. For example, Milgram had students walk down a street and extend a hand of friendship to people in a city or small town (Milgram, 1977). Over two-thirds of those

Cognitive overload occurs when people are bombarded by too much stimulation. The large numbers of people, wide variety of buildings, and many different noises of a modern city can cause cognitive overload and make adjustment difficult.

approached in the small town accepted a handshake, while only a third of those in the large city did. A stranger trying to be friendly was probably not a very important stimulus for many of the people in the city, and they simply ignored him or her. Cochise reported that to his surprise, the people of New York largely ignored him despite his Indian outfit and guns. We might even expect that he would receive the same treatment today were he to walk down the streets of Manhattan in an Apache garb.

Another response that Milgram noted was that city dwellers tended to depersonalize and deindividuate the other people in their environment. People are identified with and responded to as roles rather than people. Thus a person will respond to all strangers in one way, to all police officers in another way, and to all bus drivers in still another way. By placing people into categories and responding to the category, a person does not respond to everyone in a separate way. While this depersonalization may help reduce the variety of incoming stimuli, it leads to the characterization of the city dweller as cold and unfriendly. Further, the city dweller is less likely to offer help to deindividuated others. In Chapter 14, we discussed the case of Kitty Genovese, who was attacked and killed while 38 people looked on and did nothing to help. In another demonstration of the guardedness of city dwellers, Altman, Levine, and Nadien (1970) had individual students approach apartment residents in Manhattan and in a small town. The students explained that they had lost the address of a friend who lived nearby and asked to use the resident's telephone. Male students were refused entry into 86 percent of the Manhattan apartments and only 50 percent of the small-town apartments. Female students were not allowed into 40 percent of the Manhattan apartments, while only 6 percent of the small-town apartments refused them entry. We might argue that the city dwellers were doing the proper thing and looking out for their own welfare. The point, however, is that there was significantly less helping in the city, even if this is a wise course of action.

Clearly the city has both its bitter and sweet aspects. A government commission investigating French cities felt that the bad aspects far outweighed the advantages and recommended that newer cities in France not be allowed to grow beyond 200,000 (Kandell, 1977). This certainly seems to be a drastic measure. A wiser approach may be to use the knowledge we have gained through environmental research to control and direct the growth of our cities. For example, some cities have made shopping malls in downtown areas and have limited the amount of automobile traffic in these places. These steps reduce noise and air pollution in the area and give residents a rather quiet place to congregate and interact. Clearly, other actions can be taken to reduce the hazards of city living while still preserving the vitality and excitement of urban diversity.

SUMMARY

1. **Environmental psychology** examines the relationships between people and their environment. The findings from this field may help show how people can form a harmonious partnership with their environment.

2. **Territoriality** involves claiming control or ownership over a certain area or object. Humans have three types of territory: **primary territories** are owned by them and are central to their lives; **secondary territories** are not owned, but they are the focus of a strong emotional attachment; **public territories** are areas that people control only when they occupy the space.

3. **Personal space** is the area immediately around the person, over which he or she feels ownership. Unlike territory, which involves a fixed

piece of property, personal space moves with the individual. The amount of space that people consider personal is affected by the type of interaction they are engaged in, their sex, and their cultural background. Violations of personal space cause people to feel stressed and anxious.

4. Density is a physical measure of the amount of space available to a person in a particular setting. High density does not necessarily have negative effects on humans. Crowding is a psychological state that may or may not be associated with high density. Research has found that crowding results in stress, reduced task performance, and hostility.

5. Sound is a physical property caused by changes in air pressure. Noise, on the other hand, is a psychological concept that includes sound that is unpleasant, bothersome, and interferes with important activities. Exposure to loud sounds can cause physical damage to people's ears and can increase the risk of cardiovascular diseases, ulcers, and headaches. Noise that is unpredictable and uncontrollable can have negative effects on task performance and social interactions.

6. People are often unaware of air pollution because they cannot see or smell some of the most dangerous pollutants. Some studies have shown that people do not perform as well in polluted air as in clean air.

7. Weather also affects our performance and social behavior. Performance suffers in very hot and very cold conditions. Moderately high temperatures have been linked to increased aggression, although aggression declines in extremely hot conditions.

8. Much of our physical environment has been built with our own hands. Research has found that the design of buildings and rooms can influence peoples' behavior. For example, the shape and color of rooms and furniture can influence our social behaviors and personal comfort; high-rise buildings that have a lot of indefensible space are unpleasant environments for people; and residents feel more control over their lives in suite-type dormitories than in long-corridor dormitories.

9. Cities present a great deal of excitement and diversity. However, in some cases there can be too much stimulation, leading people to experience cognitive overload. Cognitive overload may cause people to become less open to social contact, and they may seem unfriendly to strangers.

SUGGESTED READINGS

The following book is about Nino Cochise:

COCHISE, C. N., and GRIFFITH, A. K. *The first hundred years of Nino Cochise.* New York: Abelard-Schuman, 1971.

ALTMAN, I., and CHEMERS, M. *Culture and environment.* Monterey, Calif.: Brooks/Cole, 1980. A very interesting discussion relating culture to the way people perceive and use their environment.

BAUM, A., and SINGER, J. (Eds.). *Advances in environmental psychology* (Vol. 3); *Energy: Psychological perspectives.* Hillsdale, N.J.: Erlbaum Associates, 1981. Presents a series of original chapters discussing the energy problem and how psychology can be used to help people conserve energy.

HOLAHAN, C. *Environmental psychology.* New York: Random House, 1982. A textbook that provides a broad view of the field of environmental psychology. Easy to read and up to date.

Journal of Social Issues, 37 (1), 1981: *Environmental stress.* This issue of the journal is devoted to the topic of environmental stress. It presents some interesting articles on stress resulting from noise, pollution, crowding, and heat.

WICKER, A. *An introduction to ecological psychology.* Monterey, Calif.: Brooks/Cole, 1979. This volume examines the area of ecological psychology, which involves studying people in their natural settings.

APPENDIX: Statistical Methods

M. ELIZABETH WETMORE

Students often complain that multiple-choice tests do not fairly measure their knowledge. They feel shortchanged, not only in their classes, but also in the entrance exams that determine whether or not they can go to college in the first place. Such tests always seem to be asking about things that students do not know, while not asking about things that they do know. An alternative is to give an open-ended test. A teacher might, for instance, ask students to write down everything that they remember about a lesson. How would students respond to such open-ended questions? Would performance on multiple-choice entrance exams be similar to performance on open-ended questions? Psychologists are now investigating these and other questions about open-ended exams. In doing so, they take advantage of statistics, a branch of mathematics used to describe data and to draw conclusions based on data. You don't have to be an expert in math to understand statistics, but you do have to learn a special vocabulary. To make statistics and their use more interesting and understandable, we will analyze data from an actual experiment on open-ended exams.

Twenty-five students from introductory psychology courses at the University of Virginia took part in an experiment investigating how students learn from textbooks (Wetmore, 1982). The students were asked to read a selection from an introductory biology textbook. This selection contained 54 ideas. The students were told to read the selection at whatever speed they felt comfortable and to do whatever they normally do when reading a homework assignment for the first time. After they were through reading, they were asked to recall in their own words everything they could remember from what they had just read. These lists were then analyzed to see how many of the 54 ideas each student recalled. Table 1 shows the number of ideas recalled by each student. Statistics can help us understand this data. We will use one branch of statistics to describe the data and then another branch to draw conclusions from the data.

DESCRIPTIVE STATISTICS

Descriptive statistics are tools for summarizing data so that the data can be more easily understood. The data may be any set of measurements taken of a group of objects, people, or events.

Frequency Distributions

A frequency distribution is one way of summarizing data; it reduces individual scores into groups of scores. To do this, we simply select a

TABLE A–1

Subject Number	Number of Ideas Recalled
1	37
2	31
3	33
4	36
5	28
6	44
7	43
8	20
9	21
10	37
11	36
12	32
13	35
14	31
15	31
16	40
17	41
18	27
19	25
20	30
21	38
22	30
23	30
24	30
25	41

Rank Order of Raw Scores			
20	30	35	40
21	30	36	41
25	31	36	41
27	31	37	43
28	31	37	44
30	32	38	
30	33		

TABLE A-3

Frequency distribution for scores in Table A-1	
Class Interval	Number of Scores in Each Interval
20–24	2
25–29	3
30–34	9
35–39	6
40–44	5

set of intervals and count how many scores fall into each one.

We can make a frequency distribution for the data presented in Table A-1 in two steps: (1) arrange (or rank order) the scores from lowest to highest as shown in Table A-2; (2) using an interval of 5, list the number of scores in each interval. These two steps produce the frequency distribution shown in Table A-3.

Such a frequency distribution can often be better understood if shown on a graph rather than in a table. The two most commonly used graphs are the frequency histogram and the frequency polygon.

Once a frequency distribution has been made, most of the work of making both a frequency histogram and a frequency polygon has been done. Histograms are made by placing the intervals along the horizontal axis and marking the frequencies along the vertical axis. A histogram for the data presented in Table A-3 can be seen in Figure A-1.

Another way of showing frequency distributions in graph form is to use a frequency polygon. Polygons are made by connecting a series of points representing the frequency of scores in each interval. A polygon for the data presented in Table A-3 can be seen in Figure A-2.

FIGURE A–1

A frequency histogram for data in Table A-3. The numbers under each bar indicate an interval of exam scores. The height of the bar indicates the number of scores (frequency) in each interval.

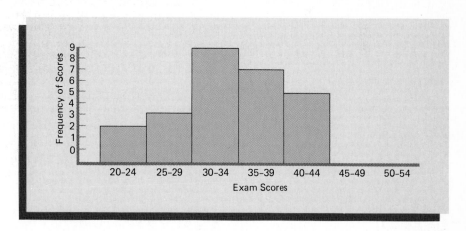

FIGURE A–2

A frequency polygon for data in Table A-3. The points represent the number of scores in each interval.

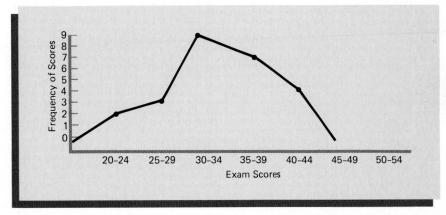

The frequency distribution, histogram, and polygon for the data presented in Table A-1 show at a glance that the scores were well below the highest possible score of 54. They ranged from the low 20s to the mid-40s, with the most frequent scores in the low 30s. Students apparently had trouble recalling all the ideas. But let's look more closely before drawing conclusions.

Measures of Central Tendency

Frequency distributions, histograms, and polygons all summarize whole distributions. Sometimes, however, single numbers are easier to compare. Statisticians therefore summarize properties of distributions with single numbers. An interesting property is a **measure of central tendency**, a score value that represents the mathematical center of a group of scores, or, to put it another way, a score that represents in some sense the "typical" score. Three different statistics are used to describe the central tendency of a distribution: the mean, the median, and the mode.

The **mean** is the most widely used measure of central tendency. It is commonly called the average and is determined by adding all the scores in the sample and dividing by the total number of scores in the sample. The mean number of ideas recalled in Table A-1 is 33.08. It was determined by adding all the students' scores to get 827 and dividing by 25 (the number of students in the sample).

The **median** is the score that divides a distribution in half. Look back at the rank ordering of scores in Table A-2. In this case the median is 32, because there are as many scores ranked above it as ranked below it. In other words, 50 percent of the scores fall above 32 and 50 percent fall below.

The **mode** is commonly called the most typical score. It is simply the score that occurs most often in a sample. You can see in Table A-2 that 30 is the most frequent score for number of ideas recalled. Therefore, 30 is the mode of this data.

Measures of Variation

Measures of central tendency do not always tell us all we need to know about a distribution. They do not tell us, for example, how different the scores are from one another; that is, they do not show variation in scores. Several distributions could have the same mean, but differ in their variation. Table A-4 shows examples for three subsets of data taken from Table A-1.

TABLE A–4

	Subset 1		Subset 2		Subset 3	
	Subject Number	Number of Ideas Recalled	Subject Number	Number of Ideas Recalled	Subject Number	Number of Ideas recalled
	1	37	6	44	11	36
	2	31	7	43	12	32
	3	33	8	20	13	35
	4	36	9	21	14	31
	5	28	10	37	15	31
Mean		33.00		33.00		33.00
Range		9.00		24.00		5.00
Variance		10.80		110.00		4.40
Standard Deviation		3.29		10.50		2.10

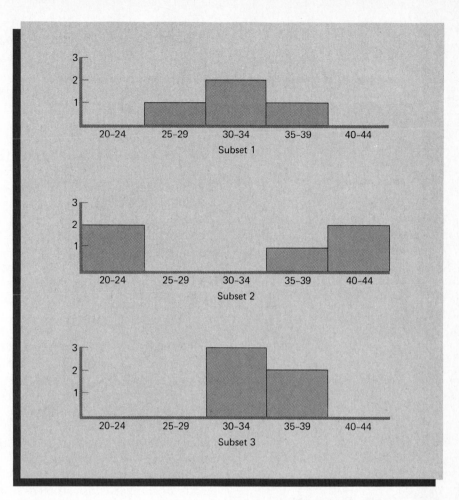

Subset 1

Subset 2

Subset 3

TABLE A–5

	d (Difference from Mean)	d (Difference squared)
37–33	4	16
31–33	−2	4
33–33	0	0
36–33	3	9
28–33	−5	25
44–33	11	121
40–33	7	49
36–33	3	9
41–33	8	64
37–33	4	16
35–33	2	4
27–33	−6	36
25–33	−8	64
31–33	−2	4
30–33	−3	9
38–33	5	25
31–33	−2	4
30–33	−3	9
43–33	10	100
20–33	−13	169
30–33	−3	9
30–33	−3	9
32–33	−1	1
21–33	−12	144
41–33	8	64
		964
	$\frac{964}{25} = 38.56$	

All three of these subsets have a mean of 33, but they differ greatly in their variation. The subjects in subset 3 have scores that are relatively close to one another, the subjects in subset 1 have scores that are slightly farther from one another, and the subjects in subset 2 have scores that are quite different from one another. The histograms in Figure A-3 show this more clearly. Three statistics are used most often to describe variation. These are called the range, the variance, and the standard deviation.

The simplest measure of variation is the **range,** the difference between the largest and smallest number in the distribution. The range for the data presented in Table A-1 is 24 ($44 - 20 = 24$).

The range uses only extreme scores. A more common measure, the **variance,** uses every score to compute a single number to summarize the variation. It is the average squared difference of each number in the sample from the mean of all numbers in the sample. To compute the variance for the data in Table A-1, we first subtract the mean of 33 from each score and square the difference. We then find the average or mean of these squared differences; this is the sum of the squared differences divided by the number of squared differences. In this case, variance of the number of ideas recalled $= \dfrac{964}{25} = 38.56$.

The **standard deviation** is simply the square root of the variance. Therefore, the standard deviation for the number of ideas recalled (Table A-5) is $\sqrt{38.56} = 6.21$. The standard deviation is often used to express how far any given score is from the mean of a set of scores. For example, in Table A-1, subjects 8 and 9, with respective scores of 20 and 21, are more than one standard deviation below the mean. Subjects 6 and 7, with respective scores of 44 and 43, are more than one standard deviation above the mean.

Subject Number	SAT Verbal Score
1	530
2	620
3	580
4	640
5	380
6	530
7	760
8	560
9	580
10	690
11	720
12	560
13	660
14	560
15	610
16	690
17	650
18	590
19	560
20	560
21	710
22	780
23	580
24	630
25	630

Mean = 614.4
Standard Deviation = 83.19

INFERENTIAL STATISTICS

Statistics can be used to organize and describe data, but they have another very important use. Psychologists often make educated guesses, or **hypotheses,** about their data. They use inferential statistics to test those hypotheses. We might, for example, try to form an hypothesis to explain why most scores in the present data were well below the total possible score of 54. One hypothesis is that the experiment used poor students. The experiment used a sample of college students, which is a subset of all college students. The hypothesis is that the sample does not represent enough good students from the population of all college students. Table A-6 provides data that allow us to test this hypothesis. The table shows SAT verbal scores for the sample of students who gave the original data in Table A-1. We can compare this sample to the national population by using a special distribution that is discussed in the next section.

Normal Distribution

When we take a large number of measurements of almost any characteristic or event, we come up with a **normal distribution,** which represents the assumption that most measurements taken of a characteristic or event will be close to average, some measurements will be a small distance from average, and few measurements will be very far from average. For example, people's heights are approximately normally distributed; most people have a height close to average, some people have a height slightly above or below average, and very few people have a height greatly above or below average. This is also true of people's weights, their IQs, and many of the behaviors studied by psychologists.

The normal distribution can be plotted as a frequency polygon called the **normal curve,** which is symmetrical and shaped like a bell. The mean, median, and mode of a normal curve have the same value, which corresponds to the highest point on the curve.

We can make a normal curve if we know the mean and standard deviation of a set of scores. The national mean for college-bound students taking the SAT verbal subtest is 424, and the standard deviation is 110. Figure A-4 shows the normal curve for the SAT verbal subtest on the College Boards Entrance Examination.

FIGURE A–4

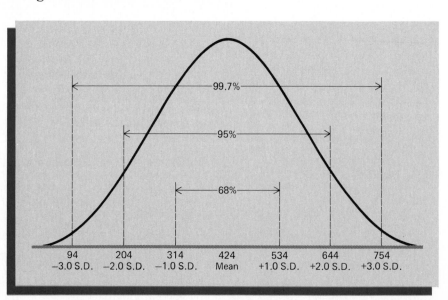

	94	204	314	424	534	644	754
	−3.0 S.D.	−2.0 S.D.	−1.0 S.D.	Mean	+1.0 S.D.	+2.0 S.D.	+3.0 S.D.

| | Area Under Normal Curve as Proportion of Total Area | | |
Standard Deviation	Area to the Left of This Value Indicates the Proportion of People Who Score *Lower* Than This Score	Area to the Right of This Value Indicates the Proportion of People Who Score *Higher* Than This Score	Area Between This Value and the Mean Indicates the Proportion of People Whose Scores Fell Between This Score and the Mean
−3.0	.001	.999	.499
−2.5	.006	.994	.494
−2.0	.023	.977	.477
−1.5	.067	.933	.433
−1.0	.159	.841	.341
−.50	.309	.691	.191
0.0	.500	.500	.000
+0.5	.691	.309	.191
+1.0	.841	1.59	.341
+1.5	.933	.067	.433
+2.0	.977	.023	.477
+2.5	.994	.006	.494
+3.0	.999	.001	.499

As shown above, 68 percent of all measurements are between one standard deviation below the mean and one standard deviation above the mean. We can see in Figure A-4 that 68 percent of all college-bound students score between 314 and 534 on the SAT verbal subtest. A more detailed listing of areas under portions of the normal curve can be found in Table A-7.

Now let's compare the scores in Table A-6 with the national scores. The mean score in Table A-6 is 614. We can see in Figure A-4 that this mean is a little over 1.5 standard deviations *above* the national mean score of 424. Table A-7 shows that only .067 of the area under the normal curve lies to the right of 1.5 standard deviations above the mean. This indicates that only 6.7 percent of college-bound students score higher than 1.5 standard deviations above the mean. The results are therefore contrary to our hypothesis. The sample was *not* made up of only poor students. In fact, the students were very good compared to the national population. The high quality of the students is further shown in the next section, which describes a way to compare each individual with the population.

Standard Scores

Often we want to know how a particular person scores in relation to other people. For example, you may have taken the SAT verbal subtest yourself and may want to know how you performed relative to the average college-bound student. To do this, you could compute your standard score and, using Table A-7, see what percentage of students scored lower and higher than you.

A **standard score** is a single number that expresses where a score lies relative to a population. For example, subject number 17 in Table A-6 got a score of 650 on the SAT verbal subtest. To compute his or her standard score, you simply subtract the mean from his or her score and divide by the standard deviation. (Recall that the national mean was 424 and the standard deviation was 110.)

Standard score for score of 650:

$$= \frac{650 - 424}{110}$$

$$= \frac{226}{110} = 2.05 \text{ standard deviation units from the mean}$$

$$= 2.05 \text{ standard score}$$

Using column one of Table A-7, we see that subject number 17 scored higher than 97.7 percent of all college-bound students. Column two indicates that only 2.3 percent scored higher, and column three indicates that 43 percent of the national population received a score falling between this subject's score and the national mean score.

By contrast, subject number 5 received a score of 380:

$$= \frac{380 - 424}{110}$$

$$= \frac{-44}{110} = -.4 \text{ standard deviations}$$

$$= -.4 \text{ standard score}$$

Using Table A-7 again, we see that subject number 5 scored higher than only 30.9 percent, 69 percent scored higher, and 19 percent of the national population received a score between this score and the national mean score.

You can use standard scores to compare each individual in Table A-6 with the national population. These comparisons will show clearly that we have no basis for saying that good students were underrepresented.

Statistical Significance

Perhaps students scored low because they did not study enough. From this we could form the hypothesis that extra study will improve performance. Table A-8 provides data for testing this hypothesis. The students who gave the data in Table A-8 read the passage, rated the importance of each idea in the passage, and then read it again before they tried to recall it. Let's call this the *experimental group*. The students who gave the data in Table A-1 read the passage once and then tried to recall it. We will call this group of students the *control group*. Students had an equal chance of being assigned to the experimental group or to the control group, and both groups were treated identically except for the different amounts of study. We can test our hypothesis about studying by comparing the data from the two groups.

One of the descriptive statistics that we discussed earlier provides a good comparison. The mean number of ideas recalled for the experimental group was 36 ideas. The mean for the control group was 33 ideas. It appears that having students study more improves comprehension and memory of ideas. But we cannot accept this without first performing a test of **statistical significance,** which determines whether the difference in the mean performance of these two groups reflects a true difference between the groups or is simply a result of sampling error. The difference would be due to **sampling error** if by chance we happened to get better readers in the experimental group than in the control group, or if we happened to get more students in the experimental group who knew a great deal about biology.

A test of statistical significance gives us a precise way to evaluate an obtained difference between sample means. To test statistical significance, we compute a test statistic that takes into account both the size

TABLE A-8

Data from Experimental Group	
Subject Number	Number of Ideas Recalled
26	32
27	41
28	40
29	43
30	35
31	39
32	34
33	36
34	28
35	40
36	37
37	41
38	44
39	37
40	41
41	25
42	30
43	47
44	42
45	39
46	25
47	31
48	27
49	26
50	42

Mean = 36.08
Standard Deviation = 6.33

of the difference in the means and the variation of the means being compared. To compute this statistic we must know not only the difference between the means, but the variation of the mean scores as well.

Standard Error of the Mean. If we draw several samples from the same population and compute the mean of each sample on some characteristic, the means of these samples will be different. Random samples drawn from a population vary simply due to chance. The **standard error of the mean** indicates the variation of a sample mean and tells how likely it is that the sample mean represents the population mean.

To determine the standard error of the mean, we simply divide the standard deviation of a sample by the square root of the number of subjects in the sample. The standard error of the mean for the data in Table A-1 is

$$\frac{6.21}{\sqrt{25}} = \frac{6.21}{5} = 1.24$$

The standard error of the mean for the data in Table A-8 is

$$\frac{6.33}{\sqrt{25}} = \frac{6.33}{5} = 1.27$$

The standard error of the mean will decrease with an increase in sample size. Thus, the mean of a large sample is more likely to be representative of the population mean.

From the standard error of the means, we can compute a **standard error of the difference between two means.** It is computed by finding the square root of the sum of the standard errors. The standard error of the difference between the means in the present experiment is

$$\sqrt{1.24 + 1.27} = \sqrt{2.5} = 1.58$$

Once we know the standard error of the difference between two means, we can compute the test statistic, the ratio of the difference between the means to the standard error of the difference between the means.

$$\text{test statistic} = \frac{\text{difference between means}}{\begin{array}{c}\text{standard error of the}\\ \text{difference between the means}\end{array}}$$

A ratio of 2.0 or more generally indicates a statistically significant difference between means, or a true difference between groups, not simply a sampling error.

A test statistic of 2.0 is selected because a value that large or larger can occur by chance less than 5 in 100 times. We treat the test statistic as a standard score. Looking at column two in Table A-7, we can see that the probability of obtaining a standard score two deviations above the mean is .023, and the chance of obtaining a standard score two standard deviations below the mean is also .023. The total probability, therefore, is .046. This means that, if we get a test statistic of 2.0, we are likely to say there is a difference between the population means (when there really isn't one) only 5 out of 100 times; 95 percent of the time we will be correct.

Recall our hypothesis that having students study more will improve their recall. This hypothesis appears to be correct. The mean of the experimental group was 36 and the mean of the control group was 33. Now, using a test statistic, let's see if this difference is statistically significant.

$$\text{test statistic} = \frac{\text{difference between means}}{\begin{array}{c}\text{standard error of the}\\ \text{difference between the means}\end{array}}$$

$$= \frac{36 - 33}{1.58} = \frac{3}{1.58} = 1.90$$

Since this value is less than 2.0, we must conclude that the difference between the means is not statistically significant. We *cannot* say with 95 percent certainty that having college students study the passage more improves their comprehension and recall of those ideas.

A nonsignificant test statistic means that we must withhold conclusion. It means that we must design more sensitive tests if we are still interested in the original hypothesis. For example, we might have another experimental group study even harder. However, in the present comparison, considerably more studying produced only three more ideas on the average. Therefore, it may be better to consider other hypotheses.

One alternative is that scores were low because students left out unimportant ideas. Deese (1981) supported this hypothesis to some extent, but he also showed that students omitted many important ideas. In fact, the data available at the present time suggest that students do not respond extremely well to open-ended questions about lessons. Apparently, they need more structure than that provided by open-ended tests.

Another question that one can ask about open-ended tests is how they relate to multiple-choice tests. We will take up this question in the next section.

Correlation

Correlation is a procedure for describing the relationship between two sets of paired scores. The sets are said to be positively correlated if high scores in one set are paired with high scores in the other set, while low scores are paired with low scores. Height and weight, for example, are positively correlated; tall people tend to weigh more, and short people tend to weigh less. The sets are said to be negatively correlated if high scores in one set are paired with low scores in the other. Reading ability and reading time, for example, are negatively correlated; more able readers require less time to read a passage. The two sets are said to be independent or uncorrelated if there is no such relationship. The number of letters in a person's last name and his or her IQ, for example, are uncorrelated; there is no relationship between these two sets of data.

We can quickly determine if two sets of scores are correlated by drawing a **scatter plot.** We place one variable (height) on the horizontal axis of a graph, and the other (weight) on the vertical axis. Then we plot a person's score on one variable along the horizontal axis and his or her score on the second variable along the vertical axis. We draw a dot where the two scores intersect. Figure A-5 shows a scatter plot of two variables that have a perfect positive correlation. Figure A-6 shows a scatter plot of two variables that have a perfect negative correlation. Figure A-7 shows a scatter plot of two variables that are totally uncorrelated.

Let's examine a scatter plot of the present data to compare SAT scores, which are based upon multiple-choice test results, with open-ended test scores. There is obviously not a perfect correlation between these two variables, but there does appear to be a slight positive correlation. Those students who recalled a larger number of ideas also tend to be those students who received a higher SAT verbal subtest score, and those students who recalled fewer ideas tend to be those students who received a lower SAT verbal subtest score.

To more precisely describe the relationship between two sets of scores, we use a **correlation coefficient,** which ranges from +1.0 to -1.0. A perfect positive correlation receives a +1.0, while a perfect negative correlation receives a -1.0. Most correlation coefficients, however, fall between

FIGURE A–5

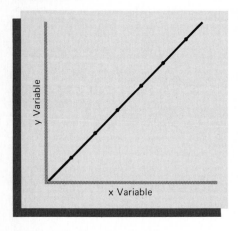

FIGURE A–6

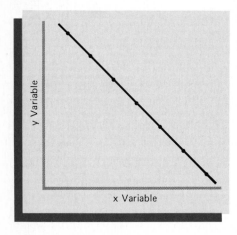

FIGURE A–7

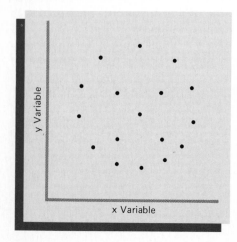

TABLE A-9

Subject Number	Number of Ideas Recalled	Difference from Mean	SAT Verbal Subtest Score	Difference from Mean
1	37	4	530	−84
2	31	−2	620	6
3	33	0	580	−34
4	36	3	640	26
5	28	−5	380	−234
6	44	11	530	−84
7	43	10	760	146
8	20	−13	560	−54
9	21	−12	580	−34
10	37	4	690	76
11	36	3	720	106
12	32	−1	560	−54
13	35	2	660	46
14	31	−2	560	−54
15	31	−2	610	−4
16	40	7	690	76
17	41	8	650	36
18	27	−6	590	−24
19	25	−8	560	−54
20	30	−3	560	−54
21	38	5	710	96
22	30	−3	780	166
23	30	−3	580	−34
24	30	−3	630	16
25	41	8	630	16

TABLE A-10

Subject Number	Product of the Differences
1	4 × −84 = −336
2	−2 × 6 = −12
3	0 × −34 = 0
4	3 × 26 = 78
5	−5 × −234 = 1170
6	11 × −84 = −924
7	10 × 146 = 1460
8	−13 × −54 = 702
9	−12 × −34 = 408
10	4 × 76 = 304
11	3 × 106 = 318
12	−1 × −54 = 54
13	2 × 46 = 92
14	−2 × −54 = 108
15	−2 × −4 = 8
16	7 × 76 = 532
17	8 × 36 = 288
18	−6 × −24 = 144
19	−8 × −54 = 432
20	−3 × −54 = 162
21	5 × 96 = 480
22	−3 × 166 × −498
23	−3 × −34 = 102
24	−3 × 16 = −48
25	8 × 16 = 128
	5152

+1.0 and −1.0 because few things are perfectly correlated. If two sets of scores are uncorrelated, the correlation coefficient will equal 0.

The Product-Moment Correlation. The most widely used index of correlation is called the **product-moment correlation** coefficient. We can compute this coefficient in five steps. Let's compute the coefficient for the present data to see if there is a relationship between number of ideas recalled in a textbook selection and SAT verbal subtest scores (Tables A-1 and A-6). First we must determine the differences of all the scores in each set from their respective means (see Table A-9). Remember that the mean number of ideas recalled was 33 and the mean SAT verbal subtest score was 614. Second, we must determine the sum of the products of the differences. See Table A-10. Third, we compute the standard deviations for both sets of scores. In this case, we have already computed them. Remember that the standard deviation for the number of ideas recalled was 6.21, and the standard deviation for the SAT verbal subtest scores was 83.19. Fourth, we multiply the product of the two standard deviations by the number of subjects in the sample.

$$25(6.21 \times 83.19) =$$

$$25(516.61) = 12915.15$$

Fifth, we divide this number into the sum of the products of the differences.

$$\frac{5152}{12915} = .399$$

As we predicted from the scatter plot in Figure A-8, this is not a perfect correlation, but it is a moderate positive correlation. For the number of

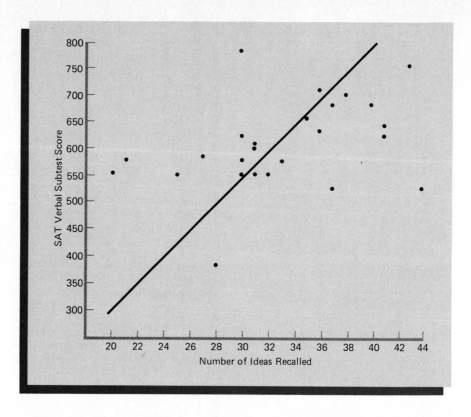

subjects in this sample, it is statistically significant at the .05 level. This means that performance on the SAT verbal subtest score does appear to be similar to performance on open-ended tests, and we are 95 percent certain that this correlation did not occur simply due to sampling error or chance.

Statistics go hand in hand with research designs. Chapter 1, for example, discusses the use of correlations with specific designs, and it goes over the logic of drawing conclusions from correlations. The more you learn about experimental designs, the more you will understand statistics. And the more you learn about statistics, the more you will understand research designs. You will do well, therefore, to refer back to this appendix when you read Chapter 1 and other chapters that take up specific research designs.

In summary, students question the accuracy of highly structured multiple-choice exams. The research reviewed here suggests, however, that going to the opposite extreme of open-ended tests is not the answer. The research suggests further that scores on very structured and very unstructured exams are correlated. Teachers are as eager as students to improve exams—if you have some ideas, speak up. Your ideas could become the bases for future experiments.

SUMMARY

1. Statistics is a branch of mathematics used by psychologists to describe data and to draw conclusions based on data.

2. Descriptive statistics are tools for summarizing data taken on a group of objects, people, or events.

3. A frequency distribution is a useful way of summarizing data. It tells how many scores fall into each of the intervals chosen to describe the data.

4. A **measure of central tendency** is a score value that represents the center of a group of scores. The **mean,** the **median,** and the **mode** are used to describe the central tendency of a distribution.

5. **Measures of variation** tell us how different the scores in a distribution are from one another. The **range,** the **variance,** and the **standard deviation** are used to describe the variation of a distribution.

6. **Inferential statistics** are used to test hypotheses made by psychologists.

7. The **normal distribution** represents the assumption that most measurements taken on a characteristic or event will be close to average, some measurements will be a small distance from average, and few measurements will be very far from average.

8. **Standard scores** are used when we want to know how a particular person scores in relation to other persons on some characteristic or event. They express the value of a score relative to the mean and the standard deviation of its distribution.

9. A **test of statistical significance** is performed to determine if the difference in the mean performance of two groups reflects a true difference between groups or is simply a result of sampling error.

10. **Correlation** is a procedure for describing the linear relationship between two sets of paired scores. A correlation coefficient tells us whether or not we can predict one measure knowing another, but does not indicate that one variable causes another.

SUGGESTED READINGS

CALFEE, R. C. *Human experimental psychology.* New York: Holt, Rinehart and Winston, 1975. Calfee teaches students to think like experimental psychologists. He immerses students in problems that force them to combine experimental psychology with statistical design and analysis.

FREEDMAN, D., PISANI, R., and PURVES, R. *Statistics.* New York: W. W. Norton and Co., Inc., 1978. Freedman et al. explain the basic ideas of statistics in nonmathematical terms through the use of real examples.

HAYS, W. L. *Statistics for the social sciences* (2nd ed.). New York: Holt, Rinehart and Winston, 1973. Hays presents a more advanced introduction to probability and statistics. This text goes into more detail than most introductory texts and places greater emphasis on the theoretical than on the computational aspects of statistics.

MOSTELLER, F., ROURKE, R. E. K., and THOMAS, G. B., JR. *Probability with statistical applications* (2nd ed.). Reading, Mass.: Addison-Wesley, 1970. Mosteller et al. explain the theory of probability and apply this theory to statistical theory. Two courses in high-school algebra are required to understand this text.

ROBINSON, P. W. *Fundamentals of experimental psychology: A comparative approach* (2nd ed.). Englewood Cliffs, N.J.: Prentice-Hall, 1981. Robinson emphasizes procedural aspects of psychological investigations. He also provides complete step-by-step examples of how to statistically analyze data from many types of experimental designs.

GLOSSARY

Abnormal behavior. Behavior may be labeled abnormal when it is unusual, causes distress to others, and makes it difficult for a person to adjust to his or her environment.

Absolute refractory period. A period after a cell has fired, during which it will not fire again—it usually lasts for about 1 millisecond.

Absolute threshold. The least amount of a certain stimulus energy that can be detected.

Accommodation. Term used by Piaget to refer to the process of adjusting one's schema to fit environmental demands. Compare with *assimilation*.

Acetylcholine (ACh). A chemical transmitter in neurons that tends to transmit fast-acting, excitatory messages.

Achievement motive (nAch). Motive to do things as rapidly and/or as well as possible.

Achievement tests. Designed to measure a person's current knowledge and skills—reflect what has been learned in the past.

Addiction. The physical dependence on a substance, so that the body develops a need for the drug. The body builds up a tolerance for a dose of the drug and needs ever-increasing doses. If the drug is not taken, people experience the painful symptoms of withdrawal, which may include headaches, cramps, nausea, uncontrollable trembling, and restlessness.

Adolescence. Extends from about age 12 to the late teens, is a time of passage from childhood to adulthood.

Affective disorders. A group of disorders involving problems with emotions and mood. People are said to be suffering from an affective disorder when their moods, such as depression, take over and they have trouble functioning because of them.

Affiliation motive. Motive or desire to associate with, be around other people.

Afterimage. Visual experience that continues after the stimulus has ceased; occurs because some activity continues in the retina after seeing the stimulus. The afterimage consists of the opposite color of what was seen in the original stimulus: blue for yellow, red for green, black for white.

Aggression cues. Stimuli that a person has learned to associate with aggression (examples are guns or knives); when these cues are present in the environment they tend to elicit aggression.

Aggression motive. Motive, whether innate or learned, to attack objects or other organisms.

Alcoholics. People who are addicted to alcohol; they have an uncontrollable urge to drink, and, because of increasing tolerance, must continue to increase their consumption of alcohol.

Allele. A single gene may occur in one of several different forms called alleles; alleles may be dominant or recessive.

Alternate states of consciousness. Mental states that differ, as measured by a specific pattern of physiological and subjective responses.

Amnesia. A selective forgetting of past events. Some forms of amnesia are caused by physical injuries, such as a blow to the head. *Psychogenic amnesia* means that the cause of the memory loss is stress rather than physical injury.

Amniocentesis. Process in which fluid is taken from a mother's womb to test for Down's syndrome and other genetic disorders.

Amplitude. Distance between the top and bottom of a sound wave; amplitude increases as sounds get louder.

Anal stage. During second and third years, the main focus of pleasure shifts from the mouth to the anal area. A major battle between child and parents occurs during this stage over the issue of toilet training.

Analytic introspection. Method used in structuralism; a way of isolating the elementary sensations of which experiences are made.

Androgens. Male hormones secreted by the testes that increase male sex drive and influence the development of secondary sex characteristics.

Anorexia nervosa. A condition in which a person loses his or her appetite, eats little, and slowly begins to starve.

Antianxiety drugs. Minor tranquilizers that reduce anxiety and tension without causing drowsiness or a loss of mental alertness. Most popular are Valium, Librium, and Miltown.

Antidepressant drugs. Drugs that work by lifting the person's spirits and increasing his or her activity level. Two examples are Tofranil and Elavil.

Antipsychotic drugs. Major tranquilizers that are used to calm and relieve the delusions of schizophrenics. Two most commonly used are Thorzaine and Stlezine.

Antisocial personality disorder. Disorder in which people perform violent and hurtful acts without the least bit of guilt or regret, are incapable of forming close relationships, and are manipulative and insincere.

Anvil. One of three small bones in the middle ear, it transmits sounds from the eardrum to the inner ear.

Anxiety disorders. A group of conditions in which people feel anxiety that is far out of proportion to the situations they are in; their responses interfere with normal daily functioning.

Apgar scoring system. Scale used to assess the condition of newborns; low scores show possible neurological damage.

Aptitude tests. Try to predict capacity for future performance.

Aqueous humor. Clear fluid that carries nourishment to the cornea of the eye.

Ascending nerves. Carry sensory information up the spinal cord to specific areas of the brain.

Assimilation. Term used by Piaget to refer to the process of interpreting events in a way that fits existing ideas (or schema). Compare with *accommodation*.

Attachment. Tendency of youngsters to seek closeness to certain people.

Attention. Paying mind to important stimuli and ignoring irrelevant ones; a selective process in memory.

Attitudes. Learned, relatively enduring feelings about objects, events, or issues.

Attribution. The process of inferring characteristics of people from their observable behavior; our way of explaining the behavior of others.

Autokinetic effect. The tendency for a stationary light viewed against darkness to look as if it is moving; the light seems to glide, jerk, and swoop through space.

Autonomic nervous system. Functional subdivision of the nervous system; regulates glands and organs. Divided into sympathetic and parasympathetic divisions.

Aversive conditioning. Type of behavior therapy often used to break bad habits such as smoking and drinking; in this type of therapy the person receives unpleasant consequences for undesired behavior. This may mean taking a drug (Antibuse) that will make them sick if they drink, or making them smoke so much and so quickly that they become sick.

Avoidance training. Occurs when a subject learns to make a response to avoid a negative reinforcer.

Axon. Long fiber that carries neural impulses away from the cell body of the neuron to the terminal branches to be passed on to other neurons.

Axon terminal. A tiny knob at the end of an axon's terminal branch.

Barbiturates. Depressant drugs that slow the body functions, reduce anxiety, and have a relaxing effect.

Basal ganglia. Four masses of gray matter in the brain that control background muscle tone and large, general muscle movements—part of the motor system.

Basilar membrane. Located inside the cochlea in the inner ear, it is attached to the oval window at one end and the tip of the cochlea at the other end. Vibrations in the oval window cause hair cells on the basilar membrane to move. When these hair cells are bent, they send nerve impulses to the brain that are experienced as sound.

Behavioral assessment. Assessment by means of examining a person's present behavior to predict future actions. Can also be used to assign traits to people.

Behavioral medicine. New field in medicine; focus is on the effects of stress and better ways of dealing with it.

Behavioral sinks. Develop as a result of overcrowding; they aggravate all forms of pathology that can be found within a group.

Behaviorism. Approach to psychology, based on the premise that human behavior can be described by focusing only on the observable stimulus and response.

Binocular cues. Cues to depth perception that we use when we are looking with both eyes.

Binocular disparity. This is the experience of seeing a different view from each of our eyes; two views are fused by the brain and produce depth perception.

Biofeedback. Technique that provides people with feedback on their physiological functions (such as heart rate and blood pressure) so that they can learn to control these functions and achieve a more relaxed state.

Biofeedback therapy. A type of therapy designed to help people control their physiological functions without the use of drugs or other biotherapy techniques. Helps people reduce tension and stress, reduce phobic reactions, and control headaches. Has also been combined with other psychotherapies. See also *biofeedback*.

Biotherapy. The use of drugs, surgery, or electric shock, with or without accompanying psychotherapy, to induce behavior change.

Bipolar cells. Cells in the retina, connected to rods and cones; actively participate in the process of coding or interpreting the information contained in light. One-to-one connections to cones; one-to-many connections to rods.

Bipolar disorder. A disorder in which the person alternates between manic and depressive stages. Often the extremes of each mood state appear for only a short time and the person generally behaves normally when between states.

Blind spot. Area in the retina that is blind because it is where the optic nerve exits from the retina.

Body language. Communication through body movement.

Boilermaker's deafness. Partial hearing loss caused by spending long periods of time around loud noises (above 85 decibels).

Bone conduction. Another way that sound is transmitted; when a person speaks, the jaw bones conduct vibrations to the cochlea. We hear our own voice through bone-conducted and air-conducted sounds; we hear others' voices only through air-conducted sounds.

Brainstem. Midbrain and hindbrain combined.

Broca's aphasia. Speech that is slow, labored, and slightly distorted; caused by injury to Broca's area in the cortex.

Calories. Units of energy produced when food is oxidized or burnt by the body.

Case history. Method used in psychology that looks in depth at a few individuals or at the effects of a single event.

Cataracts. Widespread disease affecting vision; a condition characterized by cloudy lenses; can result in blindness if lenses are not removed surgically.

Catecholamines. Chemical transmitters in neurons that tend to transmit slow-acting, inhibitory messages.

Catharsis. Release of tension through aggression.

Cerebellum. Part of the hindbrain; made up of two wrinkled hemispheres. Coordinates the force, range, and rate of body movements.

Cerebral cortex (cerebrum). Two wrinkled hemispheres that are part of the forebrain; governs our most advanced human capabilities, including abstract reasoning and speech.

Chemical transmitters. Chemicals that carry messages between neurons; some are excitatory, some inhibitory.

Chemotherapy. Treatment of disorders through the use of drugs; a form of biotherapy.

Chromosomes. Threadlike chains of genes; humans have 23 pairs of chromosomes.

Chunking. Process of grouping elements such as letters or words into units (or chunks) that function as wholes. Memory span consists of 7 ± 2 chunks.

Clairvoyance. The perception of an object, action, or event by means of ESP.

Classical conditioning. The process by which an originally neutral stimulus comes to elicit a response that was originally given to another stimulus. It takes place when the neutral stimulus is repeatedly paired with the other stimulus.

Client-centered therapy. Created by Carl Rogers, aimed at providing the proper setting for the self-growth of the client. Since the client (rather than the therapist) determines what will be discussed during therapy, it is referred to as client-centered therapy.

Clinical psychology. Subfield of psychology dedicated to the diagnosis and treatment of emotional and behavioral disorders.

Cochlea. Part of the inner ear; a tube coiled in on itself about three turns, like a spiral around a central core. Contains the basilar membrane inside it.

Cognitive dissonance. State that occurs when a person's attitudes, beliefs, and behaviors are in conflict. In order to relieve the dissonance, the person will try to change the cognitions so that they will again be in agreement.

Cognitive learning theory. Attempts to explain the function of thought processes in learning.

Cognitive map. A mental picture. In the Tolman and Honzik experiment described in Chapter 5, the rats had learned a cognitive map of the maze.

Cognitive overload. An inability to respond to stimuli because there are too many events occurring in the environment.

Cognitive psychology. Subfield of psychology concerned with the mental events that intervene between stimuli and responses.

Cohabitation. Relationship between two unmarried people who live together.

Cold spots. Areas on the skin where only cold is felt, even if stimulated by a warm object (when this occurs it is called *paradoxical cold*).

Colorblindness. Inability to see or distinguish between colors. There are several types of color blindness: red-green, blue-yellow, and total color blindness.

Community psychology. Subfield of psychology dedicated to promoting mental health at the community level; seeks to prevent and treat psychological problems by working to evaluate and to improve community organizations.

Complex tones. Sounds containing many frequencies.

Compulsion. Irrational behavior or ritual that people cannot control; often they do not know why they need to do this. See also *obsession*, which involves thought rather than behavior.

Concrete operational stage. One of Piaget's stages of cognitive development; lasts from 7 years to 12 years of age. Main theme is extending mental operations from concrete objects to purely symbolic terms.

Conditioned response (CR). A learned response to a conditioned stimulus (CS). Usually a less strong response than an unconditioned response (UR).

Conditioned stimulus (CS). Stimulus to which a subject learns to respond, through repeated pairings with an unconditioned stimulus (US).

Cones. Light receptors in the eye; located mostly in the fovea, are best for seeing details, and are responsible for color vision.

Conscious element of personality. According to Freud, this includes whatever the person is perceiving or thinking at the moment.

Consciousness. The perception of what passes in a person's own mind (Locke's definition).

Continuous reinforcement schedule. Subject receives a reinforcer for every correct response.

Control group. The group of subjects in an experiment that is treated exactly the same as the experimental group(s) except that the control group is not exposed to the independent variable and thus serves as the basis for comparison.

Conversion disorder. One of the somatoform disorders, usually involving one specific symptom. The most common symptoms are paralysis of a limb, loss of sensation in a part of the body, blindness, and deafness. There is no organic basis to this disorder.

Conformity. Occurs when a person changes his or her behavior or attitudes as a result of real or imagined group pressures, despite personal feelings to the contrary.

Cornea. Part of the eye, it is transparent, shaped like a crystal ball.

Corpus callosum. Large cable of nerve fibers that connects the two cerebral hemispheres.

Correlation. A measure of the extent to which variables change together. If two variables increase and decrease at the same time, they are positively correlated; if one increases while the other decreases, they are negatively correlated. This does not necessarily indicate a cause-and-effect relationship between the variables, however.

Correlation coefficient. Tells whether or not one can predict one measure knowing another, but does not indicate that one variable *causes* another.

Counseling and school psychology. Subfield of psychology that helps people with social, educational, and job or career adjustments.

Critical period. A stage of development during which the organism must have certain experiences or it will not develop normally.

Cross-sectional research. Research in which people of all different ages are tested in various ways; compare with *longitudinal research*, in which the one group is tested continually over a period of time, at different ages.

Crowding. Feeling or psychological state that often, but not always, accompanies high density.

Crystallized intelligence. Specific mental skills, such as one's vocabulary.

Dancing reflex. Causes infants to prance with their legs in a "tip-toe" stepping motion when they are held upright with feet touching a surface.

Dark adaptation. Downward adjustment of sensitivity to light; occurs in the rods when one enters a dark room, for example.

Decibel. Unit for measuring loudness;

each tenfold increase in sound level adds 10 decibels.

Defense mechanisms. Ways of coping with anxiety; an unconscious distortion of reality in order to defend against anxiety. See displacement; projection; rationalization; reaction formation; repression; sublimation; and suppression.

Deindividuation. Occurs in groups when people tend to lose their personal identity and assume the identity of the group.

Delta waves. High voltage, extremely low-frequency brain waves characteristic of stage-4 sleep.

Delusions. Irrational beliefs that are held in spite of contrary evidence, that have no base in reality. For example, the delusion of grandeur is the belief that the person is special or different from other people (one may think one is Napoleon or Joan of Arc, for instance).

Demand characteristics. Elements in a questionnaire or experiment that communicate what behavior is expected from the subjects.

Dendrites. Short fibers extending out from the body of a neuron, which receive impulses from other neurons and carry them to the cell body.

Density. A measure of the number of people in a given area. Not to be confused with crowding, which is a psychological state rather than a physical measure.

Deoxyribonucleic acid (DNA). Controls the way in which protein chains are built, and, thus, contain the basic blueprints for life; genes are made up of DNA.

Dependent variable. The variable that is measured in an experiment.

Depolarization. Occurs when a neuron is sending or receiving a neural impulse.

Depressants. Drugs that slow body functions or calm nervous excitement; examples are alcohol, nicotine, and heroin.

Depression. A disorder in which there is a loss of interest in most activities, including eating or sex; lack of concentration; inability to sleep. May lead to suicide in its extreme forms. See also *bipolar disorder*.

Descending nerves. Carry commands down the spinal cord to move muscles.

Descriptive statistics. Tools for summarizing data taken of a group of objects, people, or events.

Development. A process by which the genes that an organism inherits from its parents come to be expressed as specific physical and behavioral characteristics.

Developmental psychology. Subfield of psychology that examines the function of age on behavior. Examines the age at which people should be performing certain behaviors and how events that occur at various ages affect behavior.

Difference threshold. Smallest difference in intensity that can be noticed between two stimuli.

Discrimination. (1) Occurs when subjects learn to respond only to certain stimuli, but not to other, similar stimuli.

Discrimination. (2) Negative, often aggressive, behavior aimed at the target of prejudice.

Displaced aggression. Taking out one's anger and/or frustration on someone or something other than the actual cause of one's anger.

Displacement. A defense mechanism that involves redirecting an emotion from the person who caused it to another, safer or more available, target.

Dissociative disorders. Characterized by "tuning out" or dissociating a part of the person from the situation at hand. It is almost as if part of the person has split off and taken on its own identity.

Door-in-the-face approach. Persuasive technique based on the fact that people who at first refuse a large request will be more likely after that to comply with a smaller request.

Doppler shift. Occurs as cars zoom by on a racetrack; as they go by, the engine sound drops sharply to a lower pitch. Sound waves bunch up as cars approach on a racetrack and spread out as cars speed away. The bunched-up waves have a shorter distance between their wave crests (higher frequency); the spread-out waves have a longer distance between their wave crests (lower frequency).

Double-bind conflict. Results when children receive contradictory messages from their parents, messages that create a "no-win" situation for them—no matter what they do, they are wrong.

Double-blind control. Procedure used in an experiment in which neither subject nor experimenter is aware of how the independent variable is being manipulated.

Double helix. Model of the structure of DNA molecules, similar to a spiral staircase, the steps of which contain a genetic code.

Down's syndrome. Disorder characterized by mental retardation and altered physical appearance; caused by genetic mutation that adds an extra chromosome to the twenty-first pair, giving the child 47 chromosomes.

Dream interpretation. Part of Freud's technique of psychoanalysis; involves helping clients to understand the latent content of their dreams, which represents the repressed feelings that are being expressed.

Dreams. Series of images, thoughts, and emotions that occur during sleep.

Drive. A tension or state that results when a need is not met; it compels the organism to satisfy the need.

DSM III. Stands for Diagnostic and Statistical Manual, third edition, which was published in 1979. It is one of the most commonly used systems for classifying abnormal behavior, and was developed by the American Psychiatric Association.

Dualism. The theory that the mind and brain are separate entities. (See also *monism.*)

Dyspareunia. A sexual disorder in which females experience pain during intercourse.

Ear canal. Tube-like passage that funnels sound to the eardrum.

Eardrum. A fine membrane stretched over the inner end of the ear canal; vibrates when sound waves strike it.

Ego. According to Freud, a second dimension of personality, which works to control the impulses of the id; tries to satisfy the desires of the id by dealing with the environment.

Electra complex. According to Freud, during the phallic stage girls discover that they are biologically inferior to boys because they lack a penis. They envy their father's penis and become attracted to him, fantasizing about having a male baby by their father.

Electroconvulsive therapy (ECT). A technique of biotherapy in which electric shock is administered to the patient's brain, causing epileptic-like convulsions. Has been shown to have short-term benefits for those suffering from depressive disorders.

Electromagnetic spectrum. Forms the entire range of wavelengths of electromagnetic radiation; wavelengths corresponding to visible colors cover only a small part of this spectrum.

Embryo. Term for a human organism from the third week through the eighth week in the uterus.

Emotions. Affective stages or feelings, accompanied by physiological changes, that often influence behavior.

Encode. To select and represent information in a specific form (verbally, visually) in memory.

Encounter group (also called sensitivity group). Aims at expanding personal awareness and growth rather than treating emotional disorders. Such groups try to rid people of their interpersonal "hang-ups." Variations include marathon groups and nude encounter groups.

Endocrine system. Major coordinating system that regulates body chemistry.

Engineering psychology. Subfield of psychology that is concerned with making human contact with tools and machines as comfortable and as error free as possible.

Environmental psychology. Subfield of psychology that analyzes how behavior is influenced by environmental factors such as architecture, weather, space, crowding, noise, and pollution.

Episodic memory. A person's memories about events, including the time and place they occurred.

Equilibrium. Sense of overall body orientation (for example, the difference between standing upright or tilting backwards).

Escape training. Occurs when, through the use of negative reinforcement, a subject learns to make a response to remove a stimulus (such as a shock).

Estrogen. Female sex hormone. The level of estrogen is at its highest during the period of ovulation, and determines the onset of menstruation and the period of fertility. Estrogen also influences the development of secondary sex characteristics.

Ethologists. Scientists who study animal behavior in natural settings.

Experiment. An investigation in which a researcher directly manipulates one variable while measuring the effects on some other variable.

Experimental psychology. Subfield of psychology that examines the behaviors and cognitions (thoughts) that are related to learning, memory, perception, motivation, and emotion.

Experimenter bias. Expectations on the part of the person running an experiment that subjects will behave in a certain way—these behaviors can affect the subjects as well as the perceptions of the experimenter.

Extinction. A gradual falling off or decrease in a response when the conditioned stimulus (CS) is repeatedly presented alone, without the unconditioned stimulus (US). In operant conditioning, a falling off of a response when it is no longer followed by a reinforcer.

Extrasensory perception (ESP). The reception of information by means other than our usual senses of hearing, sight, taste, touch, and smell.

Family therapy. A type of psychotherapy that involves the whole family, rather than just one member of it, since it is often the family system as a whole that can create stress and contribute to the development of psychological disorders.

Farsightedness. Occurs when an eye is flattened in shape, like a vertical egg; farsighted people see far objects well, but see near objects poorly.

Fear. Reaction to a specific danger in the environment.

Fetus. Human organism from the third month through to the time of birth.

Field experiment. An experiment performed in a natural setting rather than in the controlled setting of the laboratory.

Fight-or-flight response. Response of the sympathetic division of the autonomic nervous system, involves increased oxygen consumption, respiratory rate, heart rate, blood pressure, and muscle tension.

Figure. An object standing out against a background or against its surroundings.

Figure-ground reversal (or multistable perception). Occurs when figure and ground in a picture suddenly reverse; what was seen as figure is seen as background, and vice versa.

Fissure of Rolando (central fissure). One of three fissures of the cerebral cortex.

Fissure of Sylvius (lateral fissure). One of three fissures in the cerebral cortex.

Fixed-interval schedule. Reinforces the first response made after a certain time interval (after 5 minutes, or after 2 weeks). Produces a slow rate of responding immediately after a reinforcer is received, building up to a high rate of response as the end of the time interval is reached.

Fixed-ratio schedules. Reinforce the first response after a certain number of responses have been made. Produces a fast, steady rate of responding.

Fluid intelligence. General mental skills, such as the ability to make inferences, or deductive reasoning.

Foot-in-the-door approach. Persuasive technique that gets people to agree first to a small request, then later they are more willing to agree to a second request.

Forebrain. The part of the brain that develops from the top core of the embryo brain; contains the hypothalamus, thalamus, and the cerebrum.

Forensic psychology. Subfield of psychology concerned with behaviors that relate to our legal system—forensic psychologists work with judges and lawyers who are trying to improve the reliability of witnesses and jury decisions; also consulted on the mental competency of accused people.

Forgetting. An inability to remember or retrieve information from memory.

Formal operational stage. One of Piaget's stages of cognitive development; lasts from about 13 years of age through adulthood. Main theme is the ability to consider many possible solutions to a problem and the ability to systematically test those possibilities.

Fovea. Center area of the retina where vision is best; contains most of the cones on the retina.

Free association. Freud's method of having patients express every thought (no matter how unimportant or irrelevant) that came into their mind during the therapy session.

Free association test. Procedure in which a person looks at, or listens to, a target word, and then reports other words that come to mind.

Frequency distribution. Tells how many scores fall into each of the intervals chosen to describe the data.

Frequency histogram. Way to show frequency distribution in graph form; intervals are placed along the horizontal axis, frequencies along the vertical axis.

Frequency of sound waves. Number of wavecrests that occur in a second. Changes in pitch correspond to changes in frequency.

Frequency polygon. Way to show frequency distribution in graph form; line graph connecting a series of points representing the frequency of scores in each interval.

Frontal lobe. One of four lobes in the cerebral cortex; receives sensory impulses after they have been processed by other lobes and sends out commands to muscles to make voluntary movements.

Fugue. Involves loss of memory and also physical flight, in which the person wanders away from his or her home for a matter of an hour or, in some cases, for years.

Functionalism. An approach to psychology that emphasizes the function of thought; led to important applications in education and the founding of educational psychology, a subfield of psychology.

Frustration. Basically, the result of being blocked from getting what you want when you want it.

Functional fixedness. A kind of negative set that reduces our ability to learn new uses of something that has served a specific function in the past.

Fundamental attribution error. Attributing an attitude based only on a person's behavior failing to give sufficient weight to the situation in which that behavior occurred.

Gametes. Sex cells; female gamete is an ovum, male gamete is a sperm. Each gamete has 23 chromosomes; ovum and sperm combine to form a zygote.

Gender identity disorder. A disorder that occurs in childhood, when a child rigidly adopts the role and outlook of the opposite sex.

General adaptation syndrome. Stress response noted by Hans Selye, occurs in three phases—alarm reaction, stage of resistance, and stage of exhaustion.

Generalization. See *stimulus generalization, response generalization.*

Generalized anxiety disorder. A disorder in which people experience overwhelming anxiety, but cannot identify its source.

Genes. The basic units of heredity. Located on the chromosomes.

Genetics. The study of how traits are inherited.

Genital stage. Begins at puberty with the start of sexual tension. Basic goals are to marry, raise a family, and become involved in a life's work.

Genotype. Unique set of genes that we inherit from our parents.

Gestalt psychology. German school of psychology based on the premise that we experience wholes, or gestalts, rather than separate sensations.

Gestalt therapy. Developed by Fritz Perls, proposes that unconscious thoughts and emotions (background) may lead to behaviors (figure) that are inappropriate to the situation. Encourages people to take responsibility for their actions in the present, while understanding the emotions that are influencing them.

Glaucoma. Eye disease that causes pressure to build up inside the eye; most common cause of blindness.

Glove anesthesia. People with this symptom report losing all sensation in a hand, although they have normal sensation in the arm. This is physically impossible given the system of nerves in the hand and arm; glove anesthesia is a conversion disorder.

Glucoreceptors. Cells in the hypothalamus that monitor the glucose content of the blood. If the blood is low in glucose, the glucoreceptors send out signals that cause hunger and motivate us to eat.

Gonads. Reproductive organs that secrete sex hormones. Called ovaries in females, testes in males. Sex hormones control ovulation, pregnancy, and the menstrual cycle in females, and the production of sperm in males, as well as regulating secondary sex characteristics in both sexes.

Grammar. A set of rules for combining language symbols to form sentences.

Grasp reflex. Causes infants to close their fingers tightly around an object that touches the palm.

Ground. The background or surroundings against which an object stands out.

Group. Two or more persons who are interacting with one another in such a manner that each person influences and is influenced by each other person.

Group polarization effect. Groups tend to polarize people and move them to believe more strongly in the position that they first held.

Group therapy. Involves 1 (sometimes 2) therapists and from 6 to 12 clients; clients receive feedback from others in the group as well as from the therapist. Many different therapeutic techniques may be used in group therapy.

Groupthink. Occurs when group members become so concerned with reaching agreement of all members of the group that they fail to critically evaluate their ideas.

Growth hormone. Secreted by the pituitary gland, controls development of the skeleton; too little causes dwarfism, too much, giantism.

Hallucination. Involves having a sensory experience without the external stimuli that would have caused it. Hallucinations can involve vision, hearing, taste, touch, and smell, but the most common types involve people "hearing" voices that are not there.

Hallucinogens. Drugs such as LSD, STP, mescaline, and peyote, which cause people to see visions and illusions.

Hammer. One of three small bones in the middle ear, transmits sounds from the eardrum to the inner ear.

Hedonic relevance. Refers to the degree to which an actor's behavior is rewarding or costly to the observer.

Hertz. One cycle per second of a sound wave.

Hierarchy. An organization that arranges information into levels of categories and subordinate categories.

Hindbrain. The part of the brain that develops from the bottom core in the embryonic neural tube; contains the medulla, pons, and cerebellum.

Holophrastic speech. Use of single words to express phrases. For example, "out" might mean "I want to go out."

Homeostasis. The attempt by the body to maintain a constant internal state.

Homosexuality. The sexual desire for those of the same sex as oneself.

Hormones. Chemical messengers released by the glands into the bloodstream. Either directly change their target tissue or cause it to release other hormones that change tissues elsewhere in the body.

Humanistic psychology. Movement formed by Carl Rogers, Abraham Maslow, and Rollo May which rejects Freudian view of people; argues that people are basically good and worthy of respect; stresses the creative aspect of people in reaching their true potential.

Hypnagogic images. Hallucinations that occur during the drowsy interval before sleep.

Hypnosis. A state of consciousness induced by the words and actions of a hypnotist, whose suggestions are readily accepted by the subject.

Hypothalamus. Part of the forebrain; controls body temperature and the rate at which we burn fat and carbohydrates, among other functions.

Hypothesis. An idea that is tested experimentally; an assumption that is based on theory.

Id. According to Freud, part of the personality made up of instinctual drives that serve as the basic motivation for all our behavior.

Identification. Process of acquiring personality and social behaviors by taking on characteristics of others.

Identity crisis. Term used by Erikson to describe what occurs during adolescence; refers to the search at this age for an identity, which involves trying out and testing different roles.

Imitation. Acquisition of knowledge and behavior by watching other people act and then doing the same thing ourselves.

Impotence. A sexual disorder in which males are unable to have an erection or maintain one long enough for ejaculation.

Imprinting. Attachment formed by duckling for almost any moving object that it first sees (usually, of course, its mother); imprinting occurs during a *critical period* of the first 14 hours to 2 days of life.

Indefensible spaces. Areas in an apartment complex that are not open to observation, such as enclosed stairways and alleys; such areas invite intruders and breed crime.

Independent variable. The variable that is manipulated in an experiment.

Industrial psychology. Subfield of psychology concerned with selecting, training, and managing employees.

Infantile autism. Infants who from a very early age are withdrawn, do not react to others, and become attached to inanimate objects rather than to people.

Inferential statistics. Used to test hypotheses made by psychologists.

Informational pressure. A type of influence a group has, based on the group's value as a source of information.

Insanity. A legal term, not a psychological one. Based on the McNaghten rule, which says that a person must be able to determine right from wrong at the time of the crime before he or she can be judged responsible and therefore guilty. Someone who has been judged incapable of determining right from wrong will be found not guilty by reason of insanity.

Insight. The discovery of relationships that lead to the solution of a problem. Insight learning is the sudden and irreversible learning of a solution to a problem.

Instincts. Innate or inborn predispositions to act in specific ways.

Intelligence. The capacity to learn.

Intelligence quotient (IQ). Mental age divided by chronological age and multiplied by 100.

Interaction distance. Amount of space between people in various situations; differs with the relationship between people and the kind of interaction they're engaged in.

Interference theory. The theory that we forget information because other information gets in the way. See also *proactive inhibition, retroactive inhibition.*

Internalization. The process of bringing behavior under the control of inner, personal standards that make people obey rules even if there are no external restraints.

Interview. Assessment technique that involves direct questioning of a person. Unstructured interview consists of planned questions to start, but interviewer is free to develop the conversation as he wishes. Structured interview consists of a set of specific questions asked according to a set plan.

Iris. Flat, doughnut-shaped network of muscles behind the aqueous humor of the eye.

Key-word method. Mnemonic system of using imagery to learn foreign vocabulary; consists of forming an image that will act as a link between the key word and the other word we want to remember.

Kinesis. The study of body language, or communication through body movement.

Laboratory experiment. An experiment performed in a controlled environment created for the experiment.

Latency stage. Lasts from sixth year to puberty. Children lose interest in sex-related activities and focus energy on schoolwork and hobbies, among other things.

Latent content of dreams. A hidden content determined by unconscious impulses. Freud says the latent content of dreams often involves an unacceptable desire that would create pain or anxiety if it were expressed directly, so it is disguised in a dream.

Latent learning. Refers to learning that does not show itself immediately in performance.

Law of brightness constancy. States that we see an object's brightness as constant when the amount of light striking it changes.

Law of nearness or proximity. One

of the Gestalt laws of organization; states that we group elements that are close together.

Law of shape constance. States that we see an object's shape as constant when the object's slant changes, or when we view it from a different angle.

Law of similarity. One of the Gestalt laws of organization; states that we group elements that are similar, or look alike.

Law of size constancy. States that we see an object's size as constant even if the object's distance from us changes.

Leader. The person in a group who has the most amount of influence.

Learned helplessness. A response to prolonged stress; the feeling that one's actions do not affect one's environment or what happens to one. Can lead to apathy and depression.

Learning. The process by which experience or practice results in a relatively permanent change in what one is capable of doing.

Learning set. Occurs when one's previous experience makes one ready to solve a particular type of problem.

Lens. Part of the eye that is located directly behind the pupil; helps the cornea focus light onto the back of the eye.

Libido. Energy force that propels people to satisfy the drive for survival (includes eating, drinking, and sexual activity).

Light adaptation. Upward adjustment in sensitivity to light; occurs in the cones when one suddenly goes from a dark room into bright sunlight, for example.

Limbic system. Functional subdivision of the nervous system; controls emotions, memories, and goal-directed behavior.

Linear perspective. Monocular cue to depth; artists use it to create the impression of depth in their paintings. See Figure 3–20 for an example.

Locus of control. According to Rotter, people learn general expectancies about whether the source of control of what happens to them is outside them or inside them. Internals believe they control their own fate; externals believe luck and chance control their fate.

Longitudinal fissure. One of three fissures in the cerebral cortex; separates the two cerebral hemispheres.

Longitudinal research. Research in which the same person or group of people is tested over a period of time. An example would be studying the same group of people from their birth until they were in their twenties. Compare with *cross-sectional research*, in which a number of people of different ages are tested at one time.

Long-term memory. Holds information that is transferred from short-term memory; it can last a lifetime.

Mania. A disorder in which people feel full of energy, but find it difficult to stay with any one project for long, are easily distracted, have an increased sex drive, and need less sleep than usual. See also *bipolar disorder*.

Manifest content of dreams. The portion of the dream that the person remembers. Contrast with latent content, which is the hidden element determined by impulses of which the person is unaware.

Mantra. A secret word, sound, or phrase used in Transcendental Meditation.

Masturbation. The self-manipulation of one's genitals.

Maturation. The unfolding of genetically determined abilities.

Mean. Often called the average; is determined by adding all the scores in a sample and dividing by the total number of scores in the sample.

Measure of central tendency. Score value that represents the mathematical center of a group of scores.

Median. The score that divides a distribution in half—there are as many scores ranked above it as below it.

Meditation. A state of consciousness similar to hypnosis, except that the hypnotist's authority is transferred to the meditators themselves.

Medulla. Lowest part of the hindbrain; slender tube housing nerve centers that control breathing, heartbeat, and posture.

Membrane potential. An electric tension that exists in a neuron between the cell's inside and outside environment. Also called *polarization*.

Memory. A system that allows people to retain information over time.

Memory span. The number of items that we can read through one time and then recall in sequence with no mistakes.

Memory trace. The change that occurs as a result of memorizing.

Menarche. The beginning of menstruation, which marks the onset of puberty for girls.

Mental sets. A readiness to view a problem in a particular way—a readiness to see certain relationships.

Metabolic rate. Rate at which food is transformed by the body into energy.

Midbrain. The part of the brain that develops from the middle core of the embryo brain; contains the reticular formation.

Minnesota Multiphasic Personality Inventory (MMPI). One of the most popular personality questionnaires, used by clinicians. Designed to identify specific psychological disorders. Consists of 550 statements to which people can respond true, false, or cannot say. Aimed at identifying 10 different disorders.

Mnemonics. Systems created to aid memory; examples are the key-word method and verbal mediation.

Mode. Often called the most typical scores, it is the score that occurs most often in a sample.

Modeling. Used as a therapeutic technique to teach new behaviors or strengthen existing ones. Also used to reduce a number of phobias, by showing the model interacting with the feared object.

Monism. The theory that the mind and brain are one organic whole. (See also *dualism*.)

Monocular cues. Cues to depth perception that operate even when only one eye is used.

Moro reflex (also called the **startle reflex**). Causes a motor reaction of infants' arms, legs, and trunk in response to a sudden loud noise or loss of support.

Motion sickness. A dizzy, nauseous feeling caused mainly by disagreements between vision and vestibular information.

Motive. A condition that energizes and directs the behavior of an organism.

Motor cortex. Part of the cerebral cortex; located in front of the central fissure. Controls motor responses of the body.

Motor system. Functional subdivision of the nervous system; includes basal ganglia, cerebellum, and the motor cortex. Controls voluntary muscle movements.

Multiple personalities. A disorder in which one person assumes two or more personalities. Each personality has its complete set of memories, and one is often "unaware" of the existence of the other.

Multistable perceptions (also called **figure-ground reversal**). Occurs when a picture shows alternating appearances; what was seen as figure becomes the background, and vice versa.

Mutation. Abnormal chromosome structure, responsible for such diseases as Down's syndrome.

Myelin sheath. A fatty covering of some axons, which allows neural impulses to be conducted faster.

Myelinization. Development of myelin sheaths during infancy, childhood, and adolescence.

Mysticism. The view that alternate state experiences are a response to an external reality that exists beyond the visible and understandable universe.

Narcotics. Drugs that in small doses

reduce pain, cause drowsiness, and give a feeling of happiness and well-being. Examples are morphine, heroine, and opium.

Naturalistic observation. Research method that involves studying people's reactions to naturally occurring events in natural settings.

Nearsightedness. Occurs when an eye is elongated like a horizontal egg; nearsighted people see near objects well, but see far objects poorly.

Negative reinforcement. Occurs when a stimulus is taken away or stopped.

Negative set. A mental set that reduces the chance of learning a new relationship.

Neurons. Cells in the nervous system that receive and send impulses.

Neurosis. A broad pattern of psychological disorders characterized by anxiety, fear, and self-defeating behaviors.

Noise. A psychological concept; unwanted sound, sound that is unpleasant, bothersome, or actually physiologically harmful.

Nonverbal communication. Communication through facial expression, gesture, body movement, etc.

Normal curve. Symmetrical, bell-shaped curve that occurs when a normal distribution is plotted as a frequency polygon.

Normal distribution. Represents the assumption that most measurements taken will be close to average, some will be a small distance from average, and few will be very far from average. People's height, weight, IQs show this distribution.

Normative social pressure. A type of group pressure based on the desire to belong to the group.

Norms. Rules that govern specific behavior and apply to all members of the group.

Obedience. The following of direct and explicit orders of a person in a position of authority.

Obesity. In humans, being more than 15 percent over the "ideal" weight, given the person's height and overall body build.

Observational learning. Learning by watching other people and observing the consequences of their actions. This type of learning occurs without external reinforcement or without even performing the behavior.

Obsession. Recurring, irrational thought that cannot be controlled or banished from one's mind. See also *compulsion*, which involves behavior rather than thought.

Occipital lobe. One of four lobes in the cerebral cortex; receives visual impulses from the eyes.

Oedipus complex. According to

Freud, boy desires sexual relationship with mother, but is afraid his father will find out and castrate him as punishment. In order to get rid of these fears, boy identifies with and tries to be like his father. Identification with father helps form the superego because boy internalizes the father's values.

Ophthalmoscope. Uses mirrors or prisms to direct light through the pupil so that eye doctors can examine the eye's internal structures.

Oral stage. Infant is born with general desire for physical pleasure, which is focused in the mouth region; these impulses are satisfied by eating, sucking, and biting. This is a stage of total dependency on the parents.

Oscilloscope. Device for converting sound waves to visible waves.

Olfactory cells. Odor-sensitive cells contained in the passageway between the nose and the throat.

Operant conditioning. A type of learning that occurs when desired responses are rewarded or reinforced and undesired responses are ignored or punished.

Otoliths. Organs that signal head orientation with respect to gravity.

Oval window. A membrane stretched over the opening of the inner ear.

Ovaries. Female reproductive glands, which secrete estrogen into the bloodstream.

Ovulation. In women, the time when the egg is available to be fertilized, and secretion of estrogen is at its highest; occurs once a month.

Pancreas. A large gland located behind the stomach; as part of the endocrine system, it controls the level of sugar in the blood by secreting insulin and glucagon.

Papillae. Small elevations on the tongue; contain our taste sensors, called taste buds.

Paradoxical cold. Occurs when a warm object stimulates a cold spot on the skin—cold is felt.

Paradoxical warmth. Occurs when a cold object stimulates a warm spot on the skin—warmth is felt.

Paranoid. People suffering from delusions of persecution are called paranoid; they believe that people are "out to get" them and interpret others' actions as plots against them.

Parapsychologists. Those who study ESP and PK.

Parasympathetic division. Part of the autonomic nervous system; functional subdivision of the nervous system; controls the relaxation responses.

Parathyroid glands. Four pea-shaped glands next to the thyroid in the throat; part of the endocrine system. Produce a hormone that causes leth-

argy when its level is too high, and muscle spasms when its level is too low.

Parietal lobe. One of four lobes in the cerebral cortex; responds to touch, pain, and temperature.

Partial reinforcement schedule. Subject is reinforced every few responses or every once in awhile, but not for every response.

Peak experiences. Fleeting moments in people's lives where they feel truly spontaneous and unconcerned with time or other physical constraints. A feeling of being totally absorbed in the situation, in the moment, without cares from the past or concern for the future.

Peripheral vision. Using the sides of one's eyes (and thus depending on the rods rather than the cones) to see something—usually occurs at night or in dim light.

Personal space. An area directly surrounding one's body that is regarded as one's personal territory.

Personality. The unique set of behaviors (including thoughts and emotions) and enduring qualities that influence the way a person adjusts to the environment.

Personality assessment. The description and measurement of individual characteristics.

Personality disorders. Rigid and maladaptive ways of dealing with the environment, characterized by a general approach to dealing with events rather than by any one specific behavior. The example discussed in the text is the *antisocial personality disorder*, which is the type of personality disorder most often found in Western society.

Personality psychology. Subfield of psychology that focuses on individual differences and on explaining and predicting the unique ways that people respond to their environment.

Phallic stage. According to psychoanalytic theory begins at the age of four; focus of pleasure is the genital organs. Trauma at this stage is called Oedipus complex for boys, Electra complex for girls.

Phenotype. The way one's genotype (genetic inheritance) is expressed in observable characteristics.

Phobia. A phobia is an irrational fear of an object or event. The fear is attached to a specific, identifiable object; phobics can control their anxiety by avoiding that object or situation.

Phosphenes. Visual sensations arising from spontaneous discharges of light-sensitive neurons in the eyes.

Physiological psychology. Subfield of psychology that examines the areas of learning, memory, perception, motivation, and emotion by studying the neurobiological events that underlie them.

Pinna. The outer flap of the ear.

Pitch. Difference between low and high notes. Changes in pitch correspond to changes in frequency of sound waves.

Pituitary gland. Small gland that lies in a recess at the base of the brain and is connected to the hypothalamus, which controls it. Part of the endocrine system, it is often called the master gland because it has such wide-ranging effects. Secretes many different types of hormones, which control growth and sexual reproduction, among other things.

Placebo. In drug studies, a drug substitute made from inactive materials that is given to the control group in drug research.

Placebo effect. A situation in which a treatment that has no curative value of its own has a healing effect because of the patient's belief in its effectiveness.

Placenta. A special filter used to exchange food and wastes between an embryo and his or her mother.

Pleasure principle. This is what guides the id, the immediate satisfaction of drives without regard to reality, logic, or manners.

Polarization. An electric tension that exists in a neuron between the cell's inside and outside environment. Also called *membrane potential.*

Polygenic traits. Traits that are determined by the action of more than one gene pair. Most human traits are polygenic.

Polygraph. Also called a lie detector. Records changes in heart rate, blood pressure, respiration, and galvanic skin response. Lies are identified when there is a change from baseline responses to neutral questions to a heightened response to questions about critical events.

Pons. Part of the hindbrain; a tube formed by a massive cable of nerve fibers. Connects the medulla to the midbrain.

Positive reinforcement. Occurs when a positive stimulus is added to the environment.

Posthypnotic suggestions. Suggestions made to a subject while hypnotized, which are to be carried out after hypnosis has ended.

Precognition. Perception of future thoughts, events, or actions.

Preconscious element of personality. According to Freud, the preconscious is essentially one's memory, including thoughts that people may not be aware of but that they can retrieve from memory.

Prefrontal lobotomy. Surgical technique for treating extreme psychological disorders. Involves cutting con-

nections between the thalamus and the frontal lobes. Seldom used today, only when all other methods have failed.

Prejudice. An unjustified negative attitude toward an individual based solely on that person's membership in a group.

Preoperational stage. One of Piaget's stages of cognitive development; lasts from 2 years to 7 years of age. Main theme is discovering mental operations, which are plans, strategies, and rules for solving problems and for classifying.

Preparedness. The idea that animals are more prepared to make certain responses than others, and may find other responses more difficult to make.

Primacy effect. In impression formation, the fact that people tend to base their impressions on what they hear first.

Primary motives. Motives such as hunger, thirst, and the need for air and rest. These motives are usually unlearned, common to all animals, and vital for the survival of the organism or the species.

Primary reinforcer. Events or objects that are reinforcing in and of themselves (such as food).

Primary sexual characteristics. Traits directly concerned with sexual reproduction; the production of live ovum by girls and live sperm by boys.

Primary territories. Owned and controlled by people; these territories are central to their lives.

Proactive inhibition. Interference of previous learning with memory for new learning.

Problem drinkers. People who often drink too much and whose drinking has undesirable effects on their lives or on others. See also *alcoholics.*

Projection. Defense mechanism that involves seeing our own shortcomings or undesirable traits in other people rather than in ourselves.

Projective tests. Based on Freud's theory that people will project unconscious desires onto ambiguous and non-threatening stimuli. The stimuli can be an incomplete sentence or a picture. People's responses are analyzed to see what they tell about them.

Proxemics. Study of personal space.

Psychiatric nurse. A registered nurse who has received special training in dealing with psychological disorders.

Psychiatric social worker. Someone who has an M.A. in social work and has served an internship.

Psychiatrist. A medical doctor who has received an M.D. degree and has taken part in a residency program in emotional disorders; the only type of

therapist who can prescribe drugs or conduct psychosurgery.

Psychoactive drugs. Drugs that produce subjective effects: depressants, stimulants, and hallucinogens.

Psychoanalysis. Freud's technique of treating anxiety disorders by helping people recognize and deal with their repressed feelings.

Psychoanalyst. A psychiatrist who has had a great deal of training in psychoanalytic techniques, and has often undergone psychoanalysis himor herself.

Psychokinesis (PK). Direct mental influence over physical objects or processes.

Psychological test. A test designed to identify individual differences among people; tests have been developed to measure attitudes, abilities, achievement, and personality traits.

Psychology. The scientific study of behavior and the applications gained from that knowledge.

Psychology of minorities. Subfield of psychology that examines behavior of people in minority groups, including women who are minorities in some contexts.

Psychopharmacology. The study of drugs to treat psychological disorders.

Psychophysics. Studies the relationship between physical energies and psychological experiences.

Psychophysiological disorder. Often referred to as psychosomatic illness; an actual physical illness in which stress is a contributing factor. An example is a peptic ulcer.

Psychosis. A disturbance caused by unresolved conflicts that is so great that the person can no longer deal with reality.

Psychosurgery. Various techniques of biotherapy involving surgery to the brain. The best known is the *prefrontal lobotomy*, in which connections are cut between the thalamus and the frontal lobes. Seldom used today, only when all other methods have failed.

Psychotherapy. The use of psychological techniques by a professionally trained person to help a client change unwanted behavior and adjust to his or her environment. In short, the use of language to make positive changes in the life of another.

Puberty. The time in adolescence when sexual reproduction becomes possible.

Public territories. Territories that do not involve feelings of ownership, but people feel that they control them while they are occupying them; an example is a table at a restaurant.

Punishment. A stimulus that decreases the likelihood of a response

when it is added to an environment. Compare with *reinforcement.*

Pupil. An opening in the iris of the eye; looks like a black spot in the center of the iris.

Pure tones. Sounds containing a single frequency.

Pyramidal cells. Giant cells of the motor cortex, which send a long axon through the brain down to neurons, in the spinal cord. Control precise movements such as those of hand movements and speech.

Randomization. Procedure used in an experiment by which subjects are randomly assigned to either the control group or the experimental group(s). It ensures that each person has an equal chance of being assigned to each group, thus making it highly probable that subject differences will be equally distributed between groups.

Range. A measure of variation, the difference between the largest and smallest number in the distribution.

Rational Emotive Therapy (RET). Type of therapy developed by Albert Ellis; focuses on the present and on the client's irrational beliefs. Therapist plays a much more directive and even challenging role than in most other therapies.

Rationalization. A defense mechanism that involves justifying one's behavior by finding logical or desirable reasons for it.

Reaction formation. Defense mechanism that conceals unacceptable impulses by expressing instead the opposite impulse.

Reality principle. This is what guides the ego; it tries to satisfy the desires of the id by taking into account the possibilities of reward and punishment that exist in the situation.

Recall tests. Measure a person's ability to reproduce material. *Cued recall* is when part of the material is provided as a cue for the rest; *free recall* is when no cues are provided and any order of recall is allowed.

Recognition tests. Measure a person's ability to pick the correct answer when several answers are given; often occur in the form of multiple-choice questions on tests.

Reconstruction. The organization and recoding (often done unconsciously) of memory over time; may lead to distortions of memory.

Reflex. Automatic action that requires no conscious effort.

Rehearsal. Process of repeating information in order to retain it in short-term memory or transfer it to long-term memory.

Reinforcement. An event whose occurrence just after a response increases the likelihood that the re-

sponse will be repeated. See *positive, negative reinforcement;* compare with punishment.

Relative refractory period. Period during which a cell will only fire in response to an extra-strong impulse; lasts for a few milliseconds.

Relaxation response. Phrase used by Benson to refer to the physiological patterns observed during meditation; a decrease in oxygen consumption, respiratory rate, heart rate, blood pressure, and muscle tension.

Reliability of a test. Means that you get the same results on the test every time you administer it.

REM rebound. Sharp increase of REM sleep after going through a period of sleep deprivation.

REM sleep. Stage of sleep marked by rapid eye movements (REMs) and dreams.

Repression. A defense mechanism that involves blocking or keeping unpleasant thoughts or memories from conscious awareness. Differs from suppression in that it is an unconscious process, suppression is a conscious process.

Response generalization. Means giving different, but similar, responses to the same stimulus.

Resting state. Occurs whenever a neuron is not sending or receiving neural impulses.

Retention. Process of holding information in memory.

Reticular activating system (RAS). Functional subdivision of the nervous system; activates all regions of the brain for incoming sensory impulses, plays an important part in alertness and selective attention.

Retina. Tissue covering most of the eye's interior wall; contains rods and cones.

Retrieval. Process of getting information out of memory.

Retrieval cues. Aids to retrieval that are often encoded with the information to be remembered; an example would be category names.

Retroactive inhibition. Interference of new learning with memory for previous learning.

Ribonucleic acid (RNA). Messenger molecules sent out by DNA to control how specific kinds of protein chains are made.

Rods. Light receptors located on the periphery or sides of the retina; they are best for seeing in dim light.

Roles. Group rules that apply only to people in certain positions; roles define the obligations and expectations of that specific position.

Rooting reflex. Causes infants to turn their head toward anything that touches their cheek.

Savings. The difference between one's

original learning time and the relearning time; measured by a savings test.

Savings tests. Measure people's ability to take advantage of what they have learned before in order to relearn material faster.

Scapegoating. Singling out a person or a minority group as the target (scapegoat) for aggression and hostility, when the real target is too powerful to be attacked.

Schema (plural, schemata). Term used by Piaget to refer to a mental structure that organizes responses to experiences.

Schizophrenia. A group of disorders characterized by disorganization in thoughts, perceptions, communication, emotions, and motor activity.

Sclera. The white opaque outer wall of the eye.

Secondary reinforcers. Events or objects that are reinforcing only after they have been paired with other, primary reinforcers. Money is a good example of a secondary reinforcer.

Secondary sexual characteristics. Traits typical of a sex, but not directly concerned with reproduction; for girls, the development of breasts and pubic hair; for boys, growth of the scrotum, pubic hair, and a beard.

Secondary territories. Not "owned by people," and not as central to their lives; examples are the neighborhood street, the social or country club, or even a regular seat in a classroom.

Self-actualization. Process by which a person strives to learn, create, and work to the best of his or her ability.

Self-concept. Consists of our judgments and attitudes about our behavior, abilities, and even our appearance; it is our answer to the question, "Who am I?"

Self-fulfilling prophecy. An expectation that leads one to behave in ways that will cause that expectation to come about.

Semantic memory. A person's general background knowledge about words, symbols, concepts, and rules.

Semicircular canals. Three arching structures in the inner ear that detect changes in head position.

Sensorimotor stage. One of Piaget's stages of cognitive development, extends from birth to about 2 years of age. Main theme is discovering relationships between sensations and motor behavior.

Sensory deprivation. The absence of almost all sensory stimulation.

Sensory memory. Holds sensations briefly so that they can be identified; lasts from 1 to 2 seconds.

Sex-linked traits. Occur when the gene for a trait is located on the chromosome that determines one's sex (in humans, on the X chromosome in pair

23). Examples are color blindness and hemophilia.

Shaping. A procedure used in operant conditioning in which each part of a behavior is reinforced that eventually leads to the whole behavior that is desired.

Short-term memory. Holds information that has been transferred out of sensory memory; lasts about 30 seconds unless information is repeated or rehearsed.

Single-gene traits. Some genes determine specific traits all on their own, rather than in combination with other genes. An example is eye color.

Sleep. A period of rest for the body and mind, during which bodily functions are partially suspended and sensitivity to external stimuli is diminished, but readily or easily regained.

Sleep spindles. Medium-voltage, medium-frequency brain waves characteristic of stage-2 sleep.

Sleeper effect. The fact that over time, the credibility of a communicator makes no difference in people's attitudes; seems to occur because people tend to separate the source from the message as time passes.

Social comparison. Using social reality to evaluate oneself—comparing oneself against the beliefs, attitudes, and behaviors of other people.

Social facilitation. Occurs because the presence of other people tends to arouse people; this arousal creates an additional pool of energy that aids the performance of well-learned behaviors.

Social loafing. Peoples' motivation to work decreases when they are in groups where their individual performance cannot be observed; the larger the group, the easier to reduce effort without being detected.

Social motives. Motives that come from learning and social interaction rather than based on biological needs (see primary motives). These motives include affiliation, aggression, and achievement.

Social psychology. The scientific study of the way in which people are affected by social situations and social relationships; the scientific study of the way most people act most of the time.

Social reality. Beliefs, attitudes, and behaviors of other people.

Social skill training. Aimed at teaching people to exercise control over their social environment and thus avoid a state of learned helplessness.

Somatization disorder. One of the somatoform disorders. Characterized by vague but dramatic complaints such as headaches, nausea, vomiting, stomach pains, and tiredness. There is no organic basis for these problems,

although people suffering from this disorder actually do feel sick—they are not pretending.

Somatoform disorders. Group of disorders in which people feel ill or show other symptoms such as blindness or paralysis, but there is no organic damage.

Somatosensory cortex. Part of the cerebral cortex; located behind the central fissure. Controls sensory responses of the body.

Somatotype. A person's body build. Sheldon characterized people as either endomorphic (soft, round, fat), mesomorphic (muscular, hard, rectangular), or ectomorphic (tall, thin, fragile).

Sound. A physical property caused by changes in air pressure; measured in decibels (db.). Contrast with *noise*, which is a psychological concept.

Spinal cord. A cable of long nerve fibers running from the brainstem down through the backbone to the lower back, through which ascending nerves carry sensory information up to the brain and descending nerves carry commands down from the brain to move muscles.

Spontaneous recovery. Occurs when a response reappears without any retraining, after having been extinguished.

Standard deviation. Measure of variation, the square root of the *variance*; often used to express how far any given score is from the mean of a set of scores.

Standard error of the difference between two means. Computed by finding the square root of the sum of the standard errors of the means.

Standard error of the mean. Shows the variation of a sample mean and tells how likely it is that the sample mean represents the population mean.

Standard score. A single number that expresses where a score lies relative to a population. Expresses the value of a score relative to the mean and the standard deviation of its distribution.

Standardized achievement tests. Tests that have been given to many people so that one person's score can be evaluated with respect to a large population.

Statistical significance. Means that a difference in scores is a true difference, not a result of sampling e-ror.

Statistics. A branch of mathematics used by psychologists to describe data and to draw conclusions based on data.

Stimulants. Drugs that excite body functions; examples are caffeine, amphetamines, and cocaine.

Stimulus generalization. Occurs

when responses are made to stimuli that are similar to, but not the same as, the original conditioned stimulus (CS).

Stimulus-seeking motive. Motive to explore and manipulate new objects, to increase stimulation and arousal.

Stirrup. One of three small bones in the middle ear; transmits sounds from the eardrum to the inner ear.

Stress. General response of the body to any demand made on it.

Structuralism. An approach to psychology based on identifying the elements of human experience and finding out how those elements are combined into thoughts and feelings.

Sublimation. Defense mechanism that involves rechanneling the energy associated with one emotion or event into a seemingly unrelated activity.

Sucking reflex. Causing sucking in infants when anything touches the lips.

Superego. According to Freud, the superego represents our conscience, including the moral values of right and wrong instilled in us by our parents.

Suppression. A defense mechanism that involves consciously blocking or avoiding unpleasant thoughts. Differs from repression in that it is a conscious process, repression is unconscious.

Survey. Method used in psychology; uses questionnaires that are given to large samples of people.

Sympathetic division. Part of the autonomic nervous system; functional subdivision of the nervous system; controls the fight-or-flight responses.

Synapse. A junction between two neurons.

Synaptic space. A very small gap between the axon terminal of one cell and the dendrite of the next cell.

Synaptic transmission. Occurs as a neural impulse; moves from one neuron to another.

Synaptic vesicles. Tiny oval sacs on the axon terminal filled with a chemical transmitter substance.

Systematic desensitization. Type of behavior therapy that is based on the assumption that it is impossible to be relaxed and anxious at the same time. Clients are taught deep muscle relaxation; they then pair this with feared or stressful events or objects, with the idea that the relaxation response will overcome the fear reaction. It is often used to treat phobias.

T-groups. A type of group therapy that focuses on how people function in groups rather than on emotional disorders. Widely used in industrial and educational settings to aid group performance.

Taste buds. Taste sensors contained in papillae on the tongue.

Telepathy. The perception of another's

mental state or emotion by means of ESP.

Temporal lobe. One of four lobes in the cerebral cortex; receives sound and smell impulses and has centers that control speech.

Territoriality. The claiming of control or ownership of areas or objects.

Test statistic. Ratio of the difference between the means to the standard error of the difference between the means.

Testes. Male reproductive gland, which secretes androgens into the bloodstream.

Texture gradient. Monocular cue to depth. As we look at something with texture, the nearer elements are spaced farther apart than the more distant elements. Some examples are shown in Figure 3–20.

Thalamus. Two egg-shaped structures that are part of the forebrain. Often called a relay station because sensory pathways from all over the body pass through it.

Theory. Explanation about why behavior occurs; theories generate hypotheses that can be tested experimentally.

Theta waves. Low-voltage, low-frequency brain waves characteristic of stage-1 sleep.

Thyroid glands. Large, butterfly-shaped gland in the front and sides of the throat; part of the endocrine system. Produces thyroxin, a hormone that determines the rate at which food is transformed in the body into energy.

Thyroxin. Hormone produced by the thyroid glands; determines the rate at which food is transformed in the body into energy.

Tip-of-the-tongue (TOT) phenomenon. A state of being on the verge of recalling something; often subjects say that the word or whatever they are trying to record is "on the tip of the tongue."

Token economy. A behavioral technique often used in institutional settings such as mental hospitals and prisons. People taking part are given rewards, such as poker chips, for performing certain desired behaviors. They can use the tokens to purchase a variety of things that they want.

Tonic neck reflex. Causes infants who are on their back to move their arms and legs into a "fencing" position when the head is turned to one side.

Trace-decay theory. The theory that memory traces fade away in time if their strength is not maintained through use.

Traits. Fairly permanent qualities that people possess to a greater or lesser degree.

Tranquilizers. Depressant drugs that slow the body functions, reduce anxiety, and have a relaxing effect.

Transcendental Meditation (TM). A simplified Yoga technique that allows people to meditate after a short training course.

Transference. Part of Freud's technique of psychoanalysis; occurs when clients transfer to the therapist feelings that were originally aimed at their parents. In this way they are able to work them through on a rational, conscious level.

Transpersonal psychology. Tries to increase people's self-awareness through a mixture of psychological theory, religion, and modern philosophy. Its aim is to increase personal growth in many different ways and on different levels.

Transsexual. A person who has undergone a sex-change operation that changes the anatomical features to be like those of the opposite sex.

Two-point threshold. The least distance between two stimuli that can be perceived as separate on the skin.

Type A behavior. Coronary-prone behavior pattern; a response to stress that involves becoming more active, more competitive, more "driven."

Unconditional positive regard. Part of client-centered therapy, in which the therapist tries to create a condition of unconditional positive regard by accepting and caring for clients no matter what feelings or behaviors are revealed in the session.

Unconditioned response (UR). An automatic or reflexive reaction to a stimulus.

Unconditioned stimulus (US). Something that automatically or reflexively causes a response.

Unconscious. According to Freud, a storehouse of unacceptable images, including past events, current impulses, and desires of which one is not aware. See also *conscious, preconscious.*

Uterus (womb). A hollow, muscular organ in which a mother carries a fetus in the 9 months before birth.

Vaginismus. A sexual disorder in which the involuntary tightening of the vagina makes sexual intercourse impossible.

Validity of a test. Means that the test actually measures what you say it measures; best way to tell this is to see if the results of the test successfully predict the type of behavior in which you are interested.

Variable-interval schedule. Reinforces the first response made after varying time intervals (the first interval might be 5 minutes, then 9 minutes, then 1 minute, etc.). Produces a slow, steady rate of response.

Variable-ratio schedule. Reinforces the first response made after a varying number of responses (the tenth response; the fourth response after that; the twelfth response after the previous response, etc.). Produces a rapid, steady rate of responding.

Variance. Measure of variation, the average squared difference of each number in a sample from the mean of all numbers in the sample.

Verbal mediation. Mnemonic system in which one relates new material to verbal mediators, which are words that are easy to remember.

Vestibular system. An inner-ear structure that detects body orientation and changes in body orientation.

Visual angle. Angle between lines formed by the top and bottom of an object one is looking at. The visual angle gets smaller as an object moves farther away, which means that the retinal image of the object also gets smaller.

Visual cliff. Apparatus used to test depth perception in infants.

Vitreous humor. Semiliquid gel that fills the eye's main chamber and gives it a spherical shape.

Voice stress analyzer. Records amount of voice tremor, which may be affected by stress. A decrease in voice tremor indicates tension, and, presumably, the fact that the person is lying.

Warm spots. Areas on the skin where only hot is felt, even if stimulated by a cold object (when this occurs it is called *paradoxical warmth*).

Waveform. Shape of a sound wave; changes in waveform allow us to distinguish between the sound of a piano and a violin, for instance.

Wernicke's aphasia. Speech that includes wrong words and nonsense words, shifting from topic to topic. Caused by injury to Wernicke's area in the cortex.

Zygote. A cell formed by the union of an ovum and a sperm.

Yerkes-Dodson principle. The theory that the most effective level of arousal for performance depends on the difficulty of the task.

Zener cards. Special cards used to test for ESP.

REFERENCES

ABRAMSON, L., SELIGMAN, M., and TEASDALE, J. Learned helplessness in humans. Critique and reformation. *Journal of Abnormal Psychology*, 1978, *87*, 49–74.

ABRAMSON, P., PERRY, L., ROTHBLATT, A., SEELEY, T., and SEELEY, D. Negative attitudes toward masturbation and pelvic vasocongestion: The thermographic analysis. *Journal of Research in Personality*, 1981, *15*, 497–509.

ADAMS, G., and HUSTON, T. Social perception of middle-aged persons varying in physical attractiveness. *Developmental Psychology*, 1975, *11*, 657–658.

ADORNO, T. W., FENKEL-BRUNSWICK, E., LEVINSON, D. J., and SANFORD, R. N. *The authoritarian personality*. New York: Harper & Row, 1950.

AGRAS, W. S. Behavior therapy in management of chronic schizophrenia. *American Journal of Psychiatry*, 1967, *124*, 240–243.

AGRAS, S., SYLVESTER, D., and OLIVEAU, D. The epidemiology of common fears and phobias. *Comprehensive Psychiatry*, 1969, *10*, 151–156.

AIELLO, J. R., and AIELLO, T. The development of personal space: Proxemic behavior of children 6 through 16. *Human Ecology*, 1974, *2*(3), 177–189.

AINSWORTH, M. D. The development of infant-mother interactions among the Ganda. In D. M. Foss (Ed.), *Determinants of infant behavior* (Vol. 2). New York: Wiley, 1963.

AINSWORTH, M. D. The development of infant-mother attachment. In B. Caldwell and H. Ricciuti (Eds.), *Review of child development research* (Vol. 3). Chicago: University of Chicago Press, 1973.

AINSWORTH, M., SALTER, D., and WITTIG, B. A. Attachment and exploratory behavior of one-year-olds in a strange situation. In B. M. Foss (Ed.), *Determinants of infant behavior* (Vol. 4). New York: John Wiley, 1967.

AKISKAL, H. S., and MCKINNEY, W. T., JR. Overview of recent research in depression. *Archives of General Psychiatry*, 1975, *32*, 285–305.

ALLPORT, F. H. *Social psychology*. Cambridge, Mass.: Riverside Press, 1924.

ALLPORT, G. *Personality: A psychological interpretation*. New York: Holt, Rinehart and Winston, 1937.

ALLPORT, G. W. *The nature of prejudice*. New York: Doubleday-Anchor, 1958.

ALLPORT, G. W., and ODBERT, H. S. Trait names: A psycholexical study. *Psychological Monographs*, 1936, *47* (1, Whole No. 211).

ALTMAN, I. *The environment and social behavior*. Monterey, Calif.: Brooks/Cole, 1975.

ALTMAN, I., and CHEMERS, M. *Culture and environment*. Monterey, Calif.: Brooks/Cole, 1980.

ALTMAN, I., and VINSEL, A. Personal space: An analysis of E. T. Hall's proxemics framework. In I. Altman and J. Wehwill (Eds.), *Human behavior and environment: Advances in theory and research* (Vol. 1). New York: Plenum, 1977.

ALTMAN, I., LEVINE, M., and NADIEN, J. Unpublished results cited in S. Milgram, "The experience of living in cities." *Science*, 1970, *167*, 1461–1468.

ALTMAN, I., VINSEL, A., and BROWN, B. Dialectic conceptions in social psychology: An application to social penetration and privacy regulation. In L. Berkowitz (Ed.), *Advances in experimental social psychology* (Vol. 14). New York: Academic Press, 1981.

ALTUS, W. D. Birth order, intelligence and adjustment. *Psychological Reports*, 1959, *5*, 502.

ALTUS, W. D. Birth order and its sequelae. *Science*, 1966, *151*, 44–49.

AMERICAN PSYCHIATRIC ASSOCIATION. *Diagnostic and statistical manual of mental disorders* (3rd ed.). Washington, D.C.: American Psychiatric Association, 1979.

ANDERSON, J. R., and BOWER, G. H. *Human associative memory*. Washington, D.C.: Winston, 1973.

ANDERSON, W. F., and DIACOMAKOS, E. G. Genetic engineering in mammalian cells. *Scientific American*, 1981, *245*, 106–121.

ANDERSSON, B., and LARSSON, S. Influence of local temperature changes in the preoptic area and rostral hypothalamus on the regulation of food and water intake. *Acta Physiologica Scandinavica*, 1961, 15–89.

ANDERSSON, B., and LARSSON, S. Physiological and pharmacological aspects of the control of hunger and thirst. *Acta Physiologica Scandinavica*, 1961, 188–201.

ANDREW, J. D. W. The achievement motive and advancement in two types of organizations. *Journal of Personality and Social Psychology*, 1967, *6*, 163–168.

ANSPACHER, C. Rock really does deafen. *San Francisco Chronicle*, January 26, 1972, p. 1.

APGAR, V. A proposal for a new method of evaluation of the newborn infant. *Current Researches in Anesthesia and Analgesia*, 1953, *32*, 260–267.

APPLEYARD, D., and LINTELL, M. The environmental quality of city streets: The Residents' point of view. In W. Mitchell (Ed.), *Environmental design: Research and practice*. Los Angeles: University of California/EDRA, 1972.

ARENBERG, D. Regression analyses of verbal learning on adult age at two anticipation intervals. *Journal of Gerontology*, 1967, *22*, 411–414.

ARGYLE, M. The psychology of interpersonal behavior. Baltimore: Penguin, 1967.

ARGYLE, M., and DEAN, J. Eye-contact, distance and affiliation. *Sociometry*, 1965, *28*, 289–304.

ARGYLE, M., and MCHENRY, R. Do spectacles really affect judgements of intelligence? *British Journal of Social and Clinical Psychology*, 1971, *10*, 27–29.

ARNOLD, M. B. *Emotion and personality* (2 vols.). New York: Columbia University Press, 1960.

ARONSON, E. *The social animal* (2nd ed.). San Francisco: Freeman, 1976.

ARONSON, E., and CARLSMITH, J. M. The effect of the severity of threat on the devaluation of forbidden behavior. *Journal of Abnormal and Social Psychology*, 1963, *66*, 584–588.

ARONSON, E., and LINDER, D. E. Gain and loss of esteem as determinants of interpersonal attractiveness. *Journal of Experimental Social Psychology*, 1965, *1*, 156–171.

ARONSON, E., and MILLS, J. The effect of severity of initiation on liking for a group. *Journal of Abnormal and Social Psychology*, 1959, *59*, 177–181.

ASCH, S. Forming impressions of personality. *Journal of Abnormal and Social Psychology*, 1946, *41*, 258–290.

ASCH, S. Effects of group pressure upon the modification and distortion of judgment. In H. Guetzkow (Ed.), *Groups, leadership and men.* Pittsburgh: Carnegie Press, 1951.

ASCH, S. *Social psychology.* Englewood Cliffs, N.J.: Prentice-Hall, 1952.

ASCH, S. Studies of independence and conformity: I. A minority of one against a unanimous majority. *Psychological Monographs*, 1956, *70*, No. 9.

ATKINSON, R. C. Mnemontechnics in second-language learning. *American Psychologist*, 1975, *30*, 821–828.

ATKINSON, R. C., and SHIFFRIN, R. M. The control of short-term memory. *Scientific American*, 1971, *224*, 82–90.

ATKINSON, R. C., and SHIFFRIN, R. M. Human memory: A proposed system and its control processes. In Bower, G. H. (Ed.), *Human memory: Basic processes.* New York: Academic Press, 1977.

ATTNEAVE, F. Multistability in perception. In R. Held and W. Richards (Eds.), *Recent progress in perception.* San Francisco: Freeman, 1976.

AYLLON, T., and AZRIN, N. H. *The token economy: A motivational system for therapy and rehabilitation.* New York: Appleton-Century-Crofts, 1968.

AYRES, C. E. Instinct and capacity: I. The instinct of belief-in-instincts. *Journal of Philosophy*, 1921, *18*, 561–566.

BACH-Y-RITA, P. *Brain mechanisms in sensory substitution.* New York: Academic Press, 1972.

BACH-Y-RITA, P. Sensory substitution in rehabilitation. In L. Illis, M. Sedwick, and H. Granville (Eds.), *Rehabilitation of the neurological patient.* Oxford: Blackwell Press, 1982, pp. 361–383.

BACH, G., and WYDEN, P. *The intimate enemy: How to fight fair in love and marriage.* New York: Avon, 1968.

BACHRACH, A. J., ERWIN, W., and MOHR, J. P. The control of eating behavior in an anorexic by operant conditioning techniques. In L. P. Ullman and L. Krasner (Eds.), *Case studies in behavior modification.* New York: Holt, Rinehart and Winston, 1965, 153–163.

BADIAJ, P., CULBERTSON, S., and HARSH, J. Choice of longer or stronger signalled shock over shorter or weaker unsignalled shock. *Journal of the Experimental Analysis of Behavior*, 1973, *19*, 25–32.

BALES, R. F., and SLATER, P. Role differentiation in small decision-making groups. In T. Parson and R. F. Bales (Eds.), *Family, socialization and interaction processes.* Glencoe, Ill.: Free Press, 1955.

BANDURA, A. Social learning through imitation. In M. R. Jones (Ed.), *Nebraska symposium on motivation.* Lincoln, Neb.: University of Nebraska Press, 1962.

BANDURA, A. Behavior modification through modeling procedures. In L. Krosner and L. P. Ullman (Eds.), *Research in behavior modification.* New York: Holt, Rinehart, and Winston, 1965.

BANDURA, A. Social learning interpretation of psychological dysfunctions. In P. London and D. Rosenhan (Eds.), *Foundations of abnormal psychology.* New York: Holt, Rinehart and Winston, 1968.

BANDURA, A. Social-learning theory of identificatory processes. In D. A. Goslin (Ed.), *Handbook of socialization theory and research.* Chicago: Rand McNally, 1969.

BANDURA, A. *Aggression: A social learning analysis.* New York: Holt, Rinehart and Winston, 1973.

BANDURA, A. *Social learning theory.* Englewood Cliffs, N.J.: Prentice-Hall, 1977.

BANDURA, A., and MENLOVE. Factors determining vicarious extinction of avoidance through symbolic modeling. *Journal of Personality and Social Psychology*, 1968, *8*, 99–108.

BANDURA, A., and WALTERS, R. H. *Social learning and personality development.* New York: Holt, Rinehart and Winston, 1963.

BANDURA, A., ROSS, D., and ROSS, S. A. Transmission of aggression through imitation of aggressive models. *Journal of Abnormal and Social Psychology*, 1961, *63*, 575–582.

BANDURA, A., ROSS, D., and ROSS, S. A. Imitation of film-mediated aggressive models. *Journal of Abnormal and Social Psychology*, 1963, *66*, 3–11. (a)

BANDURA, A., ROSS, D., and ROSS, S. A. Vicarious reinforcement and imitative learning. *Journal of Abnormal and Social Psychology*, 1963, *67*, 601–607. (b)

BANKS, W., and McQUATER, G. Achievement motivation and black children. *IRCD Bulletin*, *11*, 1976, 1–8.

BANKS, W., McQUATER, G., and HUBBARD, J. Task-liking and intrinsic-extrinsic achievement orientations in black adolescents. *Journal of Black Psychology*, 1977, *3*, 61–71.

BARBER, T. X. Antisocial and criminal acts induced by hypnosis: A review of experimental and clinical findings. *Archives of General Psychiatry*, 1961, *5*, 301–312.

BARBER, T. X. *LSD, marihuana, yoga, and hypnosis.* Chicago: Aldine, 1970.

BARBER, T. X., and GLASS, L. B. Significant factors in hypnotic behavior. *Journal of Abnormal and Social Psychology*, 1962, *64*, 222–228.

BARD, P. Studies in the cortical representation of somatic sensibility. *Harvey Lectures*, 1938, *33*, 143–169.

BARDWICK, C. *The psychology of women: A study of bio-cultural conflicts.* New York: Harper and Row, 1971.

BARKER, M. Planning for environmental indices: Observer appraisals of air quality. In K. Craik and E. Zube (Eds.), *Perceiving environmental quality.* New York: Plenum Press, 1976.

BARON, R. A., and BELL, P. A. Aggression and heat: The influence of ambient temperature, negative affect, and a cooling drink on physical aggression. *Journal of Personality and Social Psychology*, 1976, *33*, 245–255. (a)

BARON, R., and BELL, P. A. Physical distance and helping: Some unexpected benefits of "crowding in" on others. *Journal of Applied Social Psychology*, 1976, *6*, 95–104. (b)

BARON, R. A., and LAWTON, S. F. Environmental influences on aggression: The facilitation of modeling effects by high ambient temperatures. *Psychonomic Science*, 1972, *26*, 180–182.

BAR-TAL, D. Prosocial behavior: Theory and research. Washington, D.C.: Hemisphere, 1976.

BAR-TAL, D., and SAXE, L. Perceptions of similarly and dissimilarly attractive couples and individuals. *Journal of Personality and Social Psychology*, 1976, *33*, 772–781.

BARUCH, G. K., and BARNETT, R. C. On the well-being of adult women. In L. A. Bond and J. C. Rosen (Eds.), *Competence and coping during adulthood.* Hanover, N.H.: University Press of New England, 1980.

BATESON, G., JACKSON, D. D., HALEY, J., and WEAKLAND, J. Toward a theory of schizophrenia. *Behavioral Science*, 1956, *1*, 251–264.

BAUM, A., and GREENBERG, C. Waiting for a crowd: The behavioral and perceptual effects of anticipated crowding. *Journal of Personality and Social Psychology*, 1975, *32*, 667–671.

BAUM, A., and VALINS, S. *Architecture and social behavior: Psychological studies in social density.* Hillsdale, N.J.: Erlbaum, 1977.

BAUM, A., SINGER, J., and BAUM, C. Stress and the environment. *Journal of Social Issues*, 1981, *37*, 4–35.

BAUMAN, K., and WILSON, R. Sexual behavior of unmarried university students in 1968 and 1972. *Journal of Sex Research*, 1974, *10*, 327–333.

BAUMEISTER, R., and COOPER, J. Can the public expectation of emotion cause that emotion? *Journal of Personality*, 1981, *49*, 49–59.

BAUMRIND, D. Authoritarian vs. authoritative control. *Adolescence*, 1968, *3*, 255–272.

BAUMRIND, D. Current patterns of parental authority. *Developmental Psychology Monograms*, 1971, *1*, 1–103.

BAUMRIND, D. Reciprocal rights and responsibilities in parent-child relations. In J. Rubinstein and B. D. Brent (Eds.), *Taking sides: Clashing views on controversial psychological issues.* Guilford, Conn.: Dushkin, 1982.

BECK, A. T. *Depression: Clinical, experimental and theoretical aspects.* New York: Harper & Row, 1967.

BECK, A. T., and YOUNG, J. E. College blues. *Psychology Today*, 1978, *12*, 80–92.

BECK, A. T., RUSH, J. A., SHAW, B. R., and EMERY, G. *Cognitive therapy of depres-*

sion: A treatment manual. Copyright A. T. Beck, M. D., 1978.

BECK, R. C. Motivation: Theories and principles. Englewood Cliffs, N.J.: Prentice-Hall, 1978.

BECKER, L., and SELIGMAN, C. Welcome to the energy crisis. Journal of Social Issues, 1981, 37, 1–7.

BEIER, E. G. Nonverbal communication: How we send emotional messages. Psychology Today, October 1974, 53–56.

BELL, P. Physiological, comfort, performance and social effects of heat. Journal of Social Issues, 1981, 37, 71–94.

BELL, A. P., and WEINBERG, M. S. Homosexualities. New York: Simon & Schuster, 1978, 442.

BEM, D. J., and ALLEN, A. On predicting some of the people some of the time: The search for cross-situational consistencies in behavior. Psychological Review, 1974, 81, 506–520.

BENSON, H. The relaxation response. New York: Morrow, 1975.

BENTLER, P., and PRINCE, C. Psychiatric symptomology in transvestites. Journal of Clinical Psychology, 1970, 26, 434–435.

BERCEL, N. A. A study of the influence of schizophrenic serum on the behavior of the spider: Zilla-X-notata. In D. D. Jackson (Ed.), The etiology of schizophrenia. New York: Basic Books, 1960.

BERGER, P. A. Medical treatment of mental illness. Science, 1978, 200, 974–981.

BERGIN, A. E. The evaluation of therapeutic outcomes. In A. E. Bergin and S. L. Garfield (Eds.), Handbook of psychotherapy and behavior change: An empirical analysis. New York: Wiley, 1971.

BERKOWITZ, L. Aggression: A social psychology analysis. New York: McGraw-Hill, 1962.

BERKOWITZ, L. The concept of aggressive drive: Some additional considerations. In L. Berkowitz (Ed.), Advances in experimental social psychology (Vol. 2). New York: Academic Press, 1965.

BERLYNE, D. E. Perceptual curiosity, exploratory behavior, and maze learning. Journal of comparative and Physiological Psychology, 1957, 50, 228–232.

BERLYNE, D. E. The influence of complexity and novelty in visual figures on orienting responses. Journal of Experimental Psychology, 1958, 55, 289–296.

BERLYNE, D. E. The justifiability of the concept of curiosity. Paper delivered at the XIX International Congress of London, 1969.

BERNARD, Instinct. New York: Holt, Rinehart and Winston, 1924.

BERSCHEID, E., and WALSTER, E. Interpersonal attraction. Reading, Mass.: Addison-Wesley, 1978.

BEST, P. J., and RANCK, J. B., JR. The reliability of the relationship between hippocampal unit activity and sensory-behavioral events in the rat. Experimental Neurology, 1982, 75, 652–664.

BETTELHEIM, B. The informed heart. New York: Harper & Row, 1960.

BICKMAN, L., TEGER, A., GABRIELE, T., McLAUGHLIN, C., BERGER, M., and SUNADAY, E. Dormitory density and helping behavior. Environment and Behavior, 1973, 5, 465–490.

BINDRIM, A report on a nude marathon. The effect of physical nudity upon the practice interaction in the marathon group. Psychotherapy: Theory, Research and Practice, 1968, 5, 180–188.

BINET, A., and SIMON, T. New methods for the diagnosis of the intellectual levels of subnormals. Annals of Psychology, 1905, 11, 191.

BIRDWHISTELL, R. L. Some body motion elements accompanying spoken American English. In L. Thayer (Ed.), Communication: Concepts and perspectives. Wash., D.C.: Spartan Books, 1967.

BJORKSTEN, J. The cross-linkage theory of aging. Journal of the American Geriatrics Society, 1968, 16, 408–427.

BJORNTORP, P. Disturbances in the regulation of food intake. Advances in Psychosomatic Medicine, 1972, 7, 116–127.

BLACKWELL, B. Biofeedback in a comprehensive behavioral medicine program. Biofeedback and Self-Regulation, 1981, 6, 445–472.

BLAIR, S. M. Psychiatric diagnosis (letter). Science, 1973, 180, 363.

BLASKOVITCH, J., GINSBURG, G. P., and HOWE, R. C. Blackjack and the risky shift: II. Monetary stakes. Journal of Experimental Social Psychology, 1975.

BLAU, F. D. Women in the labor force: An overview. In J. Freeman (Ed.), Women: A feminist perspective, Palo Alto, Calif.: Mayfield, 1975.

BLENKER, M. Social work and family relationships in later life with some thoughts on filial maturity. In E. Shanas and G. Streif (Eds.), Social structure and the family. Englewood Cliffs, N.J.: Prentice-Hall, 1965.

BLOOM, L. M., HOOD, L., and LIGHTBOWN, P. Imitation in language development: If, when and why. Cognitive Psychology, 1974, 6, 380–420.

BLUM, B. Psychoanalytic theories of personality. New York: McGraw-Hill, 1953.

BOCHNER, S., and INSKO, C. A. Communicator discrepancy, source credibility, and opinion change. Journal of Personality and Social Psychology, 1966, 4, 614–621.

BONDFORD, L., GIBB, T., and BENNE, K. (Eds.). T-group theory: Laboratory method. New York: Wiley, 1964.

BOOTZIN, R. R., and MAX, D. Learning and behavioral theories of anxiety and stress. In I. L. Kutash and L. B. Schlesinger (Eds.), Pressure point: Perspectives on stress and anxiety. San Francisco: Jossey-Bass, 1981.

BOSSARD, J. Residential propinquity as a factor in marriage selection. American Journal of Sociology, 1932, 38, 219–224.

BOTWINICK, J. Intellectual abilities. In J. E. Birren and K. W. Schaie (Eds.), Handbook of the psychology of aging. New York: Van Nostrand, 1977.

BOUCHER, J. D., and EKMAN, P. Facial areas and emotional information. Journal of Communication, 1975, 25, 21–29.

BOWER, G. Mood and memory. Psychology Today, June, 1981.

BOWER, G. H., and CLARK, M. C. Narrative stories as mediators for serial learning. Psychonomic Science, 1969, 14, 181–182.

BOWER, G. H., and KARLIN, M. B. Depth of processing pictures of faces and recognition memory. Journal of Experimental Psychology, 1974, 103, 751–757.

BOWER, G. H., CLARK, M., WINZENZ, D., and LESGOLD, A. Hierarchical retrieval schemes in recall of categorized word lists. Journal of Verbal Learning and Verbal Behavior, 1969, 8, 323–343.

BOWER, T. Blind babies see with their ears. New Scientist, Feb. 1977, 255–257.

BOWLBY, J. Attachment and loss (Vol. 2): Separation, anxiety and anger. New York: Basic Books, 1973.

BRACKBILL, Y. Extinction of the smiling response in infants as a function of reinforcement schedule. Child Development, 1958, 29, 115–124.

BRADY, J. V., PORTER, R. W., CONRAD, D. G., and MASON, J. W. Avoidance behavior and the development of gastroduodenal ulcers. Journal of the Experimental Analysis of Behavior, 1958, 11, 69–73.

BRAMEL, D., JAUB, B., and BLUM, B. An observer's reaction to the suffering of his enemy. Journal of Personality and Social Psychology, 1968, 8, 384–392.

BRAMMER, L. M., and SHOSTROM, E. L. Therapeutic psychology: Fundamentals of counseling and psychotherapy (3rd ed.). Englewood Cliffs, N.J.: Prentice-Hall, 1977.

BRASHLER, W. Josh Gibson: A life in the Negro Leagues. New York: Harper & Row, 1978.

BRAY, D. W., and HOWARD, A. Career success and life satisfaction of middle-aged managers. In L. A. Bond and J. C. Rosen (Eds.), Competence and coping during adulthood. Hanover, N.H.: University Press of New England, 1980.

BRECHNER, K., and LINDER, D. A social trap analysis of energy distribution systems. In A. Baum and J. Singer (Eds.), Advances in environmental psychology (Vol. 3). Hillsdale, N.J.: Erlbaum, 1981.

BREHM, J. W., and Aderman, D. On the relationship between empathy and the actor versus observer hypothesis. Journal of Research in Personality, 1977, 11, 340–346.

BREHM, J., and CROCKER, J. An experiment on hunger. In J. Brehm and A. Cohen (Eds.), Explorations in cognitive dissonance. New York: Wiley, 1962.

BRIM, O. G., JR. Theories of the male midlife crisis. Counseling Psychologist, 1976, 6, 2–9.

BROADBECK, J. Neural control of hunger, appetite and satiety. *Yale Journal of Biological Medicine*, 1957, *29*, 565–574.

BROADBENT, D. *Decision and Stress*. New York: Academic Press, 1971.

BROCK, T. Communicator-recipient similarity and decision change. *Journal of Personality and Social Psychology*, 1965, *1*, 650–654.

BROVERMAN, J. K., VOGEL, S. R., BROVERMAN, D. M., CLARKSON, F. G., and ROSENKANTZ, P. S. Sex-role stereotypes: A current appraisal. *Journal of Social Issues*, 1972, *28*, 59–78.

BROWN, G. W., HARRIS, T., and COPELAND, J. R. Depression and loss. *British Journal of Psychiatry*. 1977, *130*, 1–18.

BROWN, P. K., and WALD, G. Visual pigments in single rod and cones of the human retina. *Science*, 1964, *144*, 45–52.

BROWN, R. *Social psychology*, New York: Free Press, 1965.

BROWN, R., CAZDEN, C. B., and BELLUGI, U. The child's grammar from I to III. In Hill, J. P. (Ed.), *Minnesota symposium on child psychology*. Vol. 2. Minneapolis: University of Minnesota Press, 1969.

BROWN, R. W., and McNEILL, D. The "tip of-the-tongue" phenomenon. *Journal of Verbal Learning and Verbal Behavior*, 1966, *5*, 325–337.

BRUNER, J. S., and KOSLOWSKI, B. Visually preadapted constituents of manipulatory action. *Perception*, 1972, *1*, 1–122.

BRY, A. *60 hours that transform your life: est*. New York: Avon Books, 1976.

BUCKHOUT, R. Eyewitness testimony. *Scientific American*, December, 1974.

BUGLIOSI, V., and GENTRY, C. *Helter skelter: The true story of the Manson murders*. New York: Norton, 1974.

BUNNY, W. E., JR., GOODWIN, F. K., MURPHY, D. L., and BORGE, G. F. The "switch process" in manic-depressive illness: I and II. *Archives of General Psychiatry*, 1972, *27*, 295–302.

BURGESS, E., and WALLIN, P. *Engagement and marriage*. Philadelphia: Lippincott, 1953.

BURNAM, M. A., PENNEBAKER, J. W., and GLASS, D. C. Time consciousness, achievement striving, and the type A coronary-prone behavior pattern. *Journal of Abnormal Psychology*. 1975, *84*, 76–79.

BURNSTEIN, E., VINOKUR, A., and TROPE, Y. Interpersonal comparison versus persuasive argumentation: A more direct test of alternative explanations for group-induced shifts in individual choice. *Journal of Experimental Social Psychology*, 1973, *9*, 236–245.

BURNSTEIN, S. Persuasion as argument processing. In M. Brandstatter, J. Davis, and G. Stocker-Kreichgaver (Eds.), *Group decision processes*. London: Academic Press, in press.

BURT, C. The genetic determination of differences in intelligence: A study of monozygotic twins reared together and apart.

British Journal of Psychology, 1966, *57*, 137–153.

BUTLER, R., and ALEXANDER, H. Daily patterns of visual exploratory behavior in the monkeys. *Journal of Comparative and Physiological Psychology*, 1955, *48*, 257–249.

BYRNE, D. *The attraction paradigm*. New York: Academic Press, 1971.

BYRNE, D., BASKETT, C. D., and HODGES, L. Behavioral indicators of interpersonal attraction. *Journal of Abnormal and Social Psychology*, 1971, *1*, 137–149.

BYRNE, D., and KELLEY, K. *An introduction to personality* (3rd ed.). Englewood Cliffs, N.J.: Prentice-Hall, 1981.

CADORET, R. J. Psychopathology in adopted-away offspring of biological parents with antisocial behavior. *Archives of General Psychiatry*, 1978, *35*, 176–184.

CADORET, R. J., and WINOFUR, G. X-linkage in manic-depressive illness. *Annual Review of Medicine*, 1975, *26*, 21–25.

CALHOUN, J. Population density and social pathology. *Scientific American*, 1962, *206*, 139–148.

CAMERON, N. *Personality development and psychopathology*. Boston: Houghton-Mifflin, 1963.

CAMPBELL, F. W. The transmission of spatial information through the visual system. In F. O. Schmitt and F. G. Worden (Eds.), *The neurosciences: Third study program*. Cambridge, Mass.: M.I.T. Press, 1974.

CAMPOS, J. L., LANGER, A., and KROWITZ, A. Cardiac responses on the visual cliff in prelocomotor human infants. *Science*, 1970, *170*, 196–197.

CANDLAND, D. K. *Psychology: The experimental approach*. New York: McGraw-Hill, 1968.

CANESTRARI, R. E. Paced and self-paced learning in young and elderly adults. *Journal of Gerontology*, 1963, *18*, 165–168.

CANNON, W. *Bodily changes in pain, hunger, fear and rage*. New York: Appleton-Century-Crofts, 1929.

CANNON, W. B. The emergency function of the adrenal medulla in pain and the major emotions. *American Journal of Physiology*, 1914, *33*, 356–372.

CANNON, W. B., and WASHBURN, A. An explanation of hunger. *American Journal of Physiology*, 1912, *29*, 441–454.

CANTRIL, H. *The pattern of human concerns*. New Brunswick, N.J.: Rutgers University Press, 1965.

CAPPON, D. Mental health in the high rise. *Canadian Journal of Public Health*, 1971, *62*, 426–431.

CARLSMITH, J. M., ELLSWORTH, P. C., and ARONSON, E. *Methods of research in social psychology*. Reading, Mass.: Addison-Wesley, 1976.

CARLSON, N. *Physiology of behavior*. Boston, Mass.: Allyn & Bacon, 1977.

CARLSON, V. R. Instructions and perceptual constancy judgements. In W. Epstein (Ed.), *Stability and constancy in visual perception: Mechanisms and processes*. New York: Wiley, 1977.

CARPENTER, F. *The Skinner primer*. New York: Free Press, 1974.

CARPENTER, G. C. Visual regard of moving and stationary faces in early infancy. *Merrill-Palmer Quarterly*, 1974, *20*, 181–194.

CARVER, C., and GLASS, D. Coronary-prone behavior pattern and interpersonal aggression. *Journal of Personality and Social Psychology*, 1978, *36*, 361–366.

CASTANEDA, C. *Journey to Ixtlan: The lessons of Don Juan*. New York: Simon & Schuster, 1972.

CASPER, R. C., and DAVIS, J. M. On the course of anorexia nervosa. *American Journal of Psychiatry*, 1977, *134*, 974–978.

CASTILLO, M., and BUTTERWORTH, G. Neonatal localization of a sound in visual space. *Perception*, 1981, *10*, 331–338.

CASTLEMAN, M. Why teenagers get pregnant. *The Nation*, November 26, 1977, 549–552.

CATTELL, R. B. *The culture free intelligence test*. Champaign, Ill.: Institute for Personality and Ability Testing, 1949.

CATTELL, R. B. *The scientific analysis of personality*. Harmondsworth, England: Penguin Books, 1965.

CATTELL, R. *Personality and mood by questionaire*. San Francisco: Jossey-Bass, 1973.

CAUTELA, J. R. Covert conditioning: Assumptions and procedures. *Journal of Mental Imagery*, 1977, *1*, 53–64.

CAVAN, S. *Liquor license*. Chicago: Aldine, 1966.

CHEN, S. C. Social modification of the activity of ants in nest building. *Physiological Zoology*, 1937, *10*, 420–437.

CHOMSKY, N. *Reflections on language*. New York: Pantheon, 1975.

CIALDINI, R. Reciprocal concessions procedure for inducing compliance: The door-in-the-face technique. *Journal of Personality and Social Psychology*, 1975, *31*, 206–215.

CLARK, K. B., and CLARK, M. P. Racial identification and preferences in Negro children. In T. M. Newcomb and E. L. Hartley (Eds.), *Readings in social psychology*. New York: Holt, Rinehart and Winston, 1947, 169–178.

CLARKE, A. An examination of the operation of residual propinquity as a factor of mate selection. *American Sociological Review*, 1952, *27*, 17–22.

CLAVAN, S. The impact of social class and social trends on the role of grandparents. *The Family Coordinator*, 1978, *27*, 351–358.

CLAPTON, W. *Personality and career change. Industrial Gerontology*, 1973, *17*, 9–17.

CLECKLEY, H. *The mask of sanity* (5th ed.). St. Louis, Mo.: Mosby, 1976.

CLIFFORD, M., and WALSTER, E. The effect of physical attractiveness on teacher expectation. *Sociology of Education*, 1973, *46*, 248.

COCHISE, C. N., and GRIFFITH, A. K. *The first 100 years of Nino Cochise.* New York: Abelard-Schuman, 1971.

COE, W. C. The problem of relevance versus ethics in researching hypnosis and antisocial conduct. *Annals of the New York Academy of Sciences*, 1977, *296*, 90–104.

COFER, C. *Motivation and Emotion.* Glenview, Ill.: Scott, Foresman, 1974.

COHEN, A. Communication discrepancy and attitude change: A dissonance theory. *Journal of Personality*, 1959, *27*, 386–396.

COHEN, D. *Dreams, visions, and drugs: A search for other realities.* New York: Franklin Watts, 1976.

COHEN, L. D., KIPNES, D., KUNKLE, E. G., and KUBZANSKY, P. E. Observations of a person with congenital insensitivity to pain. *Journal of Abnormal and Social Psychology*, 1955, *51*, 333–338.

COHEN, S. Environmental load and the allocation of attention. In A. Baum and S. Valins (Eds.), *Advances in environmental research.* Hillsdale, N.J.: Erlbaum, 1977.

COHEN, S. Sensory changes in the elderly. *American Journal of Nursing*, 1981, *81*, 1851–1880.

COHEN, S., and WEINSTEIN, T. Nonauditory effects of noise on behavior and health. *Journal of Social Issues*, 1981, *37*, 36–70.

COHEN, S., GLASS, D. C., and SINGER, J. E. Apartment noise, auditory discrimination, and reading ability in children. *Journal of Experimental Social Psychology*, 1973, *9*, 407–422.

COHEN, S., EVANS, G., KRANTZ, D., STOKOLS, D., and KELLY, S. Aircraft noise and children: Longitudinal and cross-sectional evidence of adaptation to noise and the effectiveness of noise abatement. *Journal of Personality and Social Psychology*, 1981.

COLE, C. S., and COYNE, J. C. Situational specificity of laboratory-induced learned helplessness. *Journal of Abnormal Psychology*, 1977, *86*, 615–623.

COLEMAN, J. C., BUTCHER, J. N., and CARSON, R. C. *Abnormal psychology in modern life* (6th ed.). Glenview, Ill.: Scott, Foresman, 1980.

COLLINS, A. M., and QUILLIAN, M. R. Retrieval time from semantic memory. *Journal of Verbal Learning and Verbal Behavior*, 1969, *8*, 240–247.

COLLINS, B. *Public and private conformity: Competing explanations by improvisation, cognitive dissonance, and attribution theories.* Andover, Mass.: Warner Modular Publications, 1973.

COMMITTEE OF VETERANS AFFAIRS. *Legacies of Vietnam: Comparative adjustment of veterans and their peers.* Washington, D.C.: U. S. G. P. O., 1981.

CONRAD, R. Acoustic confusions in immediate memory. *British Journal of Psychology*, 1964, *55*, 75–84.

CONE, J., and HAYES, S. *Environmental problems and behavioral solutions.* Monterey, Calif.: Brooks/Cole, 1980.

CONROY, J., and SUNDSTROM, E. Territorial dominance in dyadic conversation as a function of similarity of opinion. *Journal of Personality and Social Psychology*, 1977, *39*, 570–576.

CONWAY, J. Behavioral self-control of smoking through aversive conditioning and self-management. *Journal of Consulting and Clinical Psychology*, 1977, *45*, 348–357.

COOK, S. W. Interpersonal and attitudinal outcomes in cooperating interracial groups. *Journal of Research and Development in Education*, 1978, *12*.

COOPER, H. Statistics combining independent studies: A meta-analysis of sex differences in conformity research. *Journal of Personality and Social Psychology*, 1979, *37*, 131–146.

COOPER, J., and AXSON, D. Effort justification in psychotherapy. In G. Weary and H. Mirels (Eds.), *Emerging integrations of clinical and social psychology*, 1982.

COOPER, J., and FAZIO, R. The formation and persistence of attitudes that support intergroup conflict. In W. Austin and S. Worchel (Eds.), *The social psychology of intergroup relations.* Monterey, Calif.: Brooks/Cole, 1979.

COOPER, J., and WORCHEL, S. Role of undesired consequences in arousing cognitive dissonance. *Journal of Personality and Social Psychology*, 1970, *16*, 199–206.

COOPER, J., DARLEY, J. M., and HENDERSON, J. T. On the effectiveness of deviant and conventionally appearing communicators: A field experiment. *Journal of Personality and Social Psychology*, 1974, *29*, 752–757.

COOPER, R., and ZUBEK, J. Effects of enriched and restricted early environments on the learning ability of bright and dull rats. *Canadian Journal of Psychology*, 1958, *12*, 159–164.

COREN, S., and GIRUS, J. S. *Seeing is deceiving.* Hillsdale, N.J.: Erlbaum, 1978.

COREY, G., and COREY, M. S. *Groups: Process and practice.* Monterey, Calif.: Brooks/Cole, 1977.

CORNSWEET, T. N. *Visual perception.* New York: Academic Press, 1970.

COSTA, P. T., JR., and MCCRAE, R. R. Still stable after all these years: Personality as a key to some issues in aging. In P. B. Baltes and O. G. Brim, Jr. (Eds.), *Life-span development and behavior* (Vol. 3). New York: Academic Press, 1980.

COTMAN, C. W., and MCGAUGH, J. L. *Behavioral neuroscience.* New York: Academic Press, 1980.

COTTRELL, N. Social facilitation. In C. McClintock (Ed.), *Experimental social psychology.* New York: Holt, Rinehart and Winston, 1972.

COX, F. D. *Youth, marriage and the seductive society.* Dubuque, Iowa: William C Brown, 1974.

COYNE, J. Toward an interactional description of depression. *Psychiatry*, 1976, *39*, 14–27. (b)

COYNE, J. Depression and the response of others. *Journal of Abnormal Psychology*, 1976, *85*, 186–193. (a)

COYNE, J., and LAZARUS, R. Cognition, stress, and coping: A transactional perspective. In I. Kutash and L. Schlesinger (Eds.), *Pressure point: Perspectives on stress and anxiety.* San Francisco: Jossey-Bass, 1981.

CRAIG, C., and MCCANN, J. Developing strategies for influencing residential consumption of electricity. *Journal of Environmental Systems*, 1980, *9*, 175–188.

CRAIK, F. I. M., and LOCKHART, R. S. Levels of processing: A framework for memory research. *Journal of Verbal Learning and Verbal Behavior*, 1972, *11*, 671–684.

CRANO, W., and MELLON, P. Causal inference of teachers' expectations in childrens' academic performance across logged panel analysis. *Journal of Educational Psychology*, 1978, *70*, 39–49.

CRANDALL, V. Achievement. In H. Stevenson (Ed.), *Child psychology.* Chicago, Ill.: University of Chicago Press, 1963.

CRISP, A. H., PALMER, R. L., and KALUCY, R. S. How common is anorexia nervosa? A prevalence study. *British Journal of Psychiatry*, 1976, *128*, 549–554.

CROCKENBURG, S. B. Creativity tests: A boon or boondoggle for education? *Review of Educational Research*, 1972, *42*, 27–45.

CRONBACK, L. J., and SNOW, R. E. *Aptitudes and instructional methods.* New York: Irvington, 1977.

CRUTCHFIELD, R. S. Conformity and character. *American Psychologist*, 1955, *10*, 191–198.

CSIKSZENTMIHALYI, M. Flow: Studies of enjoyment (Report No. RO1 HM22–883–02). Washington, D.C.: U.S. Public Health Service, 1974.

CURTISS, S. *Genie: A psycholinguistic study of a modern-day "wild child."* New York: Academic Press, 1977.

CUTTING, J. E., and PROFFITT, D. R. Gait perception as an example of how we may perceive events. In R. D. Walk and H. L. Pick, Jr. (Eds.), *Intersensory perception and sensory integration.* New York: Plenum, 1981.

DANIELS, J. *The man of Independence.* Philadelphia, Penn.: Lippincott, 1950.

DARLEY, J., and COOPER, J. The "Clean for Gene" phenomenon: Deciding to vote for or against a candidate on the basis of the physical appearance of his supporters. *Journal of Applied Social Psychology*, 1972, *2*, 24–33.

DARLEY, J. M., and LATANE, B. Bystander intervention in emergencies: Diffusion of responsibility. *Journal of Personality and Social Psychology*, 1968, *8*, 377–383.

DAVENPORT, Y. B., ADLAND, M. L., GOLD, P. W., and GOODWYN, F. K. Manic-depressive illness: Psycho-dynamic features of multigenerational families. *American Journal of Orthopsychiatry*, 1979, *49*, 24–35.

DAVIDSON, W. S. II. Studies of aversive conditioning for alcoholics: A critical review of theory and research methodology. *Psychological Bulletin*, 1974, *81*, 571–581.

DAVIS, C. M. Self-selection of diet by newly weaned infants. *American Journal of Diseases of Children*, 1928, *36*, 651–679.

DAVIS, J. A two-factor theory of schizophrenia. *Journal of Psychiatric Research*, 1974, *11*, 25–29.

DAVIS, J., and LAMBERTH, J. Affective arousal and energization properties of positive and negative stimuli. *Journal of Experimental Psychology*, 1974, *103*, 196–200.

DAVIS, J., BRAY, R., and HOLT, R. The empirical study of decision processes in juries. In J. Tapp and F. Levine (Eds.), *Law, justice and the individual in society: Psychological and legal issues.* New York: Holt, Rinehart & Winston, 1977.

DAVIS, J., GALLAGHER, R., and LADOVE, R. Food intake controlled by a blood factor. *Science*, 1967, *156*, 1247–1248.

DAVIS, J., CAMPBELL, C., GALLAGHER, R., and ZUKRAKOV, M. Disappearance of a humoral satiety factor during food deprivation. *Journal of Comparative and Physiological Psychology*, 1971, *75*, 476–482.

DAVISON, G. C., and NEALE, J. M. Abnormal psychology (2nd ed.). New York: Wiley, 1978.

DEAUX, K. *The behavior of women and men.* Belmont, Calif.: Brooks/Cole, 1976.

DEESE, J. Influence of inter-item associative strength upon immediate free recall. *Psychological Reports*, 1959, *5*, 305–312.

DEESE, J. *The structure of associations in language and thought.* Baltimore, Md.: Johns Hopkins University Press, 1965.

DEESE, J. Text structure, strategies, and comprehension in learning from textbooks. In Robinson, J. (Ed.), *Research in Science Education: New Questions, New Directions.* BSCS, Boulder, Colorado, 1980.

DEINER, E. Deindividuation: Causes and consequences. *Social Behavior and Personality*, 1977, *5*, 143–155.

DEINER, E., FRASER, S. C., BEAMAN, A. L., and KELEM, R. T. Effects of deindividuation variables on stealing among Halloween trick-or-treaters. *Journal of Personality and Social Psychology*, 1976, *33*, 178–183.

DELGADO, J. M. R. Emotional behavior in animals and humans. *Psychiatric Research Reports*, 1960, *12*, 259–266.

DEMBER, W. A new look in motivation. *American Scientist*, 1965, *53*, 409–427.

DEMENT, W. C. *Some must watch while some must sleep.* New York: Norton, 1974.

DE MEYER, M. K. The nature of the neuropsychological disability in autistic children. In E. Schopler and R. J. Reichler (Eds.), *Psychopathology and child development.* New York: Plenum Press, 1976, 93–114.

DENNEY, N. W. Classification abilities in the elderly. *Journal of Gerontology*, 1974, *29*, 309–314.

DENNIS, W. Does culture appreciably affect patterns of infant behavior? *Journal of Social Psychology*, 1940, *12*, 305–317.

DENNIS, W. *Children of the crèche.* Englewood Cliffs, N.J.: Prentice-Hall, 1973.

DENNY, D., and Sullivan, B. Desensitization and modeling treatments of spider fear using two types of scenes. *Journal of Consulting and Clinical Psychology*, 1976, *44*, 573–579.

DEPUE, R. A., and EVANS, R. The psychobiology of depressive disorders. In B. H. Maher (Ed.), *Progress in experimental personality research* (Vol. 8). New York: Academic Press, 1976.

DER-KARABETRAN, A., and SMITH, A. Sex-role stereotyping in the United States: Is it changing? *Sex Roles*, 1977, *3*, 193–198.

DESOR, T. Toward a psychological theory of crowding. *Journal of Personality and Social Psychology*, 1972, *21*, 79–83.

DE VRIES, H. A. Physiological effects of an exercise training regimen upon men aged 52 to 88. *Journal of Gerontology*, 1970, *25*, 325–336.

DE VRIES, H. A. Physiology of exercise and aging. In D. S. Woodruff and J. E. Birren (Eds.), *Aging: Scientific perspectives and social issues.* New York: Van Nostrand, 1975.

DIACONIS, P. Statistical problems in ESP research. *Science*, 1978, *201*, 131–136.

DIES, R., and GREENBURG, B. Effects of physical contact in an encounter group context. *Journal of Consulting and Clinical Psychology*, 1976, *44*, 400–405.

DiMENTO, J. Making usable information on environmental stressors: Opportunities for the research and policy communities. *Journal of Social Issues*, 1981, *37*, 172–205.

DITTES, J., and KELLEY, H. H. Effects on different conditions of acceptance upon conformity to group norms. *Journal of Abnormal and Social Psychology*, 1956, *53*, 100–107.

DOBELLE, W. H. Current status of research on providing sight to the blind by electrical stimulation of the brain. *Journal of Visual Impairment and Blindness*, 1977, *71*, 290–297.

DOLLARD, J., DOOB, L., MILLER, N., MOWRER, O., and SEARS, R. *Frustration and aggression.* New Haven, Conn.: Yale University Press, 1939.

DONNERSTEIN, E., and WILSON, D. W. Effects of noise and perceived control on ongoing and subsequent aggressive behavior. *Journal of Personality and Social Psychology*, 1976, *34*, 774–781.

DOSEY, M. A., and MEISELS, M. Personal space and self-protection. *Journal of Personality and Social Psychology*, 1969, *11*, 93–97.

DOTY, R. L. Changes in the intensity and pleasantness of human vaginal odors during the menstrual cycle. *Science*, 1975, *190*, 1316–1318.

DRUG ABUSE COUNCIL. *The facts about "drug abuse."* New York: The Free Press, 1980.

DUNHAM, H. W. *Community and schizophrenia: An epidemiological analysis.* Detroit: Wayne State University Press, 1965.

DUNKER, K. On problem solving. *Psychological Monographs*, 1945, *58*, 5 (Whole No. 270).

DUNPHY, D. C. The social structure of urban adolescent peer groups. *Sociometry*, 1963, *26*, 230–246.

DURLAK, J. Comparative effectiveness of paraprofessional and professional helpers. *Psychological Bulletin*, 1979, *86*, 80–92.

DUSTIN, R., and GEORGE, R. *Action counseling for behavior change* (2nd ed.). Cranston, R. I.: Carroll Press, 1977.

DUTTON, D. G., and ARON, A. P. Some evidence for heightened sexual attraction under conditions of high anxiety. *Journal of Personality and Social Psychology*, 1974, *30*, 510–517.

EBBINGHAUS, H. *Memory: A contribution to experimental psychology* (H. A. Ruger and C. E. Bussenius, trans.). New York: Teachers College, 1885.

EBENHOLTZ, S. M. Hysteresis effects in the vergence control system: Perceptual implications. In D. F. Fisher, R. A. Monty, and J. W. Senders (Eds.), *Eye movements: Cognition and visual perception.* Hillsdale, N.J.: Erlbaum, 1981.

EBENHOLTZ, S. M., and SHEBILSKE, W. L. The doll reflex: Ocular counterrolling with head-body tilt in median plane. *Vision Research*, 1975, *15*, 713–717.

ECCLES, J. C. *The understanding of the brain.* New York: McGraw-Hill, 1973.

EDNEY, J. J. Territoriality and control: a field experiment. *Journal of Personality and Social Psychology*, 1975, *31*, 1108–1115.

EFRAN, M. G. The effect of physical appearance on the judgement of guilt, interpersonal attraction, and severity of recommended punishment in a simulated jury task. *Journal of Research in Personality*, 1974, *8*, 45–54.

EHRLICH, P. *The population bomb.* New York: Ballantine Books, 1968.

EIBL-EIBESFELDT, I. *Ethology: The biology of behavior.* (E. Klinghammer, trans.). New York: Holt, Rinehart and Winston, 1970.

EISDORFER, C. Arousal and performance: Experiments in verbal learning and a tentative theory. In G. A. Talland (Ed.), *Human aging and behavior*. New York: Academic Press, 1968.

EKMAN, P., and FRIESEN, W. V. Constants across cultures in the face and emotion. *Journal of Personality and Social Psychology*, 1971, *17*, 124–129.

EKMAN, P., FRIESEN, W., and ANCOLI, S. Facial signs of emotional experience. *Journal of Personality and Social Psychology*, 1980, *39*, 1125–1134.

EKMAN, P., SORENSON, E. R., and FRIESEN, W. V. Pan-cultural elements in facial displays of emotion. *Science*, 1969, *164*, 86–88.

ELKIND, D. Growing up faster. *Psychology Today*, February 1979, 38–45.

ELLIS, A. *Reason and emotion in psychotherapy*. New York: Lyle Stuart, 1962.

ELLIS, A., and GRIEGER, R. *RET: Handbook of rational-emotive therapy*. New York: Springer, 1977.

ELLIS, H. Mescal: A study of a divine plant. *Popular Science Monthly*, 1902, *41*, 52–71.

ELLSWORTH, P., and TOURANGEAU, R. Our failure to disconfirm what nobody ever said. *Journal of Personality and Social Psychology*, 1981, *40*, 363–369.

ENGEN, T. Why the aroma lingers on. *Psychology Today*, May 1980, 138.

EPSTEIN, N., and JACKSON, E. An outcome study of short-term communication training with married couples. *Journal of Consulting and Clinical Psychology*, 1978, *46*, 207–212.

EPSTEIN, W. The process of "taking into account" in visual perception. *Perception*, 1973, *2*, 267–285.

EPSTEIN, Y. Crowding, stress and human behavior. *Journal of Social Issues*, 1981, *37*, 126–145.

ERIKSON, E. H. Identity and the life cycle: Selected papers. *Psychological Issues*, 1959, *1*, 50–100.

ERIKSON, E. H. *Childhood and society*. New York: Norton, 1963.

ERLENMEYER-KIMLING, L., and JARVIK, L. F. Genetics and intelligence: A review. *Science*, 1963, *142*, 1477–1479.

ESTES, T. H., and SHEBILSKE, W. L. Comprehension: Of what the reader sees of what the author says. In M. L. Kamil and S. J. Moe (Eds.), *Twenty-ninth yearbook of the national reading conference*, 1980, 99–104.

EVANS, G., and JACOBS, S. Air pollution and human behavior. *Journal of Social Issues*, 1981, 95–125.

EVANS, G. W., and HOWARD, R. B. Personal space. *Psychological Bulletin*, 1973, *80*, 334–344.

EXNER, J. *The Rorschach: A comprehensive system*. New York: John Wiley, 1974.

EYSENCK, H. J. The effects of psychotherapy: An evaluation. *Journal of Consulting Psychology*, 1952, *16*, 319–324.

EYSENCK, H. J. *The I. Q. argument: Race, intelligence, and education*. La Salle,
Ill.: Open Court Publishing Company, 1971.

FANTZ, R. L. Patterns of vision in newborn infants. *Science*, 1963, *140*, 296–297.

FARINA, A., GHLIA, D., BOUDREAU, L. A., ALLEN, J. G., and SHERMAN, M. Mental illness and the impact of believing others know about it. *Journal of Abnormal Psychology*, 1971, *77*, 1–5.

FARIS, R. E. L., and DUNHAM, H. W. *Mental disorders in urban areas: An ecological study of schizophrenia and other psychoses*. Chicago: University of Chicago Press, 1939.

FARRON, D. C., and RAMEY, C. T. Infant day care and attachment behaviors toward mothers and teachers. *Child Development*, 1977, *48*, 1112–1116.

FAZIO, R., and ZANNA, M. Direct experience and attitude-behavior consistency. In L. Berkowitz, *Advances in Experimental Social Psychology* (Vol. 14), New York: Academic Press, 1981.

FEATHER, N. T. Reactions to male and female success and failure in sex-linked occupations: Impressions of personality, causal attributions, and perceived likelihood of different consequences. *Journal of Personality and Social Psychology*, 1975, *31*, 20–31.

FELDMAN, M. W., and LEWONTIN, R. C. The heritability hang-up. *Science*, 1975, *190*, 1163–1168.

FERGUSON, M. *The brain revolution: The frontiers of mind research*. New York: Taplinger, 1973.

FERRELL, R. *Off the record*. New York: Harper & Row, 1980.

FERRERO, G. *Criminal man according to the classification of Cesare Lombroso*. New York: Putnam's, 1911.

FESTINGER, L. A theory of social comparison processes. *Human Relations*, 1954, *7*, 117–140.

FESTINGER, L. *A theory of cognitive dissonance*. Stanford, Calif.: Stanford University Press, 1957.

FESTINGER, L., and CARLSMITH, M. Cognitive consequences of forced compliance. *Journal of Abnormal and Social Psychology*, 1959, *58*, 203–210.

FESTINGER, L., SCHACHTER, S., and BACK, K. *Social pressures in informal groups: A study of a housing community*. Stanford, Calif.: Stanford University Press, 1950.

FIEDLER, F. The trouble with leadership training is that it doesn't train leaders. *Psychology Today*, 1973, *6*, 23–30.

FIEDLER, F. The contingency model and the dynamics of the leadership process. In L. Berkowitz (Ed.), *Advances in experimental social psychology* (Vol 2). New York: Academic Press, 1978.

FIEDLER, F. E. *Leadership*, New York: General Learning Press, 1971.

FISHBEIN, M. Attitudes towards objects as predictions of single and multiple behavioral criteria. *Psychological Review*, 1974, *81* (1), 59–74.

FISHBEIN, M., and AZJEN, I. *Belief, attitude, intention, and behavior: An introduction to theory and research*. Reading, Mass.: Addison-Wesley, 1975.

FISHER, J., and BYRNE, D. Too close for comfort: Sex differences in response to invasions of personal space. *Journal of Personality and Social Psychology*, 1975, *32*, 15–21.

FISHER, J., NADLER, A., and WHITCHER, S. Recipient reactions to aid: A conceptual review and a new theoretical framework. Unpublished manuscript. University of Connecticut, Storrs, 1980.

FLOWERS, M. L. A lab test of some implications of Janis' groupthink hypothesis. *Journal of Personality and Social Psychology*, 1977.

FOX, G. L. The family's influence on adolescent sexual behavior. *Children Today*, May–June 1979, 21–25.

FOZARD, J. L., WOLF, E., BELL, B., McFARLAND, R. A., and PODOLSKY, S. Visual perception and communication. In J. E. Birren and K. W. Schaie (Eds.), *Handbook of the psychology of aging*. New York: Van Nostrand, 1977.

FRANKENBURG, W. K., and DODDS, J. B. The Denver developmental screening test. *Journal of Pediatrics*, 1967, *71*, 181–191.

FRASER, S., GOUGE, C., and BILLIG, M. Risky shifts, cautious shifts and group polarization. *European Journal of Social Psychology*, 1971.

FREDERICK, C. J. Current trends in suicidal behavior in the United States. *American Journal of Psychotherapy*, 1978, *32* (2), 172–200.

FREDERIKSEN, C. H. Effects of context-induced processing operations on semantic information acquired from discourse. *Cognitive Psychology*, 1975, *1*, 139–166.

FREEDMAN, J., and FRASER, S. Compliance without pressure: The foot-in-the-door technique. *Journal of Personality and Social Psychology*, 1966, *4*, 195–202.

FREEDMAN, J., HESHKA, S., and LEVY, A. Population density and pathology: Is there a relationship? *Journal of Experimental Social Psychology*, 1975, *11*, 539–552.

FREEDMAN, J., KLEVANSKY, S., and EHRLICH, P. The effect of crowding on human task performance. *Journal of Applied Social Psychology*, 1971, *1*, 7–25.

FREEDMAN, J. L., and DOOB, A. N. *Deviancy*. New York: Academic Press, 1968.

FRENCH, E. G. Effects of interaction of motivation and feedback on task performance. In Atkinson, J. W. (Ed.), *Motives in fantasy, action, and society*. New York: Van Nostrand, 400–408.

FREUD, S. *The interpretation of dreams, Vols. IV, V*. London: Hogarth Press, 1900 (standard edition, 1953).

FREUD, S. *New introductory lectures on psycho-analysis*. New York: Norton, 1933.

FRIEDMAN, M., and ROSENMAN, R. H. *Type A behavior and your heart.* New York: Knopf, 1974.

FRIEZE, I., PARSONS, J. E., JOHNSON, P. B., RUBLE, D. N., and ZELLMAN, G. L. *Women and sex roles: A social psychological perspective.* New York: Norton, 1978.

FROMM, E. *Man for himself.* New York: Holt, Rinehart and Winston, 1955.

FROMM, E. *The art of loving.* New York: Harper & Row, 1956.

GALANTER, E. Contemporary psychophysics. In R. Brown et al. (Eds.), *New directions in psychology.* New York: Holt, Rinehart and Winston, 1962, pp. 89–156.

GALIZIO, M., and HENDRICK, C. Effect of musical accompaniment on attitude: The guitar as a prop for persuasion. *Journal of Applied Social Psychology,* 1972, *2*, 350–359.

GALTON, F. Psychometric experiments. *Brain,* 1879, *2*, 149–162.

GARCIA, J., and KOELLING, R. A. Relation of cues to consequences in avoidance learning. *Psychonomic Science,* 1966, *4*, 123–124.

GARDNER, B. T., and GARDNER, R. A. Evidence for sentence constituents in the early utterances of child and chimpanzee. *Journal of Experimental Psychology: General,* 1975, *104*, 244–267.

GARDNER, R. A., and GARDNER, B. T. Teaching sign language to a chimpanzee. *Science,* 1969, *165*, 664–672.

GARFIELD, S. L., and BERGIN, A. E. (Eds.), *Handbook of psychotherapy and behavior change* (2nd ed). New York: Wiley, 1978.

GARNER, W. Good patterns have few alternatives. *American Scientist,* 1970, *58*, 34–42.

GATCHEL, R. Perceived control: A review and evaluation of therapeutic implications. In Baum, A., and Singer, J. *Advances in environmental psychology.* Hillsdale, N.J.: Erlbaum, 1980.

GEBHARD, A. Incidence of overt homosexuality in the United States and Western Europe. In J. M. Livingood (Ed.), *National Institute of Mental Health task force on homosexuality: Final report and background papers.* Rockville, Md.: National Institute of Mental Health, 1972.

GEEN, R. G., and QUANTY, M. The catharsis of aggression: An evaluation of a hypothesis. In L. Berkowitz (Ed.), *Advances in experimental social psychology* (Vol. 10). New York: Academic Press, 1977.

GELDARD, F. A. *The human senses.* New York: Wiley, 1972.

GELENBERG, A. J. The rational use of psychotropic drugs: Prescribing antidepressants. *Drug Therapy,* 1979, *9*, 95–112.

GELLER, S. H., ENDLER, N. S., and WIESENTHAL, D. L. Conformity as a function of task generalization and relative competence. *European Journal of Social Psychology,* 1973, *3*, 53–62.

GEORGE, R., and CRISTIANI, T. *Theory, methods, and process of counseling and psychology.* Englewood Cliffs, N.J.: Prentice-Hall, 1981.

GERARD, H. B., WILHELMY, R. A., and CONNOLLEY, E. S. Conformity and group size. *Journal of Personality and Social Psychology,* 1968, *8*, 79–82.

GERBNER, G., and GROSS, L. The scary world of TV's heavy viewer. *Psychology Today,* 1976, *89*, 41–45.

GERGEN, K. *The concept of self.* New York: Holt, Rinehart, and Winston, 1971.

GERGEN, K., and GERGEN, M. International assistance from a psychological perspective. *Yearbook of world affairs,* 1971 (Vol. 25.), London: Institute of World Affairs, 1972.

GESCHWIND, N. Specializations of the human brain. *Scientific American,* 1979, *241*, 180–199.

GEWIRTZ, J. L. The course of infant smiling in four child-rearing environments in Israel. In B. M. Foss (Ed.), *Determinants of infant behavior* (Vol. 3). London: Methuen, 1965.

GEWIRTZ, J. L., and BAER, D. M. The effect of brief social deprivation on behaviors for a social reinforcer. *Journal of Abnormal Social Psychology,* 1958, 165–172. (b)

GEWIRTZ, J. L., and BAER, D. M. Deprivation and satiation of social reinforcers as drive conditions. *Journal of Abnormal Social Psychology,* 1958, 165–172. (a)

GIBSON, J. J. Optical motions and transformation as stimuli for visual perception. *Psychological Review,* 1957, *64*, 288–295.

GIBSON, J. J. *The ecological approach to visual perception.* Boston: Houghton Mifflin, 1979.

GILBERT, W., and VILLA-KOMAROFF, L. Useful proteins from recombinant bacteria. *Scientific American,* 1980, *242*, 74–94.

GILCHRIST, A. Perceived achromatic color as a function of ratios within phenomenal planes. Ph.D. thesis. Rutgers University, 1975.

GILLAM, B. Geometrical illusions. *Scientific American,* 1980, *242*, 102–111.

GILLIN, J. C., KAPLAN, J., STILLMAN, R., and WYATT, R. J. The psychedelic model of schizophrenia: The case of *N,N*-dimethyltryptamine. *American Journal of Psychiatry,* 1976, *133*, 203–208.

GINTER, G., and LINDSKOLD, S. Rate of participation and expertise as factors influencing leader choice. *Journal of Personality and Social Psychology,* 1975, *32*, 1085–1089.

GLASS, D., and SINGER, J. *Urban stress: Experiments on noise and social stressors.* New York: Academic Press, 1972.

GLASS, D. C. *Behavior patterns, stress, and coronary disease.* Hillsdale, N.J.: Erlbaum, 1977.

GLASS, D. C., SINGER, J. E., and PENNEBAKER, J. Behavioral and physiological effects of uncontrollable environmental events. In D. Stokols (Ed.), *Perspectives on Environment and Behavior,* 1977, *5*, 131–149.

GLASS, D. C., SNYDER, M. L., and HOLLIS, J. F. Time urgency and the type A coronary-prone behavior pattern. *Journal of Applied Social Psychology,* 1974, *4*, 125–140.

GLASS, L., KIRSCH, M., and PARRIS, F. Psychiatric disturbance associated with Erhard Seminars Training: I. A report of cases. *American Journal of Psychiatry,* 1977, *134*, 245–247.

GLENN, M. D. Psychological well-being in the post-parental stage: Some evidence from national surveys. *Journal of Marriage and the Family,* 1975, *32*, 105–110.

GLICK, I. O., WEISS, R. S., and PARKES, C. M. *The first year of bereavement.* New York: Wiley, 1974.

GOETHALS, G. R., and DARLEY, J. M. Social comparison theory: An attributional approach. In J. M. Suls and R. L. Miller (Eds.), *Social comparison processes: Theoretical and empirical perspectives.* Washington, D.C.: Hemisphere/Halsted, 1977.

GOETHALS, G. R., and NELSON, R. Similarity in the influence process: The belief-value distinction. *Journal of Personality and Social Psychology,* 1973, *25*, 117–122.

GOETHALS, G. R., and WORCHEL, S. *Adjustment and human relations.* New York: Knopf, 1981.

GOETHALS, G., and ZANNA, M. The role of social comparison in choice shifts. *Journal of Personality and Social Psychology,* 1979, *37*, 1469–1476.

GOLD, R. Hypothalamic obesity: The myth of the ventromedial nucleus. *Science,* 1973, *182*, 488–490.

GOLDBAND, S. Stimulus specificity of physiological response to stress and the Type A coronary-prone behavior pattern. *Journal of Personality and Social Psychology,* 1980, *39*, 670–679.

GOLDBERG, P. A. Are women prejudiced against women? *Trans-action,* 1968, *5*, 28–30.

GOLDFRIED, M. R., and DAVISON, G. C. *Clinical behavior therapy.* New York: Holt, Rinehart and Winston, 1976.

GOLDMAN, J., and OLEZAK, P. Psychosocial maturity and interpersonal attraction. *Journal of Research in Personality,* 1976, *10*, 146–154.

GOLDMAN, R., JAFFA, M., and SCHACHTER, S. Yom Kippur, Air France, dormitory food, and the eating behavior of obese and normal persons. *Journal of Personality and Social Psychology,* 1968, *10*, 117–123.

GOLDSTEIN, M. J. The relationship between coping and avoiding behavior and response to fear-arousing propaganda. *Journal of Abnormal and Social Psychology,* 1959, *58*, 247–252.

GOLIMBIEWSKI, R., and BLUMBURG, A. *Sensitivity training and the laboratory approach.* Itasca, Ill.: Peacock Press, 1973.

GOODWIN, D. W. Alcoholism and heredity. *Archives of General Psychiatry, 36,* 57–61.

GORDON, S., and SCALES, P. The myth of the normal sexual outlet. *Journal of Pediatric Psychology,* 1977, *2,* 101–103.

GOTTESMAN, I. I., and SHIELDS, J. *Schizophrenia and genetics: A twin study vantage point.* New York: Academic Press, 1972.

GRAHAM, S. The sociological approach to epidemiology. *American Journal of Public Health,* 1974, *64,* 1046–1049.

GRAEN, G., ALVARES, K., ORRIS, J., and MARTELLA, J. Contingency model of leadership effectiveness: Antecedent and evidential results. *Psychology Bulletin,* 1970, *74,* 284–296.

GRAY, J. *The psychology of fear and stress.* New York: McGraw-Hill, 1971.

GREEN, D., MILLER, N., and GERARD, V. Personality traits and adjustment. In H. Gerard and N. Miller, *School desegregation: A long-range study.* New York: Plenum Press, 1975.

GREENBERG, D. J., and O'DONNELL, W. J. Infancy and the optional level of stimulation. *Child Development,* 1972, *43,* 639–645.

GREENBERG, M. A theory of indebtedness. In K. Gergen, M. Greenberg, and R. Willis (Eds.), *Social exchange: Advances in theory and research.* New York: Plenum, 1980.

GREGG, C., CLIFTON, R. K., and HAITH, M. M. A possible explanation for the frequent failure to find cardiac orienting in the newborn infant. *Developmental Psychology,* 1976, *12,* 75–76.

GRIFFITT, W., and VEITCH, R. Hot and crowded: Influence of population density and temperature on interpersonal affective behavior. *Journal of Personality and Social Psychology,* 1971, *17,* 92–98.

GRIM, R., KOHLBERG, L., and WHITE, S. Some relationships between conscience and attentional processes. *Journal of Personality and Social Psychology,* 1968, *8,* 239–253.

GUILFORD, J. P. *The nature of human intelligence.* New York: McGraw-Hill, 1967.

GUILLEMINAULT, C., and DEMENT, W. C. Amnesia and disorders of excessive daytime sleepiness. In R. R. Drucher-Colin and J. L. McGaugh (Eds.), *Neurobiology of sleep and memory.* New York: Academic Press, 1977.

GUSTAVSON, C. R., GARCIA, J., HANKINS, W. G., and RUSINIAK, K. W. Coyote predation control by aversive conditioning. *Science,* 1974, *184,* 581–583.

GYNTHER, M., and GREEN, S. Accuracy may make a difference, but does difference make for accuracy? A response to Prichard and Rosenblatt. *Journal of Consulting and Clinical Psychology,* 1980, *48,* 268–272.

HABER, R. N. Eidetic images. *Scientific American,* 1969, *220,* 36–55.

HAGESTAD, G. O. Role change and socialization in adulthood: The transition to the empty nest. Unpublished manuscript, The Pennsylvania State University, 1980.

HAITH, M. M., and CAMPOS, J. J. Human infancy. *Annual Review of Psychology,* 1977, *28,* 251–293.

HALEY, J. *Leaving home: The therapy of disturbed young people.* New York: McGraw-Hill, 1980.

HALL, C. *The meaning of dreams.* New York: McGraw-Hill, 1966.

HALL, C., and LINDZEY, G. *Theories of personality* (3rd ed.). New York: Wiley, 1978.

HALL, E. T. *The silent language.* New York: Fawcett, 1959.

HAMMEN, C. L., and PETERS, S. D. Differential responses to male and female depressive reactions. *Journal of consulting and clinical psychology,* 1977, *45,* 994–1001.

HANES, B., PRAWAT, R. S., and GRISSOM, S. Sex-role perceptions during adolescence. *Journal of Educational Psychology,* 1979, *71,* 850–855.

HANSEL, C. E. M. *ESP and parapsychology: A critical re-evaluation.* New York: Prometheus Books, 1980.

HARLOW, H. F. The formation of learning sets. *Psychological Review,* 1949, *56,* 51–65.

HARLOW, H. *Learning to love.* San Francisco: Albion, 1971.

HARLOW, H. F., and SUOMI, S. J. Nature of love simplified. *American Psychologist,* 1970, *25,* 161–168.

HARLOW, H. F., and ZIMMERMAN, R. R. Affectional responses in the infant monkey. *Science,* 1959, *130,* 421–432.

HARLOW, H., HARLOW, M. K., and MEYER, D. R. Learning motivated by a manipulation drive. *Journal of Experimental Psychology,* 1950, *40,* 228–234.

HARMON, L. D. The recognition of faces. *Scientific American,* November, 1973.

HARRIMAN, A. The effect of preoperative preference for sugar over salt upon compensatory salt selection by adrenalectomized rats. *Journal of Nutrition,* 1955, *57,* 271–276.

HARRIS, D. B. Problems in formulating a scientific concept of development. In D. B. Harris (Ed.), *The concept of development.* Minneapolis: University of Minnesota Press, 1957.

HARTSHORNE, H., and MAY, M. A. *Studies in the nature of character* (Vol. 1). *Studies in deceit.* New York: Macmillan, 1928.

HASDORF, A. H., OSGOOD, D. E., and ONO, H. The semantics of facial expressions and the prediction of the meanings of stereoscopically fused facial expressions. *Scandinavian Journal of Psychology,* 1966, *7,* 179–188.

HASHIM, S. A., and VAN ITALLIE, T. B. Studies in normal and obese subjects with a monitored food dispensary device. *Annals of the New York Academy of Science,* 1965, *131,* 654–661.

HATHAWAY, S., and MCKINLEY, J. A multiphasic personality schedule (Minnesota): III. The measurement of symptomatic depression. *Journal of Psychology,* 1942, *14,* 73–84.

HATHAWAY, S. R., and MCKINLEY, J. C. *MMPI Manual.* New York: Psychological Corporation, 1943.

HAYES, C. *The ape in our house.* New York: Harper & Row, 1951.

HEBB, D. O. Drives and the C. N. S. (conceptual nervous system). *Psychological Review,* 1955, *62,* 243–254.

HEBERLEIN, T. A., and BLACK, J. S. Attitudinal specificity and the prediction of behavior in a field setting. *Journal of Personality and Social Psychology,* 1976, *33,* 474–479.

HECKEL, R. V., and HIERS, J. M. Social distance and locus of control. *Journal of Clinical Psychology,* 1977, *33,* 469–471.

HEIDER, F. Attitudes and cognitive organization. *Journal of Personality,* 1946, *21,* 107–112.

HELLER, K., and MONAHAN, J. *Psychology and community change.* Homewood, Ill.: Dorsey, 1977.

HELMS, D. B., and TURNER, J. S. *Exploring child behavior.* New York: Holt, Rinehart and Winston, 1981.

HENNING, M., and JARDIN, A. *The managerial woman.* New York: Doubleday, 1976.

HERGENHAN, B. *An introduction to theories of personality.* Englewood Cliffs, N.J.: Prentice-Hall, 1980.

HERON, W. Cognitive and physiological effects of perceptual isolation. In P. Solomon et al. (Eds.), *Sensory deprivation.* Cambridge, Mass.: Harvard University Press, 1961.

HERRNSTEIN, R. J. *IQ in the meritocracy.* Boston: Atlantic Monthly Press, 1973.

HESS, E. H. "Imprinting" in animals. *Scientific American,* 1958, *286,* 81–90.

HESS, E. H. Attitude and pupil size. *Scientific American,* 1965, *212,* 46–54.

HETHERINGTON, A., and RANSON, S. Experimental hypothalamohypapyseal obesity in the rat. *Proceedings for the Society of Experimental Biology and Medicine,* 1939, *41,* 465–466.

HETHERINGTON, E. M., COX, M., and COX, R. The aftermath of divorce. In J. H. Stevens, Jr. and M. Matthew (Eds.), Mother-child, father-child relations. Washington, D.C.: National Association for the Education of Young Children, 1978.

HIROTO, D. S. Locus of control and learned helplessness. *Journal of Experimental Psychology,* 1974, *102,* 187–193.

HOBSON, J. A., and MCCARLEY, R. W. The brain as a dream state generator: An activation-synthesis hypothesis of the dream process. *American Journal of Psychiatry,* 1977, *134,* 1335–1348.

HOCHBERG, J. E. *Perception.* Englewood Cliffs, N.J.: Prentice-Hall, 1978.

HOCHREICH, D. J., and ROTTER, J. B. Have college students become less trusting? *Journal of Personality and Social Psychology*, 1970, *15*, 211–214.

HODGKINS, J. Influence of age on the speed of reaction and movement in females. *Journal of Gerontology*, 1962, *17*, 385–389.

HOEBEL, B. G., and TEITELBAUM, P. Hypothalamic control of feeding and self-stimulation. *Science*, 1962, *61*, 189–193.

HOFFMAN, L. W., and NYE, F. I. *Working mothers*. San Francisco: Jossey-Bass, 1974.

HOFLING, C. K. *Textbook of Psychiatry for medical practice*, 3rd ed. Philadelphia: Lippincott, 1975.

HOFLING, C. K., BROTZMAN, E., DALRYMPLE, S., GRAVES, N., and PIERCE, C. M. An experimental study in nurse-physician relationships. *The Journal of Nervous and Mental Disease*, 1966, *143* (2), 171–180.

HOKANSON, J. E., and SHELTERS, S. The effect of overt aggression on physiological arousal level. *Journal of Abnormal and Social Psychology*, 1961, *63*, 446–448.

HOKANSON, J., BURGESS, M., and COHEN, M. Effect of displaced aggression on systolic blood pressure. *Journal of Abnormal and Social Psychology*, 1963, *67*, 214–218.

HOLDEN, C. Nader on mental health centers: A movement that got bogged down. *Science*, 1972, *177*, 413–415.

HOLDEN, C. Lie detectors: PSE gains audience despite critics' doubt. *Science*, 1975, *190*, 359–362.

HOLLANDER, E. *Leadership dynamics*. New York: Free Press, 1978.

HOLLANDER, E. P., and JULIAN, J. W. A further look at leader legitimacy, influence, and innovation. In L. Berkowitz (Ed.), *Group process*. New York: Academic Press, 1978.

HOLLINGSHEAD, A. B., and REDLICH, F. C. *Social class and mental illness, a community study*. New York: Wiley, 1958.

HOLMES, D. S. Investigations of repression: Differential recall of material experimentally or naturally associated with ego threat. *Psychological Bulletin*, 1974, *81*, 632–653.

HOLMES, D., FROST, R., and LUTZ, D. Multiple sessions of systolic blood pressure biofeedback: Its effects on ability to control systolic pressure during training, after training, and its effects on pulse rate. *Journal of Research in Personality*, 1981, *15*, 30–44.

HOLMES, T., and MASUDA, M. Life change and illness susceptibility. In B. Dohrenwend and B. Dohrenwend (Eds.), *Stressful life events: Their nature and effects*. New York: Wiley, 1974.

HOLMES, T. H., and RAHE, R. H. The social readjustment rating scale. *Journal of Psychosomatic Research*, 1967, *11*, 213–318.

HOLT, A. *Animal drive and the learning process, an essay toward radical empiricism* (Vol. I). New York: Holt, Rinehart and Winston, 1931, p. 4.

HOLTZMAN, W. New developments in Holtzman inkblot techniques. In P. McReynolds (Ed.), *Advances in Psychological Assessment* (Vol. 3). San Francisco: Jossey-Bass, 1975.

HOMANS, G. *Social behavior in its elementary forms* (Rev. ed.). New York: Harcourt Brace Jovanovich, 1974.

HONIGFELD, G. Non-specific factors in treatment. I. Review of placebo reactions and placebo reactors. *Diseases of the Nervous System*, 1964, *25*, 145–156.

HOOK, E. B. Behavioral implications of the human XYY genotype. *Science*, 1973, *179*, 131–150.

HORN, J. L. Human ability systems. In P. B. Baltes (Ed.), *Life-span development and behavior* (Vol. 1). New York: Academic Press, 1978.

HORN, J. L., and DONALDSON, G. Cognitive development II: Adulthood development of human abilities. In O. G. Brim, Jr. and J. Kagan (Eds.), *Constancy and change in human development: A volume of review essays*. Cambridge, Mass.: Harvard University Press, 1980.

HORN, J. M., LOEHLIN, J. C., and WILLERMAN, L. Intellectual resemblance among adoptive and biological relatives: The Texas adoption project. *Behavior Genetics*, 1979, *9*, 177–208.

HORNER, M. S. Sex differences in achievement motivation in competitive and noncompetitive situations. Doctoral dissertation, University of Michigan, 1968.

HORNER, M. S. *Feminine personality and conflict*. Monterey, Calif.: Brooks/Cole, 1970.

HORNEY, K. *The neurotic personality of our time*. New York: Norton, 1937.

HOROWITZ, M. J., DUFF, D. F., and STRATTON, L. O. Archives of General Psychiatry (Vol. II). American Medical Association, December 1964.

HORTON, D. L., and TURNAGE, T. W. *Human learning*. Englewood Cliffs, N.J.: Prentice-Hall, 1976.

HORTON, R. W. An empirical investigation of variation in students' premarital sex standards and behavior. *Diss. Ab. Int'l.*, 1973, *34*, 1385–1386.

HOVLAND, C. I., LUMSDAINE, A., and SHEFFIELD, F. *Experiments on mass communication*. Princeton, N.J.: Princeton University Press, 1949.

HOVLAND, C. I., and WEISS, W. The influence of source credibility on communication effectiveness. *The Public Opinion Quarterly*, 1952, *15*, 635–650.

HOWARD, D. *Territory in bird life*. New York: Dutton, 1972.

HOWELLS, L., and BECKER, S. Seating arrangement and leadership emergence. *Journal of Abnormal and Social Psychology*, 1962, *64*, 148–150.

HUBEL, D. H., and WIESEL, T. N. Receptive fields and functional architecture in two nonstriate visual areas (18 and 19) of the cat. *Journal of Neurophysiology*, 1965, *28*, 229–289.

HUBEL, D. H., and WIESEL, T. N. The period of susceptibility to the physiological effects of unilateral eye closure in kittens. *Journal of Physiology*, 1970, *206*, 419–436.

HULICKA, I. M., and GROSSMAN, J. L. Age-group comparisons for the use of mediators in paired associate learning. *Journal of Gerontology*, 1967, *22*, 46–51.

HULTSCH, D. F. Adult age differences in free classification and free recall. *Developmental Psychology*, 1971, *4*, 338–342.

HULTSCH, D. F., and DEUTSCH, F. *Adult Development and Aging*. New York: McGraw-Hill, 1981.

HUNT, M. *Sexual Behavior in the 1970s*. Chicago: Playboy Press, 1974.

HURVICH, L. M., and JAMESON, D. Opponent processes as a model of neural organization. *American Psychologist*, 1974, *29*, 88–102.

HUSBAND, R. W. Cooperation versus solitary problem solution. *Journal of Social Psychology*, 1940, *11*, 405–409.

HUXLEY, A. D. *The doors of perception*. New York: Harper & Row, 1952.

HYGGE, S., and OHMAN, S. Modeling processes in the acquisition of fears: Vicarious electrodermal conditioning to fear-relevant stimuli. *Journal of Personality and Social Psychology*, 1978, *36*, 271–279.

HYMAN, R. The case against parapsychology. *The Humanist*, 1977, *37*, 47–49.

ISAACSON, R. L. When brains are damaged. *Psychology Today*, 1970, *3*, 38–42.

ISEN, A. Success, failure, attention, and reaction to others: The warm glow of success. *Journal of Personality and Social Psychology*, 1970, *15*, 294–301.

ITTLESON, W. H., PROSHANSKY, H. M., RIVLIN, L. G., and WINKEL, G. An introduction to environmental psychology. New York: Holt, Rinehart and Winston, 1974.

IVEY, A., and SIMEK-DOWNING, L. *Counseling and psychology*. Englewood Cliffs, N.J.: Prentice-Hall, 1980.

IZARD, C. Differential emotions theory and the facial feedback hypothesis of emotion activation: Comments in Tourajeau and Ellsworth's "The role of facial response in the experience of emotion." *Journal of Personality and Social Psychology*, 1981, *40*, 350–354.

IZARD, C. E. *Human emotions*. New York: Plenum Press, 1977, p. 340.

JAFFE, J., PETERSON, R., and HODGSON, R. Addictions, issues and answers. Holland: Multimedia Publications, 1980.

JAMES, R. Status and competence of jurors. *American Journal of Sociology*, 1959, *64*, 563–570.

JAMES, W. What is emotion? *Mind*, 1884, *19*, 188–205.

JAMES, W. *The principles of psychology.* New York: Holt, Rinehart and Winston, 1890, *12*, 160, 232.

JAMES, W. The varieties of religious experience. New York: Modern Library, 1967 (Originally published, 1902).

JANIS, I. L. Groupthink. *Psychology Today,* 1971, *5* (6), 43–46ff.

JANIS, I. L. *Victims of groupthink: A psychological study of foreign policy decisions and fiascoes.* Boston: Houghton-Mifflin, 1972.

JANIS, I. L., and FESHBACH, S. Effects of fear-arousing communication. *Journal of Abnormal and Social Psychology,* 1953, *48,* 78–92.

JANIS, I. L., KAYE, D., and KIRSCHNER, P. Facilitating effects of "eating-while-reading" on responsiveness to persuasive communications. *Journal of Personality and Social Psychology,* 1965, *1,* 181–186.

JANOWITZ, H. D. Role of gastrointestinal tract in the regulation of food intake. In C. F. Code (Ed.), *Handbook of physiology: Alimentary canal, I.* Washington, D.C.: American Physiological Society, 1967, 219–224.

JECKER, J., and LANDY, D. Liking a person as a function of doing him a favor. *Human Relations,* 1969, *22,* 371–378.

JENKINS, C. D. Recent evidence supporting psychologic and social risk factors for coronary disease. *New England Journal of Medicine,* 1976, *294,* 987–994.

JENSEN, A. R. How much can we boost IQ and scholastic achievement? *Harvard Educational Review,* 1969, *39,* 1–123.

JENSEN, A. R. *Educability and group differences.* New York: Harper & Row, 1973.

JEROME, E. A. Age and learning-experimental studies. In J. E. Birren (Ed.), *Handbook of aging and the individual.* Chicago: University of Chicago Press, 1959.

JERSILD, A. T., and HOLMES, F. B. Children's fears. *Child development monograph,* No. 20. New York: Teachers' College, Columbia University, 1935.

JESSOR, S., and JESSOR, R. Transition from virginity to nonvirginity among youth: A social-psychological study over time. *Developmental Psychology,* 1975, *11,* 473–484.

JOHANSSON, G. Visual motion perception. In R. Held and W. Richards (Eds.), *Recent progress in perception.* San Francisco: Freeman, 1976.

JONES, E. *The life and work of Sigmund Freud* (Vol. 3). New York: Basic Books, 1957.

JONES, E. E., and DAVIS, K. From acts to dispositions: The attribution process in person perception. In L. Berkowitz (Ed.), *Advances in experimental social psychology* (Vol. 2). New York: Academic Press, 1965.

JONES, E. E., and HARRIS, V. A. The attribution of attitudes. *Journal of Experimental Psychology,* 1967, *3,* 1–24.

JONES, E. E., and McGILLIS, D. Correspondent interferences and the attribution cube: A comparative reappraisal. In J. H. Harvey, W. J. Ickes, and R. F. Kidd (Eds.), *New directions in attribution research* (Vol. 1). Hillsdale, N.J.: Erlbaum, 1976.

JONES, E. E., and NISBETT, R. E. The actor and the observer: Divergent perceptions of the causes of behavior. In E. E. Jones, D. Kanouse, H. H. Kelley, R. E. Nisbett, S. Valins, and B. Weiner (Eds.), *Attribution: Perceiving the causes of behavior.* Morristown, N.J.: General Learning Press, 1972, pp. 79–94.

JONES, E., WOOD, G., and QUATTRONE, G. Perceived variability of personal characteristics in in-groups and out-groups: The role of knowledge and evaluation. *Personality and Social Psychology Bulletin,* 1981, *7,* 523–528.

JONES, E., and WORTMAN, C. *Ingratiation: An attributional approach.* Morristown, N.J.: General Learning Press, 1973.

JONES, E., ROCK, L., SHAVER, K. G., GOETHALS, G. R., and WARD, L. M. Pattern of performance and ability attribution: An unexpected primacy effect. *Journal of Personality and Social Psychology,* 1968, *10,* 317–340.

JONES, E. E., WORCHEL, S., GOETHALS, G. R., and GRUMET, J. F. Prior expectancy and behavioral extremity as determinants of attitude attribution. *Journal of Experimental Social Psychology,* 1971, *7,* 59–80.

JONES, H. E., and CONRAD, H. S. The growth and decline of intelligence: A study of a homogeneous group between the ages of ten and sixty. *Genetic Psychology Monographs,* 1933, *13,* 223–298.

JONES, R. A., and BREHM, J. W. Persuasiveness of one and two-sided communications as a function of awareness there are two sides. *Journal of Experimental Social Psychology,* 1970, *6,* 47–56.

JULIAN, J. W., REGULO, C. R., and HOLLANDER, E. P. Effects of prior agreement from others on task confidence and conformity. *Journal of Personality and Social Psychology,* 1968, *9,* 171–178.

KAGAN, J. What is intelligence? *Social Policy,* 1973, *4,* 88–94.

KAGAN, J., and FREEMAN, M. Relation of childhood intelligence, maternal behaviors, and social class to behavior during adolescence. *Child Development,* 1963, *34,* 899–911.

KAGAN, J., and MOSS, H. *Birth to maturity.* New York: Wiley, 1962.

KAGAN, J., KEARSLEY, R. B., and ZELANZO, P. R. The effects of infant day care on psychological development. *Educational Quarterly,* 1977, *1,* 109–142.

KAHANA, B., and KAHANA, E. Theoretical and research perspectives on grandparenthood. *Aging and Human Development,* 1971, *2,* 261–268.

KALISH, R. A., and REYNOLDS, D. K. Death and ethnicity: A psychocultural study. Los Angeles: University of Southern California Press, 1976.

KAMIN, L. J. Heredity, intelligence, politics and society. Invited address, Eastern Psychological Association, Washington, 1973.

KAMIN, L. J. Heredity, intelligence, politics, and psychology. In N. J. Block and G. Dworkin (Eds.), *The IQ controversy.* New York: Pantheon, 1976.

KAMIN, L. J. Psychology as social science: The Jensen affair, ten years after. Presidential address, Eastern Psychological Association, Philadelphia, 1979.

KANDELL, J. French rank crime high on their list of major worries. *The New York Times,* August 7, 1977, p. 13.

KANGELARI, S., ABRAMOVICH-POLYAKOV, D., and RUDENKO, V. The effects of noise and vibration on morbidity rates (Russia). *Gigiena Truda: Professional 'Nye Zabolevaniy,* 1966, *6,* 47–49.

KAPLAN, H. S. *The new sexual therapy: Active treatment of sexual dysfunctions.* New York: Brunner-Mazel, 1974.

KARLINS, M., COFFMAN, J., and WALTERS, G. On the fading of social stereotypes: Studies in three generations of college students. *Journal of Personality and Social Psychology,* 1969, *13,* 1–16.

KATCHADOURIAN, H. A. *The biology of adolescence.* San Francisco: Freeman, 1977.

KATZ, I. The socialization of academic motivation in minority group children. In D. Levine (Ed.), *Nebraska symposium on motivation* (Vol. 15). Lincoln, Neb.: University of Nebraska Press, 1967, 133–191.

KAZDIN, A. E. The rich rewards of rewards. *Psychology Today,* 1976, 10 (6), 98, 101–102, *105,* 114.

KEELE, S. W., and ELLS, J. G. Memory characteristics of kinesthetic information. *Journal of Motor Behavior,* 1972, *4,* 127–134.

KEESEY, R. E., and POWLEY, T. L. Hypothalamic regulation of body weight. *American Scientist,* 1975, *63,* 558–565.

KEHOE, J. E., FEYER, A. M., and MOSES, J. L. Second-order conditioning of the rabbits' nictitating membrane response as a function of the CS2-CS1 and CS-1-VS intervals. *Animal Learning and Behavior,* 1981, *9,* 304–315.

KELLER, H. *The story of my life.* New York: Doubleday, 1954.

KELLER, M. Treatment for depression varies. In a series by Dava Sobel, *New York Times,* Dec. 2, 1981.

KELLEY, H. The process of causal attribution. *American Psychologist,* 1973, *28,* 107–128.

KELLEY, H., and MICHELE, S. Attribution theory and research. *Annual Review of Psychology,* 1980, *31,* 457–502.

KELLEY, H. H. Two functions of reference groups. In G. E. Swanson, T. M. Newcomb, and E. L. Hartley (Eds.), *Readings in social psychology* (2nd ed.). New York: Holt, Rinehart and Winston, 1952.

KELLEY, H. H. Attribution theory in social psychology. In D. Levine (Ed.), *Nebraska Symposium on Motivation*, 1967, *15*, 192–238.

KELLEY, H. H. *Attribution in social interaction.* Morristown, N.J.: General Learning Press, 1971.

KELLOGG, T. H. The histrionic element of mental disease. *New York Medical Journal*, 1902, *LXXVI*, 107–110.

KELLY, E. *Clown.* Englewood Cliffs, N.J.: Prentice-Hall, 1954.

KELMAN, H. C., and HOVLAND, C. I. "Reinstatement" of the communicator in delayed measurement of opinion change. *Journal of Abnormal and Social Psychology*, 1953, *48*, 326–335.

KENT, R., and FOSTER, S. Direct observational procedure: Methodological issues in naturalistic settings. In A. Ciminero, K. Calhoun, and H. Adams (Eds.). *Handbook of behavioral assessment.* New York: Wiley, 1977.

KERR, N., and BRUUN, S. Ringelmann revisited: Alternative explanations for the social loafing effect. *Personality and Social Psychology Bulletin*, 1981, *7*, 224–231.

KETY, S. S., ROSENTHAL, D., WENDER, P., and SCHULSINGER, F. The type and prevalence of mental illness in the biological and adoptive families of adopted schizophrenics. In D. Rosenthal and S. S. Kety (Eds.), *The transmission of schizophrenia.* New York: Pergamon Press, 1968.

KEYES, R. *The height of your life.* Boston: Little, Brown, 1980.

KIESLER, C. A., and KIESLER, S. B. Group pressure and conformity. In J. Mills (Ed.), *Experimental social psychology.* New York: Macmillan, 1969.

KILHAM, W., and MANN, L. Level of destructive obedience as a function of transmitter and executant roles in the Milgram obedience paradigm. *Journal of Personality and Social Psychology*, 1974, *29*, 696–702.

KINSEY, A. C., POMEROY, W. B., and MARTIN, C. E. *Sexual behavior in the human male.* Philadelphia: Saunders, 1948.

KINSEY, A. C., POMEROY, W. B., MARTIN, C. E., and GEBHARD, P. H. *Sexual behavior in the human female.* Philadelphia: Saunders, 1953.

KINTSCH, W. *The representation of meaning in memory.* New York: Wiley, 1974.

KINZEL, A. S. Body buffer zone in violent prisoners. *American Journal of Psychiatry*, 1970, *10*, 263–270.

KLECK, R. E., and RUBENSTEIN, C. Physical attractiveness, perceived attitude similarity, and interpersonal attraction in an opposite-sex encounter. *Journal of Personality and Social Psychology*, 1975, *31*, 107–114.

KLEITMAN, N. *Sleep and wakefulness.* Chicago, Ill.: University of Chicago Press, 1963.

KLINE, P. *Fact and fancy in Freudian theory.* London: Methuen, 1972.

KNITTLE, J. L. Early influences on development of adipose tissue. In G. A. Bray (Ed.), *Obesity in perspective.* Washington, D.C.: U. S. Government Printing Office, 1975.

KNOX, V. J., CRUTCHFIELD, L., and HILGARD, E. R. The nature of task interference in hypnotic dissociation: An investigation of hypnotic behavior. *International Journal of Clinical and Experimental Hypnosis*, 1975, *23*, 305–323.

KOESTLER, A. *The ghost in the machine.* New York: Macmillan, 1967.

KOHLBERG, L. The development of children's orientations toward a moral order. I. Sequence in the development of moral thought. *Vita Humana*, 1963, *6*, 11–33.

KOHLBERG, L. *Stages in the development of moral thought and action.* New York: Holt, Rinehart and Winston, 1969.

KOHLBERG, L. Revisions in the theory and practice of moral development. *New Directions for Child Development*, 1978, *2*, 83–88.

KOHLER, W. *The mentality of apes.* New York: Harcourt Brace Jovanovich, 1925.

KOHN, I., FRANCK, K., and FOX, A. Defensible space modifications in row-house communities. *National Science Foundation Report*, 1975.

KOHN, M. L. Class, family, and schizophrenia: A reformulation. *Social Forces*, 1972, *50*, 295–313.

KOLODNY, R., MASTERS, W., HENDRYX, J., and TORO, G. Plasma testosterone levels and semen analysis in male homosexuals. *New England Journal of Medicine*, 1971, *285*, 1170–1174.

KONECNI, V. J. Annoyance, type and duration of postannoyance activity, and aggression: The "catharsis effect." *Journal of Experimental Psychology: General*, 1975, *104*, 76–102.

KONECNI, V. J. The role of aversive events in the development of intergroup conflict. In W. Austin and S. Worchel (Eds.), *The Social Psychology of Intergroup Behavior.* Monterey, Calif.: Brooks/Cole, 1979.

KONECNI, V. J., and DOOB, A. N. Catharsis through displacement of aggression. *Journal of Personality and Social Psychology*, 1972, *23*, 379–387.

KONECNI, V. J., LIBAUSER, L., MORTON, H., and EBBESEN, E. B. Effects of a violation of personal space on escape and helping responses. *Journal of Experimental Social Psychology*, 1975, *11*, 288–299.

KORCHIN, S. *Modern clinical psychology.* New York: Basic Books, 1976.

KORNHABER, R., and SCHROEDER, H. Importance of model similarity on extinction of avoidance behavior in children. *Journal of Consulting and Clinical Psychology*, 1975, *43*, 601–607.

KOSSLYN, S. M. The medium and the message in mental imagery: A theory. *Psychological Review*, 1981, *88*, 46–66.

KOSSLYN, S. M., BALL, T. M., and REISER, B. J. Visual images preserve spatial information: Evidence from studies of image

scanning. *Journal of Experimental Psychology: Human Perception and Performance*, 1978, *4*, 47–60.

KRAEMER, H. C., BECKER, H. B., BRODIE, H. X. H., DOERING, C. H., MOOS, R. H., and HAMBURG, D. Orgasmic frequency and plasma testosterone levels in normal human males. *Archives of Sexual Behavior*, 1976, *5*, 125–132.

KRAFT, C. L., and ELWORTH, C. L. Measurement of aircrew performance: The flight deck workload and its relation to pilot performance. (NTIS70–19779/AD699934–DTIC), 1969.

KRAMER, M. *Psychiatric services and the changing institution scene, 1952–1985.* National Institute of Mental Health, 1977 (DHEW publication #Adm 77–433).

KRASNER, L. The operant approach in behavior therapy. In A. Bergin and S. Garfield (Eds.) *Handbook of psychotherapy and behavior change.* New York: Wiley, 1971.

KRECH, D., CRUTCHFIELD, R., and BALLACHEY, E. *Individual in society: A textbook of social psychology.* New York: McGraw-Hill, 1962.

KREPS, J. M. (Ed.). *Women and the American economy.* Englewood Cliffs, N.J.: Prentice-Hall, 1976.

KRUPAT, E. *Psychology is social.* 2nd ed. Glenview, Ill.: Scott, Foresman, 1982.

KUBLER-ROSS, E. *On death and dying.* New York: Macmillan, 1969.

KUBLER-ROSS, E. *Questions and answers on death and dying.* New York: Macmillan, 1974.

KUHN, M., and McPARTLAND, T. An empirical investigation of self-attitudes. *American Social Review*, 1954, *19*, 68–76.

LACKEY, E., and NASS, G. A. A comparison of sexual attitudes and behavior in an international sample. *Journal of Marriage and the Family*, 1969, *31*, 364–379.

LAGONE, J. Healing the hostages. *Discover.* New York: Time, Inc., March 1981.

LAING, R. D. Is schizophrenia a disease? *International Journal of Social Psychiatry*, 1964, *10*, 184–193.

LAMB, H. R., and ZUSMAN, J. Primary prevention in perspective. *American Journal of Psychiatry*, 1979, *136*, 12–17.

LAMM, H., and MYERS, D. Group-induced polarization of attitudes and behavior. In L. Berkowitz (Ed.), *Advances in Experimental Social Psychology, Vol. 11.* New York: Academic Press, 1978.

LANDESMAN-DWYER, S., KELLER, S. L., and STREISSGUTH, A. P. Naturalistic observations of newborns: Effects of maternal alcohol intake. Paper presented at the American Psychological Association Annual Meeting, San Francisco, 1977.

LANGER, E. J., and RODIN, J. The effects of choice and enhanced personal responsibility for the aged: A field experiment in an institutional setting. *Journal of Personality and Social Psychology*, 1976, *34*, 191–198.

LAPIERE, R. T. Attitudes vs. actions. *Social Forces*, 1934, *13*, 230–237.

LASH, J. P. *Helen and teacher: The story of Helen Keller and Anne Sullivan Macy.* New York: Dell, 1980.

LASKA, S. B., and MICKLIN, M. The knowledge dimension of occupational socialization: Role models and their social influences. *Youth and Society*, 1979, *10*, 360–378.

LASSWELL, H. D. The structure and function of communication in society. In L. Bryson (Ed.), *Communication of ideas.* New York: Harper & Row, 1948.

LATANÉ, B., and DARLEY, J. M. *The unresponsive bystander: Why doesn't he help?* New York: Appleton-Century-Crofts, 1970.

LATANÉ, B., WILLIAMS, K., and HARKINS, S. Many hands make light the work: The causes and consequences of social loafing. *Journal of Personality and Social Psychology*, 1979, *37*, 822–832.

LAWSON, E. Hair color, personality, and the observer. *Psychological Reports*, 1971, *28*, 311–322.

LAZARSFELD, P. F., BERELSON, B., and GAUDET, H. *The people's choice.* 2nd ed. New York: Columbia University Press, 1948.

LAZARUS, R. Little hassles can be hazardous to health. *Psychology Today*, July 1981.

LAZARUS, R., and LAUNIER, R. Stress-related transactions between person and environment. In L. Pervin and M. Lewis (Eds.), *Perspectives in Interactional Psychology*, New York: Plenum Press, 1978.

LAZARUS, R. S. Emotions and adaptation: Conceptual and empirical relations. In W. J. Arnold (Ed.), *Nebraska Symposium on Motivation.* Lincoln, Neb.: University of Nebraska Press, 1968.

LAZELL, E. W., and PRINCE, L. H. A study of the causative factors of dementia Praecox. *U. S. Veterans Bureau Medical Bulletin*, 1929, *114*, 241–248.

LEBON, G. *The crowd* (trans.) London: Allen & Unwin, 1903.

LECUYER, R. Space dimensions, the climate of discussion and group decisions. *European Journal of Social Psychology*, 1975, *5*, 509–514.

LECUYER, R. Social organization and spatial organization. *Human Relations*, 1976, *19*, 1045–1060.

LEE, T. Perceived distance as a function of direction in the city. *Environment and Behavior*, 1970, *2*, 40–51.

LEFEVRE, C. The mature woman as a graduate student. *School Review*, 1972, *80*, 281–297.

LEIBERMAN, A. F. Preschooler's competence with a peer: Relations with attachment and peer experience. *Child Development*, 1977, *48*, 1277–1287.

LEMERE, F., and VOEGTLIN, W. L. An evaluation of the aversion treatment of alcoholism. *Quarterly Journal of Studies on Alcohol*, 1950, *11*, 199–204.

LENNEBERG, E. H. *Biological foundations of language.* New York: Wiley, 1967.

LERNER, I. M., and LIBBY, W. L. *Heredity, evolution and society.* San Francisco: Freeman, 1976.

LEVENTHAL, H., SINGER, R., and JONES, S. The effects of fear and specificity of recommendation upon attitudes and behavior. *Journal of Personality and Social Psychology*, 1965, *2*, 20–29.

LEVINSON, D. J. *The seasons of a man's life.* New York: Knopf, 1978.

LEVINSON, P., and FLYNN, J. The objects attacked by cats during stimulation of the hypothalamus. *Animal Behavior*, 1965, *13*, 217–220.

LEVY, L., and ROWITZ, L. *The ecology of mental disorder.* New York: Behavioral Publications, 1973.

LEWIN, K. Environmental forces in child behavior and development. In C. Murchison (Ed.), *A handbook of child psychology.* Worcester, Mass.: Clark University Press, 1931.

LEWIN, K. Forces behind food habits and methods of change. *Bulletin of the National Research Council*, 1943, *108*, 35–65.

LEWIN, K., LIPPITT, R., and WHITE, R. Patterns of aggressive behavior in experimentally created social climates. *Journal of Psychology*, 1939, *10*, 271–299.

LEWINSOHN, P. H. A behavioral approach to depression. In R. J. Friedman and M. M. Katz (Eds.), *The psychology of depression: Contemporary theory and research.* Washington, D.C.: Winston-Wiley, 1974.

LEWINSOHN, P. M., MISCHEL, W., CHAPLIN, W., and BARTON, R. Social competence and depression: The role of illusory self-perceptions. *Journal of Abnormal Psychology*, 1980, *89*, 203–212.

LEWIS, J., BADDELEY, A. D., BONHAM, K. G., and LOVETT, D. Traffic pollution and mental efficiency. *Nature*, 1970, *225*, 96.

LEWIS, S., LANGAN, C., and HOLLANDER, E. P. Expectations of future interaction and the choice of less desirable alternatives in conformity. *Sociometry*, 1972, *35*, 440–447.

LEY, D., and CYBRIWSKY, R. Urban graffiti as territorial markers. *Annals of the Association of American Geographers*, 1974, *64*, 491–505.

LICHTENSTEIN, E., HARRIS, D., BIRCHLER, G., WAHL, J., and SCHMAHL, D. Comparison of rapid smoking, warm, smoky air, and attention placebo in modification of smoking behavior. *Journal of Consulting and Clinical Psychology*, 1973, *40*, 92–98.

LIDZ, T. The family language and the transmission of schizophrenia. In D. Rosenthal and S. Kety (Eds.), *The transmission of schizophrenia.* New York: Pergamon Press, 1968.

LIEBER, A., and SHERIN, C. Homicides and the lunar cycle: Toward a theory of lunar influence on human emotional disturbance. *American Journal of Psychiatry*, 1972, *129*, 69–74.

LIEBERMAN, M. A., YALOM, I. D., and MILES, M. B. *Encounter groups: First facts.* New York: Basic Books, 1973.

LIEBERT, R. M., and BARON, R. A. Some immediate effects of televised violence on children's behavior. *Developmental Psychology*, 1972, *6*, 469–475.

LIEBERT, R. M., NEALE, J. M., and DAVIDSON, E. S. *The early window: Effects of television on children and youth.* Elmsford, N.Y.: Pergamon Press, 1973.

LIEM, J., and LIEM, R. Life events, social supports, and physical and psychological well-being. Paper presented at American Psychological Association meeting, Washington, D.C., 1976.

LILLY, J. C. Mental effects of reduction of ordinary levels of physical stimuli on intact healthy persons. *Psychiatric Research Reports*, 1956, *5*, 1–9.

LIMBER, J. The genesis of complex sentences. In T. E. Moore (Ed.), *Cognitive development and the acquisition of language.* New York: Academic Press, 1973.

LIMBER, J. Language in child and chimp? *American Psychologist*, 1977, *32*, 280–295.

LINDER, D. E., and WORCHEL, S. Opinion change as a result of effortfully drawing a counter-attitudinal conclusion. *Journal of Experimental Social Psychology*, 1970, *6*, 432–448.

LIPSCOMB, D. M. Ear damage from exposure to rock and roll music. *Archives of Otolaryngology*, 1969, *90*, 545–555.

LISLE, L. *Portrait of an artist: A biography of Georgia O'Keefe.* New York: Washington Square Press, 1980.

LITTLE, K. B. Personal space. *Journal of Experimental Social Psychology*, 1965. *1*, 237–347.

LOCKE, J. An essay concerning human understanding (Vol. 1). New York: Dover, 1959 (Originally published, 1690).

LOEHLIN, J. C., and NICHOLS, R. C. *Heredity, environment and personality.* Austin, Texas: University of Texas Press, 1976.

LOFTUS, E. F. Leading questions and the eyewitness. *Cognitive Psychology*, 1975, *1*, 560–572.

LOFTUS, E. F. *Eyewitness testimony.* Cambridge, Mass.: Harvard University Press, 1981.

LOFTUS, E. F., and PALMER, J. Reconstruction of automobile destruction: An example of interaction between language and memory. *Journal of Verbal Learning and Verbal Behavior*, 1974, *13*, 585–589.

LONGSTRETH, L. E., LONGSTRETH, G. V., RAMIREZ, C., and FERNANDEZ, G. The ubiquity of Big Brother. *Child Development*, 1975, *46*, 769–772.

LOPATA, H. Z. Self-identity in marriage and widowhood. *Sociological Quarterly*, 1973, *14*, 407–418. (a)

LOPATA, H. Z. Social relations of black and white widowed women in a northern metropolis. *American Journal of Sociology*, 1973, *74*, 1003–1010. (b)

LOPATA, H. Z. *Widowhood in an American city.* Cambridge, Mass.: Schenkman, 1973. (c)

LoPICCOLO, J. The professionalization of sex therapy: Issues and problems. In J. LoPiccolo and L. LoPiccolo, *Handbook of sex therapy.* New York: Plenum Press, 1978, 511–526.

LORAYNE, H., and LUCAS, J. *The memory book.* New York: Ballantine Books, 1974.

LORENZ, K. *On aggression.* New York: Harcourt Brace Jovanovich, 1966.

LOTTER, V. Factors related to outcome in autistic children. *Journal of Autism and Childhood Schizophrenia,* 1974, *4,* 263–277.

LOVAAS, O. I. *The autistic child.* New York: Halsted, 1977.

LOWE, C. A., and KASSIN, S. M. Biased attributions for political messages: The role of involvement. Paper presented at Eastern Psychological Association meeting, 1948.

LOWELL, E. L. The effect of need for achievement on learning and speed of performance. *Journal of Psychology,* 1952, *33,* 31–40.

LOWENTHAL, M. F. Some potentialities of a life-cycle approach to the study of retirement. In F. M. Carp (Ed.), *Retirement.* New York: Behavioral Publications, 1972.

LOWENTHAL, M. F. Toward a sociopsychological theory of change in adulthood and old age. In J. E. Birren and K. W. Schaie (Eds.), *Handbook of the psychology of aging.* New York: Van Nostrand, 1977.

LOWENTHAL, M. F., and CHIRIBOGA, D. Social stress and adaptation: Toward a life-course perspective. In C. Eisdorfer and M. P. Lawton (Eds.), *The psychology of adult development and aging.* Washington, D.C.: American Psychological Association, 1973.

LOWREY, G. H. *Growth and development of children.* Chicago: Year Book Med. Pub., Inc., 1978.

LUBORSKY, L., and SPENCE, D. P. Quantitative research on psychoanalytic therapy. In S. L. Garfield and A. E. Bergin (Eds.), *Handbook of psychotherapy and behavior change: An empirical analysis* (2nd ed.). New York: Wiley, 1978.

LUCAS, O. N. The use of hypnosis in hemophilia dental care. *Annals of the New York Academy of Science,* 1975 (January 20), *240,* 263–266.

LURIA, A. R. *The mind of a mnemonist: A little book about a vast memory* (L. Solotaroff, trans.). New York: Basic Books, 1968.

LYKKEN, D. The GSR in the detection of guilt. *Journal of Applied Psychology,* 1959, *43,* 385–388.

LYKKEN, D. T. Guilty knowledge test: The right way to use a lie detector. *Psychology Today,* March 1975,‾ 56–60.

MACCOBY, E. E., and JACKLIN, C. N. *The psychology of sex differences.* Stanford, Calif.: Stanford University Press, 1974.

MACDONALD, M. L., LIDSKY, T. I., and KERN, J. M. Drug-instigated affects. In A. P. Goldstein and F. H. Kanfer (Eds.), *Maximizing treatment gains: Transfer enhancement in psychotherapy.* New York: Academic Press, 1979, pp. 429–444.

MACDONALD, M. L., and TOBIAS, L. L. Withdrawal causes relapse? Our response. *Psychological Bulletin,* 1976, *83,* 448–451.

MACKWORTH, N. Researches on the measurement of human performance. In H. Sinaiko (Ed.), *Selected papers on human factors in the design and use of control systems.* New York: Dover, 1961.

MACNICHOL, E. F. Three-pigment color vision. *Scientific American,* 1964, *211,* 48–56.

MAHER, B. *Principles of psychopathology.* New York: McGraw-Hill, 1966.

MAHER, B. A. Delusional thinking and cognitive disorder. Paper presented at annual meeting of the American Psychological Association, 1970.

MAIER, N. R. F. Reasoning in humans. II: The solution of a problem and its appearance in consciousness. *Journal of Comparative Psychology,* 1931, *12,* 181–194.

MAIER, S., and SELIGMAN, M. Learned helplessness: Theory and evidence. *Journal of Experimental Psychology: General,* 1976, *105,* 3–46.

MALAMUD, W. The psychoneuroses. In J. McV. Hunt (Ed.), *Personality and the behavior disorders* (Vol. 2). New York: Ronald Press, 1944, pp. 833–860.

MALINOWSKI, B. *Sex and repression in savage society.* New York: Meridian Press, 1927.

MANN, L. The effect of stimulus queues on queue-joining behavior. *Journal of Personality and Social Psychology,* 1977, *35,* 337–342.

MANN, L., NEWTON, J., and INNES, J. A test between deindividuation and emergent norm theories of crowd aggression. *Journal of Personality and Social Psychology,* 1982, *42,* 260–272.

MANZ, W., and LUECK, H. Influence of wearing glasses on personality ratings: Cross-cultural validation of an old experiment. *Perceptual and Motor Skills,* 1968, *27,* 704.

MARGOLIS, A. The black student in political strife. *Proceedings of the 79th Annual Convention of the American Psychological Association,* 1971, *6,* 395–396.

MARKS, W. B., DOBELLE, W. H., and MACNICHOL, E. F., JR. Visual pigments of single primate cones. *Science,* 1964, *143,* 1181–1183.

MARSHALL, J. *Law and psychology in conflict.* New York: Doubleday, 1969.

MARTENS, R., and LANDERS, P. Evaluation potential as a determinant of coaction effects. *Journal of Experimental Social Psychology,* 1972, *8,* 347–359.

MARTIN, B. *Abnormal Psychology: Clinical and scientific perspectives* (2nd ed.). New York: Holt, Rinehart and Winston, 1981.

MARTINDALE, D. Torment in the tower. *Chicago,* April 1976, 96–101.

MARTINDALE, D. A. Territorial dominance behavior in dyadic verbal interactions. *Proceedings of the American Psychological Association,* 79th Annual Convention, 1971, *6,* 305–306.

MASLACH, C. Negative emotional biasing of unexplained arousal. In C. Izard (Ed.), *Emotion, personality and psychopathology.* New York: Plenum, 1979.

MASLOW, A. H. *Toward a psychology of being* (2nd ed.). New York: D. Van Nostrand, 1968.

MASLOW, A. H. *Motivation and personality* (2nd ed.). New York: Harper & Row, 1970.

MASSARO, D. W. Perceptual auditory images. *Journal of Experimental Psychology,* 1970, *85,* 411–417.

MASSON, M. E. J., and McDANIEL, M. A. The role of organizational processes in long-term retention. *Journal of Experimental Psychology: Human Learning and Memory,* 1981, *7,* 100–110.

MASTERS, W., and JOHNSON, V. *Human sexual response.* Boston: Little, Brown, 1966.

MASTERS, W., and JOHNSON, V. *The pleasure bond.* Boston: Little, Brown, 1975.

MASTERS, W. H., and JOHNSON, V. E. *Human sexual inadequacy.* Boston: Little, Brown, 1970.

MASTERS, W. H., and JOHNSON, V. E. *Homosexuality in perspective.* Boston: Little, Brown, 1979.

MATHER, J. A., and LACKNER, J. R. Adaptation to visual displacement: Contribution of proprioceptive, visual, and attentional factors. *Perception,* 1981, *10,* 367–374.

MATHEWS, K., HELMREICH, R., BEANE, W., and LUCKER, G. Pattern A, achievement striving, and scientific merit: Does pattern A help or hinder? *Journal of Personality and Social Psychology,* 1980, *39,* 962–967.

MATHEWS, K. E., and CANNON, L. K. Environmental noise level as a determinant of helping behavior. *Journal of Personality and Social Psychology,* 1975, *24,* 323–350.

MATIN, L. Visual location and eye movements. In W. A. Wagenaar, A. H. Wertheim, and H. W. Leibowitz (Eds.), *Symposium on the study of motion perception.* New York: Plenum, 1981.

MATIN, L., and MACKINNON, E. G. Autokinetic movement: Selective manipulation of directional components by image stabilization. *Science,* 1964, *143,* 147–148.

MAYER, L. A. That confounding enemy of sleep. *Fortune,* June 1975.

McARTHUR, L. A. The lesser influence of consensus than distinctiveness information on causal attributions: A test of the person-thing hypothesis. *Journal of Personality and Social Psychology,* 1976, *33,* 733–742.

McBRIDE, G., KING, M. G., and JAMES, J. W. Social proximity effects on galvanic skin responses in adult humans. *Journal of Psychology*, 1965, *61*, 153–157.

McBURNEY, D. H., and COLLINGS, V. B. *Introduction to sensation/perception*. Englewood Cliffs, N.J.: Prentice-Hall, 1977.

McCARTHY, D., and SAEGERT, S. Residential density, social overload and social withdrawal. *Human Ecology*, 1978, *6*, 253–272.

McCLELLAND, D. C. Some social consequences of achievement motivation. In M. R. Jones (Ed.), *Nebraska Symposium on Motivation*, 1955. Lincoln, Neb.: University of Nebraska Press, 1955.

McCLELLAND, D. C., ATKINSON, J. W., CLARK, R. A., and LOWELL, E. I. *The achievement motive*. New York: Appleton-Century-Crofts, 1953.

McCLELLAND, L. A. *Crowding and social stress*. Unpublished doctoral dissertation, University of Michigan, 1974.

McCLELLAND, L. A., and COOK, S. Promoting energy conservation in master-metered apartments through group financial incentives. *Journal of Applied Social Psychology*, 1980, *10*, 20–31.

McCLOSKEY, M., and SANTEE, J. Are semantic memory and episodic memory distinct systems? *Journal of Experimental Psychology: Human Learning and Memory*, 1981, *7*, 66–71.

McGUIRE, W. The effectiveness of supportive and refutational defenses in immunization and restoring beliefs against persuasion. *Sociometry*, 1961, *24*, 184–197.

McGUIRE, W. The nature of attitude, and attitude change. *The handbook of social psychology* (Vol. 3). Reading, Mass.: Addison-Wesley, 1968.

McKENNA, R. J. Some effects of anxiety level and food cues on the eating behavior of obese and normal subjects. *Journal of Personality and Social Psychology*, 1972, *22*, 311–319.

McMULLEN, S., and ROSEN, R. The use of self-administered masturbation training in the treatment of primary dysfunction. *Journal of Consulting and Clinical Psychology*, 1979, *47*, 912–918.

McPHERSON, B., and GUPPY, N. Pre-retirement life-style and the degree of planning for retirement. *Journal of Gerontology*, 1979, *34*, 254–263.

McTEER, W. *The scope of motivation*. Monterey, Calif.: Brooks/Cole, 1972.

McWATERS, B. An outline of transpersonal psychology: Its meaning and relevance for education. In T. Roberts (Ed.), *Four psychologies applid to education*. New York: Schenkman, 1975.

MEAD, M. *Coming of age in Samoa*. Chicago: University of Chicago Press, 1928.

MEAD, M. *Sex and temperament in three primitive societies*. New York: Morrow, 1935.

MEDVEDEV, Z. A. Aging and longevity: New approaches and new perspectives. *The Gerontologist*, 1975, *15*, 196–201.

MEE, C. L. *Seizure*. New York: Jove, 1978.

MEHRABIAN, A. Nonverbal communication. *Nebraska Symposium on Motivation*, Lincoln, Neb.: University of Nebraska Press, 1971.

MEHRABIAN, A., and WEINER, M. Decoding of inconsistent communications. *Journal of Personality and Social Psychology*, 1967, *6*, 109–114.

MELTZOFF, J., and KORNREICH, M. *Research in psychotherapy*. New York: Atherton, 1970.

MENDEL, G. Letter to Carl Nagele (1867). In M. Gabriel and S. Fogel (Eds.), *Great experiments in biology*. Englewood Cliffs, N.J.: Prentice-Hall, 1955.

MIDDLEMIST, R. D., KNOWLES, E. S., and MATTER, C. F. Personal space invasions in the lavatory: Suggestive evidence for arousal. *Journal of Personality and Social Psychology*, 1976, *33*, 541–546.

MILGRAM, S. Behavioral study of obedience. *Journal of Abnormal and Social Psychology*, 1963, *67*, 376.

MILGRAM, S. Liberating effects of group pressure. *Journal of Personality and Social Psychology*, 1965, *1*, 127–134.

MILGRAM, S. The experience of living in cities. *Science*, 1970, *167*, 1461–1468.

MILGRAM, S. *The individual in a social world*. Reading, Mass.: Addison-Wesley, 1977.

MILLER, A. G. Actor and observer perceptions of the learning of a task. *Journal of Experimental Social Psychology*, 1977, *11*, 95–111.

MILLER, B. C. A multivariate developmental model of marital satisfaction. *Journal of Marriage and the Family*, 1976, *38*, 643–657.

MILLER, G. A. The magical number seven plus or minus two: Some limits on our capacity for processing information. *Psychological Review*, 1956, *62*, 81–97.

MILLER, G. A., GALANTER, E., and PRIBRAM, K. H. *Plans and the structure of behavior*. New York: Holt, Rinehart and Winston, 1960.

MILLER, M. *Plain speaking*. New York: Berkeley, 1973.

MILLER, N. E. Experimental studies of conflict. In J. McV. Hunt (Ed.), *Personality and the behavior disorders* (Vol. 1). New York: Ronald Press, 1944.

MILLER, N. E., and BUGELSKI, R. Minor studies of aggression: II: The influence of frustrations imposed by the in-group on attitudes expressed toward the out-group. *Journal of Psychology*, 1948, *25*, 437–453.

MILLER, N. E., and DiCARA, L. Instrumental learning of heart-rate changes in curarized rats: Shaping and specificity to discriminative stimulus. *Journal of Comparative and Physiological Psychology*, 1967, *63*, 12–19.

MILLON, T. *Modern psychopathology*. Philadelphia: Saunders, 1969.

MILNER, D. Racial prejudice. In J. Turner and H. Giles (Eds.), *Intergroup Behavior*. Chicago: University of Chicago Press, 1981.

MINTZ, N. C. Effects of aesthetic surroundings: II. Prolonged and repeated experience in a "beautiful" and an "ugly" room. *Journal of Psychology*, 1956, *41*, 459–466.

MINUCHIN, S., ROSMAN, B. L., and BAKER, L. *Psychosomatic families*. Cambridge, Mass.: Harvard University Press, 1978.

MISCHEL, W. *Personality and assessment*. New York: Wiley, 1968.

MISCHEL, W. Toward a cognitive social learning reconceptualization of personality. *Psychological Review*, 1973, *80*, 252–283.

MISCHEL, W. *Introduction to personality* (2nd ed.). New York: Holt, Rinehart, and Winston, 1976.

MISCHEL, W. On the future of personality measurement, *American Psychologist*, 1977, *32*, 246–254.

MITCHELL, K. M., BOZARTH, J. D., and KRAUFF, C. C. A reappraisal of the therapeutic effectiveness of accurate empathy, nonpossessive warmth, and genuineness. In A. S. Gurman and A. M. Razin (Eds.), *Effective psychotherapy: A handbook of research*. New York: Pergamon Press, 1977.

MOEDE, W. Die Richtlinien der Leisturgs-Psychologie. *Industrielle Psychotechnik*, 1927, *4*, 193–207.

MONSON, T., and SNYDER, M. Actors, observers, and the attribution process: Toward a reconceptualization. *Journal of Experimental Social Psychology*, 1977, *13*, 89–111.

MOODY, R. *Life after life*. New York: Bantam, 1975.

MOORE, M. L. *Realities in childbearing*. Philadelphia: Saunders, 1978.

MORAY, N. Attention in dichotic listening: Affective cues and the influence of instructions. *Quarterly Journal of Experimental Psychology*, 1959, *11*, 56–60.

MORGAN, T. The psychophysiology of learning. In S. S. Stevens (Ed.), *Handbook of experimental psychology*. New York: Wiley, 1951.

MORRIS, W. N., WORCHEL, S., BOIS, J. L., PEARSON, J. A., ROUNTREE, C. A., SAMAHA, G. M., WACHTLER, J., and WRIGHT, S. L. Collective coping with stress: Group reactions to fear, anxiety, and ambiguity. *Journal of Personality and Social Psychology*, 1976, *33*, 674–679.

MORTENSEN, C. *Communication: The study of human interaction*. New York: McGraw-Hill, 1972.

MOSCOVICI, S., and ZAVALLONI, M. The group as a polarizer of attitudes. *Journal of Personality and Social Psychology*, 1969, *12*, 125–135.

MOSS, M., and AREND, R. Self-directed contact desensitization. *Journal of Consulting and Clinical Psychology*, 1977, *45*, 730–738.

MOWAT, F. *Never cry wolf*. Boston: Atlantic Monthly Press, Little, Brown, 1963.

MUELLER, C., and DONNERSTEIN, E. The effects of humor-induced arousal upon aggressive behavior. *Journal of Research in Personality*, 1977, *11*, 73–82.

MUHELMAN, J. T., BRUKER, C., and INGRAM, C. M. The generosity shift. *Journal of Personality and Social Psychology*, 1976, *34*, 344–351.

MURRAY, H. *Explorations in personality.* New York: Oxford University Press, 1938.

MURRAY, J. R., POWERS, E. A., and HAVIGHURST, R. J. Personal and situational factors producing flexible careers. *The Gerontologist*, 1971, *11*, 4–12.

MURSTEIN, B. I. Physical attractiveness and marital choice. *Journal of Personality and Social Psychology*, 1972, *22*, 8–12.

MUSSEN, P. H., and JONES, M. C. Self-conceptions, motivations, and interpersonal attitudes of late and early maturing boys. *Child Development*, 1957, *28*, 243–256.

NAHEMOW, L., and LAWTON, M. P. Similarity and propinquity in friendship formation. *Journal of Personality and Social Psychology*, 1975, *32*, 205–213.

NAIL, P., LEVY, L., RUSSIN, R., and CRANDELL, R. Time estimation and obesity. *Personality and Social Psychology Bulletin*, 1981, *7*, 139–146.

NAPIER, R., and GERSHENFELD, M. *Groups: Theory and experience.* Boston: Houghton Mifflin, 1981.

NASH, R. *Wilderness and the American mind.* New Haven, Conn.: Yale University Press, 1967.

NATHAN, P. E. Alcoholism. In H. Leitenberg (Ed.), *Handbook of behavior modification and behavior therapy.* Englewood Cliffs, N.J.: Prentice-Hall, 1976.

NELSON, L. P., and NELSON, V. Religion and death anxiety. Paper presented at Society for the Scientific Study of Religion and Religious Research Association, San Francisco, 1973.

NEUGARTEN, B. L. The awareness of middle age. In B. L. Neugarten (Ed.), *Middle age and aging.* Chicago: University of Chicago Press, 1968.

NEUGARTEN, B. L. Dynamics of transition of middle age to old age. *Journal of Geriatric Psychiatry*, 1970, *4*, 71–87.

NEUGARTEN, B. L., and HAGESTAD, G. O. Age and the life course. In R. H. Binstock and E. Shanas (Eds.), *Handbook of aging and the social sciences.* New York: Van Nostrand Reinhold, 1976.

NEUGARTEN, B. L., and WEINSTEIN, K. K. The changing American grandparent. *Journal of Marriage and the Family*, 1964, *26*, 199–204.

NEWCOMER, J. Sonicguide: Its use with public school blind children. *Journal of Visual Impairment and Blindness*, 1977, *71*, 268–271.

NEWMAN, O. *Defensible space.* New York: Macmillan, 1972.

NEWMAN, O. *Design guidelines for creating defensible space.* Washington, D.C.: U. S. Government Printing Office, 1975.

NEW YORK TIMES NEWS SERVICE. Depression linked to specific gene. *New York Times*, Sunday, Nov. 29, 1981.

NIIJIMA, A. Afferent impulse charges from glucoreceptors in the liver of the guinea pig. *Annals of the New York Academy of Sciences*, 1969, *157* (2), 690–700.

NISBETT, R. E. Taste, deprivation, and weight determinants of eating behavior. *Journal of Personality and Social Psychology*, 1968, *10*, 107–116.

NISBETT, R. E. Hunger, obesity, and the ventromedial hypothalamus. *Psychological Review*, 1972, *79*, 433–453.

NISBETT, R. E., and BORGIDA, E. Attribution and the psychology of prediction. *Journal of Personality and Social Psychology*, 1975, *32* (5), 932–943.

NISBETT, R., and ROSS, L. *Human inference: Strategies and shortcomings of social judgment.* Englewood Cliffs, N.J.: Prentice-Hall, 1980.

NOESJIRWAN, J. Contrasting cultural patterns of interpersonal closeness in doctors' waiting rooms in Sydney and Jakarta. *Journal of Cross-Cultural Psychology*, 1977, *8*, 359–368.

NORMAN, D. A. Memory, knowledge, and the answering of questions. In R. L. Solso (Ed.), *Contemporary issues in cognitive psychology.* Washington, D.C.: Winston, 1973.

NORMAN, D. A., and RUMELKART, D. E. *Exploration in cognition.* San Francisco: Freeman, 1975.

OLSEN, K. M. Social class and age-group differences in the timing of family status changes: A study of age norms in American society. Unpublished doctoral dissertation, University of Chicago, 1969.

OLSHAN, N. H. *Power over your pain without drugs.* New York: Rawson, Wade, 1980.

O'NEAL, E., BRUNAULT, M., CARIFIO, M., TRAUTWINE, R., and EPSTEIN, J. Effect of insult upon personal space. *Journal of Nonverbal Behavior*, 1980, *5*, 56–62.

ORNE, M. T. On the social psychology of the psychological experiment: With particular reference to demand characteristics and their implications. *American Psychologist*, 1962, *17*, 776–783.

ORNE, M. T. Social control in the psychological experiment: Antisocial behavior and hypnosis. *Journal of Personality and Social Psychology*, 1965, *1*, 189–200.

ORNE, M. T. On the simulating subject as a quasi-control group in hypnosis research: What, why, and how. In E. Fromm and R. E. Shor (Eds.), *Hypnosis: Research development and perspectives.* Chicago: Aldine, 1972.

ORNSTEIN, R. E., *The psychology of consciousness* (2nd ed.). New York: Harcourt Brace Jovanovich, 1977.

ORNITZ, E. M. The modulation of sensory input and motor output in autistic children. In E. Scholpler and R. J. Reichler (Eds.), *Psychopathology and child development.* New York: Plenum Press, 1976, 115–133.

OSGOOD, C. E. Dimensionality of the semantic space for communication via facial expressions. *Scandinavian Journal of Psychology*, 1966, *7*, 1–30.

OWEN, D. R. The 47, XYY male: A review. *Psychological Review*, 1972, *78*, 209–233.

PAGE, H. A., ELFNER, L. F., and JARNISON, N. Autokinetic effect as a function of intermittency of the light source. *Psychol. Rec.*, 1966, *16*, 189–192.

PARKE, D., BERKOWITZ, D., LEYENS, J. P., WEST, S. G., and SEBASTIAN, J. R. Some effects of violent and nonviolent movies on the behavior of juvenile delinquents. *Advances in Experimental Social Psychology*, 1977, *10*, 139–169.

PARKES, C. M., and BROWN, R. Health after bereavement: A controlled study of young Boston widows and widowers. *Psychosomatic Medicine*, 1972, *34*, 449–461.

PASAMANICK, B., and LILIENFELD, A. Association of maternal and fetal factors with the development of mental deficiency: I. Abnormalities in the prenatal and perinatal periods. *Journal of The American Medical Association*, 1955, *159*, 155–160.

PATTERSON, F. G. The gestures of a gorilla: Language acquisition in another pongid. *Brain and Language*, 1978, *5*, 72–97.

PATTERSON, G. R. A performance theory for coercive family interaction. In R. B. Cairns (Ed.), *Social interaction: Analysis and illustrations.* Hillsdale, N.J.: Erlbaum, 1979.

PATTERSON, M. Interpersonal distance, affect and equilibrium theory. *Journal of Social Psychology*, 1977, *101*, 205–214.

PAUL, S. M. Movement and madness: Toward a biological model of schizophrenia. In J. D. Master and M. E. P. Seligman (Eds.), *Psychopathology: Experimental models.* San Francisco: Freeman, 1977, pp. 358–386.

PAULUS, P., McCAIN, G., and COX, V. Death rates, psychiatric commitments, blood pressure and perceived crowding as a function of institutional crowding. *Environmental Psychology and Nonverbal Behavior*, 1978, *3*, 107–116.

PAVIO, A. Comparisons of mental clocks. *Journal of Experimental Psychology: Human Perception and Performance*, 1978, *4*, 61–71.

PAVLOV, I. P. *Conditioned reflexes.* New York: Oxford University Press, 1927.

PELLEGRINI, R. Impressions of male personality as a function of beardedness. *Psychology*, 1973, *10*, 29.

PENFIELD, W. *The mastery of the mind: A critical study of consciousness and the human brain.* Princeton, N.J.: Princeton University Press, 1975.

PENFIELD, W., and RASMUSSEN, T. *The cerebral cortex of man.* New York: Macmillan, 1950.

PENICK, S. B., SMITH, G. P., WIENEKE, K., JR., and HINKLE, L. E., JR. An experimental evaluation of the relationship between hunger and gastric motility. *American Journal of Psychology,* 1963, 421–426.

PENNEBAKER, J. W. Perceptual and environmental determinants of coughing. *Basic and Applied Social Psychology,* 1980, *1,* 83–91, 94.

PENNEBAKER, J., and SKELTON, A. Selective monitoring of physical sensations. *Journal of Personality and Social Psychology,* 1981, *41,* 213–223.

PEPLER, R. Performance and well-being in heat. In J. Hardy (Ed.), *Temperature: Its measurement and control in science and industry,* *3,* Part 3. New York: Van Nostrand Reinhold, 1963.

PEREZ, J. *Family counseling.* New York: Van Nostrand, 1979.

PERLS, F. S. *Ego, hunger and aggression: The beginning of Gestalt therapy.* New York: Random House, 1969.

PERLS, F. S. *Gestalt therapy verbatim.* Lafayette, Calif.: Real People Press, 1969.

PERLS, F. S. Four lectures. In J. Fagan and I. L. Sheperd (Eds.), *Gestalt therapy now.* Palo Alto, Calif.: Science and Behavior Books, 1970.

PEROVE, D. R., and SPIELBERGER, C. D. Anxiety and the perception of punishment. *Mental Hygiene,* 1966, *50,* 390–397.

PESSIN, J. The comparative effects of social and mechanical stimulation on memorizing. *American Journal of Psychology,* 1933, *45,* 263–270.

PETERSON, J. A., and PAYNE, B. *Love in the later years.* New York: Associated Press, 1975.

PETERSON, L. R., and PETERSON, M. J. Short-term retention of individual items. *Journal of Experimental Psychology,* 1959, *58,* 193–198.

PHARES, E. J. *Locus of control in personality.* Morristown, N.J.: General Learning Press, 1976.

PIAGET, J. *The moral judgement of the child.* New York: Harcourt Brace Jovanovich, 1932.

PIAGET, J. *The child's conception of the world.* London: Routledge, 1960.

PILIAVIN, I., RODIN, J., and PILIAVIN, J. Good Samaritanism: An underground phenomenon? *Journal of Personality and Social Psychology,* 1969, *13,* 289–299.

PLANNED PARENTHOOD. 11 million teenagers: What can be done about the epidemic of adolescent pregnancies in the United States? New York: PPFA, 1976.

PLOMIN, R., and DeFRIES, J. C. Genetics and intelligence: Recent data. *Intelligence,* 1980, *4,* 15–24.

PLUTCHIK, R. *Emotion: A psychoevolutionary analysis.* New York: Harper & Row, 1980.

PODD, M. H. Ego identity status and morality: The relationship between two developmental constructs. *Developmental Psychology,* 1972, *6,* 497–507.

POLLEN, D. A., and RONNER, S. F. Spatial computation performed by simple and complex cells in the visual cortex of the cat. *Vision Research,* 1982, *22,* 101–118.

POPLIN, D. *Social problems.* Glenview, Ill.: Scott, Foresman, 1978.

POPULATION REFERENCE BUREAU, 1977 *World population data sheet.* Washington, D.C.: Population Reference Bureau, 1977.

PORTEOUS, J. D. *Environment and behavior.* Reading, Mass.: Addison-Wesley, 1977.

PORTUGES, S. H., and FESHBACH, N. D. The influence of sex and social class upon imitations of teachers by elementary school children. *Child Development,* 1972, *43,* 981–989.

POULTON, E. A new look at the effects of noise: A rejoinder. *Psychological Bulletin,* 1978, *85,* 1068–1079.

POULTON, E. Composite model for human performance in continuous noise. *Psychological Review,* 1979, *86,* 361–375.

POWLEY, T., and KEESEY, R. Relationship of body weight to the lateral hypothalamic feeding syndrome. *Journal of Comparative and Physiological Psychology,* 1970, *70,* 25–36.

PREMACK, A. J., and PREMACK, D. Teaching language to an ape. *Scientific American,* November 1972.

PREMACK, D. *Intelligence in ape and man.* Hillsdale, N.J.: Erlbaum, 1976.

PRENTICE-DUNN, S., and ROGERS, R. Effects of deindividuating situational cues and aggressive models on subjective deindividuation and aggression. *Journal of Personality and Social Psychology,* 1980, *39,* 104–113.

President's Commission on Mental Health, 1978, Report to the President, Washington, D.C.: U. S. Gov. Printing Office, 1978.

President's Council on Environmental Quality. Environmental Protection Agency, Washington, D.C.: U.S. Government Printing Office, 1978.

PRESSER, H. B. Social consequences of teenage child-bearing. In W. Petersen and L. Day (Eds.), *Social demography: The state of the art.* Cambridge, Mass.: Harvard University Press, 1977.

PRIBRAM, K. Some observations on the organization of studies of mind, brain, and behavior. In N. E. Zinberg (Ed.), *Alternate states of consciousness: Multiple perspectives on the study of consciousness.* New York: Free Press, 1977.

PROFFITT, D. R., and CUTTING, J. E. An invariant for wheel-generated motions and the logic of its determination. *Perception,* 1980, *9,* 435–449.

QUATTRONE, G., and JONES, E. The perception of variability with in-groups and out-groups: Implications for the law of small numbers. *Journal of Personality and Social Research,* 1980, *38,* 141–152.

RAPOPORT, R., and RAPOPORT, R. N. *Dual career families.* Baltimore: Penguin, 1971.

RAVEN, J. C. *Progressive matrices.* London: Lewis, 1947.

RAYNOR, J. O. Relationships between achievement-related motives, future orientation, and academic performance. *Journal of Personality and Social Psychology,* 1970, *15,* 28–33.

READ, P. P. *Alive: The story of the Andes survivors.* Philadelphia: Lippincott, 1974.

REICHEL, D., and GELLER, E. Applications of behavioral analysis for conserving transportation energy. In A. Baum and J. Singer (Eds.), *Advances in environmental psychology* (Vol. 3). Hillsdale, N.J.: Erlbaum, 1981.

RESCORLA, R. A., and HOLLAND, P. C. Behavioral studies of associative learning in animals. *Annual Review of Psychology,* 1982, *33,* 265–308.

RESTAK, R. *The brain: The last frontier.* Garden City, New York: Doubleday, 1979.

REYAIJMAKERS, J. G. W., and SHIFFRIN, R. M. Search of associative memory. *Psychological Review,* 1981, *88,* 93–134.

RICE, B. Rattlesnakes, french fries, and pupillometric oversell. *Psychology Today,* 1974, *7* (9), 55–59.

RICE, B. The new truth machine. *Psychology Today,* 1978, *12,* 61–78.

RILEY, M. W., JOHNSON, M. E., and FONER, A. (Eds.), *Aging and society: A sociology of age stratification.* New York: Russell Sage Foundation, 1972.

RIMLAND, B. *Infantile autism: The syndrome and its implications for a neural theory of behavior.* New York: Appleton-Century-Crofts, 1964.

RIMM, D. C., and MASTERS, J. C. *Behavior therapy: Techniques and empirical findings.* New York: Academic Press, 1979.

RINGNESS, T. A. *The affective domain in education.* Boston: Little, Brown, 1975.

RITCHIE, G. G. (with Elizabeth Sherrill). *Return from tomorrow.* Waco, Texas: Chosen Books, 1978.

RITZER, G. *Working: Conflict and change* (2nd ed.). Englewood Cliffs, N.J.: Prentice-Hall, 1977.

ROBERTSON, J. F. Significance of grandparents: Perception of young adult grandchildren. *The Gerontologist,* 1976, *16,* 137–140.

ROCK, I. In defense of unconscious inference. In W. Epstein (Ed.), *Stability and constancy in visual perception: Mechanisms and processes.* New York: Wiley, 1977.

ROCK, I., and HARRIS, C. S. Vision and touch. *Scientific American,* 1967, *216,* 96–104.

RODIN, J. Causes and consequences of time perception differences in overweight and normal weight people. *Journal of Per-*

sonality and Social Psychology, 1975, *31,* 898–910.

RODIN, J. The effects of stimulus-bound behavior on biological self-regulation: Feeding, obesity and external control. In G. Schwartz and D. Shapiro (Eds.), *Consciousness and Self-Regulation,* New York: Plenum Press, 1977.

RODIN, J. Understanding obesity: Defining the samples. *Personality and Social Psychology Bulletin,* 1981, *7,* 147–151.

RODIN, J., and BAUM, A. Crowding and helplessness: Potential consequences of density and loss of control. In A. Baum and Y. Epstein (Eds.), *Human response to crowding.* New York: Halsted, 1978.

RODIN, J., and LANGER, E. Long-term effects of a control-relevant intervention with the institutionalized aged. *Journal of Personality and Social Psychology,* 1977, *35,* 891–902.

RODIN, J., SOLOMON, S., and METCALF, J. Role of control in mediating perceptions of density. *Journal of Personality and Social Psychology,* 1978, *36,* 988–999.

ROETHLISBERGER, F., and DICKSON, W. *Management and the worker.* Cambridge, Mass.: Harvard University Press, 1939.

ROGERS, C. *Counseling and psychotherapy: Newer concepts in practice.* Boston: Houghton Mifflin, 1942.

ROGERS, C. *Client-centered Therapy.* Boston: Houghton Mifflin, 1951.

ROGERS, C. *On becoming a person: A therapist's view of psychotherapy.* Boston: Houghton Mifflin, 1970.

ROGERS, C., and DYMOND, A. *Psychotherapy and personality change.* Chicago: University of Chicago Press, 1954.

ROOS, P. Jurisdiction: An ecological concept. *Human Relations,* 1968, 75–84.

ROSE, A. *Union solidarity.* Minneapolis: University of Minnesota Press, 1952.

ROSE, S. *The conscious brain.* New York: Knopf, 1973.

ROSEN, M. A dual model of obsessional neurosis. *Journal of Consulting and Clinical Psychology,* 1975, *43,* 453–459.

ROSEN, R., and ROSEN, L. *Human sexuality.* New York: Knopf, 1981.

ROSEN, S., BERGMAN, M., PLESTOR, D., EL-MOFTY, A., and SATTI, M. Presbycosis study of a relatively noise-free population in the Sudan. *Annals of Otology, Rhinology and Laryngology,* 1962, *71,* 727–743.

ROSENBLATT, P. C., and BUDD, L. B. Territoriality and privacy in married and unmarried couples. *Journal of Social Psychology,* 1977, *31,* 240–242.

ROSENHAN, D. L. On being sane in insane places. *Science,* 1973, *179,* 250–258.

ROSENHAN, D. L. The contextual nature of psychiatric diagnosis. *Journal of Abnormal Psychology,* 1975, *84,* 462–474.

ROSENTHAL, D. *Genetic theory and abnormal behavior.* New York: McGraw-Hill, 1970.

ROSENTHAL, R. *Experimenter effects in behavioral research.* New York: Appleton-Century-Crofts, 1966.

ROSENTHAL, R. The Pygmalion effect lives. *Psychology Today,* 1973, 56–63.

ROSENTHAL, R., and JACOBSON, L. F. Teacher expectations for the disadvantaged. *Scientific American,* 1968, *4,* 19–23.

ROSENTHAL, R., and JACOBSON, L. *Pygmalion in the classroom: Teacher expectation and pupils' intellectual development.* New York: Holt, Rinehart and Winston, 1968.

ROSENTHAL, T., and BANDURA, A. Psychological modeling: Theory and practice. In S. L. Garfield and A. E. Bergin (Eds.), *Handbook of psychotherapy and behavior change: An empirical analysis* (2nd ed.). New York: Wiley, 1978.

ROSENZWEIG, M. R. Environmental complexity, cerebral change and behavior. *American Psychologist,* 1966, *21,* 321–332.

ROSS, L. The intuitive psychologist and his shortcomings: Distortions in the attribution process. In L. Berkowitz (Ed.), *Advances in experimental social psychology* (Vol. 10). New York: Academic Press, 1977.

ROSS, L., BIERBRAUER, G., and HOFFMAN, S. The role of attribution processes in conformity and dissent: Revisiting the Asch situation. *American Psychologist,* 1976, *31,* 148–157.

ROTHBART, M. K. Birth order and mother-child interaction in an achievement situation. *Journal of Personality and Social Psychology,* 1971, *17,* 113–120.

ROTTER, J. B. Generalized expectancies for internal vs. external control of reinforcement. *Psychological Monographs,* 1966, *80* (1), 1–28.

ROTTER, J. B. A new scale for the measurement of interpersonal trust. *Journal of Personality,* 1967, *35,* 651–665.

ROTTER, J. B. Some problems and misconceptions related to the construct of internal versus external control of reinforcement. *Journal of Consulting and Clinical Psychology,* 1975, *43,* 56–67.

ROTTER, J. B., and HOCHREICH, D. J. *Personality.* Glenview, Ill.: Scott, Foresman, 1975, 159.

ROUTTENBERG, A. The two-arousal hypothesis: Reticular formation and limbic system. *Psychological Review,* 1968, *75,* 51–80.

ROYCE, J. R., STAYTON, W. R., and KINKADE, R. G. Experimental reduction of autokinetic movement. *American Journal of Psychology,* 1962, *75,* 221–231.

ROZIN, P., and KALAT, J. W. Specific hungers and poison avoidance as adaptive specializations of learning. *Psychological Review,* 1971, *78,* 459–486.

RUBIN, A. *Liking and loving: An invitation to social psychology.* New York: Holt, Rinehart and Winston, 1973.

RUBIN, I. Sex after forty and after seventy. In R. Brecher and E. Brecher (Eds.), *An analysis of human sexual response.* New York: Signet, 1966.

RUBIN, J. Increased self-acceptance: A means of reducing prejudice. *Journal of Personality and Social Psychology,* 1967, *5,* 233–238.

RUBIN, J. A., PROVENZANO, F. J., and LURIA, A. The eye of the beholder: Parents' views on sex of newborns. *American Journal of Orthopsychiatry,* 1974, *44,* 512–519.

RUBIN, Z., PEPLAU, L. A., and HILL, C. T. Loving and leaving: Sex differences in romantic attachments. Unpublished manuscript, Brandeis University, 1978.

RUFF, H. A., and BIRCH, H. G. Infant visual fixation: The effect of concentricity, curvilinearity, and the number of directions. *Journal of Experimental Child Psychology,* 1974, *17,* 460–473.

RUMBAUGH, D. M. (Ed.). *Language learning by a chimpanzee: The Lana project.* New York: Academic Press, 1977.

RUSSEK, M. Hepatic receptors and the neurophysiological mechanisms controlling feeding behavior. In S. Ehrenpreis (Ed.), *Neurosciences research* (Vol. 4). New York: Academic Press, 1971.

RUSSELL, F. *Tragedy in Dedham.* New York: McGraw-Hill, 1962.

RUTTER, M. The development of infantile autism. *Psychological Medicine,* 1974, *4,* 147–163.

RUX, J. M. Widows and widowers: Instrumental skills, socioeconomic status, and life satisfaction. Unpublished doctoral dissertation, Pennsylvania State University, 1976.

RUYS, T. Windowless offices. *Man-Environment Systems,* 1971, *1,* 549.

RYKMAN, R. M. *Theories of personality.* New York: Van Nostrand, 1979.

SACKS, J. S. S. Recognition memory for syntactic and semantic aspects of connected discourse. *Perception and Psychophysics,* 1967, *2,* 437–442.

SAKURAI, M. M. Small group cohesiveness and detrimental conformity. *Sociometry,* 1975, *38,* 340–357.

SANDERS, E. Charlie and the devil. *Esquire,* Nov. 1974, 105–111.

SARASON, I. Test anxiety, stress and social support. *Journal of Personality,* 1981, *49,* 101–114.

SARASON, I. G. Test anxiety and the self-disclosing coping model. *Journal of Consulting and Clinical Psychology,* 1975, *43,* 148–153.

SARASON, I. G., and SARASON, B. R. *Abnormal psychology* (3rd ed.). Englewood Cliffs, N.J.: Prentice-Hall, 1980.

SARNOFF, I., and ZIMBARDO, P. G. Anxiety, fear and social affiliation. *Journal of Abnormal and Social Psychology,* 1961, *62,* 356–363.

SCARR, S., and WEINBERG, R. A. Intellectual similarities within families of both adopted and biological children. *Intelligence,* 1977, *1,* 187–191.

SCARR-SALAPATEK, S. Race, social class, and IQ. *Science,* 1971, *174,* 1285.

SCARR-SALAPATEK, S. Genetics and the development of intelligence. In F. Horowitz

(Ed.), *Review of child development research* (Vol. 4). Chicago: University of Chicago Press, 1975.

SCHACHT, T., and NATHAN, P. But is it good for psychologists? Appraisal and status of DSM-III. *American Psychologist*, 1977, *32*, 1017–1025.

SCHACTER, D. L. The hypnagogic state: A critical review of the literature. *Psychological Bulletin*, 1976, *83*, 452–481.

SCHACHTER, S. Deviation, rejection and communication. *Journal of Abnormal and Social Psychology*, 1951, *46*, 190–207.

SCHACHTER, S. *The psychology of affiliation.* Stanford, Calif.: Stanford University Press, 1959.

SCHACHTER, S. *Emotion, obesity, and crime.* New York: Academic Press, 1971. (a)

SCHACHTER, S. Some extraordinary facts about obese humans and rats. *American Psychologist*, 1971, 129–144. (a)

SCHACHTER, S., and FRIEDMAN, L. N. The effects of work and cue prominence on eating behavior. In S. Schachter and J. Rodin (Eds.), *Obese humans and rats.* Hillsdale, N.J.: Erlbaum, 1974.

SCHACHTER, S., and GROSS, L. P. Manipulated time and eating behavior. *Journal of Personality and Social Psychology*, 1968, *10*, 98–106.

SCHACHTER, S., and LATANE, B. Crime, cognition, and the autonomic nervous system. In D. Levine (Ed.), *Nebraska Symposium on Motivation*, 1964, 221–273.

SCHACHTER, S., and SINGER, J. F. Cognitive, social and physiological determinants of emotional state. *Psychological Review*, 69, *337*, 379–399.

SCHACHTER, S., and WHEELER, L. Epinephrine, chlorpromazine and amusement. *Journal of Applied Social Psychology*, 1962, *65*, 121–128.

SCHAFFER, H. R., and EMERSON, P. E. The development of social attachments in infancy. *Monographs of the Society for Research in Child Development*, 1964, *29* (3, Serial No. 94).

SCHAIE, K. W., and LABOUVIE-VIEF, G. Generational and ontogenetic components of change in adult cognitive behavior: A fourteen-year cross-sequential study. *Journal of Developmental Psychology*, 1974, *10*, 305–320.

SCHALLER, M. Chromatic vision in human infants: Conditioned operant fixation to "hues" of varying intensity. *Bulletin of the Psychonomic Society*, 1975, *6*, 39–42.

SCHANK, R. Identification of conceptualizations underlying natural language. In R. Schank and K. Colby (Eds.), *Computer models of thought and language.* San Francisco: Freeman, 1973.

SCHEIN, E. H. How "career anchors" hold executives to their career paths. *Personnel*, 1975, *52*, 11–24.

SCHILLER, P., and WIENER, M. Binocular and stereoscopic viewing of geometric illusions. *Perceptual and Motor Skills*, 1962, *15*, 739–747.

SCHLESINGER, J. *A thousand days.* Boston: Houghton Mifflin, 1965.

SCHLOSSBERG, H. Three dimensions of emotion. *Psychological Review*, 1954.

SCHWARTZ, G. E. Biofeedback, self-regulation, and the patterning of physiological processes. *American Scientist*, 1975, *63*, 314–324.

SCOVERN, A. W., and KILMANN, P. R. Status of electroconvulsive therapy: Review of the outcome literature. *Psychological Bulletin*, 1980, *87*, 260–303.

SEARS, P. S., and BARBEE, A. H. Career and life satisfactions among Terman's gifted women. In J. C. Stanley, W. C. George, and C. H. Solano (Eds.), *The gifted and the creative: Fifty-year perspective.* Baltimore: Johns Hopkins University Press, 1977.

SEARS, R. R. Sources of life satisfactions of the Terman gifted man. *American Psychologist*, 1977, *32*, 119–128.

SEARS, R. R., WHITING, J. W. M., NOWLIS, J., and SEARS, P. S. Child rearing antecedents of aggression and dependency in young children. *Genetic Psychology Monographs*, 1953, *47*, 135–234.

SECUNDA, S. K., KATZ, M. M., FRIEDMAN, R. J., and SCHUYLER, D. *Special report 1973: The depressive disorders.* Washington, D.C.: U.S. Government Printing Office, 1973 (DHEW Publication No. 739157).

SEEMAN, M., and EVANS, J. W. Alienation and learning in a hospital setting. *American Sociological Review*, 1962, *27*, 772–783.

SEGAL, M. W. Alphabet and attraction: An unobtrusive measure of the effect of propinquity in a field study. *Journal of Personality and Social Psychology*, 1974, *30*, 654–657.

SEGHERS, C. Color in the office. *The Management Review*, 1948, *37*, 452–453.

SELIGMAN, C., and DARLEY, J. Feedback as a means of decreasing residential energy consumption. *Journal of Applied Psychology*, 1977, *62*, 363–368.

SELIGMAN, C., and HUTTON, R. Evaluating energy conservation programs. *Journal of Social Issues*, 1981, *37*, 51–72.

SELIGMAN, C., KRISS, M., DARLEY, J., FAZIO, R., BECKER, L., and PRYOR, J. Predicting residential energy consumption from homeowners' attitudes. *Journal of Applied Social Psychology*, 1979, *9*, 70–90.

SELIGMAN, M. *Helplessness.* San Francisco: Freeman, 1975.

SELIGMAN, M. E. P. Depression and learned helplessness. In R. J. Friedman and M. M. Katz (Eds.), *The psychology of depression: Contemporary theory and research.* Washington, D.C.: Winston-Wiley, 1974.

SELIGMAN, M. E. P. *Helplessness: On depression development and death.* San Francisco: Freeman, 1975.

SELIGMAN, M. E. P., MALER, S. F., and GEER, J. The alleviation of learned helplessness

in the dog. *Journal of Abnormal Psychology*, 1968, *78*, 256–262.

SELYE, H. *The stress of life* (rev. ed.). New York: McGraw-Hill, 1976.

SHAKOW, D. Segmental set: The adaptive process in schizophrenia. *American Psychologist*, 1977, *32*, 129–139.

SHAPIRO, A. Placebo effects in medicine, psychotherapy, and psychoanalysis. In A. Bergen and S. Garfield (Eds.), *Handbook of psychotherapy and behavior change.* New York: Wiley, 1971.

SHAPIRO, D. A biofeedback strategy in the study of consciousness. In N. E. Zinberg (Ed.), *Alternate states of consciousness: Multiple perspectives on the study of consciousness.* New York: Free Press, 1977.

SHAPIRO, J. *Methods of group psychotherapy and encounter.* Itasca, Ill.: Peacock Press, 1978.

SHAVER, K. *An introduction to attribution processes.* Cambridge, Mass.: Winthrop, 1973.

SHAW, M. *Group dynamics: The psychology of small group behavior* (3rd ed.). New York: McGraw-Hill, 1981.

SHAW, M. E. A comparison of two types of leadership in various communication nets. *Journal of Abnormal and Social Psychology*, 1955, *50*, 127–134.

SHEBILSKE, W. L. Structuring an internal representation of text: A basis for literacy. In P. A. Kolers, M. E. Wrolstad, and H. Bouma (Eds.), *Processing of visible language* (Vol. 2). New York: Plenum, 1980.

SHEBILSKE, W. L., and EBENHOLTZ, S. M. Ebbinghaus derived-list experiments reconsidered. *Psychological Review*, 1971, *78*, 553–555.

SHEBILSKE, W. L., and REID, L. S. Reading eye movements, macro-structure and comprehension processes. In P. A. Kolers, M. E. Wrolstad, and H. Bouma (Eds.), *Processing visible language* (Vol. 1). New York: Plenum, 1979.

SHEBILSKE, W. L., and ROTONDO, J. H. Typographical and spatial cues that facilitate learning from textbooks. *Visible Language*, 1981, *15*, 41–54.

SHEBILSKE, W. L. Visuomotor coordination in visual direction and position constancies. In W. Epstein (Ed.), *Stability and constancy in visual perception: Mechanisms and processes.* New York: Wiley, 1977.

SHEBILSKE, W. L. Visual direction illusions in everyday situations: Implications for sensorimotor and ecological theories. In D. F. Fisher, R. A. Monty, and J. W. Senders (Eds.), *Eye movements: Cognition and visual perception.* Hillsdale, N.J.: Erlbaum, 1981.

SHELDON, W. H. The varieties of temperament: A psychology of constitutional differences. New York: Harper & Row, 1942.

SHELDON, W., HART, E., and McDERMOTT, E. *Varieties of delinquent youth: An in-*

troduction to constitutional psychiatry. New York: Harper & Row, 1949.

SHERAS, P., and WORCHEL, S. *Clinical psychology: A social psychological approach.* New York: Van Nostrand, 1979.

SHERIF, M. *The psychology of social norms.* New York: Harper & Row, 1936.

SHERIF, M., HARVEY, O., WHITE, B., HOOD, W., and SHERIF, C. *Intergroup conflict and cooperation: The Robber's Cove experiment.* Norman, Okla.: Institute of Group Relations, University of Oklahoma, 1961.

SHERMAN, A. R. In vivo therapies for phobic reactions, instrumental behavior problems, and interpersonal and communication problems. In A. P. Goldstein and F. H. Kanfer (Eds.), *Maximizing treatment gains: Transfer enhancement in psychotherapy.* New York: Academic Press, 1979.

SHERROD, D. Crowding, perceived control and behavioral aftereffects. *Journal of Applied Social Psychology,* 1974, *4,* 171–186.

SHERTZER, B., and STONE, S. C. *Fundamentals of counseling* (2nd ed.). Boston: Houghton Mifflin, 1974.

SHIELDS, J. *Monozygotic twins brought up apart and brought up together.* London: Oxford University Press, 1962.

SHOCKLEY, W. Dysgenics, geneticity, and raceology: A challenge to the intellectual responsibility of educators. *Phi Delta Kappa,* 1972, *53,* 297–307.

SHOR, R. E., and ORNE, E. C. *The Harvard group scale of hypnotic susceptibility: Form A.* Palo Alto, Calif.: Consulting Psychologists Press, 1962.

SHOTLAND, R. L., and STRAW, M. K. Bystander response to an assault: When a man attacks a woman. *Journal of Personality and Social Psychology,* 1976, *34,* 990–999.

SHURLEY, J. *Proceedings of the third world Congress of psychiatry* (Vol. 3). Toronto, Ontario: University of Toronto Press, 1963.

SIEGEL, R. K. Hallucinations. *Scientific American,* 1977, *237,* 132–139.

SIGALL, H., and OSTROVE, N. Beautiful but dangerous: Effects of offender attractiveness and nature of crime on juridic judgments. *Journal of Personality and Social Psychology,* 1975, *31,* 410–414.

SILVERMAN, L. H. Psychoanalytic theory: "The reports of my death are greatly exaggerated." *American Psychologist,* 1976, *31,* 621–637.

SINEX, F. M. The mutation theory of aging. In M. Rockstein (Ed.), *Theoretical aspects of aging.* New York: Academic Press, 1974.

SINGER, J. L. *The inner world of daydreaming.* New York: Harper & Row, 1975.

SINGER, J., BRUSH, C., and LUBLIN, S. Some aspects of deindividuation: Identification and conformity. *Journal of Experimental Social Psychology,* 1965, *1,* 356–378.

SISTRUNK, F., and McDAVID, J. W. Sex variable in conforming behavior. *Journal of Personality and Social Psychology,* 1971, *17,* 200–207.

SIZEMORE, C., and PITTILLO, E. *I'm Eve.* Garden City, N.Y.: Doubleday, 1977.

SKINNER, B. F. *Walden two.* New York: Macmillan, 1948.

SKINNER, B. F. *Science and human behavior.* New York: Macmillan, 1953.

SKINNER, B. F. *Verbal behavior.* New York: Appleton-Century-Crofts, 1957.

SKINNER, B. F. Pigeons in a pelican. *American Psychologist,* 1960, *15,* 28–37.

SKINNER, B. F. *The behavior of organisms.* Englewood Cliffs, N.J.: Prentice-Hall, 1938, 1966.

SKINNER, B. F. *About behaviorism.* New York: Knopf, 1974.

SKINNER, B. F. The ethics of helping people. In L. Wispe (Ed.), *Sympathy, altruism, and helping behavior.* New York: Academic Press, 1978.

SLOBIN, D. I. *Psycholinguistics.* Chicago: Scott, Foresman, 1971.

SMITH, C. P., RYAN, E. R., and DIGGINS, D. R. Moral decision making: Cheating on examinations. *Journal of Personality,* 1972, *40,* 640–660.

SMITH, M. L. and GLASS, G. V. Meta-analysis of psychotherapy outcome studies. *American Psychologist,* 1977, *32,* 752–760.

SMITH, T., and BREHM, S. Person perception and the type A coronary-prone behavior pattern. *Journal of Personality and Social Psychology,* 1981, *40,* 1137–1149.

SOAL, S. G., and BATEMAN, F. *Modern experiments in telepathy.* New Haven, Conn.: Yale University Press, 1954.

SOBEL, E. F. Countertransference issues with the later life patient. *Contemporary Psychoanalysis,* 1980 (April), Vol. *16* (2), 211–222.

SOMMER, R. *Personal space: The behavioral basis of design.* Englewood Cliffs, N.J.: Prentice-Hall, 1969.

SOMMER, R., and ROSS, H. Social interaction on a geriatric ward. *International Journal of Social Psychiatry,* 1958, *4,* 128–133.

SOMMERSSCHIELD, H., and REYHER, J. Posthypnotic conflict, repression, and psychopathology. *Journal of Abnormal Psychology,* 1973, *82,* 278–290.

SORENSEN, R. C. *Adolescent sexuality in contemporary America.* New York: World, 1973.

SORRENTINO, R. M., and BOUTILLIER, R. G. The effect of quantity and quality of verbal interaction on ratings of leadership ability. *Journal of Experimental Social Psychology,* 1956, *52,* 296–305.

SPARK, G. M., and BRODY, E. M. The aged are family members. *Family Process,* 1970, *9,* 195–210.

SPEARMAN, C. *The abilities of man.* New York: Macmillan, 1927.

SPEISMAN, J. C., LAZARUS, R. S., MORDKOFF, A. M., and DAVIDSON, L. A. The experimental reduction of stress based on ego-defense theory. *Journal of Abnormal and Social Psychology,* 1964, *68,* 367–380.

SPERLING, G. The information available in brief visual presentations. *Psychological Monographs,* 1960, *74* (11, Whole No. 498).

SPERRY, R. W. Perception in the absence of neocortical commissures. In *Perception and its disorders* (Res. Publ. A.R.N.M.D., Vol. 48). New York: The Association for Research in Nervous and Mental Disease, 1970.

SPITZER, R. L. On pseudoscience in science, logic in remission, and psychiatric diagnosis: A critique of D. L. Rosenhan's "on being sane in insane places." *Journal of Abnormal Psychology,* 1975, *84,* 442–452.

SPITZER, R. L. More on pseudoscience in science and the case for psychiatric diagnosis: A critique of D. L. Rosenhan's "on being sane in insane places," and "the contextual nature of psychiatric diagnosis," *Archives of General Psychiatry,* 1976, *33,* 459–470.

SROUFE, L. A. Emotional development in infancy. In J. Osofsky (Ed.), *Handbook of infancy.* New York: Wiley, 1978.

SROUFE, L., and WATERS, E. The ontogenesis of smiling and laughter: A perspective on the organization of development in infants. *Psychological Review,* 1976, *83,* 173–189.

STAFFORD, R., BACKMAN, E., and DIBONA, P. The division of labor among cohabiting and married couples. *Journal of Marriage and the Family,* 1977, *39,* 43–58.

STAFFORD-CLARK, D., and SMITH, A. C. *Psychiatry for students* (5th ed.). London: Allen & Unwin, 1978.

STEIN, A. *Lovers, friends, slaves.* New York: Berkley, 1974.

STEINER, I. D. *Group process and productivity.* New York: Academic Press, 1972.

STENDLER, C. B. Critical periods in socialization and overdependency. *Child Development,* 1952, *23,* 1–2.

STERNBERG, S. High-speed scanning in human memory. *Science,* 1966, *153,* 652–654.

STEWART, A., and SALT, P. Life stress, lifestyles, depression and illness in adult women. *Journal of Personality and Social Psychology,* 1981, *40,* 1063–1069.

STINNETT, N., CARTER, L. M., and MONTGOMERY, J. E. Older persons' perceptions of their marriages. *Journal of Marriage and the Family,* 1972, *34,* 665–670.

STINNETT, N., and WALTERS, J. *Relationships in marriage and family.* New York: Macmillan, 1977.

STOKOLS, D. On the distinction between density and crowding: Some implications for future research. *Psychological Review,* 1972, *79,* 275–278.

STONE, J., COHEN, F., and ADLER, N. *Health psychology.* San Francisco: Jossey-Bass, 1979.

STONER, J. A comparison of individual and group decisions, including risk. Unpublished master's thesis, School of Industrial Management, M. I. T., 1961.

STREIF, G. F., and SCHNEIDER, G. J. Retirement in American society: Impact and process. Ithaca, New York: Cornell University Press, 1971.

STRELOW, E. R., KAY, N., and KAY, K. Binaural sensory aid: Case studies of its use by two children. *Journal of Visual Impairment and Blindness*, 1978, *72*, 1–9.

STRODBECK, F., and MANN, R. Sex-role differentiation in jury deliberations. *Sociometry*, 1956, *19*, 3–11.

STRONGMAN, K. T. *The psychology of emotion*. New York: Wiley, 1973.

STRUPP, H. H., and HADLEY, S. W. Specific versus nonspecific factors in psychotherapy: A controlled study of outcome. *Archives of General Psychiatry*, *36* (10), 1125–1136.

STUART, P., TAYLOR, A., and GAMMON, C. B. Effects of type and dose of alcohol on human physical aggression. *Journal of Personality and Social Psychology*, 1975, *32*, 169–175.

SUEDFELD, P. The benefits of boredom: Sensory deprivation reconsidered. *American Scientist*, January–February 1975.

SUEDFELD, P. Aloneness as a healing experience. In L. A. Peplau and D. Perlman (Eds.), *Loneliness: A sourcebook of current theory, research, and therapy*. New York: Wiley-Interscience, 1981.

SUGARMAN, A., QUINLAN, D., and DEVENIS, L. Anorexia nervosa as a defense against anaclitic depression. *The International Journal of Eating Disorders*, D. Van Nostrand, Autumn, 1981, Vol. 1.

SUNDSTROM, E. Crowding as a sequential process: Review of research on the effects of population density on humans. In A. Baum and Y. Epstein (Eds.), *Human response to crowding*. Hillsdale, N.J.: Erlbaum, 1978.

SUOMI, S. J. Peers, play, and primary prevention in primates. In *proceedings of the third Vermont conference on the primary prevention of psychopathology: Promoting social competence and coping in children*. Hanover, N.H.: University Press of New England, 1977.

SUOMI, S. J., and HARLOW, H. F. The facts and functions of fear. In M. Zuckermann, C. D. Spielberger (Eds.), *Emotions and anxiety: New concepts, methods, and applications*. Hillsdale, N.J.: Erlbaum, 1976.

SUSSMAN, M. B., and BURCHINAL, L. Kin family network: Unheralded structure in current conceptualizations of family functioning. *Marriage and Family Living*, 1962, *24*, 231–240.

SWENSON, R. *Interpersonal relations*. Glenwood, Ill.: Scott, Foresman, 1973.

SWAIN, D. The fantasy-reality distinction in televised violence: Modifying influences on children's aggression. *Journal of Research in Personality*, 1981, *15*, 323–330.

SZASZ, T. S. *The myth of mental illness: Foundations of a theory of personal conduct*. New York: Harper & Row, 1961.

SZASZ, T. S. *Ideology and insanity: Essays on the psychiatric dehumanization of a man*. Garden City, New York: Anchor Books, 1970.

TAJFEL, H. Social stereotypes and social groups. In J. Turner and H. Giles (Eds.), *Intergroup behavior*. Chicago: University of Chicago Press, 1981.

TANNER, J. M. *Foetus into man: Physical growth from conception to maturity*. Cambridge, Mass.: Harvard University Press, 1978.

TANNER, J. Sequence, tempo, and individual variation in growth and development of boys and girls aged twelve to sixteen. In J. Kagan and R. Coles (Eds.), *Twelve to sixteen: Early adolescence*. New York: Norton, 1972.

TARLER-BENLOLO, L. The role of relaxation in biofeedback training. *Psychological Bulletin*, *85*, 1978, 727–755.

TARRIS, D., and OFFIR, C. *The longest war: Sex differences in perspective*. New York: Harcourt Brace Jovanovich, 1977.

TART, C. T. Putting the pieces together: A conceptual framework for understanding discrete states of consciousness. In N. E. Zinberg (Ed.), *Alternate states of consciousness: Multiple perspectives on the study of consciousness*. New York: Free Press, 1977.

TARTTER, V. C., and KNOWLTON, K. C. Perception of sign language from an array of 27 moving spots. *Nature*, 1981, *289*, 676–678.

TAYLOR, R. E. Hinckley case might revive insanity issue. *Wall St. Journal*, April 28, 1981, 33.

TAYLOR, S. P., VARDARIS, R. M., RAWITCH, A. B., GAMMON, C. B., and CRANSTON, J. W. The effects of alcohol and delta-p-tetrahydrocannibol on human physical aggression. *Aggressive Behavior*, 1976, *2*, 153–162.

TAYLOR, S. The plea of insanity and its use in criminal cases. *New York Times*, July 27, 1981.

TAYLOR, S., and THOMPSON, S. Stalking the elusive "vividness" effect. *Psychological Review*, 1982, *89*, 155–181.

TEEVAN, R. C., and McGHEE, P. E. Childhood development of fear of failure motivation. *Journal of Personality and Social Psychology*, 1972, *21*, 345–348.

TEMPLAR, D. I. Death anxiety in religiously very involved persons. *Psychological Reports*, 1972, *31*, 361–362.

TERMAN, L. A preliminary study in the psychology and pedagogy of leadership. *Pedagogical Seminary*, 1904, *4*, 413–451.

TERMAN, L. M. *The measurement of intelligence*. Boston: Houghton Mifflin, 1916.

TERMAN, L. M., and MERRILL, M. A. *Measuring intelligence*. Boston, Mass.: Houghton Mifflin, 1937.

TERRANCE, H. S., PETITTO, L. A., SANDERS, R. J., and BEVER, T. G. Can an ape create a sentence? *Science*, 1979, *206*, 891–901.

THIGPEN, C. H., and CLECKLEY, H. M. *The three faces of Eve*. New York: Popular Library, 1974.

THOMAN, E. B., LIEDERMAN, P. H., and OLSON, J. P. Neonate-mother interaction during breast feeding. *Developmental Psychology*, 1972, *6*, 110–118.

THOMAS, M. H., HORTON, R. W., LIPPINCOTT, E. C., and DRABMAN, R. S. Desensitization to portrayals of real-life aggression as a function of exposure to television violence. *Journal of Personality and Social Psychology*, 1977, *35*, 450–458.

THOMPSON, J. Development of facial expression of emotion in blind and seeing children. *Archives of Psychology*, 1941, *37*, No. 264.

THORNDIKE, E. L. *Animal intelligence*. New York: Macmillan, 1911.

THORNDIKE, E. L. *The psychology of learning*. New York: Teachers College, 1913.

THORNDIKE, E. L. *The fundamentals of learning*. New York: Teachers College, 1932.

THORNDIKE, P. W. Cognitive structures in comprehension and memory of narrative discourse. *Cognitive Psychology*, 1977, *9*, 77–110.

THURSTONE, L. L. *Theories of intelligence*. Scientific Monthly, 1946, *62*, 101–112.

TIMBERLAKE, W., WAHL, G., and KING, D. Stimulus and response contingencies in the misbehavior of rats. *Journal of Experimental Psychology: Animal Behavior Processes*, 1982, *8*, 62–85.

TIME. Parental line: Same old birds and bees. December 25, 1978, 60.

TINBERGEN, N. *The study of instinct*. New York: Oxford University Press, 1951.

TOLMAN, E. C., and HONZIK, C. H. Introduction and removal of reward, and maze performance in rats. *University of California Publications in Psychology*, 1930, *4*, 257–275.

TOMKINS, S. Script theory: Differential magnification of affects. In V. Howe and R. Dienstbier (Eds.), *Nebraska symposium on motivation* (Vol. 26), Lincoln, Neb.: Nebraska University Press, 1979.

TOMKINS, S. The role of facial response in the experience of emotion: A reply to Tourangeau and Ellsworth. *Journal of Personality and Social Psychology*, 1981, *40*, 355–357.

TOMKINS, S. S., and McCORTER, R. What and where are the primary affects? Some evidence for a theory. *Perceptual and Motor Skills*, 1964, *18*, 119–158.

TOYNBEE, A. *A study of history* (Vol. 1). New York: Oxford University Press, 1965.

TRAVIS, L. The effect of a small audience upon eye-hand coordination. *Journal of Abnormal and Social Psychology*, 1925, *20*, 142–146.

TREISMAN, A. M. Contextual cues in selective listening. *Quarterly Journal of Experimental Psychology*, 1960, *12*, 242–248.

TRIBICH, D., and MESSER, S. Psychoanalytic character type and status of authority as determiners of suggestibility. *Journal of Consulting and Clinical Psychology*, 1974, *42*, 842–848.

TRIPLETT, N. The dynamogenic factors in pace-making and competition. *American Journal of Psychology*, 1898, *9*, 507–533.

TRIPP, C. *The homosexual matrix*. New York: McGraw-Hill, 1975.

TROLL, L. E. The family of later life: A decade review. *Journal of Marriage and the Family*, 1971, *33*, 263–290.

TRUAZ, C. B., and MITCHELL, A. Research on certain therapist interpersonal skills in relation to process and outcome. In A. E. Bergin and S. L. Garfield (Eds.), *Handbook of psychotherapy and behavior change*. New York: Wiley, 1971, pp. 299–344.

TRYON, R. C. Genetic differences in maze-learning abilities in rats. In *39th Yearbook, Part I*. National Society for the Study of Education. Chicago: University of Chicago Press, 1940.

TSANG, R. C. Hunger motivation in gastrectomized rats. *Journal of Comparative Psychology*, 1–17.

TULVING, E. Episodic and semantic memory. In E. Tulving and W. Donaldson (Eds.), *Organization of memory*. New York: Academic Press, 1972.

TULVING, E., and PEARLSTONE, Z. Availability versus accessibility of information in memory for words. *Journal of Verbal Learning and Verbal Behavior*, 1966, *5*, 381–391.

TURNER, C. W., and BERKOWITZ, L. Identification with film aggressor (overt role taking) and reactions to film violence. *Journal of Personality and Social Psychology*, 1972, *21*, 256–264.

TURNER, J. The experimental social psychology of intergroup behavior. In J. Turner and H. Giles (Eds.), *Intergroup behavior*. Chicago: University of Chicago Press, 1981.

TURNER, T. A drink a day keeps the doctor away. In *Family Weekly*. New York: Family Weekly, 23.

UNDERWOOD, B., BERENSON, J., BERENSON, R., CHERGET, K., WILSON, D., KULIK, J., MOORE, B., and WENZEL, G. Attention, negative affect, and altruism: An ecological validation. *Personality and Social Psychology Bulletin*, 1977, *3*, 54–58.

U.S. RIOT COMMISSION. *Report of the National Advisory Commission on Civil Disorders*. New York: Bantam Books, 1968.

VAILLANT, G. E. *Adaptation to life*. Boston: Little, Brown, 1977.

VALINS, S. Cognitive effects of false heart rate feedback. *Journal of Personality and Social Psychology*, 1966, *4*, 400–408.

VALINS, S. Persistent effects of information about internal reactions: Ineffectiveness of debriefing. In H. London and R. Nisbett (Eds.), *The cognitive alteration of feeling states*. Chicago: Aldine, 1972.

VAN BESKIRK, S. S. A two-phase perspective on the treatment of anorexia nervosa. *Psychological Bulletin*, 1977, *84*, 529–538.

VEITCH, R., and GRIFFIT, W. Good news, bad news: Affective and interpersonal effects. *Journal of Applied Social Psychology*, 1976, *6*, 69–75.

VERINIS, J., and ROLL, S. Primary and secondary male characteristics: The hairiness and large penis stereotypes. *Psychological Reports*, 1970, *26*, 123–126.

VON FRISCH, K. Decoding the language of the bee. *Science*, 1974, *185*, 663–668.

WAGEMAKER, H., JR., and CADE, R. The use of hemodialysis in chronic schizophrenia. *American Journal of Psychiatry*, 1977, *134*, 684–685.

WALK, R. D., and GIBSON, E. J. A comparative and analytical study of visual depth perception. *Psychological Monographs*, 1961, *75*.

WALLACE, B. *Applied hypnosis: An overview*. Chicago: Nelson-Hall, 1979.

WALLACE, R. Physiological effects of transcendental meditation. *Science*, 1970, *167*, 1751–1754.

WALLACE, W. H., TURNER, S. H., and PERKINS, C. C. *Preliminary studies of human information storage*, Signal Corps Project No. 132C, Institute for Cooperative Research, University of Pennsylvania, December, 1957.

WALLACH, H. Brightness constancy and the nature of achromatic colors. *Journal of Experimental Psychology*, 1948, *38*, 310–324.

WALLACH, H., and O'CONNEL, D. N. The kinetic depth effect. *Journal of Experimental Psychology*, 1953, *45*, 205–217.

WALLACH, M., KAGAN, N., and BEM, D. Group influence on individual risk taking. *Journal of Abnormal and Social Psychology*, 1962, *65*, 75–86.

WALLIN, P. A Guttman scale for measuring women's neighborliness. *American Journal of Sociology*, 1953, *59*, 243–246.

WALLIN, P., and VOLLMER, H. M. Marital happiness of parents and their children's attitudes to them. *American Sociological Review*, 1953, *18*, 424–431.

WALSTER, E., ARONSON, V., ABRAHAMS, D., and ROTTMAN, L. Importance of physical attractiveness in dating behavior. *Journal of Personality and Social Psychology*, 1966, *4*, 508–516. (a)

WALSTER, E., ARONSON, E., and ABRAHAMS, D. On increasing the persuasiveness of a low prestige communicator. *Journal of Experimental Social Psychology*, 1966, *2*, 325–342. (b)

WALTER, G. H., and ASHTON, P. The relationship of teacher-offered empathy, genuineness, and respect to pupil classroom behavior. Paper presented at the American Educational Research Association, Boston, 1980.

WATERS, H. F., and MALAMUD, P. Drop that gun, captain video. *Newsweek*, March 10, 1975, *85*, 81–82.

WATSON, J. B., and RAYNER, R. Conditioned emotional reactions. *Journal of Experimental Psychology*, 1920, *3*, 1–14.

WATSON, J. D., and CRICK, F. H. C. Molecular structure of nucleic acid: A structure for deoxyribose nucleic acid. *Nature*, 1953, *171*, 737–783.

WATSON, R. I. Investigation into deindividuation using a cross-cultural survey technique. *Journal of Personality and Social Psychology*, 1973, *25*, 342–345.

WAUGH, N. C., and NORMAN, P. A. Primary memory. *Psychological Review*, 1965, *72*, 89–104.

WEGNER, D. M., and VALLICHER, R. R. *The self in social psychology*. New York: Oxford University Press, 1981.

WEISS, J. M. Psychological factors in stress and disease. *Scientific American*, June 1972.

WEITZENHOFFER, A. M., and HILGARD, E. R. *Stanford hypnotic susceptibility scales, form C*. Palo Alto, Calif.: Consulting Psychologists Press, 1962.

WELCH, R. B. *Perceptual modification*. New York: Academic Press, 1978.

WELLS, A. *Mass media and society* (2nd ed.). Palo Alto, Calif.: Mayfield, 1975.

WELSH, B. Extra-auditory health effects of industrial noise: Survey of foreign literature. Aerospace Medical Research Laboratory, Aerospace Medical Division, Air Force Systems Command, Wright-Patterson, June, 1979.

WEST, D. *The young offender*. Harmondsworth, England: Penguin, 1967.

WETMORE, M. E. The relationship between perceived text structure, familiarity of content, and recall of expository text. Unpublished doctoral dissertation, University of Virginia.

WHEELER, L., DECI, E., REIS, H., and ZUCKERMAN, B. *Interpersonal influence*. Boston: Allyn & Bacon, 1978.

WHITE, C. Unpublished doctoral dissertation. Catholic University, Washington, D.C.

WHITE, R. W. Lives in progress: A study of the national growth of personality (3rd ed.). New York: Holt, Rinehart and Winston, 1975.

WHYTE, W. *The organization man*. New York: Simon & Schuster, 1956.

WICKELGREN, W. A. *Learning and memory*. Englewood Cliffs, N.J.: Prentice-Hall, 1977.

WICKELGREN, W. A. *Cognitive psychology*. Englewood Cliffs, N.J.: Prentice-Hall, 1979.

WICKER, A. *An introduction to ecological psychology.* Monterey, Calif.: Brooks/Cole, 1979.

WICKLUND, R. A., and BREHM, J. W. Perspectives on cognitive dissonance. Hillsdale, N.J.: Erlbaum, 1976.

WIDOM, C. S. A methodology for studying noninstitutionalized psychopaths. In R. R. Hare and D. Schalling (Eds.), *Psychopathic behavior: Approaches to research.* Chichester, England: John Wiley, 1978, 71–84.

WIEL, A. T. The marriage of the sun and moon. In N. E. Zinberg (Ed.), *Alternate states of consciousness: Multiple perspectives on the study of consciousness.* New York: Free Press, 1977.

WILDER, D. A., and ALLEN, V. L. The effect of absent social support on conformity. Paper presented at the meeting of the Midwestern Psychological Association, Chicago, May 1973.

WILKENS, W. Expectancy of therapeutic gain: An empirical and conceptual critique. *Journal of Consulting and Clinical Psychology,* 1973, *40,* 69–77.

WILLERMAN, B., and SWANSON, L. Group prestige in voluntary organizations. *Human Relations,* 1953, *6,* 57–77.

WILSON, G. Arousal properties of red versus green. *Perceptual and Motor Skills,* 1966, *23,* 947–949.

WINTERBOTTOM, M. R. The relation childhood training in independence to achievement motivation. Unpublished doctoral dissertation, University of Michigan, 1953.

WIRTENBURG, T., and NAKAMURA, C. Education: Barrier or boon to changing occupational roles of women. *Journal of Social Issues,* 1976, *32,* 165–179.

WOLMAN, B. B., DALE, L. A., SCHMEIDLER, G. R., and ULLMAN, M. (Eds.), *Handbook of parapsychology,* New York: Van Nostrand, 1977.

WOLPE, J. *Psychotherapy by reciprocal inhibition.* Stanford, Calif.: Stanford University Press, 1958.

WOLPE, J. The experimental foundations of some new psychotherapeutic methods. In A. J. Bachrach (Ed.), *Experimental foundations of clinical psychology.* New York: Basic Books, 1962.

WOLPE, J. *The practice of behavior therapy.* New York: Pergamon Press, 1974.

WOODRUFF, D. S. *Can you live to be 100?* New York: Chatham Square Press, 1977.

WORCHEL, P. Trust and distrust. In W. Austin and S. Worchel, *The social psychology of intergroup relations.* Monterey, Calif.: Brooks/Cole, 1979.

WORCHEL, S., and ANDREOLI, V. Facilitation of social interaction through deindividuation of the target. *Journal of Personality and Social Psychology,* 1978, *36,* 549–557.

WORCHEL, S., and BURNHAM, C. A. Reduction of autokinesis with information about the registration of eye position. *American Journal of Psychology,* 1967, *80,* 434–437.

WORCHEL, S., and COOPER, J. *Understanding social psychology.* Homewood, Ill.: Dorsey Press, 1979.

WORCHEL, S., and LOLLIS, M. Reactions to territorial contamination as a function of culture. *Personality and Social Psychology Bulletin,* 1982.

WORCHEL, S., and TEDDLIE, C. The experience of crowding: A two-factor theory. *Journal of Personality and Social Psychology,* 1976, *34,* 30–40.

WORCHEL, S., and YOHAI, S. M. L. The role of attribution in the experience of crowding. *Journal of Experimental Social Psychology,* 1979, *15.*

WORCHEL, S., ANDREOLI, V., and FOLGER, R. Intergroup cooperation and intergroup attraction: The effect of previous interaction and outcome of combined effort. *Journal of Experimental Social Psychology,* 1977, *13,* 131–140.

WORCHEL, S., AXSOM, D., FERRIS, F., SAMAHA, G., and SCHWEITZER, S. Determinants of the effects of intergroup cooperation on intergroup attraction. *Journal of Conflict Resolution,* 1978, *xxii,* 429–439.

WRIGHT, H. F. *Recording and analyzing child behavior.* New York: Harper & Row, 1967.

WRIGHT, J. D. Are working women really more satisfied? Evidence from several national surveys. *Journal of Marriage and the Family,* 1978, *40,* 301–313.

WYDEN, B. Growth: 45 crucial months. *Life,* December 1971, 93–95.

WYER, R., HENNINGER, M., and HINKLE, R. An informational analysis of actors' and observers' belief attributions in a role-playing situation. *Journal of Experimental Social Psychology,* 1977, *13,* 199–217.

MALCOLM X and ARTHUR HALEY. *The autobiography of Malcolm X.* New York: Ballantine, 1973.

YALOM, I. D. The theory and practice of group psychotherapy (2nd ed.). New York: Basic Books, 1975.

YALOM, I. D., and LIEBERMAN, A. A study of encounter group casualities. *Archives of General Psychiatry,* 1971, *25,* 16–30.

YEKOVICH, F. R., and THORNDYKE, P. W. An evaluation of alternative functional models of narrative schemata. *Journal of Verbal Learning and Verbal Behavior,* 1981, *20,* 454–469.

ZAGER, L., and MEGARGEE, E. Seven MMPI alcohol and drug abuse scales: An empirical investigation of their interrelationships, convergent and discriminant validity, and degree of racial bias. *Journal of Personality and Social Psychology,* 1981, *40,* 532–544.

ZAJONC, R. Attitudinal effects of mere exposure. *Journal of Personality and Social Psychology,* 1968, *9,* 1–27.

ZAJONC, R. B. Social facilitation. *Science,* 1965, *149,* 269–274.

ZIEGLER, H., and KARTEN, H. Central trigeminal structures and the lateral hypothalamus syndrome in the rat. *Science,* 1974, *186,* 636–637.

ZILBOORG, G., and HENRY, G. W. A history of medical psychology. New York: Norton, 1941.

ZILLMAN, D. Excitation transfer in communication-mediated aggressive behavior. *Journal of Experimental Social Psychology,* 1971, *7,* 419–434.

ZILLMAN, D. *Hostility and aggression.* Hillsdale, N.J.: Erlbaum, 1979.

ZILLMAN, D., JOHNSON, R. C., and DAY, K. D. Attribution of apparent arousal and proficiency of recovery from sympathetic activation affecting excitation transfer to aggressive behavior. *Journal of Experimental Social Psychology,* 1974, *10,* 503–515.

ZIMBARDO, P. The human choice: Individuation, reason and order versus individuation, impulse and chaos. In W. J. Arnold and D. Levine (Eds.), *Nebraska Symposium on Motivation,* 1969, Lincoln, Neb.: University of Nebraska Press, 1970.

ZIMBARDO, P. The psychological power and pathology of imprisonment. Statement prepared for the U.S. House of Representatives Committee on the Judiciary (Subcommittee No. 3, Robert Kastemeyer, Chairman, hearings on prison reform). Unpublished paper, Stanford University, 1971.

ZIMBARDO, P., and EBBESEN, E. *Influencing attitudes and changing behavior.* Reading, Mass.: Addison-Wesley, 1970.

ZINBERG, N. E. The study of consciousness states: Problems and progress. In N. E. Zinberg (Ed.), *Alternate states of consciousness: Multiple perspectives on the study of consciousness.* New York: Free Press, 1977.

ZUBEK, J. P. L., BAYER, A., and SHEPARD, J. M. Relative effects of prolonged social isolation and confinement: Behavioral and EEG changes. *Journal of Abnormal Psychology,* 1969, *74,* 625–631.

ZUCKER, S. H., and ALTMAN, R. An on-the-job training program for adolescent trainable retardates. *Training School Bulletin,* 1973, *70,* 106–110.

ZUCKERMAN, M. Variables affecting deprivation results. In J. P. L. Zubek (Ed.), *Sensory deprivation: Fifteen years of research.* New York: Appleton-Century-Crofts, 1969.

ZUCKERMAN, M., PERSKY, H., LINK, K., and BASU, G. Experimental and subject factors determining responses to sensory deprivation, social isolation and confinement. *Journal of Abnormal Psychology,* 1968, *73,* 183–194.

ZURCHER, L. *The mutable self: A self-concept for social change.* Beverly Hills, Calif.: Sage Publications, 1977.

ACKNOWLEDGMENTS

Figures, Tables, Text

Fig. 2.5: *Scientific American.* **Fig. 2.7:** Reprinted with permission of Macmillan Publishing Co., Inc., from *The Cerebral Cortex of Man* by Wilder Penfield and Theodore Rasmussen. Copyright © 1950 by Macmillan Publishing Co., Inc., renewed 1978 by Theodore Rasmussen.

Fig. 3.26: Rock, I., and Harris, C. S. Vision and touch. *Scientific American,* 1967 *216,* 96–104.

Fig. 4.2: Cotman, C.W., and McGaugh, J. L., *Behavioral Neuroscience.* New York: Academic Press, 1980, p. 612. **Fig. 4.3:** Reproduced from *Some Must Watch While Some Must Sleep* by William C. Dement, by permission of W. W. Norton & Company, Inc. Copyright © 1972, 1974, 1976, by William C. Dement. **Fig. 4.4:** Reprinted with permission of Macmillan Publishing Co., Inc., from *Alternate States of Consciousness: Multiple Perspectives on the Study of Consciousness* by Norman E. Zinberg, Ed. Copyright © 1977 by The Free Press, A Division of Macmillan Publishing Co., Inc. **Fig. 4.9:** Heron, W. Cognitive and physiological effects of perceptual isolation. In P. Solomon et al. (Eds.), *Sensory deprivation.* Cambridge, Mass.: Harvard University Press, 1961. **Fig. 4.10:** From Svedfeld, P. The benefits of boredom: Sensory deprivation reconsidered in *American Scientist,* Jan./Feb., 1975, p. 67.

Table 5.1: Luchins, *Psychological Monographs.* **Fig. 5.8:** From Tolman and Honzik, *Introduction and Removal of Reward, and Maze Performance in Rats.* Reproduced by permission of the University of California Press. **Fig. 5.9:** Schaie, K. W., Labouvie, G., and Buech, B. V. Generational and cohort specific differences in adult cognitive functioning: A fourteen-year study of independent samples. *Developmental Psychology,* 1973, *9,* 151–160. **Fig. 5.10:** Form Board Test, VZ-1; Educational Testing Service, 1962. Vocabulary Test, V-5; Educational Testing Service, 1962. Used by permission. **Fig. 5.11:** Horn, J. L., and Donaldson, G. Cognitive development II: Adulthood development of human abilities. In O. G. Brim, Jr. and J. Kagan (Eds.), *Constancy and change in human development: A volume of review essays,* Cambridge, Mass.: Harvard University Press, 1980.

Fig. 6A: Bower, G. Mood and memory. *Psychology Today,* June, 1981. **Fig. 6.2:** Sperling, G. The information available in brief visual presentations. *Psychological Monographs,* 1960, *74* (11, 498). **Table 6.2:** Brown, R. W., and McNeill, D. The "tip-of-the-tongue" phenomenon. Journal of Verbal Learning and Verbal Behavior, 1966, *5,* 325–337. **Fig. 6.3:** From Peterson and Peterson, Short-term retention of individual items. In the *Journal of Experimental Psychology,* 1959, *58,* 193–198. Copyright © 1959 by the American Psychological Association. Reprinted by permission. **Fig. 6.4:** Reprinted from the Quarterly Journal of Experimental Psychology Society. **Fig. 6.5:** From Kosslyn *et al.,* Visual images preserve metric spacial information. *Journal of Experimental Psychology:* Human Perception and Performance, 1978, *4,* 47–60. Copyright © 1978 by the American Psychological Association. Reprinted by permission. **Fig. 6.6:** Collins, A. M., and Quillian, M. R. Retrieval time from semantic memory. *Journal of Verbal Learning and Verbal Behavior,* 1969, *8,* 240–247. **Fig. 6.7:** Thorndike, P. W. Cognitive structures in comprehension and memory of narrative discourse. *Cognitive Psychology,* 1977, *9,* 77–110. **Fig. 6.8:** Allport, G. W. The nature of prejudice. New York: Doubleday-Anchor, 1958. **Fig. 6.9:** S. Sternberg, "High-Speed Scanning in Human Memory", in *Science,* Vol. 153, pp. 652–654, August 1966. Copyright © 1966 by the American Association for the Advancement of Science.

Fig. 7.1: Frankenburg, W. K., and Dodds, J. B. The Denver development screening test. *Journal of Pediatrics,* 71(1967), pp. 181–191. **Table 7.1:** From Apgar *Anesthesia and Analgesia,* 32:260, 1953. Apgar *Journal American Medical Association,* 168:1985, 1958. **Table 7.2:** From *Psycholinguistics* by Dan I. Slobin. Copyright © 1971 Scott, Foresman and Company. Reprinted by permission. **Fig. 7.3:** Wright, H. F. *Recording and analyzing child behavior.* New York: Harper & Row, 1967.

Table 8.1: From L. Kohlberg, *Stages in the Development of Moral Thought and Action.* N.Y.: Holt, Rinehart and Winston, 1969. Used with permission. **Fig. 8.1:** Tanner, J. M. *Foetus into man: Physical growth from conception to maturity.* Cambridge, Mass.: Harvard University Press, 1978. **Table 8.3:** Murray, J. R., Powers, E. A., and Havighurst, R. J. Personal and situational factors producing flexible careers. The *Gerontologist,* 1971, *11,* 4-12.

Table 9.1: Schachter, S., and Gross, L. P. Manipulated time and eating behavior. *Journal of Personality and Social Psychology,* 10, 1968, 98–106. **Table 9.2:** Reprinted with permission of (PEI) Books, Inc. From *Sexual Behavior in the 1970s* by Morton Hunt. Copyright © 1974 by Morton Hunt. **Fig. 9.3:** Tanner, J. Sequence, tempo, and individual variation in growth and development of boy and girls aged twelve to sixteen. In J. Kagan and R. Coles (Eds.), *Twelve to sixteen: Early adolescence.* New York: Norton, 1972. **Table 9.3:** Schachter, S. *The Psychology of Affiliation.* Stanford, CA: Stanford University Press, 1959. **Fig. 9.5:** Parke, D., Berkowitz, L., Leyens, J. P., West, S. G., and Sebastian, R. J. Some effects of violent and nonviolent movies on the behavior of juvenile delinquents. *Advances in Experimental Social Psychology,* 1970, *10,* 139–169.

Fig. 10.1: After Speisman, J. C., Lazarus, R. S., Mordkoff, A. M., and Davison, L. Experimental reduction of stress based on ego-defense theory. *Journal of Abnormal and Social Psychology,* 68, 1964, 367–380. **Table 10.1:** Reprinted with permission of S. S. Tomkins and R. McCarter and *Psychological Reports.* From Tomkins, S. S., and McCarter, R. What and where are the primary affects? Some evidence for a theory. *Perceptual and Motor Skills,* 1964, *18,* 119–158. **Table 10.2:** Reprinted with permission from *Journal of Psychosomatic Research,* 11: pp. 213–218, T. H. Holmes and R. H. Rahe, "The Social Readjustment Rating Scale," Copyright © 1967, Pergamon Press, Ltd. **Fig. 10.2:** Hess, E. H. Attitude and pupil size, *Scientific American,* 1965, *212,* 46–54.

Table 11.1: Rotter, J. B. Generalized expectancies for internal vs external control of reinforcement. *Psychological Monographs,* 1966, *80* (1), 1–28. **Fig. 11.2:** Cattell, R. B. *The scientific analysis of personality.* Harmondsworth, England: Penguin Books, 1965. **Fig. 11.9:** Holden, C. Nader on mental health centers: A movement that got bogged down. *Science,* 1972, *177,* 413–415.

Table 13.1: Wolpe, J. *Psychotherapy by Reciprocal Inhibition.* Stanford, CA: Stanford University Press, 1958.

Fig. 14.2: Rosenthal, R., and Jacobson, L. F. Teacher expectations for the disadvantaged. *Scientific American,* 1968, *4,* 19–23. **Fig. 14.3:** Latane, B., and Darley, J.M. *The Unresponsive Bystander:* Why dosen't he help? Adapted by permission of Prentice-Hall, Inc. **Fig. 14.1:** Reprinted by permission of Elsevier North Holand, Inc., from "The influence of source credibility on communication effectiveness" by Hovland and Weiss in *The Public Opinion Quarterly,* Vol. 15, pp. 635–650. Copyright © 1952 by The Trustees of Columbia University.

Table 15.1: Milgram, S. Behavioral study of obedience. *Journal of Abnormal and Social Psychology,* 1963, *67,* 376. **Fig. 15.2:** Asch, S. Effects of group pressure upon the modification and distortion of judgment. In H. Guetzkow (Ed.), *Groups, leadership and men.* Pittsburgh: Carnegie Press, 1951. **Table 15.2:** From *The Height of Your Life* by Ralph Keyes. Copyright © 1980 by Ralph Keyes. By permission of Little, Brown and Company.

Fig. 16.1: From Horwitz, M. J., Duff, D. F., and Stratton, L. O. Redrawn by permission from *Archives of General Psychiatry*, December 1964, Vol. 11. Copyright © 1964, American Medical Association. **Fig. 16.2:** Michael Argyle and Janet Dean, "Eye-contact, Distance and Affiliation," *Sociometry*, Vol. 28, 1965, Figure 2 on p. 300. **Fig. 16.3:** Calhoun, J. Population density and social pathology. *Scientific American*, 1962, *206*, 139–148. **Fig. 16.4:** Baum, A., and Valins, S. *Architecture and social behavior: Psychological studies in social density*. Hillsdale, N.J.: Erlbaum, 1977.

Photographs
3 Chris Regas 4 The Bettmann Archive, Inc. 5 Margaret Zear 6 New York Public Library 7 (bottom) Mary Evans Picture Library, Sigmund Freud Copyrights 8 Kathryn Millan © 1982 11 Sybil Shelton, Monkmeyer 12 Atari, Inc. 13 (left) Sybil Shelton, Monkmeyer (right) United Press International 15 Ray Ellis, Photo Researchers, Inc. 16 Ken Karp 19 Federal Bureau of Prisons 21 Ken Karp 22 Mimi Forsyth, Monkmeyer 25 Strix Pix, Monkmeyer

33 Henry Grossman 35 (a,b,c) Peter Brunjes 40 © Lester V. Bergman & Associates 47 Fred Burrell 49 (left) Richard Hutchings, Photo Researchers, Inc. (right) Wasyl Szkodzinsky, Photo Researchers, Inc. 54 (left & right) Photos courtesy of M. M. Grumbach, U. of California, San Francisco 55 Bruce Roberts, Photo Researchers, Inc. 56 United Press International

62 NASA 63 NASA 69 Spatially quantized images by Ed, Manning, c/o Blocpix ® Images, 972 E. Broadway, Stratford, CT. 06497 71 Scientific Publishing Co., Baltimore, Maryland 73 Fritz Goro, Life Magazine, © Time, Inc. 75 Photo by M. Elizabeth Wetmore 76 William Vandivert 77 Marc Anderson 78 NASA 79 (A) Carl Purcell, Photo Researchers, Inc. (B) Peter B. Kaplan, Photo Researchers, Inc. (C) Russ Kinne, Photo Researchers, Inc. 81 David J. Maenza, The Image Bank 86 Stan Pantovic, Photo Researchers, Inc. 87 Will McIntyre, Photo Researchers, Inc. 88 Richard Hutchings, Photo Researchers, Inc. 90 Sensory Aids Corp. of Bensenville 91 Sensory Aids Corp. of Bensenville

99 Photo by Jack Jeffers 107 Laimute E. Druskis 109 New York University, **Fig. 4-1** 115 Jan Halaska, Photo Researchers, Inc. 117 (top) Bill Anderson, Monkmeyer (margin) Charles Gatewood 120–21 *Scientific American*, 1977, *237*, No. 4; p. 134 123 United Press International 125 Ray Ellis, Photo Researchers, Inc.

137 American Foundation for the Blind 141 © Ed Cesar from National Audubon Society, Photo Researchers, Inc. 145, **Fig. 5-5** Eliot Elisofon, Life Magazine © 1958 Time, Inc. 147 Jan Halaska, Photo Researchers, Inc. 148 (left) United Press International (right) Resorts International Hotel Casino 150 Springer, Bettmann Film Archive 151 Ken Karp 155 Ken Karp 157. **Fig. 5-7:** Lilo Hess Three Lions, Inc. 160 H. F. Harlow, University of Wisconsin Primate Labora-

tory 164 Ken Karp 167 Van Bucher, Photo Researchers, Inc.

175 United Press International 182 Georg Gerster, Rapho/Photo Researchers, Inc. 185 Miami Dade Community College 187 United Press International 190 University of Miami 194 Wide World Photos 199 The University of Texas at Austin News and Information Service 203 Leon D. Harmon; Bell Laboratories and *Scientific American*

209 Susan Curtiss, *Genie: A Psycholinguistic Study of a Modern-day "Wild Child,"* N.Y.: Academic Press, 1978. 213 (top right) Russ Kine, Photo Researchers, Inc. Other photos from Rugh P. Shettles, 1971 216 Ken Karp 218 Ken Karp 219 William Vandivert 221 (top) David Linton, *Scientific American* (bottom) Edward Lettau, Photo Researchers, Inc. 223 George Zimbel, Monkmeyer 224 Sam Falk, N.Y.T. Pictures 227 Erika Stone, Photo Researchers, Inc. 229 R. A. and B. T. Gardner 230 W. Zehr, Alpha/FPG 231 Harry F. Harlow, University of Wisconsin Primate Laboratory 234 (bottom) Hallinan, Alpha/FPG (top) Jan Lukas, Rapho/Photo Researchers, Inc. 236 (left) Susan Johns, Rapho/Photo Researchers, Inc. (right) Bob Smith Rapho/Photo Researchers, Inc. 237 Wasyl Szkodzinsky, Photo Researchers, Inc.

243 United Press International 245 David S. Strickler, Monkmeyer 250 Ken Karp 255 (top) Mimi Forsyth, Monkmeyer (bottom) Ken Karp 256 Laimute Druskis 260 Hugh Rogers, Monkmeyer 261 Suzanne Szasz, Photo Researchers, Inc. 263 United Press International 264 Jeep Hunter, Photo Researchers, Inc. 266 (left) Suzanne Szasz, Photo Researchers, Inc. (right) Hella Hammid, Rapho/Photo Researchers, Inc. 267 (left) Ken Karp (right) Ken Karp, Sirovich Senior Center 269 Hella Hammid, Rapho/Photo Researchers, Inc.

275 Sygma, Jean-Pierre Laffont 278 Phyllis Greenberg, Photo Researchers, Inc. 279 Josephus Daniels, Photo Researchers, Inc. 283 S. Weiss, Photo Researchers, Inc. 285 Jan Lukas, Photo Researchers, Inc. 290 Alex Webb, Magnum 291 Courtesy Harry F. Harlow, University of Wisconsin Primate Laboratory 293 Gamma, Jean Pierre Laffont 296 Bob Combs, Photo Researchers, Inc. 297 Albert Bandura 300 U. S. Supreme Court

306 Ann Meuer, Photo Researchers, Inc. 307 Lawrence D. Thornton, Frederic Lewis, Inc. 310 Los Angeles Police Department 319 Max Tharpe, Monkmeyer 321 Ken Karp 323 British Official Photograph: Crown copyright reserved. Issued for British Information Services by Photographs Division, Central Office of Information, London 328 (top) Myron Wood, Photo Researchers, Inc. (bottom) Erika Stone, Photo Researchers, Inc. 330 Paul S. Conklin, Monkmeyer 333 Walter Reed Army Institute of Research 334 United Press International

345 Library of Congress 348 National Library of Medicine 352 The Bettmann

Archive, Inc. 353 *Doonesbury* by Garry Trudeau 357 Teri Leigh Stratford, Photo Researchers, Inc. 360 Wide World Photos 363 Ken Karp 366 Elliot Erwitt 372 Freda Leinwand, Monkmeyer 375 Teri Leigh Stratford, Photo Researchers, Inc.

383 United Press International 386 United Press International 393 Arthur Tress, Photo Researchers, Inc. 400 United Press International 402 Allen Green 411 (left and right) United Press International 415 Barclay Martin, *Abnormal Psychology: Clinical Scientific Perspectives*, 2nd Ed. New York: Holt Rinehart Winston, 1981 420 United Press International

427 C. Sizemore & E. Petillo, *I'm Eve*, Garden City, N.Y.: Doubleday 1977 429 (margin) The American Museum of Natural History (top) Historical Pictures Service, Inc, Chicago 433 Thomas S. England, Photo Researchers, Inc. 439 Susan Rosenberg 441 Susan Rosenberg 442 Susan Rosenberg 446 Shirley Miller Higgins 447 Susan Rosenberg 449 Ken Karp 451 Thomas S. England, Photo Researchers, Inc. 453 Catherine Ursillo, Photo Researchers, Inc.

463 United Press International 466 Ken Karp 467 Christa Armstrong, Photo Researchers, Inc. 469 Bruce Roberts, Rapho/Photo Researchers, Inc. 471 Teri Leigh Stratford, Photo Researchers, Inc. 474 Peace Corps, Belize, Pickorell 477 United Press International 479 (left) Marc P. Anderson (right) Ken Karp 481 Mimi Forsyth, Monkmeyer 482 Ken Karp 484 (right) Sybil Shackman, Monkmeyer (left) David S. Strickler, Monkmeyer 485 David S. Strickler, Monkmeyer 490 Jan Halaska, Photo Researchers, Inc. 492 Wil Blanch, dpi 493 Stan Goldblatt, Photo Researchers, Inc.

499 Photo courtesy of James "Cool Papa" Bell 501 Robert A. Isaacs, Photo Researchers, Inc. 502 Keith Gunnar, Photo Researchers, Inc. 504 United Press International 507 Sherry Suris, Rapho/Photo Researchers, Inc. 510 William Vandivert 514 Ken Karp 516 United Press International 518 Walker Research, Inc. 521 Philip G. Zimbardo 525 American Telegraph and Telephone Photo Center 527 Photo courtesy of Bill Yancey 528 Dick Hanley, Photo Researchers, Inc. 530 United Press International 531 Louis Fernandez 532 Marc Anderson 533 Ken Karp 535 Ken Karp

541 C. N. Cochise and A. K. Griffith. *The First One Hundred Years of Nino Cochise.* N.Y.: Abelard-Schuman, 1971. 543 (left) Russ Kinne, Photo Researchers, Inc. (right) Edward P. Lincoln, Photo Researchers, Inc. 547 Russ Kinne, Photo Researchers, Inc. 548 Henry E. Bradshaw, Photo Researchers, Inc. 549 United Nations 552 Chris Reeberg, dpi 557 United Nations 558 Chas Orrico, Alpha/F.P.G. 562 Tom McHugh, Photo Researchers, Inc. 563 Ned Haines, Rapho/Photo Researchers, Inc. 564 Mimi Forsyth, Monkmeyer 568 United Press International 569 C. Vergara, Photo Researchers, Inc. 571 Jim Howard, Alpha/F.P.G. 638 Frances Worchel

NAME INDEX

Cooper, J., 314, 456, 464, 475, 487, 534
Cooper, R., 57
Coren, S., 80
Corey, G., 450
Corey, M. S., 450
Costa, P. T., Jr., 258
Cotman, C. W., 47, 50, 52, 102, 111, 122
Cottrell, N., 529
Cox, F. D., 251
Cox, M., 250
Cox, V., 558
Coyne, J., 329, 403
Coyne, J. C., 404
Craik, F. I. M., 178, 186
Crandall, V., 368
Crano, W., 482
Crick, Francis, 53
Crisp, A. H., 394
Cristiani, T., 443, 451
Crockenburg, S. B., 166
Crocker, J., 475
Cronbach, L. J., 235
Crouch, Hondo, 1–3
Crutchfield, L., 123
Csikszentmihalyi, M., 114
Culbertson, S., 329
Curtiss, Susan, 210, 215, 216, 222
Cybriwsky, R., 546

Dale, L. A., 130
Daniels, J., 344
Darley, John M., 487, 489, 501, 502
Darwin, Charles, 317, 318
Davidson, 141
Davis, C. M., 283
Davis, J., 282, 414, 523
Davis, J. M., 394
Davis, K., 478
Davis, Walt, 360
Davison, G. C., 397, 398, 428, 446, 447
Dean, J., 551, 553
Deaux, K., 505
Debora, 252
Deese, J., 177, 191, 582
DeFries, J. C., 169
Dember, W., 291
Dement, W. C., 111
DeMeyer, M. K., 393
Dennis, W., 230, 231
Denny, D., 265, 445
Dentsch, D. F., 244
Depue, R. A., 405
Der-Karabetran, A., 505
Deser, T., 566
Deutsch, F., 252
de Vries, H. A., 260
Dewey, John, 6
Diacomakos, E. G., 56
Diaconis, P., 128
DiCara, L., 155
Dickson, W., 503
Diener, 521
Dies, R., 455
Diggins, D. R., 247
DiMento, J., 560

Dittes, J., 510
Dix, Dorothea, 429
Dobelle, W. H., 73, 90
Dodosh, 455
Dollard, John, 295–96, 534
Donaldson, G., 165–66
Donnerstein, E., 299
Doob, A. N., 296, 508
Dosey, M. A., 552
Doty, R. L., 287
Duff, D. F., 550
Dunham, H. W., 391
Dunker, K., 391
Dunphy, D. C., 251
Dustin, R., 447
Dutton, D. G., 324, 325
Dymond, A., 440

Ebbesen, E., 465
Ebbinghaus, H., 186
Ebenholtz, S. M., 198
Eccles, Sir John, 102
Edney, J. J., 549
Efran, M. G., 487
Egath, 177
Ehrlich, Paul, 554
Eibl-Eibesfeldt, I., 318
Eisdorfer, C., 265
Ekman, P., 317, 318
Elkind, D., 261
Elfner, L. F., 81
Ellis, Albert, 442
Ellis, Havelock, 103
Ells, J. G., 181
Ellsworth, P., 320
Emerson, P. E., 231, 232
Endler, N. S., 511
Engen, T., 181
Epstein, N., 450
Epstein, W., 76
Epstein, Y., 558
Erikson, Erik, 248–49, 252, 257–58, 268
Erlenmeyer-Kimling, L., 168
Erwin, W., 394
Escher, Maurits C., 74
Estes, T. H., 191
Evans, G., 564
Evans, G. W., 550
Evans, J. W., 368
Evans, R., 405
Evans, 409
Eysenck, Hans J., 169, 457

Factor, 571
Fantz, Robert L., 221
Farran, D. C., 232
Fazio, R., 472, 534
Feather, N. T., 301
Feldman, M. W., 168
Fenkel-Brunswick, E., 531
Ferguson, M., 123
Ferrell, R., 367
Ferrero, G., 349
Ferris, F., 535
Feschbach, S., 471
Feshbach, N. D., 235
Festinger, L., 472, 475, 486, 501
Fiedler, F., 518–20
Fishbein, M., 472

Fisher, J., 493, 553
Flowers, M. L., 526
Foley, 450
Folger, R., 535
Foner, A., 261
Forgus, 346
Foster, S., 371
Fox, G. L., 251
Fox, Terry, 360
Fozard, J. L., 259
Fraser, S., 471
Frederick, C. J., 403
Frederickson, C. H., 189
Freedman, J., 471, 556, 558
Freedman, J. L., 508
Freeman, M., 249
French, E. G., 293
Freud, Sigmund, 7–9, 108, 233, 248, 295, 321, 337, 338, 352–59, 390, 397, 399, 437, 438
Friedman, L. N., 285
Friedman, M., 335
Friesen, W. V., 317
Frieze, I., 301, 505
Fromm, Erich, 323, 324
Frost, Robert, 549

Galanter, E., 176
Gall, Franz Joseph, 348
Galton, Sir Francis, 163, 188
Garcia, Joh, 141
Gardner, R. A., 228
Gardner, B. T., 228
Garfield, S. L., 386
Gatchel, R., 456
Gebhard, A., 290
Geen, R. G., 296
Geldard, F. A., 80
Gelenberg, A. J., 435
Geller, S. H., 511
Genovese, Kitty, 488–89
George, R., 443, 447, 451
Gerard, H. B., 511
Gerbner, G., 467
Gergen, K., 493
Gergen, M., 493
Gershenfeld, M., 517
Geschwind, N., 50
Gewirtz, J. L., 230, 232, 293
Gibson, J. E., 219, 220
Gibson, J. J., 76, 79
Gilbert, W., 56
Gilchrist, A., 77
Gillam, B., 80
Gillin, J. C., 102
Ginsburg, G. P., 524
Ginter, G., 517
Girgus, J. S., 80
Glass, D. C., 336, 561, 562
Glass, G. V., 457
Glass, L., 335
Glass, L. B., 123
Glenn, M. D., 258
Glick, I. O., 269
Goethals, G. R., 451, 470, 501–2, 524–25
Gold, R., 282
Goldberg, P. A., 531
Goldfried, M. R., 446
Goldman, J., 484

Goldstein, M. J., 286
Golembiewski, R., 455
Goodwin, D. W., 419
Gordon, S., 251
Gottesman, I. I., 413
Graen, G., 520
Graham, S., 329
Green, D., 362
Greenberg, B., 455
Greenberg, M., 493
Greenbert, D. J., 221
Gregg, C., 221
Grieger, R., 442
Griffit, W., 483, 565
Griffith, A. K., 541, 558, 566
Grim, R., 247
Grissom, S., 252
Gross, 431
Gross, L., 467
Gross, L. P., 284
Grossman, J. L., 265
Gruder, 468, 492
Guilford, J. P. 163
Guilleminault, C., 111
Guppy, N., 268
Gurdon, J. B., 56
Gustavson, C. R., 141

Hadley, S. W., 457
Hagestad, G. O., 258, 267
Haith, M. M., 221
Haley, J., 450
Hall, C., 350, 364
Hall, E. T., 320, 550, 552
Hammen, C. L., 403
Hanes, B., 252
Hariton, 115
Harkins, S., 529
Harlow, Harry F., 160, 231, 291, 293, 322, 324
Harlow, M. K., 291
Harriman, A., 283
Harris, C. S., 92
Harris, D. B., 244
Harsh, J., 329
Harsuick, 553
Hartl, E., 349
Hartshorne, H., 347
Hashim, S. A., 285
Hasson, 193
Hathaway, S. R., 373
Hausel, 129
Havighurst, R. J., 262
Hayes, Cathy, 228
Hayes, Keith, 228
Hayes, S., 560, 564
Hearst, Patricia, 334
Hebb, D. O., 322
Heckel, R. J., 552
Heider, F., 468
Heller, K., 454
Helms, D. B., 251
Henning, M., 256
Henninger, M., 480
Henry, G. W., 389
Hering, E., 73
Heron, W., 127
Herrnstein, R. J., 169
Hess, E. H., 233
Hetherington, A., 250, 282

McKinley, J. C., 373
MacKinnon, 80
Mackworth, N., 565
McMullen, S., 289
M'Naghten, Daniel, 386
McNeill, D., 194
MacNichol, E. F., 73
McPherson, B., 268
McQuarter, G., 301, 302
McTeer, W., 281
McWaters, B., 453
Maharishi Mehesh Yogi, 125
Maher, B. A., 415
Maier, N. R. F., 161
Maier, S., 336
Malamud, H. F., 298
Malamud, W., 399
Malinowski, B., 359
Mann, L., 511, 514
Mann, R., 523
Manson, Charles, 381–83
Marks, W. B., 73
Martens, R., 529
Martindale, D. A., 329, 549
Maslach, C., 314
Maslow, Abraham, 280, 361–62
Massaro, D. W., 180
Masters, J. C., 445
Masters, William, 288, 291, 408–9
Masuda, M., 326
Mathews, K., 336
Matin, L., 80, 92
Matthews, K. E., 563
Maury, Alfred, 112
Max, D., 397
May, M. A., 347
Mayer, L. A., 111
Mayer-Gross, 409
Mead, M., 359
Medvedev, Z. A., 263
Megargee, E., 374
Mehrabian, Albert, 320
Meisels, M., 552
Mellon, P., 482
Meltzoff, J., 455
Mendel, Gregor, 55, 57
Menlove, 447
Messer, S., 356
Metcalf, J., 330
Meyer, D. R., 291
Meyers, D., 524
Michele, S., 476
Micklin, M., 252
Miks, M. B., 455
Milgram, Stanley, 512–15, 521, 571, 572
Miller, A. G., 351
Miller, B. C., 267
Miller, G. A., 176, 186
Miller, Merle, 344, 345, 347, 350, 355, 361
Miller, N. E., 155, 331, 534
Millon, T., 428, 432, 433
Mills, J., 473
Milner, D., 531–33
Mintz, N. C., 567
Minuchin, S., 394
Mischel, W., 351, 367
Mitchell, A., 440
Mitchell, K. M., 440, 457
Mohr, J. P., 394
Monahan, J., 454

Moniz, Egas, 430, 432
Monson, T., 480
Montgomery, J. E., 267
Moody, Raymond, 105–7
Moore, M. L., 251
Moray, N., 183
Morgan, T., 300
Mortensen, C., 320
Moscovici, S., 524
Moss, H., 210
Moss, M., 445
Mowat, F., 546
Mueller, C., 299
Murray, Harry, 299
Murray, J. R., 262
Murstein, B. I., 488
Mussen, P. H., 249

Nadien, J., 572
Nadler, A., 493
Nail, P., 285
Nakamura, 505
Napier, R., 517
Nash, R., 542
Nass, 251
Nathan, P. E., 386, 444
Neale, J. M., 397, 398, 428, 447
Nelson, L. P., 270
Nelson, R., 470
Neugarten, B. L., 258, 259, 266, 267
Newcomer, James, 91
Newman, O., 568–69
Newton, Isaac, 71
Nichols, R. C., 168
Nijima, A., 282
Nisbett, R. E., 284, 285, 351, 480
Noesjirwan, J., 551
Norman, D. A., 189, 193, 202
Norman, D. A., 186
Nydegger, 253
Nye, F. I., 255

Odbert, H. S., 351
O'Donnell, W. J., 221
Offir, C., 289
Ohman, S., 397
Olczak, P., 484
Olsen, K. M., 253
Olshan, N. H., 129
O'Neal, E., 551
Orne, E. C., 123–24
Orne, M. T., 371
Ornitz, E. M., 393
Ostrove, N., 487
Ovid, 325
Owen, D. R., 54

Page, H. A., 81
Paicheler, 524
Palmer, E. F., 191
Parke, D., 298
Parkes, C. M., 269
Pasamanick, B., 215
Patterson, Francine, 229
Patterson, G. R., 237
Paul, S. M., 414
Paulus, P., 558
Pavlov, Ivan, 138–43
Payne, B., 267
Pearlstone, Z., 193

Pellegrini, R., 487
Penfield, Wilder, 42, 102
Penick, S. B., 281
Pennebaker, J. W., 314, 336
Peplau, L. A., 323;
Perez, J., 450
Perkins, C. C., 200
Perls, Fritz, 112, 440–41
Perove, D. R., 249
Pessin, J., 528
Peters, S. D., 403
Peterson, J. A., 267
Peterson, L. R., 180–81
Peterson, M. J., 180–81
Peterson, R., 418
Petrucci, Daniel, 56
Phares, E. J., 368–69
Piaget, Jean, 222–26, 246
Pierce, 408
Piliavin, I., 489, 491
Piliavin, J., 489
Pinel, Philippe, 428–29
Pitillo, E., 425–27
Plomin, R., 169
Plutchik, R., 311, 312
Podd, M. H., 246–47
Pollen, 69
Poplin, D., 554
Porteous, J. D., 545
Portuges, S. H., 235
Poulton, E., 563
Powers, E. A., 262
Powley, T. L., 282, 283
Prawat, R. S., 252
Premack, Ann, 228
Premack, David, 228
Prentice-Dunn, S., 521
Presser, H. B., 251
Pribam, Karl, 102
Prince, L. H., 414

Quanty, M., 296
Quattrone, G., 533
Quillian, M. R., 188

Raaijmakers, J. G. W., 193
Rahe, R. H., 326–27
Ramey, C. T., 232
Randi, 130
Ransom, S., 282
Rappaport, R., 256, 260
Rappaport, R. N., 256, 260
Raven, J. C., 166
Rawitz, L., 391
Raynor, J. O., 300
Raynor, R., 7
Read, P. P., 274
Recorla, R. A., 143
Redlich, F. C., 391
Reid, L. S., 189
Reinhold, 435
Reiser, B. J., 184
Restak, R., 408
Reynolds, D. K., 268–70
Rhine, Joseph Banks, 129
Rice, B., 310, 470
Riley, M. W., 261
Rimm, D. C., 445
Ringelmann, 529
Ringness, T. A., 235
Ritchie, George G., 97–100, 103, 105, 110–12

Ritzer, G., 262
Robertson, J. F., 266
Rock, I., 76, 92
Rodin, J., 284, 285, 330, 331, 489, 556
Roethlisberger, F., 503
Rogers, Carl, 362–64, 439–40
Rogers, R., 521
Roll, S., 487
Ronner, 69
Rorschach, Hermann, 375
Rose, A., 500
Rose, S., 102
Rosen, L., 288
Rosen, M., 398
Rosen, R., 288, 289
Rosen, S., 561
Rosenblatt, P. C., 549
Rosenhan, D. L., 387–88
Rosenman, R. H., 335
Rosenthal, D., 404
Rosenthal, R., 25, 387, 414, 482
Rosenthal, T., 447
Rosenzweig, M. R., 216
Rosman, B. L., 394
Ross, D., 297
Ross, H., 567
Ross, L., 351, 479, 509
Ross, S. A., 297
Roth, 409
Rothbart, M. K., 237
Rotondo, J. H., 200
Rotter, Julian, 367–68
Rous, 546
Routtenberg, A., 393
Royce, J. R., 80
Rozin, P., 283
Rubenstein, C., 486
Rubin, I., 267
Rubin, J., 440
Rubin, J. A., 235
Rubin, Zick, 323
Rudolph, Wilma, 360
Ruff, H. A., 221
Rumbaugh, D. M., 228
Rumelkart, D. E., 189
Russek, M., 282
Russell, Francis, 175
Rutter, M., 392
Rux, J. M., 269
Ruys, T., 566
Ryan, E. R., 247
Rykman, R. M., 350, 359, 364

Saegert, S., 568
Sakurai, M. M., 510
Salk, 261
Salt, P., 329
Samaha, G., 535
Sanders, E., 406
Sanford, R. N., 531
Santee, J., 188
Sarason, B. R., 385
Sarason, I. G., 294, 385, 396, 399
Scales, P., 251
Scarr, S., 168
Scarr-Salaptek, S., 169
Schacht, T., 386
Schachter, S., 284, 285, 293, 294, 312–15, 323, 508
Schacter, D. L., 113

SUBJECT INDEX

abnormal psychology (psychological
    disorders), 384–421
  alcohol and drug addiction, 417–21
  childhood disorders, 392–94
  classification of, 385–86
  cognitive model of, 390
  definitions of, 384–88
  early views of, 388–89
  insanity as a legal term, 386–87
  labeling, 387–88
  learning model of, 390
  medical model of, 389, 432
  medical student syndrome, 391–92
  neurotic behavior. *See* neurotic behavior
  personality disorders, 416–17
  psychoanalytic model of, 389–90
  psychosis, 409–16. *See also* schizophrenia
  scope of, 385
  system model of, 391
absolute refractory period, 35
absolute threshold, 64
accidents, unconscious impulses and, 353–54
accommodation:
  of lens, 66
  in Piaget's model, 223
acetylcholine, 37
achievement motive, 299–302, 376
  basis for, 300
  characteristics of people scoring high on,
    300–301
  measuring, 300
  sex and racial differences in, 301–2
achievement tests, 162
addiction. *See* drug addiction
adolescence, 244–52
  anorexia nervosa in, 394
  career choices in, 251–52
  moral development in, 246–47
  peer groups in, 250–51
  personality development in, 247–249
  physical changes in, 244, 249
  sexual behavior in, 251
  social development in, 249–51
adopted children studies of IQ, 168–69
adulthood. *See* late adulthood; middle
    adulthood; young adulthood
advertising, attitude change and, 470
affective disorders, 401–6
  depression, 401–6
  mania and bipolar disorders, 405–6
affiliation motive, 292–94
afterimage, 73
age:
  fears related to, 321–22
  IQ and, 163–66

aggression, 249–99
  arousal and, 298–99
  catharsis effect of, 296
  displaced, 295
  frustration-aggression theory of, 295–96,
    534
  heat and, 565
  instinct theories of, 295
  media violence and, 298
  moon's influence on, 565–66
  personal space and, 550–51
  social-learning theory of, 296–98
aggression cues, 296
aging. *See also* late adulthood
  biological theories of, 263
  sensory changes and, 264
air pollution, 563–64
air-traffic controllers, 329
alarm reaction, 325–26
alcohol, 116–17
  fetal development and, 215
alcoholism, 418–19
  aversion therapy for, 141, 444
alleles, 57
altered states of consciousness, 96–131
  daydreams, 114–15
  defined, 100–101
  drug-induced states, 115–22
  hypnosis, 122–24
  meditation, 124–27
  methods for studying, 103–5
  near-death experiences, 105–7
  philosophies and theories of mind and,
    102–3
  sensory deprivation, 126–27
  sleep and dreams, 107–12
  visions during drowsiness, 113–14
American Psychiatric Association, 385, 434
American Psychological Association, 27
Ames room, 75–76
amnesia, psychogenic, 400
amniocentesis, 54–55
amphetamines, 37, 117, 419
amplitude of sound waves, 85
anal explusive personality, 357
anal retentive personality, 357
anal stage, 356–57
analytic introspection, 5
androgens, 286
anger, 296
  dying and, 269
animals:
  communication systems of, 228
  language learning abilities of, 228–29
animism, 224

anorexia nervosa, 394
antianxiety drugs, 434–35
antidepressant drugs, 435
antipsychotic drugs, 435
antisocial personality, 416–17
anvil, 82
anxiety, 390. *See also* fear
  basic, 359–60
  neurotic, 321
  objective, 321
  rational emotive therapy and, 442–43
  retrieval and, 194–95
anxiety disorders, 395–98
  generalized anxiety disorder, 395–96
  obsessive-compulsive disorders,
    397–98
  phobias, 396–97
  psychoanlysis for, 438
Apgar scores, 215
aphasia, 50
appraisal, emotions and, 315
approach-approach conflict, 331
approach-avoidance conflict, 332
aptitude tests, 162. *See also* intelligence
  tests
aqueous humor, 65–66
architecture, 566–70
arousal:
  aggression and, 298–99
  eating and, 285–86
  love and, 324–25
  performance and, 322–23
ascending nerves, 44
assessment:
  behavioral, 371
  personality. *See* personality assessment
assimilation, in Piaget's model, 223
Association for the Psychophysiological
    Study of Sleep, 111
athletes, organ inferiority in, 360
attachment, 231–33
  love and, 323
attention:
  crowding and focus of, 556
  encoding and, 182–84, 198–200
  hypnosis and, 123
  noise and focus of, 563
  selective, 46
attitudes, 465–75
  behavior and, 472
  change in, 468–71
  cognitive dissonance and, 472–75
  components of, 465
  development of, 465–67
  prejudice. *See* prejudice

attraction, interpersonal, 483–88
    physical attractiveness and, 486–88
    proximity and, 485–86
    reward and, 483–84
    similarity and, 484–85
attributions, 476–82
    actor and observer difference in, 480
    biases in, 478–81
    fundamental attribution error, 479
    hedonic relevance and, 478–79
    internal versus external cues of behavior
        and, 476–77
    physical appearance as basis for, 486–88
    primacy effects and, 480–81
    specific, 477–78
auditory hypnagogic images, 113
authoritarian parents, 249
authoritative parents, 250
authority, obedience to, 512–13
autistic children, 392–93, 446
autokinetic effect, 80–81
autonomic nervous system, 47–48
autosexual behavior, 288–89
aversion therapy, 141
aversive conditioning, 443–44
avoidance-avoidance conflict, 331–32
avoidance training, 146
axons, 34–35
axon terminal, 36

babbling, 226–27
babies. *See* infants
backward masking, 180
barbiturates, 419
basal ganglia, 49
basic anxiety, 359–60
basic hostility, 360
basilar membrane, 83, 84
Bay of Pigs incident (1961), 526
beauty:
    interpersonal attraction and, 486–88
    of rooms, 567
Bedlam, 388
behavioral assessment, 371
behavioral neuroscience, 34
behavioral sinks, 555
behaviorism, 6–7
behavior modification, 365
behavior therapies, 443–48
    aversive conditioning, 443–44
    modeling, 447–48
    operant conditioning therapies, 445–47
    systematic desensitization, 444–45
beliefs, 465
bias(es):
    in attribution, 478–81
    experimenter, 25
binocular disparity, 78
biofeedback, 111, 155
biofeedback therapy, 436
biological factors. *See also* genetics
    in depression, 404–5
    schizophrenia and, 413–14
    in sexual behavior, 286–87
biotherapy, 430, 432–37
    chemotherapy, 434–37
    definition of, 428
    electroconvulsive therapy, 432–33
    medical model as basis of, 432
    psychosurgery, 434

bipolar disorders, 406
    lithium treatment for, 435
birth order, 237
blindness, glaucoma as cause of, 66
blind children, emotional expression of, 318
blind people:
    sense of touch of, 89–91
    sensory substitution systems for, 90–91
blind spot, 66
blocking movements, 553
blood-sugar level, hunger and, 281–82
body hair, attributions based on, 487
body language, emotions and, 320
body orientation, 92–93
body temperature, hunger and, 282–83
body types, personality and, 349–50
body weight, hunger and, 283
boilermaker's deafness, 85
bone conduction, 83
bones of infants, 216
botulism, 37
brain:
    anatomy of, 38–42, 44
    at birth, 216
    language control centers of, 50
    limbic system of, 46–47
    neurons, 34–37
    reticular activating system (RAS), 46
    split, 43
    visual pathways to, 67–70
brainstem, 40
branching programs, 155
brightness constancy, law of, 77
Broca's aphasia, 50
Broca's area, 50
buildings, 567–70

caffeine, 117, 419
California Psychological Inventory (CPI),
    374–75
calories, 283
cannabis (marijuana), 420–21
Cannon-Bard theory of emotions, 312
captivity, stress of, 334
career choices, in adolescence, 251–52
career commitments, 254–57
careers:
    in middle adulthood, 262
    in psychology, 14–15
career women, 254–56, 262
caring, love and, 323
case history, 19–20
"castrating female" syndrome, 358
castration anxiety, 357, 358
cataracts, 66
catecholamines, 37
catharsis, 296
central fissure, 41
central nervous system, 44. *See also* brain;
    spinal cord
central trait, 348
cerebellum, 39–40, 49
cerebral cortex (cerebrum), 41–42
    of newborns, 216
cerebral hemispheres, 41–43
change, stress and, 326–29
chemical transmitters, 36–37. *See also*
    neurotransmitters
chemotherapy (drug therapy), 430, 434–47
    for schizophrenia, 435

childhood, 222–37
    anal stage of, 356–57
    cognitive development in, 222–26
    language development in, 226–29
    latency stage of, 358
    neo-Freudian view of, 359–61
    personality and social development in,
        229–37, 356
    phallic stage of, 357–58
    physical growth in, 222
    in psychoanalytic theory, 356–59
    psychological disorders of, 392–94
children. *See also* childhood
    birth order of, 237
    compulsive behaviors of, 397–98
    noise and, 562
    operant conditioning and, 153–55
    rights of, 260–61
choices, conflict involved in making, 331
chromosomes, 53
    bipolar disorders and, 406
    mutations and, 54–55
    sex-linked traits and, 57
chronological age, mental age and, 163
chunking, 186
cities, 570–72
clairvoyance tests, 130
classical conditioning, 138–44
    discrimination, 143
    establishing a response, 140–41
    higher-order, 143–44
    losing a response, 142
    Pavlov's experiments, 139–40
    stimulus generalization, 143
clearness, as depth cue, 78
client-centered therapy, 364, 439–40
clinical psychologists, 431, 500
clinical psychology, 14–15
cliques, 251
cloning, 56
cocaine, 37, 117–18, 419
cochlea, 83
codes. *See also* encoding
    verbal, 184
    visual, 184
cognitive development, 222–26
    concrete operational stage of, 225
    formal operational stage of, 225–26
    in late adulthood, 264–65
    Piaget's approach to, 222–23
    preoperational stage of, 224–25
    sensorimotor stage of, 223–24
cognitive dissonance, 472–75, 534–35
cognitive learning theory, 157–62, 366. *See
    also* cognitive theory
    insight, 157–58
    latent learning, 158–60
    learning sets, 160–62
cognitive map, 159–60
cognitive overload, 571
cognitive psychology, 11–12
cognitive theory. *See also* cognitive learning
    theory
    of abnormal psychology, 390
    of depression, 403–4
    of emotions, 312–15
    of obsessive-compulsive disorders, 398
    of schizophrenia, 414–15
cohabitation, 252
cohesiveness, group therapy and, 448
cold spots, 89

ear canal, 82
eardrums, 82
ears, 82–83
eating behavior. *See also* anorexia nervosa; hunger
  body weight and, 283
  learning and, 283–84
  liver and, 282
  obesity and, 284–86
ecological psychology, 391
ecological theory of size constancy, 76–77
ectomorphs, 349
educational psychologists, 500
effect, law of, 144
effort justification:
  dissonance theory and, 473–74
  psychotherapy and, 456
ego, 354–55
egocentrism of children, 224
Elavil, 435
elderly people. *See* aging; late adulthood; old people
Electra complex, 358
electric shock therapy, 429–30
electroconvulsive therapy (ECT), 430, 432–33
electromagnetic spectrum, 71
embarrassment, 314
embryo, 212
emotional appeals, in advertising, 470
emotions, 308–25. *See also specific emotions*
  appraisal and, 315
  body language and, 320
  Cannon-Bard theory of, 312
  cognitive theories of, 312–15
  Darwin's evolutionary theory of, 317
  definition of, 308
  facial expressions and, 318–20
  fear and anxiety, 321–23
  James-Lange theory of, 309–11
  love, 323–25
  motives differentiated from, 308
  nonverbal communication of, 316–20
  physiology of, 308–9
  in schizophrenia, 412
  two-factor theory of, 312–15
empiricism, 211
empty chair technique, 441
empty next syndrome, 258
encoding, 181–85
  improving your memory and, 198–201
  in long-term memory, 184–85
  organization and, 200
  in short-term memory, 182–84
encoding strategies, 367
encounter groups, 454–55
endocrine system, 34, 50–52
endomorphs, 349
energy conservation, 544
engineering psychology, 16
environment (environmental influences), 542–72. *See also* physical space
  air pollution, 563–64
  buildings, 567–70
  cognitive development and, 226
  development and, 210
  early social responses and, 230–31
  energy conservation and, 544
  noise, 559–63

prenatal, 214–15
  rooms, 566–67
  urban, 570–72
  weather, 564–66
environmental psychology, 17, 543–45
  policy making and, 560
episodic memory, 187–88
  retrieval from, 193
equilibrium, 92
Eros, 354
escape training, 146
ESP (extrasensory perception), 129–30
estrogen, 52, 287
ethical issues:
  genetics and, 56
  research methods and, 26–27
  research on obedience and, 514–15
examinations, reviewing for, 201–2
excitement phase of sexual response, 288
exercise programs, 260
exhaustion, stage of, 326
expectancies, 367
experimental psychology, 10–12
experimenter bias, 25
experiments, 23–27
  laboratory versus field, 27
external ear, 82
extinction:
  in classical conditioning, 142
  in operant conditioning, 152
extrasensory perception (ESP), 129–30
extroversion, 359
eyes, 65–69. *See also* vision
  light and dark adaptation of, 69
  pathways to the brain, 67–70

facial expressions, emotions and, 318
facial hair, attributions based on, 487
family commitments:
  in late adulthood, 266–67
  in middle adulthood, 260–61
  in young adulthood, 252–53
family cycle, 253
family therapy, 450
farsightedness, 66
fat cells, obesity and, 285
fear(s). *See also* anxiety; phobias
  affiliation motive and, 293–94
  age-related, 321–22
  definition of, 321
  functions of, 322
  of imagined situations, 322
  results of, 322–23
  systematic desensitization therapy for, 141
fear appeals, in advertising, 470
feature detectors, 70
feelings. *See* emotions
fetus, 212–15
field experiments, 27
fight-or-flight response, 126, 155
figure, 74
figure-ground reversal, 74
first impressions, self-fulfilling prophecy and, 481–82
fissure of Rolando, 41
fissure of Sylvius, 41
fixation:
  at anal stage, 357

at oral stage, 356
  at phallic stage, 358
fixed-interval schedule, 147
fixed-ratio schedules, 148
flexor-cross-extensor reflex, 45
flexor reflex, 45
flight. *See also* fight-or-flight response
  as response to invasion of personal space, 553
fluid intelligence, 164–66
foot-in-the-door technique, 471
forebrain, 40
forensic psychology, 17
forgetting, 196–98. *See also* amnesia
  interference theory of, 197–98
  trace decay theory of, 196–97
formal operational stage, 225–26
fovea, 66–67
free association, 352, 437–38
free association test, 188
free recall test, 177, 188
frequencies of sounds, 83–85
frequency distributions, 574–76
frequency theory of hearing, 84
Freudian slips, 353
Freudian theory. *See* psychoanalytic theory
frontal lobe, 41
frustration, 295
frustration-aggression, 295–96, 534
fugue, psychogenic, 400–401
functional fixedness, 161–62
functionalism, 6
fundamental arrangement of, 567

gain-loss effect, 484
galvanic skin response (GSR), lie detection and, 310
gametes, 53
Garcia effect, 141
gender identity disorders, 407
general adaptation syndrome, 325–26
General Aptitude Test Battery (GATB), 162
generalized anxiety disorder, 395–96
generativity, 257
genes, 53
  mutator, 55
genetic engineering, 56
genetics (genetic factors), 52–58
  depression and, 404–5
  development and, 210
  early social responses and, 230
  IQ and, 168–69
  laws of inheritance of characteristics or traits, 55, 57
genital stage, 358
genotype, 53
geometrical illusions, 80
Gestalt laws of organization, 74
Gestalt psychology, 6
Gestalt therapy, 440–41
glaucoma, 66, 419
glove anesthesia, 399
glucagon, 52
glucoreceptors, 282
glucose level, hunger and, 282
gonads, 52
grammar, 228
grandeur, delusions of, 410–11
grandparents, 266–67

sublimation, as defense mechanism, 338–39
sucking reflex, 217
suggestibility:
  hypnotic, 123
  sensory deprivation and, 128
suicide, depression and, 128
superego, 355–58
suppression, as defense mechanism, 338
surveys, 20–21
sympathetic division, 47
sympathetic nervous system, 308
synapse, 36
synaptic transmission, 36–38
syphilis, fetal development and, 214
systematic desensitization, 444–45
systematic desensitization therapy, 141
systems model of abnormal psychology, 391

Tactile Visual Substitution System (TVSS),
  90
task specialist, 516
taste, 87
  aging and, 264
  smell and, 88
TAT (Thematic Apperception Test), 300,
  376–77
teachers:
  operant conditioning's implications for,
  153
  personality and social development and,
  235
teaching machines, 154
teenagers. See adolescence
telepathy tests, 129–30
temperature:
  behavioral effects of, 565
  body, hunger and, 282–83
  perception of, 89
  taste and, 87
temporal lobe, 41–42
tension, frustration-aggression theory and,
  295–96
territoriality, 545–49
testes, 52, 286
testosterone, 52
tests, 21–22
  achievement, 300
  aptitude, 162. See also intelligence tests
  clairvoyance, 130
  free association, 188
  free recall, 188
  intelligence. See intelligence tests
  of memory, 176–78
  precognition, 130
  projective, 375–77
  recall, 177
  recognition, 177
  reliability of, 371
  requirements of, 370–71
  savings, 177
  scholastic aptitude, 169
  scrambled sentences, 189
  standardized, 162
  telepathy, 129–30
  validity of, 371
  of witnesses memory, 196
test-tube babies, 56

texture, depth perception and, 78–79
texture gradient, 79
T-group, 364, 454
thalamus, 40, 312
Thalidomide, 214
Thanatos, 354
Thematic Appreciation Test (TAT), 300,
  375–77
theories, 18–19
therapists:
  effectiveness of therapy and, 457
  types of, 430–31
therapy, 428–57. See also biotherapy;
  psychotherapy
  biofeedback, 436
theta waves, 108
Thorazine, 435
thought: disorganization of, in
  schizophrenia, 410–11
threats, cognitive dissonance theory and,
  475
thyroid glands, 51
Thyroxin, 51
tip-of-the-tongue phenomenon, 193–94
Titchner illusion, 80
Tofranil, 435
token economy, 154, 365, 445–47
tones, 85
tonic neck reflex, 217
touch, sense of, 89–91, 264
trace decay, 196
traits:
  central, 348
  definition, 350–51
  identification of, 351
trait theories:
  of personality, 350–52
  of leadership, 516
tranquilizers, 419, 430
  major (antipsychotic drugs), 435
  minor (antianxiety drugs), 434–35
Transcendental Meditation (TM), 124–25
transference, in psychoanalysis, 438
transpersonal psychology, 453–54
transsexualism, 407–8
trephining, 428
trichromatic receptor theory, 73
tunnel vision, 322
twin studies:
  of IQ, 168
  of schizophrenia, 413
two-factor theory of emotion, 312–15
two-point threshold, 90
Type A behavior, 335–36
type theories of personality, 348–50

ulcers, stress and, 332–33, 335
unconditional positive regard, 363–64, 440
unconditioned response (UR), 139–43
unconditioned stimulus (UR), 139–43
unconscious, the, 353–54, 437
unconscious impulses, 353–54
unconscious inference theory of size
  constancy, 76, 77
unidentified flying objects, autokinetic effect
  and, 80
unpredictability, stress and, 329–30

unstructured interview, 372
uplifts, 327–29
urban environment, 570–72

vaginismus, 408
validity:
  of interviews, 372
  of tests, 371
Valium, 434, 435
variable-interval schedules, 147–48
variable-ratio schedules, 148
variables, independent and dependent, 23
variance, 577
vascular theory of temperature perception,
  89
venereal diseases (VD), 214, 251
verbal codes, 184
verbal mediation, 201
vestibular system, 92
Vienna Psycho-Analytic Society, 359
violence, on television, 298
vision, 65–81
  aging and, 264
  color, 69–73
  depth perception, 78–79
  organization in, 74–77
  peripheral, 67
visions, during drowsiness, 113–14
visual angle, 75
visual cliff experiments, 219–20
visual codes, 184
visual illusions, 79–81
visual memory, 178–80
vitreous humor, 66
voice stress analyzer, 311
volley principle, 84–85

warm spots, 89
waveform, 85
weather, 564–66
weight, hunger and, 283
Wernicke's aphasia, 50
witnesses:
  computers for improving memory of, 203
  test of memory of, 196
witness testimony:
  leading questions and, 191
  memory standardization and, 192
  reconstruction of memory and, 191
women, working, 254–56, 262
work groups, norms of, 503
World War II, attitude changes during, 468

Yerkes-Dodson principle, 322–23
yoga, 124, 453–54
young adulthood, 252–57
  family commitments in, 252–53
  occupational commitments in, 254–57

Zener cards, 129, 130
Zen meditation, 124
Zhun/twa culture, 384
Zollner illusion, 80
zygote, 53

ABOUT THE AUTHORS

STEPHEN WORCHEL is a professor of psychology at the University of Virginia. He received his B.A. at the University of Texas at Austin and his Ph.D. at Duke University. Before coming to the University of Virginia, he taught at North Carolina Central University and the University of North Carolina at Chapel Hill. While this text was being written, he spent a year in Athens Greece as a Senior Fulbright Editor of the *Personality and Social Psychology Bulletin*, Advisory Editor to the *Psychological Abstracts*, and Editorial Consultant to *Basic and Applied Social Psychology* and *Environmental Psychology and Nonverbal Behavior*. Steve Worchel does research on environmental issues, intergroup relations, and group dynamics. He has published more than fifty articles and chapters and co-authored *Understanding Social Psychology, Adjustment and Human Relations, Clinical Psychology: A Social Psychological Approach,* and *The Social Psychology of Intergroup Relations*.

WAYNE SHEBILSKE is an Associate Professor of Psychology at the University of Virginia. He received his B.A., M.S., and Ph.D. degrees at the University of Wisconsin. He has published basic research papers on space perception, with an emphasis on effects of eye movement anomalies; reading, with an emphasis on learning from textbooks; and development, with an emphasis on minor physical anomalies. While this text was being written, he spent a year at the Behavioral Research Directorate, Human Engineering Laboratory, Aberdeen Proving Ground, Maryland. His research goals during that time included reducing illusions that cause plane crashes, improving methods for teaching advanced reading skills, and developing techniques for improving textbooks and technical manuals. The University of Virginia honored him in 1982 for his excellence in undergraduate advising, and the Office of Career Planning and Placement praised his new course, Careers for Psychology Majors.

Wayne Shebilske   Stephen Worchel